CRIMINAL
PROCEDURE
IN CANADA

CRIMINAL PROCEDURE IN CANADA

Steven Penney

Faculty of Law
University of Alberta

Vincenzo Rondinelli

Of the Ontario Bar

James Stribopoulos

Osgoode Hall Law School
at York University

 LexisNexis®

Criminal Procedure in Canada

© LexisNexis Canada Inc. 2011

December 2011

All rights reserved. No part of this publication may be reproduced or stored in any material form (including photocopying or storing it in any medium by electronic means and whether or not transiently or incidentally to some other use of this publication) without the written permission of the copyright holder except in accordance with the provisions of the *Copyright Act*. Applications for the copyright holder's written permission to reproduce any part of this publication should be addressed to the publisher. Warning: The doing of an unauthorized act in relation to a copyrighted work may result in both a civil claim for damages and criminal prosecution.

Library and Archives Canada Cataloguing in Publication

Penney, Steven, 1968-
    Criminal procedure in Canada / Steven Penney, Enzo Rondinelli and James Stribopoulos.

Includes bibliographical references and index.
ISBN 978-0-433-45521-9

    1. Criminal procedure--Canada. I. Rondinelli, Enzo II. Stribopoulos, James III. Title.

KE9260.P45 2011   345.71'05   C2011-905571-6
KF9620.ZA2P45 2011

Published by LexisNexis Canada, a member of the LexisNexis Group
LexisNexis Canada Inc.
123 Commerce Valley Dr. E., Suite 700
Markham, Ontario
L3T 7W8

Customer Service
Telephone: (905) 479-2665 • Fax: (905) 479-2826
Toll-Free Phone: 1-800-668-6481 • Toll-Free Fax: 1-800-461-3275
Email: customerservice@lexisnexis.ca
Web Site: www.lexisnexis.ca

Printed and bound in Canada.

For Melissa, Brodie, Cooper and Violet. SP

For my parents, Egidio and Anna. VR

For Georgina, Oscar and Claire. JS

FOREWORD

The publication of *Criminal Procedure in Canada* is the culmination of an ambitious project to house under one roof all aspects of criminal procedure which govern the investigation, detection and prosecution of crime in Canada. Criminal lawyers, criminal law academics and criminal law students are all beneficiaries of this first truly comprehensive treatise on what is self-described as a "tough subject for the uninitiated".

The introductory portion of the text, which deals with "Overview and Basic Concepts" is a breathtaking dash through virtually "all you ever wanted to know about criminal procedure in Canada". The authors, who combine a rare blend of academic analysis and scholarship with practical in-court experience, provide a useful primer for the uninitiated which, nevertheless, contains sufficient detail to provide meaningful assistance to practitioners, journalists, court watchers and invaluable lessons for members of law enforcement.

The reader is almost immediately struck by the depth and breadth of the research upon which the manuscript is based. The extensive footnotes complement rather than compete with the text and provide a worthwhile review, not only of the relevant jurisprudence, but as well, a précis of significant historical and current academic articles. The authors are neither timid nor equivocal in the expression of their views by critically analyzing judicial reasoning, in demanding a more disciplined focus on underlying policies, in questioning the expansion of police powers and in their lament for the trend toward limiting meaningful *Charter* scrutiny.

Following the extensive overview, which could conceivably have been published separately as a freestanding guide, the authors embark upon a detailed analysis of "Criminal Investigations", "Pre-trial Procedures", "The Trial" and "Post-Trial Procedures". The comprehensive and exhaustive treatment of virtually every significant aspect of criminal procedure guarantees its place as an indispensable addition to every criminal law library and, at the same time, precludes the realistic possibility of any rival publication in the foreseeable future. The Table of Contents, which canvasses every issue "fit to print", is tantamount to an extensive index of almost every potential procedural issue which the practitioner is likely to confront. Yet at every turn, the text provides clarity and insight while dynamically issuing challenges to rarely disputed entrenched principles. Perhaps the enduring contribution of this text is that it offers a springboard for creative thinking on procedural issues by providing a convenient and thorough examination of the material while exploring deficiencies in the existing case law.

The wealth of information which is provided in an exceptionally readable and organized format ensures that *Criminal Procedure in Canada* will become required reading in short order and will undoubtedly add several pounds to the weight of trial bags carried by conscientious criminal lawyers across the country.

Brian H. Greenspan

October 2011

PREFACE

The inspiration for this project was our collective experience as criminal procedure teachers, scholars and practitioners. Although there are a number of existing textbooks on criminal procedure in Canada, we believe there is a pressing need for a fresh approach.

Canadian criminal procedure is an especially challenging subject for the novice. The main source of confusion is the absence of any central repository for the myriad rules governing the criminal process. A comprehensive legislated code of criminal procedure is long overdue in Canada. Unfortunately, that sort of wholesale law reform seems unlikely. As a result, piecing together a complete picture of the criminal process will continue to require recourse to a variety of sources: the *Canadian Charter of Rights and Freedoms*; a number of legislative enactments (most importantly, the *Criminal Code*); the case law interpreting and applying the relevant constitutional and statutory provisions; and an extensive body of judge-made "common law".

This book's principal aim is to present the rules emanating from these sources in a clear, cohesive and comprehensive manner. There are three main features of the book that we believe assist in doing just that.

First, rather than organizing the subject around particular statutory or constitutional provisions, we have chosen a chronological structure. The relevant rules and procedures are introduced and explained in the very same sequence that a person investigated and prosecuted would ordinarily experience them. We believe that this format results in a more logical and intuitive organization, useful to both novices and experts.

Second, recognizing the *Charter*'s revolutionary impact on the criminal process, we have woven our discussion of it into the very fabric of the book. In other words, the *Charter* is not treated like an insular event with its implications simply tacked on at the end of each chapter. Instead, its innumerable effects are addressed seamlessly throughout the book.

Third, rather than writing a book directed exclusively at novices or experts, we have attempted to do both. Our aim has been to write a text that will be equally useful to students, lawyers and judges — giving the novice the context necessary to appreciate the significance of the detail, while digging deep on specifics so that experts will still find the book a useful resource. We have consequently tried to keep the text concise and uncluttered, while reserving much of the finer detail and supporting references for the footnotes.

All of that said, we have aimed to do more than simply describe the law governing the Canadian criminal process. Where there are gaps in the existing doctrine (and there are many) we make suggestions as to how they could best be filled. We also offer constructive criticism of existing rules in hopes of advancing future reform. These proposals and critiques are informed by our own research and experience, as well as by a rich tradition of criminal procedure scholarship (both legal and socio-legal) in Canada, the United States and elsewhere. We are particularly grateful to the many excellent scholars of Canadian criminal procedure upon whose work we have relied throughout the book.

This book has taken nearly five years to write. As we have discovered, writing a textbook on a topic as expansive as criminal procedure is a monumental undertaking. A project of this nature would simply not be possible without the assistance and support of a great many people.

We would like to thank all of the students who have assisted us in carrying out the extensive research that was necessary to complete this project. From the Faculty of Law at the University of Alberta, that has included: John Devlin, Julia Herscovitch, Mathieu LaFleche, Melissa Fleck, Jonathan Maryniuk, Sarah McClune and Caeleigh Shier. From Osgoode Hall Law School that has included: Jen Aubrey, Richard Diniz, Maija Martin, Kristen Morris, Audrey Ngo-Lee, Matthew Shogiley, Stephen Simpson and Lori Anne Thomas.

In addition, we would also very much like to thank LexisNexis Canada and their wonderful staff for their considerable help in making this project a reality. In particular, we would like to thank Sheila Nemet-Brown for her patience and unceasing encouragement as this project slowly progressed from idea to completed manuscript. We would also like to thank our editors at LexisNexis Canada: Dale Clarry, Tina Eng, Edward Mansia, Cynthia Notamarco and Karin Stephens, for their excellent editorial work on the manuscript.

We would also like to thank the following for research grants that have greatly aided our work: the Foundation for Legal Research, the Borden Ladner Gervais LLP Research Fellowship Program, the University of Alberta, the University of Alberta Faculty of Law, Harry Arthurs and Osgoode Hall Law School.

Lastly, it is necessary to say a word about the timeliness of the research found in this book. Unfortunately, criminal procedure is a moving target. Every day, important decisions are released by the courts, and every year Parliament enacts new legislation that makes both small and large changes to criminal procedure. Readers should therefore note that the research in this textbook is intended to reflect the law as it stood in May 2011.

Steven Penney

Vincenzo Rondinelli

James Stribopoulos

September 2011

ABOUT THE AUTHORS

Steven Penney, B.A. (Alberta), LL.B. (Alberta), LL.M. (Harvard), is a Professor at the University of Alberta, Faculty of Law, where he researches and teaches in the areas of criminal procedure, evidence, substantive criminal law, privacy, and law and technology. His articles have appeared in numerous publications, including the *American Journal of Criminal Law*, the *Journal of Criminal Law and Criminology*, *McGill Law Journal*, *Osgoode Hall Law Journal*, *Queen's Law Journal*, *Supreme Court Law Review*, *Alberta Law Review*, *Canadian Criminal Law Review* and the *Criminal Law Quarterly*. He has also written several book chapters and is co-editor of *Evidence: A Canadian Casebook*. He has previously been Associate Professor, Faculty of Law, University of New Brunswick; Visiting Professor, Faculty of Law, University of Western Ontario; and law clerk to Mr. Justice Gérard V. La Forest of the Supreme Court of Canada.

Vincenzo Rondinelli, LL.B. (Osgoode), LL.M. (Osgoode), is a criminal defence lawyer in Toronto with a busy and specialized criminal appellate practice. He has appeared at all levels of the courts, including the Supreme Court of Canada and argues appeals regularly before the Ontario Court of Appeal. He joined the adjunct faculty at Osgoode Hall Law School in 2003 and is currently Co-Director of the Criminal Intensive Program and co-instructor in the Forensic Science & the Law course. He has published scholarly articles in the *Criminal Reports*, *Criminal Law Quarterly* and the *Criminal Lawyers' Association Newsletter*. He is certified by the Law Society of Upper Canada as a Specialist in Criminal Law.

James Stribopoulos, B.A. (York), LL.B. (Osgoode), LL.M. (Columbia), J.S.D. (Columbia), is an Associate Professor at Osgoode Hall Law School where he teaches criminal law, criminal procedure and evidence in Osgoode's JD Program, while also serving as Director of the Moot Court Program and Co-Director of the Part-Time LL.M. Program Specializing in Criminal Law. He conducts research and publishes in the areas of criminal law, criminal procedure, evidence, comparative criminal procedure, constitutional law, advocacy, legal ethics, the legal profession and the legal process. His research and teaching are informed by his extensive practical experience as a criminal trial and appellate lawyer. As an appellate lawyer, he has argued appeals regularly before the Court of Appeal for Ontario and the Supreme Court of Canada. In association with Kapoor Barristers, he continues to maintain a small appellate court practice with a focus on *Charter* litigation.

TABLE OF CONTENTS

Part III Pre-Trial Procedures

TABLE OF CASES

INTRODUCTION

1. DEFINING "CRIMINAL PROCEDURE"

The term "criminal procedure" is the catchall phrase used to describe the various legal rules that make up the entire criminal process. These rules range in scope from the powers possessed by police in investigating crimes to the appeal procedures available once an individual has been convicted and sentenced — as well as everything in between.

Canadian criminal procedure is a tough subject for the uninitiated. Unlike some civil law jurisdictions, Canada has no comprehensive code of criminal procedure. As a result, understanding the legal framework that governs the criminal process requires one to draw on a number of disparate sources: legislation (both federal[1] and provincial), rules of court, the common law and constitutional law.

From a constitutional standpoint, the *Canadian Charter of Rights and Freedoms*[2] is of fundamental importance. Since its introduction in 1982, the *Charter* has transformed the criminal process, pushing the rights of those suspected and accused of crime to the forefront of public and legal discourse. Today, understanding criminal procedure requires one to become familiar not only with the *Charter*'s text, but also the never-ending stream of judicial pronouncements interpreting and applying its open-ended and value laden guarantees.

This book synthesizes information from each of these sources in order to provide readers with a clear, concise and yet comprehensive overview of the entire process and each of the major stages within it. At the outset, however, a caveat is necessary.

2. CAVEAT: LAW VS. REALITY

This is a book about legal rules. For the most part, it describes how the criminal justice system is *supposed* to work. However, as with all human systems,[3] there is a divide between the formal rules of the criminal process and the actual behaviour of those participating in it.[4] One of the great benefits of *Charter*

---

[1] Federally, the most important piece of legislation is undoubtedly the *Criminal Code*, R.S.C. 1985, c. C-46 [*Criminal Code*].

[2] Part I of the *Constitution Act, 1982*, being Schedule B to the *Canada Act 1982* (U.K.), 1982, c. 11 [*Charter*].

[3] See Catherin Casey, "Bureaucracy Re-enchanted? Spirits, Experts and Authority in Organizations" (2004) 11 Organization 58.

[4] See generally, Jerome H. Skolnick, *Justice Without Trial: Law Enforcement in Democratic Society* (New York: MacMillan, 1994). In a Canadian context, see Richard V. Ericson, *Reproducing Order: A Study of Police Patrol Work* (Toronto: University of Toronto Press, 1982); Richard V. Ericson & Patricia M. Baranek, *Ordering of Justice: A Study of Accused Persons as Dependants in the Criminal Process* (Toronto: University of Toronto Press, 1982); Richard V. Ericson, *Making Crime: A Study of Detective Work* (Toronto: Butterworths, 1981).

litigation is that it can sometimes bring illegal practices out into the open by providing both a forum (the criminal trial) and an incentive (an exclusionary remedy) for some of those affected by official malfeasance to raise such complaints publicly. Unfortunately, many parts of the system are not at all transparent, which means that "short cuts, deviations and outright rule violations"[5] can too often escape detection and, therefore, a remedy.[6]

Unfortunately, no aspect of the criminal justice system is immune from this problem. Much of the work performed by actors within the system is never subjected to public scrutiny. So, for example, if the police unlawfully detain an innocent person who is ultimately released without charge, there will be no court appearance, no criminal trial and therefore no real chance for legal accountability.[7] Similarly, if a prosecutor suppresses evidence that must be disclosed to the accused, the accused is unlikely to discover it, and again the rule violation would likely escape detection. Finally, if a defence lawyer unethically and illegally helps a guilty accused to concoct false testimony, it is unlikely that the prosecutor will uncover the impropriety by cross-examination.

All of that said, to the extent that rule violations are discoverable, discovered and capable of legal proof, this book does provide a roadmap for sorting out their legal implications. Building on existing law, it also makes suggestions on how the law of criminal procedure might be improved to bring more violations to light and minimize future occurrences. Lastly, where the parameters of existing rules are unclear or controversial, we propose interpretations or reforms that we hope will achieve better accommodations between the many, often-conflicting interests at stake in the criminal justice process.

3. ORGANIZATION OF THIS BOOK

To best assist readers in understanding the legal rules governing the criminal process, this book is organized in the same way that a person investigated and prosecuted would ordinarily experience them. Following this introduction, the book is divided into five parts.

Part I (Chapter 1) provides an overview of the criminal process and introduces and explains a number of foundational concepts that will be relevant throughout the remainder of the book.

Part II deals with Criminal Investigations. It focuses on the key legal powers used by police to investigate crime: Detention and Arrest (Chapter 2); Search and Seizure (Chapter 3); and Questioning (Chapter 4).

---

5   Malcolm M. Feeley, "Two Models of the Criminal Justice System: An Organizational Perspective" (1972-1973) 7 Law and Sociology Review 407 at 417.

6   *Ibid.*, at 422.

7   See generally, Steven Penney, "Taking Deterrence Seriously: Excluding Unconstitutionally Obtained Evidence Under Section 24(2) of the Charter" (2004) 49 McGill L.J. 105 at 120-24 (detailing the ineffectiveness of non-exclusionary remedies for police misconduct available outside of accused's criminal trial).

Part III deals with Pre-Trial Procedures. It focuses on events transpiring after arrest but before trial. It includes: Intake Procedures (Chapter 5); Bail (Chapter 6); Disclosure (Chapter 7); Prosecutorial Function (Chapter 8); Elections, Preliminary Inquiries and Preferring the Indictment (Chapter 9); and *Charter* Remedies (Chapter 10).

Part IV deals with The Trial. It focuses on topics most pertinent to the actual litigation of a criminal accusation, including: Informations and Indictments (Chapter 11); Territorial Limits (Chapter 12); Temporal Limits (Chapter 13); The Plea (Chapter 14), Jury Selection (Chapter 15); and Trial Procedure (Chapter 16).

Finally, Part V deals with Post-Trial Procedures. This involves consideration of two topics: Sentencing (Chapter 17) and Appeals (Chapter 18).

PART I

OVERVIEW AND BASIC CONCEPTS

CHAPTER 1

AN OVERVIEW OF CRIMINAL PROCEDURE AND BASIC CONCEPTS

1. INTRODUCTION

§1.1 This chapter will begin by providing readers with a very basic overview of the Canadian criminal process.

§1.2 It will next introduce readers to the competing theoretical accounts of the criminal process. As will be explained, a theoretical frame can be invaluable in assessing the impact of actual developments. In particular, the competing theoretical lenses are useful in assessing the impact of the *Canadian Charter of Rights and Freedoms*[1] on the Canadian criminal justice system.

§1.3 As will become apparent, the *Charter*'s effects have been felt in every facet of the criminal process. As a result, its presence will be pervasive throughout this book. Nevertheless, before moving to the specifics, it is useful to gain a broader understanding of the *Charter* and its impact. In this chapter, this will be accomplished by considering the state of civil liberties in the Canadian criminal justice system before the *Charter*, then exploring the text and purpose behind this revolutionary constitutional reform.

§1.4 In this chapter we also address important foundational questions about the *Charter* that transcend any particular section of this book, such as to whom it applies (*i.e.*, government, its legislation and its agents) and the extent to which it applies beyond Canada's borders.

§1.5 This chapter will then begin the process of explaining some of the basic nuts and bolts of criminal procedure in Canada. In this regard, we address the division of jurisdictional responsibilities within the criminal justice system as between the federal and provincial governments.

§1.6 Lastly, this chapter will identify and explain the various sources of the rules of criminal procedure in Canada.

---

[1] Part I of the *Constitution Act, 1982*, being Schedule B to the *Canada Act 1982* (U.K.), 1982, c. 11 [*Charter*].

2.   OVERVIEW OF THE CANADIAN CRIMINAL PROCESS

§1.7 A succinct overview of any complex system must necessarily generalize (and even simplify) some important details. We hope that the following summary will nonetheless help readers (especially novices) to gain some perspective on the whole of the Canadian criminal process.

(1)   Detection and Investigation

§1.8 Not all crimes result in the laying of formal charges. Many crimes go undetected, while others are simply not reported. If a victim of or witness to a crime reports it to police, an investigation of some form will be initiated.

§1.9 The scope and extent of a police investigation can vary, usually in direct correlation to the seriousness of the offence involved. Understandably, given the limits on police resources, a case of vandalism will usually not be investigated with the same rigour and resources as a murder.

§1.10 It is important to note as well that not all investigations are initiated by a victim or witness complaint. With so-called "consensual crimes", for example narcotics, prostitution, gambling and obscenity offences, the police initiate most (although not all) investigations.

§1.11 In addition, although much of law enforcement is reactive, a fair amount also results from proactive policing. To deter crime and provide citizens with a sense of security, police often deploy in particular areas to interact with people and make their presence felt.[2] This is sometimes referred to as "community policing", and its use is on the rise in Canada.[3]

§1.12 It is during the investigative stage that the police will question witnesses, detain suspects, conduct searches and seizures, and question suspects. There are complex sets of rules (legislative, common law and constitutional) that provide the legal parameters for each of these important police functions. They are far too involved to summarize here and are dealt with in great detail in Part I of the book. Suffice to say that, on a formal level at least, the police's goal in performing each of these functions is to collect enough evidence to lay a criminal charge.

(2)   Initiating the Process

§1.13 If the police decide that they have sufficient evidence to bring charges — this normally requires reasonable and probable grounds to believe that an indi-

---

[2]   For a judicial recognition that policing in Canada can be both reactive and proactive in nature, see *Brown v. Durham (Regional Municipality) Police Force*, [1998] O.J. No. 5274, 131 C.C.C. (3d) 1 at paras. 66-68 (Ont. C.A.).

[3]   See Curt T. Griffiths, Richard B. Parent & Brian Whitelaw, *Community Policing in Canada* (Scarborough: Nelson Thomson, 2001) at 19, 178-200. See also Paul F. McKenna, *Foundations of Community Policing in Canada* (Toronto: Prentice Hall, 2000) at 294-334.

vidual has committed an offence — they have several options on how to proceed.

§1.14 It is worth noting, however, that simply because the police have the requisite evidence to lay charges does not mean they must. For example, they may want to continue to gather evidence to fortify their case without alerting the target to the fact that he or she is under investigation. There is nothing preventing the police from delaying the formal initiation of the criminal process based on this sort of tactical consideration.

§1.15 In addition, the police have considerable discretion in deciding whether or not to bring formal charges. Even though police may possess the requisite grounds to initiate a prosecution, they may decide against doing so. If the police conclude that a prosecution is not in the public interest, they may choose to forego formal charges and employ more informal means to resolve a particular problem.

§1.16 Quite obviously, the decision not to bring charges will usually be reserved for very minor transgressions of the law. For example, with a youthful first offender caught stealing a small inexpensive item (*i.e.*, a chocolate bar), the police may decide that the better course of action is to issue a warning and alert the young person's parents.[4]

(a)   Compelling Attendance in Court

§1.17 If the police intend to charge someone for a less serious offence and judge that the person is unlikely to commit further offences while awaiting trial and will attend court as required, they may initiate the process without holding the person in custody. Instead of arresting the person to be charged, for example, police may obtain a "summons" from a justice to compel the person to appear in court. Persons who are arrested may be released on the spot after being issued an "Appearance Notice" or "Promise to Appear". Alternatively, arrestees may be released at the police station after giving an "Undertaking" that may include conditions, for example, that they not have any contact with the alleged victim. Each of these documents requires the person to appear in court on a specific date to answer to the charge(s).[5]

(b)   Swearing the Information and Confirming or Issuing Process

§1.18 If the accused is not arrested and held by police, before his or her first court appearance a police officer will "swear the information". This involves the officer taking an oath and confirming that he or she has reasonable and probable

---

[4]   See *Youth Criminal Justice Act*, S.C. 2002, c. 1, Part 1, which specifically contemplates the use of such "extrajudicial measures" for dealing with minor acts of criminal wrongdoing by young people.

[5]   Note that each of the documents discussed in this section may set out more than one charge against an individual and may include multiple instances of one offence (*e.g.*, two or more charges of assault) as well as multiple offences (*e.g.*, two charges of assault and one charge of uttering threats).

grounds to believe that the individual to be charged committed the offence set out in the information.

§1.19 The "information" is the document that formally begins the accused's prosecution. It specifies the charge(s) against the accused and provides particulars of the allegation(s), including the means of commission, the victim's name, and the date and place of the alleged offence(s).

§1.20 The justice receiving the information will then question the officer about the circumstances to confirm that there is enough evidence to support the allegations (*i.e.*, a *prima facie* case). If satisfied that such evidence exists, the justice will confirm the process previously issued by the police (the Appearance Notice, Promise to Appear, or Undertaking) or issue a summons. If the justice concludes the evidence is inadequate, he or she may cancel the process already issued by police (notifying the person not to attend court) or refuse to issue a summons.

§1.21 In some circumstances, for example, where the whereabouts of an accused are not known, the police may wish to secure an arrest warrant for that person. This will enable any police officer who encounters the suspect to arrest him or her. To obtain an arrest warrant, the police must first swear the information. If the justice decides that the evidence is sufficient, he or she will then issue the warrant.

(c) Arrest

§1.22 When the offence is more serious or the police are concerned that the individual to be charged either poses a risk to public safety or will not attend court as required, an arrest will be undertaken. Arrest involves the police actually taking physical control (or custody) over the person of an accused and bringing him or her before the court. To arrest for an indictable offence a police officer must have reasonable and probable grounds to believe that the individual has committed the offence. For summary offences (less serious crimes) a police officer must find the accused in the act of committing the crime to carry out an arrest or alternatively secure an arrest warrant.

§1.23 In cases where an arrest is made without first securing an arrest warrant, the information will be sworn after the individual's arrest but before his or her first court appearance. When a person is arrested without a warrant a justice will *not* question the officer swearing the information regarding the adequacy of the evidence. Instead, the arrestee will be brought before a justice for a bail hearing.

(3) Types of Offences

§1.24 Unlike in the United States, in Canada we no longer speak of criminal offences in terms of "felonies" and "misdemeanours". Our first *Criminal Code*, enacted in 1892,[6] did away with these common law classifications. Today, the

---

[6]   1892, 55-56 Vict., c. 29.

Criminal Code creates three different types of offences: indictable, summary and hybrid.

(a)　Indictable Offences

§1.25 Indictable offences are the most serious in our criminal law. The maximum punishments for these offences can vary, from life imprisonment (*e.g.*, murder), 14 years' imprisonment (*e.g.*, aggravated assault), 10 years' imprisonment (*e.g.*, assault causing bodily harm), five years' imprisonment (*e.g.*, dangerous driving) and two years' imprisonment (*e.g.*, cheating at play).

§1.26 Not only do indictable offences vary in potential punishment, they also vary in applicable procedure depending on which of the three types of indictable offences is charged. For the first (and most common) type, the accused is usually entitled to have a preliminary inquiry and be tried in superior court by a judge and a jury, though he or she may choose other modes of trial (described briefly in Part 2(5)(*b*), below).

§1.27 The second type of indictable offence consists of those listed in section 469 of the *Criminal Code*.[7] These are the most serious crimes known to our law, including murder, treason and (perhaps anachronistically) "alarming Her Majesty". These offences are known as "exclusive jurisdiction" offences because they must be tried in the superior courts of criminal jurisdiction. A superior court judge usually tries exclusive jurisdiction offences with a jury, normally after an accused has had a preliminary inquiry in provincial court.

§1.28 Somewhat confusingly, indictable offences of the third type are known as "absolute jurisdiction" offences. These less serious offences (*e.g.*, theft under $5,000 and keeping a gaming house) are listed in section 553 of the *Criminal Code*. Persons charged with one of these offences have no right to be tried in the superior court (with or without a jury). Instead, they are normally tried in provincial court (where there are no juries) in what is known as a "bench trial".

(b)　Summary Offences

§1.29 Compared to indictable offences, summary offences are less serious (*e.g.*, causing a disturbance and communicating for the purpose of prostitution). They are subject to the distinctive (though broadly similar) procedural rules set out in Part XXVII of the *Criminal Code*. Unless otherwise provided, the maximum punishment for summary offences is six months imprisonment and/or a fine not exceeding $5,000. When charges are dealt with summarily they are normally tried by a provincial court judge presiding alone.

§1.30 Some of the terminology is different when dealing with summary offences as opposed to indictable matters. First, the person charged is referred to as the "defendant" not the "accused".[8] Second, the charging document through-

---

[7]　R.S.C. 1985, c. C-46.
[8]　Note that in other parts of this book we use the terms "accused" and "defendant" interchangeably.

out the proceedings is the information. In contrast, in indictable matters, if the charge is not resolved in provincial court and the case makes its way to superior court then the information is replaced by an "indictment". Finally, with summary matters the person charged is not "acquitted" (the terminology used in indictable cases) but the charge is instead "dismissed".

§1.31 In summary conviction cases, the defendant need not personally appear in court but can instead appear by agent (*e.g.*, a friend, family member, paralegal or lawyer). In indictable matters, the accused must personally appear, except where an accused has followed the procedure necessary to designate counsel to appear on his or her behalf for administrative appearances.[9]

(c) Hybrid Offences

§1.32 The vast majority of crimes are hybrid offences (also known as "dual procedure"). With these offences the Crown may choose whether to proceed summarily or by indictment. How the Crown elects to proceed is entirely a matter within its discretion and will generally not be interfered with by the court.[10] The Crown's election will in turn determine the accused person's trial options, if any. The different options are explained below.

§1.33 The timing of the Crown's election varies from jurisdiction to jurisdiction. In some places, the Crown makes its election on the first appearance. In others, the Crown will often not make its formal election until much later in the proceedings (although it usually informally communicates its intention to the accused early in the proceedings).

§1.34 As noted above, arrest powers vary depending on whether the offence being dealt with is indictable or summary. In short, the police have more expansive arrest powers for the former, and more restrictive powers for the latter. Hybrid offences are deemed to be indictable until the Crown makes its formal election in court.[11] As a result, for hybrid offences police possess the more robust arrest powers reserved for indictable offences.

(4) Intake Procedures

(a) Arraignment within 24 Hours

§1.35 The *Criminal Code* requires that persons arrested and held in police custody be brought before a justice without unreasonable delay, and in any event within 24 hours. Before doing so, police often attempt to interrogate them to obtain self-incriminating statements for use at trial. A failure to bring an accused to court in a timely manner may violate the *Canadian Charter of Rights and*

---

[9]   See *Criminal Code*, R.S.C 1985, c. C-46, s. 650.01.
[10]   See *R. v. Abarca*, [1980] O.J. No. 1581, 57 C.C.C. (2d) 410 (Ont. C.A.).
[11]   See *Interpretation Act*, R.S.C. 1985, c. I-21, s. 34(1)(*a*).

Freedoms,[12] jeopardizing the admissibility of any statements obtained, in more extreme cases, even resulting in a stay (judicial dismissal) of the prosecution.

§1.36 When the accused appears in court he or she will be "arraigned". This means that the charges contained in the information will be read to the accused person.

(b)   Bail Hearing

§1.37 At the bail hearing (also known as "judicial interim release"), a justice decides whether the accused should be released (and if so, on what conditions) pending the determination of the charge. In theory, bail should be addressed at the accused's first court appearance. Unfortunately, delays are common; in some urban areas it may take several appearances for an accused person to have a bail hearing.

§1.38 On a formal level at least, there is a presumption in favour of granting bail for most offences. But for a few (such as murder) that presumption is reversed, requiring the accused to overcome it to be released.

§1.39 Regardless of which presumption applies, the criteria for deciding bail are the same. An individual may be detained pending trial based on any one of three statutorily prescribed grounds. The primary ground is concerned with the likelihood that an accused will attend court to answer to the charge. The secondary ground is directed at the protection or safety of the public, and whether an accused would pose a substantial risk of committing further offences or interfering with the administration of justice if released. The tertiary ground is concerned with maintaining confidence in the administration of justice and is reserved for those relatively rare cases where the offence charged is serious, the Crown has overwhelming evidence making a conviction likely and a very long sentence is inevitable.

§1.40 A justice has wide latitude in deciding how the concerns that animate the bail criteria might be addressed, short of ordering detention. Release can take varying forms, from a release on an undertaking to attend court without conditions, a recognizance with stringent conditions, the use of "sureties" (persons who agree to supervise the accused) and a substantial cash deposit.

(c)   Prosecutorial Discretion

§1.41 At some point, a prosecutor will review the decision by police to lay a charge. The timing of that review varies across Canada. In some provinces this review takes place before an accused person appears in court to answer to the charge. This is referred to as "pre-charge" screening. In most provinces, however, the review occurs after the information is sworn and the accused has appeared in court. This is referred to as "post-charge" screening.

---

[12]   Part I of the *Constitution Act, 1982*, being Schedule B to the *Canada Act 1982* (U.K.), 1982, c. 11.

§1.42 Prosecutors in Canada are independent of the police. Although there are slight differences in the tests used in the provinces to decide whether to prosecute, the main consideration in every jurisdiction is whether or not a conviction is likely. If unlikely, prosecutors are ethically obligated (as "ministers of justice") to bring the prosecution to a halt by withdrawing the charge. Consequently, it is not uncommon for the police to conclude that they possess the requisite grounds to lay a charge but for the charge to nevertheless not be laid or be withdrawn because a prosecutor decides that the evidence is not strong enough to prove the case beyond a reasonable doubt in court.

§1.43 Additionally, even where the evidence is strong enough to prosecute, a prosecutor may decide that a prosecution is simply not in the public interest and decide against prosecuting for this reason. In such circumstances, a prosecutor's withdrawal of charges may be prefaced on requiring an accused person to complete some form of alternative measures, for example, by doing some volunteer work, writing an essay, making a charitable donation, attending for counselling or the like. In youth court proceedings alternative measures of this kind are quite common, especially for first time offenders.

(d) Disclosure

§1.44 At a relatively early stage in the court proceedings (before the accused is called upon to elect the mode of trial, see below) an accused person is entitled to receive, and the Crown has a corresponding duty to provide, disclosure of all relevant information in its possession or under its control relating to the charge. There is a corresponding obligation on the police to deliver all relevant information and materials to the Crown, so that the Crown can fulfill its disclosure obligations.

§1.45 To comply with its obligations the Crown must provide all statements obtained from persons who have provided relevant information to the authorities, even if they are not proposed as Crown witnesses. Where statements do not exist, other information such as notes should be produced. If there are no notes, all information in the prosecution's possession relating to any relevant evidence the person could give should be supplied. The Crown may, however, withhold information over which it claims privilege. Nevertheless, such claims must themselves be disclosed to the defence who can challenge their validity before the trial judge.

§1.46 The prosecution's failure to disclose that which it should may have serious consequences. If the non-disclosure is inadvertent, an adjournment of the proceedings is likely. If deliberate suppression is shown, the prosecution could very well be stayed (*i.e.*, discontinued by order of the court).

(5) Pre-Trial Procedures

(a) The Accused's Election

§1.47 Unless the offence is either one of "exclusive" or "absolute" jurisdiction (see Part 3(*a*), above), an accused charged with an indictable offence (including a hybrid offence that the Crown has elected to try by indictment) may choose his or her mode of trial. Defendants charged with summary conviction offences do not have an election; as mentioned, they are normally tried by a provincial court judge.

§1.48 An accused with an election has three options: (*i*) a bench trial before a provincial court judge; (*ii*) a preliminary inquiry in provincial court, followed by a trial in superior court before a judge and jury; or (*iii*) a preliminary inquiry in provincial court, followed by a trial in superior court before a judge alone.

(b) The Preliminary Inquiry

§1.49 If an accused is charged with an indictable offence and elects to have a preliminary inquiry, it will normally take place before a provincial court judge. Preliminary inquiries serve both charge screening and discovery functions.

§1.50 With respect to the screening function, the Crown must adduce enough evidence to satisfy the judge that a properly instructed jury *could* convict the accused of the offence charged. If the judge is so satisfied, the accused will be "committed" to stand trial on the charge. In effect, the charge will be transferred to superior court for trial. If, on the other hand, the judge is not satisfied that the standard has been met, the accused must be "discharged". In most cases, this effectively ends the prosecution of the charge.

§1.51 At the preliminary inquiry the accused will have the opportunity to cross-examine the Crown's witnesses and call his or her own witnesses to testify. It is in this sense that the preliminary inquiry serves a discovery function, allowing the accused to gain greater insight into the Crown's case.

(c) Pre-Trial Applications

§1.52 Unlike civil litigation, the criminal process is largely self-actuating. After intake procedures are completed, the case will ordinarily be scheduled (or "set-down") for trial. Once a criminal charge is laid, established procedures and the section 11(*b*) *Charter* guarantee of a trial within a reasonable time ensure that the case moves forward to its ultimate conclusion. Thus, with few exceptions (for instance, the accused's election of the mode of trial) the court will not wait for counsel to initiate the next step in the process. If the accused or Crown want something out of the ordinary, they must usually make an application to the court.

§1.53 Pre-trial applications take varying forms. Most common are applications to adjourn the proceedings, call evidence regarding a complainant's prior sexual history, seek the release of an exhibit for forensic testing, sever charges from a multiple count information or indictment, sever accused where more than one accused is charged in the same information or indictment, seek a change of the trial venue to a different jurisdiction, challenge prospective jurors for cause, seek disclosure that the Crown refuses to provide, seek a stay of proceedings based on an allegation of deliberate non-disclosure or abuse of process, exclude evidence at trial based on the allegation that the evidence was obtained in a manner that violated the accused's *Charter* rights, or seek a declaration that the offence charged is unconstitutional. This is not, however, an exhaustive list.

§1.54 Case law usually specifies to whom a particular type of application should be brought. For example, a provincial court judge presiding over a preliminary inquiry lacks jurisdiction to grant a remedy under the *Charter*. As a result, *Charter* applications must usually be brought before the trial judge. At the same time, superior court judges are always said to possess jurisdiction to grant *Charter* remedies, so if the trial court is not yet in sight (for example, the accused's case is still in provincial court awaiting a preliminary inquiry), a *Charter* application may be brought in superior court to alleviate any harm that would be occasioned by delay.

§1.55 The procedural rules governing pre-trial applications, such as those specifying the form of any required notice, prescribing the materials that must be filed in support of different applications and setting down time periods for the filing of notice and supporting materials, are promulgated by the courts, with different rules applicable in the provincial and superior courts of each province.

(6) Plea-bargaining and the Guilty Plea

§1.56 At least formally, the criminal justice system is structured as if a trial on the merits is the means by which criminal charges are resolved. In reality, the vast majority of accused persons (by some estimates more than 90 per cent) plead guilty at some stage in the process, thereby dispensing with the need for a trial and bringing the case to an end. Most guilty pleas result from some type of "plea-bargain" between the person charged and a prosecutor. The term "plea-bargain" refers to any agreement by the accused to plead guilty in return for some promise or benefit.

§1.57 Plea-bargains can vary considerably in their formality and complexity. At one end of the spectrum, the defence lawyer and prosecutor may agree to seek a particular punishment after a short conversation. At the other, plea agreements may be reduced to writing, result in carefully negotiated accounts of the underlying facts, include the reduction or addition of charges and even require the accused to testify against an accomplice.

§1.58 Arguably, no aspect of our contemporary criminal process is more controversial than plea-bargaining. At the same time, the practice is widely accepted because of a firmly entrenched assumption that without considerably greater resources the criminal justice system would grind to a halt without it.

(7) The Trial

§1.59 Absent a guilty plea, a trial will determine whether or not the accused is guilty or not guilty of the charge set out in the information or indictment. In the Canadian criminal justice system there are two closely related and fundamental principles that animate the entire trial process. First, the accused is presumed to be innocent. The presumption of innocence is both statutorily mandated[13] and constitutionally guaranteed.[14] Second, to displace the presumption of innocence, the Crown must prove the accused's guilt beyond a reasonable doubt.

§1.60 As in other common law jurisdictions, Canadian criminal procedure makes a distinction between the "trier of fact" and the "trier of law." It is the "trier of fact" who decides whether or not the prosecution has established its case beyond a reasonable doubt. In a judge alone trial the judge decides both questions of law and questions of fact. In other words, the judge is both the trier of law and the trier of fact.

§1.61 In a jury trial, the judge gives the jury an "instruction" setting out the law. The jury is only concerned with deciding the facts and whether they establish the offence charged as explained by the judge. As a result, in a jury trial, the judge is the trier of law and the jury is the trier of fact.

§1.62 At the beginning of the trial the accused is "arraigned", which as mentioned above entails the formal charges being read aloud. At this point the accused will enter a plea with respect to each charge, normally either "guilty" or "not guilty". If the person charged pleads not guilty to any of the charges the trial will proceed.

§1.63 In a jury trial, the next step is to select a jury of 12 from persons summoned to the court on a random basis. Prospective jurors may be challenged "for cause", which can result in their dismissal on the basis of partiality, for example, because of their exposure to prejudicial pre-trial publicity or bias against members of the accused's race. In addition, each party also has a number of "peremptory challenges", which empowers it to remove prospective jurors without providing a reason. The number of peremptory challenges varies with the seriousness of the offence.

§1.64 After jury selection, the prosecution makes its opening statement, usually providing an overview of the evidence it intends to call and an explanation of what it expects the evidence will prove. Opening statements are less common in bench trials, especially in the provincial court where the proceedings are speedier and less formal.

§1.65 The prosecution then proceeds to call its evidence. Each witness is summoned individually, sworn or affirmed, and then subject to direct questioning by the prosecutor. The defence is then given an opportunity to cross-examine each witness. The Crown is entitled to re-examine the witness with respect to any-

---

[13]   *Criminal Code*, R.S.C. 1985, c. C-46, s. 6(1)(*a*).
[14]   *Canadian Charter of Rights and Freedoms*, Part I of the *Constitution Act, 1982*, being Schedule B to the *Canada Act 1982* (U.K.), 1982, c. 11, s. 11(*d*).

thing new arising from cross-examination. During the examination of witnesses, exhibits may also be introduced. By agreement, the parties can also dispense with the formal proof of facts. Such factual agreements may be stated on the record or reduced to writing and filed as an exhibit.

§1.66 At the completion of the prosecution's case, the defence may bring a motion for a "directed verdict". Such a motion requires the judge to decide, without assessing the credibility of any witnesses, whether the Crown's evidence *could* convince a properly instructed jury acting reasonably to convict the accused of a particular charge. If this minimal burden is not met, the judge will direct a verdict of "not guilty" on that charge.

§1.67 Absent a successful motion for a directed verdict, the defence will be required to decide whether or not it wishes to call any evidence. There is no obligation on the defence to call evidence. If the defence chooses to call evidence the same procedure that applied to Crown witnesses is undertaken in reverse: direct examination by defence counsel, cross-examination by the prosecutor, and re-examination by defence counsel. The accused is entitled to testify in his or her defence but is not obligated to do so. The right of an accused to remain silent at trial is constitutionally protected.[15]

§1.68 At the completion of the evidence each side may make its closing submissions to the trier of fact. If the defence has called evidence it must go first; if not, it may go last. In a jury trial, after final submissions the judge instructs the jury on the law. The jury then retires to the jury room where it will be sequestered until it reaches its verdict. The verdict must be unanimous on each charge. If the jury is unable to agree, a mistrial will be declared and the case may be retried.

§1.69 In a bench trial, a judge may render his or her judgment immediately or after a short adjournment. In either situation the judge is required to give reasons in order to enable meaningful review by an appellate court. Alternatively, the judge may decide to adjourn the case for a longer period to consider his or her verdict and prepare reasons. On the return of the case to court, the judge may either issue written reasons to be read in court and released to the parties or deliver oral reasons from the bench.

(8) Sentencing

§1.70 If the accused is found guilty of the charge he or she will be sentenced as soon as practicable. In Canada, the judge is solely responsible for determining the sentence even where a jury decided guilt or innocence.

§1.71 Judges typically have great flexibility in deciding the appropriate sentence. Normally, the maximum permissible sentence for an offence is set out by the legislative provision that creates it. In theory, judges have the discretion to

---

[15] *Canadian Charter of Rights and Freedoms*, Part I of the *Constitution Act, 1982*, being Schedule B to the *Canada Act 1982* (U.K.), 1982, c. 11, s. 11(*c*).

sentence an offender up to the maximum permitted by law. In practice, this discretion is confined by the principles of sentencing and case law.[16]

§1.72 There are few minimum punishments in Canadian criminal law. Some rare examples include murder (automatic life sentence) and drunk driving (minimum $600 fine). There is, however, a noticeable legislative trend toward increasing the number of minimum sentences.

§1.73 Subject to any prescribed minimum or maximums, judges have a number of sentencing options, including discharging an offender absolutely or conditionally, placing an offender on probation, fining an offender, imprisoning an offender, ordering that a sentence of imprisonment be served intermittently or in the community, prescribing minimum periods of parole ineligibility, and fining an offender or ordering the forfeiture of his or her property.[17]

(9) Appeals

§1.74 The accused may appeal both the finding of guilt and the sentence. Conviction appeals may be based on questions of law, fact, or mixed law and fact. The prosecution may also appeal an acquittal (unlike in the United States) as well as the sentence. Unlike the accused, however, in appeals against acquittals the Crown is restricted to appealing on the basis of questions of law alone.

§1.75 The routes of appeal vary depending on whether the offence is summary or indictable. With the former, the initial appeal is heard by a judge of the superior trial court, with a further appeal to the provincial court of appeal requiring the latter court's leave. With indictable matters, however, an appeal lies directly to the court of appeal in the province. Both summary and indictable matters may be appealed from the court of appeal to the Supreme Court of Canada. Leave from the Supreme Court is required for such appeals unless a judge in the court of appeal dissented on a question of law, in which case the appeal is heard "as of right".

§1.76 A convicted offender sentenced to jail may bring an application for bail pending the determination of his or her appeal. If the offender shows that the proposed appeal has merit, the appeal court will decide the application with reference to the ordinary bail criteria discussed above.

3.   THEORETICAL ACCOUNTS OF THE CRIMINAL PROCESS

§1.77 In addition to understanding the nuts and bolts of the criminal process, it is also useful to view that process from a more theoretical perspective. Although theory simplifies the details of the actual process, it enables us to see larger

---

[16]   Until recently, sentencing principles were found almost exclusively in the case law. Some of the most basic principles have now been codified. See *Criminal Code*, R.S.C. 1985, c. C-46, ss. 718, 718.01, 718.1, 718.2 and 718.21.

[17]   Note, however, that there are limits on how some of these potential punishments may be combined. See Chapter 17, which deals with Sentencing.

themes and trends and measure specific developments against a broader template. In other words, theory supplies a tool that assists us in understanding the entire criminal process, a lens through which one can see beyond specific details or individual cases in order to take in the whole.

(1) Packer: Crime Control vs. Due Process

§1.78 Nearly 50 years ago, Herbert Packer, an American legal scholar, offered what remains the dominant theoretical account of the criminal process. Packer argued that the criminal process is most usefully described as being in a perpetual state of tension as between two competing models or poles, which he defined as the "Crime Control Model" and the "Due Process Model".[18]

§1.79 Packer's models were not meant to describe the criminal justice system in any particular jurisdiction. Instead, they were an attempt to "abstract two separate value systems that compete for attention in the operation of the criminal process".[19] In other words, for Packer, the criminal process is best understood as a series of compromises or choices as between the values that populate the two competing models he defines. In describing these models Packer drew upon two evocative metaphors: the "assembly line" (Crime Control) and the "obstacle course" (Due Process).

§1.80 The Crime Control Model's chief concern is the efficient repression of criminal conduct. Efficiency is optimized through an administrative and managerial approach. Informal fact-finding procedures controlled by police and prosecutors are preferred over formal procedures overseen by the courts. As a result, police should be have broad and largely unfettered powers to detain, search and interrogate suspects, so they can efficiently separate the innocent from the guilty as early as possible in the process. Once they have done so, the system should move the undoubtedly guilty individuals who remain as quickly as possible toward conviction and punishment. Pre-trial release should be rare, as it only serves to discourage the timely resolution of charges by guilty defendants. It is this unceasing focus on efficiency in the processing of the guilty that makes the assembly line metaphor an apt descriptor of the Crime Control Model.

§1.81 The Crime Control Model's emphasis on efficiency in convicting and punishing the guilty also means that evidence that is illegally or unconstitutionally obtained should always be admissible. The search for truth should take precedence over concerns about the manner in which evidence was acquired. Under the Crime Control Model, the criminal process is viewed as an inappro-

---

18 See generally, Herbert L. Packer, "Two Models of the Criminal Process" (1964) 113 U. Pa. L. Rev. 1. See also Herbert L. Packer, *The Limits of the Criminal Sanction* (Stanford: Stanford University Press, 1968).

19 Herbert L. Packer, "Two Models of the Criminal Process" (1964) 113 U. Pa. L. Rev. 1 at 5. It is worth noting, however, that Packer does concede that the legal backdrop he has in mind is the legal system in the United States, in other words, an adversarial system operating with a constitutional bill of rights.

priate forum for identifying and remedying police and prosecutorial misconduct. Criminal trials should not get bogged down with such collateral matters and should instead focus on convicting and punishing the guilty.

§1.82 The emphasis on efficiency also means that whenever possible criminal cases should be resolved by way of guilty pleas thereby avoiding wasteful and time consuming trials. Recall that under the Crime Control Model, the innocent are assumed to have been screened out of the process early on either by police or, failing that, prosecutors.

§1.83 On this view, the need for appellate review is marginal. In general, appeals should be discouraged. After conviction the emphasis should be on swift punishment, not review. Appeals should therefore be restricted to correcting mistakes that are so grossly serious that they undermine the reliability of the verdict.

§1.84 Justice Learned Hand, who penned the following warning nearly 90 years ago, effectively captures the sentiment that informs the Crime Control Model:

> Our dangers do not lie in too little tenderness to the accused. Our procedure has been always haunted by the ghost of the innocent man convicted. It is an unreal dream. What we need to fear is the archaic formalism and the watery sentiment that obstructs, delays, and defeats the prosecution of crime.[20]

§1.85 The Due Process Model is not simply the converse of the Crime Control Model. For example, the Due Process Model does not deny the social desirability of repressing crime. It approaches that goal, however, with an emphasis on a set of values that differs substantially from those that populate the Due Process Model.

§1.86 Unlike the Crime Control Model, which emphasizes efficiency and places great faith in police officers and prosecutors, the Due Process Model is informed by considerable scepticism. First, there is scepticism regarding the utility of the criminal sanction as an instrument for social control. Next, there is scepticism regarding the effectiveness of informal fact-finding procedures and the supposed infallibility of official actors within the criminal justice system. The result is a strong preference for procedures that are both adversarial and judicial in their structure.

§1.87 Under the Due Process Model, the individual who comes up against the apparatus of the criminal justice system is seen as vulnerable and in need of protection from the excesses of those responsible for investigating and prosecuting crime. On this view, the potential for abuse of official power pervades every part of the criminal process, from investigation to appeal. Such abuses may lead to wrongful convictions, *i.e.*, the conviction of a person who did not commit the offence charged. Under the Due Process model, the only antidote to this danger is scrupulously fair procedures. In contrast to the preoccupation with efficiency that informs the Crime Control Model, the Due Process Model is obsessed with quality control. Quality control is achieved by strict adherence to legal rules and

---

[20] *United States v. Garsson*, 291 F. 646 at 649 (N.Y. Dist. Ct. 1923).

procedures that confine, structure and check the exercise of discretion by criminal justice officials, including police officers, prosecutors and judges. Hence, the obstacle course metaphor.

§1.88 The Due Process Model is not solely concerned with preventing wrongful convictions, however. Under this model, "the means" of the criminal process matter just as much as "the ends". "Legal guilt" and "factual guilt" are equally important concerns. Consequently, it is not enough to show that an accused person committed the crime charged, it is also necessary to establish that the process followed in acquiring the evidence and trying the allegation was procedurally sound.

§1.89 Criminal trials are therefore considered appropriate forums to pursue claims of police and prosecutorial misconduct. Sensible remedies for such misconduct include the exclusion of improperly obtained evidence or, in more extreme cases, the dismissal of charges. In addition, because police misconduct does not necessarily lead to criminal charges, other remedies are also required, including tort, internal discipline and robust civilian oversight.

§1.90 Under the Due Process Model trials are not perceived as an undesirable burden. Rather, they are seen as the logical and proper culmination of the criminal process. Guilty pleas, in contrast, are frowned upon for at least two reasons. First, they preclude the discovery and remedying of procedural irregularities. Second, they court the risk that innocent persons might plead guilty to obtain some advantage (such as a more timely resolution of the case or a reduced sentence). Given these dangers, guilty pleas should be rare and be subject to safeguards to ensure that the accused is acting in a voluntary and informed manner.

§1.91 Scepticism also animates the appellate procedures contemplated by the Due Process Model. Convicted defendants should have easy access to appellate relief, including the assistance of counsel on appeal without regard to financial resources. Given the fallibility of everyone involved in the criminal process, including trial courts, appellate courts must be possessed with broad remedial authority to not only correct factual errors but to also vindicate procedural protections.

§1.92 If we were to choose an epigraph for the Due Process Model it would be the oft-quoted claim by Justice Felix Frankfurter that: "The history of liberty is the history of the observance of procedural safeguards."[21]

(2) Packer Under Attack

§1.93 Packer's account of the criminal process as involving a series of choices as between two bipolar models has been subject to increasing criticism over the last 50 years. Although the perspective of critics has varied, the complaints reflect a growing consensus that Packer's models are inadequate.

---

[21]   *McNabb v. United States*, 318 U.S. 332 at 347 (1942), *per* Frankfurter J., dissenting.

(a)   The Empirical Challenge

§1.94 Although writing in the 1960s, Packer insightfully recognized that empiricism was beginning to challenge the view, dominant until then, that the criminal process was fairly described in the formal legal rules that govern the apprehension, screening and trial of persons suspected of crime. For example, Packer acknowledged that the criminal process "consists at least as importantly of patterns of official activity that correspond only in the roughest kind of way to the prescriptions of procedural rules".[22] Beyond this, however, Packer's focus was predominately on the formal rules and how those rules would be differently constituted under the competing models he describes.

§1.95 There has since been an explosion of research examining the gap between the formal legal rules and the realities of criminal justice practices.[23] This research suggests that the gap can sometimes be very wide indeed. As Professor Roach notes, "empirical studies have illustrated that police, prosecutors, judges, and defence counsel share common organizational interests that defy the contrasting ideologies of crime control and due process. These professionals are bureaucrats who habitually cooperate to maximize their own organizational interests, not warriors for crime control or due process."[24]

(b)   Critical Legal Studies: Due Process is for Crime Control

§1.96 Seizing on the empirical research, some Critical Legal Studies scholars have hypothesized that official deviation is no accident. They contend that both courts and legislatures create rules and procedures that are deliberately elastic, providing official actors with considerable discretion that is largely immune from meaningful scrutiny. On this view, the legal rules are little more than cover for what in practice is mostly unchecked power. In other words, they contend, "due process is for crime control".[25]

§1.97 This thesis gained some traction among legal scholars in the immediate aftermath of the *Charter*. On this view, while seeming to limit state action, the *Charter* has actually served an enabling function. It has done so by giving more power to economic and political elites, while reinforcing, if not widening, existing social and economic divisions within Canadian society, all under the cloak of rights rhetoric.[26] On this account, the *Charter* is not "a tool to control the dis-

---

[22]   Herbert L. Packer, "Two Models of the Criminal Process" (1964) 113 U. Pa. L. Rev. 1 at 2.

[23]   See generally, Jerome H. Skolnick, *Justice Without Trial: Law Enforcement in Democratic Society* (New York: MacMillan, 1994). In a Canadian context, see Richard V. Ericson, *Reproducing Order: A Study of Police Patrol Work* (Toronto: University of Toronto Press, 1982); Richard V. Ericson & Patricia M. Baranek, *The Ordering of Justice: A Study of Accused Persons as Dependants in the Criminal Process* (Toronto: University of Toronto Press, 1982); Richard V. Ericson, *Making Crime: A Study of Detective Work* (Toronto: Butterworths, 1981).

[24]   Kent Roach, *Due Process and Victims' Rights: The New Law and Politics of Criminal Justice* (Toronto: University of Toronto Press, 1999) at 20.

[25]   Doreen J. McBarnet, "Arrest: The Legal Context of Policing" in Simon Holdaway & M.R. Chatteron, eds., *The British Police* (London: Arnold, 1979) at 156.

[26]   See Allan C. Hutchison & Andrew Petter, "Private Rights/Public Wrongs: The Liberal Lie of the Charter" (1988) 38 U.T.L.J. 278; Richard V. Ericson, *Making Crime: A Study of Detective*

cretion of government and legal agents, but a means to enable, justify and legitimate their discretionary power."[27]

§1.98 In a Canadian context, the "due process is for crime control" thesis has been criticized for lacking balance. It ignores many due process developments, undeniably beneficial to disadvantaged accused, which were unlikely to have taken place without the *Charter* (for example, the generous right to disclosure established to reduce the risk of wrongful convictions).[28]

(c) Victims' Rights

§1.99 Packer's binary model has also been criticized for conceiving of the criminal process as a binary struggle between the state and the accused. [29] On Packer's account, victims barely merit mention.[30] The historic alienation of victims by the criminal process is now widely acknowledged.[31] Over the past 30 years, scholars and advocacy groups have chronicled this unfairness and advocated for reforms that would place victims' interests on equal footing with concerns about crime control and due process.[32]

§1.100 Many such reforms have been implemented.[33] For example, every province and territory now has some form of victims' rights legislation.[34] Although these Acts vary in content, each requires that victims be kept abreast of developments regarding the investigation or prosecution of their case. Unfortunately, in most provinces there is no enforcement mechanism for these "rights". As one judge noted about Ontario's legislation, "It is nothing more than a statement of government policy wrapped in the language of legislation".[35]

Work (Toronto: University of Toronto Press, 1993) at 11-12, 219; Richard V. Ericson & Kevin D. Haggerty, *Policing the Risk Society* (Toronto: University of Toronto Press, 1997) at 64-66. See also generally, Michael Mandel, *The Charter of Rights and the Legalization of Politics in Canada*, rev. ed. (Toronto: Thompson Educational Publishing, 1994).

[27] Richard V. Ericson, *The Constitution of Legal Inequality* (Ottawa: Carleton University, 1983) at 28.

[28] See James Stribopoulos, "Has the *Charter* Been for Crime Control? Reflecting on 25 Years of Constitutional Criminal Procedure in Canada" in Margaret Beare, ed., *Honouring Social Justice: Honouring Dianne Martin* (Toronto: University of Toronto Press, 2009) at 351.

[29] For a review of the relevant scholarship, see Kent Roach, *Due Process and Victims' Rights: The New Law and Politics of Criminal Justice* (Toronto: University of Toronto Press, 1999) at 26-27.

[30] In his 68-page law review article, Packer mentions the "victim" only twice! See Herbert L. Packer, "Two Models of the Criminal Process" (1964) 113 U. Pa. L. Rev. 1 at 9, 12.

[31] Recognition of this historic shortcoming began in the early 1980s. See *e.g.*, The Honourable Mr. Justice Brian Dickson, "The Forgotten Party – The Victim of Crime" (1984) 18 U.B.C.L. Rev. 319.

[32] See *e.g.*, Douglas Evan Beloof, "The Third Model of Criminal Process: The Victim Participation Model" (1999) Utah L. Rev. 289.

[33] For a review of Canadian developments over the past 30 years, see Joan Barrett, "Expanding Victims' Rights in the Charter Era and Beyond" in Jamie Cameron & James Stribopoulos, eds., *The Charter and Criminal Justice: Twenty-Five Years Later* (Toronto: LexisNexis Canada, 2008) at 627.

[34] See *e.g.*, *Victims' Bill of Rights, 1995*, S.O. 1995, c. 6.

[35] *Vanscoy v. Ontario*, [1999] O.J. No. 1661 at para. 41 (Ont. S.C.J.). In this case, two victims unsuccessfully sued for non-compliance with the *Victims' Bill of Rights, 1995*, S.O. 1995, c. 6,

§1.101 More substantive reforms have also occurred. Many of these have been directed at child victims. For example, child witnesses may now testify behind a protective screen or outside the courtroom via a video link.[36] They may also have a support person present while giving evidence.[37] As well, a videotaped statement made by a child complainant within a reasonable time after the alleged offence is admissible into evidence if the witness adopts its contents while testifying.[38]

§1.102 Other reforms have been aimed at protecting victims of sexual violence. For example, sexual assault complainants now have standing to make representations to courts considering applications for production of their personal records to the accused.[39] In addition, there are now legislated restrictions in place to prevent unjustified questioning of a complainant regarding her prior sexual history[40] or sexual reputation.[41]

§1.103 More generally, courts can now preclude a self-represented accused person from personally conducting the cross-examination of any witness, including the victim.[42]

§1.104 Finally, as part of the sentencing process, victims are now entitled to file and even read a Victim Impact Statement before a court decides on the appropriate sentence for an offender and the court is obligated to inquire whether the

---

alleging that they were not notified of pending court dates and not consulted with respect to plea-bargaining agreements. The Court rejected a *Charter* challenge to s. 2(5) of the Act, which provides that: "No new cause of action, right of appeal, claim or other remedy exists in law because" of the Act. But see *The Victims' Bill of Rights*, C.C.S.M., c. V55, which entitles a victim who feels the Act has not been respected to lodge a complaint with the Director of Prosecutions in the province (s. 28(1)) and obligates the Director of Prosecutions to conduct an investigation and report the results to the victim (s. 28(2) through (5)). A victim who is dissatisfied with the results of that report may seek a review by the provincial Ombudsman (s. 30).

[36] See *Criminal Code*, R.S.C. 1985, c. C-46, s. 486.2. This provision has been upheld as constitutional by the Supreme Court of Canada. See *R. v. Levogiannis*, [1993] S.C.J. No. 70, [1993] 4 S.C.R. 475 (S.C.C.).

[37] See *Criminal Code*, R.S.C. 1985, c. C-46, s. 486.1.

[38] See *ibid.*, s. 715.1. The constitutionality of the predecessor provision was upheld by the Supreme Court of Canada. See *R. v. L. (D.O.)*, [1993] S.C.J. No. 72, [1993] 4 S.C.R. 419 (S.C.C.).

[39] See *Criminal Code*, ss. 278.1 to 278.91, which legislates a protective scheme more robust than that set down by the Supreme Court of Canada at common law in *R. v. O'Connor*, [1995] S.C.J. No. 98, [1995] 4 S.C.R. 411 (S.C.C.). The constitutionality of these provisions was then upheld by the Court, even though they appear to deviate from the criteria set down by the majority judgment in *O'Connor*. See *R. v. Mills*, [1999] S.C.J. No. 68, [1999] 3 S.C.R. 668 (S.C.C.).

[40] See *Criminal Code*, R.S.C. 1985, c. C-46, ss. 276 to 276.5, enacted in response to the Supreme Court of Canada's judgment in *R. v. Seaboyer; R. v. Gayme*, [1991] S.C.J. No. 62, [1991] 2 S.C.R. 577 (S.C.C.), declaring the predecessor provision unconstitutional. These provisions have now been upheld as constitutional by the Supreme Court of Canada. See *R. v. Darrach*, [2000] S.C.J. No. 46, [2000] 2 S.C.R. 443 (S.C.C.).

[41] See *Criminal Code*, R.S.C. 1985, c. C-46, s. 277.

[42] See *ibid.*, s. 486.3. There is a presumption in favour of such an order where the witness is under 18 years of age (s. 486.3(1)) or is the complainant in a criminal harassment prosecution (s. 486(4)) and there is authority to make such an order in all other cases where the court considers it necessary "to obtain a full and candid account from the witnesses of the acts complained of" (s. 486.3(2)).

victim has been apprised of this right.[43] These are all welcome and important reforms.

§1.105 Some commentators contend, however, that the reforms have not gone far enough. The solution, in their view, is to interpret the *Charter* to offer more robust protection for victims' privacy and equality rights.[44] Professor Young goes so far as to suggest that a constitutional amendment might be necessary.[45]

§1.106 At the same time, there are those who argue that victims have already come to wield too much influence over the criminal process.[46] On this view, "a criminal trial is about determining guilt and just punishment of accused, not about personal redress for victims".[47] Constitutionally mandating a greater role for victims, it is feared, "would hopelessly burden and confuse an already over-taxed and under-resourced criminal justice system".[48]

§1.107 Between these two extremes is Professor Roach. He observes that in recent years the interests of victims have often been co-opted by politicians anx-ious to score easy political points with an electorate clamouring for law and or-der. The result, he argues, is the "criminalization of politics", a phenomenon that promotes "the power of the traditional agents of crime control – legislatures, police, and prosecutors – while not necessarily empowering crime victims and potential victims".[49] Exploited in this way, victims' rights are put to work for crime control. As a result, Professor Roach advocates for a new "non-punitive" model of victims' rights, which moves beyond past struggles between due proc-ess and crime control and looks toward a "more holistic integration of criminal justice with social, political, cultural and economic justice".[50] In other words, Professor Roach favours a vision of victims' rights imbued with the conciliatory aims of restorative justice.

(d) Restorative Justice

§1.108 Arguably, the most ambitious challenge to Packer's bipolar account has come from proponents of restorative justice. They reject Packer's claim that the criminal process inevitably entails "a struggle from start to finish".[51] That idea is

---

[43] See *Criminal Code*, R.S.C. 1985, c. C-46, ss. 722 and 722.2.

[44] See *e.g.*, Joan Barrett, "Expanding Victims' Rights in the Charter Era and Beyond" in Jamie Cameron & James Stribopoulos, eds., *The Charter and Criminal Justice: Twenty-Five Years Later* (Toronto: LexisNexis Canada, 2008).

[45] See Alan Young, "Crime Victims and Constitutional Rights" (2005) 49 Crim. L.Q. 432.

[46] See Don Stuart, "Charter Protection against Law and Order: Victims' Rights and Equality Rhetoric" in Jamie Cameron, ed., *The Charter's Impact on the Criminal Justice System* (To-ronto: Carswell, 1996); David M. Paciocco, "Competing Constitutional Rights in an Age of Deference: A Bad Time To Be Accused" (2001) 14 S.C.L.R. (2d) 111; David M. Paciocco, "Why the Constitutionalization of Victim Rights Should Not Occur" (2005) 49 Crim. L.Q. 393.

[47] Don Stuart, *Charter Justice in Canadian Criminal Law*, 4th ed. (Toronto: Thomson Carswell, 2005) at 40.

[48] *Ibid.*, at 41.

[49] Kent Roach, *Due Process and Victims' Rights: The New Law and Politics of Criminal Justice* (Toronto: University of Toronto Press, 1999) at 5.

[50] *Ibid.*, at 8.

[51] Herbert L. Packer, "Two Models of the Criminal Process" (1964) 113 U. Pa. L. Rev. 1 at 2.

at the foundation of Packer's theory of a system in perpetual conflict between irreconcilable poles, with crime control and due process locked in an intractable struggle.

§1.109 Proponents of restorative justice seek a wholesale transformation of our existing criminal justice practices.[52] They favour a move away from the current emphasis on competing legal interests that are negotiated by professional justice system participants preoccupied with notions of retribution, guilt, blame and punishment.

§1.110 As its name implies, the restorative justice approach instead envisions a system that focuses on restoring relationships damaged by crime, including not only victims but also offenders and affected communities. Restorative justice practices aim to bring these constituencies together and make them whole through mutual understanding, accountability, forgiveness and compassion.[53]

§1.111 Restorative justice practices may take a variety of forms. Over the last 20 years, some of these practices have made substantial inroads in Canada.[54] One of the best examples is judges' use of circle sentencing for Aboriginal offenders convicted of serious crimes.[55] Still others are the result of legislated changes, for example, allowing for the diversion of accused persons out of the formal court process and into alternative measures programs.[56]

§1.112 Advocates claim that restorative justice practices may confer benefits on everyone affected by crime. For victims, they offer opportunities to ask questions of the wrongdoer, better understand the cause of the offence, play a role in deciding the outcome and experience reconciliation and healing. For offenders, they provide opportunities to understand the harm caused to the victim, express

---

[52]   See generally, John Braithwaith, *Restorative Justice and Responsive Regulation* (Oxford: Oxford University Press U.S., 2002); Daniel W. Van Ness & Karen Heetderks Strong, *Restoring Justice: An Introduction to Restorative Justice*, 3d ed. (Ohio: Anderson Publishing Co., 2006). For a Canadian perspective, see Law Commission of Canada, *Transforming Relationships through Participatory Justice* (Ottawa: Minister of Public Works and Government Services, 2003).

[53]   See Howard Zehr, *Changing Lenses: A New Focus for Crime and Justice* (Scottdale, Pennsylvania and Waterloo, ON: Herald Press, 1990) at 181, who explains that retributive justice sees crime as "a violation of the state, defined by lawbreaking and guilt" whereas restorative justice "sees things differently. Crime is a violation of people and relationships. It creates obligations to make things right. Justice involves the victim, the offender and the community in a search for solutions which promote repair, reconciliation, and reassurance."

[54]   See generally, Bruce P. Archibald, "Co-ordinating Canada's Restorative and Inclusionary Models of Criminal Justice: the Legal Profession and the Exercise of Discretion under a Reflexive Rule of Law" (2005) 9 Can. Crim. L. Rev. 215.

[55]   Beyond the ordinary courtroom participants (judge, prosecutor, defence lawyer, offender), circle sentencing normally also includes members of the offender's family, the victim and members of his or her family, and members of the community, which can include respected elders. See *R. v. Moses*, [1992] Y.J. No. 50, 71 C.C.C (3d) 347 (Y.T. Terr. Ct.), which is generally recognized as the first sentencing circle undertaken in Canada. The practice has grown ever since. See Heino Lilles, "Circle Sentencing: Part of the Restorative Justice Continuum" in Allison Morris & Gabrielle Maxwell, *Restorative Justice for Juveniles: Conferencing, Mediation and Circles* (Portland, OR: Hart, 2001) at 161.

[56]   In the case of adults, see *Criminal Code*, R.S.C. 1985, c. C-46, s. 717. With respect to youths, see *Youth Criminal Justice Act*, S.C. 2002, c. 1, Part 1, ss. 4 through 12.

remorse, make amends, seek forgiveness and achieve reconciliation, all of which may assist in their rehabilitation and reintegration into the community. And for communities, restorative justice practices provide a forum for people to express their concerns about crime, address offenders directly, reaffirm community values, recognize and redress underlying causes of crime, lay the groundwork for reintegrating the offender and take steps to reduce future criminality.

§1.113 Restorative justice also has its detractors. Perhaps the most searing criticism is that its goals are simply unrealistic, especially for serious crimes. For many victims and their families retribution equals justice.[57] Indeed, much recent psychological research confirms that people have widely-shared and deep-seated retributive intuitions of justice; that is, the view that offenders should be *punished* in proportion to the moral magnitude of their wrongdoing.[58]

4. THE *CHARTER*: A RIGHTS REVOLUTION BEGINS

§1.114 Since its enactment in 1982, the *Charter*[59] has transformed the Canadian legal landscape. Arguably, no area of law has been affected more than criminal procedure. The *Charter*'s legal rights provisions (sections 7 through 14) impose constitutional restraints upon the investigative powers of police, which are supplemented by guarantees aimed at ensuring fair treatment for individuals once they are detained or charged with a crime. These guarantees, combined with express remedial provisions (section 24(1)), including the discretion vested in courts to exclude unconstitutionally obtained evidence (section 24(2)) and to invalidate unconstitutional laws (section 52), have occasioned what has been termed "a due process revolution".[60]

(1) Civil Liberties Before the *Charter*[61]

§1.115 The *Charter* represents such a profound break from the past that what preceded it is often overlooked. Nonetheless, a full understanding the *Charter*'s impact on the criminal process requires a brief look backward. Before 1982, individual rights in Canada were not found in any formal constitutional document. The *British North America Act, 1867*[62] did little more than facilitate Confederation. As its preamble made clear, the new Dominion was to have "a

---

[57]   See Annalise Acorn, *Compulsory Compassion: A Critique of Restorative Justice* (Vancouver: UBC Press, 2004).

[58]   See generally, Kevin M. Carlsmith & John M. Darley, "Psychological Aspects of Retributive Justice", in M.P. Zanna, ed., *Advances in Experimental Social Psychology*, vol. 40 (San Diego, CA: Elsevier, 2008) at 193.

[59]   *Canadian Charter of Rights and Freedoms*, Part I of the *Constitution Act, 1982*, being Schedule B to the *Canada Act 1982* (U.K.), 1982, c. 11.

[60]   Kent Roach, "The Attorney General and the Charter Revisited" (2000) 50 U.T.L.J. 1 at 5. It is a revolution that Roach asserts "has fundamentally altered the law and discourse that governs the criminal process".

[61]   This section draws heavily on James Stribopoulos, "In Search of Dialogue: The Supreme Court, Police Powers, and the *Charter*" (2005) 31 Queen's L.J. 1 at 6-13.

[62]   See the *Constitution Act, 1867* (U.K.), 30 & 31 Vict., c. 3, reprinted in R.S.C. 1985, App. II, No. 5 [previously known as the *British North America Act, 1867*].

Constitution similar in Principle to that of the United Kingdom."[63] In other words, the English tradition of a common law based constitution was to be maintained in Canada.[64]

§1.116 The *Canadian Bill of Rights*[65] of 1960 changed very little. Although it granted several rights to those suspected and accused of crime,[66] as a mere federal enactment it lacked constitutional status. This ultimately undermined its impact, as the judiciary (understandably) felt some uncertainty and ambivalence toward it.[67] Consequently, protection of civil liberties before the *Charter* very much depended on the common law constitution.

§1.117 The English Constitution was said to protect individual liberty through the rule of law. It did so by insisting that any interference with an individual's freedom of movement (or property) be premised on express legal authority.[68] On this approach, "liberty is residual, in the sense that everything which is not expressly forbidden . . . is permitted . . . [with the burden] . . . on the government or public authority to justify coercion".[69]

§1.118 This idea — since labelled the "principle of legality"[70] — has a long history: it can be traced back to Blackstone,[71] *Entick v. Carrington*[72] and the *Magna Carta*.[73] It spawned a rule of statutory construction requiring that any legislative encroachment on an individual's historic common law rights of liberty or property be set out "plainly, if not in express words at least by clear implication and beyond reasonable doubt".[74] Accordingly, ambiguities were to be resolved in favour of the individual.[75]

---

[63]   *Ibid.*

[64]   See *Manitoba (Attorney General) v. Canada (Attorney General); Canada (Attorney General) v. Newfoundland (Attorney General); Quebec (Attorney General) v. Canada (Attorney General)*, [1981] S.C.J. No. 58, [1981] 1 S.C.R. 753 at 805 (S.C.C.). See generally, Peter W. Hogg, *Constitutional Law of Canada*, 4th ed., vol. 1 (Toronto: Carswell, 1997) at 1-2 to 1-5.

[65]   *Canadian Bill of Rights*, S.C. 1960, c. 44, R.S.C. 1985, Appendix III [*Canadian Bill of Rights*].

[66]   *Ibid.*, s. 1(*a*), and the various subsections within s. 2.

[67]   See *R. v. Therens*, [1985] S.C.J. No. 30, [1985] 1 S.C.R. 613 at 638-39 (S.C.C.), *per* LeDain J. (explaining this experience). As Professor Tarnopolsky noted, the response of the courts to the *Bill* was "to ignore or explain away its existence." See Walter Surma Tarnopolsky, *The Canadian Bill of Rights*, 2d ed. (Toronto: McClelland & Stewart, 1975) at 14.

[68]   As Dicey explained: "The right to personal liberty as understood in England means in substance a person's right not to be subjected to imprisonment, arrest, or other physical coercion in any manner that does not admit of legal justification." See Albert V. Dicey, *Introduction to the Study of the Law of the Constitution*, 10th ed. (London: Macmillan, 1961) at 207-208. Elsewhere in his text Dicey drew no distinction between a man's "body or goods". *Ibid.*, at 188.

[69]   T.R.S. Allan, "Constitutional Rights and Common Law" (1991) 11 Oxford J. Legal Stud. 453 at 457.

[70]   See Leonard Herschel Leigh, *Police Powers in England and Wales*, 2d ed. (London: Butterworths, 1985) at 32-33.

[71]   See William Blackstone, *Commentaries on the Laws of England, A Facsimile of the First Edition of 1765-1769*, vol. 1 (Chicago: University of Chicago Press, 1979) at 130-31.

[72]   (1765), 19 State Trials 1029 at 1067, 95 E.R. 807.

[73]   See *Magna Carta*, 9 Hen. III, c. 29, art. 39.

[74]   Roy Wilson & Brian Galpin, *Maxwell on the Interpretation of Statutes*, 10th ed. (London: Sweet & Maxwell, 1953) at 286. Wilson & Galpin have collected numerous cases at 275-78.

[75]   See also Sir Rupert Cross, John Bell & Sir George Engle, *Statutory Interpretation*, 3d ed. (London: Butterworths, 1995) at 165-66, 175-80. See *e.g.*, *Morris v. Beardmore*, [1981] A.C. 446 at

§1.119 The rule of law, including the principle of legality, was imported into Canada along with the rest of the English common law constitution.[76] Most famously, it undergirded the Supreme Court of Canada's celebrated civil liberties decisions of the 1950s, in which the Court stood against the persecution of Jehovah's Witnesses by the Duplessis government in Quebec.[77] These cases made clear that in Canada, as in England, "[n]o public officer has any power beyond what the law confers upon him . . . the law puts a definite boundary around each official beyond which he acts at his peril."[78]

§1.120 Just like courts in England, the Supreme Court of Canada built on the principle of legality by adopting a rule of strict construction for statutes that limit individual rights. It recognized "that if real ambiguities are found, or doubts of substance arise . . . then that statute should be applied in such a manner as to favour the person against whom it is sought to be enforced."[79] This rule

---

455, 461-63, (H.L.). More recently, see *R. v. Secretary of State for the Home Department; Ex parte Simms*, [2000] 2 A.C. 115 at 130 (H.L.). Exceptions were occasionally made. For example, the House of Lords cited national security in agreeing to relax this principle in interpreting a wartime regulation. This move was met with a strongly worded, and now celebrated, dissent by Lord Atkin. He reminded the other judges that it is their function, in times of war or peace, to "stand between the subject and any attempted encroachments on his liberty by the executive, alert to see that any coercive action is justified in law". *Liversidge v. Anderson*, [1942] A.C. 206 at 244 (H.L). As Lord Diplock later observed, "the time has come to acknowledge openly that the majority of this House in *Liversidge v. Anderson* were expediently and, at the time, perhaps, excusably, wrong and the dissenting speech of Lord Atkin was right." *R. v. Inland Revenue Commissioners; Ex parte Rossminster*, [1980] A.C. 952 at 1011 (H.L.). Lord Atkin's statement regarding the function of courts within the English constitutional system more generally has been repeatedly reaffirmed by English judges. See *e.g.*, *R. v. Home Secretary; Ex parte Khawaja*, [1984] A.C. 74 at 110-11 (H.L.).

[76] It was much later, however, before the Supreme Court expressly acknowledged that, "the principle of the rule of law is clearly a principle of our Constitution." See *Reference re: Manitoba Language Rights*, [1985] S.C.J. No. 36, [1985] 1 S.C.R. 721 at 751 (S.C.C.). See also *Manitoba (Attorney General) v. Canada (Attorney General); Canada (Attorney General) v. Newfoundland (Attorney General); Quebec (Attorney General) v. Canada (Attorney General)*, [1981] S.C.J. No. 58, [1981] 1 S.C.R. 753 at 805 (S.C.C.); *Reference re Secession of Quebec*, [1998] S.C.J. No. 61, [1998] 2 S.C.R. 217 at 247-63 (S.C.C.).

[77] See *Chaput v. Romain*, [1955] S.C.J. No. 61, [1955] S.C.R. 834 (S.C.C.); *Lamb v. Benoît*, [1959] S.C.J. No. 13, [1959] S.C.R. 321 (S.C.C.); *Roncarelli v. Duplessis*, [1959] S.C.J. No. 1, [1959] S.C.R. 121 (S.C.C.).

[78] Frank R. Scott, *Civil Liberties and Canadian Federalism* (Toronto: University of Toronto Press, 1959) at 48.

[79] *Marcotte v. Canada (Deputy Attorney General)*, [1974] S.C.J. No. 142, [1976] 1 S.C.R. 108 at 115 (S.C.C.). In more recent years this principle has been circumscribed. Under the contemporary approach to statutory interpretation, textual ambiguities are to be resolved in favour of the individual only after the provision is read in light of its legislative context and purpose. See *Bell ExpressVu Limited Partnership v. Rex*, [2002] S.C.J. No. 43, [2002] 2 S.C.R. 559 at para. 26 (S.C.C.); *R. v. Paré*, [1987] S.C.J. No. 75, [1987] 2 S.C.R. 618 (S.C.C.).

of construction was not limited to cases involving individual liberty,[80] but was applied equally where property rights alone were implicated.[81]

§1.121 Unfortunately, reliance on the principle of legality to safeguard civil liberties suffered from two serious shortcomings. First, provided it did so in clear and precise terms, Parliament was free to legislate away freedom, and on occasion it did just that.[82] Second, given that illegally obtained evidence was almost always admissible,[83] the vindication of rights depended on civil suits and police complaint procedures. A combination of high costs and low damage awards deterred most potential civil claimants.[84] In addition, those most likely to be affected by police abuses were also the least likely to have the wherewithal to pursue a civil action or a formal complaint.[85] As a result, in situations where the principle of legality was violated there was rarely any remedy for the affected individual.

(2) The *Charter*: The Legal Rights Guarantees and Their Purpose

§1.122 The *Charter* occasioned a sea change by recognizing basic constitutional rights and coupling these guarantees to express remedial provisions. The practical implications for the criminal justice system of this shift cannot be over-

---

[80] For cases invoking the principle to protect liberty interests, see *Marcotte v. Canada (Deputy Attorney General)*, [1974] S.C.J. No. 142, [1976] 1 S.C.R. 108 (S.C.C.); *R. v. Noble*, [1977] S.C.J. No. 68, [1978] 1 S.C.R. 632 at 638 (S.C.C.); *Beatty v. Kozak*, [1958] S.C.J. No. 9, [1958] S.C.R. 177 at 190 (S.C.C.), affg [1957] S.J. No. 1, 7 D.L.R. (2d) 88 (Sask. C.A.); *Shim v. R.*, [1938] S.C.J. No. 16, [1938] S.C.R. 378 at 380-81 (S.C.C.).

[81] For cases invoking the principle to protect property interests, see *Costello v. Calgary (City)*, [1983] S.C.J. No. 4, [1983] 1 S.C.R. 14 at 21-27 (S.C.C.); *R. v. Colet*, [1981] S.C.J. No. 2, [1981] 1 S.C.R. 2 at 10 (S.C.C.); *Laidlaw v. Toronto (Metropolitan)*, [1978] S.C.J. No. 32, [1978] 2 S.C.R. 736 at 748 (S.C.C.); *Prince George (City) v. Payne*, [1977] S.C.J. No. 53, [1978] 1 S.C.R. 458 at 463 (S.C.C.); *Wells v. Newfoundland*, [1999] S.C.J. No. 50, [1999] 3 S.C.R. 199 at 218 (S.C.C.).

[82] The most obvious examples involve the invocation of the *War Measures Act*, R.S.C. 1927, c. 206 to intern persons "of the Japanese race" during the Second World War. Its use for these purposes was upheld: see *Co-Operative Committee on Japanese Canadians v. Canada (Attorney General)*, [1946] J.C.J. No. 3, [1947] A.C. 87 (P.C.).

[83] See *R. v. Wray*, [1970] S.C.J. No. 80, [1971] S.C.R. 272 at 293 (S.C.C.), recognizing a very narrow discretion to exclude evidence. See also *R. v. Hogan*, [1974] S.C.J. No. 116, [1975] 2 S.C.R. 574 at 584 (S.C.C.), rejecting the exclusion of evidence as a remedy for violations of the *Canadian Bill of Rights*, S.C. 1960, c. 44, R.S.C. 1985, Appendix III. There were only two real exceptions: (*i*) the exclusion of involuntary confessions (see *R. v. Boudreau*, [1949] S.C.J. No. 10, [1949] S.C.R. 262 (S.C.C.)); and (*ii*) a legislated requirement that in order for wiretap evidence to be admissible it had to be lawfully obtained (see *Criminal Code*, R.S.C. 1970, c. C-34, s. 178.16(1)(*a*)).

[84] See Paul C. Weiler, "The Control of Police Arrest Practices: Reflections of a Tort Lawyer" in Allen M. Linden, ed., *Studies in Canadian Tort Law* (Toronto: Butterworths, 1968) 416 at 448-49.

[85] Paul C. Weiler, "The Control of Police Arrest Practices: Reflections of a Tort Lawyer" in Allen M. Linden, ed., *Studies in Canadian Tort Law* (Toronto: Butterworths, 1968) 416 at 462. See also Andrew Goldsmith, "Necessary But Not Sufficient: The Role of Public Complaints Procedures in Police Accountability" in Philip C. Stenning, ed., *Accountability for Criminal Justice: Selected Essays* (Toronto: University of Toronto Press, 1995) 110 at 124.

stated. The legal rights guarantees set down minimum constitutional requirements for both the investigative and adjudicative phases of the criminal process.
These guarantees demand a basic level of fairness for those suspected or accused
of crime. The *Charter* is not, however, the sum total of criminal process rights in
Canada. As the Supreme Court has explained, "it represents a bare minimum
below which the law must not fall. A necessary corollary of this statement is that
the law, whether by statute or common law, can offer protections beyond those
guaranteed by the *Charter*."[86]

§1.123 The starting point is section 7 of the *Charter*. It guarantees to "everyone" the "right to life, liberty and security of the person and the right not to be
deprived thereof except in accordance with the principles of fundamental justice." Section 7 is the gateway to the other legal rights guarantees. The Supreme
Court of Canada has explained that these other provisions (sections 8 through
14) build upon section 7 by addressing "specific deprivations of the 'right' to
life, liberty and security of the person in breach of the principles of fundamental
justice, and as such, violations of s. 7."[87] This does not mean that the specific
guarantees in sections 8 through 14 exhaust the content of the principles of fundamental justice. Rather, the Court has repeatedly held that unless a claim falls
squarely within a very specific guarantee in sections 8 through 14, additional
protection may still be found in section 7. Under this "residual theory" of section
7, what the principles of fundamental justice require may exceed the specific
guarantees contained in sections 8 through 14.[88]

§1.124 Consequently, section 7 looms in the background of all legal rights
claims, supplying an overarching guarantee of both substantive and procedural
fairness.[89] Nevertheless, from a practical standpoint it is the specific guarantees
that are usually most important.

§1.125 The investigative process rights are set out in section 8 ("the right to be
secure against unreasonable search or seizure"), section 9 ("the right not to be
arbitrarily detained or imprisoned") and section 10 (rights triggered on arrest or
detention, including "(*a*) to be informed promptly of the reasons therefor; (*b*) to
retain and instruct counsel without delay and to be informed of that right; and (*c*)

[86] *R. v. Oickle*, [2000] S.C.J. No. 38, [2000] 2 S.C.R. 3 at para. 31 (S.C.C.).
[87] *Reference re Motor Vehicle Act (British Columbia)*, [1985] S.C.J. No. 73, [1985] 2 S.C.R. 486
at 502 (S.C.C.).
[88] *R. v. Lyons*, [1987] S.C.J. No. 62, [1987] 2 S.C.R. 309 at 353-54 (S.C.C.); *Thomson Newspapers Ltd. v. Canada (Director of Investigation and Research, Restrictive Trade Practices Commission)*, [1990] S.C.J. No. 23, [1990] 1 S.C.R. 425 at 536-39 (S.C.C.); *R. v. Hebert*, [1990]
S.C.J. No. 64, [1990] 2 S.C.R. 151 at 162-64, 176-78 (S.C.C.); *R. v. Généreux*, [1992] S.C.J.
No. 10, [1992] 1 S.C.R. 259 at para. 102 (S.C.C.); *R. v. Morales*, [1992] S.C.J. No. 98, [1992] 3
S.C.R. 711 at 727 (S.C.C.); *R. v. Pearson*, [1992] S.C.J. No. 99, [1992] 3 S.C.R. 665 at 682-89
(S.C.C.); *Dehghani v. Canada (Minister of Employment and Immigration)*, [1993] S.C.J. No.
38, [1993] 1 S.C.R. 1053 at 1076 (S.C.C.); *R. v. Rose*, [1998] S.C.J. No. 81, [1998] 3 S.C.R.
262 at 315 (S.C.C.).
[89] See *Reference re Motor Vehicle Act (British Columbia)*, [1985] S.C.J. No. 73, [1985] 2 S.C.R.
486 at 498-504, 511-13 (S.C.C.), wherein the Court rejected the view that "the principles of
fundamental justice" are synonymous with "natural justice" or "procedural due process" only,
thereby opening the door to substantive review of legislation under s. 7.

to have the validity of the detention determined by way of *habeas corpus* and to be released if the detention is not lawful.")

§1.126 With respect to the adjudicative process, there are a host of rights guaranteed by section 11 to ensure fair treatment for "any person charged with an offence", including:

(*a*) to be informed without unreasonable delay of the specific offence;

(*b*) to be tried within a reasonable time;

(*c*) not to be compelled to be a witness in proceedings against that person in respect of the offence;

(*d*) to be presumed innocent until proven guilty according to law in a fair and public hearing by an independent and impartial tribunal;

(*e*) not to be denied reasonable bail without just cause;

(*f*) except in the case of an offence under military law tried before a military tribunal, to the benefit of trial by jury where the maximum punishment for the offence is imprisonment for five years or a more severe punishment;

(*g*) not to be found guilty on account of any act or omission unless, at the time of the act or omission, it constituted an offence under Canadian or international law or was criminal according to the general principles of law recognized by the community of nations;

(*h*) if finally acquitted of the offence, not to be tried for it again and, if finally found guilty and punished for the offence, not to be tried or punished for it again; and

(*i*) if found guilty of the offence and if the punishment for the offence has been varied between the time of commission and the time of sentencing, to the benefit of the lesser punishment.

§1.127 There is also a right guaranteed in section 13 to testimonial "use immunity" for witnesses. It provides that a witness "has the right not to have any incriminating evidence so given used to incriminate the witness in any other proceedings, except in a prosecution for perjury or for the giving of contradictory evidence".

§1.128 A party or witness who does not "understand or speak the language in which the proceedings are conducted or who is deaf" is also conferred the right under section 14 "to the assistance of an interpreter".

§1.129 Finally, section 12 grants to everyone "the right not to be subjected to any cruel or unusual treatment or punishment".

§1.130 The constitutional guarantees found in the *Charter* are not, however, absolute. Beyond internal qualifiers within specific guarantees (for example, "unreasonable" in section 8 or "arbitrarily" in section 9), every right or freedom in the *Charter* may also be subject to any further limitations that the government is able to justify under section 1.[90] That section provides that the rights and free-

---

[90] Limitations on some *Charter* rights, however, may be extremely difficult to justify. For example, in *Reference re Motor Vehicle Act (British Columbia)*, [1985] S.C.J. No. 73, [1985] 2

doms guaranteed by the *Charter* are subject "to such reasonable limits prescribed by law as can be demonstrably justified in a free and democratic society".[91]

§1.131 As the pre-*Charter* experience illustrates, rights are hollow without meaningful remedies. The *Charter*'s full effect can only be understood by remembering the generous remedial authority it confers on courts. First, there is the express declaration in the *Constitution Act, 1982*[92] that it is the "supreme law of Canada, and any law that is inconsistent with the provisions of the Constitution is, to the extent of the inconsistency, of no force or effect". The *Charter* is part of the *Constitution Act, 1982*, so its status as part of Canada's supreme law is similarly entrenched.

§1.132 That general statement of constitutional supremacy is then combined with express remedial powers. Where a *Charter* right or freedom has been infringed or denied, there is authority vested in courts of "competent jurisdiction" under section 24(1) to grant any remedy "the court considers appropriate and just in the circumstances". As Justice McIntyre put it: "It is difficult to imagine language which could give the court a wider and less fettered discretion."[93]

§1.133 Section 24(2) of the *Charter* also specifically empowers courts to exclude unconstitutionally obtained evidence if satisfied that, "having regard to all the circumstances, the admission of it in the proceedings [could] bring the administration of justice into disrepute." This discretionary exclusionary power positions the *Charter* in the middle ground between the conflicting extremes of Packer's due process and crime control poles.

§1.134 The due process revolution occasioned by the *Charter* is the direct result of its legal rights guarantees and its generous remedial provisions. Because of them, the protection of civil liberties in Canada has grown well beyond the

---

S.C.R. 486 at para. 83 (S.C.C.), the Supreme Court of Canada suggested that a violation of s. 7 could only be justified under s. 1 in "exceptional conditions such as natural disasters, the outbreak of war, epidemics, and the like". See also *R. v. Heywood*, [1994] S.C.J. No. 101, [1994] 3 S.C.R. 761 at paras. 71-72 (S.C.C.). This reluctance also extends to s. 8, where the courts have noted that it would be very difficult to justify an "unreasonable" search or seizure as a "reasonable limit...in a free and democratic society". See *Lavallee, Rackel & Heintz v. Canada (Attorney General); White, Ottenheimer & Baker v. Canada (Attorney General); R. v. Fink*, [2002] S.C.J. No. 61, [2002] 3 S.C.R. 209 at para. 46 (S.C.C.); *Baron v. Canada*, [1993] S.C.J. No. 6, [1993] 1 S.C.R. 416 at 453 (S.C.C.); *Hunter v. Southam (sub nom. Canada (Combines Investigation Acts, Director of Investigation and Research) v. Southam Inc.)*, [1984] S.C.J. No. 36, [1984] 2 S.C.R. 145 at 169-70 (S.C.C.) [*Hunter v. Southam*]; *R. v. Noble*, [1984] O.J. No. 3395, 16 C.C.C. (3d) 146 at para. 59 (Ont. C.A.).

91 The Supreme Court has prescribed a test for assessing whether encroachments on *Charter* protected rights or freedoms are justifiable under s. 1. The test has two parts. First, the objective that the limitation is designed to serve must be sufficiently important to warrant overriding a constitutionally protected right or freedom. Next, the measures must meet a proportionality requirement. This requires that: (*i*) the measures adopted must be rationally connected to the objective; (*ii*) the means chosen should impair as little as possible the right or freedom in question; and (*iii*) the measures' *Charter*-limiting effects must be proportionate to the importance of the legislative objective. See *R. v. Oakes*, [1986] S.C.J. No. 7, [1986] 1 S.C.R. 103 (S.C.C.).

92 *Constitution Act, 1982*, being Schedule B to the *Canada Act 1982* (U.K.), 1982, c. 11, s. 52.

93 *R. v. Mills*, [1986] S.C.J. No. 39, [1986] 1 S.C.R. 863 at para. 279 (S.C.C.).

minimal protection provided by the principle of legality at common law. Today, Canadian courts are empowered to do two extraordinarily important things that were not possible before the *Charter*. First, courts can now assess the adequacy of legislative enactments that interfere with fundamental individual rights (for example, liberty and privacy) against minimum constitutional standards. If the impugned legislation falls below the *Charter*'s basic requirements and cannot be justified under section 1, then the offending law must be declared unconstitutional. Second, criminal trial courts are now authorized to scrutinize investigations and prosecutions and ensure that they meet basic constitutional standards. Consequently, the means by which the police acquire the evidence against an accused person can be challenged in individual cases and if a rights violation is made out the evidence may be excluded.

§1.135 When it comes to the day-to-day operation of the criminal justice system, permitting the exclusion of unconstitutionally obtained evidence is hugely significant. Without a potential exclusionary remedy, in the pre-*Charter* days, criminal defendants had little incentive to bring official abuses to light. This led to a widely held view that Canadian police rarely violated the law in discharging their duties.[94] Following the *Charter*'s enactment, however, the large number of cases brought forward seeking the exclusion of unconstitutionally obtained proved otherwise. As Professor Yves-Marie Morissette has pointed out, "the irregular methods must have existed on a similar and perhaps even greater scale before . . . . In this regard, the *Charter* has been an eye-opener."[95]

§1.136 That said, explaining the *Charter*'s revolutionary effects with reference only to its contents would tell only half of the story. The judiciary's attitude toward the document has been at least as important. Had Canada's judges taken a narrow and legalistic view of the *Charter*'s provisions (as some judges did early on[96]), they would have undoubtedly stifled its full due process potential. But unlike their response to the *Canadian Bill of Rights*,[97] judges embraced the *Charter*. In doing so, they followed the lead taken by the Supreme Court of Canada in its 1984 decision of *Hunter v. Southam*,[98] the first of the Court's decisions interpreting section 8. Speaking for a unanimous Court, Chief Justice Dickson observed that when a constitution is combined with a Bill of Rights, "[i]ts function is to provide a continuing framework . . . for the unremitting pro-

---

[94] See *e.g.*, J.L. Clendenning, "Police Power and Civil Liberties" (1966) 4 Osgoode Hall L.J. 174 at 185.

[95] Yves-Marie Morissette, "The Exclusion of Evidence Under the *Canadian Charter of Rights and Freedoms*: What to Do and What Not to Do" (1984) 29 McGill L.J. 521 at 535.

[96] See *e.g.*, *R. v. Altseimer*, [1982] O.J. No. 3480, 1 C.C.C. (3d) 7 (Ont. C.A), where Zuber J., at para. 20, in a now famous quote, remarked "that the *Charter* does not intend a transformation of our legal system or the paralysis of law enforcement".

[97] See Part 4(1), above, in particular §1.116.

[98] *Hunter v. Southam (sub nom. Canada (Combines Investigation Acts, Director of Investigation and Research) v. Southam Inc.)*, [1984] S.C.J. No. 36, [1984] 2 S.C.R. 145 (S.C.C.).

tection of individual rights and liberties."[99] Under such a system, he noted, "[t]he judiciary is the guardian of the constitution."[100]

§1.137 The Chief Justice then explained how the *Charter*'s guarantees should be interpreted.[101] He began by reaffirming the "living tree" analogy (which pre-dated the *Charter*)[102] indicating that the Constitution was "capable of growth and development over time to meet new social, political and historical realities often unimagined by its framers,"[103] — a goal which required a "broad, purposive analysis".[104] Before expanding on what this interpretive approach entails, Chief Justice Dickson made the following crucial observation:

> I begin with the obvious. The *Canadian Charter of Rights and Freedoms* is a purposive document. Its purpose is to guarantee and to protect, within the limits of reason, the enjoyment of the rights and freedoms it enshrines. It is intended to constrain governmental action inconsistent with those rights and freedoms; it is not in itself an authorization for governmental action. In the present case this means . . . that in guaranteeing the right to be secure from unreasonable searches and seizures, s. 8 acts as a limitation on whatever powers of search and seizure the federal or provincial governments already and otherwise possess. It does not in itself confer any powers, even of "reasonable" search and seizure, on these governments.[105]

§1.138 The Court then went on to explain the "purposive" interpretive approach for understanding particular *Charter* guarantees,[106] which it elaborated upon further in later cases.[107] Under this method, dictionary definitions are to be avoided. Instead, the words used are to be read in a manner that best achieves the purpose underlying the guarantee. In identifying that purpose, the court may look to the larger objectives of the *Charter*, the actual language used to express the right, the historical origins of the guarantee (including its drafting history) and its interrelationship to the other constitutional provisions. The Supreme Court has instructed that, ultimately, the interpretation should be "a generous rather than a

---

[99]   *Ibid.*, at 155 (S.C.R.).

[100] *Ibid.*

[101] *Ibid.*

[102] *Ibid.*, at 155-56 (S.C.R.). The "living tree" metaphor began its ascent into Canadian constitutional law under the *British North America Act* (see the *Constitution Act, 1867* (U.K.), 30 & 31 Vict., c. 3, reprinted in R.S.C. 1985, App. II, No. 5). See *Reference re: British North America Act, 1867 s. 24*, [1929] J.C.J. No. 2, [1930] A.C. 124 at 136 (P.C.), *per* Viscount Sankey. By maintaining this approach under the *Charter*, the Court closed the door on the future use of American theories of interpretation like "original intent" and "original understanding." See Ian Binnie, "Constitutional Interpretation and Original Intent" (2004) 23 Sup. Ct. L. Rev. 345.

[103] *Hunter v. Southam (sub nom. Canada (Combines Investigation Acts, Director of Investigation and Research) v. Southam Inc.)* [1984] S.C.J. No. 36, [1984] 2 S.C.R. 145 at 155 (S.C.C.).

[104] *Ibid.*, at 156 (S.C.R.).

[105] *Ibid.*, at 156-57 (S.C.R.).

[106] *Ibid.*, at 157 (S.C.R.). The Court identified the protection of reasonable privacy expectations as the purpose of s. 8.

[107] See generally, *R. v. Big M Drug Mart Ltd.*, [1985] S.C.J. No. 17, [1985] 1 S.C.R. 295 at 344 (S.C.C.); *R. v. Therens*, [1985] S.C.J. No. 30, [1985] 1 S.C.R. 613 at 641 (S.C.C.); *Reference re Motor Vehicle Act (British Columbia)*, [1985] S.C.J. No. 73, [1985] 2 S.C.R. 486 at 500-501 (S.C.C.). See also Peter W. Hogg, "The Charter of Rights and American Theories of Interpretation" (1987) 25 Osgoode Hall L. J. 87 at 102-104.

legalistic one, aimed at fulfilling the purpose of the guarantee and securing for individuals the full benefit of the *Charter*'s protection."[108] At the same time, the Court has cautioned that "it is important not to overshoot the actual purpose of the right or freedom in question, but to recall that the *Charter* was not enacted in a vacuum, and must therefore ... be placed in its proper linguistic, philosophic and historical contexts".[109]

§1.139 The passage from *Hunter v. Southam* reproduced above also made clear that the *Charter* and its legal rights provisions (in particular sections 8 and 9), impose limits on, and are not sources of, police powers. In making this critical observation about the *Charter*'s purpose, the Court implicitly reaffirmed the continued importance of the principle of legality.

§1.140 In subsequent cases, the Supreme Court of Canada has summed up the overarching purpose of the legal rights guarantees in starkly due process terms. For example, in *R. v. Hebert*,[110] Justice McLachlin (as she then was), observed for the Court that "it is to the control of the superior power of the state *vis-à-vis* the individual who has been detained by the state, and thus placed in its power, that section 7 and the related provisions that follow are primarily directed."[111] Even more emphatic was Justice Wilson's claim that these provisions are "designed *inter alia* to circumscribe [the] coercive powers of the state within the boundaries of justice and fairness to the individual. They are the most formidable defences the individual can marshal against abuses of state power."[112]

§1.141 The *Charter*'s extensive and specific effects on the criminal investigative and adjudicative processes are dealt with in detail in the chapters that follow. Before addressing its various impacts, however, there are a few more matters relating to its general application that warrant mention in this introduction.

(3) Application of the *Charter*

(a) Generally

§1.142 Section 32(1) of the *Charter* provides that the *Charter* applies "to the Parliament and government of Canada"[113] and "to the legislature and government

---

[108] *R. v. Big M Drug Mart Ltd.*, [1985] S.C.J. No. 17, [1985] 1 S.C.R. 295 at 344 (S.C.C.).
[109] *Ibid.* More recently, see *R. v. Grant*, [2009] S.C.J. No. 32 at para. 17, [2009] 2 S.C.R. 353 (S.C.C.) explaining that "while the twin principles of purposive and generous interpretation are related and sometimes conflated, they are not the same The purpose of a right must always be the dominant concern in its interpretation; generosity of interpretation is subordinate to and constrained by that purpose .... While a narrow approach risks impoverishing a *Charter* right, an overly generous approach risks expanding its protection beyond its intended purposes."
[110] [1990] S.C.J. No. 64, [1990] 2 S.C.R. 151 (S.C.C.).
[111] *Ibid.*, at 179 (S.C.R.).
[112] *R. v. DeBot*, [1989] S.C.J. No. 118, [1989] 2 S.C.R. 1140 at 1173 (S.C.C.), Wilson J., concurring.
[113] *Canadian Charter of Rights and Freedoms*, Part I of the *Constitution Act, 1982*, being Schedule B to the *Canada Act 1982* (U.K.), 1982, c. 11, s. 32(1)(a).

of each province".[114] Legislation is of course the principal means by which governments act. As a result, all legislation must comply with the *Charter*. A legislative enactment that fails to do so and that cannot be justified under section 1 is unconstitutional. Faced with such a law, a court would be required to declare it of no force or effect under section 52(1) of the *Constitution Act, 1982*.[115]

§1.143 Quite obviously, legislation alone does not constitute government. Government is made up of people who derive their public authority from legislation. The implication of this, as explained by Professor Hogg, is that "any body exercising statutory authority, for example, the Governor in Council, or Lieutenant Governor in Council, ministers, officials, municipalities, administrative tribunals and police officers, is also bound by the *Charter*."[116]

§1.144 Professor Hogg includes police officers in this list because they derive their status from legislation. For example, the authority of Royal Canadian Mounted Police officers ("RCMP") comes from their appointment as peace officers pursuant to the terms of the *Royal Canadian Mounted Police Act*.[117] The same is true of police officers belonging to municipal or provincial police forces, given that they obtain their official status from, and are subject to, provincial police acts.[118] In addition, police officers derive a great many of their specific powers from legislation, both federal and provincial, as well as the common law. In short, within the criminal justice system at least, police officers are the embodiment of government and their actions are therefore subject to the *Charter*.

(b) Private Actors Exercising Public Powers

§1.145 More difficult are the actions of entities or individuals having a more marginal connection to government. The challenge for the courts has been to delineate the boundary between "private" and "public" in a highly regulated world where law seems to touch on every facet of human activity. The Supreme Court has held that even where a non-governmental entity discharges functions that have a public dimension, it does not automatically follow that the *Charter* applies to each and every aspect of such an organization's activities. For example, in *McKinney v. University of Guelph*,[119] the Court refused to apply the *Charter* to a university's mandatory retirement policy. In coming to this conclusion, the Court acknowledged that government controls much of the environment universities operate in. Nevertheless, the Court noted that universities function

---

[114] *Ibid.*, s. 32(1)(*b*).
[115] See *Eldridge v. British Columbia (Attorney General)*, [1997] S.C.J. No. 86, [1997] 3 S.C.R. 624 at para. 20 (S.C.C.) [*Eldridge*].
[116] Peter W. Hogg, *Constitutional Law of Canada*, 4th ed., vol. 1 (Toronto: Carswell, 1997) at 34-11. Consequently, for example, the *Charter* applies to municipalities and their by-laws, given that they derive their authority entirely from provincial statutes. See *Ramsden v. Peterborough (City)*, [1993] S.C.J. No. 87, [1993] 2 S.C.R. 1084 (S.C.C.); *Godbout v. Logueuil (City)*, [1997] S.C.J. No. 95, [1997] 3 S.C.R. 844 (S.C.C).
[117] R.S.C. 1985, c. R-10.
[118] See *e.g.*, *Police Services Act*, R.S.O. 1990, c. P.15.
[119] [1990] S.C.J. No. 122, [1990] 3 S.C.R. 229 (S.C.C.) [*McKinney*].

as autonomous bodies and emphasized the fact that there was "no statutory requirement imposing mandatory retirement on the universities".[120] In *Stoffman v. Vancouver General Hospital*,[121] the Court came to essentially the same conclusion regarding a hospital's mandatory retirement policy. The Court came to the opposite conclusion in *Douglas/Kwantlen Faculty Assn. v. Douglas College*,[122] where a college's constituent statute made clear that the college was not an autonomous body but rather "a Crown agency established by the government to implement government policy."[123]

§1.146 More recently, in *Eldridge*,[124] the Supreme Court of Canada held that the *Charter* applied to a hospital's policy not to provide sign-language interpreters to deaf persons seeking medical services. Unlike in *Stoffman*, where the mandatory retirement policy was merely a matter of "internal hospital management", in *Eldridge* the *Charter* was held to apply because there was a "precisely-defined connection" between the hospital and the "implementation of a specific statutory scheme or a government program", namely, the provision of medical services.[125]

§1.147 In situations where an individual or entity is carrying out a statutorily delegated power or function, the Supreme Court has not hesitated in holding that the *Charter* applies to the discharge of the delegated authority.[126] So, for example, in *Slaight Communications*,[127] the *Charter* was held to apply to an adjudicator in his exercise of powers conferred by statute. This is an entirely sensible conclusion. Were it otherwise, government could simply insulate its actions from *Charter* scrutiny by delegating its powers to private actors.[128]

---

[120] *Ibid.*, at 273-74 (S.C.R.).

[121] [1990] S.C.J. No. 125, [1990] 3 S.C.R. 483 (S.C.C.) [*Stoffman*].

[122] [1990] S.C.J. No. 124, [1990] 3 S.C.R. 570 (S.C.C.).

[123] *Ibid.*, at 584 (S.C.R.). The Court pointed out that under the enabling legislation the college's board members, who ran the university's operations, were "not only appointed and removable at pleasure by the government; the government may at all times by law direct its operation. Briefly stated, it is simply part of the apparatus of government both in form and in fact In carrying out its functions, therefore, the college is performing acts of government...." *Ibid.*

[124] *Eldridge v. British Columbia (Attorney General)*, [1997] S.C.J. No. 86, [1997] 3 S.C.R. 624 at para. 20 (S.C.C.).

[125] *Ibid.*, at paras. 44-51.

[126] See *Slaight Communications Inc. v. Davidson*, [1989] S.C.J. No. 45, [1989] 1 S.C.R. 1038 (S.C.C.) [*Slaight Communications*] (*Charter* applies to adjudicator who derives authority from legislation); *Blencoe v. British Columbia (Human Rights Commission)*, [2000] S.C.J. No. 43, [2000] 2 S.C.R. 307 (S.C.C.) (*Charter* applies to Human Rights Commission exercising statutorily conferred authority); *Black v. Law Society Alberta*, [1989] 1 S.C.R. 591, [1989] 1 S.C.R. 591 (S.C.C.) (*Charter* applies to provincial law society's decision to restrict access to province by out of province law firms, given that it derived its authority to regulate the legal profession from a provincial statute); *Miron v. Trudel*, [1995] S.C.J. No. 44, [1995] 2 S.C.R. 418 (S.C.C.) (*Charter* was held to apply to the terms of an automobile insurance policy between and individual and a private insurance company where those terms were mandated by provincial legislation).

[127] *Slaight Communications Inc. v. Davidson*, [1989] S.C.J. No. 45, [1989] 1 S.C.R. 1038 (S.C.C.).

[128] Justice La Forest made this point regarding *Slaight Communications* in *McKinney v. University of Guelph*, [1990] S.C.J. No. 122, [1990] 3 S.C.R. 229 at 265 (S.C.C.), stating: "The arbitrator was, therefore, part of the governmental administrative machinery for effecting the specific purpose of the statute. It would be strange if the legislature and the government could evade their *Charter* responsibility by appointing a person to carry out the purposes of the statute."

§1.148 These decisions are important for criminal procedure primarily because of the recent and rapid rise of the private security industry.[129] Private security officials now undertake a great deal of "policing" in Canada. From in-house security departments at large corporations, to theft prevention officers in retail establishments, to security guards at public housing facilities and shopping malls, private police are ubiquitous.[130] It is not surprising then that every province now has legislation regulating this industry.[131] This begs the question, does the *Charter* apply to private security personnel?

§1.149 As a general matter, the answer is "No."[132] As the Supreme Court of Canada explained in *R. v. Buhay*:[133]

> Private security guards are neither government agents nor employees, and apart from a loose framework of statutory regulation, they are not subject to government control. Their work may overlap with the government's interest in preventing and investigating crime, but it cannot be said that the security guards were acting as delegates of the government carrying out its policies or programs.[134]

In *Buhay*, two security guards employed at the Winnipeg bus depot unlocked and searched the contents of a rented locker. The guards were not acting with any legal authority in doing so, nor were they acting at the suggestion or behest of the police. (The potential for otherwise private citizens to become state agents to whom the *Charter* applies is discussed in the next section.) Although there is legislation in Manitoba governing the private security industry, it confers no search and seizure powers on private security personnel.[135] Consequently, the security guards were acting in an entirely private capacity in opening the bus locker. In these circumstances, the conclusion that the *Charter* did not apply to their actions seems perfectly sensible.

§1.150 More uncertain is whether the *Charter* applies to private individuals, including security guards, when they act pursuant to specific legislative authority. Early cases suggested that it does. For example, in *R. v. Lerke*,[136] the Alberta Court of Appeal held that the *Charter* applied to a tavern manager who carried out a "citizen's arrest" pursuant to provincial legislation and the *Criminal Code*. Chief Justice Laycraft concluded that "the arrest of a citizen is a governmental function whether the person making the arrest is a peace officer or a private citi-

---

[129] Between 1991 and 2001, the private security industry in Canada grew 69 per cent, nearly five times the rate of growth in employment for all Canadian industries during the same period. See Trevor Sanders, "Rise of the Rent-a-Cop: Private Security in Canada, 1991-2001" (2005) 47 Can. J. of Criminology and Criminal Justice 175.

[130] See Law Commission of Canada, *In Search of Security: The Roles of Public Police and Private Agencies – Discussion Paper* (Ottawa: Law Commission of Canada, 2002) at 10-11.

[131] See *e.g.*, *Private Security and Investigative Services Act, 2005*, S.O. 2005, c. 34, which essentially creates a licensing regime for security guards and private investigators.

[132] See generally, *Retail, Wholesale and Department Store Union, Local 580[R.W.D.S.U.] v. Dolphin Delivery Ltd.*, [1986] S.C.J. No. 75, [1986] 2 S.C.R. 573 (S.C.C.) [*Dolphin Delivery*].

[133] [2003] S.C.J. No. 30, [2003] 1 S.C.R. 631 (S.C.C.) [*Buhay*].

[134] *Ibid.*, at para. 28.

[135] *Private Investigators and Security Guards Act*, R.S.M. 1987, c. P132.

[136] [1986] A.J. No. 27, 24 C.C.C. (3d) 129 (Alta. C.A.) [*Lerke*].

zen."[137] In the result, the Court concluded that a search carried out incidental to that arrest was unreasonable and violated section 8 of the *Charter*.

§1.151 Unfortunately, there is now conflicting *obiter dicta* from the Supreme Court regarding the correctness of the holding in *Lerke*. For example, in *Dolphin Delivery Ltd.*,[138] Justice McIntyre cited with approval a passage from Professor Hogg's text[139] that provided, in part, that: "... the *Charter* would apply to a private person exercising the power of arrest that is granted to 'any one' by the *Criminal Code*".[140] More recently, however, in *Buhay*, quoting in part from *McKinney*, Justice Arbour noted that while private security officers "arrest, detain and search individuals on a regular basis", the exclusion of private activity from the *Charter* "was a deliberate choice which must be respected".[141]

§1.152 The suggestion from *Buhay* that the *Charter* does not apply to private security guards carrying out arrests and searches is difficult to reconcile with the Court's past judgments applying the *Charter* to persons exercising statutorily delegated powers.[142] It also ignores the fact that the authority of private citizens to arrest is derived directly from statute. Given the increasing reliance on private security personnel in Canada and the ease with which government could confer further law enforcement powers on this sector, the Court should make clear that when exercising legislated powers (like "citizen's arrest"), private individuals discharge a discrete governmental function and are subject to the *Charter* in so doing.[143]

(c)   State Agents

§1.153 The Supreme Court of Canada has held that the *Charter* applies to the actions of private individuals who assist the police in response to a specific di-

---

[137] *Ibid.*, at para. 15. See also *R. v. Shafie*, [1989] O.J. No. 102, 47 C.C.C. (3d) 27 (Ont. C.A.) (citing *Lerke* with approval but refusing to extend it to a situation where there is a detention but no actual arrest) But see *R. v. J. (A.M.)*, [1999] B.C.J. No. 1367, 137 C.C.C. (3d) 213 at paras. 32-38 (B.C.C.A.) (concluding that the *Charter* should not apply to a citizen's arrest without referring to *Lerke*).

[138] [1986] S.C.J. No. 75, [1986] 2 S.C.R. 573 (S.C.C.).

[139] Peter W. Hogg, *Constitutional Law of Canada*, 2d ed. (Toronto: Carswell, 1985).

[140] [1986] S.C.J. No. 75, [1986] 2 S.C.R. 573 at 602-603 (S.C.C.).

[141] *R. v. Buhay*, [2003] S.C.J. No. 30 at para. 31, [2003] 1 S.C.R. 631 (S.C.C.). The Court in *Buhay* does not cite *Lerke* in order to expressly disapprove of it. Interestingly, it specifically acknowledged the significance of *Lerke* in an earlier judgment. See *R. v. Asante-Mensah*, [2003] S.C.J. No. 38 at para. 77, [2003] 2 S.C.R. 3 (S.C.C.) ("On the facts, we are not called on in this case to address the question whether a citizen's arrest could be construed as state action for purposes of the *Charter*, as held by the Alberta Court of Appeal in *Lerke* ... and, if so, what consequences might flow from that ruling.").

[142] See cases discussed above at §1.146 to §1.147.

[143] See *R. v. Dell*, [2005] A.J. No. 867, 199 C.C.C. (3d) 110 (Alta. C.A.) (concluding that *Buhay* does *not* implicitly overrule *Lerke* but refusing to extend the *Charter*'s application to investigative detentions undertaken by private citizens). But see *R. v. Skeir*, [2005] N.S.J. No. 209, 196 C.C.C. (3d) 353 at paras. 10-21 (N.S.C.A.), leave to appeal refused [2005] S.C.C.A. No. 367 (S.C.C.) (reading *Buhay* as holding that the *Charter* does not apply to a citizen's arrest). See also *R. v. S. (N.)*, [2004] O.J. No. 290 (Ont. C.A.) (a short endorsement that appears to come to the same conclusion regarding *Buhay*'s effect).

rection or request. In such circumstances, the individual becomes a state agent subject to the *Charter*.[144]

§1.154 In *R. v. Broyles*,[145] the Supreme Court set down a test for deciding when someone has assumed the role of a state agent. In that case, the accused was in custody on a forgery charge but the police also suspected him of a murder. The police arranged for a friend of the accused to visit him at the detention centre and equipped the friend with a body-pack recording device. During the conversation, the friend encouraged the accused to ignore his lawyer's advice that he should remain silent and elicited a critical admission. A key issue on appeal was whether the friend was acting as a state agent, such that the exchange would be subject to section 7 *Charter* standards.[146] In deciding that question, the Court explained:

> Only if the relationship between the informer and the state is such that the exchange between the informer and the accused is materially different from what it would have been had there been no such relationship should the informer be considered a state agent for the purposes of the exchange. I would accordingly adopt the following simple test: would the exchange between the accused and the informer have taken place, in the form and manner in which it did take place, but for the intervention of the state or its agents?[147]

§1.155 Applying that test, the Supreme Court easily concluded that the accused's friend was acting as a state agent. It pointed to the fact that the police were responsible for arranging the visit and had effectively instructed the friend to elicit information about the homicide. The Court was satisfied that had the authorities not intervened, the conversation "would either not have occurred at all, or else would have taken a materially different course."[148]

§1.156 In *R. v. M. (M.R.)*,[149] the Court applied the *Broyles* test to a search of a student by a school vice-principal. The vice-principal had reason to believe that the student was planning to sell drugs at a school dance. When the vice-principal saw the student arrive at the school on the evening of the dance, he called police before summoning the student to his office. A police officer arrived and briefly spoke with the vice-principal before the two men entered the office. The officer stood by quietly while the vice-principal spoke to the student and then searched him, discovering a bag of marijuana. The student was immediately arrested.

---

[144] See *R. v. Broyles*, [1991] S.C.J. No. 95, [1991] 3 S.C.R. 595 (S.C.C.) [*Broyles*]; *R. v. M. (M.R.)*, [1998] S.C.J. No. 83, [1998] 3 S.C.R. 393 at paras. 26-30 (S.C.C.); *R. v. Buhay*, [2003] S.C.J. No. 30 at paras. 25-31, [2003] 1 S.C.R. 631 (S.C.C.).

[145] [1991] S.C.J. No. 95, [1991] 3 S.C.R. 595 (S.C.C.).

[146] The Supreme Court has held that the state cannot subvert a detainee's right to silence by engaging in acts of subterfuge designed to undermine the individual's choice not to speak. See *R. v. Hebert*, [1990] S.C.J. No. 64, [1990] 2 S.C.R. 151 (S.C.C.). The right to silence and the Court's decision in *Hebert* are discussed in Chapter 4, Part 5.

[147] *R. v. Broyles*, [1991] S.C.J. No. 95, [1991] 3 S.C.R. 595 at 608 (S.C.C.).

[148] *Ibid.*, at 613 (S.C.R.).

[149] [1998] S.C.J. No. 83, [1998] 3 S.C.R. 393 (S.C.C.).

§1.157 The Court accepted the concession that schools, school administrators and teachers are part of government for section 32 *Charter* purposes.[150] It also needed to decide whether the vice-principal was a police agent, however, because if he was, the search would be subject to more exacting section 8 requirements than those applying to education officials searching for school disciplinary purposes.[151]

§1.158 Applying the *Broyles* test, the Court queried whether the search would have taken place, in the form and manner in which it did, but for the involvement of the police.[152] The Court concluded that it would have. It reasoned that "[t]he mere fact that there was cooperation between the vice-principal and the police and that an officer was present during the search is not sufficient to indicate that the vice-principal was acting as an agent of the police. . . . There is no evidence of an agreement or of police instructions to [the vice-principal] that could create an agency relationship."[153]

§1.159 The Court applied the *Broyles* test again in *Buhay*[154] (which was discussed immediately above in Part 4(3)(*b*)). After the security guards found the drugs, they returned them to the locker, locked it and called police. The police subsequently opened the locker without assistance from the guards. The Court concluded that the guards were not state agents during their initial search of the locker. The Court emphasized "that the security guards acted totally independently of the police in their initial search ... [they] started an investigation on their own initiative, without any instructions or directions from the police."[155]

§1.160 In *Buhay*, the Court also rejected the notion that routine cooperation between the security guards and police gave rise to a "standing" agency relationship. The Court explained that:

> Volunteer participation in the detection of crime by private actors, or general encouragements by the police authorities to citizens to participate in the detection of crime, will not usually be sufficient direction by the police to trigger the application of the *Charter*. Rather, the intervention of the police must be specific to the case being investigated.[156]

(d) Applies (Almost) Only in Canada

§1.161 Section 32 is silent regarding the *Charter*'s geographic limits. As noted, it simply provides that it applies "to the Parliament and government of Canada"[157] and "to the legislature and government of each province".[158] Nevertheless,

---

[150] *Ibid.*, at paras. 24-25 (S.C.J.).
[151] The differing constitutional standards applicable to police searches for law enforcement purposes as compared to searches by school officials for student disciplinary purposes are discussed in detail in Chapter 3, Part 2(5)(*d*)(iii)c.
[152] *R. v. M. (M.R.)*, [1998] S.C.J. No. 83 at para. 29, [1998] 3 S.C.R. 393 (S.C.C.).
[153] *Ibid.*, at para. 28 (S.C.J.).
[154] *R. v. Buhay*, [2003] S.C.J. No. 30, [2003] 1 S.C.R. 631 (S.C.C.).
[155] *Ibid.*, at para. 29 (S.C.J.).
[156] *Ibid.*, at para. 30 (S.C.J.).
[157] *Canadian Charter of Rights and Freedoms*, Part I of the *Constitution Act, 1982*, being Schedule B to the *Canada Act 1982* (U.K.), 1982, c. 11, s. 32(1)(*a*).

emphasizing the importance of national sovereignty and international comity and relying on international law principles that generally forbid nation states from applying their laws beyond their borders, the Supreme Court has effectively concluded that the *Charter* will almost never apply outside Canada.

§1.162 Given the plain language in section 32, the Supreme Court rather easily held in *R. v. Harrer*[159] that the *Charter* did not apply to the taking of a statement by U.S. authorities in the United States. In that case, American officials initially questioned Ms. Harrer about her immigration status. When questioning shifted to her suspected criminal activities in Canada, the officers did not give her a second right to counsel warning, as required by section 10(*b*) of the *Charter*. However, given that the *Charter* did not apply, this had no effect on the admissibility of her statements at her Canadian criminal trial. According to the Court, what was determinative was "the simple fact that the United States immigration officials and the Marshals were not acting on behalf of any of the governments of Canada, the provinces or the territories, the state actors to which, by virtue of s. 32(1) the application of the *Charter* is confined."[160]

§1.163 More difficult was *R. v. Terry*,[161] a case involving American police detectives who, acting in direct response to a specific request by Canadian law enforcement officials, interrogated a suspect held in the United States regarding a murder that had taken place in Canada. The issue was whether in these circumstances the *Charter* applied to the actions of the American police detectives. A unanimous Supreme Court of Canada concluded that it did not. In so holding, it emphasized principles of state sovereignty and international comity and the importance of respecting "the settled rule that a state is only competent to enforce its laws within its own territorial boundaries".[162] The Court also rejected that an agency relationship existed between Canadian police and their American counterparts, explaining that the "personal decision of a foreign officer or agency to assist the Canadian police cannot dilute the exclusivity of the foreign state's sovereignty within its territory, where its law alone governs the process of enforcement. The gathering of evidence by these foreign officers or agency is subject to the rules of that country and none other."[163]

§1.164 In *R. v. Cook*,[164] however, the Supreme Court of Canada seemed to carve out a modest exception to the general rule that precludes the *Charter*'s application beyond Canada's borders. Two Canadian police detectives travelled to the United States to question a suspect in New Orleans being held for extradition in relation to a murder in Vancouver. The officers obtained a statement from the accused without properly complying with section 10(*b*) of the *Charter*. In concluding that the *Charter did* apply to the Canadian police detectives, the major-

---

[158] *Ibid.*, s. 32(1)(*b*).
[159] [1995] S.C.J. No. 81, [1995] 3 S.C.R. 562 (S.C.C.).
[160] *Ibid.*, at para. 12 (S.C.J.).
[161] [1996] S.C.J. No. 62, [1996] 2 S.C.R. 207 (S.C.C.).
[162] *Ibid.*, at para. 14 (S.C.J.).
[163] *Ibid.*, at para. 19 (S.C.J.).
[164] [1998] S.C.J. No. 68, [1998] 2 S.C.R. 597 (S.C.C.) [*Cook*].

ity in *Cook* emphasized the principle of international law that permits states to assume jurisdiction based on nationality, in this case the nationality of the two Canadian police detectives.[165] As a result, it held that "the *Charter* applies on foreign territory in circumstances where the impugned act falls within the scope of s. 32(1) of the *Charter* on the jurisdictional basis of the nationality of the state law enforcement authorities engaged in governmental action, and where the application of *Charter* standards will not conflict with the concurrent territorial jurisdiction of the foreign state."[166] Under this test, the *Charter* would apply to Canadian police officers operating abroad except to the extent that its application would interfere with the legal sovereignty of the country where they are carrying out their duties.

§1.165 Unfortunately, the conceptual clarity that emerged from *Cook* seemed to disappear with the Supreme Court of Canada's subsequent judgment in *R. v. Hape*.[167] In that case, a money laundering investigation took RCMP officers to Turks and Caicos where, with the assistance and permission of local law enforcement, the Canadian officers twice surreptitiously entered and searched Mr. Hape's business premises. The issue before the Court was whether these warrantless searches violated Mr. Hape's section 8 *Charter* right to be secure against unreasonable or seizure.

§1.166 Unfortunately, rather than simply applying the test supplied by *Cook*,[168] the majority in *Hape* decided to overrule it. Where *Cook* went wrong, reasoned the majority in *Hape*, was in its failure to appreciate the importance of the ability to enforce a remedy as a precondition for the *Charter*'s application. As Justice LeBel explained for the majority:

> ... the *Charter* cannot be applied if compliance with its legal requirements cannot be enforced. Enforcement of compliance with the *Charter* means that when state agents act, they must do so in accordance with the requirements of the *Charter* so as to give effect to Canadian law as it applies to the exercise of the state power at issue. However, as has already been discussed, Canadian law cannot be enforced in another state's territory without that state's consent. Since extraterritorial enforcement is not possible, and enforcement is necessary for the *Charter* to apply, extraterritorial application of the *Charter* is impossible.[169]

If the *Charter* applied, Justice LeBel continued, it required the RCMP to obtain a warrant unavailable under Turks and Caicos law. "It would constitute blatant interference with Turks and Caicos sovereignty," he wrote, "to require that

---

[165] *Ibid.*, at paras. 41-42 (S.C.J.).

[166] *Ibid.*, at para. 48 (S.C.J.).

[167] [2007] S.C.J. No. 26, [2007] 2 S.C.R. 292 (S.C.C.) [*Hape*].

[168] In *R. v. Hape*, [2007] S.C.J. No. 26, [2007] 2 S.C.R. 292 at para. 181 (S.C.C.), *per* Binnie J., concurring, would have resolved the case by simply applying the Court's prior holding in *Cook*. He reasoned that the searches and seizures conformed with the law in Turks and Caicos and therefore applying the *Charter* to these activities would be at odds with the second requirement set down in *Cook*, that the actions not interfere with the concurrent territorial jurisdiction of the foreign state.

[169] [2007] S.C.J. No. 26 at para. 85, [2007] 2 S.C.R. 292 (S.C.C.).

country's legal system to develop a procedure for issuing a warrant in the circumstances simply to comply with the dictates of the *Charter*."[170]

§1.167 With respect, the majority in *Hape* created a false dilemma. Applying the *Charter* to the actions of the RCMP in *Hape* would not necessitate legislative action on the part of any foreign government. Rather, Canada's Parliament could simply pass legislation to allow Canadian police to apply for and obtain a Canadian warrant authorizing their extraterritorial investigative activities. A legislative precondition for issuing any such warrant could be compliance with the law of the foreign state and the co-operation of local officials. Such a scheme could track minimum *Charter* requirements for reasonable searches and seizures under section 8, while fully respecting the sovereignty of the foreign states in which Canadian police would be operating. Unfortunately, the majority in *Hape* does not avert to this possible solution to the dilemma it identifies.

§1.168 Instead, the majority in *Hape* decided to substantially scale back the *Charter*'s potential for extraterritorial application. It set down a very restrictive test for deciding whether the *Charter* applies beyond Canada's borders:

> The first stage is to determine whether the activity in question falls under section 32(1) such that the *Charter* applies to it. At this stage, two questions reflecting the two components of s. 32(1) must be asked. First, is the conduct at issue that of a Canadian state actor? Second, if the answer is yes, it may be necessary, depending on the facts of the case, to determine whether there is an exception to the principle of sovereignty that would justify the application of the *Charter* to the extraterritorial activities of the state actor. In most cases, there will be no such exception and the *Charter* will not apply.[171]

Thankfully, the Court did caution in *Hape* that the importance of international comity cannot be used to justify Canadian participation in activities of a foreign state or its agents that are contrary to Canada's international obligations. It noted that the deference required by the principle of comity "ends where clear violations of international law and fundamental human rights begin".[172] It took very little time at all for the Supreme Court to put this very narrow exception to work.

§1.169 *Canada (Justice) v. Khadr*[173] involved a Canadian citizen held by United States forces at Guantanamo Bay in Cuba on murder and terrorism charges. Mr. Khadr was questioned in Guantanamo by agents of the Canadian Security Intelligence Service (CSIS). CSIS shared the fruits of this questioning with American officials. Mr. Khadr's lawyers brought a section 7 *Charter* application in Canada seeking to compel Canadian officials to disclose documents in their possession relevant to the charges he was facing in the American proceedings.

§1.170 Following *Hape*, in *Khadr* the Supreme Court reasoned that if "the Guantanamo Bay process under which Mr. Khadr was being held was in con-

---

[170] *Ibid.*, at para. 86 (S.C.J.).
[171] *Ibid.*, at para. 113 (S.C.J.).
[172] *Ibid.*, at para. 52 (S.C.J.). See also paras. 51 and 101.
[173] [2008] S.C.J. No. 28, [2008] 2 S.C.R. 125 (S.C.C.) [*Khadr*].

formity with Canada's international obligations, the *Charter* has no application and Mr. Khadr's application for disclosure cannot succeed. ... However, if Canada was participating in a process that was violative of Canada's binding obligations under international law, the *Charter* applies to the extent of that participation."[174]

§1.171 In *Khadr*, the Supreme Court was not required to decide the legality of the process at Guantanamo Bay. Instead, it simply pointed to the fact that the United States Supreme Court had already found the impugned procedures illegal under U.S. law and contrary to the requirements of the *Geneva Conventions*. As a consequence, the *Charter* applied "to the extent that the conduct of Canadian officials involved it in a process that violated Canada's international obligations".[175] The Court therefore concluded that Canada has an obligation under section 7 of the *Charter* to provide disclosure to Mr. Khadr in order to mitigate the effect of Canada's participation in the Guantanamo Bay interrogation process.[176]

§1.172 No doubt, a situation like that which arose in *Khadr* is unlikely to be repeated. Under *Hape*, international comity concerns will almost always trump the extraterritorial application of the *Charter*. The situation in *Khadr* was unusual in the extreme. How likely is it that a future claimant will have the benefit of a pronouncement from the highest court in the foreign jurisdiction where Canadian officials were operating characterizing what took place as unlawful under the laws of that state and international law?

(e) Remedying Unfairness When the Charter Does Not Apply

§1.173 As explained in the last two sections, the *Charter* does not generally apply to non-governmental persons or to investigative activities taking place beyond Canada's borders. If the *Charter* does not apply, then a remedy under section 24 of the *Charter* is not available. This does not, however, necessarily mean that there will be no opportunity to redress any resulting unfairness.

§1.174 In those cases where the Supreme Court has concluded that the *Charter* did not apply to the acquisition of evidence, it has consistently acknowledged that a trial judge has the authority to exclude the evidence where its admission would result in an unfair trial.[177] The Court has identified both the common law rules of evidence and sections 7 and 11(*d*) of the *Charter* — which obligate a trial judge to ensure a fair trial — as the sources for this remedial authority.[178]

§1.175 It is not yet entirely clear when the admission of evidence that was *not* obtained in a manner that violated the *Charter* will serve to render a trial unfair.

---

[174] *Ibid.*, at para. 19 (S.C.J.).
[175] *Ibid.*, at para. 26 (S.C.J.).
[176] *Ibid.*, at para. 34 (S.C.J.).
[177] See *R. v. Harrer*, [1995] S.C.J. No. 81 at paras. 13-24, [1995] 3 S.C.R. 562 (S.C.C.); *R. v. Terry*, [1996] S.C.J. No. 62 at paras. 25-26, [1996] 2 S.C.R. 207 (S.C.C.); *R. v. Hape*, [2007] S.C.J. No. 26 at paras. 91 and 100, [2007] 2 S.C.R. 292 (S.C.C.); *R. v. Buhay*, [2003] S.C.J. No. 30 at para. 40, [2003] 1 S.C.R. 631 (S.C.C.).
[178] *Ibid.*

In those cases where the Court has acknowledged that trial judges have this authority, it has yet to conclude that it should have been exercised.[179] In *R. v. Harrer*,[180] a case where U.S. authorities took a statement from the accused, the Supreme Court explained that simply because evidence was acquired in a manner that would not meet *Charter* standards does not necessarily mean that its admission into evidence will render a trial unfair.[181] Instead, the Court recognized that "different balances may be achieved in different countries, all of which are fair."[182] At the same time, the Court cautioned that:

> ... Canada is not bound by the law of other countries in conducting trials in this country. We must, in determining whether evidence should be admitted into evidence, be guided by our sense of fairness as informed by the underlying principles of our own legal system as it applies to the specific context of the case.
>
> ...
>
> At the end of the day, a court is left with a principled but fact-driven decision. ... I agree that one should not be overly fastidious or adopt a chauvinistic attitude in assessing practices followed in other countries but, given the few cases on the matter, I am not at this stage prepared to accept that the unfairness must be such as to shock the conscience to warrant rejection. Simply, what we seek is a fair trial in the specific context, and I am by no means sure this requirement can be satisfied by the rejection of foreign evidence only in the most egregious circumstances.[183]

In those cases involving the taking of statements by American police officers following the proper administration of *Miranda*[184] warnings, the Court has easily concluded that admitting the evidence would not undermine trial fairness.[185]

§1.176 The result was similar in *Hape*, where the Crown sought to introduce the fruits of two warrantless searches by RCMP officers that took place in Turks and Caicos. The Court concluded that the admission of the evidence did not result in an unfair trial. In coming to this conclusion the Court emphasized that the evidence was not self-incriminating and that the Canadian police were acting under the supervision of local law enforcement, had a genuine and reasonable belief that they were complying with the local law and did not acquire the evidence in a manner that diminished its reliability.[186] Further, the Court noted that it had no basis to conclude "that the procedural requirements for a lawful search

---

[179] *Ibid.*

[180] [1995] S.C.J. No. 81, [1995] 3 S.C.R. 562 (S.C.C.).

[181] *R. v. Harrer*, [1995] S.C.J. No. 81 at paras. 14-15, [1995] 3 S.C.R. 562 (S.C.C.).

[182] *Ibid.*, at para. 14 (S.C.J.).

[183] *Ibid.*, at paras. 16-18.

[184] See *Miranda v. Arizona*, 384 U.S. 436 (1966) [*Miranda*], which set down the now famous caution that American police officers are obligated to provide before conducting a custodial interrogation.

[185] In these cases, although the strict requirements of s. 10(*b*) of the *Charter* were not satisfied, the individuals were properly apprised of their right to counsel under U.S. constitutional law. See *R. v. Harrer*, [1995] S.C.J. No. 81 at para. 4, [1995] 3 S.C.R. 562 (S.C.C.); *R. v. Terry*, [1996] S.C.J. No. 62 at paras. 3-4, [1996] 2 S.C.R. 207 (S.C.C.).

[186] *R. v. Hape*, [2007] S.C.J. No. 26 at para. 120, [2007] 2 S.C.R. 292 (S.C.C.).

and seizure under Turks and Caicos law fail to meet basic standards commonly accepted by free and democratic societies."[187]

§1.177 It remains to be seen what factors the Supreme Court will emphasize in assessing whether the admission of evidence acquired by private actors operating in Canada (for example, security guards) would result in an unfair trial. In the only case of that kind to come before the Court the issue did not need to be resolved.[188] Following the reasoning in *Hape*, the Court will likely focus on the conduct that led to the acquisition of the evidence and the reliability of the evidence obtained. So, for example, where a private actor deliberately engaged in unlawful or otherwise abusive or improper conduct in obtaining the evidence then this will counsel in favour of exclusion. If the evidence itself is unreliable (for example, a coerced confession), then this too should probably lead to exclusion.[189] On the other hand, where the evidence was obtained in good faith or without illegality and its reliability is not in doubt, admission seems likely.

5. JURISDICTION OVER CRIMINAL PROCEDURE AND CRIMINAL PROSECUTIONS

§1.178 The federal and provincial governments share responsibility over criminal procedure. This is partly a product of the division of responsibility set out in the express terms of the *Constitution Act, 1867*[190] and partly a result of agreements between the federal and provincial governments to delegate exclusively federal powers to the provinces.

(1) Federal Constitutional Authority

§1.179 Section 91(27) of the *Constitution Act, 1867* gives the Parliament of Canada exclusive authority over "The Criminal Law ... including ... Procedure in Criminal Matters".[191] Consequently, Parliament alone has the power to define what constitutes a crime and establish the rules relating to the operation of the criminal process.

§1.180 What qualifies as "criminal law" has proven a vexing constitutional question. The Supreme Court has indicated that for a law to qualify it must meet

---

[187] *Ibid.*

[188] See *R. v. Buhay*, [2003] S.C.J. No. 30, [2003] 1 S.C.R. 631 at para. 40 (S.C.C.). The case was resolved based exclusively on the subsequent actions of police, making it unnecessary for the Court to decide whether the conduct of the security guards, who entered a locked bus locker without any legal authority, was such that the evidence acquired would need to be excluded because its admission would undermine the fairness of the trial.

[189] See *R. v. Grandinetti*, [2005] S.C.J. No. 3, [2005] 1 S.C.R. 27 at para. 36 (S.C.C.) (suggesting that statements coerced by private actors might be excluded under common law and *Charter* abuse of process doctrine); *R. v. Wells*, [2003] B.C.J. No. 927, 174 C.C.C. (3d) 301 at para. 64, 181 B.C.A.C. 271, 12 C.R. (6th) 185 (B.C.C.A.) (noting that courts may exclude statements coerced by private actors under both their "discretion to exclude evidence, the probative value of which is outweighed by it prejudicial effect" and their "power and discretion . . . to ensure the fair trial of an accused"). See also Chapter 4, Part 2(2), especially §4.16.

[190] (U.K.), 30 & 31 Vict., c. 3 [Reprinted in R.S.C. 1985, App. II, No. 5].

[191] *Ibid.*, s. 91(27).

three prerequisites: (*i*) a valid criminal law purpose; (*ii*) backed by a prohibition; (*iii*) combined with a penalty.[192] The most difficult element is the first: determining what qualifies as a valid criminal law purpose. On that all important question the Supreme Court has given less than precise direction, instructing that: "[p]ublic peace, order, security, health, morality: these are the ordinary though not exclusive ends served by [criminal] law".[193] Beyond defining crimes, Parliament's constitutional authority also extends to enacting "legislation designed for the prevention of crime as well as to punishing crime".[194] What Parliament cannot do under section 91(27) is use its constitutional authority improperly, in constitutional parlance "colourably", to invade areas of provincial legislative competence.[195]

§1.181 Because of section 91(27), Parliament also has authority over "Procedure in Criminal Matters." At times the Supreme Court of Canada has interpreted this language narrowly, for example, in declaring that Parliament is limited to legislating in regard to "the steps to be taken in prosecutions and other criminal proceedings before the courts."[196] Since then, however, the Supreme Court has rejected the view that "criminal procedure" is confined to "that which takes place in the courtroom on a prosecution"[197] and has instead acknowledged that it also "encompasses such things as the rules by which, according to the *Criminal Code*, police powers are exercised, the right to counsel, search warrants, interim release, procuring attendance of witnesses".[198]

§1.182 Consequently, Parliament's authority under section 91(27) empowers it to enact legislation addressing all aspects of criminal procedure, from investigations to appeals and everything in between. In other words, if it wanted to, Parliament could enact a comprehensive code of criminal procedure. Unfortunately it has not yet done so. As explained in more detail in Part 6(2), below, although

---

[192] See *Reference re: Firearms Act (Can.)*, [2000] S.C.J. No. 31, [2000] 1 S.C.R. 783 at para. 27 (S.C.C.). See also *R. v. Malmo-Levine; R. v. Caine*, [2003] S.C.J. No. 79, [2003] 3 S.C.R. 571 at para. 74 (S.C.C.).

[193] *Reference re: Dairy Industry Act (Canada) s. 5(a)*, [1948] S.C.J. No. 42, [1949] S.C.R. 1 at 50 (S.C.C.), *per* Rand J., affd (*sub nom. Canadian Federation of Agriculture v. Quebec (Attorney General)* [1950] J.C.J. No. 1, [1951] A.C. 179 (P.C.). See also *Boggs v. R.*, [1981] S.C.J. No. 6, [1981] 1 S.C.R. 49 at 60-66 (S.C.C.); *R. v. Malmo-Levine; R. v. Caine*, [2003] S.C.J. No. 79, [2003] 3 S.C.R. 571 at paras. 73-74 (S.C.C.); *Labatt Brewing Co. v. Canada*, [1979] S.C.J. No. 134, [1980] 1 S.C.R. 914 at 933 (S.C.C.).

[194] *R. v. Goodyear Tire and Rubber Co. of Canada*, [1956] S.C.J. No. 8, [1956] S.C.R. 303 at 308 (S.C.C.).

[195] *Scowby v. Glendinning*, [1986] S.C.J. No. 57, [1986] 2 S.C.R. 226 at 237 (S.C.C.).

[196] *Quebec (Attorney General) v Canada (Attorney General)*, [1945] S.C.J. No. 26, [1945] S.C.R. 600 at 603 (S.C.C.).

[197] *Di Iorio v. Montreal (City) Common Jail*, [1976] S.C.J. No. 113, [1978] 1 S.C.R. 152 at 209 (S.C.C.).

[198] *Ibid.* See also *Scowby v. Glendinning*, [1986] S.C.J. No. 57, [1986] 2 S.C.R. 226 at para. 13 (S.C.C.) (holding that questions regarding the boundaries of arrest or detention for criminal law enforcement purposes fall within the federal government's exclusive authority over criminal law or procedure; *Quebec (Attorney General) v. Lechasseur (Quebec Youth Court Judge)*, [1981] S.C.J. No. 82, [1981] 2 S.C.R. 253 at 262 (S.C.C.) (holding that initiation of the criminal process by the laying of an information is part of criminal procedure.

the *Criminal Code*[199] includes a number of procedural provisions, they are far from comprehensive. Regrettably, they are also scattered throughout the *Code*, often intermingled with various substantive provisions.

§1.183 Parliament also has the authority to establish, maintain and manage "penitentiaries" under section 91(28) of the *Constitution Act, 1867*. In modern times, Parliament has used this power to create a federal correctional and parole system.[200] Under the *Criminal Code*, offenders who are sentenced to a period of imprisonment of two years or more enter the federal correctional system.[201]

§1.184 The constitutional division of powers also gives the federal government an important power to make judicial appointments. Though the provincial superior courts are constituted and maintained by the provinces, section 96 of the *Constitution Act, 1867* gives the Governor General (*de facto*, the Prime Minister) the exclusive authority to appoint the judges of these courts. As explained in the next Part, these courts play a critical role in the administration of the criminal justice system.

§1.185 Finally, the *Constitution Act, 1867* reserves for Parliament the power to create a "General Court of Appeal for Canada."[202] Pursuant to that authority Parliament created the Supreme Court of Canada,[203] which under the *Criminal Code* serves as the ultimate court of appeal for criminal cases.[204]

(2) Provincial Constitutional Authority

§1.186 Section 92(14) of the *Constitution Act, 1867* confers exclusive authority on the provinces to make laws in relation to "The Administration of Justice in the Province, including the Constitution, Maintenance, and Organization of Provincial Courts, both of Civil and of Criminal Jurisdiction...".[205] As the Supreme Court of Canada has noted, "[i]mplicit in the grant to the provinces of exclusive legislative authority in respect of Administration of Justice and in the grant to the federal government of exclusive legislative authority in respect of criminal law and procedure is an acceptance of a certain degree of overlapping."[206]

§1.187 Under section 92(14) of the *Constitution Act, 1867*, law enforcement is primarily the responsibility of the provinces. In each province, the Attorney General is the Crown's chief law enforcement officer. He or she has broad responsibilities for most aspects of the administration of criminal justice, including the court system, the police, criminal investigation and prosecutions, and corrections. (The Solicitor General in the province often has overlapping obligations in some of these areas, for example, policing and corrections.) The police

---

[199] R.S.C. 1985, c. C-46.

[200] See *Corrections and Conditional Release Act*, S.C. 1992, c. 20.

[201] See *Criminal Code*, R.S.C. 1985, c. C-46, s. 743.1.

[202] *Constitution Act, 1867* (U.K.), 30 & 31 Vict., c. 3, s. 101.

[203] See *Supreme Court Act*, R.S.C. 1985, c. S-26.

[204] See *Criminal Code*, R.S.C. 1985, c. C-46, ss. 691-696.

[205] *Constitution Act, 1867* (U.K.), 30 & 31 Vict., c. 3, s. 92(14).

[206] *Di Iorio v. Montreal (City) Common Jail*, [1976] S.C.J. No. 113, [1978] 1 S.C.R. 152 at 207 (S.C.C.).

forces within any given province are ultimately answerable to the Attorney General, as are the provincial Crown attorneys, who conduct most of the prosecutions that take place in Canada's criminal courts.[207] (The jurisdictional basis for the provinces to prosecute criminal offences is addressed immediately below in Part 5(3).)

§1.188 In each of the provinces, this constitutional authority has led to the introduction of policing statutes. These enactments facilitate the creation of municipal police forces and, in Ontario and Quebec, provincial police forces as well.[208] In the remaining provinces, the Royal Canadian Mounted Police (RCMP) undertake policing in rural areas and municipalities that do not have their own police forces. This is accomplished by means of contractual arrangements between the RCMP and provincial and municipal governments.[209] The RCMP is also responsible for policing in all three territories.

§1.189 There is a fair amount of overlap between the policing activities of municipal and provincial police forces and the RCMP. Even in those provinces that have provincial and municipal police forces, the RCMP still conducts investigations respecting other federal enactments beyond the *Criminal Code*. In Ontario, for example, which has a provincial police force and an abundance of municipal police agencies, the RCMP investigates and charges offences under the *Controlled Drugs and Substances Act*.[210] At the same time, provincial and municipal police forces routinely investigate and charge "criminal offences" not contained in the *Criminal Code*, for example, offences under the *Controlled Drugs and Substances Act*. In short, even though the division of powers is important to the creation and maintenance of Canada's police forces, when it comes to the investigation of crime, there is much overlap.

§1.190 Relying on their authority over the "Administration of Justice in the Province", the provinces have also enacted legislation governing the appointment and management of Crown attorneys, who are responsible for prosecuting most *Criminal Code* offences.[211] (Prosecutorial authority is discussed in greater detail immediately below in Part 5(3).)

§1.191 Section 92(14) of the *Constitution Act, 1867* also gives the provinces responsibility for the "Constitution, Maintenance, and Organization of Provincial Courts, both of Civil and of Criminal Jurisdiction." Each of the provinces

---

[207] *Ibid.*, at 206-207 (S.C.R.). See also *Reference re: Adoption Act (Ontario)*, [1938] S.C.J. No. 21, [1938] S.C.R. 398 at 403 (S.C.C.).

[208] See *e.g.*, *Police Services Act*, R.S.O. 1990, c. P.15. Both Ontario and Quebec have provincial police forces, the remaining provinces do not (though the Royal Newfoundland Constabulary operates as a provincial police force in portions of Newfoundland and Labrador).

[209] Federally, these arrangements are facilitated by the *Royal Canadian Mounted Police Act*, R.S.C. 1985, c. R-10, s. 20. These are matched by corresponding provisions in the provincial police Acts See *e.g.*, *Police Act*, R.S.A. 2000, c. P-17, ss. 21 and 22.

[210] S.C. 1996, c. 19. The RCMP also investigates and charges the offences of conspiracy to traffic or import a controlled substance, which are technically *Criminal Code* offences. See *Criminal Code*, R.S.C. 1985, c. C-46, s. 465(1)(*c*).

[211] See *e.g.*, *Crown Attorneys Act*, R.S.O. 1990, c. C.49.

has exercised this authority to enact legislation creating a provincial court,[212] a superior trial court[213] and a superior appellate court.[214]

§1.192 The *Criminal Code* confers authority on these various courts to discharge particular functions within the criminal justice system.[215] For example, the provincial (inferior) courts are where all accused persons will make their first court appearance,[216] have their bail hearing[217] and have their preliminary inquiry.[218] It is also where most accused persons are tried.[219] Judges of the provincial (inferior) courts are appointed by the government of the province.

§1.193 The *Criminal Code* also confers many responsibilities on the superior trial courts. For example, these courts review bail determinations made in the provincial courts,[220] serve as the trial court in many cases,[221] serve as the initial appellate court for summary conviction offences[222] and review decisions made by inferior courts, tribunals or officials that are not otherwise subject to review or appeal. This review function is accomplished through the extraordinary remedies of *habeas corpus, prohibition, certiorari* and *mandamus*.[223]

§1.194 More generally, superior courts are said to have "inherent jurisdiction", which means that unlike most other courts, including the Supreme Court of Canada, they are not dependent on a particular statute for their authority. Their powers are inherent and as such they perform a supervisory function over infe-

---

[212] See *e.g.*, *Courts of Justice Act*, R.S.O. 1990, c. 43, ss. 34 through 48. Similarly, see *Provincial Court Act*, R.S.A. 2000, c. P-31.

[213] See *e.g.*, *Courts of Justice Act*, R.S.O. 1990, c. 43, ss. 10 through 17. Similarly, see *Court of Queen's Bench Act*, R.S.A. 2000, c. C-31.

[214] See *e.g.*, *Courts of Justice Act*, R.S.O. 1990, c. 43 ss. 2 through 9. Similarly, see *Court of Appeal Act*, R.S.A. 2000, c. C-30. Note, however, that the existence of the superior courts is not contingent on provincial statutes; they are instead constituted by s. 129 of the *Constitution Act, 1867* (U.K.), 30 & 31 Vict., c. 3 [Reprinted in R.S.C. 1985, App. II, No. 5], which maintained those courts that were in existence at the time of Confederation.

[215] The Supreme Court of Canada has upheld as constitutional the delegation by Parliament of its power to enforce federal laws, like the *Criminal Code*, to the provincially constituted courts. See *Valin v. Langlois*, [1879] S.C.J. No. 2, 3 S.C.R. 1 (S.C.C.); *Re Vancini*, [1904] S.C.J. No. 21, 34 S.C.R. 621 (S.C.C.).

[216] See *Criminal Code*, R.S.C. 1985, c. C-46. s. 503(1)(*a*).

[217] See *ibid.*, s. 515.

[218] See *ibid.*, s. 536.

[219] See *ibid.*, ss. 469 and 553.

[220] See *ibid.*, ss. 493, 520 and 521.

[221] The jurisdiction of the superior courts over criminal offences is detailed in Part 2(3)(*a*), above.

[222] See *Criminal Code*, R.S.C. 1985, c. C-46, s. 812.

[223] See Part XXVI of the *Criminal Code*, ss. 774 through 784. These "extraordinary remedies", also known as the "prerogative writs", may be described as follows: (*i*) *habeas corpus* is used to challenge the legality of an individual's detention, it requires the person with custody of an individual to bring him or her before the court and to explain the legal justification for the detention, for example by producing the warrant, *etc.*; (*ii*) prohibition is sought to block an official or inferior court or tribunal from performing an illegal action, if it issues it prohibits the official to whom it is directed from doing the impugned act; (*iii*) *certiorari* is used to review the jurisdictional authority of an official or inferior court or tribunal, it issues if it is shown that the official, court or tribunal was acting without or in excess of its jurisdiction; (*iv*) *mandamus* is used to review the failure of an official or inferior court or tribunal to act in circumstances where it is legally obligated to do so, if it issues it commands the official, inferior court or tribunal to perform the particular action that is its responsibility to undertake.

rior courts.[224] As the Supreme Court has explained, in "Canada, the provincial superior court is the only court of general jurisdiction and as such is the centre of the judicial system. None of our statutory courts has the same core jurisdiction as the superior court and therefore none is as crucial to the rule of law."[225]

§1.195 Judges of the provincial appellate courts are also deemed to be superior court judges and thus enjoy the same inherent powers vested in the superior trial court.[226] Similar to superior court judges, judges of the appellate courts are also appointed by the Governor General (*de facto*, the Prime Minister) under section 96 of the *Constitution Act, 1867*.

§1.196 Under the *Criminal Code*, most appellate responsibilities are granted to the provincial appellate courts. For example, these courts review bail decisions made in the superior courts relating to the most serious criminal offences.[227] Most importantly, the provincial appellate courts serve as the ultimate appeal court in each province for criminal matters, with summary conviction appeals coming to them with leave[228] and appeals in indictable matters being heard by them as of right.[229]

§1.197 Section 92(6) of the *Constitution Act, 1867* also gives the provinces authority over "Reformatory Prisons in and for the Province". Every province has created provincial corrections and parole systems.[230] Under the terms of the *Criminal Code*, offenders sentenced to less than two years of imprisonment will serve their sentence in provincial correctional facilities.[231]

§1.198 A discussion of provincial authority in the field of criminal law and procedure would be incomplete without mention of section 92(15) of the *Constitution Act, 1867*. It empowers the provinces to enact laws for the "The Imposition of Punishment by Fine, Penalty, or Imprisonment for enforcing any Law of the Province made in relation to any Matter coming within any of the Classes of Subjects enumerated in this Section." In essence, section 92(15) enables the provinces to create penalties for violations of provincial statutes. Without such a power, the authority of the provinces over their various heads of power would be rather ineffective.

---

[224] See generally, *MacMillan Bloedel v. Simpson*, [1995] S.C.J. No. 101, [1995] 4 S.C.R. 725 at paras. 15, 27-38 (S.C.C.).

[225] *Ibid.*, at para. 37 (S.C.R.). The role of the superior courts is so important and their constitutional foundation so entrenched that their jurisdiction to try indictable offences existing at the time of Confederation may not be legislatively removed. See *McEvoy v. New Brunswick (Attorney General)*, [1983] S.C.J. No. 51, [1983] 1 S.C.R. 704 (S.C.C.). But see *Reference re Young Offenders Act (P.E.I.)*, [1990] S.C.J. No. 60, [1991] 1 S.C.R. 252 (S.C.C.) (upholding the conferral of exclusive jurisdiction over indictable matters involving "young offenders" to "youth courts" on the basis that there was no special jurisdiction over young persons at the time of Confederation).

[226] See *e.g.*, *Courts of Justice Act*, R.S.O. 1990, c. 43, ss. 2(1) and 13(2). Similarly, see *Court of Queen's Bench Act*, R.S.A. 2000, c. C-31, s. 2(1).

[227] See *Criminal Code*, R.S.C. 1985, c. C-46, s. 680.

[228] See *Criminal Code*, s. 839.

[229] See *Criminal Code*, ss. 686 and 687.

[230] See *e.g.*, *Ministry of Correctional Services Act*, R.S.O. 1992, c. M.22.

[231] See *Criminal Code*, R.S.C. 1985, c. C-46, s. 743.1.

§1.199 On a number of occasions the Supreme Court of Canada has relied on section 92(15) in upholding provincial legislation that clearly overlapped with federal criminal law.[232] In doing so, the Court has drawn some rather subtle distinctions. For example, in *Bédard v. Dawson*,[233] a case involving a Quebec statute that authorized judges to issue orders closing "disorderly houses", the Supreme Court explained that the legislation is "aimed at suppressing conditions calculated to favour the development of crime rather than at the punishment of crime. This is an aspect of the subject in respect of which the provinces seem to be free to legislate."[234]

§1.200 In contrast, in *R. v. Westendorp*,[235] a unanimous Supreme Court invalidated a municipal by-law that made it an offence for a person to remain on the street for the purposes of prostitution or to approach another person on the street for that purpose. The Court pointed out that the by-law was not aimed at regulating street traffic more generally but was "patently an attempt to control or punish prostitution".[236] This was very different from *Bédard*, said the Court, "where the provincial legislation under attack there was justified as concerned with the control and enjoyment of property."[237] Professor Hogg points to *Westendorp* as an important reminder that in order to be upheld under section 92(15) a provincial enactment must be firmly "anchored in property and civil rights or some other head of provincial power".[238]

(3) Shared Prosecutorial Authority

§1.201 It is now well established that the provinces have jurisdiction to prosecute most *Criminal Code* offences.[239] The uncontested source of that authority is the definition of "Attorney General" found in the *Criminal Code*. That term is

---

[232] See *Prince Edward Island (Secretary) v. Egan*, [1941] S.C.J. No. 20, [1941] S.C.R. 396 (S.C.C.) (upholding a provincial law that automatically suspended the licence of any driver convicted of impaired driving under the *Criminal Code*); *O'Grady v. Sparling*, [1960] S.C.J. No. 48, [1960] S.C.R. 804 (S.C.C.) and *R. v. Mann*, [1966] S.C.J. No. 3, [1966] S.C.R. 238 (S.C.C.) (upholding provincial offence of careless driving despite existence of federal criminal offence of dangerous driving); *R. v. Stephens*, [1960] S.C.J. No. 49, [1960] S.C.R. 823 (S.C.C.) (upholding provincial offence of failing to remain at the scene of an accident despite very similar offence in the *Criminal Code*); *R. v. Smith*, [1960] S.C.J. No. 47, [1960] S.C.R. 776 (S.C.C.) (upholding provincial offence of including false information in a prospectus despite very same offence in *Criminal Code*); *Nova Scotia (Board of Censors) v. McNeil*, [1978] S.C.J. No. 25, [1978] 2 S.C.R. 662 (S.C.C.) (provincial film censorship scheme upheld despite existence of obscenity offences in the *Criminal Code*).
[233] [1923] S.C.J. No. 30, [1923] S.C.R. 681 (S.C.C.) [*Bédard*].
[234] *Ibid.*, at 684 (S.C.R.).
[235] [1983] S.C.J. No. 6, [1983] 1 S.C.R. 43 (S.C.C.).
[236] *Ibid.*, at para. 13 (S.C.J.).
[237] *Ibid.*, at para. 16 (S.C.J.).
[238] Peter W. Hogg, *Constitutional Law of Canada*, 4th ed., vol. 1 (Toronto: Carswell, 1997) at 18-32.
[239] While Parliament has exclusive authority under s. 91(27) of the *Constitution Act, 1867* to prosecute *Criminal Code* (and other federal) offences, it may delegate this power to the provinces. See *Canada (Attorney General) v. Canadian National Transportation Ltd.*, [1983] S.C.J. No. 73, [1983] 2 S.C.R. 206 (S.C.C.); *R. v. Wetmore (County Court Judge)*, [1983] S.C.J. No. 74, [1983] 2 S.C.R. 284 (S.C.C.); *R. v. S.(S.)*, [1990] S.C.J. No. 66, [1990] 2 S.C.R. 254 (S.C.C.).

defined as generally meaning "the Attorney General or Solicitor General *of the province* in which those proceedings are taken and includes his or her lawful deputy."[240]

§1.202 Consequently, on a formal level, the Attorney General in each province has the authority to prosecute *Criminal Code* offences. In practice, the Attorney General delegates this authority to provincial Crown attorneys who are responsible for prosecuting most *Criminal Code* offences. As explained in far greater detail in Chapter 8, however, federal prosecutors also prosecute criminal offences. Briefly, in the territories, federal prosecutors prosecute all offences; in the provinces, they prosecute a few *Criminal Code* offences and most non-*Code* offences. There are also circumstances where the Attorney General of Canada is given concurrent prosecutorial authority along with the Attorney General in the particular province where the offence is alleged to have taken place. These further exceptions all involve situations in which federal authorities would have a special interest given that the offences will often be a matter of national and not simply local concern.

6.   SOURCES OF CRIMINAL PROCEDURE

§1.203 Unfortunately, unlike in some civil law jurisdictions, there is no comprehensive code of criminal procedure in Canada. Rather, the rules that govern the various phases of the Canadian criminal process come from three basic sources: the *Charter*, legislation and the common law. We draw upon these sources throughout this book in the course of describing the rules applying to each phase of the criminal process. It will be helpful, however, to make a few general comments about these sources here.

(1)   The *Charter*

§1.204 As discussed above in Part 4, the *Charter* is an important source of rules regarding the Canadian criminal process. As we stressed in that section, these rules flow not just from the *Charter*'s express wording (which in many cases is vague and open-ended) but also from their interpretation by the courts. For example, as detailed in Chapter 4, the Supreme Court of Canada has used the concise language of section 10(*b*) of the *Charter* (giving detainees the right to counsel and the right to be informed of that right) to erect a detailed scheme regulating police questioning. Similarly, as we discuss in Chapter 3, from the even more succinct language of section 8 ("Everyone has the right to be secure against unreasonable search or seizure") the courts have generated a complex and expansive set of rules regulating all manner of intrusions into individuals' privacy. We stress again, here, however, that these rules represent "a bare minimum below which the law must not fall".[241] In other words, both Parliament (through legislation) and judges (through the common law) may craft (and

---

[240] *Criminal Code*, R.S.C. 1985, c. C-46, s. 2 [emphasis added].
[241] *R. v. Oickle*, [2000] S.C.J. No. 38, [2000] 2 S.C.R. 3 at para. 31 (S.C.C.).

sometimes have crafted) criminal procedure rules that are more protective of the individual than those mandated by the *Charter*.

(2) Statutes

§1.205 There are a number of statutes that supply rules relevant to the criminal process. Just as with the *Charter*, statutory provisions must be read in conjunction with decided cases that have interpreted their meaning.

§1.206 Without a doubt, the most important criminal law statute is the *Criminal Code*.[242] The *Code* contains a number of procedural provisions that are relevant to every phase of the criminal process, though as mentioned in Part 5(1), above, these provisions are scattered throughout the statute and fall short of constituting a comprehensive code of criminal procedure.

§1.207 Other statutes also contain provisions relevant to criminal procedure. For example, some enactments creating criminal offences also include procedural provisions. The *Controlled Drugs and Substances Act*[243] is a good example. Not only does it create offences relating to possessing, trafficking and importing controlled substances, it also sets out specialized search and seizure powers applying to drug investigations.[244]

§1.208 Some other criminal statutes that do not create offences, like the *Youth Criminal Justice Act*,[245] also contain procedural provisions. That statute, which operates in conjunction with the substantive provisions found in the *Criminal Code*, contains a host of procedural provisions designed to address the unique vulnerabilities and circumstances of youth. These include enhanced protection for the right to counsel and taking of statements,[246] a more liberal bail regime[247] and a distinct set of sentencing principles and punishments.[248]

§1.209 Because criminal procedure falls exclusively under Parliament's constitutional authority, it is rare for provincial legislation to have any direct bearing on the criminal process. There are, however, areas where provincial legislation will necessarily overlap with federal criminal legislation. The best example of this involves matters relating to the use of roadways by motorists. Each province has legislation regulating the licensing of motorists and the registration of vehicles and prescribing the rules of the road.[249] At the same time, Parliament has seen fit to criminalize certain pernicious activities associated with driving, creating

---

[242] R.S.C. 1985, c. C-46.

[243] S.C. 1996, c. 19.

[244] *Ibid.*, s. 11. See also *Income Tax Act*, R.S.C. 1985 c. 1 (5th Supp.), s. 231.3 (creating a procedure for the issuance of search warrants to locate and seize evidence relevant to violations of that Act).

[245] S.C. 2002, c. 1.

[246] *Ibid.*, ss. 25, 146-147.

[247] *Ibid.*, s. 33.

[248] *Ibid.*, ss. 38 through 109.

[249] See *e.g.*, *Highway Traffic Act*, R.S.O. 1990, c. H.8 or *Traffic Safety Act*, R.S.A 2000, c. T-6.

offences such as dangerous driving,[250] impaired driving[251] and leaving the scene of an accident.[252] As the Supreme Court has acknowledged, safety on Canada's roadways is achieved through "an interlocking scheme of federal and provincial legislation".[253] Consequently, it is not uncommon for encounters that begin as a routine traffic safety stop under the authority of provincial traffic legislation to end with a charge under the *Criminal Code*. Navigating the legal implications of such encounters may sometimes require recourse to the relevant provincial traffic legislation, *Charter* jurisprudence regarding the limits on police investigative powers, and the relevant provisions of the *Criminal Code*.

(3) Rules of Court

§1.210 Parliament has conferred authority on the three levels of court in each province — the appellate court, superior trial court and provincial court — to create rules of court to manage criminal proceedings before them.[254] These rules must be published in the *Canada Gazette*.[255] This authority has been exercised to varying degrees and the rules promulgated are often available on the websites maintained by the various courts in each of the provinces and territories.[256]

§1.211 These rules of court regulate pleadings, practice and procedure in criminal matters. For example, in the trial courts, these rules may specify how much notice must be provided to an opposing party for the various types of applications that are routinely brought in criminal cases (for example, bail reviews, adjournments, *Charter*, particulars and severance). They may require certain materials to be filed in support of such applications and prescribe the form and content of those materials. The same is true of the rules established by the appellate courts, which set down filing deadlines, specify the form and content of notices of appeal and other relevant documents, and prescribe what must be filed by way of supporting documentation in order for an appeal to be heard.

§1.212 The rules that apply in the various levels of court in each of the provinces are beyond the scope of this book. Nevertheless, when it comes to nuts and bolts issues, such as when notice must be given, and the form and content of what needs to be filed, the relevant rules of court must be consulted to ensure compliance with any specified procedural requirements.

---

[250] *Criminal Code*, R.S.C. 1985, c. C-46, s. 249(1)(*a*).

[251] *Ibid.*, s. 253.

[252] *Ibid.*, s. 252.

[253] *R. v. Orbanski; R. v. Elias*, [2005] S.C.J. No. 37, [2005] 2 S.C.R. 3 at para. 27 (S.C.C.).

[254] See *Criminal Code*, R.S.C. 1985, c. C-46, s. 482. Although the superior court of criminal jurisdiction and every provincial court of appeal has the authority to create its own rules (*ibid.*, s. 482(1)), the power vested in the provincial and territorial courts to do so is subject to the approval of the lieutenant governor in council of the relevant jurisdiction (*ibid.*, s. 482(2)).

[255] *Criminal Code*, s. 482(4).

[256] In Ontario, for example, see *Ontario Court of Appeal Criminal Appeal Rules*, SI/93-169, *Superior Court of Justice Criminal Proceedings Rules*, SI/92-99, *Rules of the Ontario Court of Justice in Criminal Proceedings*, SI/97-133.

(4)   The Common Law

(a)   Defining the "Common Law"

§1.213 The "common law" is a term used to describe two related types of law created by judges. Both are important sources of rules regarding the criminal process. First, there are the decisions of judges interpreting and applying either legislative or constitutional provisions. For example, in the course of delivering reasons a judge may say something relevant to understanding section 8 of the *Charter* or a particular legislated search and seizure power. Such a decision may clarify the rules governing police search and seizure powers. Taken together, all such decisions form part of the "common law". In this category, an important limitation on how far judges can go in creating new law is the plain meaning and purpose of the legislative or constitutional text being interpreted.[257]

§1.214 A second and more traditional definition of the "common law" refers to the decisions of judges that are not anchored in any constitutional or legislative text. Judges developed this body of law over time, using established tools of legal reasoning, with each written decision on a particular topic serving to develop the existing law through a gradual and incremental process.[258] In this second category, the theoretical limits on how far judges can go in creating law comes from the institutional constraints on the judiciary in a constitutional democracy. On a number of occasions the Supreme Court has acknowledged these functional limitations.[259] For example, on behalf of the Court, Justice Iacobucci explained that:

---

[257] For an explanation of the Supreme Court's interpretive approach to *Charter* guarantees, see Part 4(2), above, in particular §1.136 to §1.140. In the context of statutory interpretation, the Court has repeatedly endorsed the view that "the words of an Act are to be read in their entire context and in their grammatical and ordinary sense harmoniously with the scheme of the Act, the object of the Act, and the intention of Parliament." See *Bell ExpressVu Limited Partnership v. Rex*, [2002] S.C.J. No. 43, [2002] 2 S.C.R. 559 at para. 26 (S.C.C.). See also *Stubart Investments Ltd. v. Canada*, [1984] S.C.J. No. 25, [1984] 1 S.C.R. 536 at 578 (S.C.C.), *per* Estey J.; *Québec (Communauté urbaine) v. Corp. Notre-Dame de Bon-Secours*, [1994] S.C.J. No. 78, [1994] 3 S.C.R. 3 at 17 (S.C.C.); *Re Rizzo & Rizzo Shoes Ltd.*, [1998] S.C.J. No. 2, [1998] 1 S.C.R. 27 at para. 21 (S.C.C.); *R. v. Gladue*, [1999] 1 S.C.R. 688 at para. 25; *R. v. Araujo*, [2000] 2 S.C.R. 992 at para. 26; *R. v. Sharpe*, [2001] S.C.J. No. 3, [2001] 1 S.C.R. 45 at para. 33 (S.C.C.), *per* McLachlin C.J.C.; *Chieu v. Canada (Minister of Citizenship and Immigration)*, [2002] S.C.J. No. 1, [2002] 1 S.C.R. 84 at para. 27 (S.C.C.).

[258] See generally, Melvin Aron Eisenberg, *The Nature of the Common Law* (Cambridge, MA and London: Harvard University Press, 1988) who explains the common law ideal of "doctrinal stability", which finds expression in the concept of *stare decisis*. According to Eisenberg, "the courts must establish and apply rules that are supported by the general standards of society or the special standards of the legal system, and must adopt a process of reasoning that is replicable by the profession". *Ibid.*, at 47. Eisenberg goes on to provide a useful taxonomy of the various modes of common law legal reasoning, which include: (*i*) Reasoning from Precedent; (*ii*) Reasoning from Principle; (*iii*) Reasoning by Analogy; (*iv*) Reasoning from Doctrines Established in the Professional Literature; (*v*) Reasoning from Hypotheticals. *Ibid.*, at 50 to 103.

[259] See *Watkins v. Olafson*, [1989] S.C.J. No. 94, [1989] 2 S.C.R. 750 at 760-61 (S.C.C.) ("Where the matter is one of a small extension of existing rules to meet the exigencies of a new case and the consequences of the change are readily assessable, judges can and should vary existing principles. But where the revision is major and its ramifications complex, the courts must proceed with great caution."). See also *Winnipeg Child and Family Services (Northwest Area) v. D.F.G.*,

... in a constitutional democracy such as ours it is the legislature and not the courts which has the major responsibility for law reform; and for any changes to the law which may have complex ramifications, however necessary or desirable such changes may be, they should be left to the legislature. The judiciary should confine itself to those incremental changes which are necessary to keep the common law in step with the dynamic and evolving fabric of our society.[260]

§1.215 In the context of criminal procedure, this idea of judicial restraint in developing the common law was very strong in the pre-*Charter* era. Although the *Criminal Code* dealt with some very basic issues, like the authority of the police to arrest[261] and to search with warrants,[262] many important details about the parameters of police authority went undefined. Despite this ambiguity, the courts were reluctant to fill the gaps by creating new common law police powers. One exception was the recognition of a power to search persons arrested despite the absence of any authority for this practice in the *Criminal Code*. To the extent that such a power was recognized before the *Charter*, it was said to derive from the "common law".[263] Civil and criminal cases addressing that power, however, were quite rare,[264] so its exact parameters were far from clear.[265] *Charter* challenges ultimately forced the Supreme Court to confront these gaps and finally led it to sketch out the details of this important police power.[266] The *Charter*'s unintended impact on how the "common law" is now understood in Canada is addressed immediately below in Part 6(4)(*b*).

(b) The Ancillary Powers Doctrine

§1.216 One of the more unexpected by-products of *Charter* litigation has been how it has served to reveal serious deficiencies in the scattered collection of statutory and common law rules that make up the law of police powers in Canada. Despite general pronouncements about the need to avoid far-reaching changes to the common law,[267] over the past 25 years the Supreme Court has been much more willing to use its "common law" law-making authority to authorize previously unrecognized investigative powers.

[1997] S.C.J. No. 96, [1997] 3 S.C.R. 925 at para. 18 (S.C.C.); *Bow Valley Husky (Bermuda) Ltd. v. Saint John Ship Building Ltd.*, [1997] S.C.J. No. 111, [1997] 3 S.C.R. 1210 at para. 93 (S.C.C.), *per* McLachlin J. (as she then was); *R. v. Cuerrier*, [1998] S.C.J. No. 64, [1998] 2 S.C.R. 371, 127 C.C.C. (3d) 1 at para. 43 (S.C.C.), *per* McLachlin J. (as she then was), concurring.

[260] *R. v. Salituro*, [1991] S.C.J. No. 97, [1991] 3 S.C.R. 654 (S.C.C.).

[261] *Criminal Code*, R.S.C. 1970, c. C-34, ss. 449-450.

[262] *Ibid.*, at s. 443.

[263] See Report of the Canadian Committee on Corrections, *Toward Unity: Criminal Justice and Corrections* (Ottawa: Queen's Printer, 1969) at 61-63 (Chair: Roger Ouimet). See *e.g.*, *R. v. Brezack*, [1949] O.J. No. 492, [1949] O.R. 888 (Ont. C.A.).

[264] The Supreme Court only addressed the existence of this power for the first time after the *Charter*. See *Cloutier v. Langlois*, [1990] S.C.J. No. 10, [1990] 1 S.C.R. 158 (S.C.C.).

[265] In dealing with strip-searches incidental to arrest, the Supreme Court recently acknowledged much of this. See *R. v. Golden*, [2001] S.C.J. No. 81, [2001] 3 S.C.R. 679 at para. 67 (S.C.C.).

[266] The Court has now dealt with various aspects of the power, discussed in much greater detail in Chapter 3, Part 4.

[267] See §1.214 above and supporting references.

§1.217 The device developed by the Supreme Court for creating new "common law" police powers is known as the "ancillary powers doctrine". It allows for the recognition of police powers by deploying what is essentially a cost-benefit analysis. This law-making device involves two steps. First, the court asks whether the impugned actions of police fall within the scope of their broad duties.[268] Assuming the answer is "yes",[269] the second step involves a weighing of the apparent benefits (usually for law enforcement and public safety) against any interference with individual liberty. If the benefits are characterized as outweighing the costs, the action is said to be "justifiable" and a new police power is born.[270]

§1.218 The Supreme Court first used the ancillary powers doctrine to create a new police power in *R. v. Dedman.*[271] In that case, a slim (five judge) majority of the Supreme Court seized on what was then an obscure decision of the English Court of Criminal Appeal. In *R. v. Waterfield,*[272] the English court had merely used the two-part test referred to above to decide whether a police officer was acting in "execution of his duty" — an element of the offence charged in that case.[273] In *Dedman,* however, a majority of the Supreme Court of Canada transformed the test into a basis for recognizing an entirely new police power: the authority of police to conduct sobriety check-stops of motorists.

§1.219 The legitimacy of this transformation was rejected by Chief Justice in his scathing dissent in *Dedman.* The majority's approach, was "nothing short of a fiat for illegality on the part of the police whenever the benefit of police action appeared to outweigh the infringement of individual's rights."[274] For him, it was

---

[268] The source of police duties is derived from legislation, usually the legislation governing the police in the particular jurisdiction, and tends to define police duties in expansive terms such as "preserving the peace", "preventing crimes and other offences" and "apprehending criminals and other offenders". See *e.g., Police Services Act,* R.S.O. 1990, c. P15, s. 42.

[269] It invariably will be, unless the officer is involved in some entirely illegitimate activity completely unrelated to his or her official duties. See *Brown v. Durham (Regional Municipality) Police Force,* [1998] O.J. No. 5274, 131 C.C.C. (3d) 1 at 116-117 (Ont. C.A.).

[270] See *R. v. Dedman,* [1985] S.C.J. No. 45, [1985] 2 S.C.R. 2 (S.C.C.). See also *R. v. Mann,* [2004] S.C.J. No. 49, [2004] 3 S.C.R. 59 at para. 24 (S.C.C.).

[271] [1985] S.C.J. No. 45, [1985] 2 S.C.R. 2 (S.C.C.) [*Dedman*].

[272] [1964] 1 Q.B. 164 (Ct. Crim. App.).

[273] The relevant passage from *R. v. Waterfield,* [1964] 1 Q.B. 164 at 170-71 (Ct. Crim. App.) provides: "In most cases it is probably more convenient to consider what the police constable was actually doing and in particular whether such conduct was prima facie an unlawful interference with a person's liberty or property If so, it is then relevant to consider whether (a) such conduct falls within the general scope of any duty imposed by statute or recognised at common law and (b) whether such conduct, albeit within the general scope of such a duty, involved an unjustifiable use of police powers associated with the duty. Thus, while it is no doubt right to say in general terms that police constables have a duty to prevent crime and a duty, when crime is committed, to bring the offender to justice, it is also clear from the decided cases that when the execution of these general duties involves interference with the person or property of a private person, the powers of constables are not unlimited."

[274] *R. v. Dedman,* [1985] S.C.J. No. 45, [1985] 2 S.C.R. 2 at 15 (S.C.C.) (quoting *Reference re: Judicature Act (Alberta), s. 27(1),* [1984] S.C.J. No. 64, [1984] 2 S.C.R. 697 at 718-19 (S.C.C.), Dickson C.J.C., dissenting). As Justice Patrick Healy has correctly pointed out, the ancillary powers doctrine crept into our law like "something of a Trojan-horse for the expansion of police powers": Patrick Healy, "Investigative Detention in Canada" [2005] Crim. L.R. 98 at 107.

"the function of the legislature, not the courts, to authorize . . . police action that would otherwise be unlawful as a violation of rights traditionally protected at common law."[275]

§1.220 The law-making authority that *Dedman* recognized lay dormant for close to two decades. In the interim, the Supreme Court of Canada repeatedly refused to recognize new police powers in response to *Charter* challenges under section 8, thereby engaging Parliament in a form of dialogue that led to the creation of a number of much needed legislated search powers.[276] During this period, the Supreme Court sent strong signals that it would not again use the ancillary powers doctrine to create new police powers. As Justice La Forest explained on behalf of the majority in *R. v. Wong:*[277]

> The common law powers of search were extremely narrow, and the courts have left it to Parliament to extend them where need be ... it does not sit well for the courts, as the protectors of our fundamental rights, to widen the possibility of encroachments on these personal liberties. It falls to Parliament to make incursions on fundamental rights if it is of the view that they are needed for the protection of the public in a properly balanced system of criminal justice.[278]

§1.221 This changed with the Court's 2004 decision in *R. v. Mann,*[279] where the Supreme Court used the ancillary powers doctrine to recognize an investigative detention and protective search power.[280] The use of the ancillary power doctrine to create new police powers has been widely criticized by commentators.[281] Crit-

---

[275] *R. v. Dedman,* [1985] S.C.J. No. 45, [1985] 2 S.C.R. 2 at 15 (S.C.C.).

[276] See James Stribopoulos, "In Search of Dialogue: The Supreme Court, Police Powers, and the *Charter*" (2005) 31 Queen's L.J. 1 at 6-13. The one exception was the recognition of a police power to enter private premises to investigate disconnected 911 calls. See *R. v. Godoy,* [1998] S.C.J. No. 85, [1999] 1 S.C.R. 311 (S.C.C.). This power is discussed in detail in Chapter 3, Part 4(5).

[277] [1990] S.C.J. No. 118, [1990] 3 S.C.R. 36 (S.C.C.).

[278] *Ibid.,* at 56 (S.C.R.).

[279] [2004] S.C.J. No. 49, [2004] 3 S.C.R. 59 (S.C.C.).

[280] *R. v. Mann,* [2004] S.C.J. No. 49, [2004] 3 S.C.R. 59 (S.C.C.), is discussed in detail in Chapter 2, Part 4(3)(*a*) dealing with Detention and Arrest. Ironically, the Court failed to acknowledge in *Mann* the extensive body of case law, clearly and consistently holding that at *common law* there is no power to detain for investigative purposes short of actual arrest. See *R. v. Hicks,* [1988] O.J. No. 957, 42 C.C.C. (3d) 394 at 400 (Ont. C.A.), affd on other grounds [1990] S.C.J. No. 7, [1990] 1 S.C.R. 120, 54 C.C.C. (3d) 575 (S.C.C.); *R. v. Moran,* [1987] O.J. No. 794, 36 C.C.C. (3d) 225 at 258 (Ont. C.A.), leave to appeal refused [1988] S.C.C.A. No. 213 (S.C.C.); *R. v. Esposito,* [1985] O.J. No. 1002, 24 C.C.C. (3d) 88 at 94 (Ont. C.A.), leave to appeal refused [1986] S.C.C.A. No. 63, [1986] 1 S.C.R. viii (S.C.C.); *R. v. Dedman,* [1981] O.J. No. 2993, 59 C.C.C. (2d) 97 at 108-109 (Ont. C.A.), affd on other grounds [1985] S.C.J. No. 45, [1985] 2 S.C.R. 2 (S.C.C.); *R. v. O'Donnell; R. v. Cluett,* [1982] N.S.J. No. 542, 3 C.C.C. (3d) 333 at 347-48 (N.S.C.A.), revd on other grounds [1985] S.C.J. No. 54, 21 C.C.C. (3d) 318 (S.C.C.); *R. v. Guthrie,* [1982] A.J. No. 29 69 C.C.C. (2d) 216 at 218-19 (Alta. C.A.); *R. v. Moore,* [1978] S.C.J. No. 82, [1979] 1 S.C.R. 195, 43 C.C.C. (2d) 83 at 89-90 (S.C.C.); *Rice v. Connolly,* [1966] 2 Q.B. 414 at 419 (Div. Ct.); *Kenlin v. Gardner,* [1967] 2 Q.B. 510 (Div. Ct.); *Koechlin v. Waugh,* [1957] O.J. No. 105, 118 C.C.C. 24 at 26-27 (Ont. C.A.).

[281] See generally, Howard Chisvin, "R. v. Dedman: Annotation" (1985) 34 M.V.R. 165; Glen Luther, "Police Power and *The Charter of Rights and Freedoms*: Creation or Control" (1986) 51 Sask. L. Rev. 117: R.J. Delisle, "Judicial Creation of Police Powers" (1993) 20 C.R. (4th) 29;

ics argue that the Court's use of the ancillary powers doctrine to create new police powers conflicts sharply with the traditional view of the common law. As mentioned, common law courts had traditionally insisted that any interference with individual liberty or property rights be premised on clear legal authority. Absent such authority, the common law erred on the side of individual freedom, a notion that came to be termed the "principle of legality".[282] Critics further asserted that when appellate courts exceed their institutional capacities and take on an inherently legislative role, the rules they create often fail to provide sufficient guidance to those who must apply and enforce the law on the ground: police and the lower courts.[283] This ambiguity in turn may increase the risk of unjustified and abusive intrusions on individual liberty and privacy.[284]

§1.222 Nevertheless, *Mann* seemed to signal that any reluctance the Supreme Court had periodically expressed about creating new police powers had fallen to the wayside. Since *Mann*, the Court has used the ancillary powers doctrine to recognize a host of unprecedented police powers, including:

Heather Pringle, "The Smoke and Mirrors of Godoy: Creating Common Law Authority While Making Feeney Disappear" (1999) 21 C.R. (5th) 227; Don Stuart, "Time to Recodify Criminal Law and Rise Above Law and Order Expediency: Lessons from the Manitoba Warriors Prosecution" (2000) 28 Man. L.J. 89; Aman S. Patel, "Detention and Articulable Cause: Arbitrariness and Growing Judicial Deference to Police Judgment" (2000) 45 Crim. L.Q. 198; Steve Coughlan, "Search Based on Articulable Cause: Proceed with Caution or Full Stop?" (2002) 2 C.R. (6th) 49; Lesley A. McCoy, "Liberty's Last Stand? Tracing the Limits of Investigative Detention" (2002) 46 Crim. L.Q. 319; Peter Sankoff, "Articulable Cause Based Searches Incident to Detention – This *Cooke* May Spoil the Broth" (2002) 2 C.R. (6th) 41; James Stribopoulos, "A Failed Experiment? Investigative Detention: Ten Years Later" (2003) 41 Alta. L. Rev. 335; Lesley A. McCoy, "Some Answers from the Supreme Court on Investigative Detention ... and Some More Questions" (2004) 49 Crim. L.Q. 268; Tim Quigley, "Mann It's a Disappointing Decision" (2004) 21 C.R. (6th) 41; Tim Quigley, "Brief Investigatory Detentions: A Critique of *R. v. Simpson*" (2004) 41 Alta. L. Rev. 93; Patrick Healy, "Investigative Detention in Canada" [2005] Crim. L.R. 98; Joseph R. Marin, "R. v. Mann: Further Down the Slippery Slope" (2005) 42 Alta. L. Rev. 1123; James Stribopoulos, "In *Search* of Dialogue: The Supreme Court, Police Powers and the Charter" (2005) 31 Queen's L.J. 1; Christina Skibinsky, "Regulating Mann in Canada" (2006) 69 Sask. L. Rev. 197; James Stribopoulos, "The Limits of Judicially Created Police Powers: Investigative Detention After *Mann*" (2007) 52 Crim. L.Q. 299; Steve Coughlan, "Common Law Police Powers and the Rule of Law" (2007) 47 C.R. (6th) 266; James Stribopoulos, "Sniffing Out the Ancillary Powers Implications of the Dog Sniff Cases" (2009) 47 S.C.L.R. (2d) 35; Don Stuart, "The Unfortunate Dilution of Section 8 Protection: Some Teeth Remain" (1999) 25 Queen's L.J. 65; Don Stuart, "Godoy: The Supreme Court Reverts to the Ancillary Powers Doctrine to Fill a Gap in Police Power" (1999) 21 C.R. (5th) 225. However, in fairness, Don Stuart seems to have changed his mind recently about the ancillary powers doctrine. See Don Stuart, "Charter Standards for Investigative Powers: Have the Courts Got the Balance Right?" in Jamie Cameron & James Stribopoulos, eds., *The Charter and Criminal Justice: Twenty-Five Years Later* (Markham: LexisNexis Canada, 2008) 4.

[282] For a detailed discussion of the principle of legality, including its origins and its recognition in Canadian law, see Part 4(1), above.

[283] See generally, James Stribopoulos, "The Limits of Judicially Created Police Powers: Investigative Detention After *Mann*" (2007) 52 Crim. L.Q. 299.

[284] See, for example, Lesley A. McCoy, "Some Answers from the Supreme Court on Investigative Detention ... and Some More Questions" (2004) 49 Crim. L.Q. 268; Joseph R. Marin, "R. v. Mann: Further Down the Slippery Slope" (2005) 42 Alta. L. Rev. 1123; James Stribopoulos, "The Limits of Judicially Created Police Powers: Investigative Detention After *Mann*" (2007) 52 Crim. L.Q. 299.

(*i*) a power to ask drivers questions about alcohol consumption and request their participation in sobriety tests without first complying with s. 10(*b*) of the *Charter*;[285]

(*ii*) a power to conduct criminal investigative roadblock stops where such a stop is tailored to the information possessed by police, the seriousness of the offence being investigated and the temporal and geographic connection between the situation being investigated and the timing and location of the roadblock;[286] and

(*iii*) a power to use a drug detecting dog to sniff at an individual, as well as his or her belongings, where the police have reasonable grounds to suspect the individual is carrying narcotics, in order to confirm or refute that suspicion.[287]

In the decisions recognizing this last power — *R. v. Kang-Brown*[288] and *R. v. M. (A.)*[289] — the judicial debate over the legitimacy and efficacy of using the ancillary powers doctrine to create new police powers was rekindled. Though a slim majority of the Court was happy to continue with the *Dedman/Mann*[290] approach, in his concurring reasons in *Kang-Brown*, Justice LeBel (joined by Justices Fish, Abella and Charron) demurred, refusing to recognize a common law power to use drug-sniffing dogs. In a judgment strongly reminiscent of the warnings of Justices Dickson and La Forest in the late 1980s and early 1990s, he rejected the idea that it was the Court's role to fill gaps in police powers. He wrote:

> The common law has long been viewed as a law of liberty. Should we move away from that tradition, which is still part of the ethos of our legal system and of our democracy? This case is about the freedom of individuals and the proper function of the courts as guardians of the Constitution. I doubt that it should lead us to depart from the common law tradition of freedom by changing the common law itself to restrict the freedoms protected by the Constitution under s. 8 of the *Charter*.[291]

---

[285] *Canadian Charter of Rights and Freedoms*, Part I of the *Constitution Act, 1982*, being Schedule B to the *Canada Act 1982* (U.K.), 1982, c. 11; *R. v. Orbanksi; R. v. Elias*, [2005] S.C.J. No. 37, [2005] 2 S.C.R. 3 (S.C.C.). The detention portion of this power is discussed in Chapter 2, Part 4(2)(*e*), and the questioning component is discussed in Chapter 4, Part 3(4)(*g*).

[286] *R. v. Clayton*, [2007] S.C.J. No. 32, [2007] 2 S.C.R. 725 (S.C.C.). This power is discussed in Chapter 2, Part 4(3)(*b*). Although LeBel and Fish JJ. had expressed strong scepticism about this sort of *ad hoc* law-making in their dissenting judgment in *R. v. Orbanksi; R. v. Elias*, [2005] S.C.J. No. 37, [2005] 2 S.C.R. 3 (S.C.C.), their vote in favour of recognizing a police power at "common law" to conduct roadblocks for criminal investigative purposes in *Clayton*, seemed to signal a change of heart.

[287] See *R. v. Kang-Brown*, [2008] S.C.J. No. 18, [2008] 1 S.C.R. 456 (S.C.C.); *R. v. M. (A.)*, [2008] S.C.J. No. 19, [2008] 1 S.C.R. 569 (S.C.C.). Discussed in Chapter 3, Part 4(4).

[288] [2008] S.C.J. No. 18, [2008] 1 S.C.R. 456 (S.C.C.).

[289] [2008] S.C.J. No. 19, [2008] 1 S.C.R. 569 (S.C.C.).

[290] *R. v. Dedman*, [1985] S.C.J. No. 45, [1985] 2 S.C.R. 2 at 15 (S.C.C.); *R. v. Mann*, [2004] S.C.J. No. 49, [2004] 3 S.C.R. 59 (S.C.C.).

[291] *R. v. Kang-Brown*, [2008] S.C.J. No. 18 at para. 12, [2008] 1 S.C.R. 456 (S.C.C.).

Echoing the academic criticism of *Mann*, Justice LeBel noted that "the courts are ill-equipped to develop an adequate legal framework for the use of police dogs."[292]

§1.223 It is difficult to quarrel with these observations about the historic importance of the common law in protecting liberty and the need for courts to act with restraint before recognizing new police powers, especially where those powers would have complex and far-reaching consequences. The only troubling aspect of Justice LeBel's analysis is his failure to convincingly explain why it was appropriate in *Mann* and *Clayton* to use the ancillary powers doctrine in this way, whereas it was inappropriate to do so in *Kang-Brown* and *M. (A.)*. The complexity of the various issues raised by investigative detention power (for example, the use of force to effect such detentions, the temporal and geographic limits on them, the difficulty in reconciling this power with the right to counsel on detention found in section 10(*b*) and what, if any, corresponding obligations the power might impose on those detained, *etc.*[293]) suggests that, if anything, the dog sniff power is better suited for recognition under the ancillary powers doctrine than were investigative detentions.

§1.224 In his concurring reasons in *Kang-Brown*, Justice Binnie (joined by Chief Justice McLachlin) took exception to this sudden trepidation on the part of Justices LeBel, Fish, Abella and Charron. For Justice Binnie, the use of the ancillary powers doctrine to create new police powers is part of a long tradition of "incremental" expansion of the common law. That doctrine simply provides courts with a methodology, like many judge-created methodologies used by common law courts over time, to develop the law in a particular area.[294]

§1.225 The problem with this view is that it largely ignores the fact that there is nothing at all "incremental" about how new police powers are created under the cost-benefit analysis supplied by the ancillary powers doctrine. The truth is, our courts have used the doctrine to create police powers out of whole cloth. These new powers have no linkage to earlier judgments, and sometimes serve to implicitly overrule cases that pronounced on the absence of any such power (investigative detention providing the best example).

§1.226 That said, Justice Binnie was right to point out that Justice LeBel's approach could potentially breed even greater uncertainty. Unless the Court reverses itself fully on the ancillary powers doctrine, litigants would have no way of knowing what approach the Court might be inclined to employ in a given case, one in which it is receptive to creating new police powers or one in which it insists on deferring such law-making responsibilities to Parliament.[295] For Justice Binnie, the question was long ago settled. The only way forward, he insists,

---

[292] *Ibid.*, at para. 15 (S.C.J.).

[293] See generally, James Stribopoulos, "The Limits of Judicially Created Police Powers: Investigative Detention After *Mann*" (2007) 52 Crim. L.Q. 299. Each of these issues is discussed in detail in Chapter 2, Part 4(3)(*a*).

[294] *R. v. Kang-Brown*, [2008] S.C.J. No. 18 at paras. 50-51, [2008] 1 S.C.R. 456 (S.C.C.).

[295] *Ibid.*, at para. 22 (S.C.J.).

is for the courts to "proceed incrementally with the *Waterfield/Dedman* analysis of common law police powers rather than try to re-cross the Rubicon to retrieve the fallen flag of the *Dedman* dissent."[296]

§1.227 The ancillary powers doctrine may thus be at a crossroads. If the Court continues on its current path, prosecutors will continue to be able to argue for the recognition of new common law police powers, they will often succeed and Parliament will largely be absolved of any responsibility to define and regulate new police powers. Alternatively, we could see a return to the era when Parliament and the courts adhered more closely to their traditional, dialogical roles: the former promulgating new police powers and the latter interpreting their scope and scrutinizing them for constitutional compliance. We hope that the Supreme Court chooses the latter road.

---

[296] *Ibid.*, at para. 51. For a critique of Binnie J.'s use of the "crossing the Rubicon" metaphor as especially inappropriate in light of the historic importance of judges overruling wrongly decided cases, see James Stribopoulos, "Sniffing Out the Ancillary Powers Implications of the Dog Sniff Cases" (2009) 47 S.C.L.R. (2d) 35 at 50-51.

PART II

CRIMINAL INVESTIGATIONS

Chapter 2

DETENTION AND ARREST

1. INTRODUCTION

§2.1 It is impossible to overstate the importance of individual liberty. As Justice Iacobucci observed, "[a]t the heart of a free and democratic society is the liberty of its subjects".[1] One of the most important aspects of individual liberty is the right to move about freely without unjustified state interference. Nevertheless, even in the freest of societies, public safety concerns will sometimes justify state interference with an individual's freedom of movement. Everyone's freedom would suffer if the state lacked the legal tools necessary to apprehend and imprison those who perpetrate crime. As a result, like all rights, liberty is not absolute. Striking the right balance between freedom of movement and public safety is no easy task. This chapter explains how Canadian law attempts to balance these important but competing interests.

§2.2 This chapter begins with a brief history of how Anglo-Canadian law has attempted to protect freedom of movement. It then introduces and explains section 9 of the *Charter*,[2] which provides that "[e]veryone has the right not to be arbitrarily detained or imprisoned." That provision supplies the constitutional framework for regulating the ways in which the state may interfere with the individual's liberty. The chapter concludes by explaining the contemporary detention powers possessed by Canadian police, including the arrest power.

2. PROTECTING LIBERTY BEFORE THE *CHARTER*: DETENTION AND ARREST HISTORICALLY

§2.3 In England, the historic importance of protecting liberty can be traced all the way back to the *Magna Carta*.[3] In that document, one finds the seeds of what would become the key legal safeguard for nearly eight centuries,[4] namely, the

---

[1] See *R. v. Hall*, [2002] S.C.J. No. 65 at para. 47, [2002] 3 S.C.R. 309 (S.C.C.), *per* Iacobucci J., dissenting.

[2] *Canadian Charter of Rights and Freedoms*, Part I of the *Constitution Act, 1982*, being Schedule B to the *Canada Act 1982* (U.K.), 1982, c. 11 [*Charter*].

[3] 9 Hen. III, c. 29.

[4] See *Magna Carta*, 9 Hen. III, c. 29. The *Magna Carta* was drafted in 1215. Article 39 provided: "No Freeman shall be taken, or imprisoned, or be disseised of his ... Liberties ... or be outlawed or exiled, or any otherwise destroyed; nor we will not pass upon him or condemn him, but by lawful Judgement of his Peers, or by the Law of the Land. We will sell to no man, we will not deny or defer to any man either Justice or Right."

idea that liberty could only be interfered with when justified by law.[5] In time, this prohibition on unlawful deprivations of liberty came to be known as the "principle of legality". The origins, operation and limitations of this principle are explained in greater detail in Chapter 1, Part 4(1).

§2.4 At common law, there was only one recognized means by which state officials could suspend an individual's liberty: arrest. It was the prevalence of complaints about false imprisonment that provided the forum for the evolution of arrest law. Civil suits brought by persons claiming to be victims of improper arrests led courts to create more precise legal rules.[6] Thus, by the eighteenth century the rules of arrest at common law were well settled. A suspected felon could be arrested without a warrant first being procured. A constable had both a right and a duty to arrest if he had reasonable grounds to believe that a felony had been committed and that the party to be arrested was guilty of the crime. In addition, an arrest was permitted in order to prevent the commission of a felony.[7]

§2.5 In contrast, neither private citizen nor public officer could make an arrest for a misdemeanour without first obtaining a warrant. A narrow exception to this general prohibition existed, however. A warrantless arrest was permissible if the misdemeanour involved a breach of the peace, or if there were grounds for believing that a breach of the peace was about to occur or be renewed in an arresting officer's presence.[8] In all other cases, for instance where the breach of the peace had already subsided, a misdemeanour arrest was only possible after obtaining a warrant from a magistrate.[9]

§2.6 In Canada, the first *Criminal Code* included an arrest power.[10] Even though no statute expressly abolished the common law powers of arrest, this was the effect of other *Code* provisions. First, the original *Criminal Code* abandoned common law felonies and misdemeanours in favour of statutorily prescribed summary and indictable offences. In addition, in time, the *Criminal Code* did

---

[5]　　Albert V. Dicey, the revered English constitutional law scholar, explained this common law principle as follows: "The right to personal liberty as understood in England means in substance a person's right not to be subjected to imprisonment, arrest, or other physical coercion in any manner that does not admit of legal justification. .... personal freedom in this sense of the term is secured in England by the strict maintenance of the principle that no man can be arrested or imprisoned except in due course of law, *i.e.* .. under some legal warrant or authority... ." See Albert V. Dicey, *Introduction to the Study of the Law of the Constitution*, 8th ed. (London: Macmillan, 1915) at 198, 203-204.

[6]　　William S. Holdsworth, *A History of English Law*, 3d ed., vol. 3 (Boston: Little Brown and Co., 1922) at 599-600.

[7]　　See *Samuel v. Payne* (1780), 1 Dougl. K.B. 359; *Leachinsky v. Christie*, [1946] K.B. 124 at 128-29 (C.A.), affd [1947] A.C. 573 (H.L.). Also see *R. v. Dedman*, [1985] S.C.J. No. 45, [1985] 2 S.C.R. 2 (S.C.C.), *per* Dickson C.J.C., dissenting; Glanville W. Williams, "Arrest for Felony at Common Law" [1954] Crim. L.R. 408.

[8]　　See *Leachinsky v. Christie*, [1946] K.B. 124 at 128-29 (C.A.), affd [1947] A.C. 573 (H.L.). Also see Glanville Williams, "Arrest for Breach of the Peace," [1954] Criminal L. Rev. 578 at 578. But see *Atwater v. City of Lago Vista*, 532 U.S. 318 at 326-45 (2001) (concluding that there was a lack of consensus at common law as to whether a breach of the peace was a precondition for a warrantless misdemeanour arrest).

[9]　　See *Cooke v. Nethercote* (1835), 172 Eng. Rep. 1443 at 1445; *Regina v. Tooley* (1710), 92 Eng. Rep. 349 at 352; *Mathews v. Biddullph* (1841), 133 Eng. Rep. 1195.

[10]　See *Criminal Code, 1892*, S.C. 1892, c. 29, s. 552.

away with convictions for common law offences.[11] The necessary implication of these developments was the elimination of common law arrest powers in Canada.[12] Today, arrest powers are derived exclusively from statute. These statutory powers are explained in Part 4(4), below.

§2.7 Before the *Charter*, Canadian police were said to lack any power to interfere with an individual's liberty short of arrest. A long string of cases[13] and commentary[14] repeatedly reaffirmed the view that the police had only two legal options when dealing with a suspected wrongdoer: arrest or release.[15] The reality on the ground, however, was much different. Police frequently detained people short of arrest in the course of investigating crime and maintaining public order.[16] Unfortunately, such unlawful detentions were only very rarely subject to legal scrutiny. As explained more fully in Chapter 1, Part 4(1), before the enactment of the *Charter*, the protection of individual liberty against unjustified state intrusion was more theoretical than real. There were ostensibly two key protections in place during this period, the principle of legality and the *Canadian Bill of Rights*[17] of 1960. Each suffered from the same fatal shortcoming: an absence of meaningful remedies.

§2.8 Under the principle of legality, people unlawfully detained or arrested had limited recourse. Although in theory they could sue in tort, low damage awards and the risk of being saddled with the other side's costs if unsuccessful deterred most potential litigants.[18] In addition, given the absence of a power to exclude illegally obtained evidence, unlawful detentions were practically immune from

---

[11] *Criminal Code*, R.S.C. 1985, c. C-46, s. 9(*a*) [*Code*].

[12] Robert Wood, "Powers of Arrest in Canada Under Federal Law" (1970) 9 West. Ont. L. Rev. 55 at 65-66. Also see Commission of Inquiry Concerning Certain Activities of the R.C.M.P., *National Security: The Legal Dimensions* (Ottawa: Ministry of Supply and Services, 1980) at 75.

[13] See *e.g.*, *R. v. Esposito*, [1985] O.J. No. 100 2, 24 C.C.C. (3d) 88 at 94 (Ont. C.A.), leave to appeal refused [1986] S.C.C.A. No. 63, [1986] 1 S.C.R. viii (S.C.C.).

[14] See *e.g.*, Canada, Law Commission of Canada, *Arrest, Working Paper 41* (Ottawa: Supply & Services Canada, 1985) at 33, 37.

[15] As explained below, this has now changed. In recent years, Canadian courts have invoked the ancillary powers doctrine to assert their law-making authority at common law and recognize a number of new police detention powers. (The ancillary powers doctrine was explained and critiqued in Chapter 1, Part 6(4)(*b*).)

[16] See Alan Young, "All Along the Watchtower: Arbitrary Detention and the Police Function" (1991) 29 Osgoode Hall L.J. 329.

[17] S.C. 1960, c. 44, R.S.C. 1985, Appendix III [*Canadian Bill of Rights*].

[18] See Paul C. Weiler, "The Control of Police Arrest Practices: Reflections of a Tort Lawyer" in Allen M. Linden, ed., *Studies in Canadian Tort Law* (Toronto: Butterworths, 1968) 416 at 448-49.

scrutiny at criminal trials.[19] Consequently, cases involving successful claims of unlawful detention and arrest were extraordinarily rare.[20]

§2.9 In addition, although the principle of legality demanded clear legal authority for any interference with individual liberty, it did not empower courts to evaluate the substance of laws. As long as it did so in unambiguous terms, Parliament could authorize deprivations of liberty on the most arbitrary of bases; think of the internment of Japanese-Canadians during the Second World War under the authority of the *War Measures Act*.[21] Unfortunately, the principle of legality did not supply courts with the authority to remedy this sort of legislated injustice.[22]

§2.10 The experience under the *Canadian Bill of Rights* was no better. Although section 2(*a*) mandated that laws not be construed to permit "arbitrary detention, imprisonment or exile,"[23] that provision, just like much of the document, was largely ineffective.[24] Claims of arbitrary detention rarely arose because, as we have seen, criminal courts had no authority to grant meaningful remedies.[25] And, despite the fact that the *Canadian Bill of Rights* was ultimately interpreted as permitting courts to declare inconsistent laws "inoperative", such cases were exceptionally uncommon.[26] The *Canadian Bill of Rights* did nothing, for example, to stem the federal government's reliance during the 1970 FLQ crisis on the *War Measures Act*, which authorized arrests based on suspicion and detention without charge or release for up to 28 days.[27]

---

[19]   See *R. v. Wray*, [1970] S.C.J. No. 80, [1971] S.C.R. 272 at 293 (S.C.C.), recognizing only a limited discretion in trial judges to exclude evidence if its admission would operate unfairly, but indicating that this would only be the case where the evidence is gravely prejudicial, its admissibility is tenuous and its probative value with respect to the main issue before the court is trifling.

[20]   There are very few reported judgments. For a rare example of a successful civil suit, see *Koechlin v. Waugh*, [1957] O.J. No. 105, 118 C.C.C. 24 (Ont. C.A.).

[21]   R.S.C. 1927, c. 206.

[22]   The *War Measures Act*, R.S.C. 1927, c. 206, authorized the internment of members "of the Japanese race" during the Second World War. Its use for these purposes was upheld in *Co-Operative Committee on Japanese Canadians v. A.G. (Canada)*, [1947] A.C. 87 (P.C.).

[23]   *Canadian Bill of Rights*, S.C. 1960, c. 44, R.S.C. 1985, Appendix III, s. 2(*a*).

[24]   The ineffectiveness of the *Canadian Bill of Rights* more generally was discussed in Chapter 1, Part 4(1). The experience with s. 2(*a*) was no different. As Professor Tarnopolsky noted "[t]here are only a few reported cases in which this clause was raised but it did not directly affect the result in any instance". See Walter Surma Tarnopolsky, *The Canadian Bill of Rights*, 2d rev. ed. (Toronto: McClelland & Stewart, 1975) at 235.

[25]   See *R. v. Hogan*, [1974] S.C.J. No. 116, [1975] 2 S.C.R. 574 at 584 (S.C.C.), rejecting the exclusion of evidence as a remedy for violations of the *Canadian Bill of Rights*.

[26]   See *R. v. Drybones*, [1969] S.C.J. No. 83, [1970] S.C.R. 282 (S.C.C.), where a majority of the Court interpreted s. 2 of the *Canadian Bill of Rights* as conferring this authority.

[27]   See generally, John T. Saywell, *Quebec 70: A Documentary Narrative* (Toronto: University of Toronto Press, 1971).

3. CONSTITUTIONAL LIMITATIONS ON DETENTION AND ARREST: SECTION 9 OF THE *CHARTER*

§2.11 Section 9 of the *Charter* provides that "[e]veryone has the right not to be arbitrarily detained or imprisoned." Read in conjunction with the cases that have interpreted its meaning, section 9 sets down the minimum constitutional standards for regulating state interference with individual liberty. In this regard, the provision plays two critically important functions. First, it permits constitutional scrutiny of the decision to detain in individual cases. Accordingly, when a police officer detains or arrests, section 9 supplies a basis for assessing the constitutionality of that encounter. Second, section 9 permits courts to assess the substance of statutory and common law powers authorizing detention. In other words, it prescribes minimum constitutional standards that must be met by any law empowering state officials to interfere with people's freedom of movement.

§2.12 What section 9 demands in each of these contexts will be explained below. For now, a bit more background on the purpose of the guarantee and its origins will be helpful in placing section 9 in its proper historic and political context.

(1) The Purpose and Drafting History of Section 9 of the *Charter*

§2.13 Section 9 of the *Charter* has been before the Supreme Court of Canada on countless occasions. Unfortunately, it was only in 2009 that the Court finally identified the purpose underlying the guarantee. In *R. v. Grant*,[28] the Court recognized that:

> The purpose of s. 9, broadly put, is to protect individual liberty from unjustified state interference .... "liberty", for *Charter* purposes, is not "restricted to mere freedom from physical restraint", but encompasses a broader entitlement "to make decisions of fundamental importance free from state interference" .... Thus, s. 9 guards not only against unjustified state intrusions upon physical liberty, but also against incursions on mental liberty by prohibiting the coercive pressures of detention and imprisonment from being applied to people without adequate justification. The detainee's interest in being able to make an informed choice whether to walk away or speak to the police is unaffected by the manner in which the detention is brought about.[29]

The Supreme Court's long delay in identifying the purpose of section 9 was conspicuous. With so many years passing without clear recognition of the guarantee's purpose, there had been considerable confusion about its requirements.[30] As is explained more fully below, *Grant* has brought some much-needed clarity and the future of this important *Charter* guarantee now looks much brighter.

---

[28] [2009] S.C.J. No. 32, [2009] 2 S.C.R. 353 (S.C.C.) [*Grant*].

[29] *Ibid.*, at para. 20 (S.C.C.).

[30] On the interpretive problems created by the Supreme Court's failure to expressly recognize s. 9's purpose, see James Stribopoulos, "The Forgotten Right: Section 9 of the Charter, Its Purpose and Meaning" (2008) 40 S.C.L.R. (2d) 211.

§2.14 A significant source of this confusion was the language adopted for the constitutional standard found in section 9: "arbitrarily". As is explained below in Part 3(4), until *Grant*, a recurring interpretive challenge was giving meaning to that term. The drafting history that led to section 9 of the *Charter* is worth remembering, as it sheds light on how those who framed the provision envisioned its operation, including what they understood "arbitrarily" would mean. This can be of assistance in resolving disagreements about the requirements of the guarantee that will undoubtedly arise in future cases.[31]

§2.15 At least superficially, section 9 of the *Charter* can be traced directly to section 2(*a*) of the *Canadian Bill of Rights*.[32] As noted above, that section provided that "no law of Canada shall be construed or applied so as to ... authorize or effect the arbitrary detention, imprisonment or exile of any person." The fact that "arbitrariness" figures prominently in both provisions is no accident. Each was influenced by Article 9(1) of the *International Declaration of Human Rights*,[33] which provides that "[n]o one shall be subjected to arbitrary arrest, detention or exile." In addition, in 1966, after the *Canadian Bill of Rights* but long before the *Charter*, the *International Covenant on Civil and Political Rights*[34] came into effect. Article 9(1) of that treaty states:

> Everyone has the right to liberty and security of person. No one shall be subjected to arbitrary arrest or detention. No one shall be deprived of his liberty except on such grounds and in accordance with such procedure as are established by law.[35]

§2.16 During the constitutional negotiations between the provincial and federal governments in 1980, section 9 faced serious challenges that nearly resulted in the guarantee taking on a much less effective form. In response to strong objections from the provinces to the wording in the August 1980 draft,[36] the federal government significantly redrafted what would become section 9. In the draft of October 1980,[37] section 9 was changed to read:

> 9. Everyone has the right not to be detained or imprisoned except on grounds, and in accordance with procedures, established by law.

---

[31] See *Reference re Motor Vehicle Act (British Columbia) s. 94(2)*, [1985] S.C.J. No. 73, [1985] 2 S.C.R. 486 at 504-509 (S.C.C.) (holding that courts may consider testimony before the Special Joint Committee in interpreting the *Charter*, but cautioning that because of the multiplicity of actors involved in negotiation, drafting and adoption, the words of a few civil servants cannot be considered determinative and should therefore be given "minimal weight").

[32] S.C. 1960, c. 44, R.S.C. 1985, Appendix III.

[33] Adopted and proclaimed by General Assembly resolution 217 A (III) of December 10, 1948.

[34] *International Covenant on Civil and Political Rights*, G.A. Res. 2200, 21 GAOR, Supp. (No. 16) 52, U.N. Doc. A/6316 (1966).

[35] *Ibid.*, Art. 9(1).

[36] See Provincial Proposal, August 29, 1980, reproduced in Anne F. Bayefsky, *Canada's Constitution Act 1982 & Amendments: A Documentary History*, vol. 2 (Toronto: McGraw-Hill, 1989) at 683-85. The provinces unanimously sought the deletion of s. 7, and — with the exception of New Brunswick and Newfoundland — sought changes to the wording of ss. 8 and 9.

[37] See October 1980 Draft of the *Charter*, *ibid.*, at 743.

§2.17 For the provinces, the goal of these changes was to "clarify and limit the scope of legal rights".[38] This led to language that would have done little more than codify the principle of legality ("except on grounds, and in accordance with procedures, established by law").[39]

§2.18 A number of organizations that made representations before the Special Joint Committee were critical of the October 1980 draft. These groups expressed grave doubts about the wording of section 9 found in the October 1980 draft.[40] They correctly pointed out that as revised, the section left open the potential for legislation authorizing detentions and imprisonments on patently arbitrary and discriminatory bases.[41] The federal government responded positively to these criticisms and in its next draft adopted wording identical to what would become the final version of section 9 of the *Charter*.[42]

§2.19 In putting forward these "major changes", Jean Chrétien (then federal Minister of Justice and Attorney General) explained that legality would not be conclusive proof of constitutionality. Rather, a law authorizing detention will also need to meet the substantive test of "not being arbitrary".[43] Later, when questions were raised as to whether legality should be specifically mentioned in section 9, a Deputy Minister of Justice assured the Committee that such a change was unnecessary because if a detention "were illegal, ... against the law, then it would be annulled by the courts for that very reason."[44] To the limited extent that the "framers' intent" may be gleaned from such historical materials,[45] it would appear to have been assumed that illegal detentions would necessarily be considered arbitrary under section 9 of the *Charter*. As discussed in Part

---

[38] *Ibid.*, at 681.

[39] As discussed in Chapter 3, Part 2(1), this mirrors the drafting history of s. 8 of the *Charter*.

[40] See Canada, *Minutes of Proceedings and Evidence of the Special Joint Committee of the Senate and of the House of Commons on the Constitution of Canada*, vol. 1, No. 7 at 11-12, 15-16, 27-29 (November 18, 1980) (Canadian Civil Liberties Association), vol. 1, No. 7 at 89-90, 92 (November 18, 1980) (Canadian Jewish Congress), vol. 1 No. 15 at 8, 15, 18 (November 28, 1980) (Canadian Bar Association).

[41] *Ibid.*

[42] See January 1981 draft of the *Charter*, ss. 8, 9 and 24, reproduced in Anne F. Bayefsky, *Canada's Constitution Act 1982 & Amendments: A Documentary History*, vol. 2 (Toronto: McGraw-Hill, 1989) at 771.

[43] *Ibid.*, at 11. See also Canada, *Minutes of Proceedings and Evidence of the Special Joint Committee of the Senate and of the House of Commons on the Constitution of Canada*, No. 36 at 10-11 (January 12, 1981) (Jean Chrétien, Minister of Justice at that time, explained that the changes to s. 9 were made in direct response to the concerns expressed — the objective being "to strengthen the protection of human rights and freedoms").

[44] Canada, *Minutes of Proceedings and Evidence of the Special Joint Committee of the Senate and of the House of Commons on the Constitution of Canada*, No. 46 at 116-117 (January 27, 1981) (see questions by Senator Asselin and the responses of the Deputy Minister of Justice, Mr. Tassé).

[45] See *Reference re Motor Vehicle Act (British Columbia) s. 94(2)*, [1985] S.C.J. No. 73, [1985] 2 S.C.R. 486 at 504-509 (S.C.C.) (holding that courts may consider testimony before the Special Joint Committee in interpreting the *Charter*, but cautioning that because of the multiplicity of actors involved in negotiation, drafting and adoption, the words of a few civil servants cannot be considered determinative and should therefore be given "minimal weight").

3(4)(*a*), it was not until *R. v. Grant* that this principle was accepted by the Supreme Court of Canada.

(2)   The Elements of Section 9

§2.20 As mentioned, section 9 provides that "[e]veryone has the right not to be arbitrarily detained or imprisoned." There are three elements to any section 9 violation: (*i*) state action (*ii*) resulting in an individual being "detained or imprisoned" (*iii*) in an "arbitrary" manner. If each is established,[46] the affected individual may apply for relief under one of the *Charter*'s remedial provisions, which are discussed in Chapter 10.[47] The state action requirement is discussed in Chapter 1, Part 4(3), given that it is relevant to all *Charter* claims, not just those relating to section 9. The remainder of this section will therefore focus on the second and third elements.

(3)   Triggering Section 9: Detained or Imprisoned

§2.21 An individual must either be "detained or imprisoned" to receive the protection of section 9. The concept of imprisonment is straightforward. As a result, we will deal with it first before addressing the far more contentious question of detention.

(a)   The Meaning of "Imprisoned"

§2.22 It is obvious when an individual is being "imprisoned". The presence of prison bars, locked doors, prison uniforms and jail guards clearly signify a deprivation of liberty that is sufficiently prolonged to warrant the more onerous label implied by that term. As the Supreme Court recently explained, "'[i]mprisonment' connotes total or near-total loss of liberty."[48] As a result, without any discussion of this threshold requirement,[49] the Supreme Court has routinely relied upon section 9 of the *Charter* to scrutinize the constitutionality of legislation that could result in a person being confined in jail.[50]

---

[46]   This assumes that the infringement is not undertaken pursuant to a law that authorizes arbitrary detention or imprisonment that is justified under s. 1 of the *Charter*. Examples of laws violating s. 9 but being upheld under s. 1 of the *Charter* are discussed below in Part 4(2)(*a*) through (*g*).

[47]   In criminal cases, this will usually entail an application by the defendant for the exclusion of evidence under s. 24(2) of the *Charter*.

[48]   *R. v. Grant*, [2009] S.C.J. No. 32, [2009] 2 S.C.R. 353 at para. 29 (S.C.C.).

[49]   Given that anyone imprisoned is necessarily detained, the need for a definition of imprisonment in this context is questionable.

[50]   See *e.g.*, *Charkaoui v. Canada (Citizenship and Immigration)*, [2007] S.C.J. No. 9, [2007] 1 S.C.R. 350 (S.C.C.) [*Charkaoui*] (challenging the security certificate scheme); *R. v. Heywood*, [1994] S.C.J. No. 101, [1994] 3 S.C.R. 761 (S.C.C.) (challenging the offence of vagrancy by loitering near playgrounds); *R. v. Morales*, [1992] S.C.J. No. 98, [1992] 3 S.C.R. 711 (S.C.C.) (challenging the public safety and public interest bases for denying bail); *R. v. Pearson*, [1992] S.C.J. No. 99, [1992] 3 S.C.R. 665 (S.C.C.) (challenging the reversal of the burden on bail hearings for drug offences); *R. v. Swain*, [1991] S.C.J. No. 32, [1991] 1 S.C.R. 933 (S.C.C.) (challenging the automatic committal to custody of those found not guilty by reason of insanity); *R. v. Beare; R. v. Higgins*, [1987] S.C.J. No. 92, [1988] 2 S.C.R. 387 (S.C.C.) (challenging the

(b) The Meaning of "Detained"

(i) Introduction

§2.23 Deciding whether or not there has been a "detention" for *Charter* purposes, in contrast, can be challenging. In making this determination, much will depend on where a particular encounter is situated along the spectrum of potential interactions between the police and the public. Most such interactions are entirely benign and will not qualify; imagine a simple exchange of pleasantries between a police officer and a member of the public. At the other end of the spectrum, certain interactions are inherently coercive and necessarily entail a "detention". For example, if the police carry out a formal arrest the individual arrested is clearly detained.[51] Unfortunately, between these two extremes there will be a great many encounters that are far more difficult to categorize.

§2.24 Whether or not there has been a "detention" is critically important for *Charter* purposes. Not only is "detention" a trigger for the constitutional protection provided by section 9, it is also one of the threshold requirements for engaging the safeguards found in section 10 of the *Charter*, which become operative "on arrest or *detention*." Consequently, when it comes to the constitutional regulation of the relationship between the individual and the state, detention is key to unlocking a host of important *Charter* rights.

§2.25 Not surprisingly then, whether dealing with a suspect who is encountered on the street or at the stationhouse, the police will often have good tactical reasons for avoiding a detention as long as possible. Absent detention, police enjoy considerable freedom in questioning suspects.[52] Questioning may produce evidence of wrongdoing, either because the answers are incriminating or they reveal the location of physical evidence or contraband.

§2.26 If the detention threshold is crossed, however, the constitutional implications are significant. First, if the police lack the requisite legal grounds to detain, section 9 of the *Charter* will be violated. (This will be explained below in Part 3(4)(*a*).) Second, detention also triggers informational duties under section 10 of the *Charter*. A detained suspect must be informed of the reasons for detention (section 10(*a*)) and apprised of the right to consult counsel (section 10(*b*)). (These guarantees are explained fully in Chapter 4.) This information may alert

---

fingerprinting of persons charged or arrested); *R. v. Smith*, [1987] S.C.J. No. 36, [1987] 1 S.C.R. 1045 (S.C.C.) (challenging the mandatory minimum sentence for importing a narcotic); *R. v. Milne*, [1987] S.C.J. No. 73, [1987] 2 S.C.R. 512 (S.C.C.) (challenging the continued detention as a dangerous offender where the index offence has since been repealed); *R. v. Lyons*, [1987] S.C.J. No. 62, [1987] 2 S.C.R. 309 (S.C.C.) (challenging the imposition of indeterminate sentences of imprisonment under the dangerous offender regime).

[51] In *R. v. Grant*, [2009] S.C.J. No. 32, [2009] 2 S.C.R. 353 at para. 34 (S.C.C.), the Supreme Court noted that "[a]t one end of the spectrum of possibilities, detention overlaps with arrest or imprisonment and the *Charter* will clearly apply."

[52] Other than the *Charter*, the only significant restraint on police questioning of adult suspects stems from the common law voluntary confessions rule. See generally, *R. v. Oickle*, [2000] S.C.J. No. 38, [2000] 2 S.C.R. 3 (S.C.C.). This rule is discussed in Chapter 4, Part 2. In short, that rule requires that before any statement made by an accused to a person in authority is admitted into evidence it must be proven voluntary.

suspects to their potential jeopardy and cause them to stop talking. As a result, until they are ready to effect an arrest the police will often want to avoid a detention.[53] It is the courts, however, not the police, which ultimately decide whether and when the detention threshold was crossed in a given case.

§2.27 It was a case involving section 10(*b*), the right to counsel, that first raised the meaning of detention before the Supreme Court. In *R. v. Therens*,[54] police subjected a motorist to a breath demand under the *Criminal Code*.[55] He was taken back to the police station, took and failed a breathalyzer test, and was arrested. At the time of the demand, police did not apprise him of his right to counsel, which section 10(*b*) requires on "detention".

§2.28 The issue before the Court in *Therens* was whether the motorist was "detained" following the breath demand but before his arrest. The Court had previously held[56] that breath demands do not trigger a detention under section 2(*c*)(ii) of the *Canadian Bill of Rights*,[57] which provides the "right to retain and instruct counsel without delay" to persons "arrested *or detained*".[58] The fact that it was an offence to refuse to comply with these demands did not mean that a person subject to such a demand was legally detained.[59] Detention, under the *Canadian Bill of Rights*, was limited to situations of "actual physical restraint."[60]

§2.29 In *Therens*,[61] Justice Le Dain concluded that the meaning of detention under the *Canadian Bill of Rights* was not controlling under the *Charter*. Rather, he reasoned that detention under the *Charter* should be read more broadly.[62] In addition to physical constraint, he asserted, a detention also arises when police assume "control over the movement of a person by a demand or direction which

---

53 See Casey Hill, "Investigative Detention: A Search / Seizure by Any Other Name?" (2008) 40 S.C.LR. (2d) 179 at 204, who notes that there is "a situational incentive for the police to provide the suspect less, rather than more, information about the transaction under investigation as the investigator's questions attempt to draw out information about the suspect's recent whereabouts, association with others, route, *etc.*, committing the detainee to an account for evaluation against the officer's possessed and incoming information."

54 [1985] S.C.J. No. 30, [1985] 1 S.C.R. 613 (S.C.C.) [*Therens*].

55 *Criminal Code*, R.S.C. 1970, c. C-34, s. 235(1). Today, see *Criminal Code*, R.S.C. 1985, c. C-46, as amended, s. 254(3).

56 *R. v. Chromiak*, [1979] S.C.J. No. 116, [1980] 1 S.C.R. 471 (S.C.C.).

57 S.C. 1960, c. 44.

58 *Canadian Bill of Rights*, S.C. 1960, c. 44, s. 2(ii) [emphasis added].

59 *R. v. Chromiak*, [1979] S.C.J. No. 116, [1980] 1 S.C.R. 471 at 478 (S.C.C.).

60 *Ibid.*

61 [1985] S.C.J. No. 30, [1985] 1 S.C.R. 613 (S.C.C.).

62 In so concluding, he emphasized "that the *Charter* must be regarded, because of its constitutional character, as a new affirmation of rights and freedoms and of judicial power and responsibility in relation to their protection." (*R. v. Therens*, [1985] S.C.J. No. 30, [1985] 1 S.C.R. 613 at 638 (S.C.C.), *per* Le Dain J. dissenting (on other grounds)). He also went on to explain two further reasons for rejecting the narrow definition from *Chromiak*. First, he acknowledged that the judiciary had felt rather restrained in its use of the *Canadian Bill of Rights*, given that it was simply legislation and therefore lacked constitutional status. *Ibid.* In addition, given that the *Canadian Bill of Rights* did not include any equivalent to s. 1 of the *Charter*, a narrow interpretation of "detention" was the only means by which the Court in *Chromiak* could place reasonable limits on the right to counsel. *Ibid.*, at 639 (S.C.R.). Of course, s. 1 of the *Charter* now permits the Supreme Court to balance individual and state interests more transparently.

may have significant legal consequence and which prevents or impedes access to counsel."[63] Given the legal duty on the motorist to accompany the police officer for the purposes of administering a breath test, this would have been enough to dispose of the appeal. But Justice Le Dain went a step further, holding that a detention may sometimes arise even when there is neither physical restraint nor "criminal liability for failure to comply" with a legal duty.[64] He explained:

> In my opinion, it is not realistic, as a general rule, to regard compliance with a demand or direction by a police officer as truly voluntary, in the sense that the citizen feels that he or she has the choice to obey or not .... Most citizens are not aware of the precise legal limits of police authority. Rather than risk the application of physical force or prosecution for wilful obstruction, the reasonable person is likely to err on the side of caution, assume lawful authority and comply with the demand. The element of psychological compulsion, in the form of a reasonable perception of suspension of freedom of choice, is enough to make the restraint of liberty involuntary. Detention may be effected without the application or threat of application of physical restraint if the person concerned submits or acquiesces in the deprivation of liberty and reasonably believes that the choice to do otherwise does not exist.[65]

Not long after *Therens* was decided, its definition of "detention" for section 10 *Charter* purposes was transplanted to section 9. The Supreme Court concluded that there is "no reason in principle why the general approach to the meaning of detention reflected in those cases should not be applied to the meaning of 'detained' in s. 9."[66]

§2.30 *Therens* thus had the effect of recognizing three categories of detention, now pertinent for both sections 9 and 10 of the *Charter*: (*i*) psychological restraint (with legal compulsion); (*ii*) psychological restraint (without legal compulsion); and (*iii*) physical restraint.[67]

---

[63] *R. v. Therens*, [1985] S.C.J. No. 30, [1985] 1 S.C.R. 613 at 642 (S.C.C.), Le Dain J., dissenting (on other grounds). All eight judges in *Therens* agreed that the accused was detained, however, only three others expressly adopted Le Dain J.'s reasoning. A unanimous Court subsequently endorsed Le Dain J.'s approach. See *R. v. Thomsen*, [1988] S.C.J. No. 31, [1988] 1 S.C.R. 640 at 649 (S.C.C.) [*Thomsen*]. The *Therens* approach to defining detention has since been repeatedly affirmed by the Court. See *R. v. Simmons*, [1988] S.C.J. No. 86, [1988] 2 S.C.R. 495 (S.C.C.); *R. v. Feeney*, [1997] S.C.J. No. 49, [1997] 2 S.C.R. 13 at 55 (S.C.C.); *R. v. Prosper*, [1994] S.C.J. No. 72, [1994] 3 S.C.R. 236 at 272-73; *Dehghani v. Canada (Minister of Employment and Immigration)*, [1993] S.C.J. No. 38, [1993] 1 S.C.R. 1053 at 1065-1066 (S.C.C.).

[64] *R. v. Therens*, [1985] S.C.J. No. 30, [1985] 1 S.C.R. 613 at 644 (S.C.C.).

[65] *Ibid*. This is in keeping with the Supreme Court's eventual recognition in *Grant* that the purpose of s. 9 is both to protect "physical liberty" as well as "mental liberty". See *R. v. Grant*, [2009] S.C.J. No. 32, [2009] 2 S.C.R. 353 at para. 20 (S.C.C.).

[66] *R. v. Hufsky*, [1988] S.C.J. No. 30, [1988] 1 S.C.R. 621 at 632 (S.C.C.). See also *R. v. Ladouceur*, [1990] S.C.J. No. 53, [1990] 1 S.C.R. 1257 at 1277 (S.C.C.).

[67] See *R. v. Therens*, [1985] S.C.J. No. 30, [1985] 1 S.C.R. 613 at 641-44 (S.C.C.), Le Dain J., dissenting; *R. v. Thomsen*, [1988] S.C.J. No. 31, [1988] 1 S.C.R. 640 at 648-49 (S.C.C.). In *R. v. Grant*, [2009] S.C.J. No. 32, [2009] 2 S.C.R. 353 at para. 30 (S.C.C.), the Court specifically reaffirmed these three categories of detention first recognized in *Therens*.

§2.31 In *Grant*, the Supreme Court recently reaffirmed the continued relevance of these three categories, while providing some long overdue guidance with respect to category *(ii)*, cases of psychological restraint not involving legal compulsion.[68] We discuss each of these categories immediately below.

(ii) Psychological Restraint with Legal Compulsion

§2.32 In principle, it should be easy to decide if a suspect was psychologically restrained by the threat of legal sanctions. As explained in *Therens*, this form of detention arises whenever a person may be punished for failing to comply with police directives. In that case, the Court accordingly held that drivers subject to breath sample demands are detained.[69] This follows, given that drivers who refuse to comply with a lawful demand are guilty of a criminal offence.[70] The Court later held that a detention occurs whenever police stop a vehicle for any purpose,[71] a conclusion that applies equally to the driver and any passengers who happen to be travelling in the vehicle when it is pulled over.[72]

§2.33 Even though every motor vehicle stop constitutes a "detention", the Supreme Court of Canada has refrained from applying the same constitutional standards to all stops. As explained below in Part 4(2), vehicle stops motivated by traffic safety concerns are subject to less exacting constitutional standards. The Court has done this by upholding legislated overrides of section 9 (and section 10(*b*)) as reasonable limits under section 1 of the *Charter*.

§2.34 Unfortunately, on other occasions, the Court has dealt with the impracticality of fully applying *Charter* standards by straining the meaning of detention. For example, customs and immigration officials have broad powers to detain, search and question people entering and leaving Canada.[73] As in the case of ve-

---

[68]   The Court specifically identified and reaffirmed the categories of detention first recognized in *R. v. Therens*, [1985] S.C.J. No. 30, [1985] 1 S.C.R. 613 (S.C.C.). See *R. v. Grant*, [2009] S.C.J. No. 32, [2009] 2 S.C.R. 353 at para. 30 (S.C.C.).

[69]   See also *R. v. Trask*, [1985] S.C.J. No. 31, [1985] 1 S.C.R. 655 (S.C.C.); *R. v. Rahn*, [1985] S.C.J. No. 32, [1985] 1 S.C.R. 659 (S.C.C.); *R. v. Schmautz*, [1990] S.C.J. No. 21, [1990] 1 S.C.R. 398 (S.C.C.).

[70]   See *Criminal Code*, R.S.C. 1985, c. C-46, s. 254(5).

[71]   *R. v. Orbanski; R. v. Elias*, [2005] S.C.J. No. 37, [2005] 2 S.C.R. 3 at para. 31 (S.C.C.). See also *R. v. Hufsky*, [1988] S.C.J. No. 30, [1988] 1 S.C.R. 621 (S.C.C.) (stopping of vehicles a detention within the meaning of s. 9 of the *Charter*); *R. v. Clayton*, [2007] S.C.J. No. 32, [2007] 2 S.C.R. 725 at para. 66 (S.C.C.), *per* Binnie J., concurring (same). These detentions fall under the "psychological restraint with legal compulsion" category because provincial highway traffic statutes typically make it an offence for a driver to fail to stop when directed to do so by police. See *e.g.*, *Traffic Safety Act*, R.S.A. 2000, c. T-6, ss. 157 and 166; *Highway Traffic Act*, R.S.O. 1990, c. H.8, s. 216.

[72]   Most courts have sensibly held that vehicle passengers are also detained when the driver is pulled over by police. The detention of passengers in these circumstances would technically fall into the category of psychological restraint without legal compulsion. See *R. v. Harris*, [2007] O.J. No. 3185, 49 C.R. (6th) 220 at paras. 18-19 (Ont. C.A.). See also *Brendlin v. California*, 127 S.Ct. 2400 (2007). *Contra*, *R. v. Bradley*, [2008] N.S.J. No. 268, 2008 NSCA 57 (N.S.C.A.).

[73]   See *Customs Act*, R.S.C. 1985, c. 1 (2nd Supp.), ss. 98, 99.1, 99.2, 99.3; *Immigration and Refugee Protection Act*, S.C. 2001, c. 27, s. 16.

hicle stops, failure to cooperate constitutes an offence.[74] The Court has found, however, that people stopped for routine questioning and searches at border crossings are not detained for *Charter* purposes.[75] Detention arises only when people are suspected of having committed an offence and subjected to lengthier and more intrusive inquiries.[76]

§2.35 This approach has been rightly criticized for stretching the plain meaning of "detention" beyond its breaking point.[77] It would have been preferable if the Court had instead reached the same result by applying section 1 of the *Charter*. As discussed in the context of roadside detentions in Part 4(2), below, there is little to be gained (and much to be lost) in providing the full panoply of *Charter* rights to people subject to preliminary, routine inquiries at border crossings.

(iii) Psychological Restraint without Legal Compulsion

a. *Therens* Endorses an Objective Test

§2.36 In *Therens*,[78] the Supreme Court of Canada recognized that psychological compulsion could result in detention. The test it identified is whether the individual affected acquiesces to a deprivation of liberty and reasonably believes that the choice to do otherwise does not exist.[79]

§2.37 On its face, the test is paradoxical: it deems people to be "detained" for *Charter* purposes even though their liberty is not limited by law. Despite their (reasonable) belief that they must comply with police requests, they actually have no legal obligation to do so. (We thus sometimes refer to this category as "non-legal" psychological detention.) As the Court explained in *Grant*,[80] "an individual confronted by state authority ordinarily has the option to choose simply to walk away."[81]

---

[74] See *Customs Act*, R.S.C. 1985, c. 1 (2nd Supp.), s. 153.1; *Immigration and Refugee Protection Act*, S.C. 2001, c. 27, ss. 127, 128.

[75] See *R. v. Simmons*, [1988] S.C.J. No. 86, [1988] 2 S.C.R. 495 (S.C.C.); *R. v. Jacoy*, [1988] S.C.J. No. 83, [1988] 2 S.C.R. 548 (S.C.C.); *Dehghani v. Canada (Minister of Employment and Immigration)*, [1993] S.C.J. No. 38, [1993] 1 S.C.R. 1053 (S.C.C.) (detention not arising from secondary examination). See also *R. v. Sekhon*, [2009] B.C.J. No. 855, 2009 BCCA 187 at paras. 69-77 (B.C.C.A.), leave to appeal refused [2009] B.C.J. No. 855 (S.C.C.) (no detention arising from routine questioning and routine search of vehicle); *R. v. Hardy*, [1995] B.C.J. No. 2570, 103 C.C.C. (3d) 289 at paras. 28-52 (B.C.C.A.) (detention not arising from secondary examination or destructive luggage search); *R. v. Vandenbosch*, [2007] M.J. No. 346 (Man. C.A.), leave to appeal refused [2007] S.C.C.A. No. 554 (S.C.C.) (applying customs detention jurisprudence to prison visitors).

[76] See *R. v. Simmons*, [1988] S.C.J. No. 86, [1988] 2 S.C.R. 495 at 521 (S.C.C.) (detention arose when suspect strip-searched); *R. v. Jacoy*, [1988] S.C.J. No. 83, [1988] 2 S.C.R. 548 at 557-58 (S.C.C.) (detention arose when decision made to strip-search suspect if necessary).

[77] See Eric Colvin & Tim Quigley, "Developments in Criminal Law and Procedure: The 1988-89 Term" (1990) 1 S.C.L.R. 187 at 224-25; Tim Quigley, *Procedure in Canadian Criminal Law*, 2d ed. (looseleaf) (Toronto: Thomson Carswell, 2006) § 5.3(c)(i).

[78] *R. v. Therens*, [1985] S.C.J. No. 30, [1985] 1 S.C.R. 613 (S.C.C.).

[79] *Ibid.*, at 644 (S.C.R.). In *R. v. Grant*, [2009] S.C.J. No. 32, [2009] 2 S.C.R. 353 at paras. 28-32 (S.C.C.), the Court reaffirmed that this remains the controlling test.

[80] *R. v. Grant*, [2009] S.C.J. No. 32, [2009] 2 S.C.R. 353 (S.C.C.).

[81] *Ibid.*, at para. 21 (S.C.C.).

§2.38 How has this situation arisen? We can imagine a legal regime requiring police to tell people whether they are legally obliged to cooperate. Before stopping and questioning, for example, police would have to tell suspects that they are either (*i*) being detained under law for a particular purpose (with an explanation as to what they are legally required to do and what they are free to refuse to do); or (*ii*) not being detained and free to leave or remain silent.[82]

§2.39 Neither Parliament nor the courts, however, have seen fit to impose such a regime.[83] Instead, they have sanctioned a state of affairs in which police are permitted (as a general rule) to approach people and ask them questions without any particularized suspicion and without any need to inform them of their legal status or rights. As the Supreme Court explained in *Grant*:

> Section 9 of the *Charter* does not require that police abstain from interacting with members of the public until they have specific grounds to connect the individual to the commission of a crime. Nor does s. 10 require that the police advise everyone at the outset of any encounter that they have no obligation to speak to them and are entitled to legal counsel.[84]

Given this legal milieu, it is not surprising that the Supreme Court of Canada has recognized that people often assume that they must comply with police requests.[85] Nor is it surprising, given the imbalance of power and potential for abuse inherent in such encounters, that the Court has found that a "detention" may occur for *Charter* purposes even in circumstances where an individual has no legal obligation to remain in the company of police and would be legally justified in walking away.

§2.40 When it comes to psychological detention, the challenge is demarcating the line between consensual and coerced encounters. This is no easy task. Encounters between individuals and the police are rich in their diversity. Many are relatively innocuous, often involving nothing more than passing conversation.[86] Such exchanges become more invasive, however, when consent and conversation are replaced by coercion and interrogation. As noted, for non-legal psycho-

---

[82]   See Law Reform Commission of Canada, *Arrest* (Report 29) (Ottawa: The Commission, 1986) at 20; Stephen Coughlan, "Police Detention for Questioning: A Proposal" (1986) 28 Crim. L.Q. 170; Alan D. Gold, "Perspectives on Section 10(*b*): The Right to Counsel under the *Charter*" (1993) 22 C.R. (4th) 370 at 374.

[83]   The *Grant* Court did counsel police that if they are "uncertain whether their conduct is having a coercive effect on the individual, it is open to them to inform the subject in unambiguous terms that he or she is under no obligation to answer questions and is free to go." *R. v. Grant*, [2009] S.C.J. No. 32, [2009] 2 S.C.R. 353 at para. 32 (S.C.C.).

[84]   *R. v. Grant*, [2009] S.C.J. No. 32, [2009] 2 S.C.R. 353 at para. 38 (S.C.C.). See also *R. v. Suberu*, [2007] O.J. No. 317, 218 C.C.C. (3d) 27 at para. 3 (Ont. C.A.), affd [2009] S.C.J. No. 33, [2009] 2 S.C.R. 460 (S.C.C.).

[85]   *R. v. Therens*, [1985] S.C.J. No. 30, [1985] 1 S.C.R. 613 (S.C.C.).

[86]   See *R. v. Mann*, [2004] S.C.J. No. 49, [2004] 3 S.C.R. 59 at para. 19 (S.C.C.); *R. v. Rajaratnam*, [2006] A.J. No. 137, 214 C.C.C. (3d) 547 at para. 13 (Alta. C.A.) ("the law has not yet reached a point that a compulsion to comply will be inferred whenever a police officer requests information, for that would mean police could never ask questions"). See also *R. v. Grafe*, [1987] O.J. No. 796, 60 C.R. (3d) 242 (Ont. C.A.); *United States of America c. Alfaro*, [1992] J.Q. no 831, 75 C.C.C. (3d) 211 at 236 (Que. C.A.); *R. v. Elshaw*, [1991] S.C.J. No. 68, [1991] 3 S.C.R. 24 at 53-70 (S.C.C.), *per* L'Heureux-Dubé J., dissenting.

logical detention, the turning point is the moment when suspects submit to police authority under the reasonable belief that they cannot do otherwise.[87]

§2.41 Unfortunately, *Therens* failed to provide any concrete guidance to assist lower courts in distinguishing consensual from coerced encounters. Without it, lower courts, invariably seeing only cases involving factually guilty claimants,[88] have sometimes refrained from labelling ambiguously coercive encounters as detentions.[89]

b. *Grant* Identifies a List of Relevant Factors

§2.42 In *Grant*, the Supreme Court of Canada expressly reaffirmed *Therens*'s definition of detention, including the category of psychological restraint without legal compulsion.[90] Under *Grant*, the ultimate question remains "whether the police conduct would cause a reasonable person to conclude that he or she was not free to go and had to comply with the police direction or demand."[91] But recognizing that this form of detention had "proven difficult to define consistently",[92] the Court added a considerable measure of gloss. In so doing, however, it subtly narrowed the definition's scope. Emphasizing a point absent from *Therens*, the Court stated that, "not every trivial or insignificant interference with liberty attracts *Charter* scrutiny"; rather, only the person "whose liberty is *meaningfully* constrained has genuine need of the additional rights accorded by the *Charter* to people in that situation."[93] The coupling of "detention" with "imprisonment" in section 9, the Court explained, suggests that detention arises "when the deprivation of liberty may have legal consequences."[94]

§2.43 The Court in *Grant* also stressed that the *Therens* test is objective, meaning that a police officer's subjective intentions are not relevant in deciding if

---

[87]   *R. v. Therens*, [1985] S.C.J. No. 30, [1985] 1 S.C.R. 613 at 644 (S.C.C.).

[88]   See James Stribopoulos, "The Forgotten Right: Section 9 of the Charter, Its Purpose and Meaning" (2008) 40 S.C.L.R. (2d) 2117 at 237-39 (discussing selection bias ensuing from the fact that courts are presented only with encounters where evidence is obtained, placing pressure to uphold police actions to ensure conviction of the factually guilty).

[89]   *Ibid.*, at 239-45 (discussing this trend, especially in the Ontario Court of Appeal). See *e.g.*, *R. v. Lawrence*, [1990] O.J. No. 1648, 59 C.C.C. (3d) 55 (Ont. C.A.), where a police officer, investigating a reported break-in, drove his police cruiser onto the sidewalk to block Ms. Lawrence from proceeding further on her bicycle. She was questioned for 25 minutes regarding where she lived. The officer disbelieved her and asked to look in her backpack, she complied, revealing evidence that implicated her in a break-in. She was then placed in the rear of the cruiser. The Court found that she was only detained *after* being placed in the police cruiser.

[90]   *R. v. Grant*, [2009] S.C.J. No. 32, [2009] 2 S.C.R. 353 at paras. 28-32 (S.C.C.).

[91]   *Ibid.*, at para. 31.

[92]   *Ibid.*

[93]   *Ibid.*, at para. 26 [emphasis added]. The Court quoted here with approval from *R. v. Mann*, [2004] S.C.J. No. 49, [2004] 3 S.C.R. 59 (S.C.C.), where Iacobucci J. noted (at para. 26) that: "... the police cannot be said to 'detain', within the meaning of ss. 9 and 10 of the *Charter*, every suspect they stop for purposes of identification, or even interview. The person who is stopped will in all cases be 'detained' in the sense of 'delayed', or 'kept waiting.' But the constitutional rights recognized by ss. 9 and 10 of the *Charter* are not engaged by delays that involve no significant physical or psychological restraint."

[94]   *R. v. Grant*, [2009] S.C.J. No. 32 at para. 29, [2009] 2 S.C.R. 353 (S.C.C.).

there was a detention.[95] The suspect's "particular circumstances and perceptions",[96] however, may be relevant "in assessing the reasonableness of any perceived power imbalance between the individual and the police, and thus the reasonableness of any perception that he or she had no choice but to comply with the police directive."[97] The claimant's testimony will usually be the best source of such evidence, the Court noted, but since the test is objective a claimant's failure to testify is not fatal to finding a detention.[98]

§2.44 With this backdrop in place, the Court proceeded to identify a host of factors to consider when deciding whether a non-legal psychological detention occurred. First, it emphasized the importance of determining a police officer's purpose in approaching or questioning the claimant. If this purpose was non-adversarial, a finding of detention is unlikely. For example, the Court stated that no detention would arise where police respond to an emergency call, even if they assume control over the situation or interfere with a person's freedom of movement.[99] Similarly, there is no detention when police approach bystanders in the wake of an accident or crime to obtain preliminary information for their investigation.[100] Deprivations of liberty that result from such encounters are not "significant enough to attract *Charter* scrutiny because they do not attract legal consequences for the concerned individuals."[101]

§2.45 According to the Court, neighbourhood policing initiatives (where police focus on meeting community needs and maintaining order) fall in the non-adversarial category. It rightly acknowledged, however, that this sort of proactive policing can "subtly merge with the potentially coercive police role of investigating crime and arresting suspects so that they may be brought to justice."[102]

§2.46 The Court contrasted these kinds of non-adversarial encounters with situations where police have a "focused suspicion".[103] While focused suspicion

---

[95]   *Ibid.*, at para. 32 (S.C.R.). The majority acknowledged that the officer's subjective intentions will be relevant in deciding upon the appropriate remedy under s. 24(2) of the *Charter* if a violation is made out. *Ibid.* In contrast, Binnie J. emphasized the importance of considering the subjective mindset of the police in deciding whether or not a detention has taken place. See *R. v. Grant*, [2009] S.C.J. No. 32, [2009] 2 S.C.R. 353 (S.C.C.), *per* Binnie J., concurring.

[96]   *Ibid.*

[97]   *Ibid.*

[98]   *Ibid.*, at para. 50 (S.C.R.).

[99]   *Ibid.*, at para. 36 (S.C.R.).

[100]   *Ibid.*, at para. 37 (S.C.R.).

[101]   *Ibid.*, at para. 36 (S.C.R.).

[102]   *Ibid.*, at para. 40 (S.C.R.). This observation by the Court reveals a perceptive appreciation of some of the realities of community policing. See Stephen D. Mastrofski, "Community Policing As Reform: A Cautionary Tale" in Jack R. Green and Stephen D. Mastrofksi, eds., *Community Policing: Rhetoric Or Reality* (New York: Praeger, 1988) 46 at 53 (noting that "aggressive order maintenance strategies" are often part and parcel of community policing efforts and can include "rousting and arresting people thought to cause public disorder, field interrogations and roadblock checks, surveillance of suspicious people, vigorous enforcement of public order and nuisance laws, and, in general, much greater attention to the minor crimes and disturbances thought to disrupt and displease the civil public").

[103]   *R. v. Grant*, [2009] S.C.J. No. 32, [2009] 2 S.C.R. 353 at para. 41 (S.C.C.).

does not in itself give rise to a detention, "police must be mindful that, depending on how they act and what they say, the point may be reached where a reasonable person, in the position of that individual, would conclude he or she is not free to choose to walk away or decline to answer questions."[104]

§2.47 The second factor the Court identified was the duration of the encounter.[105] The shorter the interaction, the less likely it is to be labelled a detention. The longer the encounter, in contrast, the more likely a reasonable person would feel unable to walk away.

§2.48 Third, the Court noted that physical contact between the police officer and the individual affected is a relevant consideration. But as with other variables, its significance hinges on context. The Court gave the example of a police officer "placing" his or her hand on someone's arm:

> If sustained, it might well lead a reasonable person to conclude that his or her freedom to choose whether to cooperate or not has been removed. On the other hand, a fleeting touch may not, depending on the circumstances, give rise to a reasonable conclusion that one's liberty has been curtailed.[106]

§2.49 Finally, the Court recognized that in some situations, "a single forceful act or word may be enough to cause a reasonable person to conclude that his or her right to choose how to respond has been removed."[107] No reasonable person, for example, would feel free to walk away after a police officer points at him or her and issues an authoritative command to "Get out of your car!"[108]

§2.50 In conclusion, the Court in *Grant* set out the following useful summary:[109]

> ... In cases where there is no physical restraint or legal obligation, it may not be clear whether a person has been detained. To determine whether the reasonable person in the individual's circumstances would conclude that he or she had been deprived by the state of the liberty of choice, the court may consider, *inter alia*, the following factors:
>
> (a) The circumstances giving rise to the encounter as would reasonably be perceived by the individual: whether the police were providing general assistance; maintaining general order; making general inquiries regarding a particular occurrence; or, singling out the individual for focused investigation.
>
> (b) The nature of the police conduct, including the language used; the use of physical contact; the place where the interaction occurred; the presence of others; and the duration of the encounter.

---

[104] *Ibid.*

[105] *Ibid.*, at para. 42 (S.C.R.).

[106] *Ibid.* As we discuss below in Part 3(3)(*b*)(iv), anything more than a fleeting touch would likely result in detention by means of physical restraint.

[107] *R. v. Grant*, [2009] S.C.J. No. 32, [2009] 2 S.C.R. 353 at para. 42 (S.C.C.).

[108] See *e.g., R. v. Chaisson*, [2006] S.C.J. No. 11, [2006] 1 S.C.R. 415 (S.C.C.) (restoring trial judge's finding that detention arose when accused complied with police direction to "get out" of his parked car).

[109] *R. v. Grant*, [2009] S.C.J. No. 32, [2009] 2 S.C.R. 353 at para. 44 (S.C.C.).

(c) The particular characteristics or circumstances of the individual where relevant, including age; physical stature; minority status; level of sophistication.

§2.51 In considering these factors, trial judges must keep in mind "all the circumstances of the case"[110] and engage in "a realistic appraisal of the entire interaction as it developed, not a minute parsing of words and movements."[111] But while the trial judge's findings of fact are owed deference on appeal, the "application of the law to the facts is a question of law."[112] Given the number of factors that a trial judge must take into account, the potential for reviewable error seems considerable.

§2.52 Applying the factors discussed above, the Supreme Court concluded that there was a detention in *Grant*. Mr. Grant, a young black man, was walking on the sidewalk of a Toronto street at midday when, according to two plainclothes police officers, his manner and clothing attracted their attention. The plainclothes officers requested that a nearby uniformed officer "have a chat" with Mr. Grant. The uniformed officer approached Mr. Grant head-on and stopped directly in his path. The officer asked Mr. Grant "what was going on", and requested his name and address. In response, Mr. Grant produced a provincial health card. At one point, Mr. Grant, behaving nervously, adjusted his jacket, prompting the officer to tell him to "keep his hands in front of him". By this time, the two plainclothes officers had also approached, flashed their badges and stood behind the uniformed officer. Pointed questions followed, with Mr. Grant being asked if he was carrying anything that he "shouldn't have", an exchange that culminated in Mr. Grant admitting that he was in possession of marijuana and a firearm, and being arrested.

§2.53 The Court found that the preliminary approach and general questioning of Mr. Grant was not enough to trigger a detention because "a reasonable person would not have concluded he or she was being deprived of the right to choose how to act".[113] But a detention arose, the Court ruled, when the uniformed officer told him to "keep his hands in front of him".[114] While in some cases such a statement might be viewed merely as a "precautionary directive",[115] here the encounter was "inherently intimidating".[116] This conclusion was buttressed, the Court reasoned, by the arrival of two additional police officers who flashed their badges before taking up "tactical positions", the fact that Mr. Grant was being singled out, the posing of probing, interrogative questions, and Mr. Grant's youth and inexperience.

---

[110] *Ibid.*, at para. 43 (S.C.R.).
[111] *Ibid.*, at para. 32 (S.C.R.).
[112] *Ibid.*, at para. 43 (S.C.R.). See also *ibid.*, at para. 32 (S.C.R.).
[113] *Ibid.*, at para. 47 (S.C.R.).
[114] *Ibid.*, at paras. 48-52 (S.C.R.).
[115] *Ibid.*, at para. 48 (S.C.R.).
[116] *Ibid.*, at para. 50 (S.C.R.).

§2.54 Contrast this with the facts in *R. v. Suberu*,[117] a companion case to *Grant*. There, a police officer attended at a liquor store (LCBO) in response to reports that two suspects were attempting to use a stolen credit card. On entering the store, the officer saw another police officer speaking with a store employee and another man. At this point, Mr. Suberu walked past the officer toward the exit and told him, "he did this, not me, so I guess I can go."[118] The officer followed Mr. Suberu outside and said, "Wait a minute. I need to talk to you before you go anywhere."[119] While Mr. Suberu was seated in the driver's seat of a van, but turned outward, facing the officer, there was a brief exchange during which the officer asked about Mr. Suberu's relationship to the man inside the store, where the two men had come from and who owned the van. As they spoke, the officer received further information over his radio linking the van and Mr. Suberu to the use of a stolen credit card at other locations earlier in the day (a Wal-Mart and an LCBO store). The officer then asked for Mr. Suberu's identification and vehicle ownership. As he did so, he saw shopping bags inside the van from Wal-Mart and the LCBO and arrested Mr. Suberu.

§2.55 Applying the *Grant* factors, the Supreme Court upheld the trial judge's conclusion that Mr. Suberu was *not* detained before his arrest.[120] The Court began by noting that when police believe a crime has recently been committed, they "may engage in preliminary questioning of bystanders without giving rise to a detention under sections 9 and 10 of the *Charter*."[121] While the "line between general questioning and focused interrogation amounting to detention may be difficult to draw in particular cases",[122] the Court concluded that the trial judge's "findings on the facts, supported by the evidence",[123] lead to the conclusion that the officer's questions were merely "exploratory" and he had "not yet zeroed in on the individual as someone whose movements must be controlled."[124]

§2.56 The Court also considered the words used by the officer ("Wait a minute, I need to talk to you before you go anywhere"). On their face, the Court observed, these words were equivocal. On the one hand, they might mean "I need to talk to you to get more information"; on the other, they could be interpreted "as an order not to leave, suggestive of putting Mr. Suberu under police control."[125] The Court preferred the former interpretation, emphasizing that the officer made no move to obstruct Mr. Suberu's movements, Mr. Suberu remained seated in the van while he spoke with the officer and the encounter was "very brief".[126]

---

[117]   [2009] S.C.J. No. 33, [2009] 2 S.C.R. 460 (S.C.C.).
[118]   *Ibid.*, at para. 9 (S.C.J.).
[119]   *Ibid.*
[120]   *Ibid.*, at para. 35 (S.C.J.).
[121]   *Ibid.*, at para. 28 (S.C.J.).
[122]   *Ibid.*, at para. 29 (S.C.J.).
[123]   *Ibid.*
[124]   *Ibid.*, at paras. 29-31 (S.C.J.).
[125]   *Ibid.*, at para. 33 (S.C.J.).
[126]   *Ibid.*

§2.57 The trial judge's conclusion, the Court reasoned, was also supported by the lack of evidence regarding Mr. Suberu's "personal circumstances, feelings or knowledge."[127] Because he did not testify, "there was no evidence as to whether he subjectively believed that he could not leave."[128] Without such evidence, the Court was left with the evidence of the police officer who testified that he was merely "exploring the situation", Mr. Suberu never told him he did not wish to speak, and their conversation was not "strained".[129]

§2.58 The Court thus dismissed the claim that Mr. Suberu's section 10(*b*) *Charter* rights were violated by the officer, who had proceeded to question him without apprising him of his right to counsel.

c. Uncertainty after *Grant*, a Proposal for Reform

§2.59 *Grant* has its doctrinal virtues. Its multi-factor approach for assessing whether or not there has been a psychological detention is flexible and nuanced. But as two of us have argued in greater detail elsewhere,[130] it fails to give police sufficient guidance on the scope of their authority. In our view, this uncertainty is likely to have three unfortunate effects. First, it will cause too many errors; that is, cases where police incorrectly decide (in relation to what the courts will or would have found) that a detention has or has not arisen. Second, in the face of this uncertainty, police will more often than not assume that a detention has *not* occurred and (if they are wrong) thereby deprive those detained of their rights under sections 9 and 10 of the *Charter*. Finally, in applying *Grant*, lower courts will too often take an overly deferential approach toward police decision-making.

§2.60 How might this situation be improved? In short, the courts should interpret and apply *Grant* in a manner that provides as much *ex ante* certainty to police as possible. In that regard, the experience in provincial appellate courts after *Therens*[131] is instructive. Shortly after *Therens* was decided, the Ontario Court of Appeal articulated a test for detention that is similar in many ways to the approach in *Grant*. In *R. v. Moran*,[132] Justice Martin set out a list of relevant criteria in a case involving an accused interviewed by police at the stationhouse on two separate occasions during the course of a homicide investigation.[133] The *Moran*

---

[127] *Ibid.*, at para. 34 (S.C.J.).

[128] *Ibid.*

[129] *Ibid.*

[130] See Steven Penney & James Stribopoulos, "'Detention' under the *Charter* after *R. v. Grant* and *R. v. Suberu*" (2010) 51 S.C.L.R. (2d) 439.

[131] [1985] S.C.J. No. 30, [1985] 1 S.C.R. 613 (S.C.C.). See *R. v. Moran*, [1987] O.J. No. 794, 36 C.C.C. (3d) 225 at 258-59 (Ont. C.A.), leave to appeal refused [1988] S.C.C.A. No. 213, [1988] 1 S.C.R. xi (S.C.C.). This approach is similar to that taken in the United States in determining whether the suspect is in "custody" for the purposes of the *Miranda* warning. See *Miranda v. Arizona*, 384 U.S. 437 (1966); *Berkemer v. McCarty*, 468 U.S. 420 (1984); *Stansbury v. California*, 511 U.S. 318 at 323 (1994); Wayne R. LaFave, Jerold H. Israel and Nancy J. King, *Criminal Procedure*, 3d ed. (St. Paul, Minn.: West Group, 2000) § 6.6.

[132] [1987] O.J. No. 794, 36 C.C.C. (3d) 225 at 258-59 (Ont. C.A.), leave to appeal refused [1988] S.C.C.A. No. 213, [1988] 1 S.C.R. xi (S.C.C.) [*Moran*].

[133] *Ibid.*, at 258-59 (S.C.R.), where Martin J. identified the following criteria:

criteria were adopted by most courts of appeal[134] and applied to many different types of police-suspect encounters, including the questioning of pedestrians.[135]

§2.61 At first glance, the *Moran* approach appears at least as open-ended and indeterminate as *Grant*. A close look at the jurisprudence, however, reveals that most often (including in *Moran* itself) detention turned on the (related) fourth, fifth and sixth factors; namely, the stage of the investigation, the degree of suspicion attaching to the accused and the nature of the questioning.[136]

---

1. The precise language used by the police officer in requesting the person who subsequently becomes an accused to come to the police station, and whether the accused was given a, choice or expressed a preference that the interview be conducted at the police station, rather than at his or her home;

2. Whether the accused was escorted to the police station by a police officer or came himself or herself in response to a police request;

3. Whether the accused left at the conclusion of the interview or whether he or she was arrested;

4. The stage of the investigation, that is, whether the questioning was part of the general investigation of a crime or possible crime or whether the police had already decided that a crime had been committed and that the accused was the perpetrator or involved in its commission and the questioning was conducted for the purpose of obtaining incriminating statements from the accused;

5. Whether the police had reasonable and probable grounds to believe that the accused had committed the crime being investigated;

6. The nature of the questions: whether they were questions of a general nature designed to obtain information or whether the accused was confronted with evidence pointing to his or her guilt;

7. The subjective belief by an accused that he or she is detained, although relevant, is not decisive, because the issue is whether he or she reasonably believed that he or she was detained. Personal circumstances relating to the accused, such as low intelligence, emotional disturbance, youth and lack of sophistication are circumstances to be considered in determining whether he had a subjective belief that he was detained.

[134] See *R. v. Johns*, [1998] O.J. No. 445, 14 C.R. (5th) 302 at para. 23 (Ont. C.A.); *R. v. Voss*, [1989] O.J. No. 1124, 33 O.A.C. 190 (Ont. C.A.); *R. v. Caputo*, [1997] O.J. No. 857, 114 C.C.C. (3d) 1 at 11 (Ont. C.A.); *R. v. H. (C.R.)*, [2003] M.J. No. 90 174 C.C.C. (3d) 67 at paras. 27-30 (Man. C.A.); *R. c. Amyot*, [1990] J.Q. no 1061, 58 C.C.C. (3d) 312 (Que. C.A.); *R. v. V. (T.A.)*, [2001] A.J. No. 1679, 48 C.R. (5th) 366 at para. 18 (Alta. C.A.); *R. c. Gaudette*, [2006] J.Q. no 8112, 2006 QCCA 1004 at para. 37 (Que. C.A.); *R. v. C. (S.)*, [1989] N.J. No. 81, 74 Nfld. & P.E.I.R. 252 (Nfld. C.A.); *R. v. Groat*, [2006] B.C.J. No. 109, 205 C.C.C. (3d) 542 (B.C.C.A.); *R. v. Priddle*, [2003] B.C.J. No. 2671, 2003 BCCA 637 (B.C.C.A.).

[135] See e.g., *R. v. B. (L.)*, [2007] O.J. No. 3290, 227 C.C.C. (3d) 70 (Ont. C.A.); *R. v. H. (C.R.)*, [2003] M.J. No. 90, 2003 MBCA 38 (Man. C.A.); *R. v. Grafe*, [1987] O.J. No. 796, 36 C.C.C. (3d) 267 (Ont. C.A.); *R. v. Hall*, [1995] O.J. No. 544, 22 O.R. (3d) 289 (Ont. C.A.); *R. v. V. (T.A.)*, [2001] A.J. No. 679, 48 C.R. (5th) 366 (Alta. C.A.).

[136] For example, writing for the Manitoba Court of Appeal in *R. v. H. (C.R.)*, [2003] M.J. No. 90, 2003 MBCA 38 (Man. C.A.), Steele J. held that police did not detain a pedestrian even though they asked for his identification and checked his name against a computer database. See also *R. v. B. (L.)*, [2007] O.J. No. 3290, 227 C.C.C. (3d) 70 at para. 67 (Ont. C.A.) (request for pedestrian's identity and running of database check did not trigger detention). Subsequently, Steele J. concluded in *R. v. Dolynchuck*, [2004] M.J. No. 135, 184 C.C.C. (3d) 214 at para. 32 (Man. C.A.), leave to appeal refused [2004] S.C.C.A. No. 271 (S.C.C.), that police did detain the accused when they questioned him in a parking lot after receiving a tip that he had been driving while impaired. Police had more than a mere suspicion that he had committed this offence, indicated that they would have detained him for investigative purposes after they confirmed his identity and asked him a question ("were you driving?"), the answer to which provided proof of an element of the offence. Police had "already decided that a crime had been committed and

§2.62 Before *Grant*, a detention was usually found when police identified the accused as the likely perpetrator and conducted questioning with a view to inducing self-incriminating statements.[137] When both of these conditions were present, a detention was usually triggered even when suspects were told that they were free to leave or to decline answering questions.[138] Conversely, when one of these conditions was *not* present (such as in the case of accusatory questioning), a detention was usually not found even if police had grounds to detain or arrest at the conclusion of questioning.[139] It thus appeared that while courts formally applied an open-ended, "totality of the circumstances" approach, like that endorsed in *Grant*, the results in actual cases were dictated by a (relatively) "bright-line" standard. In all but a few cases, detention was found when (and only when), police attempted to elicit incriminating statements from the likely perpetrator of the offence under investigation.[140]

§2.63 To be clear, we do not mean to argue that the *Moran* criteria, as narrowed and refined in subsequent cases, should be resurrected to replace the various factors identified in *Grant*. In fact, as we detail below, the controlling considerations that emerged in *Moran* are under-inclusive because they fail to provide any protection where the police have no offence in mind but are instead engaged in an invasive fishing expedition, as they were in *Grant*.[141] The *Moran* factors were

---

that the accused was the perpetrator" and their question was designed to obtain "incriminating statements".

137 See *e.g.*, *R. v. Voss*, [1989] O.J. No. 1124, 33 O.A.C. 190 at 204 (Ont. C.A.) ("the police investigation changed from one of trying to determine a cause of death to one of trying to get information from a man who is alleged to have and has admitted to having assaulted his wife in order to determine if he was implicated in the death"); *R. v. Pomeroy*, [2008] O.J. No. 2550, 2008 ONCA 521 at para. 37 (Ont. C.A.) ("The focus of the interview was to gain general information as part of the investigation of the 'suspicious death'; the questioning was not conducted for the purpose of obtaining incriminating statements from the appellant."); *R. v. Caputo*, [1997] O.J. No. 857, 114 C.C.C. (3d) 1 at para. 27 (Ont. C.A.) ("The questioning up to that point appears to have been general in nature and directed toward obtaining a witness statement from the appellant. He had not yet been confronted with evidence pointing to his guilt or to the contradictions between his statements and the other evidence that was being gathered as the investigation continued.").

138 See *R. v. Johns*, [1998] O.J. No. 445, 14 C.R. (5th) 302 at para. 28 (Ont. C.A.); *R. v. Teske*, [2005] O.J. No. 3759 at para. 55 (Ont. C.A.); *R. v. Rajaratnam*, [2006] A.J. No. 1373, 214 C.C.C. (3d) 547 at para. 17, 43 C.R. (6th) 280 Alta. C.A.); *R. v. Lee*, [2007] A.J. No. 1183, 2007 ABCA 337, 417 A.R. 331 (Alta. C.A.).

139 See *R. v. Pomeroy*, [2008] O.J. No. 2550, 2008 ONCA 521, 91 O.R. (3d) 261 at para. 37 (Ont. C.A.); *R. v. Hall*, [2004] O.J. No. 5007, 193 O.A.C. 7 at para. 22 (Ont. C.A.); *R. v. B. (L.)*, [2007] O.J. No. 3290, 86 O.R. (3d) 730 at paras. 56-57 (Ont. C.A.).

140 This test is similar to that set out in *R. v. Hawkins*, [1993] S.C.J. No. 50, [1993] 2 S.C.R. 157, 20 C.R. (4th) 55 (S.C.C.), but without reference to the intention of police to arrest or charge suspects. See also Tim Quigley, *Procedure in Canadian Criminal Law*, 2d ed. (looseleaf) (Toronto: Thomson Carswell, 2005) § 5.3(c)(ii); David M. Tanovich, "Rethinking the Meaning of Detention: The Doctrine of 'Preliminary Investigatory Detention' is Not Appropriate" (1992) 7 C.R. (4th) 374 at 380; Don Stuart, *Charter Justice in Canadian Criminal Law*, 4th ed. (Toronto: Thomson Carswell, 2005) at 326-27; Steven Penney, "What's Wrong with Self-Incrimination? The Wayward Path of Self-Incrimination Law in the Post-Charter Era, Part 2: Self-Incrimination in Police Investigations" (2004) 48 Crim. L.Q. 280 at 284-85, 320-21.

141 This is the principal reason why we also disagree with Binnie J.'s proposed approach for defining detention, which would emphasize the perception and intention of police. See *R. v. Grant*, [2009] S.C.J. No. 32, [2009] 2 S.C.R. 353 at para. 180 (S.C.C.), Binnie J., concurring. We

developed with section 10 of the *Charter* in mind and are most relevant to formal, "sit down" interviews conducted at a police station or other suitable locations. They were not designed to address the section 9 liberty interests implicated by impromptu, "in the field" inquiries of pedestrians, motorists and the like. We reference *Moran*'s treatment only to stress that not all factors under a multi-factor approach are deserving of equal emphasis. By focusing on the key variables identified in *Grant*, courts can both give police clear guidance, as well

---

worry that in the hands of lower court judges, a police officer's assertion that "I didn't suspect the accused of anything, I was just having a chat" would too easily allow highly coercive encounters to avoid being labelled detentions. We are especially concerned about certain so-called "community policing programs", like the Toronto Anti-Violence Intervention Strategy (TAVIS). TAVIS is a relatively recent initiative of the Toronto Police Service. Its stated purpose ("an intensive, violence reduction and community mobilization strategy intended to reduce crime and increase safety in our neighbourhoods") is laudable. See Toronto Police Service, TAVIS, available online at <http://www.torontopolice.on.ca/tavis>. In practice, however, it involves large teams of police officers proactively policing "high-crime" neighbourhoods and engaging in aggressive stop and frisk practices. Those stopped are asked to produce identification and are routinely searched. Individuals who are in possession of drugs or weapons are arrested, as are those for whom there are outstanding warrants or who happen to be breaching the terms of a bail or probation order. For others, the encounter often only ends after the police have completed a "contact card," known within the Toronto Police Service as a "208 card." See Timothy Appleby, "New police strategy designed to blanket high-violence areas", *Globe and Mail*, February 13, 2006, A1; Moira Welsh, "Elite Toronto police squad goes looking for trouble," *Toronto Star* (February 8, 2010) available online at: <http://www.thestar.com/special sections/raceandcrime/article/761310--elite-toronto-police-squad-goes-looking-for-trouble>. The use of these cards was explained by LaForme J. in *R. v. Ferdinand*, [2004] O.J. No. 3209, 21 C.R. (6th) 65 at paras. 12-16 (Ont. S.C.J.):

> A 208 card is approximately 3" by 5" and is printed on both sides, commencing with the words, "Person Investigated". It records information obtained from a person who is stopped by the police that includes information such as, "name, aliases, date of birth, colour, address, and contact location including the time". On the back it has entries for things such as: "associates" and "associated with: gang, motorcycle club, Drug Treatment Court". The police then input the information from the completed 208 cards into a police computer database for their future reference.
>
> . . .
>
> There is no evidence that any police officer advises, or has ever advised, any person stopped that they have a right not to answer any questions from this card and that they are free to leave if they wish. The testimony of the two young men from the neighbourhood is that: The police "always stop them, and always search them", and they are not told they do not have to answer. They add that, persons stopped by these two officers always answer questions and submit to searches because they believe they have to, and that it does not do any good not to.

It is fair to say that Justice LaForme was troubled by the way in which these cards were being used. In a rather prescient comment, he noted that the "impression that one could draw from the information sought on these 208 cards — along with the current manner in which they are being used — is that they could be a tool utilized for racial profiling." *Ibid.*, at para. 19 (C.R.).

In 2010, the *Toronto Star* gained access, by means of a freedom of information request, to the data compiled by Toronto police using the 208 cards. See *Toronto Police Services Board v. Ontario (Information and Privacy Commissioner)*, [2009] O.J. No. 90, 93 O.R. (3d) 563 (Ont. C.A.). After analyzing the data, which includes racial descriptors of the persons stopped and questioned, the *Star* reports that black males between the ages of 15 and 24 years are 2.5 times more likely to be stopped and documented than white males the same age. See Jim Rankin, "Race Matters: Blacks documented by police at high rate" *Toronto Star* (February 6, 2010), online: <http://www.thestar.com/specialsections/raceandcrime/article/761343--race-matters-blacks-documented-by-police-at-high-rate>.

as achieve a more optimal accommodation between the conflicting interests implicated by police-citizen encounters.

§2.64 Of course, this begs the questions, which of the *Grant* factors are most important to achieving this accommodation and what guidance should courts give to the police in future cases? In the aftermath of *Grant*, we would emphasize two variables:

(1) *The language used to initiate the encounter.* Permissive language would be far less likely to result in a detention than obligatory language. For example, in the context of a street stop, "I'd like to speak with you" or "Would you mind if I asked you some questions?" would be unlikely to result in a detention. A detention would likely arise, in contrast, from "Stay right there!", "Freeze!", or "Show me some identification!"[142] Similarly, for "sit down" interviews, "I'd like to speak with you at a time and place of your choosing" is less likely to trigger detention than, "We want you to come with us to the police station to talk about this right now."[143]

(2) *The nature of any ensuing questioning.* Purely exploratory questions are unlikely to trigger detention, for example, a police officer who approaches a person on the street and asks, "How are things?" or an officer who responds to an emergency call and asks someone present "What's going on?" or "Do you know what happened here?" In contrast, if a person is approached and asked for identification before being quizzed about where they are coming from, what they are doing, where they are going, whether they are carrying a weapon or contraband, *etc.*, a detention is the undoubted result. In the latter circumstances, few reasonable people would feel free to walk away. Similarly, in a more formal interview context, a detention would not likely arise from open-ended, non-accusatory questions designed to gather preliminary information; whereas questions designed to

---

[142] Unfortunately, *R. v. Grant*, [2009] S.C.J. No. 32, [2009] 2 S.C.R. 353 (S.C.C.) did not address whether a police demand for identification results in a detention. When police asked Mr. Grant for his name and address, he produced his provincial health card without a police request, so the question did not arise. A number of pre-*Grant* cases suggest that such a request does not result in a detention. See *R. v. B. (L.)*, [2007] O.J. No. 3290, 86 O.R. (3d) 730 (Ont. C.A.); *R. v. Hall*, [1995] O.J. No. 544, 22 O.R. (3d) 289 at paras. 21-23 (Ont. C.A.); *R. v. H. (C.R.)*, [2003] M.J. No. 90, 174 C.C.C. (3d) 67 at paras. 33-36 (Man. C.A.). Post-*Grant*, it remains to be seen how this question will be resolved. Obviously, police must be free to approach people and engage them in conversation, which includes the social pleasantry of asking someone's name. Few would feel compelled to remain in a police officer's presence because of such a routine and benign question. But a police request for identification is undoubtedly different. Given a police officer's position of authority, most people would not hesitate in complying with what they would reasonably perceive as a demand. And, surely, once a police officer is holding your identification (especially if while doing so they are simultaneously peppering you with questions regarding where you are coming from, where you are going, whether you have anything in your possession that you should not, *etc.*), most reasonable people would not think that they are free to leave.

[143] See *R. v. Moran*, [1987] O.J. No. 794, 36 C.C.C. (3d) 225 at 258 (Ont. C.A.), leave to appeal refused [1988] S.C.C.A. No. 213, [1988] 1 S.C.R. xi (S.C.C.) (stressing scrutiny of language used in requesting person to come to the police station and "whether the accused was given a choice or expressed a preference that the interview be conducted at the police station, rather than at his or her home").

elicit self-incriminating evidence from someone strongly suspected of committing a crime likely would.

§2.65 The first of these variables targets the liberty interests inherent in section 9;[144] the second aims to protect the interests inhering in section 10(*b*) — preventing inquisitorial abuses and compelled self-incrimination.[145] Each also allows police to seek preliminary investigative information without significant restraint. It follows that a detention should usually be found when *either* of these factors points in that direction. If courts were to require both, one of these *Charter*-protected interests would frequently be left unprotected. Without factor (1), as long as they do not engage in interrogation-like questioning, police could coercively restrain people's freedom without reasonable suspicion that they have committed a crime. And without factor (2), as long as they do not coercively restrain people's freedom, police could conduct accusatory (and potentially abusive) interrogations, again without reasonable suspicion and without extending the protections of the right to counsel.

§2.66 In addition to enabling a better balance between individual and law enforcement interests, our proposal gives police much more concrete guidance than the open-ended *Grant* factors. In short, it tells them that if they don't want to detain they should *use permissive language and refrain from interrogating*. Conversely, it warns them that if they use compulsory language to initiate encounters with suspects or engage in the functional equivalent of an interrogation, they will likely have triggered a detention and must thus comply with sections 9, 10(*a*) and (subject to any changes to the law that we advocate for below) 10(*b*) of the *Charter*. In other words, they must have reasonable grounds to suspect an individual of being involved in a recently committed or unfolding criminal offence, tell that person why they have been detained, and inform them of their right to retain and instruct counsel without delay. (The requirements for a lawful investigative detention are explained in detail below in Part 4(3).)

§2.67 As mentioned, the Court suggested in *Grant* that if the police want to avoid engaging these various *Charter* rights there is a relatively simple solution: tell the affected individual in unambiguous terms that he or she is under no obligation to answer questions and is free to go. This suggestion, we caution, should be read very strictly. In the context of brief "in the field" inquiries, such a state-

---

[144] *Canadian Charter of Rights and Freedoms*, Part I of the *Constitution Act, 1982*, being Schedule B to the *Canada Act 1982* (U.K.), 1982, c. 11. In *R. v. Grant*, [2009] S.C.J. No. 32, [2009] 2 S.C.R. 353 at para. 20 (S.C.C.), the Court finally took the opportunity to expressly acknowledge the purpose underlying this important *Charter* right, which it recognized as being, "broadly put ... to protect individual liberty from unjustified state interference." Rather remarkably, even though s. 9 of the *Charter* had been before the Court on 24 prior occasions, it has never before expressly identified its purpose. See James Stribopoulos, "The Forgotten Right: Section 9 of the Charter, Its Purpose and Meaning" (2008) 40 S.C.L.R. (2d) 211 at 214-23.

[145] See *R. v. Suberu*, [2009] S.C.J. No. 33, [2009] 2 S.C.R. 460 at para. 40 (S.C.C.); *R. v. Manninen*, [1987] S.C.J. No. 41, [1987] 1 S.C.R. 1233 at 1242-1243 (S.C.C.); *R. v. Brydges*, [1990] S.C.J. No. 8, [1990] 1 S.C.R. 190 at 203, 206, 215 (S.C.C.); *R. v. Bartle*, [1994] S.C.J. No. 74, [1994] 3 S.C.R. 173 at 191 (S.C.C.); *R. v. Prosper*, [1994] S.C.J. No. 72, [1994] 3 S.C.R. 236 at 271 (S.C.C.). For further discussion of the purposes of s. 10(*b*) of the *Charter*, see Chapter 3, Part 4(3).

ment would likely be enough to convey to most people that they are truly not required to cooperate. In the context of accusatory questioning at the police station (and perhaps other "sit down" interviews), something more may be required to impress upon suspects that they are not under legal constraint.[146] It would be prudent, for example, to require suspects in such circumstances to read, understand and sign a statement (perhaps repeatedly in the case of lengthy interviews), clearly explaining that they are legally entitled to leave or remain silent.

(iv) Physical Restraint

§2.68 As noted in *Therens*,[147] *Thomsen*[148] and recently reiterated in *Grant*,[149] an individual subject to physical restraint is detained for *Charter* purposes. There is little jurisprudence on the meaning of this category of detention, likely because "physical restraint" is usually obvious. Though no court has ventured to define it, the category appears to be limited to situations where police take physical control over a suspect by manually handling him or her in a manner that is more than fleeting or trifling.[150]

§2.69 With the Supreme Court's recent decision in *Grant*, the amount of contact necessary before a physical detention results is unfortunately left less than clear. In that case, discussed in detail immediately above, in identifying considerations relevant to whether or not there has been a *psychological detention*, the Court listed physical contact between a police officer and a suspect as one of many variables. In that regard, the Court specifically mentions a police officer "placing" a hand on a suspect. According to the Court, a "fleeting touch" would be insufficient to trigger a psychological detention but "[i]f sustained" it could be enough.[151]

§2.70 Although the Court was right in *Grant* to note that a fleeting touch is probably not enough to result in a detention, any physical contact between a police officer and a suspect that is more sustained or significant than that should undoubtedly be characterized as a *physical detention*.[152] So, for example, if a police officer grasps an individual's arm,[153] handcuffs a suspect[154] or directs an

---

[146] See §2.62, above, and the cases cited in the supporting footnotes for decisions (finding detention in the context of accusatory "sit down" interviews despite police statements that suspects were free to leave or remain silent).

[147] [1985] S.C.J. No. 30, [1985] 1 S.C.R. 613 (S.C.C.).

[148] [1988] S.C.J. No. 31, [1988] 1 S.C.R. 640 at 648-49 (S.C.C.).

[149] [2009] S.C.J. No. 32, [2009] 2 S.C.R. 353 at para. 25 (S.C.C.).

[150] See e.g., R. v. DeBot, [1989] S.C.J. No. 118, [1989] 2 S.C.R. 1140 at 1152, 1161 (S.C.C.) (suspect ordered to stand "spread eagle" against a wall and empty his pockets was detained).

[151] R. v. Grant, [2009] S.C.J. No. 32, [2009] 2 S.C.R. 353 at para. 42 (S.C.C.).

[152] In R. v. Feeney, [1997] S.C.J. No. 49, [1997] 2 S.C.R. 13 at para. 56 (S.C.C.), for example, the Supreme Court of Canada held that the accused was detained when police shook his leg and told him to get out of bed.

[153] See e.g., R. v. Hanano, [2007] M.J. No. 11 at para. 6, 2007 MBQB 9 (Man. Q.B.), detention found where a police officer "took hold" of a suspect's arms.

[154] See e.g., R. v. Greaves, [2004] B.C.J. No. 1953 at para. 18, 189 C.C.C. (3d) 305 (B.C.C.A.), leave to appeal refused [2004] S.C.C.A. No. 522 (S.C.C.) where the Court rather understanda-

individual into the backseat of a police cruiser,[155] a physical detention obviously results. In such circumstances, engaging in a concurrent analysis as to whether there was a psychological detention is unnecessary. Once a police officer takes physical control of a suspect, no reasonable person could possibly conclude that he or she is still free to walk away.[156]

§2.71 It follows that non-consensual searches of a suspect's clothing or body entail a physical detention.[157] Similarly, non-consensual searches of a suspect's personal belongings, such as handbags or suitcases, also trigger detention, so long as the search is performed in the suspect's presence.[158] In and of themselves, consent searches do not trigger detention.[159]

§2.72 Detention by physical restraint does not likely extend to situations where police have arguably constrained a suspect's freedom of movement without manually handling his or her person or property. Cases where pedestrians have argued that police positioned themselves or their vehicles to prevent them from leaving, for example, have typically been decided on the basis of psychological detention (without legal compulsion).[160] Courts have similarly rejected claims that physical detention arises when police obtain legal authority to arrest or detain but choose not (at least temporarily) to exercise that authority.[161]

§2.73 This is as it should be. Without a requirement of actual contact, the physical restraint category becomes too indeterminate. The two categories of

---

bly spent no time considering the threshold question of whether there was a "detention" in a case where the police handcuffed a suspect).

[155] See *R. v. Elshaw*, [1991] S.C.J. No. 68, [1991] 3 S.C.R. 24 (S.C.C.), where the majority acted on a concession by the Crown, based on the reasoning of the courts below, that Mr. Elshaw was detained when he was placed in the rear of a police van by one of the investigating officers. See also *R. v. Lawrence*, [1990] O.J. No. 1648, 59 C.C.C. (3d) 55 (Ont. C.A.), finding that the accused was detained when she was directed into the rear of a police cruiser by the investigating officer prior to her formal arrest.

[156] In *R. v. Feeney*, [1997] S.C.J. No. 49, [1997] 2 S.C.R. 13 at para. 56 (S.C.C.), for example, the Supreme Court of Canada held that the accused was detained when police shook his leg and told him to get out of bed.

[157] See *R. v. DeBot*, [1989] S.C.J. No. 118, [1989] 2 S.C.R. 1140 at 1146 (S.C.C.); *R. v. Greffe*, [1990] S.C.J. No. 32, [1990] 1 S.C.R. 755 at 793-94 (S.C.C.); *R. v. Simmons*, [1988] S.C.J. No. 86, [1988] 2 S.C.R. 495 at 521 (S.C.C.); *R. v. V. (T.A.)*, [2001] A.J. No. 1679, 48 C.R. (5th) 366 at para. 21 (Alta. C.A.).

[158] See *R. v. Rube*, [1992] B.C.J. No. 105, 10 B.C.A.C. 48 (B.C.C.A.). As discussed above, at §2.34 to §2.35, in the customs and border crossing context, routine searches of person or property do not trigger s. 10 detention.

[159] See *R. v. Jeanes*, [2009] O.J. No. 364, 2009 ONCA 96 (Ont. C.A.); *R. v. Rube*, [1992] B.C.J. No. 105, 10 B.C.A.C. 48 (B.C.C.A.); *R. v. Vandenbosch*, [2007] M.J. No. 346, 52 C.R. (6th) 191 (Man. C.A.), leave to appeal refused [2007] S.C.C.A. No. 554 (S.C.C.); *R. v. Hall*, [2004] O.J. No. 5007, 193 O.A.C. 7 at para. 23 (Ont. C.A.); *R. v. Nicholas*, [2004] O.J. No. 725, 182 C.C.C. (3d) 393 (Ont. C.A.); *R. v. Hardy*, [1995] B.C.J. No. 2570, 103 C.C.C. (3d) 289 (B.C.C.A.). The requirements for a valid consent search are discussed in Chapter 3, Part 2(4)(c).

[160] See *R. v. Grant*, [2006] O.J. No. 2179, 38 C.R. (6th) 58 at para. 8 (Ont. C.A.), affd [2009] S.C.J. No. 32, [2009] 2 S.C.R. 353 (S.C.C.) without addressing this discrete issue. See also *R. v. B. (L.)*, [2007] O.J. No. 3290, 49 C.R. (6th) 245 at para. 64, 86 O.R. (3d) 730, 227 O.A.C. 132, 227 C.C.C. (3d) 70 (Ont. C.A.).

[161] See *R. v. Pomeroy*, [2008] O.J. No. 2550, 2008 ONCA 521 at para. 20 (Ont. C.A.); *R. v. Hall*, [2004] O.J. No. 5007, 193 O.A.C. 7 at para. 22 (Ont. C.A.).

psychological detention discussed above are flexible enough to capture any situation where we would wish to recognize a detention without bodily interference.

(4) Determining Whether Detention or Imprisonment is Arbitrary

§2.74 Once it is established that an individual was "detained or imprisoned" section 9 of the *Charter* is engaged. The guarantee, however, only prohibits "arbitrary" deprivations of liberty. This begs the question, what makes a detention or imprisonment arbitrary? There are two types of claims that can be raised under section 9.

§2.75 Most common are challenges directed at the decision to detain or imprison in specific cases. As we shall see in the next section, thanks to the Supreme Court's recent decision in *Grant*,[162] these sorts of claims are now relatively straightforward, at least from a legal standpoint.

§2.76 The second category of section 9 *Charter*[163] claims is less common, involving challenges to the law authorizing detention or imprisonment. If the responsible law contains criteria or procedures that are in themselves arbitrary, it will violate section 9 and will therefore be null and void unless it can be saved under section 1 of the *Charter*. If a state official detains or imprisons in reliance on an unconstitutional enactment, then the resulting interference with liberty is by implication also unconstitutional.

§2.77 We will consider each category of section 9 *Charter* claims in the following two sections.

(a) Challenging Detention or Imprisonment in Specific Cases

§2.78 The most common section 9 *Charter* challenge is aimed at the decision to detain or imprison in a specific case. In *Grant*, the Supreme Court of Canada finally made clear that any unlawful interference with liberty is necessarily arbitrary and contrary to section 9 of the *Charter*. As the Court explained:

> The s. 9 guarantee against arbitrary detention is a manifestation of the general principle, enunciated in s. 7, that a person's liberty is not to be curtailed except in accordance with the principles of fundamental justice. As this Court has stated: "This guarantee expresses one of the most fundamental norms of the rule of law. The state may not detain arbitrarily, but only in accordance with the law": *Charkaoui v. Canada (Citizenship and Immigration)*, 2007 SCC 9, [2007] 1 S.C.R. 350, at para. 88. Section 9 serves to protect individual liberty against unlawful state interference. <u>A lawful detention is not arbitrary within the meaning of s. 9 (*Mann*, at para. 20), unless</u>

---

[162] *R. v. Grant*, [2009] S.C.J. No. 32, [2009] 2 S.C.R. 353 (S.C.C.).
[163] *Canadian Charter of Rights and Freedoms*, Part I of the *Constitution Act, 1982*, being Schedule B to the *Canada Act 1982* (U.K.), 1982, c. 11.

the law authorizing the detention is itself arbitrary. *Conversely, a detention not authorized by law is arbitrary and violates s. 9.*[164]

Importantly, the Supreme Court in *Grant* also explained that earlier appellate court decisions suggesting that an unlawful detention is not necessarily arbitrary should no longer be followed.[165]

§2.79 The Supreme Court's decision to equate any unlawful detention as necessarily violating section 9 of the *Charter* makes good sense. First, this conclusion is in keeping with the drafting history reviewed in Part 3(1), above, which demonstrates that the *Charter*'s framers envisioned that illegal encroachments on liberty would be considered arbitrary under section 9.[166] This interpretation is also in keeping with the purpose of section 9, which the Supreme Court identified in *Grant* as being to protect individual liberty from unjustified state interference.[167] Insisting that detention be based on lawful authority best serves that goal and is consistent with the principle of legality, a key component of the Anglo-Canadian common law constitution.[168] Finally, as the Supreme Court noted in *Grant*, this approach sensibly mirrors what the Court has done under section 8 of the *Charter*, where lawful authority is also a precondition for a "reasonable", and thus constitutional, search or seizure.[169]

---

[164] [2009] S.C.J. No. 32, [2009] 2 S.C.R. 353 at para. 54 (S.C.C.) [emphasis added].

[165] *Ibid.*, at para. 55. The Court specifically cited *R. v. Duguay*, [1985] O.J. No. 2492, 18 C.C.C. (3d) 289 at 296 (Ont. C.A.), affd [1989] S.C.J. No. 4, [1989] 1 S.C.R. 93 (S.C.C.), which had held that not every unlawful detention is necessarily arbitrary and required a consideration of the detaining officer's mindset, an oblique motive would result in finding an arbitrary detention but an honest mistake based on grounds just short of those required by the law might not. The *Duguay* approach had been widely followed. See *R. v. Brown*, [1987] N.S.J. No. 22, 33 C.C.C. (3d) 54 at 67-68 (N.S.C.A.); *Freeman v. West Vancouver (District)*, [1992] B.C.J. No. 2146, 19 B.C.A.C. 81 at para. 29 (B.C.C.A.); *R. v. Campbell*, [2003] M.J. No. 207, 175 C.C.C. (3d) 452 at paras. 39-42 (Man. C.A.); *R. v. Perello*, [2005] S.J. No. 60, 193 C.C.C. (3d) 151 at para. 40 (Sask. C.A.); *R. v. Pimentel*, [2000] M.J. No. 256, 145 Man. R. (2d) 295 (Man. C.A.), leave to appeal refused [2000] S.C.C.A. No. 359 (S.C.C.). But see *R. v. Simpson*, [1994] N.J. No. 69, 88 C.C.C. (3d) 377 at 388 (Nfld. C.A.), revd in the result only [1995] S.C.J. No. 12, [1995] 1 S.C.R. 449, 95 C.C.C. (3d) 96 (S.C.C.) (implicitly questioning this approach but without referring to *Duguay*). Also see *R. v. Porquez*, [1991] A.J. No. 103, 114 A.R. 1 (Alta. C.A.), leave to appeal refused [1991] S.C.C.A. No. 289, 137 N.R. 160*n* (S.C.C.) (holding that an arrest in the absence of reasonable and probable grounds violated s. 9 of the *Charter* without ever addressing the subjective mindset of the arresting officers). The *Duguay* approach had also been criticized by commentators. See Don Stuart, *Charter Justice in Canadian Criminal Law*, 3d ed. (Toronto: Carswell, 2001) at 263. James Stribopoulos, "The Forgotten Right: Section 9 of the Charter, Its Purpose and Meaning" (2008) 40 S.C.L.R. (2d) 211 at 218-31.

[166] See Part 3(1), above, especially at §2.19.

[167] *R. v. Grant*, [2009] S.C.J. No. 32, [2009] 2 S.C.R. 353 at para. 20 (S.C.C.).

[168] The protection of individual liberty, historically, by means of the principle of legality, was discussed above in Part 2.

[169] See *R. v. Grant*, [2009] S.C.J. No. 32, [2009] 2 S.C.R. 353 at para. 56 (S.C.C.) citing *R. v. Collins*, [1987] S.C.J. No. 15, [1987] 1 S.C.R. 265 (S.C.C.). In *Collins*, at 278 (S.C.R.), the Supreme Court explained that a "search will be reasonable if it is authorized by law, if the law itself is reasonable and if the manner in which the search was carried out is reasonable." See also *R. v. Evans*, [1996] S.C.J. No. 1, [1996] 1 S.C.R. 8 at 22 (S.C.C.). The legality precondition for a reasonable search or seizure is discussed more fully in Chapter 3, Part 2(5)(*a*), specifically §3.104 and §3.105.

§2.80 Once it is determined that police detained a suspect, it will therefore often be sensible to begin the section 9 analysis by asking if the police acted lawfully in doing so. This requires close scrutiny of the detaining officer's actions as against the legal authority under which he or she purported to be acting. (Police powers to interfere with liberty are introduced and explained below in Part 4.)

§2.81 But compliance with the law's formal requirements does not necessarily exhaust the potential for section 9 *Charter* claims in the case-specific category. Beyond illegality, the Supreme Court of Canada has also recognized that section 9 of the *Charter* is violated if an arrest is undertaken "because a police officer was biased towards a person of a different race, nationality or colour, or that there was a personal enmity between a police officer directed towards the person arrested."[170] This rule applies to all detentions, not just those culminating in arrest. It is difficult to imagine anything more arbitrary than a detention undertaken for a discriminatory[171] or other improper[172] purpose.

§2.82 This acknowledgment by the Supreme Court is welcome. In Canada, it is now widely recognized that the exercise of police discretion may sometimes be motivated, consciously or subconsciously, by nefarious considerations like an individual's age, economic circumstances, ethnicity or race.[173] For example, in recent years a growing body of evidence has emerged that strongly suggests that both Aboriginals[174] and African-Canadians[175] are detained by police at dispropor-

---

[170] *R. v. Storrey*, [1990] S.C.J. No. 12, [1990] 1 S.C.R. 241 at 251-52 (S.C.C.).

[171] Of course, if a police officer is motivated by some bias that implicates one of the prohibited grounds of discrimination under s. 15(1) of the *Charter*, then that section would also be violated.

[172] See *Brown v. Durham (Regional Municipality) Police Force*, [1998] O.J. No. 5274, 131 C.C.C. (3d) 1 at 116-17 (Ont. C.A.), leave to appeal refused [1999] S.C.C.A. No. 87 (S.C.C.) [*Brown*] (in the "improper purposes" category the Court sensibly includes "purposes which are illegal, purposes which involve the infringement of a person's constitutional rights and purposes which have nothing to do with the execution of a police officer's public duty."). See also *R. v. Nolet*, [2010] S.C.J. No. 24, [2010] 1 S.C.R. 851, 2010 SCC 24 at paras. 32-41(S.C.C.).

[173] See Richard V. Ericson, *Reproducing Order: A Study of Police Patrol Work* (Toronto: University of Toronto Press, 1982) (noting that the police tend to proactively stop young males of lower socio-economic status and that, depending on the region, race may also play a role — for example, blacks in certain urban areas or Native Canadians in rural areas on the Prairies at 16-17, 200-201).

[174] See Public Inquiry into the Administration of Justice and Aboriginal People, *Report of the Aboriginal Justice Inquiry of Manitoba. Volume 1: The Justice System and Aboriginal People* (Winnipeg: Queen's Printer, 1991) at 595; Report of the Task Force on the Criminal Justice System and Its Impact on the Indian and Metis People of Alberta, *Justice on Trial* (Edmonton: Task Force, 1991) at 2-5, 2-46 to 2-51.

[175] See *Report of the Commission on Systemic Racism in the Ontario Criminal Justice System* (Toronto: Queen's Printer for Ontario, 1995) at 349-60. See Scot Wortley, "The Usual Suspects: Race, Police Stops and Perceptions of Criminal Injustice", Paper Presented at the 48th Annual Conference of the American Society of Criminology, Chicago, November, 1997); Carl E. James, "'Up to No Good': Black on the Streets and Encountering Police" in Vic Satzewich, ed., *Racism & Social Inequality in Canada: Concepts, Controversies & Strategies of Resistance* (Toronto: Thompson Educational Publishing, 1998) at 157; Robynne Neugebauer, "Kids, Cops, and Colour: The Social Organization of Police-Minority Youth Relations" in Robynne Neugebauer, ed., *Criminal Injustice: Racism in the Criminal Justice System* (Toronto: Canadian Scholars Press, 2000) at 1; Jim Rankin *et al.*, "Police Target Black Drivers", *Toronto Star*, October 20, 2002) online: <http://www.thestar.com/specialsections/raceandcrime/article/761200--

tionately higher rates than members of other racial groups.[176] Responding to this evidence, two provincial appellate courts have recently acknowledged the existence of racial profiling.[177] The Ontario Court of Appeal has adopted the following definition of racial profiling:

> Racial profiling is criminal profiling based on race. Racial or colour profiling refers to that phenomenon whereby certain criminal activity is attributed to an identified group in society on the basis of race or colour resulting in the targeting of individual members of that group. In this context, race is illegitimately used as a proxy for the criminality or general criminal propensity of an entire racial group.[178]

The Ontario Court of Appeal has explained that racial profiling is not only the result of overt racism, noting that:

> The attitude underlying racial profiling is one that may be consciously or unconsciously held. That is, the police officer need not be an overt racist. His or her conduct may be based on subconscious racial stereotyping.[179]

Of course, establishing that race improperly[180] influenced a police officer's decision to detain or arrest is no easy task,[181] so cases in which such claims have succeeded continue to remain extraordinarily rare.[182]

---

police-target-black-drivers ContentServer?pagename=thestar/Layout/Article_PrintFriendly&c=Article&cid=1026146624189>. See Ron Melchers, "Do Toronto Police Engage in Racial Profiling?" (2003) 45 Can. J. Crim. 347. But see also Scot Wortley, "Data, Denials, and Confusion: The Racial Profiling Debate in Toronto" (2003) 45 Can. J. Crim. 367.

[176] See also William J. Closs & Paul F. McKenna, "Profiling a problem in Canadian police leadership: the Kingston Police data collection project" (2006) 49 Canadian Public Administration 143, detailing the most recent and, arguably, most comprehensive Canadian study. For an excellent summary of the compelling evidence that racial profiling is a reality in Canada, see David M. Tanovich, *The Colour of Justice: Policing Race in Canada* (Irwin: Toronto, 2006).

[177] See *R. v. Brown*, [2003] O.J. No. 1251, 64 O.R. (3d) 161 at paras. 7-9 (Ont. C.A.); *R. v. H. (C.R.)*, [2003] M.J. No. 90, 173 Man. R. (2d) 113 at para. 49 (Man. C.A.). On the topic of racial profiling in Canada more generally, see David M. Tanovich, *The Colour of Justice: Policing Race in Canada* (Toronto: Irwin Law, 2006).

[178] *R. v. Richards*, [1999] O.J. No. 1420, 26 C.R. (5th) 286 at para. 24 (Ont. C.A.), quoting the definition put forward by the African Canadian Legal Clinic. The Court subsequently adopted this definition as authoritative. See *R. v. Brown*, [2003] O.J. No. 1251, 64 O.R. (3d) 161 at para. 7 (Ont. C.A.).

[179] *R. v. Brown*, [2003] O.J. No. 1251, 64 O.R. (3d) 161 at para. 8 (Ont. C.A.).

[180] In some circumstances it is perfectly legitimate for police to rely upon an individual's race in deciding to effect a stop. See Samuel R. Gross & Debra Livingston, "Racial Profiling Under Attack" (2002) 102 Colum. L. Rev. 1413 at 1415 ("it is not racial profiling for an officer to question, stop, search, arrest, or otherwise investigate a person because his race or ethnicity matches information about a perpetrator of a specific crime that the officer is investigating. That use of race — which usually occurs when there is a racially specific description of a criminal — does not entail a global judgment about a racial or ethnic group as a whole."). But see David M. Tanovich, "Moving Beyond 'Driving While Black:' Race, Suspect Description and Selection" (2004-2005) 36 Ottawa L. Rev. 315, cautioning against placing too much weight on racial descriptors because, often generic, they can all too easily justify the indiscriminate detention of racialized persons.

[181] See generally, David M. Tanovich, "E-Racing Racial Profiling" (2004) 41 Alta. L. Rev. 905 (chronicling many of the practical obstacles to proving such claims and suggesting ways in which they might be overcome).

[182] See *e.g.*, *R. v. Peck*, [2001] O.J. No. 4581 (Ont. S.C.J.).

(b)   Challenging Legislation Authorizing Detention or Imprisonment

§2.83 The second category of section 9 *Charter* claims involves challenges to legislation. Section 9 has been used to challenge the constitutionality of a wide array of legislative provisions authorizing detention or imprisonment, including provincial laws empowering police to detain motorists at checkpoints and through roving and random stops,[183] and *Criminal Code* provisions permitting the indefinite imprisonment of persons designated as dangerous offenders.[184]

§2.84 In these cases it has usually been the presence of too little or too much discretion in the statutory authority conferred that has proven determinative. Legislation that mandates a loss of liberty without the need to consider any rational criteria or standards has been held to operate "arbitrarily".[185] The Supreme Court has rightly recognized that "it is the absence of discretion which would, in many cases, render arbitrary the law's application."[186] At the same time the Court has found legislation at odds with section 9 of the *Charter* when it confers unfettered discretion on state agents to detain individuals. In such circumstances, "[a] discretion is arbitrary... [because] ... there are no criteria, express or implied,

---

[183] See *R. v. Hufsky*, [1988] S.C.J. No. 30, [1988] 1 S.C.R. 621 (S.C.C.); *R. v. Ladouceur*, [1990] S.C.J. No. 53, [1990] 1 S.C.R. 1257 (S.C.C.); *R. v. Wilson*, [1990] S.C.J. No. 54, [1990] 1 S.C.R. 1291 (S.C.C.). In these cases, provincial legislation authorizing police to stop motorists was found to be inconsistent with s. 9 as it did not provide any criteria to guide police in deciding whom to stop, effectively granting unfettered discretion. But after citing statistical evidence documenting the catastrophic effect of impaired and unlicensed drivers, the Court upheld the power to conduct organized check stops and random roving stops as reasonable limits in a free and democratic society under s. 1. However, such stops are only permissible under s. 1 if their purpose is limited to checking licences, insurance, driver sobriety and the mechanical fitness of vehicles. Any probing beyond these limited purposes is, in theory, prohibited (see *R. v. Ladouceur*, [1990] S.C.J. No. 53, [1990] 1 S.C.R. 1257 at 1287 (S.C.C.); *R. v. Mellenthin*, [1992] S.C.J. No. 100, [1992] 3 S.C.R. 615 at 628 (S.C.C.)) and may transform a stop from an encounter that was constitutionally permissible at its inception into an arbitrary detention. But see *Brown v. Durham (Regional Municipality) Police Force*, [1998] O.J. No. 5274, 131 C.C.C. (3d) 1 at 116-17 (Ont. C.A.), leave to appeal refused [1999] S.C.C.A. No. 87 (S.C.C.) (holding that an ulterior motivation for such a stop, for instance, the pursuit of other investigative interests, does not automatically render the detention arbitrary provided that the ulterior purpose is not itself unconstitutional — for instance, a stop undertaken for the purpose of effecting an unconstitutional search). See also *R. v. Nolet*, [2010] S.C.J. No. 24, [2010] 1 S.C.R. 851, 2010 SCC 24 (S.C.C.) (holding that provided the police act within the confines of their regulatory authority, the fact that an officer also harbours criminal suspicions that are furthered through his or her use of the regulatory authority does not *per se* result in a *Charter* violation).

[184] See *R. v. Milne*, [1987] S.C.J. No. 73, [1987] 2 S.C.R. 512 (S.C.C.) and *R. v. Lyons*, [1987] S.C.J. No. 62, [1987] 2 S.C.R. 309 at 347 (S.C.C.), which upheld the dangerous offender scheme because it "narrowly defines a class of offenders with respect to whom it may properly be invoked, and prescribes quite specifically the conditions under which an offender may be designated as dangerous." Also see *R. v. Luxton*, [1990] S.C.J. No. 87, [1990] 2 S.C.R. 711 at 722-23 (S.C.C.), upholding the sentencing scheme for first degree murder on a similar basis).

[185] See *R. v. Swain*, [1991] S.C.J. No. 32, [1991] 1 S.C.R. 933 at 1013 (S.C.C.) (the *Criminal Code* provisions requiring trial judges to automatically commit those found not guilty by reason of insanity to strict custody, without considering their particular mental health circumstances were found to be unconstitutional under s. 9).

[186] *R. v. Lyons*, [1987] S.C.J. No. 62, [1987] 2 S.C.R. 309 at 348 (S.C.C.).

which govern its exercise."[187] (The specifics of those cases dealing with motor vehicle stopping powers are discussed below in Part 4(3).)

§2.85 Beyond identifying minimum constitutional requirements for legislative standards that authorize an interference with liberty, the Supreme Court recently added a procedural layer to section 9. In *Charkaoui v. Canada (Citizenship and Immigration)*,[188] the Court was faced with a constitutional challenge to the security certificate scheme found in the *Immigration and Refugee Protection Act*.[189] The Court found a number of *Charter* violations, including a breach of section 9. According to the Court, by precluding foreign nationals subject to security certificates from seeking judicial review of the reasons for their detention for at least 120 days, the legislative scheme ran afoul of section 9. The Court emphasized that there was no compelling reason justifying the delay. This violated section 9 because it amounted to a "complete denial of a timely detention review."[190] How quickly such review must take place in order to comply with section 9 of the *Charter* was left for another day; what is clear, based on the Court's judgment, is that 120 days is clearly too long.

4. POLICE DETENTION AND ARREST POWERS

§2.86 The authority of police to interfere with people's freedom of movement is detailed in this Part. We begin by reviewing the powers possessed by police to detain short of arrest; thereafter we discuss the arrest powers in the *Criminal Code*.[191] Given that unlawfully interfering with liberty necessarily violates section 9 of the *Charter* (see Part 3(4)(*a*), above), assessing whether or not a police officer acted lawfully in carrying out a detention or arrest, is essential in assessing the constitutionality of such encounters. In other words, to avoid a constitutional violation, police restraints of liberty must come within the parameters of one or more of the powers detailed below. Of course, if there is no "detention" (as defined in Part 3(3)(*b*), above), the encounter is not subject to *Charter* scrutiny and the powers identified below are not relevant.

(1) Detention Powers

§2.87 Most of the powers discussed below emerged after the enactment of the *Charter*, mostly through the courts' use of the ancillary powers doctrine to recognize new "common law" detention powers. As discussed in Chapter 1, Part

---

[187] *R. v. Hufsky*, [1988] S.C.J. No. 30, [1988] 1 S.C.R. 621 at 633 (S.C.C.). See also *R. v. Ladouceur*, [1990] S.C.J. No. 53, [1990] 1 S.C.R. 1257 at 1276 (S.C.C.); *R. v. Morales*, [1992] S.C.J. No. 98, [1992] 3 S.C.R. 711 at 740 (S.C.C.); *R. v. Pearson*, [1992] S.C.J. No. 99, [1992] 3 S.C.R. 665 at 700 (S.C.C.) (noting that "detention is arbitrary if it is governed by unstructured discretion").

[188] [2007] S.C.J. No. 9, [2007] 1 S.C.R. 350 (S.C.C.).

[189] S.C. 2001, c. 27.

[190] *Charkaoui v. Canada (Citizenship and Immigration)*, [2007] S.C.J. No. 9, [2007] 1 S.C.R. 350 at 403 (S.C.C.).

[191] R.S.C. 1985, c. C-46.

6(4)(*b*), this practice has been criticized by commentators, and in some cases, even by members of the Supreme Court of Canada.

(2) The Power to Detain Motorists for Traffic Safety Purposes

§2.88 Before the *Charter*, the legal authority of police to stop motorists was uncertain. In most provinces, provincial traffic legislation provided no such power. Nor did such a power exist at common law.[192] Developments at common law and under provincial traffic legislation have since served to change this.

§2.89 Today, in every province and territory the police have the power to conduct both proactive and reactive traffic safety stops. In the proactive category, police are empowered to stop vehicles at fixed-point check stops or through roving and random stops in order to confirm the driver's sobriety, inspect driving related documents (*e.g.*, driver's licence, vehicle registration and proof of insurance) and examine the vehicle for mechanical fitness. In the reactive category, police have the power to stop a motorist who they reasonably suspect to be impaired or who they observe committing a moving violation contrary to provincial traffic legislation. (They may also stop motorists for criminal investigative purposes under the authority of the *Criminal Code*'s arrest powers and the various common law detention powers discussed elsewhere in this chapter.)

(a) Checkpoint Traffic Safety Stops

§2.90 A police power to conduct fixed-point check stops of motorists was first recognized by Supreme Court of Canada in *R. v. Dedman*.[193] Such stops need not be based on any degree of suspicion that a particular motorist is in breach of the law. In that case, a slim majority of the Court relied upon the English case of *R. v. Waterfield*[194] to grant police a power at common law to conduct random stops at sobriety checkpoints (The test from *Waterfield* has come to be known as the ancillary powers doctrine, and its use to create police powers was examined in Chapter 1, Part 6(4)(*b*).)

§2.91 In *Dedman*, after acknowledging that sobriety checkpoints involve an interference with liberty, the Court applied the two-part *Waterfield* test to recognize an entirely new police power.[195] Under the first prong — whether the police action fell within the ambit of a police duty — the Court upheld random stops at sobriety checkpoints on the basis of the duty of police to prevent crime and protect life and property by controlling traffic. The application of the second prong — whether the police action involves an unjustifiable use of police power —

---

[192] See Paul C. Weiler, "The Control of Police Arrest Practices: Reflections of a Tort Lawyer" in Allen M. Linden, ed., *Studies in Canadian Tort Law* (Toronto: Butterworths, 1968) at 416, where the author, writing in the late 1960s, observed that the police routinely operate outside the law, giving as an example the "mass stopping of automobiles to check for impaired drivers." *Ibid.*, at 437.

[193] [1985] S.C.J. No. 45, [1985] 2 S.C.R. 2 (S.C.C.) [*Dedman*].

[194] [1963] 3 All E.R. 659 (Ct. Crim. App.).

[195] [1985] S.C.J. No. 45, [1985] 2 S.C.R. 2 at 32-36 (S.C.C.).

turned on whether it was "necessary for the carrying out of the particular police duty and ... reasonable, having regard to the nature of the liberty interfered with and the importance of the public purpose served by the interference."[196] This was a simple cost-benefit analysis. On the cost side of the ledger, the Court acknowledged that checkpoint stops are entirely arbitrary and could therefore cause drivers some psychological discomfort. But these effects would be minimized, it reasoned, by the publicity accompanying such programs, their "relatively short duration", and the merely "slight inconvenience" that they cause to motorists.[197] On the benefit side, the Court simply noted that due to "the seriousness of the problem of impaired driving, there can be no doubt about the importance and necessity of a program to improve the deterrence of it."[198]

§2.92 As *Dedman*[199] made its way through the lower courts, Ontario amended its *Highway Traffic Act*[200] to grant police express statutory authority to conduct traffic stops. The relevant provision (section 189(*a*)1) provided that a police officer "may require a driver of a motor vehicle to stop", and obligated the driver "when signalled" to "immediately come to a safe stop."[201] (Each of the provinces has since followed suit, amending provincial traffic acts to create an analogous police power.[202]) As worded, the provision grants police unfettered authority in deciding whom to stop.

§2.93 In *R. v. Hufsky*,[203] this provision was challenged as being contrary to the right not to be arbitrarily detained under section 9 of the *Charter*. Police at a fixed checkpoint randomly stopped the accused. The Court unanimously concluded that the impugned provision was inconsistent with section 9 because it did not specify any criteria for deciding which drivers to stop, leaving the police with absolute discretion.[204] Nevertheless, after citing the Crown's voluminous evidence documenting the high toll of injury, death and property damage exacted by impaired, unlicensed and uninsured drivers, and after noting that such offences are difficult to detect through observation alone, the Court upheld the power as demonstrably justifiable under section 1 of the *Charter*.[205]

§2.94 The decision in *Hufsky* did away with the publicity requirement that the Supreme Court in *Dedman* appeared to recognize as a precondition for sobriety checkpoint stops. In *Hufsky*, the Court explained that such a requirement was no longer necessary because checkpoint stops had become notorious.[206]

---

[196] *Ibid.*, at 35 (S.C.R.).

[197] *Ibid.*, at 36 (S.C.R.).

[198] *Ibid.*, at 35-36 (S.C.R.).

[199] [1985] S.C.J. No. 45, [1985] 2 S.C.R. 2 (S.C.C.).

[200] R.S.O. 1980, c. 198.

[201] *Ibid.*, s. 189a(1), which was added to the Act by the *Highway Traffic Amendment Act, 1981 (No. 3)*, S.O. 1981, c. 72, s. 2. This provision remains in force; see now *Highway Traffic Act*, R.S.O. 1990, c. H.8, s. 216(1).

[202] See *e.g.*, *Traffic Safety Act*, R.S.A. 2000, c. T-6, s. 166.

[203] [1988] S.C.J. No. 30, [1988] 1 S.C.R. 621 (S.C.C.) [*Hufsky*].

[204] *Ibid.*, at 632-33 (S.C.R.).

[205] *Ibid.*, at 633-37 (S.C.R.).

[206] *Ibid.*, at 637 (S.C.R.).

(b) *Roving and Random Traffic Safety Stops*

§2.95 Unfortunately, the Court in *Hufsky* (discussed immediately above) did not indicate whether the section 1 justification extended to roving and random stops. After two years of uncertainty, the answer came in *R. v. Ladouceur*.[207] There the police stopped the appellant's car at random in order to check his documentation. His licence had been suspended, and he was charged accordingly. The case turned on how far the Court was willing to go to hold that the authority to arbitrarily detain motorists granted by Ontario's traffic legislation (explained immediately above) was justified under section 1 of the *Charter*. Unlike in *Hufsky*, this time around the Court was sharply divided.

§2.96 A five-member majority found that the violation was justified under the section 1 *Oakes* test.[208] Relying on the same materials filed in *Hufsky*, the majority easily found the required pressing and substantial concern for overriding a constitutional right. It then reasoned that roving and random stops would enhance the deterrence of drunk, unlicensed and uninsured drivers by increasing the threat of detection. As a result, such stops were rationally connected to the objective. And in concluding that they satisfied the minimal impairment requirement, it noted that they "must be of *relatively* short duration";[209] they required the "production of only a few documents";[210] a driver was "*generally* ... questioned in his or her own vehicle or at worst, when there is an infraction, in the police cruiser";[211] and there was "*seldom* a need to bring the driver to the police station."[212] Fears that this police power could too easily abused were dismissed as "unfounded".[213] The majority wrote:

> There are mechanisms already in place which prevent abuse. Officers can stop persons only for legal reasons, in this case reasons related to driving a car such as checking the driver's licence and insurance, the sobriety of the driver and the mechanical fitness of the vehicle. Once stopped the only questions that may justifiably be asked are those related to driving offences. Any further, more intrusive procedures could only be undertaken based upon reasonable and probable grounds. Where a stop is found to be unlawful, the evidence from the stop could well be excluded under s. 24(2) of the *Charter*.[214]

---

[207] [1990] S.C.J. No. 53, [1990] 1 S.C.R. 1257 at 1276 (S.C.C.) [*Ladoceur*].
[208] See *R. v. Oakes*, [1986] S.C.J. No. 7, [1986] 1 S.C.R. 103 (S.C.C.). The *Oakes* test for justifying the override of a *Charter* right under s. 1 was discussed in Chapter 1, Part 4(2) §1.130.
[209] [1990] S.C.J. No. 53, [1990] 1 S.C.R. 1257 at 1286 (S.C.C.) [emphasis added].
[210] *Ibid.*
[211] *Ibid.* [emphasis added].
[212] *Ibid.* [emphasis added]. See also *R. v. Smith*, [1996] O.J. No. 372, 105 C.C.C. (3d) 58 at 73 (Ont. C.A.).
[213] *R. v. Ladouceur*, [1990] S.C.J. No. 53, [1990] 1 S.C.R. 1257 at 1287 (S.C.C.).
[214] *Ibid.* Following *R. v. Mann*, [2004] S.C.J. No. 49, [2004] 3 S.C.R. 59 (S.C.C.), "reasonable suspicion" would now seem to be enough to prolong the detention and, possibly, also conduct a protective pat down search. See *e.g.*, *R. v. Nguyen*, [2008] S.J. No. 799, 240 C.C.C. (3d) 39 (Sask. C.A.), abandoned [2009] S.C.C.A. No. 5 (S.C.C.).

§2.97 These limits on the acceptable purposes for such stops and the types of questions that may be asked are not found anywhere in the Act. Rather, without any explanation, the Court simply read them into the impugned provision as part of its section 1 analysis. As the above quotation makes clear, the Court anticipated that compliance with these limits would be enforced on a case-by-case basis by applying the exclusionary remedy under section 24(2) of the *Charter*.[215]

§2.98 In our view, the majority in *Ladouceur*[216] unduly downplayed the risk of abusive roadside detentions. Of particular concern is the leeway that the decision provides for "pretextual" stops. Under the guise of routine safety checks, police (who typically perceive themselves as being involved in a competitive, crime-fighting endeavour[217]) may, under *Ladouceur*, stop motorists on the basis of unsubstantiated hunches. Such stops then give police the chance to develop grounds to justify further probing. If that fails, they may seek permission to search and worry later (if at all) about how to admit the fruits of the search if contraband is found.[218]

§2.99 The dissenting justices in *Ladouceur*, in contrast, doubted that adding a power to conduct roving random stops would significantly enhance the deterrence provided by fixed-point stops. How many innocent drivers would be stopped, they questioned, to catch the few who are drunk, unlicensed, or uninsured? For the dissenters, the cost was too great:

> [T]he roving random stop would permit any individual officer to stop any vehicle, at any time, at any place. The decision may be based on any whim. Individual officers will have different reasons. Some may tend to stop younger drivers, others older cars, and so on. Indeed, ... racial considerations may be a factor too.[219]

When *Ladouceur* was decided there was almost no empirical basis for fears that racial bias might influence police detention decisions. As noted in Part 3(4)(*a*), above, a growing body of evidence has since emerged showing that police disproportionately detain Aboriginals and African-Canadians.[220] In light of that evidence, it would now seem that the majority's optimism in *Ladouceur* was

---

[215] See *e.g.*, *R. v. Mellenthin*, [1992] S.C.J. No. 100, [1992] 3 S.C.R. 615 (S.C.C.) (concluding that the exclusion of cannabis resin was appropriate, where police stopped the appellant at a sobriety checkpoint and without reasonable cause asked him probing questions regarding the contents of gym bag located in the vehicle. The Court characterized an "attempt to extend the random stop programs to include a right to search without warrant or without reasonable grounds" as a "serious *Charter* violation." *Ibid.*, at 490 (S.C.R.)).

[216] [1990] S.C.J. No. 53, [1990] 1 S.C.R. 1257 (S.C.C.).

[217] For insight into this self-perception on the part of Canadian police, see Greg Marquis, "Power from the Street: The Canadian Municipal Police" in R.C. Macleod & David Schneiderman, eds., *Police Powers in Canada: The Evolution and Practice of Authority* (Toronto: University of Toronto Press, 1994) 24 at 30-31.

[218] Given that many vehicle passengers will be found to lack a constitutionally protected privacy expectation, they are particularly vulnerable to such tactics. See *R. v. Belnavis*, [1997] S.C.J. No. 81, [1997] 3 S.C.R. 341 (S.C.C.). This problem is discussed in detail in Chapter 3, Part 2(4)(*b*)(iv).

[219] *R. v. Ladouceur*, [1990] S.C.J. No. 53, [1990] 1 S.C.R. 1257 at 1267 (S.C.C.).

[220] In particular, see §2.281 and §2.282, above, and the supporting footnotes.

misplaced, and that the dissent's concerns were well founded. We hope that the Court will reconsider its section 1 analysis in light of this new evidence. Until then, the open-ended power of proactive road safety stops remains, as does its potential for abuse.

(c) Reactive Stops for Particularized Traffic Safety Reasons

§2.100 From a constitutional standpoint, reactive vehicle stops raise different considerations than proactive ones. Although the legality of reactive stops may also depend on provincial traffic legislation granting unfettered authority to stop vehicles (see Parts 4(2)(*a*) and (*b*), immediately above), stops made for a legitimate, particularized reason (for example, because police have reasonable grounds to suspect the driver is impaired or have witnessed a traffic infraction) are not *per se* arbitrary under section 9.[221] This is quite different from the sorts of random stops that the Court upheld as justifiable under section 1 of the *Charter* in *Hufsky* and *Ladouceur* (discussed above). That said, if police exceed the scope of their lawful powers in a particular case, then as discussed in Part 3(4)(*a*), above, the detention will necessarily be arbitrary and violate section 9 of the *Charter*.

(d) Limits on Traffic Safety Stops and Criminal Investigative Purposes

§2.101 As discussed in Part 4(2)(*b*), above, the unfettered authority of Canadian police to conduct motor vehicle stops for traffic safety purposes creates a serious risk of abuse. Formally, at least, this authority is subject to strict limitations. During such stops, police may question the occupants of the vehicle about driving related matters. But as the Saskatchewan Court of Appeal has noted, "[t]he courts have, on a number of occasions, made it clear that an investigation or inquiry into the possible possession of contraband is not permissible as part of 'general inquiries in vehicle stops,' absent other grounds for the inquiry."[222]

§2.102 The "other grounds" may come from plain view or plain smell (olfactory) observations the police are entitled to make as they interact with a motorist

---

[221] See *R. v. Wilson*, [1990] S.C.J. No. 54 at para. 13, [1990] 1 S.C.R. 1291 (S.C.C.). The Court explained that where the "police offer grounds for stopping a motorist that are reasonable and can be clearly expressed (the articulable cause referred to in the American authorities), the stop should not be regarded as random. As a result, although the appellant was detained, the detention was not arbitrary in this case and the stop did not violate s. 9 of the *Charter*."

[222] *R. v. Rutten*, [2006] S.J. No. 65, 205 C.C.C. (3d) 504 at para. 29 (Sask. C.A.) (finding that the appellant's rights under ss. 8 and 10(*b*) of the *Charter* were violated where police stopped him for speeding and began questioning him regarding the possibility that he was transporting contraband before seeking and obtaining an invalid consent to search); *Canada (Attorney General) v. Mouland*, [2007] S.J. No. 532, 53 M.V.R. (5th) 11 (Sask. C.A.) (same). See also *R. v. Ladouceur*, [1990] S.C.J. No. 53, [1990] 1 S.C.R. 1257 at 1287 (S.C.C.); *R. v. Mellenthin*, [1992] S.C.J. No. 100, [1992] 3 S.C.R. 615 at 624 (S.C.C.) ("Random stop programs must not be turned into a means of either conducting an unfounded general inquisition or an unreasonable search.").

at the roadside for traffic safety purposes.[223] Absent such readily apparent grounds, however, further criminal investigative inquiries by police incidental to a routine traffic stop, for example, by searching the vehicle or prolonging the encounter longer than necessary for traffic safety purposes to ask questions probing possible criminal activity, will likely run afoul of one or more of sections 8, 9 or 10(*b*) of the *Charter*.

§2.103 That said, the Supreme Court of Canada held in *R. v. Nolet*[224] that police are entitled to harbour ulterior criminal investigative purposes for a traffic stop.[225] Provided that police are truly motivated by traffic safety concerns for the entire duration of the traffic safety-grounded detention, the fact that they are simultaneously interested in discovering criminal evidence will not in itself invalidate the detention.[226] Guided by earlier appellate decisions to the same effect, many police forces have taken full advantage of this rule, training their officers on how to use routine traffic stops to develop the grounds needed to probe further for criminal activities, especially the transporting of illegal drugs.[227]

§2.104 In conducting such "dual purpose" investigations, however, police must be careful not to exceed the limits of their regulatory authority in pursuing criminal suspicions. If they do so, they will violate the *Charter*.[228]

§2.105 The Supreme Court has instructed that a reviewing court should proceed step-by-step through an encounter between the police and the individual subject to a vehicle stop, to assess whether, as the situation developed, the police stayed within their authority, having regard to the information lawfully obtained at each stage of their inquiry.[229] In *Nolet*, for example, a police officer randomly stopped

---

[223] See *R. v. Mellenthin*, [1992] S.C.J. No. 100, [1992] 3 S.C.R. 615 (S.C.C.). The Court noted that it is permissible for police to visually inspect a vehicle interior and to use a flashlight to do so at night. *Ibid.*, at 623. By analogy, like plain view observations, plain smell olfactory observations would seem to be permissible. See *R. v. Nguyen*, [2008] S.J. No. 799 at para. 14, 240 C.C.C. (3d) 39 (Sask. C.A.), abandoned [2009] S.C.C.A. No. 5 (S.C.C.) noting that "an odour of contraband of sufficient strength" would be sufficient to justify prolonging a traffic stop to investigate further the officer's reasonable suspicion that the motorist is in possession of contraband. See *e.g.*, *R. v. Pearson*, [2009] A.J. No. 693, 9 Alta. L.R. (5th) 319 (Alta. Q.B.) (faint scent of raw marijuana emanating from vehicle stopped for speeding provided reasonable suspicion required to prolong roadside detention and to use drug sniffer dog). The plain view doctrine is discussed in detail in Chapter 3, Part 3(6).

[224] [2010] S.C.J. No. 24, [2010] 1 S.C.R. 851, 2010 SCC 24 (S.C.C.) [*Nolet*].

[225] *Ibid.* See also *R. v. Brown*, [1987] N.S.J. No. 22, 33 C.C.C. (3d) 54 (N.S.C.A.); *R. v. Duncanson*, [1991] S.J. No. 373, 12 C.R. (4th) 86 (Sask. C.A.), affd [1992] S.C.J. No. 31, [1992] 1 S.C.R. 836, 12 C.R. (4th) 98 (S.C.C.). But see *R. v. Guénette*, [1999] J.Q. no 760, 136 C.C.C. (3d) 311 (Que. C.A.).

[226] See [2010] S.C.J. No. 24 at paras. 32-41, [2010] 1 S.C.R. 851, 2010 SCC 24 (S.C.C.).

[227] See *e.g.*, *R. v. Calderon*, [2004] O.J. No. 3474, 188 C.C.C. (3d) 481 (Ont. C.A.). See also David M. Tanovich, "Operation Pipeline and Racial Profiling" (2002) 1 C.R. (6th) 52. Unless evidence is found, however, these cases rarely receive any public attention. For a rare exception, see Rod Mickleburgh, "RCMP Reach Settlement With Off-Duty Policeman" *The Globe and Mail* (January 20, 2005) at A6.

[228] See *R. v. Nolet*, [2010] S.C.J. No. 24 at para. 39, [2010] 1 S.C.R. 851, 2010 SCC 24 (S.C.C.) [*Nolet*] ("[i]f the *Charter* is violated, it makes little difference ... that the police had in mind multiple purposes A valid regulatory purpose, whether predominant or not, would not sanitize or excuse a *Charter* violation").

[229] *Ibid.*, at paras. 4, 23 (S.C.J.).

a commercial truck to make inquiries authorized by provincial regulatory legislation. After determining that the documents produced by the appellants were
inadequate, the officer searched the vehicle, again under the authority of the
provincial statute. Inside the truck cab, behind the driver's seat, the officer discovered a duffel bag. As relevant trucking documents were often kept in that
manner, and as, at a touch, it appeared to contain paper, he opened it to find
$115,000 bundled in small denominations. As this was typical of drug transac-
tions, he arrested the appellant for possession of the proceeds of crime. A search
of the truck incidental to that arrest revealed a hidden compartment containing
392 pounds of packaged of marijuana. The fact that the officer had earlier suspected that the vehicle might be transporting illegal drugs, the Supreme Court
reasoned, did not detract from the legitimacy of this search.[230] Given the inconsistencies found in the relevant documentation, it was reasonable for police to
rely on the authority to search granted by the provincial regulatory statute governing commercial trucking to look inside the bag for documents that would
help prove the suspected regulatory infractions.[231]

§2.106 Contrast this with *R. v. Ladouceur*,[232] a decision used by the Court in
Nolet as an example of a constitutionally flawed, pre-textual detention.[233] In
Ladouceur, police set up a random stop program to detect both highway infractions and contraband. The checkpoint was staffed not only with police, but also
at times with sniffer dogs, customs and immigration officials, wildlife officers,
and law enforcement agents. This program, the Court explained in *Nolet*, "was
designed as a 'comprehensive check for criminal activity' ... and was therefore
fatally flawed from the outset."[234]

(e)   Sections 10(a) and 10(b) of the Charter Incidental to Traffic Safety Stops

§2.107 Unfortunately, the cases discussed above did not explain how police
were to reconcile their power to detain motorists with their obligations under
section 10 of the *Charter*, which are triggered by "detention". Because motor
vehicle stops constitute a "detention" (see Part 3(3)(*b*)(ii)), section 10 would
seem to apply, thus requiring police to promptly apprise motorists of the reasons
for detention (section 10(*a*)) and the right to retain and instruct counsel without
delay and to be informed of that right (section 10(*b*)). (The requirements of section 10(*a*) and 10(*b*) of the *Charter* more generally are fully explained in Chapter 4, Part 3.)

§2.108 Fulfilling the informational duty imposed by section 10(*a*) incidental to
a traffic stop is easily accomplished. A police officer must simply tell detained
motorists why they have been pulled over. For example, "I stopped you because

---

[230] *Ibid.*, at paras. 32-41 (S.C.J.).
[231] *Ibid.*, at para. 44 (S.C.J.).
[232] [2002] S.J. No. 343, 165 C.C.C. (3d) 321 (Sask. C.A.) [*Ladoceur*].
[233] *R. v. Nolet*, [2010] S.C.J. No. 24 at para. 25, [2010] 1 S.C.R. 851, 2010 SCC 24 (S.C.C.).
[234] *Ibid.*, at para. 25 (S.C.J.).

you were speeding" is sufficient to satisfy the requirements of section 10(*a*). In contrast, a police officer would appear to violate the guarantee by simply asking a driver "Do you know why I pulled you over?"[235]

§2.109 Unfortunately, the Supreme Court in *Nolet* did not address what effect ulterior criminal investigative interests (discussed immediately above, in Part 4(2)(*d*)) might have on the obligations of police under section 10 of the *Charter*. For example, if one of the reasons for the detention is the officer's ulterior criminal investigative suspicion, must that secondary purpose for the stop be revealed to the person detained? The plain meaning of section 10(*a*) suggests that it should be.

§2.110 The right to counsel found in section 10(*b*) is more complicated. After two decades of conflicting jurisprudence,[236] the Supreme Court held in *R. v. Orbanski; R. v. Elias*[237] that the right to counsel does *not* apply at the roadside when the police are conducting road-safety inquiries, for example, questioning a driver about alcohol consumption or requesting that the driver participate in so-briety tests. According to the Court, the right to counsel is implicitly overridden in such circumstances by the "operating requirements"[238] of the "interlocking scheme of federal and provincial legislation"[239] governing motor vehicle travel.[240] In other words, the right is overridden because of the impracticality of imple-menting it at the roadside.

§2.111 The Court in *Orbanski & Elias* held that this override of section 10(*b*) is justified under section 1 of the *Charter*. In coming to this conclusion, it noted that reducing the carnage caused by impaired driving constitutes a compelling

---

[235] An argument that having engaged in a particular form of wrongdoing (*i.e.*, speeding) the de-tained individual would necessarily know why they were being detained has been rejected by the Supreme Court. See *R. v. Borden*, [1994] S.C.J. No. 82, [1994] 3 S.C.R. 145 at 417 (S.C.C.). In that case, the Court noted that the "the logical extension of this argument would be that the protections afforded by the Charter no longer apply whenever the person arrested is guilty of the offence for which he or she has been detained."

[236] A number of appellate courts held that before requesting that a driver answer questions regard-ing alcohol consumption or participate in coordination tests, the police must comply with s. 10(*b*) of the *Charter*. See *R. v. Gallant*, [1989] A.J. No. 311, 95 A.R. 101 (Alta. C.A.), leave to appeal refused [1989] S.C.C.A. No. 409, 104 A.R. 240n (S.C.C.); *R. v. Hill*, [1990] P.E.I.J. No. 124, 86 Nfld. & P.E.I.R. 197 (P.E.I.C.A.); *R. v. Oldham*, [1996] N.B.J. No. 399, 181 N.B.R. (2d) 321, 109 C.C.C. (3d) 392 (N.B.C.A.); *R. v. Baroni*, [1989] N.S.J. No. 242, 49 C.C.C. (3d) 553 (N.S.C.A.); *R. v. Orbanski*, [2003] M.J. No. 99, 173 Man. R. (2d) 132 (Man. C.A.), affd (*sub nom. R. v. Orbanski; R. v. Elias*) [2005] S.C.J. No. 37, [2005] 2 S.C.R. 3, 2005 SCC 37 (S.C.C.). In contrast, other courts held that the common law power to detain motorists at sobriety check stops constituted a reasonable limit on the right to counsel under s. 1 of the *Charter*, so that the right to counsel did not apply. See *R. v. Sullivan*, [1989] C.M.A.J. No. 8, 22 MV.R. (2d) 261 (Ct. Martial App. Ct.); *R. v. Sundquist*, [2000] S.J. No. 299, 145 C.C.C. (3d) 145 (Sask. C.A.). Still other courts had pointed to provincial legislation in coming to the same conclusion. See *R. v. Saunders*, [1988] O.J. No. 397, 41 C.C.C. (3d) 532 (Ont. C.A.).

[237] *R. v. Orbanski; R. v. Elias*, [2005] S.C.J. No. 37, [2005] 2 S.C.R. 3, 2005 SCC 37 (S.C.C.) [*Orbanski & Elias*].

[238] *Ibid.*, at paras. 37, 39 (S.C.J.).

[239] *Ibid.*, at para. 27 (S.C.J.).

[240] *Ibid.*, at para. 43 (S.C.J.).

state objective.[241] It explained that questioning drivers' about their alcohol consumption and requesting their participation in roadside sobriety tests is rationally connected to that objective.[242] Finally, the Court emphasized that infringement of the right to counsel was no more than necessary to meet the objective. In that respect, the Court indicated that while the right to counsel is overridden, any responses given by the motorists to police questions or the results of any roadside sobriety tests can only be used as an investigative tool to confirm or refute the officer's suspicion that the driver might be impaired; it cannot be used as direct evidence to incriminate the driver.[243]

§2.112 The Supreme Court has also upheld the override of section 10(*b*) in the context of roadside breath tests. In *Thomsen*,[244] the Court held that what was then section 234.1 (and is now section 254(2)) of the *Criminal Code*,[245] the provision authorizing police to demand that a driver furnish a breath sample into a roadside screening device where they suspect a driver has alcohol in his body, by necessary implication, limited the right to counsel. Nevertheless, for reasons analogous to those cited in *Orbanksi & Elias*, the Court concluded that the violation was justified under section 1 of the *Charter*. If a motorist fails the roadside screening test the result is not admissible at a later trial. Rather, the failed test merely provides police with a basis for making a breathalyzer demand under section 254(3) of the *Criminal Code*.[246]

§2.113 The rationale for overriding the right to counsel would seem to apply equally to any traffic stop motivated by road safety concerns, not just those carried out to investigate driver sobriety. For example, drivers pulled over for speeding, other moving violations, or simply to confirm that their licence or insurance is in order, are not entitled to be apprised of their right to counsel. In such circumstances, the right to counsel is implicitly overridden by the provincial traffic provisions authorizing the stop. For the same reasons endorsed in *Thomsen* and *Orbanksi & Elias*, such an override should be justified under section 1 of the *Charter*.[247]

---

[241] *Ibid.*, at para. 55. (S.C.J.)

[242] *Ibid.*, at para. 56 (S.C.J.).

[243] *Ibid.*, at para. 58 (S.C.J.). See also *R. v. Milne*, [1996] O.J. No. 1728, 107 C.C.C. (3d) 118 at 128-31(Ont. C.A.), leave to appeal refused [1996] S.C.C.A. No. 353, [1996] 3 S.C.R. xiii (S.C.C.); *R. v. Coutts*, [1999] O.J. No. 2013, 45 O.R. (3d) 288 (Ont. C.A.); *R. v. Ellerman*, [2000] A.J. No. 150, [2000] 6 W.W.R. 704 (Alta. C.A.); and *R. c. Roy*), [1997] J.Q. no 1074, 117 C.C.C. (3d) 243 (Que. C.A.). This aspect of *Orbanski & Elias* is criticized in Chapter 4, Part 3(4)(*g*), in particular §4.97 and supporting footnotes.

[244] [1988] S.C.J. No. 31, [1988] 1 S.C.R. 640 at 648-49 (S.C.C.).

[245] R.S.C. 1970, c. C-34.

[246] See *R. v. Milne*, [1996] O.J. No. 1728, 107 C.C.C. (3d) 118 (Ont. C.A.), leave to appeal refused [1996] S.C.C.A. No. 353, [1996] 3 S.C.R. xiii (S.C.C.) (concluding that the results of the roadside breath screening cannot be used to establish the charges of impaired driving or "over 80" at trial) and *R. v. Coutts*, [1999] O.J. No. 2013, 45 O.R. (3d) 288 (Ont. C.A.) (rejecting the use of these results to refute an "evidence to the contrary" defence advanced at trial).

[247] See *R. v. Harris*, [2007] O.J. No. 3185, 225 C.C.C. (3d) 193 at paras. 47-48 (Ont. C.A.); *R. v. Ellerman*, [2000] A.J. No. 150, [2000] 6 W.W.R. 704 (Alta. C.A.). See also the discussion in Chapter 4, Part 3(4)(*g*).

§2.114 The situation is different, however, where the purpose of the stop is not road safety. Police must comply with section 10(*b*) of the *Charter* when they either stop motorists for purely criminal investigative purposes or, having initially stopped for road safety reasons, begin a purely criminal inquiry unrelated to traffic safety.[248]

(f) Case-by-Case Explication of Associated Powers

§2.115 As the discussion above illustrates, the development of police powers to detain motorists has been far from straightforward. With some of these powers originating at common law (under the ancillary powers doctrine), others flowing from open-ended grants of authority under provincial traffic legislation and still others stemming from *Criminal Code* impaired driving provisions, there remains a fair bit of uncertainty regarding the exact parameters of police authority in this area.

§2.116 The Supreme Court of Canada acknowledged this uncertainty in *Orbanski & Elias*.[249] According to the Court, some degree of ambiguity is unavoidable because it "is both impossible to predict all the aspects of such encounters and impractical to legislate exhaustive details as to how they must be conducted".[250] For the Court, the solution to this uncertainty is to rely on the common law as a guide to resolving unanswered questions.[251] For example, in *Orbanski & Elias*, the Court suggested that the scope of police power to make impaired driving inquiries during roadside detention should be decided by a "case-specific" reasonableness inquiry.[252] Quoting from an Ontario Court of Appeal decision, the Court concluded that such inquiries will be reasonable if they "can be performed at the site of the detention, with dispatch, with no danger to the safety of the detainee and with minimal inconvenience to the detainee."[253] In other words, the exact contours of police authority will vary depending on the facts of each case.

§2.117 This approach is far from ideal. Without reasonably clear rules to guide their actions *ex ante*, police will frequently stretch the boundaries of their powers past the breaking point. Without clarity on the limits of investigative powers and the consequences of exceeding them, the fact that a court might later find a

---

[248] See *R. v. Calderon*, [2004] O.J. No. 3474, 188 C.C.C. (3d) 481 (Ont. C.A.) (vehicle initially stopped for speeding eventually searched based on police suspicion that occupants were transporting drugs, s. 10(*b*) violated (along with ss. 8 and 9) when police sought consent to search trunk without apprising occupants of their right to counsel). See also *R. v. Rutten*, [2006] S.J. No. 65, 205 C.C.C. (3d) 504 at para. 50 (Sask. C.A.) (s. 10(*b*) *Charter* violated when driver "not advised of this right *before* the officers questioned him about the presence of drugs in the vehicle and sought his consent to search the vehicle for drugs." [emphasis added]). But see *R. v. Omelusik*, [2003] B.C.J. No. 1237, 182 B.C.A.C. 315 (B.C.C.A.) (no violation of ss. 10(*a*) or 10(*b*) because delay in administering warnings was very brief and the impracticality of consulting counsel at the roadside).

[249] [2005] S.C.J. No. 37, [2005] 2 S.C.R. 3, 2005 SCC 37 (S.C.C.) [*Orbanski & Elias*].

[250] *Ibid.*, at para. 45 (S.C.J.).

[251] See *ibid.*, at para. 45 (S.C.J.).

[252] *Ibid.*, at paras. 47, 49-50 (S.C.J.).

[253] *Ibid.*, at para. 46 (S.C.J.), quoting from *R. v. Smith*, [1996] O.J. No. 372 at para. 28, 105 C.C.C. (3d) 58 (Ont. C.A.).

constitutional violation and (perhaps) exclude evidence obtained thereby can do little to deter rule-breaking.[254] Further, even assuming that police will diligently try to conform to the rules, the ubiquity, complexity and ambiguity of the decisions emanating from the case-specific approach make it extremely difficult for them to do so.[255] Although no legislative scheme could ever address every potential eventuality, statutory guidance could go a considerable distance toward structuring and confining police discretion in a manner that would reduce the potential for abuse.[256] Unfortunately, as long as the Court remains willing to fill the gaps, legislatures will have little incentive to regulate this important area of interaction between the police and the public.[257]

(3) Detention for Criminal Investigative Purposes

§2.118 When state actors wish to interfere with an individual's liberty or privacy interests for the purposes of a criminal investigation, the law usually demands greater justification than it does for regulatory matters (such as traffic safety, discussed above). This enhanced protection is warranted, it has been said, by the fact that criminal investigation and prosecution typically causes people to suffer greater disapprobation and punishment.[258] However, as we examine below, the various criminal investigation detention powers available to law enforcement, it will become apparent that the degree of protection granted varies considerably depending on the nature and strength of both the state's crime control interest and the individual's interests in liberty and privacy.

(a) Investigative Detention

§2.119 Prior to 1993, Canadian law was clear: police had no power to detain short of carrying out a formal arrest.[259] (Arrest powers are detailed below in Part

---

[254] See Steven Penney, "Taking Deterrence Seriously: Excluding Unconstitutionally Obtained Evidence Under Section 24(2) of the *Charter*" (2004) 49 McGill L.J. 105 at 116-17.

[255] See William C. Heffernan and Richard W. Lovely, "Evaluating the Fourth Amendment Exclusionary Rule: The Problem of Police Compliance with the Law" (1991) 24 Mich. J.L. Reform 311 at 320-21.

[256] See Kenneth C. Davis, *Police Discretion* (St. Paul: West Publishing Co., 1975), who long ago recognized the dangers of too little and too much discretion, arguing: "Unnecessary discretion must be eliminated. But discretion often is necessary and often must be preserved. Necessary discretion must be properly confined, structured and checked." *Ibid.*, at 170.

[257] For an elaboration on this critique, see James Stribopoulos, "In *Search* of Dialogue: The Supreme Court, Police Powers and the *Charter*" (2005) 31 Queen's L.J. 1.

[258] See *Thomson Newspapers Ltd. v. Canada (Director of Investigation and Research, Restrictive Trade Practices Commission)*, [1990] S.C.J. No. 23, [1990] 1 S.C.R. 425 at 476-77 (S.C.C.).

[259] See *R. v. Hicks*, [1988] O.J. No. 957, 42 C.C.C. (3d) 394 at 400 (Ont. C.A.), affd on other grounds [1990] S.C.J. No. 7, [1990] 1 S.C.R. 120, 54 C.C.C. (3d) 575 (S.C.C.); *R. v. Moran*, [1987] O.J. No. 794, 36 C.C.C. (3d) 225 at 258 (Ont. C.A.), leave to appeal refused [1988] S.C.C.A. No. 213 (S.C.C.); *R. v. Esposito*, [1985] O.J. No. 100 2, 24 C.C.C. (3d) 88 at 94 (Ont. C.A.), leave to appeal refused [1986] S.C.C.A. No. 63, [1986] 1 S.C.R. viii (S.C.C.); *R. v. Dedman*, [1985] S.C.J. No. 45, [1985] 2 S.C.R. 2 (S.C.C.); *R. v. O'Donnell; R. v. Cluett*, [1982] N.S.J. No. 542, 3 C.C.C. (3d) 333 at 347-48 (N.S.C.A.), revd on other grounds [1985] S.C.J. No. 54, [1985] 2 S.C.R. 216, 21 C.C.C. (3d) 318 (S.C.C.); *R. v. Guthrie*, [1982] A.J. No. 29, 69 C.C.C. (2d) 216 at 218-19 (Alta. C.A.); *R. v. Moore*, [1978] S.C.J. No. 82, [1979] 1 S.C.R. 195,

4(4).) This changed with the Ontario Court of Appeal's decision in *R. v. Simpson*.[260]

§2.120 After applying the ancillary powers doctrine (explained in detail in Chapter 1, Part 6(4)(*b*)), the court in *Simpson* used the ancillary powers doctrine to recognize a power to briefly detain when police have "articulable cause" to believe that the person is involved in criminal activity.[261]

§2.121 The investigative detention power recognized in *Simpson* was ultimately endorsed by appellate courts across the country.[262] It took 11 years, however, for the Supreme Court of Canada to finally give it its stamp of approval. Acknowledging that "police officers must be empowered to respond quickly, effectively, and flexibly to the diversity of encounters experienced daily on the front lines of policing,"[263] in *R. v. Mann*,[264] the Court applied the ancillary powers doctrine to recognize an investigative detention power.

§2.122 In *Mann*, the Court held that an individual may be briefly detained where police have reasonable grounds to suspect a clear nexus between the individual being detained and a recently committed or still unfolding criminal offence.[265] An investigative detention that is carried out in accordance with this

---

43 C.C.C. (2d) 83 at 89-90 (S.C.C.); *Rice v. Connolly*, [1966] 2 Q.B. 414 at 419 (Div. Ct.); *Kenlin v. Gardner*, [1967] 2 Q.B. 510 (Div. Ct.); *Koechlin v. Waugh*, [1957] O.J. No. 105, 118 C.C.C. 24 at 26-27 (Ont. C.A.); Alan Young, "All Along The Watchtower: Arbitrary Detention and the Police Function" (1991) 29 Osgoode Hall L.J. 329 at 330, 343; David C. McDonald, *Legal Rights in the Canadian Charter of Rights and Freedoms*, 2d ed. (Toronto: Carswell, 1989) at 303-304; Canada, Law Commission of Canada, *Arrest, Working Paper 41* (Ottawa: Supply & Services Canada, 1985) at 33, 37; Steve Coughlan, "Police Detention: A Proposal" (1985) 28 Crim. L.Q. 64 at 66, 77.

[260] [1993] O.J. No. 308, 79 C.C.C. (3d) 482 (Ont. C.A.) [*Simpson*].

[261] *Ibid.*, at 499-502 (C.C.C.).

[262] See *R. v. Ferris*, [1998] B.C.J. No. 1415, 126 C.C.C. (3d) 298 (B.C.C.A.), leave to appeal refused [1998] S.C.C.A. No. 424 (S.C.C.); *R. v. Dupuis*, [1994] A.J. No. 1011, 162 A.R. 197 (Alta. C.A.); *R. v. Lake*, [1996] S.J. No. 886, 113 C.C.C. (3d) 208 (Sask. C.A.); *R. v. G. (C.M)*, [1996] M.J. No. 428, 113 Man. R. (2d) 76 (Man. C.A.); *R. c. Pigeon*, [1993] J.Q. no 1683, 59 Q.A.C. 103 (Que. C.A.); *R. v. Carson*, [1998] N.B.J. No. 482, 39 M.V.R. (3d) 55 (N.B.C.A.); *R. v. Chabot*, [1993] N.S.J. No. 465, 86 C.C.C. (3d) 309 (N.S.C.A.); *R. v. Burke*, [1997] N.J. No. 187, 118 C.C.C. (3d) 59 (Nfld. C.A.).

[263] *R. v. Mann*, [2004] S.C.J. No. 49 at para. 16, [2004] 3 S.C.R. 59 (S.C.C.).

[264] [2004] S.C.J. No. 49, [2004] 3 S.C.R. 59 (S.C.C.).

[265] *Ibid.*, at paras. 34, 45 (S.C.R.). Unfortunately, the Court could have been clearer on whether the investigative detention power identified was limited to crimes actually known to police or whether it also extends to crimes that are reasonably suspected. The latter explanation makes much more sense as it allows police to respond to events that they observe while on patrol, giving rise to a reasonably based suspicion that criminality may be afoot. See *R. v. Nesbeth*, [2008] O.J. No. 3086, 238 C.C.C. (3d) 567 at para. 18 (Ont. C.A.), leave to appeal refused [2009] S.C.C.A. No. 10 (S.C.C.) ("While the court in *Mann* speaks of reasonable grounds to suspect that the individual is connected to 'a particular crime', in my view, it is not necessary that the officers be able to pinpoint the crime with absolute precision."); *R. v. Yeh*, [2009] S.J. No. 582, 2009 SKCA 112, [2009] 11 W.W.R. 193 at para. 84 (Sask. C.A.) ("'a particular crime,' read in context, reflects the idea that the police may not detain an individual out of a general sense he or she might be doing something unlawful. ... police suspicions must relate to specific criminal wrongdoing").

common law power, the Court explained, is not "arbitrary" and thus does not infringe section 9 of the *Charter*.[266]

(i) Reasonable Suspicion

§2.123 The reasonable suspicion standard endorsed in *Mann* is unfortunately difficult to define with precision. The Supreme Court has made clear that a "reasonable suspicion" requires "the police officer's subjective belief to be backed by objectively verifiable indications."[267] In other words, the test has both a subjective and objective component.[268]

§2.124 The best explanation places the standard along a spectrum, with absolute certainty and proof beyond a reasonable doubt at one end and a mere hunch or barren suspicion at the other. On this approach, "'reasonable suspicion' means something more than a mere suspicion and something less than a belief based upon reasonable and probable grounds."[269] As a result, a "hunch based on intuition", even one gained by experience, does not amount to reasonable suspicion.[270]

§2.125 In deciding whether or not the standard is met, the Court in *Mann* instructed, a court must consider the "totality of the circumstances".[271] This means that the collective significance of all of the circumstances confronting police must be considered in light of common sense and practical experience; individual pieces of evidence should not be viewed in isolation or discounted without due regard to the entire context.[272] As a result, there are few hard and fast rules — the analysis is unavoidably fact driven. Nevertheless, some concrete guidance has emerged.

---

[266] *R. v. Mann*, [2004] S.C.J. No. 49, [2004] 3 S.C.R. 59 at para. 20 (S.C.C.).

[267] *R. v. M. (A.)*, [2008] S.C.J. No. 19, [2008] 1 S.C.R. 569 at para. 80 (S.C.C.).

[268] *R. v. Mann*, [2004] S.C.J. No. 49, [2004] 3 S.C.R. 59 (S.C.C.), acknowledging as much in describing the analogous "articulable cause" standard (*ibid.*, at para. 27 (S.C.R.)), a standard that the Court identified as equivalent to the reasonable suspicion standard (*ibid.*, at para. 33 (S.C.R.)).

[269] *R. v. Kang-Brown*, [2008] S.C.J. No. 18, [2008] 1 S.C.R. 456 (S.C.C.), *per* Binnie J., at para. 75 and *per* Deschamps J., at paras. 164-165 (S.C.R.), dissenting. The Court has explained that reasonable suspicion crystallizes at a point along the spectrum *somewhat* lower than the "reasonable and probable grounds" required for a conventional arrest. See *R. v. Mann*, [2004] S.C.J. No. 49, [2004] 3 S.C.R. 59 at para. 27 (S.C.C.) (noting that the analogous articulable standard is "clearly a threshold *somewhat* lower than the reasonable and probable grounds required for lawful arrest" (emphasis added)). See also *R. v. Aslam*, [2006] B.C.J. No. 3152, 149 C.R.R. (2d) 43 at para. 6 (B.C.C.A.); *R. v. Greaves*, [2004] B.C.J. No. 1953 at para. 41, 189 C.C.C. (3d) 305 (B.C.C.A.), leave to appeal refused [2004] S.C.C.A. No. 522 (S.C.C.); *R. v. Houben*, [2006] S.J. No. 715, 214 C.C.C. (3d) 519 at para. 45 (Sask. C.A.).

[270] *R. v. Mann*, [2004] S.C.J. No. 49, [2004] 3 S.C.R. 59 at para. 30 (S.C.C.). See *R. v. Kang-Brown*, [2008] S.C.J. No. 18, [2008] 1 S.C.R. 456 (S.C.C.), *per* Binnie J. at para. 76 and *per* Deschamps J., at para. 165, dissenting; *R. v. M. (A.)*, [2008] S.C.J. No. 19, [2008] 1 S.C.R. 569 at para. 91 (S.C.C.), *per* Binnie J.

[271] *R. v. Mann*, [2004] S.C.J. No. 49, [2004] 3 S.C.R. 59 at para. 34 (S.C.C.).

[272] See *R. v. Bramley*, [2009] S.J. No. 219, 67 C.R. (6th) 293 at paras. 47, 60 (Sask. C.A.).

§2.126 For example, the Court in *Mann* warned police that a suspect's presence in a "so-called high crime area" is not by itself a basis for detention.[273] Similarly, the fact that an individual is nervous when approached by police does not, on its own, give rise to reasonable suspicion.[274] Nor does reasonable suspicion of criminality arise simply because a person chooses to assert his or her constitutional rights, for example, by walking away from police or refusing consent to search.[275]

§2.127 On the other hand, running away from police, when combined with other objectively suspicious circumstances, can justify a detention;[276] so can the odour of freshly-smoked marijuana emanating from a vehicle (since it may indicate either that someone in the vehicle is in possession of the drug or that the driver is impaired).[277] Finally, pre-*Mann* case law suggests that although the police are not entitled to search or arrest based only on an anonymous tip predicting that a suspect will be in possession of contraband at a specified time and place, such a tip is sufficient justification for an investigative detention.[278]

§2.128 More controversial is the use of profiles. For example, with the assistance of their American counterparts, police in Canada have developed a drug courier profile to target motorists for increased scrutiny during traffic stops.[279] Similar profiles have been developed to target travellers as they move through transportation hubs such as airports and bus depots.[280] As described in the re-

---

[273] *R. v. Mann*, [2004] S.C.J. No. 49, [2004] 3 S.C.R. 59 at para. 47 (S.C.C.). See *e.g.*, *R. v. O. (N.)*, [2009] A.J. No. 213, 2 Alta. L.R. (5th) 72 at para. 40 (Alta. C.A.) ("Even though some apartment buildings in a neighbourhood may be known to the police as havens of drug activity, that does not mean that anyone who enters any apartment building in an ill-defined area or neighbourhood can objectively be suspected of criminal activity.")

[274] *R. v. Kang-Brown*, [2008] S.C.J. No. 18, [2008] 1 S.C.R. 456 at para. 96 (S.C.C.), *per* Binnie J. ("I do not think that [nervousness] on its own ... is a sufficient marker of unusual conduct to afford grounds of reasonable suspicion, nor taken with the other factors (or 'indicia') mentioned by Sergeant MacPhee [*i.e.*, staring at police] does it, in my opinion, reach that level.").

[275] *R. v. Kang-Brown*, [2008] S.C.J. No. 18, [2008] 1 S.C.R. 456 at para. 92 (S.C.C.), *per* Binnie J. (explaining that "Individuals should not be penalized for asserting their constitutional rights."). See *e.g.*, *R. v. Ferdinand*, [2004] O.J. No. 3209, 21 C.R. (6th) 65 (Ont. S.C.J.), where accused walking away from police officer when he approached was held not to give rise to reasonable suspicion of criminality.

[276] See *R. v. Nesbeth*, [2008] O.J. No. 3086, 238 C.C.C. (3d) 567 at para. 17 (Ont. C.A.), leave to appeal refused [2009] S.C.C.A. No. 10 (S.C.C.) (detention justified where the detainee was encountered late at night in the stairwell of a building known to be a high-crime area and immediately bolted when he saw uniformed police officers, threw a shopping cart at police as they gave chase to block their progress and threw away a knapsack that he had been tightly holding up until then); *R. v. Cooper*, [2005] N.S.J. No. 102, 195 C.C.C. (3d) 162 at para. 44 (N.S.C.A.) (detention of vehicle passenger involved in police pursuit justified where suspect exited car while it was travelling at 20 kilometres per hour and ran through backyards to evade police).

[277] See *R. v. Webster*, [2008] B.C.J. No. 2234, 238 C.C.C. (3d) 270 at para. 31 (B.C.C.A.).

[278] See *R. v. Lewis*, [1998] O.J. No. 376, 122 C.C.C. (3d) 481 at para. 27 (Ont. C.A.) ("The tip and the verification of the details in the tip while not amounting to reasonable grounds for arrest, did provide the officers with articulable cause to briefly detain the respondent to investigate the allegations made by the tipster....")

[279] See §2.103, above, and the supporting footnotes.

[280] *R. v. Kang-Brown*, [2008] S.C.J. No. 18, [2008] 1 S.C.R. 456 at paras. 47, 79, 82-84, 88 (S.C.C.) *per* Binnie J., describing the "Operation Jetway" program involved in that case and expressing scepticism as to the probative value of some of the purported indicators, *i.e.*, whether

ported cases, the purported "indicators" of drug couriers include the use of a rented, out-of-province vehicle and the presence in the passenger compartment of cell phones, pagers, road maps, fast-food wrappers and luggage.

§2.129 Some courts have been persuaded that the presence of such "indicators" is sufficient to ground the reasonable suspicion necessary to justify an investigative detention.[281] In *R. v. Calderon*,[282] however, the Ontario Court of Appeal disagreed. The majority noted that these so-called "indicators" were in fact "neutral" and "might be found in any car."[283] In fact, the officers conceded that they had used the profile on countless prior occasions without success. Justice Laskin thus concluded for the majority that given "the neutrality and apparent unreliability of these indicators, I fail to see how their presence could amount to reasonable grounds for detention."[284]

§2.130 The decision in *Calderon* is undoubtedly correct. The problem with investigative profiles is their failure to account for the incidence of these same variables in the larger (law-abiding) population. Without reliable data on the likelihood of innocent motorists sharing the same characteristics identified by the drug-courier profile, the presence of the indicators is empirically meaningless. This failing, known as the "base rate fallacy", is endemic to all investigative profiles.[285] Courts must be cognizant of it before too readily concluding that the presence of profile "indicators" constitutes reasonable suspicion.

§2.131 Courts should also be reluctant to extend too much deference to police officer's experience, training and judgment in interpreting suspects' ambiguous or neutral conduct.[286] As much empirical scholarship suggests, in exercising broad, discretionary powers, police rely as much on occupational culture and other informal norms as on formal legal rules.[287] Without firm and objective strictures on their powers, police too often rely on conscious and unconscious stereotypes, including those based on race and ethnicity.[288] Research also suggests that warrantless police powers, like the investigative detention power, are

---

an individual makes eye contact with police, whether a bus ticket is purchased with cash at the last minute, *etc*. In contrast, Deschamps J. (joined by Rothstein J.) concluded that these variables did give rise to reasonable suspicion. See *R. v. Kang-Brown*, [2008] S.C.J. No. 18, [2008] 1 S.C.R. 456 at para. 187 (S.C.C.), *per* Deschamps J.

[281] See *e.g.*, *R. v. Bramley*, [2009] S.J. No. 219, 67 C.R. (6th) 293 (Sask. C.A.).

[282] *R. v. Calderon*, [2004] O.J. No. 3474, 188 C.C.C. (3d) 481 (Ont. C.A.).

[283] *Ibid.*, at para. 72 (O.J.). Justice Weiler dissented. She concluded that the collection of circumstances gave rise to reasonably based suspicion and justified the detentions.

[284] *R. v. Calderon*, [2004] O.J. No. 3474, 188 C.C.C. (3d) 481 at para. 72 (Ont. C.A.).

[285] See Alan D. Gold, *Expert Evidence in Criminal Law: The Scientific Approach*, 2d ed. (Toronto: Irwin, 2009), Chapter 7.

[286] Such deference was arguably extended, for example, by the dissenting judges in *R. v. Kang-Brown*, [2008] S.C.J. No. 18, [2008] 1 S.C.R. 456 (S.C.C.), *per* Deschamps J., at para. 205, dissenting and *per* Bastarache J., at paras. 249-250, dissenting.

[287] See Richard V. Ericson, *Reproducing Order: A Study of Police Patrol Work* (Toronto: University Toronto Press, 1982); Debra Livingston,"A Gang Loitering, the Court, and Some Realism about Police Patrol" [1999] Sup. Ct. Rev. 141.

[288] See David M. Tanovich, *The Colour of Justice: Policing Race in Canada* (Toronto: Irwin Law, 2006) at 135-37.

considerably more likely to be used against innocent persons than powers re-quiring prior judicial approval.[289]

(ii) Protective Pat-down Search Power

§2.132 In *R. v. Mann*,[290] the Supreme Court held that where an individual is lawfully detained for investigative purposes, that person may also be subject to a limited protective pat-down search. According to the Court, "[s]uch a search power does not exist as a matter of course; the officer must believe on reason-able grounds that his or her own safety, or the safety of others, is at risk."[291] Un-der this power, the police are only entitled to pat-down a suspect to ensure that he or she is not carrying weapons. In other words, it is a protective power, not intended as a means of searching for and gathering evidence. The protective search power created in *Mann* and its limits are explained in greater detail in Chapter 3, Part 4(3) (that chapter deals with Search and Seizure).

(iii) Sections 10(a) and 10(b) of the Charter Incidental to Investigative Detention

§2.133 Despite 11 years of rather intense litigation between *Simpson*[292] and *Mann*,[293] there was unfortunately no clear and consistent answer from appellate courts as to whether the rights found in section 10 of the *Charter* apply when an individual is subject to investigative detention.[294] (The requirements of section 10(*a*) and 10(*b*) of the *Charter* more generally are fully explained in Chapter 4, Part 3.)

§2.134 In *Mann*, the Supreme Court thankfully made clear that section 10(*a*) of the *Charter* does apply. The Court explained that the police must tell the person "in clear and simple language"[295] of the reasons for the detention. Unfortunately,

---

[289] See Max Minzner, "Putting Probability Back into Probable Cause," *Cardozo Legal Studies Research Paper No. 240* (July 9, 2008), online: Social Science Research Network <http://papers.ssrn.com/sol3/papers.cfm?abstract_id=1157111> at 13-14 (summarizing data from various sources indicating that success rates for warrantless searches are typically well be-low 50 per cent).

[290] [2004] S.C.J. No. 49, [2004] 3 S.C.R. 59 (S.C.C.).

[291] *Ibid.*, at para 40.

[292] [1993] O.J. No. 308, 79 C.C.C. (3d) 482 (Ont. C.A.).

[293] [2004] S.C.J. No. 49, [2004] 3 S.C.R. 59 at para. 47 (S.C.C.).

[294] See *R. v. V. (T.A.)*, [2001] A.J. No. 1679, 48 C.R. (5th) 366 (Alta. C.A.) (essentially holding that s. 10(*b*) did not apply). But see *R. v. Lewis*, [1998] O.J. No. 376, 122 C.C.C. (3d) 481 at para. 28 (Ont. C.A.) ("Without deciding whether every investigative detention requires compli-ance with s. 10(b), I would hold that this investigative detention, which encompassed a search of the respondent's luggage, gave rise to an obligation that the police inform the respondent of his right to counsel.").

[295] [2004] S.C.J. No. 49, [2004] 3 S.C.R. 59 at para. 21 (S.C.C.). See also *R. v. Nguyen*, [2008] O.J. No. 219, 231 C.C.C. (3d) 541 (Ont. C.A.) (finding that s. 10(*a*) was violated when a police offi-cer present at a home where a marijuana grow operation was found intercepted the appellant af-ter he pulled into the driveway, told him "Police, stop" and then immediately asked him if he lived at the residence without first informing him of the reason for his detention. The Court concluded that this violation of s. 10(*a*) "cannot be considered a trivial matter." *Ibid.*, at para. 21 (C.C.C.).)

the same was not true with respect to section 10(*b*). Although the Supreme Court cautioned in *Mann* that the police should not use compliance with that right as an excuse to unduly and artificially prolong an investigative detention, it deliberately deferred for another day the more pressing question of whether or not the right applies.[296] It took five more years of uncertainty before that day arrived.[297]

§2.135 In *R. v. Suberu*,[298] the Supreme Court of Canada definitively held that, "subject to concerns for officer or public safety",[299] police must tell people subject to investigative detention about their right to retain and instruct counsel immediately upon detention and do everything required under section 10(*b*) to facilitate that right.[300] It summarily dismissed the suggestion that a suspension of the right to counsel during such detentions was justified under section 1 of the *Charter*, which subjects section 10(*b*) and other *Charter* rights to reasonable limits prescribed by law as can be "demonstrably justified in a free and democratic society."[301] "Because the definition of detention, as understood in these reasons, gives the police leeway to engage members of the public in non-coercive, exploratory questioning without necessarily triggering their *Charter* rights relating to detention," the Court reasoned, "s. 1 need not be invoked in order to allow the police to effectively fulfill their investigative duties."[302] (The meaning of "detention" after *Grant* and *Suberu* is discussed above in Part 3(3)(*b*).)

§2.136 Nevertheless, when the detention threshold is crossed it remains to be determined how the police are expected to facilitate contact with counsel during street-level investigative detentions. We also worry that the implementation of the right to counsel will artificially prolong street-level detentions and transform them into *de facto* arrests, the precise danger that the Court cautioned against in *Mann*. Finally, we fear that the challenge posed by section 10(*b*) *Charter* claims may encourage courts, invariably only seeing the factually guilty, to strain to avoid finding a "detention" so as to excuse non-compliance with section 10(*b*). Although this would give police room to engage in initial questioning of persons they stop in suspicious circumstances, it also runs the risk of watering down the meaning of "detention" so far that it eliminates any meaningful protection from

---

[296] [2004] S.C.J. No. 49, [2004] 3 S.C.R. 59 at para. 22 (S.C.C.).

[297] The uncertainty flowed from conflicting judgments as to the applicability of the right. See, for example, *R. v. Greaves*, [2004] B.C.J. No. 1953 at paras. 82-85, 189 C.C.C. (3d) 305 (B.C.C.A.), leave to appeal refused [2004] S.C.C.A. No. 522 (S.C.C.) (holding that the right applied). But see *R. v. Suberu*, [2007] O.J. No. 317, 218 C.C.C. (3d) 27 (Ont. C.A.), affd on other grounds [2009] S.C.J. No. 33, [2009] 2 S.C.R. 460 (S.C.C.) (effectively holding that the right does not apply).

[298] [2007] O.J. No. 317, 218 C.C.C. (3d) 27 (Ont. C.A.), affd on other grounds [2009] S.C.J. No. 33, [2009] 2 S.C.R. 460 (S.C.C.).

[299] *Ibid.*, at para. 2 (S.C.R.).

[300] *Ibid.*, at para. 42. See also *R. v. Strachan*, [1988] S.C.J. No. 94, [1988] 2 S.C.R. 980 at 998-99 (S.C.C.) (s. 10 warnings must be given immediately upon detention but may be delayed in situations where police need to gain control over a dangerous situation); *R. v. DeBot*, [1989] S.C.J. No. 118, [1989] 2 S.C.R. 1140 at 1163-64 (S.C.C.), *per* Wilson J. (same).

[301] *R. v. Suberu*, [2009] S.C.J. No. 33, [2009] 2 S.C.R. 460 at para. 63 (S.C.C.).

[302] *Ibid.*, at para. 45.

unjustified police stops. For all these reasons, two of us have argued elsewhere that the more sensible solution would be a brief override of the right to counsel under section 1 of the *Charter* incidental to a lawful investigative detention, at least to the extent necessary for police to engage in *brief* and *preliminary* questioning.[303]

§2.137 What precisely do we mean by "brief" and "preliminary"? Courts have been reluctant to impose a quantitative limit on the length of investigative detentions,[304] and we do not propose one here. However, absent exceptional circumstances, a detention lasting longer than 20 minutes would seem to be excessive.[305] On this approach, questioning that is the functional equivalent of an interrogation would also exceed the scope of investigative detention. As under the approach to detention we propose above (see Part 3(3)(*b*)(iii)c), an investigative detention (and the accompanying suspension of the right to counsel) would expire when police decide that the individual probably committed an offence and ask questions designed to induce self-incriminating answers. These are precisely the circumstances when suspects need the protection of the right to counsel.[306]

(iv) Duties on the Person Detained

§2.138 Although the cases don't explicitly say as much, it seems obvious that a person subject to investigative detention is legally obligated to acquiesce to police authority and remain with police until instructed that he or she is free to go. Failing to do so would arguably constitute the offence of obstructing police.[307] Such a duty and potential criminal liability for non-compliance would seem to depend on two preconditions. First, the detention must be lawful (*i.e.*, police must have the requisite grounds to detain); there can be no obligation to submit

---

[303] See Steven Penney & James Stribopoulos, "'Detention' under the *Charter* after *R. v. Grant* and *R. v. Suberu*" (2010) 51 S.C.L.R. (2d) 439.

[304] See *e.g.*, *R. v. Greaves*, [2004] B.C.J. No. 1953 at paras. 50-55, 189 C.C.C. (3d) 305 (B.C.C.A.), leave to appeal refused [2004] S.C.C.A. No. 522 (S.C.C.) (40-minute detention lawful as accused's evasive and inconsistent responses regarding his identity gave rise to reasonable grounds to suspect him of attempting to obstruct justice). See also *United States v. Place*, 462 U.S. 696 at 709, n.10 (1983) (a time limit would interfere with the ability of the "authorities to graduate their responses to the demands of any particular situation").

[305] In its Model Code the Institute adopts a 20-minute rule. See American Law Institute, *A Model Code Of Pre-Arraignment Procedure* (Philadelphia: American Law Institute, 1975) at 283.

[306] See Steven Penney, "What's Wrong with Self-Incrimination? The Wayward Path of Self-Incrimination Law in the Post-Charter Era, Part 2: Self-Incrimination in Police Investigations" (2004) 48 Crim. L.Q. 280 at 321.

[307] See *Criminal Code*, R.S.C. 1985, c. C-46, s. 129(*a*). See *e.g.*, *R. v. Waugh*, [2010] O.J. No. 425, 251 C.C.C. (3d) 139 (Ont. C.A.), leave to appeal refused [2010] S.C.C.A. No. 127, [2010] 2 S.C.R. ix (S.C.C.). In *Waugh*, the accused was found guilty of obstructing police for refusing to acquiesce to police demands when they attempted to impound his uninsured vehicle. Although there was no statutory authority to impound a vehicle in such circumstances in Ontario, the Court, after applying the ancillary powers doctrine, found such a power at common law and based the accused's conviction on his failure to acquiesce to police authority pursuant to that newly minted common law power. The rather obvious rule of law problems that this sort of retroactive imposition of criminal responsibility creates was unfortunately not addressed by the Court.

to an illegal interference with one's liberty. Second, the detaining officer must have complied with section 10(*a*) of the *Charter*; an individual cannot be expected to acquiesce to police authority unless told that he or she is being placed under investigative detention and apprised of the reason(s) why.

§2.139 Beyond submitting to police authority, the detained individual does not appear to have any further obligations. The Supreme Court made clear in *Mann* that investigative detention "does not impose an obligation on the detained individual to answer questions posed by the police."[308] Whether the Court meant to include the most basic of questions, such as "What's your name?" is not explicitly addressed. Nevertheless, this is how the British Columbia Court of Appeal has read *Mann*, suggesting in *obiter* that there is no legal obligation on detainees to identify themselves to police.[309]

(v) Use of Force Incidental to Investigative Detentions

§2.140 Section 25(1) of the *Criminal Code*[310] provides that police officers may use "as much force as necessary" when "authorized by law to do anything" if the officer "acts on reasonable grounds", and would now seem to license the use of all "necessary" force in effecting a lawful investigative detention.

§2.141 Unfortunately, the case law provides very little explanation as to the sort of force that police are permitted to use incidental to an investigative detention. On more than a few occasions, the courts have noted (uncritically) that police used physical force to restrain uncooperative detainees.[311] Provided that police use only as much force as "necessary", section 25(1) would clearly provide a justification for police in such circumstances. For example, in a pre-*Mann* case, the Ontario Court of Appeal held that if a suspect does not "submit to lawful detention", then the officer is entitled to "pursue him" and, when caught, to "physically restrain" him.[312]

§2.142 Courts have also approved the use of handcuffs during investigative detentions where police have reasonably based safety concerns; again, section 25(1) would seem to provide authority for this.[313] That said, courts should be careful to avoid endorsing the use of handcuffs as a matter of course during all investigative detentions. Routine handcuffing is unwarranted and would result in

---

[308] *R. v. Mann*, [2004] S.C.J. No. 49, [2004] 3 S.C.R. 59 at para. 45 (S.C.C.).

[309] *R. v. Greaves*, [2004] B.C.J. No. 1953 at para. 50, 189 C.C.C. (3d) 305 (B.C.C.A.), leave to appeal refused [2004] S.C.C.A. No. 522 (S.C.C.).

[310] R.S.C. 1985, c. C-46.

[311] See *R. v. Clayton*, [2007] S.C.J. No. 32, [2007] 2 S.C.R. 725 at paras. 10-12 (S.C.C.); *R. v. Duong*, [2006] B.C.J. No. 1452, 142 C.R.R. (2d) 261 at paras. 30-32 (B.C.C.A.); *R. v. Greaves*, [2004] B.C.J. No. 1953 at paras. 18, 55, 59, 189 C.C.C. (3d) 305 (B.C.C.A.), leave to appeal refused [2004] S.C.C.A. No. 522 (S.C.C.).

[312] *R. v. Wainwright*, [1999] O.J. No. 3539, 68 C.R.R. (2d) 29 at 30 (Ont. C.A.).

[313] See *R. v. O. (N.)*, [2009] A.J. No. 213, 2 Alta. L.R. (5th) 72 at paras. 9-10, 45 (Alta. C.A.); *R. v. Greaves*, [2004] B.C.J. No. 1953 at paras. 55, 59, 189 C.C.C. (3d) 305 (B.C.C.A.), leave to appeal refused [2004] S.C.C.A. No. 522 (S.C.C.); *R. v. Duong*, [2006] B.C.J. No. 1452, 142 C.R.R. (2d) 261 at paras. 28, 57 (B.C.C.A.).

the unnecessary erosion of an important distinction between brief investigative detentions and conventional arrests.

(vi) Length of Detentions

§2.143 In *Mann*, the Court emphasized that investigative detentions "should be brief in duration."[314] Unfortunately, the decision did not shed much light on what that actually means in practice. Subsequent cases have not done much better, with the length of detentions usually only receiving passing mention in a court's recitation of the facts.[315]

§2.144 The same challenge has arisen under the analogous "stop-and-frisk" power recognized by the United States Supreme Court ("the *Terry* doctrine").[316] In the U.S., it remains unclear how much time can pass before a "detention" will be characterized as an "arrest" requiring probable cause.[317] Instead, the United States Supreme Court has embraced a case-by-case approach, explaining that:

> In assessing whether a detention is too long in duration to be justified as an investigative stop, we consider it appropriate to examine whether the police diligently pursued a means of investigation that was likely to confirm or dispel their suspicions quickly, during which time it was necessary to detain the defendant. ... A court making this assessment should take care to consider whether the police are acting in a swiftly developing situation, and in such cases the court should not indulge in unrealistic second-guessing.[318]

In adopting this approach, the Court rejected "a *per se* rule that a 20-minute detention is too long to be justified under the *Terry* doctrine".[319] It feared that a time limit would interfere with the ability of the "authorities to graduate their responses to the demands of any particular situation".[320]

---

[314] *R. v. Mann*, [2004] S.C.J. No. 49, [2004] 3 S.C.R. 59 at paras. 22, 45 (S.C.C.).

[315] But see *R. v. Greaves*, [2004] B.C.J. No. 1953 at paras. 50-55, 189 C.C.C. (3d) 305 (B.C.C.A.), leave to appeal refused [2004] S.C.C.A. No. 522 (S.C.C.), a case where the Court dealt squarely with the length of the detention, which lasted 40 minutes. The Court concluded that the length of the detention was justified, although it acknowledged that the accused had no legal obligation to answer police questions or prove his identity, his evasive and inconsistent responses regarding his identity gave rise to reasonable grounds to detain him on suspicion of attempting to obstruct justice.

[316] See *Terry v. Ohio*, 392 U.S. 1 (1968) [*Terry*]. In *Terry*, the United States Supreme Court recognized that police are entitled to stop a person who they reasonably suspect is engaged in criminal behaviour, and to frisk that person for a weapon, if the officer also has reason to believe that he is dealing with an armed and dangerous individual.

[317] See *Michigan v. Summers*, 452 U.S. 692 (1981); *United States v. Sharpe*, 470 U.S. 675 (1985). But see *United States v. Place*, 462 U.S. 696 (1983) (insinuating that 90 minutes might be outside the limit at 709-10). But see *United States v. Montoya de Hernandez*, 473 U.S. 531 (1985) [*Montoya de Hernandez*] (upholding 18-hour investigative detention of suspected alimentary canal smuggler). See generally Wayne R. LaFave, "'Seizures' Typology: Classifying Detentions of the Person to Resolve Warrant, Grounds and Search Issues" (1984) 17 U. Mich. L. Rev. 417.

[318] *United States v. Sharpe*, 470 U.S. 675 at 686 (1985).

[319] *Ibid.*

[320] *United States v. Place*, 462 U.S. 696 at 709, footnote 10 (1983).

§2.145 A flexible fact-specific standard, however, carries its own drawbacks. First, as the American Law Institute explained in endorsing a 20-minute rule, "[i]t is important that a police officer have a clear notion of how long he may hold a person and when he must tell that person he is free to go".[321] Failing that, the Institute warned, the meaning of "brief" "might in certain circumstances plausibly appear to an officer to be a period of one or two hours."[322] Second, under a flexible standard, courts will be more inclined to accept that the police acted appropriately. The cases invariably seen by the courts are the ones where the delay paid off and where hindsight tends to push the court toward a conclusion that the police acted reasonably. Over time, the danger is that courts will extend the duration of stops so far that the line between investigative detentions and conventional arrests will be practically eliminated.[323] This is undoubtedly a danger that Canadian courts must be careful to avoid.

(vii)   Moving the Detainee

§2.146 In *Mann*, the Supreme Court did not address whether, and to what extent, the police might have the authority to move those subject to investigative detention. Subsequent cases have only indirectly addressed the issue. For example, in cases involving the detention of motorists, the police routinely (and rather sensibly) direct detainees to exit their vehicles[324] or place them in the back of a police cruiser.[325] Unfortunately, courts usually only make passing reference to these practices in their recitation of the facts, rarely commenting on their permissibility. In a rare (pre-*Mann*) case where the movement of a suspect was mentioned, the Ontario Court of Appeal suggested that it is permissible for police to move those detained at least short distances.[326]

§2.147 Courts should be careful not to accede too readily to the authority of police to move those detained any more than *very short* distances. Licensing more than that would serve to unduly prolong what are supposed to remain brief encounters and risk transforming investigative detentions into *de facto* arrests.

---

[321] American Law Institute, *A Model Code of Pre-Arraignment Procedure* (Washington, D.C.: 1975) at 283. In its Model Code the Institute adopts a 20-minute rule (*ibid.*, § 110.2(1)).

[322] *Ibid.*

[323] See *e.g.*, *United States v. Montoya de Hernandez*, 473 U.S. 531 (1985) (where the detention of a suspected alimentary canal smuggler for 18 hours was upheld under the *Terry* doctrine).

[324] See *R. v. Bramley*, [2009] S.J. No. 219, 67 C.R. (6th) 293 at para. 12 (Sask. C.A.); *R. v. Clayton*, [2007] S.C.J. No. 32, [2007] 2 S.C.R. 725 at paras. 6, 10 (S.C.C.); *R. v. Duong*, [2006] B.C.J. No. 1452, 142 C.R.R. (2d) 261 at para. 4 (B.C.C.A.); *R. v. Martens*, [2008] A.J. No. 894, 76 M.V.R. (5th) 163 (Alta. C.A.), leave to appeal refused [2008] S.C.C.A. No. 440 (S.C.C.).

[325] *R. v. Martens*, [2008] A.J. No. 894, 76 M.V.R. (5th) 163 (Alta. C.A.), leave to appeal refused [2008] S.C.C.A. No. 440 (S.C.C.).

[326] See *e.g.*, *R. v. Lewis*, [1998] O.J. No. 376, 122 C.C.C. (3d) 481 (Ont. C.A.). In *Lewis*, a suspect initially detained in an airport concourse was then moved about 20 feet by police to a private room. The Court characterized the decision to move the suspect as "appropriate" (*Ibid.*, at para. 27 (C.C.C.)).

(b)   Roadblock Stops

§2.148 Applying the ancillary powers doctrine, in *R. v. Clayton*[327] the Supreme Court of Canada recognized that the police would occasionally be justified in employing a roadblock for criminal investigative purposes. In *Clayton*, police were responding to a 911 call, which reported that four of about 10 "black guys" in a parking lot in front of a strip club were openly displaying handguns. The caller identified four vehicles. The dispatcher put out a "gun call" and a number of police officers immediately responded to the location. Within five minutes, two police constables travelling in a marked police cruiser positioned their vehicle at the rear exit of the club's parking lot. Almost immediately, a car drove toward the exit. It was not one of the four cars referred to by the 911 caller. Nevertheless, the officers stopped the car, having decided that they would stop any vehicle that happened to exit the parking lot of the strip club. Farmer was driving the car and Clayton was the only passenger. Both men were directed out of the vehicle. After exiting the car, Clayton soon took flight and was subdued by police; he was found to be in possession of a loaded handgun. The main issue on appeal was whether the use of a roadblock was permissible in these circumstances.

§2.149 The Supreme Court of Canada was unanimous in overturning the judgment of the Court of Appeal for Ontario, which had concluded that the ancillary powers doctrine did not authorize police to stop every vehicle leaving the parking lot. Writing for six of the judges, Justice Abella concluded as follows:

> In the totality of the circumstances, therefore, the initial detention in this case was reasonably necessary to respond to the seriousness of the offence and the threat to the police's and public's safety inherent in the presence of prohibited weapons in a public place, and was temporally, geographically and logistically responsive to the circumstances known by the police when it was set up. The initial stop was consequently a justifiable use of police powers associated with the police duty to investigate the offences described by the 911 caller and did not represent an arbitrary detention contrary to s. 9 of the *Charter*.[328]

§2.150 Ultimately, future cases will turn on a fact-specific application of the ancillary powers doctrine. In deciding whether or not to employ a roadblock for criminal investigative purposes, the police would be wise to consider the seriousness of the offence(s) being investigated (less serious and non-violent crimes would probably not qualify). In addition, the police must also be careful to ensure that any roadblock that is deployed is both temporally and geographically connected to the situation that is being investigated. The more removed a roadblock is in time and place from the crime being investigated, the greater the risk that a reviewing court will conclude that it represented an unjustifiable use of police power and therefore fails the second prong of analysis under the ancillary powers doctrine.

---

[327]   [2007] S.C.J. No. 32, [2007] 2 S.C.R. 725 (S.C.C.).
[328]   *Ibid.*, at para. 41 (S.C.R.).

(4)   Arrest Powers

§2.151 Police arrest powers have long been codified in Canada.[329] When it comes to arrests for criminal offences, the *Criminal Code* contains a comprehensive set of police powers. The reader should note, however, that these are not the only arrest powers possessed by police. Though it is beyond the scope of this book, each of the provinces has also specified certain circumstances in which police may arrest for violations of provincial offences.[330] Each of the *Criminal Code* arrest powers is detailed below.

(a)   Defining Arrest (and Keeping it Distinct from Investigative Detention)

§2.152 Defining the concept of "arrest" is important for two reasons. First, properly categorizing a police-citizen encounter is key to assessing its legality and (by necessary implication) its constitutionality under section 9 of the *Charter*. This is because police can conduct an investigative detention based on a less exacting standard (reasonable suspicion) than that required for an arrest (reasonable and probable grounds). Second, as discussed in Chapter 4, "arrest" is one of the two events that trigger the rights set out in section 10 of the *Charter* (the other being "detention", the meaning of which is discussed in Part 3(3)(*b*), above). Fortunately, the courts have adopted a single definition of arrest that governs both the power to arrest and the constitutional obligations that apply once an arrest is undertaken.

§2.153 According to the case law, an arrest "consists of the actual seizure or touching of a person's body with a view to his detention" or, alternatively, the pronouncing of "words of arrest" if "the person sought to be arrested submits to the process and goes with the arresting officer."[331] The failure to use the word "arrest" is not determinative; rather it is the substance of the encounter that matters most — that is, the use of language that reasonably leads an individual to conclude that he or she is in police custody and not free to leave.[332]

§2.154 An arrest has the potential to be much more intrusive, however, than the definitions alone suggest. If the subject offers resistance or attempts to flee, police officers are licensed to use as much force as they consider necessary to ef-

---

[329] The authority to arrest was dealt with in Canada's first Criminal Code. See *Criminal Code, 1892*, S.C. 1892, c. 29, s. 552.

[330] See *e.g.*, *Traffic Safety Act*, R.S.A. 2000, c. T-6, s. 169; *Highway Traffic Act*, R.S.O. 1990, c. H.8, s. 217.

[331] *R. v. Whitfield*, [1969] S.C.J. No. 66, [1970] S.C.R. 46 at 48 (S.C.C.). See also *R. v. Asante-Mensah*, [2003] S.C.J. No. 38, [2003] 2 S.C.R. 3 at paras. 42-45 (S.C.C.).

[332] *R. v. Latimer*, [1997] S.C.J. No. 11, [1997] 1 S.C.R. 217 (S.C.C.). The Court in *Latimer* held that accused, for whom police had reasonable and probable grounds to arrest but who was told he was "being detained for investigation" (*ibid.*, at 225 (S.C.R.)), was placed under *de facto* arrest, as the words used by police made it clear to accused that he was in police custody and he thereafter acquiesced to police authority. *Ibid.*, at 230-32 (S.C.R.). See also *R. v. Asante-Mensah*, [2003] S.C.J. No. 38, [2003] 2 S.C.R. 3 at para. 46 (S.C.C.).

fect an arrest. In certain circumstances, they may even use lethal force.[333] In addition, the use of handcuffs to restrain those arrested is a standard police practice.[334] So is the incidental search, which can vary in intrusiveness from a mere pat-down to complete strip search in some cases.[335] Finally, in the period following an arrest, fingerprints and photographs will also be taken.[336] The hallmarks of an arrest are therefore a prolonged loss of one's freedom of movement (either through acquiescence or physical restraint) coupled with a marked reduction in autonomy and personal privacy.

§2.155 Before moving to examine the specific arrest powers in the *Criminal Code*, it is important to stress the differences between investigative detention (discussed in Part 4(3)(*a*), above) and arrest. As the United States Supreme Court has observed:

> An arrest is a wholly different kind of intrusion upon individual freedom ...
> It is the initial stage of a criminal prosecution. It is intended to vindicate so-
> ciety's interest in having its laws obeyed, and it is inevitably accompanied
> by future interference with the individual's freedom of movement, whether
> or not trial or conviction ultimately follows.[337]

As mentioned, there is a risk that investigative detention, which is supposed to be brief and comparatively unintrusive, may come to resemble *de facto* arrests. This would be most unfortunate. If courts were to authorize the police to routinely handcuff those detained for investigative purposes, to hold those detained for extended periods, to move those held to different locations (like the stationhouse) and to carry out intrusive personal searches, then investigative detentions would in time become indistinguishable from conventional arrests. This would mean that arrest-like encounters would have been licensed by the courts on the basis of a considerably lesser standard than that which Parliament has legislatively mandated for arrests: reasonable and probable grounds. In effect, such a change would impose the harsh consequences of arrest on a much greater number of innocent people.[338] As a result, we hope that the courts, as custodians of this police power, will be fastidious in maintaining a clear distinction between investigative detentions and conventional arrests.[339]

---

[333] See *Criminal Code*, R.S.C. 1985, c. C-46, s. 25(4).

[334] See *Fraser v. Soy* (1918), [1918] N.S.J. No. 5, 30 C.C.C. 367 (N.S.C.A.); *Hamilton v. Massie*, [1889] O.J. No. 143, 18 O.R. 585 (Ont. C.A.). Both cases acknowledge a common law power on the part of the police to use handcuffs to restrain those arrested.

[335] The scope and limits of search incidental to arrest are discussed in detail in Chapter 3, Part 4(2).

[336] See *Identification of Criminals Act*, R.S.C. 1985, c. I-1. Also see *R. v. Beare; R. v. Higgins*, [1987] S.C.J. No. 92, [1988] 2 S.C.R. 387 (S.C.C.) (upholding the constitutionality of this legislation). But if the police choose to compel an accused's appearance in court through less intrusive means, the taking of fingerprints and photographs can be delayed. See §2.187.

[337] *Terry v. Ohio*, 392 U.S. 1 at 26 (1968).

[338] See generally, James Stribopoulos, "The Limits of Judicially Created Police Powers: Investigative Detention After Mann" (2007) 52 Crim. L.Q. 299.

[339] See *R. v. Plummer*, [2011] O.J. No. 2034, 2011 ONCA 350 (Ont. C.A.), wherein Sharpe J.A., in a concurring judgment, in which Laskin J.A. joined, addressed the importance of not expanding the protective search power that can accompany some investigative detentions, by explaining, at para. 76 (O.J.): "A search incidental to an investigative detention is defined and limited by the

(b)　Citizen's Arrest

§2.156 Section 494(1)(*a*) introduces the arrest powers in the *Criminal Code* by recognizing the authority to carry out a "citizen's arrest". The provision allows "[a]ny one", police officers included, to arrest without warrant "a person whom he finds committing an indictable offence".[340] The term "finds committing" has been interpreted by the Supreme Court as meaning "apparently committing".[341] This requires that the "arresting party comes upon someone *in the very act of committing an offence.* In other words, criminal activity must be taking place in the presence of the arresting party."[342] In addition, if there are reasonable grounds to believe that an individual has committed a "criminal offence"[343] and is escaping from and being freshly pursued by those with lawful authority to arrest, then section 495(1)(*b*) authorizes a warrantless arrest.[344] Finally, subsection 494(2) confers an analogous power to arrest on owners or custodians of property if they find someone committing, or (again) apparently committing, a criminal offence in relation to that property.[345]

§2.157 If an arrest is undertaken under any of these provisions, the person carrying out the arrest is then obligated to "forthwith deliver the person to a peace officer."[346] This does not mean instantly but merely as soon as is reasonably possible under all the circumstances.[347]

---

immediate concerns of officer safety. This reflects an important difference between the narrowly focussed and strictly limited protective search that may accompany an investigative detention, and the broader power to search consequent to a lawful arrest. It is necessary to maintain that distinction and to confine the scope of a search incidental to an investigative detention within strict limits. Here, the police did not arrest the appellant, presumably because they did not think they had grounds for an arrest. As the appellant points out, there is an understandable tendency to expand a narrow rule to endorse the police conduct being challenged, since the case before the court will always be one where the search actually yielded a weapon or some other valuable evidence. This is a tendency that the courts should resist."

[340]　*Criminal Code*, R.S.C. 1985, c. C-46, s. 494(1)(*a*).

[341]　See *R. v. Biron*, [1975] S.C.J. No. 64, [1976] 2 S.C.R. 56 at 72 (S.C.C.), where the Court read the analogous language in what is now s. 495(1)(*b*) of the *Criminal Code*, "a person whom he finds committing" as being the equivalent of "apparently committing". See also *R. v. Abel*, [2008] B.C.J. No. 197, 229 C.C.C. (3d) 465 at paras. 31, 63 (B.C.C.A.); *R. c. Sirois*, [1999] Q.J. No. 1079 at para. 13 (C.A.); *R. v. Roberge*, [1983] S.C.J. No. 25, [1983] 1 S.C.R. 312 at 324 (S.C.C.).

[342]　*R. v. Abel*, [2008] B.C.J. No. 197, 229 C.C.C. (3d) 465 at para. 31 (B.C.C.A.) [emphasis in original].

[343]　The use of the term "criminal offence" means that the power extends to both indictable and summary conviction offences. See *Plested v. McLeod* (1910), 3 Sask. L.R. 374 at 378 (Sask. C.A.); *R. v. Johnson* (1924), 42 C.C.C. 279 (Man. C.A.).

[344]　*Criminal Code*, R.S.C. 1985, c. C-46, s. 494(1)(*b*). "Fresh pursuit" requires that the pursuit be conducted with reasonable diligence, so that pursuit and capture along with the commission of the offence may be considered as forming part of a single transaction. See *R. v. Macooh*, [1993] S.C.J. No. 28, [1993] 2 S.C.R. 802 at 816-17 (S.C.C.). But see *R. v. Dean*, [1965] O.J. No. 1129, [1966] 3 C.C.C. 228 at 231 (Ont. C.A.).

[345]　*Criminal Code*, R.S.C. 1985, c. C-46, s. 494(2). See *R. v. Cunningham*, [1979] M.J. No. 355, 49 C.C.C. (2d) 390 at 394 (Man. Co. Ct.).

[346]　*Criminal Code*, R.S.C. 1985, c. C-46, s. 494(3).

[347]　*R. v. Cunningham*, [1979] M.J. No. 355, 49 C.C.C. (2d) 390 at 395 (Man. Co. Ct.).

§2.158 Given that it is rare for the police to be present when an offence is committed they will usually not look to section 494, but to section 495, for their authority to arrest.

(c) Arrests for Indictable Offences Based on Reasonable Grounds

§2.159 The most important arrest power is contained in section 495(1)(a). Under its terms, a police or other peace officer[348] may arrest without a warrant a person whom, "on reasonable grounds, he believes has committed or is about to commit an indictable offence."[349] This provision is essential to the police, who must usually form their grounds for arrest based on information supplied to them by the public. It allows an officer "to act on his belief, if based on reasonable and probable grounds."[350] In addition, it also licenses a proactive response, so that a police officer can arrest an individual who has taken the preparatory steps toward committing a crime rather than awaiting its actual commission.[351]

§2.160 The reasonable and probable grounds standard has been defined as "an honest belief in the guilt of the accused based upon a full conviction, founded upon reasonable grounds, of the existence of a state of circumstances, which, assuming them to be true, would reasonably lead any ordinarily prudent and cautious man, placed in the position of the accuser, to the conclusion that the person charged was probably guilty of the crime imputed."[352] In other words, the standard has both subjective and objective components. Not only must the arresting officer personally believe that he or she possesses the required grounds to arrest, those grounds must be objectively established, in the sense that a rea-

---

[348] "Peace officer" is defined rather expansively under s. 2 of the *Criminal Code*, R.S.C. 1985, c. C-46, essentially to include anyone who discharges a public law enforcement function, including a "police officer, police constable, bailiff, constable, or other person employed for the preservation and maintenance of the public peace or for the service or execution of civil process". *Ibid.*

[349] *Criminal Code*, R.S.C. 1985, c. C-46, s. 495(1)(a). The provision begins by also indicating that a peace officer may arrest without warrant "a person who has committed an indictable offence". This introductory language would appear to validate arrests, provided that guilt is subsequently established. See Canada, Law Commission of Canada, *Arrest, Working Paper 41* (Ottawa: Supply & Services Canada, 1985) at 48. But these words have been effectively read out of s. 495(1)(a). See *R. v. Storrey*, [1990] S.C.J. No. 12, [1990] 1 S.C.R. 241 at 249 (S.C.C.), indicating that what is now 495(1)(a), "makes it clear that the police were required to have reasonable and probable grounds that [the accused] had committed the offence".

[350] *R. v. Biron*, [1975] S.C.J. No. 64, [1976] 2 S.C.R. 56 at 72 (S.C.C.). Prior to 1985, s. 495(1)(a) specified that an officer must have "reasonable *and probable* grounds"; see *Bail Reform Act*, R.S.C. 1970, c. 2 (2nd Supp.), s. 450(1)(a). Following a recommendation by the Law Reform Commission of Canada, the word "probable" was removed. See *Criminal Code*, R.S.C. 1985, c. C-46, deleting the reference to "probable" in ss. 495(1)(a), 495(1)(c) and 495(2)(d). Since then it has been held that, "reasonableness comprehends a requirement of probability. The meaning of the section has not changed with the amendment." See *R. v. Smellie*, [1994] B.C.J. No. 2850, 95 C.C.C. (3d) 9 at 17 (B.C.C.A.), leave to appeal refused [1995] S.C.C.A. No. 64, 97 C.C.C. (3d) vi (S.C.C.).

[351] See *R. v. Beaudette*, [1957] O.J. No. 440, 118 C.C.C. 295 (Ont. C.A.).

[352] *Hicks v. Faulkner* (1878), 8 Q.B.D. 167 at 171, *per* Hawkins J. (Div. Ct.), affd (1882), 46 L.T. 130 (C.A.). See also *Herniman v. Smith*, [1938] A.C. 305 at 316 (H.L.). This definition was adopted by the Supreme Court of Canada in *Nelles v. Ontario*, [1989] S.C.J. No. 86, [1989] 2 S.C.R. 170 at 193 (S.C.C.).

sonable person standing in the shoes of the officer would believe that there were reasonable and probable grounds to make an arrest.[353]

§2.161 The Supreme Court has elaborated on the meaning of the reasonable and probable grounds standard by placing it along a spectrum. According to the Court, it imports a standard of reasonable probability, which entails something less than proof beyond a reasonable doubt or a *prima facie* case[354] but something more substantial than reasonable suspicion,[355] and much further along the spectrum than mere possibility or suspicion.[356] Based on this approach the standard is said to be met at "the point where credibly-based probability replaces suspicion."[357]

§2.162 As with reasonable suspicion (discussed above in Part 4(3)(*a*)(i)), whether or not the reasonable and probable grounds standard is satisfied ultimately turns on the facts. The courts have established few bright line rules. To date, the most concrete guidance has been a few rather obvious admonishments to police. In deciding whether or not to arrest, the police have been told to investigate thoroughly, consider all available information and disregard only that which they have good reason to believe is unreliable.[358] With few exceptions,[359] the courts have demonstrated a consistent reluctance to propose any rigid criteria as to what will constitute sufficient grounds for an arrest. The usual approach for the courts is to recite the facts involved in the case and then announce whether or not those particular facts constitute reasonable and probable grounds.

§2.163 This is not intended as a criticism. To the contrary, although an enumeration of relevant factors on some generalized level of abstraction is possi-

---

[353] *R. v. Storrey*, [1990] S.C.J. No. 12, [1990] 1 S.C.R. 241 at 250-51 (S.C.C.). See also *R. v. Feeney*, [1997] S.C.J. No. 49, [1997] 2 S.C.R. 13 at 40 (S.C.C.), concluding that "[a]ny finding that the subjective test is not met will generally imply that the objective test is not met, unless the officer is to be considered to have an unreasonably high standard."

[354] See *R. v. DeBot*, [1989] S.C.J. No. 118, [1989] 2 S.C.R. 1140 at 1166 (S.C.C.). See also *R. v. Storrey*, [1990] S.C.J. No. 12, [1990] 1 S.C.R. 241 at 250-51 (S.C.C.).

[355] See §2.124, above, and supporting footnotes.

[356] *Baron v. Canada*, [1993] S.C.J. No. 6, [1993] 1 S.C.R. 416 at 448 (S.C.C.).

[357] *Hunter v. Southam (sub nom. Canada (Combines Investigation Acts, Director of Investigation and Research) v. Southam Inc.)*, [1984] S.C.J. No. 36, [1984] 2 S.C.R. 145 at 167 (S.C.C.). The standard is discussed in more detail in Chapter 3, Parts 2(5)(*b*)(ii) and 3(3)(*a*).

[358] See *Chartier v. Quebec (Attorney General)*, [1979] S.C.J. No. 56, [1979] 2 S.C.R. 474 at 499 (S.C.C.). See also *R. v. Storrey*, [1990] S.C.J. No. 12, [1990] 1 S.C.R. 241 at 249-51 (S.C.C.); *Oniel v. Toronto (Metropolitan) Police Force*, [2001] O.J. No. 90, 195 D.L.R. (4th) 59 at 85 (Ont. C.A.), leave to appeal refused [1998] S.C.C.A. No. 68 (S.C.C.); *R. v. Golub*, [1997] O.J. No. 3097, 117 C.C.C. (3d) 193 at 203 (Ont. C.A.), leave to appeal refused [1997] S.C.C.A. No. 571 (S.C.C.); *R. v. Hall*, [1995] O.J. No. 544, 39 C.R. (4th) 66 at 73-75 (Ont. C.A.); *R. c. Proulx*, [1993] J.Q. no 422, 81 C.C.C. (3d) 48 at 51 (Que. C.A.).

[359] For example, absent confirmation of details other than those describing innocent and commonplace conduct, a tip from an untested, anonymous informant cannot, standing alone, supply adequate grounds for an arrest. See *R. v. Lewis*, [1998] O.J. No. 376, 122 C.C.C. (3d) 481 at 490 (Ont. C.A.); *R. c. Bennett*, 1996] J.Q. no 545, 108 C.C.C. (3d) 175 at 181-85 (Que. C.A.). In addition, the odour of burnt marijuana alone has been held inadequate to justify an arrest. See *R. v. Polashek*, [1999] O.J. No. 968, 134 C.C.C. (3d) 187 at 194 (Ont. C.A.); *R. v. Janvier*, [2007] S.J. No. 646, 227 C.C.C. (3d) 294 (Sask. C.A.).

ble,[360] there is an undoubted cost for the certainty that such an approach might purchase; namely, denying police the flexibility they need to respond to the myriad factual situations they confront in the field. As the United States Supreme Court stated in dealing with the analogous standard under the Fourth Amendment: "[p]robable cause is a fluid concept — turning on the assessment of probabilities in particular factual contexts — not readily, or even usefully, reduced to a neat set of legal rules."[361]

(d)   Arrests for Summary Offences

§2.164   The arrest power for summary offences is set out in section 495(1)(*b*) of the *Criminal Code*, which authorizes police and other peace officers to arrest without a warrant "a person whom he finds committing a criminal offence." Given sections 494(1)(*a*) and 495(1)(*b*), this provision is redundant as it relates to indictable offences. Its sole function is to bestow a limited power on police officers to arrest individuals who are discovered committing, or as interpreted by the Supreme Court of Canada, *apparently committing* summary conviction offences.[362] If a police officer does not witness the offence then he or she must procure a warrant before carrying out an arrest.[363] (Of course, where the police wish to charge an individual with a summary offence they have a number of options for compelling that person's attendance in court short of arrest. These various options are explained below in Part 4(4)(*h*).)

(e)   Arrests for Outstanding Warrants

§2.165   The final provision in the series is section 495(1)(*c*), which authorizes police and other peace officers to arrest if they have "reasonable grounds to believe that a warrant of arrest or committal" is outstanding within the "territorial jurisdiction in which the person is found."[364]

§2.166   This provision allows an officer who has the requisite grounds to arrest to obtain a warrant and have it registered on the Canadian Police Information Computer, so that any other police officers who encounter the subject can also effect an arrest.

---

[360]   For such an effort, see American Law Institute, *A Model Code of Pre-Arraignment Procedure* (Washington, D.C.: 1975) ss. 120.1(2), (3). For an exhaustive list of the type of factors and information that may provide cause for an arrest, see Wayne R. LaFave, *Arrest: The Decision to Take a Suspect into Custody* (Boston: Little, Brown & Co., 1965) at 244-99.

[361]   *Illinois v. Gates*, 426 U.S. 213 at 232 (1983). The Supreme Court of Canada has characterized the two standards as "identical". *Canada (Combines Investigation Acts, Director of Investigation and Research) v. Southam Inc.*, [1984] S.C.J. No. 36, [1984] 2 S.C.R. 145 at 167 (S.C.C.).

[362]   *R. v. Biron*, [1975] S.C.J. No. 64, [1976] 2 S.C.R. 56 at 71-75 (S.C.C.). It will be remembered from Chapter 1, Part 2(3)(*b*), that there are relatively few "summary offences" when it comes to police arrest powers. With respect to hybrid offences, until the Crown elects to proceed summarily, they are deemed to be indictable offences and thereby attract the far more generous indictable offence arrest power. See *Interpretation Act*, R.S.C. 1985, c. I-21, s. 34(1)(*a*).

[363]   See Bruce P. Archibald, "The Law of Arrest" in Vincent M. Del Buono, ed., Criminal Procedure in Canada: Studies (Toronto: Butterworths, 1982) 125 at 138; *R. v. Stevens*, [1976] N.S.J. No. 476, 33 C.C.C. (2d) 429 at 434 (N.S.C.A.).

[364]   *Criminal Code*, R.S.C. 1985, c. C-46, s. 495(1)(*c*).

§2.167 Arrest warrants are obtained pursuant to section 507 of the *Criminal Code*. The process by which arrest warrants are obtained is explained in detail in Chapter 5, Part 4.

§2.168 Once an arrest warrant is issued, any police officer with knowledge of the warrant who encounters the individual named in it is authorized to arrest pursuant to section 495(1)(*c*).

§2.169 The authority conferred under this provision does not depend upon actual possession of the warrant or knowledge of its contents. When acting under this paragraph, "the duty of the arresting officer is fully discharged by telling the arrested person the reason for his arrest is the existence of an outstanding warrant."[365]

(f)   Arrests for Breach of the Peace

§2.170 Lastly there is the power in section 31(1) of the *Criminal Code* to arrest any person a police officer or another peace officer "finds committing" a "breach of the peace or who, on reasonable grounds, he believes is about to join in or renew a breach of the peace."[366] According to the authorities, a "breach of the peace" includes "riots, tumults, or actual physical violence".[367]

§2.171 The Law Reform Commission recommended the elimination of this power because it is premised on an "exceedingly vague" standard.[368] It also gives rise to post-arrest confusion, as there is no offence in the *Criminal Code* of "breaching the peace", as there was at common law. It is therefore unclear as to how long an individual can be held following such an arrest and what procedures, if any, can be carried out as an incident thereto.[369] That lack of certainty makes this provision especially vulnerable to a challenge under section 9 of the *Charter*. Without clear direction to police as to how long they can hold those arrested pursuant to this power, the liberty of the individual affected seems to turn on little more than the whim of the arresting officer; it is difficult to conceive of a power to detain more arbitrary than that. (The requirements of section 9 of the *Charter* were detailed above in Part 3(4)(*b*).)

§2.172 Unfortunately, because arrests under section 31(1) do not give rise to any charge or court proceeding, the extent to which police make recourse to this power is unknown. Quite obviously, the low visibility of section 31(1) breach of

---

[365] *R. v. Gamracy*, [1973] S.C.J. No. 100, [1974] S.C.R. 640 at 643 (S.C.C.) (interpreting s. 29 of the *Criminal Code)*. But see the *Charter* s. 10(a) guaranteeing on arrest or detention the right "to be informed promptly of the *reasons* therefor" [emphasis added].

[366] *Criminal Code*, R.S.C. 1985, c. C-46, s. 31(1).

[367] *Frey v. Fedoruk*, [1950] S.C.J. No. 21, [1950] S.C.R. 517 at 524, 529 (S.C.C.). See also Glanville L. Williams, "Arrest for Breach of the Peace" [1954] Crim. L. Rev. 578 at 578, indicating that a "breach of the peace" includes riots, unlawful assemblies or simply fighting; *R. v. Howell*, [1982] Q.B. 416, 78 Cr. App. R. 31 at 37 (C.A.) (same).

[368] Canada, Law Commission of Canada, *Arrest, Working Paper 41* (Ottawa: Supply & Services Canada, 1985) at 62.

[369] See *R. v. Lefebvre*, [1982] B.C.J. No. 1038, 1 C.C.C. (3d) 241 at 244 (B.C. Co. Ct.), affd (1984), [1984] B.C.J. No. 3153, 15 C.C.C. (3d) 503 (B.C.C.A.); *R. v. Januska*, [1996] O.J. No. 2883, 106 C.C.C. (3d) 183 (Ont. Gen. Div.).

peace arrests is a further cause for concern regarding the potential for abuse of this power.

(g) Entering a Dwelling-House to Arrest: Feeney Warrants

§2.173 In *R. v. Feeney*,[370] the Supreme Court of Canada revisited the common law governing the authority of police to enter a private residence to affect an arrest.[371] The Court held that section 8 of the *Charter* — the right to be secure against unreasonable search or seizure — requires that, absent hot pursuit, before police enter a residence to effect an arrest, they obtain prior judicial authorization for the entry. To comply with section 8, such a warrant should only issue if there are reasonable grounds for the arrest and reasonable grounds to believe that the person will be found at the address named. The Court subsequently stayed the effect of its decision in *Feeney* for six months, in order to permit the government to enact this sort of warrant scheme.[372]

§2.174 Parliament responded by enacting section 529 of the *Criminal Code*. When issuing an arrest warrant, that section gives authority to the justice to also authorize the police to enter "a dwelling-house described in the warrant for the purpose of arresting or apprehending the person if the judge or justice is satisfied by information on oath in writing that there are reasonable grounds to believe that the person is or will be present in the dwelling-house."[373] In addition, where a conventional arrest warrant has already been obtained for an indictable offence, the police may apply for a Form 7.1 warrant to authorize their entry into a residence to effect an arrest on making a similar showing.[374] In either situation, if a police officer believes it would be impracticable to personally attend before a justice to seek either type of warrant, an application may be made over the phone or by fax.[375]

§2.175 The need for a warrant applies whether the police wish to arrest a suspect at his or her residence or at the residence of some third party. The Court of Appeal for Ontario has held that there is nothing in section 529 or in *Feeney* to suggest that a warrant is not required for an arrest in the dwelling-house of a third party.[376] The police will not require a warrant to enter a third party's resi-

---

[370] [1997] S.C.J. No. 49, [1997] 2 S.C.R. 13 (S.C.C.).

[371] At common law the police could enter a private residence to effect an arrest if the following preconditions were satisfied: (*i*) the officer had reasonable grounds to believe that the person sought was within the premises; (*ii*) proper announcement was made; (*iii*) the officer believed reasonable grounds for the arrest existed; and (*iv*) objectively speaking, reasonable and probable grounds for the arrest did exist. See *R. v. Feeney*, [1997] S.C.J. No. 49, [1997] 2 S.C.R. 13 at para. 24 (S.C.C.). See also *Eccles v. Bourque*, [1974] S.C.J. No. 123, [1975] 2 S.C.R. 739 (S.C.C.); *R. v. Landry*, [1986] S.C.J. No. 10, [1986] 1 S.C.R. 145 (S.C.C.).

[372] *R. v. Feeney (Application)*, [1997] S.C.J. No. 80, [1997] 2 S.C.R. 117 (S.C.C.).

[373] *Criminal Code*, R.S.C. 1985, c. C-46 s. 529(1).

[374] *Ibid.*, s. 529(2).

[375] *Ibid.*, s. 529.5. Section 487.1 applies to such applications subject to any modifications that the circumstances require.

[376] See *R. v. Adams*, [2001] O.J. No. 3240, 157 C.C.C. (3d) 220 at para. 6 (Ont. C.A.).

dence, however, where the homeowner is present and gives police informed consent to enter without a warrant.[377]

§2.176 A *Feeney* warrant is time sensitive, in the sense that the person to be arrested could move and the officer's grounds could become stale. As a result, all such warrants are subject to "the condition that the peace officer may not enter the dwelling-house unless the peace officer has, immediately before entering the dwelling-house, reasonable grounds to believe that the person to be arrested or apprehended is present in the dwelling-house."[378]

§2.177 The *Criminal Code* preserves the hot-pursuit exception for entry that existed at common law.[379] According to the definition adopted by the Supreme Court, "hot-pursuit" exists where the officer is in "continuous pursuit conducted with reasonable diligence, so that pursuit and capture along with the commission of the offence may be considered as forming part of a single transaction."[380] In other words, a police officer is not required to pause and obtain a warrant where "the officer is literally at the heels of a suspect at the moment that suspect enters a dwelling-house."[381]

§2.178 Beyond hot pursuit, the relevant section also carves out a generous exigency exception. Provided a police officer has reasonable grounds to believe that the person to be arrested is present in a particular residence, he or she can dispense with the need for prior judicial approval if "by reason of exigent circumstances it would be impracticable to obtain a warrant."[382] The *Code* goes on to specify two non-exhaustive examples of "exigent circumstances"; first where police have reasonable grounds to suspect that entry is necessary to prevent imminent bodily harm or death; and second, where they have reasonable grounds to believe that evidence relating to the commission of an offence is present in the residence and entry is necessary to prevent its imminent loss or destruction.[383]

§2.179 Police entering private premises pursuant to the authority of a warrant must usually comply with an announcement requirement developed at common law. In the ordinary course, before forcing entry, the police are required to give

---

[377] See *e.g.*, *R. v. Guiboche*, [2004] M.J. No. 43, 183 C.C.C. (3d) 361 at para. 59 (Man. C.A.). On the requirements for consent to search and seize more generally, see Chapter 3, Search and Seizure, Part 2(4)(*c*).

[378] *Criminal Code*, R.S.C. 1985, c. C-46, s. 529(2).

[379] *R. v. Van Puyenbroek*, [2007] O.J. No. 4689, 226 C.C.C. (3d) 289 at para. 31 (Ont. C.A.). According to the Court in *Van Puyenbroek*, the opening words of s. 529.3(1) preserve the common law hot pursuit exception In particular, s. 529.3(1) provides that "Without limiting or restricting any power a peace officer may have to enter a dwelling-house under this or any other Act *or law*..." [emphasis added].

[380] *R. v. Macooh*, [1993] S.C.J. No. 28, [1993] 2 S.C.R. 802 (S.C.C.) adopting with approval the definition from Roger E. Salhany, *Canadian Criminal Procedure*, 5th ed. (Canada Law Book: Toronto, 1989) at 44.

[381] *R. v. Van Puyenbroek*, [2007] O.J. No. 4689, 226 C.C.C. (3d) 289 at para. 32 (Ont. C.A.).

[382] *Criminal Code*, R.S.C. 1985, c. C-46, s. 529.3(1).

[383] *Ibid.*, s. 529.3(2). For an example of exigent circumstances occasioned by the potential escape of a suspect or the loss of evidence, see *R. v. Duong*, [2002] B.C.J. No. 90, 162 C.C.C. (3d) 242 (B.C.C.A.), leave to appeal refused [2002] S.C.C.A. No. 112 (S.C.C.).

(*i*) notice of presence by knocking or ringing the doorbell, (*ii*) notice of authority, by identifying themselves as law enforcement officers and (*iii*) notice of purpose, by stating a lawful reason for entry (*i.e.*, "arrest warrant"). Minimally, they should request admission and have admission denied. The Supreme Court has recognized, however, that there will be occasions when exigent circumstances may allow police to dispense with the notice requirements. Examples provided by the court include when it is necessary to save someone within the premises from death or injury, to prevent the destruction of evidence or if in hot pursuit.[384]

§2.180 Tracking the common law, the *Feeney* warrant provisions specifically empower the justice issuing the warrant to authorize police to dispense with the announcement requirement if satisfied that there are reasonable grounds to believe that prior announcement of the entry would either expose the police or some other person to imminent bodily harm or death, or result in the imminent loss or destruction of evidence.[385] The relevant provisions also specifically authorize police officers who enter to arrest without a warrant in exigent circumstances to dispense with the announcement requirement in the same circumstances.[386]

§2.181 Finally, a justice issuing a *Feeney* warrant has the authority to include any terms and conditions within it that he or she considers advisable to ensure the entry is undertaken in a reasonable manner.[387]

(h) The Duty Not to Arrest or To Release Following Arrest — Police Bail

§2.182 Any discussion of the arrest powers in the *Criminal Code* would be incomplete without a consideration of section 495(2). This section has been described as suffering from "bewildering complexity".[388] It was added to the *Code* in the early 1970s, amidst concerns that police were exercising their arrest pow-

---

[384] See generally, *R. v. Cornell*, [2010] S.C.J. No. 31, [2010] 2 S.C.R. 142 (S.C.C.); *Eccles v. Bourque*, [1974] S.C.J. No. 123, [1975] 2 S.C.R. 739 (S.C.C.); *R. v. Feeney*, [1997] S.C.J. No. 49, [1997] 2 S.C.R. 13 (S.C.C.). See, for example, *R. v. Gimson*, [1990] O.J. No. 354, 54 C.C.C. (3d) 232 (Ont. C.A.), affd without reasons [1991] S.C.J. No. 104, [1991] 3 S.C.R. 692 (S.C.C.) (involving a no-knock entry to preserve evidence); *R. v. Genest*, [1989] S.C.J. No. 5, [1989] 1 S.C.R. 59 (S.C.C.) (involving a no-knock entry based on a legitimate fear of violence directed toward the police and third parties); *R. v. Cornell*, [2010] S.C.J. No. 31, [2010] 2 S.C.R. 142 (S.C.C.) (no-knock entry involving the execution of a search warrant where police were investigating a violent street gang and were looking for cocaine, violent nature of gang and potential destruction of cocaine were said to justify no-knock forced entry).

[385] *Criminal Code*, R.S.C. 1985, c. C-46, s. 529.4(1). Even when so authorized, however, the officers acting under the authority of such a warrant must turn their minds to whether the justification for dispensing with the knock and announce requirement persists immediately before effecting entry. See *Criminal Code*, s. 529.4(2).

[386] *Criminal Code*, s. 529.4(3).

[387] *Ibid.*, s. 529.2.

[388] Don Stuart, *Charter Justice in Canadian Criminal Law*, 3d ed. (Toronto: Carswell, 2001) at 260.

ers unnecessarily.[389] Parliament responded with the *Bail Reform Act*.[390] The principal purpose of these reforms was to minimize the unnecessary use of police arrest powers and to liberalize pre-trial release procedures more generally. (The Act's considerable effects on the Canadian bail system are detailed in Chapter 6.)

§2.183 Once a police officer decides that he or she has the required grounds to carry out an arrest, section 495(2) directs the officer not to arrest for less serious indictable offences, hybrid offences and summary conviction offences,[391] if there are reasonable grounds to believe an arrest unnecessary in the "public interest". In assessing the "public interest", an officer is directed to consider "all the circumstances", including the need to establish identity, secure or preserve evidence, or prevent the continuation of the offence or the commission of some other crime.[392] An arrest is also permissible if there are reasonable grounds to believe that the person will fail to attend court in answer to the charge.[393]

§2.184 There is an ongoing obligation on the arresting officer to release if the circumstances change,[394] as well as an obligation upon the officer in charge of the station to reconsider these same factors once an accused is back at the station-house.[395]

§2.185 Should police choose not to arrest, or to release, there are a number of less coercive means by which to secure an individual's attendance in court. Attendance may be compelled through an appearance notice,[396] a promise to ap-

---

[389] See Martin L. Friedland, *Detention Before Trial: A Study of Criminal Cases Tried in the Toronto Magistrates' Courts* (Toronto: University of Toronto Press, 1965) (during the period from 1958 to 1962 in Toronto, arrests were preferred in 91 to 97 per cent of cases, despite the ability to simply summons. *Ibid.*, at 9.) See also *Report of the Canadian Committee on Corrections, Towards Unity: Criminal Justice and Corrections* (Ottawa: Queen's Printer, 1969) at 108-15 (Chair: Roger Ouimet).

[390] R.S.C. 1970, c. 2 (2nd Supp.).

[391] See *Criminal Code*, R.S.C. 1985, c. C-46, ss. 495(2)(*a*) (offences in s. 553, *e.g.*, theft, fraud, mischief); 495(2)(*b*) (hybrid offences); 495(2)(*c*) (summary conviction offences). Also see s. 503(4), which imposes an analogous obligation to release anyone who is arrested on the basis that there were reasonable grounds to believe they were about to commit an indictable offence.

[392] *Criminal Code*, R.S.C. 1985, c, C-46, s. 495(2)(*d*)(i)-(iii). See *e.g.*, *R. v. Tomlinson*, [2009] B.C.J. No. 899, 2009 BCCA 196 (B.C.C.A.), where the Court rejected a challenge to the failure to release an accused where police refrained from releasing because their investigation remained ongoing and they were about to execute a search warrant at the arrestee's residence. The Court concluded that holding the accused in these circumstances was in the "public interest".

[393] *Criminal Code*, R.S.C. 1985, c. C-46, s. 495(2)(*e*).

[394] *Ibid.*, s. 497(1), (1.1).

[395] *Ibid.*, ss. 498(1), (1.1). The officer in charge has the added power to release for any indictable offence punishable by a maximum of not more than five years.

[396] An appearance notice is in Form 9. See *Criminal Code*, R.S.C. 1985, c. C-46, s. 493. An appearance notice may be used if the officer *does not arrest* the person because of s. 495(2) and the offence that the individual is to be charged with is either an absolute jurisdiction indictable offence listed in s. 553 (*Criminal Code*, s. 496(*a*)), a hybrid offence, *i.e.*, an offence that can be prosecuted either summarily or by indictment (*Criminal Code*, s. 496(b)), or a pure summary offence (*Criminal Code*, s. 496(*c*)).

pear,[397] a summons[398] or a recognizance entered into before the officer in charge.[399]

§2.186 Somewhat inexplicably, the *Criminal Code* sets out one last chance for release by police unconstrained by many of the preconditions found in the various sections just described. Under section 503(2), "a peace officer or an officer in charge" may release someone charged with an offence, with the exception of one of those very serious offences listed in section 469 (*i.e.*, murder), if the officer "is satisfied that the person ... should be released".[400] If this authority is exercised, the individual can be released either on a promise to appear, a recognizance or an undertaking with conditions.[401]

§2.187 Each of these various forms of police issued process will name the accused, set out the substance of the offence(s) alleged and require the accused to attend court on a date specified and thereafter as required by the court.[402] In addition, each may require the accused to attend to be fingerprinted and photographed.[403] Finally, each must set out the text for the *Criminal Code* offences of failing to attend court and failing to attend for fingerprinting or photographing, serving to put the accused on notice of the legal obligation to comply.[404] With

---

[397] A promise to appear is in Form 10. See *Criminal Code*, R.S.C. 1985, c. C-46, s. 493. A promise to appear is used in two situations where an individual *is arrested*. First, if the person is to be charged with an absolute jurisdiction, hybrid or summary offence but the arresting officer believes on reasonable grounds that the various "public interest" factors do not warrant holding the person in custody (*Criminal Code*. s. 497). Second, in the very same circumstances, the officer in charge of the station must also release but with the added power on his or her part to also do so "for any other offence that is punishable by imprisonment for five years or less" (*Criminal Code*, ss. 498(1)(*b*), 498(1.1)).

[398] A summons is in Form 6. See *Criminal Code*, R.S.C. 1985, c. C-46, s. 493. If an individual is initially arrested for an absolute jurisdiction, hybrid or summary offence or any other offence that is punishable by imprisonment for five years or less and the officer in charge believes on reasonable grounds that the various "public interest" factors do not warrant holding the person in custody, then the officer in charge must release the person with the intention of compelling their appearance in court by way of a summons. See *Criminal Code*, ss. 498(1)(*a*), 498(1.1).

[399] A recognizance entered into before the officer in charge is in Form 11. See *Criminal Code*, R.S.C. 1985, c. C-46, s. 493. A recognizance entered into before the officer in charge can be used in two situations. First, if an individual is initially arrested for an absolute jurisdiction, hybrid or summary offence or any other offence that is punishable by imprisonment for five years or less and the officer in charge believes on reasonable grounds that the various "public interest" factors do not warrant holding the person in custody, then the officer in charge must release the person on the person's entering into a recognizance for an amount not exceeding $500 that the officer directs but without deposit of money or valuable security (*Criminal Code*, ss. 498(1)(*c*), 498(1.1)). Second, in the very same circumstances just detailed, where the person arrested does not reside within the province or within 200 kilometres, then the officer in charge may also require the depositing of a sum of money or other valuable security not exceeding the amount or value $500 (*Criminal Code*, ss. 498(1)(*d*), 498(1.1))

[400] *Criminal Code*, R.S.C. 1985, c. C-46, s. 503(2). See generally, *R. v. L. (M.C.)*, [2005] O.J. No. 1500, 196 C.C.C. (3d) 571 (Ont. C.J.).

[401] *Criminal Code*, R.S.C. 1985, c. C-46, s. 503(2). An undertaking is in Form 11.1 or Form 12. See *Criminal Code*, s. 493. For the various conditions that can be included in the undertaking, see *Criminal Code*, s. 503(2.1).

[402] *Criminal Code*, R.S.C. 1985, c. C-46, s. 501(1).

[403] *Ibid.*, s. 501(3). Fingerprinting and photographing takes place under the authority of the *Identification of Criminals Act*, R.S.C. 1985, c. I-1.

[404] *Criminal Code*, R.S.C. 1985, c. C-46, s. 501(2).

each of these various forms of police issued process, the *Code* requires that an accused be requested to sign the document and be provided with a copy.[405] The accused person's failure or refusal to sign the document does not affect its validity.[406]

§2.188 With the exception of section 503(2), which confers relatively unfettered discretion, the various sections described above appear to impose a legal obligation on police either to not arrest or to release, when it appears unnecessary to hold an accused person in custody In reality, however, there are rarely ramifications for disregarding these provisions. Police decisions are deemed lawful for the purposes of an accused's trial.[407] This does not foreclose a civil suit for false imprisonment but, absent an admission that the police completely failed to consider their release obligations, success is unlikely.[408] A police officer's assertion that the decision to arrest, or not to release, was based on principled rather than punitive considerations will be difficult to refute.[409] It is not surprising then that the Law Reform Commission of Canada concluded that these provisions, deeming police conduct lawful, almost run the obligation to release "into a charade".[410]

---

[405] *Ibid.*, s. 501(4).

[406] *Ibid.*

[407] *Criminal Code*, R.S.C. 1985, c. C-46, ss. 495(3)(*a*), 497(3)(*a*), 498(3)(*a*). Also see *R. v. Cayer*, [1988] O.J. No. 1120, 66 C.R. (3d) 30 at 42 (Ont. C.A.); *R. v. Adams*, [1972] S.J. No. 295, 21 C.R.N.S. 257 (Sask. C.A.); *R. v. McKibbon*, [1973] B.C.J. No. 766, 12 C.C.C. (2d) 66 (B.C.C.A.).

[408] See *Kucher v. Guasparini*, [1998] B.C.J. No. 582 (B.C.S.C.) (for a rare example). See also *Collins v. Brantford Police Services Board*, [2001] O.J. No. 3778, 204 D.L.R. (4th) 660 at 667 (Ont. C.A.), noting that to succeed the plaintiff must establish that the arresting officer "believed on reasonable grounds that the public interest, having regard to all the circumstances, could be satisfied without arresting [the plaintiff]."

[409] Bruce P. Archibald, "The Law of Arrest" in Vincent M. Del Buono, ed., *Criminal Procedure in Canada: Studies* (Toronto: Butterworths, 1982) 125 at 143. See *e.g.*, *Abbey (Guardian ad litem of) v. Dallin*, [1991] B.C.J. No. 108 (B.C.S.C.).

[410] Canada, Law Commission of Canada, *Arrest, Working Paper 41* (Ottawa: Supply & Services Canada, 1985) at 81.

Chapter 3

SEARCH AND SEIZURE

1. INTRODUCTION

§3.1 Privacy is a pillar of freedom. Individuals understandably cherish their ability to control the dissemination of information about their personal lives. In short, privacy is integral to human autonomy and dignity. Protecting it against unjustified state intrusion is therefore an essential feature of liberty in any free society.

§3.2 Although a key aspect of individual liberty, privacy also has its dark side. Like the law-abiding, criminals value their privacy. Privacy cloaks all aspects of human activity, both the intimate and the unlawful. As a result, the state will sometimes have compelling reasons for invading privacy. Given this, an inevitable tension arises between our desire to maintain privacy because of its importance to individual freedom and the state's interest in encroaching upon it in order to protect societal interests — especially law enforcement. This chapter details how Canadian law currently attempts to strike this delicate but important balance.

§3.3 The rules governing police powers of search and seizure are arguably the most complex aspect of Canadian criminal procedure. This is due to the number of sources that must be drawn upon in order to sketch out the parameters of police authority. Unfortunately, there is no central repository for all the relevant rules. Rather, gaining a complete sense of the scope and limits on police authority to search for and seize evidence requires that a number of different sources be consulted, including myriad statutory provisions, case law interpreting these legislated police powers, and the judgments of courts that identify and define the parameters of certain "common law" search powers.

§3.4 In addition, these various sources of police authority must all be read in light of the vaguely worded constitutional guarantee found in section 8 of the *Canadian Charter of Rights and Freedoms*,[1] which provides that "[e]veryone has the right to be secure against unreasonable search or seizure." Familiarity with the Supreme Court of Canada's jurisprudence interpreting section 8 of the *Charter* is essential to gaining an understanding of the law of search and seizure.

§3.5 This chapter will draw on these various sources in an effort to piece together a complete picture of this complex area of law.

---

[1] Part I of the *Constitution Act, 1982*, being Schedule B to the *Canada Act 1982* (U.K.), 1982, c. 11 [*Charter*].

(1)   Search and Seizure at Common Law

§3.6 Limitations on the state's power to search and seize have a long history within the Anglo-American legal world. As early as 1604, in *Semayne's Case*,[2] Lord Coke pronounced his now famous declaration that "the house of everyone is to him as his castle and fortress."[3]

§3.7 The modern genesis of these protections is often traced back to *Entick v. Carrington*.[4] Like with most early search and seizure cases, the decision was the result of a civil suit. Entick sued Carrington who, along with three other men, entered his home and over several hours searched for and seized a number of his private papers. The men were acting on the orders of the newly appointed Secretary of State for the Northern Department, who had signed a warrant ostensibly authorizing the men to search Entick's home and secure evidence of sedition. Entick sued Carrington and his colleagues, arguing that they had acted unlawfully and that they were liable as trespassers. Carrington and his colleagues argued that they had acted upon the authority of a warrant issued by the Secretary of State. The main issue before the Court was whether the Secretary of State had the authority to issue such a warrant. The Court concluded that he did not and ruled for the plaintiff. In the course of delivering judgment, Chief Justice Camden made a number of now famous pronouncements about the protection afforded to the individual by the common law. For example, he stated:

> ... By the laws of England, every invasion of private property, be it ever so minute, is a trespass. No man can set his foot upon my ground without my license, but he is liable to an action, though the damage be nothing; which is proved by every declaration in trespass, where the defendant is called upon to answer for bruising the grass and even treading upon the soil. If he admits the fact, he is bound to show by way of justification, that some positive law has empowered or excused him. The justification is submitted to the judges, who are to look into the books; and if such a justification can be maintained by the text of the statute law, or by the principles of common law. If no excuse can be found or produced, the silence of the books is an authority against the defendant, and the plaintiff must have judgment.

> According to this reasoning, it is now incumbent upon the defendants to show the law by which this seizure is warranted. If that cannot be done, it is a trespass.

> Papers are the owner's goods and chattels: they are his dearest property; and are so far from enduring a seizure, that they will hardly bear an inspection; and though the eye cannot by the laws of England be guilty of a trespass, yet where private papers are removed and carried away, the secret nature of those goods will be an aggravation of the trespass, and demand more considerable damages in that respect. Where is the written law that gives any

---

2   [1604] All E.R. Rep. 62 (Ct. of K.B.).
3   *Ibid.*
4   (1765), 19 St. Tr. 1029.

magistrate such a power? I can safely answer, there is none; and therefore it is too much for us without such authority to pronounce a practice legal, which would be subversive of all the comforts of society.

But though it cannot be maintained by any direct law, yet it bears a resemblance, as was urged, to the known case of search and seizure for stolen goods.

I answer that the difference is apparent. In the one, I am permitted to seize my own goods, which are placed in the hands of a public officer, till the felon's conviction shall entitle me to restitution. In the other, the party's own property is seized before and without conviction, and he has no power to reclaim his goods, even after his innocence is cleared by acquittal.

The case of searching for stolen goods crept into the law by imperceptible practice. It is not the only case of the kind that is to be met with. No less a person than my lord Coke (4 Inst.176,) denied its legality; and therefore if the two cases resembled each other more than they do, we have no right, without an act of parliament to adopt a new practice in the criminal law, which was never yet allowed from all antiquity.

Observe too the caution with which the law proceeds in this singular case. There must be a full charge upon oath of a theft committed. The owner must swear that the goods are lodged in such place. He must attend at the execution of the warrant to shew them to the officer, who must see that they answer the description. And, lastly, the owner must abide the event at his peril; for if the goods are not found, he is a trespasser; and the officer being an innocent person, will be always a ready an convenient witness against him.

* * *

What would the parliament say, if the judges should take upon themselves to mould an unlawful power into a convenient authority, by new restrictions? That would be, not judgment, but legislation.

* * *

It is then said, that it is necessary for the ends of government to lodge such a power with a state officer; and that it is better to prevent the publication before than to punish the offender afterwards. I answer, if the legislature be of that opinion, they will revive the Licensing Act. But if they have not done that I conceive they are not of that opinion. And with respect to the argument of state necessity, or a distinction that has been aimed at between state offenses and others, the common law does not understand that kind of reasoning, nor do our books take notice of any such distinctions.

A number of foundational principles were recognized in this judgment and are reflected in the excerpts reproduced above, concepts that continue to resonate in contemporary Canadian law.

§3.8 The first principle is that state officials can only interfere with individual property rights when they are possessed with clear lawful authority to do so. This idea, which at common law applied equally to protect both individual property and liberty interests,[5] is known in contemporary terms as the "principle of legality".[6]

§3.9 Second, privacy (in this case relating to the personal nature of Entick's papers) was an important value considered worthy of protection by the common law. (We will see below how privacy returns as a central consideration in the interpretation of section 8 of the *Charter* by the Supreme Court of Canada.)

§3.10 Third, at least at early common law, the power of state officials to search for and seize evidence was extraordinarily limited. The only basis for a warrant to enter and search was where there were good grounds to believe that stolen property was secreted in a particular place. Otherwise, there was no official power to enter onto another person's property to search (although there was a limited power to do so in order to arrest[7]).

§3.11 Finally, note that the court was reluctant to accept the defendants' invitation to recognize a new search power, suggesting instead that such developments are better left for Parliament. At the end of this chapter we will see how in recent years Canadian courts have not shared this same trepidation about recognizing new "common law" search powers.[8]

(2) Search and Seizure Before the *Charter*

§3.12 In time, the reality that law enforcement required powers to search and seize in situations beyond the investigation of stolen property led to legislative action. In Canada, the first *Criminal Code* enacted in 1892 included a provision that authorized the issuance of search warrants.[9] Over the years that section has been refined by various amendments, ultimately becoming what is today section 487 of the *Criminal Code*.[10] A number of offence specific statutory search and seizure powers followed, some of which remain in the *Criminal Code* to this day.[11] (Contemporary statutory search and seizure powers are considered in Part 3, below.)

§3.13 Prior to the enactment of the *Charter* in 1982, only the principle of legality protected individuals from the state's abuse of its search and seizure powers. This principle, however, was limited in its capacity to safeguard individual rights. Although the principle required Parliament to speak clearly if it wished to

---

[5] See William Blackstone, *Commentaries on the Laws of England, A Facsimile of the First Edition of 1765-1769*, vol. 1 (Chicago: University of Chicago Press, 1979) at 130-31.

[6] See Leonard Herschel Leigh, *Police Powers in England and Wales*, 2d ed. (London: Butterworths, 1985) at 32-33. The principle of legality is explained in much fuller detail in Chapter 1, Part 4(1).

[7] That power has since been curtailed somewhat by developments under the *Charter*, which are explained in detail in Part 4(2)(*b*)(i), below.

[8] This issue is also discussed in Chapter 1, Part 4.

[9] See *Criminal Code, 1892*, S.C. 1892, c. 29, s. 569.

[10] R.S.C. 1985, c. C-46.

[11] See *Criminal Code*, R.S.C. 1985, c. C-46, s. 447(3) (authorizing police officers to seize "cocks" where they are found in "a cockpit or on premises where a cockpit is located").

authorize an intrusion on individual liberty or property interests, it did little more than that.

§3.14 This was the case for two reasons. First, the courts were not empowered to evaluate the substance of laws that interfered with individual liberty or property interests. Parliament could (and sometimes did) cloak government officials with expansive and largely unchecked authority to search for and seize evidence. "Writs of assistance", for example, authorized police, in advance, to enter and search any place that they believed contained drugs.[12] They were not required to subject any supporting grounds to review by a neutral judicial official like a justice of the peace or a judge. In the American colonies, the abuse of these writs fuelled great hostility toward the king and played a direct role in sparking the American Revolution.[13] In Canada, however, it was not armed struggle but the entrenchment of the *Charter* that brought an end to writs of assistance.[14]

§3.15 Second, even when the police disregarded limits on their authority, there were rarely any practical consequences. Civil lawsuits like *Seymane's Case* and *Entick v. Carrington* were rare and criminal courts had no real means (such as a power to exclude illegally obtained evidence[15]) to remedy rights violations. The formal limits on police authority to search and seize were therefore far from clear. Although there was a hodgepodge of statutory provisions and judicial decisions relating to search and seizure, the law in this area was not at all comprehensive.[16] Without an exclusionary rule, the question of how police acquired the evidence was rarely consequential. And, as a result, the law governing search and seizure, like the law relating to all police powers, was only infrequently the subject of litigation.[17] The few judicial comments on the limits of official police power tended to occur in criminal prosecutions where an accused was charged with interfering, obstructing or assaulting a police officer in the "execution of his duty",[18] in cases where the target of a search warrant brought an application to set a search warrant aside,[19] and (very rarely) in civil cases.[20]

---

[12] See *Narcotic Control Act*, R.S.C. 1970, c. N-1, s. 10(1), (3); *Food and Drugs Act*, R.S.C. 1970, c. F-27, s. 37(1), (3); *Customs Act*, R.S.C. 1970, c. C-40, ss. 139, 145; *Excise Tax Act*, R.S.C. 1970, c. E-13, ss. 76, 78.

[13] See generally, Leonard W. Levy, *Origins of the Bill of Rights* (New Haven: Yale University Press, 1999) at 156-68.

[14] See *R. v. Noble*, [1984] O.J. No. 3395, [1985] 48 O.R. (2d) 643, 16 C.C.C. (3d) 146 (Ont. C.A.) (concluding that the writs of assistance were unconstitutional for failing to comply with the requirements of s. 8 of the *Charter*).

[15] See Chapter 10, Part 5(2)(*a*).

[16] How the police responded to this uncertainty is also less than clear. Sociologists who have studied the police in action, however, note that "when police are not provided with explicit authority to deal effectively with the problems they encounter ... they often unwittingly become dirty workers, furtively 'doing what has to be done' through the exercise of their discretion." See George L. Kelling & Catherine M. Coles, *Fixing Broken Windows: Restoring Order and Reducing Crime in Our Communities* (New York: Free Press, 1996) at 167.

[17] This fact about the pre-*Charter* system was recently acknowledged by the Supreme Court of Canada. See *R. v. Golden*, [2001] S.C.J. No. 81, [2001] 3 S.C.R. 679 at para. 67 (S.C.C.).

[18] See *e.g.*, *R. v. Colet*, [1981] S.C.J. No. 2, [1981] 1 S.C.R. 2 (S.C.C), where the accused was charged with a number of offences, including assaulting police officers in the execution of their

2. CONSTITUTIONAL LIMITATIONS ON SEARCH AND SEIZURE: SECTION 8 OF THE *CHARTER*

§3.16 Section 8 of the *Charter* seems deceptively simple. The clause, in its totality, reads:

> Everyone has the right to be secure against unreasonable search or seizure.

(1) Origins and Drafting History of Section 8

§3.17 Section 8 has no precedent in Canadian law. Unlike many of the *Charter*'s legal rights guarantees, no analogous provision was contained in the *Canadian Bill of Rights*[21] of 1960. Of course, the inclusion of a prohibition on unreasonable search or seizure was not entirely surprising. The decision to include such a guarantee was undoubtedly influenced by the Fourth Amendment to the United States Constitution,[22] as well as Article 17 of the *International Covenant on Civil and Political Rights*.[23]

§3.18 Nevertheless, the drafting process nearly resulted in section 8 taking on an entirely different and much less effective form. In response to strong objections from the provinces to the wording in the August 1980 draft[24] of the *Char-*

---

duties, for violently resisting the execution of a warrant at his property. The Court agreed with Colet that the police were acting unlawfully and therefore not in "execution of their duty" when they entered onto his property to search for weapons under the authority of a warrant that only authorized them to "seize" weapons.

[19] Such applications are brought through the prerogative writ of *certiorari* to conduct a review of the warrant on jurisdictional grounds. See *e.g.*, *Laporte v. Laganière J.S.P.*, [1972] Q.J. No. 35, 8 C.C.C. (2d) 343 (Que. Q.B.), quashing a search warrant that purported to authorize surgery on an individual to retrieve what was suspected to be a bullet from his body. See also Part 3(3)(*d*), below.

[20] See *e.g.*, *Eccles v. Bourque*, [1974] S.C.J. No. 123, [1975] 2 S.C.R. 739 (S.C.C.), where the authority of police to search private premises to effect an arrest was addressed in the context of a civil lawsuit. This power was ultimately revised by the Supreme Court in light of s. 8 of the *Charter*. See *R. v. Feeney*, [1997] S.C.J. No. 49, [1997] 2 S.C.R. 13 (S.C.C.). These developments are dealt with in Chapter 2, Part 4(4)(*g*).

[21] S.C. 1960, c. 44, R.S.C. 1985, Appendix III.

[22] U.S. Const. amend. IV [Fourth Amendment]. The Fourth Amendment provides: "The right of the people to be secure in their persons, houses, papers, and effects, against unreasonable searches and seizures, shall not be violated, and no warrants shall issue, but upon probable cause, supported by oath or affirmation, and particularly describing the place to be searched, and the persons or things to be seized."

[23] *International Covenant on Civil and Political Rights*, December 19, 1966, 999 U.N.T.S. 171, art. 179, Can. T.S. 1976 No. 47, 6 I.L.M. 368 (entered into force March 23, 1976, accession by Canada May 19, 1976). Article 17 provides: "1. No one shall be subjected to arbitrary or unlawful interference with his privacy, family, home or correspondence, nor to unlawful attacks on his honour and reputation. 2. Everyone has the right to the protection of the law against such interference or attacks."

[24] See Provincial Proposal, August 29, 1980 reproduced in Anne F. Bayefsky, *Canada's Constitution Act 1982 & Amendments: A Documentary History*, vol. 2 (Toronto: McGraw-Hill, 1989) at 683-85.

ter, the federal government significantly reworded what would ultimately become section 8. In the draft of October 1980,[25] section 8 was changed to read:

> Everyone has the right not to be subjected to search or seizure except on grounds, and in accordance with procedures, established by law.

§3.19 For the provinces, the goal of these changes was to "clarify and limit the scope of legal rights."[26] This led to the addition of language that did little more than codify the principle of legality ("except on grounds, and in accordance with procedures, established by law").[27]

§3.20 Civil liberties and lawyers' organizations were highly critical of the October 1980 draft.[28] They pointed out, for example, that because they were the product of express legislative authority, writs of assistance would be constitutional under this version of section 8, as would any other legislated search or seizure power regardless of how unreasonable it might be. The federal government took these concerns seriously, responding in the next draft with new wording that would ultimately be the final form for section 8 of the *Charter*.[29]

(2)   The Purpose of Section 8

§3.21 The first opportunity the Supreme Court of Canada had to pour content into the relatively open-ended language of section 8 came in *Hunter v. Southam (sub nom. Canada (Combines Investigation Acts, Director of Investigation and Research) v. Southam Inc.)*.[30] Writing for a unanimous court, Justice Dickson (as he then was) began his analysis by explaining that section 8, like each of the legal rights guarantees found in the *Charter*, is a check on, and not a source of, state power. He stated:

> ... in guaranteeing the right to be secure from unreasonable searches and seizures, s. 8 acts as a limitation on whatever powers of search and seizure the federal or provincial governments already and otherwise possess. It does not itself confer any powers, even of "reasonable" search and seizure on these governments.[31]

---

25   See October 1980 Draft of the *Charter*, *ibid.*, at 743.

26   *Ibid.*, at 681.

27   *Ibid.*, at 743.

28   For example, on behalf of the Canadian Civil Liberties Association, Alan Borovoy expressed grave doubts about the wording proposed for s. 8, complaining that if left unaltered it would serve as little more than "a verbal illusion" that would "pretend to give us something" while granting "us nothing more than we already have." See Canada, Minutes of Proceedings and Evidence of the Special Joint Committee of the Senate and of the House of Commons on the Constitution of Canada, vol. 1, No. 7 at 11-12 (November 18, 1980) (Canadian Civil Liberties Association).

29   See January 1981 draft of the *Charter*, s. 8, reproduced in Anne F. Bayefsky, *Canada's Constitution Act 1982 & Amendments: A Documentary History*, vol. 2 (Toronto: McGraw-Hill, 1989) at 771.

30   [1984] S.C.J. No. 36, [1984] 2 S.C.R. 145 (S.C.C.) [*Hunter*].

31   *Ibid.*, at 156-57 (S.C.R.).

§3.22 The remainder of the interpretive task was not so easy. As Justice Dickson noted, there was not "any particular historical, political or philosophic context capable of providing an obvious gloss on the meaning of the guarantee."[32] As a result, the Court could have easily taken the position that the provision served to affirm the historical sanctity of private property at common law. But this restrictive approach was categorically rejected in favour of a "broad and liberal" purposive interpretation.[33] The right was of a "wider ambit" and did not include language that would "restrict it to the protection of property or to associate it with the law of trespass."[34]

§3.23 In coming to this conclusion, Justice Dickson found guidance in the seminal decision under the Fourth Amendment to the United States Constitution: *Katz v. United States*.[35] In *Katz*, the Supreme Court of the United States concluded that "the Fourth Amendment protects people, not places."[36] *Katz* abandoned earlier formulations of the guarantee that had defined the scope of Fourth Amendment protection by reference to the law of trespass.[37] This approach had been discredited in the United States[38] and the Supreme Court of Canada was not anxious to repeat that experience. Instead the Court, like its American counterpart, concluded that privacy — and not property — is the fountainhead of section 8 protection.[39]

§3.24 As with other *Charter* rights, however, the individual interest recognized by section 8 must be balanced against collective concerns. As Justice Dickson put it in *Hunter*, in each case "an assessment must be made as to whether in a particular situation the public's interest in being left alone by government must give way to the government's interest in intruding on the individual's privacy in order to advance its goals, notably those of law enforcement."[40] Section 8 deci-

---

32   *Ibid.*, at 154-55 (S.C.R.).
33   *R. v. Dyment*, [1988] S.C.J. No. 82, [1988] 2 S.C.R. 417 at 426 (S.C.C.). See also *R. v. Colarusso*, [1994] S.C.J. No. 2, [1994] 1 S.C.R. 20 at para. 70 (S.C.C.).
34   *Hunter v. Southam (sub nom. Canada (Combines Investigation Acts, Director of Investigation and Research) v. Southam Inc.)* [1984] S.C.J. No. 36, [1984] 2 S.C.R. 145 at 158 (S.C.C.).
35   389 U.S. 347 (1967).
36   *Ibid.*, at 351.
37   See *Olmstead v. United States*, 277 U.S. 438 (1928); *Goldman v. United States*, 316 U.S. 129 (1942).
38   See *Warden v. Hayden*, 387 U.S. 294 at 304 (1967).
39   *Hunter v. Southam (sub nom. Canada (Combines Investigation Acts, Director of Investigation and Research) v. Southam Inc.)* [1984] S.C.J. No. 36, [1984] 2 S.C.R. 145 (S.C.C.). After citing Stewart J.'s view that this was the purpose of the Fourth Amendment, Dickson J. indicated "I believe this approach is equally appropriate in construing the protections in s. 8." *Ibid.*, at 159 (S.C.R.). See also *R. v. Dyment*, [1988] S.C.J. No. 82, [1988] 2 S.C.R. 417 at 426 at 428-29 (S.C.C.). But note that in emphasizing the pre-eminence of privacy concerns in *Hunter v. Southam (sub nom. Canada (Combines Investigation Acts, Director of Investigation and Research) v. Southam Inc.)*, [1984] S.C.J. No. 36, [1984] 2 S.C.R. 145 at 159 (S.C.C.), Dickson J. indicated, "I would be wary of foreclosing the possibility that the right to be secure against unreasonable search and seizure might protect interests beyond the right of privacy, but for the purposes of the present appeal I am satisfied that its protections go at least that far."
40   *Hunter v. Southam (sub nom. Canada (Combines Investigation Acts, Director of Investigation and Research) v. Southam Inc.)* [1984] S.C.J. No. 36, [1984] 2 S.C.R. 145 at 159-60 (S.C.C.).

sions thus entail a kind of cost-benefit calculation, weighing the costs and benefits of individual privacy against society's interests in any given context, be that crime control, national security, administrative or regulated fields, and the like.[41]

(3) The Elements of Section 8

§3.25 There are three elements to any section 8 violation: (*i*) state action (*ii*) constituting a "search or seizure" (*iii*) that is "unreasonable." If any of these elements is absent, section 8 is not infringed. If each is established,[42] the applicant may apply for relief under one of the *Charter*'s remedial provisions, which are discussed in Chapter 10.[43] Because it is relevant to all *Charter* claims, the state action requirement is discussed in Chapter 1, Part 4(3). The remainder of this Part will therefore focus on the second and third elements.

(4) What is a "Search or Seizure"? The Reasonable Expectation of Privacy Test

(a) General Principles

§3.26 Assuming state action, the first question to be asked in any section 8 case is whether the applicant suffered an intrusion that may be characterized as a "search or seizure". As in the United States, this question is answered by deciding whether the state action intruded on the applicant's "reasonable expectation of privacy."[44] If not, there is no "search or seizure" and thus no violation of section 8.[45]

§3.27 In most cases, intrusions have been characterized either as a "search" or as both a "search and seizure". In *R. v. Dyment*,[46] however, the Supreme Court of Canada held that the taking of a blood sample from a defendant by a physician (who later gave the sample to police) constituted a "seizure" and not a "search".[47] Writing for the Court, Justice La Forest defined a "seizure" as "the taking of a thing from a person by a public authority without that person's consent."[48] He went on to find, however, that the seizure violated the defendant's

---

41 See Steven Penney, "Reasonable Expectations of Privacy and Novel Search Technologies: An Economic Approach" (2007) 97 J. Crim. L. & Criminology 477 at 479.

42 This assumes that the infringement is not justified by s. 1 of the *Charter*. As discussed below in Part 2(6), in the context of s. 8, s. 1 is largely redundant.

43 In criminal cases, this will most often entail an application by the defendant for the exclusion of evidence under s. 24(2) of the *Charter*.

44 *Hunter v. Southam (sub nom. Canada (Combines Investigation Acts, Director of Investigation and Research) v. Southam Inc.)* [1984] S.C.J. No. 36, [1984] 2 S.C.R. 145 at 159 (S.C.C.); *R. v. Dyment*, [1988] S.C.J. No. 82, [1988] 2 S.C.R. 417 at 426 (S.C.C.).

45 See *R. v. Wise*, [1992] S.C.J. No. 16, [1992] 1 S.C.R. 527 at 533 (S.C.C.); *R. v. M. (A.)*, [2008] S.C.J. No. 19, [2008] 1 S.C.R. 569 at para. 8 (S.C.C.), *per* Binnie J.

46 [1988] S.C.J. No. 82, [1988] 2 S.C.R. 417 (S.C.C.).

47 *Ibid.*, at 430-31 (S.C.R.).

48 *Ibid.*, at 431. See also *Thomson Newspapers Ltd. v. Canada (Director of Investigation and Research, Restrictive Trade Practices Commission)*, [1990] S.C.J. No. 23, [1990] 1 S.C.R. 425 at 505 (S.C.C.), *per* La Forest J. [*Thomson*]. The Court also made it clear in *Thomson* that a "search or sei-

reasonable expectation of privacy.[49] He made it clear, moreover, that not all non-consensual takings will be considered "seizures" under section 8. "If I were to draw the line between a seizure and a mere finding of evidence," he concluded, "I would draw it logically and purposefully at the point at which it can reasonably be said that the individual had ceased to have a privacy interest in the subject-matter allegedly seized."[50]

§3.28 Nothing actually turns, therefore, on whether an intrusion is characterized as a "search" or a "seizure".[51] Linguistically speaking, one of these terms may be better suited to the factual circumstances of a case than the other, but there is no jurisprudential difference between the two. If government intrudes on an applicant's reasonable expectation of privacy, then it has conducted a "search or seizure".[52] The court must then go on to decide whether the intrusion was "reasonable".[53]

§3.29 How then have the courts gone about deciding what constitutes a reasonable expectation of privacy? As it turns out, this is not a simple question. Broadly speaking, when a court recognizes a reasonable expectation of privacy, it is saying that section 8 limits and regulates the state's use of a particular investigative technique in a particular factual context. If there is no reasonable expectation of privacy, then absent any limits imposed by statute or another *Charter* provision, the state may use the technique without legal restriction.[54]

---

zure" occurs not only when the state directly observes or takes something attracting a reasonable expectation of privacy, but also when it compels a suspect or third party to produce documents or things (for example, by a subpoena or production order). *Ibid.*, at 505 (S.C.R.), *per* La Forest J. and 493 (S.C.R.), *per* Wilson J.

[49] *R. v. Dyment*, [1988] S.C.J. No. 82, [1988] 2 S.C.R. 417 at 434-35 (S.C.C.).

[50] *Ibid.*, at 435 (S.C.R.). Similarly, a restraint on property that might be referred to as a "seizure" in ordinary discourse is not a "seizure" under s. 8 unless it invades a reasonable expectation of privacy. See *Quebec (Attorney General) v. Laroche*, [2002] S.C.J. No. 74, [2002] 3 S.C.R. 708 at para. 53 (S.C.C.) (to be considered a constitutionally protected seizure, property must be restrained as a result of an administrative or criminal investigation and have a valid privacy interest attached to it). See also S. C. Hutchison, J. C. Morton & M. P. Bury, *Search and Seizure Law in Canada*, looseleaf (Toronto: Carswell, 1991) at 2-5; F. Chevrette & H. Cyr, "La protection en matière de fouilles, perquisitions et saisies, en matière de détention, la non-rétroactivité de l'infraction et la peine la plus douce" in G.-A. Beaudoin & E. Mendes, eds., *The Canadian Charter of Rights and Freedoms*, 3d ed. (Toronto: Carswell, 1995) 10-1 at 10-8-10-9.

[51] Accordingly, in this chapter "search", "seizure" and "search or seizure" are used interchangeably.

[52] See *R. v. Evans*, [1996] S.C.J. No. 1, [1996] 1 S.C.R. 8 at para. 11 (S.C.C.), *per* Sopinka J. ("[N]ot every form of examination conducted by the government will constitute a 'search' for constitutional purposes. On the contrary, only where those state examinations constitute an intrusion upon some reasonable privacy interest of individuals does the government action in question constitute a 'search' within the meaning of s. 8.").

[53] See *e.g.*, *R. v. Edwards*, [1996] S.C.J. No. 11, [1996] 1 S.C.R. 128 at para. 33 (S.C.C.) ("There are two distinct questions which must be answered in any s. 8 challenge. The first is whether the accused had a reasonable expectation of privacy. The second is whether the search was an unreasonable intrusion on that right to privacy.").

[54] See generally, *R. v. Duarte*, [1990] S.C.J. No. 2, [1990] 1 S.C.R. 30 at 42 (S.C.C.); *R. v. Wong*, [1990] S.C.J. No. 118, [1990] 3 S.C.R. 36 at 47 (S.C.C.).

§3.30 For example, section 8 limits law enforcement's ability to covertly intercept people's telephone conversations.[55] We reasonably expect that police will not be able to do this without a warrant. In contrast, we have no reasonable expectation that they will refrain from listening to us with their unaided ears as we speak into cellular telephones at full volume in public places. Section 8 does not place any limits (such as the need to obtain a warrant) on this latter kind of surveillance.

§3.31 The Supreme Court has attempted to set out a framework for making reasonable expectation of privacy decisions. However, this approach — the "totality of the circumstances" test[56] — is simply a list of factors for courts to consider, not a bright-line, normative standard. The relevance and weight of these factors, moreover, depends heavily on the facts of each case.[57] Further, while we examine these factors below, there is little point in setting them out in a factual vacuum. Instead, it is more productive to look closely at the way that courts have decided the reasonable expectation of privacy question in varying contexts.[58]

§3.32 That said, the Supreme Court has articulated a few general principles applicable to all reasonable expectation decisions. First, the decision must be made from an *ex ante* perspective, without regard to the fact that evidence of illegal activity was discovered. This principle was best explained in *R. v. Wong*.[59] There, police observed illegal gambling activity through a tiny video camera that they had surreptitiously placed in a hotel room wall. In finding that this invaded the defendants' reasonable expectation of privacy, Justice La Forest wrote the following for the majority of the Court:

> [T]he answer to the question whether persons who were the object of an electronic search had a reasonable expectation of privacy cannot be made to depend on whether or not those persons were engaged in illegal activities. ... If reliance were to be placed on such *ex post facto* reasoning, and the courts to conclude that persons who were the subject of an electronic search could not have had a reasonable expectation of privacy because the search revealed that they were in fact performing a criminal act, the result would inevitably be to adopt a system of subsequent validation for searches ....

> Accordingly, it follows logically ... that it would be an error to suppose that the question that must be asked in these circumstances is whether persons who engage in illegal activity behind the locked door of a hotel room have a

---

[55] See discussion below, Part 2(5)(*c*)(i).

[56] See *R. v. Edwards*, [1996] S.C.J. No. 11, [1996] 1 S.C.R. 128 (S.C.C.); *R. v. Tessling*, [2004] S.C.J. No. 63, [2004] 3 S.C.R. 432 (S.C.C.); *R. v. Patrick*, [2009] S.C.J. No. 17, [2009] 1 S.C.R. 579, 2009 SCC 17 (S.C.C.).

[57] *R. v. Tessling*, [2004] S.C.J. No. 63, [2004] 3 S.C.R. 432 at para. 31 (S.C.C.).

[58] For similar approaches, see Susanne Boucher & Kenneth Landa, *Understanding Section 8: Search, Seizure and the Canadian Constitution* (Toronto: Irwin Law, 2005), c. 3; Barbara McIsaac, Rick Shields & Kris Klein, *The Law of Privacy in Canada*, vol. 1, looseleaf (Toronto: Carswell, 2000) § 2.3.

[59] [1990] S.C.J. No. 118, [1990] 3 S.C.R. 36 (S.C.C.).

reasonable expectation of privacy. Rather, the question must be framed in broad and neutral terms so as to become whether in a society such as ours persons who retire to a hotel room and close the door behind them have a reasonable expectation of privacy.[60]

§3.33 Second, the reasonable expectation of privacy decision is a normative inquiry, not simply a descriptive one.[61] As stated in *Wong*, the fundamental question for the courts is "whether giving their sanction to the particular form of unauthorized surveillance in question would see the amount of privacy and freedom remaining to citizens diminished to a compass inconsistent with the aims of a free and open society."[62] Accordingly, while the existence of a subjective expectation of privacy may bolster an applicant's claim, its absence is not fatal. Otherwise, the state could simply advertise its intention to monitor everything capable of being monitored and effectively eviscerate any protection afforded by section 8.[63] Moreover, people who are more suspicious or aware of governmental surveillance would receive less constitutional protection than those who are more trusting or ignorant.[64] The focus of the inquiry, therefore, is whether it is "objectively reasonable" to expect that the authorities will not have free reign to use an investigative technique to gain information about us.[65]

§3.34 Section 8 claimants must nevertheless show that the state intruded into *their* privacy — not that of another person.[66] As discussed in Part 2(5)(*c*)(i), below, intrusions upon the privacy of third parties may be taken into account in assessing the reasonableness of a search of seizure. There is no "search or seizure" within the meaning of section 8, however, unless the claimant's own expectation of privacy is also violated.

---

[60]   *Ibid.*, at 49-50 (S.C.R.).

[61]   See *R. v. Tessling*, [2004] S.C.J. No. 63, [2004] 3 S.C.R. 432 at para. 42 (S.C.C.) ("Expectation of privacy is a normative rather than a descriptive standard."). See also *R. v. Patrick*, [2009] S.C.J. No. 17, [2009] 1 S.C.R. 579, 2009 SCC 17 at para. 14 (S.C.C.).

[62]   *R. v. Wong*, [1990] S.C.J. No. 118, [1990] 3 S.C.R. 36 at 46 (S.C.C.). This phraseology was borrowed from Anthony Amsterdam, "Perspectives on the Fourth Amendment" (1974) 58 Minn. L. Rev. 349 at 402.

[63]   *R. v. Patrick*, [2009] S.C.J. No. 17, [2009] 1 S.C.R. 579, 2009 SCC 17 at para. 14 (S.C.C.) ("A government that increases its snooping on the lives of citizens, and thereby makes them suspicious and reduces their expectation of privacy, will not thereby succeed in unilaterally reducing their constitutional entitlement to privacy protection."). See also Anthony Amsterdam, "Perspectives on the Fourth Amendment" (1974) 58 Minn. L. Rev. 349 at 384; Melvin Gutterman, "A Formulation of the Value and Means Models of the Fourth Amendment in the Age of Technologically Enhanced Surveillance" (1988) 39 Syracuse L. Rev. 647 at 675-76.

[64]   See *R. v. Tessling*, [2004] S.C.J. No. 63, [2004] 3 S.C.R. 432 at para. 42 (S.C.C.) ("It is one thing to say that a person who puts out the garbage has no reasonable expectation of privacy in it. It is quite another to say that someone who fears their telephone is bugged no longer has a *subjective* expectation of privacy and thereby forfeits the protection of s. 8."); Melvin Gutterman, "A Formulation of the Value and Means Models of the Fourth Amendment in the Age of Technologically Enhanced Surveillance" (1988) 39 Syracuse L. Rev. 647 at 675 ("A citizen's unfounded belief that his private activities were not protected had a 'self-determining' quality: the fourth amendment's protections as he perceived them were the maximum benefit that he could obtain.").

[65]   *R. v. Tessling*, [2004] S.C.J. No. 63, [2004] 3 S.C.R. 432 at para. 43 (S.C.C.).

[66]   *R. v. Edwards*, [1996] S.C.J. No. 11, [1996] 1 S.C.R. 128 at paras. 34-43 (S.C.C.).

(b) *Applying the Reasonable Expectation of Privacy Test*

(i) *Persons*

§3.35 Not surprisingly, invasions of people's bodily integrity almost always constitute a "search or seizure" under section 8. Such intrusions may cause physical[67] and psychological[68] harm and reveal sensitive information that may be misused by authorities.[69] There are two types of bodily searches: (*i*) the taking from a person of bodily substances, impressions and images; and (*ii*) searches of a person's body and personal effects for evidence or weapons.

§3.36 The taking of bodily substances for forensic analysis will usually invade a reasonable expectation of privacy. The Supreme Court has found such invasions when authorities extract bodily samples for toxicological[70] and DNA identification analysis.[71] Section 8 applies, moreover, even when police acquire bodily samples from medical personnel who have taken them for medical purposes.[72] Recognizing a reasonable expectation of privacy in these circumstances not only protects people's bodily integrity, it also maintains their trust and confidence in their health care providers. This confidentiality ensures that people will not be deterred from seeking treatment out of a fear that damaging information will be disclosed to police or other authorities.[73]

---

[67] *R. v. Greffe*, [1990] S.C.J. No. 32, [1990] 1 S.C.R. 755, 55 C.C.C. (3d) 161 (S.C.C.) (rectal examination to search for heroin); *Laporte v. Laganière J.S.P.*, [1972] Q.J. No. 35, 8 C.C.C. (2d) 343 (Que. Q.B.) (surgical recovery of bullet located inside suspect's body).

[68] See *R. v. Greffe*, [1990] S.C.J. No. 32, [1990] 1 S.C.R. 755, 55 C.C.C. (3d) 161 (S.C.C.); *R. v. Golden*, [2001] S.C.J. No. 81, [2001] 3 S.C.R. 679 at para. 83 (S.C.C.) (strip searches are "often a humiliating, degrading and traumatic experience for individuals subject to them").

[69] See *e.g.*, *R. v. Dyment*, [1988] S.C.J. No. 82, [1988] 2 S.C.R. 417 at 432-34 (S.C.C.); *R. v. B. (S.A.)*, [2003] S.C.J. No. 61, [2003] 2 S.C.R. 678 at para. 50 (S.C.C.).

[70] See *R. v. Dersch*, [1993] S.C.J. No. 116, [1993] 3 S.C.R. 768 (S.C.C.); *R. v. Dyment*, [1988] S.C.J. No. 82, [1988] 2 S.C.R. 417 (S.C.C.); *R .v. Pohoretsky*, [1987] S.C.J. No. 26, [1987] 1 S.C.R. 945 (S.C.C.); *R. v. Colarusso*, [1994] S.C.J. No. 2, [1994] 1 S.C.R. 20 (S.C.C.). These cases all involved blood samples, but courts have come to the same conclusion with respect to breath and urine samples. See *R. v. Wills*, [1992] O.J. No. 294, 70 C.C.C. (3d) 529 at 540 (Ont. C.A.) ("Given the personal privacy interests which underlie s. 8 of the Charter, I see no reason to differentiate between the taking of a person's breath and the taking of a person's blood or urine, insofar as the applicability of s. 8 is concerned. The state capture, for investigative purposes, of the very breath one breathes constitutes a significant state intrusion into one's personal privacy.").

[71] *R. v. Borden*, [1994] S.C.J. No. 82, [1994] 3 S.C.R. 145 (S.C.C.); *R. v. Stillman*, [1997] S.C.J. No. 34, [1997] 1 S.C.R. 607 (S.C.C.). See also *R. v. Dorfer*, [1996] B.C.J. No. 332, 104 C.C.C. (3d) 528 at paras. 30-40 (B.C.C.A.) (taking of bodily substances produced by prisoner's dental treatment and preserved for law enforcement purposes triggers reasonable expectation of privacy).

[72] See *R. v. Dyment*, [1988] S.C.J. No. 82, [1988] 2 S.C.R. 417 (S.C.C.); *R. v. Dersch*, [1993] S.C.J. No. 116, [1993] 3 S.C.R. 768 (S.C.C.). The Court came to the same conclusion when police obtained blood samples from a coroner. See *R. v. Colarusso*, [1994] S.C.J. No. 2, [1994] 1 S.C.R. 20 (S.C.C.).

[73] See Tracey M. Bailey & Steven Penney, "Healing not Squealing: Recent Amendments to Alberta's *Health Information Act*" (2007) 15 Health L. Rev. 3 at 8"; *R. v. Dyment*, [1988] S.C.J. No. 82, [1988] 2 S.C.R. 417 at 433-34 (S.C.C.); *R. v. Colarusso*, [1994] S.C.J. No. 2, [1994] 1 S.C.R. 20 (S.C.C.); *R. v. Dersch*, [1993] S.C.J. No. 116, [1993] 3 S.C.R. 768 (S.C.C.).

§3.37 Convicted offenders, however, have no reasonable expectation that their identities, as inscribed in DNA extracted from bodily substances, will remain secret from law enforcement.[74] In *R. v. Rodgers*,[75] the Supreme Court thus concluded that the taking of such samples and the identifying genetic profiles derived from them for inclusion in a national database did not violate section 8.[76]

§3.38 There is typically no reasonable expectation of privacy, moreover, in bodily substances that are not extracted by another person. It has been held, for example, that police did not violate section 8 when they seized a sample of a suspect's blood from his vehicle after an accident.[77] In such cases, courts have typically found that the suspect had "abandoned" the substance and thus relinquished any privacy interest in it.[78]

§3.39 Two exceptions to this principle should be kept in mind. First, while abandonment may extinguish any privacy interest in the substance, the suspect may have a reasonable expectation of privacy in the place where the substance is seized. Police may not, for example, conduct a warrantless search of a suspect's home to seize discarded bodily substances for DNA analysis. Second, suspects may retain a privacy interest in bodily substances discarded while in custody. In *R. v. Stillman*,[79] a bare majority of the Supreme Court held that a suspect in custody did not abandon a mucous-containing tissue when he threw it in the trash. Since he had refused to voluntarily provide bodily samples, and since people in custody can do little to prevent the seizure of extruded bodily substances, the Court held that the warrantless seizure of the tissue violated section 8.[80] Lower

---

[74] See *R. v. Rodgers*, [2006] S.C.J. No. 15, [2006] 1 S.C.R. 554 at paras. 5, 43 (S.C.C.). This legislation is discussed below, Part 3(7)(*a*)(ii).

[75] [2006] S.C.J. No. 15, [2006] 1 S.C.R. 554 (S.C.C.).

[76] *Ibid.* As discussed below, Part 2(5)(*d*)(iii), prisoners, persons on probation and parole, and persons found not criminally responsible by reason of mental disorder, may have a "diminished" expectation of privacy in relation to the taking of bodily substances for drug testing. See also *R. v. Newell*, [2009] N.J. No. 60, 243 C.C.C. (3d) 33 (N.L.C.A.) (accused's reasonable expectation of privacy not breached when police used DNA sample ordered after conviction to match with crime scene for another incident even though conviction and order overturned on appeal).

[77] *R. v. LeBlanc*, [1981] N.B.J. No. 273, 64 C.C.C. (2d) 31 (N.B.C.A.), leave to appeal refused [1982] S.C.C.A. No. 334 (S.C.C.). See also *R. v. Love*, [1994] A.J. No. 847 (Alta. Q.B.) (mucous-containing tissue seized from garbage in motel room).

[78] See *R. v. Stillman*, [1997] S.C.J. No. 34, [1997] 1 S.C.R. 607 at para. 62 (S.C.C.) ("where an accused who is not in custody discards a [tissue] or cigarette butt, the police may ordinarily collect and test these items without any concern about consent"); *R. v. Arp*, [1998] S.C.J. No. 82, [1998] 3 S.C.R. 339 (S.C.C.), affg [1997] B.C.J. No. 1193, 116 C.C.C. (3d) 168 (B.C.C.A.) (no search when police gathered DNA from suspect's discarded cigarette butt after non-custodial interview). See also *R. v. Delaa*, [2006] A.J. No. 948 (Alta. Q.B.) (no search when undercover officer obtained suspect's gum by pretending to conduct a gum-tasting survey).

[79] [1997] S.C.J. No. 34, [1997] 1 S.C.R. 607 (S.C.C.).

[80] *Ibid.*, at paras. 52-63 (S.C.R.). The Court would have admitted the DNA evidence obtained from the mucous, however, under s. 24(2) of the *Charter*, in part because the seizure did not "interfere with the appellant's bodily integrity, nor cause him any loss of dignity." *Ibid.*, at para. 128 (S.C.R.). See also *R. v. Nguyen*, [2002] O.J. No. 3, 57 O.R. (3d) 589 (Ont. C.A.) (taking of gum from defendant in custody prior to entering a courthouse violated s. 8).

courts have interpreted this holding very narrowly, however, finding abandonment in a wide variety of custodial and quasi-custodial settings.[81]

§3.40 In the context of bodily substances, the Supreme Court's abandonment doctrine is at once more and less protective than it should be. Though people who are in custody have little choice but to leave behind traces of their genetic code, the situation is not much different for those who are not in custody. DNA may be extracted from an increasing variety and diminishing quantity of bodily substances.[82] It is consequently becoming easier and easier to obtain DNA from places and objects attracting no reasonable expectation of privacy. In these circumstances, it makes little sense to draw a constitutional distinction between warrantless seizures of discarded bodily samples in custodial and non-custodial settings, especially considering that police are more likely to have reasonable grounds to obtain a warrant to seize samples in the former situation than in the latter.[83] So long as police do not otherwise invade a reasonable expectation of privacy, they should be permitted to seize abandoned DNA, whether or not the suspect is in custody.

§3.41 Police should not have *carte blanche*, however, to use abandoned DNA for any purpose whatsoever.[84] DNA can reveal a great deal more than identity.[85] While we may unavoidably (and unwittingly) leave traces of our genetic code in places attracting no reasonable expectation of privacy, the state should not be free to use it to divine our propensity for disease, mental illness, criminality and

---

[81] See *R. v. F. (D.M.)*, [1999] A.J. No. 1086, 139 C.C.C. (3d) 144 at paras. 61-69 (Alta. C.A.) (no search when police took cigarette butts discarded during questioning at a police station, as the suspect was not detained and could have taken them with him when he left); *R. v. Marini*, [2005] O.J. No. 6197, 71 W.C.B. (2d) 727 (Ont. S.C.J.) (no search when DNA obtained from pop cans discarded by accused in courthouse); *R. v. Johnson*, [2004] M.J. No. 109 (Man. Q.B.) (no search when police took cigar left by accused on an ashtray outside the courthouse).

[82] See Andrei Semikhodskii, *Dealing with DNA Evidence: A Legal Guide* (New York: Routledge-Cavendish, 2007) at 96-101; June Mary Z. Makdisi, "Genetic Privacy: New Intrusion a New Tort?" (2001) 34 Creighton L. Rev. 965 at 972-74; U.S. Department of Justice, National Commission on the Future of DNA Evidence, *The Future of Forensic DNA Testing: Predictions of the Research and Development Working Group* (Rockville, MD: National Institute of Justice, 2000).

[83] These grounds could be used to obtain either a search warrant (to seize the abandoned item) or a DNA sample warrant (to seize fresh samples directly from the suspect). See *R. v. Stillman*, [1997] S.C.J. No. 34, [1997] 1 S.C.R. 607 (S.C.C.); *Criminal Code*, R.S.C. 1985, c. C-46, s. 487.05.

[84] See generally, *R. v. Rodgers*, [2006] S.C.J. No. 15, [2006] 1 S.C.R. 554 at para. 43 (S.C.C.) (a convicted offender "has lost any reasonable expectation of privacy in the *identifying information* derived from DNA sampling in the same way as he has lost any expectation of privacy in his fingerprints, photograph or any other identifying measure taken under the authority of the *Identification of Criminals Act*.") [emphasis in original]. See also Margaret H. McKay, "Genetic Material and Section 8: The Other Side of *Stillman*" (1998) 8 W.R.L.S.I. 139 at 149.

[85] See *R. v. B. (S.A.)*, [2003] S.C.J. No. 61, [2003] 2 S.C.R. 678 at para. 48 (S.C.C.); *R. v. Rodgers*, [2006] S.C.J. No. 15, [2006] 1 S.C.R. 554 at para. 39 (S.C.C.). See also Julianne Parfett, "Canada's DNA Databank: Public Safety and Private Costs" (2002) 29 Man. L.J. 33; Steven Penney & Jonathan Maryniuk, "Forensic DNA Identification and Canadian Criminal Law" (2008) Hosei Riron (J. Law & Politics, Japan) 91 at 109-10.

the like. The courts should therefore clarify that the abandonment doctrine applies only to the use of bodily substances for legitimate investigative purposes.[86]

§3.42 Police may also wish to obtain impressions from or images of a person's body for identification purposes.[87] So long as such takings involve some kind of compulsion, they invade a reasonable expectation of privacy.[88] While legislation compelling persons charged with certain offences to submit to fingerprinting withstood constitutional challenge,[89] the taking of fingerprints after an unlawful arrest violates section 8.[90] Police are free, however, to capture images of non-intimate parts of a suspect's body, provided that no compulsion is involved and the imaging is not an element of a broader surveillance technique that itself engages a reasonable expectation of privacy.[91]

§3.43 Not surprisingly, the probing of a person's body for evidence or weapons will almost always invade a reasonable expectation of privacy. As discussed in Part 4, below, this expectation may be diminished in certain circumstances, and the protection offered by section 8 may accordingly be curtailed. It is safe to say,

---

[86] This situation is analogous to the Supreme Court's consent search doctrine, discussed below, Part 2(4)(*c*). Briefly, while people may expressly or implicitly consent to certain intrusions on their privacy, the state may only use information gained from the intrusion for purposes consistent with that consent. Police accordingly invade a reasonable expectation of privacy when they use this information for other purposes. See *R. v. Evans*, [1996] S.C.J. No. 1, [1996] 1 S.C.R. 8 (S.C.C.); *R. v. Dyment*, [1988] S.C.J. No. 82, [1988] 2 S.C.R. 417 at 431 (S.C.C.); *R. v. Colarusso*, [1994] S.C.J. No. 2, [1994] 1 S.C.R. 20 at 58-61 (S.C.C.); *R. v. Borden*, [1994] S.C.J. No. 82, [1994] 3 S.C.R. 145 at paras. 37-41 (S.C.C.); *R. v. Arp*, [1998] S.C.J. No. 82, [1998] 3 S.C.R. 339 at paras. 89-90 (S.C.C.), affg [1997] B.C.J. No. 1193, 116 C.C.C. (3d) 168 (B.C.C.A.).

[87] Specifically, police may wish to: (*i*) authenticate a person's identity by comparing a unique bodily characteristic (such as a fingerprint) with a sample from a trusted database; (*ii*) place images of identifying features (such as fingerprints, mug shots, tattoos or scars) in a database for future crime detection purposes; or (*iii*) link a suspect with a crime by comparing a unique bodily feature (such as fingerprints or dental formations) with an impression found on evidence.

[88] *R. v. Feeney*, [1997] S.C.J. No. 49, [1997] 2 S.C.R. 13 at para. 60 (S.C.C.) (taking of fingerprints); *R. v. Stillman*, [1997] S.C.J. No. 34, [1997] 1 S.C.R. 607 (S.C.C.) (taking of dental impressions).

[89] *R. v. Beare; R. v. Higgins*, [1987] S.C.J. No. 92, [1988] 2 S.C.R. 387 (S.C.C.). In *Beare*, the accused challenged the constitutionality of the fingerprinting provisions of the *Identification of Criminals Act*, R.S.C. 1985, c. I-1, primarily on the basis that they violated s. 7 of the *Charter*. The Court also held, however, that the provisions did not violate s. 8. *Ibid.*, at 414 (S.C.R.). See also *R. v. Stillman*, [1997] S.C.J. No. 34, [1997] 1 S.C.R. 607 at paras. 45, 90 (S.C.C.) (noting minimal intrusiveness of fingerprinting). The Act also authorizes police to take photographs as well as "such other measurements, processes and operations having the object of identifying persons as are approved [by regulations]." *Ibid.*, s. 2(1). While the *Beare* Court did not specifically rule on the question, it suggested that these procedures were also constitutional. *Ibid.*, at 404 (S.C.R.). For further discussion, see below, Part 3(7)(*d*).

[90] *R. v. Feeney*, [1997] S.C.J. No. 49, [1997] 2 S.C.R. 13 at para. 60 (S.C.C.). See also *R. v. Dore*, [2002] O.J. No. 2845, 166 C.C.C. (3d) 225 at paras. 53-86 (Ont. C.A.) (retention of fingerprints subsequent to acquittal violates s. 8 if applicant makes timely request for removal and no compelling state interest in retention).

[91] See below, Part 2(4)(*b*)(v).

however, that any physical search of the body (such as a frisk, strip or bodily cavity search) will constitute a "search" for section 8 purposes.[92]

(ii) Private, Personal Property

§3.44 Like bodily searches, searches of items carried by or belonging to a person that conceal other personal property or information will usually invade a reasonable expectation of privacy. The courts have accordingly (and unsurprisingly) held that section 8 protects against searches of bags,[93] wallets,[94] computers[95] and communications devices.[96] It also regulates the observation or taking of confidential documents from people in possession of them, including personal items (such as diaries[97]) and business and financial records.[98] Whether such documents retain an expectation of privacy when in possession of third parties is discussed below in Part 2(4)(*b*)(vi) (which deals with privacy in information).

§3.45 People claiming section 8 protection for private, personal property must demonstrate a proprietary or possessory interest in the item, however.[99] As with bodily substances, this interest may be lost through abandonment. For example, in *R. v. Patrick*,[100] the Supreme Court ruled that although the contents of household garbage may reveal intimate information, any reasonable expectation of privacy is extinguished by leaving garbage bags for collection at the perimeter

---

[92] See generally, *R. v. Mann*, [2004] S.C.J. No. 49, [2004] 3 S.C.R. 59 at para. 56 (S.C.C.); *R. v. Golden*, [2001] S.C.J. No. 81, [2001] 3 S.C.R. 679 at para. 89 (S.C.C.); *R. v. Greffe*, [1990] S.C.J. No. 32, [1990] 1 S.C.R. 755 (S.C.C.).

[93] See *e.g.*, *R. v. Mohamad*, [2004] O.J. No. 279, 182 C.C.C. (3d) 97 at 106 (Ont. C.A.) (briefcase); *R. v. Chui*, [1996] A.W.L.D. 718 (Alta. Q.B.) (luggage).

[94] See *e.g.*, *R. v. Gregoire*, [2005] A.J. No. 529, 2005 ABQB 340 (Alta. Q.B.).

[95] See *e.g.*, *R. v. Morelli*, [2010] S.C.J. No. 8, [2010] 1 S.C.R. 253, 2010 SCC 8 at paras. 1-3 (S.C.C.) (implicitly recognizing reasonable expectation of privacy in personal computer and files contained therein).

[96] See *e.g.*, *R. v. Bacon*, [2010] B.C.J. No. 48, 2010 BCPC 1 at para. 47 (B.C. Prov. Ct.).

[97] *R. v. M. (D.)*, [2000] O.J. No. 3114, [2000] O.T.C. 640 at para. 43 (Ont. S.C.J.). See also *R. v. Shearing*, [2002] S.C.J. No. 59, [2002] 3 S.C.R. 33 at para. 167 (S.C.C.) (substantial privacy interest in locked diary).

[98] See *R. v. Black*, [2002] N.S.J. No. 576, 213 N.S.R. (2d) 60 at para. 71 (N.S.C.A.) ("commercial records must meet the 'personal and confidential' standard" for there to be a reasonable expectation of privacy). See also *Lavallee, Rackel & Heintz v. Canada (Attorney General); White, Ottenheimer & Baker v. Canada (Attorney General); R. v. Fink*, [2002] S.C.J. No. 61, [2002] 3 S.C.R. 209 at para. 35 (S.C.C.) [*Lavallee*] (reasonable expectation of privacy in documents held by one's lawyer); *R. v. Jarvis*, [2002] S.C.J. No. 76, [2002] 3 S.C.R. 757 at paras. 96-98 (S.C.C.) (reasonable expectation of privacy in financial documents). However, as discussed in more detail below, Part 2(5)(*d*)(iii)a, there may be a diminished expectation of privacy in documents, business and tax records kept pursuant to regulatory schemes.

[99] See *R. v. Belnavis*, [1997] S.C.J. No. 81, [1997] 3 S.C.R. 341 at para. 24 (S.C.C.) (defendant could not demonstrate interest in garbage bags found in vehicle); *R. v. Edwards*, [1996] S.C.J. No. 11, [1996] 1 S.C.R. 128 at para. 44 (S.C.C.) (no expectation of privacy in seized drugs when defendant denied ownership). See also *R. v. Sandhu*, [1993] B.C.J. No. 1279, 82 C.C.C. (3d) 236 at para. 102 (B.C.C.A.). The question of whether and in what circumstances people retain a reasonable expectation of privacy in documents in the possession of third parties is discussed below, Part 2(4)(*b*)(vi).

[100] [2009] S.C.J. No. 17, [2009] 1 S.C.R. 579 (S.C.C.).

of one's property.[101] Similarly, courts have held that suspects have abandoned items by walking away from them in the presence of police and disclaiming ownership when questioned,[102] by intentionally throwing them away while being pursued by police,[103] by leaving them in a police vehicle[104] or leaving items in a hotel room after checking out.[105]

§3.46 There is, however, a difference between simply leaving one's property unattended and the sort of deliberate action required for abandonment. For example, in *R. v. M. (A.)*,[106] Justice Binnie noted that students did not abandon their privacy interests in the concealed contents of backpacks left unattended in the school gymnasium.[107] Similarly, people may retain a reasonable expectation of privacy in property that has been lost or stolen. In *R. v. Law*,[108] police recovered a stolen, opened safe. The Supreme Court held that while police were entitled to fingerprint the safe and examine it for the purposes of furthering the investigation of its theft, they violated section 8 when they looked through documents found in the safe for evidence that its owners were involved in tax fraud.[109]

§3.47 Not surprisingly, the Supreme Court has also decided that property placed in a bus depot locker attracts a reasonable expectation of privacy.[110] Though the bus company owned the locker and had the ability to open it at any time, the defendant was entitled to expect that this would happen only if the items "appeared to pose a threat to the security of the bus depot."[111]

§3.48 In *R. v. Kang-Brown*[112] and *R. v. M. (A.)*,[113] the Court held that the use of trained dogs to detect the odour of illegal drugs emanating from personal property also invades a reasonable expectation of privacy.[114] In *Kang-Brown*, an un-

---

101 *R. v. Patrick*, [2009] S.C.J. No. 17, [2009] 1 S.C.R. 579 (S.C.C.). See also *R. v. Kennedy*, [1996] O.J. No. 4401, 95 O.A.C. 321 at paras. 4-5 (Ont. C.A.) (no expectation of privacy in garbage placed outside of apartment for collection); *R. v. Krist*, [1995] B.C.J. No. 1606, 62 B.C.A.C. 133 at para. 28 (B.C.C.A.) (no privacy interest in garbage bags left outside home for collection); *R. c. Allard*, [2006] J.Q. no 3377, 2006 QCCQ 3080 (Que. Crim. Ct.) (same).

102 *R. v. B. (L.)*, [2007] O.J. No. 3290, 227 C.C.C. (3d) 70 at para. 71 (Ont. C.A.).

103 *R. v. Nesbeth*, [2008] O.J. No. 3086, 238 C.C.C. (3d) 567 at para. 23 (Ont. C.A.), leave to appeal refused [2009] S.C.C.A. No. 10 (S.C.C.); *R. v. Collins*, [1999] N.J. No. 44, 133 C.C.C. (3d) 8 at para. 74 (Nfld. C.A.).

104 *R. v. Hilts*, [1997] A.J. No. 516, 203 A.R. 161 (Alta. Prov. Ct.).

105 *R. v. Butterworth*, [1997] M.J. No. 129 (Man. Prov. Ct.).

106 [2008] S.C.J. No. 19, [2008] 1 S.C.R. 569 (S.C.C.).

107 *Ibid.*, at para. 48 (S.C.R.), *per* Binnie J., concurring. See also *R. v. M. (A.)*, [2008] S.C.J. No. 19, [2008] 1 S.C.R. 569 at para. 158 (S.C.C.), *per* Bastarache J., dissenting.

108 [2002] S.C.J. No. 10, [2002] 1 S.C.R. 227 (S.C.C.).

109 *Ibid.*, at paras. 17-28. See also *R. v. Spinelli*, [1995] B.C.J. No. 2123, 101 C.C.C. (3d) 385 at para. 36 (B.C.C.A.), *per* Southin J., concurring (police entitled to search a vehicle reported stolen for evidence relating to the theft, but not for evidence that owner has possibly committed a crime).

110 *R. v. Buhay*, [2003] S.C.J. No. 30, [2003] 1 S.C.R. 631 (S.C.C.).

111 *Ibid.*, at para. 21. See also *R. v. Meyers*, [1987] A.J. No. 328, 58 C.R. (3d) 176 (Alta. Q.B.) (expectation of privacy in hospital staff lockers).

112 [2008] S.C.J. No. 18, [2008] 1 S.C.R. 456, 2008 SCC 18 (S.C.C.).

113 [2008] S.C.J. No. 19, [2008] 1 S.C.R. 569 (S.C.C.).

114 As discussed more fully below, Part 4(4), however, in both cases a majority of the Court found that the reliable and contraband-specific nature of sniff searches justified their (warrantless) use

dercover police officer monitoring an intercity bus terminal for drug couriers approached the defendant, asked him a few questions and asked to see the contents of his bag. After the defendant revoked his initial consent, a dog and handler were summoned. The dog signalled the presence of drugs in the bag, the defendant was arrested and drugs were found. In *M. (A.)*, police conducted a sweep of a high school with a drug-sniffing dog at the request of the school's principal. The defendant was arrested after the dog signalled the presence of drugs in a backpack left unattended in the gymnasium.

§3.49 In *Kang-Brown*, all nine judges agreed that the dog's "sniff" constituted a search under section 8 of the *Charter*.[115] Such sniffs, the Court reasoned, reveal precise and reliable information about the interior contents of personal belongings.[116] The fact that the dog makes a positive indication (and police subsequently search the item) only when it detects contraband,[117] in the Court's view, does not detract from the reasonableness of the suspect's privacy expectation.[118] The revealed information forms part of the "biographical core" of information protected by section 8, *i.e.*, information relating to the "intimate details" of a person's "lifestyle and personal choices".[119]

§3.50 The same reasoning was used by the majority in *R. v. M. (A.)*.[120] But writing for herself and Justice Rothstein in dissent, Justice Deschamps argued that the combination of the school's advertised "zero-tolerance" drug policy, the "tightly controlled" nature of the school environment, the destructive effect of drugs in schools, and the unattended state of the suspect's backpack reduced his privacy expectation to zero.[121]

---

on the basis of reasonable suspicion. See *R. v. Kang-Brown*, [2008] S.C.J. No. 18, [2008] 1 S.C.R. 456, 2008 SCC 18 (S.C.C.) at para. 58 (S.C.R.), *per* Binnie J., at paras. 191-193 (S.C.R.), *per* Deschamps J., dissenting and at paras. 234-244 (S.C.R.), *per* Bastarache J., dissenting; *R. v. M. (A.)*, [2008] S.C.J. No. 19, [2008] 1 S.C.R. 569 (S.C.C.), at paras. 8-13, 42, 74, 81-90 (S.C.R.), *per* Binnie J., at paras. 159-160 (S.C.R.), *per* Bastarache J., dissenting.

[115] *R. v. Kang-Brown*, [2008] S.C.J. No. 18, [2008] 1 S.C.R. 456, 2008 SCC 18 (S.C.C.).

[116] *R. v. Kang-Brown*, [2008] S.C.J. No. 18, [2008] 1 S.C.R. 456, 2008 SCC 18 (S.C.C.), at para. 58 (S.C.R.), *per* Binnie J., at para. 175 (S.C.R.), *per* Deschamps J., dissenting, and at para. 227 (S.C.R.), *per* Bastarache J., dissenting.

[117] In rare circumstances, an accurate positive indication may indicate the possession of a legal substance, such as licensed medical marijuana. See *R. v. Kang-Brown*, [2008] S.C.J. No. 18, [2008] 1 S.C.R. 456 at para. 175, 2008 SCC 18 (S.C.C.), *per* Deschamps J., dissenting. It is also possible, of course, that persons in physical possession of an illegal drug may be innocent of any offence, for example, if they were not aware of such presence and hence lacked *mens rea*.

[118] *R. v. Kang-Brown*, [2008] S.C.J. No. 18, [2008] 1 S.C.R. 456 at para. 175, 2008 SCC 18 (S.C.C.), *per* Deschamps J., dissenting. See also *R. v. M. (A.)*, [2008] S.C.J. No. 19, [2008] 1 S.C.R. 569 at paras. 69-73 (S.C.C.), *per* Binnie J. The United States Supreme Court has reached the opposite conclusion. See *Illinois v. Caballes*, 543 U.S. 405 (2005) (dog sniffs detect only the presence or absence of contraband and are thus not searches under the Fourth Amendment); *United States v. Place*, 462 U.S. 696 (1983) (same).

[119] *R. v. Kang-Brown*, [2008] S.C.J. No. 18, [2008] 1 S.C.R. 456 at para. 227, 2008 SCC 18 (S.C.C.), *per* Bastarache J., dissenting.

[120] [2008] S.C.J. No. 19, [2008] 1 S.C.R. 569 (S.C.C.), at paras. 38, 66-76, *per* Binnie J. and at paras. 157-158, *per* Bastarache J., dissenting.

[121] *Ibid.*, at paras. 121-123, 129-140, *per* Deschamps J., dissenting.

§3.51 Canine sniffs should be held to trigger a reasonable expectation of privacy in certain circumstances. But in our view the Supreme Court may have defined those circumstances too broadly.[122] Canine sniffs may cause a variety of privacy-related harms. If conducted without adequate justification, suspects may understandably find them to be disruptive, scary, intimidating, embarrassing, unfair and discriminatory. There is consequently ample reason to prohibit police from conducting such searches at their sole discretion.[123]

§3.52 That said, when police conduct dog sniffs of anonymous property without interacting with suspects, there is less reason for concern. In many such cases, the only "harm" caused to the possessors of the property is the discovery of contraband. As mentioned, a majority of the Court in *Kang-Brown* and *M. (A.)* recognized the discovery of criminal information as an intrusion potentially worthy of protection under section 8 of the *Charter*.[124] This is perplexing. In a high proportion of cases, a well-trained dog will only signal (and spark a physical search by police) when contraband is present.[125] The fraction of innocent persons subjected to physical searches in these circumstances would surely be much lower than that associated with search warrants backed by reasonable and probable grounds.[126] But why should a guilty person's interest in avoiding detection and punishment be protected under section 8? A possible answer, unstated by the Court, is its reluctance to give police an unfettered and powerful tool to enforce an arguably unwise law (the marijuana possession prohibition). Whatever the merits and demerits of such subterranean lawmaking, we urge against recognizing a reasonable expectation of privacy for investigative techniques revealing *only* information about criminal activity (and causing no other privacy-related harms). Such a principle may thwart the investigation of serious crimes with minimal benefit to the privacy of law-abiding Canadians.

(iii) Private, Real Property

§3.53 As discussed in the introduction to this chapter, the common law protected privacy mainly through the vehicle of property rights, and especially

---

[122] See Steven Penney, "Conceptions of Privacy: A Comment on *R. v. Kang-Brown* and *R. v. A.M.*" (2008) 46 Alta. L. Rev. 203.

[123] See James Stribopoulos, "Sniffing Out the Ancillary Powers Implications of the Dog Sniff Cases" (2009) 47 S.C.L.R. (2d) 35 at 38-40.

[124] *R. v. Kang-Brown*, [2008] S.C.J. No. 18, [2008] 1 S.C.R. 456 at para. 175, 2008 SCC 18 (S.C.C.), *per* Deschamps J., dissenting; *R. v. M. (A.)*, [2008] S.C.J. No. 19, [2008] 1 S.C.R. 569 at paras. 69-73 (S.C.C.), *per* Binnie J. See also *R. v. Gomboc*, [2010] S.C.J. No. 55, [2010] 3 S.C.R. 211 (S.C.C.), at para. 80, *per* Abella J., concurring and at para. 130, *per* McLachlin C.J.C. and Fish J., dissenting.

[125] See Sherri Davis-Barron, "The Lawful Use of Drug Detector Dogs" (2007) 52 Crim. L.Q. 345 at 366. Undoubtedly the prosecution should bear the burden of showing that the error rate of a dog and its handler is reasonably low.

[126] As mentioned below, Part 3(3)(*a*), at a maximum, the reasonable and probable grounds standard requires only that police show that it is more likely than not that evidence will be found.

through its concern for the sanctity of the home.[127] The importance of residential privacy has also been a theme of section 8 jurisprudence. The most common type of residential search is the entry by police into the interior of a home to examine its contents. This obviously invades a reasonable expectation of privacy.[128] As we have seen, section 8 also protects the privacy of hotel rooms, even when the registered guest invites strangers to enter.[129] Commercial premises also attract a reasonable expectation of privacy,[130] unless an invitation to enter has been extended to members of the general public.[131]

§3.54 As mentioned above, however, for any of these intrusions the applicant must prove that his or her *own* expectation of privacy was invaded. In *R. v. Edwards*,[132] the accused could not establish that he had a sufficient privacy interest in his girlfriend's apartment to engage the protection of section 8. He stayed at the apartment only occasionally, did not contribute substantially to rent or expenses, and lacked the authority to admit or exclude others.[133] Courts applying *Edwards* have thus typically rejected section 8 claims made by visitors,[134] landlords,[135] former residents[136] and even occupants' children.[137]

---

[127] See generally, *Eccles v. Bourque*, [1974] S.C.J. No. 123, [1975] 2 S.C.R. 739 (S.C.C.); *R. v. Colet*, [1981] S.C.J. No. 2, [1981] 1 S.C.R. 2 (S.C.C.).

[128] See *R. v. Silveira*, [1995] S.C.J. No. 38, [1995] 2 S.C.R. 297 (S.C.C.); *R. v. Kokesch*, [1990] S.C.J. No. 117, [1990] 3 S.C.R. 3 (S.C.C.).

[129] See *R. v. Wong*, [1990] S.C.J. No. 118, [1990] 3 S.C.R. 36 at 50-51 (S.C.C.). See also *R. v. Mercer*, [1992] O.J. No. 137, 70 C.C.C. (3d) 180 at paras. 14, 23 (Ont. C.A.), leave to appeal refused [1992] S.C.C.A. No. 231 (S.C.C.).

[130] See *Hunter v. Southam (sub nom. Canada (Combines Investigation Acts, Director of Investigation and Research) v. Southam Inc.)*, [1984] S.C.J. No. 36, [1984] 2 S.C.R. 145 (S.C.C.) (search of corporate offices for documents); *R. v. Rao*, [1984] O.J. No. 3180, 12 C.C.C. (3d) 97 at 123 (Ont. C.A.) ("the warrantless search of a person's office requires justification in order to meet the constitutional standard of reasonableness secured by s. 8 of the *Charter*"). As discussed below, Part 2(5)(*d*)(iii)b, the reasonable expectation of privacy in business premises may be diminished in the context of regulatory investigations.

[131] See *R. v. Fitt*, [1995] N.S.J. No. 83, 96 C.C.C. (3d) 341 at para. 19 (N.S.C.A.), affd *(sub nom. R. v. Fitt; R. v. Kouyas)*, [1996] S.C.J. No. 6, [1996] 1 S.C.R. 70 (S.C.C.); *R. v. Kouyas*, [1994] N.S.J. No. 567, 136 N.S.R. (2d) 195 (N.S.C.A.), affd *(sub nom. R. v. Fitt; R. v. Kouyas)*, [1996] S.C.J. No. 6, [1996] 1 S.C.R. 70 (S.C.C.). See also *R. v. Grant*, [1993] S.C.J. No. 98, [1993] 3 S.C.R. 223 at 241 (S.C.C.).

[132] [1996] S.C.J. No. 11, [1996] 1 S.C.R. 128 (S.C.C.).

[133] *R. v. Edwards*, [1996] S.C.J. No. 11, [1996] 1 S.C.R. 128 at paras. 47-50 (S.C.C.). See also *R. v. Guiboche*, [2004] M.J. No. 43, [2004] 8 W.W.R. 425 (Man. C.A.), leave to appeal refused [2004] S.C.C.A. No. 177, [2004] 3 S.C.R. viii (S.C.C.) (no expectation of privacy in the accused's father's house, where the accused had not lived for at least seven years). The *Edwards* Court also decided that applications to exclude evidence under s. 24(2) of the *Charter* may not be based on violations of the rights of third parties. This aspect of the decision is discussed below, Chapter 10, Part 2.

[134] See *R. v. Nguyen*, [1996] A.J. No. 119, 177 A.R. 396 (Alta. Q.B.) (casual visitor has no expectation of privacy in another person's residence); *R. v. Khuc*, [2000] B.C.J. No. 50, 142 C.C.C. (3d) 276 (B.C.C.A.) (babysitter has no expectation of privacy); *R. v. Jamieson*, [2004] O.J. No. 1780, [2004] O.T.C. 369 (Ont. S.C.J.) (nurse caring for/babysitting child has no expectation of privacy); *R. v. Sparvier*, [2001] S.J. No. 652, 2001 SKQB 485 (Sask. Q.B.) (girlfriend has no expectation of privacy in boyfriend's home); *R. v. Vu*, [1999] B.C.J. No. 707, 121 B.C.A.C 66 (B.C.C.A.) (family member of landlord has no reasonable expectation of privacy); *R. v. Charle-*

§3.55 Despite the strong privacy interest in the home's interior, police may be able to gain limited access to it on the basis of the occupant's implicit consent. In *R. v. Evans*,[138] the Supreme Court decided that police have an "implied licence" to knock on the door of a home.[139] The majority held, however, that this licence is limited to "those activities that are reasonably associated with the purpose of communicating with the occupant".[140] The defendant's reasonable expectation of privacy was violated, therefore, when police knocked on his door with the intention of smelling for the odour of marijuana.[141] If police were allowed to do this, Justice Sopinka wrote in his plurality reasons, they could conduct arbitrary "spot checks" of homes for criminal activity, for example in neighbourhoods "with a high incidence of crime".[142] If their only intention is to ask questions, in contrast, any evidence they discern with their senses is in "plain view" (or "plain smell") and consequently does not attract a reasonable expectation of privacy.[143]

---

bois, [2007] O.J. No. 1668, 2007 ONCJ 190 (Ont. C.J.) (no expectation of privacy in acquaintance's backyard).

[135] See *R. v. Pugilese*, [1992] O.J. No. 450, 8 O.R. (3d) 259 (Ont. C.A.) (landlord has no privacy interest in tenant's residence).

[136] See *R. v. Brooks*, [1998] O.J. No. 3913, 113 O.A.C. 201 (Ont. C.A.), revd on other grounds [2000] S.C.J. No. 12, [2000] 1 S.C.R. 237 (S.C.C.) (no expectation of privacy in former residence); *R. v. Tam*, [1993] B.C.J. No. 781 (B.C.S.C.) (no expectation of privacy in abandoned home used for the sole purpose of commissioning a serious crime); *R. v. Kinkead*, [1999] O.J. No. 1458, 96 O.T.C. 161 (Ont. S.C.J.) (no expectation of privacy in former girlfriend's residence in which accused had partially resided).

[137] *R. v. G. (L.)*, [1996] O.J. No. 2204, 37 C.R.R. (2d) 76 (Ont. Prov. Div.) (scope of youth's privacy dictated by an arrangement with his mother regarding exclusive possession of his room); *R. v. Rai*, [1998] B.C.J. No. 2187, [1998] B.C.J. No. 2187 (B.C.S.C.); *R. v. F.(D.M.)*, [1999] A.J. No. 1086, 139 C.C.C. (3d) 144 (Alta. C.A.) (scope of youth's privacy in room determined by parents); *R. v. K. (I.D.)*, [2002] B.C.J. No. 2884, 2002 BCPC 536 (B.C. Youth Ct.) (expectation of privacy in youth's room in foster home); *R. v. Scheck*, [2002] B.C.J. No. 1671, 2002 BCSC 1046 (B.C.S.C.) (no expectation of privacy in youth's room in grandmother's house); *R. v. Figueroa*, [2002] O.J. No. 3138, [2002] O.T.C. 553 (Ont. S.C.J.) (no expectation of privacy in youth's room that was commonly accessed household area).

[138] [1996] S.C.J. No. 1, [1996] 1 S.C.R. 8 (S.C.C.).

[139] *Ibid.*, at para. 13 (S.C.R.), *per* Sopinka J.

[140] *Ibid.*, at para. 15, *per* Sopinka J. Justice Sopinka wrote for three judges in a seven judge panel. La Forest J. indicated that he was in "substantial agreement" with Sopinka J. *Ibid.*, at para. 1 (S.C.R.), *per* La Forest J., concurring. See also *R. v. Sandhu*, [1993] B.C.J. No. 1279, 22 C.R. (4th) 300 at para. 47 (B.C.C.A.), *per* Prowse J. (police violated s. 8 by listening to "normal" volume conversation from outside of closed front door); Reneé Pomerance, "Parliament's Response to *R. v. Feeney*: A New Regime for Entry and Arrest in Dwelling Houses" (1998) 13 C.R. (5th) 84 at para. 9.

[141] *R. v. Evans*, [1996] S.C.J. No. 1, [1996] 1 S.C.R. 8 at paras. 16-21 (S.C.C.), *per* Sopinka J. The dissenting judges found, in contrast, that the terms of the implied licence are not exceeded by the police's intention to make sensory observations at the door. *Ibid.*, at paras. 40-58 (S.C.R.), *per* Major J., dissenting.

[142] *Ibid.*, at para. 20 (S.C.R.), *per* Sopinka J. This speaks to the concern that in some circumstances, failing to recognize a reasonable expectation of privacy may enhance the risk of discriminatory profiling on the basis of race, ethnicity or socioeconomic status.

[143] The plain view doctrine is discussed below, Part 3(6). See also *R. v. Laurin*, [1997] O.J. No. 905, 113 C.C.C. (3d) 519 (Ont. C.A.) (no expectation of privacy in odour emanating from apartment hallway); *R. v. Sawicki*, [1999] Y.J. No. 55 (Y.T. Terr. Ct.) (expectation of privacy

§3.56 Police may also have implicit permission to enter into private buildings when they suspect that a crime has been or is occurring there.[144] This permission is only effective if they believe that the owner of the property is not the perpetrator.[145] Similarly, as discussed below, in limited circumstances police may enter into a home to ensure the safety of its occupants.[146] In neither situation, however, may police actively search for evidence against the occupants. They may intrude only to the extent necessary to achieve the purpose of the entry; but in so doing, they may seize any evidence in plain view.[147]

§3.57 The zone of privacy attaching to the home extends to observations of its exterior and the areas surrounding it,[148] at least when police enter onto private property to make close observations of buildings and other structures.[149] The

---

triggered when licence to knock withdrawn). Justice Sopinka suggested in *R. v. Evans*, [1996] S.C.J. No. 1, [1996] 1 S.C.R. 8 at para. 21 (S.C.C.), that any approach of a dwelling "for the purpose of securing evidence against the occupant" invades reasonable expectation of privacy. Interpreted broadly, this would prohibit the questioning of residents at their homes in the hope that their responses could be incriminating. In our view, this cannot be what Justice Sopinka meant. In and of itself, this kind of questioning cannot be a "search", as it does not implicate the privacy of the home. See *R. v. LeClaire*, [2005] N.S.J. No. 547, 208 C.C.C. (3d) 559 at para. 15 (N.S.C.A.), leave to appeal refused [2006] S.C.C.A. No. 63 (S.C.C.) ("it is permissible for the police to approach a residence with a bona fide investigative inquiry and that the communicative nature of the activity takes it out of the realm of a search according to the principles in *Evans*"); *R. v. Van Wyk*, [1999] O.J. No. 3515 at para. 33 (Ont. C.J.), affd [2002] O.J. No. 3144 (Ont. C.A.), and [2002] O.J. No. 3145 (Ont. C.A.) ("Where the sole purpose of the police officer is to ask questions of the homeowner, nothing can be gathered by the government, in the sense of unwitting disclosure by the occupant, until he or she chooses to speak. The police intent of facilitating communication, even investigative questioning, does not exceed the bounds of the implied right to approach and knock and is, accordingly, not trespassory or in breach of s. 8 of the *Charter*.").

144 See *R. v. Mulligan*, [2000] O.J. No. 59, 142 C.C.C. (3d) 14 (Ont. C.A.); *R. v. Dreysko*, [1990] A.J. No. 982, 110 A.R. 317 (Alta. C.A.) (police entered home that had clearly been broken into); *R. v. Hern*, [1994] A.J. No. 83, 149 A.R. 75 (Alta. C.A.) (police entered home that appeared to be broken into to search for suspects); *R. v. Bastiero*, [2006] O.J. No. 3246, 2006 ONCJ 290 (Ont. C.J.) (after discovering blood on the driveway and in a damaged car, there were no exigent circumstances or implied licence to justify police entering a suspect's backyard); *R. v. Lotozky*, [2006] O.J. No. 2516, 81 O.R. (3d) 335 (Ont. C.A.) (entrance onto driveway open to public justifiable under implied licence doctrine).

145 *R. v. Mulligan*, [2000] O.J. No. 59, 142 C.C.C. (3d) 14 at para. 31(Ont. C.A.).

146 See below, Part 4(5).

147 See the discussion of the plain view doctrine in Part 3(6), below.

148 At common law, the term "curtilage" denotes the area outside the residence that is considered to be part of the home for various legal purposes. See *Black's Law Dictionary*, 8th ed. (St. Paul, Minn.: West Publishing Co., 2004) ("The land or yard adjoining a house, usually within an enclosure...."). See also *Criminal Code*, R.S.C. 1985, c. C-46, s. 2; *R. v. Kelly*, [1999] N.B.J. No. 98, 169 D.L.R. (4th) 720 at para. 41 (N.B.C.A.).

149 See *R. v. Plant*, [1993] S.C.J. No. 97, 84 C.C.C. (3d) 203 at 291 (S.C.C.); *R. v. Grant*, [1993] S.C.J. No. 98, [1993] 3 S.C.R. 223 at 240-41 (S.C.C.); *R. v. Wiley*, [1993] S.C.J. No. 96, [1993] 3 S.C.R. 263 at 273 (S.C.C.); *R. v. Kokesch*, [1990] S.C.J. No. 117, [1990] 3 S.C.R. 3 at 14 (S.C.C.), *per* Dickson C.J.C., dissenting. Each of these cases involved the entry by police onto the suspect's property to inspect the outside of the home for evidence of marijuana growing. See also *R. v. Kaltsidis*, [2007] O.J. No. 1400 (Ont. S.C.J.) (reasonable expectation of privacy in a partially fenced carport); *R. v. Curic*, [1999] O.J. No. 5786 (Ont. C.J.) (reasonable expectation of privacy in porch).

Supreme Court ruled in *R. v. Patrick*,[150] however, that police did not invade the accused's reasonable expectation of privacy by reaching over his property line to obtain garbage left for collection.[151]

§3.58 Courts have also held that naked-eye observations of private property from conventional vantage points (such as public roads) do not invade a reasonable expectation of privacy.[152] It is not as clear, however, whether police may observe private land from unconventional vantage points. A number of courts have considered, for example, whether police need warrants to make observations from overflying aircraft. In *R. v. Kelly*,[153] the Court held that the naked-eye aerial surveillance of a residential garden from any altitude invades a reasonable expectation of privacy.[154] But more recently, courts have held that aerial surveillance will only engage section 8 if it enables close-range observations of a kind normally unavailable to the flying public.[155]

---

[150] [2009] S.C.J. No. 17, [2009] 1 S.C.R. 579 (S.C.C.).

[151] *Ibid.*, at paras. 41-52 (S.C.R.) (Binnie J. noted that he did "not think constitutional protection should turn on whether the bags were placed a few inches inside the property line or a few inches outside it"). *Patrick* is discussed further below, Part 2(4)(*b*)(iii).

[152] See *R. v. Patriquen*, [1994] N.S.J. No. 573, 36 C.R. (4th) 363 (N.S.C.A.), affd [1995] S.C.J. No. 84, [1995] 4 S.C.R. 42 (S.C.C.) (no reasonable expectation of privacy in private wooded clearing five minutes from road); *R. v. Lauda*, [1998] O.J. No. 71, 37 O.R. (3d) 513 (Ont. C.A.), affd [1998] S.C.J. No. 71, [1998] 2 S.C.R. 683 (S.C.C.) (no expectation of privacy in use of another's abandoned land); *R. v. Truong*, [2005] O.J. No. 4200 (Ont. S.C.J.) (entry onto private land equivalent to observation from neighbouring property and hence no reasonable expectation of privacy). *Contra R. v. Kelly*, [1999] N.B.J. No. 98, 169 D.L.R. (4th) 720 at paras. 49-50 (N.B.C.A.) ("lawful occupants have an expectation of privacy in all open spaces within their residential lots that is qualitatively sufficient to invest them with s. 8 protection against unlawful aerial as well as terrestrial searches").

[153] [1999] N.B.J. No. 98, 169 D.L.R. (4th) 720 (N.B.C.A.).

[154] *R. v. Kelly*, [1999] N.B.J. No. 98, 169 D.L.R. (4th) 720 at paras. 43-53 (N.B.C.A.) (observations from helicopter flying at altitude of 30 feet).

[155] See *R. v. Kwiatkowski*, [2010] B.C.J. No. 428, 252 C.C.C. (3d) 426 (B.C.C.A.) (no violation of reasonable expectation of privacy in telescopically-enhanced observation of translucent greenhouses on acreage from a helicopter flying at 1,000 feet adjacent to, but not above, property); *R. v. Cook*, [1999] A.J. No. 527, 245 A.R. 8 at paras. 56-63 (Alta. Q.B.) (observations from 100 feet, but not 1,000 feet, invaded a reasonable expectation of privacy); *R. v. Kuitenen*, [2001] B.C.J. No. 1292, 2001 BCSC 677 at para. 28 (B.C.S.C.) (reasonable expectation of privacy violated because of "inordinately low altitude of the flights"); *R. v. Poncelet*, [2008] S.J. No. 222, 2008 SKQB 157, 318 Sask. R. 50 (Sask. Q.B.) (low flying helicopter observations permitting precise observation invaded reasonable expectation of privacy); *R. c. Giroux*, [2004] J.Q. no 11085, [2005] R.J.Q. 659 (Que. Ct.) (no violation of a reasonable expectation of privacy when police made naked-eye observations from plane at 500 feet). This approach is similar to that adopted in the United States. The Supreme Court there has held that there is no reasonable expectation of privacy if the airspace is "publically navigable" and the search not "physically intrusive": *California v. Ciraolo*, 476 U.S. 207 at 213 (1986) (no violation in unaided visual surveillance from 1,000 feet of a backyard enclosed by high double fences). See also *Dow Chem. Co. v. United States*, 476 U.S. 227 (1986) (no violation in use of high-resolution mapping camera at 12,000, 3,000, and 1,200 feet to photograph industrial facilities shielded from ground-level observation); *Florida v. Riley*, 488 U.S. 445 (1989) (no violation in unaided visual surveillance of partially-covered greenhouse from 400 feet).

§3.59 Police may also use remote sensors to obtain information about activity occurring inside an enclosed structure. In *R. v. Tessling*,[156] the Supreme Court held that the use of an infrared camera to detect the high intensity lamps used for hydroponic marijuana cultivation did not invade a reasonable expectation of privacy.[157] Because the camera was only able to discern crude patterns of heat distribution, the Court held, it revealed nothing of the occupant's "biographical core of personal information."[158] Though he could not prevent heat from escaping,[159] and though the camera revealed more information than was apparent to the naked eye, it nonetheless "record[ed] only information exposed to the public".[160]

§3.60 The key questions left unresolved by *Tessling* are whether and to what extent police may use tools to: (*i*) gain a better vantage point (such as cranes, ladders, or aircraft) to make unaided sensual observations; (*ii*) enhance sensual observations (for example with telescopic lenses); or (*iii*) accomplish both (*i*) and (*ii*). Following *Tessling*, courts considering these questions are likely to focus on the nature of the information that the investigative technique reveals. In doing so, they should also carefully consider the consequential effects of either applying or not applying section 8 to an investigative technique. The camera used in *Tessling* was not troubling because it did not reveal information that might cause law abiding people to either avoid beneficial activities or spend wastefully on defensive privacy measures; nor did it seem likely to encourage discriminatory profiling.[161]

§3.61 However, if an area of private, real property is typically used for intimate, lawful activity, and occupants have taken reasonable measures to shield it from public view, police should not be free to use technological means to defeat those measures. Warrants should accordingly be required for intrusive surveillance of the fenced-in, private land immediately surrounding a residence.[162] People do not expect as much privacy in their backyards, pools and gardens as in the interiors of their homes, but they do use these areas for sensitive activities. Police would thus require warrants to observe these areas using either telescopic enhancement or continuous video recording. Warrants would not be required, however, to make naked-eye observations or take non-telescopic still photographs from ei-

---

[156] [2004] S.C.J. No. 63, [2004] 3 S.C.R. 432 (S.C.C.).
[157] *Ibid.*
[158] *Ibid.*, at para. 63 (S.C.R.), citing *R. v. Plant*, [1993] S.C.J. No. 97, 84 C.C.C. (3d) 203 at 293 (S.C.C.).
[159] *R. v. Tessling*, [2004] S.C.J. No. 63, [2004] 3 S.C.R. 432 at paras. 39-41 (S.C.C.).
[160] *Ibid.*, at para. 47 (S.C.R.).
[161] Steven Penney, "Reasonable Expectations of Privacy and Novel Search Technologies: An Economic Approach" (2007) 97 J. Crim. L. & Criminology 477 at 509-11. For another view, see Stephen Coughlan and Marc S. Gorbet, "Nothing Plus Nothing Equals... Something? A Proposal for FLIR Warrants on Reasonable Suspicion" (2005) 23 C.R. (6th) 239.
[162] See generally, James Stribopoulos, "Reasonable Expectations of Privacy & 'Open Fields': Taking the American 'Risk Analysis' Head On" (1999) 25 C.R. (5th) 351 at 359-61.

ther high altitudes or conventionally accessible vantage points, such as adjoining buildings.[163]

§3.62 There is always a risk, of course, that private citizens will use technologies to intrude into others' property.[164] This does not mean, however, that police should be entitled to do so without restriction. Currently, the costs of this type of surveillance are large enough to make the prospect of widespread, suspicionless monitoring of private land unlikely. Technological advances, however, are likely to diminish these costs, potentially quite dramatically.[165] In this milieu, the warrant requirement provides a vital check on law enforcement's ability to engage in abusive and potentially discriminatory surveillance.[166]

§3.63 Most recently, the Supreme Court held in *R. v. Gomboc*[167] that a homeowner's reasonable expectation of privacy was not invaded when, at the police's request, an electricity service provider installed a device on his power line to measure the flow of electricity into his home.[168] The majority divided, however, on the reasons for this conclusion. Justice Deschamps found for a plurality that the case was undistinguishable from *R. v. Plant*.[169] Recall that in that decision (discussed in Part 2(4)(*a*), above), the Court held that electrical consumption records maintained by the utility for billing purposes did not trigger section 8 protection because the information did not invade the homeowner's "biographical core". Though the device used in *Gomboc* produced a more detailed measurement of hourly electricity usage than the records in *Plant*, Justice Deschamps found that it did not reveal intimate details of household activities.[170] This, combined with the fact that disclosure of electrical consumption to police was legis-

---

[163] See *R. v. Bagnell*, [2004] N.S.J. No. 228, 2004 NSPC 29 (N.S. Prov. Ct.) (unaided observation of suspect's property from neighbour's premises does not invade a reasonable expectation of privacy).

[164] In some cases, such prying may constitute a tort. See *Lipiec v. Borsa*, [1996] O.J. No. 3819 at para. 16 (Ont. Gen. Div.) (use of video camera for constant surveillance of neighbour's backyard was "an intentional invasion of the defendants' right to privacy"). See also *Saelman v. Hill*, [2004] O.J. No. 2122 (Ont. S.C.J.); *Jones v. Tsige*, [2011] O.J. No. 1273, 2011 ONSC 1475 (Ont. S.C.J.); *Milner v. Manufacturers Life Insurance Co. (c.o.b. Manulife Financial)*, [2005] B.C.J. No. 2632, 2005 BCSC 1661 (B.C.S.C.); John G. Fleming, *The Law of Torts*, 9th ed. (Sydney: LBC Information Services, 1998) at 667-68; Russell Brown, "Rethinking Privacy: Exclusivity, Private Relation and Tort Law" (2006) 43 Alta. L. Rev. 589 at 593-94.

[165] See generally, A. Michael Froomkin, "The Death of Privacy?" (2000) 52 Stan. L. Rev. 1461 at 1475-78.

[166] This is not to say, however, that this kind of surveillance should require police to establish reasonable and probable grounds. While these are the only type of warrants currently available for this type of surveillance (see *Criminal Code*, R.S.C. 1985, c. C-46, s. 487.01), it would likely be constitutionally acceptable to conduct technologically-assisted visual surveillance of private land on the basis of reasonable suspicion. See discussion below, Part 2(4)(*b*)(v).

[167] [2010] S.C.J. No. 55, [2010] 3 S.C.R. 211 (S.C.C.).

[168] *Ibid.* See also *R. v. Cheung*, [2007] S.J. No. 187, 2007 SKCA 51 (Sask. C.A.); *R. v. Luong*, [2010] O.J. No. 86, 2010 ONSC 84 (Ont. S.C.J.).

[169] [1993] S.C.J. No. 97, 84 C.C.C. (3d) 203 (S.C.C.).

[170] [2010] S.C.J. No. 55 at paras. 7-15, 36-40, [2010] 3 S.C.R. 211 (S.C.C.), *per* Deschamps J.

latively permitted,[171] led her to conclude that there was no reasonable expectation of privacy in the circumstances.[172]

§3.64 In her concurring reasons, Justice Abella agreed that there was no reasonable expectation of privacy. But absent the legislation expressly permitting disclosure, she would have found otherwise.[173] In her view, the fact that the device revealed that the home was likely being used for marijuana cultivation was sufficiently invasive to trigger section 8's protections.[174] In dissent, Chief Justice McLachlin and Justice Fish agreed with Justice Abella on the invasiveness of the device.[175] It was also capable, they added, of enabling "predictions regarding the probable activities taking place within a home,"[176] including "whether anyone is home, the approximate time at which the occupants go to bed and wake up, and guesses as to particular appliances being used."[177] They found, however, that the legislation did not extinguish the homeowner's reasonable expectation of privacy.[178]

§3.65 In our view, Justice Deschamps's reasons are the most compelling. As she documented, the evidentiary record showed that the device revealed very little about what was going on inside the home, other than the probable presence of a marijuana grow op.[179] As we have argued in relation to the dog sniff cases in Part 2(4)(*b*)(ii), above, this is not the type of information that should attract a reasonable expectation of privacy.

(iv) Vehicles

§3.66 As a rule, vehicle interiors attract a reasonable expectation of privacy.[180] This rule is subject to two exceptions. First, as with residential searches, this expectation attaches not to the vehicle itself, but rather to an individual's interest in it. Drivers will almost always have such an interest, but passengers may or may not, depending on the circumstances.[181] In *R. v. Belnavis*,[182] a majority of the Supreme Court held that a passenger did not, as she had no relationship with the

---

171 The effect of privacy-related legislation on the s. 8 reasonable expectation of privacy question is further explored below, Part 2(4)(*b*)(v).
172 [2010] S.C.J. No. 55 at paras. 31-33, 41-43, [2010] 3 S.C.R. 211 (S.C.C.).
173 *Ibid.*, at paras. 82-95 (S.C.J.), *per* Abella J., concurring.
174 *Ibid.*, at para. 81 (S.C.J.).
175 *Ibid.*, at paras. 105, 124, 129 (S.C.J.), *per* McLachlin C.J.C., dissenting.
176 *Ibid.*, at para. 128 (S.C.J.).
177 *Ibid.*, *per* McLachlin C.J.C., dissenting.
178 *Ibid.*, at paras. 138-142 (S.C.J.).
179 *Ibid.*, at paras. 7-15 (S.C.J.), *per* Deschamps J.
180 See *R. v. Belnavis*, [1997] S.C.J. No. 81, [1997] 3 S.C.R. 341 at para. 19 (S.C.C.); *R. v. Nolet*, [2010] S.C.J. No. 24, [2010] 1 S.C.R. 851, 2010 SCC 24 at paras. 30-31, 43 (S.C.C.) (reasonable expectation of privacy extends to commercial vehicles and to sleeping area of tractor-trailer cab, though in both cases the expectation is minimal).
181 *R. v. Belnavis*, [1997] S.C.J. No. 81, [1997] 3 S.C.R. 341 at paras. 19-23 (S.C.C.).
182 [1997] S.C.J. No. 81, [1997] 3 S.C.R. 341 (S.C.C.).

car's owner and exerted no control over it.[183] A spouse or passenger sharing driving duties and expenses, in contrast, would likely be protected by section 8.[184]

§3.67 Unfortunately, this exception is likely to foster an overly aggressive (and potentially discriminatory) approach to the detention and searching of vehicles with multiple passengers.[185] Consider a police officer who conducts a legitimate, random vehicle stop. The car is expensive and is occupied by several young, casually dressed, Aboriginal or African-Canadian men.[186] There is no evidence of criminal activity, but the officer nonetheless conducts a thorough search of the car's interior, including the glove compartment, trunk and areas under the seats. Illegal drugs are found. The officer clearly exceeded his or her power to conduct an incidental search, thus violating the driver's section 8 right. At the driver's trial, the drugs would probably be excluded under section 24(2) of the *Charter*. But according to *Belnavis*, unless the passengers are able to demonstrate a specific privacy interest in the vehicle or its contents, they can neither claim a section 8 violation nor seek to exclude the drugs. Knowing this, the officer is more likely to conduct the illegal search, since not searching will uncover no evidence, but searching may reveal evidence admissible against the passengers.[187] *Belnavis* should thus be overruled. As a matter of policy and common sense, passengers should generally be considered to have the same expectation of privacy as drivers.[188]

---

[183] *Ibid.*, at paras. 22 (S.C.R.). See also *R. v. Hyatt*, [2003] B.C.J. No. 63, 171 C.C.C. (3d) 409 at paras. 38-41 (B.C.C.A.).

[184] [1997] S.C.J. No. 81, [1997] 3 S.C.R. 341 at para. 24 (S.C.C.). See also *R. v. Luc*, [2004] S.J. No. 542, 188 C.C.C. (3d) 436 (Sask. C.A.), leave to appeal refused [2004] S.C.C.A. No. 480 (S.C.C.) (reasonable expectation of privacy for passenger who had rented vehicle); *R. v. Rossbach*, [2004] B.C.J. No. 2447, 2004 BCPC 424 at para. 67 (B.C. Prov. Ct.) (same); *R. v. France*, [2002] N.W.T.J. No. 36, 2002 NWTSC 32 at para. 60 (N.W.T.S.C.) (same). Passengers may also claim a reasonable expectation of privacy in relation to either personal items located inside a vehicle or areas of the vehicle within their control. See *R. v. Belnavis*, [1997] S.C.J. No. 81, [1997] 3 S.C.R. 341 at para. 24 (S.C.C.); *R. v. Poulin*, [2004] O.J. No. 1354 at paras. 81-82 (Ont. S.C.J.) (passenger had reasonable expectation of privacy in area beneath seat); *R. v. Logan*, [2005] A.J. No. 490, 388 A.R. 255 at para. 81 (Alta. Q.B.) (same).

[185] See generally, Ursula Hendel & Peter Sankoff, "*R. v. Edwards*: When Two Wrongs Might Just Make a Right" (1996) 45 C.R. (4th) 330.

[186] The problem of racial profiling is discussed in Chapter 2, Part 3(4)(*a*). See also *R. v. Landry*, [1986] S.C.J. No. 10, [1986] 1 S.C.R. 145 at 186 (S.C.C.), *per* La Forest J., dissenting (a broad, discretionary power "is unlikely to be used as much against the economically favoured or powerful as against the disadvantaged"); *R. v. Belnavis*, [1997] S.C.J. No. 81, [1997] 3 S.C.R. 341 at para. 66 (S.C.C.), *per* La Forest J., dissenting (same).

[187] See Steven Penney, "Taking Deterrence Seriously: Excluding Unconstitutionally Obtained Evidence Under Section 24(2) of the *Charter*" (2004) 49 McGill L.J. 105 at 125; *R. v. Edwards*, [1996] S.C.J. No. 11, [1996] 1 S.C.R. 128 (S.C.C.), *per* La Forest J., concurring; Jonathan Dawe, "Standing to Challenge Searches and Seizures Under the *Charter:* The Lessons of the American Experience and Their Application to Canadian Law" (1993) 52 U.T. Fac. L. Rev. 39 at 68-71; Kent Roach, *Constitutional Remedies in Canada*, looseleaf, at paras. 10.450-10.570 (Aurora, ON: Canada Law Book, 1994).

[188] See Don Stuart, "The Unfortunate Dilution of Section 8 Protection" (1999) 25 Queen's L.J. 65 at 71-76; *R. v. Belnavis*, [1997] S.C.J. No. 81, [1997] 3 S.C.R. 341 (S.C.C.), *per* La Forest J., dissenting. Of course, there could be justifiable exceptions, for instance, where the passenger's connection is especially transient, for example, a customer riding in a taxicab or a commuter

§3.68 The second exception relates to the nature of the privacy interest inside a vehicle. As discussed in Chapter 2, Part 4(2), police have a virtually unfettered discretion to stop vehicles to investigate driving offences. The power to search a vehicle's interior as an incident of that investigation, however, is initially limited to observations of the driver for signs of impairment, the inspection of driving documents and plain view observations of the passenger compartment.[189] Given the highly regulated nature of driving, there is in effect no reasonable expectation privacy with respect to these intrusions.[190] In addition, if police obtain reasonable grounds for any driving-related offences in exercising this incidental search power, they may search for further evidence of such offences, even if they also hope to uncover evidence of other offences.[191]

§3.69 This exception is also potentially troublesome. Police should not be given free rein to search bags, luggage and other closed containers in vehicles whenever someone commits a driving infraction. Such searches should be limited to items that could provide evidence necessary to prove offences that police have grounds to believe have been committed. For example, police should not be permitted to open closed containers inside vehicles simply because a driver fails to produce a valid licence, vehicle registration or proof of insurance. In all but rare cases, the failure to produce the required documentation, coupled with information from government records, should be sufficient to prove these offences. Further searches in these circumstances should generally be considered "pre-textual"; that is, searches conducted for the exclusive purpose of discovering evidence of unrelated (usually criminal) offences.[192]

§3.70 On the other hand, when acting with express legislative authority, police are entitled to conduct searches specifically tailored to discover evidence that may be necessary to prove reasonably suspected driving offences, even if the "predominant" motive for the search is to obtain evidence of unrelated criminal offences.[193] In *R. v. Nolet*,[194] for example, a police officer randomly stopped a commercial truck to make inquiries authorized by provincial regulatory legislation. After determining that the documents produced by the appellants were inadequate, the officer searched the vehicle, again under the authority of the

---

riding on a public bus. In most other circumstances, however, the *Belnavis* rule simply invites the potential for significant abuse.

[189] *R. v. Mellenthin*, [1992] S.C.J. No. 100, [1992] 3 S.C.R. 615 at 623-25 (S.C.C.). See also *R. v. Belnavis*, [1997] S.C.J. No. 81, [1997] 3 S.C.R. 341 at para. 28 (S.C.C.); *R. v. Carlston*, [2003] S.J. No. 708, 238 Sask. R. 183 (Sask. C.A.).

[190] See *R. v. Hufsky*, [1988] S.C.J. No. 30, [1988] 1 S.C.R. 621 at 638 (S.C.C.) ("the demand by the police officer ... that the appellant surrender his driver's licence and insurance card for inspection did not constitute a search within the meaning of s. 8 because it did not constitute an intrusion on a reasonable expectation of privacy").

[191] *R. v. Nolet*, [2010] S.C.J. No. 24, [2010] 1 S.C.R. 851, 2010 SCC 24 at para. 28 (S.C.C.).

[192] See generally, *R. v. Law*, [2002] S.C.J. No. 10, [2002] 1 S.C.R. 227 (S.C.C.) (police violated owner's reasonable expectation of privacy by looking through documents in stolen safe for purpose unrelated to theft investigation).

[193] *R. v. Nolet*, [2010] S.C.J. No. 24, [2010] 1 S.C.R. 851, 2010 SCC 24 at paras. 39, 43 (S.C.C.).

[194] [2010] S.C.J. No. 24, [2010] 1 S.C.R. 851, 2010 SCC 24 (S.C.C.).

provincial statute. Inside the truck cab, behind the driver's seat, the officer discovered a duffel bag. As relevant trucking documents were often kept in that manner, and as, at a touch, it appeared to contain paper, he opened it to find $115,000 bundled in small denominations. As this was typical of drug transactions, he arrested the appellant for possession of the proceeds of crime. A search of the truck incidental to that arrest revealed a hidden compartment containing 392 pounds of marijuana. The fact that the officer had earlier suspected that the vehicle might be transporting illegal drugs, the Supreme Court reasoned, did not detract from the legitimacy of this search.[195] Given the inconsistencies found in the relevant documentation, it was reasonable for police to rely on the authority to search granted by the provincial regulatory statute governing commercial trucking to look inside the bag for documents that would help prove the suspected regulatory infractions.[196]

(v) Public Spaces

§3.71 The unaided, visual surveillance of people in public spaces does not invade a reasonable expectation of privacy. Police are therefore entitled to watch us (whether covertly or openly) as we walk down streets, drive along roads and shop in stores.[197] In some circumstances, however, section 8 may limit the use of technologies to enhance this kind of surveillance. In *R. v. Wise*,[198] the Supreme Court decided that the installation of a radio-tracking device on a vehicle constituted a search. It noted, however, that driving is a heavily regulated activity[199] and that the use of the device was only a "very rudimentary extension of physical surveillance."[200] It consequently held that the invasion of privacy was minimal[201] and suggested that it would likely be constitutional for a warrant to issue authorizing the use of such tracking devices based on "reasonable suspicion," a lesser standard than that required for conventional warrants. At the time, however, the *Criminal Code* contained no such warrant power.[202]

---

[195] *R. v. Nolet*, [2010] S.C.J. No. 24, [2010] 1 S.C.R. 851 at paras. 32-41, 2010 SCC 24 (S.C.C.).

[196] *Ibid.*, at para. 44 (S.C.R.).

[197] See *R. v. Shortreed*, [1990] O.J. No. 145, 54 C.C.C. (3d) 292 (Ont. C.A.) (consent not needed for police to take photograph in public). The same principle applies in civil cases. See *Druken v. R.G. Fewer and Associates Inc.*, [1998] N.J. No. 312, 171 Nfld. & P.E.I.R. 312 at para. 43 (Nfld. T.D.).

[198] [1992] S.C.J. No. 16, [1992] 1 S.C.R. 527 (S.C.C.).

[199] *Ibid.*, at 533-35 (S.C.R.).

[200] *Ibid.*, at 535 (S.C.R.).

[201] *Ibid.*, at 534-36 (S.C.R.). Notably, the Crown had conceded that the installation of the beeper violated section 8. *Ibid.*, at 532 and 538 (S.C.R.). Not surprisingly, the Court concluded that despite the violation, the trial judge should not have excluded evidence obtained from the beeper. *Ibid.*, at 539-48 (S.C.R.).

[202] *Ibid.*, 548-49 (S.C.R.). As discussed below, Part 3(9)(a), Parliament subsequently enacted a provision (*Criminal Code*, R.S.C. 1985, c. C-46, s. 492.1) authorizing the issuance of tracking warrants on the basis of reasonable suspicion.

§3.72 Courts have also considered whether the continuous video monitoring of public areas can invade a reasonable expectation of privacy. In *R. v. Wong*,[203] Justice La Forest noted that surreptitious video surveillance represents a grave threat to privacy.[204] However, as mentioned in Part 2(4)(*a*), above, the camera in *Wong* was used to covertly monitor and record activities in a hotel room, which attracted a robust level of privacy protection. Similarly, the video monitoring of the inside of public washroom cubicles has been held to violate section 8.[205] In contrast, courts have held that no reasonable expectation of privacy was infringed by video monitoring of the exterior of a home[206] or business,[207] an apartment entrance lobby,[208] an interview in a police station[209] or the common area of a public washroom.[210]

§3.73 Notably, the video surveillance in each of these cases was conducted as part of a specific investigation. The decisions accordingly turned largely on the sensitivity of the activities taking place in the place being monitored and the extent to which these activities were open to public scrutiny. Authorities are increasingly using video surveillance, however, in less targeted ways, such as the continuous monitoring or recording of activities on public streets and parks.[211] The courts have not yet decided whether, or in what circumstances, this kind of surveillance invades a reasonable expectation of privacy. When they do, they should not focus on the nature of the monitored activities, which are by definition exposed to the public.[212] Instead, they should consider the effect that continuous, systematic video monitoring may have on law-abiding people's behaviour.[213] These schemes may employ networks of high-resolution cameras that can follow and record people's movements and behaviours in fine detail, over

---

[203] [1990] S.C.J. No. 118, [1990] 3 S.C.R. 36 (S.C.C.).

[204] *Ibid.*, at 47-48 (S.C.R.).

[205] *R. v. Silva*, [1995] O.J. No. 3840, 26 O.R. (3d) 554 (Ont. Gen. Div.).

[206] *R. v. Bryntwick*, [2002] O.J. No. 3618, 55 W.C.B. (2d) 207 (Ont. S.C.J.).

[207] *R. c. Elzein*, [1993] J.Q. no 802, 82 C.C.C. (3d) 455 (Que. C.A.), leave to appeal refused [1993] 4 S.C.R. v (S.C.C.).

[208] *R. c. Joyal*, [1995] J.Q. no 692, 43 C.R. (4th) 317 (Que. C.A.).

[209] *R. v. Bell*, [1996] O.J. No. 5199 (Ont. Prov. Div.); *R. v. Ramsoondar*, [2001] O.J. No. 897, 14 M.V.R. (4th) 33 at para. 19 (Ont. C.J.).

[210] *R. v. LeBeau*, [1988] O.J. No. 51, 41 C.C.C. (3d) 163 (Ont. C.A.).

[211] See Robert W. Hubbard, Susan Magotiaux & Matthew Sullivan, "The State Use of Closed Circuit TV: Is There a Reasonable Expectation of Privacy in Public? (2004) 49 Crim. L.Q. 222 at 223-24, 234-35; Dean Wilson & Adam Sutton, "Watched Over or Over-watched? Open Street CCTV in Australia" (2004) 37 Aust. & N.Z. J. Criminology 211 at 213.

[212] See Robert W. Hubbard, Susan Magotiaux & Matthew Sullivan, "The State Use of Closed Circuit TV: Is There a Reasonable Expectation of Privacy in Public? (2004) 49 Crim. L.Q. 222 at 230, 244.

[213] See, *ibid.*, at 242-46; Elizabeth Paton-Simpson, "Privacy and the Reasonable Paranoid: The Protection of Privacy in Public Places" (2000) 50 U.T.L.J. 305; Office of the Privacy Commissioner of Canada, *Opinion: Video Surveillance* by Gérard V. La Forest (April 5, 2002), online: <http://www.privcom.gc.ca/media/nr-c/opinion_020410_e.asp>; Marc Jonathan Blitz, "Video Surveillance and the Constitution of Public Space: Fitting the Fourth Amendment to a World that Tracks Image and Identity" (2004) 82 Texas L. Rev. 1349 at 1463-65.

large areas and for extended time periods.[214] These capabilities may chill inno-cent (but stigmatizing) behaviour[215] and facilitate discriminatory profiling and harassment.[216] Systematic video surveillance programs should thus be found to invade a reasonable expectation of privacy.[217]

(vi)   Third Party Records

§3.74 Police often seek information about suspects from records kept by third parties. The United States Supreme Court has concluded that information volun-tarily provided to others attracts no reasonable expectation of privacy.[218] Our own Supreme Court has taken a taken a different approach, holding in *R. v. Plant*[219] that such information will be protected under section 8 if it relates to a "biographical core of personal information which individuals in a free and de-mocratic society would wish to maintain and control from dissemination to the state."[220] In *Plant*, police obtained electrical consumption records of a residence suspected of housing a marijuana grow operation. The acquisition of the records, Justice Sopinka held for the majority, "cannot reasonably be said to reveal inti-mate details of the appellant's life since electricity consumption reveals very little about the personal lifestyle or private decisions of the occupant of the resi-dence."[221]

§3.75 Similarly, the Supreme Court held that a police request for a driver's li-censing documents during a traffic stop does not engage section 8. According to the Court, there "is no such intrusion where a person is required to produce a licence or permit or other documentary evidence of a status or compliance with some legal requirement that is a lawful condition of the exercise of a right or privilege."[222] As a general rule, however, this requirement does not extend to

---

[214] See Christopher Slobogin, "Public Privacy: Camera Surveillance of Public Places and the Right to Anonymity" (2002-2003) 72 Miss. L.J. 213 at 220.

[215] See, *ibid.*, at 240-45, 251.

[216] See Stephen J. Fay, "Tough on Crime, Tough on Civil Liberties: Some Negative Aspects of Britain's Wholesale Adoption of CCTV Surveillance During the 1990s" (1998) 12 Int'l Rev. L. Comp. & Tech. 315 at 324; Clive Norris & Gary Armstrong, *The Unforgiving Eye: CCTV Sur-veillance in Public Places* (Hull: University of Hull, 1997) at 6-7.

[217] See Office of the Privacy Commissioner of Canada, *Opinion: Video Surveillance* by Gérard V. La Forest (April 5, 2002), online: <http://www.privcom.gc.ca/media/nr-c/opinion_020410 _e.asp> (installation of camera and monitoring of a public street violated section 8). It may not be appropriate, however, to demand strict compliance with the usual s. 8 "reasonableness" stan-dards of prior authorization and reasonable and probable grounds. For discussions of the consti-tutional regulation of public video surveillance programs, see Derek Lai, "Public Video Surveillance by the State: Policy, Privacy Legislation, and the *Charter*" (2007) 45 Alta. L. Rev. 43; Christopher Slobogin, "Public Privacy: Camera Surveillance of Public Places and the Right to Anonymity" (2002-2003) 72 Miss. L.J. 213.

[218] See *United States v. Miller*, 425 U.S. 435 (1976) (banking records); *Smith v. Maryland*, 442 U.S. 735 (1979) (telephone records).

[219] [1993] S.C.J. No. 97, 84 C.C.C. (3d) 203 (S.C.C.).

[220] *Ibid.*, at 293 (C.C.C.).

[221] *Ibid.*

[222] *R. v. Hufsky*, [1988] S.C.J. No. 30, [1988] 1 S.C.R. 621 at para. 23 (S.C.C.).

passengers. In *R. v. Harris*,[223] the Ontario Court of Appeal held that it violated the section 8 requirement for police to ask a passenger his name for the purpose of conducting a Canadian Police Information Computer (CPIC) check to ascertain whether he had a criminal record or was subject to any court orders. Police can make such requests only for the purposes of investigating offences leading to the stop or charging the passenger with traffic offences, such as failure to wear a seatbelt.[224]

§3.76 Records containing sensitive information will usually be protected under section 8. People have a reasonable expectation of privacy, for instance, in most documents possessed by their lawyers,[225] therapists,[226] health care providers[227] and welfare agencies.[228] The status of financial and other commercial records is less certain. While members of the Supreme Court have asserted that bank account information can attract a reasonable expectation of privacy,[229] a majority of the Court has yet to resolve the question. Lower courts have come to varying conclusions, but the consensus appears to be that detailed and extensive financial

223 [2007] O.J. No. 3185, 225 C.C.C. (3d) 193 (Ont. C.A.).

224 *Ibid.*, at para. 40 (C.C.C.). Given that there was no lawful basis for this search the Court found that it violated s. 8. The Court distinguished cases where requests for identification of individuals who were not "detained" were upheld under the *Charter*. See *R. v. Grafe*, [1987] O.J. No. 796, 36 C.C.C. (3d) 267 (Ont. C.A.); *R. v. Hall*, [1995] O.J. No. 544, 22 O.R. (3d) 289 (Ont. C.A.).

225 See *Lavallee, Rackel & Heintz v. Canada (Attorney General); White, Ottenheimer & Baker v. Canada (Attorney General); R. v. Fink*, [2002] S.C.J. No. 61, [2002] 3 S.C.R. 209 at para. 35 (S.C.C.) ("A client has a reasonable expectation of privacy in all documents in the possession of his or her lawyer, which constitute information that the lawyer is ethically required to keep confidential, and an expectation of privacy of the highest order when such documents are protected by the solicitor-client privilege.").

226 *R. v. O'Connor*, [1995] S.C.J. No. 98, [1995] 4 S.C.R. 411 at para. 99 (S.C.C.) ("the determination of when a reasonable expectation of privacy actually exists in a particular record (and, if so, to what extent it exists) is inherently fact- and context-sensitive, this may include records that are medical or therapeutic in nature, school records, private diaries, and activity logs prepared by social workers, to name just a few"). See also *R. v. Mills*, [1999] S.C.J. No. 68, [1999] 3 S.C.R. 668 at paras. 82-85 (S.C.C.).

227 See *R. v. Dersch*, [1993] S.C.J. No. 116, [1993] 3 S.C.R. 768 at 778 (S.C.C.) ("the appellant had a reasonable expectation that the specific medical information revealed by Dr. Gilbert, including the blood alcohol test results, would be kept confidential by the doctors and the hospital"); *Canadian AIDS Society v. Ontario*, [1995] O.J. No. 236,1 25 O.R. (3d) 388 (Ont. Gen. Div.), affd [1996] O.J. No. 4184, 31 O.R. 798 (Ont. C.A.), leave to appeal refused [1997] S.C.C.A. No. 33, 107 O.A.C. 80 (S.C.C.) (reasonable expectation of privacy in identity of HIV positive blood donors).

228 See *R. v. Chambers*, [1997] M.J. No. 428, 122 Man. R. (2d) 125 (Man. Q.B.) (expectation of privacy in information given to city's Social Services Department).

229 In *Schreiber v. Canada (Attorney General)*, [1998] S.C.J. No. 42, [1998] 1 S.C.R. 841 (S.C.C.), the Supreme Court of Canada considered whether the seizure of a suspect's foreign banking records violated s. 8 of the *Charter*. The majority concluded that the Canadian government's request for foreign assistance did not engage s. 8; it declined to consider whether a warrantless search of a suspect's domestic banking records would have attracted a reasonable expectation of privacy. In his concurring reasons, Lamer C.J.C. indicated that he would have answered "yes" to this question. *Ibid.*, at para. 22 (S.C.R.). In his dissent, Iacobucci J. concluded that the suspect did have a reasonable expectation of privacy in his foreign banking records. *Ibid.*, at para. 55 (S.C.R.).

records are protected by section 8,[230] whereas basic account information may not be.[231]

§3.77 In deciding whether third party records attract a reasonable expectation of privacy, courts should be mindful of the federal *Personal Information Protection and Electronic Documents Act*[232] and its provincial counterparts.[233] These statutes require private sector organizations to maintain the confidentiality of personal information that they collect, subject to various exceptions (including several enabling disclosure to police).[234] Their effect on the reasonable expectation of privacy analysis, however, is limited. Recall that in *R. v. Gomboc*[235] (discussed in Part 2(4)(*b*)(iii), above), the Supreme Court of Canada divided three ways on the question of how to interpret a provincial regulation permitting the disclosure of electrical consumption records. But a majority agreed that legislative and contractual provisions are not determinative of the reasonable expectation of privacy question.[236]

§3.78 We agree. As a constitutional provision, section 8's requirements cannot be dictated by statute or contract. As Justice Deschamps put it in *Gomboc*:

---

[230] See *R. v. Eddy*, [1994] N.J. No. 142, 119 Nfld. & P.E.I.R. 91 at para. 183 (Nfld. T.D.) (s. 8 triggered when police requested identity of account owner and whether any transactions had occurred on a particular date); *Gernhart v. Canada*, [1999] F.C.J. No. 1669, 181 D.L.R. (4th) 506 (F.C.A.) (*Income Tax Act* provision, which mandated disclosure of appealed returns to Tax Court violated s. 8 as, by virtue of Court's rules, returns became public documents); *R. v. Academy Doors and Windows Ltd.*, [2004] O.J. No. 5805 at para. 72 (Ont. C.J.) (reasonable expectation of privacy in banking documents relating to corporation); *R. v. Chusid*, [2001] O.J. No. 4741, 57 O.R. (3d) 20 at para. 46 (Ont. S.C.J.) ("Banking records are formed in a confidential relationship between the individual and a banking institution, and *prima facie* attract a reasonable expectation of privacy.").

[231] See *R. v. Lillico*, [1994] O.J. No. 4521, 92 C.C.C. (3d) 90 (Ont. Gen. Div.), affd [1999] O.J. No. 95 (Ont. C.A.) (police request for information relating to a single cheque and subsequent account activity did not invade reasonable expectation of privacy); *R. v. Quinn*, [2006] B.C.J. No. 1170, 209 C.C.C. (3d) 278 at paras. 89-93 (B.C.C.A.) (no search when police sought name associated with account number). As discussed below, Part 3(4), Parliament has recently introduced a provision empowering authorities to obtain basic account information on the reasonable suspicion standard. See *Criminal Code*, R.S.C. 1985, c. C-46, s. 487.013. In so doing, it has arguably recognized that such information attracts at least a minimal expectation of privacy.

[232] S.C. 2000, c. 5 [PIPEDA].

[233] See *Personal Information Protection Act*, S.B.C. 2003, c. 63; *Personal Information Protection Act*, S.A. 2003, c. P-6.5; *An Act respecting the protection of personal information in the private sector*, R.S.Q., c. P-39.1. See generally, *R. v. Mahmood*, [2008] O.J. No. 3922, 236 C.C.C. (3d) 3 at para. 56 (Ont. S.C.J.), reconsideration denied [2009] O.J. No. 3192, 194 C.R.R. (2d) 180 (Ont. S.C.J.) (finding of reasonable privacy expectation in phone records "legislatively supported by Parliament's enactment of PIPEDA, which prevents the disclosure by the service provider of personal information relating to subscribers in the absence of lawful authority").

[234] See *e.g.*, PIPEDA, ss. 7(3)(*c.1*); *Personal Information Protection Act*, S.B.C. 2003, c. 63; *Personal Information Protection Act*, S.A. 2003, c. P-6.5, s. 20(*f*); *An Act Respecting the Protection of Personal Information in the Private Sector*, R.S.Q., c. P-39.1, ss. 18(2)-(3).

[235] [2010] S.C.J. No. 55, [2010] 3 S.C.R. 211 (S.C.C.).

[236] *Ibid.*, at paras. 33-34 (S.C.R.), *per* Deschamps J. and para. 115 (S.C.R.), *per* McLachlin C.J.C. and Fish J., dissenting.

... [T]he fact that the person claiming an expectation of privacy in information ought to have known that the terms governing the relationship with the holder of that information allowed disclosure may not be determinative. Rather, the appropriate question is whether the information is the sort that society accepts should remain out of the state's hands because of what it reveals about the person involved, the reasons why it was collected, and the circumstances in which it was intended to be used.[237]

§3.79 The fact that a statute or contract permits disclosure to police, in other words, does not necessarily mean that section 8 has been complied with. As Chief Justice McLachlin and Justice Fish stated in *Gomboc*, "legislation is only one factor that is to be considered when determining whether an expectation of privacy is objectively reasonable and it may be insufficient to negate an expectation of privacy that is otherwise particularly compelling."[238]

§3.80 But if legislation permitting disclosure is not conclusive on the section 8 question, neither is legislation prohibiting it. As the Nova Scotia Court of Appeal noted in *R. v. Chehil*,[239] the broad definitions of "personal information" in the privacy statutes encompass information that might not be considered intimate or revealing enough to attract a reasonable expectation of privacy under the *Charter*.[240] There, the Court held that police did not invade an airplane passenger's reasonable expectation of privacy by obtaining information (his name, flight number, payment method and baggage allotment) from the airline that did not expose intimate details of his lifestyle or personal choices.[241]

§3.81 The expectation of privacy attaching to even highly sensitive information may be lost if it is disclosed to a third party in inherently non-confidential circumstances. In *R. v. Regan*,[242] for example, journalists who had interviewed sexual assault complainants for the purposes of a television documentary were compelled to testify by the defendant at a preliminary inquiry.[243] The Court held that the information revealed in these interviews did not attract a reasonable expectation of privacy, since "the very purpose of the interviews was to prepare a publicly broadcast news report about the subject."[244]

---

[237] *Ibid.*, at para. 34 (S.C.R.).

[238] *Ibid.*, at para. 115 (S.C.R.), *per* McLachlin C.J.C. and Fish J., dissenting. Of course, legislative provisions permitting such disclosures are themselves subject to scrutiny under s. 8. See generally, *ibid.*, at para. 58 (S.C.R.), *per* Deschamps J. (noting that the legislation was not subject to a *Charter* challenge; *Royal Bank v. Welton*, [2009] O.J. No. 209, 306 D.L.R. (4th) 487 (Ont. C.A.), leave to appeal refused [2009] S.C.C.A. No. 111 (S.C.C.) (rejecting a s. 8 *Charter* challenge aimed at the exceptions found in ss. 7(3)(d) and (*h.2*) of PIPEDA).

[239] [2009] N.S.J. No. 515, 248 C.C.C. (3d) 370 (N.S.C.A.).

[240] *Ibid.*, at paras. 23-25 (C.C.C.).

[241] *Ibid.*, at paras. 51-56 (C.C.C.).

[242] [1997] N.S.J. No. 69, 113 C.C.C. (3d) 237 (N.S.C.A.), leave to appeal refused [1997] S.C.C.A. No. 129, 42 C.R.R. (2d) 188 (S.C.C.).

[243] *Ibid.*

[244] *Ibid.*, at para. 34 (C.C.C.). See also *R. v. Hughes*, [1998] B.C.J. No. 1694 (B.C.S.C.) (no reasonable expectation of privacy in reporter's interview notes as material was intended to be reported).

§3.82 An issue likely to become increasingly prominent is whether the collection and indexing of disparate pieces of non-intimate information is capable of invading a reasonable expectation of privacy. The growing digitization of searchable, private and public sector information databases have facilitated this technique, often called "data mining".[245] The Supreme Court of Canada in *Smith v. Canada (Attorney General)*[246] considered a small-scale data-mining program. There, the Court tersely affirmed a decision upholding the constitutionality of a federal government program enabling the cross-departmental sharing of customs information to detect fraudulent Employment Insurance claims. The courts below had held that air travellers entering Canada have no reasonable expectation of privacy in the information that they are compelled to disclose (name, date of birth, postal code, dates departed from and returned to Canada, and purpose of travel) and that employment insurance officials were thus free to systematically match this information with their own records to identify beneficiaries who unlawfully claimed benefits for periods in which they were not present in Canada.[247]

§3.83 As with public video surveillance, viewed in isolation, the individual pieces of information acquired by data-mining programs will not often reveal much about an individual's "personal lifestyle or private decisions."[248] But by aggregating data from a vast number of sources over time, data mining may paint a detailed portrait of a person's associations and habits. In the absence of regulation, police may use this information in abusive and discriminatory ways.[249] The state's use of broad, systematic data-mining techniques should thus be considered to invade a reasonable expectation of privacy.[250]

---

[245] See generally, Daniel J. Solove, "Digital Dossiers and the Dissipation of Fourth Amendment Privacy" (2002) 75 S. Cal. L. Rev. 1083.

[246] [2001] S.C.J. No. 85, [2001] 3 S.C.R. 902 (S.C.C.), affg [2000] F.C.J. No. 174, 252 N.R. 172 (F.C.A.), affg CUB-44824 (U.I.C. Umpire).

[247] *Ibid.*

[248] See *R. v. Plant*, [1993] S.C.J. No. 97, 84 C.C.C. (3d) 203 at 293 (S.C.C.).

[249] See Daniel J. Solove, "Digital Dossiers and the Dissipation of Fourth Amendment Privacy" (2002) 75 S. Cal. L. Rev. 1083 at 1084-85; Wayne N. Renke, "Who Controls the Past Now Controls the Future: Counter-Terrorism, Data Mining and Privacy" (2006) 43 Alta. L. Rev. 779 at 804.

[250] Wayne N. Renke, "Who Controls the Past Now Controls the Future: Counter-Terrorism, Data Mining and Privacy" (2006) 43 Alta. L. Rev. 779 at 800-809; Office of the Privacy Commissioner of Canada, *Opinion: CCRA Passenger Name Record* by Gérard V. La Forest (April 5, 2002) (proposal for long-term retention of detailed information travel information from airline passengers entering Canada likely infringes s. 8), online: <http://www.privcom.gc.ca/media/nrc/opinion_021122_lf_e.asp>. As with public video surveillance, data-mining programs may require a different approach to the assessment of "reasonableness" under s. 8. See Wayne N. Renke, "Who Controls the Past Now Controls the Future: Counter-Terrorism, Data Mining and Privacy" (2006) 43 Alta. L. Rev. 779 at 810-21.

(vii) Communications

§3.84 The privacy interest attaching to private communications is very strong.[251] Even before the *Charter*, Parliament introduced legislation criminalizing unauthorized wiretapping and subjecting its authorization to onerous conditions.[252] It came as no surprise, therefore, that after the *Charter*'s passage, the Supreme Court of Canada held that the covert interception of private communications invades a reasonable expectation privacy.[253] Somewhat more surprising was the Court's finding in *R. v. Duarte*[254] that this expectation exists even where one of the parties to the communication (such as an informer or undercover police officer) is aware of the interception.[255] At the time, the *Criminal Code* did not require authorizations for such intercepts,[256] and the United States Supreme Court had held that the Fourth Amendment did not apply to them.[257] In *United States v. White*,[258] the Court held that if the law "gives no protection to the wrongdoer whose trusted accomplice is or becomes a police agent, neither should it protect him when that same agent has recorded or transmitted the conversations which are later offered in evidence to prove the State's case."[259] Writing for the Supreme Court of Canada in *Duarte*, Justice La Forest rejected this approach, asserting that while section 8 does not protect people from the risk that their confidants will turn out to be informers, it does prohibit the state from arbitrarily making a "permanent electronic record" of their conversations.[260] Courts have also held that text-based communication technologies, such as email, attract a reasonable expectation of privacy.[261]

---

[251] See Steven Penney, "Reasonable Expectations of Privacy and Novel Search Technologies: An Economic Approach" (2007) 97 J. Crim. L. & Criminology 477 at 492-93; Steven Penney "Updating Canada's Communications Surveillance Laws: Privacy and Security in the Digital Age" (2008) 12 Can. Crim. L. Rev 115 at 129-30.

[252] *Protection of Privacy Act*, S.C. 1973-74, c. 50, s. 2. See now *Criminal Code*, R.S.C. 1985, c. C-46, Part VI, which is discussed below, Part 3(8).

[253] See *R. v. Duarte*, [1990] S.C.J. No. 2, [1990] 1 S.C.R. 30 at 42 (S.C.C.) ("surreptitious electronic surveillance of the individual by an agency of the state constitutes an unreasonable search or seizure under s. 8 of the Charter"); *R. v. Wiggins*, [1990] S.C.J. No. 3, [1990] 1 S.C.R. 62 (S.C.C.); *R. v. Thompson*, [1990] S.C.J. No. 104, [1990] 2 S.C.R. 1111 at 136-37 (S.C.C.).

[254] [1990] S.C.J. No. 2, [1990] 1 S.C.R. 30 (S.C.C.).

[255] *Ibid.*

[256] See *Criminal Code*, R.S.C. 1970, c. C-34, s. 178.11.

[257] *United States v. White*, 401 U.S. 745 (1971) (plurality) (no expectation of privacy when defendant communicates with informant surreptitiously carrying a "wire" transmitting conversations to police).

[258] 401 U.S. 745 (1971).

[259] *Ibid.*, at 752.

[260] *R. v. Duarte*, [1990] S.C.J. No. 2, [1990] 1 S.C.R. 30 at 48 (S.C.C.). Note, however, that s. 8 is not violated when someone privy to an illegally recorded communication testifies at trial as to their recollection of the communication, even if the participant's memory has been refreshed by reference to the tainted recording. But it is violated when portions of an illegally obtained recording or transcript that a witness does not recall are adduced in evidence. See *R. v. Fliss*, [2002] S.C.J. No. 15, [2002] 1 S.C.R. 535 (S.C.C.).

[261] See *R. v. Weir*, [1998] A.J. No. 155, [1998] 8 W.W.R. 228 at paras. 70-77 (Alta. Q.B.), affd [2001] A.J. No. 869, 156 C.C.C. (3d) 188 (Alta. C.A.). See also *Warshak v. United States*, 2007

§3.85 It will not always be reasonable to expect, however, that an electronic communication will not be intercepted or recorded by state agents. For example, section 8 does not protect the privacy of 911 calls.[262] In some circumstances, communications made in custodial settings may also be exempted from section 8 protection. Police may surreptitiously record interviews with suspects,[263] but they may not do so with respect to prisoners' telephone conversations.[264] The courts have split, however, on the question of whether non-privileged telephone communications may be intercepted when prisoners are informed that their conversations may be monitored.[265]

§3.86 There are also divergent decisions on whether radio-based communications devices, such as pagers, cordless telephones and wireless phones, are protected under section 8.[266] Because communications transmitted by older versions of these devices could often be intercepted by commercially available receivers, a number of courts held that they did not attract a reasonable expectation of privacy, either under Part VI of the *Criminal Code*, section 8 of the *Charter*, or both.[267] Contemporary radio-based communications are much harder to

---

U.S. App. LEXIS 14297 (6th Cir.) (email stored by service provider attracts reasonable expectation of privacy); Robert W. Hubbard, Peter DeFreitas & Susan Magotiaux, "The Internet: Expectations of Privacy in a New Context" (2002) 45 Crim. L.Q. 170 at 196-97. Email will not always attract a reasonable expectation of privacy, however. It has been held, for example, that, having been warned that the employer's email system was not to be used for unauthorized purposes and would be monitored, government employees had no reasonable expectation in the privacy in emails sent over this system. See *Briar v. Canada (Treasury Board)*, 2003 PSSRB 3 (Can. P.S.S.R.B.). Courts and adjudicators have come to similar conclusions in non-*Charter* cases. See *Re Owens-Corning Canada Inc. and C.E.P., Loc. 728 (Gorgichuk)* (2002), 113 L.A.C. (4th) 97 at para. 74; *Milsom v. Corporate Computers Inc.*, [2003] A.J. No. 516, 2003 ABQB 296 at para. 41 (Alta. Q.B.); *Dorrian v. Canadian Airlines International Ltd.*, [1997] C.L.A.D. No. 607.

[262] See *R. v. Robertshaw*, [1996] O.J. No. 1540 at para. 26 (Ont. Gen. Div.); *R. v. Latham*, [1993] O.J. No. 4534 (Ont. Gen. Div.).

[263] See *R. v. S. (S.)*, [1997] O.J. No. 79, 23 O.T.C. 290 (Ont. Gen. Div.); *R. v. Jenkins*, [2000] O.J. No. 5225 (Ont. S.C.J.).

[264] See *R. v. Williamson*, [1998] A.J. No. 652, 123 C.C.C. (3d) 540 (Alta. Q.B.).

[265] See *R. v. Olson*, [1993] B.C.J. No. 2529, 37 B.C.A.C. 155 (B.C.C.A.) (no reasonable expectation of privacy); *R. v. Bartkowski*, [2004] B.C.J. No. 2950, 2004 BCSC 44 (B.C.S.C.) (same); *R. v. McIsaac*, [2005] B.C.J. No. 946, 2005 BCSC 385 (B.C.S.C.) (same); *R. v. Rodney*, [1991] B.C.J. No. 2018, 65 C.C.C. (3d) 304 (B.C.S.C.) (reasonable expectation of privacy); *R. v. Williamson*, [1998] A.J. No. 652, 218 A.R. 332 at para. 65 (Alta. Q.B.) (same). See also *R. v. Bobier*, [1998] S.J. No. 654 at para. 36 (Sask. Prov. Ct.) (private citizen has a reasonable expectation of privacy in telephone conversations with a prisoner who was warned that calls would be monitored).

[266] See Steven Penney, "Updating Canada's Communications Surveillance Laws: Privacy and Security in the Digital Age" (2008) 12 Can. Crim. L. Rev. 115 at 124-25.

[267] See *R. v. Penna*, [1997] B.C.J. No. 3014 at paras. 13-19 (B.C.S.C.) (cordless landline telephone); *R. v. Watts*, [2000] B.C.J. No. 2721 at paras. 6-12 (B.C. Prov. Ct.) (same); *R. c. Solomon*, [1992] J.Q. no 2371, 77 C.C.C. (3d) 264 at 283-84 (Que. Mun. Ct.) (wireless telephone); *R. v. Wong*, [1993] B.C.J. No. 2634 at para. 11 (B.C.S.C.) (same); *R. v. Lubovac*, [1989] A.J. No. 1170, 52 C.C.C. (3d) 551 at 557 (Alta. C.A.), leave to appeal refused [1989] S.C.C.A. No. 463, 53 C.C.C. (3d) vii (S.C.C.) (pager); *R. c. Nin*, [1985] J.Q. no 155, 34 C.C.C. (3d) 89 at 91-94 (Que. Ct. Sess.) (same).

intercept,[268] and courts have accordingly held that they attract a reasonable expectation of privacy.[269]

§3.87 Courts have also recognized a reasonable expectation of privacy in the non-content "transmission" information[270] attaching to electronic communications.[271] Transmission data is typically acquired from third parties, such as telecommunications service providers. While not as intimate as communications content, transmission information can reveal a great deal about criminal suspects, including the identity of the persons and organizations that they communicate with, the frequency, duration and timing of those communications, and the location of the communicators.[272] Recognizing a reasonable expectation of privacy in this information is therefore appropriate.[273] While the transmission data attached to any single communication is not likely to be intimate, personal

---

[268] See Steven Penney, "Updating Canada's Communications Surveillance Laws: Privacy and Security in the Digital Age" (2008) 12 Can. Crim. L. Rev. 115 at 124.

[269] See *R. v. Cheung*, [1995] B.C.J. No. 1751, 100 C.C.C. (3d) 441 at para. 17 (B.C.S.C.) (wireless telephone); *R. v. Larson*, [1996] A.J. No. 959 at para. 29 (Alta. Prov. Ct.) (same); *R. c. Harbour*, [1995] A.Q. no. 1165 at paras. 74-79 (Que. S.C.) (same); *R. v. Wong*, [1993] B.C.J. No. 2634 at para. 24 (B.C.S.C.) (same). See *R. v. Penna*, [1997] B.C.J. No. 3014 at para. 13 (B.C.S.C.); *R. v. Watts*, [2000] B.C.J. No. 2721 at para. 9 (B.C. Prov. Ct.).

[270] Transmission data, sometimes referred to as "envelope" information, refers to addressing and other information attached to a communication that is the functional equivalent of the information contained on the outside of a letter mail envelope. See Orin S. Kerr, "Internet Surveillance After the *USA Patriot Act*: The Big Brother That Isn't" (2003) 97 Nw. U. L. Rev. 607 at 611-16; Robert W. Hubbard, Peter DeFreitas & Susan Magotiaux, "The Internet: Expectations of Privacy in a New Context" (2002) 45 Crim. L.Q. 170 at 190.

[271] Before the enactment of s. 492.2 of the *Criminal Code* in 1993, discussed below, Part 3(8), courts had held that telephone transmission data attracted a reasonable expectation of privacy when it related to local calls (which were not logged by the phone company for billing purposes) but not when it related to long-distance calls (which were so logged). See *R. v. Griffith*, [1988] O.J. No. 1659, 44 C.C.C. (3d) 63 (Ont. Dist. Ct.); *R. v. Mikituk*, [1992] S.J. No. 235, 101 Sask. R. 286 (Sask. Q.B.); *R. v. Khiamal*, [1990] A.J. No. 279, 73 Alta. L.R. (2d) 359 (Alta. Q.B.). The great majority of courts that have since considered the matter have held that all telephone transmission information attracts a reasonable expectation of privacy. See *Cody c. R.*, [2007] Q.J. No. 11001, 228 C.C.C. (3d) 331 at para. 25 (Que. C.A.); *R. v. Nguyen*, [2004] B.C.J. No. 247, 20 C.R. (6th) 151 at para. 15 (B.C.S.C.); *R. v. Hackert*, [1997] O.J. No. 6384 (Ont. Gen. Div.); *R. v. Bryan*, [1999] O.J. No. 5074, 70 C.R.R. (2d) 305 (Ont. S.C.J.); *R. v. Mahmood*, [2008] O.J. No. 3922, 236 C.C.C. (3d) 3 at paras. 55-82 (Ont. S.C.J.), reconsideration denied [2009] O.J. No. 3192, 194 C.R.R. (2d) 180 (Ont. S.C.J.); *R. v. Pal*, [2007] B.C.J. No. 2193, 2007 BCSC 1494 (B.C.S.C.); *R. v. Lee*, [2007] A.J. No. 1473, 88 Alta. L.R. (4th) 231 at para. 283 (Alta. Q.B.). For decisions to the contrary, see *R. v. Brown*, [2000] O.J. No. 1177 (Ont. S.C.J.); *Smith v. Maryland*, 442 U.S. 735 (1979).

[272] See *R. v. Mahmood*, [2008] O.J. No. 3922, 236 C.C.C. (3d) 3 at para. 77 (Ont. S.C.J.), reconsideration refused [2009] O.J. No. 3192, 194 C.R.R. (2d) 180 (Ont. S.C.J.) ("no doubt that the cell phone records obtained ... could and did reveal personal information that contained at least some of the elements of biographical core, in terms of providing some general identification of movement, of personal associations, and of frequency of contact with associated persons").

[273] See Steven Penney, "Updating Canada's Communications Surveillance Laws: Privacy and Security in the Digital Age" (2008) 12 Can. Crim. L. Rev. 115 at 145-46. Parliament implicitly recognized a reasonable expectation of privacy in telephone transmission data in passing s. 492.2 of the *Criminal Code*, R.S.C. 1985, c. C-46, which is discussed below, Part 3(9)(*b*).

or stigmatizing,[274] when aggregated from multiple communications, it may paint a detailed portrait of a person's "lifestyle or private decisions".[275] Giving police unrestricted access to this information could chill lawful and socially beneficial communications, induce wasteful spending on privacy protection measures and facilitate discriminatory profiling.[276]

§3.88 There is no jurisprudential consensus, however, on whether the "subscriber" information associated with electronic communications attracts a reasonable expectation of privacy.[277] Analogous to the name, address and number associated with a conventional landline telephone number (whether publicly listed or not), police often need this information to acquire either the content or transmission information attaching to a suspect's electronic communications. A generation ago, this was rarely a problem. Armed with a suspect's name, address or telephone number, police could easily obtain the other two items from the local monopoly service provider, even if the subscriber's number was not listed in a public directory.[278] Today the situation is much more complicated. There are many more communications technologies, service providers and legal restrictions on the disclosure of customers' personal information. If a service provider refuses to disclose a customer's subscriber information, police must rely on a court order to compel them to do so. A search warrant or production order will suffice, but in either case police must satisfy the onerous reasonable and probable grounds standard. As mentioned, telephone subscriber information may

---

[274] See Stanley A. Cohen, *Privacy, Crime and Terror: Legal Rights and Security in a Time of Peril* (Markham, ON: LexisNexis Butterworths, 2005) at 494-96.

[275] *R. v. Plant*, [1993] S.C.J. No. 97, 84 C.C.C. (3d) 203 at 293 (S.C.C.).

[276] See Steven Penney, "Updating Canada's Communications Surveillance Laws: Privacy and Security in the Digital Age" (2008) 12 Can. Crim. L. Rev. 115 at 145-46.

[277] See *R. v. Nguyen*, [2004] B.C.J. No. 247, 20 C.R. (6th) 151 at paras. 23-24 (B.C.S.C.) (reasonable expectation that service provider would keep mobile phone number confidential); *Re C. (S.)*, [2006] O.J. No. 3754, 71 W.C.B. (2d) 241 (Ont. C.J.) (reasonable expectation that service provider would keep Internet customer's name and address confidential); *R. v. Cuttell*, [2009] O.J. No. 4053, 247 C.C.C. (3d) 424 (Ont. C.J.) (reasonable expectation of privacy in subscriber information linked to Internet address); *R. v. Kwok*, [2008] O.J. No. 2414 (Ont. C.J.) (same); *R. v. Hutchings*, [1996] B.C.J. No. 3060, 111 C.C.C. (3d) 215 at paras. 22-26 (B.C.C.A.) (declining to find a reasonable expectation of privacy in telephone numbers, but noting that there was no evidence that the suspect's number was unlisted); *R. v. Brown*, [2000] O.J. No. 1177 at para. 63 (Ont. S.C.J.) (no reasonable expectation of privacy in mobile phone subscriber records); *R. v. Stucky*, [2006] O.J. No. 108, [2006] O.T.C. 30 (Ont. S.C.J.) (no reasonable expectation of privacy in identifying information of postal box customer); *R. v. Friers*, [2008] O.J. No. 5646, 2008 ONCJ 740 (Ont. C.J.) (no reasonable expectation of privacy in account information associated with subscriber's Internet address); *R. v. Wilson*, [2009] O.J. No. 1067 (Ont. S.C.J.) (same); *R. v. McGarvie* (2009), 2009 CarswellOnt 500 (Ont. C.J.) (same); *R. v. Ward*, [2008] O.J. No. 3116 (Ont. C.J.) (same); *R. v. McNeice*, [2010] B.C.J. No. 2131, 2010 BCSC 1544 (B.C.S.C.) (same); *R. v. Brousseau*, [2010] O.J. No. 5793, 2010 ONSC 6753 (Ont. S.C.J.) (same); *R. v. Spencer*, [2009] S.J. No. 798, 2009 SKQB 341 (Sask. Q.B.) (same); *R. v. Vasic*, [2009] O.J. No. 1968 (Ont. S.C.J.) (no reasonable expectation of privacy in subscriber information linked to Internet address where customer service agreement expressly denied confidentiality).

[278] See Robert W. Hubbard, Susan Magotiaux & Xenia Proestos, "The Limits of Privacy: Police Access to Subscriber Information in Canada" (2002) 46 Crim. L.Q. 361 at 362-63.

likely be obtained on the basis of reasonable suspicion.[279] However, as mentioned, police commonly seek to obtain subscriber information to establish the grounds for obtaining these orders.[280]

§3.89 We thus caution against recognizing an expectation of privacy for subscriber information.[281] It is difficult to see how a customer's name, address[282] or the identifying information attaching to a communications mechanism (such as a telephone number or email address) would reveal intimate details of people's lifestyles or personal choices, even if the information is not publicly available.[283] Of course, subscriber information may be linked with other sources of personal information to compile detailed and intimate profiles of people's lifestyles and behaviour.[284] But so long as they do not systematically troll for this information as part of a broader data-mining effort,[285] police should not be required to have either individualized suspicion or a warrant to obtain it. Such conditions would severely hamper police efforts to combat crime on and offline.

(c)   Waiving the Right to Privacy: Searches and Seizures on Consent

§3.90 If police investigative activities encroach upon a reasonable expectation of privacy then section 8's reasonableness requirements are engaged. (These standards are considered in detail below.) As with any *Charter* right, people are entitled to waive the protections afforded by section 8.[286] Such waivers are also characterized as "consent" searches or seizures because their legality turns on

---

[279]   See below, Part 3(9)(*b*).

[280]   See Robert W. Hubbard, Susan Magotiaux & Xenia Proestos, "The Limits of Privacy: Police Access to Subscriber Information in Canada" (2002) 46 Crim. L.Q. 361 at 363, 372-73.

[281]   For an extended version of this argument, see Steven Penney, "Updating Canada's Communications Surveillance Laws: Privacy and Security in the Digital Age" (2008) 12 Can. Crim. L. Rev. 115 at 154-58.

[282]   This would include any unique physical or "virtual" address (such as an Internet protocol address) identifying an individual communications device. See Robert W. Hubbard, Peter De-Freitas & Susan Magotiaux, "The Internet: Expectations of Privacy in a New Context" (2002) 45 Crim. L.Q. 170 at 196; Robert W. Hubbard, Susan Magotiaux & Xenia Proestos, "The Limits of Privacy: Police Access to Subscriber Information in Canada" (2002) 46 Crim. L.Q. 361 at 387. On the legal issues implicated by compelling the disclosure of IP addresses in the civil context, see *BMG Canada Inc. v. John Doe*, [2005] F.C.J. No. 858, [2005] 4 F.C.R. 81 (F.C.A.).

[283]   Robert W. Hubbard, Susan Magotiaux & Xenia Proestos, "The Limits of Privacy: Police Access to Subscriber Information in Canada" (2002) 46 Crim. L.Q. 361 at 370-71, 373, 383-87. This is not to say that an individual's identity can never attract a reasonable expectation of privacy. In some circumstances, its disclosure may itself reveal intimate, personal information, such as the fact that a person has received medical treatment or legal advice. See Tracey M. Bailey & Steven Penney, "Healing not Squealing: Recent Amendments to Alberta's *Health Information Act*" (2007) 15 Health L. Rev. 3.

[284]   See Stanley A. Cohen, *Privacy, Crime and Terror: Legal Rights and Security in a Time of Peril* (Markham, ON: LexisNexis Butterworths, 2005) at 533.

[285]   See discussion above, Part 2(4)(*b*)(vi).

[286]   On the standard for the waiver of *Charter* rights see generally, *R. v. Clarkson*, [1986] S.C.J. No. 20, [1986] 1 S.C.R. 383 (S.C.C.). See also *R. v. Evans*, [1991] S.C.J. No. 31, [1991] 1 S.C.R. 869 at 892-94 (S.C.C.); *R. v. Tran*, [1994] S.C.J. No. 16, [1994] 2 S.C.R. 951 at para. 78 (S.C.C.).

the subject's agreement to forego the constitutional protections that would otherwise apply. As Justice Doherty explained in *R. v. Wills*, [287] when "one consents to the police taking something that they otherwise have no right to take, one relinquishes one's right to be left alone by the state and removes the reasonableness barrier imposed by section 8 of the *Charter*."[288] Because consent searches or seizures are by definition warrantless, the burden of establishing a valid waiver will fall on the party seeking to justify it, which will almost always be the Crown.[289]

§3.91 If an individual's consent is determined to be valid, then the protections afforded by section 8 of the *Charter* are waived. If, on the other hand, a purported consent is determined to be deficient, absent any other legal authority, the resulting search or seizure will very likely be characterized as "unreasonable" for section 8 *Charter* purposes.

(i)   The Requirements for a Valid Consent

§3.92 There are three requirements for a valid consent to a search or seizure. First, the person giving the consent must have the authority to do so. Obviously, an individual is only entitled to waive their own privacy interests, not those of a third party. Consequently, the police must make some effort to ensure that the person from whom consent is sought has the authority to grant it.[290]

§3.93 Second, the consent must be voluntary.[291] As with confessions, to be considered "voluntary", consent "must not be procured by intimidating conduct or by force or threats of force by the police."[292] In addition, the giver of consent must also have the capacity to waive his or her privacy rights. As with the con-

---

[287] [1992] O.J. No. 294, 70 C.C.C. (3d) 529 (Ont. C.A.).

[288] *Ibid.*, at para. 48 (O.J.).

[289] See *Hunter v. Southam (sub nom. Canada (Combines Investigation Acts, Director of Investigation and Research) v. Southam Inc.)*, [1984] S.C.J. No. 36, [1984] 2 S.C.R. 145 at 161 (S.C.C.); *R. v. Wills*, [1992] O.J. No. 294, 70 C.C.C. (3d) 529 (Ont. C.A.). This presumption of unreasonableness for warrantless searches or seizures is explained in the next Part.

[290] *R. v. Wills*, [1992] O.J. No. 294, 70 C.C.C. (3d) 529 (Ont. C.A.). See also *R. v. Blinch*, [1993] B.C.J. No. 1608, 83 C.C.C. (3d) 158 at 169-70 (B.C.C.A.). If police err regarding an individual's apparent authority to authorize a search, the reasonableness of the mistake will militate in favour of admission under s. 24(2) of the *Charter*. Such an error will not, however, serve to make lawful the purported consent offered by someone who had no authority to grant it. See *R. v. Mercer; R. v. Kenny*, [1992] O.J. No. 137, 70 C.C.C. (3d) 180 (Ont. C.A.); *R. v. Brilhante*, [2001] O.J. No. 1987, 83 C.R.R. (2d) 349 (Ont. S.C.J.).

[291] See *R. v. Mellenthin*, [1992] S.C.J. No. 100, [1992] 3 S.C.R. 615 at 624-25 (S.C.C.); *R. v. Clement*, [1996] S.C.J. No. 69, [1996] 2 S.C.R. 289 (S.C.C.); *R. v. Borden*, [1994] S.C.J. No. 82, [1994] 3 S.C.R. 145 at 162 (S.C.C.).

[292] See *R. v. Goldman*, [1979] S.C.J. No. 136, [1980] 1 S.C.R. 976 at 1006 (S.C.C.). See also *R. v. Wills*, [1992] O.J. No. 294, 70 C.C.C. (3d) 529 (Ont. C.A.). See *e.g.*, *R. v. Login*, [2006] O.J. No. 680, 138 C.R.R. (2d) 254 (Ont. C.J.) (consent not voluntary when given by accused while under unlawful arrest, after having gun pointed at him, while his family was being detained and he was in police car after strip search in full view of his neighbours).

fessions rule, the individual must have an "operating mind".[293] An extremely intoxicated person, for example, might be found to lack the capacity to give a valid consent to search.[294]

§3.94 Third, the consent must be "informed". This requires the individual to have enough information to allow a "meaningful" choice as to whether to permit the search or seizure.[295] What exactly does this entail?

§3.95 First, an informed consent requires compliance with section 10(*b*) of the *Charter*. As a consequence, any person "detained" or "arrested" under the *Charter*[296] must be told that he or she has the right to retain and instruct counsel without delay and to be informed of that right.[297] If this right is violated, any purported consent is automatically vitiated.[298] For example, because motorists searched following traffic stops are always "detained" for *Charter* purposes, any failure to comply with the right to counsel would consequently render unconstitutional any accompanying consent searches.[299]

§3.96 Second, an informed consent requires that the subject be aware of the right to refuse permission for the search or seizure. In other words, an individual cannot be said to give an *informed* consent if he or she is ignorant of the choice to do otherwise.[300] Strictly speaking, this does not necessarily require police to apprise suspects of their right to refuse. If the police fail to do so, however, it will be extremely difficult for the Crown to prove that the suspect knew of this right and nevertheless decided to forego it.[301]

---

[293] The operating mind requirement of the confessions rule is discussed in detail in Chapter 4, Part 2(3)(*a*).

[294] See generally, *R. v. Clarkson*, [1986] S.C.J. No. 20, [1986] 1 S.C.R. 383 (S.C.C.).

[295] See *R. v. Borden*, [1994] S.C.J. No. 82, [1994] 3 S.C.R. 145 at 161-62 (S.C.C.). See also *R. v. Arp*, [1998] S.C.J. No. 82, [1998] 3 S.C.R. 339 at para. 87 (S.C.C.) ("persons consenting must be aware of their rights and as far as possible the consequences of their consent").

[296] What will constitute a "detention" under the *Charter* is considered in detail in Chapter 2, Part 2(3)(*b*).

[297] Section 10(*b*) of the *Charter* is discussed in detail in Chapter 4, Part 3(4).

[298] See *R. v. DeBot*, [1989] S.C.J. No. 118, [1989] 2 SC.R. 1140 (S.C.C.), holding that the right to counsel must be complied with "where the lawfulness of the search is dependent on the detainee's consent." *Ibid.*, para. 3, *per* Lamer J. concurring.

[299] See *e.g.*, *R. v. Calderon*, [2004] O.J. No. 3474, 188 C.C.C. (3d) 481 para. 85 (Ont. C.A.) (finding a purported consent invalid where it was obtained following a traffic stop without first appraising the driver and passenger of their s. 10(*b*) *Charter* rights). On the definition of "detention" and why motor vehicle stops necessarily qualify, see Chapter 2, Part 3(3)(*b*)(ii). It is an open question whether passengers riding in a vehicle stopped by police are similarly "detained". Although it seems somewhat obvious that they would be, the question remains somewhat unsettled. See *R. v. Harris*, [2007] O.J. No. 3185, 225 C.C.C. (3d) 193 at paras. 18-22 (Ont. C.A.) (signalling that passengers are most likely detained during a traffic stop but declining to decide the issue). This issue is discussed in further detail in Chapter 2, Part 3(3)(*b*)(ii).

[300] See *R. v. Mellenthin*, [1992] S.C.J. No. 100, [1992] 3 S.C.R. 615 at 624 (S.C.C.), wherein the Court noted that it was, "... incumbent upon the Crown to adduce evidence that the person detained had indeed made an informed consent to the search based upon an awareness of his rights to refuse to respond to the questions or to consent to the search."

[301] See *R. v. Lewis*, [1998] O.J. No. 376, 122 C.C.C. (3d) 481 at para. 12 (Ont. C.A.) ("If the police do not tell a person of the right to refuse to give a consent to a search, the police run the very real risk that any apparent consent given will be found to be no consent at all for the purposes of

§3.97 Third, an informed consent requires the individual to be aware of the potential consequences of the search or seizure. This means that that the person must know: (*i*) the investigative purposes for which consent is being sought; and (*ii*) that anything found could be used against him or her to substantiate a criminal charge.[302] In *R. v. Borden*,[303] for example, the accused was under arrest for a sexual assault that had taken place at a motel involving an exotic dancer. The attack did not involve intercourse or ejaculation. Unbeknownst to the accused, the police also suspected that he was involved in the rape of an elderly woman. The police requested a blood sample from the accused. The wording of the written consent signed by him referred the taking of his blood by police for "purposes relating to their investigations".[304] The use of the plural was not accidental, as the police intended to use the sample to investigate the attack on the elderly woman. That ulterior purpose was never disclosed to the accused. The Supreme Court concluded that this non-disclosure not only violated the accused's section 10(*a*) *Charter* right (which obliges police to inform those detained of the "reasons" for their detention[305]), but also served to undermine the validity of the accused's consent for the taking of his blood. Writing for the majority, Justice Iacobucci explained as follows:

> The degree of awareness of the consequences of the waiver of the s. 8 right required of an accused in a given case will depend on its particular facts. Obviously, it will not be necessary for the accused to have a detailed comprehension of every possible outcome of his or her consent. However, his or her understanding should include the fact that the police are also planning to use the product of the seizure in a different investigation from the one for which he or she is detained. Such was not the case here. Therefore, I conclude that the police seized the respondent's blood in relation to the offence forming the subject matter of this charge.[306]

---

s. 8. ... Where the police do not inform a person of the right to refuse to consent to a search, it is certainly open to a trial judge to conclude that the person was unaware of the right to refuse and could not, therefore, give an informed consent."). See also *R. v. Rutten*, [2006] S.J. No. 65, 205 C.C.C. (3d) 504 at para. 38 (Sask. C.A.); *R. v. Luc*, [2004] S.J. No. 542, 188 C.C.C. (3d) 436 (Sask. C.A.), leave to appeal refused [2004] S.C.C.A. No. 480 (S.C.C.); *R. v. Lam*, [2003] B.C.J. No. 2565, 180 C.C.C. (3d) 279 at para. 35 (B.C.C.A); *R. v. Coggan*, [1999] N.B.J. No. 476, 218 N.B.R. (2d) 369 at para. 14 (N.B.Q.B.). But see *R. v. Clement*, [1996] S.C.J. No. 69, [1996] 2 S.C.R. 289 (S.C.C.) (consent valid as the "appellant testified that he knew that the police had no right to search his car"); *R. v. Kennedy*, [2000] B.C.J. No. 1167, 147 C.C.C. (3d) 144 (B.C.C.A.) (accused not told of right to refuse police request to look inside his home for a wanted person but ultimately refused police request to look in basement, a fact that was emphasized in finding that the accused knew of the right to refuse and therefore initial consent was held to be valid). See also *R. v. Head*, [1994] B.C.J. No. 2522, 52 B.C.A.C. 121 (B.C.C.A.) (trial judge's finding of valid consent upheld despite police failure to tell accused of right to refuse).

302 See *R. v. Wills*, [1992] O.J. No. 294, 70 C.C.C. (3d) 529 (Ont. C.A.).

303 [1994] S.C.J. No. 82, [1994] 3 S.C.R. 145 (S.C.C.).

304 *Ibid.*, at para. 21 (S.C.J.).

305 This right is discussed in detail in Chapter 4, Part 3(3).

306 [1994] S.C.J. No. 82 at para. 40, [1994] 3 S.C.R. 145 (S.C.C.). The Court also rejected the Crown's argument that because Borden had left his semen at the scene of the attack on the eld-

§3.98 To obtain an informed consent, however, police need only disclose "those anticipated purposes known to the police at the time the consent was given".[307] Thus, the Supreme Court concluded in *R. v. Arp*[308] that police were entitled to use hair samples provided freely and unconditionally by Mr. Arp during an earlier investigation when he became a suspect in a different investigation almost thirty months later. As the Court explained:

> ... if neither the police nor the consenting person limit the use which may be made of the evidence then, as a general rule no limitation or restriction should be placed on the use of that evidence.[309]

§3.99 Lastly, informed consent requires police to be forthright regarding their legal position. *R. v. O'Connor*[310] involved a search of a suspect's truck based on his purported consent. The accused had initially refused police requests to search the vehicle. In response, officers told him that unless he consented they would apply for a search warrant and that its execution might take place at a time inconvenient for him. Shortly thereafter the accused consented. When police sought the accused's consent, they recognized that they lacked the requisite grounds to obtain a warrant. Although the officers were careful to only tell the accused that they would *apply* for a warrant, in assessing the validity of this purported consent the Ontario Court of Appeal focussed rightly on what the accused would have understood. Although what police told the accused was literally accurate, the information they provided would have left him with the erroneous impression that police could obtain a warrant, when in fact they could not. According to the Court, once the police raised the possibility of obtaining a warrant, "it was incumbent upon them to fully and fairly apprise the appellant of the correct situation, including the fact that they did not have sufficient grounds to obtain a warrant."[311]

---

erly woman, he must have known that the police might use his blood sample to connect him to that offence. The problem with such an approach, the Court reasoned, is that it would lead to different levels of *Charter* protection depending on a suspect's guilt or innocence. It also involves a form of *ex post facto* reasoning, allowing the results of an improper search to be used to then justify it — an approach that has been repeatedly repudiated by the Court in its s. 8 jurisprudence. *Ibid.*, at para. 37. See also the discussion above, Part 2(4)(*a*).

[307] [1998] S.C.J. No. 82 at para. 88, [1998] 3 S.C.R. 339 (S.C.C.).

[308] [1998] S.C.J. No. 82, [1998] 3 S.C.R. 339 (S.C.C.).

[309] *Ibid.*, at para. 87 (S.C.J.). Depending on the context, however, limitations may be implicit. For example, blood given on consent to medical personal is subject to an implicit limitation that it will only be used for medical purposes. As a result, its subsequent taking by police would require further consent or some other lawful authority. See *e.g.*, *R. v. Tran*, [2001] O.J. No. 3056, 156 C.C.C. (3d) 1 at para. 29 (Ont. C.A.). To avoid factual contests about the existence and terms of purported consent searches, police should ensure whenever possible that any consent granted be reduced to writing, including specifications as to the precise scope of the consent.

[310] [2002] O.J. No. 4410, 170 C.C.C. (3d) 365 (Ont. C.A.).

[311] *Ibid.*, at para. 75. See also *R. v. Bergauer-Free*, [2009] O.J. No. 3340, 68 C.R. (6th) 362 at paras. 54-57 (Ont. C.A.) (purported consent not effective where it resulted from police telling accused that if he did not consent to search a canine unit would be summoned; police did not disclose that they had no authority to hold the appellant pending the arrival of the canine unit).

(ii)   Withdrawal and Refusal of Consent

§3.100 Since consent is premised on the will of the individual, the person giving it should also be entitled to withdraw it. Provided that evidence or contraband has not yet been located, a reassertion of one's right to privacy should bring any search on consent to an abrupt end. As is explained in Part 3(6), below, where so-called "plain-view" seizures are explained, once incriminating evidence is located the authority of police to search and seize would no longer depend on the affected individual's consent. Therefore, the withdrawal of consent at such a very late stage should have no practical or legal effect.

§3.101 An individual's refusal to consent to a search will often raise suspicions on the part of police that the person has something to hide. Nevertheless, a refusal of consent does not provide legal grounds to believe that an individual is concealing illegality. Were it otherwise, police lacking grounds to search could seek consent and, as a result, either obtain permission to search or grounds to search. In this scenario, the right to be free from unreasonable search or seizure would be illusory.[312] For this reason, the Supreme Court of Canada has rightly indicated that a refusal of consent cannot supply the required grounds to search.[313]

(5)   When is a "Search or Seizure" Unreasonable?

(a)   General Principles

§3.102 As discussed, it is only state encroachments on a reasonable expectation of privacy that engage the protection of section 8. Such intrusions qualify as a "search or seizure". To establish a violation of section 8, however, the applicant must also demonstrate that the search or seizure was "unreasonable". Of course, "unreasonable" is not self-defining. Over the last 25 years, however, the Supreme Court of Canada has said much to help courts decide whether privacy intrusions were "reasonable" under section 8.

§3.103 The historic importance of search warrants under Anglo-Canadian law figured prominently in the Supreme Court's early efforts to give "unreasonable" meaning. In *Hunter*,[314] the Court pointed both to that history and American jurisprudence to conclude that a search or seizure that takes place without a warrant

---

[312] For the same reason, the Supreme Court of Canada has held that suspects' reliance on the right to refuse to answer police questions cannot be used against them at trial. See *R. v. Chambers*, [1990] S.C.J. No. 108, [1990] 2 S.C.R. 1293 (S.C.C.).

[313] See *R. v. Kang-Brown*, [2008] S.C.J. No. 18, [2008] 1 S.C.R. 456 at para. 92, 2008 SCC 18 (S.C.C.), *per* Binnie J. (rejecting claim that accused's objection to police searching his bag supplied reasonable suspicion that contraband was concealed within); *R. v. Ferdinand*, [2004] O.J. No. 3209, 21 C.R. (6th) 65 (Ont. S.C.J.) (reasonable suspicion not arising from accused walking away from police when approached).

[314] *Hunter v. Southam (sub nom. Canada (Combines Investigation Acts, Director of Investigation and Research) v. Southam Inc.*, [1984] S.C.J. No. 36, [1984] 2 S.C.R. 145 at 161 (S.C.C.).

is presumptively unreasonable.[315] Accordingly, the party seeking to justify a warrantless search (normally the prosecution) always bears the burden of establishing that it is "reasonable" under section 8 of the *Charter*.[316] In contrast, where the constitutionality of a search pursuant to warrant is being challenged, the burden remains where it is normally in *Charter* matters: on the party asserting the violation (usually the accused).[317]

§3.104 The general analytical framework for deciding the reasonableness of a search or seizure under section 8 of the *Charter* is as follows. To be considered "reasonable", a search or seizure must: (*i*) be authorized by a law; (*ii*) that law must itself be reasonable; and (*iii*) the search or seizure must be carried out in a reasonable manner.[318] Section 8 challenges may accordingly be brought on any of these three fronts.

§3.105 The starting point for any section 8 analysis is therefore a consideration of the lawful authority for a particular search or seizure. That authority may come either from a statute or the common law.[319] If police search or seize in circumstances where they lack or exceed their lawful powers then section 8 of the *Charter* is necessarily violated. In *R. v. Stillman*,[320] for example, the Court held that the common law power to search incident to arrest did not allow police to extract bodily substances from the person arrested.[321] Because no legislation authorized such takings at the time, the search violated section 8.[322] The question of whether particular kinds of searches are authorized by statute or at common law is addressed in Parts 3 and 4, below.

§3.106 Assuming that the police have acted under the colour of legal authority, an applicant may nevertheless argue that the particular law that authorized the search or seizure is unconstitutional on its face. To succeed, the applicant must show that the search or seizure power created by the law is unreasonable as a

---

[315] *Ibid.*, at 161 (S.C.R.).

[316] *Ibid.* See also *R. v. Nolet*, [2010] S.C.J. No. 24, [2010] 1 S.C.R. 851, 2010 SCC 24 at para. 21 (S.C.C.).

[317] See *R. v. Collins*, [1987] S.C.J. No. 15, [1987] 1 S.C.R. 265 at 277-78 (S.C.C.).

[318] *R. v. Collins*, [1987] S.C.J. No. 15, [1987] 1 S.C.R. 265 at 278 (S.C.C.). See also *R. v. Caslake*, [1998] S.C.J. No. 3, [1998] 1 S.C.R. 51 at para. 10 (S.C.C.); *R. v. Nolet*, [2010] S.C.J. No. 24, 2010 SCC 24 at para. 21 (S.C.C.). Early on, some provincial courts of appeal had held that unlawful searches are not necessarily "unreasonable" within the meaning of s. 8. See *R. v. Heisler*, [1984] A.J. No. 1008, 11 C.C.C. (3d) 475 (Alta. C.A.); *R. v. Harris*, [1987] O.J. No. 394, 57 C.R. (3d) 356 (Ont. C.A.), leave to appeal dismissed [1987] S.C.C.A. No. 395 (S.C.C.). The Supreme Court has now definitively concluded that if statutory or common law does not give police the authority to conduct a particular search, then the search is illegal and necessarily violates s. 8. *R. v. Collins*, [1987] S.C.J. No. 15, [1987] 1 S.C.R. 265 at 278 (S.C.C.); *R. v. Kokesch*, [1990] S.C.J. No. 117, [1990] 3 S.C.R. 3 at 18 (S.C.C.); *R. v. Stillman*, [1997] S.C.J. No. 34, [1997] 1 S.C.R. 607 at para. 50 (S.C.C.); *R. v. Caslake*, [1998] S.C.J. No. 3, [1998] 1 S.C.R. 51 at para. 12 (S.C.C.).

[319] See *R. v. Wiley*, [1993] S.C.J. No. 96, [1993] 3 S.C.R. 263 at 273 (S.C.C.).

[320] [1997] S.C.J. No. 34, [1997] 1 S.C.R. 607 (S.C.C.).

[321] *Ibid.*, at paras. 42-43, 49 (S.C.R.). The power to search incident to arrest is discussed below, Part 4(2).

[322] *Ibid.*, at para. 50 (S.C.R.).

matter of general application. Immediately below, we address the minimum constitutional standards for assessing the reasonableness of laws authorizing searches or seizures in a variety of contexts. Obviously, if the law under which the authorities acted is found to be unconstitutional then their actions will be considered unlawful and unreasonable. Good faith reliance by the police on a search power later determined to be invalid will be relevant, however, to a court's decision whether or not to exclude evidence under section 24(2) of the *Charter*. This issue is discussed in Chapter 10.

§3.107 Lastly, it may be argued that a facially valid search power was applied in an unconstitutional manner in a particular case because police violated a condition imposed by a statute, the common law or the *Charter*.[323] Such searches may be characterized as infringing either the "authorized by law" requirement or the "reasonable manner" requirement.[324] In *R. v. Collins*,[325] for example, the Supreme Court found that in the absence of specific information affording reasonable and probable grounds to believe that a suspect was concealing drugs inside her mouth it was unreasonable for police to violently grab her by the neck to prevent her from swallowing them.[326] The Court concluded that the search was both unlawful and conducted in an unreasonable manner.[327] Courts have come to similar conclusions in residential search cases where police used excessive force[328] or allowed the news media to film the execution of the search inside a home.[329]

§3.108 As explained by the Supreme Court in *Hunter*,[330] context is all-important in assessing the reasonableness of a law authorizing a search or seizure. As mentioned, section 8 requires courts to balance individual privacy against public interests. Section 8's requirements will accordingly vary depending on the nature and strength of these competing interests.

§3.109 That said, in *Hunter* the Court established what can usefully be thought of as three "default" minimum requirements for reasonableness under section 8:

---

[323] See generally, *R. v. Caslake*, [1998] S.C.J. No. 3, [1998] 1 S.C.R. 51 at para. 12 (S.C.C.).

[324] See generally, *R. v. DeBot*, [1989] S.C.J. No. 118, [1989] 2 S.C.R. 1140 at para. 6 (S.C.C.) ("The 'manner' in which the search is conducted relates to the physical way in which it is carried out."). See also *R. v. Kang-Brown*, [2008] S.C.J. No. 18, [2008] 1 S.C.R. 456 at para. 60, 2008 SCC 18 (S.C.C.) (suggesting that a search without lawful authority was unreasonable under both the first and third *Collins* prongs.)

[325] [1987] S.C.J. No. 15, [1987] 1 S.C.R. 265 at 278 (S.C.C.).

[326] *Ibid.*, at 278-79 (S.C.R.). Had such grounds been present, the seizure would have been authorized by a statutory search power. *Ibid.*, at 278 (S.C.R.). Since the trial judge erred in failing to consider the import of hearsay evidence in forming such grounds, the Court ordered a new trial to determine whether reasonable and probable grounds in fact existed.

[327] *Ibid.*, at 279 (S.C.R.) ("Without [evidence of reasonable and probable grounds], it is clear that the trial judge was correct in concluding that the search was unreasonable because unlawful and carried out with unnecessary violence."). See also *R. v. Caslake*, [1998] S.C.J. No. 3, [1998] 1 S.C.R. 51 (S.C.C.).

[328] See *e.g.*, *R. v. Genest*, [1989] S.C.J. No. 5, [1989] 1 S.C.R. 59 (S.C.C.).

[329] See *e.g.*, *R. v. West*, [1997] B.C.J. No. 2755, 122 C.C.C. (3d) 218 (B.C.C.A.).

[330] *Hunter v. Southam (sub nom. Canada (Combines Investigation Acts, Director of Investigation and Research) v. Southam Inc.*, [1984] S.C.J. No. 36, [1984] 2 S.C.R. 145 (S.C.C.).

- The law should require that searches be authorized by warrant except in circumstances where it is not feasible to obtain one.

- The standard for searching should be reasonable and probable grounds, established on oath, to believe that a crime has been committed and that the search will reveal evidence of that crime.

- The law should require that someone capable of acting judicially (*i.e.*, a judge or justice of the peace) be the one to decide adequacy of the grounds for issuing the warrant.[331]

§3.110 The three "*Hunter* standards", as they are often called, may be collapsed into two: (*i*) prior authorization, *i.e.*, a warrant issued by an impartial arbiter; and (*ii*) reasonable and probable grounds. As default standards, they will apply unless one or both are shown to be inappropriate in the circumstances.[332] For example, in *Hunter*, Justice Dickson noted that the reasonable and probable grounds requirement might not be appropriate where "the state's interest is not simply law enforcement as, for instance, where state security is involved, or where the individual's interest is not simply his expectation of privacy as, for instance, when the search threatens his bodily integrity...".[333] This implies, and subsequent case law has confirmed, that the standard for justifying a search may be raised or lowered based on a weighing of state and individual interests in a particular context. The post-*Hunter* jurisprudence has also made clear that warrantless searches may be found to be reasonable under section 8, even in cases where it would have been feasible to obtain one. As the Supreme Court has stressed, courts making reasonableness decisions must consider a multitude of factors "in light of the particular factual situation presented."[334] The various circumstances in which this has occurred are canvassed in detail below in Parts 2(5)(*c*) to (*d*).

(b) The Hunter Standards

(i) Prior Authorization

§3.111 As stressed in *Hunter*, the purpose of section 8 is to prevent unjustified searches "before they happen", not to simply decide, after the fact, "whether

---

[331] *Ibid.* A fourth minimum standard, discussed below, Part 2(5)(*c*), was established in *Baron v. Canada*, [1993] S.C.J. No. 6, [1993] 1 S.C.R. 416 (S.C.C.). It requires that all warrant-based search powers give the issuing authority the discretion to impose any additional conditions necessary to render the search reasonable in the particular circumstances at hand.

[332] See *R. v. Simmons*, [1988] S.C.J. No. 86, [1988] 2 S.C.R. 495 at para. 47 (S.C.C.) ("departures from the *Hunter v. Southam Inc.* standards that will be considered reasonable will be exceedingly rare."). As discussed below, Part 2(5)(*d*), this prediction has been proven to be flawed.

[333] *Hunter v. Southam (sub nom. Canada (Combines Investigation Acts, Director of Investigation and Research) v. Southam Inc.)*, [1984] S.C.J. No. 36, [1984] 2 S.C.R. 145 at 168 (S.C.C.).

[334] *Canadian Broadcasting Corp. v. New Brunswick (Attorney General)*, [1991] S.C.J. No. 88, [1991] 3 S.C.R. 459 at 478 (S.C.C.).

they ought to have occurred."[335] This is best accomplished by obliging police to get a warrant. Police are strongly motivated to uncover evidence of crime. If they are wholly free to decide when and how to search, they will systematically favour this interest over suspects' privacy. By requiring this decision to be approved by someone who is impartial as between these interests, warrants improve the odds that an appropriate balance will be struck between them. As Justice Dickson put it in *Hunter*:

> The purpose of a requirement of prior authorization is to provide an opportunity, before the event, for the conflicting interests of the state and the individual to be assessed, so that the individual's right to privacy will be breached only where the appropriate standard has been met, and the interests of the state are thus demonstrably superior. For such an authorization procedure to be meaningful it is necessary for the person authorizing the search to be able to assess the evidence as to whether that standard has been met, in an entirely neutral and impartial manner.[336]

§3.112 *Hunter* also provided guidance for deciding whether the person authorizing a search is "neutral and impartial".[337] He or she "need not be a judge, but he [or she] must at a minimum be capable of acting judicially."[338] The provisions of the *Combines Investigation Act*[339] at issue in *Hunter* gave the authority to approve searches to officials with both investigative and adjudicative powers.[340] Their investigative role, the Court concluded, was incompatible with the inherently independent, judicial function demanded by the prior authorization requirement.[341] The search power was therefore found to infringe section 8.

§3.113 Warrants issued under the *Criminal Code* and other criminal law statutes must be issued by members of the judiciary, *i.e.*, justices of the peace, provincial court judges and superior court judges.[342] Categorically speaking, each of these adjudicators meets the "neutral and impartial" standard.[343] Courts have occasionally held, however, that justices of the peace (JPs) were not performing

---

[335] *Hunter v. Southam (sub nom. Canada (Combines Investigation Acts, Director of Investigation and Research) v. Southam Inc.)*, [1984] S.C.J. No. 36, [1984] 2 S.C.R. 145 at 160 (S.C.C.).

[336] *Ibid.*, at 161-62 (S.C.R.).

[337] *Ibid.*, at 162 (S.C.R.).

[338] *Ibid.*

[339] R.S.C. 1970, c. C-23.

[340] *Hunter v. Southam (sub nom. Canada (Combines Investigation Acts, Director of Investigation and Research) v. Southam Inc.)*, [1984] S.C.J. No. 36, [1984] 2 S.C.R. 145 at 162-64 (S.C.C.).

[341] *Ibid.*, at 165 (S.C.R.).

[342] See *e.g.*, *Criminal Code*, R.S.C. 1985, c. C-46, s. 487 (authorizing issuance of search warrants by a "justice," which s. 2 of the *Code* defines as "a justice of the peace or a provincial court judge"). See below, Part 3(3).

[343] See generally, *R. v. Valente (No. 2)*, [1983] O.J. No. 2971, 2 C.C.C. (3d) 417 (Ont. C.A.), affd [1985] S.C.J. No. 77, [1985] 2 S.C.R. 673 (S.C.C.) (provincial court is independent tribunal); *R. v. Universal Spa Ltée*, [1986] Q.J. No. 2256, 33 C.C.C. (3d) 535 (Que. C.A.) (justices of the peace are capable of being impartial and independent); *R. v. Lippé*, [1990] S.C.J. No. 128, [1991] 2 S.C.R. 114 (S.C.C.) (part-time municipal court judges are capable of impartiality and independence); *Ell v. Alberta*, [2003] S.C.J. No. 35, [2003] 1 S.C.R. 857 (S.C.C.) (legislation allowing government to remove justices of the peace for failing to meet qualifications does not interfere with their independence).

their roles in an independent manner.[344] For example, in one jurisdiction JPs were assisting police in redrafting warrant applications in violation of section 8.[345]

§3.114 Pointing to high application success rates, some have argued that warrants fail to serve as a truly independent check on police discretion.[346] By necessity, most warrant applications are made on an *ex parte* basis.[347] Issuing judges thus hear only law enforcement's side of the story. Many warrants, moreover, are issued by JPs, who do not typically hear criminal trials and are therefore less familiar than judges with the privacy rights claims frequently asserted there. Some commentators have thus suggested that JPs systematically favour crime control interests.[348]

§3.115 There is likely some truth to this. As compared to contested, adversarial proceedings, *ex parte* hearings are less likely to generate correct decisions. There is a danger, moreover, that JPs who repeatedly hear applications from the same police agencies and officers may unduly sympathize with their perspective and fail to scrutinize applications rigorously.

---

[344] See *R. v. Baylis*, [1988] S.J. No. 414, 43 C.C.C. (3d) 514 (Sask. C.A.) (justice of the peace lacked impartiality because she was a member of the Corps of Commissionaires responsible for enforcing traffic regulations); *R. v. Anderson*, [1990] S.J. No. 298, 84 Sask. R. 299 (Sask. Q.B.) (suspicion of partiality in justice of the peace visiting detachment in which he used to be commanding officer to grant a warrant); *R. v. Haley*, [1995] N.S.J. No. 269, 142 N.S.R. (2d) 107 (N.S.C.A.) (limited participation of a justice in warrant application does not compromise impartiality); *R. v. Kelly*, [1995] B.C.J. No. 1369, 99 C.C.C. (3d) 367 (B.C.C.A.) (a justice including certain facts in warrant application orally obtained from police does not compromise independence); *R. v. Magee*, [1988] A.J. No. 61, [1988] 3 W.W.R. 169 (Alta. Q.B.) (being accommodating to police does not suggest partiality); *R. v. Malik*, [2002] B.C.J. No. 3215, 2002 BCSC 1731 (justice's impartiality was tainted by police obtaining a provisional opinion of whether evidence was sufficient for a successful search warrant); *R. v. Hallman*, [2001] B.C.J. No. 1966, 88 C.R.R. (2d) 111 at para. 24 (B.C.S.C.) (justice's impartiality was tainted by both suggesting and personally writing in changes to the police's search warrant application); *R. v. Thurston*, [1998] O.J. No. 1731 at paras. 29-30 (Ont. Prov. Div.) (same). See also *R. v. Valente*, [1985] S.C.J. No. 77, [1985] 2 S.C.R. 673 (S.C.C.) (outlining general requirements for impartiality of judges under s. 11(*d*) of the *Charter*).

[345] *R. v. Gray*, [1993] M.J. No. 248, 85 Man. R. (2d) 211 (Man. C.A.).

[346] See Casey Hill, "The Role of Fault in Section 24(2) of the *Charter*" in Jamie Cameron, ed., *The Charter's Impact on the Criminal Justice System* (Toronto: Carswell, 1996) at 57; Casey Hill, Scott Hutchison & Leslie Pringle, "Search Warrants: Protection or Illusion? (2000) 28 C.R. (5th) 89; Law Reform Commission of Canada, *Police Powers: Search and Seizure in Criminal Law Enforcement*, Working Paper No. 30 at 83-89 (Ottawa: Law Reform Commission of Canada, 1983).

[347] See *e.g.*, *Criminal Code*, R.S.C. 1985, c. C-46, s. 487. This is to prevent the destruction of evidence that would often ensue if suspects had advance warning of impending searches. See Christopher Slobogin, "Subpoenas and Privacy" (2005) 54 DePaul L. Rev. 805 at 810-11. Judges have a discretion, however, to order an *inter partes* hearing when this danger is not present, as when the information sought is in the possession of an innocent third party. See *R. v. B. (S.A.)*, [2003] S.C.J. No. 61, [2003] 2 S.C.R. 678 at para. 56 (S.C.C.).

[348] See Richard V. Ericson, *Making Crime: A Study of Detective Work* (Toronto: Butterworths, 1981) at 152-54.

§3.116 The flaws of the warrant process, however, should not be overstated.[349] As discussed in more detail below, the *Criminal Code* and *Charter* set out a number of preconditions to the granting of warrants that encourage issuing authorities to take their oversight responsibilities seriously. Judges and JPs who slight these obligations risk the embarrassment of having their decisions regularly overturned on review. And compared to the pre-*Charter* era, today JPs are more likely to serve as a check on police power.[350] More and more types of warrants must now be granted by provincial or superior court judges.[351]

§3.117 The most important protection provided by warrants, however, is the cost associated with preparing applications. Police have limited resources and are reluctant to devote them to weak applications that are unlikely to be approved. As compared to warrantless search powers, warrants force police to take more care to ensure that they have adequate grounds to search.[352] This incentive to self-screen may contribute more to high approval rates than any systematic bias in favour of crime control.[353]

(ii)   Standard of Justification: Reasonable and Probable Grounds

§3.118 As Justice Dickson stressed in *Hunter*, it is not enough for police to have a "reasonable belief that evidence *may* be uncovered in the search."[354] They must demonstrate that the discovery of evidence is *likely*. Justice Dickson defined the standard as follows:

> The state's interest in detecting and preventing crime begins to prevail over the individual's interest in being left alone at the point where credibly-based probability replaces suspicion. History has confirmed the appropriateness of this requirement as the threshold for subordinating the expectation of privacy to the needs of law enforcement. ... [R]easonable and probable grounds, established upon oath, to believe that an offence has been committed and that there is evidence to be found at the place of the search, consti-

---

[349] See James Stribopoulos, "Unchecked Power: The Constitutional Regulation of Arrest Reconsidered" (2003) 48 McGill L.J. 225 at 286-87.

[350] See Anthony N. Doob, Patricia M. Baranek & Susan M. Addario, *Understanding Justices: A Study of Canadian Justices of the Peace* (Toronto: Centre of Criminology, University of Toronto, 1991) at 25 (72 per cent of justices surveyed perceived their role as being "to serve as a buffer between the police and the ordinary citizen"); Casey Hill, Scott Hutchison & Leslie Pringle, "Search Warrants: Protection or Illusion? (2000) 28 C.R. (5th) 89; Law Reform Commission of Canada, *Police Powers: Search and Seizure in Criminal Law Enforcement*, Working Paper No. 30 at 83-89 (Ottawa: Law Reform Commission of Canada, 1983) (finding 47 per cent refusal rate for telewarrant applications in Ontario).

[351] See *e.g.*, *Criminal Code*, R.S.C. 1985, c. C-46, ss. 183 (wiretap authorizations), 487.05 (DNA sample warrants), 487.01 (general investigative warrants).

[352] William J. Stuntz, "Warrants and Fourth Amendment Remedies" (1991) 77 Va. L. Rev. 881 at 908, 920-25, 927; H. Richard Uviller, *Tempered Zeal: A Columbia Law Professor's Year on the Streets with the New York City Police* (Chicago: Contemporary Books, 1988) at 25.

[353] See Donald Dripps, "Living With *Leon*" (1986) 95 Yale L.J. 906 at 926.

[354] *Hunter v. Southam (sub nom. Canada (Combines Investigation Acts, Director of Investigation and Research) v. Southam Inc.)*, [1984] S.C.J. No. 36, [1984] 2 S.C.R. 145 at 167 (S.C.C.) [emphasis added].

tutes the minimum standard, consistent with s. 8 of the *Charter*, for authorizing search and seizure.[355]

§3.119 In subsequent judgments, the Supreme Court has explained that the "reasonable and probable grounds to believe" standard imports a standard of reasonable belief or reasonable probability, which entails something less than proof beyond a reasonable doubt or a *prima facie* case[356] but something more than mere possibility or suspicion.[357] As the Court noted in the quoted passage from *Hunter*, the standard is met at the point "where credibly-based probability replaces suspicion".[358] This is a mixed subjective and objective standard. It is not enough that the person carrying out the search believes he or she has the requisite grounds, "a reasonable person placed in the position of the officer must be able to conclude that there were indeed reasonable and probable grounds".[359] (The "reasonable and probable grounds" standard is discussed more fully below in Part 3(3)(*a*), as it is the controlling standard for the issuance of search warrants.)

(c) Situations Where Reasonableness Demands More than Hunter Requires

§3.120 As we have seen, *Hunter* established the presumption that reasonableness requires prior authorization on the basis of reasonable and probable grounds. In some situations, however, more exacting standards have been demanded for laws authorizing searches or seizures. In some cases, section 8 will require that police satisfy additional prerequisites before obtaining a warrant or conducting a warrantless search. In others, issuing authorities must impose conditions on the manner in which the search is executed. In still other cases, reviewing courts may find that in executing an otherwise valid search, police infringed an implicit condition of a search warrant or warrantless search power, such as avoiding excessive force, harassment or intimidation. All warrant-based search powers, moreover, must leave issuing authorities with a residual discretion to impose prerequisites and conditions.[360] If not, they are unconstitutional on

---

[355] *Ibid.*, at 167-68 (S.C.R.). See also *R. v. Morelli*, [2010] S.C.J. No. 8, [2010] 1 S.C.R. 253 at para. 39 (S.C.C.). In *Hunter v. Southam (sub nom. Canada (Combines Investigation Acts, Director of Investigation and Research) v. Southam Inc.*), [1984] S.C.J. No. 36, [1984] 2 S.C.R. 145 at 167 (S.C.C.), Justice Dickson noted that this standard is equivalent to the "probable cause" standard set out in the Fourth Amendment. Despite the clarity of Justice Dickson's pronouncement, the courts have not always interpreted "reasonable and probable grounds" as requiring applicants to prove that the discovery of evidence is more likely than not. This and other issues surrounding the meaning of the standard are discussed below, Part 3(3)(*a*).

[356] See *R. v. DeBot*, [1989] S.C.J. No. 118, [1989] 2 S.C.R. 1140 at 1166 (S.C.C.); *R. v. Storrey*, [1990] S.C.J. No. 12, [1990] 1 S.C.R. 241 at 250-51 (S.C.C.).

[357] See *Baron v. Canada*, [1993] S.C.J. No. 6, [1993] 1 S.C.R. 416 at 448 (S.C.C.).

[358] *Hunter v. Southam (sub nom. Canada (Combines Investigation Acts, Director of Investigation and Research) v. Southam Inc.*), [1984] S.C.J. No. 36, [1984] 2 S.C.R. 145 at 167 (S.C.C.).

[359] *R. v. Storrey*, [1990] S.C.J. No. 12, [1990] 1 S.C.R. 241 at 251 (S.C.C.).

[360] *Baron v. Canada*, [1993] S.C.J. No. 6, [1993] 1 S.C.R. 416 (S.C.C.) (statutory provision requiring that judge "shall" issue warrant if prerequisites fulfilled violated s. 8). See also *Descôteaux*

their face and it need not be shown that prerequisites or conditions were needed in a given case.[361]

§3.121 As discussed immediately below, additional requirements are most likely to be imposed in cases involving either: (*i*) especially sensitive privacy interests or (*ii*) interests other than the privacy of the target of the search. These issues are most likely to be present in searches involving electronic communications or professional privilege and confidentiality.

(i) Electronic Communications

§3.122 As mentioned, the state's interception of private, electronic communications poses an especially grave threat to privacy. The courts have accordingly stressed that such interceptions should be conducted only when necessary to combat serious threats to the public order.[362] As discussed in more detail in Part 3(8), below, Part VI of the *Criminal Code*[363] imposes a number of constraints on wiretapping that go beyond *Hunter's* basic preconditions of prior authorization on the basis of reasonable and probable grounds. The reasonableness of *Criminal Code* Part VI authorizations may nevertheless become an issue in two situations.

§3.123 The first involves authorizations that may invade the privacy of large numbers of non-suspects. In such cases, conditions must be imposed to minimize these invasions.[364] In *R. v. Thompson*,[365] police obtained an authorization to intercept conversations made at any pay phone that might conceivably be used by the targets of the investigation. Writing for a majority of the Supreme Court, Justice Sopinka concluded that "at a minimum" the authorization should have provided that pay phone conversations "not be intercepted unless there were reasonable and probable grounds for believing that a target was using the telephone at the time that the listening device was activated."[366]

§3.124 The second situation arises when one of the statutory restrictions on wiretapping going beyond the basic *Hunter* requirements is removed. The Supreme Court has repeatedly mentioned these protections in upholding the constitutionality of Part VI of the *Criminal Code*.[367] In particular, it intimated in *R. v.*

---

v. Mierzwinski, [1982] S.C.J. No. 43, [1982] 1 S.C.R. 860 (S.C.C.) (pre-*Charter* case interpreting s. 487 of the *Criminal Code* as leaving issuing authorities with the discretion not to issue a warrant even if statutory prerequisites are fulfilled).

[361] *Baron v. Canada*, [1993] S.C.J. No. 6, [1993] 1 S.C.R. 416 at 436-40 (S.C.C.).

[362] See *R. v. Duarte*, [1990] S.C.J. No. 2, [1990] 1 S.C.R. 30 (S.C.C.).

[363] R.S.C. 1985, c. C-46.

[364] See *R. v. Thompson*, [1990] S.C.J. No. 104, [1990] 2 S.C.R. 1111 (S.C.C.). See also *R. v. Finlay and Grellette*, [1985] O.J. No. 2680, 23 C.C.C. (3d) 48 (Ont. C.A.), leave to appeal refused [1986] 1 S.C.R. ix (S.C.C.).

[365] [1990] S.C.J. No. 104, [1990] 2 S.C.R. 1111 (S.C.C.).

[366] *Ibid.*, at 1145 (S.C.R.).

[367] See *R. v. Duarte*, [1990] S.C.J. No. 2, [1990] 1 S.C.R. 30 at 45 (S.C.C.); *R. v. Garofoli*, [1990] S.C.J. No. 115, [1990] 2 S.C.R. 1421 at 1444 (S.C.C.).

Araujo[368] that "investigative necessity" is constitutionally required for wiretap authorizations.[369] As discussed in more detail in Part 3(8)(*b*), below, this requires police to show that "other investigative procedures have been tried and have failed, other investigative procedures are unlikely to succeed or the urgency of the matter is such that it would be impractical to carry out the investigation of the offence using only other investigative procedures."[370] Parliament has nevertheless eliminated the investigative necessity requirement for "criminal organization" and "terrorism" offences,[371] and lower courts have rejected suggestions that this violates section 8.[372]

§3.125 It is difficult to reconcile these decisions with the Supreme Court's (admittedly *obiter*) statement in *Araujo*. There are good policy reasons, moreover, to require investigative necessity for all covert interceptions. If police are investigating sophisticated criminals or terrorists, it will usually be easy to show that conventional investigative methods are unlikely to succeed.[373] The definitions of some of the criminal organization and terrorism offences, however, are extremely broad.[374] Police will consequently often be able to intercept the communications of unsophisticated suspects who would have been vulnerable to conventional investigative techniques.[375] If investigative necessity is not constitutionally required in such cases, then it is probably not required in any others.

---

[368] [2000] S.C.J. No. 65, [2000] 2 S.C.R. 992 (S.C.C.).

[369] *Ibid.*, at para. 26 (S.C.R.) ("... [W]e must not forget that the text of s. 186(1) represents a type of constitutional compromise. In particular, the investigative necessity requirement embodied in s. 186(1) is one of the safeguards that made it possible for this Court to uphold these parts of the *Criminal Code* on constitutional grounds.").

[370] *Criminal Code*, R.S.C. 1985, c. C-46, s. 186(1)(*b*).

[371] *Ibid.*, s. 186(1.1).

[372] See *R. v. Doiron*, [2007] N.B.J. No. 189, 2007 NBCA 41 (N.B.C.A.), leave to appeal refused [2007] S.C.C.A. No. 413 (S.C.C.) (criminal organizations); *R. v. Pangman*, [2000] M.J. No. 300, 147 Man. R. (2d) 93 (Man. Q.B.) (same); *R. c. Doucet*, [2003] J.Q. no 18497, 18 C.R. (6th) 103 (Que. S.C.) (same).

[373] As discussed below, Part 3(8)(*b*), the Supreme Court has defined "investigative necessity" in a flexible and pragmatic fashion that takes into account the fact that the higher levels of sophisticated criminal organizations are often difficult to penetrate by conventional means. See *R. v. Araujo*, [2000] S.C.J. No. 65, [2000] 2 S.C.R. 992 (S.C.C.).

[374] See Don Stuart, "Time to Recodify Criminal Law and Rise Above Law and Order Expediency: Lessons from the Manitoba Warriors Prosecution" (2000) 28 Man. L.J. 89; Kent Roach, "The New Terrorism Offences and the Criminal Law" in Ronald J. Daniels, Patrick Macklem & Kent Roach, ed. *The Security of Freedom: Essays on Canada's Anti-Terrorism Bill* (Toronto: University of Toronto Press, 2001) 151. See also *R. v. Terezakis*, [2007] B.C.J. No. 1592, 223 C.C.C. (3d) 344 (B.C.C.A.), leave to appeal refused [2007] S.C.C.A. No. 487, 226 C.C.C. (3d) vi*n* (S.C.C.) (upholding constitutionality of s. 467.13); *R. v. Lindsay*, [2009] O.J. No. 2700, 245 C.C.C. (3d) 301 (Ont. C.A.), leave to appeal refused [2009] S.C.C.A. No. 540 (S.C.C.) (upholding the constitutionality of s. 467.12).

[375] See Nathan Whitling, "Wiretapping, Investigative Necessity, and the *Charter*" (2002) 46 Crim. L.Q. 89 at 118-19; Steven Penney, "National Security Surveillance in an Age of Terror: Statutory Powers & *Charter* Limits" (2010) 48 Osgoode Hall L.J. 247 at 233-66.

(ii)   Professional Privilege and Confidentiality

§3.126 The *Hunter* requirements may also be supplemented when a search threatens to disrupt a confidential, professional relationship. Searches of lawyers' offices, for instance, may disclose documents protected by lawyer-client privilege.[376] Before the *Charter*, the Supreme Court interpreted the *Criminal Code*'s warrant provisions so as to provide stringent protections for lawyer-client privilege.[377] Police had to show investigative necessity and ensure that potentially privileged documents would be sealed pending a judicial determination of the merits of any privilege claim.[378] Parliament later enacted detailed procedures regulating the seizure of documents from lawyers' offices.[379] The Supreme Court found, however, that the legislation authorized the "potential breach of solicitor-client privilege without the client's knowledge, let alone consent."[380] As a consequence, the Court struck it down and set out detailed rules governing law office searches pending the introduction of new legislation.[381] The most important of these rules dictate that:

(a)   warrants cannot be issued for documents known to be privileged;

(b)   police must demonstrate investigative necessity;

(c)   seized documents must be sealed until a judge can determine whether privilege exists; and

---

[376] It is important to note that unlike other information attracting a reasonable expectation of privacy, with limited exceptions, privileged information may *never* be obtained by police, even if there are reasonable and probable grounds to believe that it will provide evidence of an offence. See *Lavallee, Rackel & Heintz v. Canada (Attorney General); White, Ottenheimer & Baker v. Canada (Attorney General); R. v. Fink*, [2002] S.C.J. No. 61, [2002] 3 S.C.R. 209 at para. 24 (S.C.C.). On lawyer-client privilege generally, see Alan W. Bryant, Sidney N. Lederman & Michelle K. Fuerst, *Sopinka, Lederman & Bryant: The Law of Evidence in Canada*, 3d ed. (Markham, ON: LexisNexis Canada, 2009) 924-75; David M. Paciocco & Lee Stuesser, *The Law of Evidence*, 5th ed. (Toronto: Irwin Law, 2008) at 222-35; Alan W. Mewett & Peter J. Sankoff, *Witnesses*, vol. 2, looseleaf (Toronto: Carswell, 1991) at 49ff.

[377] See *Descôteaux v. Mierzwinski*, [1982] S.C.J. No. 43, [1982] 1 S.C.R. 860 (S.C.C.).

[378] *Ibid.*, at 887-96.

[379] *Criminal Law Amendment Act*, R.S.C. 1985, c. 27 (1st Supp.), s. 71. See now *Criminal Code*, R.S.C. 1985, c. C-46, s. 488.1.

[380] *Lavallee, Rackel & Heintz v. Canada (Attorney General); White, Ottenheimer & Baker v. Canada (Attorney General); R. v. Fink*, [2002] S.C.J. No. 61, [2002] 3 S.C.R. 209 at para. 39 (S.C.C.).

[381] *Lavallee, Rackel & Heintz v. Canada (Attorney General); White, Ottenheimer & Baker v. Canada (Attorney General); R. v. Fink*, [2002] S.C.J. No. 61, [2002] 3 S.C.R. 209 at paras. 48-49 (S.C.C.). Parliament has not yet responded with new legislation. See also *Festing v. Canada (Attorney General)*, [2003] B.C.J. No. 404 at para. 24, 172 C.C.C. (3d) 321 (B.C.C.A.) (*Lavallee* rules may apply to "any place where privileged documents may reasonably be expected to be located"); *R. v. Ritter*, [2006] A.J. No. 791, 2006 ABPC 162 at paras. 62-64 (Alta. Prov. Ct.) (merely placing "solicitor-client privilege" stickers on property does not entitle one to *Lavallee* protections); *R. v. Qureshi*, [2006] A.J. No. 1759, 2006 ABQB 727 (Alta. Q.B.) (files of private investigator working for lawyer not protected by solicitor-client privilege).

(d)   before the search is executed, every effort must be made to contact affected clients and their lawyers, failing which the search should be overseen by a law society representative.[382]

§3.127 Unlike legal documents, privilege does not generally attach to confidential materials kept by other professionals, such as journalists[383] and health care providers.[384] The courts have recognized, however, that searches and seizures of such materials implicate important societal interests that must be considered in issuing and executing search warrants. The Supreme Court has noted, for instance, that journalists play a "vitally important role" in disseminating the news.[385] The Court has also recognized the importance of maintaining the confidentiality of sources in assisting journalists to uncover wrongdoing in matters of public interest.[386] Courts must be mindful of these interests, as well as the constitutional guarantee of freedom of the press,[387] in deciding whether to: (*i*) refuse to issue a warrant despite the fulfillment of the *Hunter* requirements; or (*ii*) impose any minimizing conditions.[388] Such conditions may include giving the media an opportunity to contest the validity of the warrant before either its issuance or execution; requiring the police applying for the warrant to demonstrate investigative necessity; requiring police executing the warrant to minimize any impedance of the media organization's operations; and directing that any documents

---

[382]   *Ibid.*, at para. 49. See also *Re Law Society of Upper Canada*, [2006] O.J. No. 4915, 2006 ONCJ 470 (Ont. C.J.) (computer technician permissible substitute for law society representative who refused to co-operate).

[383]   See *R. v. National Post*, [2010] S.C.J. No. 16, [2010] 1 S.C.R. 477, 2010 SCC 16 (S.C.C.).

[384]   See *R. v. Serendip Physiotherapy Clinic*, [2004] O.J. No. 4653, 189 C.C.C. (3d) 417 at para. 17 (Ont. C.A.), leave to appeal refused [2004] S.C.C.A. No. 585 (S.C.C.). Privilege may be found to exist, however, in relation to a particular document on a case-by-case basis. See Alan W. Bryant, Sidney N. Lederman & Michelle K. Fuerst, *Sopinka, Lederman & Bryant: The Law of Evidence in Canada*, 3d ed. (Markham, ON: LexisNexis Canada, 2009) 1005-1029; David M. Paciocco & Lee Stuesser, *The Law of Evidence*, 5th ed. (Toronto: Irwin Law, 2008) at 254-59. See also *R. v. Gruenke*, [1991] S.C.J. No. 80, [1991] 3 S.C.R. 263 at 35-41 (S.C.C.) (recognizing case-by-case privilege for religious communications).

[385]   *Canadian Broadcasting Corp. v. New Brunswick (Attorney General)*, [1991] S.C.J. No. 88, [1991] 3 S.C.R. 459 at 475 (S.C.C.) [*CBC v. New Brunswick*].

[386]   *R. v. National Post*, [2010] S.C.J. No. 16, 2010 SCC 16 at paras. 28-30, 33-34 (S.C.C.).

[387]   See *Canadian Charter of Rights and Freedoms*, Part I of the *Constitution Act, 1982*, being Schedule B to the *Canada Act 1982* (U.K.), 1982, c. 11 [*Charter*], s. 2(*b*) ("Everyone has the following fundamental freedoms: ... freedom of thought, belief, opinion and expression, including freedom of the press and other media of communication.").

[388]   See *Canadian Broadcasting Corp. v. New Brunswick (Attorney General)*, [1991] S.C.J. No. 88, [1991] 3 S.C.R. 459 at 480-81 (S.C.C.); *Canadian Broadcasting Corp. v. Lessard*, [1991] S.C.J. No. 87, [1991] 3 S.C.R. 421 at 445 (S.C.C.) [*Lessard*]; *R. v. National Post*, [2010] S.C.J. No. 16, [2010] 1 S.C.R. 477, 2010 SCC 16 at para. 31 (S.C.C.).

seized by sealed on request.[389] The Supreme Court has stopped short, however, of requiring investigative necessity or any other mandatory conditions.[390]

§3.128 The Court has also declined to recognize either a class privilege or constitutional immunity protecting the confidentiality of journalistic sources.[391] Instead, it has ruled that such sources may be protected under a case-by-case "Wigmore" privilege[392] that may, "in a proper case [be] asserted against the issuance or execution of a search warrant."[393] In most cases, the decision whether to permit a search that could reveal the identity of a confidential source will turn on a balancing of the public's interest in fostering confidentiality against countervailing public interests such as the investigation of crime.[394] This calculus will include a weighing of "the nature and seriousness of the offence under investigation, and the probative value of the evidence sought to be obtained, measured against the public interest in respecting the journalist's promise of confidentiality."[395] It may also include consideration of the purpose of the investigation, as

---

[389] *Canadian Broadcasting Corp. v. Lessard*, [1991] S.C.J. No. 87, [1991] 3 S.C.R. 421 at 445 (S.C.C.); *Canadian Broadcasting Corp. v. New Brunswick (Attorney General)*, [1991] S.C.J. No. 88, [1991] 3 S.C.R. 459 at 481 S.C.C.); *R. v. National Post*, [2010] S.C.J. No. 16, 2010 SCC 16 at paras. 80-87 (S.C.C.).

[390] *Canadian Broadcasting Corp. v. New Brunswick (Attorney General)*, [1991] S.C.J. No. 88, [1991] 3 S.C.R. 459 at 478 (S.C.C.); *Canadian Broadcasting Corp. v. Lessard*, [1991] S.C.J. No. 87, [1991] 3 S.C.R. 421 at 446 (S.C.C.). The Court did state in *Lessard*, however, that "in most cases" applicants will be expected to indicate "that there was either no alternative source of information to the police or, if there were, that the information sought could not be obtained from that alternative source". The failure to do so, moreover, "is certainly a basis upon which the justice of the peace could refuse to issue the search warrant." *Ibid.* See also *R. v. Canadian Broadcasting Corp.*, [2001] O.J. No. 706, 52 O.R. (3d) 757 (Ont. C.A.).

[391] *R. v. National Post*, [2010] S.C.J. No. 16, 2010 SCC 16 at paras. 37-49 (S.C.C.).

[392] In *R. v. National Post*, [2010] S.C.J. No. 16, 2010 SCC 16 at para. 53 (S.C.C.), the Court described the "Wigmore criteria" as follows:

> First, the communication must originate in a confidence that the identity of the informant will not be disclosed. Second, the confidence must be essential to the relationship in which the communication arises. Third, the relationship must be one which should be "sedulously fostered" in the public good ("Sedulous[ly]" being defined in the *New Shorter Oxford English Dictionary on Historical Principles* (6th ed. 2007), vol. 2, at p. 2755, as "diligent[ly] ... deliberately and consciously."). Finally, if all of these requirements are met, the court must consider whether in the instant case the public interest served by protecting the identity of the informant from disclosure outweighs the public interest in getting at the truth.

See also *Wigmore on Evidence* (McNaughton Rev. 1961), vol. 8, at § 2285; Alan W. Bryant, Sidney N. Lederman & Michelle K. Fuerst, *The Law of Evidence in Canada*, 3d ed. (Markham: LexisNexis Canada, 2009) at paras. 14.19 *et seq.*; David M. Paciocco & Lee Stuesser, *The Law of Evidence*, 5th ed. (Toronto: Irwin Law, 2008) at 254-59.

[393] *R. v. National Post*, [2010] S.C.J. No. 16, [2010] 1 S.C.R. 477 at para. 52 (S.C.C.). See also *Wasylyshen v. Canadian Broadcasting Corp.*, [2005] A.J. No. 1685, 385 A.R. 343 (Alta. Q.B.); *O'Neill v. Canada (Attorney General)*, [2006] O.J. No. 4189, 213 C.C.C. (3d) 389 (Ont. S.C.J.), supp. reasons [2007] O.J. No. 496 (Ont. S.C.J.); *Privacy Protection Act*, 42 U.S.C. § 2000aa (2007) (limiting circumstances where law enforcement may obtain warrants to search journalists).

[394] *R. v. National Post*, [2010] S.C.J. No. 16, [2010] 1 S.C.R. 477 at para. 58 (S.C.C.). The onus for establishing the Wigmore criteria lies with the person claiming the privilege. *Ibid.*, at para. 60 (S.C.R.).

[395] *R. v. National Post*, [2010] S.C.J. No. 16, [2010] 1 S.C.R. 477 at para. 61 (S.C.C.).

where authorities conduct a search to intimidate a journalist into forgoing an investigation that might embarrass police or government.[396]

§3.129 Applying these factors in *R. v. National Post*,[397] the Supreme Court ruled that a warrant to seize an allegedly forged document from a journalist was properly issued despite the fact that forensic analysis of it might reveal the identity of a confidential source. Since the document was allegedly the very *actus reus* of the offence being investigated, the Court reasoned, the identity of the person who gave it to the journalist had "no continuing claim to the protection of the law".[398]

§3.130 Searches of confidential health records may also merit additional protection under section 8.[399] As with searches of journalistic materials, however, courts have not recognized any class privilege or imposed any mandatory conditions.[400]

(d) Situations Where Reasonableness Requires Less than the Hunter Standards

§3.131 As we have seen, the default requirements of reasonableness under section 8 of the *Charter* are a warrant (where feasible) and reasonable and probable grounds to believe that evidence will be found before the warrant issues. Just as these basic requirements may be supplemented by additional protections, there are also circumstances where a search or seizure will be reasonable even though it departs from one or both of these conditions. As noted above, the application of less rigorous standards for assessing laws that authorize searches or seizures has usually resulted from the combined effect of two factors: a diminished privacy expectation and a compelling state interest other than criminal law enforcement.

---

[396] *R. v. National Post*, [2010] S.C.J. No. 16, [2010] 1 S.C.R. 477 at para. 62 (S.C.C.). See also *O'Neill v. Canada (Attorney General)*, [2006] O.J. No. 4189, 213 C.C.C. (3d) 389 at paras. 154-59 (Ont. S.C.J.), supp. reasons [2007] O.J. No. 496 (Ont. S.C.J.) (search warrant executed for improper motive of pressuring journalist to reveal confidential source).

[397] [2010] S.C.J. No. 16, [2010] 1 S.C.R. 477 (S.C.C.).

[398] *R. v. National Post*, [2010] S.C.J. No. 16, [2010] 1 S.C.R. 477 at para. 77 (S.C.C.).

[399] See *e.g.*, *R. v. O. (J.)*, [1996] O.J. No. 4799 (Ont. Gen. Div.) (warrant for psychiatric records must contain measures to protect patients' privacy).

[400] See *R. v. Serendip Physiotherapy Clinic*, [2004] O.J. No. 4653, 189 C.C.C. (3d) 417 at paras. 34-41 (Ont. C.A.), leave to appeal refused [2004] S.C.C.A. No. 585 (S.C.C.) (searches of health records do not generally require additional conditions, with the exception of privileged documents and, possibly, psychiatric records). See also Alan W. Bryant, Sidney N. Lederman & Michelle K. Fuerst, *Sopinka, Lederman & Bryant: The Law of Evidence in Canada*, 3d ed. (Markham, ON: LexisNexis Canada, 2009) at 1021-1029.

(i)   Searches Based on Reasonable Suspicion

§3.132 As mentioned, in *Hunter*,[401] Justice Dickson suggested that the default standard of justification for searches (reasonable and probable grounds) may have to be raised or lowered depending on the interests involved.[402] Courts have yet to recognize any circumstances warranting a higher standard, but in recent years they have upheld a number of search powers on the lower standard of "reasonable suspicion".[403] Though resting on a lesser degree of probability than "reasonable and probable grounds",[404] "reasonable suspicion" must nonetheless be grounded on "objectively discernable facts".[405] A "hunch based on intuition", even one gained by experience, is not objectively reasonable.[406] A court (whether authorizing the search *ex ante* or *ex post*) must be able to "make an independent assessment of the facts upon which the suspicion is based."[407] (The reasonable suspicion standard is discussed more fully in Chapter 2, Part 4(3)(*a*)(i), as it is also the controlling standard for investigative detention.)

§3.133 The reasonable suspicion standard has been used for both statutory and common law search powers. Many of these powers are discussed in detail in Parts 3 and 4, below. Here we focus on the *Criminal Code* search powers using

---

[401]   *Hunter v. Southam (sub nom. Canada (Combines Investigation Acts, Director of Investigation and Research) v. Southam Inc.)*, [1984] S.C.J. No. 36, [1984] 2 S.C.R. 145 (S.C.C.).

[402]   *Ibid.*, at 168 (S.C.R.) ("Where in the state's interest is not simply law enforcement as, for instance, where state security is involved, or where the individual's interest is not simply his expectation of privacy as, for instance, when the search threatens his bodily integrity, the relevant standard might well be a different one.").

[403]   In the *Criminal Code* and other statutes, the "reasonable suspicion" standard is typically expressed as "reasonable grounds to suspect" or "suspects on reasonable grounds." See *e.g.*, *Criminal Code*, R.S.C. 1984, c. C-46, ss. 254(2), 492.1, 492.2, 487.013; *Customs Act*, R.S.C. 1985, c. 1 (2nd Supp.), ss. 98, 99, 99.2; *Corrections and Conditional Release Act*, S.C. 1992, c. 20, s. 49; *Proceeds of Crime (Money Laundering) and Terrorism Financing Act*, S.C. 2000, c. 17, ss. 15(1), 17(1). The courts have variously expressed the same standard in the context of common law search and detention powers as "reasonable suspicion", "reasonable grounds to suspect", "articulable cause", and "reasonable grounds to detain". See *R. v. Kang-Brown*, [2008] S.C.J. No. 18, [2008] 1 S.C.R. 456, 2008 SCC 18 at para. 76 (S.C.C.), *per* Binnie J., at para. 164 (SCC), *per* Deschamps J., dissenting; *R. v. Jacques*, [1996] S.C.J. No. 88, [1996] 3 S.C.R. 312 at para. 24 (S.C.C.); *R. v. Mann*, [2004] S.C.J. No. 49, [2004] 3 S.C.R. 59 at paras. 31-33 and 45 (S.C.C.).

[404]   See *R. v. Kang-Brown*, [2008] S.C.J. No. 18, [2008] 1 S.C.R. 456, 2008 SCC 18 at para. 75 (S.C.C.); Peter Sankoff & Stéphane Perrault, "Suspicious Searches: What's so Reasonable about Them?" (1999) 24 C.R. (5th) 123 at 125-26.

[405]   *R. v. Simpson*, [1993] O.J. No. 308, 12 O.R. (3d) 182 (Ont. C.A.). See also *R. v. Jacques*, [1996] S.C.J. No. 88, [1996] 3 S.C.R. 312 at para. 24 (S.C.C.); *R. v. Mann*, [2004] S.C.J. No. 49, [2004] 3 S.C.R. 59 at para. 27, 43 (S.C.C.); *R. v. M. (A.)*, [2008] S.C.J. No. 19, [2008] 1 S.C.R. 569, 2008 SCC 19 at para. 80 (S.C.C.), *per* Binnie J.

[406]   *R. v. Mann*, [2004] S.C.J. No. 49, [2004] 3 S.C.R. 59 at para. 30 (S.C.C.). See also *R. v. Kang-Brown*, [2008] S.C.J. No. 18, [2008] 1 S.C.R. 456, 2008 SCC 18 at para. 76 (S.C.C.), *per* Binnie J., at para. 165, *per* Deschamps J., dissenting; *R. v. M. (A.)*, [2008] S.C.J. No. 19, 2008 SCC 19 at para. 91 (S.C.C.), *per* Binnie J.; *R. v. Simpson*, [1993] O.J. No. 308, 79 C.C.C. (3d) 482 at para. 61 (Ont. C.A.).

[407]   *R. v. Lal*, [1998] B.C.J. No. 2446, 113 B.C.A.C. 47 at para. 23 (B.C.C.A.), leave to appeal to S.C.C. refused [1999] S.C.C.A. No. 28 (S.C.C.), cited in *R. v. Kang-Brown*, [2008] S.C.J. No. 18, [2008] 1 S.C.R. 456, 2008 SCC 18 at para. 77 (S.C.C.), *per* Binnie J.

the reasonable suspicion standard that have been or are likely to be challenged under section 8 of the *Charter*.

§3.134 Sections 492.1 and 492.2 were added to the *Criminal Code* in 1993. They authorize the issuance of warrants for "tracking devices" and "number recorders", respectively. As mentioned,[408] section 492.1 was Parliament's response to *R. v. Wise*,[409] where the Supreme Court had suggested that reasonable suspicion would have been sufficient to justify the installation and monitoring of a rudimentary tracking device.[410] The provision appears to sanction the use of much more intrusive devices, however. Contemporary Global Positioning System devices (GPS) and wireless telephone networks allow authorities to track people's movements with increasing efficiency and precision.[411] Though there is a paucity of authority on point, the courts have appeared to assume that reasonable suspicion is sufficient to justify such surveillance under section 8.[412]

§3.135 The constitutionality of section 492.2, in contrast, has been directly considered. It allows police to acquire the transmission data associated with telephone communications,[413] including the numbers and locations of phones connecting to the target phone. Though there is some contrary authority,[414] in the most recent cases, the courts have concluded that the use of the reasonable suspicion standard in this context complies with section 8.[415]

§3.136 In 2004, Parliament added section 487.013 to the *Code*. It authorizes courts to order financial institutions to disclose a person's name, account number and certain other account information (not including details of transactions) on the basis of reasonable suspicion. As with section 492.2, courts are likely to uphold the use of the reasonable suspicion standard.[416]

---

[408] See discussion above, Part 2(4)(*b*)(v).

[409] [1992] S.C.J. No. 16, [1992] 1 S.C.R. 527 (S.C.C.).

[410] *Ibid.*, at 548-49 (S.C.R.).

[411] See Steven Penney, "Reasonable Expectations of Privacy and Novel Search Technologies: An Economic Approach" (2007) 97 J. Crim. L. & Criminology 477 at 513-17.

[412] See *R. v. T. & T. Fisheries Inc.*, [2005] P.E.I.J. No. 74 (P.E.I. Prov. Ct.) (s. 492.1 warrant used by police to install and monitor GPS tracking device); *R. v. Bacon*, [2010] B.C.J. No. 48, 2010 BCPC 1 at para. 69 (B.C. Prov. Ct.) (noting that the reasonable suspicion standard is based on the diminished expectation of privacy in vehicles); *R. v. Scott*, [2009] B.C.J. No. 1459, 2009 BCPC 235 at paras. 8-13 (B.C. Prov. Ct.) (police had reasonable suspicion to install tracking warrant under s. 492; no violation of s. 8).

[413] Transmission information is discussed above, Part 2(4)(*b*)(vii).

[414] See *R. v. Hackert*, [1997] O.J. No. 6384 (Ont. Gen. Div.); *R. v. Nguyen*, [2004] B.C.J. No. 247, 20 C.R. (6th) 151 (B.C.S.C.).

[415] See *R. v. Cody*, [2007] Q.J. No. 11001, 228 C.C.C. (3d) 331 at paras. 5-8 (Que. C.A.); *Griffin v. R.*, [2008] Q.J. No. 3589, 237 C.C.C. (3d) 374 at paras. 92-95 (Que. C.A.), revd on other grounds (*sub nom. R. v. Griffin*) [2009] S.C.J. No. 28, [2009] 2 S.C.R. 42 (S.C.C.). See also *R. v. Mahmood*, [2008] O.J. No. 3922, 236 C.C.C. (3d) 3 at paras. 138-45 (Ont. S.C.J.), reconsideration denied [2009] O.J. No. 3192, 194 C.R.R. (2d) 180 (Ont. S.C.J.).

[416] See *R. v. Mahmood*, [2008] O.J. No. 3922, 236 C.C.C. (3d) 3 at para. 138 (Ont. S.C.J.), reconsideration denied [2009] O.J. No. 3192, 194 C.R.R. (2d) 180 (Ont. S.C.J.) (suggesting without deciding that, as with s. 492.2, Parliament's use of reasonable suspicion in this context is reasonable).

§3.137 In our view, all of these provisions are reasonable under section 8. Though the information they make available attracts a reasonable expectation of privacy, it is not so revealing as to justify overturning the balance that Parliament has deliberately struck between privacy and crime control.[417] Used in conjunction with modern information processing technologies, these provisions do allow police to systematically gather information about people's associations and habits.[418] Much of this information, however, can be obtained through investigative methods that do not engage section 8, such as physical surveillance and undercover questioning.[419] None of the provisions allows police to obtain highly sensitive information, such as communications content, diaries, health records or financial statements.

§3.138 Police typically use these orders, moreover, at the early stages of an investigation, when they have not yet established reasonable and probable grounds.[420] They often use the information acquired, along with other information, to justify more intrusive investigative techniques, such as wiretaps or search warrants. Requiring reasonable grounds would thus greatly diminish the usefulness of these orders. They would either be unavailable (when reasonable grounds did not exist) or redundant (when police had reasonable grounds to justify more intrusive searches).

§3.139 Further, requiring prior authorization, even on the standard of reasonable suspicion, greatly minimizes the risk of discriminatory profiling.[421] To justify the resources needed to apply for a warrant, and convince the issuing authority that reasonable suspicion exists, police must gather concrete, objective evidence that evidence of criminal activity may be uncovered. This makes it all but impossible to engage in indiscriminate fishing expeditions for suspicious patterns or associations.

§3.140 Lastly, some deference should be paid to Parliament's choice to use the reasonable suspicion standard. Section 8 may justify displacing legislative judgments as to the proper balance between privacy and crime control, especially when the social costs of a search power are likely to be disproportionately borne by minorities.[422] These provisions, however, are the product of democratically-accountable decisions to afford a specific level of protection to particular

---

[417] This argument is developed more fully in Steven Penney, "Reasonable Expectations of Privacy and Novel Search Technologies: An Economic Approach" (2007) 97 J. Crim. L. & Criminology 477 at 495-500 and Steven Penney, "Updating Canada's Communications Surveillance Laws: Privacy and Security in the Digital Age" (2008) 12 Can. Crim. L. Rev 115 at 147.

[418] Steven Penney, "Reasonable Expectations of Privacy and Novel Search Technologies: An Economic Approach" (2007) 97 J. Crim. L. & Criminology 477 at 500-506.

[419] See *Cody v. R.*, [2007] Q.J. No. 11001, 228 C.C.C. (3d) 331 at para. 26 (Que. C.A.)

[420] *Ibid.*, at para. 26 (C.C.C.).

[421] See Steven Penney, "Reasonable Expectations of Privacy and Novel Search Technologies: An Economic Approach" (2007) 97 J. Crim. L. & Criminology 477 at 526-27.

[422] *Ibid.*, at 502-506.

types of personal information.[423] In the absence of evidence that the provisions will be systematically abused, these decisions should be allowed to stand.

(ii) Searches Incident to Arrest and Detention

§3.141 Police may also conduct warrantless searches as an "incident" to a number of arrest and detention powers. We discuss the scope and constitutionality of incidental searches executed pursuant to these common law search powers in Part 4, below.

§3.142 There are also several statutory warrantless search powers flowing from detention or arrest. As discussed in more detail in Part 3(7)(*b*), below, drivers suspected of being impaired may be compelled to provide breath samples (and in some circumstances, blood samples) for blood alcohol analysis.[424] Police must have objective grounds for suspicion to exercise these powers, but they need not obtain a warrant. Surprisingly, the Supreme Court has never expressly decided whether this is reasonable under section 8. It has apparently simply assumed that they are.[425] In other contexts, the Court has noted that motor vehicle travel is highly regulated, that drivers accordingly have a diminished expectation of privacy and that deterring impaired driving is a particularly pressing legislative objective.[426] Requiring a warrant, moreover, could frustrate the police's ability to obtain reliable samples and needlessly prolong the detention of innocent drivers.[427]

(iii) Searches for Non-criminal Investigative Purposes

§3.143 Deviations from the *Hunter* standards are more common outside the realm of the ordinary criminal investigative process. While we have grouped these cases into discrete categories, they share a common feature. In each, the state's interest goes beyond criminal law enforcement, while the individual's privacy expectations are somewhat diminished. In such cases, the courts have often upheld under section 8 both warrantless searches and searches based on standards lower than reasonable and probable grounds.

---

[423] See generally, Peter W. Hogg & Allison A. Bushell, "The *Charter* Dialogue Between Courts and Legislatures (Or Perhaps The *Charter of Rights* Isn't Such a Bad Thing After All)" (1997) 35 Osgoode Hall L.J. 75 at 89-90.

[424] See *Criminal Code*, R.S.C. 1985, c. C-46, s. 254.

[425] See *R. v. Bernshaw*, [1994] S.C.J. No. 87, [1995] 1 S.C.R. 254 (S.C.C.).

[426] See *R. v. Thomsen*, [1988] S.C.J. No. 31, [1988] 1 S.C.R. 640 at 653-56 (S.C.C.); *R. v. Hufsky*, [1988] S.C.J. No. 30, [1988] 1 S.C.R. 621 at 636-37 (S.C.C.); *R. v. Ladouceur*, [1990] S.C.J. No. 53, [1990] 1 S.C.R. 1257 at 1279-86 (S.C.C.); *R. v. Orbanski*; *R. v. Elias*, [2005] S.C.J. No. 37, [2005] 2 S.C.R. 3 at para. 55 (S.C.C.). See also *R. v. Bernshaw*, [1994] S.C.J. No. 87, [1995] 1 S.C.R. 254 at paras. 98-101 (S.C.C.), *per* L'Heureux-Dubé J., concurring.

[427] See generally, *R. v. Thomsen*, [1988] S.C.J. No. 31, [1988] 1 S.C.R. 640 at 654 (S.C.C.) [*Thomsen*].

a.   Regulatory Searches

§3.144 Activities subject to regulatory oversight often attract a diminished expectation of privacy. In *Thomson*,[428] the Supreme Court considered a provision permitting competition regulators to compel the production of documents without prior authorization or evidentiary justification. In upholding the legislation under section 8, the Court characterized it as "administrative" or "regulatory" in nature.[429] Writing for the majority, Justice La Forest explained:

> In a modern industrial society, it is generally accepted that many activities in which individuals can engage must nevertheless to a greater or lesser extent be regulated by the state to ensure that the individual's pursuit of his or her self-interest is compatible with the community's interest in the realization of collective goals and aspirations. In many cases, this regulation must necessarily involve the inspection of private premises or documents by agents of the state. [430]

It follows that there is only a minimal expectation of privacy in respect of premises or documents used or produced in the course of activities which, though lawful, are subject to state regulation. State inspection of premises and documents is a routine and expected feature of participation in such activity.[431]

§3.145 Justice La Forest also noted that evidence of wrongdoing in regulatory cases is often exceptionally difficult to uncover. Insisting on compliance with *Hunter* in such cases would frustrate the government's ability to regulate in the public interest.[432] The fact that some regulatory offences provide for imprisonment, moreover, does not in itself demand prior authorization on reasonable grounds. As Justice La Forest concluded in *Thomson*, this possibility does not alter the "essential character" of the legislation as regulatory in nature.[433]

§3.146 Not all regulatory searches are exempt from the *Hunter* requirements, however. In each case, reasonableness must be assessed in light of the intrusiveness of the search, the nature of the regulatory scheme, and the purpose of the investigation. *Hunter* itself, for instance, involved a regulatory search that the Court decided required prior authorization on the basis of reasonable and prob-

---

[428]   *Thomson Newspapers Ltd. v. Canada (Director of Investigation and Research, Restrictive Trade Practices Commission)*, [1990] S.C.J. No. 23, [1990] 1 S.C.R. 425 (S.C.C.).

[429]   *Ibid.*, at 506 (S.C.R.).

[430]   *Ibid.*

[431]   *Ibid.*, at 506-507 (S.C.R.).

[432]   *Thomson Newspapers Ltd. v. Canada (Director of Investigation and Research, Restrictive Trade Practices Commission)*, [1990] S.C.J. No. 23, [1990] 1 S.C.R. 425 at 526 (S.C.C.) [*Thomson*]. See also *R. v. McKinlay Transport Ltd.*, [1990] S.C.J. No. 25, [1990] 1 S.C.R. 627 at 648 (S.C.C.).

[433]   *Thomson Newspapers Ltd. v. Canada (Director of Investigation and Research, Restrictive Trade Practices Commission)*, [1990] S.C.J. No. 23, [1990] 1 S.C.R. 425 at 509 (S.C.C.) [*Thomson*]. For further discussions of the distinction between regulatory and criminal legislation, see *Thomson, ibid.*, at 510-11 (S.C.R.); *R. v. Wholesale Travel Group Inc.*, [1991] S.C.J. No. 79, [1991] 3 S.C.R. 154 at paras. 143-45 (S.C.C.); *R. v. Jarvis*, [2002] S.C.J. No. 76, [2002] 3 S.C.R. 757 at paras. 59-62 (S.C.C.); *R. v. Hydro-Québec*, [1997] S.C.J. No. 76, [1997] 3 S.C.R. 213 at paras. 39-49 (S.C.C.); *R. v. Pontes*, [1995] S.C.J. No. 70, [1995] 3 S.C.R. 44 at paras. 20-26 (S.C.C.).

able grounds. As Justice La Forest noted in *Thomson*,[434] the legislation at issue in *Hunter* authorized warrantless searches of business and residential premises.[435] Such searches, he reasoned, are much more likely to threaten personal privacy than production orders for business documents.[436] Such documents "do not normally contain information about one's lifestyle, intimate relations or political or religious opinions."[437]

§3.147 Subsequent cases have confirmed that the compelled production of business and tax records does not generally require either prior authorization or objective grounds for suspicion. The Supreme Court has upheld such powers in the context of industrial competition,[438] income tax,[439] fisheries[440] and securities;[441] and lower courts have upheld them in a number of other circumstances.[442]

---

[434] [1990] S.C.J. No. 23, [1990] 1 S.C.R. 425 at 520-21 (S.C.C.).

[435] See also *R. v. McKinlay Transport Ltd.*, [1990] S.C.J. No. 25, [1990] 1 S.C.R. 627 at 649 (S.C.C.), *per* Wilson J. ("while a taxpayer may have little expectation of privacy in relation to his business records relevant to the determination of his tax liability, he has a significant privacy interest in the inviolability of his home"); *Baron v. Canada*, [1993] S.C.J. No. 6, [1993] 1 S.C.R. 416 at 444-45 (S.C.C.) (power to search any "building, receptacle or place" for evidence of tax offences must comply with *Hunter* requirements).

[436] *Thomson Newspapers Ltd. v. Canada (Director of Investigation and Research, Restrictive Trade Practices Commission)*, [1990] S.C.J. No. 23, [1990] 1 S.C.R. 425 at 521-22 (S.C.C.) [*Thomson*]; *R. v. McKinlay Transport Ltd.*, [1990] S.C.J. No. 25, [1990] 1 S.C.R. 627 at 649 (S.C.C.). See also *British Columbia Securities Commission v. Branch*, [1995] S.C.J. No. 32, [1995] 2 S.C.R. 3 at para. 60 (S.C.C.) ("The demand for the production of documents contained in the summonses is one of the least intrusive of the possible methods which might be employed to obtain documentary evidence."); *Baron v. Canada*, [1993] S.C.J. No. 6, [1993] 1 S.C.R. 416 at 649-50 (S.C.C.); *143471 Canada Inc. v. Quebec (Attorney General); Tabah v. Quebec (Attorney General)*, [1994] S.C.J. No. 45, [1994] 2 S.C.R. 339 at 381 (S.C.C.), *per* Cory J.

[437] *Thomson Newspapers Ltd. v. Canada (Director of Investigation and Research, Restrictive Trade Practices Commission)*, [1990] S.C.J. No. 23, [1990] 1 S.C.R. 425 at 517 (S.C.C.) [*Thomson*]. See also *British Columbia Securities Commission v. Branch*, [1995] S.C.J. No. 32, [1995] 2 S.C.R. 3 at para. 62 (S.C.C.); *143471 Canada Inc. v. Quebec (Attorney General); Tabah v. Quebec (Attorney General)*, [1994] S.C.J. No. 45, [1994] 2 S.C.R. 339 at 377 (S.C.C.), *per* Cory J.

[438] *Thomson Newspapers Ltd. v. Canada (Director of Investigation and Research, Restrictive Trade Practices Commission)*, [1990] S.C.J. No. 23, [1990] 1 S.C.R. 425 (S.C.C.) [*Thomson*].

[439] See *R. v. McKinlay Transport Ltd.*, [1990] S.C.J. No. 25, [1990] 1 S.C.R. 627 (S.C.C.); *Del Zotto v. Canada (Minister of National Revenue - M.N.R.)*, [1997] F.C.J. No. 795, 147 D.L.R. (4th) 457 (F.C.A.), *per* Strayer J., dissenting, revd *(sub nom. Del Zotto v. Canada)* [1999] S.C.J. No. 1, [1999] 1 S.C.R. 3 (S.C.C.) (a subpoena ordering the production of documents needed to administer the *Income Tax Act* does not constitute an unreasonable seizure).

[440] See *R. v. Fitzpatrick*, [1995] S.C.J. No. 94, [1995] 4 S.C.R. 154 at paras. 49-51 (S.C.C.). As discussed more fully in Chapter 4, Part 6(2), *Fitzpatrick* was argued on the basis of s. 7 principle against self-incrimination, not s. 8. In rejecting the s. 7 challenge, however, the Court noted that there was a diminished expectation of privacy in statutorily compelled fishing records.

[441] See *British Columbia Securities Commission v. Branch*, [1995] S.C.J. No. 32, [1995] 2 S.C.R. 3 at paras. 51-64 (S.C.C.). See also *Mitton v. British Columbia (Securities Commission)*, [2001] B.C.J. No. 665, 82 C.R.R. (2d) 60 (B.C.S.C.) (securities legislation enabling searches of business premises constitutional); *British Columbia (Securities Commission) v. S. (B.D.)*, [2003] B.C.J. No. 979, 2003 BCCA 244 at paras. 31-35 (B.C.C.A.) (legitimacy of orders for securities documents confirmed).

[442] See *Re Belgoma Transportation Ltd. and Ontario (Director of Employment Standards)*, [1985] O.J. No. 2598, 51 O.R. (2d) 509 (Ont. C.A.) (employment standards); *R. v. Ezzeddine* (1996) [1996] A.J. No. 338, 38 Alta. L.R. (3d) 385 (Alta. Q.B.) (bankruptcy).

§3.148 Even though *Hunter* does not apply in these situations, investigators must be able to show that the records are "relevant to a lawful inquiry".[443] This in turn requires the regulator to be "sufficiently precise and clear in terms of its identification of the documents".[444] This does not preclude random audits, however, which may be necessary to maximize compliance.[445]

§3.149 Courts have also typically upheld powers to inspect businesses for regulatory purposes. In *Comité paritaire de l'industrie de la chemise v. Potash; Comite paritaire de l'industrie de la chemise v. Selection Milton*,[446] the Supreme Court rejected a section 8 challenge to a provision authorizing the warrantless and suspicionless inspection of workplaces for compliance with employment standards legislation.[447] As in the case of production orders, section 8 requires only that the inspection be carried out in good faith and in accordance with the purposes of the regulatory scheme.[448] This applies, the Court held, even if the inspection takes place in a home where employees are working.[449]

§3.150 The *Hunter* prerequisites are more likely to apply when regulators seek evidence establishing penal liability. In *R. v. Jarvis*[450] and *R. v. Ling*,[451] the Su-

---

443 *Thomson Newspapers Ltd. v. Canada (Director of Investigation and Research, Restrictive Trade Practices Commission)*, [1990] S.C.J. No. 23, [1990] 1 S.C.R. 425 at 531, 532 (S.C.C.) [*Thomson*].

444 *Ibid.*, at 532 (S.C.R.).

445 See *R. v. McKinlay Transport Ltd.*, [1990] S.C.J. No. 25, [1990] 1 S.C.R. 627 at 648 (S.C.C.), per Wilson J.; *R. v. Fitzpatrick*, [1995] S.C.J. No. 94, [1995] 4 S.C.R. 154 at para. 50 (S.C.C.); *R. v. Jarvis*, [2002] S.C.J. No. 76, [2002] 3 S.C.R. 757 at paras. 50-51 (S.C.C.); *Comité paritaire de l'industrie de la chemise v. Potash; Comite paritaire de l'industrie de la chemise v. Selection Milton*, [1994] S.C.J. No. 7, [1994] 2 S.C.R. 406 at para. 86 (S.C.C.).

446 [1994] S.C.J. No. 7, [1994] 2 S.C.R. 406 (S.C.C.).

447 *Ibid.*, at 422-23 (S.C.R.). See also *R. v. Grosky*, [1991] M.J. No. 397, [1991] 5 W.W.R. 547 (Man. Q.B.) (legislation permitting searches of fuel tanks); *Ontario Chrysler (1977) Ltd. v. Ontario (Director of the Consumer Protection Division of the Ministry of Consumer & Commercial Relations)*, [1990] O.J. No. 114, 72 O.R. (2d) 106 (Ont. C.A.) (examination and copying of documents in *Business Practices Act* investigation); *R. v. Kent*, [1991] N.S.J. No. 423, 109 N.S.R. (2d) 335 (N.S.C.A.) (inspection of boat for invalid lobster traps), *R. v. Leahy*, [2004] N.S.J. No. 485, 229 N.S.R. (2d) 32 (N.S. Prov. Ct.) (examination of fishing boat and seizure of records); *R. v. Quesnel*, [1985] O.J. No. 2725, 53 O.R. (2d) 338 (Ont. C.A.), leave to appeal refused [1986] 1 S.C.R. xiii (S.C.C.) (inspection of farms to ensure compliance with *Farm Products Marketing Act*); *R. v. McGowan Motors Ltd.*, [1994] P.E.I.J. No. 8, 13 C.E.L.R. (N.S.) 161 (P.E.I.C.A.) (search powers under environmental legislation); *R. v. Sutikno*, [2006] O.J. No. 5538 (Ont. C.J.) (searches to ensure compliance with massage parlour regulations); *Ozubko v. Manitoba Horse Racing Commission*, [1986] M.J. No. 500, 43 Man.R. (2d) 253 (Man. C.A.), leave to appeal refused [1987] S.C.C.A. No. 204 (S.C.C.) (searches of horse track property to enforce licensing).

448 *Comité paritaire de l'industrie de la chemise v. Potash; Comite paritaire de l'industrie de la chemise v. Selection Milton*, [1994] S.C.J. No. 7, [1994] 2 S.C.R. 406 at 425 (S.C.C.).

449 *Ibid.*, at 424 (S.C.R.). See also *R. v. Bichel*, [1986] B.C.J. No. 491, 4 B.C.L.R. (2d) 132 (B.C.C.A.) (home inspections that enforce zoning by-laws do not violate s. 8); *R. v. Bolczak*, [2005] M.J. No. 299, 198 Man.R. (2d) 1 (Man. Q.B.) (limited regulatory searches can occur in a sleeper berth of a semi-trailer, which is a "dwelling place"). In other contexts, some courts have found that regulatory inspections of residences require a warrant. See *R. v. Huttman*, [1996] A.J. No. 988, 191 A.R. 184 (Alta. Prov. Ct.) (warrantless entries of private dwellings pursuant to *Meat Inspection Act*, R.S.A. 1980 c. M-10, unconstitutional); *R. v. Sheppard*, [1984] N.J. No. 17, 46 Nfld. & P.E.I.R. 189 (Nfld. C.A.) (warrant needed to search homes for illegal meat).

450 [2002] S.C.J. No. 76, [2002] 3 S.C.R. 757 (S.C.C.).

preme Court considered provisions requiring taxpayers to answer questions and provide documents related to income tax reporting.[452] Tax authorities conducting conventional audits, the Court concluded, may use these powers freely. But once the "predominant purpose" of the investigation becomes an inquiry into penal liability, they may no longer compel answers and must obtain warrants to seize documents.[453] It is only where taxpayers face the possibility of criminal punishments, the Court reasoned, that they enter into an "adversarial relationship" with the state.[454] In deciding whether such a relationship arose, courts must consider whether authorities had reasonable grounds to believe that a criminal offence was committed, attempted to collect evidence of *mens rea* and shifted primary responsibility for the investigation from auditors to criminal investigators.[455] Evidence obtained before the advent of the adversarial relationship, however, may be used in any criminal investigation and prosecution.[456]

§3.151 The "predominant purpose" test is both unworkable and unjustified.[457] "Totality of the circumstances" tests are notoriously difficult to apply *ex ante*.[458] Not surprisingly, the jurisprudence on the question has been highly variable.[459] Since no single factor is determinative, how are regulators to decide at one point they must obtain a warrant? This decision may be especially difficult in regula-

---

[451] [2002] S.C.J. No. 75, [2002] 3 S.C.R. 814 (S.C.C.).

[452] *Income Tax Act*, R.S.C. 1985, c. 1 (5th Supp.), ss. 231.1(1) and 231.2(1).

[453] *R. v. Jarvis*, [2002] S.C.J. No. 76, [2002] 3 S.C.R. 757 at paras. 2, 46, 88, and 99 (S.C.C.).

[454] *Ibid.*, at paras. 84, 88 (S.C.R.).

[455] *Ibid.*, at paras. 89-92 (S.C.R.).

[456] *Ibid.*, at paras. 95-97 (S.C.R.).

[457] See Steven Penney, "What's Wrong with Self-Incrimination? The Wayward Path of Self-Incrimination Law in the Post-*Charter* Era: Part III: Compelled Communications, the Admissibility of Defendants' Previous Testimony, and Inferences from Defendants' Silence" (2004) 48 Crim. L.Q. 474 at 503.

[458] See Antonin Scalia, "The Rule of Law as a Law of Rules" (1989) 56 U. Chi. L. Rev. 1175 at 1182 (through the "totality of the circumstances" test "equality of treatment is difficult to ... achieve; predictability is destroyed; judicial arbitrariness is facilitated; judicial courage is impaired"); Carol S. Steiker, "Second Thoughts About First Principles" (1994) 107 Harv. L. Rev. 820 at 854-855 (rules generally "preferred over standards because they 'reduce the danger of official arbitrariness or bias'"); Yael Aridor Bar-Ilan, "Justice: When Do We Decide?" (2007) 39 Conn. L. Rev. 923 at 941-42 ("ex post analysis leaves to some totality of the circumstances the resolution of future cases, without any guidelines and framework on which to determine such cases.").

[459] See *R. v. Dial Drug Stores Ltd.*, [2001] O.J. No. 159, 52 O.R. (3d) 367 (Ont. C.J.), revd [2003] O.J. No. 754, 63 O.R. (3d) 529 (Ont. S.C.J.) (investigations into possible tax offences are criminal nature); *Kligman v. Canada (Minister of National Revenue – M.N.R.)*, [2004] F.C.J. No. 639, 2004 FCA 152 (F.C.A.) (an investigation becomes criminal in nature if a decision to proceed with such an investigation could have been made; otherwise, multiple factors are determinative); *R. v. Chusid*, [2001] O.J. No. 4741, 57 O.R. (3d) 20 at paras. 60-61 (Ont. S.C.J.) (an audit becomes a criminal investigation when there is a reasonable and probable belief an offence has been committed); *R. v. Norway Insulation Inc.*, [1995] O.J. No. 1073, 23 O.R. (3d) 432 (Ont. Gen. Div.) (investigation becomes criminal once it is concluded that there is "sufficient evidence" of an offence); *R. v. Coghlan*, [1993] O.J. No. 1599, [1994] 1 C.T.C. 164 (Ont. Prov. Div.) (a matter becomes criminal once Revenue Canada decides to lay charges).

tory schemes combining inspection and investigation functions in one department or class of official.[460]

§3.152 More important, as the Supreme Court has repeatedly recognized, income tax and business records attract only a minimal expectation of privacy.[461] If it does not unduly violate individual privacy to seize them when there are no grounds for suspicion (*i.e.*, in a random audit), how can it do so when there are (*i.e.*, in a criminal investigation)? If anything, greater protection is warranted in the former situation than the latter. To conclude otherwise is to favour the privacy of the "likely guilty" over that of the "likely innocent". *Jarvis* and *Ling* should thus be overruled. The warrantless seizure of business and tax records to further criminal inquiries should not be held to violate section 8 of the *Charter*.

b. Border Control and Public Transportation Networks

§3.153 As noted, the Court suggested in *Hunter* that reasonableness might have to be assessed differently "where state security is involved".[462] In *R. v. Simmons*,[463] the Court seized upon this *dictum* in finding that people crossing Canada's borders have a diminished expectation of privacy.[464] Sovereign states, Chief Justice Dickson wrote for the majority, have a legitimate interest "in preventing the entry of undesirable persons and prohibited goods, and in protecting tariff revenue."[465] This interest justified the warrantless and suspicionless frisk and luggage searches authorized by customs legislation.[466] Strip searches at border crossings, in contrast, require reasonable suspicion (but not prior authorization).[467] The Court intimated, but did not decide, that "highly invasive" searches,

---

[460] See David Stratas, "'Crossing the Rubicon': The Supreme Court and Regulatory Investigations" (2003) 6 C.R. (6th) 74 at 80.

[461] See *R. v. McKinlay Transport Ltd.*, [1990] S.C.J. No. 25, [1990] 1 S.C.R. 627 at 650 (S.C.C.), *per* Wilson J.; *R. v. Jarvis*, [2002] S.C.J. No. 76, [2002] 3 S.C.R. 757 at para. 95 (S.C.C.); *143471 Canada Inc. v. Quebec (Attorney General); Tabah v. Quebec (Attorney General)*, [1994] S.C.J. No. 45, [1994] 2 S.C.R. 339 at 379 (S.C.C.), *per* Cory J. and 366 (S.C.R.), *per* La Forest J., dissenting.

[462] *Hunter v. Southam (sub nom. Canada (Combines Investigation Acts, Director of Investigation and Research) v. Southam Inc.)* [1984] S.C.J. No. 36, [1984] 2 S.C.R. 145 at 168 (S.C.C.) [*Hunter*].

[463] [1988] S.C.J. No. 86, [1988] 2 S.C.R. 495 (S.C.C.).

[464] *Ibid.*, at 528 (S.C.R.).

[465] *Ibid.*, at 527-28 (S.C.R.).

[466] *Ibid.*, at 529 (S.C.R.).

[467] *Ibid.*, at 529-30 (S.C.R.). In *Simmons*, the statute gave suspects the right to "require the officer to take him or her before a police magistrate or justice of the peace or before the collector or chief officer at the port or place who shall, if he or she sees no reasonable cause for search, discharge the person." Though this provision does not satisfy the *Hunter* prior authorization requirement, the Court held that it was "not unreasonable". It went on to hold (in self-described *obiter*), however, that the failure to inform the suspect of either this right or the right to counsel under s. 10(*b*) of the *Charter* rendered the search unreasonable. *Ibid.*, at 530-31(S.C.R.). The current legislation gives suspects the right to have the search approved by the "senior officer" on duty, but it does not demand that suspects be informed of this right. See *Customs Act*, R.S.C. 1985, c. 1 (2nd Supp.), s. 98. See *R. v. Granston*, [2000] O.J. No. 2437, 146 C.C.C. (3d) 411 at para. 44 (Ont. C.A.) ("In my view, it is essential that this right [of review by a senior officer] be

such as those involving bodily cavities, X-rays or emetics, might merit additional protection.[468] The Court subsequently found, however, that subjecting a traveller suspected of ingesting drugs to a "bedpan vigil" was analogous to a strip search; it could thus be conducted without a warrant on the basis of reasonable suspicion.[469] The same reduced section 8 standards justify legislative powers that authorize warrantless searches of vehicles near border crossings.[470]

§3.154 Courts have also found that air travellers have a diminished expectation of privacy in luggage and other goods transported on domestic flights. Airline passengers have no reasonable expectation that their luggage will not be randomly (or otherwise) searched for explosives, weapons or other items posing a threat to security or safety.[471] While section 8 is not violated if such searches uncover other illegal items, searches conducted for non-security purposes must conform to the usual *Hunter* standards.[472]

§3.155 The distinction between security and non-security purposes may also be relevant in the context of searches of passengers and items flowing through other domestic public transportation networks. In *R. v. Kang-Brown*,[473] members of the Supreme Court of Canada expressed differing views on the question of whether domestic bus terminals were analogous to border crossings.[474] A majority of the Court found, however, that police need reasonable suspicion — the same standard applying in other domestic contexts — before subjecting bus passengers and their belongings to canine sniff searches for illegal drugs.[475] The

---

clearly understood by someone detained at the border."); *R. v. Bryson*, [1991] B.C.J. No. 3926 (B.C.S.C.) (detainees must be told of their right of review, not merely directed to the text of the *Customs Act*).

[468] *R. v. Simmons*, [1988] S.C.J. No. 86, [1988] 2 S.C.R. 495 at 517 (S.C.C.). See also *R. v. Monney*, [1999] S.C.J. No. 18, [1999] 1 S.C.R. 652 at para. 46 (S.C.C.); *R. v. Oluwa*, [1996] B.C.J. No. 1065, 107 C.C.C. (3d) 236 at paras. 63-64 (B.C.C.A.).

[469] *R. v. Monney*, [1999] S.C.J. No. 18, [1999] 1 S.C.R. 652 at paras. 39-48 (S.C.C.).

[470] *R. v. Jacques*, [1996] S.C.J. No. 88, [1996] 3 S.C.R. 312 (S.C.C.) (upholding s. 99(1)(*f*) of the *Customs Act*, R.S.C. 1985, c. 1 (2nd Supp.), which authorizes a customs official to detain and search when he or she "suspects on reasonable grounds" that an offence has been committed).

[471] See *R. v. Lewis*, [1998] O.J. No. 376, 122 C.C.C. (3d) 481 at para. 40 (Ont. C.A.) ("The respondent had to know that his luggage could be examined and searched at random by state authorities for security purposes before it was placed or taken on the airplane."); *R. v. Truong*, [2002] B.C.J. No. 1067, 168 C.C.C. (3d) 132) at para. 9 (B.C.C.A.).

[472] See *R. v. Truong*, [2002] B.C.J. No. 1067, 168 C.C.C. (3d) 132) at paras. 9-21 (B.C.C.A.); *R. v. Lewis*, [1998] O.J. No. 376, 122 C.C.C. (3d) 481 at para. 12 (Ont. C.A.); *R. v. Sandhu*, [1992] B.C.J. No. 913 (B.C.S.C.), affd [1993] B.C.J. No. 1279 (B.C.C.A.), leave to appeal to S.C.C. refused [1993] S.C.C.A. No. 348 (S.C.C.); *R. v. Cody*, [2003] N.J. No. 335, 233 Nfld. & P.E.I.R. 73 (N.L. Prov. Ct.).

[473] [2008] S.C.J. No. 18, [2008] 1 S.C.R. 456, 2008 SCC 18 (S.C.C.).

[474] *Ibid.*, at paras. 69-72 (SCC), *per* Binnie J., (distinguishing border searches from domestic searches), at 228-31 (SCC), *per* Bastarache J., dissenting (stating that the diminished expectation of privacy attaching to transportation hubs relates to both security and general crime control).

[475] See *R. v. Kang-Brown*, [2008] S.C.J. No. 18, [2008] 1 S.C.R. 456, 2008 SCC 18 at para. 58 (S.C.C.), *per* Binnie J., at paras. 191-193 (SCC), *per* Deschamps J., dissenting, at paras. 234-244 (SCC), *per* Bastarache J., dissenting. For further discussion of canine searches, see below, Part 4(4).

situation might be different, Justice Binnie suggested, if the sniffs had been directed at "explosives, guns or other public safety concerns."[476]

c.   Prisons, Schools and Workplaces

§3.156 Not surprisingly, courts have held that prisoners have a markedly reduced expectation of privacy. In *Weatherall v. Canada (Attorney General)*,[477] the Supreme Court found that legislation authorizing suspicionless frisk searches and the inspection of prison cells did not violate section 8, even where such searches were performed by female guards on male inmates.[478] "Imprisonment necessarily entails surveillance," Justice La Forest wrote for the Court, which is necessary "for the security of the institution."[479] Offenders serving sentences outside of prison also have diminished privacy rights, but any intrusions must be reasonable and proportionate to the risk posed to the safety of the community.[480]

§3.157 More controversially, the Supreme Court decided in *R. v. M. (M.R.)*[481] that schoolchildren have a diminished expectation of privacy while at school.[482] In that case, the vice-principal of a junior high school was informed that a student might be selling drugs at the school. He called the police and searched the student in the presence of a police officer. Drugs were found and the student was arrested. The Court concluded that the vice-principal was not acting as an agent of police[483] and that *Hunter*'s requirements did not therefore apply.[484] Though the

---

[476] *R. v. Kang-Brown*, [2008] S.C.J. No. 18, [2008] 1 S.C.R. 456, 2008 SCC 18 at para. 18 (S.C.C.), *per* Binnie J.

[477] [1993] S.C.J. No. 81, [1993] 2 S.C.R. 872 (S.C.C.).

[478] *Ibid.*

[479] *Ibid.*, at 877 (S.C.R.). See also *R. v. Golden*, [2001] S.C.J. No. 81, [2001] 3 S.C.R. 679 at paras. 97-98 (S.C.C.) (noting that arrestees in short-term detention in police cells may have a higher expectation of privacy than prison inmates, especially with respect to strip searches for non-violent offences); *Mazzei v. British Columbia (Director of Adult Forensic Services)*, [2006] B.C.J. No. 1410, 2006 BCCA 321, 228 B.C.A.C. 129 (B.C.C.A.) (no violation of s. 8 when Review Board ordered mentally disordered person detained in psychiatric facility to submit to random drug testing).

[480] See generally, *R. v. Shoker*, [2006] S.C.J. No. 44, [2006] 2 S.C.R. 399 at para. 25 (S.C.C.).

[481] [1998] S.C.J. No. 83, [1998] 3 S.C.R. 393 (S.C.C.).

[482] *R. v. M. (M.R.)*, [1998] S.C.J. No. 83, [1998] 3 S.C.R. 393 (S.C.C.). See also *R. v. Z. (S.M.)*, [1998] M.J. No. 587, 21 C.R. (5th) 170 at para. 21 (Man. C.A.) ("The expectation of privacy which a student has with respect to his locker is at the lower end of the scale."); *R. v. S. (M.W.)*, [2005] B.C.J. No. 1270, 2005 BCPC 213 (B.C. Prov. Ct. (Youth Div.)) (lower expectation of privacy in locker than on person); *R. v. M.(A.)*, [2006] O.J. No. 1663, 79 O.R. (3d) 481 at para. 49 (Ont. C.A.), affd [2008] S.C.J. No. 19, [2008] 1 S.C.R. 569 (S.C.C.) ("a student's backpack should be afforded at least the same degree of respect as an adult's briefcase"). For criticism of *R. v. M. (M.R.)*, see Wayne MacKay "Don't Mind Me, I'm from the R.C.M.P.: *R. v. M. (M.R.)* — Another Brick in the Wall Between Students and Their Rights" (1997) 7 C.R. (5th) 24; Don Stuart, "The Unfortunate Dilution of Section 8 Protection: Some Teeth Remain" (1999) 25 Queen's L.J. 65-94.

[483] The Court assumed, but did not definitively decide, that s. 8 applied to the principal's actions because public schools are subject to the *Charter*. *R. v. M. (M.R.)*, [1998] S.C.J. No. 83, [1998] 3 S.C.R. 393 at paras. 24-25, 30 (S.C.C.). When school officials act as police agents, the usual *Hunter* standards apply. *R. v. M. (M.R.)*, [1998] S.C.J. No. 83, [1998] 3 S.C.R. 393 at para. 56 (S.C.C.). The concept of state agency is explained in detail in Chapter 1, Part 4(3).

[484] *R. v. M. (M.R.)*, [1998] S.C.J. No. 83, [1998] 3 S.C.R. 393 at para. 45 (S.C.C.).

governing legislation gave school officials no express power to search, the Court reasoned that "[n]onetheless, the responsibility placed upon the teachers, and principals to maintain proper order and discipline in the school and to attend to the health and comfort of students by necessary implication authorizes searches of students."[485] In light of concerns for safety and discipline, teachers and administrators may conduct warrantless searches "if there are reasonable grounds to believe that a school rule has been or is being violated, and that evidence of the violation will be found in the location or on the person of the student searched."[486]

§3.158 The Court later rejected the argument, however, that the exigencies of school safety and discipline justified the use of drug-sniffing dogs in the absence of reasonable suspicion.[487] In *R. v. M. (A.)*,[488] a majority of the Court stressed that students have no lesser expectation of privacy than others in relation to searches conducted by *police* (or their dogs).[489] "The difference between a police search and an investigation by school authorities was of critical importance to the Court's decision in *M. (M.R.)*," Justice Binnie wrote, and "... is of importance here as well."[490] As in the case of sniffs in bus depots, however, he hinted that the situation might be different if the investigation had been directed at "explosives, guns or other public safety issues."[491]

(6) Section 1 of the *Charter*

§3.159 Section 8 violations are almost never justified under section 1,[492] which subjects all *Charter* rights to "such reasonable limits prescribed by law as can be demonstrably justified in a free and democratic society." The reason for this is simple. Unlike some other *Charter* rights, section 8 does not entitle people to an unfettered zone of individual liberty. As we have seen, it only gives them a right to be secure against "unreasonable" searches or seizures. It is difficult to imagine how an unreasonable search could nevertheless constitute a "reasonable limit" under section 1.[493] In other words, with respect to section 8, the balancing

---

[485] *Ibid.*, at para. 51 (S.C.R.).

[486] *Ibid.*, at para. 48 (S.C.R.). See also *ibid.*, at para. 50 (S.C.R.). The Court noted that to be reasonable under s. 8, such searches must be "conducted in a sensitive manner and be minimally intrusive." *Ibid.*, at para. 54 (S.C.R.). See also *R. v. Thanganadan*, [2004] O.J. No. 2560, 2004 ONCJ 82 at 34 (Ont. C.J.) (mere suspicion of breaching school regulations falls short of the "modified standard" threshold to conduct a warrantless search).

[487] See also *R. v. Kang-Brown*, [2008] S.C.J. No. 18, [2008] 1 S.C.R. 456, 2008 SCC 18 at paras. 71-72 (S.C.C.), *per* Binnie J. For further discussion of canine searches, see below, Part 4(4).

[488] [2008] S.C.J. No. 19, [2008] 1 S.C.R. 569, 2008 SCC 19 (S.C.C.).

[489] *Ibid.*, at paras. 35, 45-47 (SCC), *per* Binnie J.

[490] *R. v. M. (A.)*, [2008] S.C.J. No. 19, [2008] 1 S.C.R. 569, 2008 SCC 19 at para. 46 (S.C.C.).

[491] *Ibid.*, at para. 3 (SCC), *per* Binnie J. See also *ibid.*, at para. 37 (SCC).

[492] See *contra R. v. Pelletier*, [1989] S.J. No. 420, 50 C.C.C. (3d) 22 (Sask. Q.B.).

[493] See *Lavallee, Rackel & Heintz v. Canada (Attorney General); White, Ottenheimer & Baker v. Canada (Attorney General); R. v. Fink*, [2002] S.C.J. No. 61, [2002] 3 S.C.R. 209 at para. 46 (S.C.C.); *Baron v. Canada*, [1993] S.C.J. No. 6, [1993] 1 S.C.R. 416 at 453 (S.C.C.); *Hunter v. Southam (sub nom. Canada (Combines Investigation Acts, Director of Investigation and Research) v. Southam Inc.)*, [1984] S.C.J. No. 36, [1984] 2 S.C.R. 145 at 169-70 (S.C.C.) [*Hunter*].

between state and individual interests that usually takes place under section 1 of the *Charter* is already incorporated into the reasonableness standard found within the constitutional guarantee itself. As a result, it would be redundant to apply section 1 to a section 8 violation.

3. STATUTORY SEARCH POWERS

(1) Introduction

§3.160 Federal and provincial statutes set out a broad variety of search powers. A thorough review of all these powers is beyond the scope of this chapter. Instead, we focus in this part on the search and seizure powers contained in the *Criminal Code* and those found in other federal enactments commonly resorted to by the police in conducting criminal investigations.

§3.161 Some of the legislated search powers reviewed in this part are quite old, originating in much earlier versions of our *Criminal Code*. Many others, however, are relatively new. Throughout the 1990s, as the Supreme Court of Canada held that specific investigative techniques intruded upon reasonable privacy expectations and therefore had to comply with the minimum requirements of section 8 of the *Charter*, Parliament responded with legislative provisions to authorize these techniques in terms that, for the most part, track *Hunter*'s minimum requirements.[494] This period of robust constitutional dialogue relating to police powers was, however, short-lived.[495]

---

[494] There are numerous examples of this sort of dialogue. See *Criminal Code*, R.S.C. 1985, c. C-46, s. 487.05, creating a legislated scheme for DNA warrants (added by *An Act to amend the Criminal Code and the Young Offenders Act (forensic DNA analysis)*, S.C. 1995, c. 27, s. 1) in response to *R. v. Borden*, [1994] S.C.J. No. 82, [1994] 3 S.C.R. 145 (S.C.C.); *Criminal Code*, s. 487.091, creating a legislated scheme for the issuance of body impression warrants (added by the *DNA Identification Act*, S.C. 1998, c. 37) in response to *R. v. Stillman*, [1997] S.C.J. No. 34, [1997] 1 S.C.R. 607 (S.C.C.); *Criminal Code*, s. 492.1(1), creating legislative scheme for the issuance of warrants to place electronic tracking devices on vehicles (added by *An Act to amend the Criminal Code, the Crown Liability and Proceedings Act and the Radiocommunication Act*, S.C. 1993, c. 40, s. 18), in response to *R. v. Wise*, [1992] S.C.J. No. 16, [1992] 1 S.C.R. 527 (S.C.C.); *Criminal Code*, ss. 184.1 and 184.2, creating a legislated scheme for participant surveillance and to ensure the safety of police officers involved in dangerous undercover operations (added by *An Act to amend the Criminal Code, the Crown Liability and Proceedings Act and the Radiocommunication Act*, S.C. 1993, c. 40, s. 4) in response to *R. v. Duarte*, [1990] S.C.J. No. 2, [1990] 1 S.C.R. 30 (S.C.C.) and *R. v. Wiggins*, [1990] S.C.J. No. 3, [1990] 1 S.C.R. 62 (S.C.C.); *Criminal Code*, s. 487.01, creating a legislative scheme for a general warrant to authorize the use of any investigative device, technique or procedure, expressly mentioning video-surveillance (added by *An Act to amend the Criminal Code, the Crown Liability and Proceedings Act and the Radiocommunication Act*, S.C. 1993, c. 40, s. 15), in response to *R. v. Duarte*, [1990] S.C.J. No. 2, [1990] 1 S.C.R. 30 (S.C.C.) and *R. v. Wong*, [1990] S.C.J. No. 118, [1990] 3 S.C.R. 36 (S.C.C.); *Criminal Code*, s. 487.11 and s. 11(7) of the *Controlled Drugs and Substances Act*, S.C. 1996, c. 19, as amended, authorizing warrantless searches if the grounds for a search with a warrant exist but due to exigent circumstances it is not feasible to obtain one (added by the *Criminal Law Improvement Act, 1996*, S.C. 1997, c. 18) in response to comments by the Court in *R. v. Silveira*, [1995] S.C.J. No. 38, [1995] 2 S.C.R. 297 (S.C.C.); *Criminal Code*, ss. 529 and 529(1), creating a legislative scheme for the issuance of a warrant to

§3.162 There are also a number of offence-specific search and seizure powers contained in the *Criminal Code*, including sections 117.02 (weapons in place other than dwelling-house); 117.04 (preventive weapons searches); 199(1) to (2) (gaming and bawdy house searches); 254(2) to (4) (breath or blood demands with respect to alcohol related driving offences); 339(3) (stolen timber); 447(2) (seizure of cocks found in a cockpit); 462 (seizure of counterfeit money). Some of these legislated search powers are discussed in greater detail below.

§3.163 As discussed in Part 2(5), above, if the lawful parameters of these powers are exceeded then the police act unlawfully and thus violate section 8. Section 8 is similarly infringed if the conduct of the authorities is technically in compliance with the parameters of a legislated power but the manner in which a search or seizure is carried out is unreasonable.

(2) Searches in Exigent Circumstances

§3.164 Many of the legislated search powers just noted pre-date the *Charter*. While some have been amended in an attempt to comply with the minimum requirements of section 8 of the *Charter*,[496] others are constitutionally suspect because they authorize the police to search without any need to first obtain a warrant.[497] Rather than declare such powers invalid, however, in the past the Supreme Court has preferred to read them down so that their availability is limited to situations where exigent circumstances make it impracticable to obtain a warrant.[498]

§3.165 The Supreme Court has indicated that such circumstances "will generally be held to exist if there is an imminent danger of the loss, removal, destruction or disappearance of the evidence if the search or seizure is delayed"[499] in order to obtain a warrant. A mere possibility that evidence may be lost is not sufficient.[500] And, quite obviously, exigent circumstances will not arise if the police have deliberately structured their actions in a manner calculated to create

---

enter a dwelling-house to effect an arrest (added by *An Act to amend the Criminal Code and the Interpretation Act (powers to arrest and enter dwellings)*, S.C. 1997, c. 39, s. 2) in response to *R. v. Feeney*, [1997] S.C.J. No. 49, [1997] 2 S.C.R. 13 (S.C.C.).

[495] Eventually, the Supreme Court became much more proactive in filling gaps in police search powers, with the result being a lack of legislative activity by Parliament. For a discussion of these developments more generally and the larger implications of same, see Chapter 1, Part 6(4)(*b*). See also James Stribopoulos, "In Search of Dialogue: The Supreme Court, Police Powers and the *Charter*" (2005) 31 Queen's L.J. 1.

[496] For example, *Criminal* Code, R.S.C. 1985, c. C-46, ss. 117.02(1), 117.04(2), 199(1) to (2)).

[497] See *e.g.*, *Criminal Code,* s. 339(3).

[498] *R. v. Grant*, [1993] S.C.J. No. 98, [1993] 3 S.C.R. 223 (S.C.C.).

[499] *Ibid.*, at 241-42 (S.C.R.). See also *R. v. Bowen-Courville*, [2007] O.J. No. 180 (Ont. S.C.J.) (exigent circumstances that justify a warrantless search cannot be claimed if they occurred after the search began).

[500] See *R. v. Feeney*, [1997] S.C.J. No. 49, [1997] 2 S.C.R. 13 at para. 52 (S.C.C.).

the very urgency that is then claimed as the justification for dispensing with the warrant requirement.[501]

§3.166 Exigent circumstances may justify warrantless searches of vehicles.[502] As discussed in Chapter 2, Part 4(2), though police investigating driving-related offences require neither a warrant nor individualized suspicion to stop a vehicle, they may conduct only a limited search for evidence relating to those offences. However, if they have reasonable and probable grounds to believe that the vehicle contains evidence relating to other offences, they may be able to conduct a more extensive search without a warrant.[503] As Justice Martin noted in *R. v. Rao*,[504] "the mobility of ... vehicles would, in most cases, make the requirement of a warrant impracticable."[505] Unlike the United States Supreme Court,[506] however, Canadian courts have not created a "blanket" vehicle exception to the warrant requirement. In each case police must determine whether it is truly "impracticable to obtain a warrant."[507] In making this decision, it must also be kept in mind that most warrants may be obtained under an expedited "telewarrant" process.[508]

§3.167 In response to these decisions, Parliament added express exigent circumstances exceptions to a number of statutory search powers,[509] including some authorizing searches inside homes.[510] Each of these provisions allows police to

---

[501] See *R. v. Silveira*, [1995] S.C.J. No. 38, [1995] 2 S.C.R. 297 (S.C.C.), *per* La Forest J. dissenting in the result.

[502] See *R. v. Grant*, [1993] S.C.J. No. 98, [1993] 3 S.C.R. 223 at 242-43 (S.C.C.).

[503] As discussed below, Part 4(2)(*b*)(ii), police may also conduct a general search of the vehicle if they arrest an occupant, given the expansive power to search incidental to arrest.

[504] [1984] O.J. No. 3180, 12 C.C.C. (3d) 97 at 123 (Ont. C.A.).

[505] *Ibid.*, at 114 (C.C.C.).

[506] *Carroll v. United States* (1924), 267 U.S. 132; *United States v. Ross* (1982), 102 S. Ct. 2157.

[507] *R. v. Grant*, [1993] S.C.J. No. 98, [1993] 3 S.C.R. 223 at 242 (S.C.C.). See also *Canada (Attorney General) v. D. (I.D.)*, [1987] S.J. No. 653, 38 C.C.C. (3d) 289 at 297 (Sask. C.A.).

[508] See *S. (V.) v. Alberta (Director of Child Welfare)*, [2004] A.J. No. 1474, 373 A.R. 201 at para. 37 (Alta. Q.B.) (telewarrant ought to be obtained where there is no immediate danger to life or safety); *R. v. Jamieson*, [2002] B.C.J. No. 1476, 166 C.C.C. (3d) 501 at paras. 32-36 (B.C.C.A.) (adequate time to obtain a telewarrant does not invalidate a warrantless search justified by exigent circumstances); *R. v. Phillips*, [2004] B.C.J. No. 2919, 2004 BCSC 1797 at para. 20 (B.C.S.C.) (urgency or exigent circumstances are not prerequisites to issuing telewarrant); *R. v. Erickson*, [2003] B.C.J. No. 2982, 19 C.R. (6th) 367 at paras. 29-35 (B.C.C.A.) (same); *R. v. Martens*, [2004] B.C.J. No. 2300, 2004 BCSC 1450 at paras. 214-235 (B.C.S.C.) (same); *R. v. Lewis*, [2004] N.S.J. No. 186, 223 N.S.R. (2d) 394 at para. 24 (N.S. Prov. Ct.) (telewarrant should have been obtained despite the officer being alone, without backup and a possibility of evidence disappearing); *R. v. Gobert*, [2007] S.J. No. 222, 2007 SKPC 31 (Sask. Prov. Ct.) (detecting an odour of narcotics does not render it impractical to obtain telewarrant).

[509] See *Criminal Law Improvement Act, 1996*, S.C. 1997, c. 18, s. 46; *An Act to amend the Criminal Code and the Interpretation Act*, S.C. 1997, c. 39, s. 2; *Firearms Act*, S.C. 1995, c. 39 and *Criminal Code*, ss. 487.11 (exigent circumstances exceptions for warrants to search any "building, receptacle or place" under s. 487 and tracking warrants under s. 492.1) and 117.02 (exigent circumstances exception for firearm offence searches of a "person", "vehicle" or "place or premises other than a dwelling-house"); *Controlled Drugs and Substances Act*, S.C. 1996, c. 19, s. 11(7) (exigent circumstances exception for warrants to search any "place" or "person").

[510] See *R. v. McCormack*, [2000] B.C.J. No. 143, 143 C.C.C. (3d) 260 (B.C.C.A.) (in exigent circumstances, police may enter and secure a residence awaiting the arrival of a search warrant);

search without a warrant if "the conditions for obtaining a warrant exist," but by reason of "exigent circumstances" it would not be practical to obtain one.[511]

§3.168 As discussed below,[512] police have other powers to enter homes without a warrant in exigent or otherwise urgent circumstances. These are not search powers *per se*, but they do permit police to invade privacy in ways that would otherwise violate section 8. In exercising these powers, police may seize evidence in plain view and search as an incident to any lawful arrest.[513] Police may make a warrantless arrest inside a residence, for example, when in "hot pursuit" of a suspect[514] or to prevent either "imminent bodily harm or death"[515] or the "imminent loss or imminent destruction of the evidence."[516]

§3.169 If exigent circumstances are lacking, however, the search powers conferred by these provisions should not be resorted to. Instead, if the police wish to proceed lawfully and constitutionally they will normally need to obtain a warrant. Generally, warrants to carry out a conventional "search" are obtained under section 487 of the *Criminal Code*.

(3) Conventional Search Warrants (*Criminal Code*, Section 487)

§3.170 Search warrants are indispensable investigative tools allowing police to uncover and preserve evidence relevant to events that may have give rise to criminal liability. The most frequently used warrant provision is section 487(1) of the *Criminal Code*, which reads as follows:

R. v. Duong, [2002] B.C.J. No. 90, 162 C.C.C. (3d) 242 (B.C.C.A.), leave to appeal refused [2002] S.C.C.A. No. 112 (S.C.C.) (destruction of evidence qualifies as exigent circumstances justifying a warrantless search of a residence). Before these amendments, the Supreme Court had held that there was no statutory power to search the *inside* of a residence, even in exigent circumstances. In *R. v. Silveira*, [1995] S.C.J. No. 38, [1995] 2 S.C.R. 297 at para. 140 (S.C.C.), police entered and secured a residence while awaiting the arrival of a warrant. They believed that this was required to prevent the loss and destruction of evidence. At the time of entry, there was considerable evidence that police had reasonable and probable grounds to obtain a warrant, and they subsequently obtained one and executed it. The Crown conceded, and the majority accepted, that this was "a form of search not authorized by law" and thus violated section 8. See also *ibid.*, at para. 49 (S.C.R.), *per* La Forest J., dissenting ("absent clear statutory language ... police have no power to enter a dwelling-house to conduct a search without a warrant").

[511] Though these provisions remove the usual requirement of prior authorization, they do not remove the usual requirement for justification based on the relevant legal standard. See *Criminal Code*, ss. 487.11 and 117.02; *Controlled Drugs and Substances Act*, S.C. 1996, c. 19, s. 11(7).

[512] See discussion below, Part 4(2)(*b*)(i).

[513] See *R. v. Schulz*, [2001] B.C.J. No. 2164, 159 B.C.A.C. 146 (B.C.C.A.); *R. v. Golub*, [1997] O.J. No. 3097, 117 C.C.C. (3d) 193 (Ont. C.A.), leave to appeal refused [1997] S.C.C.A. No. 571 (S.C.C.). The "plain view" seizure power is discussed below, Part 3(6). The search incidental to arrest power is discussed below, Part 4(2).

[514] See *R. v. Macooh*, [1993] S.C.J. No. 28, [1993] 2 S.C.R. 802 at paras. 34-35 (S.C.C.); *R. v. Feeney*, [1997] S.C.J. No. 49, [1997] 2 S.C.R. 13 at paras. 47-51 (S.C.C.).

[515] *Criminal Code*, R.S.C. 1985, c. C-46, s. 529.3(2)(*a*).

[516] *Ibid.*, s. 529.3(2)(*b*).

A justice[517] who is satisfied by information on oath in Form 1 that there are reasonable grounds to believe that there is in a building, receptacle or place

    (*a*) anything on or in respect of which any offence against this Act or any other Act of Parliament has been or is suspected to have been committed,

    (*b*) anything that there are reasonable grounds to believe will afford evidence with respect to the commission of an offence, or will reveal the whereabouts of a person who is believed to have committed an offence, against this Act or any other Act of Parliament,

    (*c*) anything that there are reasonable grounds to believe is intended to be used for the purpose of committing any offence against the person for which a person may be arrested without warrant, or

    (*c.1*) any offence-related property,

may at any time issue a warrant authorizing a peace officer or a public officer who has been appointed or designated to administer or enforce a federal or provincial law and whose duties include the enforcement of this Act or any other Act of Parliament and who is named in the warrant

    (*d*) to search the building, receptacle or place for any such thing and to seize it, and

    (*e*) subject to any other Act of Parliament, to, as soon as practicable, bring the thing seized before, or make a report in respect thereof to, the justice or some other justice for the same territorial division in accordance with section 489.1.[518]

§3.171 Where it is impracticable for police to apply for a search warrant by attending in person before a justice, section 487.1 of the *Code* allows an officer to apply for a warrant by telephone or other means of telecommunications. The criteria for an information submitted by telephone or other means of telecommunications are set out in section 487.1(4). The information will include a statement of the circumstances that make it impracticable for the peace officer to attend personally before the justice;[519] a statement of the indictable offence alleged, the place to be searched and the items liable to seizure; a statement of the peace officer's grounds for believing that such items will be found in the place to be searched; and a statement as to any prior application for a warrant in respect of the same matter. Authority to issue the warrant is contained in section

---

[517] Section 2 of the *Criminal Code* defines a "justice" as a "justice of the peace or a provincial court judge ...".

[518] *Criminal Code*, R.S.C. 1985, c. C-46, s. 487(1) applies to proceedings under any federal statute regardless of whether or not that statute also contains its own search and seizure provisions. See *R. v. Multiform Manufacturing Co.*, [1990] S.C.J. No. 83, [1990] 2 S.C.R. 624 (S.C.C.).

[519] In *R. v. Erickson*, [2003] B.C.J. No. 2982, 19 C.R. (6th) 367 at paras. 33-34 (B.C.C.A.), the British Columbia Court of Appeal concluded that "impracticable" means something less than impossible and imports a large measure of practicality, what may be termed common sense.

487.1(5). There must be reasonable grounds for dispensing with personal attendance by the peace officer.[520]

§3.172 A justice or judge may, on application made pursuant to section 487.3 of the *Criminal Code* at the time of the issuance of the search warrant or at any time thereafter, make a "sealing order" prohibiting access to and the disclosure of any information relating to the search warrant. The party seeking a sealing order must demonstrate that public access to the documentation would subvert the ends of justice.[521] The issuing justice or judge has the discretion to lift the sealing order originally made to maintain the protection of the innocent, preserve the accused's right to a fair trial or safeguard the privacy interests of third parties.[522]

(a)   Reasonable and Probable Grounds

§3.173 Section 487(1) incorporates the minimum standards mandated by section 8 of the *Charter*, that is, that a judicial officer may only issue a warrant if satisfied that there are reasonable grounds, established upon oath, that an offence *has* been committed and that relevant evidence or contraband *will* be found in the "building, receptacle or place" to be searched.[523] The "reasonable grounds to believe" or "reasonable and probable grounds to believe" standard is the linchpin for most statutory search powers. As a result, the discussion of it in this section applies equally to all other statutory search powers that incorporate this standard.

§3.174 Historically, the reasonable and probable grounds standard has been defined as "an honest belief in the guilt of the accused based upon a full conviction, founded upon reasonable grounds, of the existence of a state of circumstances, which, assuming them to be true, would reasonably lead any ordinarily prudent and cautious man, placed in the position of the accuser, to the conclusion that the person charged was probably guilty of the crime imputed."[524]

§3.175 The Supreme Court has elaborated upon the meaning of the reasonable and probable grounds standard by placing it along a spectrum. According to the Court, "reasonable and probable grounds" imports a standard of reasonable probability, which entails something less than proof beyond a reasonable doubt or a *prima facie* case[525] but something more than mere possibility or sus-

---

[520]   See *R. v. Pedersen*, [2004] B.C.J. No. 229, [2004] B.C.J. No. 229 (B.C.C.A.).

[521]   *Nova Scotia (Attorney General) v. McIntyre*, [1982] S.C.J. No. 1, [1982] 1 S.C.R. 175 (S.C.C.).

[522]   *R. v. Eurocopter Canada Ltd.*, [2003] O.J. No. 4238, 180 C.C.C. (3d) 15 (Ont. S.C.J.).

[523]   See *R. v. Morelli*, [2010] S.C.J. No. 8, [2010] 1 S.C.R. 253, 2010 SCC 8 at para. 39 (S.C.C.); also *R. v. Grant*, [1993] S.C.J. No. 98, [1993] 3 S.C.R. 223 at 253 (S.C.C.); *R. v. Multiform Manufacturing Co.*, [1990] S.C.J. No. 83, [1990] 2 S.C.R. 624 at 631 (S.C.C.).

[524]   *Hicks v. Faulkner* (1878), 8 Q.B.D. 167 at 171 (Div. Ct.), *per* Hawkins J., affd (1882), 46 L.T. 130 (C.A.). See also *Herniman v. Smith*, [1938] A.C. 305 at 316 (H.L.). This definition was adopted by the Supreme Court of Canada in *Nelles v. Ontario*, [1989] S.C.J. No. 86, [1989] 2 S.C.R. 170 at 193 (S.C.C.).

[525]   See *R. v. DeBot*, [1989] S.C.J. No. 118, [1989] 2 S.C.R. 1140 at 1166, 52 C.C.C. (3d) 193 (S.C.C.). See also *R. v. Storrey*, [1990] S.C.J. No. 12, [1990] 1 S.C.R. 241 at 250-51 (S.C.C.).

picion[526] or even reasonable suspicion.[527] Based on this approach, the standard is said to be met at "the point where credibly-based probability replaces suspicion."[528] Some courts have treated this as the equivalent of "more likely than not" standard, while some commentators have suggested that it signifies a lesser degree of probability than that.[529]

§3.176 This ambiguity has never been fully resolved. As Justice La Forest once lamented, it "comprises something more than mere surmise, but determining with any useful measure of precision what it means beyond that poses rather intractable problems both for the police and the courts."[530] To date, the most concrete guidance from Canadian courts has come in the form of a few rather obvious admonishments to police. In deciding whether or not they possess reasonable and probable grounds, the police have been told to investigate thoroughly, consider all available information and disregard only information that they have good reason to believe is unreliable.[531] With few exceptions,[532] the courts have demonstrated a consistent reluctance to propose any rigid criteria as to what will constitute reasonable and probable grounds.

§3.177 This is not intended as a criticism. To the contrary, although an enumeration of relevant factors on some generalized level of abstraction may be possible, there is an undoubted cost for the certainty that such an approach might purchase. The development of more rigid criteria may have the undesirable effect of denying police the flexibility they need to respond to myriad factual situations they confront in the field. The United States Supreme Court acknowledged this reality in dealing with the analogous "probable cause" standard under the Fourth Amendment.[533] That court indicated, "probable cause is a fluid con-

---

[526] *Baron v. Canada*, [1993] S.C.J. No. 6, [1993] 1 S.C.R. 416 at 448, 99 D.L.R. (4th) 350 (S.C.C.).

[527] See *R. v. Kang-Brown*, [2008] S.C.J. No. 18, [2008] 1 S.C.R. 456 at para. 75 (S.C.C.) (explaining that "'reasonable suspicion' means something more than a mere suspicion and something less than a belief based upon reasonable and probable grounds.").

[528] *Hunter v. Southam (sub nom. Canada (Combines Investigation Acts, Director of Investigation and Research) v. Southam Inc.)* [1984] S.C.J. No. 36, [1984] 2 S.C.R. 145 at 167, [1984] 6 W.W.R. 577 (S.C.C.).

[529] See R.E. Salhany, *Canadian Criminal Procedure*, 6th ed., looseleaf, § 3.1140 (Aurora, ON: Canada Law Book, 2005).

[530] *R. v. Landry*, [1986] S.C.J. No. 10, [1986] 1 S.C.R. 145 at 180, 26 D.L.R. (4th) 368 (S.C.C.) *per* La Forest J., dissenting.

[531] See *Chartier v. Quebec (Attorney General)*, [1979] S.C.J. No. 56, [1979] 2 S.C.R. 474 at 499, 104 D.L.R. (3d) 321 (S.C.C.) [*Chartier*]. See also *R. v. Storrey*, [1990] S.C.J. No. 12, [1990] 1 S.C.R. 241 at 249-51 (S.C.C.); *Oniel v. Toronto (Metropolitan) Police Force*, [2001] O.J. No. 90, 195 D.L.R. (4th) 59 at 85 (Ont. C.A.); *R. v. Golub*, [1997] O.J. No. 3097, 34 O.R. (3d) 743 at 751, 117 C.C.C. (3d) 193 (Ont. C.A.); *R. v. Hall*, [1995] O.J. No. 544, 39 C.R. (4th) 66 at 75, 79 O.A.C. 24 (Ont. C.A.); *R. v. Proulx*, [1993] J.Q. no 422, 81 C.C.C. (3d) 48 at 51, 54 Q.A.C. 241 (Que. C.A.).

[532] See *R. v. Kang-Brown*, [2008] S.C.J. No. 18, [2008] 1 S.C.R. 456 at para. 96 (S.C.C.) (indicating that an individual's refusal of consent does not furnish grounds to search). Similarly, the odour of burnt marijuana alone has been held inadequate to justify a search. See *R. v. Polashek*, [1999] O.J. No. 968, 172 D.L.R. (4th) 350 at 358, 134 C.C.C. (3d) 187 (Ont. C.A.). See also *R. v. Janvier*, [2007] S.J. No. 646, 227 C.C.C. (3d) 294 (Sask. C.A.).

[533] *Illinois v. Gates*, 462 U.S. 213, 103 S. Ct. 2317 (1983).

cept — turning on the assessment of probabilities in particular factual contexts — not readily, or even usefully, reduced to a neat set of legal rules."[534]

§3.178 All of this favours strict adherence to the warrant requirement in circumstances where it is feasible for police to obtain one. In other words, the uncertainty inherent in the reasonable and probable grounds standard, coupled with the partisan perspective of police, makes mistakes somewhat inevitable and provides a compelling justification for the check provided by requiring police to subject their grounds for searching to prior judicial scrutiny.

§3.179 Despite the inherent uncertainty of the standard, the Supreme Court of Canada has provided some useful guidance on how an issuing judge should approach the task of assessing whether police have reasonable and probable grounds to search. For example, the Court has made clear that "a mere conclusory" tip from a confidential informant would never be enough.[535] More generally, the Court has directed that the "totality of circumstances" must always be considered in assessing the existence of reasonable and probable grounds to search.[536] The Supreme Court has noted that at least three general factors need to be taken into account in assessing the totality of the circumstances. These factors have come to be known as the "three Cs", comprising: (*i*) whether the information predicting the commission of a criminal offence is *compelling*; (*ii*) if that information was based on a "tip", whether the source of the tip is *credible*; and (*iii*) whether the information has been *corroborated* by police investigation prior to making the decision to conduct the search.[537]

§3.180 The Court has been especially cautious when it comes to information supplied by anonymous tipsters (those whose identities are not even known to police) or untried informants, indicating that in "such circumstances the quality of the information and corroborative evidence may have to be such as to compensate for the inability to assess the credibility of the source."[538] The Ontario Court of Appeal has gone even further, suggesting that "[a]bsent confirmation of details other than [those] which describe innocent and commonplace conduct, information supplied by an untested, anonymous informant cannot, standing alone, provide reasonable grounds".[539]

---

[534] *Ibid.*, at 232. The Supreme Court of Canada has characterized the two standards as "identical". See *Hunter v. Southam (sub nom. Canada (Combines Investigation Acts, Director of Investigation and Research) v. Southam Inc.)*, [1984] S.C.J. No. 36, [1984] 2 S.C.R. 145 at 167, [1984] 6 W.W.R. 577 (S.C.C.).

[535] See *R. v. Greffe*, [1990] S.C.J. No. 32, [1990] 1 S.C.R. 755 at 792 (S.C.C.). See also *R. v. Garofoli*, [1990] S.C.J. No. 115, [1990] 2 S.C.R. 1421 at para. 81 (S.C.C.).

[536] See *e.g.*, *R. v. DeBot*, [1989] S.C.J. No. 118, [1989] 2 S.C.R. 1140 at 1168 (S.C.C.). See also *R. v. Greffe*, [1990] S.C.J. No. 32, [1990] 1 S.C.R. 755 at 790 (S.C.C.).

[537] *R. v. DeBot*, [1989] S.C.J. No. 118, [1989] 2 S.C.R. 1140 at 1168 (S.C.C.).

[538] *Ibid.*, at para. 58 (S.C.R.).

[539] *R. v. Lewis*, [1998] O.J. No. 376, 38 O.R. (3d) 540 at 547, 122 C.C.C. (3d) 481 (Ont. C.A.). See also *R. c. Bennett*, [1996] J.Q. no 545, 108 C.C.C. (3d) 175 at 181, 185, 49 C.R. (4th) 206 (Que. C.A.).

§3.181 Finally, the Supreme Court has repeatedly emphasized that the results of a particular search or seizure cannot be used to assess whether or not there were reasonable and probable grounds to justify it.[540] This is entirely in keeping with the Court's recognition, discussed above, that the very purpose of section 8 of the *Charter* and the warrant requirement is to prevent unreasonable searches before they occur rather than attempting to sort them out after-the-fact.[541]

(b) The Application Process, Hearsay and Confidential Informants

§3.182 A warrant application begins with a law enforcement officer (the "informant") swearing an Information to Obtain a Search Warrant (the "information").[542] In addition to stating that he or she has reasonable grounds to believe that a crime has been committed and that the specified items may afford relevant evidence of that crime and are in the place to be searched, the informant must also set out his or her grounds for so believing. It is permissible, and quite often unavoidable, for the informant to rely on hearsay information in applying for a search warrant.[543]

§3.183 There is a weighty onus on the informant to provide full and frank disclosure to the issuing justice.[544] Nevertheless, an informant may choose not to

---

[540] See *Hunter v. Southam (sub nom. Canada (Combines Investigation Acts, Director of Investigation and Research) v. Southam Inc.)*, [1984] S.C.J. No. 36, [1984] 2 S.C.R. 145 at 160-61(S.C.C.) [*Hunter*]; *R. v. Dyment*, [1988] S.C.J. No. 82, [1988] 2 S.C.R. 417 at 430 (S.C.C.); *R. v. Wong*, [1990] S.C.J. No. 118, [1990] 3 S.C.R. 36 at para. 19 (S.C.C.); *R. v. Garofoli*, [1990] S.C.J. No. 115, [1990] 2 S.C.R. 1421 at para. 86 (S.C.C.); *R. v. Greffe*, [1990] S.C.J. No. 32, [1990] 1 S.C.R. 755 at 790, 798 (S.C.C.); *R. v. Kokesch*, [1990] S.C.J. No. 117, [1990] 3 S.C.R. 3 at para. 49 (S.C.C.).

[541] See above, Part 2(5)(*b*).

[542] See *Criminal Code*, R.S.C. 1985, c. C-46, Form 1. Unfortunately, these terms are also used in other contexts. For example, the charging document for the initiation of criminal proceedings is also known as an "information" (see *Criminal Code*, s. 506, Form 2) and the person who swears it is also referred to as an "informant". In addition, as we shall see below, an individual who supplies information to police in confidence is also normally referred to as an "informant". For obvious reasons, the multiple uses of this same term can result in a fair amount of confusion.

[543] See *R. v. DeBot*, [1989] S.C.J. No. 118, [1989] 2 S.C.R. 1140 at para. 59 (S.C.C.); *R. v. Garofoli*, [1990] S.C.J. No. 115, [1990] 2 S.C.R. 1421 at para. 81 (S.C.C.); *R. v. Agensys International Inc.*, [2004] O.J. No. 2721, 187 C.C.C. (3d) 481 at paras. 43, 48 (Ont. C.A.). See also *R. v. Collins*, [1987] S.C.J. No. 15, [1987] 1 S.C.R. 265 at para. 37 (S.C.C.) (coming to the exact same conclusion with respect to the reasonable and probable grounds required to search under a warrantless search power).

[544] See generally, *R. v. Araujo*, [2000] S.C.J. No. 65, [2000] 2 S.C.R. 992 at paras. 46-47 (S.C.C.), where the Court indicated:

> The legal obligation on anyone seeking an ex parte authorization is full and frank disclosure of material facts ... So long as the affidavit meets the requisite legal norm, there is no need for it to be as lengthy as *À la recherche du temps perdu*, as lively as the Kama Sutra, or as detailed as an automotive repair manual. All that it must do is set out the facts fully and frankly for the authorizing judge in order that he or she can make an assessment of whether these rise to the standard required in the legal test for the authorization. Ideally, an affidavit should be not only full and frank but also clear and concise. It need not include every minute detail of the police investigation over a number of months and even of years.

identify a particular source and instead identify such a person as a "confidential informant".[545] A confidential informant is someone who supplies information to law enforcement either on the express or implied understanding that the police will shield his or her identity.[546] In recognition of their value to the administration of justice, the law generally insulates the identity of confidential informants from disclosure by subjecting it to a privilege[547] that can normally only be waived with their consent.[548]

§3.184 If the privilege is claimed but the identity of the confidential informant is revealed in the information (for example, because knowing who the informant is may be essential for the issuing justice to meaningfully assess the adequacy of the supporting grounds), an order sealing the search warrant information may be sought.[549] The information must, however, set out grounds to justify such a sealing order in the circumstances.[550]

A corollary to the requirement of an affidavit being full and frank is that it should never attempt to trick its readers. At best, the use of boiler-plate language adds extra verbiage and seldom anything of meaning; at worst, it has the potential to trick the reader into thinking that the affidavit means something that it does not. Although the use of boiler-plate language will not automatically prevent a judge from issuing an authorization (there is, after all, no formal legal requirement to avoid it), I cannot stress enough that judges should deplore it. There is nothing wrong — and much right — with an affidavit that sets out the facts truthfully, fully, and plainly. Counsel and police officers submitting materials to obtain wiretapping authorizations should not allow themselves to be led into the temptation of misleading the authorizing judge, either by the language used or strategic omissions.

See also *R. v. Morelli*, [2010] S.C.J. No. 8, [2010] 1 S.C.R. 253, 2010 SCC 8 at para. 44 (S.C.C.).

[545] See *R. v. Hardy*, [1994] B.C.J. No. 1281, 45 B.C.A.C. 146 at 149 (B.C.C.A.) ("It is well recognized that information which might identify a confidential informant need not be disclosed to the Justice of the Peace or at trial."). See also *R. v. Solloway*, [1930] O.J. No. 111, 53 C.C.C. 271 (Ont. C.A.); *R. v. Blain*, [1960] S.J. No. 112, 127 C.C.C. 267 (Sask. C.A.).

[546] See *Bisaillon v. Keable*, [1983] S.C.J. No. 65, [1983] 2 S.C.R. 60 at 105 (S.C.C.), where the Court noted that:

The rule gives a peace officer the power to promise his informers secrecy expressly or by implication, with a guarantee sanctioned by the law that this promise will be kept even in court, and to receive in exchange for this promise information without which it would be extremely difficult for him to carry out his duties and ensure that the criminal law is obeyed.

See also *R. v. Basi*, [2009] S.C.J. No. 52, [2009] 3 S.C.R. 389, 2009 SCC 52 at para. 36 (S.C.C.).

[547] *R. v. Basi*, [2009] S.C.J. No. 52, [2009] 3 S.C.R. 389, 2009 SCC 52 at paras. 36-37 (S.C.C.). See also *R. v. Hunter*, [1987] O.J. No. 328, 57 C.R. (3d) 1 at 5-6 (Ont. C.A.); *R. v. Scott*, [1990] S.C.J. No. 132, [1990] 3 S.C.R. 979 at 994 (S.C.C.).

[548] According to the Supreme Court, "informer privilege belongs jointly to the Crown and to the informant. Neither can waive it without the consent of the other." See *R. v. Basi*, [2009] S.C.J. No. 52, [2009] 3 S.C.R. 389, 2009 SCC 52 at para. 40 (S.C.C.). As a result, the Crown cannot, without the informer's consent, waive the privilege either expressly or by implication by not raising it. See *Bisaillon v. Keable*, [1983] S.C.J. No. 65, [1983] 2 S.C.R. 60 at 94 (S.C.C.). There is only one exception to the privilege — the "innocence at stake" exception. In order to raise the exception "there must be a basis on the evidence for concluding that disclosure of the informer's identity is necessary to demonstrate the innocence of the accused" (*R. v. Leipert*, [1997] S.C.J. No. 14, [1997] 1 S.C.R. 281 at para. 21 (S.C.C.)).

[549] See *Criminal Code*, R.S.C. 1985, c. C-46, s. 487.3, which specifically entitles an issuing justice to make an order sealing the search warrant information where disclosure of the information

§3.185 Although accused persons are ultimately entitled to disclosure of the information sworn to obtain a warrant so that they can make full answer and defence to a criminal charge,[551] such access is then subject to the authority of the court to edit out references that would serve to identify a confidential informant.[552] On subsequent review, in deciding whether and to what extent the privilege applies, the judge must conduct an *in camera* hearing, at which only the putative informer and the Crown are permitted to attend.[553] In order to protect the interests of the excluded accused, a judge is required to adopt all reasonable measures to permit defence counsel to make meaningful submissions regarding what occurs in their absence.[554] This may include inviting submissions on the scope of the privilege — including argument as to who constitutes a confidential informant entitled to the privilege — and its application in the circumstances of the case. Defence counsel may be invited as well to suggest questions to be put by the trial judge to any witness that will be called at the *ex parte* proceeding.[555] In appropriate cases, fairness may require the court to provide the defence with a redacted or summarized version of the evidence presented *ex parte* — edited to eliminate any possibility of disclosing the informant's identity — so as to permit the trial judge to receive additional submissions from the defence on whether the privilege applies in the particular circumstance of the case.[556] In particularly difficult cases, the trial judge may even appoint an *amicus curiae* to attend the *ex parte* proceeding to provide assistance in navigating the claim of privilege.[557]

§3.186 If the Crown fears that the court's decision could compromise the confidential informant's identity, it has several options. First, it may elect to reveal the informant's identity (with his or her consent). Second, it may choose to treat the search as though it was warrantless and attempt to justify it on that basis. Finally, the Crown may simply decide to stay or withdraw the charge(s).[558]

---

would "compromise the identity of a confidential informant" and outweighs the importance of public access to the information. *Ibid.*, s. 487.3(2)(*a*).

[550] See generally, *Toronto Star Newspapers Ltd. v. Ontario*, [2005] S.C.J. No. 41, [2005] 2 S.C.R. 188 (S.C.C.), emphasizing that because such orders are contrary to the open court principle those who seek them must explicitly justify them.

[551] See generally, *Dersch v. Canada (Attorney General)*, [1990] S.C.J. No. 113, [1990] 2 S.C.R. 1505 (S.C.C.).

[552] See *R. v. Garofoli*, [1990] S.C.J. No. 115, [1990] 2 S.C.R. 1421 at 1458 (S.C.C.) wherein Justice Sopinka noted that "[e]diting ... is essential in cases in which confidential information is included in the affidavit filed in support of an authorization." He added, "In determining what to edit, the judge will have regard for the rule against disclosure of police informants." That said, where the informant is anonymous, in the sense that his or her identity is not even known to the police, special caution is required because it will be unknown to everyone involved what disclosure might serve to identify him or her. See *R. v. Leipert*, [1997] S.C.J. No. 14, [1997] 1 S.C.R. 281 at para. 31 (S.C.C.).

[553] See *R. v. Basi*, [2009] S.C.J. No. 52, [2009] 3 S.C.R. 389, 2009 SCC 52 at paras. 38, 44, 53 (S.C.C.).

[554] *Ibid.*, at para. 55 (SCC).

[555] *Ibid.*, at para. 56 (SCC).

[556] *Ibid.*, at para. 57 (SCC).

[557] *Ibid.*, at para. 58 (SCC).

[558] See *R. v. Hunter*, [1987] O.J. No. 328, 57 C.R. (3d) 1 (Ont. C.A.), the Ontario Court of Appeal's judgment was subsequently expressly approved of by the Supreme Court. See *R. v. Scott*,

(c) Manner of Execution

§3.187 When executing a search warrant the police must comply with the requirements of section 29(1) of the *Criminal Code*, which provides that: "It is the duty of every one who executes a process or warrant to have it with him, where it is feasible to do so, and to produce it when requested to do so." The Supreme Court has explained that the purpose of this requirement "is to allow the occupant of the premises to be searched to know why the search is being carried out, to allow assessment of his or her legal position and to know as well that there is a colour of authority for the search, making forcible resistance improper."[559] According to the Court, that purpose is fulfilled if the warrant is in the possession of at least one of the executing officers; every officer participating in a warrant's execution is not required to have a copy.[560]

§3.188 Search warrants should normally be executed during the day.[561] In fact, pursuant to section 488 of the *Criminal Code*, daytime execution of search warrants is the rule and night searches are the exception requiring justification and specific authorization.[562]

§3.189 There are also "knock and announce" requirements that the police must normally comply with when executing a search warrant. In the ordinary course, before forcing entry, the police are required to give: (*i*) notice of presence by knocking or ringing the doorbell; (*ii*) notice of authority, by identifying themselves as law enforcement officers; and (*iii*) notice of purpose, by stating a lawful reason for entry (*i.e.*, "search warrant"). At a minimum they should request admission and have admission denied.[563]

§3.190 The Supreme Court has recognized, however, that there will be occasions when exigent circumstances may allow police to dispense with the "knock and announce" requirements. If the police depart from those requirements, they will bear the onus of establishing the necessity of doing so. This entails showing that they had reasonable grounds to be concerned about either the possibility of harm to themselves or occupants or the destruction of evidence. The greater the departure from the principles of announced entry, the heavier the onus on the

---

[1990] S.C.J. No. 132, [1990] 3 S.C.R. 979 (S.C.C.); *R. v. Leipert*, [1997] S.C.J. No. 14, [1997] 1 S.C.R. 281 (S.C.C.).

[559] *R. v. Cornell*, [2010] S.C.J. No. 31, [2010] 2 S.C.R. 142, 2010 SCC 31 at para. 43 (S.C.C.).

[560] *Ibid.* In *Cornell*, however, the four judges in the majority disagreed with the three dissenting judges as to whether the requirements of s. 29(1) were met in that case. For the majority, although none of the members of the tactical team who initially entered the residence had a copy of the warrant in their possession, s. 29(1) was complied with because the primary investigator, who was just a short distance up the street and arrived within four minutes of the initial entry, was in possession of the warrant. *Ibid.*, at paras. 38-43 (SCC). For the dissenting judges, however, this did not amount to compliance with s. 29(1). See *R. v. Cornell*, [2010] S.C.J. No. 31, [2010] 2 S.C.R. 142, 2010 SCC 31 at paras. 53, 120 (SCC), *per* Fish J., dissenting.

[561] *Criminal Code*, R.S.C. 1985, c. C-46, s. 2 defines "day" as the period between 6:00 a.m. and 9:00 p.m.

[562] *R. v. Sutherland*, [2000] O.J. No. 4704, 150 C.C.C. (3d) 231 (Ont. C.A.).

[563] See *Eccles v. Bourque*, [1974] S.C.J. No. 123, [1975] 2 S.C.R. 739 at 747 (S.C.C.). See also *R. v. Cornell*, [2010] S.C.J. No. 31, [2010] 2 S.C.R. 142, 2010 SCC 31 at para. 18 (S.C.C.).

police to justify their approach. The evidence to justify such behaviour must be apparent in the record and available to the police at the time they acted. The Crown cannot rely on *ex post facto* justifications.[564]

§3.191 When executing a search warrant, the police may use reasonable force to gain entry to the premises.[565] Further, upon entry, the police are entitled to "control the premises" to ensure the safety of themselves and others and to prevent the destruction of evidence.[566] Of course, once such concerns are alleviated, the execution of a warrant alone does not provide the police with a free-standing detention power.[567] In other words, in order to continue lawfully detaining persons who happen to be present, the police must have some other legal basis for doing so, for example, a lawful investigative detention or arrest. (The legal requirements for conducting an investigative detention or arrest are detailed in Chapter 2.)

§3.192 Similarly, the execution of a section 487 search warrant does not automatically entitle the police to search people who happen to be found at the premises being searched.[568] A personal search of an individual who happens to be present at the location being searched would require some other legal justification. For example, if the police possess reasonable and probable grounds to arrest an individual then they would be legally entitled to search their person incidental to the arrest. (Search incidental to arrest is discussed in Part 4(2), below).

§3.193 Section 489(1) of the Code authorizes the person executing the warrant to seize, in addition to the things specifically mentioned in the warrant, anything that the person believes on reasonable grounds has been obtained, has been used or will afford evidence in respect of an offence against the *Criminal Code* or any other Act of Parliament. In other words, the police are not required to ignore other evidence or contraband that they happen to come across while executing a

---

[564] *R. v. Cornell*, [2010] S.C.J. No. 31, [2010] 2 S.C.R. 142, 2010 SCC 31 at para. 20 (S.C.C.) (police justified in dispensing with knock and announce requirements where they reasonably believed that a violent criminal gang was secreting cocaine in the targeted residence, risk of violence and fact that cocaine could easily be destroyed both justified unannounced forced entry). See also *R. v. Gimson*, [1990] O.J. No. 354, 54 C.C.C. (3d) 232 (Ont. C.A.), affd without reasons [1991] S.C.J. No. 104, [1991] 3 S.C.R. 692 (S.C.C.) (upholding a no-knock entry to preserve evidence); *R. v. Genest*, [1989] S.C.J. No. 5, [1989] 1 S.C.R. 59 at 90 (S.C.C.) (upholding a no-knock entry based on a legitimate fear of violence directed toward the police and third parties, but emphasizing that: "The Crown must, however, lay the evidentiary framework to support the conclusion that there were grounds to be concerned about the possibility of violence."

[565] *Criminal Code*, R.S.C. 1985, c. C-46, s. 25(1). See also *R. v. Genest*, [1989] S.C.J. No. 5, [1989] 1 S.C.R. 59 (S.C.C.); *R. v. Gimson*, [1991] S.C.J. No. 104, [1991] 3 S.C.R. 692 (S.C.C.).

[566] *R. v. Silveira*, [1995] S.C.J. No. 38, [1995] 2 S.C.R. 297 (S.C.C.); *R. v. Strachan*, [1988] S.C.J. No. 94, [1988] 2 S.C.R. 980 (S.C.C.).

[567] See *R. v. Gogol*, [1994] O.J. No. 61, 27 C.R. (4th) 357 (Ont. Prov. Ct.) (no detention power incidental to execution of search warrant); *R. v. Kirby*, [2001] M.J. No. 593, [2001] M.J. No. 593 at para. 71 (Man. Prov. Ct.) (same).

[568] See *Laporte v. Laganière J.S.P.*, [1972] Q.J. No. 3518, C.R.N.S. 357 (Que. S.C.); *R. v. Thompson*, [1996] O.J. No. 1501, 30 W.C.B. (2d) 485 (Ont. Prov. Div.).

search warrant simply because it is not mentioned in the warrant. Nevertheless, there are limits on the authority of police to seize other items; these are discussed below in Part 3(6) in addressing the "plain view" seizure power.

§3.194 Whether the scope of the authority to search a residence provided by a warrant extends to vehicles parked on the property or nearby remains an open question.[569] Ideally, a properly drafted search warrant would specifically refer to any vehicles that are expected to be at the residence to be searched.

§3.195 The *Criminal Code* also provides specific rules for the search and seizure of computer data. Section 487(2.1) and (2.2) empower police, based on reasonable grounds to believe, to search and seize data found on a computer system. The person in "possession or control" of any building or place that is subject to the search must permit the person carrying out the search to use the computer system, obtain a hard copy of the data or to use any copying equipment at the place to make copies of the data.

(d) Challenging the Warrant and Searches Pursuant to Warrants

§3.196 Search warrants are subject to a presumption of validity.[570] That presumption, however, can be rebutted. The validity of a search warrant may be challenged by way of a writ of *certiorari* or by means of a *Charter* application. Before the *Charter*, the writ of *certiorari* supplied the only means for challenging a search warrant. The writ is rather limited in scope, however, as it merely allows a superior court to quash a warrant where there has been jurisdictional error.[571] A *Charter* application is not subject to the same jurisdictional constraints. As a result, today writs of *certiorari* are only rarely used to challenge warrants. These applications are typically brought prior to any charges being laid and normally in effort to gain the return of items seized.[572] In circumstances where charges are laid, it is usually far more sensible for an accused to challenge the validity of a warrant as part of a section 8 *Charter* application at trial,[573] typically coupled with a request to have any evidence obtained through the execution of the warrant excluded under section 24(2).

§3.197 A person who is the target of a search warrant does not have automatic standing. To quash a search warrant and request the return of items seized, the applicant must establish a proprietary or possessory interest in the items. As discussed in Part 2(4), above, a person claiming a violation of section 8 of the

---

[569] *R. v. Benz*, [1986] O.J. No. 227, 27 C.C.C. (3d) 454 (Ont. C.A.). *Contra, R. v. Vu*, [2004] B.C.J. No. 824, 184 C.C.C. (3d) 545 (B.C.C.A.).

[570] *R. v. Collins*, [1987] S.C.J. No. 15, [1987] 1 S.C.R. 265 (S.C.C.).

[571] See generally, *R. v. Church of Scientology of Toronto*, [1987] O.J. No. 64, 31 C.C.C. (3d) 449 (Ont. C.A.), leave to appeal refused [1987] S.C.C.A. No. 257, [1987] 1 S.C.R. vii (S.C.C.); *R. v. Times Square Bookstore*, [1985] O.J. No. 177, 21 C.C.C. (3d) 503 (Ont. C.A.); *Re Print Three Inc. and The Queen*, [1985] O.J. No. 2580, 20 C.C.C. (3d) 392 (Ont. C.A.).

[572] See *e.g., R. v. Branton*, [2001] O.J. No. 1445, 154 C.C.C. (3d) 139 (Ont. C.A.).

[573] See *R. v. Zevallos*, [1987] O.J. No. 663, 37 C.C.C. (3d) 79 (Ont. C.A.), which makes this very point.

Charter must have a reasonable expectation of privacy in the place searched or the item seized.[574]

§3.198 Regardless the route of attack taken — that is, by way of prerogative writ or *Charter* application — the test for the court reviewing the validity of a search warrant is the same. The reviewing court will consider both the facial (the warrant itself) and sub-facial (the information)[575] validity of the warrant.

§3.199 For the sub-facial part of the review, false, misleading or unconstitutionally obtained information must be excised from the information. The validity of the warrant is then determined based on any non-excised material as well as, in some cases, new evidence adduced at the hearing.[576] Specifically, such new evidence may be used to "amplify" the record (*i.e.*, to show the true state of police knowledge at the time they made the original application) as long as: (*i*) police did not deliberately attempt to mislead the issuing justice; and (*ii*) amplification does not subvert the prior authorization requirement.[577] As the Supreme Court cautioned in *R. v. Araujo*:[578]

> The danger inherent in amplification is that it might become a means of circumventing a prior authorization requirement. Since a prior authorization is fundamental to the protection of everyone's privacy interests ... amplification cannot go so far as to remove the requirement that the police make their case to the issuing judge, thereby turning the authorizing procedure into a sham. On the other hand, to refuse amplification entirely would put form above substance in situations where the police had the requisite reasonable and probable grounds ... but had, in good faith, made some minor, technical error in the drafting of their affidavit material.[579]

§3.200 More recently, in *R. v. Morelli*,[580] the Supreme Court stressed that amplification evidence "is not a means for the police to adduce additional information so as to retroactively authorize a search that was not initially supported by reasonable and probable grounds."[581] Amplification, in other words, cannot be used to retroactively authorize a warrant that was not substantively justified at the time it was applied for.

---

[574] See generally, *R. v. Edwards*, [1996] S.C.J. No. 11, [1996] 1 S.C.R. 128 (S.C.C.); *R. v. Belnavis*, [1997] S.C.J. No. 81, [1997] 3 S.C.R. 341 (S.C.C.).

[575] Sub-facial conditions include whether the information was based on material non-disclosure or deliberate or reckless misrepresentation of facts.

[576] See *R. v. Grant*, [1993] S.C.J. No. 98, [1993] 3 S.C.R. 223 at 251 (S.C.C.); *R. v. Plant*, [1993] S.C.J. No. 97, 84 C.C.C. (3d) 203 at 216 (S.C.C.); *R. v. Evans*, [1996] S.C.J. No. 1, [1996] 1 S.C.R. 8 at para. 26 (S.C.C.); *R. v. Kokesch*, [1990] S.C.J. No. 117, [1990] 3 S.C.R. 3; *R. v. Araujo*, [2000] S.C.J. No. 65, [2000] 2 S.C.R. 992 at para. 58 (S.C.C.); *R. v. Morelli*, [2010] S.C.J. No. 8, [2010] 1 S.C.R. 253 at paras. 41, 45 (S.C.C.).

[577] See *R. v. Araujo*, [2000] S.C.J. No. 65, [2000] 2 S.C.R. 992 at para. 55-59 (S.C.C.); *R. v. Morelli*, [2010] S.C.J. No. 8, [2010] 1 S.C.R. 253 at para. 41 (S.C.C.).

[578] *R. v. Araujo*, [2000] S.C.J. No. 65, [2000] 2 S.C.R. 992 (S.C.C.).

[579] See *ibid.*, at para. 59 (S.C.R.). See also *R. v. Morelli*, [2010] S.C.J. No. 8, [2010] 1 S.C.R. 253 at paras. 41-43 (S.C.C.).

[580] [2010] S.C.J. No. 8, [2010] 1 S.C.R. 253 (S.C.C.).

[581] *Ibid.*, at para. 42 (S.C.R.).

§3.201 Once the offending evidence has been excised and the amplified record considered, the reviewing court is not to undertake a *de novo* review, substituting its view for that of the authorizing judge. Instead, as the Supreme Court has explained, the warrant should be upheld if the reviewing court "concludes that the authorizing judge could have granted the authorization".[582] The test, in other words, is "whether there was reliable *evidence that might reasonably be believed on the basis of which the authorization could have issued*".[583]

§3.202 A search warrant issued pursuant to section 487 of the *Criminal Code* requires that a justice or judge be satisfied that there are reasonable grounds to believe that specified items are connected to an offence. While the suspected offence must be named in the information to obtain the warrant, it need not be particularized as specifically as would be required by a charging document such as an information or indictment.[584]

§3.203 Similarly, the items to be searched for need not be described with absolute precision in either the information or the warrant. That said, the items cannot be described so broadly as to authorize a fishing expedition.[585] The warrant must specify the things to be searched for with sufficient precision that it would be reasonably clear to both the police and the target what can be sought and taken.

§3.204 Given the duty on an informant to make "full and frank" disclosure to the issuing justice of all materials facts,[586] an accused challenging a search warrant may understandably wish to cross-examine the affiant. However, cross-examination of the affiant is not automatic. Instead, the accused must seek leave from the presiding judge. Before permission will be granted, a basis must be shown by the accused for the view that the cross-examination will elicit testimony tending to discredit the existence of one of the preconditions to the authorization, for example, the existence of reasonable and probable grounds.[587]

§3.205 A conclusion that an affiant has acted in bad faith and deliberately misled the issuing justice will often result in a warrant being quashed and the evidence acquired being excluded. In fact, even a careless or sloppy approach may lead to this same result.[588] That said, there is no hard and fast rule to this effect.

---

[582] *R. v. Garofoli*, [1990] S.C.J. No. 115, [1990] 2 S.C.R. 1421 at 1452 (S.C.C.). See also *R. v. Araujo*, [2000] S.C.J. No. 65, [2000] 2 S.C.R. 992 at paras. 52-54 (S.C.C.); *R. v. Morelli*, [2010] S.C.J. No. 8, [2010] 1 S.C.R. 253 at para. 40 (S.C.C.).

[583] *R. v. Araujo*, [2000] S.C.J. No. 65, [2000] 2 S.C.R. 992 at para. 54 (S.C.C.) [emphasis in original]. See also *R. v. Morelli*, [2010] S.C.J. No. 8, [2010] 1 S.C.R. 253 at para. 40 (S.C.C.).

[584] See *R. v. Yorke*, [1992] N.S.J. No. 474, 77 C.C.C. (3d) 529 (N.S.C.A.), affd [1993] S.C.J. No. 109, [1993] 3 S.C.R. 647 (S.C.C.).

[585] See generally, *R. v. Church of Scientology of Toronto* (1987), [1987] O.J. No. 64, 31 C.C.C. (3d) 449 (Ont. C.A.), leave to appeal refused [1987] 1 S.C.R. vii (S.C.C.); *R. v. Gillis* (1982), 1 C.C.C. (3d) 545 (Que. S.C.).

[586] See generally, *R. v. Araujo*, [2000] S.C.J. No. 65, [2000] 2 S.C.R. 992 at paras. 46-47 (S.C.C.).

[587] See *R. v. Garofoli*, [1990] S.C.J. No. 115, [1990] 2 S.C.R. 1421 at 1465 (S.C.C.). See also *R. v. Pires; R. v. Lising*, [2005] S.C.J. No. 67, [2005] 3 S.C.R. 343 (S.C.C.).

[588] See generally, *R. v. Hosie*, [1996] O.J. No. 2175, 107 C.C.C. (3d) 385 (Ont. C.A.). See also *R. v. Sutherland*, [2000] O.J. No. 4704, 52 O.R. (3d) 27, 150 C.C.C. (3d) 231 at paras. 29-32 (Ont.

As the Ontario Court of Appeal has noted, "even fraud in the obtaining of the warrant does not automatically invalidate the warrant."[589] "The improper material is excised," the Court continued, "and a determination made as to whether 'sufficient reliable information' remains."[590]

§3.206 Finally, it is important to remember (as discussed above in Part 3(3)(*c*)) that even a search pursuant to a valid warrant may be challenged based on the way it was executed. A search conducted in an abusive manner, for example, where the authorities use gratuitous force or cause unnecessary property damage, may result in a violation of section 8 of the *Charter*.[591] That said, as the Supreme Court recently pointed out in *R. v. Cornell*,[592] "the question for the reviewing judge is not whether every detail of the search, viewed in isolation, was appropriate."[593] The question, instead, is "whether the search overall, in light of the facts reasonably known to the police, was reasonable."[594]

§3.207 In conducting such reviews, judges have often been reluctant to second-guess what they consider to be tactical decisions by police. For example, in *Cornell*, the Supreme Court divided 4:3 in upholding a search where heavily-armed police wearing body armour and balaclavas made a forced and unannounced entry into a residence. Having concluded that the police were justified in entering without "knocking and announcing", the majority felt that it should not "micromanage the police's choice of equipment".[595] This conclusion attracted a strong dissent.[596] Absent some specific justification,[597] the dissenting judges convincingly argued that allowing police officers to cover their faces when executing a search warrant is nothing more than gratuitous intimidation, a form of psychological violence that could in itself render a search unreasonable. They rightly worried about the potential for unchecked abuses if state officials are permitted to wield their coercive powers anonymously.[598] In time, we hope

---

C.A.); *R. v. Branton*, [2001] O.J. No. 1445, 53 O.R. (3d) 737 at para. 30 (Ont. C.A.); *R. v. Morelli*, [2010] S.C.J. No. 8, [2010] 1 S.C.R. 253, 2010 SCC 8 at paras. 100-103 (S.C.C.).

[589]   *R. v. Budd*, [2000] O.J. No. 4649, 150 C.C.C. (3d) 108 at para. 21(Ont. C.A.).

[590]   *Ibid*. See also *R. v. Bisson*, [1994] S.C.J. No. 112, [1994] 3 S.C.R. 1097 (S.C.C.).

[591]   *R. v. Stillman*, [1997] S.C.J. No. 34, [1997] 1 S.C.R. 607, 113 C.C.C. (3d) 321 at 338 (S.C.C.); *Cloutier v. Langlois*, [1990] S.C.J. No. 10, 53 C.C.C. (3d) 257 at 278 (S.C.C.); *R. v. Genest*, [1989] S.C.J. No. 5, [1989] 1 S.C.R. 59, 45 C.C.C. (3d) 385 at 407-409 (S.C.C.). But see *R. v.* [2010] 2 S.C.R. 142, [2010] S.C.J. No. 31, 2010 SCC 31 (S.C.C.).

[592]   [2010] S.C.J. No. 31, [2010] 2 S.C.R. 142, 2010 SCC 31 at para. 43 (S.C.C.).

[593]   *Ibid*., at para. 31 (SCC).

[594]   *Ibid*.

[595]   *Ibid*.

[596]   Fish, Binnie and LeBel JJ. dissented, with Fish J. writing reasons on behalf of the dissenting judges.

[597]   Fish J. gave a number of examples, where police may cover their faces "to protect the officers' faces in case of a chemical fire — for example, when they raid a suspected drug lab — or when they contemplate the use of flashbangs or pepper spray to overcome anticipated resistance. Alternatively, balaclavas may be worn to protect the identity of officers still involved in an ongoing undercover investigation." *R. v. Cornell*, [2010] S.C.J. No. 31, [2010] 2 S.C.R. 142, 2010 SCC 31 at para. 115 (S.C.C.), *per* Fish. J., dissenting.

[598]   *R. v. Cornell*, [2010] S.C.J. No. 31, [2010] 2 S.C.R. 142, 2010 SCC 31 at paras. 115-119 (S.C.C.), *per* Fish J., dissenting.

that the Court will reconsider the unduly deferential approach exhibited in the majority judgment. Under the *Charter*, it is precisely the function of our courts to scrutinize the decisions of state officials affecting constitutionally protected interests, especially when those judgments lack any apparent justification.

(e)   Return of Seized Material

§3.208 Following the execution of a search warrant, sections 489.1 and 490 of the *Criminal Code* provide a comprehensive scheme for supervising and ensuring the return of items seized.[599] Following the seizure, the peace officer is required to prepare a report for the justice of the peace or the provincial court judge who issued the warrant detailing both the items that have been returned to their lawful owners and the items sought to be further detained. The report must be completed "as soon as practicable"[600] but need not be under oath.[601] In *R. v. Guiller*,[602] Justice Borins held that a breach of these mandatory provisions resulted in a violation of section 8 of the *Charter*.[603]

§3.209 Upon completion of the report, a justice can, pursuant to section 490, either order that the items be returned to the owner or person lawfully entitled to possession or be detained pending completion of an investigation or court proceeding.[604] Either a peace officer or a prosecutor may make an application for continued detention pursuant to section 490. As investigations and prosecutions have become more complex, extensions of the initial three-month period provided for by section 490(1)(*b*) are commonly sought and ordinarily granted.[605]

(4)   Production Orders

§3.210 Production orders available pursuant to section 487.012 or section 487.013 of the *Criminal Code* are relatively new investigative search powers.

---

[599] This section applies equally to warrantless search powers exercised by the authorities, so for example, search incidental to a lawful arrest. See *R. v. Backhouse*, [2005] O.J. No. 754, 194 C.C.C. (3d) 1 (Ont. C.A.).

[600] In *R. c. Bérubé*, [1999] J.Q. no 2608, 139 C.C.C. (3d) 304 (Que. C.A.), leave to appeal refused [1999] C.S.C.R. no 482, 140 C.C.C. (3d) vi (S.C.C.), the Court concluded that a nine-day delay in filing the report did not invalidate the search.

[601] See *R. v. Radok*, [1988] B.C.J. No. 1905, 44 C.C.C. (3d) 317 (B.C.S.C.); *Alder v. Attorney General for the Province of Alberta*, [1977] A.J. No. 756, 37 C.C.C. (2d) 234 (Alta. T.D.).

[602] [1985] O.J. No. 2442, 25 C.R.R. 273 at 292-3 (Ont. Dist. Ct.).

[603] See also *R. v. Keifer*, [1990] O.J. No. 2126 (Ont. Gen. Div.); *R. v. MacNeil*, [1994] N.S.J. 179 (N.S.S.C.); *R. v. Noseworthy*, [1995] O.J. No. 1759 (Ont. Gen. Div.). For a contrary view, see *R. v. C. (S.C.E.)*, [1998] B.C.J. No. 1446 (B.C. Prov. Ct.). See also *R. v. Backhouse*, [2005] O.J. No. 754, 194 C.C.C. (3d) 1 at para. 115 (Ont. C.A.) (acknowledging that it was unlawful for police not to file a return with respect to property that was lawfully seized but refraining from deciding whether it was necessarily unreasonable under s. 8 of the *Charter*).

[604] For a detailed discussion of these provisions, see *R. v. Mac*, [1995] O.J. No. 604, 97 C.C.C. (3d) 115 (Ont. C.A.).

[605] *Criminal Code*, R.S.C. 1985, c. C-46, s. 490(2) allows for a period of retention of a further nine-month period, and s. 490(3) provides for a period longer than one year from the date of seizure.

Section 487.012 provides for a production order whereby a justice of the peace or judge can compel a third party who is not under investigation to produce documents or data relevant to the commission of a crime for use by the authorities. Should a lawyer be subject to a production order, section 487.012(4) provides that the order may contain terms and conditions to protect privileged communications.

§3.211 Despite the high costs that a third party may incur in complying with a production order, the Supreme Court of Canada has concluded that the production order scheme in the *Code* does not confer any jurisdiction on the courts to make an order directing that the authorities compensate the target for any costs incurred in abiding by the order.[606] Instead, under section 487.015(4)(*b*) courts have the authority to grant exemptions from such orders where they would impose a potentially unreasonable burden on the recipient. According to the Supreme Court, to obtain an exemption:

> ... the financial consequences must be so burdensome that it would be unreasonable in the circumstances to expect compliance....What is reasonable will be informed by a variety of factors, including the breadth of the order being sought, the size and economic viability of the object of the order, and the extent of the order's financial impact on the party from whom production is sought. Where the party is a repeated target of production orders, the cumulative impact of multiple orders may also be relevant.[607]

§3.212 In essence, production orders are warrants. Section 487.012(3) requires the issuing justice of the peace or judge to be satisfied based on information on oath that there are reasonable grounds to believe that the documents or data will afford evidence respecting the commission of an offence. As with search warrants, the standard is one of credibly based probability. Mere suspicion or hypothesis falls short of the minimally acceptable constitutional standard.[608] The retention procedures mandated in sections 489.1 and 490 discussed above in Part 3(3)(*e*) apply in respect of documents or data produced under this section.[609]

§3.213 Whereas section 487.012 provides for general production orders, section 487.013 allows for the making of a more specific production order dealing with account information of a person named in the order from financial institutions and certain other members of the financial industry. Section 487.013(4) requires the issuing justice of the peace or judge to be satisfied on information on oath that there are reasonable grounds to suspect that the documents or data will assist in the investigation of the offence. As discussed in Part 2(5)(*d*)(i), above, given the more limited nature of the information that may be obtained under this provision, Parliament's use of the lower standard of reasonable suspicion (as opposed to the usual reasonable and probable grounds) likely complies with

---

[606] See *Tele-Mobile Co. v. Ontario*, [2008] S.C.J. No. 12, [2008] 1 S.C.R. 305 (S.C.C.).
[607] *Ibid.*, at para. 67 (S.C.R.).
[608] *R. v. Dunphy*, [2006] O.J. No. 850 (Ont. S.C.J.).
[609] *Criminal Code*, R.S.C. 1985, c. C-46, s. 487.012(6).

section 8 of the *Charter*. The issuing justice of the peace or judge also has the power to revoke, vary, or renew the order upon application by the peace officer named in the order.

(5) General Warrants

§3.214 In 1993, section 487.01 was added to the *Criminal Code* to provide for the issuance of "general warrants". These warrants, which may only be granted by provincial and superior court judges, may authorize police to use "any device or investigative technique or procedure or do any thing described in the warrant that would, if not authorized, constitute an unreasonable search or seizure ...".[610] A precondition for granting such a warrant is that there be no other provision in the *Code* or another Act of Parliament by which to authorize the intrusion.[611] The *Code* expressly provides that these warrants cannot be used to interfere with the bodily integrity of any person.[612] Moreover, the issuing judge must be satisfied that issuing the warrant is in "the best interests of the administration of justice".[613] Lastly, general warrants to conduct video surveillance must comply with the additional conditions imposed by Part VI of the *Code*.[614]

§3.215 Some of the salient aspects of the provisions of section 487.01 were summarized by the Ontario Court of Appeal in *R. v. Noseworthy*[615] as follows:

(a) The power to issue warrants under the section is limited to provincial court judges and superior court judges. It is not extended to justices of the peace.

(b) An issuing judge is not bound by the strictures of other warrant provisions, but rather is governed by "the best interests of the administration of justice".

(c) Whereas s. 487 is limited to searching a building, receptacle or a place for a specified thing and to bringing that thing or reporting with respect to it to the court, s. 487.01 authorizes a court to issue a warrant to "use any device or investigative technique or procedure or do any thing described in the warrant". Thus, s. 487.01 is both more specific and more general than s. 487.

(d) The section authorizes warrants relating to offences not yet committed.

---

[610] *Criminal Code*, s. 487.01(1).

[611] *Criminal Code* s. 487.01(1)(*c*). Non-compliance with this requirement will mean that any warrant issued is invalid. See *R. v. Brooks*, [2003] O.J. No. 3757, 178 C.C.C. (3d) 361 (Ont. C.A.).

[612] *Criminal Code*, s. 487.01(2). It should be noted, however, that the *Code* does include a comprehensive DNA warrant scheme that does permit for the seizure of bodily substances, including hair, saliva and blood for forensic DNA purposes. That scheme is considered in detail below in Part 3(7)(*a*)(i).

[613] *Criminal Code*, s. 487.01(*b*).

[614] See *Criminal Code*, s. 487.01(5) and discussion below, Part 3(8). At the time of *R. v. Wong*, [1990] S.C.J. No. 118, [1990] 3 S.C.R. 36 (S.C.C.), s. 487.01 of the *Criminal Code*, which provides for the authorization for video surveillance, was not in force. In part, s. 487.01 was a statutory response to *Wong*.

[615] [1997] O.J. No. 1946, 33 O.R. (3d) 641 (Ont. C.A.).

(e) Apart from its location in proximity to "device or investigative technique or procedure", there is nothing in the context to suggest that "any thing" should be read *ejusdem generis*. More specifically, "any thing" is not modified by the word "similar" or the phrase "of the same nature" or anything resembling them.

(f) Unlike s. 487, s. 487.01(3) and (4) provide that the judge may make the issuance of the warrant conditional upon such terms and conditions as she or he considers advisable.

(g) Section 487.01 does not provide simply for seizing things which are evidence, contraband or instrumentalities, but rather it provides for the doing of any thing which will yield information concerning an offence, thus paralleling the breadth of the informational privacy interests protected by s. 8 of the *Charter*: see *R. v. Plant*, [1993] 3 S.C.R. 281 at pp. 296-97.[616]

§3.216 With its broad application, section 487.01 allows for anticipatory searches for something not presently at the specific location to be searched. As in *Noseworthy*, where a general warrant was held to be valid in authorizing the re-seizure of items upon their return to the target individual's counsel at the offices of the RCMP, the items were previously seized pursuant to an invalid warrant.

§3.217 General warrants may also be anticipatory in the sense that they are issued in contemplation of an offence being committed in the future. For example, in *R. v. Harrison*,[617] police obtained a general warrant to conduct a surreptitious perimeter search of the accused's residence using a drug detection dog in investigating a potential marijuana grow operation. It is important to note that the requirement of section 488 of the *Criminal Code* that search warrants be executed by day unless otherwise authorized does not apply to the execution of general warrants. It is easy to see how covert police investigations would be severely hampered if they were limited to being conducted during broad daylight. Nevertheless, where a general warrant authorizes the covert entry and search of a location, the *Code* mandates that warrant also specify that notice of the entry and search be given within a time after its execution that the issuing judge considers reasonable in the circumstances.[618]

§3.218 When coupled with assistance orders issued under section 487.02 of the *Criminal Code*, general warrants can be used to employ the assistance of third parties in a criminal investigation. In *Canada Post Corp. v. Canada (Attorney General)*,[619] a general warrant and assistance order were issued to require em-

---

[616] *Ibid.*, at para. 11 (O.J.).
[617] [2005] O.J. No. 4707 (Ont. S.C.J.).
[618] *Criminal Code*, s. 487.01(5.1).
[619] [1995] O.J. No. 126, 95 C.C.C. (3d) 568 (Ont. Gen. Div.).

ployees of Canada Post to photocopy the outside of envelopes and packages delivered through the mail to a certain post office box.[620]

(6) Plain View Seizures

§3.219 Police officers are not required to ignore evidence of criminality that they unexpectedly happen upon. The police officer who pulls over a motorist for a moving violation and while speaking with the driver observes the butt of a handgun protruding out from under a floor mat, is lawfully entitled to seize the gun. The authority for such a seizure is the "plain view doctrine".

§3.220 The plain view doctrine is best understood as an instantiation of the reasonable expectation of privacy principle. On this view, police do not need a legal basis to make plain view seizures as items subject to the doctrine by definition attract no reasonable expectation of privacy; after all, they are in *plain view*.

§3.221 The Supreme Court of Canada has recognized that there are some important preconditions on the availability of the plain view seizure power at common law. First, the seizing officer must have a prior *lawful* justification to intrude into the place where the seizure occurs. In other words, the officer must already legally be in the location at which he or she makes the plain view observation leading to the seizure.[621] Second, the discovery of evidence or contraband must be inadvertent. A "plain view" seizure cannot be planned. The police officer must happen upon the item to be seized and its evidentiary or illicit nature must be immediately obvious. If the significance of the thing seized depends on further examination or closer scrutiny, then the plain view doctrine does not apply and some other legal justification for the seizure would be necessary.[622]

§3.222 In addition to the common law, there are also some statutory provisions that bear upon the authority of the police to seize evidence in plain view. Section 489(1) of the *Criminal Code* and section 11(8) of the *Controlled Drugs and Substances Act*[623] specifically authorize a police officer who is executing a warrant under either of these enactments, or who is otherwise lawfully present in a place and in execution of his or her duties (section 489(2)) to seize any thing the officer believes on reasonable grounds has been obtained by or used in the commission of an offence or that will afford evidence in respect of an offence.

---

[620] *Ibid.* See also *R. v. National Post*, [2010] S.C.J. No. 16, [2010] 1 S.C.R. 477 at paras. 89-90 (S.C.C.) (issuance of assistance order compelling newspaper editor to "take such steps as are necessary" to give effect to search warrant did not violate s. 8 of the *Charter*).

[621] See *R. v. Buhay*, [2003] S.C.J. No. 30, [2003] 1 S.C.R. 631 at para. 37 (S.C.C.) (describing as the plain view doctrines "central feature, that the police officers have a prior justification for the intrusion into the place where the 'plain view' seizure occurred"); *R. v. Law*, [2002] S.C.J. No. 10, [2002] 1 S.C.R. 227 at para. 27 (S.C.C.) (suggesting that the officer must be "lawfully positioned" at the time of the discovery for reliance on this power).

[622] See *R. v. Law*, [2002] S.C.J. No. 10, [2002] 1 S.C.R. 227 at para. 27 (S.C.C.) (noting that the evidence must be discovered "inadvertently").

[623] S.C. 1996, c. 19.

§3.223 In our view, these provisions entitle a police officer to seize evidence and contraband that he or she inadvertently stumbles upon while in a place that he or she is otherwise lawfully entitled to be in. They give police a power, in other words, to seize evidence or contraband in "plain view"; in essence codifying the common law authority that has been repeatedly recognized by the Supreme Court.[624]

§3.224 Our interpretation of these provisions has met with some judicial scepticism, however. For example, the Ontario Court of Appeal has questioned, albeit in *obiter*, whether "the complexities of the plain view doctrine should be read into the language of s. 489(2)."[625] By implication, this same doubt would probably also transfer over to section 11(8) of the *Controlled Drugs and Substances Act*, which shares the very same wording.

§3.225 In preferring the view that the legislated seizure powers found in section 489(2) of the *Code* and section 11(8) of the *Controlled Drugs and Substances Act* simply codify the common law's plain view seizure power, we are concerned that if not subject to the common law's lawful presence and inadvertence requirements, these statutory provisions would have the effect of creating rather sweeping *search* powers. On such an interpretation, we worry that the right to be *secure* against unreasonable search or seizure would be needlessly imperilled.

§3.226 Take the example of a police officer specifically authorized by a warrant to enter a residence to search for and seize a stolen bicycle. The nature of what is authorized surely constrains where and how the officer may search. For example, a bicycle cannot be secreted inside a suspect's dresser drawer. Should a police officer executing such a warrant find narcotics inside a dresser drawer, this seizure should not be justifiable under section 11(8) of the *Controlled Drugs and Substances Act*. Yet, should the courts fail to incorporate the common law's lawful presence and inadvertence requirements into these statutory provisions, then that would indeed be the effect. The officer's seizure of the drugs, even though he or she was searching somewhere that he or she really had no justification looking under the terms of the warrant (*i.e.*, inside the dresser) would be lawful. In our view, these provisions should not be given an interpretation such as this, as it would effectively justify invasive searches that go well beyond the scope of the specific licence to search that is provided by a warrant.

(7) Search and Seizure of Bodily Samples and Impressions

§3.227 As mentioned, there are several statutory search powers permitting authorities to take bodily samples and impressions for various purposes.

---

[624] The exact relationship between the statutory and common law plain view powers remains unclear. See *e.g.*, *R. v. F. (L.)*, [2002] O.J. No. 2604, 166 C.C.C. (3d) 97 (Ont. C.A.).

[625] *R. v. B. (E.)*, [2011] O.J. No. 1042, 2011 ONCA 194 at para. 77 (Ont. C.A.). However, the Court refrained from deciding the s. 8 issue based on the meaning of s. 489(2) and instead concluded that even assuming a violation the evidence would still have been admissible under s. 24(2).

(a) Forensic DNA Samples

§3.228 With the 1988 murder conviction of Colin Pitchfork in England,[626] "DNA fingerprinting" burst onto the forensics scene as a revolutionary criminal investigative tool. Since then, DNA evidence has proved to be a boon not only for detecting criminal perpetrators, but uncovering wrongful convictions.[627] To further the beneficial use of DNA as a crime scene investigation tool while at the same time limiting its potential to infringe privacy rights, Parliament has enacted legislation dealing with the seizure of DNA samples from individuals. The *Criminal Code* contains two sets of provisions dealing with DNA: firstly, a DNA search warrant regime and, secondly, the collection of DNA samples for data banking purposes.

(i) DNA Search Warrants

§3.229 Since 1995, police have been authorized to obtain warrants to collect DNA samples from suspects. The DNA warrant scheme is only applicable to the investigation of certain enumerated "designated offences".[628] The application for a DNA search warrant is heard *ex parte*[629] by a provincial court judge who may grant the warrant if there are reasonable grounds to believe that: (*i*) a bodily substance has been found that is associated with the commission of the designated offence; (*ii*) a person was party to the offence; and (*iii*) DNA analysis will be probative to the issue of whether the bodily substance is associated with the donor.[630] In addition, the judge must be satisfied that issuing the warrant "is in the best interests of the administration of justice".[631]

§3.230 Section 487.06 outlines three acceptable methods for the extraction of DNA from the donor: (*i*) plucking hair, (*ii*) taking buccal swabs from the mouth and (*iii*) taking blood by pricking the skin with a sterile lancet. While the provision does not expressly authorize the use of force, it does require the person executing the search to inform the suspect of his or her authority "... to use as much force as is necessary for the purpose of taking the samples."[632] This has been interpreted to give police the authority to use force, if necessary, to execute the warrant, but only to a degree proportionate to the circumstances.[633]

---

[626] *R. v. Pitchfork*, [2009] EWCA Crim. 963 (C.A.).

[627] See Jim Dwyer, Peter Neufeld & Barry Scheck, *Actual Innocence: When Justice Goes Wrong and How to Make it Right* (New York: New American Library, 2003).

[628] *Criminal Code*, s. 487.04.

[629] The judge has the discretion to order an *inter partes* hearing when appropriate. See *R. v. B. (S.A)*, [2003] S.C.J. No. 61, [2003] 2 S.C.R. 678 at paras. 38, 46 (S.C.C.); *R. v. Feeney*, [2001] B.C.J. No. 311, 41 C.R. (5th) 326 at paras. 31-40 (B.C.C.A.); *R. v. F. (S.)*, [2000] O.J. No. 60, 141 C.C.C. (3d) 225 (Ont. C.A.).

[630] *Criminal Code*, s. 487.05(1).

[631] *Ibid.*

[632] *Criminal Code*, s. 487.07(1)(*d*).

[633] *R. v. F. (S.)*, [2000] O.J. No. 60, 141 C.C.C. (3d) 225 at para. 105 (Ont. C.A.).

§3.231 Once a DNA sample is obtained, section 487.08 of the *Criminal Code* restricts the use that can be made of any samples seized or the DNA test results, which can only be used for forensic DNA analysis in the course of an investigation of a designated offence. Section 487.09 mandates the destruction of the bodily substance seized as well as the results of the forensic DNA analysis when: (*i*) there is no match between crime scene DNA and the suspect's DNA; (*ii*) the suspect is acquitted of the designated offence; or (*iii*) after certain time periods have elapsed (unless a new information is laid or an indictment is preferred or a judge concludes that the sample might reasonably be required in another investigation or prosecution of a designated offence).

§3.232 In *R. v. B. (S.A.)*,[634] the Supreme Court of Canada gave a constitutional seal of approval to the DNA search warrant legislative scheme.[635] The Court held that the provisions appropriately balance the public interest in law enforcement and the privacy rights of individuals, including concerns about human dignity, physical integrity and controlling the release of personal information.

(ii)   National DNA Data Bank

§3.233 Canada's National DNA Data Bank was established through the enactment of the *DNA Identification Act*,[636] which was proclaimed in force on June 30, 2000. The data bank is comprised of two principal indices. The Crime Scene index is an electronic index composed of DNA profiles obtained from crime scene investigations. The Convicted Offender Index contains an electronic index of DNA profiles collected from offenders convicted of designated primary[637] and secondary[638] offences listed in section 487.04 of the *Criminal Code*. The procedures for collecting the samples are similar to those authorized pursuant to the DNA warrant scheme. The main purpose of the data bank is to help law enforcement agencies identify persons alleged to have committed designated offences.[639]

§3.234 The *Criminal Code* establishes the process that can lead to a judicial order authorizing the taking of bodily samples from designated convicted offenders for DNA data banking purposes. The "primary designated" offences are broken down into two categories. Upon a finding of guilt for primary designated

---

[634]   [2003] S.C.J. No. 61, [2003] 2 S.C.R. 678 (S.C.C.).

[635]   *Ibid.*

[636]   S.C. 1998, c. 37, as amended by S.C. 2000, c. 10.

[637]   *Criminal Code*, s. 487.04. Primary designated offences encompass the most serious of violent offences including murder, manslaughter and sexual offences.

[638]   *Criminal Code*, s. 487.04. Secondary designated offences are not restricted to violent offences and include failure to stop at scene of accident, arson and certain drug offences under the *Controlled Drugs and Substances Act*, S.C. 1996, c. 19. Secondary designated offences also include a much broader class of offences; any offence that may be prosecuted by indictment for which the maximum punishment is imprisonment for five years or more.

[639]   *DNA Identification Act*, S.C. 1998, c. 37, s. 3.

offences listed in section 487.04(a),[640] a DNA data bank order will automatically issue. For primary designated offences listed in section 487.04(*a*)(i),[641] a DNA data bank order will presumptively issue unless the judge is satisfied that the impact on the offender's privacy and security of the person would be "grossly disproportionate to the public interest in the protection of society and the proper administration of justice, to be achieved through the early detection, arrest and conviction of offenders."[642] Orders are rarely denied under this category.[643] However, in *R. v. C. (R.)*,[644] the Supreme Court held that judges considering whether or not to grant such an order must give special consideration to young offenders and the purposes of the applicable youth criminal justice legislation.[645] The Court emphasized that in creating a separate criminal justice system for young persons, Parliament has recognized that they are to be treated differently by the courts due to differences in vulnerability, maturity, experience and other factors related to their youth.[646]

§3.235 In the case of a secondary designated offence, the Crown must ask a judge to exercise his or her discretion under section 487.051(3)(*b*). The order may be granted if the judge is satisfied that it is in the best interests of the administration of justice to do so. In making this decision, the judge must consider the criminal record of the individual, the nature of the offence, the circumstances surrounding its commission and the impact such an order would have on the person's privacy and security in their person.[647] Orders under this section will also issue in most cases. As Justice Rosenberg noted in *R. v. F. (P.R.); R. v. Hendry; R. v. M. (G.A.); R. v. W. (W.D.)*,[648] "[P]articularly if the offender has a record that includes offences described as primary designated offences, I would think it exceptional that the order not be made."[649] The *Code* also includes retroactive provisions making a limited category of offenders convicted before the

---

[640] The list includes the most serious of violent offences such as murder, manslaughter, robbery and aggravated sexual assault.

[641] This list includes offences such as sexual assault, terrorist offences and child pornography offences.

[642] *Criminal Code*, s. 487.051(2). Though this provision does not, unlike the provision dealing with secondary designated offences, refer judges to any specific factors to consider in making this decision, courts have held that they should consider the same factors. See *R. v. C. (R.)*, [2005] S.C.J. No. 62, [2005] 3 S.C.R. 99 at para. 30 (S.C.C.); *R. v. Jordan*, [2002] N.S.J. No. 20, 1 C.R. (6th) 141 at para. 62 (N.S.C.A.).

[643] *R. v. F. (P.R.); R. v. Hendry; R. v. M. (G.A.); R. v. W. (W.D.)*, [2001] O.J. No. 5084, 161 C.C.C. (3d) 275 at 289-90 (Ont. C.A.).

[644] [2005] S.C.J. No. 62, [2005] 3 S.C.R. 99 (S.C.C.).

[645] See *R. v. B. (K.)*, [2003] O.J. No. 3553, 179 C.C.C. (3d) 413 at 416 (Ont. C.A.); *R. v. R. (T.S.)*, [2005] A.J. No. 1053, 371 A.R. 353 at para. 10 (Alta. C.A.).

[646] See also *R. v. B. (K.)*, [2003] O.J. No. 3553, 179 C.C.C. (3d) 413 (Ont. C.A.).

[647] *Criminal Code*, s. 487.051(3)(*b*).

[648] [2001] O.J. No. 5084, 161 C.C.C. (3d) 275 (Ont. C.A.).

[649] *Ibid.*, at 290 (C.C.C.); *R. v. Jordan*, [2002] N.S.J. No. 20, 1 C.R. (6th) 141 at paras. 77-78 (N.S.C.A.); *R. v. B. (K.)*, [2003] O.J. No. 3553, 179 C.C.C. (3d) 413 at 416 (Ont. C.A.); *R. v. Durham*, [2007] B.C.J. No. 606, 2007 BCCA 190 at para. 12 (B.C.C.A.); *R. v. North*, [2002] A.J. No. 696, 165 C.C.C. (3d) 393 (Alta. C.A.).

coming into force of the *DNA Identification Act* eligible to have their profiles included in the databank.[650]

§3.236 Like the DNA warrant regime, the DNA data bank legislation has survived *Charter* scrutiny.[651] The Supreme Court held in *R. v. Rodgers*,[652] that the scheme strikes an appropriate balance between the public interest in the effective identification of persons convicted of serious offences and the rights of individuals to physical integrity and privacy.[653] As mentioned in Part 2(4)(*b*)(ii) above, the Court concluded that convicted offenders have no reasonable expectation of privacy with respect to their identities; it also found that the legislation provided sufficient protection against the use of their DNA for other purposes.[654]

(b) *Breath and Blood Samples in Impaired Driving Context*

§3.237 Drinking and driving investigations rely, for the most part, on either breath samples or blood samples being seized from a driver.[655] The *Criminal Code* provides authority to seize breath samples in two ways: section 254(2)(*b*) (a screening demand) and section 254(3)(*a*)(i) (a breathalyzer demand). Blood may be seized pursuant to section 254(3)(*a*)(ii) (a blood sample demand) and section 256 (a blood sample warrant). These provisions do not allow police to force a person, physically or otherwise, to submit to these takings.[656] Instead, section 254(5) of the *Criminal Code* creates a distinct offence for refusing to provide such a sample. In addition, section 258(3) provides that in certain drinking and driving prosecutions, evidence that the accused, without reasonable excuse, failed or refused to comply with a breath or blood demand, is admissible and the court may draw an adverse inference from such evidence. While sections 254(2) and 254(3) of the *Criminal Code* grant statutory authority for the seizure of either a breath or blood sample, a demand made pursuant to either section must be a lawful one, otherwise the seizure will run afoul of section 8 of the *Charter*.[657]

---

[650] *Criminal Code*, s. 487.055.
[651] *R. v. Rodgers*, [2006] S.C.J. No. 15, [2006] 1 S.C.R. 554 (S.C.C.).
[652] *Ibid.*
[653] *Ibid.*
[654] *Ibid.*, at paras. 35-55.
[655] *Criminal Code*, s. 258(2) provides that no person is required to give a sample of a bodily substance other than breath or blood.
[656] *R. v. Knox*, [1996] S.C.J. No. 89, [1996] 3 S.C.R. 199 at para. 12 (S.C.C.). Blood sample warrants issued under *Criminal Code*, s. 256, however, are generally executed without the individual's consent. The section authorizes a justice to issue a warrant to draw blood from an individual who is incapable of consenting where there are reasonable and probable grounds to believe that a person has, within the preceding four hours, committed the offence of impaired driving, and was involved in an accident resulting in the death of another person or in bodily harm to himself or herself or to any other person.
[657] See *R. v. Haas*, [2005] O.J. No. 3160, 200 C.C.C. (3d) 81 (Ont. C.A.), leave to appeal refused [2005] S.C.C.A. No. 423 (S.C.C.); *R. v. Pierman*, [1994] O.J. No. 1821, 92 C.C.C. (3d) 160 (Ont. C.A.), affd *(sub nom. R. v. Dewald)*, [1996] S.C.J. No. 5, [1996] 1 S.C.R. 68, 103 C.C.C. (3d) 382 (S.C.C.).

§3.238 Impaired driving cases are undoubtedly the most litigated and judicially considered area of our criminal law. As such, the intricacies of the statutory regime for breath and blood samples in the context of drinking and driving offences are beyond the scope of this chapter.[658] It is important to note, however, the distinction in standards between demands made for breath samples versus breathalyzer demands. Section 254(2) of the *Criminal Code* allows a police officer, on mere suspicion that a driver has alcohol in his or her body, to demand that the driver provide a sample of breath into an approved screening device.[659] That reasonable suspicion need only relate to the existence of alcohol in the body. The officer need not believe that the driver has committed a criminal offence.[660] If the driver registers a "fail" on the roadside screening device, that result alone, or in combination with other observations made by the police officer, may provide reasonable and probable grounds to conclude that the driver has committed a drinking and driving offence. On that conclusion, an officer may then arrest the driver and lawfully make a breathalyzer demand under section 254(3)(*a*)(i) of the *Criminal Code*. The requisite reasonable and probable grounds entail both subjective and objective components. The police officer must subjectively believe that the driver has committed the offence and there must be corresponding objectively reasonable grounds justifying this belief.[661]

§3.239 Where police seek a blood sample under section 254(3)(*a*)(ii) of the *Criminal Code* rather than a breath sample, the police officer must have reasonable grounds to believe that, because of the physical condition of the driver, he or she may be incapable of providing breath samples or that it would be impracticable to obtain breath samples. Only a qualified medical practitioner may take these blood samples and he or she must be satisfied that the taking of the samples would not endanger the life or health of the driver. As with demands made for breath samples, a demand for blood requires the requisite reasonable and probable grounds both from a subjective and objective standpoint.[662]

(c) Bodily Samples in Driving under the Influence of Drugs Cases

§3.240 Recently, Bill C-2[663] ushered in new law enforcement measures aimed at the investigation and prosecution of driving offences while under the influence

---

[658] For a full discussion of the relevant case law and legislation dealing with this complex area of the law, see Joseph F. Kenkel, *Impaired Driving in Canada, 2009 Edition* (Markham: LexisNexis Canada, 2008); Alan D. Gold, *Defending Drinking and Driving Cases 2010* (Toronto: Thomson Carswell, 2010).

[659] *R. v. Einarson*, [2004] O.J. No. 852, 70 O.R. (3d) 286 (Ont. C.A.).

[660] *R. v. Lindsay*, [1999] O.J. No. 870, 134 C.C.C. (3d) 159 (Ont. C.A.).

[661] *R. v. Bernshaw*, [1994] S.C.J. No. 87, [1995] 1 S.C.R. 254, 95 C.C.C. (3d) 193 at para. 48 (S.C.C.).

[662] *R. v. Salmon*, [1999] B.C.J. No. 2893, 141 C.C.C. (3d) 207 (B.C.C.A.), leave to appeal refused [2000] S.C.C.A. No. 510 (S.C.C.).

[663] Bill C-2, An Act to amend the Criminal Code and to make consequential amendments to other Acts (*Tackling Violent Crime Act*, 2nd Sess., 39th Parl. (received Royal Assent February 28, 2008)).

of drugs (DUID). Section 254(2)(*a*) of the *Criminal Code* now authorizes a peace officer, who has reasonable grounds to suspect that the person has a drug in his or her body and has operated a motor vehicle within the preceding three hours, to demand that a person perform *forthwith* physical coordination tests prescribed by regulation[664] "to enable the peace officer to determine" whether a further demand under section 254(3.1) may be made. Section 254(3.1) provides:

> (3.1) If a peace officer has reasonable grounds to believe that a person is committing, or at any time within the preceding three hours has committed, an offence under paragraph 253(1)(*a*) as a result of the consumption of a drug or of a combination of alcohol and a drug, the peace officer may, by demand made as soon as practicable, require the person to submit, as soon as practicable, to an evaluation conducted by an evaluating officer to determine whether the person's ability to operate a motor vehicle, a vessel, an aircraft or railway equipment is impaired by a drug or by a combination of alcohol and a drug, and to accompany the peace officer for that purpose.

The tests and procedures that the evaluating officer is authorized to conduct are set out in the Regulations.[665]

§3.241 Section 254(3.4) also provides the authority for the evaluating officer to demand a sample of either oral fluid or urine, or samples of blood. A demand for bodily samples, however, can occur only after the evaluating officer has completed the preceding evaluation and forms reasonable grounds to believe that the person's ability to operate a motor vehicle is impaired by a drug or combination

---

[664] *Evaluation of Impaired Operation (Drugs and Alcohol) Regulations*, SOR/2008-196. Section 2 the Regulations provides that the physical coordination tests to be conducted under paragraph 254(2)(*a*) of the *Criminal Code* are the following standard field sobriety tests: (a) the horizontal gaze nystagmus test; (b) the walk-and-run test; and (c) the one-leg stand test.

[665] *Ibid.* Section 3 of the Regulations provide that the tests to be conducted and the procedures to be followed during an evaluation under s. 254(3.1) of the *Criminal Code* are:
>   (*a*) a preliminary examination, which consists of measuring the pulse and determining that the pupils are the same size and that the eyes track an object equally;
>   (*b*) eye examinations, which consist of
>   (i)   the horizontal gaze nystagmus test,
>   (ii) the vertical gaze nystagmus test, and
>   (iii) the lack-of-convergence test;
>   (*c*) divided-attention tests, which consist of
>   (i)   the Romberg balance test,
>   (ii) the walk-and-turn test referred to in paragraph 2(*b*),
>   (iii) the one-leg stand test referred to in paragraph 2(*c*), and
>   (iv) the finger-to-nose test, which includes the test subject tilting the head back and touching the tip of their index finger to the tip of their nose in a specified manner while keeping their eyes closed;
>   (*d*) an examination, which consists of measuring the blood pressure, temperature and pulse;
>   (*e*) an examination of pupil sizes under light levels of ambient light, near total darkness and direct light and an examination of the nasal and oral cavities;
>   (*f*) an examination, which consists of checking the muscle tone and pulse; and
>   (*g*) a visual examination of the arms, neck and, if exposed, the legs for evidence of injection sites.

of alcohol and a drug.[666] Section 254(5) makes it an offence to refuse, without reasonable excuse, to comply with any of the officer's demands made under section 254.

(d) Fingerprints and Other Body Impressions

§3.242 As one of the most valuable and oldest criminal investigative tools, fingerprinting has long been part of the criminal justice system. The *Identification of Criminals Act*[667] provides for compulsory fingerprinting and photographing under certain conditions, most commonly, when a person is charged with or has been convicted of an indictable offence.[668] As mentioned, in *R. v. Beare; R. v. Higgins*,[669] the Supreme Court of Canada upheld the constitutionality of this legislation.[670]

§3.243 The Act is entirely silent on whether or not the police are entitled to retain the photographs or fingerprints of an accused where the charge(s) are withdrawn, stayed or result in an acquittal. The Ontario Court of Appeal has held that section 8 is not violated simply because the authorities do not automatically destroy the photographs or fingerprints of such individuals. Nevertheless, the Court did conclude that where such an individual makes a request for the destruction of his or her fingerprints or photographs it would be unreasonable and contrary to section 8 of the *Charter* for the authorities to retain them. In other words, a request for destruction following the withdrawal, staying or dismissal of the charge(s) imposes a constitutional obligation on the authorities to comply.[671]

§3.244 In addition to the *Identification of Criminals Act*, the *Criminal Code* provides for the obtaining of fingerprints for investigative purposes. Under section 487.092, a justice of the peace or a provincial court judge may issue a warrant authorizing a peace officer to obtain from a suspect a handprint, fingerprint, footprint, foot impression, teeth impression or "other print or impression of the body or any part of the body". The warrant will only issue if the judicial officer is satisfied that there are reasonable grounds to believe that an offence has been committed, that information concerning the offence will be obtained by the print or impression, and that it is in the best interests of the administration of justice to issue the warrant. The section is not only broad in the types of permissible im-

---

[666] Section 254(3.4) of the *Criminal Code*.

[667] R.S.C. 1985, c. I-1.

[668] The Act also allows for the compulsory taking of fingerprints and photographs of persons charged with or convicted of an offence under the *Security of Information Act*, R.S.C. 1985, c. O-5, any person apprehended under the *Extradition Act*, S.C. 1999, c. 18 and any person who is in lawful custody pursuant to the anti-terrorist provisions of the *Criminal Code*, R.S.C. 1985, c. C-46.

[669] [1987] S.C.J. No. 92, [1988] 2 S.C.R. 387 (S.C.C.).

[670] *Ibid.*, at paras. 60-61.

[671] See *R. v. Dore*, [2002] O.J. No. 2845, 166 C.C.C. (3d) 225 (Ont. C.A.).

pressions to be obtained but also with respect to applicable offences, covering offences against the *Criminal Code* and "any other Act of Parliament".

§3.245 Despite its breadth, section 487.092 has garnered very little judicial consideration. On a practical level, however, the warrant's utility is easily discerned. For example, in a situation where bloodstain pattern analysis of a crime scene reveals barefoot and footwear transfer impressions, impressions taken from a suspect can be instrumental for comparative purposes. It is of note that section 487.092 contains no express use-of-force authority where the individual refuses to acquiesce and passively permit a print or impression to be obtained.[672] Further, the section does not provide for a separate offence for refusing to provide a print or impression, nor does the section allow for an adverse inference to be drawn by a trier-of-fact for the individual's failure to comply with a lawful demand.[673]

(8) Interception of Private Communications

§3.246 As discussed above in Part 2(5)(*c*)(i), the surreptitious electronic surveillance of an individual by the state constitutes a search and seizure within the meaning of section 8 of the *Charter*.[674] The legislation governing such surveillance is found in Part VI of the *Criminal Code*.[675] Part VI prohibits the electronic interception of "private communications"[676] unless the interception is: (*i*) consented to by one of the parties to the communication;[677] (*ii*) made by police pur-

---

[672] Although s. 25 of the *Criminal Code* may likely authorize the use of force in executing such a warrant.

[673] As noted above, both options are available in the drinking and driving context.

[674] *R. v. Duarte*, [1990] S.C.J. No. 2, [1990] 1 S.C.R. 30 at 42 (S.C.C.).

[675] For a thorough examination of the intricacies of Part VI, see Robert Hubbard, Scott Fenton & Peter Brauti, *Wiretapping and Other Electronic Surveillance: Law and Procedure* (Aurora, ON: Canada Law Book, 2000).

[676] *Criminal Code*, s. 184(1) ("Every one who, by means of any electro-magnetic, acoustic, mechanical or other device, wilfully intercepts a private communication is guilty of an indictable offence and liable to imprisonment for a term not exceeding five years."). Section 183 of the *Code* defines "private communication" as "any oral communication, or any telecommunication, that is made by an originator who is in Canada or is intended by the originator to be received by a person who is in Canada and that is made under circumstances in which it is reasonable for the originator to expect that it will not be intercepted by any person other than the person intended by the originator to receive it, and includes any radio-based telephone communication that is treated electronically or otherwise for the purpose of preventing intelligible reception by any person other than the person intended by the originator to receive it." This definition echoes the "reasonable expectation of privacy" test under s. 8 of the *Charter*. "Telecommunication" is in turn defined by s. 35(1) of the *Interpretation Act*, R.S.C. 1985, c. I-21, as "the emission, transmission or reception of signs, signals, writing, images, sounds or intelligence of any nature by any wire, cable, radio, optical or other electromagnetic system, or by any similar technical system" [emphasis added]. Part VI of the *Criminal Code* thus applies to the interception of communications carried over most electronic communications technologies, including wireless telephones, as well as email and other text-based communications devices. See Steven Penney, "Updating Canada's Communications Surveillance Laws: Privacy and Security in the Digital Age" (2008) 12 Can. Crim. L. Rev 115 at 125-26.

[677] *Criminal Code*, s. 184(2)(*a*) ("Subsection (1) does not apply to (*a*) a person who has the consent to intercept, express or implied, of the originator of the private communication or of the person

suant to a court authorization;[678] (*iii*) made by operators or regulators of communications networks in course of maintaining or protecting those networks;[679] or (*iv*) made by police in order to prevent one of the parties to the communication from causing immediate, serious harm.[680]

§3.247 The most important of these exceptions, for our purposes, is the authorization exception. In comparison to ordinary search warrants, the requirements for obtaining wiretap authorizations are significantly more onerous. The application must receive written approval from a senior governmental official; the authorization is available only for certain serious offences[681] and may be issued only by a superior court judge (except in Quebec);[682] the judge may impose terms and conditions on its execution;[683] the maximum period of interception (for most offences) is 60 days;[684] it is an offence to use or disclose intercepted private communications for any purpose not related to law enforcement or the operation of communications networks;[685] the target of the interception must be notified (in most circumstances) within 90 days after the expiry of the warrant;[686] and the responsible minister must make an annual report to Parliament providing detailed statistics on the use of wiretapping by federal authorities.[687]

§3.248 Most critically, the police must convince the judge that issuing the authorization "would be in the best interests of the administration of justice" and that "other investigative procedures have been tried and have failed, other investigative procedures are unlikely to succeed or the urgency of the matter is such

---

intended by the originator thereof to receive it"). While the general interception prohibition (and its accompanying criminal penalties) does not apply when one of the parties is aware of the interception, since 1990 police have been required to obtain warrants to conduct consent surveillance in most circumstances as result of the decision in *R. v. Duarte*, [1990] S.C.J. No. 2, [1990] 1 S.C.R. 30 (S.C.C.), discussed above, Part 2(4). In response to *Duarte*, Parliament amended the *Code* to allow police to obtain warrants to conduct consent interceptions. See *Criminal Code*, s. 184.2. Unlike authorizations given under s. 186, consent authorizations are not restricted to investigating the enumerated offences in s. 183 of the *Criminal Code*, but may be obtained for any federal offence. Following *Duarte*, the *Code* was also amended to permit warrantless consent intercepts by police in order to ensure the safety of undercover agents. Private communications intercepted under this provision, however, are inadmissible as evidence except in proceedings relating to the infliction (or attempted or threatened infliction) of bodily harm upon the agent. If no such violence occurs, any intercepted private communications must be destroyed. See *Criminal Code*, s. 184.1.

[678] *Criminal Code*, s. 184(2)(*b*).

[679] *Ibid.*, ss. 184(2)(*c*)-(3).

[680] *Ibid.*, s. 184.4.

[681] *Ibid.*, s. 183.

[682] *Ibid.*, s. 185(1).

[683] *Ibid.*, s. 186(4)(*d*).

[684] *Ibid.*, s. 186(4)(*e*).

[685] *Ibid.*, s. 193.

[686] *Ibid.*, s. 196(1).

[687] *Ibid.*, s. 195. See Public Safety and Emergency Preparedness Canada, *Annual Report on the use of Electronic Surveillance — 2005* (Ottawa: Minister of Public Safety and Emergency Preparedness, 2006), online: <http://www.publicsafety.gc.ca/abt/dpr/le/elecsur_05-eng.asp>.

that it would be impractical to carry out the investigation of the offence using only other investigative procedures."[688] Each concept is considered below.

(a) Best Interests of the Administration of Justice

§3.249 Although Part VI of the *Criminal Code* does not expressly require a showing of reasonable grounds, the Supreme Court held in *Duarte* that the "best interests of the administration of justice" prerequisite "imports as a minimum requirement that the issuing judge must be satisfied ... that the authorization sought will afford evidence of that offence."[689] This aligns Part VI with the *Hunter* requirements under section 8 of the *Charter*.[690]

§3.250 More specifically, in applying for a Part VI authorization, police must name and provide the addresses and occupations of "known" targets, *i.e.*, people whose communications police have "reasonable grounds to believe may assist" in their investigation.[691] The communications of persons not named in the authorization may be intercepted only if their existence was not known to police at the time of the application.[692] Similarly, police must describe the "nature and location" of any "known" places where the interceptions are to occur;[693] communications made at other locations may be intercepted pursuant to a "resort to" clause.[694] "Resort to" clauses typically involve the authorization to intercept a target's communications at phones and locations other than those that the individual would normally use, such as payphones or phones belonging to friends or family. These clauses, however, should require that selective monitoring must be employed to minimize such interceptions and such interceptions must cease when a target of the investigation is not involved in the communication.

(b) Investigative Necessity

§3.251 Section 185(1)(*h*) of the *Criminal Code* requires that an application for a wiretap authorization be accompanied by an affidavit in which the affiant deposes to the investigative necessity of a wiretap. In issuing a search warrant, an authorizing judge must be satisfied that such necessity exists.[695] In *R. v. Araujo*,[696] the Supreme Court of Canada was called upon to resolve the contin-

---

[688] *Criminal Code*, s. 186(1).

[689] *R. v. Duarte*, [1990] S.C.J. No. 2, [1990] 1 S.C.R. 30 at 45 (S.C.C.). See also *R. v. Araujo*, [2000] S.C.J. No. 65, [2000] 2 S.C.R. 992 at para. 20 (S.C.C.); *R. v. Garofoli*, [1990] S.C.J. No. 115, [1990] 2 S.C.R. 1421 at 1444 (S.C.C.).

[690] *R. v. Garofoli*, [1990] S.C.J. No. 115, [1990] 2 S.C.R. 1421 at 1443-45 (S.C.C.).

[691] *Criminal Code*, s. 185(1)(*e*).

[692] The communications of unknown persons may be intercepted pursuant to a "basket" clause in the authorization. See *R. v. Chesson*, [1988] S.C.J. No. 70, [1988] 2 S.C.R. 148 at para. 21 (S.C.C.).

[693] *Criminal Code*, s. 185(1)(*e*).

[694] See *R. v. Moore*, [1993] B.C.J. No. 1073, 81 C.C.C. (3d) 161 (B.C.C.A.), affd [1995] S.C.J. No. 24, [1995] 1 S.C.R. 756 (S.C.C.).

[695] *Criminal Code*, s. 186(1)(*b*).

[696] [2000] S.C.J. No. 65, [2000] 2 S.C.R. 992 (S.C.C.).

ued uncertainty that surrounded its own and lower courts' decisions on the meaning of the investigative necessity requirement. Some courts had suggested that wiretapping can only be permitted as an investigative method of "last resort".[697] Other courts (including the court below in *Araujo*) had required only that wiretapping be the "most efficacious way" of investigating the offence.[698]

§3.252 The Supreme Court preferred an interpretation falling somewhere between these two extremes. "[P]ractically speaking," it held, there must be "no other reasonable alternative method of investigation."[699] This is not equivalent, the Court stressed, to a "last resort" standard.[700] The test can be satisfied, in other words, by demonstrating that "normal investigative techniques are unlikely to succeed," for example, by failing to: (*i*) reveal "key information";[701] (*ii*) penetrate "a large-scale crime organization, ... a close-knit family ... or a drug conspiracy";[702] or (*iii*) overcome "counter-surveillance methods".[703] Nor should investigative necessity be equated to a "most efficacious" standard.[704] To do so would, in the Court's words, "replace a standard of necessity with one of opportunity at the discretion of law enforcement bodies."[705]

§3.253 Despite its disapproval of the Court of Appeal's interpretation of the investigative necessity requirement, the Supreme Court agreed that the police had satisfied it on the facts. The affidavit demonstrated that the targets of the investigation were the ringleaders of a drug trafficking ring, that they commonly used counter-surveillance techniques, that physical surveillance and the execution of search warrants had been tried and failed, and that the use of informants and undercover agents would likely be dangerous and ineffective.[706]

§3.254 As noted in Part 2(5)(*c*)(i), above, there is no requirement to show investigative necessity for authorizations sought in relation to criminal organiza-

---

[697] *R. v. Duarte*, [1990] S.C.J. No. 2, [1990] 1 S.C.R. 30 at 55 (S.C.C.). See also *R. v. Commisso*, [1983] S.C.J. No. 67, [1983] 2 S.C.R. 121 at 135 (S.C.C.), *per* Dickson J., dissenting; *R. v. Thompson*, [1990] S.C.J. No. 104, [1990] 2 S.C.R. 1111 at 1160 (S.C.C.), *per* La Forest J., dissenting; *R. v. Finlay*, [1985] O.J. No. 2680, 23 C.C.C. (3d) 48 at 69 (Ont. C.A.).

[698] *R. v. Araujo*, [1998] B.C.J. No. 1558, 127 C.C.C. (3d) 315 at para. 30 (B.C.C.A.), affd [2000] S.C.J. No. 65, [2000] 2 S.C.R. 992 (S.C.C.). See also *R. v. Paulson*, [1995] B.C.J. No. 691, 97 C.C.C. (3d) 344 (B.C.C.A.); *R. v. Cheung*, [1997] B.C.J. No. 2282, 119 C.C.C. (3d) 507 (B.C.C.A.), leave to appeal refused [1997] S.C.C.A. No. 596 (S.C.C.).

[699] *R. v. Araujo*, [2000] S.C.J. No. 65, [2000] 2 S.C.R. 992 at paras. 29, 35 (S.C.C.). See also *R. v. Todoruk*, [1992] B.C.J. No. 2651, 78 C.C.C. (3d) 139 at 145 (B.C.S.C.); *R. v. Smyk*, [1993] M.J. No. 483, 86 C.C.C. (3d) 63 at 74 (Man. C.A.); *R. v. Shalala*, [2000] N.B.J. No. 14, 224 N.B.R. (2d) 118 at para. 87 (N.B.C.A.).

[700] *R. v. Araujo*, [2000] S.C.J. No. 65, [2000] 2 S.C.R. 992 at para. 33 (S.C.C.).

[701] *Ibid.*

[702] *Ibid.*

[703] *Ibid.*

[704] *Ibid.*, at para. 39 (S.C.R.).

[705] *Ibid.*

[706] *Ibid.*, at paras. 41-43. Despite its conclusion that investigative necessity was demonstrated, the Court criticized the affiant's (potentially misleading) use of "boiler-plate" language, excess verbiage and reliance on the knowledge of other officers. *Ibid.*, at paras. 45-49.

tion or terrorism offences.[707] Nor is there such requirement for the issuance of a one-party consent authorization under section 184.2 of the *Code*.

(9) Other Forms of Electronic Surveillance

§3.255 The advancement of technology continues to provide new tools for both criminals to perpetrate wrongdoing and police to detect and deter it. In response to these technologies and the courts' use of section 8 of the *Charter* to limit law enforcement's ability to use them, Parliament has in recent decades sought to regulate the use of a variety of novel electronic surveillance techniques. We have already discussed the general warrant provision, section 487.01 of the *Code*, which allows police to conduct video and other forms of surveillance not otherwise authorized by statute.[708] We discuss a number of more specific provisions immediately below.

(a) Tracking Devices

§3.256 As mentioned in Part 2(5)(*d*)(i), above, the use of tracking devices is regulated by section 492.1 of the *Criminal Code*. A "tracking device" means "any device that, when installed in or on any thing, may be used to help ascertain, by electronic or other means, the location of any thing or person."[709] A tracking device warrant may be issued by a justice of the peace or a provincial court judge who is satisfied that there are "reasonable grounds to suspect" that an offence under the *Criminal Code* or any other Act of Parliament has been, or will be, committed and that the information that is relevant to the commission of the offence, including the whereabouts of any person, can be obtained through the use of a tracking device. Although police may obtain successive warrants, each is valid for a maximum of 60 days.[710]

§3.257 There are two main questions arising from this provision. The first, whether the use of the "reasonable suspicion" standard complies with section 8 of the *Charter*; this was discussed in Part 2(5)(*d*)(i), above. The second is whether section 492.1 authorizes the monitoring of tracking devices that were not installed by government agents, such as those included in certain wireless telephones and vehicles. As seen above, the provision permits police to "install, maintain, and remove" the device as well as to "monitor" it. While this implies that police must install the device, the definition of "tracking device" ("any device that, *when installed in or on any thing*, may be used to help ascertain ... [its] location"[711]) implies that police may take advantage of devices installed for non-

---

[707] *Criminal Code*, ss. 185(1.1) and 186(1.1). The constitutionality of this omission is also discussed above, Part 2(5)(*c*)(i).

[708] See above, Part 3(5).

[709] *Criminal Code*, s. 492.1(4).

[710] *Criminal Code*, ss. 492.1(2) and (3). Section 492.1(5) also empowers a justice to authorize the covert removal of the device.

[711] Emphasis added.

law enforcement purposes. From a policy perspective, there is little reason to differentiate between devices installed by police and those used by commercial service providers provided that, in the case of privately installed devices, judicial authorization is sought for their use by police.[712]

(b)   Number Recorders

§3.258 As mentioned in Part 2(5)(*d*)(i), above, section 492.2 of the *Criminal Code* authorizes the issuance of digital "number recorder" warrants and production orders. The section defines a "number recorder" as "any device that can be used to record or identify the telephone number or location of the telephone from which a telephone call originates, or at which it is received or is intended to be received."[713] Such a warrant, when issued, will authorize police to "install, maintain and remove a number recorder in relation to any telephone or telephone line" as well to as "monitor, or to have monitored, the number recorder."[714] A production order directs "person or body that lawfully possesses records of telephone calls originated from, or received or intended to be received at, any telephone give the records, or a copy of the records, to a person named in the order."[715] As with tracking device warrants, police may obtain successive warrants, each of which is valid for a maximum of 60 days.[716]

§3.259 To obtain a warrant or production order, police need only satisfy a justice that there are "reasonable grounds to suspect" that an offence under the *Criminal Code* or any other Act of Parliament has been or will be committed.[717] As mentioned in Part 2(5)(*d*)(i), above, most courts have concluded that reasonable suspicion justifies this kind of surveillance under section 8 of the *Charter*. Section 492.2 also raises a question of ordinary statutory interpretation; namely, precisely what types of information does it allow police to obtain? It obviously includes the unique number identifier associated with the telephones dialled or received by the target phone.[718] The provision has also been interpreted to authorize the recording of the date, time and duration of calls made and received.[719] It should not be read, however, to permit the capture of any other digits or num-

---

[712] See Steven Penney, "Reasonable Expectations of Privacy and Novel Search Technologies: An Economic Approach" (2007) 97 J. Crim. L. & Criminology 477 at 527 n. 231.

[713] *Criminal Code*, s. 492.2(4).

[714] *Criminal Code*, s. 492.2(1).

[715] *Criminal Code*, s. 492.2(2).

[716] *Criminal Code*, ss. 492.2(3).

[717] *Criminal Code*, s. 492.2(1).

[718] See Robert Hubbard, Scott Fenton & Peter Brauti, *Wiretapping and Other Electronic Surveillance: Law and Procedure* (Aurora, ON: Canada Law Book, 2000) at § 5.12.1.1; Steven Penney, "Updating Canada's Communications Surveillance Laws: Privacy and Security in the Digital Age" (2008) 12 Can. Crim. L. Rev 115 at 148.

[719] See *Cody c. R.*, [2007] Q.J. No. 11001, 228 C.C.C. (3d) 331 at para. 15 (Que. C.A.).

ber-based codes inputted into or received by the target phone, especially if those digits comprise confidential passwords or personal identification numbers.[720]

§3.260 As mentioned, the definition of a number recorder specifically refers to the "location" of telephones connecting with the target telephone. In the case of conventional landline phones, this is the registered billing address associated with the phone. The courts have also interpreted section 492.2 to allow police to obtain information on the physical location of mobile phones at the times that calls are made or received.[721]

§3.261 Lastly, while there is some contrary authority,[722] it is likely that police may use section 492.2 to obtain subscriber information (*i.e.*, the name and address of the registered user) either for the targeted phone or the phone connecting to it.[723] Without subscriber information for both the target and connecting phones, police may not be able to determine the identities of the people using them.

(10) Searches and Seizures in Relation to Drugs

§3.262 Search warrants are commonly issued with respect to drug investigations. The statutory authority for these warrants is found in both the *Criminal Code*[724] and the *Controlled Drugs and Substances Act*.[725] Section 11 of the CDSA governs the criteria for the issuance of a search warrant. The section reads:

> 11. (1) A justice who, on *ex parte* application, is satisfied by information on oath that there are reasonable grounds to believe that
>
> (*a*) a controlled substance or precursor in respect of which this Act has been contravened,
>
> (*b*) any thing in which a controlled substance or precursor referred to in paragraph (*a*) is contained or concealed,
>
> (*c*) offence-related property, or
>
> (*d*) any thing that will afford evidence in respect of an offence under this Act or an offence, in whole or in part in relation to a contravention of this Act, under section 354 or 462.31 of the *Criminal Code*

---

[720] See Robert Hubbard, Scott Fenton & Peter Brauti, *Wiretapping and Other Electronic Surveillance: Law and Procedure* (Aurora, ON: Canada Law Book, 2000) at § 5.12.1.1; Steven Penney, "Updating Canada's Communications Surveillance Laws: Privacy and Security in the Digital Age" (2008) 12 Can. Crim. L. Rev 115 at 148.

[721] See *Griffin c. R.*, [2008] Q.J. No. 3589, 237 C.C.C. (3d) 374 at paras. 92-94 (Que. C.A.), revd on other grounds *(sub nom. R. v. Griffin)*, [2009] S.C.J. No. 28, [2009] 2 S.C.R. 42 (S.C.C.); *Cody c. R.*, [2007] Q.J. No. 11001, 228 C.C.C. (3d) 331 at paras. 14-27 (Que. C.A.).

[722] *R. v. Nguyen*, [2004] B.C.J. No. 248, 20 C.R. (6th) 135 at paras. 42-46 (B.C.S.C.).

[723] See *R. v. Mahmood*, [2008] O.J. No. 3922, 236 C.C.C. (3d) 3 at paras. 50, 150 (Ont. S.C.J.), reconsideration denied [2009] O.J. No. 3192, 194 C.R.R. (2d) 180 (Ont. S.C.J.).

[724] See *Criminal Code*, R.S.C. 1985, c. C-46, ss. 487 and 487.01, which are discussed above in Parts 3(3) and 3(5).

[725] S.C. 1996, c. 19 [CDSA].

is in a place may, at any time, issue a warrant authorizing a peace officer, at any time, to search the place for any such controlled substance, precursor, property or thing and to seize it.

§3.263 As with warrants issued under section 487 of the *Criminal Code*, the CDSA provides for the use of telewarrants.[726] Also similar to section 487 warrants, police may seize items that are not specifically named in a CDSA warrant. The partial codification of the "plain view doctrine" in section 11(6) and (8) of the CDSA grants police the authority to seize non-specified items if the seizing officer "believes on reasonable grounds" that the evidence relates to an "offence".[727] The plain view seizure power is discussed above in Part 3(6).

§3.264 There are, however, significant differences between CDSA search warrants and those under section 487 of the *Criminal Code*. First, the CDSA gives police the express authority to use "as much force as is necessary" in executing a section 11 CDSA warrant.[728] Secondly, police may search persons found in the place set out in the warrant if the police have "reasonable grounds to believe" that individual has on their person any controlled substance, precursor, property or thing set out in the warrant.[729] Thirdly, a CDSA search warrant may be executed "at any time"[730] thereby avoiding the daytime only restriction that generally restricts the execution of section 487 *Criminal Code* warrants.

§3.265 The CDSA also contains a provision authorizing a warrantless search "if the conditions for obtaining a warrant exist but by reason of exigent circumstances it would be impracticable to obtain one."[731] This is the legislated exigency exception, similar to the *Criminal Code* exception found in section 487.11. The exigency exceptions are discussed in far greater detail in Part 3(2), above. Items seized pursuant to a CDSA warrant are subject to reporting requirements under section 13 of the CDSA. While the *Criminal Code* reporting provisions detailed above in Part 3(3) apply to "offence-related" property seized under the CDSA,[732] the CDSA provides specific reporting provisions to deal with seized controlled substances. Section 13(4) requires a peace officer who seizes a controlled substance to notify a justice *and* the Minister of Health, as soon as is reasonable in the circumstances, of the place searched, the controlled substance seized and the place where it is being detained. Quite obviously, unlike the *Criminal Code* retention provisions, the CDSA provides no mechanism for the return of controlled substances to those from whom they were seized.

---

[726] CDSA, s. 11(2).
[727] The use of the word "offence" suggests that the seizure is not restricted to drug offences.
[728] CDSA, s. 12(*b*).
[729] CDSA, s. 11(5).
[730] CDSA, s. 11.
[731] CDSA, s. 11(7).
[732] CDSA, 13(2).

(11) Search and Seizure Powers in International Investigations

§3.266 The increasingly transnational nature of crime and terrorism has placed a premium on international co-operation in criminal investigations and prosecutions. Traditionally, *letters rogatory* submitted by a court seeking assistance from a court in a foreign state served as the main mechanism for international assistance. Today, international comity is much more regulated, whether by treaty or Acts of Parliament. Two particular pieces of legislation that provide for statutory search and seizure powers and have significant international ramifications are the *Mutual Legal Assistance in Criminal Matters Act*[733] and the *DNA Identification Act*.[734]

(a) Mutual Legal Assistance in Criminal Matters Act

§3.267 In 1988, Parliament enacted the *Mutual Legal Assistance in Criminal Matters Act* to specifically govern the process by which Canadian authorities receive from and provide assistance to other countries in the gathering of evidence in criminal investigations. The Act gives legal effect to requests made by a foreign state or entity pursuant to a treaty, a one-off "administrative arrangement",[735] or a designation under the Act.[736] While section 6(2) of the Act allows for assistance in matters amounting to a summary conviction violation or a provincial offence, the section mandates that such assistance will only be given in "exceptional circumstances".

§3.268 Sections 10 through 16 of the Act govern searches and seizures made in Canada at the request of a state or entity. Section 10 of the Act incorporates the provisions of the *Criminal Code* as applicable to searches and seizures. The following aspects of the search warrant provisions found in the Act are of particular importance:

    (i) The application must be made to a superior court judge.[737]

    (ii) A search warrant may not only issue in relation to an offence that has been committed, but may also issue for "... information that may reveal the whereabouts of a person who is suspected of having committed the offence ..."[738]

    (iii) A search warrant will not issue if it would be more appropriate, in the circumstances, to make an order under section 18(1) of the Act. Section 18(1) of the Act is in effect, a subpoena power akin to issuing a *subpoena duces tecum* in that such an order may require an individual to give evidence under oath and produce documents.[739]

---

[733] R.S.C. 1985, c. 30 (4th Supp.).
[734] S.C. 1998, c. 37.
[735] *Mutual Legal Assistance in Criminal Matters Act*, R.S.C. 1985, c. 30 (4th Supp.), s. 6(2).
[736] *Mutual Legal Assistance in Criminal Matters Act*, s. 4(1).
[737] *Mutual Legal Assistance in Criminal Matters Act*, s. 12(1).
[738] *Mutual Legal Assistance in Criminal Matters Act*, ss. 12(1)(*a*) and (*b*).
[739] *Mutual Legal Assistance in Criminal Matters Act*, s. 12(1)(*c*).

(*iv*) The execution of a search warrant may be made subject to any conditions that the issuing justice considers "desirable", including conditions relating to the time or manner of its execution.[740]

(*v*) The issuing judge is required to set a date for a hearing, known as a "sending hearing", to consider the execution of the warrant. A notice that sets out the time, place, purpose and scope of the hearing is included on the warrant itself.[741] In executing the warrant, the peace officer must provide a copy of the warrant to the occupant in charge of the searched premises. If no such person is present, the peace officer shall post the warrant in a prominent place within the premises.[742]

(*vi*) Section 13 allows for a "plain view" seizure power similar to that provided by section 489 of the *Criminal Code*, but only in respect of evidence relating to an offence under "an Act of Parliament". Hence, if the warrant is being executed pursuant to a request from the United States in relation to a specified offence, the police do not have the authority to seize an item discovered that is only evidence of a separate offence committed in the United States.

(*vii*) Section 13.1 grants the authority to issue a general warrant similar to the power in section 487.01 of the *Criminal Code*.

(*viii*) Section 15 of the Act governs the "sending hearing" held before the issuing judge or a judge of the same court. The presiding judge may make an order to send the item to the requesting state or entity unless *(i)* he or she is not satisfied that the warrant was executed according to its terms and conditions or, *(ii)* he or she is satisfied that a sending order should not be made.[743]

(b) *DNA Data Bank Legislation*

§3.269 Forensic DNA data banks are becoming commonplace throughout the world. As these data banks increase in population, so too does the interest of sharing such information amongst countries. Indeed, section 6 of the *DNA Identification Act*[744] allows for communication of information contained in the National DNA Data Bank to foreign states. In April 2002, Canada entered into a bilateral agreement with Interpol, which allows Canadian law enforcement au-

---

[740] *Mutual Legal Assistance in Criminal Matters Act*, s. 12(2).

[741] *Mutual Legal Assistance in Criminal Matters Act*, ss. 12(3) and (4).

[742] *Mutual Legal Assistance in Criminal Matters Act*, ss.12(5) and (6).

[743] In *United States of America v. Price*, [2007] O.J. No. 2673, 225 C.C.C. (3d) 307 (Ont. C.A.), leave to appeal refused [2007] S.C.C.A. No. 430 (S.C.C.), the Ontario Court of Appeal held that the discretion bestowed on the judge by operation of s. 15 of the *DNA Identification Act*, S.C. 1998, c. 37, is broad enough to allow the judge to exercise his or her discretion to make a sending order despite a finding that the search warrant had not been executed according to its terms and conditions. This discretion, however, is not unlimited. As the Court stated at para. 18, "The judge must rigorously scrutinize the manner in which the warrant was executed to determine whether there was any significant or meaningful failure to execute the warrant according to its terms. If there was, the wording of the section requires the judge to refuse to make a sending order."

[744] S.C. 1998, c. 37.

thorities the ability to exchange DNA Data Bank data with 178 signing countries.[745] Consequently, individuals who have provided samples to the National DNA Data Bank are susceptible to being drawn into criminal investigations in foreign countries that may have very different constitutional protections or standards of investigation than Canada. The possibility that an international false match could occur and result in a complex extradition hearing trying to "convince" a foreign state that they got the "wrong" person was borne true in 2003 when an English man was falsely implicated in a murder committed in Italy.[746] The English man was arrested in Liverpool and extradition hearings commenced after a crime scene sample found in Italy "matched" the man's DNA profile held in the United Kingdom's Data Bank. After it was determined that the man had never been to Italy and had been at work at the time of the murder, a second DNA test was conducted and the man was cleared. But query the potential for a miscarriage of justice if the English man did not have a compelling alibi?

4. COMMON LAW SEARCH POWERS

(1) Introduction

§3.270 At least on a formal level, police powers to search and seize were extraordinarily limited at common law. This was the product of a more general reluctance on the part of English jurists to recognize police powers that would encroach on individual property and liberty interests. It was the insistence on express legal authority for such intrusions that served as the hallmark of "rights" under the English common law constitution.[747] It will be remembered, for example, that in refusing to uphold the search and seizure carried out in *Entick v. Carrington*,[748] Chief Justice Camden queried:

> What would the parliament say, if the judges should take upon themselves
> to mould an unlawful power into a convenient authority, by new restric-
> tions? That would be, not judgment, but legislation.[749]

As a result, most authority to search and seize evidence in England resulted from parliamentary enactments. Ultimately these various enactments were replaced with the *Police and Criminal Evidence Act 1984* (PACE).[750]

---

[745] National DNA Data Bank Advisory Committee 2002-2003 Annual Report, online:
<http://www.rcmp-grc.gc.ca/dnaac-adncc/annurp/2002-2003-annurp-eng.htm>.

[746] See *Liverpool Daily Post, Cleared Murder Accused Victim of DNA Blunder* (March 10, 2003), online: <http://icliverpool.icnetwork.co.uk/0100news/0100regionalnews/tm_method=full%26objectid= 12718961%26siteid=50061-name_page.html>.

[747] See generally, Douglas E. Edlin, "Rule Britannia" (2002) 52 U.T.L.J. 313.

[748] (1765), 19 St. Tr. 1029.

[749] *Ibid.* See also Part 1(1), above.

[750] Based on the recommendations of the Royal Commission on Criminal Procedure, the English Parliament replaced what had grown into a fragmented system with a comprehensive code of police powers, the *Police and Criminal Evidence Act 1984*, (U.K.), 1984, c. 60. See generally, Leonard Herschel Leigh, *Police Powers in England and Wales*, 2d ed. (London: Butterworths,

§3.271 In Canada, comprehensive legislative reform has never come. Due to the absence of an exclusionary rule before 1982 there were relatively few opportunities for Canadian courts to develop police powers at "common law". As explained above, the *Charter* finally changed this. Section 24(2) meant that police illegality could have significant consequences: the exclusion of evidence where the police acted in a legally grey area and a court concluded that their conduct ran afoul of constitutional standards.

§3.272 The *Charter*'s exclusionary remedy brought with it considerable pressure on the Supreme Court of Canada to use its authority to fill the countless gaps in police search powers. At least during the *Charter*'s first decade the Supreme Court actively resisted suggestions that it do so. For example, in *R. v. Wong*,[751] writing for the Court, Justice La Forest explained:

> The common law powers of search were extremely narrow, and the courts have left it to Parliament to extend them where need be ... As Kaufman J.A., speaking for the Quebec Court of Appeal, has stated on this point ...
>
> > The law may well be unsatisfactory, but that is not for us to say, nor ... is it for the courts to fill in lacunae, however desirable such a course may seem. That must be left to the legislator."[752]

§3.273 As was explained in greater detail in Chapter 1, Part 6(4)(*b*), over the last 20 years the Supreme Court has increasingly ignored its own early warnings about the perils of acceding to requests that it create new police powers. As will become apparent below, the Court has repeatedly used the "ancillary powers doctrine" (also known as the "*Waterfield* test") to not only expand on the one common law search power that pre-dated the *Charter* (search incidental to arrest) but to also recognize a number of additional search powers at "common law". Each of these "common law" search powers will be considered in this part.

§3.274 One final caveat should be noted before moving forward. In the process of developing common law powers of search and seizure, the Supreme Court of Canada has only rarely averted to the minimum standards mandated by section 8 of the *Charter*. Nevertheless, given the Court's repeated instruction that the common law must be developed in accordance with the *Charter*'s minimum standards[753] it seems fair to assume that each of these powers complies with sec-

---

1985) at 32-44; Tim Newburn & Robert Reiner, "50th Anniversary Article: From P.C. Dixon to Dixon PLC: Policing and Police Powers Since 1954" (2004) Crim. L. Rev. 601 at 605.

[751] [1990] S.C.J. No. 118, [1990] 3 S.C.R. 36 (S.C.C.).

[752] *Ibid.*, at 56 (S.C.R.).

[753] See *Retail, Wholesale and Department Store Union, Local 580 [R.W.D.S.U.] v. Dolphin Delivery Ltd.*, [1986] S.C.J. No. 75, [1986] 2 S.C.R. 573 at 603, 33 D.L.R. (4th) 174 (S.C.C.); *Cloutier v. Langlois*, [1990] S.C.J. No. 10, [1990] 1 S.C.R. 158 at 184, 53 C.C.C. (3d) 257; *R. v. Salituro*, [1991] S.C.J. No. 97, [1991] 3 S.C.R. 654 at 675, 68 C.C.C. (3d) 289 (S.C.C.); *R. v. Swain*, [1991] S.C.J. No. 32, [1991] 1 S.C.R. 933 at 978-79, 63 C.C.C. (3d) 481 (S.C.C.); *Dagenais v. Canadian Broadcasting Corp.*, [1994] S.C.J. No. 104, [1994] 3 S.C.R. 835 at paras. 69-73, 94 C.C.C. (3d) 289 (S.C.C.); *Hill v. Church of Scientology of Toronto*, [1995]

tion 8.[754] As discussed in Part 2(5)(*a*), above, if the lawful parameters of these powers are exceeded, then the police act unlawfully and thus violate section 8. Section 8 is similarly infringed if the conduct of the authorities is technically in compliance with the parameters of a common law power but the manner in which a search or seizure is carried out is itself unreasonable.

(2) Search Incidental to Arrest

§3.275 Although the *Criminal Code* has long included arrest powers, it has always been silent on the existence of an accompanying power to search those arrested. Nevertheless, long before the *Charter*, Canadian courts had recognized that such a power existed at common law.[755] Civil and criminal cases addressing that power, however, were quite rare, so its exact parameters were less than clear.[756] It was the *Charter*'s exclusionary rule that finally required the Supreme Court to sketch out the details of this police power.[757] Over the last 25 years, the Supreme Court of Canada has acknowledged the existence of a common law power to search incidental to arrest and has said much to define its contours.

§3.276 The Supreme Court has held that this power is contingent upon a *lawful* arrest.[758] In other words, if the police lack the requisite grounds to carry out an arrest (normally because they lack reasonable and probable grounds to believe that the person arrested has committed a crime) the power to search does not arise. This means that if the arrest is unlawful then any search that accompanies it will also be unlawful and thus contrary to section 8.[759] As a result, a sensible starting point for scrutinizing any search incidental to arrest is an analysis of the basis for the arrest itself (see Chapter 2, Part 4).

S.C.J. No. 64, [1995] 2 S.C.R. 1130 at paras. 83-98, 126 D.L.R. (4th) 129; *R. v. Golden*, [2001] S.C.J. No. 81, [2001] 3 S.C.R. 679 at 726-27, 159 C.C.C. (3d) 449 (S.C.C.).

[754] The need to expressly address the constitutional implications of the police powers created by the Court's application of the *Waterfield* test was a point of disagreement between the majority in *R. v. Clayton*, [2007] S.C.J. No. 32, [2007] 2 S.C.R. 725 (S.C.C.) and Binnie J. (joined by Fish and LeBel JJ.).

[755] Such a power was recognized in English decisions dating back to the nineteenth century, see *Bessell v. Wilson* (1853), 118 E.R. 518, 17 J.P. 52 (Q.B.); *Leigh v. Cole* (1853), 6 Cox. C.C. 329. These cases were ultimately followed in Canada. See *Yakimishyn v. Bileski*, [1946] M.J. No. 11, 86 C.C.C. 179 at 181 (Man. K.B.); *R. v. Brezack*, [1949] O.J. No. 492, 96 C.C.C. 97 at 101 (Ont. C.A.). See also Report of the Canadian Committee on Corrections, *Toward Unity: Criminal Justice and Corrections* (Ottawa: Queen's Printer, 1969) at 61-63 (Chair: Roger Ouimet).

[756] The Supreme Court recently acknowledged much of this in dealing with strip-searches incidental to arrest. See *R. v. Golden*, [2001] S.C.J. No. 81, [2001] 3 S.C.R. 679 at para. 67, 159 C.C.C. (3d) 449 (S.C.C.).

[757] So, for example, it was only after the *Charter*, in *Cloutier v. Langlois*, [1990] S.C.J. No. 10, [1990] 1 S.C.R. 158 (S.C.C.), that the Supreme Court of Canada first addressed this power.

[758] See *Cloutier v. Langlois*, [1990] S.C.J. No. 10, [1990] 1 S.C.R. 158 at 180-81(S.C.C.); *R. v. Stillman*, [1997] S.C.J. No. 34, [1997] 1 S.C.R. 607 at para. 27 (S.C.C.).

[759] As the Court indicated in *R. v. Stillman*, [1997] S.C.J. No. 34, [1997] 1 S.C.R. 607 at para. 27 (S.C.C.): "No search, no matter how reasonable, may be upheld under this common law power where the arrest which gave rise to it was arbitrary or otherwise unlawful." *Ibid.*, at para. 27 (S.C.R.).

§3.277 The Supreme Court has made clear that as long as an arrest is lawful, the search incidental to arrest power arises. Triggering this power does not depend on the existence of any additional grounds beyond those justifying the arrest.[760] As a result, at least superficially, this search power does not seem to comply with the minimum constitutional requirements set down in *Hunter*. Nevertheless the Supreme Court has upheld this common law power, explaining that it is constitutionally "justifiable because the arrest itself requires reasonable and probable grounds (under s. 494 of the Code) or an arrest warrant (under s. 495)."[761] The exigencies inherent in arrest, which occasions an immediate need to secure weapons and evidence, make it sensible to dispense with the need for prior judicial authorization as a precondition for searches incidental to arrest.

§3.278 The fact that an arrest is lawful, however, is not determinative of the legality of a resulting search. To come under the authority of this common law power, the police must truly be searching for purposes relating to the arrest.[762] In other words, "the search must have been conducted as an 'incident' to the lawful arrest,"[763] in that one of the purposes for the search must be "the discovery of an object that may be a threat to the safety of the police, the accused or the public, or that may facilitate escape or act as evidence against the accused".[764] As the Supreme Court explained in *Caslake*:

> ... The restriction that the search must be "truly incidental" to the arrest means that the police must be attempting to achieve some valid purpose connected to the arrest. Whether such an objective exists will depend on what the police were looking for and why. There are both subjective and objective aspects to this issue. In my view, the police must have one of the purposes for a valid search incident to arrest in mind when the search is conducted. Further, the officer's belief that this purpose will be served by the search must be a reasonable one.[765]

§3.279 In *Caslake*, for example, the accused was arrested while driving his car. The vehicle was towed to a garage, across the street from the police detachment. Six hours later the arresting officer searched the vehicle. The search revealed $1,400 in cash and two small packages of cocaine. The accused was charged accordingly. When this search was challenged at trial the officer testified that it had not been undertaken to locate evidence. Rather, he maintained that the purpose of the search was to complete an inventory of the vehicle's condition and contents as mandated by RCMP policy. There was, however, no statutory or common law authority for such an inventory search. For the Court, even though this search could have been objectively justifiable as a search incident to arrest,

---

[760] *Cloutier v. Langlois*, [1990] S.C.J. No. 10, [1990] 1 S.C.R. 158 at 179-81 (S.C.C.).

[761] *R. v. Caslake*, [1998] S.C.J. No. 3, [1998] 1 S.C.R. 51 at para. 13 (S.C.C.). See also *R. v. Nolet*, [2010] S.C.J. No. 24, [2010] 1 S.C.R. 851, 2010 SCC 24 at para. 51 (S.C.C.).

[762] *R. v. Caslake*, [1998] S.C.J. No. 3, [1998] 1 S.C.R. 51 at para. 15 (S.C.C.).

[763] *R. v. Stillman*, [1997] S.C.J. No. 34, [1997] 1 S.C.R. 607 at para. 27 (S.C.C.).

[764] *Cloutier v. Langlois*, [1990] S.C.J. No. 10, [1990] 1 S.C.R. 158 at 186 (S.C.C.).

[765] *R. v. Caslake*, [1998] S.C.J. No. 3, [1998] 1 S.C.R. 51 at para. 19 (S.C.C.).

the absence of the requisite subjective mindset on the part of the officer conducting the search was fatal. Chief Justice Lamer explained:

> In my view, it would be contrary to the spirit of the *Charter*'s s. 8 guarantee of security against unreasonable searches or seizures to allow searches incident to arrest which do not meet both the subjective and objective criteria. This Court cannot characterize a search as being incidental to an arrest when the officer is actually acting for purposes unrelated to the arrest. That is the reason for the subjective element of the test. The objective element ensures that the police officer's belief that he or she has a legitimate reason to search is reasonable in the circumstances.[766]

§3.280 Due to these limitations, where a person is arrested for reasons other than the commission of an offence, the scope of the incidental search power will be circumscribed by the reasons for arrest. So, for example, where an individual is arrested while driving a car because of a warrant relating to outstanding traffic fines, the potential scope of any incidental search will be limited to safety concerns and will not extend to the discovery or preservation of evidence. This is because there is no offence for which the accused is being arrested and therefore no justification to search for evidence. In such a case, once the police have ensured their own safety, there could be nothing to justify searching any further.[767]

§3.281 In short, the scope of what is permissible by way of search incident to arrest is a function of the underlying justifications for this search power, namely ensuring the safety of the police, the person arrested and the public; and the discovery and preservation of evidence.[768] The extent to which the police may search under the authority of this power depends on the individual police officer's subjective view of how to best achieve these goals and the objective reasonableness of that belief in the circumstances. On a practical level, of course, the objective reasonableness of a police officer's actions will only become legally relevant if the search is ultimately challenged in court. In other words, it is ultimately the court's call whether the decision to search in a given case was objectively reasonable in the circumstances in light of the justifications for search incident to arrest. This approach has the benefit of flexibility but it also makes it difficult to provide very many hard and fast rules about search incidental to arrest. Nevertheless, a close reading of the case law does provide some essential guidance.

---

[766] *Ibid.*, at para. 21 (S.C.R.). See also *R. v. Nolet*, [2010] S.C.J. No. 24, [2010] 1 S.C.R. 851, 2010 SCC 24 at para. 53 (S.C.C.) (inventory search of tractor-trailer violated s. 8 even though earlier arrest for drug trafficking would have justified search as an incident to arrest).

[767] See *R. v. Caslake*, [1998] S.C.J. No. 3, [1998] 1 S.C.R. 51 at paras. 18, 22 (S.C.C.). See also *R. v. Belnavis*, [1996] O.J. No. 1853, 107 C.C.C. (3d) 195 at 213 (Ont. C.A.), affd on other grounds [1997] S.C.J. No. 81, [1997] 3 S.C.R. 341 (S.C.C.). See *e.g.*, *R. v. Bulmer*, [2005] S.J. No. 437, 198 C.C.C. (3d) 363 (Sask. C.A.) (search of vehicle following arrest of driver on outstanding warrant for seatbelt infraction could not be justified as a search incident to arrest and therefore violated s. 8 of the *Charter*).

[768] See *R. v. Caslake*, [1998] S.C.J. No. 3, [1998] 1 S.C.R. 51 at para. 17 (S.C.C.); *R. v. Nolet*, [2010] S.C.J. No. 24, [2010] 1 S.C.R. 851, 2010 SCC 24 at para. 49 (S.C.C.).

(a) **Searches of the Person**

§3.282 To begin, the person of the individual arrested can obviously be searched incidental to a lawful arrest. In *Cloutier v. Langlois*,[769] the Supreme Court endorsed the use of a "frisk" search which it described as a "relatively non-intrusive procedure: outside clothing is patted down to determine whether there is anything on the person of the arrested individual. Pockets may be examined but the clothing is not removed and no physical force is applied. The duration of the search is only a few seconds."[770] Of course, where there is an arrest, the detention itself will last much longer. It is the pat-down search that the Court expected would be very brief.

§3.283 There are strict limits, however, on the amount of interference with the person of an individual the search incident to arrest power will justify. Although the Supreme Court rejected a *Charter* challenge to legislation authorizing the police to fingerprint and photograph individuals they arrest,[771] it has been reluctant to use its authority to expand the common law search incident to arrest power to license more intrusive procedures.

§3.284 For example, in *R. v. Stillman*,[772] the Supreme Court of Canada declined a request that it expand this common law power to authorize the taking of dental impressions or bodily samples (*i.e.*, hair, blood, saliva or urine) from a person who is arrested. In coming to this conclusion, it stressed that the power to search as an incident of arrest is predicated on narrow grounds, and in particular on the need to preserve evidence.[773] Bodily impressions and samples, it noted "are usually in no danger of disappearing."[774] (The taking of body impressions and samples is now possible by warrant due to amendments to the *Criminal Code*, discussed above in Part 3(7)).

§3.285 Police are permitted, however, to conduct strip searches incidental to arrest in limited circumstances. A "strip search" is a search that involves "the removal or rearrangement of some or all of the clothing of a person so as to permit a visual inspection of a person's private areas, namely genitals, buttocks, breasts (in the case of a female), or undergarments."[775] Unlike the seizure of bodily samples, it is much easier to imagine circumstances in which the failure to strip search a person arrested could jeopardize the safety of both the police and

---

[769] [1990] S.C.J. No. 10, [1990] 1 S.C.R. 158 (S.C.C.).

[770] *Ibid.*, at 186 (S.C.R.).

[771] See *R. v. Beare; R. v. Higgins*, [1987] S.C.J. No. 92, [1988] 2 S.C.R. 387 (S.C.C.) and the discussion above, Part 3(7)(*d*).

[772] [1997] S.C.J. No. 34, [1997] 1 S.C.R. 607 (S.C.C.).

[773] *Ibid.*, at paras. 41-42, 49 (S.C.R.). Of course, there are statutory provisions addressing the seizure of breath samples for breathalyzer analysis in the impaired driving context (see s. 254(3)(*a*) and (*b*) of the *Criminal Code*, R.S.C. 1985, c. C-46) and the taking of hair, blood and saliva samples pursuant to the DNA warrant scheme (ss. 487.04 to 487.09 of the *Criminal Code*). Both are also discussed above in Part 3(7).

[774] *Ibid.*, at para. 49.

[775] *R. v. Golden*, [2001] S.C.J. No. 81, [2001] 3 S.C.R. 679 at para. 47, 159 C.C.C. (3d) 449 (S.C.C.).

other persons in police custody and potentially lead to the destruction of valuable evidence. As a result, in *R. v. Golden*[776] the Court rejected the suggestion that section 8 of the *Charter* required that strip searches always be preceded by a warrant.

§3.286 Nevertheless, in *Golden*, the Court acknowledged that the intrusiveness of such searches — which it described as "inherently humiliating and degrading ... regardless of the manner in which they are carried out" — required the imposition of additional safeguards.[777] The Court held that the police may only conduct a strip search following an arrest when, in addition to the grounds for a lawful arrest, they have reasonable and probable grounds to believe that a strip search is necessary in the circumstances to either secure a weapon or preserve evidence.[778] In addition, the Court held that in the absence of "exigent circumstances" strip searches should only be conducted in the privacy of a police station. Strip searches in the field are only justifiable where "there is a demonstrated necessity and urgency to search for weapons or objects that could be used to threaten the safety of the accused, the arresting officers or other individuals. The police would also have to show why it would have been unsafe to wait and conduct the strip search at the police station rather than in the field."[779]

§3.287 Finally, borrowing extensively from the legislative scheme in the United Kingdom, the Court identified a number of factors to be kept in mind in order to ensure that strip searches are carried out in a reasonable manner. The list includes concerns such as:[780]

- whether the search will be conducted in a manner that respects the health and safety of all involved;
- whether a supervisory officer authorized the search;
- whether steps have been taken to ensure that the officer carrying out the search is of the same gender as the person searched;
- whether the number of officers involved is no more than is reasonably necessary in the circumstances;
- whether any force used is the minimum necessary;
- whether the search is carried out so that no one other than those involved in the search can observe the search;
- whether the search is conducted as quickly as possible and in a way that ensures that the person is not completely undressed at any one time;
- whether the search involves only visual inspection of genital and anal areas without physical contact; and

---

[776] [2001] S.C.J. No. 81, [2001] 3 S.C.R. 679, 159 C.C.C. (3d) 449 (S.C.C.).
[777] *Ibid.*, at paras. 87, 90 (S.C.R.).
[778] *Ibid.*, at para. 99 (S.C.R.).
[779] *Ibid.*, at para. 102 (S.C.R.).
[780] *Ibid.*, at para. 101 (S.C.R.).

• if visual inspection reveals the presence of a weapon or evidence secreted in a body cavity (not including the mouth) will the individual be given the option to remove the object himself or herself or have the object removed by a trained medical profession.

§3.288 Strip searches are different than body cavity searches. As the Supreme Court made clear in *Golden*, body cavity searches are "more intrusive" as they "involve a *physical* inspection of the detainee's genital or anal regions".[781] Beyond this, however, the Supreme Court has quite deliberately refrained from reaching out to decide whether search incident to arrest could ever justify a body cavity search, choosing instead to wait until that question is directly before it.[782] That said, it seems extraordinarily unlikely that the Court would extend search incident to arrest this far. It will be remembered, for example, that in *Stillman* the Court refrained from expanding this power to include the authority to seize bodily samples. In doing so it emphasized the intrusiveness of such seizures.[783] Given that body cavity searches are comparatively far more invasive, it is difficult to imagine the Court coming to a different conclusion with respect to them. The absence of such a common law power, combined with the fact that there is presently no statutory authority to conduct such searches, means that such searches are constitutionally impermissible.[784] As a result, the only option that might be available to the authorities when an individual is believed to be secreting contraband inside their body is to conduct a passive "bedpan vigil". Doing so, however, requires that the authorities have an existing legal basis to detain the person, such as an arrest based on reasonable and probable grounds that the person is in possession of a controlled substance.[785]

§3.289 Finally, it should be noted that in *Golden* the Court explained that while "the mouth is a body cavity, it is not encompassed by the term 'body cavity search'. Searches of the mouth do not involve the same privacy concerns, al-

---

[781] *Ibid.*, at para. 47 (S.C.R.) [emphasis added].

[782] *R. v. Stillman*, [1997] S.C.J. No. 34, [1997] 1 S.C.R. 607 at para. 87 (S.C.C.). See also *R. v. Simmons*, [1988] S.C.J. No. 86, [1988] 2 S.C.R. 495 at 517 (S.C.C.). See also *R. v. Greffe*, [1990] S.C.J. No. 32, [1990] 1 S.C.R. 755 (S.C.C.) (where the Supreme Court decided a s. 8 case involving a rectal search exclusively on the basis of s. 24(2), the s. 8 violation being assumed).

[783] *R. v. Stillman*, [1997] S.C.J. No. 34, [1997] 1 S.C.R. 607 at para. 42 (S.C.C.).

[784] Of course, statutory authority would be the starting point. Any legislative scheme would also have to meet the other requirements of s. 8. In that regard, the Supreme Court said the following in *R. v. Golden*, [2001] S.C.J. No. 81, [2001] 3 S.C.R. 679 at para. 87, 159 C.C.C. (3d) 449 (S.C.C.):"More intrusive searches of the person such as this involve a higher degree of infringement of personal dignity and privacy as well as additional medical concerns and, accordingly, a higher degree of justification will be required before such a search can be carried out. In addition, more intrusive searches will be subject to greater constraints as to the manner in which they may be reasonably performed."

[785] See *e.g.*, *R. v. Monney*, [1999] S.C.J. No. 18, [1999] 1 S.C.R. 652 (S.C.C.), rejecting a s. 8 challenge where customs officials detained a suspected alimentary canal smuggler entering Canada for the purpose of conducting a so-called "bedpan vigil". In that case, however, there was a specific provision in the *Customs Act*, R.S.C. 1985, c. 1 (2nd Supp.), that the Court said authorized this detention and search. See discussion above, Part 2(5)(*d*)(iii)b.

though they may raise other health concerns for both the detainee and for those conducting the search."[786] In drawing this distinction, the Court may have been influenced by *obiter* in one of its earlier decisions, which suggests that where a police officer is possessed of reliable and "very specific information" that a person is secreting evidence in his or her mouth, it would not be contrary to section 8 of the *Charter* for police to explore that possibility, including through the use of a choke hold to prevent that person from swallowing the evidence.[787]

(b)   Searches Beyond the Person

§3.290 More difficult is deciding how far beyond the person of an individual the search incidental to arrest may extend. American courts have long struggled with this question. The clearest guidance offered by the United States Supreme Court is to indicate that police have "ample justification" to search "the area from within which [the arrestee] ... might gain possession of a weapon or destructible evidence".[788] That Court noted, however, that there is "no comparable justification ... for routinely searching any room other than that in which an arrest occurs — or, for that matter, for searching through all the desk drawers or other closed or concealed areas in that room itself."[789] This was unfortunately the high water mark of clarity on this question. Since then, mostly due to exceptions carved out in the context of automobile searches, the American jurisprudence has provided less than certain guidance on this question.[790]

§3.291 The Supreme Court of Canada has avoided setting down categorical rules on the potential scope of searches incidental to arrest. Instead, it stressed the importance of examining two variables: the timing and location of the search relative to the arrest that is said to justify it. As the Court explained in *R. v. Caslake*:[791]

> Delay and distance do not automatically preclude a search from being incidental to arrest, but they may cause the court to draw a negative inference. However, that inference may be rebutted by a proper explanation.[792]

The Court deliberately refrained, however, from setting down a firm deadline. Instead, it indicated that:

> As a general rule, searches that are truly incidental to arrest will usually occur within a reasonable period of time after the arrest. A substantial delay

---

[786] *R. v. Golden*, [2001] S.C.J. No. 81, [2001] 3 S.C.R. 679 at para. 47, 159 C.C.C. (3d) 449 (S.C.C.).

[787] *R. v. Collins*, [1987] S.C.J. No. 15, [1987] 1 S.C.R. 265 at 278 (S.C.C.).

[788] *Chimel v. California*, 395 U.S. 752 at 763 (1969).

[789] *Ibid.*

[790] See *e.g.*, *New York v. Bolton*, 453 U.S. 454 (1981) (holding that where a police officer has lawfully arrested the occupant of an automobile, he may conduct a search of the passenger compartment of the vehicle as an incident thereto — in *Bolton*, the four occupants were outside of the car and in police custody when the officer returned to the vehicle to search the vehicle, including searching the pocket of a jacket found in the car).

[791] [1998] S.C.J. No. 3, [1998] 1 S.C.R. 51 (S.C.C.).

[792] *Ibid.*, at para. 25 (S.C.R.).

does not mean that the search is automatically unlawful, but it may cause the court to draw an inference that the search is not sufficiently connected to the arrest. Naturally, the strength of the inference will depend on the length of the delay, and can be defeated by a reasonable explanation for the delay.[793]

§3.292 So, for example, in *Caslake* the Supreme Court suggested that the six-hour delay in searching the vehicle in that case, would not, in and of itself, have been problematic. This was because there were only two police officers on duty in the rural area where the arrest occurred, with one of them preoccupied with other policing commitments. These are circumstances that the Supreme Court suggested could justify the long delay between arrest and search.[794] (Recall that the problem with the search in *Caslake* was that it was undertaken to complete an inventory of the vehicle's contents due to RCMP policy and not for any purposes related to the arrest itself.)

§3.293 The Ontario Court of Appeal has even held that a search "incidental" to arrest may sometimes precede the formal arrest, provided that the authorities have the requisite grounds to arrest at the time of the search.[795] In other words, if the police have the grounds to arrest (for example, because there are reasonable and probable grounds to believe that the subject is in possession of a controlled substance) then they may search that person under the authority of this common law power. If a search reveals evidence or contraband that fortifies the officer's grounds, then the arrest can follow. If it does not, then the police may decide to let the person go. In either case, the search is only legally permissible where the police have the requisite reasonable and probable grounds to arrest *before* embarking on the search. The results can never be used to justify a search that was undertaken on the bases of deficient grounds.[796] Finally, it should be noted that if the delay between search and arrest becomes too great, a court might subsequently view the search as too attenuated from the arrest to be justified under the search "incident" to arrest power.[797]

§3.294 The distance factor dictates that the greater the physical separation between an arrest and the location being searched, the more difficult it will become to justify a search as being "incidental" to that arrest. Many cases will be obvious. For example, where an individual is arrested while holding a bag,[798]

---

[793] *Ibid.*, at para. 24 (S.C.R.).

[794] *Ibid.*, at para. 28 (S.C.R.). See also *R. v. Nolet*, [2010] S.C.J. No. 24, [2010] 1 S.C.R. 851, 2010 SCC 24 at para. 50 (S.C.C.) (two-hour delay from arrest to search of tractor-trailer not problematic).

[795] *R. v. DeBot*, [1986] O.J. No. 994, 30 C.C.C. (3d) 207 at 223-25 (Ont. C.A.), affd (1989), [1989] S.C.J. No. 118, [1989] 2 S.C.R. 1140, 52 C.C.C. (3d) 193 (S.C.C.) but without addressing this discrete issue.

[796] *Ibid.*

[797] See *e.g.*, *R. v. Tomaso*, [1989] O.J. No. 593, 70 C.R. (3d) 152 (Ont. C.A.).

[798] See *R. v. Clough*, [2000] B.C.J. No. 2618 at para. 32, 2000 BCPC 160 (B.C. Prov. Ct.) (search of handbag upheld under search incidental to arrest power, "as [the accused] was holding on to the bag at the time of the arrest"; *R. v. Gallant*, [2006] N.B.J. No. 138, 2006 NBQB 114 (N.B.Q.B.) (search of bag carried by accused at time of arrest upheld under search incidental to arrest power); *R. v. Gurr*, [2007] B.C.J. No. 1480, 2007 BCSC 979 (B.C.S.C.) (same); *R. v.*

purse,[799] knapsack,[800] briefcase,[801] suitcase[802] or package,[803] an incidental search of such receptacles is easily justified by their physical proximity and connection to the person being arrested.

§3.295 Much more difficult are searches of electronic devices that a person is carrying when arrested, for example, a cell phone, a smartphone or a personal computer. Police are undoubtedly entitled to seize such items incidental to arrest where they have reason to believe that they may afford evidence relevant to the offence. What remains somewhat unsettled is whether the police can then proceed to examine the data contained on such devices pursuant to the search incidental to arrest power or whether this sort of further probing should be preceded by a warrant.

§3.296 There are conflicting decisions on this important question. Some courts have held that provided the police subjectively believe that such a device contains evidence and that belief is objectively reasonable in the circumstances, its contents may be searched incidental to arrest.[804] However, the vast majority of

---

Miller, [2003] O.J. No. 3544 (Ont. C.J.) (same); *R. v. Boudreau*, [2006] B.C.J. No. 1354, 2006 BCSC 914 (B.C.S.C.) (search of bag located in backseat of car driven by accused at time of her arrest upheld under search incidental to arrest power).

799   See, *R. v. Andrew*, [1986] B.C.J. No. 3233, 26 C.C.C. (3d) 111 (B.C.S.C.) and *R. v. Martens*, [2004] B.C.J. No. 2300, 2004 BCSC 1450 (B.C.S.C.), both upholding searches of purses carried at the time of arrest under the incidental search power.

800   See *R. v. Lewis*, [2007] N.S.J. No. 18, 217 C.C.C. (3d) 82 (N.S.C.A.) (search of backpack worn by accused arrested for narcotics possession properly searched pursuant to search incidental to arrest power); *R. v. Dickinson*, [2005] B.C.J. No. 311, 2005 BCPC 41 (B.C. Prov. Ct.) (at police detachment, police search backpack worn by accused at time of arrest, search upheld under search incident to arrest power).

801   See *R. v. Mohamad*, [2004] O.J. No. 279, 182 C.C.C. (3d) 97 (Ont. C.A.) (upholding search of briefcase incidental to accused's arrest).

802   See *R. v. Kang-Brown*, [2005] A.J. No. 1110, 31 C.R. (6th) 231, 203 C.C.C. (3d) 132 (Alta. Q.B.), revd on other grounds [2008] S.C.J. No. 18, [2008] 1 S.C.R. 456 (S.C.C.) (search of traveller's luggage following his arrest upheld under search incidental to arrest power); *R. v. Martens*, [2004] B.C.J. No. 2300, 2004 BCSC 1450 (B.C.S.C.) (upholding a search of two suitcases located in the accused's car at the time of her arrest); *R. v. Hoang*, [2000] A.J. No. 1630, 284 A.R. 201 (Alta. Prov. Ct.) (upholding search of suitcase, after accused consented to dog sniff of his luggage and dog responded positively for narcotics in suitcase); *R. v. Rajaratnam*, [2005] A.J. No. 1346, 388 A.R. 69 (Alta. Q.B.) (same); *R. v. Mercer*, [2004] A.J. No. 634, 362 A.R. 136 (Alta. Prov. Ct.) (search of luggage belonging to accused upheld following his arrest based on a positive reaction by drug-sniffer dog to luggage).

803   See *R. v. Park*, [1999] N.W.T.J. No. 105 (N.W.T. Terr. Ct.) (accused arrested for possession of drugs, search of package carried by accused at time of arrest and believed to contain drugs upheld under search incidental to arrest power).

804   See *R. v. Giles*, [2007] B.C.J. No. 2918, 2007 BCSC 1147 (B.C.S.C.) (upholding the retrieval of emails from a BlackBerry® device seized incidental to arrest as lawful under the search incidental to arrest power, rejecting an argument that this required a warrant). See also *R. v. Fearon*, [2010] O.J. No. 5745 at para. 51, 2010 ONCJ 645 (Ont. C.J.) (upholding search of cell phone's contents incidental to arrest, emphasizing that police had basis to believe phone contained evidence of offence and rejecting the claim that a warrant was necessary, noting that: "the expectation of privacy in the information contained in the cell phone is more akin to what might be disclosed by searching a purse, a wallet, a notebook or briefcase found in the same circumstances"); *R. v. Otchere-Badu*, [2010] O.J. No. 901, 2010 ONSC 1059 (Ont. S.C.J.) (same). But see *R. v. Polius*, [2009] O.J. No. 3074, 196 C.R.R. (2d) 288 (Ont. S.C.J.) (holding

courts that have considered the issue have tended to hold that anything more than a cursory inspection of such devices, for the purpose of quickly assessing whether a device may have evidentiary significance and should therefore be seized, requires a warrant.[805] The Ontario Court of Appeal appears to be leaning strongly toward the latter view. In *R. v. Manley*,[806] the Court rejected the appellant's claim that police violated his section 8 *Charter* rights when, following his arrest, they examined the contents of his cell phone. In upholding this search, the Court emphasized that the accused had been arrested for break and enter and, when arrested, was in possession of a number of unusual and suspicious items. The police had information from a confidential informant that in the past the accused had stolen cell phones. According to the Court, ownership of the cell phone was relevant to the offences for which the accused had been arrested. That combination of circumstances was said to provide the police with a lawful basis for conducting a cursory search of the cell phone to determine whether it had been stolen.[807] It was during just such a search that police discovered an incriminating photograph on the phone. On these facts, the Court upheld the trial judge's decision that the cursory search of the cell phone was lawful. In doing so, however, the Court emphasized that "in a case where there was no reason to doubt the arrested party's ownership of the phone and no link between ownership and the offence for which the person was arrested, a search of the stored data in the phone could not be justified on the basis that the police were simply trying to determine who owned the phone."[808]

§3.297 In *Manley*, the Ontario Court of Appeal expressly refrained from pronouncing more generally on the scope of police authority to search the data in smartphones or cell phones seized incidental to arrest. Nevertheless, in *obiter* Justice Sharpe made the following important observation:

> ... I would observe it is apparent that the traditional rules defining the powers of the police to conduct a search incident to arrest have to be interpreted and applied in a manner that takes into account the facts of modern technology. While I would not apply *Polius* in the particular circumstances of this case, I am far from persuaded that *Polius* was wrongly decided or that it ought to be overruled. Cell phones and other similar handheld communication devices in common use have the capacity to store vast amounts of highly sensitive personal, private and confidential information – all manner of private voice, text and e-mail communications, detailed personal contact lists, agendas, diaries and personal photographs. An open-ended power to search without a warrant all the stored data in any cell phone found in the

that anything more than a cursory examination of such a device exceeds the search incidental to arrest power and, absent exigent circumstances, requires a search warrant). See also *R. v. Finnikin*, [2009] O.J. No. 6016, 2009 CanLII 82187 (Ont. S.C.J.) (same).

805 See *R. v. Polius*, [2009] O.J. No. 3074, 196 C.R.R. (2d) 288 at paras. 52-57 (Ont. S.C.J.). See also *R. v. Finnikin*, [2009] O.J. No. 6016, 2009 CanLII 82187 (Ont. S.C.J.) (same); *R. v. McBean*, [2011] O.J. No. 517, 2011 ONSC 878 (Ont. S.C.J.) (same).

806 [2011] O.J. No. 642, 2011 ONCA 128 (Ont. C.A.).

807 *Ibid.*, at para. 37 (O.J.).

808 *Ibid.*, at para. 38 (O.J.).

possession of any arrested person clearly raises the spectre of a serious and significant invasion of the *Charter*-protected privacy interests of arrested persons. If the police have reasonable grounds to believe that the search of a cell phone seized upon arrest would yield evidence of the offence, the prudent course is for them to obtain a warrant authorizing the search.[809]

§3.298 We agree. Given the staggering amount of personal information that such devices can potentially store, combined with the fact that they will often also contain information that implicates the privacy interests of third parties (for example, email communications) the analogy between items such as bags, suitcases or purses is inapt.[810] It remains to be seen how the Supreme Court will ultimately decide this question. Given the potential privacy implications, however, it would make much sense for the Court to follow the approach it took in *Stillman* and insist that before such a profound intrusion on privacy can be permitted, a judicial officer should be required to decide whether there are reasonable grounds to believe that such a device contains relevant evidence.

(i)   Searches of Premises (Feeney Warrants)

§3.299 If a person is arrested at home[811] or at a place of business, an extensive search of the location of the arrest is easily justified by the incidental search power. In light of this, however, police could easily time arrests to enable them to search private premises without a warrant. It was this possibility that ultimately caused the Supreme Court of Canada to revisit the common law authority of the police to enter private premises to affect an arrest.

§3.300 In *R. v. Feeney*,[812] the Supreme Court concluded that section 8 required that before the police enter a dwelling to carry out an arrest they must first obtain prior judicial approval. A judicial officer must assess not only whether there are reasonable and probable grounds to arrest, but also whether there are grounds to believe that the individual to be arrested will be located in the place to be entered. The Court recognized, however, that this warrant requirement does not apply when the police are in "hot pursuit" of someone who they have lawful grounds to arrest who then flees into a private dwelling. Ultimately, Parliament responded to *Feeney* with a legislative scheme for the issuance of warrants to enter private places to carry out arrest. This requirement was made subject to a general exigency exception, which allows the police to enter without a warrant in a variety of situations, beyond hot pursuits, where it would be impractical to expect the police to pause and obtain a warrant.[813] (The issuance of

---

[809]   *Ibid.*, at para. 39.

[810]   See generally, *R. v. Morelli*, [2010] S.C.J. No. 8, [2010] 1 S.C.R. 253 at paras. 1-3 (S.C.C.) (noting the exceptionally invasive and indiscriminate nature of computer searches).

[811]   See *e.g.*, *R. v. Kyllo*, [1999] B.C.J. No. 717 (B.C.S.C.).

[812]   [1997] S.C.J. No. 49, [1997] 2 S.C.R. 13 (S.C.C.).

[813]   See *Criminal Code*, R.S.C. 1985, c. C-46, ss. 529 and 529(1) introduced in response. The concept of "exigent circumstances" is discussed more fully above. See Part 3(2).

warrants authorizing entry into a dwelling-house to effect an arrest are discussed in detail in Chapter 2, Part 4(4)(*g*).)

§3.301 The Ontario Court of Appeal in *R. v. Golub*[814] subsequently addressed the effect of *Feeney* on the authority to search a residence incidental to an arrest. In *Golub*, the police had good reason to believe that the defendant was in possession of an illegal automatic sub-machine gun. They arrived at his residence, made telephone contact and ultimately directed him outside. He complied, but locked the door of his apartment, even after being told not to do so. When asked if anyone else was inside, he responded ambiguously. Police arrested and frisked him but did not find any weapons. Concerned that an unsecured weapon might be inside the residence, possibly along with an identified third party, police entered the residence (without a warrant) to carry out a "protective sweep". No one else was inside the apartment, but the police did find a sub-machine gun hidden on a bed beneath some covers.

§3.302 The Court noted that "searches of a home as an incident of an arrest, like entries of a home to effect an arrest, are now generally prohibited subject to exceptional circumstances where the law enforcement interest is so compelling that it overrides the individual's right to privacy within the home."[815] After citing the ancillary powers doctrine, the Court concluded that the search in this case was lawful and not contrary to section 8. In doing so, the Court recognized a "protective sweep" power associated with arrests that take place at or near a related residence. The court explained the parameters of this power as follows:

> ... where immediate action is required to secure the safety of those at the scene of an arrest, a search conducted in a manner which is consistent with the preservation of the safety of those at the scene is justified. If, in order to secure the safety of those at the scene, entry into and search of a residence is necessary, I would hold that the risk of physical harm to those at the scene of the arrest constitutes exceptional circumstances justifying the warrantless entry and search of the residence. The search must be conducted for the purpose of protecting those at the scene and must be conducted in a reasonable manner which is consistent with that purpose.

> . . .

> ... If the circumstances of an arrest give rise to a legitimate cause for concern with respect to the safety of those at the scene, reasonable steps to allay that concern may be taken. The nature of the apprehended risk, the potential consequences of not taking protective measures, the availability of alternative measures, and the likelihood of the contemplated danger actually existing, must all be considered. The officers making this assessment must, of course, do so on the spot with no time for careful reflection. In my opinion, a reasonable suspicion, based on the particular circumstances of the arrest, that someone is on the other side of a closed door with a loaded sub-machine gun, or that someone is lying injured on the other side of that door,

---

[814] [1997] O.J. No. 3097, 117 C.C.C. (3d) 193 (Ont. C.A.).
[815] *Ibid.*, at para. 41 (C.C.C.).

creates a legitimate cause for concern justifying entry and search of the apartment for persons.[816]

(ii)   Searches of Automobiles

§3.303 In Canada, unlike in the United States, searches of automobiles incidental to an arrest are not subject to any special rules. Rather, as the Supreme Court of Canada explained in *R. v. Caslake*:[817]

> The right to search a car incident to arrest and the scope of that search will depend on a number of factors, including the basis for the arrest, the location of the motor vehicle in relation to the place of the arrest, and other relevant circumstances.[818]

For example, in *Caslake*, the accused was arrested while driving his car. That vehicle had been observed in close proximity to the location where marijuana was discovered, which led to the arrest. For the Supreme Court these factors provided a sufficient connection between the arrest and the vehicle so as to justify the police in searching it.[819]

§3.304 Quite obviously, when an accused is arrested while driving or riding in a car a search of the entirety of the vehicle may very well be justified. Ultimately, however, this will depend on the reasons for the arrest. For example, if the police arrest an individual for possession of a controlled substance (as they did in *Caslake*), the possibility that drugs might be secreted within the vehicle will likely be enough to justify an extensive search, including closed compartments like the glove box and trunk, and inside bags, luggage or any other closed containers found within the vehicle. [820] In contrast, as noted above, if an arrest is undertaken because of an outstanding traffic warrant,[821] or for an offence that does not in the circumstances justify a search to locate or preserve evidence,[822]

---

[816]   *Ibid.*, at paras. 46 and 48 (C.C.C.).
[817]   [1998] S.C.J. No. 3, [1998] 1 S.C.R. 51 (S.C.C.).
[818]   *Ibid.*, at para. 23 (S.C.R.).
[819]   *Ibid.*, at para. 26 (S.C.R.). See also *R. v. Nolet*, [2010] S.C.J. No. 24, [2010] 1 S.C.R. 851, 2010 SCC 24 (S.C.C.). Recall that in both *Caslake* and *Nolet*, the difficulty was that the officer conducting the search did not subjectively avert to evidence collection in carrying out the search. Instead, the motivation was exclusively the completion of a vehicle inventory form.
[820]   See *e.g.*, *R. v. Polashek*, [1999] O.J. No. 968, 134 C.C.C. (3d) 187 (Ont. C.A.) (arrest of driver for possession of marijuana, where personal search reveals cannabis, was held to justify search of vehicle and its trunk). See also *R. v. Alkins*, [2007] O.J. No. 1348, 218 C.C.C. (3d) 97 (Ont. C.A.) (arrest of driver and vehicle occupants for weapons offences was held to justify search of vehicle, including the trunk).
[821]   See above, Part 4(2).
[822]   See *R. v. Mitchell*, [2005] N.B.J. No. 573, 204 C.C.C. (3d) 289 at para. 19, 36 C.R. (6th) 289 (N.B.C.A.) (After being stopped by police, the appellant gave a false name and was arrested for obstructing justice. The police proceeded to search the appellant's vehicle, believing that it would contain drugs. It did and the appellant was charged accordingly. On appeal, the Court indicated that the vehicle search was not authorized under the search incidental to arrest power, given that the purpose of the search did not relate to the reason for the arrest.); *R. v. Caron*, [2011] B.C.J. No. 200 at paras. 43-45, 2011 BCCA 56 (B.C.C.A.) (Accused arrested for dangerous driving, while looking in glove box for vehicle registration officer finds digital camera.

then once an individual is securely in police custody, a search of the vehicle would not seem to be justified because there really is no evidence relating to the reasons for arrest that is in need of discovery and preservation.

(3) Protective Searches During Investigative Detentions

§3.305 The common law power to detain for investigative purposes was explained in detail in Chapter 2, Part 4(3)(*a*). It will be remembered that in *R. v. Mann*,[823] the Supreme Court of Canada applied the ancillary powers doctrine to recognize an investigative detention power at common law. In short, *Mann* now supplies the legal authority to briefly detain for investigative purposes where, in the totality of circumstances, a police officer has reasonable grounds to suspect a clear nexus between the individual being detained and a recent or ongoing criminal offence.

§3.306 Although *Mann* was the first time that the Supreme Court passed on the authority of the police to detain for investigative purposes, that power originated 10 years earlier with the Ontario Court of Appeal's decision in *R. v. Simpson*.[824] *Simpson* applied the ancillary powers doctrine to create a detention power but said nothing about a corresponding search power. In the decade after *Simpson*, every appellate court in the country eventually adopted the detention power that it recognized.[825] Some of these courts went even further and created a corresponding power to search those who are detained for investigative purposes.[826] *Mann* thankfully addresses both the detention and the search power. In particular, the judgment places significant constraints on the search power,[827] limitations that were noticeably absent from some of the provincial appellate court judgments that preceded it.[828] As a result, the pre-*Mann* case law on the power

---

Officer proceeds to look at photos on the camera — in purported hope of finding a photograph of the speedometer at excessive speed. Instead, officer sees photo of accused and others holding firearms. This precipitates a more extensive search of vehicle's trunk, where officer locates large quantity of cash and handgun. Court holds that search of digital camera not authorized incidental to arrest, belief that digital camera would contain evidence of driving offence not objectively reasonable.).

[823] [2004] S.C.J. No. 49, [2004] 3 S.C.R. 59 (S.C.C.).

[824] [1993] O.J. No. 308, 79 C.C.C. (3d) 482 (Ont. C.A.).

[825] For a discussion of developments relating to investigative detention between *R. v. Simpson*, [1993] O.J. No. 308, 79 C.C.C. (3d) 482 (Ont. C.A.) and *R. v. Mann*, [2004] S.C.J. No. 49, [2004] 3 S.C.R. 59 (S.C.C.), see James Stribopoulos, "A Failed Experiment? Investigative Detention: Ten Years Later" (2003) 41 Alta. L. Rev. 335.

[826] James Stribopoulos, "A Failed Experiment? Investigative Detention: Ten Years Later" (2003) 41 Alta. L. Rev. 335 at 360-72.

[827] The Court does not expressly address s. 8 of the *Charter*. Nevertheless, it is a safe assumption that given the obligation to develop the common law in accordance with minimum *Charter* standards that the search power recognized in *R. v. Mann*, [2004] S.C.J. No. 49, [2004] 3 S.C.R. 59 (S.C.C.) must meet these standards. For a detailed discussion of why a protective search power like that recognized in *Mann* is justifiable under s. 8 of the *Charter*, see James Stribopoulos, "A Failed Experiment? Investigative Detention: Ten Years Later" (2003) 41 Alta. L. Rev. 335 at 368-72.

[828] Some provincial appellate courts failed to draw any distinction between the sort of intrusive probing for weapons and evidence permitted by the search incidental to arrest power and the au-

to search incidental to an investigative detention must be applied with great caution.

§3.307 In *Mann*, the Supreme Court held that where an individual is lawfully detained for investigative purposes, that person may also be subject to a limited protective pat-down search. According to the Court, "[s]uch a search power does not exist as a matter of course; the officer must believe on reasonable grounds that his or her own safety, or the safety of others, is at risk."[829]

§3.308 The Court concluded that the police had the requisite grounds to conduct a protective pat-down of Mann, who was detained a short distance away from a reported break and enter in progress. He very closely matched the description of the suspect. As a result, the detention in *Mann* was lawful.[830] With respect to the search, the Court said the following:

> There was a logical possibility that the appellant, suspected on reasonable grounds of having recently committed a break-and-enter, was in possession of break-and-enter tools, which could be used as weapons. The encounter also occurred just after midnight and there were no other people in the area. On balance, the officer was justified in conducting a pat-down search for protective purposes.[831]

§3.309 The police violated section 8 of the *Charter*, however, by reaching inside Mann's pocket and removing a baggie containing marijuana. In coming to this conclusion, the Court emphasized that the "trial judge found as a fact that 'there [was] nothing from which [he could] infer that it was reasonable to proceed beyond a pat down search for security reasons'."[832] In other words, further probing beyond a pat-down of a suspect is only justifiable where a police officer feels something during the initial protective search that raises reasonably based safety concerns.[833]

§3.310 Unfortunately, *Mann* left a great many issues relating to the investigative detention power unresolved, including a number of important details regard-

---

thority to search incidental to an investigative detention. See *e.g.*, *R. v. Lake*, [1996] S.J. No. 886, 113 C.C.C. (3d) 208 (Sask. C.A.).

[829] *R. v. Mann*, [2004] S.C.J. No. 49, [2004] 3 S.C.R. 59 at para. 40 (S.C.C.).

[830] *Ibid.*, at para. 47 (S.C.R.).

[831] *Ibid.*, at para. 48 (S.C.R.).

[832] *Ibid.*, at para. 49 (S.C.R.).

[833] See *R. v. Duong*, [2006] B.C.J. No. 1452 at para. 56, 142 C.R.R. (2d) 261(B.C.C.A.) upholding a search where a police officer began with a pat-down but then explored inside the detainee's pocket. The Court emphasized that: "In this case, the search progressed beyond a basic 'pat down' only when the officer felt a "hard" object that could be a weapon." See also *R. v. Greaves*, [2004] B.C.J. No. 1953, 189 C.C.C. (3d) 305 (B.C.C.A.), concluding that s. 8 of the *Charter* was violated when police exceeded the protective search power by searching inside the appellant's pockets, cigarette case and cell phone phonebook to obtain information to confirm the detainee's identity. *Ibid.*, at paras. 60-72 (C.C.C.). But see *R. v. White*, [2007] O.J. No. 1605, 85 O.R. (3d) 407 (Ont. C.A.), where the Court concluded that a police officer was justified in seizing a detainee's cell phone incidental to an investigative detention, where the detainee was speaking on the phone when police approached him and police overheard him say "they're here now" – Court concluded officer had safety justification for seizure, preventing detainee from summoning assistance.

ing the protective search power.[834] The Court undoubtedly felt constrained by its institutional obligation to only decide those questions raised by the case directly under consideration. Unfortunately, this meant that definitive answers for some rather important practical questions regarding the incidental search power remain to be decided in some future case.

§3.311 For example, the Court failed to address how the police are entitled to respond if they have well-founded safety concerns when detaining someone who happens to be carrying a bag or driving a car. Are the police entitled to search inside the bag[835] or examine the interior of a car to locate potential weapons? And, if so, how extensive can these sorts of "protective" searches be?[836]

§3.312 The Court's choice of language in describing the grounds necessary to conduct a pat-down search is also problematic. In noting that the search power created was not to be an automatic part of every investigative detention, the Court relied on the U.S. Supreme Court's decision in *Terry v. Ohio*.[837] That case concluded that pat-down searches are reasonable under the Fourth Amendment if the detaining officer "has reason to believe he is dealing with an armed and dangerous individual."[838] Unfortunately, the Supreme Court bundled the language used in that decision with the Canadian term "reasonable grounds". As a result, in two distinct places, the judgment in *Mann* indicates that a protective pat-down search is only permitted where a police officer has "reasonable

---

[834] These issues are canvassed in detail in Chapter 2, Part 4(3)(*a*)(ii). See generally, James Stribopoulos, "The Limits of Judicially Created Police Powers: Investigative Detention After *Mann*" (2007) 45 Crim. L.Q. 299.

[835] See *e.g., R. v. Peters*, [2007] A.J. No. 560, 155 C.R.R. (2d) 324 (Alta. C.A.) where the appellant was lawfully detained based on a gun call. An initial cursory look inside the appellant's knapsack revealed no weapons. A second officer testified that he had lingering concerns about the knapsack, so he searched it more carefully. This search revealed marijuana but no weapons. The Court upheld both searches as justified under the protective search power. But see *R. v. Dufault*, [2009] A.J. No. 285, 448 A.R. 365 at para. 15 (Alta. C.A.) (suggesting in *obiter* that the search of a backpack is not permissible incidental to an investigative detention).

[836] In a recent decision, the Ontario Court of Appeal refused to interfere on a Crown appeal where a trial judge found a *Charter* violation based on a search inside a motor vehicle. The two accused were lawfully detained when police responded to a 911 gun call. An initial pat-down search of each man came up negative. The trial judge concluded that, without more, a search inside the car was not justified. See *R. v. Batzer*, [2005] O.J. No. 3929, 200 C.C.C. (3d) 330 (Ont. C.A.). But see *R. v. Calderon*, [2004] O.J. No. 3474, 188 C.C.C. (3d) 481 at para. 78 (Ont. C.A.), although the majority finds that a search of the vehicle was not justified in this case, it implies that such a search could be justified if police safety as opposed to evidence acquisition is the motivation. Also see *R. v. Plummer*, [2011] O.J. No. 2034 at para. 77, 2011 ONCA 350 (Ont. C.A.), wherein the Court upheld the search of a vehicle interior Sharpe J.A. in a concurring judgment in which Laskin J.A. joined, explained: "a modest extension of the *Mann* pat-down search was justified in this case. Although the officers had the appellant under their temporary control, the situation was fluid. The appellant's earlier actions, when he appeared to conceal something in the vehicle, combined with the Officer Safety Alert indicating that he might be carrying a gun, gave rise to a legitimate serious concern that he had immediate access to a weapon that he could use if the officers were to simply release him and return to their own vehicle." See generally, Scott Latimer, "The Expanded Scope of Search Incident to Investigative Detention" (2007) 48 C.R. (6th) 201.

[837] 392 U.S. 1 (1968).

[838] *Ibid.*, at 27.

grounds to believe" that his or her safety or that of others is at risk.[839] This language seems to import the standard for conventional arrests, which makes little sense.[840] If the police have such grounds, they could arrest a suspect on a charge of weapons dangerous and then conduct a far more probing search.[841] It seems as though the Court misspoke. A protective search power that is prefaced on reasonable grounds *to believe* that a detainee is in possession of weapons provides police with virtually no added protection beyond that which they already have pursuant to the search incidental to arrest power. Given this, and for the sake of coherence, the accompanying search power, like the detention power itself, should be prefaced on reasonable grounds *to suspect* that an individual being lawfully detained is armed. The Crown in *Mann* responded to this apparent error by filing a motion for a rehearing and submitting suggested revisions for the problematic paragraphs.[842] Unfortunately, the Court dismissed that motion without reasons.[843]

§3.313 It was three years before the Supreme Court revisited investigative detention and the incidental search power. In *R. v. Clayton*,[844] the Court concluded that the police lawfully stopped the vehicle in which the two respondents were travelling. The police had responded to a 911 call that reported a group of men were brandishing firearms in a parking lot from which the respondents' vehicle emerged a few minutes later. (This aspect of the decision is discussed in detail in Chapter 2, Part 4(3)(*b*).) In addition, the majority upheld the pat-down searches that accompanied these detentions. Unfortunately, the Court did not directly address (and therefore clarify) the standard controlling when protective searches will be justified.[845]

(4) Use of Drug-Sniffing Dogs

§3.314 As explained in Part 2(4)(*b*)(i), above, in *R. v. Kang-Brown*[846] and *R. v. M. (A.)*,[847] the Supreme Court of Canada held that the use of trained dogs to de-

---

[839] *R. v. Mann*, [2004] S.C.J. No. 49, [2004] 3 S.C.R. 59 at paras. 43, 45 (S.C.C.).

[840] See *Criminal Code*, R.S.C. 1985, c. C-46, s. 495(1)(*a*), which authorizes a police officer to arrest any person "who, on reasonable grounds, he believes has committed or is about to commit an indictable offence." See also *R. v. Storrey*, [1990] S.C.J. No. 12, [1990] 1 S.C.R. 241 (S.C.C.); *R. v. Klimchuk*, [1991] B.C.J. No. 2872, 67 C.C.C. (3d) 385 at 403-406 (B.C.C.A.); and *R. v. Smellie*, [1994] B.C.J. No. 2850, 95 C.C.C. (3d) 9 at 17 (B.C.C.A.), leave to appeal refused [1995] S.C.C.A. No. 64, 97 C.C.C. (3d) vi (S.C.C.).

[841] The police are authorized to search inside a suspect's pockets incidental to an arrest. See *Cloutier v. Langlois*, [1990] S.C.J. No. 10, [1990] 1 S.C.R. 158 (S.C.C.).

[842] See Respondent's Submissions on Motion for a Re-hearing in *R. v. Mann*, S.C.C. File No. 29477.

[843] See S.C.C. Bulletin, 2004, p. 1596. (In dismissing the motion, the Court did take the opportunity to correct some of the wording found in a single sentence of its French judgment.)

[844] [2007] S.C.J. No. 32, 2007 SCC 32 (S.C.C.).

[845] The closest the Court comes in *R. v. Clayton*, [2007] S.C.J. No. 32, 2007 SCC 32 (S.C.C.) is in paras. 43 and 44 of its judgment, where it quotes with approval a passage from the Ontario Court of Appeal's judgment (*R. v. Clayton*, [2005] O.J. No. 1078 at para. 67 (Ont. C.A.)) that applies the "reasonable grounds to believe" language from *Mann*.

[846] [2008] S.C.J. No. 18, [2008] 1 S.C.R. 456, 2008 SCC 18 (S.C.C.).

[847] [2008] S.C.J. No. 19, [2008] 1 S.C.R. 569 (S.C.C.).

tect the odour of illegal drugs emanating from a person or his or her belongings encroaches upon a reasonable expectation of privacy. In other words, this constitutes a "search" for section 8 *Charter* purposes, a conclusion that triggered the "reasonableness" requirements of the guarantee, including the need for lawful authority before such searches could be constitutionally undertaken.

§3.315 There is no legislated authority for police in Canada to employ drug-sniffing dogs. In these judgments, the Court was sharply divided — 5:4 — on whether it should employ the ancillary powers doctrine to recognize such a police power or whether its creation should be left for Parliament. (The significance of this disagreement for the future use of the ancillary powers doctrine as a source of new police powers is fully explored in Chapter 1, Part 6(4)(*b*).)

§3.316 The majority concluded that the Court should use the ancillary powers doctrine to create a new police power. Four of the judges, writing in two separate sets of reasons in each case (Justice Binnie and Chief Justice McLachlin, and Justices Deschamps and Rothstein, dissenting), after applying the ancillary powers doctrine, concluded that police should have the power to conduct "sniff" searches based on "reasonable suspicion" and without requiring prior judicial authorization.[848] The majority explained the appropriateness of using the "reasonable suspicion" standard as opposed to the "reasonable and probable grounds" standard by emphasizing that dog-sniff searches are far less intrusive than other searches. For example, they can be undertaken without any need for physical contact with an individual's person or belongings and reveal comparatively little, merely the presence or absence of contraband.[849] Further, in explaining the need to dispense with the warrant requirement, the majority noted that police use these dogs in situations requiring quick action guided by on-the-spot observations, factors that make prior-judicial approval impractical.[850]

§3.317 In addition, the majority noted that insisting on strict adherence to the *Hunter* standards would make drug-sniffer dogs "superfluous and unnecessary", given that police could undertake a conventional search in circumstances where they possess reasonable and probable grounds.[851]

§3.318 In separate reasons, Justice Bastarache was prepared to go even further. He agreed that reasonable suspicion is the appropriate standard, but expressed the view that it need not always be individualized to justify the use of such dogs. Rather, a generalized suspicion, for example, that drugs are routinely being trafficked through a particular location (such as a bus depot, an airport or a school),

---

[848] *R. v. Kang-Brown*, [2008] S.C.J. No. 18, [2008] 1 S.C.R. 456, 2008 SCC 18 (S.C.C.), *per* Binnie and Deschamps JJ., dissenting.

[849] *R. v. M. (A.)*, [2008] S.C.J. No. 19, [2008] 1 S.C.R. 569 at paras. 81-82, 89 (S.C.C.), *per* Binnie J.; *R. v. Kang-Brown*, [2008] S.C.J. No. 18, [2008] 1 S.C.R. 456 at paras. 25, 58, 60, 2008 SCC 18 (S.C.C.), *per* Binnie J. and at paras. 168, 191 (S.C.R.), *per* Deschamps J., dissenting.

[850] *R. v. M. (A.)*, [2008] S.C.J. No. 19, [2008] 1 S.C.R. 569 at para. 90 (S.C.C.), *per* Binnie J.

[851] *R. v. Kang-Brown*, [2008] S.C.J. No. 18, [2008] 1 S.C.R. 456 at para. 21, 2008 SCC 18 (S.C.C.), *per* Binnie J.; see also para. 192 (S.C.R.), *per* Deschamps J., dissenting.

would be enough to justify the use of drug detecting dogs to sniff persons and their belongings in such locations.[852]

§3.319 The effect of Justice Bastarche's vote is that reasonable suspicion emerges as the controlling constitutional standard in this context. And, given that four of the justices insisted that it be of a particularized nature, the clear implication would seem to be that before police can use such dogs to sniff at an individual or his or her belongings, they must possess reasonable grounds to suspect that the person is carrying narcotics on his or her person or inside his or her belongings. Consequently, the fact that police conduct an investigative detention based on a reasonable suspicion of criminal activity is not necessarily sufficient to justify a sniff search; such searches must be grounded on a reasonable suspicion that drugs are actually present.[853]

§3.320 Further, to use a drug-sniffing dog in a particular location, the police would already need to be lawfully in that place.[854] For example, the police could not enter a home (without a search warrant) to use a drug-sniffing dog to search for narcotics based on a reasonable suspicion that drugs are secreted in the home. In other words, use of a drug-sniffing dog will not enable the police to by-pass the warrant requirement for entering into private places, such as a home or office. Of course, if the police approach the target in a public place, this same concern does not arise.

§3.321 An individual who is the target of a dog-sniff search will often be detained. (Detention is explained in Chapter 2, Part 3(3)(*b*)). As a result, when carrying out such a detention and search, the police would need to comply with sections 10(*a*) and 10(*b*) of the *Charter*. (These rights are explained in Chapter 4.) In addition, if the police lack the requisite grounds, not only will the sniff-search violate section 8 of the *Charter*, but also the detention that facilitates that search will likely violate section 9. (The requirements for a lawful investigative detention are explained in Chapter 2, Part 4(3)(*a*).)

§3.322 It is also worth noting that the Court signalled in *M. (A.)* that a less exacting standard would be warranted if the purpose for which the authorities were using a dog's olfactory powers was not merely routine crime prevention but related to a far greater and more urgent threat to public safety, for example, the presence of weapons or explosives in a particular location.[855]

---

[852] See *R. v. Kang-Brown*, [2008] S.C.J. No. 18, [2008] 1 S.C.R. 456 at paras. 214, 244-247, 2008 SCC 18 (S.C.C.), *per* Bastarche J., dissenting; *R. v. M. (A.)*, [2008] S.C.J. No. 19, [2008] 1 S.C.R. 569 at paras. 151-152, 163-164 (S.C.C.), *per* Bastarche J., dissenting.

[853] See *R. v. Schrenk*, [2010] M.J. No. 114, 254 C.C.C. (3d) 277 at 105-107 (Man. C.A.); *R. v. Yeh*, [2009] S.J. No. 582, 248 C.C.C. (3d) 125 at paras. 48-49 (Sask. C.A). Investigative detention and the "reasonable suspicion" standard are discussed more fully in Chapter 2, Part 4(3)(*a*). The limited protective search power attaching to investigative detention is discussed above in Part 4(3).

[854] *R. v. M. (A.)*, [2008] S.C.J. No. 19, [2008] 1 S.C.R. 569 at para. 13 (S.C.C.), *per* Binnie J.

[855] *Ibid.*, at para. 37 (S.C.R.), *per* Binnie J.

(5) Searches in Response to Disconnected 911 Calls and Other Emergencies

§3.323 The Supreme Court has also used the ancillary powers doctrine to recognize a police power to enter private premises in response to a disconnected 911 telephone call. In *R. v. Godoy*,[856] the police responded to a residence from which a 911 call had originated. The caller hung up before providing any reason for the call. At the residence, the appellant opened the door and reported, "there is no problem", but refused a request by police to enter. The police responded by forcing their way inside. Once there, they quickly acquired the required grounds to arrest the appellant for assaulting his wife. The appellant resisted, and was charged accordingly. At issue before the Supreme Court was the legality of the police entry on these facts. There was no statutory or common law authority for police to enter private premises in such circumstances. Not surprisingly, an application of the cost-benefit analysis mandated by the ancillary powers doctrine led the Court to recognize a new police power:

> ...to investigate the 911 call and, in particular, to locate the caller and determine his or her reasons for making the call and provide such assistance as may be required. The police authority for being on private property in response to a 911 call ends there. They do not have further permission to search premises or otherwise intrude on a resident's privacy or property. In *Dedman*, [*R. v. Dedman*, [1985] 2 S.C.R. 2]..., at p. 35, Le Dain J. stated that the interference with liberty must be necessary for carrying out the police duty and it must be <u>reasonable</u>. A reasonable interference in circumstances such as an unknown trouble call would be to locate the 911 caller in the home. If this can be done without entering the home with force, obviously such a course of action is mandated. Each case will be considered in its own context, keeping in mind all of the surrounding circumstances.[857]

§3.324 Of course, it is essential that the police have the power to enter private premises in response to disconnected 911 calls. Unfortunately, in embracing a case-by-case approach, the Court favoured flexibility over certainty — an inevitable by-product of judicial rule-making more generally. Although this leaves courts much room to manoeuvre in some future case with different facts, considerable uncertainty also results.

§3.325 For example, what if instead of a disconnected 911 call the police are faced with a report that a neighbour has overheard a man and woman arguing loudly? On these facts, if a woman answers the door but refuses entry, can the police then force their way inside? What if police respond to a report that an elderly neighbour who lives alone has not been seen or heard from in days — do these facts justify entry? It could be some time before the Supreme Court eventually sketches out the parameters of the common law emergency entry power.

---

[856] [1998] S.C.J. No. 85, [1999] 1 S.C.R. 311 (S.C.C.).
[857] *Ibid.*, at para. 22 (S.C.R.) [emphasis added].

§3.326 In the interim, a number of appellate courts have demonstrated an understandable willingness to extend the reach of *Godoy* to authorize the police to enter and search for public safety purposes more generally.[858] Of course, courts must remember to scrutinize such claims carefully so as to guard against "public safety" being used as pretext to circumvent well-established constitutional standards. To prevent this, the emergency power should be prefaced on the existence of reasonable grounds to believe that the safety of an occupant may be threatened. As *Godoy* illustrates, a disconnected 911 call will almost always provide the required objective justification. Myriad other potential circumstances could do the same.[859] Unfortunately, in the absence of clear guidelines, residents will be left guessing when they might be legally obligated to allow police to enter without a warrant. Less likely, but more troubling, is the danger that police might hesitate in other emergency situations because of uncertainty regarding their authority to force entry.[860] Hopefully, the Supreme Court will soon revisit *Godoy* and flesh out in greater detail the parameters of the emergency entry power. Even better, Parliament should intervene and provide comprehensive legislative guidance on this critically important police power.

---

[858] See *R. v. Hill*, [2006] B.C.J. No. 3043, 214 C.C.C. (3d) 492 (B.C.C.A.) (police acted lawfully and therefore did not violate s. 8 when they entered a residence in response to 911 call from neighbour reporting gunshots); *R. v. Jamieson*, [2002] B.C.J. No. 1476, 166 C.C.C. (3d) 501 (B.C.C.A.) (police acted lawfully in entering in response to a 911 call from neighbour reporting that an occupant had suffered an acid burn attack given that they were acting for safety and not investigative purposes); *R. v. Grenkow*, [1994] N.S.J. No. 577, 136 N.S.R. (2d) 264 (N.S.C.A.) (officers, in the midst of a building fire, justified in breaking down apartment door to avert further danger); *R. v. Phan*, [1996] O.J. No. 3241, 13 O.T.C. 81 (Ont. Gen. Div.) (fire inspector justified in entering a premises to investigate fire). But see *R. v. W. (D.G.)*, [2005] A.J. No. 1463, 387 A.R. 390 (Alta. Q.B.) (searches by child welfare authorities limited to extent necessary to ensure the immediate safety of children, not to be used as means to gather evidence).

[859] *Ibid.*, for cases detailing an assortment of emergency scenarios justifying police entry. See also *R. v. Nicholls*, [1999] O.J. No. 3660, 139 C.C.C. (3d) 253 at para. 12 (Ont. C.A.) wherein the court concluded that the police acted lawfully when they forced entry based on a 911 call from a relative of the appellant who reported that he posed a threat to himself and others and could not be contacted by phone. The Court rightly noted that "An informed caller from outside the apartment describing the nature of the emergency is a more reliable justification for a concern about the health and safety of the occupant of the apartment than is a disconnected telephone call".

[860] See Don Stuart, "*Godoy*: The Supreme Reverts to the Ancillary Powers Doctrine to Fill a Gap in Police Powers" (1999) 21 C.R. (5th) 225.

Chapter 4

QUESTIONING

1. INTRODUCTION

§4.1 The questioning of witnesses, suspects and others is a key component of most criminal investigations.[1] Police question people to further their investigations and obtain self-incriminating statements for use against defendants at trial. However, unlike the detention, arrest and search powers canvassed in Chapters 2 and 3, with few and limited exceptions, police do not have any legal "powers" to question people. Instead, they are simply free (subject to the limitations described below) to ask people questions, including both those not subject to any legal restraint and those who are legally detained. Detained persons may sometimes have no choice but to listen to police questions, but neither they nor non-detained persons are obliged to respond. Police have no legal power, in other words, to compel answers.[2] It is thus often said that people have a "right" to remain silent.[3]

§4.2 Police seeking to question therefore have only two options. They can either persuade people to cooperate voluntarily or trick them into speaking to covert agents. However, because police may abuse their physical and psychological advantage over suspects, the law regulates these efforts. This regulation is designed to balance the state's interest in detecting, deterring and punishing criminals against individuals' interests in avoiding cruel questioning practices, unfair self-incrimination, and in the worst-case scenario, wrongful convictions based on false confessions. As we will see, many of the controversies surrounding

---

[1]   See *Boudreau v. R.*, [1949] S.C.J. No. 10, [1949] S.C.R. 262 (S.C.C.), *per* Rand J.; *R. v. Fitton*, [1956] S.C.J. No. 70, [1956] S.C.R. 958 at 972 (S.C.C.), *per* Nolan J., at 963-64 *per* Rand J.; *R. v. Singh*, [2007] S.C.J. No. 48, [2007] 3 S.C.R. 405 at para. 28 (S.C.C.).

[2]   People who lie to police, however, may be convicted of obstructing justice. See *Criminal Code*, R.S.C. 1985, c. C-46, s. 139; *R. v. Spezzano*, [1977] O.J. No. 2183, 15 O.R. (2d) 489 (Ont. C.A.) (giving false name to police may constitute obstruction if done to thwart possible prosecution); *R. v. Hoggarth*, [1956] B.C.J. No. 108, 25 C.R. 174 (B.C.C.A.) (false statement to police without more not obstruction). But see *R. v. Dosanjh*, [2006] B.C.J. No. 2637, 2006 BCPC 449 at para. 69 (B.C. Prov. Ct.) ("There may be a live question as to whether, post-*Charter*, the telling by an accused of a deliberate falsehood to the police is an obstruction of justice").

[3]   Since police have no general power to compel answers, Ratushny argues that it is better to say that people have a "freedom" to remain silent. Ed Ratushny, *Self-incrimination in the Canadian Criminal Process* (Toronto: Carswell, 1979) at 185-86. See also *R. v. Singh*, [2007] S.C.J. No. 48, [2007] 3 S.C.R. 405 at paras. 27-28 (S.C.C.); *R. v. Turcotte*, [2005] S.C.J. No. 51, [2005] 2 S.C.R. 519 at para. 41 (S.C.C.); *R. v. Rothman*, [1981] S.C.J. No. 55, [1981] 1 S.C.R. 640 at 683 (S.C.C.).

police questioning stem from disputes over the meaning and relative importance of these interests.

§4.3 This chapter addresses the key components of this regulatory framework: the common law confessions rule and sections 10(*a*), 10(*b*) and 7 of the *Charter*.[4] By requiring the prosecution to prove that a defendant's statements to police were "voluntary", the confessions rule discourages the use of coercive tactics to induce cooperation. Section 10(*a*) of the *Charter* obliges police to tell people they have detained of the reasons for their detention. Section 10(*b*) requires police to tell detainees that they have a right to talk to a lawyer and gives detainees who wish to exercise that right a reasonable opportunity to do so before being questioned. Section 7 limits the ability of police to use covert operatives to obtain statements from people in their custody and prohibits the state, in some circumstances, from using legally-compelled statements in proceedings against the person who made them.

2.   THE CONFESSIONS RULE

(1)   Introduction

§4.4 Strictly speaking, the confessions rule is part of the law of evidence, not criminal procedure. It does not directly regulate police questioning. Instead, it prohibits the admission[5] at trial of statements[6] made by suspects to police or other "persons in authority" unless the prosecution proves beyond a reasonable doubt[7] that the statements were "voluntary".[8] Consequently, if police wish to elicit admissible statements from a suspect, they must be careful to avoid tactics that could elicit an involuntary confession.

---

[4]   *Canadian Charter of Rights and Freedoms*, Part I of the *Constitution Act, 1982*, being Schedule B to the *Canada Act 1982* (U.K.), 1982, c. 11 [*Charter*].

[5]   Statements made in violation of the confessions rule are inadmissible for all purposes, including impeaching the credibility of an accused whose testimony is inconsistent with the out of court statement. See *R. v. G. (B.)*, [1999] S.C.J. No. 29, [1999] 2 S.C.R. 475 at paras. 29-32 (S.C.C.); *R. v. Hébert*, [1954] S.C.J. No. 61, [1955] S.C.R. 120 at 134, *per* Estey J., at 147 *per* Fateaux J. (S.C.C.). See also *R. v. Calder*, [1996] S.C.J. No. 30, [1996] 1 S.C.R. 660 at para. 26 (S.C.C.).

[6]   The rule applies to any statement made to a person of authority, whether "inculpatory" or "exculpatory" on its face. See *R. v. Piché*, [1970] S.C.J. No. 59, [1971] S.C.R. 23 at 26 (S.C.C.). As Cartwright J. noted in his concurring reasons in *R. v. Piché*, it is "difficult to see how the prosecution can consistently urge that a statement forced from an accused is in reality exculpatory while at the same time asserting that its exclusion has resulted in the acquittal of the accused and that its admission might well have resulted in conviction."

[7]   See *R. v. Clear*, [2004] A.J. No. 752, 2004 ABCA 235 at para. 5 (Alta. C.A.); *R. v. Stoddart*, [2007] O.J. No. 769 at para. 3, 2007 ONCA 139 (Ont. C.A.); *R. v. Bunn*, [2001] M.J. No. 31, 2001 MBCA 12 at para. 12 (Man. C.A.).

[8]   A criminal defendant's voluntary, out-of-court statements are admissible at the instance of the prosecution by virtue of the admissions exception to the hearsay rule, which states that a party may adduce any statement by the other party. See Alan W. Bryant, Sidney R. Lederman & Michelle K. Fuerst, *Sopinka, Lederman & Bryant: The Law of Evidence in Canada*, 3d ed. (Markham, ON: LexisNexis Canada, 2009) at 361, 417. As noted by the Supreme Court in *Hodgson*, this rule rests on the assumption that "what people freely say which is contrary to their interest is probably true." *R. v. Hodgson*, [1998] S.C.J. No. 66, [1998] 2 S.C.R. 449 at para. 17 (S.C.C.).

§4.5 The confessions rule is a long-standing common law doctrine.[9] In its original form, it was designed to prevent wrongful convictions by excluding unreliable confessions.[10] It excluded only statements made by suspects because of "fear of prejudice or hope of advantage" held out by state authorities.[11] Excluding such statements, it was believed, was necessary to prevent triers-of-fact from giving them undue weight.[12]

§4.6 The contemporary Canadian version of the rule is somewhat broader in both its doctrinal scope and underlying policy justifications. Involuntariness may arise from one or more of the following: (*i*) diminished capacity; (*ii*) threats or promises; or (*iii*) oppressive interrogation conditions. In addition, even voluntary statements may be excluded if they are induced by police methods that would "shock the conscience" of the community.[13] And while the modern version of the rule continues to stress the prevention of wrongful convictions,[14] it also encompasses concerns for inhumane interrogation practices and unfair self-incrimination.[15]

(2) Person in Authority

§4.7 As mentioned, the confessions rule applies only to statements made to "persons in authority". Traditionally, this meant persons whom defendants be-

---

9   *R. v. Warickshall* (1783), 1 Leach 262, 168 Eng. Rep. 234 (K.B.); *Ibrahim v. The King*, [1914] A.C. 599 at 609 (P.C.). See generally, Steven Penney, "Theories of Confession Admissibility: A Historical View" (1998) 25 Am. J. Crim. L. 309 at 320-22.

10   See *R. v. Boudreau*, [1949] S.C.J. No. 10, [1949] S.C.R. 262 (S.C.C.), *per* Rand J.; *R. v. Fitton*, [1956] S.C.J. No. 70, [1956] S.C.R. 958 (S.C.C.); *R. v. Rothman*, [1981] S.C.J. No. 55, [1981] 1 S.C.R. 640 at 644 (S.C.C.).

11   *Ibrahim v. The King*, [1914] A.C. 599 at 609 (P.C). *Ibrahim* is the case most often cited by Canadian authorities as establishing the modern confessions rule. It was first followed by the Supreme Court in *R. v. Prosko*, [1922] S.C.J. No. 6, 63 S.C.R. 226 (S.C.C.). Courts in common law jurisdictions have been excluding confessions on this basis, however, at least since *R. v. Warickshall* (1783), 1 Leach 262, 168 Eng. Rep. 234 (K.B.). See generally, *R. v. Hebert*, [1990] S.C.J. No. 64, [1990] 2 S.C.R. 151 at 165-70 (S.C.C.).

12   In *Ibrahim v. The King*, [1914] A.C. 599 at 609 (P.C), Lord Sumner recognized that ideally, the circumstances under which a statement was made should go to weight, not admissibility. The confessions rule was, however, a necessary "rule of policy" that recognized the "danger of receiving such evidence." *Ibid.*, at 611. See also *R. v. Hodgson*, [1998] S.C.J. No. 66, [1998] 2 S.C.R. 449 at para. 60 (S.C.C.), *per* L'Heureux-Dubé J., concurring. As noted by the Supreme Court, in demonstrating first, that false confessions occur regularly, and second, that jurors find it difficult to believe that an innocent person would falsely confess, contemporary empirical research provides considerable support for this policy. See *R. v. Oickle*, [2000] S.C.J. No. 38, [2000] 2 S.C.R. 3 at paras. 34-36 (S.C.C.); Saul M. Kassin & Holly Sukel, "Coerced Confessions and the Jury: An Experimental Test of the 'Harmless Error' Rule" (1997) 21 L. & Human Behav. 27.

13   *R. v. Oickle*, [2000] S.C.J. No. 38, [2000] 2 S.C.R. 3 (S.C.C.).

14   See especially *R. v. Oickle*, [2000] S.C.J. No. 38, [2000] 2 S.C.R. 3 at paras. 34-46 (S.C.C.). See also *R. v. Singh*, [2007] S.C.J. No. 48, [2007] 3 S.C.R. 405 at para. 29 (S.C.C.) (the confessions rule "is largely informed by the problem of false confessions").

15   See *R. v. Hodgson*, [1998] S.C.J. No. 66, [1998] 2 S.C.R. 449 at paras. 18-24 (S.C.C.); *R. v. Hebert*, [1990] S.C.J. No. 64, [1990] 2 S.C.R. 151 at 171-74 (S.C.C.); *R. v. Singh*, [2007] S.C.J. No. 48, [2007] 3 S.C.R. 405 at paras. 21, 30-31 (S.C.C.).

lieved were involved in their "arrest, detention, examination or prosecution".[16] In the vast majority of cases, this test did not present courts with much difficulty. People who identified themselves to the accused as being (and actually were), police, prosecutors or prison officials were unequivocally found to be persons in authority.[17] Conversely, undercover agents (whose status was therefore unknown to the accused) were not.[18]

§4.8 Difficulty ensued, however, when it was alleged that a defendant *believed* that the questioner could influence the case, but the questioner was not a law enforcement official. In such cases, the courts adopted one of two approaches. The first ("the subjective approach"), held that the defendant's belief was sufficient to find that the questioner was a person in authority, even if that belief was wrong.[19] The rationale behind this approach is that confessions coerced by people believed to be state agents are particularly apt to be unreliable.[20] Under the second ("the subjective + objective approach"), questioners would only be found to be persons in authority if they were both believed to be *and actually were* state agents.[21] On this view, private citizens could be persons in authority, but only if they were collaborating with the authorities at the time the statements were made.[22]

---

[16] *R. v. B. (A.)*, [1986] O.J. No. 91, 26 C.C.C. (3d) 17 at 26 (Ont. C.A.). See also *R. v. Hodgson*, [1998] S.C.J. No. 66, [1998] 2 S.C.R. 449 at paras. 16 and 48 (S.C.C.); *The King v. Todd*, [1901] M.J. No. 1, 4 C.C.C. 514 at 526-27 (Man. K.B.), *per* Bain J.; *R. v. Berger*, [1975] B.C.J. No. 1181, 27 C.C.C. (2d) 357 at 385-86 (B.C.C.A.); *R. v. Paonessa*, [1982] O.J. No. 3209, 66 C.C.C. (2d) 300 at 306 (Ont. C.A.), *per* Zuber J.A., affd [1983] S.C.J. No. 46, [1983] 1 S.C.R. 660 (S.C.C.).

[17] *R. v. Collins*, [1975] A.J. No. 430, [1976] 3 W.W.R. 82 at 83 (Alta. T.D.).

[18] See *R. v. Rothman*, [1981] S.C.J. No. 55, [1981] 1 S.C.R. 640 (S.C.C.); *The King v. Todd*, [1901] M.J. No. 1, 4 C.C.C. 514 at 526-27 (Man. K.B.); *R. v. Pettipiece*, [1972] B.C.J. No. 669, [1972] 5 W.W.R. 129 (B.C.C.A.); *R. v. Towler*, [1968] B.C.J. No. 122, 5 C.R.N.S. 55 (B.C.C.A.).

[19] See *R. v. Perras*, [1973] S.C.J. No. 102, [1974] S.C.R. 659 at 672 (S.C.C.), *per* Spence J., dissenting; *R. v. Sweryda*, [1987] A.J. No. 212, 34 C.C.C. (3d) 325 (Alta. C.A.). See also Fred Kaufman, *Admissibility of Confessions*, 3d ed. (Toronto: Carswell, 1979) at 81.

[20] See Fred Kaufman, *Admissibility of Confessions*, 3d ed. (Toronto: Carswell, 1979) at 80, 89; *R. v. Collins*, [1975] A.J. No. 430, [1976] 3 W.W.R. 82 at 87 (Alta. T.D.).

[21] See *e.g.*, *R. v. Collins*, [1975] A.J. No. 430, [1976] 3 W.W.R. 82 at 91 (Alta. T.D.); *R. v. Perras*, [1973] S.C.J. No. 102, [1974] S.C.R. 659 (S.C.C.).

[22] See *e.g.*, *R. v. Trenholme* (1920), 35 C.C.C. 341 (Que. K.B.) (father of complainant was person in authority as he had real influence over prosecution); *R. v. Downey*, [1976] N.S.J. No. 467, 32 C.C.C. (2d) 511 (N.S.S.C.) (complainant was person in authority where accused was taken to speak with her by police and accused pleaded with her to drop the charges); *R. v. Perras*, [1973] S.C.J. No. 102, [1974] S.C.R. 659 at 663-64 (S.C.C.), *per* Ritchie J. (psychiatrist interviewing arrestee at a police station was a person in authority); *R. v. Sweryda*, [1987] A.J. No. 212, 34 C.C.C. (3d) 325 (Alta. C.A.) (social worker was a person in authority because she was investigating child abuse allegations and had the power to institute a prosecution). See also *R. v. B.(G.)*, [2000] O.J. No. 2963, 146 C.C.C. (3d) 465 (Ont. C.A.), leave to appeal refused [2000] S.C.C.A. No. 609 (S.C.C.) (private citizen informer was an agent of the police); *R. v. Wilband*, [1967] S.C.J. No. 2, [1967] S.C.R. 14 at 20 (S.C.C.) (psychiatrist not a person in authority because he could not "control or influence the course of...proceedings in the sense and the manner in which the course of proceedings may be controlled or influenced by persons who have a concern with the apprehension, prosecution or examination of prisoners conducted to collect evi-

§4.9 In *R. v. Hodgson*,[23] the Supreme Court rejected the subjective approach on the basis that the confessions rule is "aimed at controlling coercive state conduct".[24] It instead adopted a version of the subjective + objective approach. The person in authority requirement will be established, it held, only when the accused "*reasonably* believes the person receiving the statement is acting as an agent of the police or prosecuting authorities and could therefore influence or control the proceedings against him or her."[25]

§4.10 Like other iterations of the subjective + objective approach, under *Hodgson* the person in authority requirement would be met when there was "a relationship of agency or close collaboration between the receiver of the statement and the police or prosecution, and that relationship was known to the accused."[26] The decision could also be read, however, to find a person in authority when no such relationship existed, yet the defendant reasonably believed that it did.[27] This could occur, for example, where a non-state agent questioned the accused while convincingly impersonating a police officer.

§4.11 In our view, this is not likely what the *Hodgson* Court had in mind.[28] Though it articulated the test using the language of "reasonable belief", there is reason to think that the objective part of the test refers exclusively to the *actual* relationship between the questioner and the authorities, and not the reasonableness of the defendant's *beliefs* about that relationship. In applying the test to the facts at hand, the Court focused, on the one hand, on the true relationship between the questioner and the authorities, and on the other, on the accused's beliefs about that relationship. It did not speak of the *reasonableness* of those beliefs *per se*. "[A]nyone is capable of being a person in authority," the Court stated, "where a person becomes sufficiently involved with the arrest, detention, examination or prosecution of an accused, and the accused believes that the person may influence the process against him or her."[29] In concluding that the trial

---

dence leading to the conviction of an offence"); *R. v. Edwards*, [2004] O.J. No. 3228, 72 O.R. (3d) 135 at para. 59 (Ont. C.A.) (leaving open question of whether psychiatrist was person in authority when statements made while accused in police custody); *R. v. G. (H.A.)*, [2004] A.J. No. 1241, 2004 ABCA 322 at para. 26 (Alta. C.A.) (accused's psychiatrist acted independently of police and was not therefore a state agent); *R. v. Roadhouse*, [1933] B.C.J. No. 7 at para. 5, [1934] 1 W.W.R. 349 (B.C.C.A.) (doctor was not a person in authority because he "was not deputized by the police to act on their behalf nor was he performing any function in connection with the administration of justice").

[23] [1998] S.C.J. No. 66, [1998] 2 S.C.R. 449 at para. 34 (S.C.C.).

[24] *Ibid.*, at para. 34 (S.C.R.).

[25] *Ibid.*, at paras. 34 and 48 [emphasis added]. See also *R. v. Wells*, [1998] S.C.J. No. 67, [1998] 2 S.C.R. 517 (S.C.C.); *R. v. T. (S.G.)*, [2010] S.C.J. No. 20, [2010] 1 S.C.R. No. 688, 2010 SCC 20 at para. 22 (S.C.C.) [*T. (S.G.)*].

[26] *R. v. Hodgson*, [1998] S.C.J. No. 66, [1998] 2 S.C.R. 449 at para. 34 (S.C.C.).

[27] See *R. v. McKenzie*, [1965] A.J. No. 36, [1965] 3 C.C.C. 6 at 28 (Alta. S.C.), *per* Johnson J.A. ("If one, who has no power to control or influence the course of the proceedings by words or conduct, induces an accused to believe that he has such power, he may be held to be an agent of the prosecuting authority and, therefore, a person in authority").

[28] *R. v. Hodgson*, [1998] S.C.J. No. 66, [1998] 2 S.C.R. 449 (S.C.C.).

[29] *Ibid.*, at para. 49 (S.C.R.).

judge did not err in failing to hold a *voir dire* on voluntariness, the Court noted that there was:

> ... nothing to suggest that the complainant or her family members had spoken to the police or anyone else in authority or were even considering making a complaint. Similarly, there was nothing to suggest that the appellant subjectively believed the complainant's family to have control over criminal proceedings.[30]

This interpretation is buttressed by Justice Abella's comments for a majority of the Court in *R. v. Grandinetti*.[31] After relating *Hodgson*'s reasonable belief test, she stated the following:

> It is not enough, however, that an accused reasonably believe that a person can influence the course of the investigation or prosecution. As the trial judge correctly concluded:
>
>> [R]eason and common sense dictates that when the cases speak of a person in authority as one who is capable of controlling or influencing the course of the proceedings, it is from the perspective of someone who is involved in the investigation, the apprehension and prosecution of a criminal offence resulting in a conviction, an agent of the police or someone working in collaboration with the police. It does not include someone who seeks to sabotage the investigation or steer the investigation away from a suspect that the state is investigating.[32]

§4.12 Allowing the person in authority requirement to be satisfied by showing that an accused had a mistaken (yet reasonable) belief that the questioner was an agent of law enforcement, moreover, runs counter to the rationale for the subjective + objective approach: the deterrence of *state* (not private) misconduct. If the questioner is not in fact a state actor, then under this approach it should not matter whether the accused's contrary belief was reasonable or unreasonable.

§4.13 *Hogdson* is best interpreted, then, as conforming to the orthodox version of the subjective + objective approach. To establish the person in authority requirement, therefore, the prosecution must show that: (*i*) the suspect believed that the questioner was an agent of law enforcement; and (*ii*) the questioner actually was an agent of law enforcement. If, in the case of the second requirement, the questioner is not employed in an official law enforcement capacity, the question should be resolved in the same manner that it has been in other contexts in criminal procedure; that is, by asking whether "the exchange between the accused and the [receiver of the statement] have taken place, in the form and manner in which it did take place, but for the intervention of the state or its agents"?[33] On this view, any relationship between the receiver and the authorities

---

30 *Ibid.*, at para. 50.
31 *R. v. Grandinetti*, [2005] S.C.J. No. 3, [2005] 1 S.C.R. 27 (S.C.C.).
32 *Ibid.*, at para. 39.
33 *R. v. Broyles*, [1991] S.C.J. No. 95, [1991] 3 S.C.R. 595 at 608 (S.C.C.) (setting out the test for state agency in the context of the right to silence under s. 7 of the *Charter*). See also *R. v. M.*

that develops after the making of the statement would not make the receiver a person in authority.[34]

§4.14 Similarly, the fact that private persons may have some degree of general "influence" on the accused or the proceedings, for example by making a complaint or providing or withholding evidence, is not in itself enough to make them persons in authority.[35] In *R. v. T. (S.G.)*,[36] for example, the Supreme Court held that there was no evidence on the record that the receiver of the confession (the complainant's mother) had "any control" over the prosecution or was "operating on behalf of the investigating authorities."[37] As stated in *R. v. Broyles*,[38] private persons are state agents only if their relationship with the authorities is such that the relevant transaction was "materially different from what it would have been had there been no such relationship."[39] In such cases, a private person is effectively delegated by the authorities to perform a law enforcement function. Thus in *R. v. Wells*,[40] the Supreme Court ordered that there should be a voluntariness *voir dire* to decide the person in authority question at a new trial where the statement was made to the complainant's parents after they "visited and spoke to the police and, after that visit, planned to obtain an admission from the respondent by a trick."[41]

§4.15 The question remains, however, whether *Hodgson* adequately protects against the danger of receiving confessions coerced by non-state actors. Though the Court recognized that the person in authority rule permits the admission of dangerously unreliable confessions (such as those coerced by the infliction or threat of violence), it declined to abolish it.[42] Doing so, it claimed, "could bring

---

(M.R.), [1998] S.C.J. No. 83, [1998] 3 S.C.R. 393 at para. 29 (S.C.C.) (using the *Broyles* test to determine whether a high school principal was acting as an agent of police in searching accused student); *R. v. Buhay*, [2003] S.C.J. No. 30, [2003] 1 S.C.R. 631 at paras. 28-29 (S.C.C.) (bus station security guards who searched locker before any police involvement not state agents); *R. v. G. (H.A.)*, [2004] A.J. No. 1241, 2004 ABCA 322 at para. 26 (Alta. C.A.) (accused's psychiatrist acted independently of police and was not therefore a state agent); *R. v. Weir*, [2001] A.J. No. 869, 2001 ABCA 181 (Alta. C.A.) (Internet service provider acted as state agent when it forwarded suspect's emails to police at their request). See also the discussion below, Part 5. The general concept of state agency for *Charter* purposes, including many of the Supreme Court judgments mentioned in this footnote, is discussed in greater detail in Chapter 1, Part 4(3).

34   See *R. v. Broyles*, [1991] S.C.J. No. 95, [1991] 3 S.C.R. 595 at 608 (S.C.C.).
35   See *R. v. McKenzie*, [1965] A.J. No. 36, [1965] 3 C.C.C. 6 at 28 (Alta. S.C.); *R. v. Hodgson*, [1998] S.C.J. No. 66, [1998] 2 S.C.R. 449 at paras. 91-92 (S.C.C.), *per* L'Heureux-Dubé J., concurring.
36   [2010] S.C.J. No. 20, [2010] 1 S.C.R. 688, 2010 SCC 20 26 (S.C.C.).
37   *R. v. T. (S.G.)*, [2010] S.C.J. No. 20, [2010] 1 S.C.R. 688, 2010 SCC 20 at para. 26 (S.C.C.).
38   [1991] S.C.J. No. 95, [1991] 3 S.C.R. 595 (S.C.C.).
39   *Ibid.*, at 608 (S.C.R.).
40   [1998] S.C.J. No. 67, [1998] 2 S.C.R. 517 (S.C.C.).
41   *Ibid.*, at para. 16 (S.C.R.).
42   *R. v. Hodgson*, [1998] S.C.J. No. 66, [1998] 2 S.C.R. 449 at paras. 25-26 (S.C.C.). See also Law Reform Commission of Canada, *Report on Evidence* (Ottawa: Information Canada, 1975) at 62.

about complex and unforeseeable consequences,"[43] and should thus be the subject of Parliamentary study and consideration.[44] Pending any legislative reform, it suggested, juries should be instructed on the dangers of relying on statements coerced from individuals who are not persons in authority.[45]

§4.16 The Court curiously failed to mention another solution: using the existing judicial discretion to exclude evidence when its prejudicial effect would outweigh its probative value.[46] This discretion should be exercised when there is a reasonable possibility that the trier-of-fact would place undue weight on a

---

[43] This reluctance contrasts markedly with the Court's stance on the recognition of novel common law police powers. See Chapter 1, Part 6(4)(*b*).

[44] The Court noted, for example, that in the absence of the requirement the prosecution would face "an overwhelming burden if it had to establish the voluntariness of every statement against interest made by an accused to any person." *R. v. Hodgson*, [1998] S.C.J. No. 66, [1998] 2 S.C.R. 449 at para. 25 (S.C.C.).

[45] *R. v. Hodgson*, [1998] S.C.J. No. 66, [1998] 2 S.C.R. 449 at para. 30 (S.C.C.). The person in authority requirement has been criticized by many commentators. See *e.g.*, Peter Mirfield, "Confessions: the 'Person in Authority' Requirement" (1981) Crim. L. Rev. 92; Alan Gold, "Confession: Person in Authority" (1981) 23 Crim. L.Q. 334. Many jurisdictions have abolished it. In Australia, most jurisdictions have abolished the person in authority requirement through either judicial modification of the common law rule, legislative intervention, or both. See Peter Gillies, *Law of Evidence in Australia*, 2d ed. (Sydney: Legal Books, 1991) at 537-38 ("The Australian rule ... is broader in its scope [than the English rule] in not being confined to involuntariness resulting from the conduct of the person in authority"); *Evidence Act 1995*, 1995 (Australia), No. 2, s. 84 and *Evidence Act 1995*, 1995 (N.S.W.), No. 25, s. 84. The United States Supreme Court has held that state action is required to render confessions inadmissible under the voluntariness component of the due process clause in the Fourteenth Amendment of the federal Constitution. See *Colorado v. Connelly*, 479 U.S. 157 (1986). Several states have excluded confessions made to private actors, however, pursuant to the common law, state legislation, or state constitutional provisions. See Kimberly C. Simmons, "Coercive Conduct by Private Person as Affecting Admissibility of Confession under State Statutes or Constitutional Provisions: Post-*Connelly* Cases" (1997) 48 A.L.R. (5th) 555. In England and Wales, confessions made to private parties may be excluded if they were obtained by either "oppression" or "in consequence of anything said or done which was likely ... to render unreliable any confession which might be made by him in consequence thereof." *Police and Criminal Evidence Act 1984*, 1984 (U.K.), c. 60, s. 76(2).

[46] In *R. v. Wray*, [1970] S.C.J. No. 80, [1971] S.C.R. 272 at 293 (S.C.C.), the Court limited the scope of the discretion to cases where the evidence is "gravely prejudicial" and its probative value is "trifling". But the Court eventually came to the view that exclusion is warranted whenever the evidence's prejudicial effect is out of proportion to its probative value. See *R. v. Sweitzer*, [1982] S.C.J. No. 48, [1982] 1 S.C.R. 949 at 953 (S.C.C.); *R. v. Corbett*, [1988] S.C.J. No. 40, [1988] 1 S.C.R. 670 (S.C.C.), *per* La Forest J., dissenting on other grounds; *R. v. Potvin*, [1989] S.C.J. No. 24, [1989] 1 S.C.R. 525 (S.C.C.), *per* La Forest J., concurring; *Thomson Newspapers v. Canada (Director of Investigation and Research)*, [1990] S.C.J. No. 23, [1990] 1 S.C.R. 425 (S.C.C.), *per* La Forest J., concurring; *R. v. Seaboyer*, [1991] S.C.J. No. 62, [1991] 2 S.C.R. 577 (S.C.C.); *R. v. Mohan*, [1994] S.C.J. No. 36, [1994] 2 S.C.R. 9 (S.C.C.); *R. v. Harrer*, [1995] S.C.J. No. 81, [1995] 3 S.C.R. 562 (S.C.C.); *R. v. R.J.S.*, [1995] S.C.J. No. 10, [1995] 1 S.C.R. 451 at paras. 197 and 258 (S.C.C.); *R. v. Arp*, [1998] S.C.J. No. 82, [1998] 3 S.C.R. 339 (S.C.C.); *R. v. Jabarianha*, [2001] S.C.J. No. 72, [2001] 3 S.C.R. 430 at para. 17 (S.C.C.); *R. v. Buhay*, [2003] S.C.J. No. 30, [2003] 1 S.C.R. 631 at para. 40 (S.C.C.). See generally, Alan W. Bryant, Sidney R. Lederman & Michelle K. Fuerst, *Sopinka, Lederman & Bryant: The Law of Evidence in Canada*, 3d ed. (Markham, ON: LexisNexis Canada, 2009) at 58-63.

confession coerced by someone who is not a person in authority.[47] As the British Columbia Court of Appeal has stated:

> ... the majority opinion in *Hodgson* cannot be taken to require that all confessions to persons not in authority, regardless of whether the confession is obtained by violence or threats of violence, must be admitted into evidence. To so hold would ignore the court's discretion to exclude evidence, the probative value of which is outweighed by [its] prejudicial effect, and the power and discretion of the courts to ensure the fair trial of an accused.[48]

To the same effect, judges could exclude privately coerced confessions pursuant to their power under sections 7 and 11(*d*) of the *Charter* to exclude evidence when its admission would compromise the fairness of the trial.[49]

(3) Voluntariness

§4.17 The heart of the confessions rule is deciding whether a statement made to a person in authority is "voluntary". A notoriously nebulous concept, voluntariness encompasses a "complex of values", including ensuring reliability, preserving free choice and deterring abusive police methods.[50] As discussed more fully below, in recent years, the Supreme Court of Canada has emphasized the importance of the voluntariness inquiry in preventing the admission of false confessions that might lead to wrongful convictions.[51]

§4.18 The rule does not squarely confront any these concerns, however. As we will see, dubiously reliable statements may be voluntary,[52] and statements that are likely true may be involuntary.[53] Similarly, while the confessions rule offers

---

[47]   See Steven Penney, "What's Wrong with Self-Incrimination? The Wayward Path of Self-Incrimination Law in the Post-Charter Era, Part 2: Self-Incrimination in Police Investigations" (2004) 48 Crim. L.Q. 280 at 294-95; *R. v. Osmar*, [2007] O.J. No. 244, 2007 ONCA 50 at para. 49 (Ont. C.A.), leave to appeal refused [2007] S.C.C.A. No. 157 (S.C.C.).

[48]   *R. v. Wells*, [2003] B.C.J. No. 927, 174 C.C.C. (3d) 301 at para. 64 (B.C.C.A). In *R. v. Grandinetti*, [2005] S.C.J. No. 3, [2005] 1 S.C.R. 27 at para. 36 (S.C.C.), the Court suggested that statements coerced by private actors might also be excluded under the common law and *Charter* abuse of process doctrine.

[49]   See *e.g.*, *R. v. Harrer*, [1995] S.C.J. No. 81, [1995] 3 S.C.R. 562 at paras. 13-24 (S.C.C.); *R. v. Terry*, [1996] S.C.J. No. 62, [1996] 2 S.C.R. 207 at paras. 25-26 (S.C.C.); *R. v. Hape*, [2007] S.C.J. No. 26, [2007] 2 S.C.R. 292 at paras. 91 and 100 (S.C.C.); *R. v. Buhay*, [2003] S.C.J. No. 30, [2003] 1 S.C.R. 631 at para. 40 (S.C.C.). This power is discussed more fully in Chapter 1, Part 4(3)(*e*).

[50]   *R. v. Oickle*, [2000] S.C.J. No. 38, [2000] 2 S.C.R. 3 at para. 70 (S.C.C.), quoting *Blackburn v. Alabama*, 361 U.S. 199 at 207 (1960), *per* Warren C.J.

[51]   *R. v. Oickle*, [2000] S.C.J. No. 38, [2000] 2 S.C.R. 3 at paras. 34-46 (S.C.C.). For an overview of the state of social scientific knowledge on the role of false confessions in generating wrongful convictions, see Saul M. Kassin *et al.*, "Police-Induced Confessions: Risk Factors and Recommendations" (2010) 34 Law and Human Behaviour 49.

[52]   Prosecutors must establish the voluntariness of statements made to person in authority, for example, even if they concede that the statements are untrue. See *R. v. Piché*, [1970] S.C.J. No. 59, [1971] S.C.R. 23 (S.C.C.).

[53]   See *R. v. Murakami*, [1951] S.C.J. No. 25, [1951] S.C.R. 801 at 802 (S.C.C.); *R. v. DeClercq*, [1968] S.C.J. No. 68, [1968] S.C.R. 902 at 906 (S.C.C.); *R. v. Hodgson*, [1998] S.C.J. No. 66,

some protection against unwitting self-incrimination and cruel interrogation methods, as we will see, police are permitted to use a variety of manipulative and unpleasant means to "somehow convince the suspect that it is in his or her best interests to confess."[54]

§4.19 To decide whether a statement was made voluntarily, therefore, judges must consider a number of factors, few of which are determinative. The voluntariness inquiry is "contextual",[55] having regard to "the entire circumstances",[56] including the (objective) nature of the tactics used by police and the suspect's (subjective) reaction to those tactics.[57] That said, in the Supreme Court of Canada's leading decision on the confessions rule — *R. v. Oickle*[58] — the Court grouped the relevant factors under three distinct headings: (*i*) operating mind; (*ii*) threats or promises (otherwise known as "inducements"); and (*iii*) oppression.[59]

(a) Operating Mind

§4.20 A statement is not voluntary unless it is the product of an "operating mind".[60] This issue typically arises when the accused suffered from some kind of cognitive deficiency when making the statement. In *R. v. Whittle*,[61] the Supreme Court declared that to have an operating mind, the accused need only have "sufficient cognitive capacity to understand what he or she is saying and what is said," including "[t]he ability to understand a caution that the evidence can be used against the accused."[62] In so holding, the Court implicitly rejected previous

---

[1998] 2 S.C.R. 449 at paras. 19-20 (S.C.C.). See also Ed Ratushny, *Self-incrimination in the Canadian Criminal Process* (Toronto: Carswell, 1979) at 113-115.

54 *R. v. Oickle*, [2000] S.C.J. No. 38, [2000] 2 S.C.R. 3 at para. 57 (S.C.C.). See also *R. v. Singh*, [2007] S.C.J. No. 48, [2007] 3 S.C.R. 405 at para. 45 (S.C.C.) ("Provided that the detainee's rights are adequately protected, including the freedom to choose whether to speak or not, it is in society's interest that the police attempt to tap this valuable source"); *R. v. Hebert*, [1990] S.C.J. No. 64, [1990] 2 S.C.R. 151 at 184 (S.C.C.) ("Police persuasion, short of denying the suspect the right to choose or depriving him of an operating mind, does not breach the right to silence.").

55 *R. v. Oickle*, [2000] S.C.J. No. 38, [2000] 2 S.C.R. 3 at para. 71 (S.C.C.).

56 *Ibid.*, at para. 68.

57 See *R. v. Hodgson*, [1998] S.C.J. No. 66, [1998] 2 S.C.R. 449 at para. 15 (S.C.C.); *R. v. Fitton*, [1956] S.C.J. No. 70, [1956] S.C.R. 958 at 962 (S.C.C.); *R. v. Spencer*, [2007] S.C.J. No. 11, [2007] 1 S.C.R. 500 at paras. 13, 21 (S.C.C.); *R. v. Oickle*, [2000] S.C.J. No. 38, [2000] 2 S.C.R. 3 at para. 42 (S.C.C.). *Contra R. v. Hebert*, [1990] 2 S.C.R. 151 at 181 (apart from the operating mind requirement (which is entirely subjective), courts should determine voluntariness objectively; *i.e.*, by focussing on the conduct of police and not on the suspect's subjective perceptions).

58 [2000] S.C.J. No. 38, [2000] 2 S.C.R. 3 (S.C.C.).

59 *R. v. Oickle*, [2000] S.C.J. No. 38, [2000] 2 S.C.R. 3 at para. 48, 58, 63 (S.C.C.). See also *R. v. H. (L.K.)*, [2006] N.S.J. No. 347, 2006 NSCA 104 at para. 11 (N.S.C.A.).

60 See *Thomas c. R.*, [2005] Q.J. No. 8251, 2005 QCCA 628 at paras. 25, 39 (Que. C.A.); *R. c. Otis*, [2000] J.Q. no 4320, 151 C.C.C. (3d) 416 at para. 33 (Que. C.A.), leave to appeal refused [2001] 1 S.C.R. xvii (S.C.C.).

61 [1994] S.C.J. No. 69, [1994] 2 S.C.R. 914 (S.C.C.).

62 *Ibid.*, at 941 (S.C.R.). See also *R. v. Oickle*, [2000] S.C.J. No. 38, [2000] 2 S.C.R. 3 at para. 63 (S.C.C.). An operating mind obviously does require, however, that the suspect have a basic

suggestions that voluntariness might require a more thorough understanding of the consequences of speech.[63] Suspects need not be capable of exercising "analytical reasoning," the Court held, or making "a good or wise choice or one that is in his or her interest."[64]

§4.21 Courts have therefore held that suspects affected by intoxicating substances,[65] mental illness,[66] intellectual disabilities[67] or biochemical imbalances[68] may still be capable of making voluntary statements.[69] Though Whittle, for example, believed that voices in his head were commanding him to confess, the Court held that he was sufficiently aware of the consequences of speaking.[70] "To the extent that the inner voices prompted [him] to speak in apparent disregard of the advice of his counsel and to his detriment, because he did not care about the consequences or felt that he could not resist the urging of the voices," the Court held, "they cannot be the basis for exclusion."[71]

§4.22 It is not clear, however, whether the operating mind requirement is satisfied when suspects (mistakenly) believe that their statements are being made "off the record". Such cases typically arise when a suspect who is not cognitively impaired is cautioned about the consequences of speaking, but is subsequently led to believe that conversations with police will remain confidential. Some courts have held that this renders the confession inadmissible;[72] others have not.[73]

---

understanding of the language (*e.g.*, English) used by police. See *R. v. Kooktook*, [2006] Nu.J. No. 7, 210 C.C.C. (3d) 106 at paras. 126-130 (Nu. C.A.).

[63] See *R. v. Clarkson*, [1986] S.C.J. No. 20, [1986] 1 S.C.R. 383 at 393-95 (S.C.C.).

[64] *R. v. Whittle*, [1994] S.C.J. No. 69, [1994] 2 S.C.R. 914 at 933, 939, 941-42 (S.C.C.).

[65] See *e.g.*, *R. v. McKenna*, [1961] S.C.J. No. 45, [1961] S.C.R. 660 (S.C.C.); *R. v. McPherson*, [2000] M.J. No. 597, 2000 MBCA 157 at para. 2 (Man. C.A.); *R. v. Richard*, [1980] B.C.J. No. 1076, 56 C.C.C. (2d) 129 (B.C.C.A.); *R. v. Hartridge*, [1966] S.J. No. 202, [1967] 1 C.C.C. 346 (Sask. C.A.).

[66] See *e.g.*, *R. v. Whittle*, [1994] S.C.J. No. 69, [1994] 2 S.C.R. 914 (S.C.C.); *R. v. Nagotcha*, [1980] S.C.J. No. 19, [1980] 1 S.C.R. 714 (S.C.C.); *R. v. Santinon*, [1973] B.C.J. No. 778, 11 C.C.C. (2d) 121 (B.C.C.A.).

[67] See *e.g.*, *R. c. Otis*, [2000] J.Q. no 4320, 151 C.C.C. (3d) 416 at para. 41 (Que. C.A.), leave to appeal refused [2001] 1 S.C.R. xvii (S.C.C.).

[68] See *e.g.*, *R. v. Sabean*, [1979] N.S.J. No. 788, 35 N.S.R. (2d) 35 (N.S.S.C.); *R. v. Arkell*, [1980] B.C.J. No. 607, 54 C.C.C. (2d) 266 (B.C.C.A.).

[69] See *e.g.*, *R. v. Hayes*, [2002] N.B.J. No. 356, 2002 NBCA 80 at para. 29 (N.B.C.A.) (diabetic condition); *R. v. Bedard*, [2000] O.J. No. 3992 (Ont. C.A.) (hypoglycemia); *R. v. Taylor*, [2008] A.J. No. 723, 2008 ABCA 253 (Alta. C.A.) (same). But see *R. v. Clear*, [2004] A.J. No. 752, 2004 ABCA 235 at para. 6 (Alta. C.A.) (police knowledge of suspect's reaction when deprived of anxiety and depression medication was one of several factors that raised a question as to voluntariness).

[70] *R. v. Whittle*, [1994] S.C.J. No. 69, [1994] 2 S.C.R. 914 at 922-23, 946-47 (S.C.C.).

[71] *R. v. Whittle*, [1994] S.C.J. No. 69 at para. 54, [1994] 2 S.C.R. 914 (S.C.C.).

[72] The precise basis for exclusion has not always been made clear. In *R. v. Ford*, [1994] O.J. No. 2688, 25 C.R.R. (2d) 304 at para. 4 (Ont. C.A.), for example, the Court appeared to ground exclusion on a violation of the accused's *Charter* right to silence ("We therefore conclude that the implicit misrepresentation by the police officer induced the accused to waive his right to silence and, since the Crown cannot show good faith, that the statement should have been excluded."). In *R. v. Cameron*, [2002] O.J. No. 3545 at paras. 12-16 (Ont. S.C.J.), in contrast, exclusion was

§4.23 In our view, the question should be approached by asking whether, given the interrogators' conduct, the suspect's state of mind and the other conditions of the interrogation, the prospect of confidentiality created a risk of wrongful conviction. This could occur, for example, where interrogators specifically promise that a statement would not be used against the suspect. In such circumstances an innocent suspect might be induced to confess falsely to avoid further interrogation.[74] If, on the other hand, the suspect understands that the statements may be used against him or her, but simply wants the conversation to be unrecorded, then it would be difficult to justify exclusion.[75]

(b)   Threats or Promises (Inducements)

§4.24 We also know that a statement will be involuntary if police improperly used threats or promises to induce the defendant to speak. Not all threats or promises are improper, however. The use or threat of physical violence will always result in exclusion.[76] Save for "exceptional circumstances", so will explicit offers to procure lenient treatment.[77] But the status of more subtle inducements is

---

seemingly grounded on the confessions rule. See also *R. v. Reashore*, [1999] N.S.J. No. 469, 73 C.R.R. (2d) 258 at paras. 23-29 (N.S.S.C.) (rights to silence and counsel were violated when police failed to inform accused that they intended to elicit admissible statements from him during an "off the record" conversation); *R. v. Carey*, [2001] O.J. No. 1455 (Ont. S.C.J.) (right to silence violated); *R. v. Tran*, [1998] B.C.J. No. 2874 at paras. 38-42 (B.C.S.C.) (suggesting without deciding that assurances that statement would be off the record violated the confessions rule); *R. v. Smith*, [1989] S.C.J. No. 89, [1989] 2 S.C.R. 368 at 380 (S.C.C.), *per* La Forest J. dissenting (stating, in the context of a s. 24(2) *Charter* analysis that "...I am troubled by the fact that after the appellant had repeatedly asserted his desire to speak to his lawyer, the police did nothing to disabuse him of the notion that he could speak to the police 'off the record'").

[73]   See *R. v. Moran*, [1987] O.J. No. 794, 21 O.A.C. 257 (Ont. C.A.); *R. v. Allen*, [2007] O.J. No. 3503, 74 W.C.B. (2d) 768 (Ont. S.C.J.); *R. v. Stewart*, [1980] A.J. No. 631, 54 C.C.C. (2d) 93 (Alta. C.A.).

[74]   Richard Ofshe & Richard Leo, "The Decision to Confess Falsely: Rational Choice and Irrational Action" (1997) 74 Denv. U.L. Rev. 979 at 997-98, 1001-1003. This scenario could also be characterized as involving either an improper inducement or trickery that would "shock the community". See Parts 2(3)(*b*) and 2(4), respectively.

[75]   See *R. v. Narwal*, [2009] B.C.J. No. 1941, 2009 BCCA 410 at paras. 31-35 (B.C.C.A.); *R. v. Kiloh*, [2003] B.C.J. No. 321 at paras. 46-63 (B.C.S.C.). As discussed in Part 5(*b*), a suspect's desire to make an off the record statement should not justify the admission of an unrecorded confession.

[76]   *R. v. Oickle*, [2000] S.C.J. No. 38, [2000] 2 S.C.R. 3 at para. 48 (S.C.C.) ("obviously imminent threats of torture will render a confession inadmissible"). See also *R. v. Sabri*, [2002] O.J. No. 2202 (Ont. C.A.) (statement ruled involuntary after assault); *R. v. Rufiange*, [1963] J.Q. no 16, 43 C.R. 12 (Que. C.A.) (same); *R. v. Précourt* (1976), 39 C.C.C. (2d) 311 (Ont. C.A.) (same); *R. v. Logue*, [1968] O.J. No. 1216, [1969] 2 C.C.C. 346 (Ont. C.A.) (same); *R. v. Letendre*, [1979] B.C.J. No. 1496, 46 C.C.C. (2d) 398 (B.C.C.A.) (statement ruled involuntary because interrogator's statement that he was getting angry was a veiled threat).

[77]   See *R. v. Oickle*, [2000] S.C.J. No. 38, [2000] 2 S.C.R. 3 at para. 49 (S.C.C.). See also *R. v. T. (S.G.)*, [2008] S.J. No. 572, 2008 SKCA 119 (Sask. C.A.), revd [2010] S.C.J. No. 20, [2010] 1 S.C.R. 688, 2010 SCC 20 (S.C.C.) (statement ruled involuntary after police told accused that he might not be charged if he apologized); *R. c. Begin*, [2002] J.Q. no 3546 at para. 17 (Que. C.A.) (statement ruled involuntary after accused offered "leniency and favourable conditions of detention" in return for confession); *R. v. Leblanc*, [1972] B.C.J. No. 703, 8 C.C.C. (2d) 562 (B.C.C.A.) (statement ruled involuntary after police stated that accused would not be presented

less clear. Courts have been reluctant to prohibit specific tactics *ex ante*. Instead, they have favoured a "contextual approach" that considers "the entire circumstances" to determine whether the "will of the subject has been overborne."[78]

§4.25 Courts have thus admitted confessions despite the use of a variety of manipulative inducements, including offering psychiatric counselling;[79] threatening to investigate, question, or charge suspects' loved ones;[80] withholding contact with loved ones;[81] minimizing the moral (as opposed to legal) seriousness of the offence;[82] and suggesting that "it would be better" if the suspect confessed.[83] Similarly, courts have generally not considered appeals to religion or conscience to be improper inducements.[84]

§4.26 In *Oickle*, the Court suggested that the critical factor in evaluating an alleged inducement is whether it should be characterized as a *quid pro quo* offered in exchange for a confession.[85] It later held in *R. v. Spencer*,[86] however, that "while a *quid pro quo* is an important factor in establishing the existence of a threat or promise, it is the *strength* of the inducement, having regard to the particular individual and his or her circumstances, that is to be considered in the overall contextual analysis ... ."[87] Thus, while the police clearly offered Spencer a *quid pro quo* (withholding a visit with his girlfriend until he confessed), the Court upheld the trial judge's decision that it was not strong enough to render

---

to justice for bail hearing until he confessed). On the other hand, it is not an improper inducement to promise a suspect that he will be released if he provides a confirmable alibi: *R. v. Backhouse*, [2005] O.J. No. 754, 194 C.C.C. (3d) 1 (Ont. C.A.).

[78] *R. v. Oickle*, [2000] S.C.J. No. 38, [2000] 2 S.C.R. 3 at paras. 50, 57 and 68 (S.C.C.).

[79] *Ibid.*, at paras. 50 and 78 (S.C.R.) (suggestions that suspect needed "professional help" were acceptable because they did not constitute an offer contingent on a confession). See also *R. v. Ewert*, [1991] B.C.J. No. 3394, 68 C.C.C. (3d) 207 at 217 (B.C.C.A.), revd on other grounds [1992] S.C.J. No. 81, 76 C.C.C. (3d) 287*n* (S.C.C.); *R. v. Hatton*, [1978] O.J. No. 460, 39 C.C.C. (2d) 281 (Ont. C.A.); *R. v. Reyat*, [1993] B.C.J. No. 622, 80 C.C.C. (3d) 210 (B.C.C.A.).

[80] See *R. v. Oickle*, [2000] S.C.J. No. 38, [2000] 2 S.C.R. 3 at paras. 81-84 (S.C.C.) (threat to question fiancée); *R. v. Spencer*, [2007] S.C.J. No. 11, [2007] 1 S.C.R. 500 (S.C.C.) (threat to charge girlfriend); *R. v. Jackson*, [1977] B.C.J. No. 1117, 34 C.C.C. (2d) 35 (B.C.C.A.) (threats to charge friend).

[81] *R. v. Spencer*, [2007] S.C.J. No. 11, [2007] 1 S.C.R. 500 (S.C.C.).

[82] *R. v. Oickle*, [2000] S.C.J. No. 38, [2000] 2 S.C.R. 3 at paras. 73-77 (S.C.C.).

[83] The Supreme Court has stated that such comments require exclusion "only where the circumstances reveal an implicit threat or promise"; otherwise they will likely be considered only "moral inducements" that do not undermine voluntariness: *R. v. Oickle*, [2000] S.C.J. No. 38, [2000] 2 S.C.R. 3 at paras. 55, 79-80 (S.C.C.). See also *R. v. Hayes*, [1982] A.J. No. 1042, 65 C.C.C. (2d) 294 (Alta. C.A.); *R. v. Puffer*, [1976] M.J. No. 175, 31 C.C.C. (2d) 81 (Man. C.A.).

[84] See Fred Kaufman, *Admissibility of Confessions*, 3d ed. (Toronto: Carswell, 1979) at 179-86. As the Court explained in *R. v. Oickle*, [2000] S.C.J. No. 38, [2000] 2 S.C.R. 3 at para. 56 (S.C.C.), such statements are acceptable because "the inducement offered is not in the control of the police officers."

[85] *R. v. Oickle*, [2000] S.C.J. No. 38, [2000] 2 S.C.R. 3 at para. 57 (S.C.C.) ("The most important consideration in all cases is to look for a quid pro quo offer by interrogators, regardless of whether it comes in the form of a threat or a promise.").

[86] [2007] S.C.J. No. 11, [2007] 1 S.C.R. 500 (S.C.C.).

[87] *Ibid.*, at para. 15 (S.C.R.) [emphasis added]. See also *R. v. Jackson*, [1977] B.C.J. No. 1117, 34 C.C.C. (2d) 35 at 38 (B.C.C.A).

his statement inadmissible, especially in light of his savvy and experience in dealing with police.[88]

(c)   Oppression

§4.27 Confessions may also be excluded if they were obtained in an "atmosphere of oppression".[89] Like inducement, oppression is an expansive concept.[90] Put simply, it arises when a suspect is detained or interrogated under "inhumane conditions".[91] In *Oickle*, the Court noted that such conditions may be created by depriving suspects of necessities such as food, clothing, water, sleep or medical attention; denying them access to counsel; subjecting them to aggressive, intimidating or prolonged questioning; or confronting them with inadmissible or fabricated evidence.[92] Failing to warn suspects about their right to silence and ignoring invocations of this right may also contribute to an oppressive atmosphere.[93]

§4.28 None of these factors is determinative, however, and it is difficult to discern much consistency in either the pre- or post-*Oickle* case law. While egregious disregard for a detainee's basic physical needs will usually be considered oppressive,[94] some courts have failed to find oppression despite substantial deprivations of sleep[95] and clothing.[96] Similarly, courts have often found confessions to be voluntary despite failures to caution;[97] prolonged denials of access to

---

[88] *R. v. Spencer*, [2007] S.C.J. No. 11, [2007] 1 S.C.R. 500 at paras. 13, 20-21 (S.C.C.).

[89] *R. v. Hobbins*, [1982] S.C.J. No. 25, [1982] 1 S.C.R. 553 at 547 (S.C.C.). See also *R. v. Liew*, [1999] S.C.J. No. 51, [1999] 3 S.C.R. 227 at para. 37 (S.C.C.); *R. v. Oickle*, [2000] S.C.J. No. 38, [2000] 2 S.C.R. 3 at para. 27 (S.C.C.); *R. v. Hoilett*, [1999] O.J. No. 2358, 26 C.R. (5th) 332 (Ont. C.A.).

[90] See Alan W. Bryant, Sidney R. Lederman & Michelle K. Fuerst, *Sopinka, Lederman & Bryant: The Law of Evidence in Canada*, 3d ed. (Markham, ON: LexisNexis Canada, 2009) at 448 ("[o]ppression, like the term 'voluntariness', is a concept more easily understood by illustration than by definition"); *R. v. Alexis*, [1994] O.J. No. 2270, 35 C.R. (4th) 117 at 155 (Ont. Gen. Div.) ("oppressiveness is necessarily contextual...[t]he circumstances of each case must be scrutinized with no one factor or combination of factors reducing themselves to an automatic formula").

[91] *R. v. Oickle*, [2000] S.C.J. No. 38, [2000] 2 S.C.R. 3 at para. 60 (S.C.C.).

[92] *Ibid.*, at paras. 60-61 (S.C.R.).

[93] *R. v. Singh*, [2007] S.C.J. No. 48, [2007] 3 S.C.R. 405 at paras. 32, 53 (S.C.C.). See also *R. v. Otis*, [2000] J.Q. no 4320, 151 C.C.C. (3d) 416 at para. 56 (Que. C.A.), leave to appeal refused [2001] 1 S.C.R. xvii (S.C.C.).

[94] See *e.g.*, *R. v. Hoilett*, [1999] O.J. No. 2358, 26 C.R. (5th) 332 (Ont. C.A.).

[95] See *R. v. Ross*, [1997] O.J. No. 2316, 30 O.T.C. 247 (Ont. Gen. Div.) (oppressiveness did not arise from the police's refusal to allow an exhausted accused sleep during questioning).

[96] See *R. v. Owen*, [1983] N.S.J. No. 367, 4 C.C.C. (3d) 538 (N.S.S.C.); *R. v. McLeod*, [1983] O.J. No. 81, 6 C.C.C. (3d) 29 (Ont. C.A.); *R. v. Jackson*, [2005] A.J. No. 1726, 2005 ABCA 430 (Alta. C.A.). But see *R. v. Moore-McFarlane*, [2001] O.J. No. 4646, 56 O.R. (3d) 737 at para. 73 (Ont. C.A.) (lack of clothing one of several factors raising doubt as to voluntariness).

[97] See discussion below, Part 3.

counsel;[98] lengthy, repetitive or assertive questioning;[99] disregard of the suspect's wish to remain silent;[100] and unlawful or unreasonably lengthy detentions.[101]

§4.29 The use of trickery or deception may also yield oppression, especially when it is apt to produce a false confession. The use of false evidence, the Court noted in *Oickle*, is particularly dangerous; such evidence "is often crucial in convincing the suspect that protestations of innocence, even if true, are futile."[102]

---

[98] See *R. v. Hogan*, [1974] S.C.J. No. 116, 18 C.C.C. (2d) 65 (S.C.C.); *R. v. Emele*, [1940] S.J. No. 1, 74 C.C.C. 76 (Sask. C.A.) (one-day delay); *R. v. Letendre*, [1975] M.J. No. 30, 25 C.C.C. (2d) 180 (Man. C.A.) (institutional delay); *R. v. Settee*, [1974] S.J. No. 317, 29 C.R.N.S. 104 at 117 (Sask. C.A.); *R. v. Whynott*, [1975] N.S.J. No. 373, 27 C.C.C. (2d) 321 at 327 (N.S.C.A.); *R. v. Conkie*, [1978] A.J. No. 53, 39 C.C.C. (2d) 408 at 418 (Alta. C.A.) (police talked to accused in defiance of counsel's request); *R. v. Chow*, [1978] B.C.J. No. 1109, 43 C.C.C. (2d) 215 (B.C.C.A.) (police held accused from counsel for eight hours; counsel partially acquiesced to the delay).

[99] *R. v. Fayant*, [1983] M.J. No. 138, 6 C.C.C. (3d) 507 (Man. C.A.); *R. v. Owen*, [1983] N.S.J. No. 367, 4 C.C.C. (3d) 538 (N.S.C.A.); *R. v. McCormack*, [1984] M.J. No. 158, 12 W.C.B. 169 (Man. C.A.); *R. v. Bellos*, [1927] S.C.J. No. 13, [1927] S.C.R. 258 (S.C.C.); *R. v. Fitton*, [1956] S.C.J. No. 70, [1956] S.C.R. 958 at 964 (S.C.C.), *per* Rand J., at 972 (S.C.R.), *per* Nolan J., at 984 (S.C.R.), *per* Fateaux J.; *R. v. Singh*, [2007] S.C.J. No. 48, [2007] 3 S.C.R. 405 at para. 47 (S.C.C.). As discussed in Parts 3 and 5, respectively, ss. 10(*b*) and 7 also limit police interrogation tactics.

[100] See *R. v. Singh*, [2007] S.C.J. No. 48, [2007] 3 S.C.R. 405 (S.C.C.) (repeated questioning in face of 18 assertions of right to silence did not render confession involuntary); *R. v. Edmondson*, [2005] S.J. No. 256, 2005 SKCA 51 (Sask. C.A.), leave to appeal refused [2005] S.C.C.A. No. 273 (S.C.C.). But see *R. c. Otis*, [2000] J.Q. no 4320, 151 C.C.C. (3d) 416 (Que. C.A.), leave to appeal to S.C.C. refused, [2001] 1 S.C.R. xvii (S.C.C.) (persistent questioning of suspect with limited cognitive capacities violated s. 7 of *Charter*). For criticisms of this jurisprudence, see Dale E. Ives & Christopher Sherrin, "*R. v. Singh*: A Meaningless Right to Silence with Dangerous Consequences" (2008) 51 C.R. (6th) 250; Don Stuart, "Annotation to *Singh*" (2008) 51 C.R. (6th) 199. See also Lee Stuesser, "The Accused's Right to Silence: No Doesn't Mean No" (2002) 29 Man. L.J. 149.

[101] *R. v. Précourt*, [1976] O.J. No. 2421, 39 C.C.C. (2d) 311, 18 O.R. (2d) 174 (Ont. C.A.); *R. v. Fayant*, [1983] M.J. No. 138, 6 C.C.C. (3d) 507 (Man. C.A.); *R. v. Guerin*, [1979] J.Q. no 227, 14 C.R. (3d) 1 (Que. S.C.); *R. v. Hobbins*, [1980] O.J. No. 1279, 54 C.C.C. (2d) 353 (Ont. C.A.), affd [1982] S.C.J. No. 25, 66 C.C.C. (2d) 289 (S.C.C.); *R. v. Feeny*, [1980] J.Q. no 180, [1980] C.A. 99, appeal quashed [1981] 2 S.C.R. 130; *R. v. Hatton*, [1978] O.J. No. 460, 39 C.C.C. (2d) 281 (Ont. C.A.); *R. v. Nye*, [1958] O.J. No. 321, 29 C.R. 82 (Ont. C.A.); *R. v. Grosse*, [1983] N.S.J. No. 545, 9 C.C.C. (3d) 465 (N.S.S.C.); *R. v. Roy*, [2003] O.J. No. 4252, 15 C.R. (6th) 282 at para. 13 (Ont. C.A.). Courts have sometimes indicated, however, that confessions obtained after lengthy confinement will likely be excluded unless the Crown adduces evidence detailing suspects' treatment during this period. See *R. v. Thiffault*, [1933] S.C.J. No. 44, [1933] S.C.R. 509 (S.C.C.); *R. v. Koszulap*, [1974] O.J. No. 726, 20 C.C.C. (2d) 193 (Ont. C.A.); *R. v. Botfield*, [1973] B.C.J. No. 782, 28 C.C.C. (2d) 472 (B.C.C.A.).

[102] *R. v. Oickle*, [2000] S.C.J. No. 38, [2000] 2 S.C.R. 3 at para. 61 (S.C.C.). See also *ibid.*, at paras. 38 and 40 (S.C.R.). The traditional view had been that deception not amounting to a threat or promise could not render a confession involuntary. See *R. v. Rothman*, [1981] S.C.J. No. 55, [1981] 1 S.C.R. 640 at 673 (S.C.C.); *R. v. Alward*, [1976] N.B.J. No. 220, 32 C.C.C. (2d) 416 (N.B.C.A.), affd [1977] S.C.J. No. 63, 35 C.C.C. (2d) 392 (S.C.C.); *R. v. White*, [1908] O.J. No. 23, 15 C.C.C. 30 (Ont. C.A.); *R. v. McLeod*, [1968] O.J. No. 533, 5 C.R.N.S. 101 (Ont. C.A.); *R. v. Allen*, [1979] O.J. No. 4565, 46 C.C.C. (2d) 553 (Ont. H.C.J.); *R. v. Robertson*, [1975] O.J. No. 1658, 21 C.C.C. (2d) 385 (Ont. C.A.); *R. v. Green*, [1987] A.J. No. 561, 36 C.C.C. (3d) 137 (Alta. C.A.); *R. v. Paradis* (1976), 38 C.C.C. (2d) 455 (Que. C.A.); *R. v. Pettipiece*, [1972] B.C.J. No. 669, 18 C.R.N.S. 236 (B.C.C.A.). See generally, Ed Ratushny,

The use of this type of trickery may lead to a finding that the interrogation was oppressive and hence involuntary.

(d) Reforming the Voluntariness Test

§4.30 How well does the voluntariness test serve the interests implicated by police questioning? The test should maximize the probability of convicting the factually guilty, minimize the possibility of convicting the innocent and deter abusive interrogation practices. As the Supreme Court has recognized, of these interests, preventing the admission of false confessions that could lead to wrongful convictions should be paramount.[103] Evidence is mounting that wrongful convictions are disturbingly frequent, that a substantial proportion of wrongful convictions involve false confessions and that when admitted at trial, false confessions are likely to cause a wrongful conviction.[104] Consequently, judges should apply the voluntariness test to exclude statements that are of such questionable reliability that their admission would create a significant risk of wrongful conviction.[105]

§4.31 A rule excluding particular confessions judged to be unreliable does not do enough to prevent wrongful convictions, however. The courts should also exclude statements produced by methods that *generally* create a significant risk of false confession, even if the confession in a particular case appears trustworthy. Evidence allegedly corroborating potentially dubious confessions is often itself unreliable. Interrogators may feed innocent suspects non-public information, for example, or courts may admit dubious jailhouse informant or forensic evidence.[106] Statements produced by interrogation techniques that experience and

---

"Statements by Trickery: How Far Will They Go? Annotation to *R. v. Pettipiece*" (1972) 18 C.R.N.S. 257.

[103] See *R. v. Oickle*, [2000] S.C.J. No. 38, [2000] 2 S.C.R. 3 at paras. 32-46 (S.C.C.).

[104] See Brandon L. Garrett, "Judging Innocence" (2008) 108 Colum. L. Rev. 55 at 88-91; Steve Drizin & Richard A. Leo, "The Problem of False Confessions in the Post-DNA World" (2004) 82 N.C. L. Rev. 891. Though there is a dearth of Canadian research on the subject, there is little reason to think that the situation in the United States is markedly different, especially as Canadian interrogators receive very similar training to their American counterparts, including widespread reliance on the "Reid Technique" training program offered by John E. Reid and Associates. See *R. v. Cruz*, [2008] A.J. No. 559, 2008 ABPC 155 at para. 106 (Alta. Prov. Ct.); *R. v. Minde*, [2003] A.J. No. 1184 at para. 32 (Alta. Q.B.); *R. v. Barrett*, [1993] O.J. No. 1317, 13 O.R. (3d) 587 at para. 58 (Ont. C.A.), revd [1995] S.C.J. No. 19, [1995] 1 S.C.R. 752 (S.C.C.); *R. v. Whalen*, [1999] O.J. No. 3488 at paras. 11-15 (Ont. C.J.); *R. v. Barges*, [2005] O.J. No. 5595 at paras. 52-53, 80-81 (Ont. S.C.J.). See also Fred E. Inbau *et al.*, *Criminal Interrogation and Confessions*, 4th ed. (Boston: Jones and Bartlett, 2004).

[105] See *R. v. Oickle*, [2000] S.C.J. No. 38, [2000] 2 S.C.R. 3 at para. 68 (S.C.C.) ("... because of the criminal justice system's overriding concern not to convict the innocent, a confession will not be admissible if it is made under circumstances that raise a reasonable doubt as to voluntariness").

[106] See Brandon L. Garrett, "Judging Innocence" (2008) 108 Colum. L. Rev. 55 at 89.

study have shown are apt to produce false confessions should therefore be considered involuntary.[107]

§4.32 The voluntariness test could also be improved by injecting more precision into the "totality of the circumstances" inquiry.[108] Though the Supreme Court has identified many of the factors contributing to false confessions, it has imposed few bright-line restrictions. Consequently, when faced with a recalcitrant suspect and the pressure to solve a serious crime, police may use coercive tactics in the hope that prosecutors will later be able to convince the court that, considering all the circumstances, the confession is sufficiently reliable.

§4.33 We thus urge courts (and ideally, Parliament) to provide more concrete guidelines to police by, for example, imposing maximum limits on the length of interrogations,[109] restricting the questioning of vulnerable suspects,[110] banning the use of false evidence[111] and prohibiting specific misrepresentations as to the strength of evidence.[112] We also recommend greater sensitivity to the role that

---

[107] See Welsh S. White, "False Confessions and the Constitution: Safeguards Against Untrustworthy Confessions" (1997) 32 Harv. C.R.-C.L. L. Rev. 105 at 139-40; Steven Penney, "What's Wrong with Self-Incrimination? The Wayward Path of Self-Incrimination Law in the Post-Charter Era, Part 2: Self-Incrimination in Police Investigations" (2004) 48 Crim. L.Q. 280 at 296-97.

[108] *R. v. Oickle*, [2000] S.C.J. No. 38, [2000] 2 S.C.R. 3 at paras. 68 and 71 (S.C.C.).

[109] Psychological studies indicate that suspects subjected to lengthy and persistent interrogations may confess falsely in order to end the ordeal. See Welsh S. White, "False Confessions and the Constitution: Safeguards Against Untrustworthy Confessions" (1997), 32 Harv. C.R.-C.L. L. Rev. 105 at 143-45, who suggests a five hour time limit. See also American Law Institute, *A Model Code of Pre-Arraignment Procedure* (Philadephia: The Institute, 1975). In *R. v. Oickle*, [2000] S.C.J. No. 38, [2000] 2 S.C.R. 3 at paras. 45 and 60 (S.C.C.), the Court acknowledged that false confessions can be produced by prolonged questioning. But it set no *ex ante* limit on the length of an interrogation, stating only that lengthy questioning was one factor capable of producing an atmosphere of oppression leading to an involuntary statement. Indeed, the interrogation approved in that case lasted nearly six hours.

[110] As the Court noted in *R. v. Oickle*, [2000] S.C.J. No. 38, [2000] 2 S.C.R. 3 at para. 42 (S.C.C.), empirical evidence also suggests that false confessions are particularly likely to result from the interrogation of vulnerable suspects, such as people who are young, compliant, cognitively disabled or mentally ill. But it declined to set out standards for the questioning of such suspects. See also Richard A. Leo, "False Confessions: Causes, Consequences and Implications" (2009), 37 J. Am. Academy Psych. & Law 332 at 335-37.

[111] The Court also admitted in *R. v. Oickle*, [2000] S.C.J. No. 38, [2000] 2 S.C.R. 3 at para. 43 (S.C.C.) that fabricating evidence may convince innocent, suggestible suspects that they committed the crime. Alternatively, it may induce innocent suspects to believe their "protestations of innocence are futile." But the court refused to prohibit the practice, holding that it was only a "relevant consideration" in determining voluntariness at (para. 61).

[112] As in the case of fabricated evidence, exaggerating the strength of genuine evidence may induce a false confession by creating a false belief in guilt, a sense of futility or a desire to end a nightmarish ordeal. White argues that while general statements about the strength of the government's case are not likely to lead to false confessions by non-vulnerable suspects, specific misrepresentations "designed to convince the suspect that forensic evidence establishes his guilt" may do so and should therefore be prohibited. See Welsh S. White, "False Confessions and the Constitution: Safeguards Against Untrustworthy Confessions" (1997) 32 Harv. C.R.-C.L.L. Rev. 105 at 146-47. In *R. v. Oickle*, [2000] S.C.J. No. 38, [2000] 2 S.C.R. 3 at para. 100 (S.C.C.), police repeatedly exaggerated the accuracy of the polygraph test administered to the suspect. But the majority concluded that this did not render his confession inadmissible.

threats or promises play in inducing false confessions. Empirical research confirms what judges have long intuited: threats and promises are the most frequent cause of false confessions.[113] The Supreme Court's declaration in *Spencer* that *quid pro quo* inducements need not always lead to exclusion (particularly when offered to "savvy" suspects) thus deserves reconsideration.[114]

(4) Community Shock

§4.34 In *R. v. Oickle*,[115] the Supreme Court said that even if a confession is not found to be involuntary, it may still be excluded if it was obtained by trickery "so appalling as to shock the community."[116] There have been few cases applying this *dictum*, however, and it is difficult to conceive of tactics that would shock the community[117] but nonetheless elicit a voluntary confession.[118]

§4.35 As discussed in Part 2(2), above, the confession rule only applies to statements made to persons known by the suspect to be in a position of authority over the investigation or prosecution (*i.e.*, a "person in authority"). The community shock standard has also been applied, however, to statements made to un-

---

113 See Richard Ofshe & Richard A. Leo, "The Social Psychology of Police Interrogation: The Theory and Classification of True and False Confessions" (1997) 16 Studies in Law, Politics & Society 189.

114 *R. v. Spencer*, [2007] S.C.J. No. 11, [2007] 1 S.C.R. 500 (S.C.C.). See also Lisa Dufraimont, "Regulating Unreliable Evidence: Can Evidence Rules Guide Juries and Prevent Wrongful Convictions?" (2008) 33 Queen's L.J. 261 at 285-86; Dale E. Ives & Christopher Sherrin, "*R. v. Singh* — A Meaningless Right to Silence with Dangerous Consequences" (2007) 51 C.R. (6th) 250.

115 [2000] S.C.J. No. 38, [2000] 2 S.C.R. 3 (S.C.C.).

116 *Ibid.*, at para. 67 (S.C.R.). See also *R. v. Collins*, [1987] S.C.J. No. 15, [1987] 1 S.C.R. 265 at 286-87 (S.C.C.).

117 In *R. v. Oickle*, [2000] S.C.J. No. 38, [2000] 2 S.C.R. 3 (S.C.C.), the Court indicated that none of the following practices would shock the conscience of the community: manipulatively cultivating suspects' trust (paras. 85, 103 (S.C.R.), *per* Iacobucci J. and para. 125 (S.C.R.), *per* Arbour J., dissenting); failing to inform suspects that polygraph evidence is inadmissible (para. 91(S.C.R.)); or exaggerating the accuracy of polygraph testing (paras. 94-100(S.C.R.)). But see *R. v. Amyot*, [1990] J.Q. no 1061, 58 C.C.C. (3d) 312 at 324 (Que. C.A.); *R. v. Fowler*, [1979] N.J. No. 56, 23 Nfld. & P.E.I.R. 255 (Nfld. C.A.).

118 See *e.g.*, *R. v. T. (S.G.)*, [2008] S.J. No. 572, 2008 SKCA 119 (Sask. C.A.), revd [2010] S.C.J. No. 20, [2010] 1 S.C.R. 688, 2010 SCC 20 (S.C.C.), (upholding trial judge's finding that interrogator's fabrication of his own criminal past to establish trust with suspect would shock the community, but noting that the confession was also held to be involuntary on the basis of improper inducements); *R. v. Wiegand*, [2003] A.J. No. 401, 335 A.R. 157 (Alta. Q.B.) (use of fabricated evidence and other trickery would shock the community, but finding that trickery, oppression and lack of an operating mind rendered confession involuntary); *R. v. Heinermann*, [2003] O.J. No. 2645, [2003] O.T.C. 592 (Ont. S.C.J.) (giving suspect false impression that polygraph was infallible would shock the community, but also finding that this tactic rendered confession involuntary); *R. v. N.*, [2005] O.J. No. 357, 28 C.R. (6th) 140 (Ont. S.C.J.) (trickery would shock the community but also resulted in involuntariness); *R. v. Espadilla*, [2005] B.C.J. No. 1208, 2005 BCSC 174 (B.C.S.C.) (holding out possibility of death penalty would shock the community but also constituted improper inducement leading to involuntariness); *R. v. Rowe*, [2006] O.J. No. 1752, 208 C.C.C. (3d) 412 (Ont. C.A.) (use of spiritualist to induce confession would not shock community where accused had sought his assistance in avoiding apprehension).

dercover agents. In *R. v. Rothman*,[119] an agent posing as a fellow prisoner obtained a confession from a suspect who had previously exerted his right to remain silent. Applying the person in authority test, a majority of the Supreme Court held that the confessions rule did not apply. In his concurring opinion, Justice Lamer agreed. He suggested, however, that statements obtained by state conduct that "shocks the community" and "would bring the administration of justice into disrepute" should be excluded at trial.[120]

§4.36 As discussed in Part 5, below, the Court has since held that section 7 of the *Charter* is violated when state agents *actively elicit* statements from suspects *in police custody*. The argument that the admission of statements derived from undercover questioning would shock the community (and thus be excluded) may still be relevant, however, in two[121] circumstances: first, where undercover agents passively elicit statements from detained suspects, and second, where such agents obtain statements from suspects outside of custody.[122] The second circumstance includes elaborate operations (sometimes called "Mr. Big" schemes) designed to trick suspects into confessing to undercover police posing as gang members.[123] In none of these cases, however, has a court found that such tactics would shock the community.

---

[119] *R. v. Rothman*, [1981] S.C.J. No. 55, [1981] 1 S.C.R. 640 (S.C.C.).

[120] *Ibid.*, at 697 (S.C.R.). The trickery used by the police, in Lamer J.'s view, did not warrant exclusion. He suggested, however, that the following conduct would: permitting a police agent to pose as a priest or duty counsel to obtain a confession from a suspect or injecting a diabetic suspect with truth serum after telling him or her that the substance was insulin. "Pretending to be a hard drug addict to break a drug ring", in contrast, "would not shock the community; nor would, as in this case, pretending to be a truck driver to secure the conviction of a trafficker; in fact, what would shock the community would be preventing the police from resorting to such a trick."

[121] A third circumstance is technically (but not practically) possible; namely, where the court finds a violation of s. 7 but does not exclude the statement under s. 24(2) of the *Charter*. It is inconceivable, however, that a court would find that the admission of a statement would not "bring the administration of justice into disrepute" but conclude that the tactics producing it would nonetheless shock the community.

[122] See *R. v. McIntyre*, [1994] S.C.J. No. 52, [1994] 2 S.C.R. 480 (S.C.C.), affd [1993] N.B.J. No. 293, 135 N.B.R. (2d) 266 (N.B.C.A.); *R. v. Osmar*, [2007] O.J. No. 244, 2007 ONCA 50 at para. 48 (Ont. C.A.); *R. v. Bonisteel*, [2008] B.C.J. No. 1705, 2008 BCCA 344, 236 C.C.C. (3d) 170 (B.C.C.A.).

[123] See *e.g.*, *R. v. McIntyre*, [1994] S.C.J. No. 52, [1994] 2 S.C.R. 480, 168 N.R. 308, 153 N.B.R. (2d) 161, 392 A.P.R. 161, affd [1993] N.B.J. No. 293, 135 N.B.R. (2d) 266 (N.B.C.A.); *R. v. Osmar*, [2007] O.J. No. 244, 2007 ONCA 50, 84 O.R. (3d) 321, 220 O.A.C. 186, 217 C.C.C. (3d) 174, 44 C.R. (6th) 276 (Ont. C.A.); *R. v. Bonisteel*, [2008] B.C.J. No. 1705, 2008 BCCA 344, 236 C.C.C. (3d) 170 (B.C.C.A.); *R. v. Roberts*, [1997] B.C.J. No. 765, 90 B.C.A.C. 213, 147 W.A.C. 213 (B.C.C.A.); *R. v. Unger*, [1993] M.J. No. 363, 83 C.C.C. (3d) 228 at para. 71, 85 Man.R. (2d) 284, 41 W.A.C. 284 (Man. C.A); *United States of America v. Burns*, [1997] B.C.J. No. 1554, 117 C.C.C. (3d) 454 (B.C.C.A.), application for leave to appeal and for reconsideration dismissed, [1997] S.C.C.A. No. 515 (S.C.C.); *R. v. Grandinetti*, [2005] S.C.J. No. 3, [2005] 1 S.C.R. 27 at paras. 28-45 (S.C.C.); *R. v. Ashmore*, [2011] B.C.J. No. 75, 2011 BCCA 18 at paras 38-40 (B.C.C.A.).

(5) Evidentiary Issues

(a) The Voir Dire

§4.37 Whenever the prosecution wishes to introduce a statement made by the accused to a person in authority, the trial judge must hold a *voir dire* to decide its admissibility.[124] That said, where the defence does not request it, the failure to do so will be a reversible error only if "clear evidence existed in the record which objectively should have alerted [the judge] to the need for a *voir dire* notwithstanding counsel's silence."[125] When the prosecution proffers a statement made by the accused to a conventional person in authority, such as a police officer, the need for a *voir dire* will be obvious and one must be held regardless of a request from the accused.[126] If the receiver of the statement was not such a person, and the defence does not request a *voir dire*, the judge's obligation to hold one will be triggered by evidence that the receiver was "closely connected to the authorities".[127] In such a case, the trial judge must ask the defence if it wishes to waive the *voir dire*.[128] If a *voir dire* is held (whether due to a defence request or the court's own initiative), the defence must discharge an evidentiary burden on the person in authority issue.[129] If it does, then to admit the statement the prosecution must prove beyond a reasonable doubt *either* that the receiver was not a person in authority *or* that the statement was voluntary.[130]

(b) Proving Voluntariness: Recording and Cautioning

§4.38 Traditionally, the confessions rule *voir dire* would typically be based on the testimony of interrogators (and any other police present for the interview and relevant events leading up to it) and the defendant.[131] The version of events offered by police witnesses, however, often differed from that presented by the defendant. Not surprisingly, courts most often resolved this conflict in favour of the police.[132]

---

[124] See *R. v. Hodgson*, [1998] S.C.J. No. 66, [1998] 2 S.C.R. 449 at para. 41 (S.C.C.); *R. v. Erven*, [1978] S.C.J. No. 114, [1979] 1 S.C.R. 926 at 943 (S.C.C.), *per* Dickson, J.; *R. v. Sweezey*, [1974] O.J. No. 690, 20 C.C.C. (2d) 400 at 417-18 (Ont. C.A.).

[125] *R. v. Hodgson*, [1998] S.C.J. No. 66, [1998] 2 S.C.R. 449 (S.C.C.).

[126] See *R. v. Hodgson*, [1998] S.C.J. No. 66, [1998] 2 S.C.R. 449 at para. 45 (S.C.C.); *R. v. T. (S.G.)*, [2010] S.C.J. No. 20, 2010 SCC 20 at para. 23 (S.C.C.).

[127] *R. v. Hodgson*, [1998] S.C.J. No. 66, [1998] 2 S.C.R. 449 (S.C.C.).

[128] *Ibid.*, at para. 46 (S.C.R.).

[129] *R. v. Hodgson*, [1998] S.C.J. No. 66, [1998] 2 S.C.R. 449 at para. 37 (S.C.C.). See also *R. v. P. (R.G.)*, [1977] A.J. No. 502, 3 A.R. 524 at 542 (Alta. C.A.).

[130] *R. v. Hodgson*, [1998] S.C.J. No. 66, [1998] 2 S.C.R. 449 at paras. 37-38 (S.C.C.).

[131] See Alan W. Bryant, Sidney R. Lederman & Michelle K. Fuerst, *Sopinka, Lederman & Bryant: The Law of Evidence in Canada*, 3d ed. (Markham: LexisNexis Canada, 2009) at 476-79.

[132] See Ed Ratushny, *Self-incrimination in the Canadian Criminal Process* (Toronto: Carswell, 1979) at 107-108; Fred Kaufman, *Admissibility of Confessions*, 3d ed. (Toronto: Carswell, 1979) at 63-64 and 140-42.

§4.39 Fortunately, it is becoming increasingly common for police to make audiovisual recordings of interrogations.[133] As the Supreme Court noted in *R. v. Oickle*,[134] this practice is commendable.[135] Electronic recording provides a generally reliable record of the circumstances of interrogation for the purposes of determining admissibility on the *voir dire* and helps prevent false confessions, abusive questioning and false claims of coercion.[136] As a consequence, legislatures[137] and courts[138] in many jurisdictions have made electronic recording a prerequisite to the admission of confessions in certain circumstances.[139]

---

[133] See *R. v. Oickle*, [2000] S.C.J. No. 38, [2000] 2 S.C.R. 3 at para. 46 (S.C.C.).

[134] [2000] S.C.J. No. 38, [2000] 2 S.C.R. 3 (S.C.C.).

[135] See *R. v. Oickle*, [2000] S.C.J. No. 38, [2000] 2 S.C.R. 3 at para. 46 (S.C.C.). See also *R. v. B. (K.G.)*, [1993] S.C.J. No. 22, [1993] 1 S.C.R. 740 at 792-94 (S.C.C.); *R. v. Crockett*, [2002] B.C.J. No. 2947, 2002 BCCA 658 at paras. 17-20 (B.C.C.A.); *R. v. Barrett*, [1993] O.J. No. 1317, 82 C.C.C. (3d) 266 (Ont. C.A.), revd [1995] S.C.J. No. 19, [1995] 1 S.C.R. 752 (S.C.C.); *R. v. Vangent*, [1978] O.J. No. 3759, 42 C.C.C. 2d 313 at 328-330 (Ont. Prov. Ct.); *R. v. Lim (No. 3)*, [1990] O.J. No. 940, 1 C.R.R. (2d) 148 (Ont. H.C.J.); *R. v. Falcher*, [1994] O.J. No. 1922 (Ont. Gen. Div.); *R. v. Luong*, [1995] O.J. No. 1430 (Ont. Prov. Div.); *R. v. Nelson*, [1999] O.J. No. 4377 (Ont. S.C.J.); *R. v. Haynes*, [2001] O.J. No. 73 (Ont. S.C.J.); Ed Ratushny, *Self-incrimination in the Canadian Criminal Process* (Toronto: Carswell, 1979) at 272; Law Reform Commission of Canada, *Questioning Suspects: Working Paper No. 32* (Ottawa: Law Reform Commission of Canada, 1984) at 58; Alan Grant, "Videotaping Police Interviews: A Canadian Experiment" [1987] Crim. L. Rev. 375; Alan Young, "Adversarial Justice and the Charter of Rights: Stunting the Growth of the 'Living Tree'" (1997) 39 Crim. L.Q. 362 at 379-80; Joyce Miller, *The Audio-Visual Taping of Police Interviews with Suspects and Accused Persons by Halton Regional Police Force: An Evaluation* (Ottawa: Law Reform Commission of Canada, 1988); R. Woods, *Police Interrogation* (Toronto: Carswell, 1990) at 106; *Report to the Attorney General by the Police Commission on the Use of Video Equipment by Police Forces in British Columbia* (Victoria: British Columbia Police Commission, 1986); Tim Quigley, "Pre-trial, Trial, and Post-trial Procedure" in Don Stuart, Ronald J. Delisle & Alan Manson, eds., *Towards a Clear and Just Criminal Law: A Criminal Reports Forum* (Toronto: Carswell, 1999) 253 at 290.

[136] See *R. v. Oickle*, [2000] S.C.J. No. 38, [2000] 2 S.C.R. 3 at para. 46 (S.C.C.). See also Glanville Williams, "The Authentication of Statements to the Police" [1979] Crim. L.R. 6 at 13-22; Welsh S. White, "False Confessions and the Constitution: Safeguards Against Untrustworthy Confessions" (1997) 32 Harv. C.R.-C.L. L. Rev. 105 at 153. Audiovisual recording cannot, of course, guarantee a full and accurate record. It is possible for police to record or produce only selective portions of questioning or even to physically manipulate the recording. In most cases, however, discontinuities and manipulation are readily detectable. Empirical evidence indicates, moreover, that abuses are rare and that the presence of recording devices does not inhibit suspects from cooperating. See William A. Geller, *Police Videotaping of Suspect Interrogations and Confessions: A Preliminary Examination of Issues and Practices: A Report to the National Institute of Justice* (Washington, D.C.: United States Department of Justice 1992) at 117-19; Joyce Miller, *The Audio-Visual Taping of Police Interviews with Suspects and Accused Persons by Halton Regional Police Force, Ontario, Canada: An Evaluation* (Ottawa: Law Reform Commission of Canada, 1987) at 75-77; Paul Cassell, "*Miranda*'s Social Costs: An Empirical Reassessment" (1996) 90 Nw. U. L. Rev. 387 at 488-90.

[137] See *Illinois Code of Criminal Procedure of 1963*, 725 ILCS 5, s. 103-2.1; *Tex. Code Crim. Proc.*, art. 38.22 § 3(a)(1) (2002) (Texas); D.C. Code Ann. § 5-116.01 (LexisNexis Supp. 2007) (D.C.); Me. Rev. Stat. Ann. tit. 25, § 2803-B (2007) (Maine); N.M. Stat. § 29-1-16 (Supp. 2006) (New Mexico); Tex. Code Crim. Proc. Ann. art. 38.22, § 3 (Vernon Supp. 2007); N.C. Gen. Stat. § 15A-211 (North Carolina); *Evidence Act 2001*, s. 85A (Tasmania); *Crimes Act 1958*, s. 464H (Victoria); *Criminal Code*, s. 570D (Western Australia); *Police Administration Act*, ss. 142-143 (Northern Territory); *Criminal Procedure Act 1986*, s. 281 (New South Wales); *Summary Offences Act 1953*, s. 74D (South Australia); *Crimes Act 1914*, s. 23A(6)

§4.40 The Parliament of Canada has not yet enacted such legislation, however, and in *Oickle*, the Supreme Court stopped short of adopting such a rule.[140] But since *Oickle*, several courts have held that when recording equipment is available and police deliberately set out to interrogate a suspect in custody, the failure to record will place a "heavy burden" on the Crown to prove voluntariness beyond a reasonable doubt.[141] Other courts, however, have resisted this trend, hold-

---

(Cth.) (Australian Capital Territory); *Police Powers and Responsibilities Act 2000*, ss. 246 and 263-266 (Queensland); *Crimes Act 1914*, s. 23V (Cth.) (Australia); *Criminal Justice Act, 1984 (Electronic Recording of Interviews) Regulations, 1997*, S.I. No. 74/1997 (Ireland); *Police and Criminal Evidence Act 1984*, c. 62, s. 60 (England and Wales).

[138] See *Stephan v. State*, 711 P.2d 1156 at 1159-60 (Alaska S.C. 1985); *State v. Scales*, 518 N.W.2d 587 at 591-93 (Minn. S.C. 1994).

[139] Commentators have advocated mandatory electronic recording for many years. See the Hon. Peter deC. Cory, *The Inquiry regarding Thomas Sophonow* (November 4, 2001) at 19, online: <http://www.gov.mb.ca/justice/publications/sophonow/police/recommend.html>; *The Commission on Proceedings Involving Guy Paul Morin* (Toronto: Ministry of the Attorney General, 1998) at 1199-1206; Steven Penney, "What's Wrong with Self-Incrimination? The Wayward Path of Self-Incrimination Law in the Post-Charter Era, Part 2: Self-Incrimination in Police Investigations" (2004) 48 Crim. L.Q. 280 at 290-93; Ed Ratushny, *Self-incrimination in the Canadian Criminal Process* (Toronto: Carswell, 1979) at 272; Law Reform Commission of Canada, *Questioning Suspects: Working Paper No. 32* (Ottawa: The Commission, 1984) at 58; Alan Grant, "Videotaping Police Interviews: A Canadian Experiment" [1987] Crim. L. Rev. 375; Alan Young, "Adversarial Justice and the *Charter of Rights*: Stunting the Growth of the 'Living Tree'" (1997) 39 Crim. L.Q. 362 at 379-80; Joyce Miller, *The Audio-visual Taping of Police Interviews with Suspects and Accused Persons by Halton Regional Police Force: An Evaluation* (Ottawa: The Commission, 1988); R. Woods, *Police Interrogation* (Toronto: Carswell, 1990) at 106; *Report to the Attorney General by the Police Commission on the Use of Video Equipment by Police Forces in British Columbia* (Victoria: British Columbia Police Commission, 1986); Tim Quigley, "Pre-trial, Trial, and Post-trial Procedure" in Don Stuart, Ronald J. Delisle & Alan Manson, eds., *Towards a Clear and Just Criminal Law: A Criminal Reports Forum* (Toronto: Carswell, 1999) 253 at 290.

[140] *R. v. Oickle*, [2000] S.C.J. No. 38, [2000] 2 S.C.R. 3 at para. 46 (S.C.C.) ("This is not to suggest that non-recorded interrogations are inherently suspect; it is simply to make the obvious point that when a recording is made, it can greatly assist the trier of fact in assessing the confession.").

[141] *R. v. Moore-McFarlane*, [2001] O.J. No. 4646, 160 C.C.C. (3d) 493 at para. 65 (Ont. C.A.). See also *R. v. Swanek*, [2005] O.J. No. 493, 28 C.R. (6th) 93 (Ont. C.A.); *R. v. Ahmed*, [2002] O.J. No. 4597, 170 C.C.C. (3d) 27 at para. 14 (Ont. C.A.); *R. v. White*, [2003] O.J. No. 2458, 65 O.R. (3d) 97 at paras. 21-25 (Ont. C.A.); *R. v. Sabri*, [2002] O.J. No. 2202 at paras. 16-18 (Ont. C.A.); *R. v. Marshall*, [2005] O.J. No. 3549 at paras. 95-99 (Ont. C.A.), leave to appeal to S.C.C. refused [2006] S.C.C.A. No. 105 (S.C.C.); *R. v. Groat*, [2006] B.C.J. No. 109, 2006 BCCA 27, 205 C.C.C. (3d) 542 at para. 7 (B.C.C.A.). The taking of contemporaneous notes has been held not to be a sufficient substitute for audiovisual recording: *R. v. Moore-McFarlane*, [2001] O.J. No. 4646, 160 C.C.C. (3d) 493 at para. 62 (Ont. C.A.) (C.C.C.) ("even if 'notes were accurate concerning the content of what was said, they cannot reflect the tone of what was said and any body language that may have been employed'"). Some courts have found that a suspect's request to speak without recording justifies the admission of unrecorded confessions. See *e.g.*, *R. v. Narwal*, [2006] B.C.J. No. 526, 2006 BCSC 377 at para. 38 (B.C.S.C.), affd [2009] B.C.J. No. 1941, 2009 BCCA 410 (B.C.C.A.). Others, however, have rightly held that it does not. See *R. v. Bunn*, [2001] M.J. No. 31 at paras. 13-15 (Man. C.A.); *R. v. Cameron*, [2002] O.J. No. 3545 (Ont. S.C.J.).

ing that the failure to record is simply one factor to be considered in determining voluntariness.[142]

§4.41 We favour the former view and urge the courts to go even further. The costs of recording (financial and otherwise) are minimal and the benefits to the administration of the criminal justice system are substantial. While legislative intervention would be welcome, courts have been modifying the confessions rule for hundreds of years and have extensive knowledge of the frailties of witnesses's memories, limitations of cross-examination and role of coercive interrogation in generating false confessions and wrongful convictions. Unrecorded statements to persons in authority by suspects in police custody should not therefore be admitted at trial unless audiovisual recording was not feasible in the circumstances.[143] Given how ubiquitous, inexpensive and compact video recording devices have become, we would expect that such circumstances would be quite rare.

§4.42 Another step that police should take to assist in proving voluntariness is to give suspects a proper "caution" before questioning them. Before beginning custodial questioning, police typically inform suspects of: (*i*) their right to counsel; (*ii*) their right to remain silent and (*iii*) the fact that their statements may be used against them. Failing to issue these cautions, many courts have held, is a "major" or "important" factor militating against voluntariness.[144] It does not, however, automatically lead to exclusion; courts have held (both before[145] and after[146] the enactment of the *Charter*[147]) that a confession may still be voluntary without it.

---

[142] See *R. v. Narwal*, [2009] B.C.J. No. 1941, 2009 BCCA 410 at paras. 36-38 (B.C.C.A.); *R. v. Quinn*, [2009] B.C.J. No. 1168, 2009 BCCA 267 (B.C.C.A.); *R. v. Billings*, [2004] B.C.J. No. 1029, 2004 BCSC 456 at paras. 53-56 (B.C.S.C.); *R. v. Ducharme*, [2004] M.J. No. 60, 2004 MBCA 29 at paras. 26-47, [2004] 9 W.W.R. 218, 182 C.C.C. (3d) 243, 20 C.R. (6th) 332, 184 Man.R. (2d) 36 (Man. C.A.).

[143] This would include the audiovisual recording of the entire interrogation, including any post-admission narrative provided by the suspect. Recording this phase of the interrogation allows courts to determine if interrogators explicitly or implicitly provided the accused with non-public facts that could otherwise be viewed as corroborating the truth of the confession. See Richard A. Leo, "False Confessions: Causes, Consequences and Implications" (2009) 37 J. Am. Academy Psych. & Law 332.

[144] See *R. v. Morrison*, [2000] O.J. No. 5733 at paras. 53-60, 57 W.C.B. (2d) 161 (Ont. S.C.J.) (failure to caution suspect major factor in determining confession involuntary); *R. v. Papadopoulos*, [2006] O.J. No. 5423, 74 W.C.B. (2d) 820 (Ont. S.C.J.) ("presence or absence of a caution is but one factor, although an important one, in determining whether a statement was made voluntarily"); *R. v. Kooktook*, [2006] Nu.J. No. 7, 210 C.C.C. (3d) 106 at paras. 122-124 (Nu. C.A.) (lack of evidence as to contents of caution one factor raising doubt as to voluntariness).

[145] See *R. v. Boudreau*, [1949] S.C.J. No. 10, [1949] S.C.R. 262 at 267 (S.C.C.); *R. v. Fitton*, [1956] S.C.J. No. 70, [1956] S.C.R. 958 (S.C.C.); *R. v. Esposito*, [1985] O.J. No. 1002, 24 C.C.C. (3d) 88 (Ont. C.A.); *R. v. DeClercq*, [1968] S.C.J. No. 68, [1968] S.C.R. 902 (S.C.C.). See also Tim Quigley, "Pre-trial, Trial, and Post-trial Procedure" in D. Stuart, R.J. Delisle, & Alan Manson, eds., *Towards a Clear and Just Criminal Law: A Criminal Reports Forum* (Toronto: Carswell, 1999) 253 at 290.

[146] See *R. v. Singh*, [2007] S.C.J. No. 48, [2007] 3 S.C.R. 405 at paras. 32-33 (S.C.C.); *R. v. Morrison*, [2000] O.J. No. 5733 at paras. 53-60, 57 W.C.B. (2d) 161 (Ont. S.C.J.); *R. v. Wills*, [2006] O.J. No. 4232, 73 W.C.B. (2d) 479 at para. 127 (Ont. S.C.J.); *R. v. Papadopoulos*, [2006] O.J.

(c) Evidence Derived from Involuntary Confessions

§4.43 Involuntary confessions, while not themselves admissible, may lead to the discovery of other evidence. Depending on the circumstances, this "derivative" evidence may or may not be admissible. There are two lines of authority on this question: one dealing with statements and one with physical evidence.

(i) Statements (The "Derived Confession" Rule)

§4.44 At common law, statements made following an involuntary confession may also be considered involuntary (and thus inadmissible). Under the "derived confession" rule, such statements are excluded if "either the tainting features which disqualified the first confession continued to be present or if the fact that the first statement was made was a substantial factor contributing to the making of the second statement."[148]

§4.45 Strictly speaking, the first part of the rule is no more than a reiteration of the confessions rule: if the features that rendered the first confession involuntary were also present when the second statement was made, the second statement must also be involuntary. The second part of the rule, however, is distinct. If an otherwise voluntary confession is sufficiently connected to a prior involuntary confession, it too will be rendered involuntary and inadmissible.[149] As several courts have recognized, this is essentially a causation inquiry; the court must decide, in other words, whether the second confession would have been made "but for" the existence of the first.[150]

§4.46 Several factors may be relevant to this inquiry, including "the time span between the statements, advertence to the previous statement during questioning, the discovery of additional incriminating evidence subsequent to the first statement, the presence of the same police officers at both interrogations, and other similarities between the two circumstances."[151] Courts will also consider

---

No. 5423; 74 W.C.B. (2d) 820 (Ont. S.C.J.); *R. v. Kooktook*, [2006] Nu.J. No. 7, 210 C.C.C. (3d) 106 at paras. 122-124 (Nu. C.A.); *R. v. R.D.D.*, [2005] A.J. No. 1340, 2005 ABQB 252 at paras. 242-247 (Alta. Q.B.).

[147] As mentioned and as discussed in detail in Part 3(4), below, s. 10(*b*) of the *Charter* now expressly requires detainees to be informed of their right to counsel; failing to do so may thus be an independent ground for the exclusion of a confession.

[148] *R. v. I. (L.R.)*, [1993] S.C.J. No. 132, [1993] 4 S.C.R. 504 at 526 (S.C.C.). See also *R. v. G.(B.)*, [1999] S.C.J. No. 29, [1999] 2 S.C.R. 475 at para. 31 (S.C.C.); *R. v. T. (S.G.)*, [2010] S.C.J. No. 20, [2010] 1 S.C.R. 688, 2010 SCC 20 at paras. 28-29 (S.C.C.); *R. v. McIntosh*, [1999] O.J. No. 4842, 141 C.C.C. (3d) 97 at para. 22 (Ont. C.A.).

[149] See *R. v. Kooktook*, [2006] Nu.J. No. 7, 210 C.C.C. (3d) 106 at para. 117 (Nu. C.A.).

[150] *R. v. McIntosh*, [1999] O.J. No. 4842, 141 C.C.C. (3d) 97 at paras. 64-65, 30 C.R. (5th) 161, 128 O.A.C. 69 (Ont. C.A.), leave to appeal refused [2000] S.C.C.A. No. 81, 146 C.C.C. (3d) vi, 141 O.A.C. 197*n*, 260 N.R. 397*n* (S.C.C.); *R. v. Caputo*, [1997] O.J. No. 857, 98 O.A.C. 30, 114 C.C.C. (3d) 1 at para. 37 (Ont. C.A.).

[151] *R. v. I. (L.R.)*, [1993] S.C.J. No. 132, [1993] 4 S.C.R. 504 at 526 (S.C.C.). See also *R. v. Boudreau*, [1949] S.C.J. No. 10, [1949] S.C.R. 262 at 285-86 (S.C.C.); *R. v. Horvath*, [1979] S.C.J. No. 54, [1979] 2 S.C.R. 376 at 429 (S.C.C.); *R. v. Hobbins*, [1982] S.C.J. No. 25, [1982] 1 S.C.R. 553 at 557-58 (S.C.C.); *R. v. Wittwer*, [2008] S.C.J. No. 33, [2008] 2 S.C.R. 235, 2008

whether, before the second interrogation began, police attempted to disabuse the suspect of any influence of prior threats or promises and whether the suspect has talked to a lawyer between the two statements.[152] The presence of either or both of these factors, however, will not necessarily lead to admission. As the Supreme Court stressed in *R. v. I. (L.R.)*,[153] "[a]n explanation of one's rights either by a police officer or counsel may not avail in the face of a strong urge to explain away incriminating matters in a prior statement".[154] Efforts by police to create a "fresh start" before a subsequent interrogation will not suffice to break the causal chain if the existence of the first statement was still a "substantial factor" in the making of the second.[155]

§4.47 In *R. v. G. (B.)*,[156] the Supreme Court of Canada held that to be eligible for exclusion under the derived confession rule, the second statement need not be made to a "person in authority".[157] In *obiter* comments in *T. (S.G.)*,[158] however, a majority of the Court cast doubt on that proposition, suggesting that exclusion might not be appropriate "where, for example, the accused repeats the contents of the tainted confession to a personal friend who has no connection to the [case]."[159] Ultimately, however, the Court decided that it was not necessary to decide whether the derived confessions rule "extends to admissions made to ordinary persons."[160]

SCC 33 at paras. 23-24 (S.C.C.); *R. v. T.(S.G.)*, [2010] S.C.J. No. 20, [2010] 1 S.C.R. 688, 2010 SCC 20 at para. 29 (S.C.C.).

[152] See *R. v. McIntosh*, [1999] O.J. No. 4842, 141 C.C.C. (3d) 97 at para. 22, 30 C.R. (5th) 161, 128 O.A.C. 69 (Ont. C.A.), leave to appeal refused [2000] S.C.C.A. No. 81, 146 C.C.C. (3d) vi, 141 O.A.C. 197*n*, 260 N.R. 397*n* (S.C.C.).

[153] [1993] S.C.J. No. 132, [1993] 4 S.C.R. 504 (S.C.C.).

[154] *Ibid.*, at 527 (S.C.R.). See also *R. v. Kooktook*, [2006] Nu.J. No. 7, 210 C.C.C. (3d) 106 at para. 135 (Nu. C.A.); *R. v. Boudreau*, [1949] S.C.J. No. 10, [1949] S.C.R. 262 at 285 (S.C.C.) ("A warning under such circumstances, when already he had given information in reply to questions and when immediately after the warning he is further questioned by the same parties in a manner that directed his mind to the information already given, is quite different in its effect from a warning given before any questions are asked.")

[155] *R. v. Wittwer*, [2008] S.C.J. No. 33, [2008] 2 S.C.R. 235, 2008 SCC 33 at para. 24 (S.C.C.).

[156] [1999] S.C.J. No. 29, [1999] 2 S.C.R. 475 (S.C.C.).

[157] *Ibid.*, at para. 22 (S.C.R.).

[158] [2010] S.C.J. No. 20, [2010] 1 S.C.R. 688, 2010 SCC 20 (S.C.C.).

[159] *Ibid.*, at para. 32 (SCC). In her decision for the majority in *T. (S.G.)*, Charron J. asserted that the "the majority in *G. (B.)* expressly declined to address this point, instead excluding the second statement (made to a psychiatrist) on the basis that it would be impossible to admit the second statement without also indirectly admitting the first statement, as the second statement at issue in that case actually contained the first, inadmissible statement": *R. v. T. (S.G.)*, [2010] S.C.J. No. 20, [2010] 1 S.C.R. 688, 2010 SCC 20 at para. 31 (S.C.C.). With respect, this is not a defensible reading of *G. (B.)*. As Fish J. pointed out in his dissent in *T. (S.G.)*, since the Court in *G. (B.)* found the second statement inadmissible without deciding if its receiver was a person in authority, it must necessarily have concluded that statements made to ordinary persons can be excluded as derived confessions. See *R. v. T. (S.G.)*, [2010] S.C.J. No. 20, [2010] 1 S.C.R. 688, 2010 SCC 20 at para. 84 (S.C.C.), *per* Fish J., dissenting.

[160] *R. v. T. (S.G.)*, [2010] S.C.J. No. 20, [2010] 1 S.C.R. 688, 2010 SCC 20 at para. 33 (S.C.C.). The majority also noted that it might be possible to exclude a derived confession under s. 24(2) of the *Charter*; however, it did not explain the basis for doing so: *R. v. T. (S.G.)*, [2010] S.C.J. No. 20, [2010] 1 S.C.R. 688, 2010 SCC 20 at para. 33 (S.C.C.).

§4.48 In our view, the rule should be interpreted to permit the exclusion of statements made to ordinary persons. If not, police would be free to coerce recalcitrant suspects to confess knowing that they might consequently make admissions to family members, friends or others that they would not otherwise have made. That said, the fact that the receiver of the second statement was not a person in authority may support a finding that it was not derivative, *i.e.*, that it would have been made despite the earlier confession. For example, in deciding that the impugned statement was not derivative in *T. (S.G.)*, the Court noted that the accused made the first statement in the context of a custodial interrogation, while he made the second in the context of his response to the complainant's mother's request for permission to allow the complainant to travel with her outside the country.[161] The most important factor leading to the Court's conclusion, however, was the fact that the second statement concerned an incident "entirely unrelated" to the subject of the tainted confession.[162] On the majority's interpretation of the evidentiary record, there was no causal connection between the first and second statements.[163]

(ii) Physical Evidence and Statements Confirmed by Physical Evidence (The "St. Lawrence" Rule)

§4.49 When an involuntary confession leads to the discovery of physical evidence, courts have historically admitted both the physical evidence as well as any portion of the confession that the physical evidence corroborates.[164] So if the accused confessed involuntarily to knowing the location of a murder weapon that was subsequently found in the place that the accused described, both the accused's knowledge of the location and the weapon itself would be admissible. The contemporary vitality of the "*St. Lawrence* rule", as it is known, is doubtful.[165] In any case, several courts have held that evidence deriving from involuntary confessions may be excluded under sections 7 and section 24(2) of the *Charter*.[166]

---

[161] *R. v. T. (S.G.)*, [2010] S.C.J. No. 20, [2010] 1 S.C.R. 688, 2010 SCC 20 at para. 38 (S.C.C.).

[162] *Ibid.*

[163] Writing in dissent, Fish J. (Binnie J., concurring) took at very different view of the evidence. See *R. v. T. (S.G.)*, [2010] S.C.J. No. 20, [2010] 1 S.C.R. 688, 2010 SCC 20 at paras. 79-88 (S.C.C.), *per* Fish J., dissenting.

[164] See *R. v. St. Lawrence*, [1949] O.J. No. 447, 7 C.R. 464 at 474 (Ont. H.C.J.); *R. v. Wray*, [1970] S.C.J. No. 80, [1971] S.C.R. 272 (S.C.C.); *R. v. John*, [1971] S.C.J. No. 100, [1971] S.C.R. 781 (S.C.C.).

[165] See *R. v. Sweeney*, [2000] O.J. No. 3534, 50 O.R. (3d) 321 at paras. 47-62 (Ont. C.A.) (suggesting without deciding that involuntary statements confirmed by derivative physical evidence should generally be excluded at common law).

[166] See *R. v. S. (K.)*, [2000] O.J. No. 3534, 50 O.R. (3d) 321 at paras. 47-62 (Ont. C.A.) (confession excluded under ss. 7 and 24(2) despite being subsequently corroborated by physical evidence); *R. v. Woolley*, [1988] O.J. No. 340, 40 C.C.C. (3d) 531 (Ont. C.A.) (physical evidence discovered as a result of improper questioning may be excluded under s. 24(2) but not in this case); *R. v. Robert*, [1996] B.C.J. No. 142, 104 C.C.C. (3d) 480 at para. 82 (B.C.C.A.) (self-incriminating evidence obtained in violation of s. 7 eligible for exclusion under s. 24(2)). See also Alan W. Bryant, Sidney R. Lederman & Michelle K. Fuerst, *Sopinka, Lederman & Bryant:*

§4.50 The *St. Lawrence* rule should be substantially modified. While it does not countenance the admission of unreliable evidence in the case at hand, it does not adequately address other concerns underlying the confessions rule, including the need to deter coercive interrogation methods. If the only concern with an involuntary confession is its dubious reliability, then we should continue to admit both derivative physical evidence as well as any part of the confession confirmed thereby.[167] But neither type of evidence should be admitted where police used methods either unacceptably cruel or apt to produce false confessions generally.[168] Otherwise, police would have little reason to exercise restraint when faced with a suspect who is not amenable to lawful persuasion.[169]

3. SECTION 10 OF THE *CHARTER*

(1) Introduction

§4.51 In the United States, dissatisfaction with the confession rule's effectiveness in deterring abusive interrogation practices ultimately led the Supreme Court to interpret the Fifth Amendment's self-incrimination clause to give additional protections to persons subject to custodial interrogation.[170] The rules set out in *Miranda v. Arizona*[171] require police to warn such a person that "he has a right to remain silent, that any statement he does make may be used as evidence against him, and that he has a right to the presence of an attorney, either retained or appointed."[172] Despite criticisms of both its interpretive foundations and regulatory efficacy, the United States Supreme Court has subsequently used *Miranda* to construct a detailed scheme directing police to not only inform suspects of their rights, but also facilitate access to counsel and prevent unwitting self-

---

The Law of Evidence in Canada, 3d ed. (Markham, ON: LexisNexis Canada, 2009) at 493-97; David M. Paciocco, "Self-Incrimination and the Case to Meet: The Legacy of Chief Justice Lamer" (2000) 5 Can. Crim. L. Rev. 63 at 77.

[167] This could occur, for example, where a suspect who lacks an operating mind makes a *prima facie* unreliable confession that is later corroborated by the discovery of derivative evidence. If police did not employ abusive tactics, and there is no concern for deterring methods apt to produce unreliable confessions, there would be no reason to exclude.

[168] See Steven Penney, "What's Wrong with Self-Incrimination? The Wayward Path of Self-Incrimination Law in the Post-*Charter* Era, Part 2: Self-Incrimination in Police Investigations" (2004) 48 Crim. L.Q. 280 at 305-306.

[169] If this rule were adopted, there would be no need to invoke the *Charter* when physical evidence is discovered as a result of an involuntary confession. As the Supreme Court has noted, s. 7 offers no greater protection than the confessions rule to a detainee questioned by non-undercover police: *R. v. Singh*, [2007] S.C.J. No. 48, [2007] 3 S.C.R. 405 at paras. 25 and 39 (S.C.C.). It is difficult to conceive of circumstances that would justify (under ss. 7 and 24(2) of the *Charter*), either: (*i*) the exclusion of reliable evidence not obtained by coercion; or (*ii*) the admission of evidence (whether reliable or not) obtained through coercion.

[170] See generally, Steven Penney, "Theories of Confession Admissibility: A Historical View" (1998) 25 Am. J. Crim. L. 309 at 366-72.

[171] 384 U.S. 436 at 444 (1966).

[172] *Ibid.*, at 444.

incrimination.[173] Statements obtained in violation of these rules must be excluded at trial.[174]

§4.52 A similar regulatory regime has emerged in Canada as a result of our own Supreme Court's interpretation of sections 10(*a*) and 10(*b*) of the *Charter*.[175] These provisions give everyone "the right on arrest or detention (*a*) to be informed promptly of the reasons therefor; [and] (*b*) to retain and instruct counsel without delay and to be informed of that right ...". As with violations of other *Charter* rights, section 24(2) of the *Charter* permits the exclusion at trial of statements and other evidence obtained through a violation of these guarantees.[176]

§4.53 Much like the United States Supreme Court has done with the Fifth Amendment, to fulfill the "purpose" behind sections 10(*a*) and 10(*b*) of the *Charter*, the Canadian Supreme Court has imposed obligations on police that go beyond the express language of the provisions.[177] According to the Court, this purpose is to help suspects make informed, voluntary choices in their interactions with police.[178] The right to talk to a lawyer, as well as the right to be informed of that right, attempt to ensure that suspects are aware of their legal situation.[179] Similarly, the principal aim of the right to be told of the reasons for detention is to help suspects make informed decisions about whether to talk to police or consult with counsel and ensure that those who contact lawyers obtain appropriate advice.[180] The Court has recognized that these rights are particularly

---

[173] See *e.g.*, *Dickerson v. United States*, 530 U.S. 428 (2000).

[174] *Miranda v. Arizona*, 384 U.S. 436 at 479 (1966). Depending on the circumstances, evidence derived from a statement obtained in violation of *Miranda* may be admissible. See Wayne R. LaFave, Jerold H. Israel & Nancy J. King, *Criminal Procedure*, 3d ed. (St. Paul, Minn.: West, 2000) § 9.5.

[175] Section 2(*c*)(ii) of the *Canadian Bill of Rights*, S.C. 1960, c. 44, R.S.C. 1985, Appendix III, in effect since 1960, provides that federal legislation shall be construed so to not "deprive a person who has been arrested or detained ... of the right to retain and instruct counsel without delay". This provision has been almost completely ineffective in regulating police questioning practices, however. It applies only to legislation, and few aspects of police questioning are governed by statute. Even where s. 2(*c*)(ii) has been violated, the Supreme Court has held that there is no power to exclude evidence. See *R. v. Hogan*, [1974] S.C.J. No. 116, [1975] 2 S.C.R. 574 (S.C.C.). The ineffectiveness of the *Canadian Bill of Rights* more generally is elaborated on in Chapter 1, Part 4(1).

[176] See below, Chapter 10.

[177] See *R. v. Brydges*, [1990] S.C.J. No. 8, [1990] 1 S.C.R. 190 at 202 (S.C.C.); *R. v. Black*, [1989] S.C.J. No. 81, [1989] 2 S.C.R. 138 at 152 (S.C.C.).

[178] See *R. v. Bartle*, [1994] S.C.J. No. 74, [1994] 3 S.C.R. 173 at 193-94 (S.C.C.); *R. v. Sinclair*, [2010] S.C.J. No. 35, [2010] 2 S.C.R. 310 at paras. 24-26 (S.C.C.).

[179] See *R. v. Manninen*, [1987] S.C.J. No. 41, [1987] 1 S.C.R. 1233 at 1242-43 (S.C.C.).

[180] See *R. v. Evans*, [1991] S.C.J. No. 31, [1991] 1 S.C.R. 869 at 886-87 (S.C.C.); *R. v. Black*, [1989] S.C.J. No. 81, [1989] 2 S.C.R. 138 at 152-53 (S.C.C.); *R. v. Smith*, [1991] S.C.J. No. 24, [1991] 1 S.C.R. 714 at 728 (S.C.C.); *R. v. Borden*, [1994] S.C.J. No. 82, [1994] 3 S.C.R. 145 at 166 (S.C.C.); *R. v. Latimer*, [1997] S.C.J. No. 11, [1997] 1 S.C.R. 217 at para. 28 (S.C.C.). The Court has also suggested that s. 10(*a*) instantiates the common law principle that suspects are not required to submit to arrest unless reasons are given. See *R. v. Latimer*, [1997] S.C.J. No. 11, [1997] 1 S.C.R. 217 at para. 28 (S.C.C.) ("it would be a gross interference with individual liberty for persons to have to submit to arrest without knowing the reasons"). Section 10(*a*) may

important in preventing suspects from unwittingly making inculpatory statements.[181]

§4.54 As with the confessions rule, however, the Court has not read section 10 of the *Charter* as forbidding police from pressuring suspects to make self-incriminating statements.[182] It has instead tried to strike a balance between suspects' interest in avoiding unfair self-incrimination and the state's need to obtain confession evidence to effectively deter, prosecute and punish crime. This is a laudable goal. However, in outlining the jurisprudence surrounding sections 10(*a*) and 10(*b*) below, we urge that greater attention be paid to the need to deter abusive interrogation practices, including those apt to produce false confessions. Such attention, in our view, would improve the law in two ways: first, it would provide more precise direction for police as to their section 10(*a*) and 10(*b*) obligations; and second, it would achieve a better accommodation between the state's interest in obtaining reliable evidence and suspects' interests in avoiding inhumane treatment and wrongful convictions.

(2) Triggering Mechanisms: Arrest or Detention

§4.55 As mentioned, the rights in sections 10(*a*) and 10(*b*) are triggered when a suspect is either detained or arrested.[183] The meaning of these terms is discussed in detail in Chapter 2, Parts 3(3)(*b*) and 4(4)(*a*), respectively.

---

also reduce the likelihood of violent resistance. See *R. v. Evans*, [1991] S.C.J. No. 31, [1991] 1 S.C.R. 869 at 886-87 (S.C.C.) (arrest without explanation unlawful at common law and justifies resistance); *R. v. Kelly*, [1985] O.J. No. 2, 17 C.C.C. (3d) 419 at 424 (Ont. C.A.) (same). See also Don Stuart, *Charter Justice in Canadian Criminal Law*, 4th ed. (Toronto: Thomson Carswell, 2005) at 328.

[181] See *R. v. Manninen*, [1987] S.C.J. No. 41, [1987] 1 S.C.R. 1233 at 1242-43 (S.C.C.); *R. v. Brydges*, [1990] S.C.J. No. 8, [1990] 1 S.C.R. 190 at 203, 206, 215 (S.C.C.); *R. v. Bartle*, [1994] S.C.J. No. 74, [1994] 3 S.C.R. 173 at 191 (S.C.C.); *R. v. Prosper*, [1994] S.C.J. No. 72, [1994] 3 S.C.R. 236 at 271 (S.C.C.); *R. v. S. (R.J.)*, [1995] S.C.J. No. 10, [1995] 1 S.C.R. 451 at para. 85 (S.C.C.); *R. v. Jones*, [1994] S.C.J. No. 42, [1994] 2 S.C.R. 229 at 254-255 (S.C.C.), *per* Lamer C.J.C., dissenting. See also *R. v. Hebert*, [1990] S.C.J. No. 64, [1990] 2 S.C.R. 151 at 176 (S.C.C.) ("The detained suspect, potentially at a disadvantage in relation to the informed and sophisticated powers at the disposal of the state, is entitled to rectify the disadvantage by speaking to legal counsel at the outset, so that he is aware of his right not to speak to the police and obtains appropriate advice with respect to the choice he faces.").

[182] See generally, *R. v. Sinclair*, [2010] S.C.J. No. 35, [2010] 2 S.C.R. 310 at paras. 30-31 (S.C.C.) (disagreeing with Binnie J.'s dissenting view that one of s. 10(*b*)'s purposes is to "advise the detainee how to deal with police questions").

[183] This is one of the key differences between the Canadian and American regimes. As mentioned, *Miranda v. Arizona*, 384 U.S. 437 (1966) is triggered by "custodial interrogation", which the Court defined as "questioning initiated by law enforcement officers after a person has been taken into custody or otherwise deprived of his freedom of action in any significant way." See also *Berkemer v. McCarty*, 468 U.S. 420 (1984). As discussed below, Part 3(4)(*b*), police in Canada must (generally) issue the warnings immediately upon arrest or detention; in the United States police are not required to do so until they initiate questioning of a suspect in custody.

(3)   Section 10(*a*) of the *Charter*

§4.56 Section 10(*a*) states that anyone arrested or detained must be "informed promptly of the reasons therefor." As interpreted by the Supreme Court, this requires police to tell suspects, in "clear and simple language",[184] about every offence that they are under investigation for[185] and about any significant change in the nature of the investigation.[186] The reasons need not be lengthy or technically precise. It is sufficient if they convey the general extent of the suspect's legal jeopardy.[187] As the Supreme Court put it in *R. v. Evans*:[188]

> ... it is the substance of what the accused can reasonably be supposed to have understood, rather than the formalism of the precise words used, which must govern. The question is whether what the accused was told, viewed reasonably in all the circumstances of the case, was sufficient to permit him to make a reasonable decision to decline to submit to arrest, or alternatively, to undermine his right to counsel under s. 10(*b*).[189]

Thus, the Court in *Evans* held that police did not violate section 10(*a*) when they failed to formally warn the accused, who had initially been arrested for marijuana possession, that he was now being detained as a murder suspect. "[T]he appellant was aware," the Court concluded, "that the focus of the questioning had changed and that he was then being questioned with respect to the killings."[190]

§4.57 Standing alone, changes in interrogation strategy do not trigger a significant change in jeopardy.[191] Similarly, there is no requirement that police inform the accused of the specific allegations, information in the hands of police, identity of any deceased parties or even of the exact charges against them.[192] Provided that detainees understand the general extent of their jeopardy, the obligations under Section 10(*a*) will have been fulfilled.

---

[184] *R. v. Mann*, [2004] S.C.J. No. 49, [2004] 3 S.C.R. 59 at para. 21 (S.C.C.).

[185] *R. v. Borden*, [1994] S.C.J. No. 82, [1994] 3 S.C.R. 145 at 166 (S.C.C.) (police violated *Charter* s. 10(*a*) when they failed to tell a detained suspect who knew he was being held in relation to one sexual assault that they also suspected him of another).

[186] *R. v. Evans*, [1991] S.C.J. No. 31, [1991] 1 S.C.R. 869 at 887-88 (S.C.C.); *R. v. Black*, [1989] S.C.J. No. 81, [1989] 2 S.C.R. 138 at 153-54 (S.C.C.).

[187] See *R. v. Evans*, [1991] S.C.J. No. 31, [1991] 1 S.C.R. 869 at 888 (S.C.C.); *R. v. Smith*, [1991] S.C.J. No. 24, [1991] 1 S.C.R. 714 at 728-29 (S.C.C.).

[188] [1991] S.C.J. No. 31, [1991] 1 S.C.R. 869 (S.C.C.).

[189] *R. v. Evans*, [1991] S.C.J. No. 31, [1991] 1 S.C.R. 869 at 888 (S.C.C.).

[190] *Ibid.*, at 886-87 (S.C.R.). See also *R. v. Latimer*, [1997] S.C.J. No. 11, [1997] 1 S.C.R. 217 at para. 31 (S.C.C.) (though the accused was not specifically told that he could be charged with murder, he "understood the basis for his apprehension by the police and hence the extent of his jeopardy"); *R. v. Taylor*, [2008] A.J. No. 723, 2008 ABCA 253 at para. 22, 433 A.R. 1 (Alta. C.A.); *R. v. McIntosh*, [1999] O.J. No. 4842, 141 C.C.C. (3d) 97 at para. 49 (Ont. C.A.); *R. v. Chalmers*, [2009] O.J. No. 1254, 2009 ONCA 268 at para. 38 (Ont. C.A.).

[191] *R. v. V. (S.E.)*, [2009] A.J. No. 311, 2 Alta. L.R. (5th) 157 at para. 29 (Alta. C.A.).

[192] *Ibid.*, at para. 29 (Alta. L.R.); *R. v. Ekman*, [2003] B.C.J. No. 2097, 186 B.C.A.C. 242 at para. 91 (B.C.C.A.); *R. v. Jackson*, [2005] A.J. No. 1726, 204 C.C.C. (3d) 127 at para. 25 (Alta. C.A.).

(4) Section 10(*b*) of the *Charter*

§4.58 Section 10(*b*) is one of the most important (and frequently litigated) legal rights in the *Charter*. Its language is deceptively simple: "[e]veryone has the right on arrest or detention ... to retain and instruct counsel without delay and to be informed of that right ... ." From this single sentence, the Supreme Court has constructed an elaborate regulatory scheme that, broadly speaking, prevents police from obtaining self-incriminating information from detainees until they understand that they have a right to speak to a lawyer and, if they choose to exercise that right, are given a reasonable opportunity to do so. The major interpretive questions that have arisen from this scheme are the following:

1. What initial information must be provided to persons upon detention?

2. When must this initial information be provided?

3. What degree of understanding must detainees exhibit to be said to have been "informed" of their rights?

4. What is required for detainees to invoke their right to talk to counsel?

5. Once this right is invoked, what must police do, and refrain from doing, to facilitate access to counsel?

6. What limitations does section 10(*b*) impose on police questioning after a detainee has been afforded a reasonable opportunity to talk to a lawyer?

7. When can the failure to comply with section 10(*b*) be justified under section 1 of the *Charter*?

(a) What Information Must be Provided to Persons upon Detention?

§4.59 Section 10(*b*) expressly requires police to tell detainees that they have the right to "retain and instruct counsel." Simply put, this means that police must tell them that they may speak to a lawyer.[193] The Court has interpreted section 10(*b*) to require that detainees also be informed of any legal aid or duty counsel services available in the jurisdiction, even if they do not express any concern about being able to afford a lawyer.[194] This is to ensure that impecunious detain-

---

[193] As discussed in Part 3(4)(*e*), detainees have a right to talk to a lawyer of their choosing, provided that this occurs within a reasonable time. To date, however, courts have rejected the claim that police have a duty to tell them this. See *R. v. Grouse*, [2004] N.S.J. No. 346, 2004 NSCA 108 at paras. 22-28 (N.S.C.A.). See also *R. v. Willier*, [2008] A.J. No. 327, 230 C.C.C. (3d) 1 at para. 37 (Alta. C.A.), affd [2010] S.C.J. No. 37, [2010] 2 S.C.R. 429 (S.C.C.). Similarly, as discussed in Part 3(4)(*e*), while detainees who exercise their right to counsel are entitled to do so in private, courts have thus far held that ordinarily police need not inform them of this. See *R. v. Jackson*, [1993] O.J. No. 2511, 25 C.R. (4th) 265 at para. 24 (Ont. C.A.) (no obligation to inform unless detainee reasonably believes that privacy will not be provided and police should have been aware of that); *R. v. Butler*, [1995] B.C.J. No. 2716, 104 C.C.C. (3d) 198 (B.C.C.A.), leave to appeal to S.C.C. refused [1996] S.C.C.A. No. 90, 105 C.C.C. (3d) vi (S.C.C.) (no violation absent indication that accused misunderstood right to privacy).

[194] *R. v. Brydges*, [1990] S.C.J. No. 8, [1990] 1 S.C.R. 190 at 209-10, 212, 215 (S.C.C.); *R. v. Bartle*, [1994] S.C.J. No. 74, [1994] 3 S.C.R. 173 at 195 (S.C.C.).

ees are not deterred from taking advantage of their section 10(*b*) rights.[195] "Legal aid" refers to long-term legal assistance (usually contingent on financial qualification); "duty counsel" to immediate, temporary legal advice available irrespective of financial means.[196] Further, if duty counsel are available, police must tell detainees how to contact them.[197] Typically police give detainees either a single (toll-free) duty counsel telephone number or a list of numbers for lawyers acting as duty counsel.[198] However, police are only required to tell detainees how to access any duty counsel services available at the time of arrest.[199] There is no obligation to provide phone numbers of available duty counsel when the detention occurs during normal business hours and legal assistance is available through an easily obtainable local number.[200]

§4.60 In *R. v. Bartle*,[201] the Court determined that it is theoretically possible to waive the right to be informed of the right to counsel.[202] However, such a waiver will only be effective where there is "a reasonable basis for believing that the detainee in fact knows and has adverted to his rights, and is aware of the means by which these rights can be exercised."[203] Detainees who say that they are aware of their rights do not thereby waive them. Moreover, police must take reasonable steps to ensure that detainees are aware of all required information. Since this would effectively require police to convey the entire content of the section 10(*b*) caution, in practice the possibility of waiver is inconsequential.

(b)   When Must this Information be Provided?

§4.61 As stated in section 10(*b*), police must impart the required initial information about the right to counsel "without delay". The Supreme Court has interpreted this phrase strictly,[204] holding that the warning must be given "immediately upon detention",[205] unless it is necessary to first gain control over a

---

[195] *R. v. Brydges*, [1990] S.C.J. No. 8, [1990] 1 S.C.R. 190 at 209-10, 212, 215 (S.C.C.); *R. v. Bartle*, [1994] S.C.J. No. 74, [1994] 3 S.C.R. 173 at 195 (S.C.C.).

[196] *R. v. Bartle*, [1994] S.C.J. No. 74, [1994] 3 S.C.R. 173 at 191, 195-97 (S.C.C.). In *R. v. Prosper*, [1994] S.C.J. No. 72, [1994] 3 S.C.R. 236 (S.C.C.) the Court held that s. 10(*b*) did not require provinces to make duty counsel services available to detainees.

[197] See *R. v. Bartle*, [1994] S.C.J. No. 74, [1994] 3 S.C.R. 173 at 197 (S.C.C.).

[198] See *R. v. Bartle*, [1994] S.C.J. No. 74, [1994] 3 S.C.R. 173 at 200-201 (S.C.C.); *R. v. Cook*, [1998] S.C.J. No. 68, [1998] 2 S.C.R. 597 at para. 59 (S.C.C.); *R. v. Pozniak*, [1994] S.C.J. No. 75, [1994] 3 S.C.R. 310 at para. 11 (S.C.C.); *R. v. Harper*, [1994] S.C.J. No. 71, [1994] 3 S.C.R. 343 at para. 26 (S.C.C.); *R. v. Cobham*, [1994] S.C.J. No. 76, [1994] 3 S.C.R. 360 at para. 12 (S.C.C.).

[199] *R. v. Latimer*, [1997] S.C.J. No. 11, [1997] 1 S.C.R. 217 at paras. 32-37 (S.C.C.); *R. v. Prosper*, [1994] S.C.J. No. 72, [1994] 3 S.C.R. 236 at 259 (S.C.C.).

[200] *R. v. Latimer*, [1997] S.C.J. No. 11, [1997] 1 S.C.R. 217 at paras. 37-39 (S.C.C.).

[201] [1994] S.C.J. No. 74, [1994] 3 S.C.R. 173 (S.C.C.).

[202] *Ibid.*

[203] *Ibid.*, at 204-205 (S.C.R.).

[204] See *R. v. DeBot*, [1989] S.C.J. No. 118, [1989] 2 S.C.R. 1140 at 1163 (S.C.C.), *per* Wilson J. ("'without delay' does not permit of internal qualification").

[205] *R. v. DeBot*, [1989] S.C.J. No. 118, [1989] 2 S.C.R. 1140 at 1146 (S.C.C.).

dangerous situation.[206] This does not allow for delays to access telephones[207] or conduct searches[208] or preliminary questioning.[209]

§4.62 Further, as with the section 10(*a*) warning, police must re-issue the section 10(*b*) caution when the nature of the detention changes significantly.[210] Specifically, this obligation is triggered by a "fundamental and discrete change in the purpose of the investigation, one involving a different and unrelated offence or a significantly more serious offence than that contemplated at the time of the warning."[211] This rule ensures that detainees are able to decide whether to talk to a lawyer knowing the extent of the jeopardy they face and prevents police from manipulating detainees into waiving their right to counsel on the basis that they are facing only less serious charges.[212] Police need not repeat the section 10(*b*) caution, however, when detainees are aware of the general extent of their jeopardy.[213]

(c) What Degree of Understanding Must Detainees Exhibit to be Said to Have Been "Informed" of Their Rights?

§4.63 The rights granted by section 10(*b*) will not serve their purposes if detainees do not understand them.[214] Where a lack of understanding is claimed, two distinct constitutional arguments are possible. First, an accused may assert that police violated section 10(*b*) by failing to take reasonable steps to facilitate

---

[206] *R. v. Strachan*, [1988] S.C.J. No. 94, [1988] 2 S.C.R. 980 at 998-999 (S.C.C.); *R. v. DeBot*, [1989] S.C.J. No. 118, [1989] 2 S.C.R. 1140 at 1163-64 (S.C.C.), *per* Wilson J.

[207] See *R. v. Bartle*, [1994] S.C.J. No. 74, [1994] 3 S.C.R. 173 at para. 38 (S.C.C.).

[208] See *R. v. DeBot*, [1989] S.C.J. No. 118, [1989] 2 S.C.R. 1140 at 1163-64 (S.C.C.), *per* Wilson J.; *R. v. Strachan*, [1988] S.C.J. No. 94, [1988] 2 S.C.R. 980 at 999 (S.C.C.) (violation of s. 10(*b*) where police prevented accused from contacting counsel until after search had ended and accused had been taken to police station); *R. v. Polashek*, [1999] O.J. No. 968, 25 C.R. (5th) 183 (Ont. C.A.) (13-minute delay between initial arrest and advising of right to counsel to allow for search of accused and vehicle violated s. 10(*b*)).

[209] See *R. v. Suberu*, [2009] S.C.J. No. 33, [2009] 2 S.C.R. 460, 2009 SCC 33 at paras. 37-42 (S.C.C.) (s. 10(*b*) not suspended for investigative detention).

[210] See *R. v. Black*, [1989] S.C.J. No. 81, [1989] 2 S.C.R. 138 at 155 (S.C.C.); *R. v. Evans*, [1991] S.C.J. No. 31, [1991] 1 S.C.R. 869 at 890-93 (S.C.C.).

[211] *R. v. Evans*, [1991] S.C.J. No. 31, [1991] 1 S.C.R. 869 at 893 (S.C.C.). See also *R. v. Black*, [1989] S.C.J. No. 81, [1989] 2 S.C.R. 138 at 154 (S.C.C.); *R. v. Borden*, [1994] S.C.J. No. 82, [1994] 3 S.C.R. 145 at 165-66 (S.C.C.); *R. v. Paternak*, [1996] S.C.J. No. 108, [1996] 3 S.C.R. 607 (S.C.C.); *R. v. Burlingham*, [1995] S.C.J. No. 39, [1995] 2 S.C.R. 206 at para. 20 (S.C.C.).

[212] *R. v. Evans*, [1991] S.C.J. No. 31, [1991] 1 S.C.R. 869 at 892-93 (S.C.C.).

[213] See *R. v. V. (S.E.)*, [2009] A.J. No. 311, 2 Alta. L.R. (5th) 157 at para. 29 (Alta. C.A.) (accused learning more about allegations and information in hands of police not significant change in jeopardy); *R. v. Sinclair*, [2008] B.C.J. No. 502, 2008 BCCA 127 at para. 67 (B.C.C.A.), affd [2010] S.C.J. No. 35, [2010] 2 S.C.R. 310 (S.C.C.) (no obligation to re-warn when detainee becomes more aware of strength of case against him); *R. v. Haynes*, [1997] B.C.J. No. 2756, 121 C.C.C. (3d) 1 (B.C.C.A.) (accused aware of full extent of jeopardy throughout); *R. v. Chalmers*, [2009] O.J. No. 1254, 2009 ONCA 268 at para. 38 (Ont. C.A.) (same); *R. v. McIntosh*, [1999] O.J. No. 4842, 141 C.C.C. (3d) 97 at para. 49 (Ont. C.A.) (obligation to re-warn where accused who was not initially a suspect confesses).

[214] *R. v. Evans*, [1991] S.C.J. No. 31, [1991] 1 S.C.R. 869 at 890 (S.C.C.).

understanding of the right to counsel. If police properly convey the required information, however, they may assume that detainees understand it. The obligation to facilitate only arises when it is apparent from the circumstances that comprehension is an issue.[215] In such cases police must take reasonable steps to facilitate understanding before they attempt to obtain any self-incriminating information.[216] In *R. v. Evans*,[217] for example, the Court held that police violated section 10(*b*) by failing to do anything to explain the right to counsel to a cognitively limited detainee who indicated that he did not understand it.[218]

§4.64 The Court should go further and require police to take reasonable, proactive steps to ensure understanding even when there is no evidence of incomprehension.[219] Specifically, they should be required to ask detainees whether they understand the caution. The answer (or non-answer) to this question should then be considered in deciding whether police reasonably believed that detainees understood their rights.[220] Given that police routinely ask this question (and record any answer) in any case,[221] imposing a constitutional duty to do so should not be unduly burdensome.

---

[215] See *R. v. Baig*, [1987] S.C.J. No. 77, [1987] 2 S.C.R. 537 at 540 (S.C.C.); *R. v. Evans*, [1991] S.C.J. No. 31, [1991] 1 S.C.R. 869 at 891 (S.C.C.); *R. v. Anderson*, [1984] O.J. No. 3100, 10 C.C.C. (3d) 417 at 431 (Ont. C.A.); *R. v. Reyat*, [1993] B.C.J. No. 622, 80 C.C.C. (3d) 210, 20 C.R. (4th) 149, 14 C.R.R. (2d) 282, 40 W.A.C. 161 (B.C.C.A.), leave to appeal refused [1993] S.C.C.A. No. 239, 83 C.C.C. (3d) vi (S.C.C.). Though the Supreme Court has not expressly said so, it can be assumed that the obligation to facilitate an understanding arises when the possibility of incomprehension would be apparent to a reasonable observer. A negligent failure by police to detect comprehension issues, in other words, should constitute a violation of section 10(*b*). See Simon Verdun-Jones & Adamira Tijerino, "A Review of *Brydges* Duty Counsel Services in Canada" (Ottawa: Department of Justice Canada, 2004) at 42. Such a rule is consistent with what the Court has said on the subject, commensurate with the objectives of s. 10(*b*), and not unduly burdensome for police. See *R. v. Evans*, [1991] S.C.J. No. 31, [1991] 1 S.C.R. 869 at 891 (S.C.C.) ("where...there is a positive indication that the accused does not understand his right to counsel, the police cannot rely on their mechanical recitation of the right to the accused; they must take steps to facilitate that understanding").

[216] *R. v. Evans*, [1991] S.C.J. No. 31, [1991] 1 S.C.R. 869 at 891 (S.C.C.); *R. v. Bartle*, [1994] S.C.J. No. 74, [1994] 3 S.C.R. 173 at para. 21 (S.C.C.).

[217] [1991] S.C.J. No. 31, [1991] 1 S.C.R. 869 (S.C.C.).

[218] *R. v. Evans*, [1991] S.C.J. No. 31, [1991] 1 S.C.R. 869 (S.C.C.). See also *R. v. Vanstaceghem*, [1987] O.J. No. 509, 58 C.R. (3d) 121 (Ont. C.A.) (s. 10(*b*) includes right to be informed of right to counsel in the language that one comprehends); *R. v. Tam*, [1995] B.C.J. No. 1428, 100 C.C.C. (3d) 196 (B.C.C.A.) (violation of s. 10(*b*) where police failed to inform accused of right to counsel in Cantonese until 11 hours after it became apparent that accused did not understand his rights as read to him in English).

[219] See Tim Quigley, "Pre-trial, Trial, and Post-trial Procedure," in Don Stuart, R.J. Delisle & Alan Manson, eds., *Towards a Clear and Just Criminal Law: A Criminal Reports Forum* (Toronto: Carswell, 1999) 253 at 293-94, 298.

[220] A failure to answer would not necessarily indicate incomprehension, as in the case of a fully competent but uncooperative detainee.

[221] See *e.g.*, *R. v. V. (S.E.)*, [2009] A.J. No. 311, 2 Alta. L.R. (5th) 157 at para. 8 (Alta. C.A.); *R. v. Taylor*, [2008] A.J. No., 723, 2008 ABCA 253 at para. 5, 433 A.R. 1 (Alta. C.A.); *R. v. Sinclair*, [2008] B.C.J. No. 502, 169 C.R.R. (2d) 232 at para. 6 (B.C.C.A.), affd [2010] S.C.J. No. 35, [2010] 2 S.C.R. 310 (S.C.C.); *R. v. Green*, [2003] B.C.J. No. 2789, 2003 BCCA 639 at para. 3 (B.C.C.A.); *R. v. Leedhal*, [2002] S.J. No. 14, 213 Sask. R. 235 at para. 8 (Sask. C.A.); *R. v. Boomer*, [2001] B.C.J. No. 760, 153 C.C.C. (3d) 425 at para. 12 (B.C.C.A.); *R. v. Butler*,

§4.65 The second type of challenge is based on detainees' actual subjective capacity to understand their right to counsel (rather than the reasonableness of police efforts to facilitate understanding). Here the Supreme Court has held that section 10(*b*) requires detainees exhibit the same level of mental competence as the "operating mind" component of the confessions rule.[222] As discussed in Part 2(3)(*a*), above, this requires only that the detainee be "capable of communicating with counsel to instruct counsel, and understand the function of counsel and that he or she can dispense with counsel even if this is not in the accused's best interests."[223] Section 10(*b*) is accordingly violated if police obtain self-incriminating evidence from a detainee lacking such capacity.[224]

§4.66 Though some have argued that this standard for capacity is too low,[225] in our view it is sufficient.[226] Many detainees, including many of those unburdened by mental illness, cognitive deficits or substance-induced impairment, make ill-considered and irrational decisions to forego the right to counsel and make admissions to police.[227] Section 10(*b*) requires that detainees be informed of their rights; it does not demand that they talk to a lawyer.[228] Requiring police to convince detainees to make fully-informed, self-interested decisions about whether to talk to a lawyer would be impractical and substantially reduce access to reliable evidence of guilt, yet do little to prevent abusive questioning practices.[229]

[1995] B.C.J. No. 2716, 104 C.C.C. (3d) 198 at para. 18 (B.C.C.A.), leave to appeal refused [1996] S.C.C.A. No. 90, 105 C.C.C. (3d) vi (S.C.C.); *R. v. Schneider*, [1994] S.J. No. 415, 123 Sask. R.81 at para. 3 (Sask. C.A.).

[222] *R. v. Whittle*, [1994] S.C.J. No. 69, [1994] 2 S.C.R. 914 at 939 (S.C.C.).

[223] *R. v. Whittle*, [1994] S.C.J. No. 69, [1994] 2 S.C.R. 914 at 933 (S.C.C.). See also *R. v. G. (B.)*, [1999] S.C.J. No. 29, [1999] 2 S.C.R. 475 at para. 19 (S.C.C.); *R. v. Oickle*, [2000] S.C.J. No. 38, [2000] 2 S.C.R. 3 at para. 63 (S.C.C.). See also *Colorado v. Connelly*, 479 U.S. 157 (1986).

[224] When such evidence consists of a statement (as it often does), it will be considered involuntary under the confessions rule. See above, Part 2(3)(*a*). In such cases, a s. 10(*b*) argument will be unnecessary, since involuntary confessions (unlike statements obtained in violation of the *Charter*) are always excluded, and since the prosecution bears the burden of proof to prove voluntariness beyond a reasonable doubt, whereas the accused has the burden to both prove a violation of the *Charter* and justify exclusion under s. 24(2).

[225] See R.J. Delisle, "*Whittle* and *Tran:* Conflicting Messages on How Much an Accused Must Understand" (1994) 32 C.R. (4th) 29; Simon Verdun-Jones & Adamira Tijerino, "A Review of *Brydges* Duty Counsel Services in Canada" (Ottawa: Department of Justice Canada, 2004) at 42.

[226] See also Steven Penney, "What's Wrong with Self-Incrimination? The Wayward Path of Self-Incrimination Law in the Post-Charter Era, Part 2: Self-Incrimination in Police Investigations" (2004) 48 Crim. L.Q. 280 at 294-95 and 314-17.

[227] See Joseph D. Grano, "Introduction — The Changed and Changing World of Constitutional Criminal Procedure: The Contribution of the Department of Justice's Office of Legal Policy" (1989) 22 U. Mich. J.L. Ref. 395 at 406-408; Louis Michael Seidman, "Rubashov's Question: Self-Incrimination and the Problem of Coerced Preferences" (1990) 2 Yale J.L. & Human. 149 at 165; Albert Alschuler, "Implementing the Criminal Defendant's Right to Trial: Alternatives to the Plea Bargaining System" (1983) 50 U. Chi. L. Rev. 931 at 1007.

[228] See *R. v. Manninen*, [1987] S.C.J. No. 41, [1987] 1 S.C.R. 1233 (S.C.C.).

[229] As discussed in Part 3(4)(*e*), the standard for waiving the right to counsel after it has been invoked is appropriately higher.

§4.67 In summary, section 10(*b*) provides two layers of insurance against incomprehension of the right to counsel. First, it requires police to take reasonable steps to facilitate understanding when potential misunderstanding is objectively evident; and second, it requires detainees to exhibit a basic level of understanding before choosing whether to talk to their lawyers. Provided that police ask detainees whether they understand the caution, this regime achieves a sensible balance between the need for comprehension of the right to counsel and law enforcements need to obtain reliable evidence.

(d) What is Required for Detainees to Invoke Their Right to Talk to Counsel?

§4.68 Once the right to counsel is conveyed and understood, the issue becomes whether it is invoked. If it is, police must refrain from eliciting evidence from detainees until they have given them a "reasonable opportunity" to talk to a lawyer; if not, they may proceed to question (or otherwise acquire self-incriminating evidence from) the detainee.[230]

§4.69 Invocation requires a positive assertion of the right to speak to a lawyer.[231] Detainees have a duty to make it reasonably clear that they wish to exercise their rights.[232] So long as the police have complied with the duties set out above, and absent indications that detainees do not understand or are incapable of asserting their rights, silence will not constitute invocation.[233]

§4.70 What then does constitute invocation? Although there is no authoritative test, it appears that courts decide the question on the basis of whether police should have appreciated that the detainee wanted to talk to a lawyer. Police are not required, it has been said, to "read the mind" of the detainee.[234] For example, in response to the question of whether a detainee wished to contact a lawyer, the words "Can I think about it?" were held not to constitute invocation.[235]

§4.71 Though the police's duty to facilitate access to counsel requires invocation, the Supreme Court has implicitly required police to give detainees a

---

[230] See *R. v. Bartle*, [1994] S.C.J. No. 74, [1994] 3 S.C.R. 173 at 192 (S.C.C.); *R. v. Baig*, [1987] S.C.J. No. 77, [1987] 2 S.C.R. 537 at 540 (S.C.C.); *R. v. Evans*, [1991] S.C.J. No. 31, [1991] 1 S.C.R. 869 at 891 (S.C.C.); *R. v. Brydges*, [1990] S.C.J. No. 8, [1990] 1 S.C.R. 190 at 357 (S.C.C.).

[231] See *R. v. Tremblay*, [1987] S.C.J. No. 59, [1987] 2 S.C.R. 435 at 439 (S.C.C.); *R. v. Hollis*, [1992] B.C.J. No. 2066, 76 C.C.C. (3d) 421 at 435 (B.C.C.A.).

[232] *R. v. Hollis*, [1992] B.C.J. No. 2066, 76 C.C.C. (3d) 421 at 435 (B.C.C.A.); *R. v. Taylor*, [2008] A.J. No. 723, 2008 ABCA 253 at paras. 20-21, 433 A.R. 1 (Alta. C.A.).

[233] *R. v. Hollis*, [1992] B.C.J. No. 2066, 76 C.C.C. (3d) 421 at 435 (B.C.C.A.).

[234] *Ibid.*, at 435 (C.C.C.); *R. v. Taylor*, [2008] A.J. No. 723, 433 A.R. 1 at para. 20 (Alta. C.A.).

[235] *R. v. Green*, [2003] B.C.J. No. 2789, 2003 BCCA 639 at para. 3 (B.C.C.A.). See also *R. v. McKeen*, [2001] N.S.J. No. 44, 190 N.S.R. (2d) 322 (N.S.C.A.) (being deliberately uncooperative with arresting officer and speaking only in German, when the accused knew English, not invocation); *R. v. Leedahl*, [2002] S.J. No. 14, 213 Sask.R. 235 (Sask. C.A.) (no invocation where accused declined opportunity to talk to lawyer at roadside stop on assumption that he would get another chance later at police station).

reasonable opportunity to decide whether to exercise their rights. In *R. v. Feeney*,[236] the Court concluded that police violated section 10(*b*) when they questioned the accused immediately after giving him the caution.[237] Though he did not ask to speak to a lawyer, the Court stated that police did not give him "an adequate opportunity to *consult* with counsel."[238] Given previous holdings that the duty to provide such an opportunity arises only on request, this statement must be regarded as *per incuriam*. It makes sense, however, to require police to delay questioning until they have given suspects a reasonable opportunity to *request* counsel.[239] Indeed, we urge the Court to go one step further and require police (as they normally do in practice[240]) to ask detainees whether they wish to call a lawyer.

(e)   Once This Right is Invoked, What Must Police Do, and Refrain from Doing, to Facilitate Access to Counsel?

§4.72   When detainees first invoke the right to counsel, two police duties are triggered. First, police must provide a "reasonable opportunity" to exercise the right by giving detainees the means and time necessary to talk to a lawyer.[241] Second, police must refrain from or cease "questioning or otherwise attempting to elicit evidence from the detainee".[242] Once the "reasonable opportunity" expires, however, police may proceed with such measures, regardless of whether

---

[236] [1997] S.C.J. No. 49, [1997] 2 S.C.R. 13 (S.C.C.).

[237] *Ibid.*, at paras. 57-58 (S.C.R.).

[238] *R. v. Feeney*, [1997] S.C.J. No. 49, [1997] 2 S.C.R. 13 at para. 58 (S.C.C.) [emphasis added].

[239] See *R. v. Woods*, [1989] O.J. No. 532, 70 C.R. (3d) 45 (Ont. C.A.); *R. v. Hollis*, [1992] B.C.J. No. 2066, 17 C.R. (4th) 211 (B.C.C.A.), *per* Wood J.A.

[240] See *R. v. V. (S.E.)*, [2009] A.J. No. 311, 2 Alta. L.R. (5th) 157 at para. 8 (Alta. C.A.); *R. v. Taylor*, [2008] A.J. No. 723, 2008 ABCA 253 at para. 5 (Alta. C.A.); *R. v. Sinclair*, [2008] B.C.J. No. 502, 169 C.R.R. (2d) 232 (B.C.C.A.), affd [2010] S.C.J. No. 35, [2010] 2 S.C.R. 310 at para. 6 (S.C.C.); *R. v. Green*, [2003] B.C.J. No. 2789, 2003 BCCA 639 at para. 3 (B.C.C.A.); *R. v. Leedhal*, [2002] S.J. No. 14, 213 Sask.R. 235 at para 8 (Sask. C.A.); *R. v. Boomer*, [2001] B.C.J. No. 760, 153 C.C.C. (3d) 425 at para. 12 (B.C.C.A.); *R. v. Butler*, [1995] B.C.J. No. 2716, 104 C.C.C. (3d) 198 at para 18 (B.C.C.A.), leave to appeal refused [1996] S.C.C.A. No. 90, 105 C.C.C. (3d) vi (S.C.C.); *R. v. Schneider*, [1994] S.J. No. 415, 123 Sask.R. 81 at para. 3 (Sask. C.A.).

[241] See *R. v. Manninen*, [1987] S.C.J. No. 41, [1987] 1 S.C.R. 1233 at 1241 (S.C.C.).

[242] See *R. v. Manninen*, [1987] S.C.J. No. 41, [1987] 1 S.C.R. 1233 at 1242 (S.C.C.); *R. v. Prosper*, [1994] S.C.J. No. 72, [1994] 3 S.C.R. 236 at 269 (S.C.C.). As a rule, this bar does not apply to evidence that is not self-incriminating. Police are thus not obliged to defer most types of searches until a reasonable opportunity to talk to a lawyer has been provided. See *R. v. DeBot*, [1989] S.C.J. No. 118, [1989] 2 S.C.R. 1140 at 1146 (S.C.C.); *R. v. Lewis*, [2007] N.S.J. No. 18, 2007 NSCA 2 at para. 34 (N.S.C.A.). This opportunity may have to be given, however, when detainees have a right to seek review of the decision to search. See *R. v. Simmons*, [1988] S.C.J. No. 86, [1988] 2 S.C.R. 495 (S.C.C.) (s. 10(*b*) rights violated when accused subjected to customs strip search; had she been given the right to consult counsel, counsel could have informed of statutory right to request higher authorization for search); *R. v. DeBot*, [1989] S.C.J. No. 118, [1989] 2 S.C.R. 1140 (S.C.C.) (police obligated to suspend search incident to arrest until detainee had opportunity to retain counsel where detainee has statutory right to seek review of decision to search). See *R. v. Nelson*, [2010] A.J. No. 1329, 490 A.R. 271 (Alta. C.A.) (delay in contacting counsel did not breach s. 10(*b*) because police refrained from questioning until detainee had spoken with counsel).

detainees have talked to a lawyer.[243] Detainees must thus be "reasonably dili-gent" in exercising their right to counsel.[244] Otherwise, the Court has explained, they could unduly frustrate the ability of police to collect evidence that may not be available in perpetuity.[245]

§4.73 The question, then, is what constitutes a "reasonable opportunity"? Police must allow detainees to telephone a lawyer in private,[246] as soon as reasonably possible,[247] even if privacy is not requested.[248] If private telephone consultation is possible at the place of initial detention (or anywhere a detainee is taken before a police station), it must be provided there.[249] If not, it must be provided at the sta-tion.[250] Police may not elicit any evidence from the detainee before such access is provided.[251]

§4.74 Once police have provided private telephone access, two further ques-tions arise: (*i*) whether detainees are entitled to talk to a lawyer of their choos-ing; and (*ii*) how long must police wait for detainees to contact counsel before eliciting self-incriminating evidence from them? The Supreme Court addressed

---

[243] *R. v. Prosper*, [1994] S.C.J. No. 72, [1994] 3 S.C.R. 236 (S.C.C.).

[244] *R. v. Ross*, [1989] S.C.J. No. 2, [1989] 1 S.C.R. 3 at 11 (S.C.C.); *R. v. Tremblay*, [1987] S.C.J. No. 59, [1987] 2 S.C.R. 435 at 439 (S.C.C.).

[245] *R. v. Smith*, [1989] S.C.J. No. 89, [1989] 2 S.C.R. 368 at 385 (S.C.C.).

[246] The courts have typically held that s. 10(*b*) requires an environment "where the conversation cannot be overhead and there is no reasonable apprehension...of being overheard." *R. v. Miller*, [1990] N.J. No. 305, 87 Nfld. & P.E.I.R. 55 at 58 (Nfld. C.A.). See also *R. v. Kelly*, [1996] N.J. No. 110, 140 Nfld. & P.E.I.R. 14 (Nfld. C.A.); *R. v. LePage*, [1986] N.S.J. No. 371, 32 C.C.C. (3d) 171 (N.S.C.A.); *R. v. Kennedy*, [1995] N.J. No. 340, 103 C.C.C. (3d) 161, 135 Nfld. & P.E.I.R. 271, 420 A.P.R. 271 (Nfld. C.A.); *R. v. Playford*, [1987] O.J. No. 1107, 40 C.C.C. (3d) 142 at 158 (Ont. C.A.); *R. v. Young*, [1987] N.B.J. No. 826, 6 M.V.R. (2d) 295 (N.B.C.A.); *R. v. Cairns*, [2004] O.J. No. 210 at para. 10 (Ont. C.A.) (presence of video camera not sufficient to ground reasonable belief that privacy lacking; *R. v. Panchyshyn*, [1985] S.J. No. 411, 38 Sask.R. 239 (Sask. C.A.) (police officer's presence did not violate s. 10 when accused elected to contact father rather than counsel). See *R. v. Nelson*, [2010] A.J. No. 1329, 490 A.R. 271 at para. 20 (Alta. C.A.) ("calls made by accused persons in the presence of police are of doubtful value. The right to counsel means the right to consult in private.").

[247] See *R. v. Manninen*, [1987] S.C.J. No. 41, [1987] 1 S.C.R. 1233 at 1242 (S.C.C.) ("...there may be circumstances in which it is particularly urgent that the police continue with an investigation before it is possible to facilitate a detainee's communication with counsel"). See also *R. v. Bur-ley*, [2004] O.J. No. 319, 181 C.C.C. (3d) 463 at para. 16 (Ont. C.A.); *R. v. Nelson*, [2010] A.J. No. 1329, 490 A.R. 271 at paras. 15-23 (Alta. C.A.).

[248] See *R. v. Jackson*, [1993] O.J. No. 2511, 86 C.C.C. (3d) 233, 25 C.R. (4th) 265, 15 O.R. (3d) 709, 48 M.V.R. (2d) 277, 66 O.A.C. 64 (Ont. C.A.); *R. v. Parrill*, [1998] N.J. No. 322, 58 C.R.R. (2d) 56, 38 M.V.R. (3d) 7, 521 A.P.R. 28, 169 Nfld. & P.E.I.R. 28 (Nfld. C.A.); *R. v. Butler*, [1995] B.C.J. No. 2716, 104 C.C.C. (3d) 198 at para. 45 (B.C.C.A.), leave to appeal re-fused [1996] S.C.C.A. No. 90, 105 C.C.C. (3d) vi (S.C.C.); *R. v. McKane*, [1987] O.J. No. 557, 58 C.R. (3d) 130 (Ont. C.A.).

[249] See *R. v. Manninen*, [1987] S.C.J. No. 41, [1987] 1 S.C.R. 1233 at 1242-43 (S.C.C.); *R. v. Bur-ley*, [2004] O.J. No. 319, 181 C.C.C. (3d) 463 (Ont. C.A.).

[250] See *R. v. Lewis*, [2007] N.S.J. No. 18, 2007 NSCA 2 (N.S.C.A.) (public phone in railway sta-tion did not provide sufficient privacy, police justified in transporting accused almost immedi-ately to police station to use telephone there).

[251] *R. v. Lewis*, [2007] N.S.J. No. 18, 2007 NSCA 2 at para. 32 (N.S.C.A.); *R. v. Nelson*, [2010] A.J. No. 1329, 490 A.R. 271 (Alta. C.A.).

both in *R. v. Ross*.[252] There, two detainees were unable to contact lawyers of their choosing at 2:00 a.m. Before they were able to call their lawyers' offices in the morning, police placed them in an identification line-up. This violated section 10(*b*), the Court held, because detainees have a "right to choose their counsel".[253] They are only expected to call another lawyer if their chosen lawyer "cannot be available within a reasonable time."[254] The duration of this period, it suggested, might be foreshortened by circumstances of "urgency" or some other "compelling reason", but in this case the line-up could have easily been held "a few hours later".[255] The failure to be reasonably diligent, it should be stressed, does not extinguish the right to talk to a lawyer; it only negates the duty of police to refrain from attempting to elicit evidence from the detainee.[256] The duty of police to "hold off" may resume, however, if there is a significant change in circumstances, as where police begin to suspect that the detainee has committed a substantially different or more serious offence.[257]

§4.75 The courts have set out few hard and fast rules dictating the duration and timing of the "reasonable opportunity" to contact counsel. In each case "all of the surrounding circumstances" must be considered in deciding whether police have provided a reasonable opportunity, or conversely, whether detainees have diligently exercised their rights.[258] In *R. v. Smith*,[259] for example, the accused was first given the opportunity to contact counsel at 9:00 p.m. Unable to find his lawyer's home number, he choose not to try calling his office, telling police he would contact him in the morning. A majority of the Court held that by not attempting to call the office (and thereby possibly receiving information on how to reach his lawyer) he did not exercise reasonable diligence.[260]

---

[252] *R. v. Ross*, [1989] S.C.J. No. 2, [1989] 1 S.C.R. 3 (S.C.C.).

[253] *Ibid.*, at 11 (S.C.R.).

[254] *Ibid.*; *R. v. Traicheff*, [2010] O.J. No. 5355, 2010 ONCA 851 (Ont. C.A.) (after waiting a "reasonable period" for laywer to return call police should ask detainee if he would like to consult another lawyer (or whether he has another number for his counsel)).

[255] *R. v. Ross*, [1989] S.C.J. No. 2, [1989] 1 S.C.R. 3 at 12-13 (S.C.C.).

[256] *R. v. Smith*, [1989] S.C.J. No. 89, [1989] 2 S.C.R. 368 at 386-88 (S.C.C.).

[257] *Ibid.*, at 386 (S.C.R.). See also discussion at Part 3(4)(*b*) and Part 3(4)(*f*).

[258] *R. v. Prosper*, [1994] S.C.J. No. 72, [1994] 3 S.C.R. 236 at 269 (S.C.C.); *R. v. Sheppard*, [2005] N.J. No. 233, 2005 NLCA 45 at para. 18 (Nfld. C.A.); *R. v. Basko*, [2007] S.J. No. 564, 2007 SKCA 111 at para. 13 (Sask. C.A.); *R. v. Ngo*, [2003] A.J. No. 610, 2003 ABCA 121 at para. 25 (Alta. C.A.); *R. v. Whitford*, [1997] A.J. No. 309, 115 C.C.C. (3d) 52 at para. 7 (Alta. C.A.), leave to appeal refused [1997] S.C.C.A. No. 246 (S.C.C.); *R. v. Richfield*, [2003] O.J. No. 3230, 178 C.C.C. (3d) 23 at para. 9 (Ont. C.A.).

[259] [1989] S.C.J. No. 89, [1989] 2 S.C.R. 368 (S.C.C.).

[260] *R. v. Smith*, [1989] S.C.J. No. 89, [1989] 2 S.C.R. 368 at 385-386 (S.C.C.). This holding was sharply criticized by the dissent as well as by several commentators. See *R. v. Smith*, [1989] S.C.J. No. 89, [1989] 2 S.C.R. 368 at 378-80 (S.C.C.), *per* La Forest J., dissenting; Stephen Coughlan, "When Silence Isn't Golden: Waiver and the Right to Counsel" (1990) 33 Crim. L.Q. 43 at 55; Stanley A. Cohen, "Police Interrogation of the Wavering Suspect" (1989) 71 C.R. (3d) 148; Patrick Healy, "The Value of Silence" (1990) 74 C.R. (3d) 176 at 181-83; Don Stuart, *Charter Justice in Canadian Criminal Law*, 4th ed. (Toronto: Thomson Carswell, 2005) 352-53; Tim Quigley, *Procedure in Canadian Criminal Law*, 2d ed. (looseleaf) (Toronto: Thomson Carswell, 2006) § 7.2(c)(iii)(B).

§4.76 The duration of the "reasonable opportunity" may also be affected by the availability of duty counsel. In *R. v. Prosper*,[261] the Court concluded that while provinces had no constitutional obligation to provide duty counsel,[262] their unavailability may extend the period during which police are required to refrain from eliciting evidence from detainees to a time when "the local Legal Aid office opens, when a private lawyer willing to provide free summary advice can be reached, or when the detainee is brought before a justice of the peace for bail purposes."[263] Conversely, where duty counsel services are available, detainees unable to contact their own lawyer may be expected to use them,[264] especially where the police's ability to elicit evidence may be compromised by delay.[265]

§4.77 Before their "reasonable opportunity" expires, detainees who have not yet talked to a lawyer may "waive" their right to do so.[266] In such cases police may attempt to elicit incriminating information from them. The standard for waiver in these circumstances, however, is stringent. The prosecution must show that detainees (*i*) indicated clearly and unequivocally that they no longer wished to talk to a lawyer and (*ii*) made this decision with full knowledge of their rights and the consequences of foregoing them.[267] Further, if detainees do something to

---

261 [1994] S.C.J. No. 72, [1994] 3 S.C.R. 236 (S.C.C.).

262 *R. v. Prosper*, [1994] S.C.J. No. 72, [1994] 3 S.C.R. 236 at 265-68 (S.C.C.).

263 *Ibid.*, at 270 (S.C.R.). The Court recognized that there may be "compelling and urgent circumstances" that would relieve police of their obligation to hold off, even if duty counsel were not available. Such circumstances, however, do not arise from "mere investigatory and evidentiary expediency", as in the case of the two-hour evidentiary presumption available to the Crown in impaired driving cases pursuant to s. 258(1)(*d*) of the *Criminal Code*, R.S.C. 1985, c. C-46, *i.e.*, that a breath or blood sample reading taken within two hours of the offence is deemed to reflect the blood alcohol level at the time of the offence. *R. v. Prosper*, [1994] S.C.J. No. 72, [1994] 3 S.C.R. 236 at 270, 275 (S.C.C.).

264 See *R. v. Prosper*, [1994] S.C.J. No. 72, [1994] 3 S.C.R. 236 at 269-70 (S.C.C.) ("the existence of duty counsel services may affect what constitutes 'reasonable diligence' of a detainee in pursuing the right to counsel, which will in turn affect the length the period during which the state authorities' s. 10(b) implementational duties will require them to "hold off" from trying to elicit incriminatory evidence from the detainee"); *R. v. Richfield*, [2003] O.J. No. 3230 at para. 8 (Ont. C.A.) ("in considering whether the appellant has been given a reasonable opportunity to exercise the right to counsel and has exercised this right with reasonable diligence, the existence of 24 hour duty counsel services is a crucial factor that must be considered"); *R. v. Luong*, [2000] A.J. No. 1310, 149 C.C.C. (3d) 571 (Alta. C.A.) (new trial ordered to determine whether 15 minutes in a room equipped with phone books, a roster of duty counsel and an operating telephone afforded a reasonable opportunity).

265 *R. v. Prosper*, [1994] S.C.J. No. 72, [1994] 3 S.C.R. 236 at 270, 275 (S.C.C.) ("the fact that the evidence may cease to be available as a result of a long delay" as well as the existence of "compelling and urgent circumstances" must be considered in determining the length of the "reasonable opportunity" where duty counsel are available); *R. v. Brydges*, [1990] S.C.J. No. 8, [1990] 1 S.C.R. 190 at 216 (S.C.C.); *R. v. Basko*, [2007] S.J. No. 564, 2007 SKCA 111 at para. 16 (Sask. C.A.). As noted in *Prosper*, however (at 274 (S.C.R.)), investigative urgency does not contract the duration of detainees' reasonable opportunity to contact counsel when duty counsel are unavailable.

266 *R. v. Prosper*, [1994] S.C.J. No. 72, [1994] 3 S.C.R. 236 at 275 (S.C.C.) (s. 10(*b*) does not impose "an obligation on detainees to seek the advice of a lawyer").

267 *R. v. Ross*, [1989] S.C.J. No. 2, [1989] 1 S.C.R. 3 at 11-12 (S.C.C.); *R. v. Prosper*, [1994] S.C.J. No. 72, [1994] 3 S.C.R. 236 at 274-75 (S.C.C.); *R. v. Manninen*, [1987] S.C.J. No. 41, [1987] 1 S.C.R. 1233 at 1244; *R. v. Black*, [1989] S.C.J. No. 81, [1989] 2 S.C.R. 138 at 156-57 (S.C.C.);

suggest that they no longer wish to talk to a lawyer, police must advise them of the right "to a reasonable opportunity to contact counsel and of their obligation during this time not to elicit incriminating evidence".[268]

§4.78 Several courts of appeal have held, however, that this "*Prosper*" warning, as it has become known, need not be given to detainees who have not been reasonably diligent in attempting to contact counsel.[269] For example, in *R. v. Jones*,[270] the Court found that a *Prosper* warning was not required where the accused, who tried unsuccessfully to contact his own lawyer, refused the offer of police to call duty counsel.[271] The same result was reached in *R. v. Basko*,[272] where after two unsuccessful calls to Legal Aid (the line was busy), the accused said, "I know what they are going to tell me, so I'll call one tomorrow."[273] Police asked him if he would like to try a different lawyer, but he replied, "No, let's get it over," and submitted to the taking of breath samples.

§4.79 These decisions are difficult to reconcile with the Supreme Court's jurisprudence on diligence and waiver. As discussed, detainees must be given a reasonable opportunity to consult with counsel of choice. While the availability of duty counsel may in some cases abbreviate the duration of that opportunity, it does not extinguish it. It is thus difficult to see how Jones's failure to call duty counsel was unreasonable.[274] Similarly, while Basko had not expressed a desire to contact a specific lawyer, his decision to forego further attempts to reach duty counsel was hardly dilatory. And while both were entitled to forego consultation, waiver requires "full knowledge" of the right and an "appreciation of the consequences" of their decision.[275] Without being informed of the police's duty to hold off until his reasonable opportunity expired, how can it be said that they were fully aware of the consequences of waiver?

R. v. Brydges, [1990] S.C.J. No. 8, [1990] 1 S.C.R. 190 at 204 (S.C.C.); *R. v. Evans*, [1991] S.C.J. No. 31, [1991] 1 S.C.R. 869 at 893-94 (S.C.C.); *R. v. Smith*, [1991] S.C.J. No. 24, [1991] 1 S.C.R. 714 at 727-28 (S.C.C.); *R. v. Bartle*, [1994] S.C.J. No. 74, [1994] 3 S.C.R. 173 at 192-94, 206 (S.C.C.).

[268] *R. v. Prosper*, [1994] S.C.J. No. 72, [1994] 3 S.C.R. 236 at 274 (S.C.C.).

[269] See *R. v. Basko*, [2007] S.J. No. 564, 2007 SKCA 111 (Sask. C.A.); *R. v. Jones*, [2005] A.J. No. 1325, 2005 ABCA 289 (Alta. C.A.), leave to appeal refused [2005] S.C.C.A. No. 538 (S.C.C.); *R. v. Luong*, [2000] A.J. No. 1310, 2000 ABCA 301, 149 C.C.C. (3d) 571 (Alta. C.A.).

[270] [2005] A.J. No. 1325, 2005 ABCA 289 (Alta. C.A.), leave to appeal refused [2005] S.C.C.A. No. 538 (S.C.C.).

[271] *R. v. Jones*, [2005] A.J. No. 1325, 2005 ABCA 289 at para. 12 (Alta. C.A.), leave to appeal refused [2005] S.C.C.A. No. 538 (S.C.C.).

[272] [2007] S.J. No. 564, 2007 SKCA 111 (Sask. C.A.).

[273] *R. v. Basko*, [2007] S.J. No. 564, 2007 SKCA 111 at para. 27 (Sask. C.A.).

[274] *R. v. Jones*, [2005] A.J. No. 1325, 2005 ABCA 289 at paras. 20-30 (Alta. C.A.), leave to appeal refused [2005] S.C.C.A. No. 538 (S.C.C.), *per* Berger J.A., dissenting. See also *R. v. Luong*, [2000] A.J. No. 1310, 149 C.C.C. (3d) 571 at para. 9 (Alta. C.A.) (if police do not give detainees a reasonable opportunity to contact counsel, "an assessment as to whether due diligence was exercised ... does not arise").

[275] *R. v. Prosper*, [1994] S.C.J. No. 72, [1994] 3 S.C.R. 236 at 282 (S.C.C.).

§4.80 The diligence rule is designed to prevent dilatory detainees from frustrating legitimate investigative efforts.[276] It should not be interpreted to require them to take every conceivable measure to contact a lawyer as soon as possible. The fact that they could have done more to contact counsel before "giving up" should not therefore disentitle them to the *Prosper* warning. By informing detainees that they are entitled to a reasonable opportunity to talk to a lawyer, the warning mitigates the ability of police to pressure detainees into forgoing their rights.[277] It is also very simple for police to administer. Once they confirm that detainees no longer wish to contact counsel, police are free to continue the investigation.

§4.81 Unfortunately, the Supreme Court of Canada's decision in *R. v. Willier*[278] could be interpreted as confirming that police must give the *Prosper* warning only to detainees who diligently attempted to consult with counsel.[279] In our view, this suggestion is *obiter* and should not be read as relieving police from their duty to give the warning to non-diligent detainees who had initially wished to talk to a lawyer but failed to do so. We say this because diligence was not an issue in *Willier*. There, the accused spoke with duty counsel for three minutes after his arrest.[280] Before being interviewed by police the next morning, he called his lawyer of choice (who was not available), left a message and consulted again briefly with duty counsel. Since he was unable to consult with his preferred lawyer, he argued that police should have given him the *Prosper* warning before questioning him. In rejecting this claim, the Court held that circumstances triggering a *Prosper* warning were "fundamentally different from those in the case at hand."[281] We agree. As the Court stated, "[t]he concerns animating the provision of a *Prosper* warning do not arise when a detainee is unsuccessful in contacting a specific lawyer and simply opts to speak with another."[282]

§4.82 The real issues in *Willier* were whether the detainee was given a reasonable opportunity to talk to his preferred lawyer and whether his brief consultations with duty counsel were substantively sufficient. On the first question, the Court found that while police began questioning him only 50 minutes after he tried to speak with his chosen lawyer, he was given a reasonable opportunity to consult with counsel. Because it was the weekend, the Court noted, his lawyer was unlikely to get back to him promptly; the accused indicated, moreover, that

---

[276] See *R. v. Smith*, [1989] S.C.J. No. 89, [1989] 2 S.C.R. 368 at 385 (S.C.C.); *R. v. Whitford*, [1997] A.J. No. 309, 115 C.C.C. (3d) 52 at para. 15 (Alta. C.A.).

[277] See *R. v. Prosper*, [1994] S.C.J. No. 72, [1994] 3 S.C.R. 236 at 275 (S.C.C.) ("[T]he waiver must be free and voluntary and it must not be the product of either direct or indirect compulsion.").

[278] [2010] S.C.J. No. 37, [2010] 2 S.C.R. 429 (S.C.C.).

[279] *Ibid.*, at paras. 32, 38 (S.C.R.) (*Prosper* warning warranted only where detainee is "diligent but unsuccessful" in contacting a lawyer).

[280] *R. v. Willier*, [2010] S.C.J. No. 37, [2010] 2 S.C.R. 429 (S.C.C.).

[281] *Ibid.*, at para. 38 (S.C.R.).

[282] *Ibid.*, at para. 39 (S.C.R.).

he was satisfied with the legal advice he received.[283] As the Court stated, "the *Charter* does not guarantee detainees an absolute right to retain and instruct a particular counsel at the initial investigative stage regardless of the circumstances."[284]

§4.83 The Court confronted a very similar scenario in *R. v. McCrimmon*.[285] There, the detainee expressed a desire to speak to a particular lawyer, Cheevers. After unsuccessfully trying to contact Cheevers, police asked the detainee if he wished to speak to duty counsel. He replied, "...yes, definitely, but I prefer Mr. Cheevers."[286] He talked to duty counsel for five minutes and told police he was satisfied with the advice given. The Court had little difficulty in concluding that police had no further obligation to "hold off the interrogation until such time as Mr. Cheevers became available."[287]

§4.84 The Court in *Willier* also rejected the argument that the detainee's brief consultation with duty counsel was substantively inadequate. Section 10(*b*) does not require police to "monitor the quality" of legal advice once contact is made.[288]

§4.85 Because of concerns for privacy and lawyer-client confidentiality and privilege, the Court reasoned, police are not in a position to decide whether any advice given was sufficient. "[U]nless a detainee indicates, diligently and reasonably, that the advice he or she received is inadequate," it continued, "the police may assume that the detainee is satisfied with the exercised right to counsel and are entitled to commence an investigative interview."[289]

---

[283] See also *R. v. Jones*, [2005] A.J. No. 1325, 2005 ABCA 289 (Alta. C.A.), leave to appeal refused [2005] S.C.C.A. No. 538 (S.C.C.) (accused terminated efforts to contact counsel after seven minutes of knocking on door; police not obligated to ask whether he required further time); *R. v. Sadownik*, [1988] A.J. No. 101, 84 A.R. 91 (Alta. C.A.) (15 minutes to use phone and seven minutes to personally consult with counsel provided reasonable opportunity, as accused not interrupted and length of call determined solely by accused).

[284] *R. v. Willier*, [2010] S.C.J. No. 37, [2010] 2 S.C.R. 429 at para. 24 (S.C.C.).

[285] [2010] S.C.J. No. 36, [2010] 2 S.C.R. 402 (S.C.C.).

[286] *Ibid.*, at para. 7 (S.C.R.).

[287] *Ibid.*, at para. 19 (S.C.R.). But see *R. v. Badgerow*, [2008] O.J. No. 3416, 2008 ONCA 605 (Ont. C.A.), leave to appeal refused [2008] S.C.C.A. No. 483 (S.C.C.) (s. 10(*b*) violation where detainee spoke briefly to partner of preferred lawyer and expressed satisfaction but instructed partner to keep trying to contact preferred lawyer).

[288] *R. v. Willier*, [2010] S.C.J. No. 37, [2010] 2 S.C.R. 429 at para. 41 (S.C.C.).

[289] *Ibid.*, at para. 42 (S.C.R.). But see *R. v. Osmond*, [2007] B.C.J. No. 2132, 227 C.C.C. (3d) 375 (B.C.C.A.), leave to appeal refused [2007] S.C.C.A. No. 545 (S.C.C.) (police violated s. 10(*b*) by questioning unsophisticated murder suspect after two-minute consultation with duty counsel who, after telling him not to speak with police or other detainees, failed to give him any further advice about how to resist police pressures to speak). See also *R. v. Ashmore*, [2011] B.C.J. No. 75, 2011 BCCA 18 at para. 63 (B.C.C.A.) (noting that the reasoning in *Osmond* "may well have been brought into question by *Willier*").

(f) What Limitations Does Section 10(b) Impose on Police Questioning After a Detainee has Been Afforded a Reasonable Opportunity to Talk to a Lawyer?

§4.86 In the United States, once suspects invoke their right to counsel, police must cease questioning until a lawyer is present.[290] This rule applies whether or not suspects consult with counsel or exercise due diligence in attempting to do so.[291] No such rule exists in Canada. Once detainees have been given a single reasonable opportunity to talk to a lawyer, police may question or otherwise attempt to elicit evidence from them, even if they have not actually talked to a lawyer[292] or request further consultation.[293] Similarly, police are not required to permit detainees' lawyers to be present during questioning.[294]

§4.87 These rules are subject to a few limited exceptions. First, the Supreme Court of Canada held in *R. v. Sinclair*[295] that police must offer a second chance to talk to a lawyer when "reconsultation is necessary in order for the detainee to have the information relevant to choosing whether to cooperate with the police investigation or not."[296] We have already discussed (in Part 3(4)(*a*), above) the duty to re-issue the section 10(*b*) caution when there is a "fundamental and discrete change in the purpose of the investigation, one involving a different and unrelated offence or a significantly more serious offence than that contemplated

---

[290] *Miranda v. Arizona*, 384 U.S. 436 at 474 (1966); *Edwards v. Arizona*, 451 U.S. 477 at 484-85 (1981); *Minnick v. Mississippi*, 498 U.S. 146 at 150 (1990). This rule does not apply, however, if suspects themselves initiate further communication with police. See *Edwards v. Arizona*, *ibid.*; *Oregon v. Bradshaw*, 462 U.S. 1039 (1983).

[291] *Minnick v. Mississippi*, 498 U.S. 146 at 150 (1990).

[292] *R. v. Manninen*, [1987] S.C.J. No. 41, [1987] 1 S.C.R. 1233 (S.C.C.).

[293] See *R. v. Sinclair*, [2010] S.C.J. No. 35, [2010] 2 S.C.R. 310 (S.C.C.); *R. v. McCrimmon*, [2010] S.C.J. No. 36, [2010] 2 S.C.R. 402 (S.C.C.). See also *R. v. Baidwan*, [2003] B.C.J. No. 1439, 2003 BCCA 351, leave to appeal refused [2003] S.C.C.A. No. 377 (S.C.C.); *R. v. Wood*, [1994] N.S.J. No. 542, 94 C.C.C. (3d) 193 at 225 (N.S.C.A.), leave to appeal refused [1995] S.C.C.A. No. 41 (S.C.C.); *R. v. Logan*, [1988] O.J. No. 2107, 46 C.C.C. (3d) 354 (Ont. C.A.), affd [1990] S.C.J. No. 89 (S.C.C.); *R. v. Roper*, [1997] O.J. No. 305, 98 O.A.C. 225 (Ont. C.A.); *R. v. Gormley*, [1999] P.E.I.J. No. 80, 140 C.C.C. (3d) 110 at para. 45 (P.E.I.C.A.); *R. v. Mayo*, [1999] O.J. No. 714, 133 C.C.C. (3d) 168 (Ont. C.A.); *R. v. Ekman*, [2000] B.C.J. No. 1363, 146 C.C.C. (3d) 346 at para. 23 (B.C.C.A.); *R. v. Friesen*, [1995] A.J. No. 770, 101 C.C.C. (3d) 167 (Alta. C.A.), leave to appeal refused [1995] S.C.C.A. No. 539 (S.C.C.); *R. v. Russell*, [1998] A.J. No. 569, 62 Alta. L.R. (3d) 87 (Alta. C.A.), affd [2000] S.C.J. No. 56 (S.C.C.); *R. v. Plata*, [1999] J.Q. no. 586, 136 C.C.C. (3d) 436 (Que. C.A.); *R. v. Kerr*, [2000] B.C.J. No. 611, 32 C.R. (5th) 359 (B.C.C.A.).

[294] See *R. v. Sinclair*, [2010] S.C.J. No. 35, [2010] 2 S.C.R. 310 at paras. 33-42 (S.C.C.). See also *R. v. Ekman*, [2000] B.C.J. No. 1363, 2000 BCCA 414 (B.C.C.A.); *R. v. Ekman*, [2006] B.C.J. No. 943, 2006 BCCA 206 (B.C.C.A.); *R. v. Baidwan*, [2003] B.C.J. No. 1439, 2003 BCCA 351, leave to appeal refused [2003] S.C.C.A. No. 377 (S.C.C.); *R. v. Friesen*, [1995] A.J. No. 770, 101 C.C.C. (3d) 167 (Alta. C.A.), leave to appeal refused [1995] S.C.C.A. No. 539 (S.C.C.); *R. v. Mayo*, [1999] O.J. No. 714, 133 C.C.C. (3d) 168 (Ont. C.A.); *R. v. Osmond*, [2007] B.C.J. No. 2132, 2007 BCCA 470, 227 C.C.C. (3d) 375 (B.C.C.A.), leave to appeal refused [2007] S.C.C.A. No. 545 (S.C.C.).

[295] [2010] S.C.J. No. 35, [2010] 2 S.C.R. 310 (S.C.C.).

[296] *Ibid.*, at para. 48 (S.C.R.).

at the time of the warning."[297] *Sinclair* confirms that in such circumstances police must give a detainee who has already consulted with counsel a second
chance to do so.[298] The Court in *Sinclair* also held that a second opportunity is
warranted when police plan to subject detainees to "[n]on routine procedures,
like participation in a line-up or submitting to a polygraph".[299] In addition, the
Court concluded that police who become aware that a detainee may not have
understood "the initial s. 10(*b*) advice of his right to counsel" must provide another opportunity for consultation. Lastly, the Court held that an additional opportunity must be given if "police undermine the legal advice that the detainee
has received".[300]

§4.88 The *Sinclair* Court stressed that there may be other circumstances triggering a right to re-consult.[301] The circumstances, however, must be "objectively
observable".[302] As the Court stated, it is "not enough for the accused to assert,
after the fact, that he was confused or needed help, absent objective indicators
that renewed legal consultation was required to permit him to make a meaningful choice as to whether to cooperate with the police investigation or refuse to do
so."[303] The majority in *Sinclair* rejected Justice Binnie's suggestion[304] that police
must comply with any reasonable request for re-consultation by detainees.[305]

§4.89 To better illustrate the majority's approach, consider the facts in *Sinclair*.
After police questioned Mr. Sinclair for two and a half hours, the interrogator
told him that the evidence against him was "overwhelming", making reference
to both true and false incriminating evidence. Mr. Sinclair replied that he did not
want to talk to them and wished to see his lawyer. After the interrogator again
referred to the evidence as "absolutely overwhelming" and after further requests
by Mr. Sinclair to talk to his lawyer, he confessed. For Justice Binnie, police
were obliged under section 10(*b*) to permit re-consultation after they confronted
Mr. Sinclair with what they said was "absolutely overwhelming" evidence.[306]

---

[297] *R. v. Evans*, [1991] S.C.J. No. 31, [1991] 1 S.C.R. 869 at 893 (S.C.C.). See also *R. v. Black*,
[1989] S.C.J. No. 81, [1989] 2 S.C.R. 138 at 193-94 (S.C.C.); *R. v. Borden*, [1994] S.C.J. No.
82, [1994] 3 S.C.R. 145 at 165-66 (S.C.C.); *R. v. Paternak*, [1996] S.C.J. No. 108, [1996] 3
S.C.R. 607 (S.C.C.); *R. v. Burlingham*, [1995] S.C.J. No. 39, [1995] 2 S.C.R. 206 at para. 20
(S.C.C.).

[298] *R. v. Sinclair*, [2010] S.C.J. No. 35, [2010] 2 S.C.R. 310 at paras. 47-48, 51 (S.C.C.).

[299] *Ibid.*, at para. 50 (S.C.R.). See also *R. v. Ashmore*, [2011] B.C.J. No. 75, 2011 BCCA 18 at
paras. 66-71 (B.C.C.A.) (neither playing incriminating video to detainee nor inviting him to
participate in re-enactment constitutes new or non-routine procedure triggering right to re-
consultation); *R. v. Wu*, [2010] A.J. No. 1327, 2010 ABCA 337 at paras. 69-70 (Alta. C.A.)
(electronic recording of interview not non-routine procedure).

[300] *R. v. Sinclair*, [2010] S.C.J. No. 35, [2010] 2 S.C.R. 310 at para. 52 (S.C.C.). As discussed in
this Part, below, the undermining or denigration of the detainee's counsel may violate s. 10(*b*)
even if a further opportunity to talk to a lawyer is provided.

[301] *Ibid.*, at paras. 49, 54 (S.C.R.).

[302] *Ibid.*, at para. 55 (S.C.R.).

[303] *Ibid.*

[304] *Ibid.*, at para. 80 (S.C.R.), *per* Binnie J., dissenting.

[305] *Ibid.*, at para. 56 (S.C.R.).

[306] *Ibid.*, at para. 118 (S.C.R.), *per* Binnie J., dissenting.

The majority concluded, however, that Mr. Sinclair was always aware of his jeopardy and knew he could remain silent.[307] The pressure police put on him to confess did not overwhelm his understanding of his rights and trigger a right to further consultation with counsel.

§4.90 The majority's reasons in *Sinclair* also confirm that, in and of itself, lengthy and persistent questioning is unlikely to either give rise to a section 10(*b*) violation or a right to re-consultation.[308] This principle holds even if detainees repeatedly say that they wish to remain silent or talk to their lawyer. The majority also suggested that there was no support for the "view that the common police tactic of gradually revealing (actual or fake) evidence to the detainee in order to demonstrate or exaggerate the strength of the case against him automatically triggers the right to a second consultation with a lawyer".[309]

§4.91 In *R. v. Burlingham*,[310] the Supreme Court had previously held that police violated section 10(*b*) by "continually" questioning a detainee who told them that he did not want to speak in the absence of his lawyer.[311] However, both before and after this decision, courts have allowed extensive post-invocation questioning, even when detainees ask to speak to their lawyers or tell police that they do not want to speak.[312] The *Sinclair* majority noted that persistent or deceptive questioning may run afoul of the confessions rule;[313] though as discussed in Part 2(3), above, confessions are rarely found to be involuntary for these reasons.

---

[307] *Ibid.*, at paras. 66-74 (S.C.R.).

[308] *Ibid.*, at paras. 61-63 (S.C.R.).

[309] *Ibid.*, at para. 60 (S.C.R.).

[310] [1995] S.C.J. No. 39, [1995] 2 S.C.R. 206 (S.C.C.).

[311] *Ibid.* The Court's discussion of this point was disappointingly brief. It stated simply (at para. 13 (S.C.R.)) that police must "refrain from attempting to elicit incriminatory evidence once a detainee has asserted his or her right to counsel." The Court had never previously held, however, that this limitation is continuous. As discussed, the duty to "hold off" expires once the suspect has had a reasonable opportunity to talk to a lawyer.

[312] See *R. v. Sinclair*, [2010] S.C.J. No. 35, [2010] 2 S.C.R. 310 (S.C.C.) (no violation where police continued questioning despite five requests to speak to counsel). See also *R. v. Wood*, [1994] N.S.J. No. 542, 94 C.C.C. (3d) 193 at 225 (N.S.C.A.), leave to appeal refused [1995] S.C.C.A. No. 41, 99 C.C.C. (3d) vi (S.C.C.) (police permitted to maintain intense, three-hour interrogation after suspect had consulted with counsel and advised police that he had nothing to say); *R. v. Cuff*, [1989] N.J. No. 94, 49 C.C.C. (3d) 65 (Nfld. C.A.) (no violation of s. 10(*b*) where police questioned suspect after he had talked to a lawyer); *R. v. Emile*, [1988] N.W.T.J. No. 196, 65 C.R. (3d) 135 (N.W.T.C.A.) (police permitted to question suspect who had consulted counsel in absence of counsel and without seeking counsel's permission); *R. v. Gormley*, [1999] P.E.I.J. No. 80, 140 C.C.C. (3d) 110 (P.E.I.C.A.) (police permitted to question suspect for almost four hours despite suspect repeatedly refusing to answer questions because lawyer told him to remain silent); *R. v. Roper*, [1997] O.J. No. 305, 98 O.A.C. 225 (Ont. C.A.) (police permitted to continue questioning of suspect after he consulted counsel and counsel advised police that suspect intended to exercise right to silence); *R. v. Kerr*, [2000] B.C.J. No. 611, 32 C.R. (5th) 359 (B.C.C.A.) (same); *R. v. Mayo*, [1999] O.J. No. 714, 133 C.C.C. (3d) 168 (Ont. C.A.) (police permitted to question suspect after he had talked to lawyer despite his insistence that he did not want to talk in counsel's absence); *R. v. Ekman*, [2000] B.C.J. No. 1363, 146 C.C.C. (3d) 346 (B.C.C.A.) (same). But see *R. v. Nugent*, [1988] N.S.J. No. 186, 63 C.R. (3d) 351 (N.S.C.A.) (continued interrogation after suspect contacted counsel violated section 10(*b*)).

[313] *R. v. Sinclair*, [2010] S.C.J. No. 35, [2010] 2 S.C.R. 310 at para. 60 (S.C.C.).

§4.92 Two other holdings from *Burlingham*, however, remain largely intact. First, the Court held that police violated section 10(*b*) by repeatedly denigrating the detainee's lawyer's competence and integrity.[314] Not all negative comments run afoul of this rule, however. Section 10(*b*) only prohibits police from "belittling an accused's lawyer with the express goal or effect of undermining the accused's confidence in and relationship with defence counsel."[315] As discussed, the Court in *Sinclair* held that undermining a lawyer's advice triggers an obligation to give detainees a further opportunity to talk to a lawyer. *Sinclair* should not be read, however, to permit police to "cure" section 10(*b*) violations by providing such an opportunity. When the aim or effect of police comments is to undermine detainees' confidence in their lawyers, the damage will often be irreparable. Further, finding a section 10(*b*) violation in these circumstances, even when further consultation occurs, is necessary to dissuade police from committing a flagrant impropriety.

§4.93 The Court also held in *Burlingham* that offering a plea bargain to a detainee in the absence of his or her lawyer may violate section 10(*b*). There, police pressured the accused to accept a deal on offer for a "short period of time during which they [knew] defence counsel to be unavailable."[316] Section 10(*b*) requires any plea bargain, the Court concluded, to be offered "either to accused's counsel or to the accused while in the presence of his or her counsel, unless the accused has expressly waived the right to counsel."[317]

§4.94 The Supreme Court should rethink its jurisprudence on post-invocation questioning. The advantages of the American approach are obvious.[318] Suspects who invoke their rights to silence and counsel are particularly vulnerable to abuse.[319] Facing pressure to solve serious crimes, police may be tempted to badger, manipulate or deceive contumacious suspects into confessing. These tactics are often effective even after suspects have talked to a lawyer and been

---

[314] *R. v. Burlingham*, [1995] S.C.J. No. 39, [1995] 2 S.C.R. 206 at para. 4 (S.C.C.) (police making references to the lawyer's lack of loyalty, commitment, availability, trustworthiness and the amount of legal fees).

[315] *Ibid.*, at para. 14 (S.C.R.). See also *R. v. Friesen*, [1995] A.J. No. 770, 101 C.C.C. (3d) 167 at 175-83 (Alta. C.A.), leave to appeal refused [1995] S.C.C.A. No. 539, [1996] 2 S.C.R. vi (S.C.C.) (police telling detainee that his lawyer would likely not want to be present for his interview did not undermine right to counsel); *R. v. Crockett*, [2002] B.C.J. No. 2947, 170 C.C.C. (3d) 569 at paras. 7, 22 (B.C.C.A.) (no violation where police told detainee that his lawyer's advice to remain silent "was what a lot of lawyers said, but that a lawyer cannot see into your heart").

[316] *R. v. Burlingham*, [1995] S.C.J. No. 39, [1995] 2 S.C.R. 206 at para. 21 (S.C.C.).

[317] *Ibid.*

[318] See Lee Stuesser, "The Accused's Right to Silence: No Doesn't Mean No" (2002) 29 Man. L.J. 149 at 150; Steven Penney, "What's Wrong with Self-Incrimination? The Wayward Path of Self-Incrimination Law in the Post-Charter Era, Part 2: Self-Incrimination in Police Investigations" (2004), 48 Crim. L.Q. 280 at 318-20.

[319] See Stanley A. Cohen, "Police Interrogation of the Wavering Suspect" (1989) 71 C.R. (3d) 148; Patrick Healy, "The Value of Silence" (1990) 74 C.R. (3d) 176.

advised to remain silent.[320] A simple rule prohibiting post-invocation questioning would substantially reduce the risk of abuse.[321] It would also eliminate the ambiguities inherent in the *ex post* determination of whether police tactics produced an involuntary confession or a violation of section 10(*b*) of the *Charter*. Further, courts would no longer have to make the difficult decision about whether detainees were reasonably diligent in exercising their right to counsel.[322] Such a rule would, of course, decrease the availability of confession evidence. However, in our view, permitting police to persistently and intensively interrogate suspects who have clearly expressed a desire to remain silent and sought the protection of counsel creates too great a risk of abuse and false confessions.

(g) When Can the Failure to Comply with Section 10 be Justified under Section 1 of the Charter?

§4.95 As with other *Charter* rights, limitations on section 10 rights may be justified under section 1. In such cases, courts cannot award any *Charter* remedy (such as the exclusion of evidence). To uphold a limit on a *Charter* right, the government must show that it is both "prescribed by law" and "reasonable ... in a free and democratic society."[323] A limit will be prescribed by law if it "is expressly provided for by statute," arises by "necessary implication from the terms of a statute or from its operating requirements" or results from the "application of a common law rule."[324] Section 1 may thus be invoked when a court finds that a statutory or common law rule limits one of the rights under section 10. To prove that the rule is reasonable the Crown must show that: (*i*) it achieves a "sufficiently important" objective; (*ii*) there is a "rational connection" between the rule and the objective; (*iii*) the infringement is "no more than is necessary" to meet the objective; and (*iv*) there is proportionality between the rule's "deleterious and...salutary effects."[325]

§4.96 There have been no cases upholding limits on section 10(*a*) of the *Charter*. Limits on section 10(*b*), in contrast, have been justified in the context of

---

[320] See *Miranda v. Arizona*, 384 U.S. 436 at 444 at 470 (1966), where the Court noted that "even preliminary advice given to the accused by his own attorney can be swiftly overcome by the secret interrogation process." See also *Minnick v. Mississippi*, 498 U.S. 146 at 153-54.

[321] See *Michigan v. Harvey*, 494 U.S. 344 at 350 (1990) (holding that the *Miranda/Edwards* rule is "designed to prevent police from badgering a defendant into waiving his previously asserted *Miranda* rights").

[322] See discussion at Part 3(4)(*e*).

[323] The full text of s. 1 of the *Canadian Charter of Rights and Freedoms*, Part I of the *Constitution Act, 1982*, being Schedule B to the *Canada Act 1982* (U.K.), 1982, c. 11 [*Charter*] reads as follows: "The *Canadian Charter of Rights and Freedoms* guarantees the rights and freedoms set out in it subject only to such reasonable limits prescribed by law as can be demonstrably justified in a free and democratic society."

[324] *R. v. Therens*, [1985] S.C.J. No. 30, [1985] 1 S.C.R. 613 at 645 (S.C.C.). See also *RWDSU Loc 580 v. Dolphin Delivery Ltd.*, [1986] S.C.J. No. 75, [1986] 2 S.C.R. 573 at 599 (S.C.C.) (*Charter* applies to the common law).

[325] *R. v. Orbanski; R. v. Elias*, [2005] S.C.J. No. 37, [2005] 2 S.C.R. 3 at para. 54 (S.C.C.). See also generally, *R. v. Oakes*, [1986] S.C.J. No. 7, [1986] 1 S.C.R. 103 (S.C.C.); *Dagenais v. Canadian Broadcasting Corp.*, [1994] S.C.J. No. 104, [1994] 3 S.C.R. 835 (S.C.C.).

motor vehicle stops. Specifically, the Supreme Court has held that police need not comply with section 10(*b*) in exercising powers to briefly detain motorists to investigate driving-related offences. In *R. v. Thomsen*,[326] it concluded that the right to counsel may be denied to drivers subject to breath alcohol screening demands.[327] This denial is both "prescribed by law" (because the denial arises by necessary implication from the *Criminal Code*'s alcohol testing regime) and "reasonable" (because conferring a right to counsel at this stage would unduly diminish the deterrence of impaired driving).[328] For the same reasons, the Court has upheld the denial of the right to counsel to drivers questioned about their alcohol consumption or asked to perform physical sobriety tests.[329] Courts of appeal have similarly exempted police from cautioning drivers[330] and passen-

---

[326] [1988] S.C.J. No. 31, [1988] 1 S.C.R. 640 (S.C.C.).

[327] *Ibid.*, at 650-56 (S.C.R.). Section 254(2) of the *Criminal Code* permits police, on the basis of reasonable suspicion, to demand that a motorist provide a sample of breath for analysis by an approved screening device (ASD). To be legally effective and constitutionally sound, this demand must generally be made immediately, *i.e.*, before there is a reasonable opportunity to contact counsel. A positive result does not prove liability, but will typically give police the reasonable and probable grounds they require to demand a breathalyzer sample, which precisely determines the alcohol concentration in a person's blood. See *Criminal Code*, R.S.C. 1985, c. C-46, s. 254(3); *R. v. Woods*, [2005] S.C.J. No. 42, [2005] 2 S.C.R. 205 at paras. 13-15, 30-32, 43-44 (S.C.C.); *R. v. Latour*, [1997] O.J. No. 2445, 116 C.C.C. (3d) 279 (Ont. C.A.).

[328] *R. v. Thomsen*, [1988] S.C.J. No. 31, [1988] 1 S.C.R. 640 at 650-56 (S.C.C.). See also *R. v. Grant*, [1991] S.C.J. No. 78, [1991] 3 S.C.R. 139 (S.C.C.).

[329] *R. v. Orbanski; R. v. Elias*, [2005] S.C.J. No. 37, [2005] 2 S.C.R. 3 at paras. 54-60 (S.C.C.). See also *R. v. Smith*, [1996] O.J. No. 372, 105 C.C.C. (3d) 58 (Ont. C.A.) (denial of right to counsel at roadside stop for brief period for purposes of questioning motorist about alcohol consumption and performing physical sobriety test is reasonable limit); *R. v. Sadlon*, [1992] O.J. No. 912, 36 M.V.R. (2d) 127 (Ont. C.A.), leave to appeal refused [1992] S.C.C.A. No. 191, [1992] 3 S.C.R. viii (S.C.C.) (availability of telephone irrelevant in finding that denial of right to counsel for breath demand is reasonable limit); *R. v. Saunders*, [1988] O.J. No. 397, 41 C.C.C. (3d) 532 (Ont. C.A.) (s. 1 for override of right to counsel applies to statutory provision authorizing demand for coordination testing); *Berkemer v. McCarty*, 468 U.S. 420 (1984) (*Miranda*) does not apply to motorists subject to brief roadside questioning as such questioning does not constitute "custodial interrogation").
At the time the offences were committed in *R. v. Orbanksi; R. v. Elias*, [2005] S.C.J. No. 37, [2005] 2 S.C.R. 3 (S.C.C.), police did not have the power to compel motorists to answer questions or perform sobriety tests. They must have therefore sought motorists' voluntary cooperation. However, as discussed in Chapter 2, Part 4(2), they could randomly stop motorists to investigate driving offences (which is a form of legal psychological detention) and in the course of such an investigation ask motorists to voluntarily answer questions or voluntarily perform sobriety tests. The *Criminal Code* has since been amended to empower police to demand that motorists perform roadside physical coordination tests on reasonable suspicion. See *Criminal Code*, R.S.C. 1985, c. C-46, s. 254(2)(*a*).

[330] See *R. v. MacLennan*, [1995] N.S.J. No. 77, 138 N.S.R. (2d) 369 at para. 61 (N.S.C.A.) (driver is not entitled to right to counsel during period between detention and conclusion of inspection of documents, which must be as brief as possible); *R. v. Campbell*, [2003] M.J. No. 207, 177 Man.R. (2d) 117 at para. 49 (Man. C.A.) (police obtaining driver's licence during roadside detention without first advising driver of right to counsel not in itself violation of *Charter* s. 10(*b*)); *R. v. Ellerman*, [2006] A.J. No. 150, [2000] 6 W.W.R. 704 (Alta. C.A.) (driver not entitled to be apprised of right to counsel during routine motor vehicle stop, right overridden by s. 1 by provincial legislation authorizing police to stop motorists).

gers[331] subject to brief, lawful, roadside detentions for general vehicle offence investigations.

§4.97 Some of these cases raise questions about reading in limits to the right to counsel that are not expressly set out in legislation.[332] But the underlying policy question should not be controversial. Had any court held that the denial of the right to counsel was not "prescribed by law", legislatures would very likely have enacted provisions specifically authorizing the infringement, and the courts would have upheld them under section 1.[333] The reason for this is simple: complying with section 10(*b*) in these circumstances would prolong suspects' detention and frustrate investigations while doing little to advance the objectives of the right. In the case of roadside screening demands, so long as police follow the rules, suspects must either comply or risk criminal punishment for refusal.[334] In the vast majority of cases, talking to a lawyer would not change this situation. More importantly, affording a right to counsel at this point would do little to deter abusive interrogation practices. Brief roadside stops are not likely to involve cruel interrogation methods or generate false confessions.[335] As the United States Supreme Court observed in *Berkemer v. McCarty*,[336] the brevity and public nature of most traffic stops substantially mitigates the risk of abuse.[337]

§4.98 The situation is different for breathalyzer tests. These are usually carried out at the police station and the accompanying detention may last several hours.

---

[331] *R. v. Harris*, [2007] O.J. No. 3185, 87 O.R. (3d) 214 at paras. 45-49 (Ont. C.A.); *R. v. Bradley*, [2008] N.S.J. No. 268, 266 N.S.R. (2d) 126 at para. 16 (N.S.C.A.) (not an absolute rule that passengers automatically detained as soon as vehicle is pulled over by police).

[332] This issue was the focus of the debate between the majority and minority concurring reasons in *R. v. Orbanski; R. v. Elias*, [2005] S.C.J. No. 37, [2005] 2 S.C.R. 3 (S.C.C.). See also Tim Quigley, "Annotation" (2005) 29 C.R. (6th) 205; Don Stuart, *Charter Justice in Canadian Criminal Law*, 4th ed. (Toronto: Thomson Carswell, 2005) at 303-304.

[333] In fact, most provinces now have legislation that does specifically authorize police to stop, detain, and conduct inquiries of motorists in the course of driving-related investigations. See *e.g.*, *Highway Traffic Act*, S.M. 1985-86, c. 3, s. 76.1(1); *Highway Traffic Act*, R.S.O. 1990, c. H.8, s. 48(1). And as mentioned earlier in this Part, subsequent to *R. v. Orbanski; R. v. Elias*, [2005] S.C.J. No. 37, [2005] 2 S.C.R. 3 (S.C.C.), Parliament gave police the power to compel participation in physical coordination tests. See *Criminal Code*, R.S.C. 1985, c. C-46, s. 254(2)(*a*).

[334] See *Criminal Code*, R.S.C. 1985, c. C-46, s. 254(5).

[335] This is not to say that the courts have entirely ignored the issue of self-incrimination in the context of roadside detentions. The Supreme Court suggested in *R. v. Orbanski; R. v. Elias*, [2005] S.C.J. No. 37, [2005] 2 S.C.R. 3 at paras. 58-59 (S.C.C.), that the violation of s. 10(*b*) during roadside detentions might not be justified if the Crown attempted to prove impairment by adducing evidence created by the accused such as the results of approved screening device (ASD) tests and answers to questions about consumption. See also *R. v. Milne*, [1996] O.J. No. 1728, 107 C.C.C. (3d) 118 at 121 (Ont. C.A.); *R. v. Coutts*, [1996] O.J. No. 2013, 136 C.C.C. (3d) 225 at paras. 15-18 (Ont. C.A.). This position is curious. If evidence created by drivers during roadside detentions is admissible for the purpose of demonstrating the existence of reasonable and probable grounds (which it is), and such grounds provide the basis for breathalyzer demands (the results of which are admissible), then this evidence must be "self-incriminating" in any realistic sense of the phrase. It is thus difficult to understand why evidence collected from drivers during roadside detentions should not be admissible to prove impairment.

[336] 468 U.S. 420 (1984).

[337] *Ibid.*, at 438-39.

As with roadside screening tests, talking to a lawyer will rarely prevent the compulsion of incriminating bodily substances. But as in other custodial settings, the caution may help to deter abusive questioning practices. Complying with section 10(*b*) in these circumstances, moreover, will rarely substantially prolong the detention or detract from police's ability to obtain reliable evidence of guilt. The *Therens* Court thus rightly concluded that drivers subject to breathalyzer demands must be informed of their right to counsel under section 10(*b*).[338]

4. QUESTIONING OF YOUNG PERSONS

§4.99 In addition to the common law and *Charter* protections afforded to adults, people under the age of 18, when questioned by police, are also protected by the *Youth Criminal Justice Act* (YCJA).[339] This "enhanced procedural protection"[340] recognizes young people's vulnerability and aims to diminish the risk of false confessions, which they are more likely to make than adults.[341]

§4.100 These protections are triggered by arrest, detention or the existence of "reasonable grounds for believing" that a young person has committed an offence.[342] Any statement[343] made to a person in authority[344] in such circumstances is (subject to exceptions described below) inadmissible against the young per-

---

[338] *R. v. Therens*, [1985] S.C.J. No. 30, [1985] 1 S.C.R. 613 (S.C.C.). See also *R. v. Orbanski; R. v. Elias*, [2005] S.C.J. No. 37, [2005] 2 S.C.R. 3 at para. 57 (S.C.C.) ("there is no question that the motorist who is not allowed to continue on his way but, rather, is requested to provide a breath or blood sample, is entitled to the full protection of the *Charter* right to counsel"). See also *R. v. Woods*, [2005] S.C.J. No. 42, [2005] 2 S.C.R. 205 at paras. 35-36 (S.C.C.).

[339] S.C. 2002, c. 1, s. 146(1). See also Nicholas Bala, *Youth Criminal Justice Law* (Toronto: Irwin Law, 2003) at 245-91; Sanjeev S. Anand & James Robb, "The Admissibility of Young People's Statements Under the Proposed *YCJA* (2002) 39 Alta. L. Rev. 771.

[340] See YCJA, ss. 3(1)(*b*)(iii), 146(6). See also *R. v. H. (L.T.)*, [2008] S.C.J. No. 50, [2008] 2 S.C.R. 739 at para. 1 (S.C.C.).

[341] See *R. v. H. (L.T.)*, [2008] S.C.J. No. 50, [2008] 2 S.C.R. 739 at para. 38 (S.C.C.); *R. v. Oickle*, [2000] S.C.J. No. 38, [2000] 2 S.C.R. 3 at para. 42 (S.C.C.); *R. v. I. (L.R.)*, [1993] S.C.J. No. 132, [1993] 4 S.C.R. 504 at 522 (S.C.C.); *R. v. J. (J.T.)*, [1990] S.C.J. No. 88, [1990] 2 S.C.R. 755 at 766-67 (S.C.C.); *R. v. S. (S.)*, [2007] O.J. No. 2552, 222 C.C.C. (3d) 545 (Ont. C.A.); Nicholas Bala, *Youth Criminal Justice Law* (Toronto: Irwin Law, 2003) at 200-43; Sanjeev S. Anand & James Robb, "The Admissibility of Young People's Statements Under the Proposed *YCJA*" (2002) 39 Alta. L. Rev. 771 at 772.

[342] YCJA, s. 146(2).

[343] This includes oral and written statements, as well as any gestures or other forms of response that are an integral part of the response. See YCJA, s. 146(2); *R. v. J. (J.T.)*, [1990] S.C.J. No. 88, [1990] 2 S.C.R. 755 at 769 (S.C.C.).

[344] "Person in authority" has the same meaning here as in the context of the confessions rule. YCJA, s. 146(2). See discussion in Part 2(2). See also YCJA, s. 146(9) (person in authority does not include a parent or other person consulted under s. 146(2(*c*)); *R. v. B. (A.)*, [1986] O.J. No. 91, 26 C.C.C. (3d) 17 (Ont. C.A.), leave to appeal refused [1986] S.C.C.A. No. 203, 26 C.C.C. (3d) 17*n* (S.C.C.) (parent not "person in authority" where no realistic and close connection between decision to contact authorities and inducement of accused's statement); *R. v. B. (M.R.)*, [1998] B.C.J. No. 1197, 125 C.C.C. (3d) 335 (B.C.C.A.) (ambulance attendant administering first aid at accident scene not "person in authority").

son,[345] unless the prosecution proves beyond a reasonable doubt[346] that the following requirements have been met.

§4.101 First, the statement must be voluntary.[347] This protection is obviously redundant in light of the common law confessions rule. However, in applying the confessions rule to statements by youth, courts have paid particular attention to the vulnerability of juveniles to coercive pressures.[348] Further, unlike the confessions rule, the YCJA also gives judges a discretion to exclude statements made "under duress imposed by any person who is not, in law, a person in authority."[349]

§4.102 Second, before the statement is made, the person taking the statement must "clearly explain", in "language appropriate to [the young person's] age and understanding", that:

(i) the young person is under no obligation to make a statement,

(ii) any statement made by the young person may be used as evidence in proceedings against him or her,

(iii) the young person has the right to consult counsel[350] and a parent [or other appropriate adult[351]] ... and

(iv) any statement made by the young person is required to be made in the presence of counsel and any other person consulted ... unless the young person desires otherwise ....[352]

---

[345] As with the confessions rule, YJCA compliant statements made after inadmissible statements will also be inadmissible where: (*i*) they constituted a continuation of earlier inadmissible statements; or (*ii*) earlier inadmissible statements substantially contributed to the making of the subsequent statement. See *R. v. I. (L.R.)*, [1993] S.C.J. No. 132, [1993] 4 S.C.R. 504 (S.C.C.); *R. v. Cho*, [2001] B.C.J. No. 2437, 155 C.C.C. (3d) 558 (B.C.C.A.); *R. v. O. (D.)*, [1990] O.J. No. 1881, 41 O.A.C. 145 (Ont. C.A.). See also discussion in Part 2(5)(*c*)(i).

[346] *R. v. H. (L.T.)*, [2008] S.C.J. No. 50, [2008] 2 S.C.R. 739 at paras. 6, 46 (S.C.C.).

[347] YCJA, s. 146(2)(*a*).

[348] See Sanjeev S. Anand & James Robb, "The Admissibility of Young People's Statements Under the Proposed *YCJA* (2002) 39 Alta. L. Rev. 771 at 780-81.

[349] The accused has the burden to establish such duress. YCJA, s. 146(7). See also *R. v. C. (M.)*, [2001] N.S.J. No. 144, 157 C.C.C. (3d) 97 (N.S.C.A.) (judge erred in failing to consider whether father touching accused's cheek with cigarette constitutes duress).

[350] See also YCJA, ss. 25(1) and (2) (providing right to counsel and right to be informed thereof to young persons arrested or detained).

[351] Specifically, there is a right to consult "with a parent or, in the absence of a parent, an adult relative or, in the absence of a parent and an adult relative, any other appropriate adult chosen by the young person, as long as that person is not a co-accused, or under investigation, in respect of the same offence ...." YCJA, s. 146(2)(*c*)(ii). "Parent" is defined in s. 2(1) of the YCJA to include "any person ... under a legal duty to provide for the young person or any person who has, in law or in fact, the custody or control of the young person ...".

[352] YCJA, s. 146(2)(*b*). See also *R. v. I. (L.R.)*, [1993] S.C.J. No. 132, [1993] 4 S.C.R. 504 (S.C.C.) (young people must be told of right to consult with both parent *and* lawyer; parent not an alternative to counsel); *R. v. S. (S.)*, [2007] O.J. No. 2552, 222 C.C.C. (3d) 545 (Ont. C.A.) (telling young person of right to lawyer or parent's presence not sufficient; must be told that presence is required unless young person desires otherwise).

In relaying this information, police must take reasonable steps to ensure understanding.[353] Actual understanding, however, need not be proved.[354]

§4.103 Third, youth must be given a reasonable opportunity to consult both counsel and a parent (or other appropriate adult) before making a statement.[355] Unless the young person desires otherwise, the statement taken must be made in the presence of these people.[356] Juveniles may waive their rights to consult one of these persons or have them present during questioning, but the standard for waiver is more stringent than under section 10(*b*) of the *Charter*. The YCJA requires that such waivers be recorded either electronically or in the form of a signed statement confirming that the person has been informed of his or her rights.[357] At trial, the Crown must satisfy the court, beyond a reasonable doubt,[358] that "[the] waiver [was] premised on a true understanding of the rights involved and the consequences of giving them up."[359]

§4.104 As mentioned, failure to comply with these requirements does not inevitably lead to exclusion. First, compliance with the second and third requirements set out above is not mandatory when youth make spontaneous[360] oral statements before police have had a reasonable opportunity to fulfill their obligations. Second, judges have a discretion to admit when non-compliance with the second or third requirements amounts to a mere "technical irregularity" and admission would "not bring into disrepute the principle that young persons are entitled to enhanced procedural protection to ensure that they are treated fairly and

---

[353] See *R. v. H. (L.T.)*, [2008] S.C.J. No. 50, [2008] 2 S.C.R. 739 at paras. 22-30 (S.C.C.) (reading of standardized form not normally sufficient, police must consider educational level, language and vocabulary skills, faculties of understanding, previous experience with criminal justice system and emotional state). See also *R. v. M. (M.A.)*, [1986] B.C.J. No. 1262, 32 C.C.C. (3d) 566 (B.C.C.A.).

[354] *R. v. H. (L.T.)*, [2008] S.C.J. No. 50, [2008] 2 S.C.R. 739 at paras. 21, 30 (S.C.C.).

[355] See *R. v. S. (J.L.)*, [1995] A.J. No. 213, 97 C.C.C. (3d) 20 (Alta. C.A.) (right violated when police lied about availability of accused's mother).

[356] YCJA, s. 146(2)(*b*)(iv). See also *R. v. P. (S.)*, [1991] O.J. No. 337, 44 O.A.C. 316 (Ont. C.A.) (when invoked, right to parent's presence must be granted immediately if parent is available); *R. v. C. (M.)*, [2001] N.S.J. No. 144, 157 C.C.C. (3d) 97 (N.S.C.A.) (where accused's parent leaves during interview at no fault of police, police not obliged to reiterate caution).

[357] YCJA, s. 146(5). A judge may determine that a waiver is valid under this provision despite a "technical irregularity" if he or she is satisfied that the young person "was informed of his or her rights, and voluntarily waived them." YCJA, s. 146(6).

[358] *R. v. H. (L.T.)*, [2008] S.C.J. No. 50, [2008] 2 S.C.R. 739 at para. 39 (S.C.C.).

[359] *R. v. H. (L.T.)*, [2008] S.C.J. No. 50, [2008] 2 S.C.R. 739 at paras. 40, 46 (S.C.C.). See also *R. v. M. (E.A.D.)*, [2007] M.J. No. 471, 220 Man.R. (2d) 312 (Man. C.A.), leave to appeal refused [2008] S.C.C.A. No. 51 (S.C.C.) (waiver valid despite failing to provide opportunity to consult with counsel prior to completion of waiver form where nothing meaningful occurs before access to counsel is provided).

[360] YCJA, s. 146(3). See also *R. v. M. (D.P.)*, [1991] A.J. No. 192, [1991] W.D.F.L. 421 (Alta. C.A.) (accused's response to the question "What is going on here?" spontaneous); *R. v. Wilson*, [2001] B.C.J. No. 1190, 156 C.C.C. (3d) 74 (B.C.C.A.), affd [2002] S.C.J. No. 70, [2002] 3 S.C.R. 629 (S.C.C.) (accused's statements to guard inquiring about his distraught emotional state were "spontaneous outbursts"); *R. v. W.(J.)*, [1996] O.J. No. 3003, 109 C.C.C. (3d) 506 (Ont. C.A.) (despite no direct question to accused, statements were not spontaneous as they were in part prompted by external stimuli and any doubt should be resolved in favour of accused).

their rights protected."³⁶¹ Lastly, judges may also admit a non-compliant statement or waiver where young persons have: (*i*) represented themselves as being at least 18 years old; (*ii*) police reasonably believed that they were such an age; and (*iii*) "in all other circumstances the statement or waiver would otherwise be admissible."³⁶²

5. SECTION 7 OF THE *CHARTER* AND UNDERCOVER QUESTIONING

§4.105 Section 7 of the *Charter* gives everyone "the right to life, liberty and security of the person and the right not to be deprived thereof except in accordance with the principles of fundamental justice." One such principle, according to the Supreme Court, is the "principle against self-incrimination", which gives certain distinct types of protection to people subject to inquiries by state agents.³⁶³ Under the aegis of this principle, the Court has interpreted section 7 to protect a "right to silence"³⁶⁴ giving detainees a "right to choose" whether to speak to authorities.³⁶⁵

§4.106 When a detainee makes a statement to a person in authority, however, this right is subsumed by the confessions rule.³⁶⁶ In other words, a finding that a statement to a person in authority was neither involuntary nor a product of conduct that would "shock the community" precludes a finding of a violation under section 7. This is because any protection that section 7 provides is already provided by the confessions rule. Further, as it is easier for the defence to raise a reasonable doubt on voluntariness than prove a *Charter* violation and show that evidence obtained as a result should be excluded under section 24(2), an independent section 7 application will rarely be warranted in these circumstances.³⁶⁷

---

³⁶¹ *R. v. S. (S.)*, [2007] O.J. No. 2552, 222 C.C.C. (3d) 545 (Ont. C.A.) (failing to inform accused that it is a *requirement*, as opposed to a *right*, to have lawyer or other specified adult present when providing statement not a "technical irregularity").

³⁶² YCJA, s. 146(8).

³⁶³ See *e.g.*, *R. v. Jarvis*, [2002] S.C.J. No. 76, [2002] 3 S.C.R. 757 (S.C.C.). Other aspects of the s. 7 principle against self-incrimination are discussed below, in Part 6.

³⁶⁴ *R. v. Hebert*, [1990] S.C.J. No. 64, [1990] 2 S.C.R. 151 at para. 77 (S.C.C.).

³⁶⁵ *Ibid.*, at para. 78 (S.C.R.); *R. v. Singh*, [2007] S.C.J. No. 48, [2007] 3 S.C.R. 405 at para. 35 (S.C.C.).

³⁶⁶ *R. v. Singh*, [2007] S.C.J. No. 48, [2007] 3 S.C.R. 405 at paras. 37-41 (S.C.C.). To be precise, the Court in *Singh* referred to statements made to "obvious" persons in authority. The importance of this qualification is nebulous, however. As discussed above, in Part 2(2), a person in authority is someone who the suspect reasonably believes is in a position to influence the prosecution against him or her. Nothing in *Singh* suggests that the admission of a statement voluntarily made to such a person could infringe section 7.

³⁶⁷ See *R. v. Singh*, [2007] S.C.J. No. 48, [2007] 3 S.C.R. 405 at para. 38 (S.C.C.); *R. v. Oickle*, [2000] S.C.J. No. 38, [2000] 2 S.C.R. 3 at paras. 29-31 (S.C.C.). See also *R. v. Carpenter*, [2001] B.C.J. No. 95, 151 C.C.C. (3d) 205 at paras. 70-71, 147 B.C.A.C. 135, 241 W.A.C. 135 (B.C.C.A.); David M. Paciocco & Lee Stuesser, *The Law of Evidence*, 5th ed. (Toronto: Irwin Law, 2008) at 342-43. However, as discussed in Part 2(5)(*c*)(ii), to avoid any continuing effect of the common law "*St. Lawrence*" rule, it may be wise to apply under ss. 7 and 24(2) of the *Charter* to exclude involuntary statements corroborated by physical evidence.

Similarly, when detainees are questioned by non-undercover police, section 7 does not offer any greater protection against coercion than that provided by section 10.[368]

§4.107 The situation is different, however, when an undercover agent questions a detainee. As noted, the confessions rule does not apply when suspects do not know that their questioners are persons in authority.[369] But in *R. v. Hebert*,[370] the Court held that section 7 forbids covert state agents from actively eliciting statements from detained suspects.[371] There, a robbery suspect was arrested, cautioned and taken to the police station. He talked to a lawyer, who advised him to remain silent. Police then attempted to interview him, but he refused to make a statement. He was then placed in a cell with a police officer posing as a fellow arrestee. The officer engaged him in conversation and he made incriminating statements. Because the statements were not made to a known "person in authority", and were made after he was properly cautioned, this trickery violated neither the confessions rule nor section 10 of the *Charter*. Writing for the majority, however, Justice McLachlin (as she then was) held that the section 7 "right to silence" is violated when detained suspects are duped into foregoing their rights to silence and counsel by persons concealing their identity as law enforcement agents.[372]

§4.108 The *Hebert* rule only applies, however, if three conditions are met. First, the right applies only during detention, not when suspects are tricked into confessing to undercover agents before or after.[373] As Justice McLachlin explained in *R. v. Hebert*:

---

[368] See *R. v. Hebert*, [1990] S.C.J. No. 64, [1990] 2 S.C.R. 151 at 184 (S.C.C.); *R. v. Lepage*, [2008] B.C.J. No. 524, 2008 BCCA 132 at paras. 35-36, 425 W.A.C. 253, 232 C.C.C. (3d) 411 (B.C.C.A.), leave to appeal refused [2008] S.C.C.A. No. 249 (S.C.C.) (*Hebert* does not apply when accused questioned openly by police in course of normal arrest procedure).

[369] See discussion above, in Part 2(2). As discussed, once detained suspects have been cautioned, police are free to question them either immediately (if they do not invoke their s. 10 rights) or after suspects have had a reasonable opportunity to consult with counsel (if they do). In the latter case, police generally have no obligation to repeat the caution prior to questioning. See *R. v. Logan*, [1988] O.J. No. 2107, 46 C.C.C. (3d) 354 (Ont. C.A.), affd [1990] S.C.J. No. 89 (S.C.C.); *R. v. Emile*, [1988] N.W.T.J. No. 196, 65 C.R. (3d) 135 (N.W.T.C.A.).

[370] *R. v. Hebert*, [1990] S.C.J. No. 64, [1990] 2 S.C.R. 151 (S.C.C.).

[371] As in the case of s. 10, statements obtained in violation of this rule may be excluded pursuant to s. 24(2) of the *Charter*. See *R. v. Hebert*, [1990] S.C.J. No. 64, [1990] 2 S.C.R. 151 at 187-89 (S.C.C.).

[372] *R. v. Hebert*, [1990] S.C.J. No. 64, [1990] 2 S.C.R. 151 at 186-87 (S.C.C.). Detainees are not required to positively assert their right to silence: *R. v. Liew*, [1999] S.C.J. No. 51, [1999] 3 S.C.R. 227 at para. 44 (S.C.C.). As discussed in Chapter 10, statements obtained in violation of this rule are likely to be excluded under s. 24(2) of the *Charter*. For a criticism of the *Hebert* rule, see Steven Penney, "What's Wrong with Self-Incrimination? The Wayward Path of Self-Incrimination Law in the Post-Charter Era, Part 2: Self-Incrimination in Police Investigations" (2004) 48 Crim. L.Q. 280 at 323-29.

[373] See *R. v. Hebert*, [1990] S.C.J. No. 64, [1990] 2 S.C.R. 151 at 184 (S.C.C.); *R. v. McIntyre*, [1994] S.C.J. No. 52, [1994] 2 S.C.R. 480 (S.C.C.), affd [1993] N.B.J. No. 293, 135 N.B.R. (2d) 266 (N.B.C.A.) (s. 7 right to silence does not apply to accused who confesses to undercover agent after being released from detention); *R. v. McReery*, [1998] B.C.J. No. 1199, 16 C.R. (5th) 71 at para. 23 (B.C.C.A.), leave to appeal to appeal refused [1998] S.C.C.A. No. 253,

In an undercover operation prior to detention, the individual from whom information is sought is not in the control of the state. There is no need to protect him from the greater power of the state. After detention, the situation is quite different; the state takes control and assumes the responsibility of ensuring that the detainee's rights are respected.[374]

§4.109 Second, the person eliciting the statement must be a state agent.[375] Public officials (such as police, prosecutors and prison guards) obviously qualify.[376] As mentioned in Part 2(2), above, private persons may also be state agents if their relationship with the authorities is such that their interaction with the suspect was "materially different from what it would have been had there been no such relationship".[377] The question to be asked is "would the exchange between the accused and the informer have taken place, in the form and manner in which it did take place, but for the intervention of the state or its agents?"[378] Thus, in *R. v. Broyles*,[379] the Supreme Court found that the accused's friend acted as state agent when, at the request of police, he wore a recording device during his conversation with the accused. But for the police's involvement, Justice Iacobucci wrote for the Court, the conversation "would either not have occurred at all, or else would have taken a materially different course."[380]

---

231 N.R. 399*n* (S.C.C.) (s. 7 right to silence does not apply to accused who confesses to undercover agent before being detained); *R. v. Osmar*, [2007] O.J. No. 244, 84 O.R. (3d) 321 (Ont. C.A.), leave to appeal refused [2007] S.C.C.A. No. 157 (S.C.C.) (s. 7 right to silence does not apply to accused who confesses to undercover agent in drug treatment centre); *R. v. Bonisteel*, [2008] B.C.J. No. 1705, 236 C.C.C. (3d) 170 (B.C.C.A.) (no violation of s. 7 where accused confesses during undercover operation involving threats of physical violence and significant financial reward); *R. v. Roberts*, [1997] B.C.J. No. 765, 90 B.C.A.C. 213 (B.C.C.A.) (same); *United States of America v. Burns*, [1997] B.C.J. No. 1554, 117 C.C.C. (3d) 454 (B.C.C.A.), application for leave to appeal and for reconsideration dismissed [1997] S.C.C.A. No. 515 (S.C.C.) (no violation of s. 7 where accused confesses during undercover operation involving threats of extreme violence to accused and family); *R. v. Grandinetti*, [2005] S.C.J. No. 3, [2005] 1 S.C.R. 27 at paras. 28-45 (S.C.C.) (no violation of s. 7 where accused confesses to undercover officers posing as members of criminal organization who have influence over police).

374 *R. v. Hebert*, [1990] S.C.J. No. 64, [1990] 2 S.C.R. 151 at 184 (S.C.C.).

375 See *R. v. Hebert*, [1990] S.C.J. No. 64, [1990] 2 S.C.R. 151 at 184 (S.C.C.); *R. v. Broyles*, [1991] S.C.J. No. 95, [1991] 3 S.C.R. 595 (S.C.C.).

376 *R. v. Broyles*, [1991] S.C.J. No. 95, [1991] 3 S.C.R. 595 at 608 (S.C.C.).

377 *Ibid.*

378 *Ibid.*, at 608 (S.C.R.). See also *R. v. Kennedy*, [1996] O.J. No. 4401, 95 O.A.C. 321 (Ont. C.A.) (inmate who offered to record accused's conversations not state agent even though police gave him pen and paper and he had been providing information to police for many years); *R. v. Madeley*, [2002] O.J. No. 2410, 160 O.A.C. 346 at paras. 26-28 (Ont. C.A.), leave to appeal refused [2003] S.C.C.A. No. 50, [2003] 1 S.C.R. xiii (S.C.C.) (fellow inmate and prior acquaintance of accused who had no prior contact with police but assumed he would receive some benefit in exchange for information not state agent); *R. v. Gray*, [1991] O.J. No. 1084, 66 C.C.C. (3d) 6 (Ont. C.A.), leave to appeal refused [1991] S.C.C.A. No. 424, 69 C.C.C. (3d) *vi* (S.C.C.) (inmate who offers information about conversation with accused is not state agent where officer tells inmate that police would be interested in information but no reward offered); *R. v. Stark*, [2000] O.J. No. 1406, 145 C.C.C. (3d) 129 (Ont. C.A.), leave to appeal refused [2000] S.C.C.A. No. 326,148 C.C.C. (3d) vi (S.C.C.) (mere expression of interest by informer not enough to create agency relationship).

379 [1991] S.C.J. No. 95, [1991] 3 S.C.R. 595 (S.C.C.).

380 *Ibid.*, at 613 (S.C.R.).

§4.110 Third, the state agent must actively elicit the statement and not merely passively observe the suspect. Typically, this is determined by considering two key factors.[381] The first relates to the form of conversation that takes place between the state agent and the suspect. Active elicitation arises when the conversation is akin to an interrogation, as where agents initiate the conversation or ask leading questions.[382] Conversely, the right to silence is not infringed when agents behave as they ordinarily would in their adopted roles.[383] In *R. v. Liew*,[384] for example, the accused had a conversation with an undercover officer posing as his partner in a drug transaction.[385] The Supreme Court found that the officer did not actively elicit the statement as he neither strayed from his role nor "prompted, coaxed or cajoled the appellant to respond."[386] The second factor relates to the relationship between the agent and the suspect. The right to silence is more likely to be violated where the agent has exploited any of the suspect's vulnerabilities, obligations or trust relationships.[387]

---

[381] *Ibid.*, at 611 (S.C.R.); *R. v. Liew*, [1999] S.C.J. No. 51, [1999] 3 S.C.R. 227 at paras. 42-46 (S.C.C.). The Court noted in *Liew* (at para. 46 (S.C.R.)) that these factors "are neither exhaustive nor dispositive."

[382] *R. v. Hebert*, [1990] S.C.J. No. 64, [1990] 2 S.C.R. 151 at 185 (S.C.C.); *R. v. Broyles*, [1991] S.C.J. No. 95, [1991] 3 S.C.R. 595 at 611-12 (S.C.C.).

[383] *R. v. Broyles*, [1991] S.C.J. No. 95, [1991] 3 S.C.R. 595 (S.C.C.).

[384] [1999] S.C.J. No. 51, [1999] 3 S.C.R. 227 (S.C.C.).

[385] *Ibid.*

[386] *R. v. Liew*, [1999] S.C.J. No. 51, [1999] 3 S.C.R. 227 at para. 51 (S.C.C.). See also *R. v. Myers*, [2008] N.J. No. 52, 229 C.C.C. (3d) 293, 837 A.P.R. 5, 274 Nfld. & P.E.I.R. 5, 167 C.R.R. (2d) 332 (N.L.C.A.) (no active elicitation where agent engaged in conversation for purposes of voice identification only); *R. v. Baltrusaitis*, [2002] O.J. No. 464, 155 O.A.C. 249 at para. 22, 162 C.C.C. (3d) 539, 58 O.R. (3d) 161 (Ont. C.A.) (no active elicitation where questions were not "probing or persistent such that they could be considered inveigling or in the nature of an interrogation"; rather, they were consistent with "an average cellmate showing mild interest by asking the occasional appropriate question"); *R. v. Wolfe*, [2009] S.J. No. 627, 2009 SKQB 424 at para. 30 (Sask. Q.B.) (no active elicitation where accused's statements "completely voluntary and made spontaneously"); *R. v. J. (D.)*, [2009] O.J. No. 1187, 242 C.C.C. (3d) 400 (Ont. S.C.J.) (no active elicitation where conversation not functional equivalent of interrogation and no exploitation of trust); *R. v. Jenkins* (2002), 2002 CarswellOnt 6174 (Ont. S.C.J.) (same); *R. v. Forslund*, [2007] B.C.J. No. 755, 2007 BCSC 357 at para. 63 (B.C.S.C.) (no active elicitation as conversation "flowed naturally" to discussion of offence); *R. v. Jeffrey*, [2007] Nu.J. No. 10, 2007 NUCJ 6 at para. 298 (Nu. C.J.) (same); *R. v. Tse*, [2008] B.C.J. No. 2019, 180 C.R.R. (2d) 135 (B.C.S.C.) (active elicitation found where police used both out-of-cell interviews and undercover questioning in concerted and relentless effort to undermine accused's invocation of right to silence; functional equivalent of interrogation); *R. v. Kiloh*, [2003] B.C.J. No. 321, 2003 BCSC 209 at paras. 213-214 (B.C.S.C.) (same); *R. v. Van Osselaer*, [2000] B.C.J. No. 1652, 2000 BCSC 1065, 47 W.C.B. (2d) 178 (B.C.S.C.) (active elicitation where agent directed conversation toward accused's involvement in offence); *R. v. Chung*, [2011] B.C.J. No. 446, 2011 BCCA 131 at paras. 51-53 (B.C.C.A.) (no s. 7 breach when undercover officer passively elicited statements from appellant).

[387] *R. v. Broyles*, [1991] S.C.J. No. 95, [1991] 3 S.C.R. 595 at 611 (S.C.C.). See also *R. v. Rose*, [2005] B.C.J. No. 2457, 191 C.C.C. (3d) 399 at para. 13 (B.C.C.A.), leave to appeal refused [2005] S.C.C.A. No. 45 (S.C.C.); *R. v. Whynder*, [1996] N.S.J. No. 110, 149 N.S.R. (2d) 241 at paras. 97-98 (N.S.C.A.).

6. COMPELLED COMMUNICATIONS

§4.111 As we have seen, police have no general power to force criminal suspects to answer questions. To obtain self-incriminating evidence, they must either convince them to speak voluntarily or employ surreptitious methods such as undercover questioning or electronic surveillance. In limited circumstances, however, the law empowers authorities (though usually not police or prosecutors[388]) to compel potentially self-incriminating communications. This section discusses these powers and their statutory and constitutional limits.

(1) Testimonial Compulsion

§4.112 Criminal defendants are not compellable witnesses at their own trials.[389] But like other people, criminal suspects may be compelled to testify as witnesses in other legal proceedings, such as others' criminal trials, civil trials or regulatory inquiries. If they refuse, they may be punished for contempt. This raises the possibility that the state could do indirectly what it is forbidden to do directly: compel suspects' testimony to use against them in future criminal proceedings.

(a) Evidentiary Immunity

§4.113 Over the years, courts and legislators have adopted different strategies to prevent this kind of compulsion. At common law, witnesses were entitled to refuse to answer questions that might incriminate them.[390] This "privilege" against self-incrimination, as it is known, was abrogated by the *Canada Evidence Act*,[391] which requires witnesses to answer potentially self-incriminating questions.[392] Section 5(2) of the Act, however, prohibits the admission of

---

[388] An exception to this principal was created by the investigative hearing provisions of the *Anti-terrorism Act*, S.C. 2001, c. 41, s. 4, codified at *Criminal Code*, R.S.C. 1985, c. C-46, ss. 83.28-83.29. These provisions permitted police to apply to a judge for an order compelling persons to respond in court to questions relating to terrorism offences. Pursuant to the "sunset clause" in s. 83.32, the provisions ceased to apply as of March 1, 2007. Their constitutionality was upheld in *Re Application under s. 83.28 of the Criminal Code*, [2004] S.C.J. No. 40, [2004] 2 S.C.R. 248 (S.C.C.).

[389] Section 11(c) of the *Charter* grants a person charged with an offence the right "not to be compelled to be a witness in proceedings against that person in respect of the offence." At common law, criminal defendants were not competent to testify for either the defence or prosecution. In 1893, Parliament amended what is now s. 4(1) of the *Canada Evidence Act*, R.S.C. 1985, c. C-5, to allow accused persons to testify in their own defence. See *Canada Evidence Act, 1893*, S.C. 1893, c. 31, s. 4.

[390] See Ed Ratushny, *Self-incrimination in the Canadian Criminal Process* (Toronto: Carswell, 1979) at 78.

[391] R.S.C. 1985, c. C-5.

[392] *Canada Evidence Act*, R.S.C. 1985, c. C-5, s. 5(1) ("No witness shall be excused from answering any question on the ground that the answer to the question may tend to criminate him, or may tend to establish his liability to a civil proceeding at the instance of the Crown or of any person.") Similar rules apply to proceedings governed by the various provincial evidence statutes. See Alan W. Bryant, Sidney R. Lederman & Michelle K. Fuerst, *Sopinka, Lederman & Bryant: The Law of Evidence in Canada*, 3d ed. (Markham, ON: LexisNexis Canada, 2009) at 503-504.

compelled statements in later criminal proceedings against that witness, but only if at the time of the initial proceedings (*i*) the statements were known to be incriminating and (*ii*) the witness expressly claimed the statutory protection at the previous proceeding.[393]

§4.114 These prerequisites became moot with the enactment of section 13 of the *Charter*, which states that a "witness who testifies in any proceedings has the right not to have any incriminating evidence so given used to incriminate that witness in any other proceedings, except in a prosecution for perjury or for the giving of contradictory evidence."[394] After many years of confusion, the Supreme Court of Canada has settled on the following interpretation of this provision.[395] If defendants facing penal consequences[396] do not testify, the prosecution may not adduce their previous testimony (whether compelled or voluntary).[397] But if such defendants do testify, immunity is granted only to their previous non-voluntary testimony (*i.e.*, testimony that *could* have been compelled, whether or not it was actually compelled by a *subpoena*); previous non-

---

[393] *Canada Evidence Act*, s. 5(2) ("Where with respect to any question a witness objects to answer on the ground that his answer may tend to criminate him, or may tend to establish his liability to a civil proceeding at the instance of the Crown or of any person, and if but for this Act, or the Act of any provincial legislature, the witness would therefore have been excused from answering the question, then although the witness is by reason of this Act or the provincial Act compelled to answer, the answer so given shall not be used or admissible in evidence against him in any criminal trial or other criminal proceeding against him thereafter taking place, other than a prosecution for perjury in the giving of that evidence or for the giving of contradictory evidence."). See also *R. v. Marcoux*, [1975] S.C.J. No. 54, [1976] 1 S.C.R. 763 at 768-69 (S.C.C.); *R. v. Noël*, [2002] S.C.J. No. 68, [2002] 3 S.C.R. 433 at para. 32 (S.C.C.); *R. v. Tass*, [1946] S.C.J. No. 39, [1947] S.C.R. 103 (S.C.C.); *R. v. Boulet*, [1976] S.C.J. No. 116, [1978] 1 S.C.R. 332 (S.C.C.); *Klein v. Bell*, [1955] S.C.J. No. 19, [1955] S.C.R. 309 (S.C.C.); David M. Paciocco & Lee Stuesser, *The Law of Evidence*, 5th ed. (Toronto: Irwin Law, 2008) at 286-89.

[394] To receive the protection of s. 13, the initial testimony may have been given in any type of formal proceeding, including regulatory inquiries, bail hearings and disciplinary hearings. Section 13 does not apply, however, to informal investigative questioning. See Alan W. Bryant, Sidney R. Lederman & Michelle K. Fuerst, *Sopinka, Lederman & Bryant: The Law of Evidence in Canada*, 3d ed. (Markham, ON: LexisNexis Canada, 2009) at 506-507.

[395] See Steven Penney, "The Principle Against Self-incrimination", in S. Casey Hill *et al.*, *McWilliams' Canadian Criminal Evidence*, 4th ed., vol. 1, looseleaf (Toronto: Canada Law Book, 2011), §15:20.40.

[396] Given its reference to the word "incriminate", courts have interpreted s. 13 as protecting only testimony adduced at subsequent proceedings involving penal consequences. See *Knutson v. Saskatchewan Registered Nursing Assn*, [1990] S.J. No. 603, [1991] 2 W.W.R. 327 (Sask. C.A.) (s. 13 does not apply to non-penal disciplinary proceeding); *Re Jaballah*, [2010] F.C.J. No. 257, 2010 FC 224 at paras. 45-58 (F.C.) (s. 13 does not apply to security certificate deportation proceedings). Because corporations and other non-human persons cannot be witnesses, s. 13 does not protect them, though it does protect human defendants against the admission of their prior testimony about corporate activities. See *R. v. Amway Corp.*, [1989] S.C.J. No. 3, [1989] 1 S.C.R. 21 (S.C.C.) (s. 13 applies to corporate representatives insofar as they are personally implicated by their testimony); *British Columbia (Securities Commission) v. Branch*, [1995] S.C.J. No. 32, [1995] 2 S.C.R. 3 at paras. 42, 44 (S.C.C.) (same). See also Alan W. Bryant, Sidney R. Lederman & Michelle K. Fuerst, *Sopinka, Lederman & Bryant: The Law of Evidence in Canada*, 3d ed. (Markham, ON: LexisNexis Canada, 2009) at 515, 517; David M. Paciocco & Lee Stuesser, *The Law of Evidence*, 5th ed. (Toronto: Irwin Law, 2008) at 291.

[397] *R. v. Henry*, [2005] S.C.J. No. 76, [2005] 3 S.C.R. 609.

compellable testimony (such as that given as a defendant in pre-trial and trial proceedings) is admissible to both impeach and incriminate them.[398]

§4.115 The *Canada Evidence Act* and section 13 of the *Charter* thus grant "use immunity" to defendants' compelled previous testimony. But neither provides either "transactional immunity" (prohibiting authorities from charging witnesses with any offence relating to their testimony) or "derivative use immunity" (excluding evidence that would not have been found but for compelled testimony). However, in *R. v. S. (R.J.)*,[399] the Supreme Court ruled that the self-incrimination principle inhering in section 7 of the *Charter* gives compellable witnesses derivative use immunity for "evidence which could not have been obtained, or the significance of which could not have been appreciated, but for [their testimony]."[400] Section 7 also gives them use immunity if it is not otherwise provided.[401] Evidence covered by these immunities is inadmissible[402] against persons facing penal sanctions as well as at any other proceeding engaging the rights protected by section 7 (life, liberty or security of the person).[403] Section 7 does not give compelled witnesses transactional immunity, however. Thus, persons compelled to provide testimony in other proceedings may be still be prosecuted by way of any non-derivative (and otherwise admissible) evidence.

§4.116 In *S. (R.J.)*, the Court also held that while applicants bear the burden to prove a section 7 violation, they will typically have to show only "a plausible connection between the proposed evidence and prior testimony."[404] Thereafter the practical burden will shift to the prosecution, "since it is the Crown which can be expected to know how evidence was, or could have been, obtained."[405] In other words, once the accused establishes a plausible connection, the prosecution

---

[398] *Ibid.* See also *R. v. Nedelcu*, [2011] O.J. No. 795, 2011 ONCA 143 at para. 31 (Ont. C.A.) (examination for discovery in a civil action should not be admitted at criminal trial to impeach accused).

[399] [1995] S.C.J. No. 10, [1995] 1 S.C.R. 451 (S.C.C.).

[400] *Ibid.*, at para. 191 (S.C.R.). See also *Thomson Newspapers Corp. v. Canada (Director of Investigation and Research)*, [1990] S.C.J. No. 23, [1990] 1 S.C.R. 425 at 560-61 (S.C.C.), *per* La Forest J. [*Thomson Newspapers*].

[401] See *Re Application under s. 83.28 of the Criminal Code*, [2004] S.C.J. No. 40, [2004] 2 S.C.R. 248 at para. 79 (S.C.C.).

[402] The Court held that exclusion flowed directly from s. 7 of the *Charter*, though it suggested that the same result would likely ensue under s. 11(*d*): *R. v. S. (R.J.)*, [1995] S.C.J. No. 10, [1995] 1 S.C.R. 451 at paras. 191, 193, 196-199 (S.C.C.). More recently, the Court has held that where the admission of evidence in the proceedings would violate the *Charter*, the evidence should be excluded under s. 24(1). See *R. v. Bjelland*, [2009] S.C.J. No. 38, [2009] 2 S.C.R. 651, 2009 SCC 38 (S.C.C.); *R. v. White*, [1999] S.C.J. No. 28, [1999] 2 S.C.R. 417 at paras. 83-89 (S.C.C.); *R. v. Z. (L.)*, [2001] O.J. No. 1882, 43 C.R. (5th) 133 at para. 44, 155 C.C.C. (3d) 152, 54 O.R. (3d) 97, 146 O.A.C. 304, 83 C.R.R. (2d) 246 (Ont. C.A.).

[403] See *Re Application under s. 83.28 of the Criminal Code*, [2004] S.C.J. No. 40, [2004] 2 S.C.R. 248 at paras. 73-79 (S.C.C.) (use and derivative use immunity applies to deportation and extradition hearings). See also *British Columbia (Securities Commission) v. Branch*, [1995] S.C.J. No. 32, [1995] 2 S.C.R. 3 at para. 5 (S.C.C.) (immunity applies only where applicant "subject to penal sanctions or in any proceedings engaging s. 7 of the *Charter*").

[404] *R. v. S. (R.J.)*, [1995] S.C.J. No. 10, [1995] 1 S.C.R. 451 at para. 203 (S.C.C.).

[405] *Ibid.*

"will have to satisfy the court on a balance of probabilities that the authorities would have discovered the impugned derivative evidence absent the compelled testimony."[406]

§4.117 Evidentiary immunity is provided not only to prevent self-incrimination, but also improve adjudicative accuracy.[407] Witnesses who have committed unlawful acts will often be reluctant to testify truthfully. Prohibiting the state from using their testimony against them in future proceedings reduces the cost of truth-telling, thus increasing the yield of truthful testimony at the initial proceeding. And since many of these witnesses would not have testified truthfully without it, giving them immunity may not deprive the state of much evidence of wrongdoing. The net result is the creation of more reliable evidence than would have been available without immunity.[408]

(b) Resisting Compulsion

§4.118 The *S. (R.J.)* Court also concluded that in rare and limited circumstances compelling testimony would in itself violate section 7.[409] Even if the evidentiary fruits of compelled testimony cannot be used in future proceedings, compulsion may sometimes cause other harms. Though the questioning of witnesses in public proceedings is not akin to police interrogation,[410] it may cause unjustified embarrassment and stigmatization. Use and derivative use immunity provide some protection against this kind of abuse. If the state is prohibited from using compelled testimony or its non-discoverable fruits in future proceedings against a witness, it will generally only compel testimony if it has a legitimate reason for doing so, such as regulating economic activity, ensuring public safety or convicting others. But authorities may sometimes compel testimony for less savoury reasons, such as intimidation or harassment.[411] In addition, adverse

---

[406] *British Columbia (Securities Commission) v. Branch*, [1995] S.C.J. No. 32, [1995] 2 S.C.R. 3 at para. 5 (S.C.C.). See also *Re Application under s. 83.28 of the Criminal Code*, [2004] S.C.J. No. 40, [2004] 2 S.C.R. 248 at paras. 72-73 (S.C.C.); *R. v. Z. (L.)*, [2001] O.J. No. 1882, 43 C.R. (5th) 133 at paras. 42-44, 155 C.C.C. (3d) 152, 54 O.R. (3d) 97, 146 O.A.C. 304, 83 C.R.R. (2d) 246 (Ont. C.A.) (witness's evidence implicating accused "in all probability would not have been obtained if it had not been for [the witness's] compelled testimony at the...preliminary inquiry").

[407] See Steven Penney, "What's Wrong with Self-Incrimination? The Wayward Path of Self-Incrimination Law in the Post-Charter Era, Part 3: Compelled Communications, the Admissibility of Defendants' Previous Testimony, and Inferences from Defendants' Silence" (2004) 48 Crim. L.Q. 474 at 480-81.

[408] See *R. v. Dubois*, [1985] S.C.J. No. 69, [1985] 2 S.C.R. 350 at 384 (S.C.C.), affg [1987] A.J. No. 1047 (Alta. C.A.), *per* McIntyre J., dissenting; *R. v. Noël*, [2002] S.C.J. No. 68, [2002] 3 S.C.R. 433 at paras. 22-24 (S.C.C.); J. McNaughton, ed., *Wigmore on Evidence*, vol. 8 (Boston: Little, Brown, 1961) § 2251.

[409] *R. v. S. (R.J.)*, [1995] S.C.J. No. 10, [1995] 1 S.C.R. 451 (S.C.C.).

[410] See *R. v. S. (R.J.)*, [1995] S.C.J. No. 10, [1995] 1 S.C.R. 451 at para. 80 (S.C.C.).

[411] See *Thomson Newspapers Corp. v. Canada (Director of Investigation and Research)*, [1990] S.C.J. No. 23, [1990] 1 S.C.R. 425 at 480 (S.C.C.), *per* Wilson J.; *R. v. S. (R.J.)*, [1995] S.C.J. No. 10, [1995] 1 S.C.R. 451 at paras. 142, 319 (S.C.C.). For examples of such abuses, see Ed Ratushny, *Self-incrimination in the Canadian Criminal Process* (Toronto: Carswell, 1979) at 349, 358-84.

publicity produced by compelled evidence may contaminate fact finding in future trials.[412]

§4.119 A majority of the *S. (R.J.)* Court, however, could not agree on either the test for deciding when compulsion infringed section 7 or the appropriate remedy for a violation.[413] These questions appeared to be answered in *British Columbia Securities Commission v. Branch*.[414] There, the Court held that witnesses may not be compelled to testify if (*i*) the compelling authority's "predominant purpose" is to "obtain incriminating evidence" against the witness rather than a "legitimate public purpose;"[415] and (*ii*) that the compulsion would cause them prejudice beyond the "possible subsequent derivative use of the testimony".[416] If the witness proves that the predominant purpose of the compelled testimony is self-incrimination, the Court found, the "witness should not be compelled unless the party seeking to compel the witness justifies the compulsion" on the basis of a lack of prejudice.[417]

§4.120 However, in *Re Application under s. 83.28 of the Criminal Code*, the Court held that a witness may refuse to testify "where proceedings are undertaken or predominately used to obtain evidence for the prosecution of the witness."[418] No reference was made to the requirement in *Branch* to show prejudice.[419] Thus, while the matter is not entirely free from doubt, it appears that

---

[412] See Ed Ratushny, *Self-incrimination in the Canadian Criminal Process* (Toronto: Carswell, 1979) at 349-51, 359-61. In his concurring minority reasons in *Phillips v. Nova Scotia (Commission of Inquiry into the Westray Mine Tragedy)*, [1995] S.C.J. No. 36, [1995] 2 S.C.R. 97 at paras. 140, 145 (S.C.C.) [*Phillips*], Cory J. suggested that remedies for adverse publicity created by compelled testimony can be sought pursuant to ss. 11(*d*) and 24(1) of the *Charter*. This approach is limited by the fact that s. 11(*d*) does not apply to persons not yet "charged with an offence" who are likely to be charged later.

[413] *R. v. S. (R.J.)*, [1995] S.C.J. No. 10, [1995] 1 S.C.R. 451 at para. 278 (S.C.C.). L'Heureux-Dubé J. (Gonthier J. concurring) concluded that s. 7 is violated when the authority's predominant purpose in compelling the witness is "to build or advance its case against that witness instead of acting in furtherance of those pressing and substantial purposes validly within the jurisdiction of the body compelling the testimony." But in most cases, she asserted, the appropriate remedy would be to stay the proceedings (if and when they arise) against the witness rather than quashing the subpoena. *Ibid.*, at paras. 285-288 (S.C.R.). Iacobucci J. (La Forest, Cory, and Major JJ. concurring) agreed that the inquiry should focus on purpose, but his elaboration of the point was obscure. He declined to comment on the remedy issue. *Ibid.*, at paras. 146-154 (S.C.R.). Sopinka J. (McLachlin J. concurring) argued that a witness should be able to resist compulsion where "prejudice to his or her interests overbears the necessity of obtaining the evidence." He set out a list of factors judges should consider in balancing these interests. *Ibid.*, at para. 326 (S.C.R.). Lamer J. agreed generally with Sopinka J. on this point. *Ibid.*, at para. 4 (S.C.R.).

[414] *British Columbia Securities Commission v. Branch*, [1995] S.C.J. No. 32, [1995] 2 S.C.R. 3 (S.C.C.).

[415] *Ibid.*, at para. 7 (S.C.R.). See also *R. v. Primeau*, [1995] S.C.J. No. 33, [1995] 2 S.C.R. 60 at para. 20 (S.C.C.); *R. v. Jobin*, [1995] S.C.J. No. 31, [1995] 2 S.C.R. 78 at para. 36 (S.C.C.).

[416] *British Columbia Securities Commission v. Branch*, [1995] S.C.J. No. 32, [1995] 2 S.C.R. 3 at para. 9 (S.C.C.).

[417] *Ibid.*, at para. 11 (S.C.R.).

[418] *Re Application under s. 83.28 of the Criminal Code*, [2004] S.C.J. No. 40, [2004] 2 S.C.R. 248 at para. 71 (S.C.C.).

[419] See also *Phillips v. Nova Scotia (Commission of Inquiry into the Westray Mine Tragedy)*, [1995] S.C.J. No. 36, [1995] 2 S.C.R. 97 at paras. 82 and 85-86 (S.C.C.), *per* Cory J. (where the

section 7 gives compelled witnesses a "constitutional exemption" from testifying when *either* (*i*) the predominant purpose of compulsion is to obtain self-incriminating evidence or (*ii*) the compulsion would cause undue prejudice.[420] Such prejudice may be established where compulsion would threaten the fairness of any subsequent trial.[421]

§4.121 While the Court has not expressly said as much, it is likely that prejudice may also arise from any unjustified harassment, stigmatization or other abuse that testimonial compulsion could induce. Relevant factors here include the nature of the proceeding, its legislative and regulatory context, the degree of concretized suspicion attaching to the witness, the availability of other investigative techniques, the importance of the testimony and the procedural protections attaching to the proceedings, such as whether the hearing is held in public or *in camera*, the availability of publication bans and whether the witness has a right to be represented by counsel.[422]

§4.122 In our view, the "predominant purpose" test should be discarded. The distinction between compulsion designed to incriminate and that designed to further a legitimate policy objective is often difficult to discern.[423] Consider the

---

witness establishes that the predominant purpose of compulsion is to elicit self-incriminatory testimony, the witness is never compellable); *R. v. Jarvis*, [2002] S.C.J. No. 76, [2002] 3 S.C.R. 757 at para. 96 (S.C.C.) ("when the predominant purpose of a question or inquiry is the determination of penal liability, the 'full panoply' of *Charter* rights are engaged for the taxpayer's protection").

[420] See *R. v. Eurocopter Canada Ltd.*, [2004] O.J. No. 2120, 185 C.C.C. (3d) 233 (Ont. S.C.J.) (no exemption where witness's compelled preliminary inquiry testimony could not be used against him in foreign criminal proceedings); *R. v. Blair*, [2007] M.J. No. 86, [2007] 6 W.W.R. 168, 216 Man.R. (2d) 34, 160 C.R.R. (2d) 72 (Man. Q.B.) (no exemption where witness compelled to testify at accomplices' trial already found guilty and testimony protected from use in sentencing proceedings by s. 13); *R. v. Papadopoulos*, [2006] O.J. No. 5423, 74 W.C.B. (2d) 820 at para. 20 (Ont. S.C.J.) (no exemption where no evidence that applicant's testimony at accomplices' trial would disclose his defence); *R. v. Cadagan*, [1998] O.J. No. 3724, 165 D.L.R. (4th) 747, 55 C.R.R. (2d) 364 at para. 29 (Ont. Gen. Div.) (no exemption where predominant purpose of compelling witness's testimony at accomplice's preliminary inquiry not to incriminate even if "Crown may glean some tactical advantage by obtaining some discovery of the accused's defence"); *R. v. Almaktari*, [2007] O.J. No. 3720 (Ont. C.A.) (no exemption for witness testifying at co-accused's preliminary inquiry where testimony could assist Crown's application to admit witness's "*K.G.B.*" hearsay statement). See also David M. Paciocco & Lee Stuesser, *The Law of Evidence*, 5th ed. (Toronto: Irwin Law, 2008) at 304-305.

[421] *British Columbia Securities Commission v. Branch*, [1995] S.C.J. No. 32, [1995] 2 S.C.R. 3 at para. 9 (S.C.C.); *Phillips v. Nova Scotia (Commission of Inquiry into the Westray Mine Tragedy)*, [1995] S.C.J. No. 36, [1995] 2 S.C.R. 97 at para. 86 (S.C.C.), *per* Cory J., concurring.

[422] See *Re Application under s. 83.28 of the Criminal Code*, [2004] S.C.J. No. 40, [2004] 2 S.C.R. 248 at paras. 47-54 (S.C.C.). See also *Catalyst Fund General I Inc. v. Hollinger Inc.*, [2005] O.J. No. 2191, 255 D.L.R. (4th) 233 at para. 65, 8 B.L.R. (4th) 95, 133 C.R.R. (2d) 1 (Ont. S.C.J.), affd [2005] O.J. No. 4666 (Ont. C.A.) (in denying the applicants' request for an exemption from examination by a court-appointed inspector in shareholder proceedings, the court noted that the hearing may be held *in camera*, the "transcript kept from disclosure and potentially incriminating questions reviewed before answers are required").

[423] See Steven Penney, "What's Wrong with Self-Incrimination? The Wayward Path of Self-Incrimination Law in the Post-Charter Era, Part 3: Compelled Communications, the Admissibility of Defendants' Previous Testimony, and Inferences from Defendants' Silence" (2004) 48 Crim. L.Q. 474 at 480-91.

compulsion at issue in *British Columbia Securities Commission v. Branch*.[424] For the Supreme Court, the purpose of this compulsion was to facilitate securities regulation.[425] However, is it not more accurate to say that its purpose was to induce self-incriminating testimony to help convict and punish wrongdoers, the effect of which is to deter others and thereby promote fair and efficient trading? As Paciocco and Stuesser have noted, "it will be a rare case where the accused can show... that the predominant reasons for his compulsion is to make him speak about his own criminality."[426] The exemption decision should thus be decided solely on the issue of prejudice, including concerns for both trial fairness and inquisitorial abuse.

§4.123 Claims that compulsion would or has violated section 7 may be made at either the *subpoena* or trial stage of proceedings. Quashing the *subpoena*, and thereby exempting the witness from testifying, will be appropriate only in the "clearest of cases."[427] Courts more commonly award less drastic remedies at the *subpoena* stage, such as ordering a ban on publication to avoid influencing future jurors.[428] At the trial stage, the judge would normally stay the proceedings, though here again lesser remedies may be sufficient.[429]

(2)   Non-testimonial Compulsion

§4.124 Many regulatory statutes require people to make non-testimonial statements or maintain documentary records. Some of these prohibit this evidence from being used to incriminate persons so compelled.[430] But no such protection is given by either common law[431] or the express language of the *Canada Evidence Act*[432] or *Charter*.[433] Section 5(2) of the *Canada Evidence Act* and sections

---

[424] [1995] S.C.J. No. 32, [1995] 2 S.C.R. 3 (S.C.C.).

[425] *Ibid.*, at paras. 34-35 (S.C.R.).

[426] David M. Paciocco & Lee Stuesser, *The Law of Evidence*, 5th ed. (Toronto: Irwin Law, 2008) at 304. See also *Phillips v. Nova Scotia (Commission of Inquiry into the Westray Mine Tragedy)*, [1995] S.C.J. No. 36, [1995] 2 S.C.R. 97 at para. 85 (S.C.C.), *per* Cory J. ("the situations in which an improper purpose for compelling evidence arises may be infrequent").

[427] See *British Columbia Securities Commission v. Branch*, [1995] S.C.J. No. 32, [1995] 2 S.C.R. 3 at para. 72 (S.C.C.). See also *Catalyst Fund General I Inc. v. Hollinger Inc.*, [2005] O.J. No. 2191, 255 D.L.R. (4th) 233 at para. 70, 8 B.L.R. (4th) 95, 133 C.R.R. (2d) 1 (Ont. S.C.J.), affg [2005] O.J. No. 4666 (Ont. C.A.) (noting that "no court has yet quashed a subpoena or excused a witness from compelled testimony for the reason that the predominant purpose of an inquiry was to incriminate the witness").

[428] See *Phillips v. Nova Scotia (Commission of Inquiry into the Westray Mine Tragedy)*, [1995] S.C.J. No. 36, [1995] 2 S.C.R. 97 at paras. 34-35 (S.C.C.), *per* L'Heureux-Dubé J. and at para. 134, *per* Cory J. Other possible remedies include ordering an *in camera* hearing and delaying the taking of testimony until the conclusion of the witness's trial.

[429] See *R. c. Liakas*, [2000] J.Q. no. 498, 144 C.C.C. (3d) 359 at para. 42 (Que. C.A.); *R. v. Z. (L.)*, [2001] O.J. No. 1882, 43 C.R. (5th) 133 (Ont. C.A.).

[430] See *e.g.*, *Traffic Safety Act*, R.S.A. 2000, c. T-6, s. 11(3)(*b*).

[431] See *R. v. Walker*, [1939] S.C.J. No. 6, [1939] S.C.R. 214 (S.C.C.).

[432] R.S.C. 1985, c. C-5.

[433] *Canadian Charter of Rights and Freedoms*, Part I of the *Constitution Act, 1982*, being Schedule B to the *Canada Act 1982* (U.K.), 1982, c. 11.

11(*c*) and 13 of the *Charter* have been read to apply only to witnesses in legal proceedings.[434]

§4.125 The Supreme Court of Canada has nonetheless interpreted the principle against self-incrimination inhering in section 7 of the *Charter* as granting protection to certain self-incriminating communications "brought into existence by the exercise of compulsion by the state."[435] The principle does not, however, protect evidence produced prior to and independently of compulsion.[436] The admission of statutorily compelled communications, moreover, does not always violate section 7.[437] In deciding whether to grant protection, courts balance self-incrimination concerns against regulatory and law enforcement objectives.[438] Factors to be considered include the nature of the relationship between the parties, purpose of the compulsion, existence of coercion, effect of compulsion on the communication's reliability and potential for the abuse of state power.[439]

§4.126 Applying this matrix, the Court found in *R. v. Fitzpatrick*[440] that mandatory reporting of fish catches to regulatory authorities did not violate section 7; such reports are thus admissible in overfishing prosecutions.[441] There, prosecutors wished to adduce documentary fishing records and oral "hail reports" of daily catches that the accused was required to submit to regulatory officials. Justice La Forest reasoned that at the time the records are made, fishers and the state are not in an adversarial relationship; the predominant purpose of the record-keeping requirement is to facilitate efficient regulation, not to compel self-incrimination; fishers participate in the industry voluntarily; any incentive to falsify records exists despite the absence of use immunity; and fishers are not subject to psychological or emotional pressure or forced to divulge intimate information.[442] Further, if self-reports were inadmissible, regulators would be

---

[434] See *R. v. Fitzpatrick*, [1995] S.C.J. No. 94, [1995] 4 S.C.R. 154 at para. 19 (S.C.C.). See also David M. Paciocco, *Charter Principles and Proof in Criminal Cases* (Toronto: Carswell, 1987) at 465-66, 485-89.

[435] *British Columbia Securities Commission v. Branch*, [1995] S.C.J. No. 32, [1995] 2 S.C.R. 3 at para. 43 (S.C.C.).

[436] *Ibid.*, at paras. 43-46 (S.C.R.). See also *Thomson Newspapers Ltd. v. Canada (Director of Investigation and Research, Restrictive Trade Practices Commission)*, [1990] S.C.J. No. 23, [1990] 1 S.C.R. 425 at 608 (S.C.C.), *per* Sopinka J. and 588 (S.C.R.), *per* L'Heureux-Dubé J; *R. v. D'Amour*, [2002] O.J. No. 3103, 163 O.A.C. 164 at para. 42 (Ont. C.A.) (T4 slips are created by employers and exist independently of state compulsion); *Jackson v. Vaughan (City)*, [2010] O.J. No. 588, 2010 ONCA 118 at paras. 38-46 (Ont. C.A.) (compliance audit under *Municipal Elections Act* does not engage s. 7 as accused voluntarily chose to participate in election and proceedings were regulatory not criminal).

[437] *R. v. Fitzpatrick*, [1995] S.C.J. No. 94, [1995] 4 S.C.R. 154 at para. 21 (S.C.C.).

[438] See *R. v. Fitzpatrick*, [1995] S.C.J. No. 94, [1995] 4 S.C.R. 154 at paras. 27-30 (S.C.C.).

[439] *R. v. Fitzpatrick*, [1995] S.C.J. No. 94, [1995] 4 S.C.R. 154 at paras. 34, 44-46, 53 (S.C.C.).

[440] [1995] S.C.J. No. 94, [1995] 4 S.C.R. 154 (S.C.C.).

[441] *R. v. Fitzpatrick*, [1995] S.C.J. No. 94, [1995] 4 S.C.R. 154 at para. 54 (S.C.C.).

[442] *R. v. Fitzpatrick*, [1995] S.C.J. No. 94, [1995] 4 S.C.R. 154 at paras. 34-35, 42, 44, 52 (S.C.C.). See also *R. v. Labrador Sea Products Inc.*, [2008] N.J. No. 308, 181 C.R.R. (2d) 1 at paras. 48-53, 284 Nfld. & P.E.I.R. 240 (N.L.T.D.).

forced to use more intrusive and expensive techniques to acquire evidence of overfishing.[443]

§4.127 In *R. v. White*,[444] in contrast, the Court concluded that section 7 forbade the admission of defendants' compelled vehicle accident reports at their criminal trials.[445] The defendant was charged under the *Criminal Code* with failing to stop at the scene of an accident.[446] At trial, the prosecution attempted to introduce self-incriminating statements compelled by provincial motor vehicle legislation. That legislation purports to provide use immunity for such statements in subsequent proceedings.[447] But division of powers principles prevent this immunity from applying to federal offences.[448] Applying the factors outlined in *Fitzpatrick*, the Court noted that the police's presence creates an environment of "pronounced psychological and emotional pressure"[449] that could induce drivers to "provide a more extensive statement to police than legally required under the Act;"[450] that the reports' use in criminal prosecutions is not integral to the regulatory scheme;[451] and that the fear of criminal prosecution could induce false statements.[452]

§4.128 Lower courts have applied this jurisprudence in myriad situations. Where the obligation to provide information arises in the context of routine inspections, audits or self-reports, courts have been reluctant to find that section 7 is engaged. For example, courts have refused to extend section 7's protections to statutory powers requiring entrants to Canada to answer routine questions by customs officials[453] and requiring police to make notes of their investigative activities.[454] Section 7 is more likely to be triggered, in contrast, where the obligation arises in the context of an incident likely to generate a criminal inquiry. Courts have found, for example, that section 7 applies to the obligation of police to report using force or causing injury to civilians.[455]

---

[443] *R. v. Fitzpatrick*, [1995] S.C.J. No. 94, [1995] 4 S.C.R. 154 at paras. 47-48 (S.C.C.).

[444] [1999] S.C.J. No. 28, [1999] 2 S.C.R. 417 (S.C.C.).

[445] *Ibid.* As the Court intended, this has since prompted police to separate the taking of accident reports from their general investigative inquiries. See *e.g.*, *R. v. Gallant*, [2007] N.B.J. No. 2282, 52 M.V.R. (5th) 288 at paras. 60-61 (N.B. Prov. Ct.).

[446] *Criminal Code*, R.S.C. 1985, c. C-46, s. 252(1)(*a*).

[447] *Motor Vehicle Act*, R.S.B.C. 1979, c. 288, s. 61(7), as amended.

[448] *R. v. White*, [1999] S.C.J. No. 28, [1999] 2 S.C.R. 417 at para. 35 (S.C.C.); *R. v. Walker*, [1939] S.C.J. No. 6, [1939] S.C.R. 214 (S.C.C.). See also *Klein v. Bell*, [1955] S.C.J. No. 19, [1955] S.C.R. 309 (S.C.C.).

[449] *R. v. White*, [1999] S.C.J. No. 28, [1999] 2 S.C.R. 417 at para. 58 (S.C.C.).

[450] *Ibid.*, at para. 64 (S.C.R.).

[451] *Ibid.*, at para. 60 (S.C.R.).

[452] *Ibid.*, at para. 62 (S.C.R.). See also *R. v. Powers*, [2006] B.C.J. No. 2650, 213 C.C.C. (3d) 351 at para. 21 (B.C.C.A.), leave to appeal refused [2006] S.C.C.A. No. 452, 217 C.C.C. (3d) vi (S.C.C.); *R. v. Choy*, [2008] A.J. No. 1320, 2 Alta. L.R. (5th) 343 (Alta. Q.B.) (obligation to report injury to child in foster care triggers s. 7 as foster parent in adversarial position with state and strong motive to provide false report).

[453] *R. v. Jones*, [2006] O.J. No. 3315, 81 O.R. (3d) 481 at paras. 27-31 (Ont. C.A.).

[454] *R. v. Schertzer*, [2007] O.J. No. 3560, 161 C.R.R. (2d) 367 (Ont. S.C.J.).

[455] See *R. v. Wighton*, [2003] O.J. No. 2611, 176 C.C.C. (3d) 550, 13 C.R. (6th) 266 (Ont. C.J.); *Côté c. R.*, [2006] J.Q. no. 14437, 2006 QCCQ 13381.

§4.129 In cases where regulators have both regulatory and criminal law enforcement powers, courts must also consider whether the compulsion occurred after the investigation became an inquiry into penal liability.[456] Once this occurs, authorities may no longer compel answers and must obtain warrants to seize documents.[457] Any evidence obtained in violation of this rule may be excluded at trial pursuant to section 24(2) of the *Charter*.[458] In deciding whether a penal investigation has arisen, courts should consider whether authorities had reasonable grounds to believe that a criminal offence was committed,[459] attempted to collect evidence of *mens rea*[460] or shifted primary responsibility for the investigation from auditors to criminal investigators.[461] Furthermore, a clear decision to pursue

---

[456] *R. v. Jarvis*, [2002] S.C.J. No. 76, [2002] 3 S.C.R. 757 (S.C.C.) (evidence compelled with the purpose of determining a taxpayer's penal liability in a tax evasion investigation violates s. 7); *R. v. Ling*, [2002] S.C.J. No. 75, [2002] 3 S.C.R. 814 (S.C.C.) (same); *R. v. Kooktook*, [2006] Nu.J. No. 7, 210 C.C.C. (3d) 106 at para. 91 (Nu. C.A.) (s. 7 violated by fisheries officers engaged primarily in investigation of penal liability, not mere inspection); *R. v. Tiffin*, [2008] O.J. No. 1525, 90 O.R. (3d) 575 (Ont. C.A.), appeal to S.C.C. quashed [2008] S.C.C.A. No. 236, 236 C.C.C. (3d) 1 (S.C.C.) (no s. 7 protection where auditor's inquiries not directed "only" at determining penal liability, but rather inquired into both civil and criminal tax offenses). See also David Stratas, "'Crossing the Rubicon': The Supreme Court and Regulatory Investigations" (2003) 6 C.R. (6th) 74 at 78-80.

[457] *R. v. Jarvis*, [2002] S.C.J. No. 76, [2002] 3 S.C.R. 757 at paras. 2, 46, 88, 99 (S.C.C.); *R. v. Kooktook*, [2006] Nu.J. No. 7, 2210 C.C.C. (3d) 106 at paras. 87-91 (Nu. C.A.).

[458] *R. v. Jarvis*, [2002] S.C.J. No. 76, [2002] 3 S.C.R. 757 at para. 105 (S.C.C.).

[459] *Ibid.*, at para. 89 (S.C.R.) (reasonable and probable grounds relevant but not determinative in finding that the predominant purpose is determination of penal liability). See also *R. v. Alexander*, [2003] B.C.J. No. 1509, 184 B.C.A.C. 280 at para. 19 (B.C.C.A.) (regulatory investigation became warrantless search to determine penal liability when officer established reasonable and probable grounds); *R. v. Lempen*, [2008] N.B.J. No. 466, 338 N.B.R. (2d) 377 at para. 8 (N.B.C.A.) (existence of reasonable grounds not sufficient to trigger protection where no other evidence that purpose of investigation was determination of penal liability); *Ontario (Securities Commission) v. Robinson*, CanLII 58983 at paras. 29-31 (Ont. S.C.J.) (fact that police did not have reasonable grounds to lay charges relevant to determination that audit had not become criminal investigation); *R. v. Rice*, [2009] B.C.J. No. 2510, 250 C.C.C. (3d) 303 (B.C.C.A.) (despite existence of reasonable grounds, hunters' obligation to answer conservation officer's questions under provincial wildlife statute does not engage s. 7 as predominant purpose not to determine penal liability).

[460] *R. v. Jarvis*, [2002] S.C.J. No. 76, [2002] 3 S.C.R. 757 at para. 91 (S.C.C.). See also *Kligman v. Canada (Minister of National Revenue)*, [2004] F.C.J. No. 639, [2004] 239 D.L.R. (4th) 1 at paras. 35-37 (F.C.A.) (difficult if not impossible to show that evidence is only relevant to *mens rea*, even where primary purpose of investigation is to establish penal liability); *R. v. Lempen*, [2008] N.B.J. No. 466, 181 C.R.R. (2d) 160 at para. 13 (N.B.C.A.) (evidence collected is not relevant only to establishing *mens rea* for penal liability where also relevant to general concerns that company is reporting and paying taxes correctly); *R. v. Tiffin*, [2008] O.J. No. 1525, 90 O.R. (3d) 575 at para. 180 (Ont. C.A.), appeal to S.C.C. quashed [2008] S.C.C.A. No. 236, 236 C.C.C. (3d) 1 (S.C.C.) (not enough to show that evidence could be relevant to *mens rea* when it is also relevant to civil liability).

[461] *R. v. Jarvis*, [2002] S.C.J. No. 76, [2002] 3 S.C.R. 757 at para. 92 (S.C.C.). See also *R. v. Bjellebo*, [2003] O.J. No. 3946, 2003 D.T.C. 5659 (Ont. C.A.), leave to appeal refused [2004] S.C.C.A. No. 69 (S.C.C.) (investigation carried out by department with mandate to prosecute does not automatically trigger protection); *R. v. Tiffin*, [2008] O.J. No. 1525, 90 O.R. (3d) 575 at para. 169 (Ont. C.A.), appeal to S.C.C. quashed [2008] S.C.C.A. No. 236, 236 C.C.C. (3d) 1 (S.C.C.) (date that files are transferred from auditor to criminal investigation unit given "great weight" in determining when investigation of penal liability begins).

a criminal investigation may be sufficient on its own to show that a criminal investigation has arisen.[462] Notably, self-incriminating information acquired before (but not after) a penal investigation begins may be used in that penal investigation and is admissible at trial.[463]

§4.130 As with testimonial compulsion, the protection afforded to compelled, non-testimonial communications by section 7 of the *Charter* promotes the provision of reliable information to the state. Without evidentiary immunity, for example, people may not provide information vital to the efficacy of a regulatory scheme. Whether immunity is needed to achieve this objective, however, is a decision that should in our view generally be left to legislatures to decide.[464] The Supreme Court was thus right in *Fitzpatrick* to defer to Parliament's choice not to grant immunity. As the Court recognized, if self-reports were inadmissible, regulators would be forced to use more intrusive and expensive techniques to acquire evidence of overfishing.[465] The same logic applies to many other self-reporting schemes, such as the income tax provisions considered in *R. v. Jarvis*[466] and *R. v. Ling*.[467]

§4.131 Enhancing regulation, however, is not the only reason to provide protection against self-incrimination in this context. Non-testimonial compulsion may also raise concerns about inquisitorial abuse. Indeed, as the protections attaching to legal proceedings are absent, the range of potential abuses is greater than that in the case of testimonial compulsion. There are three types of harms: cruel interrogation practices, false confessions leading to wrongful convictions and unwarranted invasions of privacy.

§4.132 The first two harms may be considered in tandem. If suspects have no right to remain silent, authorities may be emboldened to use coercive methods to extract admissions. These methods may be intrinsically cruel, apt to induce false confessions, or both. The magnitude of these harms depends on two variables: the nature of the legal obligation to speak and the environment in which questioning takes place. Investigators clothed with broad inquisitorial powers are less

---

[462] *R. v. Jarvis*, [2002] S.C.J. No. 76, [2002] 3 S.C.R. 757 at para. 93 (S.C.C.); *Kligman v. Canada (Minister of National Revenue - M.N.R.)*, [2004] F.C.J. No. 639, 239 D.L.R. (4th) 1 at paras. 13, 28 (F.C.A.).

[463] *R. v. Jarvis*, [2002] S.C.J. No. 76, [2002] 3 S.C.R. 757 at paras. 95-97 (S.C.C.).

[464] An exception to this principle arose in *R. v. White*, [1999] S.C.J. No. 28, [1999] 2 S.C.R. 417 (S.C.C.). There, the provincial legislature's provision of use immunity for accident reports was *ultra vires* for the purposes of federal criminal proceedings. By providing immunity under s. 7, the Court effectively repaired the damage to the regulatory scheme wrought by the division of powers. In doing so, the Court had to decide not only between competing legislative objectives (encouraging accurate reporting to improve highway safety *v.* convicting criminal wrongdoers), but also between competing legislatures. There being no single state interest to defer to, the Court was forced to choose. It decided that the effective operation of the regulatory regime required the granting of immunity. Evidence necessary for criminal prosecutions could be obtained in other ways. See Steven Penney, "The Continuing Evolution of the s. 7 Self-Incrimination Principle: *R. v. White*" (1999) 24 C.R. (5th) 247.

[465] *R. v. Fitzpatrick*, [1995] S.C.J. No. 94, [1995] 4 S.C.R. 154 at para. 44 (S.C.C.).

[466] [2002] S.C.J. No. 76, [2002] 3 S.C.R. 757 (S.C.C.).

[467] [2002] S.C.J. No. 75, [2002] 3 S.C.R. 814 (S.C.C.).

likely to be satisfied by non-confessional responses than those entitled only to limited information. Similarly, questioning in environments akin to custody is more likely to involve coercion than questioning in non-custodial settings.

§4.133 In *Fitzpatrick*, the compelled information was highly specific and provided in a non-coercive setting. The accident reports mandated by the legislation considered in *White*, in contrast, are often made in coercive circumstances, such as custodial questioning ensuing from arrests for criminal offences.[468] It was consequently sensible to provide use immunity to all statements made pursuant to the statutory reporting requirement.[469] Similarly, in *Jarvis* and *Ling*, the accused were required to "answer all proper questions" relating to tax investigations.[470] While auditors asking routine questions about deduction claims or income statements would be unlikely to use coercion, criminal investigators may also use this power in settings akin to *incommunicado* interrogation. The distinction drawn in those cases between ordinary compliance audits and tax evasion investigations responds to this concern. Giving evidentiary immunity only to statements made in the course of penal investigations minimizes the risk of abuse and wrongful conviction without denying the state access to reliable, self-incriminating evidence obtained from non-coercive regulatory inquiries.

§4.134 People's privacy may be unjustifiably invaded when authorities compel non-testimonial communications from people that may harass, embarrass or stigmatize them. The protection afforded by section 7 of the *Charter* in this context largely overlaps with that granted by section 8.[471] As with section 8, the Supreme Court has interpreted section 7 to give regulators much greater latitude to invade privacy than criminal investigators.[472] In particular, for regulatory inquiries the usual requirements of prior, independent authorization and individualized suspicion are often elided.[473] In such cases, constitutionality typically turns on the importance of the compulsion to the efficacy of the regulatory scheme and the magnitude of any reasonable expectation of privacy in the communications compelled.

---

[468] *Motor Vehicle Act*, R.S.B.C. 1979, c. 288, ss. 61(1), 61(4).

[469] See *R. v. White*, [1999] S.C.J. No. 28, [1999] 2 S.C.R. 417 at paras. 64-65 (S.C.C.). As the Court intended, this has since prompted police to separate the taking of accident reports from their general investigative inquiries. See *e.g.*, *R. v. Gallant*, [2007] N.B.J. No. 2282, 52 M.V.R. (5th) 288 (N.B. Prov. Ct.).

[470] *Income Tax Act*, R.S.C. 1985, c. 1 (5th Supp.), s. 231.1(1)(*d*).

[471] See Chapter 3, Part 2(5)(*d*)(iii)a. Sections 7 and 8 both apply to the acquisition by state agents of statutorily compelled documentary records. Only s. 7 applies to the compulsion of oral statements.

[472] See Chapter 3, Part 2(5)(*d*)(iii)a.

[473] See *e.g.*, *British Columbia Securities Commission v. Branch*, [1995] S.C.J. No. 32, [1995] 2 S.C.R. 3 at paras. 52-53 (S.C.C.); *Thomson Newspapers Ltd. v. Canada (Director of Investigation and Research, Restrictive Trade Practices Commission)*, [1990] S.C.J. No. 23, [1990] 1 S.C.R. 425 at 517-18 (S.C.C.), *per* La Forest J.; *Comité paritaire de l'industrie de la chemise v. Potash*, [1994] S.C.J. No. 7, [1994] 2 S.C.R. 406 at 420-21 (S.C.C.), *per* La Forest J. and 441-44 (S.C.R.), *per* L'Heureux-Dubé J.; *R. v. McKinlay Transport Ltd.*, [1990] S.C.J. No. 25, [1990] 1 S.C.R. 627 at 645-47 (S.C.C.), *per* Wilson J.

§4.135 In *Fitzpatrick*, *Jarvis* and *Ling*, for example, the Court noted that mandatory self-reporting and record keeping were essential to efficient regulation. Fisheries management and income tax collection would not be possible if authorities either had to obtain warrants to obtain such communications or were prohibited from using them to prosecute wrongdoers.[474] In *White*, in contrast, the Court concluded that admitting vehicle accident reports in criminal prosecutions would not further the provincial legislature's goal of furthering highway safety by compiling accurate accident statistics.[475]

§4.136 The Court has also repeatedly noted that in the regulatory context, compelled information usually relates to relatively impersonal matters, such as business and financial records.[476] Such records are not likely to divulge the "state of mind, thoughts, or opinions of the individual who has submitted the records."[477] Compelling their production will therefore rarely create undue embarrassment or stigma.[478]

§4.137 To summarize, it is rarely appropriate to protect persons compelled to make non-testimonial communications from self-incrimination. Except where officials are empowered to compel statements in circumstances akin to custodial interrogation, providing immunity is not needed to prevent abusive questioning or false confessions. Courts should generally defer to the legislature's choice to favour the availability of evidence for prosecution over the incentive for truth-telling that immunity might provide, at least where they can discern a single, coherent legislative choice. It will also rarely be necessary to provide protection against self-incrimination to prevent fishing expeditions. In the regulatory context in which non-testimonial compulsion usually occurs, individuals typically do not have a sufficient expectation of privacy to warrant restrictions on inquisitorial intrusions.

---

[474] See *R. v. Jarvis*, [2002] S.C.J. No. 76, [2002] 3 S.C.R. 757 at para. 51 (S.C.C.).

[475] See *R. v. White*, [1999] S.C.J. No. 28, [1999] 2 S.C.R. 417 at para. 60 (S.C.C.).

[476] See *R. v. Jarvis*, [2002] S.C.J. No. 76, [2002] 3 S.C.R. 757 at para. 72 (S.C.C.); *R. v. Fitzpatrick*, [1995] S.C.J. No. 94, [1995] 4 S.C.R. 154 at para. 49 (S.C.C.). See also *Thomson Newspapers Ltd. v. Canada (Director of Investigation and Research, Restrictive Trade Practices Commission)*, [1990] S.C.J. No. 23, [1990] 1 S.C.R. 425 at 507 (S.C.C.), *per* La Forest J.; *143471 Canada Inc. v. Quebec (Attorney General)*, [1994] S.C.J. No. 45, [1994] 2 S.C.R. 339 at 378 (S.C.C.), *per* Cory J.; *Comité paritaire de l'industrie de la chemise v. Potash*, [1994] S.C.J. No. 7, [1994] 2 S.C.R. 406 at 420-21 (S.C.C.); *R. v. McKinlay Transport Ltd.*, [1990] S.C.J. No. 25, [1990] 1 S.C.R. 627 at 649-50 (S.C.C.).

[477] *R. v. Fitzpatrick*, [1995] S.C.J. No. 94, [1995] 4 S.C.R. 154 at para. 51 (S.C.C.). See also *Thomson Newspapers Ltd. v. Canada (Director of Investigation and Research, Restrictive Trade Practices Commission)*, [1990] S.C.J. No. 23, [1990] 1 S.C.R. 425 at 517-18 (S.C.C.), *per* La Forest J.

[478] The Court was therefore wrong, in our view, to hold in *R. v. Jarvis*, [2002] S.C.J. No. 76, [2002] 3 S.C.R. 757 (S.C.C.) that when an authority's predominant purpose is to determine penal liability, it may not examine a taxpayer's documents without a warrant. See Chapter 3, Part 2(5)(*d*)(iii)a.

PART III

PRE-TRIAL PROCEDURES

Chapter 5

INTAKE PROCEDURES

1. INTRODUCTION

§5.1 This chapter explains how an individual moves from being a suspect or arrestee, to a person formally charged with a crime and appearing in court as either a "defendant" or an "accused".[1] That is, it explains the intake procedures that control an individual's entry into the adjudicative phase of the criminal process.

§5.2 The route that an individual will typically travel to the courtroom depends on whether the police decide to carry out an arrest and hold the person in custody for a bail hearing, or decide instead to pursue less coercive options for compelling the person's attendance in court. As was explained in Chapter 2, Part 4(4)(*h*), the police have considerable discretion in that regard. Depending on how that discretion is exercised, the procedures governing the way in which an individual will come before the court and be charged with an offence will differ. These differences are explained in this chapter.

§5.3 The procedures outlined in this chapter also apply to the initiation of proceedings against young persons under the *Youth Criminal Justice Act*.[2] In that context, however, there are some important differences, mainly aimed at ensuring that a young person's parents or a responsible adult are notified of the charges.[3]

§5.4 In addition, entirely independent of the police, the *Criminal Code*[4] retains the possibility of privately laid charges. This chapter addresses how private prosecutions are initiated and details the statutory and common law limitations on such proceedings.

2. LAYING THE INFORMATION

§5.5 The first step in the formal process of initiating a criminal prosecution involves the laying of the "information" by an "informant"[5]. The information is

---

[1] As explained in Chapter 1, Part 2(3)(*b*), the *Criminal Code*, R.S.C. 1985, c. C-46, uses "defendant" for summary conviction proceedings and "accused" for indictable matters.

[2] S.C., 2002, c. 1. Section 28 of the Act makes Part XVI of the *Criminal Code* applicable to proceedings under the Act except to the extent that they are inconsistent or excluded.

[3] See *Youth Criminal Justice Act*, S.C., 2002, ss. 26 and 27.

[4] R.S.C. 1985, c. C-46 [*Code*].

[5] Unfortunately, the terms "information" and "informant" are used in a number of different contexts both in the *Criminal Code* and in the case law governing various aspects of the criminal

the document that charges someone with a criminal offence; its format is set out in Form 2 of the *Criminal Code*. The process, form and requirements are the same irrespective of the type of offence being charged — indictable, hybrid or summary.[6]

§5.6 The information is a document sworn under oath before a "justice".[7] With charges laid by the police, the informant is usually an officer assigned to court duties. The informant can, however, be "any one";[8] hence the potential for criminal charges laid by private persons (discussed in Part 5, below).

§5.7 The information sets out the key aspects of a criminal allegation, including the name of the person(s) charged and the particulars of the allegation(s), for example, the time, place and nature of the offence(s) alleged as well as the name(s) of the alleged victim(s).[9] This *ex parte* and *in camera*[10] procedure requires that the informant make a sworn declaration that he or she has "personal knowledge" or "believes on reasonable grounds" that the person to be charged committed the offence(s) specified.[11] The informant's basis for this sworn assertion may simply come from reading a report or synopsis prepared by the arresting officer.[12]

---

process. For example, the document sworn to obtain a search warrant is also known as an "information" and the person who swears it is also referred to as an "informant". See *Criminal Code*, R.S.C. 1985, c. C-46, s. 487, Form 1. In addition, as was explained in Chapter 3, Part 3(3)(*b*), a person who supplies information to police in confidence is also normally referred to as an "informant".

[6] For indictable matters see *Criminal Code*, R.S.C. 1985, c. C-46, s. 506, Form 2. The rules governing informations in summary prosecutions are essentially the same as those that apply to indictable matters. See *Criminal Code*, ss. 788 to 790, including the use of Form 2 (see s. 788(1)). More generally, s. 795 incorporates by reference the various intake procedures applicable to indictable matters to summary proceedings "so far as they are not inconsistent ... with such modifications as the circumstances require ...". See *Criminal Code*, s. 795. It will be remembered that so-called hybrid offences, those that can be prosecuted by indictment or summarily are deemed to be indictable until the Crown formally makes its election. See *Interpretation Act*, R.S.C. 1985, c. I-21, s. 34(1)(*a*). As a result, they are treated just like indictable offences in this context. The three types of offences (indictable, hybrid and summary) were each explained in detail in Chapter 1, Part 2(3).

[7] Section 2 of the *Criminal Code* provides that "justice" "means a justice of the peace or a provincial court judge". In virtually all jurisdictions, it is a justice of the peace who receives the information.

[8] *Criminal Code*, s. 504 ("[a]*ny one* who, on reasonable grounds, believes that a person has committed an indictable offence may lay an information in writing and under oath before a justice, and the justice shall receive the information...") [emphasis added].

[9] See *McHale v. Ontario (Attorney General)*, [2010] O.J. No. 2030, 2010 ONCA 361 at para. 43 (Ont. C.A.), leave to appeal refused [2010] S.C.C.A. No. 290 (S.C.C.). The requirements for informations are set out in greater detail in Chapter 11.

[10] The term "*ex parte*" means that the person to be charged is not present. The term "*in camera*" means that it takes place behind closed doors, not in open court, usually in a court office.

[11] *Criminal Code*, s. 504, Form 2. See also *R. v. Kamperman*, [1981] N.S.J. No. 494, 48 N.S.R. (2d) 317, 63 C.C.C. (2d) 531 (N.S.T.D.).

[12] *R. v. Peavoy*, [1974] O.J. No. 103, 15 C.C.C. (2d) 97 at 105-106 (Ont. H.C.J.). Note, however, that a complete absence of knowledge on the part of the informant does not affect the validity of the information. Nor can the information be attacked collaterally on this basis at the preliminary inquiry or trial. The only potential redress is a motion before the original justice to set aside the

§5.8 At this very preliminary stage, when the information is initially laid, there is no obligation on the informant to apprise the justice of the grounds supporting a charge. Rather, the *Criminal Code* mandates that the "justice shall receive the information".[13] This means that, absent some facial defect,[14] the justice must complete this "ministerial" function and receive the charge; there is no discretion to refuse it.[15] Once the facially valid information is sworn, the person named therein is "charged" with an offence.[16]

§5.9 The swearing of the information is therefore largely a *pro forma* exercise — it is not designed to serve a substantive screening function with the receiving justice ferreting out unjustified charges. Rather, as explained below, a limited

---

information or by extraordinary remedy in the superior court to quash the information. See *R. v. Whitmore*, [1987] O.J. No. 102, 41 C.C.C. (3d) 555 at 565-66 (Ont. H.C.J.), affd [1989] O.J. No. 1611, 51 C.C.C. (3d) 294 (Ont. C.A.). But see *R. v. Jones*, [1971] P.E.I.J. No. 41, 1 Nfld. & P.E.I.R. 394, 3 C.C.C. (2d) 25 (P.E.I.S.C.); *R. v. Pilcher*, [1981] M.J. No. 552, 58 C.C.C. (2d) 435 (Man. Prov. Ct.); *R. v. Kamperman*, [1981] N.S.J. No. 494, 48 N.S.R. (2d) 317, 63 C.C.C. (2d) 531 (N.S.T.D.), cases in which the information was held to be a nullity because the informant did not actually possess the requisite belief.

[13] *Criminal Code*, s. 504.

[14] A facial defect would exist if the minimal preconditions found in s. 504 were not met. For example, the section requires that it be "alleged":

    (*a*) that the person has committed, anywhere, an indictable offence that may be tried in the province in which the justice resides, and that the person

        (i) is or is believed to be, or

        (ii) resides or is believed to reside, within the territorial jurisdiction of the justice;

    (*b*) that the person, wherever he may be, has committed an indictable offence within the territorial jurisdiction of the justice;

    (*c*) that the person has, anywhere, unlawfully received property that was unlawfully obtained within the territorial jurisdiction of the justice; or

    (*d*) that the person has in his possession stolen property within the territorial jurisdiction of the justice.

So, for example, if the information does not name a particular person as accused, or if the allegation does not constitute an offence then the information should not be received. See generally, *McHale v. Ontario (Attorney General)*, [2010] O.J. No. 2030, 2010 ONCA 361 at paras. 5, 43-44 (Ont. C.A.), leave to appeal refused [2010] S.C.C.A. No. 290 (S.C.C.); *R. v. Whitmore*, [1987] O.J. No. 102, 41 C.C.C. (3d) 555 at 563-64 (Ont. H.C.J.), affd [1989] O.J. No. 1611, 51 C.C.C. (3d) 294 (Ont. C.A.). See *e.g.*, *R. v. Buchbinder; Venner v. Buchbinder*, [1985] O.J. No. 161, 20 C.C.C. (3d) 481 (Ont. C.A.) (information invalid where it purported to charge an unknown person). The territorial division requirement in s. 504(a) is a reference to the province, as opposed to the separate judicial regions within the province. As a result, a justice sitting in one judicial region is obligated to receive an information charging someone with an offence alleged in another. See *R. v. Ellis*, [2009] O.J. No. 2460, 244 C.C.C. (3d) 438 (Ont. C.A.).

[15] See *R. v. Whitmore*, [1987] O.J. No. 102, 41 C.C.C. (3d) 555 at 562-563 (Ont. H.C.J.), affd [1989] O.J. No. 1611, 51 C.C.C. (3d) 294 (Ont. C.A.); *R. v. Jean Talon Fashion Center Inc.* (1975), 22 C.C.C. (2d) 223 at 227-28 (Que. S.C.); *Casey v. Automobiles Renault Can. Ltd.*, [1963] N.S.J. No. 5, [1964] 3 C.C.C. 208 at 222-23 (N.S.S.C.), revd [1965] S.C.J. No. 33 (S.C.C.).

[16] *R. v. Kalanj*, [1989] S.C.J. No. 71, [1989] 1 S.C.R. 1594 at 1607 (S.C.C.) (addressing the question in deciding the point at which the clock begins to run under s. 11(*b*) of the *Canadian Charter of Rights and Freedoms*, Part I of the *Constitution Act, 1982*, being Schedule B to the *Canada Act 1982* (U.K.), 1982, c. 11 [*Charter*], the right once "*charged* with an offence" to be "tried be within a reasonable time").

form of judicial screening occurs when the time comes to confirm or issue process.

§5.10 Informations are ordinarily laid by way of personal attendance before a justice. However, the *Code* also allows a "peace officer"[17] to lay an information "by any means of telecommunication that produces a writing."[18] Simply put, this means that a police officer may lay an information by fax or email. If this route is taken the informant does not swear an oath *before* the justice. Instead, the informant makes a statement swearing that all matters contained in the information are true to the officer's knowledge and belief, and this is treated as the equivalent of an oath.[19] This provision is no doubt invaluable for police officers operating in remote regions where the nearest justice may be hundreds of kilometres away.

§5.11 The timing of the laying of the information depends on the manner in which the accused's attendance in court is compelled. If police issue one of their own processes for compelling appearance (*i.e.*, a promise to appear, recognizance or undertaking), the information will be laid after this is done and (usually immediately) before police apply for a court order confirming the process they have issued. If police arrest the accused and hold him or her in custody, the information will be laid after the arrest and before the accused's first court appearance. Lastly, if police seek to compel appearance through a court-issued process (*i.e.*, a summons or arrest warrant), they will lay the information (usually immediately) before applying for that process. Each of these procedures is explained in the sections below.

3. CONFIRMING OR CANCELLING POLICE ISSUED PROCESS

§5.12 As explained in detail in Chapter 2, Part 4(4)(*h*), other than for the most serious offences (such as murder), even though they intend to charge a person with a crime, the police may be obligated either not to arrest or release following an arrest. Generally speaking, police should only hold a person in custody if they have reasonable grounds to believe that either (*i*) the person's detention is necessary in the "public interest" or (*ii*) the person will fail to attend court in answer to the charge.[20] In assessing the "public interest" the police must consider "all the circumstances", including the need to establish identity, secure or preserve evidence, or prevent the continuation of the offence or the commission of some other crime.[21] (As explained more fully in Chapter 2, Part 4(4)(*h*), §2.188, there are rarely any consequences for police non-compliance with these release

---

[17] "Peace officer" is defined in s. 2 of the *Criminal Code* to include police officers as well as several other officials charged with law enforcement duties.

[18] *Criminal Code*, s. 508.1(1).

[19] *Criminal Code*, s. 508.1(2).

[20] *Criminal Code*, ss. 495(2), 497(1), (1.1), 498(1), (1.1).

[21] *Criminal Code*, ss. 495(2), 497(1), (1.1), 498(1), (1.1).

obligations, given that the police are deemed to be acting lawfully for the purpose of criminal proceedings.)

§5.13 If the police decide not to hold a person in custody, they may compel his or her attendance in court by means of an appearance notice,[22] a promise to appear[23] or a recognizance entered into before an officer in charge.[24] Where a peace officer or the officer in charge decides to release by having the accused give a promise to appear or enter a recognizance, he or she may also require the accused to enter into an undertaking with conditions.[25] In addition, in certain circumstances, a summons may be used,[26] the issuance of which is dealt with below.

§5.14 With each of these various forms of police issued process, section 505 of the *Code* requires that the information actually charging the offence be "laid before a justice as soon as practicable thereafter and in any event before the time stated in the appearance notice, promise to appear or recognizance issued to or given or entered into by the accused for his attendance in court."[27] The goal of this provision is to ensure that the information is in fact before the court when the accused attends on the date that he or she is directed to do so. However, failure to comply with section 505 does not invalidate the information or result in a loss of jurisdiction over the offence. Rather, the consequences are limited to situations where the accused does not attend court. If that happens, non-compliance with section 505 will obviate any charge of failure to appear and preclude the court from issuing an arrest warrant. If the accused does attend court, however, the deficiency in process becomes irrelevant and the court obtains jurisdiction over the accused with respect to the charge(s).[28]

§5.15 After the information is laid, the justice's role shifts from ministerial to judicial in deciding whether to confirm or cancel the process issued by police.[29]

---

[22] *Criminal Code*, s. 496. See *Criminal Code*, Form 9.
[23] *Criminal Code*, s. 497, ss. 498(1)(b), 498(1.1). See *Criminal Code*, Form 10.
[24] *Criminal Code*, ss. 498(1)(c), 498(1.1). See *Criminal Code*, Form 11.
[25] *Criminal Code*, s. 503(2.1). See *Criminal Code*, Forms 11.1 and 12.
[26] Specifically, following an arrest for an absolute jurisdiction, hybrid or summary offence or any other offence that is punishable by imprisonment for five years or less, the officer in charge of the station must release the person arrested with the intention of compelling his or her appearance in court by way of a summons, unless the officer in charge reasonably believes that detention is necessary for public interest or court attendance reasons. See *Criminal Code*, ss. 498(1)(*a*), 498(1.1.).
[27] *Criminal Code*, s. 505.
[28] See *R. v. Markovic*, [2005] O.J. No. 4286, 200 C.C.C. (3d) 449 at paras. 19-29 (Ont. C.A.), leave to appeal refused [2005] S.C.C.A. No. 530 (S.C.C.); *R. v. Naylor*, [1978] O.J. No. 1131, 42 C.C.C. (2d) 12 at 18-19 (Ont. C.A.); *R. v. Gougeon*, [1980] O.J. No. 1342, 55 C.C.C. (2d) 218 at 230-31 (Ont. C.A.). But see *R. v. Brown*, [1983] N.J. No. 3, 44 Nfld. & P.E.I.R. 38 (Nfld. C.A.) (finding that the information was a nullity). See also *R. v. Oliveira*, [2009] O.J. No. 1002, 243 C.C.C. (3d) 217 at para. 40 (Ont. C.A.) (concluding that once the accused appeared in court in answer to the charge, non-compliance with s. 505 did not affect the validity of an undertaking).
[29] See *Criminal Code*, s. 508. Although the cases all deal with the issuance of summonses or warrants under s. 507, the principle would seem to have equal application to the pre-inquiry required under s. 508 for the confirmation of police issued process. On the judicial nature of this

At this point an *in camera*[30] pre-inquiry must be conducted, at which time the justice must hear and consider *ex parte*[31] the allegations of the informant and, if considered desirable or necessary, the evidence of the witnesses.[32] The informant and any witnesses will be sworn and their evidence will be recorded.[33] The level of formality at a pre-inquiry varies depending on the justice and the circumstances of the case.[34]

§5.16 The *Code* provides that where the justice "considers that a case for doing so is made out, whether the information relates to the offence alleged in the appearance notice, promise to appear or recognizance or to an included or other

---

function, see *R. v. Whitmore*, [1987] O.J. No. 102, 41 C.C.C. (3d) 555 at 563-64 (Ont. H.C.J.), affd [1989] O.J. No. 1611, 51 C.C.C. (3d) 294 (Ont. C.A.); *R. v. Bahinipaty*, [1983] S.J. No. 322, 5 C.C.C. (3d) 439 at 445 (Sask. C.A.); *R. v. Allen*, [1974] O.J. No. 998, 20 C.C.C. (2d) 447 at 448 (Ont. C.A.); *Casey v. Automobiles Renault Can. Ltd.*, [1964] N.S.J. No. 5, [1964] 3 C.C.C. 208 at 222-23 (N.S.S.C.), revd [1965] S.C.J. No. 33 (S.C.C.).

[30] The *Code* does not specifically require that the pre-inquiry be held *in camera*, that is, behind closed doors (usually in the justice's chambers), but the analogous provision in s. 507 governing pre-inquiries for the issuances of summonses and warrants has been so interpreted. See *Southam Inc. v. Coulter (judge)*, [1990] O.J. No. 1782, 60 C.C.C. (3d) 267 (Ont. C.A.). The rationale for this holding, protecting the prospective accused against the public airing of unfounded allegations, applies equally to pre-inquiries under s. 508.

[31] *Criminal Code*, s. 508(1)(a). The *ex parte* and *in camera* nature of the pre-inquiry under the analogous s. 507 (which governs the issuance of summonses and warrants) has been upheld under the *Charter*. See *Southam Inc. v. Coulter (judge)*, [1990] O.J. No. 1782, 60 C.C.C. (3d) 267 (Ont. C.A.); *R. v. Whitmore*, [1989] O.J. No. 1611, 51 C.C.C. (3d) 294 (Ont. C.A.), affg [1987] O.J. No. 102, 41 C.C.C. (3d) 555 (Ont. H.C.J.); *R. v. Cohen*, [1976] J.Q. no. 189, 32 C.C.C. (2d) 446 at 449 (Que. C.A.), revd [1979] S.C.J. No. 50 (S.C.C.).

[32] It is a matter within the justice's discretion whether or not to hear witnesses. See *Re Tait*, [1950] B.C.J. No. 38, 98 C.C.C. 241 at 253-54 (B.C.C.A.). The obligation to "hear and consider" the allegations of the informant, however, is mandatory. See *R. v. Jeffrey*, [1976] O.J. No. 1655, 34 C.R.N.S. 283 (Ont. Prov. Ct.).

[33] *Criminal Code* s. 508(2). Case law interpreting the analogous provision in s. 507 governing the issuance of summonses and arrest warrants suggests that evidence taken should be provided to the accused upon request. See *R. v. Cohen*, [1976] J.Q. no. 189, 32 C.C.C. (2d) 446 at 451-52 (Que. C.A.), revd [1979] S.C.J. No. 50 (S.C.C.).

[34] See *R. v. Whitmore*, [1987] O.J. No. 102, 41 C.C.C. (3d) 555 at 565 (Ont. H.C.J.), affd [1989] O.J. No. 1611, 51 C.C.C. (3d) 294 (Ont. C.A.), observing that:

> In most cases, the justice conducting the pre-inquiry will issue process on hearing the allegations of the informant. ... In certain cases, e.g., a charge of driving over 80 mg. or wilful refusal to take a breathalyzer, the mere reading of the information duly sworn by an informant with personal knowledge may satisfy the justice that process should issue, given the specificity of the charge: ...
> In the vast majority of cases, the justice should question the informant, the more so where the informant has only hearsay knowledge of the charge, to decide whether process should issue. Often an inquiry of a few minutes will suffice. In other cases, the inquiry must be more detailed. If the justice is not satisfied that the informant has a sufficient factual basis justifying the issuance of process, the justice must hear the evidence of other witnesses. ... Even though an informant might have sufficient grounds to justify process, the justice may still consider it "desirable" to hear the evidence of other witnesses, especially where the witnesses are alleged accomplices, of disreputable backgrounds, or closely associated to the accused.

offence"[35] he or she is to confirm the process and endorse the information accordingly,[36] or, alternatively, cancel the police process and issue a summons or warrant in its place.[37] If a sufficient case *is not* made out, however, the justice is required to cancel the appearance notice, promise to appear or recognizance and cause the accused to be notified forthwith of the cancellation.[38]

§5.17 On its face, the controlling standard is subjective and vague, turning on whether the justice "considers that a case for doing so is made out".[39] Nevertheless, the Ontario Court of Appeal made this language more concrete by interpreting it as requiring a determination that "there is disclosed by the evidence a *prima facie* case of the offences alleged."[40] This requires that "there is some evidence against the accused on all the essential elements of the charges."[41] This reading is slightly more onerous than the interpretation given by the Supreme Court to the very same language, albeit in *obiter*, which the Court suggested requires "reasonable and probable grounds to believe that the person ... has committed the offence."[42] The standard used, however, likely makes little practical difference.

§5.18 Although in theory the pre-inquiry should serve an important vetting function (protecting individuals from unsubstantiated criminal charges), in practice the procedure tends to be *pro forma*.[43] This is unfortunate, as apart from the preliminary inquiry (which takes place in only a small minority of criminal cases) there is no other stage in the pre-trial process where a neutral arbiter

---

See also *R. v. Ingwer*, [1955] O.J. No. 611, 113 C.C.C. 361 at 65-366 (Ont. H.C.J.); *R. v. Jean Talon Fashion Center Inc.* (1975), 22 C.C.C. (2d) 223 at 228 (Que. S.C.).

[35] *Criminal Code*, s. 508(1)(*b*).

[36] *Criminal Code*, s. 508(1)(*b*)(i).

[37] *Criminal Code*, s. 508(*b*)(ii). The justice might choose to do so, for example, if he or she thinks the police were wrong to release the accused. The process governing the issuance of summonses and warrants is detailed below.

[38] *Criminal Code*, s. 508(1)(*c*). Unfortunately, the *Code* is silent on whether the police may respond to such a development by simply seeking fresh process from of a different justice. The case law dealing with s. 507, the analogous provision relating to the issuance of summonses and warrants, suggests that there is nothing inappropriate in them doing so, at least with the benefit of some new evidence. See *R. v. Allen*, [1974] O.J. No. 998, 20 C.C.C. (2d) 447 at 448 (Ont. C.A.) ("the complainant is entitled to attend before the same or another Justice of the Peace on a subsequent occasion *with additional evidence*, and to request the issue of a summons on the basis of the evidence which is presented on that subsequent day" [emphasis added]). See also *Gilbert Steel Ltd. v. Southwick*, [1967] O.J. No. 1034, [1967] 2 C.R.N.S. 46 (Ont. C.A.).

[39] *Criminal Code*, s. 508(1)(*b*). See Law Reform Commission of Canada, *Compelling Appearance, Interim Release and Pre-trial Detention* (Working Paper 57) (Ottawa: Law Reform Commission of Canada, 1988) (criticizing the ambiguity of the legislative language at 32-34).

[40] *R. v. Whitmore*, [1989] O.J. No. 1611, 51 C.C.C. (3d) 294 at 296 (Ont. C.A.), affg [1987] O.J. No. 102, 41 C.C.C. (3d) 555 (Ont. H.C.J.), interpreting the exact same language found in s. 507(1)(*b*).

[41] *R. v. Grinshpun*, [2004] B.C.J. No. 2371, 190 C.C.C. (3d) 483 at para. 33 (B.C.C.A.), leave to appeal refused [2004] S.C.C.A. No. 579 (S.C.C.) (interpreting the exact same test under s. 507.1(2)).

[42] *R. v. Storrey*, [1990] S.C.J. No. 12, [1990] 1 S.C.R. 241 at para. 14 (S.C.C.) (addressing the analogous language used in s. 507 governing the issuance of summonses and warrants).

[43] Law Reform Commission of Canada, *Controlling Criminal Prosecutions: The Attorney General and the Crown Prosecutor* (Working Paper 62) (Ottawa: Law Reform Commission of Canada, 1990) at 70.

examines the Crown's evidence and decides whether it is sufficient to merit a trial.[44] As discussed in Chapter 8, in practice the only vetting of charges in most cases is that conducted by Crown prosecutors. While they are required to perform this function impartially, the exercise of prosecutorial discretion is no substitute for independent judicial oversight.

§5.19 A breach of the pre-inquiry requirements does not invalidate the information or result in a loss of jurisdiction over the offence. Rather, the consequences are usually limited to situations where the accused does not attend court. If that happens, non-compliance with section 508 will obviate any charge of failure to appear, preclude the court from issuing an arrest warrant or from proceeding with an *ex parte* trial with respect to summary offences.[45] In those rare cases where an accused becomes aware of a significant deficiency, the Ontario Court of Appeal has suggested that an argument could be made at the first appearance that the court lacks jurisdiction over the accused. But where an accused has made several appearances before raising the issue, the court will be said to have obtained jurisdiction, and any deficiency in the confirmation of process will be rendered moot.[46] In contrast, other appellate courts have held that an appearance by the accused in court always cures any defect in the confirmation process.[47]

4.   ISSUING A SUMMONS OR A WARRANT

§5.20 Police who decide to either not arrest or arrest and release a person they intend to charge must obtain a summons from a justice to compel the person's attendance in court.[48] Police who wish to make an arrest, but have not yet done so, may also ask a justice to issue an arrest warrant.[49] This is typically done so that details of the warrant can be registered on the Canadian Police Information Computer (CPIC). Once a warrant issues, any police officer who encounters the

---

[44] See Chapter 9, dealing with preliminary inquiries.

[45] See *R. v. Gougeon*, [1980] O.J. No. 1342, 55 C.C.C. (2d) 218 at 227-28 (Ont. C.A.).

[46] *Ibid.*

[47] See *R. v. Wetmore*, [1976] N.S.J. No. 494, 32 C.C.C. (2d) 347 at (N.S.C.A.) and *R. v. McGinnis*, [1979] A.J. No. 851, 51 C.C.C. (2d) 301 at 305-306 (Alta. C.A.).

[48] Specifically, following an arrest for an absolute jurisdiction, hybrid or summary offence or any other offence that is punishable by imprisonment for five years or less, if the officer in charge of the station believes on reasonable grounds that the various "public interest" factors do not warrant holding the person in custody, then the officer in charge must release the person with the intention of compelling their appearance in court by way of a summons. See *Criminal Code*, R.S.C. 1985, c. C-46, ss. 498(1)(*a*), 498(1.1.). In addition, even where other forms of process have already issued, for example, the police previously issued an individual an appearance notice, promise to appear or had him or her enter into a recognizance before an officer in charge, or even where a summons previously issued, a justice still has the authority to issue a fresh summons if he or she has reasonable and probable grounds to believe that it is necessary in the public interest to do so. See *Criminal Code*, s. 512(1)(*b*).

[49] An arrest warrant may be obtained, however, even if police have either already arrested (and released) the person or issued a process compelling appearance, such as an appearance notice, promise to appear or recognizance. A justice may issue such a warrant when he or she has reasonable and probable grounds to believe that a warrant is necessary in the public interest. See *Criminal Code*, ss. 508(1)(*b*)(ii), 512(1)(*a*).

individual can arrest him or her even if the officer lacks any personal knowledge of the circumstances of the offence.[50] The arrest warrant is therefore an indispensable tool for law enforcement in the quest to apprehend fugitives.

§5.21 As the issuance of summonses and arrest warrants is governed by essentially the same procedure, we deal with them together here. As mentioned above (§5.11), police seeking either order must first lay an information before a justice.[51] After the information is received, the justice's role shifts from ministerial to judicial in deciding whether to issue a summons or warrant.[52] At this point, an *in camera*[53] pre-inquiry is conducted where the justice *must* hear and consider *ex parte* the allegations of the informant and, if considered desirable or necessary, the evidence of the witnesses.[54] The informant and any witnesses will be sworn and their evidence recorded.[55]

§5.22 Just like the standard that governs confirmation of police issued process, the relevant provision provides that a summons or warrant should issue if the justice "considers that a case for so doing is made out".[56] The Ontario Court of Appeal has interpreted this language as requiring a determination that "there is disclosed by the evidence a *prima facie* case of the offences alleged."[57] This requires that "there is some evidence against the accused on all the essential elements" of the charges.[58] *Obiter dictum* from the Supreme Court of Canada, however, suggests a slightly lower threshold, "reasonable and probable grounds to believe that the person to be arrested has committed the offence."[59]

---

50 *Criminal Code*, s. 495(1)(*c*).

51 *Criminal Code*, s. 507(1).

52 See *R. v. Whitmore*, [1987] O.J. No. 102, 41 C.C.C. (3d) 555 at 563-64 (Ont. H.C.J.), affd [1989] O.J. No. 1611, 51 C.C.C. (3d) 294 (Ont. C.A.); *R. v. Dowson*, [1983] S.C.J. No. 68, [1983] 2 S.C.R. 144 at 157 (S.C.C.); *R. v. Jean Talon Fashion Center Inc.* (1975), 22 C.C.C. (2d) 223 at 227-28 (Que. S.C.); *R. v. Allen*, [1974] O.J. No. 998, 20 C.C.C. (2d) 447 at 448 (Ont. C.A.); *Reeves v. Magistrate's Court (Wentworth); R. v. Reeves*, [1964] O.J. No. 763, [1964] 2 O.R. 316 at 318 (Ont. H.C.J.); *Re Tait*, [1950] B.C.J. No. 38, 98 C.C.C. 241 at 244, 248 (B.C.C.A.); *Casey v. Automobiles Renault Can. Ltd.*, [1964] N.S.J. No. 5, [1964] 3 C.C.C. 208 at 222-23 (N.S.S.C.), revd [1965] S.C.J. No. 33 (S.C.C.).

53 Although s. 507(1) does not expressly require an *in camera* proceeding, that is how the provision has been interpreted. See *Southam Inc. v. Coulter (judge)*, [1990] O.J. No. 1782, 60 C.C.C. (3d) 267 (Ont. C.A.).

54 *Criminal Code* s. 507(1)(*a*). The *ex parte* and *in camera* nature of the pre-inquiry has been upheld. See *Southam Inc. v. Coulter (judge)*, [1990] O.J. No. 1782, 60 C.C.C. (3d) 267 (Ont. C.A.); *R. v. Whitmore*, [1989] O.J. No. 1611, 51 C.C.C. (3d) 294 (Ont. C.A.), affg [1987] O.J. No. 102, 41 C.C.C. (3d) 555 (Ont. H.C.J.); *R. v. Cohen*, [1976] Q.J. No. 189, 32 C.C.C. (2d) 446 at 449 (Que. C.A.), revd [1979] S.C.J. No. 50, [1979] 2 S.C.R. 305 (S.C.C.).

55 *Criminal Code* s. 507(3). Upon request the accused is entitled to receive a copy of the evidence taken. See *R. v. Cohen*, [1976] J.Q. no. 189, 32 C.C.C. (2d) 446 at 451-52 (Que. C.A.), revd [1979] S.C.J. No. 50 (S.C.C.).

56 *Criminal Code*, s. 507(1)(*b*).

57 *R. v. Whitmore*, [1989] O.J. No. 1611, 51 C.C.C. (3d) 294 at 296 (Ont. C.A.), affg [1987] O.J. No. 102, 41 C.C.C. (3d) 555 at 568-69 (Ont. H.C.J.) (interpreting same language in s. 507(1)(*b*)).

58 *R. v. Grinshpun*, [2004] B.C.J. No. 2371, 190 C.C.C. (3d) 483 at para. 33 (B.C.C.A.), leave to appeal refused [2004] S.C.C.A. No. 579 (S.C.C.) (interpreting same test under s. 507.1(2)).

59 *R. v. Storrey*, [1990] S.C.J. No. 12, [1990] 1 S.C.R. 241 at para. 14 (S.C.C.).

§5.23 Should a justice decide that police have not established a sufficient case to justify issuing a summons or warrant, the *Code* is silent on whether or not they may simply try again before a different justice; case law suggests that they may, at least with the benefit of additional evidence.[60] Without further evidence, such a response tends to subvert the protective benefit of the pre-inquiry process, however limited it may be.

§5.24 Under section 507(1) the justice has discretion whether or not to hear from the witnesses.[61] But the requirement that the justice "*shall* ... hear and consider ... the allegations of the informant" is clearly mandatory. Some lower courts have held that the failure to abide by this requirement renders the resulting process a nullity, with the consequence that the court would not properly secure jurisdiction over the accused.[62] In contrast, at least two provincial appellate courts have held that any procedural deficiency does not result in a loss of jurisdiction over the offence, but rather, merely the person, and that it is of no consequence if the accused appears in answer to the charge.[63] The Ontario Court of Appeal has taken a middle position, holding that non-compliance with the pre-inquiry requirement entitles an accused to raise an objection on the first appearance but not thereafter.[64]

§5.25 In deciding between issuing a summons or a warrant, the justice is directed to prefer a summons, unless the evidence "discloses reasonable grounds to believe that it is necessary in the public interest to issue a warrant for the arrest of the accused."[65] The term "public interest" is not defined, but in the bail context it has been found to import an unconstitutionally vague standard.[66] Nevertheless, its use in the context of section 507 has been upheld as constitutional because its underlying purpose serves to animate the meaning of "public interest".[67] In *Budreo v. R.*,[68] the Court thus interpreted the phrase to mean "assuring that the suspect (i) will attend, and (ii) will not commit offences prior to appear-

---

60   See *R. v. Allen*, [1974] O.J. No. 998, 20 C.C.C. (2d) 447 at 448 (Ont. C.A.) ("the complainant is entitled to attend before the same or another Justice of the Peace on a subsequent occasion *with additional evidence*, and to request the issue of a summons on the basis of the evidence which is presented on that subsequent day" [emphasis added]). See also *Gilbert Steel Ltd. v. Southwick*, [1967] O.J. No. 1034, [1967] 2 C.R.N.S. 46 (Ont. C.A.).

61   See *R. v. Jean Talon Fashion Center Inc.* (1975), 22 C.C.C. (2d) 223 at 228 (Que. S.C.); *R. v. Ingwer*, [1955] O.J. No. 611, 113 C.C.C. 361 at 366 (Ont. H.C.J.).

62   See *R. v. Brown* (1975), 28 C.C.C. (2d) 398 at 408-409 (Ont. Prov. Ct.); *R. v. Jeffrey*, [1976] O.J. No. 1655, 34 C.R.N.S. 283 (Ont. Prov. Ct.).

63   See *R. v. Pottle*, [1978] N.J. No. 39, 49 C.C.C. (2d) 113 at 119-20 (Nfld. C.A.); *R. v. Hrankowski*, [1980] A.J. No. 865, 54 C.C.C. (2d) 174 at 180 (Alta. C.A.), leave to appeal refused 35 N.R. 70*n* (S.C.C.).

64   See *R. v. Gougeon*, [1980] O.J. No. 1342, 55 C.C.C. (2d) 218 at 227-28 (Ont. C.A.).

65   *Criminal Code*, s. 507(4).

66   See *R. v. Morales*, [1992] S.C.J. No. 98, [1992] 3 S.C.R. 711 (S.C.C.) (concluding that the part of the former s. 515(10)(*b*), which permitted a denial of bail "in the *public interest*", was unconstitutional because the language was so vague and imprecise that it was incapable of meaningfully framing the legal debate or structuring discretion).

67   See *Budreo v. R.*, [1996] O.J. No. 3, 104 C.C.C. (3d) 245 (Ont. Gen. Div.), affd [2000] O.J. No. 72 (Ont. C.A.).

68   *Ibid.*

ing in court .... [M]atters extraneous to compelling attendance and preventing further illegal conduct," it stressed, "can simply not be read into the provision."[69] A warrant should therefore not issue simply because an arrest will provide police with an opportunity to secure or preserve evidence relating to the offence. (In contrast, this goal remains a permissible basis *for police* to favour an arrest without warrant over some less intrusive means of securing attendance in court.[70])

§5.26 The *Code* specifically contemplates the issuance of an arrest warrant where an accused who was issued a summons, appearance notice, promise to appear or recognizance fails to attend for fingerprinting and photographing as directed,[71] fails to attend court as required[72] or where an individual appears to be evading service of a summons.[73]

§5.27 A summons issues in Form 6.[74] It indicates the offence charged and directs the accused to attend court at a time and date specified and thereafter as required by the court.[75] In addition, a summons may also require the accused person to attend to be fingerprinted and photographed.[76] It must set out the text for the *Criminal Code* offences of failing to attend court and failing to attend for fingerprinting or photographing as required, which essentially puts the recipient on notice that compliance is mandatory.[77] Finally, the summons must either be personally served on the person to whom it is directed or if that person "cannot conveniently be found", left at his or her residence with an occupant who appears at least 16 years of age.[78]

§5.28 An arrest warrant issues in Form 7.[79] It ordinarily names the person to be arrested, briefly sets out the offence charged and orders that the person named be "forthwith" arrested and brought before the court from which the warrant originated.[80] Once issued, an arrest warrant remains in force until executed; that is, until the person who is named in it is arrested.[81] Nevertheless, if the subject of

---

[69] *Ibid.*, at 308.

[70] *Criminal Code*, ss. 495(2)(*d*)(ii), 497(1)(*f*)(ii), 498(1)(ii).

[71] *Criminal Code*, s. 502. Before a warrant can issue in these circumstances, however, the police issued process must first be confirmed under s. 508. Confirmation of process is explained above in Part 3.

[72] See *Criminal Code*, s. 512(2)(*a*), (*b*).

[73] See *Criminal Code*, s. 512(2)(*c*).

[74] See *Criminal Code*, s. 493 and Form 6.

[75] See *Criminal Code*, s. 509(1).

[76] See *Criminal Code*, s. 509(2). Fingerprinting and photographing takes place under the authority of the *Identification of Criminals Act*, R.S.C. 1985, c. I-1.

[77] See *Criminal Code*, s. 509(4).

[78] See *Criminal Code*, s. 509(2).

[79] See *Criminal Code*, s. 493 and Form 7.

[80] See *Criminal Code*, s. 511(1). Although the judge or justice who issues the warrant can exercise his or her discretion to specify a period before which the warrant should not be executed. See *Criminal Code*, s. 511(3). This authority will sometimes be used by judges or justices presiding in remand court to retain jurisdiction over a person who fails to attend and afford him or her an opportunity to voluntarily attorn to the jurisdiction of the court.

[81] See *Criminal Code*, s. 511(2).

the warrant appears voluntarily in court to answer to the charge, then the warrant is deemed executed.[82]

§5.29 Special rules govern the authority of police to enter a dwelling to affect an arrest. This includes the need for a specialized warrant — a *Feeney* warrant — to authorize such entry, unless police are in hot-pursuit or otherwise dealing with exigent circumstances.[83] The authority of police to enter a residence to arrest is explained in detail in Chapter 2, Part 4(5)(g), including the process governing the issuance of *Feeney* warrants.

§5.30 A justice who issues an arrest warrant for an offence, other than for one of the most serious indictable offences (like murder), may endorse the warrant (using Form 29) so as to authorize the accused's release once the warrant is executed.[84] Even with such an endorsement, however, it is the officer in charge of the station where the accused is taken who has authority to decide whether or not to release and the form that the release should take (from a promise to appear to a recognizance, which can include an undertaking with conditions).[85] The justice's endorsement simply lifts the requirement that the individual arrested under the authority of the warrant must be taken before the court in order to be released.

5. ISSUING PROCESS FOR PRIVATELY LAID CHARGES

§5.31 As noted above, the *Code* contemplates that "any one" may lay an information charging another person with an offence.[86] This language invites the laying of charges not only by the police, but also by private individuals. Private prosecutions have a long history at common law, so the decision to maintain them under the *Criminal Code* is rather understandable.[87]

§5.32 In theory, privately laid charges provide an important check on state power. Where government officials fail to act on evidence of criminal wrongdoing, possibly because of bias or corruption, the citizen is empowered to force the airing of such allegations in a public forum.[88] That said, private prosecutions also carry an obvious risk of abuse. It is for this reason that, as we will see below, in practice the Crown can effectively bring such prosecutions to halt before the allegations see the light of day.

§5.33 Until quite recently, police laid charges and privately laid charges were treated in precisely the same manner: a justice was required to conduct the very

---

[82] See *Criminal Code*, s. 511(4).
[83] See *Criminal Code*, ss. 529 through 529.5.
[84] See *Criminal Code*, s. 507(6).
[85] See *Criminal Code*, s. 499.
[86] *Criminal Code*, s. 504.
[87] See generally, Law Reform Commission of Canada, *Private Prosecutions* (Working Paper 52) (Ottawa: Law Reform Commission of Canada, 1986).
[88] *Ibid.*, at 19-20.

same sort of pre-inquiry in deciding whether or not to issue a summons or warrant (see Part 4, above). However, in 2002 the *Code* was amended to impose additional restrictions on the issuance of process for privately laid charges. The apparent motivation for these changes was a concern that private prosecutions were too often initiated for frivolous or vexatious reasons.[89] In *McHale v. Ontario (Attorney General)*,[90] the Ontario Court of Appeal reviewed these relatively new provisions in detail and provided a useful summary on their operation.

§5.34 Today, when a justice receives an information from a private complainant it must be referred to a judge or a specially designated justice.[91] The same legislative standard that applies to police laid charges operates in this context, with the relevant provision providing that the judge or designated justice "who considers that a case for doing so is made out shall issue a summons or warrant."[92] Accordingly, before a summons or a warrant may issue for a privately laid charge, a *prima facie* case for the offence(s) alleged must be established.[93] This requires that "there is some evidence against the accused on all the essential elements of the charges."[94] Although the legal test is the same, there are a number of additional procedural requirements that must be satisfied. Under section 507.1(3), a judge or designated justice may issue a summons or warrant only if he or she:

(*a*) has heard and considered the allegations of the informant and the evidence of witnesses;

(*b*) is satisfied that the Attorney General[95] has received a copy of the information;

(*c*) is satisfied that the Attorney General has received reasonable notice of the hearing under paragraph (*a*); and

---

[89] See *McHale v. Ontario (Attorney General)*, [2010] O.J. No. 2030, 2010 ONCA 361 at para. 65 (Ont. C.A.), leave to appeal refused [2010] S.C.C.A. No. 290 (S.C.C.) [*McHale*], noting that the provision "puts in place several measures to assure scrutiny of prospective private prosecutions to stifle the procession of frivolous or vexatious prosecutions before the courts." See also *R. v. Friesen*, [2008] O.J. No. 1094, 229 C.C.C. (3d) 97 at para. 9 (Ont. S.C.J.).

[90] [2010] O.J. No. 2030, 2010 ONCA 361 (Ont. C.A.), leave to appeal refused [2010] S.C.C.A. No. 290 (S.C.C.).

[91] *Criminal Code*, s. 507.1(1). A "designated justice" means a justice designated for this purpose by the chief judge of the provincial court having jurisdiction in the matter. See *Criminal Code*, s. 507.1(10).

[92] *Criminal Code*, s. 507.1(2).

[93] *Criminal Code*, s. 507(1)(b). See *R. v. Edge*, [2004] A.J. No. 316, 21 C.R. (6th) 361 at paras. 82, 100 (Alta. Prov. Ct.) (holding that because the test is identical to that found in s. 507(4), the jurisprudence governing that provision, in particular the *prima facie* standard, applies equally to this provision).

[94] *R. v. Grinshpun*, [2004] B.C.J. No. 2371, 190 C.C.C. (3d) 483 at para. 33 (B.C.C.A.), leave to appeal refused [2004] S.C.C.A. No. 579 (S.C.C.).

[95] For the purpose of s. 507.1 "Attorney General" includes "the Attorney General of Canada and his or her lawful deputy with respect to proceedings that could have been commenced at the instance of the Government of Canada". See *Criminal Code*, s. 507.1(11).

(*d*) has given the Attorney General an opportunity to attend the hearing under paragraph (*a*) and to cross-examine and call witnesses and to present any relevant evidence at the hearing.

The clear goal of these provisions is to make the pre-inquiry a more meaningful
vehicle for vetting privately laid charges. This is accomplished by requiring *both*
that the allegations of the informant and the evidence of witnesses be heard[96] and
by permitting the Crown to be present to test the evidence. These added requirements will hopefully spare innocent individuals from enduring the stress
and inconvenience of being required to attend court in response to a meritless
charge.

§5.35 If the judge or designated justice decides against issuing a summons or
warrant, the information will be endorsed accordingly. If this happens, a further
pre-inquiry is barred for the same or an included offence "unless there is new
evidence in support of the allegation in respect of which the hearing is sought to
be held."[97] (As noted above there is no similar limitation in place when it comes
to police laid charges.[98])

§5.36 Where the judge or designated justice decides against issuing a summons
or a warrant, the informant may commence proceedings to compel him or her to
do so.[99] The vehicle for this sort of review will be an application in the superior
court seeking a writ of *mandamus* to compel the issuance of process. The responding party on such an application is the Crown.[100] Nevertheless, depending
on the circumstances, the court may require that the prospective accused be
given notice of the hearing.[101] In addition, it has been held that on such a review,
where the privacy interests of the proposed accused are at stake, the *mandamus*
hearing may be ordered to take place *in camera* — that is, with the public
excluded.[102]

§5.37 To succeed on an application for *mandamus* the informant must demonstrate that there has been jurisdictional error or that the justice did not exercise

---

[96]   See *McHale v. Ontario (Attorney General)*, [2010] O.J. No. 2030, 2010 ONCA 361 at para. 47
(Ont. C.A.), leave to appeal refused [2010] S.C.C.A. No. 290 (S.C.C.) (emphasizing the "obligation" on the justice to hear witnesses and contrasting that with the discretionary language applicable to police laid charges). See also *R. v. Edge*, [2004] A.J. No. 316, 21 C.R. (6th) 361 at
paras. 90-91 (Alta. Prov. Ct.).
[97]   *Criminal Code*, s. 507.1(7).
[98]   See §5.23, above.
[99]   *Criminal Code*, s. 507.1(5).
[100] *R. v. Friesen*, [2008] O.J. No. 1094, 229 C.C.C. (3d) 97 at paras. 18-22 (Ont. S.C.J.). See also
Southam Inc. v. Coulter (judge), [1990] O.J. No. 1782, 60 C.C.C. (3d) 267 (Ont. C.A.).
[101] *R. v. Friesen*, [2008] O.J. No. 1094, 229 C.C.C. (3d) 97 at para. 29 (Ont. S.C.J.) (holding that
"[e]ach case should be assessed according to its particular facts and an appropriate order made
by the presiding judge for service of the proposed accused where it would serve the ends of justice or the proposed accused could be served at the option of the Crown if it felt that procedural
fairness demanded it").
[102] *Ibid.*, at paras. 32 through 53. But see *R. v. Parkinson*, [2008] O.J. No. 5340 (Ont. S.C.J.) (suggesting that the better course where privacy concerns are raised is to issue a publication ban
rather than closing the courtroom to the public).

his or her discretion judicially, according to law.[103] If no such proceeding is initiated within six months of the refusal of process[104] or if the informant initiates such proceedings but is unsuccessful[105] then the information in either situation is deemed never to have been laid.

§5.38 If the judge or designated justice decides that a case for doing so is made out, a summons or a warrant may issue. (The same principles that guide the choice between issuing a summons or a warrant for police laid charges should apply equally in this context.[106]) If process does issue, once the accused appears in court the private informant will be responsible for conducting the prosecution.[107] In practice, however, once the accused appears in court the Crown invariably exercises its authority to assume carriage of such cases.[108] After it does so, the Crown has complete discretion over whether or not to proceed with the prosecution; at that point, the matter is completely beyond the control of the informant. The Crown could choose to withdraw the charge (even though the informant wants to proceed) or proceed (even though the informant wants the charge withdrawn).[109]

§5.39 Beyond withdrawal, which must await the issuance of process, the Ontario Court of Appeal has suggested that once an information is laid the "proceedings in relation to an accused ... are commenced" under section 579(1) of the *Code*, thereby triggering the Crown's statutory authority to stay the proceedings; even before the pre-inquiry gets underway.[110] This position, in our view,

---

[103] See *R. v. Grinshpun*, [2004] B.C.J. No. 2371, 190 C.C.C. (3d) 483 at para. 34 (B.C.C.A.), leave to appeal refused [2004] S.C.C.A. No. 579 (S.C.C.), referring to *R. v. Blythe*, [1973] B.C.J. No. 561, 13 C.C.C. (2d) 192 (B.C.S.C.), approved in *R. v. Fry*, [1998] B.C.J. No. 1163 (B.C.C.A.). See *e.g.*, *McHale v. Ontario (Attorney General)*, [2009] O.J. No. 5743, 251 C.C.C. (3d) 283 (Ont. S.C.J.), affd [2010] O.J. No. 2030, 2010 ONCA 361 at para. 65 (Ont. C.A.) (granting *mandamus* where the justice refused to hear the informant's allegations).

[104] *Criminal Code*, s. 507.1(5).

[105] *Criminal Code*, s. 507.1(6).

[106] See Part 4, above.

[107] The *Criminal Code* anticipates this through its definition of "prosecutor", which is defined in s. 2 as meaning "the Attorney General or, where the Attorney General does not intervene, means the person who institutes proceedings to which this Act applies, and includes counsel acting on behalf of either of them".

[108] This authority is derived from common law. See *Krieger v. Law Society of Alberta*, [2002] S.C.J. No. 45, [2002] 3 S.C.R. 372 at para. 46 (S.C.C.) (recognizing that "the core elements of prosecutorial discretion encompass ... the discretion to take control of a private prosecution"). This authority is sometimes also referenced and affirmed in provincial statutes governing Crown attorneys. See *Crown Attorneys Act*, R.S.O. 1990, c. C.49, s. 11(*d*).

[109] See generally, *Krieger v. Law Society of Alberta*, [2002] S.C.J. No. 45, [2002] 3 S.C.R. 372 at para. 46 (S.C.C.). See also *McHale v. Ontario (Attorney General)*, [2010] O.J. No. 2030, 2010 ONCA 361 at paras. 42, 57 (Ont. C.A.), leave to appeal refused [2010] S.C.C.A. No. 290 (S.C.C.); *R. v. Bradley*, [1975] O.J. No. 2374, 9 O.R. (2d) 161 at 169 (Ont. C.A.) The discretion of the Crown in this regard is discussed in greater detail in Chapter 8, which addresses the Prosecutorial Function.

[110] See *McHale v. Ontario (Attorney General)*, [2010] O.J. No. 2030, 2010 ONCA 361 at paras. 83-90 (Ont. C.A.), leave to appeal refused [2010] S.C.C.A. No. 290 (S.C.C.). See also *R. v. Pardo*, [1990] J.Q. no. 2202, 62 C.C.C. (3d) 371 (Que. C.A.) (coming to the very same conclusion under the predecessor regime).

puts form above substance.[111] As the Supreme Court of Canada warned in *R. v. Dowson*:[112]

> The power to stay is a necessary one but one which encroaches upon the citizen's fundamental and historical right to inform under oath a Justice of the Peace of the commission of a crime. Parliament has seen fit to impose upon the justice an obligation to "hear and consider" the allegation and make a determination. In the absence of a clear and unambiguous text taking away the right, it should be protected. This is particularly true when considering a text of law that is open to an interpretation that favours the exercise of that right whilst amply accommodating the policy consideration that supports the power to stay. When one adds to these considerations the fact that, apart from the court's control, the only one left is that of the legislative branch of government, given a choice, any interpretation of the law, which would have the added advantage of better ensuring the Attorney General's accountability by enhancing the legislative capacity to superintend the exercise of his power, should be preferred.[113]

§5.40 In light of these comments, if Crown prosecutors were meant to have the power to stay charges before a pre-inquiry is undertaken, one would expect that Parliament would have included express reference to such authority in section 507.1.

6.   TAKING THOSE ARRESTED BEFORE A JUSTICE WITHIN 24 HOURS

§5.41 Once arrested, a person who is not released by police must be taken before a justice "without unreasonable delay".[114] Unfortunately, the relevant section does not specify the sorts of delays that are reasonable and unreasonable.

§5.42 Delays occasioned to secure or preserve evidence would appear to be reasonable due to other provisions in the *Criminal Code* specifically authorizing the police to hold those arrested for such purposes.[115] For example, it would seem to be entirely reasonable for police to delay the first court appearance so

---

[111] At first blush, this conclusion also appears to be contrary to a prior Supreme Court's holding in *R. v. Dowson*, [1983] S.C.J. No. 68, [1983] 2 S.C.R. 144 at 157 (S.C.C.) that "[T]he Attorney General's power to stay starts as of the moment a summons or warrant is issued." In concluding that *Dowson* is not controlling, the Court in *McHale* noted that the language under the predecessor to s. 579(1) (what was then s. 508(1)), had changed, with the authority to stay previously only attaching "at any time after an indictment has been found". See *McHale v. Ontario (Attorney General)*, [2010] O.J. No. 2030, 2010 ONCA 361 at paras. 85-86 (Ont. C.A.), leave to appeal refused [2010] S.C.C.A. No. 290 (S.C.C.).

[112] [1983] S.C.J. No. 68, [1983] 2 S.C.R. 144 (S.C.C.).

[113] *Ibid.*, at 155 (S.C.R.).

[114] *Criminal Code*, s. 503(1)(a) ("where a justice is available within a period of *twenty-four hours* after the person has been arrested ... the person *shall* be taken before a justice *without unreasonable delay* and *in any event within that period*") [emphasis added].

[115] *Criminal Code*, ss. 495(2)(*d*)(ii), 497(1.1)(*a*)(ii), 498(1.1)(*a*)(ii).

that they can fingerprint and photograph the suspect, carry out an identification line-up or conduct an interrogation.[116]

§5.43 The *Code* does, however, impose a 24-hour time limit on such post-arrest police controlled detentions.[117] As Justice Martin explained on behalf of the Ontario Court of Appeal:

> ... a police officer who arrests a person does not have an unqualified right to keep such person in custody for the purposes of investigation for a period of twenty-four hours before taking such person before a Justice. Section 454(1) [now section 503(1)] of the *Criminal Code* requires the police officer who has arrested a person with or without a warrant to take such person before a Justice *without unreasonable delay* and in any event within twenty-four hours if a Justice is available within that period.[118]

In other words, 24 hours is the *outer* limit.[119] In the absence of some reasonable justification for delay,[120] the police are required to bring the accused before the court sooner rather than later.

§5.44 If police fail to respect this statutory requirement the resulting detention will become unlawful. According to the Supreme Court of Canada's recent judgment in *R. v. Grant*,[121] an unlawful detention is necessarily arbitrary and will violate section 9 of the *Charter*.[122] Important for the purposes of section 503(1)(*a*) is the Court's direction in *Grant* that earlier appellate court decisions suggesting that an unlawful detention is not necessarily arbitrary should no longer be followed.[123] As a result, earlier cases involving section 503(1)(*a*), in

---

[116] See *R. v. Storrey*, [1990] S.C.J. No. 12, [1990] 1 S.C.R. 241 (S.C.C.) (18-hour delay to conduct line-up not unreasonable); *R. v. Fayant*, [1983] M.J. No. 138, 6 C.C.C. (3d) 507 (Man. C.A.) (14-hour delay, during which accused gave a statement, not unreasonable); *R. v. Precourt*, [1976] O.J. No. 2421, 18 O.R. (2d) 714, 39 C.C.C. (2d) 311 (Ont. C.A.) (holding accused arrested at 4:30 p.m. overnight to participate in a line-up the next morning permissible; subsequent holding in police cells after court appearance was not).

[117] *Criminal Code*, s. 503(1)(*a*).

[118] *R. v. Koszulap*, [1974] O.J. No. 726, 20 C.C.C. (2d) 193 at 200-201 (Ont. C.A.) [emphasis in original]. See also *R. v. Precourt*, [1976] O.J. No. 2421, 18 O.R. (2d) 714, 39 C.C.C. (2d) 311 at 318-19 (Ont. C.A.).

[119] See *R. v. Storrey*, [1990] S.C.J. No. 12, [1990] 1 S.C.R. 241 at 256 (S.C.C.).

[120] See *R. v. W. (E.)*, [2002] N.J. No. 226, 168 C.C.C. (3d) 38 at para. 16 (Nfld. C.A.) (delay may be justified for investigative reasons but "investigation must, in fact, be underway and continuing."). There is no abstract entitlement on the part of police to hold individuals for up to 24 hours; delays must be justified. See *R. v. Holmes*, [2002] O.J. No. 4178, 169 C.C.C. (3d) 344 at para. 22 (Ont. C.A.) ("the obligation on the police under [now] s. 503(1) is to bring the arrestee before a justice without unreasonable delay. The police have no power to detain a person under this section for 24 hours for investigation. In this case, there was no evidence offered as to why the appellant was not taken before a justice of the peace.").

[121] [2009] S.C.J. No. 32, [2009] 2 S.C.R. 353 (S.C.C.).

[122] *R. v. Grant*, [2009] S.C.J. No. 32, [2009] 2 S.C.R. 353 at para. 54 (S.C.C.) ("a detention not authorized by law is arbitrary and violates s. 9").

[123] The Court specifically cited *R. v. Duguay*, [1985] O.J. No. 2492, 18 C.C.C. (3d) 289 at 296 (Ont. C.A.), affd [1989] S.C.J. No. 4 (S.C.C.), which had held that not every unlawful detention is necessarily arbitrary and required a consideration of the detaining officer's mindset, an oblique motive would result in finding an arbitrary detention but an honest mistake based on

which courts looked to the reasons why policed failed to meet the 24-hour time limit in deciding whether or not section 9 of the *Charter* was violated, should no longer be followed.[124] To the extent that the police have a good excuse for missing the deadline, such explanations should now be considered when deciding on the appropriate remedy under section 24 of the *Charter*.

§5.45 Depending on any mitigating circumstances, the legal implications if the police fail to comply with their legal obligation under section 503(1)(*a*) may be significant. For example, there is case law holding that an unlawful delay can be taken into consideration when assessing whether a statement was voluntarily given.[125] In addition, if evidence is acquired as a result of the delay then it could be excluded under section 24(2) of the *Charter*.[126] In some cases, the remedy ordered has been a substantial reduction in the sentence that would otherwise be appropriate.[127] In more extreme cases, for example, where non-compliance is the result of a larger systemic failure, a stay of the proceedings has been ordered.[128]

§5.46 As mentioned above, when an accused is arrested and held by police the information will be laid at some point prior to the first court appearance. In these circumstances there is no pre-inquiry. Instead, the accused is entitled to a bail hearing. Bail is the subject of the next chapter.

---

grounds just short of those required by the law might not. See *R. v. Grant*, [2009] S.C.J. No. 32, [2009] 2 S.C.R. 353 at para. 55 (S.C.C.).

[124] See *e.g.*, *R. v. Tam*, [1995] B.C.J. No. 1428, 100 C.C.C. (3d) 196 (B.C.C.A.) (detention unlawful but not arbitrary where requirement missed by an hour and half for good logistical reasons).

[125] See *R. v. Koszulap*, [1974] O.J. No. 726, 20 C.C.C. (2d) 193 (Ont. C.A.) (non-compliance contributed to finding of involuntariness). See also *R. v. Holmes*, [2002] O.J. No. 4178, 169 C.C.C. (3d) 344 (Ont. C.A.) (new trial ordered where trial judge failed to consider unexplained non-compliance with s. 503(1)(*a*) in ruling statement voluntary). The effect of unlawful detention in deciding voluntariness under the confessions rule is also discussed in Chapter 4, Part 2.

[126] See *R. v. Mangat*, [2006] O.J. No. 2418, 209 C.C.C. (3d) 225 (Ont. C.A.) (statement excluded after accused held in custody for just over 24 hours so police could continue interrogation); *R. v. Ansari*, [2008] B.C.J. No. 2411, 2008 BCSC 1492 (B.C.S.C.) (statement excluded where accused held in custody for just slightly over 24 hours and is purportedly "taken before" a justice by means of telephone). But see *R. v. W. (E.)*, [2002] N.J. No. 226, 168 C.C.C. (3d) 38 (Nfld. C.A.) (confession obtained during breach of s. 503(1)(*a*) and s. 9 of the *Charter* causally attenuated from violation and exclusion under s. 24(2) refused).

[127] See *R. v. Charles*, [1987] S.J. No. 489, 36 C.C.C. (3d) 286 (Sask. C.A.) (36-hour delay warrants substantial reduction in sentence); *R. v. Macpherson*, [1995] N.B.J. No. 277, 100 C.C.C. (3d) 216 (N.B.C.A.) (two-day delay warrants reduction in sentence from six to three months); *R. v. Rashid*, [2009] O.J. No. 957, 243 C.C.C. (3d) 318 (Ont. S.C.J.) (accused held for slightly more than 24 hours granted enhanced credit for pre-trial custody). But see *R. v. Nasogaluak*, [2010] S.C.J. No. 6, [2010] 1 S.C.R. 206 (S.C.C.) (questioning the need to resort to s. 24(1) to take *Charter* violations into account in sentencing). *Charter* remedies are discussed in detail in Chapter 10.

[128] See *R. v. Simpson*, [1994] N.J. No. 69, 88 C.C.C. (3d) 377 (Nfld. C.A.), revd [1995] S.C.J. No. 12, [1995] 1 S.C.R. 449 (S.C.C.) (stay upheld where accused brought before justice 48 hours after arrest as a result of a systemic failure to have justices of the peace available for such purposes on weekends). But see *R. v. Erickson*, [1984] B.C.J. No. 1768, 13 C.C.C. (3d) 269 (B.C.C.A.) (three-day delay not warranting stay given the seriousness of charges and absence of police malice).

§5.47 After an accused is taken to court the Code contemplates that any subsequent detention should be in a provincial remand centre pursuant to court order, not in police holding cells. As a result, it would be improper for police to return an individual to their custody after he or she appears in court.[129]

---

[129] See *R. v. Precourt* (1976), 18 O.R. (2d) 714, 39 C.C.C. (2d) 311 at 318-23 (Ont. C.A.).

Chapter 6

BAIL

1. INTRODUCTION

§6.1 "Bail" (or in the language of the *Criminal Code*,[1] "judicial interim release") is the term used to describe an accused person's custodial status pending trial. Other than determining guilt or innocence, whether an individual charged with a crime is released or detained before trial is undoubtedly the most important judgment in the criminal process.

§6.2 If bail is refused, the impact on detainees can be profound. They are held in maximum-security facilities, where personal searches, overcrowding and lengthy lockdowns are common.[2] In addition, pre-trial custody may jeopardize a suspect's employment, result in a loss of residence, undermine personal or family relationships and interfere with the ability to prepare a defence. Studies have also shown that those subject to pre-trial detention are more likely to plead guilty, be found guilty after trial and receive harsher sentences if convicted.[3] There is also troubling evidence that (controlling for other variables) blacks are more likely to be detained before trial than whites.[4]

---

[1] R.S.C. 1986, c. C-46 [*Code*].

[2] See *R. v. Wust*, [2000] S.C.J. No. 19, [2000] 1 S.C.R. 455 at paras. 28-31, 41 (S.C.C.); *R. v. Rezaie*, [1996] O.J. No. 4468, 112 C.C.C. (3d) 97 at para. 25 (Ont. C.A.); *R. v. McDonald*, [1998] O.J. No. 2990, 127 C.C.C. (3d) 57 at para. 48 (Ont. C.A.); *R. v. Johnson*, [2011] O.J. No. 822, 2011 ONCJ 77 at paras. 26-28 (Ont. C.J.).

[3] See generally, Report of the Canadian Committee on Corrections: Towards Unity: Criminal Justice and Corrections (Ottawa: Queen's Printer, 1969) at 101-102 (Chair: Roger Ouimet); Martin L. Friedland, *Detention Before Trial: A Study of Criminal Cases Tried in the Toronto Magistrates' Courts* (Toronto: University of Toronto Press, 1965) at 60-62, 101-102, 110-25; Gary T. Trotter, *The Law of Bail in Canada*, 3d ed. (Toronto: Thomson Carswell, 2010) at 1-37 to 1-58; Pamela Koza & Anthony N. Doob, "The Relationship of Pre-Trial Custody to the Outcome of a Trial" (1974-75) 17 Crim. L.Q. 391; Hon. Marc Rosenberg, "The Attorney General and the Administration of Criminal Justice" (2009) 34 Queen's L.J. 813 at 857-61. The Canadian judiciary has frequently recognized pre-trial detention's adverse effects. See *R. v. McDonald*, [1998] O.J. No. 2990, 127 C.C.C. (3d) 57 at paras. 32-34, 48 (Ont. C.A.); *R. v. Wust*, [2000] S.C.J. No. 19, [2000] 1 S.C.R. 455 at 470-72, 477-78 (S.C.C.); *R. v. Hall*, [2002] S.C.J. No. 65, [2002] 3 S.C.R. 309 at paras. 58-59 (S.C.C.), Iacobucci J., dissenting; *Toronto Star Newspapers Ltd. v. Canada*, [2010] S.C.J. No. 21, [2010] 1 S.C.R. 721, 2010 SCC 21 at paras. 10-11 (S.C.C.) [*Toronto Star*].

[4] See Ontario, *Commission on Systemic Racism in the Ontario Criminal Justice System* (Toronto: Queen's Printer for Ontario, 1995) at 143 (concluding that "pre-trial detention of white and black persons charged with the same offence type reveals evidence of differential treatment across the entire sample").

§6.3 Today, bail is governed by Part XVI of the *Criminal Code*, which is the direct descendent of liberalizing reforms ushered in by the *Bail Reform Act*[5] of 1970. Over the intervening years, however, there have been some significant changes, mostly prompted by decisions from the Supreme Court of Canada invaliding statutory provisions declared inconsistent with section 11(*e*) of the *Canadian Charter of Rights and Freedoms*.[6] That constitutional provision guarantees that: "[a]ny person charged with an offence has the right not to be denied reasonable bail without just cause."

§6.4 This chapter is divided into three parts. In the first part, we briefly canvas the historic evolution of bail, from its origins at common law to the present day. The second (and largest) part of the chapter provides an overview of the contemporary rules governing bail in Canada. Here, the focus will be on bail granted through the courts. As explained in Chapter 2, the decision by police to lay a criminal charge will not necessarily result in an individual being arrested and held in custody. In all but the most serious cases, the police have considerable discretion in deciding whether or not to release an individual or hold him or her in custody for a bail hearing. (So-called "police bail" was dealt with in Chapter 2, Part 4(4)(*h*), given its close relationship to police arrest powers.) In the final part of the chapter, we examine the requirements of section 11(*e*) of the *Charter* and its impact on the law of bail in Canada.

2. HISTORY

§6.5 The concept of bail can be traced to medieval England. The practice grew out of necessity. At the time, sheriffs had the responsibility of housing and feeding those charged with crimes while they awaited trial. To free themselves of this burden they began to bail prisoners to sureties. A surety was someone who agreed to take responsibility for the accused and ensure his or her attendance in court to answer the charge. The surety would usually deposit or pledge money or property and agreed to forfeit it if the accused failed to appear for trial. Unfortunately, some sheriffs exploited their control over bail for their own gain.[7]

§6.6 Early reform came in 1275 with the *Statute of Westminster*, which limited the discretion of sheriffs with respect to the bail. Although sheriffs still had the authority to fix the amount of bail required, the statute stipulated which crimes were bailable and which ones were not. Over the next two centuries the sheriff's power over bail was gradually transferred to justices of the peace through a series of statutes.[8]

---

5   S.C. 1970-71-72, c. 37.

6   Part I of the *Constitution Act, 1982*, being Schedule B to the *Canada Act 1982* (U.K.), 1982, c. 11 [*Charter*].

7   See generally, Gary T. Trotter, *The Law of Bail in Canada*, 3d ed. (Toronto: Thomson Carswell, 2010) at 1-2 to 1-4. For contemporary judicial recognition of this history, see *Toronto Star Newspapers Ltd. v. Canada*, [2010] S.C.J. No. 21, [2010] 1 S.C.R. 721, 2010 SCC 21 at para. 9 (S.C.C.).

8   Gary T. Trotter, *The Law of Bail in Canada*, 3d ed. (Toronto: Thomson Carswell, 2010) at 1-4 to 1-6.

§6.7 In Canada, the surety has continued to remain a part of the bail process to the present day. (The contemporary role of sureties in Canada is explained below in Part 3(4)). Unlike in the United States, there are no bail bondsmen in Canada. In fact, it is a crime to pay or accept a fee in return for serving as a surety.[9] As a result, this role is usually reserved for relatives or close acquaintances of the person charged.

§6.8 As mentioned, the current legislative scheme governing bail found its genesis in the *Bail Reform Act*.[10] That statute occasioned a host of changes to the *Criminal Code*, adding what is now Part XVI, which is peppered with provisions that make clear a legislated preference for pre-trial release over pre-trial detention. These changes came about in direct response to what were perceived to be major shortcomings in our former bail system.

§6.9 The work of Professor Martin Friedland provided the impetus for these changes. During the 1960s, at a time when pre-trial procedures were largely ignored by the Canadian legal academy, Professor Friedland undertook a groundbreaking study of intake and bail procedures at the Old City Hall courthouse in Toronto.[11] His findings were profoundly important to law reform in this area. For example, he found that although police officers had the discretion to release and summon those who they charged with an offence, they overwhelmingly favoured the use of arrest. His study found that over a five-year period the police arrested and held 91 to 97 per cent of individuals whom they could have released and summoned.[12] According to Professor Friedland, beyond concerns about public safety and the potential for flight, the decision of police to hold arrestees was often driven by a desire to avoid paperwork as well as a punitive mindset on the part of some officers.

[handwritten margin note: Prof Friedland .]

§6.10 Unfortunately, the situation did not improve after police brought arrestees to court for a bail hearing. At the time, bail was a highly discretionary matter. Under the controlling *Code* provision, it was presumed that an accused person would be detained prior to trial unless he or she applied for bail.[13] The *Code* gave virtually no guidance to judges or magistrates in deciding whether or not to order the accused's release.[14] Although case law had served to establish criteria

---

9   See *Criminal Code*, R.S.C. 1985, c. C-46, ss. 139(1)(*a*), (*b*) [*Code*].
10   S.C. 1970-71-72, c. 37.
11   See Martin L. Friedland, *Detention Before Trial: A Study of Criminal Cases Tried in the Toronto Magistrates' Courts* (Toronto: University of Toronto Press, 1965). The transformative impact of Professor Friedland's work has been acknowledged by the Supreme Court of Canada. See *R. v. Hall*, [2002] S.C.J. No. 65, [2002] 3 S.C.R. 309 at para. 57 (S.C.C.), Iacobucci J., dissenting and *Toronto Star Newspapers Ltd. v. Canada*, [2010] S.C.J. No. 21, [2010] 1 S.C.R. 721, 2010 SCC 21 at para. 10 (S.C.C.).
12   Martin L. Friedland, *Detention Before Trial: A Study of Criminal Cases Tried in the Toronto Magistrates' Courts* (Toronto: University of Toronto Press, 1965) at 9.
13   See *Criminal Code*, S.C. 1953-54, c. 51 (as amended by S.C. 1960-61, c. 43), s. 463(1).
14   *Ibid.*, s. 463(3) provided, "The judge or magistrate may, upon production of any material that he considers necessary upon the application, order that the accused be admitted to bail ...."

to direct the exercise of discretion, the jurisprudence eventually came to reflect a strong preference for pre-trial custody.[15]

§6.11 Professor Friedland's assessment of this evidence was damning. The bail system, he asserted, "falls far short of any reasonable standard."[16] "Little, if any thought," he added, "is given to the purposes to be accomplished by the granting or denying of bail."[17] In effect, he concluded, the system is "often subverted into a form of punishment before trial."[18]

§6.12 Many of Professor Friedland's concerns were ultimately echoed in the *Ouimet Report*,[19] whose recommendations for sweeping reforms led directly to the enactment of the *Bail Reform Act*[20] in 1970.[21] It is that statute that continues to supply the framework for the modern law of bail in Canada. Briefly stated, the *Criminal Code* now requires police to bring arrestees before a justice without unreasonable delay and directs that justice to release them unless the Crown demonstrates (on the basis of limited grounds) the necessity for continued detention.[22] The legislation promised to create, as the Supreme Court has put it, a "'liberal and enlightened system of pre-trial release'...under which an accused must normally be granted bail."[23]

§6.13 Whether this promise has been realized is far from clear. At present, approximately one in four people who are charged with a criminal offence are detained before trial.[24] There is reason to think that this percentage is too high. Revisiting the subject three decades after the *Bail Reform Act*, Professor Friedland noted the following:

> The pendulum has swung too far in the direction of requiring sureties rather than using release on one's own recognizance. In England, sureties are required in only a small fraction of the cases. About two thirds of those who

---

[15] For an overview of the case law from that period, see Gary T. Trotter, *The Law of Bail in Canada*, 3d ed. (Toronto: Thomson Carswell, 2010) at 1-8 to 1-10.

[16] Martin L. Friedland, *Detention Before Trial: A Study of Criminal Cases Tried in the Toronto Magistrates' Courts* (Toronto: University of Toronto Press, 1965) at 175.

[17] *Ibid.*

[18] *Ibid.*

[19] Report of the Canadian Committee on Corrections: Towards Unity: Criminal Justice and Corrections (Ottawa: Queen's Printer, 1969) at 101-102 (Chair: Roger Ouimet) at 108-15.

[20] S.C. 1970-71-72, c. 37.

[21] See generally, Gary T. Trotter, *The Law of Bail in Canada*, 3d ed. (Toronto: Thomson Carswell, 2010) at 1-10 to 1-13. See also *Toronto Star Newspapers Ltd. v. Canada*, [2010] S.C.J. No. 21, [2010] 1 S.C.R. 721, 2010 SCC 21 at paras. 10-13 (S.C.C.).

[22] See *Toronto Star Newspapers Ltd. v. Canada*, [2010] S.C.J. No. 21, [2010] 1 S.C.R. 721, 2010 SCC 21 at para. 13 (S.C.C.).

[23] *R. v. Morales*, [1992] S.C.J. No. 98, [1992] 3 S.C.R. 711 at para. 11 (S.C.C.), quoting *R. v. Bray*, [1983] O.J. No. 2509, 2 C.C.C. (3d) 325 at 328 (Ont. C.A.).

[24] See Juristat: Canadian Centre for Justice Statistics, *Adult Correctional Services in Canada, 1999/00* (Statistics Canada: Ottawa, 2001) (Catalogue No. 85-002-XPE01005), Vol. 21 no. 5. In fact, the rate at which accused persons in Canada are held in custody awaiting trial has been steadily increasing over the last 20 years, from 15 per 100,000 people in 1987 to 39 per 100,000 people in 2007. See generally, Cheryl Marie Webster, Anthony N. Doob & Nicole M. Myers, "The Parable of Ms. Baker: Understanding Pre-Trial Detention in Canada" (2009) 21 *Current Issues in Criminal Justice* 79.

appear for a bail hearing in Toronto today are required to find sureties and only about half of this number are actually released. The other half, it appears, could not find acceptable sureties. Less than 10% held for a bail hearing are released on their own undertaking or recognizance.

What appears to be happening is that the requirement to find sureties has taken the place of cash bail as a method of holding accused persons in custody. The majority of persons who are caught up in the criminal justice system, many of whom are not from the community where they are arrested, have difficulty finding sureties.[25]

In short, as the Ontario Court of Appeal recently acknowledged, "[t]here may now be an over reliance on sureties."[26]

3. CURRENT LEGISLATIVE SCHEME

§6.14 As discussed in detail in Chapter 5, Part 6, persons who are arrested and not released by police must normally be brought before a justice in provincial court within 24 hours.[27] Unless the accused pleads guilty or is charged with one of the offences listed in section 469 of the *Criminal Code*,[28] the justice will decide the question of bail.[29] If the accused is charged with a section 469 offence, the justice must order the accused to be detained in custody.[30] Thereafter the accused wishing to be released on bail must make an application for release in the superior court.[31] In the following sections we outline the procedures governing both regimes.

(1) Role of Justices of the Peace

§6.15 As mentioned, for all offences except murder and the other crimes listed in section 469 of the *Criminal Code*, the authority to make bail determinations is given to a "justice". Section 2 defines "justice" as including both justices of the peace and provincial court judges. As a result, in many provinces, justices of the peace are routinely tasked with deciding whether to release an accused on bail. (As explained in Part 3(10)(*b*), below, the initial bail decision may be reviewed by a superior court judge.) As a result, for many accused persons it is a justice of the peace who will decide their custodial status pending trial.

---

[25] Martin L. Friedland, "Criminal Justice in Canada Revisited" (2004) 48 C.L.Q. 419 at 433-34.
[26] *Canada (Attorney General) v. Horvath*, [2009] O.J. No. 4308, 248 C.C.C. (3d) 1 at para. 47 (Ont. C.A.)
[27] *Criminal Code*, s. 503(1)(*a*).
[28] Practically speaking, the only relevant offence in this list is murder. The other offences (treason, alarming Her Majesty, intimidating Parliament or a legislature, inciting to mutiny, sedition, piracy and piratical acts) are extremely rare.
[29] *Criminal Code*, s. 510(1). As discussed below in Part 3(5), as a consequence of adjournments this decision may not be made for several days.
[30] *Criminal Code*, s. 515(11).
[31] *Criminal Code*, s. 522(1).

§6.16 Throughout Canada, it is not a precondition to being appointed a justice of the peace that an individual be a lawyer or have a law degree.[32] Given this, it is absolutely essential that the selection process for justices of the peace be meaningful and that those appointed receive proper training.[33]

(2) Presumption in Favour of Release and the Ladder Approach

§6.17 As mentioned, the current legislative scheme favours release, at least on a formal level. In circumstances other than those enumerated in sections 469 and 515(6) of the *Criminal Code*,[34] there is a presumption that an accused should be released on an undertaking without conditions. Specifically, section 515(1) of the *Criminal Code* obliges the justice to order an accused's unconditional release unless the Crown "shows cause" why either the accused's detention in custody or that some more restrictive form of release is justified.[35] Consequently, the onus of justifying restrictions on individual liberty ordinarily rests with the prosecutor.[36]

§6.18 Unless the prosecutor shows cause why the detention in custody of the accused is justified, the *Code* contemplates what has been characterized as a "ladder" approach, with the Crown required to specifically justify more restrictive forms of release up each rung of the ladder.[37] The choices escalate from less restrictive to more restrictive, progressing from:

- an undertaking *without* conditions;[38]
- to an undertaking *with* conditions;[39]
- to a recognizance *without* sureties and *without* deposit of money, but *with* conditions;[40]

---

[32] See *e.g.*, *Justice of the Peace Act*, R.S.A. 2000, c. J-4. But see *Justices of the Peace Act*, R.S.O. 1990, c. J.4, s. 2.1, which recently added a requirement of 10 years of work experience and a post-secondary degree.

[33] See Anthony N. Doob, Patricia M. Baranek & Susan M. Addario, *Understanding Justices: A Study of Canadian Justices of the Peace* (Toronto: Centre of Criminology, University of Toronto, 1991) at 61 (noting dearth of formal training in Ontario).

[34] As is explained in Parts 3(6) and 3(7), below, for the offences listed in ss. 469 and 515(6) the onus is reversed.

[35] See *Criminal Code*, s. 515(1).

[36] See generally, *R. v. Pearson*, [1992] S.C.J. No. 99, [1992] 3 S.C.R. 665 at 691 (S.C.C.).

[37] See *Criminal Code*, s. 515(3), which directs that the "justice shall not make an order under any of paragraphs (2)(*b*) to (*e*) unless the prosecution shows cause why an order under the immediately preceding paragraph should be made." See also *R. v. Horvat*, [1972] B.C.J. No. 540, 9 C.C.C. (2d) 1 at 2 (B.C.S.C.). See also *R. v. Thompson*, [1972] B.C.J. No. 400, 7 C.C.C. (2d) 70 at 74 (B.C.S.C.).

[38] *Criminal Code*, s. 515(1). An undertaking is simply a signed document in which the accused "undertakes" (*i.e.*, pledges) to come to court as required. Unlike a "recognizance", an undertaking does not include any pledge of money or valuable security. See *Code*, Form 12.

[39] *Criminal Code*, s. 515(2)(*a*). Essentially, this is the very same sort of document explained above in note 38, except that it also includes conditions. See *Code*, Form 12. Authority over potential conditions that may be included is governed by s. 515(4), (4.1), (4.11), and (4.2). Conditions are discussed below in Part 3(3).

- to a recognizance *with* sureties and *without* deposit but *with* conditions;[41]
- *with* the prosecutor's consent, to a recognizance *without* sureties but *with* a deposit of money in an amount directed by the justice *with* conditions;[42]
- if the accused does not ordinarily reside in the province or does not ordinarily reside within 200 kilometres of the court, on entering a recognizance *with* or *without* sureties, *with* conditions and *with* a deposit of money in an amount directed by the justice.[43]

§6.19 The case law makes clear that where a cash deposit is determined to be appropriate the amount set should not be so high as to effectively amount to a detention order. In other words, the ability of the accused (and any sureties) to raise the required funds must be taken into account in deciding on the amount of

---

[40] *Criminal Code*, s. 515(2)(*b*). Unlike an undertaking, a "recognizance" involves the pledging of money. Essentially, by entering a recognizance the accused is acknowledging a debt to the Crown that will become payable if he or she fails to attend court or fails to comply with any of the specified conditions. See *Code*, Form 32. See generally, *R. v. McDonald*, [1958] O.J. No. 601, 120 C.C.C. 198 at 202-204 (Ont. C.A.).

[41] *Criminal Code*, s. 515(2)(*c*). See *Code*, Form 32. "Recognizance" is defined above in note 40. When sureties are involved, the indebtedness signified by the recognizance is essentially shared by the sureties up to the amounts that each pledges, so that if the accused fails to attend court or fails to comply with any of the specified conditions, a surety could be made to pay the sum pledged. Authority over potential conditions that may be included is governed by s. 515(4), (4.1), (4.11), and (4.2). Conditions are discussed below in Part 3(3).

[42] *Criminal Code*, s. 515(2)(*d*). Reliance on this provision is contingent on the Crown giving consent, a precondition that has been rightly described as "peculiar". See Gary T. Trotter, *The Law of Bail in Canada*, 3d ed. (Toronto: Thomson Carswell, 2010) at 6-13. If the Crown does consent, the provision allows for the accused to deposit money or valuable security (essentially to guarantee the debt pledged). The need for Crown consent under this subsection has been challenged. See *R. v. Melo*, [1996] O.J. No. 2235, 49 C.R. (4th) 184 (Ont. Gen. Div.) (upholding subsection). But see *R. v. Saunders*, [2001] B.C.J. No. 2089, 46 C.R. (5th) 395 (B.C.S.C.) (finding a violation of s. 11(*e*) of the *Charter* and reading the provision down so as not to require the Crown's consent.). Under the plain terms of the subsection, a deposit *cannot* be included along with sureties; "the provision appears to intend for a deposit *as an alternative to* sureties, not *in addition to* sureties." *R. v. Folkes*, [2007] A.J. No. 1142, 228 C.C.C. (3d) 284 at para. 25 (Alta.Q.B.) [emphasis in original]. See *R. v. Melo*, [1996] O.J. No. 2235, 49 C.R. (4th) 184 (Ont. Gen. Div.). See *Code*, Form 32. "Recognizance" is defined above in note 40. Authority over potential conditions that may be included is governed by s. 515(4), (4.1), (4.11), and (4.2). Conditions are discussed below in Part 3(3).

[43] *Criminal Code*, s. 515(2)(*e*). According to Trotter, the "form of release provided by this section is designed to be more secure." See Gary T. Trotter, *The Law of Bail in Canada*, 3d ed. (Toronto: Thomson Carswell, 2010) at 6-16. It is important to recognize that resort to this subsection is not automatic simply because an accused is not ordinarily resident in the province or resides more than 200 kilometres away. Rather, following the ladder approach mandated by s. 515(2), the justice must first be satisfied that one of the less onerous forms of release is inappropriate for such a person before resort to this subsection can be made. See Gary T. Trotter, *The Law of Bail in Canada*, 3d ed. (Toronto: Thomson Carswell, 2010) at 6-16; *R. v. Horvat*, [1972] B.C.J. No. 540, 9 C.C.C. (2d) 1 (B.C.S.C.); *R. v. Thompson*, [1972] B.C.J. No. 400, 7 C.C.C. (2d) 70 (B.C.S.C.). It has been suggested that restricting the combination of a deposit and sureties to those who reside outside of province or more than 200 kilometres may violate s. 11(*d*) of the *Charter*. See *R. v. Folkes*, [2007] A.J. No. 1142, 228 C.C.C. (3d) 284 at 296, 301 (Alta. Q.B.). See *Criminal Code*, Form 32. "Recognizance" is defined above in note 40. Authority over potential conditions that may be included is governed by s. 515(4), (4.1), (4.11), and (4.2). Conditions are discussed below in Part 3(3).

any deposit.[44] As a result, before requiring a cash deposit, a justice must inquire as to the ability of the accused or any sureties to raise the necessary funds.[45]

(3) Bail Conditions

§6.20 A justice's authority to include conditions as part of a pre-trial release order is critically important. It enables the terms of a release to be tailored to the specific circumstances of an accused and potentially alleviate concerns that might otherwise warrant pre-trial detention.[46] As explained immediately above, however, the starting point is release on an undertaking *without* conditions. Under the ladder approach, the burden is on the Crown to justify the need for more restrictive forms of release, including an undertaking or recognizance *with* conditions.[47]

§6.21 A justice who decides to release an accused pending trial has considerable discretion in ordering conditions. For example, the justice may impose conditions requiring that the accused report to a peace officer or other designated person;[48] remain within a particular territorial jurisdiction;[49] report any change of address, employment or occupation to the authorities;[50] not communicate with the victim, a witness or any other person named in the order;[51] not attend any place specified in the order except in accordance with any conditions that the justice may choose to specify;[52] and surrender his or her passport.[53]

§6.22 Beyond the specific examples enumerated in the *Code*, a justice also has a broad discretion to impose conditions specifically tailored to the particular allegations and accused. Specifically, the *Code* authorizes the justice to impose any condition that he or she "considers necessary to ensure the safety and security of any victim of or witness to the offence"[54] as well as any "other reasonable conditions" that "the justice considers desirable".[55]

§6.23 The justice's authority to fashion release conditions does however have its limits. As the Quebec Court of Appeal explained in *R. v. Keenan*,[56] at the bail stage an accused is presumed innocent. As a result, the sorts of conditions that might be appropriate as part of a probation order following a finding of guilt

---

44 See *R. v. Garrington*, [1972] O.J. No. 1965, 9 C.C.C. (2d) 472 (Ont. H.C.J.); *R. v. Cichanski*, [1976] O.J. No. 2430, 25 C.C.C. (2d) 84 (Ont. H.C.J.).

45 *R. v. Fraser*, [1982] O.J. No. 3404, 38 O.R. (2d) 172 (Ont. Dist. Ct.).

46 See Clifford Chatterton, *Bail: Law and Practice* (London: Butterworths, 1986) at 143 ("The balance of the decision whether to remand a person in custody or on bail may well rest on the ability of the court to impose meaningful conditions on bail.").

47 See §6.18, above, and supporting notes.

48 *Criminal Code*, s. 515(4)(*a*).

49 *Criminal Code*, s. 515(4)(*b*).

50 *Criminal Code*, s. 515(4)(*c*).

51 *Criminal Code*, s. 515(4)(*d*).

52 *Ibid.*

53 *Criminal Code*, s. 515(4)(*e*).

54 *Criminal Code*, s. 515(4)(*e*.1).

55 *Criminal Code*, s. 515(4)(*f*).

56 *R. v. Keenan*, [1979] J.Q. no 195, 57 C.C.C. (2d) 267 (Que. C.A.) [*Keenan*].

may exceed the bounds of an acceptable bail order.[57] Only conditions that relate to the circumstances of the alleged offence and a purpose that would otherwise justify the accused's detention pending trial are permissible.[58] For example, ensuring the accused's attendance in court, protecting the safety of the public and maintaining confidence in the administration of justice are all valid considerations to which conditions may relate.

§6.24 The case law provides guidance on the sorts of conditions that are and are not appropriate. In *Keenan*, for example, the Court invalidated a condition requiring the accused, charged with being found in a common bawdy house, to take medical treatment as directed by a physician. This condition, the Court reasoned, was not connected to a purpose relating to bail.[59]

§6.25 Conditions must also be carefully crafted to give the accused fair notice of what is required to comply. A condition prohibiting entry into a certain place to prevent future offences, for example, should define the proscribed area precisely.[60] Imprecise or ambiguous conditions should either be invalidated or interpreted in a manner favourable to the accused.[61] Further, the conditions imposed must be realistic; they should not be so stringent that compliance is practically impossible.[62]

§6.26 Although a justice has considerable discretion in ordering conditions, that authority is also subject to certain mandatory legislative directives. For example, where an accused is charged with certain enumerated offences (crimes where violence against a person was used, threatened or attempted,[63] a terrorism offence,[64] criminal harassment,[65] a commercial drug crime,[66] an offence related to

---

[57] *Ibid.*, at 276-77 (C.C.C.).

[58] *Ibid.*

[59] The Court noted that its conclusion would have been different if it the accused had been charged with communicating a venereal disease to another person and the condition directed that he take treatment in order to prevent the repetition of the offence. *R. v. Keenan*, [1979] J.Q. no 195, 57 C.C.C. (2d) 267 at 278-79 (Que. C.A.). See also Gary T. Trotter, *The Law of Bail in Canada*, 3d ed. (Toronto: Thomson Carswell, 2010) at 6-37 to 6-38, who raises the legitimate concern that without the authority to impose such treatment conditions to address bail concerns a justice may understandably feel that the only other option is to order pre-trial detention. No doubt there are few accused who would prefer pre-trial detention to mandatory treatment.

[60] See *e.g.*, *R. v. Bielefeld*, [1981] B.C.J. No. 1261, 64 C.C.C. (2d) 216 (B.C.S.C.) (upholding condition prohibiting accused from coming within one block of two cross-streets where she was alleged to have struck up a conversation with the victim regarding sex before accompanying him to a hotel where she allegedly robbed him).

[61] See *e.g.*, *R. v. Grey*, [1993] O.J. No. 251, 19 C.R. (4th) 363 (Ont. Prov. Ct.) (refusing to read condition requiring accused "to be of good behaviour" as the equivalent of a "community standard of behaviour" as this would result in an unconstitutionally vague standard, condition therefore construed as requiring violation of substantive law).

[62] See *e.g.*, *R. v. Sexton*, [1976] N.J. No. 89, 33 C.R.N.S. 307 (Nfld. Dist. Ct.) (conditions tantamount to a detention order; accused required to report to police four times per day, not to possess credit cards or more than $5 in cash and not leave his parents' residence except to attend the hospital, his lawyer's office or the police station in order to report).

[63] *Criminal Code*, s. 515(4.1)(*a*).

[64] *Criminal Code*, s. 515(4.1)(*a*.1).

[65] *Criminal Code*, s. 515(4.1)(*b*).

[66] *Criminal Code*, s. 515(4.1)(*c*).

weapons or explosives[67] or a specified offence under the *Security of Information Act*[68] relating to the disclosure of state secrets[69]) the justice must include a weapons, ammunition and explosives prohibition unless he or she "considers that such a condition is not required in the interests of the safety of the accused or the safety and security of a victim of the offence or of any other person."[70] A justice who declines to impose such a condition must give reasons for this decision.[71]

§6.27 For some of these same offences,[72] the justice is also required to consider whether it is desirable, in the interests of the safety and security of victims, witnesses and justice system participants, to include a condition that the accused abstain from communicating with them.[73] Further, the justice is conferred express authority to impose any other conditions that he or she considers necessary to ensure the safety and security of those persons.[74]

§6.28 Finally, it should be noted that the appropriate forum for challenging bail conditions is on direct review, which is discussed below in Part 3(10). An accused who is charged with failing to comply with some term in a release order is precluded from contesting the validity of that condition at a trial for breaching it.[75] This flows from the more general rule prohibiting "collateral attacks" on court orders.[76] As a result, an accused cannot simply disregard a condition that he or she considers unlawful expecting that its illegality will afford a defence if he or she is charged with breaching it.

(4) Sureties

§6.29 Although "sureties" are contemplated by the bail provisions, nothing in the *Code* defines their role and responsibilities. Nevertheless, sureties have played an important function since the very inception of bail at common law.[77] A surety is normally someone well-known to the accused, typically a family member, friend or employer, who agrees to supervise the accused to ensure that he or she attends court and complies with any conditions of release.[78] The surety's commitment is signified by acknowledging a debt to the Crown. The amount

---

[67] *Criminal Code*, s. 515(4.1)(*d*).
[68] R.S.C. 1985, c. O-5.
[69] *Criminal Code*, s. 515(4.1)(*e*).
[70] *Ibid.*
[71] *Criminal Code*, s. 515(4.12).
[72] See *Criminal Code*, s. 515(4.3).
[73] *Criminal Code*, s. 515(4.2)(*a*).
[74] *Criminal Code*, s. 515(4.2)(*b*).
[75] See *R. v. Gaudreault*, [1995] J.Q. no 1337, 105 C.C.C. (3d) 270 (Que. C.A.).
[76] The rule holds that "a court order, made by a court having jurisdiction to make it," may not be attacked "in proceedings other than those whose specific object is the reversal, variation, or nullification of the order or judgment." See *R. v. Wilson*, [1983] S.C.J. No. 88, [1983] 2 S.C.R. 594 at 599 (S.C.C.), *per* McIntyre J. See also *R. v. Litchfield*, [1993] S.C.J. No. 127, [1993] 4 S.C.R. 333 (S.C.C.).
[77] See Part 2, above, specifically §6.5.
[78] See *Canada (Attorney General) v. Horvath*, [2009] O.J. No. 4308, 248 C.C.C. (3d) 1 at para. 48 (Ont. C.A.) (noting that sureties are expected to supervise the accused).

pledged is forfeited if the accused fails to attend court or breaches the terms of release.[79]

§6.30 As mentioned, unlike in the United States, where bail bondsmen play an analogous role in return for financial compensation, in Canada it is an offence to offer or accept payment to act as a surety.[80] Here, the commitment is based on kinship or friendship,[81] which is believed to be more effective. As one court has observed, "[t]he real pull of bail, the real effective force it exerts, is that it may cause the offender to attend his trial rather than subject his nearest and dearest who has gone surety for him to undue pain and discomfort."[82]

(a) Approval of Sureties

§6.31 The responsibility for approving potential sureties belongs to the court and cannot be delegated to the Crown.[83] In practice, a surety will either be approved by the justice who presides at the bail hearing (by naming the surety when making the order granting the accused bail)[84] or by the justice who takes the recognizance entered by the surety and the accused.[85] In cases where the court ordering release approves a specific surety, there is a lack of consensus on

---

[79] Gary T. Trotter, *The Law of Bail in Canada*, 3d ed. (Toronto: Thomson Carswell, 2010) at 7-1. Historically, the surety was considered to be standing in the place of the jailer. As Mathers C.J.K.B. explained, the accused's "custody has been transferred, for his own benefit, from the gaoler of the Court to gaolers of his own choosing, who have obligated themselves by recognizance under penalty for his due appearance." *R. v. Lepicki*, [1925] M.J. No. 2, 44 C.C.C. 263 at 265 (Man. K.B.). See also *Criminal Code*, Form 32, which makes clear that the sureties are liable to make good their debt to the Crown "if the said [accused] fails in any of the conditions hereunder written."

[80] *Criminal Code*, s. 139(1).

[81] Gary T. Trotter, *The Law of Bail in Canada*, 3d ed. (Toronto: Thomson Carswell, 2010) at 7-1.

[82] *R. v. Southampton Justices, ex parte Corker* (1976), 120 S.J. 214, quoted with approval in *Canada (Attorney General) v. Horvath*, [2009] O.J. No. 4308, 248 C.C.C. (3d) 1 at paras. 40-41 (Ont. C.A.).

[83] See *R. v. Dewsbury*, [1989] O.J. No. 1252, 50 C.C.C. (3d) 163 at 166-67 (Ont. H.C.J.) (concluding that the practice in Ontario of the Crown attorney approving potential sureties is fundamentally unfair, offends the *Charter* and should end). See also *R. v. Chisholm*, [1974] O.J. No. 2308, 18 C.C.C. (2d) 509 at 510 (Ont. H.C.J.) (criticizing the practice and characterizing it as "an abdication by the Justice of the Peace of his judicial responsibilities. ... The Justice may properly receive submissions from the law officers of the Crown but must exercise the judicial function and satisfy himself of the adequacy of any surety."); *R. v. Morenstein*, [1977] O.J. No. 2605, 40 C.C.C. (2d) 131 at 132-33 (Ont. C.A. (In Chambers)) (disapproving of the suggestion that the Crown had ultimate authority over the approval of proposed sureties). See generally, Gary T. Trotter, "Fundamental Justice and the Approval of Sureties by the Crown" (1988) 30 Crim. L.Q. 238.

[84] *Criminal Code*, s. 515(2.1) now specifically authorizes the justice or judge who orders an accused released to name particular persons as sureties.

[85] Gary T. Trotter, *The Law of Bail in Canada*, 3d ed. (Toronto: Thomson Carswell, 2010) at 7-21. See also *R. v. Gillespie*, [1984] O.J. No. 177, 16 C.C.C. (3d) 140 (Ont. C.A.) (holding that there is no requirement that the same justice who presides at the bail hearing also take the recognizance).

whether the justice must see and hear from the proposed surety or can simply act on information imparted to the court.[86]

§6.32 Given that a surety is expected to supervise the accused in the community and pledges to pay a specified sum if that obligation is not faithfully discharged, the courts have recognized that not everyone is up to this task. In deciding on the appropriateness of a proposed surety, the court must consider a number of variables.

§6.33 One of the most important is the relationship between the proposed surety and the accused. As Justice Trotter explains, considerations such as "how long the surety has known the accused, whether they are related, how frequently they see each other and how close they live to one another (indeed, whether they live together)" are all relevant to assessing if the surety "can be expected to supervise an accused and take action if the accused fails to live up to the conditions of his/her release."[87] For example, if a proposed surety "barely knows the accused" or "has little contact with the accused" then they are unlikely "to be effective at supervising the accused."[88] The same is true of a close friend or family member who lives far from the accused.[89]

§6.34 Another relevant factor is the surety's character. The court will want to ensure that the proposed surety can be entrusted to conscientiously discharge his or her responsibilities. There are few hard and fast rules governing this determination.[90] Nevertheless, in practice, amidst the hustle and bustle of Canada's busy bail courts, a list originally penned in an annotation on bail many years ago supplies a concise summary of those who should generally not be permitted to serve as sureties. The list includes accomplices, persons with prior convictions for serious[91] offences, counsel for the accused (a rule intended to protect counsel from being subject to undue pressure from clients), persons who are being indemnified, persons in custody or on bail awaiting trial for a criminal offence,

---

[86] See *R. v. Brooks*, [2001] O.J. No. 1563, 153 C.C.C. (3d) 533 at para. 35 (Ont. S.C.J.), where Hill J. indicates that "There is no legal requirement that a surety be present in court and testify in order for judicial interim release to be considered." Instead, he suggests that the court may act on information supplied to the court regarding a proposed surety. *Ibid.*, at para. 38 (C.C.C.). See also *R. v. V. (J.)*, [2002] O.J. No. 1027, 163 C.C.C. (3d) 507 at para. 81 (Ont. S.C.J.). But see *R. v. M. (T.)*, [2002] A.J. No. 48, 310 A.R. 336 at para. 10 (Alta. Q.B.), suggesting that it is necessary to examine proposed sureties "under oath to ascertain the full extent of their commitment and involvement".

[87] Gary T. Trotter, *The Law of Bail in Canada*, 3d ed. (Toronto: Thomson Carswell, 2010) at 7-19.

[88] *Ibid.*

[89] *Ibid.*

[90] See Gary T. Trotter, *The Law of Bail in Canada*, 3d ed. (Toronto: Thomson Carswell, 2010) at 7-17 to 7-18, who argues that the question should be approached from a functional standpoint that is "derived from what the law expects of sureties and whether the proposed surety can realistically discharge the obligations and willingly exercise the powers of a surety."

[91] Justice Trotter rightly observes that a relatively minor and dated criminal record should not serve as a bar to standing as a surety. Gary T. Trotter, *The Law of Bail in Canada*, 3d ed. (Toronto: Thomson Carswell, 2010) at 7-18.

minors, persons already acting as sureties for another accused or a non-resident of the province.[92]

§6.35 Before the proposed surety is approved, the court will also want assurance that he or she has the financial resources to satisfy the commitment being made.[93] Expectations for supporting evidence vary widely. Some justices, for example, simply rely on the proposed surety's own description of his or her assets. Other justices, in contrast, require sworn testimony and supporting documents like pay stubs, bank statements, income tax returns and property deeds.

(b) *Withdrawal of Surety*

§6.36 The surety's responsibilities generally continue until the accused is either discharged or sentenced.[94] There are steps that a surety can take, however, to be released of his or her obligation sooner. The *Code* contemplates two distinct routes by which the surety can bring the arrangement to an end. First, the surety may apply in writing to the court to be relieved of his or her obligation under the recognizance.[95] That order authorizes the arrest of the accused.[96] Once the court receives confirmation of the accused's arrest, the recognizance is to be endorsed to that effect.[97] That endorsement serves to vacate the recognizance and discharge the surety from his or her obligations.[98] The second option available to a surety is to physically deliver the accused into the court's custody.[99] In either case, when the accused is delivered to the court, the court may either commit him or her to prison[100] or substitute any other "suitable person" as a surety.[101] Substitution does not affect the original order of release and recognizance.[102]

---

[92] Eric Armour, "Annotation: Bail in Criminal Cases" (1927) 47 C.C.C. 1 at 6. The author provides supporting citations from English case law for most of these propositions. His list also includes the following antiquated consideration: "8. A married woman unless she has separate estate." Quite obviously, this factor is an artifact of the law's subordination of women, especially married women who had no legal status separate from that of their husband. See also Eugene G. Ewaschuk, *Criminal Pleadings & Practice in Canada*, 2d ed. (looseleaf) (Aurora: Canada Law Book, 1987-) § 6:1120 (also reproducing Armour's list, absent the discriminatory disqualification of married women).

[93] The surety's assets must be in the province. See *R. v. Martin (No. 2)*, [1980] O.J. No. 2568, 57 C.C.C. (2d) 31 (Ont. C.A. (In Chambers)) (concluding that surety whose assets were out of province was not suitable, given that under the estreatment provisions in the *Code* such a surety was not put at risk of having property taken in execution in the event of a default by the accused). See also *R. v. Fleming*, [2007] B.C.J. No. 925, 238 B.C.A.C. 317 (B.C.C.A.)]

[94] *Criminal Code*, s. 764.
[95] *Criminal Code*, s. 766(1).
[96] *Criminal Code*, s. 766(2).
[97] *Criminal Code*, s. 766(3).
[98] *Criminal Code*, s. 766(4).
[99] *Criminal Code*, s. 767. Unless this is done on a day that the accused is already required to be in court and voluntarily appears, this option invites the risk that the accused will be uncooperative.
[100] *Criminal Code*, ss. 766(1), 767.
[101] *Criminal Code*, s. 767.1(1).
[102] *Criminal Code*, s. 767.1(2).

(c) Forfeiture of Recognizance

§6.37 If the accused fails to attend court or breaches any conditions of release,[103] the court will endorse the recognizance with a Certificate of Default, which will specify the nature of the default and list the names and addresses of the accused and sureties.[104] Ultimately, that certificate will be transferred to the clerk of the court. Thereafter, the Crown may apply for forfeiture of the recognizance.[105] Once such a request is made, a time and place for the hearing will be set and the accused and the sureties will be notified.[106]

§6.38 At that hearing, commonly known as an "estreatment hearing", the accused and any sureties are to be afforded an opportunity to show cause why the recognizance should not be forfeited.[107] Section 771(2) provides that after hearing from the parties, the judge presiding on the application may "in his discretion grant or refuse the application and make any order with respect to the forfeiture of the recognizance that he considers proper."[108] As this language suggests, the forfeiture of the entire amount pledged is not automatic. Rather, the judge hearing the application has considerable discretion in deciding on whether or not to order forfeiture and in what amount. A key consideration is the degree of fault on the part of the surety. As Lord Denning explained in *R. v. Southampton Justices, ex parte Green*:[109]

> If [the surety] connived at the disappearance of the accused man, or aided it or abetted it, it would be proper to forfeit the whole of the sum. If he or she was wanting in due diligence to secure his appearance, it might be proper to forfeit the whole or a substantial part of it, depending on the degree of fault. If he or she was guilty of no want of diligence and used every effort to secure the appearance of the accused man, it might be proper to remit it entirely.[110]

This passage has been repeatedly cited with approval by Canadian courts.[111] In a recent Ontario case, the Crown argued in favour of a more rigid approach: a

---

[103] The failure to attend court will be obvious and amply demonstrated by the issuance of a bench warrant for an accused's arrest. Non-compliance with a condition will usually become evident on an application to revoke the accused's bail pursuant to s. 524. The revocation of bail pursuant to that provision is explained below in Part 3(11).

[104] *Criminal Code*, s. 770, Form 33.

[105] *Criminal Code*, s. 771(1)(*a*).

[106] *Criminal Code*, s. 771(1)(*b*).

[107] *Ibid.* See *Canada (Attorney General) v. Horvath*, [2009] O.J. No. 4308, 248 C.C.C. (3d) 1 (Ont. C.A.) (explaining that "the onus is on the surety to show why the recognizance should not be forfeited" (at para. 27 (C.C.C.)) and that it is the sureties who "have the obligation to adduce credible evidence to support their position" (at para. 52 (C.C.C.))).

[108] *Criminal Code*, s. 771(2).

[109] [1975] 2 All E.R. 1073 (C.A.).

[110] *Ibid.*, at 1077-1078.

[111] See *R. v. Huang*, [1998] O.J. No. 2991, 127 C.C.C. (3d) 397 at para. 11 (Ont. C.A.); *Re Millward*, [1998] A.J. No. 922, 128 C.C.C. (3d) 67 at para. 34 (Alta. Q.B.); *R. v. Miller*, [1990] B.C.J. No. 2016 (B.C. Co. Ct.); *R. v. Sandhu*, [1984] J.Q. no 662, 38 C.R. (3d) 56 (Que. S.C.); *R. v. Andrews*, [1975] N.J. No. 26, 34 C.R.N.S. 344 at 347-48 (Nfld.T.D.).

presumption in favour of total forfeiture absent exceptional circumstances.[112] The Court of Appeal rejected this proposal.[113] Instead, after emphasizing the discretion expressly conferred by section 771(2), the importance of sureties to facilitating the *Charter* right to reasonable bail, the potential for sureties to be imprisoned if unable to pay the amount pledged on forfeiture and the reality that sureties rarely receive independent legal advice, the Court reaffirmed the continued importance of scrutinizing the surety's level of diligence.[114] Nevertheless, Justice Rosenberg explained that:

> ... the diligence of the surety is only one factor relevant to a forfeiture hearing. In the end, the judge must attempt to balance various considerations in exercising the discretion conferred by s. 771(2). I do not think it is helpful or even possible to develop an exhaustive list of the factors that the judge should take into account in exercising this discretion. Further, not all factors will be of equal relevancy or weight in all cases. A review of the cases does, however, show that there are categories of factors that the courts regularly take into account, including: the amount of the recognizance; the circumstances under which the surety entered into the recognizance, especially whether there was any duress or coercion; the surety's diligence; the surety's means; any significant change in the surety's financial position after the recognizance was entered into and especially after the breach; the surety's post-breach conduct, especially attempts to assist the authorities in locating the accused; and the relationship between the accused and the surety.[115]

§6.39 It is also open to a court to make a conditional order that the recognizance be forfeited unless the accused is taken into custody by a certain date.[116] No doubt, such an order will give a surety a compelling incentive to cooperate with the authorities in locating the accused.

§6.40 The Crown may collect any amount ordered forfeited from the accused and his or her sureties in the same manner as a civil judgment.[117] In addition, any moneys deposited toward bail may be transferred to satisfy the amount ordered forfeited.[118]

§6.41 Finally, though this seldom happens, the Crown may also seek the imprisonment of the surety if the amount ordered forfeited cannot be satisfied. To invoke this power, the Crown must apply for a hearing at which the surety will be required to show cause why he or she should not be committed to custody.[119] A surety must be given seven clear days' notice of the date and location of the

---

[112] See *Canada (Attorney General) v. Horvath*, [2009] O.J. No. 4308, 248 C.C.C. (3d) 1 (Ont. C.A.).

[113] *Ibid.*, at para. 44 (C.C.C.).

[114] *Ibid.*, at paras. 44-50 (C.C.C.).

[115] *Ibid.*, at para. 51 (C.C.C.).

[116] *Ibid.*, at para. 54 (C.C.C.).

[117] See *Criminal Code*, ss. 771(3), (3.1), 772.

[118] *Criminal Code*, s. 771(4).

[119] *Criminal Code*, s. 773(1).

hearing.[120] The judge presiding at the hearing has considerable discretion. He or she may order "the discharge of the amount for which the surety is liable"[121] or "make any order with respect to the surety and to his imprisonment that he considers proper in the circumstances".[122] In our view, the entirely unfettered discretion to imprison a defaulting surety appears to be inconsistent with the right not to be arbitrarily imprisoned guaranteed by section 9 of the *Charter* and is therefore ripe for constitutional challenge.[123]

(5) Adjournments and Delay

§6.42 On its face, section 515(1) creates the impression that an accused deserving of bail will be released within 24 hours of arrest. It is common, however, for the bail hearing to be adjourned at the accused's or prosecutor's request, though the accused must consent to any adjournment for more than three clear days.[124] If a bail hearing is adjourned, the accused is remanded in custody to a prison.[125] The Ontario Court of Appeal has noted that it is implicit "in the provisions of the *Code* and the statutory form of warrant remanding a prisoner" that an accused who is remanded in custody pending a bail hearing "is to be held in a custodial facility separate from mere holding cells connected with the police".[126] Therefore, once taken to bail court, absent a court order permitting otherwise, the police will no longer be in a position to maintain control over an accused in order to continue with an interrogation or otherwise elicit his or her cooperation in the investigation.[127]

§6.43 Where a justice adjourns the bail hearing, the *Code* permits him or her to order that the accused abstain from communicating, directly or indirectly, with any victim, witness or other person identified in the order, except in accordance with any conditions specified in the order.[128] This is meant to reduce the danger

---

[120] *Criminal Code*, s. 773(2).

[121] *Criminal Code*, s. 773(3)(*a*).

[122] *Criminal Code*, s. 773(3)(*b*).

[123] The Supreme Court of Canada has recognized that, under s. 9 of the *Charter*, "[a] discretion is arbitrary ... [because] ... there are no criteria, express or implied, which govern its exercise." *R. v. Hufsky*, [1988] S.C.J. No. 30, [1988] 1 S.C.R. 621 at 633 (S.C.C.). See generally, Chapter 2, Part 3(4)(*b*), which explains s. 9's minimum standards with respect to laws that authorize detention or imprisonment.

[124] *Criminal Code*, s. 516(1). See also the *Interpretation Act*, R.S.C. 1985, c. I-21, s. 27(1) ("clear days" excludes the days between two events, so an accused's bail hearing may be involuntarily remanded from a Monday to a Friday). See *R. v. Zarinchang*, [2010] O.J. No. 1548, 254 C.C.C. (3d) 133 at para. 39 (Ont. C.A.).

[125] *Criminal Code*, s. 516(1). This is done by way of a warrant of remand. See *Criminal Code*, Form 19. Section 2 defines "prison" as including "a penitentiary, common jail, public or reformatory prison, lock-up, guard-room or other place in which persons who are charged with or convicted of offences are usually kept in custody".

[126] *R. v. Precourt*, [1976] O.J. No. 2421, 18 O.R. (2d) 714, 39 C.C.C. (2d) 311 at 318-19 (Ont. C.A.), leave to appeal refused [1977] 1 S.C.R. xi (S.C.C.).

[127] *Ibid.*

[128] *Criminal Code*, s. 516(2). This is done by way of a warrant of remand. See *Criminal Code*, Form 19. Section 2 defines "prison" as including "a penitentiary, common jail, public or refor-

of an accused using a phone at the prison to intimidate the victim or a witness. It should be noted, however, that the condition only remains in effect while the accused is being remanded in custody for bail purposes; it ceases to have any effect once the accused is found guilty and remanded in custody pending sentencing.[129]

§6.44 The discretion to adjourn a bail hearing for up to three clear days without an accused person's consent, when combined with heavy caseloads in some jurisdictions, can lead to alarming delays before a bail hearing is held.[130] Delays in affording those arrested a bail hearing may give rise to constitutional concerns.

§6.45 The *Charter*'s prohibition on arbitrary detention (section 9) and the right not to be denied reasonable bail without just cause (section 11(*e*)) would be illusory if a chronic lack of resources resulted in long delays. As Justice Hill observed, "[t]he routine adjournment of bail hearings other than at the request of the prosecutor or the accused (Code section 516(1)), as 'not reached' cases, is an entirely unacceptable threat to constitutional rights, a denial of access to justice, and an unnecessary cost to the court system".[131]

§6.46 Given the fundamental constitutional interests at stake, it is incumbent on governments to provide adequate resources (including courtrooms, justices, prosecutors, administrative and security staff) to ensure that the *Code*'s promise of a bail hearing within 24 hours of arrest is actually realized. Sections 9 and 11(*e*) of the *Charter* are violated when an accused is forced to languish in custody awaiting a bail hearing due to inadequate resources.[132]

---

matory prison, lock-up, guard-room or other place in which persons who are charged with or convicted of offences are usually kept in custody".

[129] See *R. v. Brown*, [2000] N.S.J. No. 412, 151 C.C.C. (3d) 85 (N.S.C.A.).

[130] See Pamela Koza & Anthony N. Doob, "Some Empirical Evidence on Judicial Interim Release Proceedings" (1974-75) 17 Crim. L.Q. 258 at 266-70 (after studying 448 bail determinations, the authors concluded that most remands are requested by prosecutors, that these requests are influenced by heavy dockets and in the 72 cases remanded, 22 persons were ultimately detained after spending an average of 5.86 days in custody, while 50 individuals were released after an average of 3.86 days in custody). The problem of delay has apparently worsened over the intervening years. For example, in 2001 it took on average four days for a bail determination to be made whereas by 2006, on average, it took almost six days. See Cheryl Marie Webster, Anthony N. Doob & Nicole M. Myers, "The Parable of Ms. Baker: Understanding Pre-Trial Detention in Canada" (2009) 21(1) *Current Issues in Criminal Justice* 79 at 94-97.

[131] *R. v. V. (J.)*, [2002] O.J. No. 1027, 163 C.C.C. (3d) 507 at para. 67 (Ont. S.C.J.).

[132] See *R. v. Brown*, [2009] O.J. no. 3592, 247 C.C.C. (3d) 11 (Ont. C.A.) (long delays occasioned by a lack of adequate resources violated the accused person's ss. 9 and 11(*e*) *Charter* rights; order for costs against the Crown upheld); *R. v. Zarinchang*, [2010] O.J. No. 1548, 254 C.C.C. (3d) 133 at para. 39 (Ont. C.A.) 39 ("Unreasonably prolonged custody awaiting a bail hearing gives rise to a breach of s. 11(e) of the *Charter*."); *R. v. Jevons*, [2008] O.J. No. 4397, 2008 ONCJ 559 (Ont. C.J.) (finding a violation of s. 11(*e*) of the *Charter* where accused, due to insufficient resources, made several appearances in bail court over eight days before being released and ordering a stay of proceedings as a result.) *Charter* remedies, including the case law governing stays of proceedings as a remedy under s. 24(1), are dealt within in Chapter 10.

(6)   Reversal of the Onus under Section 515(6) of the *Code*

§6.47 As mentioned, there are two types of cases where the onus at the bail hearing is reversed. This section deals with the procedure applying to offences committed in the circumstances enumerated in section 515(6) of the *Criminal Code*. In the next section we discuss the reverse onus applying to murder and the other offences listed in section 469. Where section 515(6) applies, the accused will be detained unless, having been afforded a reasonable opportunity to do so, he or she shows cause why pre-trial detention is not justified.[133] If an accused is ordered released in any of the specified circumstances, the justice is required to provide reasons for doing so.[134]

§6.48 The list of circumstances in which the onus will be reversed has grown long. A reverse onus now applies where an accused is charged with an indictable offence while already subject to an earlier release order for another indictable offence;[135] a specified offence that is alleged to have been committed for the benefit or at the behest of a criminal organization;[136] a specified terrorism offence;[137] a specified offence under the *Security of Information Act*[138] relating to the disclosure of state secrets;[139] illegal weapons trafficking, importing or possession for the purpose of trafficking;[140] an enumerated violent crime that is alleged to have been committed with a firearm;[141] an offence involving a weapon while an accused is subject to a weapons prohibition order;[142] failing to attend court or violating the terms of an undertaking or recognizance, including failing to attend for fingerprinting or photographing as directed by a summons, appearance notice or promise to appear;[143] or trafficking, possession for the purpose of trafficking, importing/exporting or producing a controlled substance or conspiring to commit one of these offences in circumstances where the maximum potential penalty is life imprisonment.[144] Finally, irrespective of the offence charged, the onus is always reversed if the accused is not ordinarily resident in Canada.[145]

---

[133] *Criminal Code*, s. 515(6).

[134] *Criminal Code*, s. 515(6.1).

[135] *Criminal Code*, s. 516(*a*)(i).

[136] *Criminal Code*, s. 515(6)(*a*)(ii)).

[137] *Criminal Code*, s. 515(6)(*a*)(iii).

[138] R.S.C. 1985, c. O-5.

[139] *Criminal Code*, s. 515(6)(*a*)(iii) and (iv).

[140] *Criminal Code*, s. 515(6)(*a*)(vi).

[141] *Criminal Code*, s. 515(6)(*a*)(vii).

[142] *Criminal Code*, s. 515(6)(*a*)(viii).

[143] *Criminal Code*, s. 515(6)(*c*).

[144] *Criminal Code*, s. 515(6)(*d*).

[145] *Criminal Code*, s. 515(6)(*b*). A person in Canada illegally has been held not to be "ordinarily resident". See *R. v. Jonas*, [1981] O.J. No. 2442, 25 C.R. (3d) 325 (Ont. H.C.J.). In contrast, those in Canada claiming refugee status are not here illegally and, even though their status may be tenuous, should not automatically be treated as non-residents under this subsection. See *R. v. Oladipo*, [2004] O.J. No. 5028, 191 C.C.C. (3d) 237 (Ont. S.C.J.).

§6.49 The constitutionality of reversing the onus applicable at bail hearings is addressed in detail below in Part 4(2). For now, it is worth relating the Supreme Court's reasoning in *R. v. Pearson*,[146] which involved a constitutional challenge to the predecessor to section 515(6)(*d*), which reversed the onus where an accused was charged with a drug distribution offence. In rejecting the challenge, the Court noted that the concerns underlying the reversal of the onus (the increased risk of recidivism and flight associated with sophisticated and well-resourced criminal organizations), would be easily overcome by accused whose circumstances raised no such concerns. As Chief Justice Lamer explained, "[t]he 'small fry' and 'generous smoker' will normally have no difficulty justifying their release and obtaining bail."[147]

§6.50 Today, the risk of overreach for lesser drug traffickers is ameliorated somewhat as the reverse onus applies only to offences where the accused faces a maximum punishment of life imprisonment on conviction.[148] The larger point to remember from *Pearson*, however, is that where a particular case is not the archetype that led Parliament to reverse the onus, the accused required to show cause should face no great obstacle in obtaining his or her release. That said, in our view, at least some of the situations in which the onus is now reversed are constitutionally suspect. These are discussed below in Part 4(2).

(7) Section 469 Offences

§6.51 As mentioned, the offences listed in section 469 are subject to two substantial variations on the rules that ordinarily apply to bail, both of which make pre-trial release more difficult to obtain. First, bail hearings for such offences are not automatic. When an accused charged with murder or another section 469 offence is first brought to court, the justice must order that the accused be detained in custody.[149] The justice may also order that the accused abstain from communicating, directly or indirectly, with any victim, witness or other person identified in the order, except in accordance with any conditions specified in the order.[150]

§6.52 Thereafter, the accused's release may only be ordered by a judge of the superior court of criminal jurisdiction for the province in which the accused is charged. The accused must apply to that court for a bail hearing, with notice to the prosecutor. This may be done at any time before or after the accused has been ordered to stand trial.[151] Unless there is agreement otherwise, the application must be supported by evidence, normally in the form of affidavits.[152] Depending on the province, the rules of the court may specify what must be filed in

---

[146] [1992] S.C.J. No. 99, [1992] 3 S.C.R. 665 (S.C.C.).

[147] *Ibid.*, at para. 65.

[148] See *Criminal Code*, s. 515(6)(*d*); *Controlled Drugs and Substances Act*, S.C. 1996, c. 19, ss. 5-7.

[149] *Criminal Code*, s. 515(11). The accused is remanded by the justice issuing a warrant in Form 8.

[150] *Criminal Code*, s. 515(12).

[151] *Criminal Code*, s. 522.

[152] See *R. v. West*, [1972] O.J. No. 1962, 9 C.C.C. (2d) 369 at 372-73 (Ont. C.A.).

support of such an application, for example, affidavits from the accused and any proposed sureties.[153] At the hearing, the judge may also deal with bail for any other offences that the accused is charged with.[154]

§6.53 The second variation for section 469 offences is the reversal of the onus of proof. In such cases, bail will be denied unless the accused "shows cause why his detention in custody is not justified within the meaning of subsection 515(10)."[155] In murder cases, appellate courts have upheld this reversal of the burden under section 11(*e*) of the *Charter*, reasoning that since murder is the most serious offence in the *Code* and carries an automatic life sentence, the ordinary bail rules "would create an intolerable risk of continuing criminal behaviour and/or of absconding."[156] (Part 4, below, deals in detail with the requirements of section 11(*e*) of the *Charter*, including those decisions upholding the reversal of the burden for section 469 offences.)

§6.54 Finally, as in all bail hearings, if the judge refuses bail to an accused charged with a section 469 offence, he or she may also order the accused to abstain from communicating, directly or indirectly, with any victim, witness or other person identified in the order except in accordance with such conditions specified in the order as the judge considers necessary.[157]

§6.55 The combined effect of requiring an accused charged with section 469 offences to seek bail in superior court, reversing the burden of persuasion and the inherent flight risk stemming from an automatic life sentence, make bail for those charged with murder difficult[158] (though not impossible[159]) to obtain. Further, even those who manage to secure bail will necessarily spend a significant amount of time in custody between arrest and release.

(8) Criteria Governing Bail

§6.56 Irrespective of who bears the onus, the criteria governing bail remain the same. Subsection 515(10) of the *Criminal Code* is the controlling provision. It provides that the detention of an accused in custody is justified only on one or more of the following grounds:[160]

---

[153] See *e.g.*, *Superior Court of Justice Criminal Proceedings Rules*, SI/92-99, Rule 20, available online at: <http://www.ontariocourts.on.ca/scj/en/about/rules/rules.pdf>.

[154] *Criminal Code*, s. 522(6).

[155] *Criminal Code*, s. 522(2).

[156] See *R. v. Sanchez*, [1999] N.S.J. No. 142, 24 C.R. (5th) 330 at para. 29 (N.S.C.A.). See also *R. v. Bray*, [1983] O.J. No. 2509, 2 C.C.C. (3d) 325 (Ont. C.A.).

[157] *Criminal Code*, s. 522(2.1).

[158] See *e.g.*, *R. v. McCreery*, [1996] B.C.J. No. 2018, 110 C.C.C. (3d) 561 at para. 32 (B.C.S.C.) (noting that "[i]t is rare, however, for bail to be granted where the charge is murder").

[159] See *e.g.*, *R. v. Dubois*, [1983] J.Q. no 69, 8 C.C.C. (3d) 344 (Que. S.C.) (granting release to accused charged with murder nine years earlier based on absence of other charges and facts that accused was a Canadian citizen, married and ran his own business).

[160] Headings have been added for ease of reference. Courts routinely refer to the three grounds for denying bail as the "primary", "secondary" and "tertiary" grounds. See *e.g.*, *R. v. M. (E.W.)*, [2006] O.J. No. 3654, 223 C.C.C. (3) 407 at para. 11 (Ont. C.A.).

Attendance in Court: the primary ground — (*a*) where the detention is nec-essary to ensure his or her attendance in court in order to be dealt with according to law;

Public Safety: the secondary ground — (*b*) where the detention is necessary for the protection or safety of the public, including any victim of or witness to the offence, or any person under the age of 18 years, having regard to all the circumstances including any substantial likelihood that the accused will, if released from custody, commit a criminal offence or interfere with the administration of justice; and

Confidence in the Justice System: the tertiary ground — (*c*) if the detention is necessary to maintain confidence in the administration of justice, having regard to all the circumstances, including

(i) the apparent strength of the prosecution's case,

(ii) the gravity of the offence,

(iii) the circumstances surrounding the commission of the offence, including whether a firearm was used, and

(iv) the fact that the accused is liable, on conviction, for a potentially lengthy term of imprisonment or, in the case of an offence that involves, or whose subject-matter is, a firearm, a minimum punishment of imprisonment for a term of three years or more.

These subsections provide alternative bases for denying bail. In other words, any one of these factors, standing alone, will be sufficient to justify pre-trial detention. These considerations govern bail determinations from the accused's first appearance until conviction, including reviews of the initial bail determination by either the accused or the prosecution (review is dealt with below in Part 3(10)).[161] Slightly different and more onerous considerations apply for bail pending appeal (discussed in Chapter 18, Part 2(1)(*e*)). Each of the legislatively prescribed considerations under section 515(10) is explained below.

§6.57 Before turning to the relevant provisions, a few words about what, in our view, is missing from the existing criteria. It is not a precondition for denying bail or imposing restrictive bail conditions that there be reasonable and probable grounds to support the charge(s). As explained in Chapter 5, that sort of vetting does take place when police have released an accused and seek confirmation of the process they have issued to compel the accused's appearance in court. Inexplicably, there is no parallel procedure for those held for bail hearings. As mentioned, for these accused, release may be denied on the basis of only one of the grounds set out in section 515(10) of the *Code*. The apparent strength of the prosecution's case — which given the presumption of innocence should presumably play an important role in deciding bail — is considered only indirectly.[162] For example, as explained below, whether the Crown's case is strong or

---

[161] See *Criminal Code*, ss. 520, 521, 680 (setting out the review procedures). Review is dealt with in detail below in Part 3(10).

[162] For example, if the Crown's case is strong and the offence charged is serious, pre-trial release gives rise to both flight and public safety concerns. See Gary T. Trotter, *The Law of Bail in*

weak will be relevant in analyzing the potential for flight and the need to maintain confidence in the administration of justice. As a result, appellate courts have cautioned that this is "only one factor to be considered among several others."[163] In the end, release decisions motivated by fatal deficiencies in the Crown's case must still be reconciled with the established legislative criteria for granting bail.[164]

Suggestions to Parliament **§6.58** In our view, Parliament should require judicial confirmation of reasonable and probable grounds to support the charge(s) as a precondition for refusing bail or imposing restrictive bail conditions. Without such a requirement, the current scheme raises serious constitutional concerns.[165]

(a) Attendance in Court: The Primary Ground

§6.59 The primary ground, set out in section 515(10)(*a*), requires an accused's detention when "necessary to ensure his or her attendance in court in order to be dealt with according to law." A number of factors are relevant under this subsection, though none is determinative. Rather, "one must view all of the circumstances very carefully and must not make a decision lightly or based on only one factor."[166]

§6.60 One important consideration is whether the accused has roots in the community. An accused is more likely to be released if he or she has a fixed residence, a spouse or partner, children, employment, and close relatives and friends living in close proximity.[167] Unfortunately, these considerations often work against people who are already marginalized: the homeless, itinerant, unemployed and socially isolated. In some jurisdictions, bail programs (where staff essentially play the role that would normally be fulfilled by family or friends

---

Canada, 3d ed. (Toronto: Thomson Carswell, 2010) at 3-6 to 3-7, 3-19 to 3-22 and 3-34 to 3-37; Daniel Kiselbach, "Pre-Trial Criminal Procedure: Preventive Detention and the Presumption of Innocence (1989) 31 Crim. L.Q. 168 at 188-90. See also the numerous cases referred to by both authors.

[163] *R. v. Perron*, [1989] J.Q. no 852, 51 C.C.C. (3d) 518 at 529 (Que. C.A.). See also *R. v. Braun*, [1994] S.J. No. 312, 91 C.C.C. (3d) 237 at 254-55 (Sask. C.A.); *R. v. Lamothe*, [1990] J.Q. no 514, 58 C.C.C. (3d) 530 at 540 (Que. C.A.).

[164] See *e.g.*, *R. v. Khan*, [1998] M.J. No. 443, 129 C.C.C. (3d) 443 at 444-45 (Man. C.A.) (explicitly addressing each of the legislated grounds despite concluding that there is "a real possibility that the applicant will eventually be acquitted on this charge" and that release should be ordered, as otherwise the court might be "detaining a possibly innocent man in custody"). See also *R. v. Rivest*, [1996] J.Q. no 1347, 49 C.R. (4th) 392 (Que. C.A.).

[165] See James Stribopoulos, "Unchecked Power: The Constitutional Regulation of Arrest Reconsidered" (2003) 48 McGill L.J. 225.

[166] *R. v. Smith (No. 3)*, [1972] B.C.J. No. 701, 8 C.C.C. (2d) 291 at 291 (B.C.S.C.).

[167] See *e.g.*, *R. v. Powers*, [1972] O.J. No. 902, 9 C.C.C. (2d) 533 at 541 (Ont. H.C.J.) ("detention for the purpose of ensuring attendance in Court for the trial includes consideration of such things as residence, fixed place of abode, employment or occupation, marital and family status, ... proximity of close friends and relatives, character witnesses, [and] ... personal history ....").

[Handwritten annotation at top: Problem — many accused do not have pp as sureties or full time employment/family]

acting as sureties) may serve to fill this void. Unfortunately, such programs are not available in many places.[168]

§6.61 The availability of potential sureties is also an important consideration. Release is more likely if a responsible member of the community who knows the accused (for example, a family member, a friend or an employer) is willing to act as a surety and prepared to monitor the accused and ensure his or her attendance in court and compliance with any conditions of release. In contrast, if an accused is a transient with no real connection to the locale and no potential sureties, a detention order becomes far more likely.[169]

§6.62 A criminal record is also relevant under section 515(10)(*a*) because it may shed light on the accused's track record while on bail. For example, recent prior convictions for failing to attend court weigh in favour of detention.[170] Even a single such conviction, especially where an accused has no acceptable surety, might be enough to tip the scales in favour of pre-trial detention. Dated convictions for failing to attend court, however, may matter little, especially where the accused has faced criminal charges and dutifully attended court over the intervening years.[171]

§6.63 A further consideration is how the accused responds once aware that the police are interested in making an arrest. If an accused takes flight and becomes a fugitive, this militates in favour of detention. In contrast, "surrender, without flight, is an acknowledgement by ... [an accused that he or she is] ... prepared to be dealt with according to the law and bears in their favour on the primary ground."[172]

§6.64 Finally, the strength of the Crown's case and the potential for a lengthy period of imprisonment may combine to make a compelling case for pre-trial detention on the primary ground.[173] That said, at the relatively early stage of a

---

[168] See generally, Gary T. Trotter, *The Law of Bail in Canada*, 3d ed. (Toronto: Thomson Carswell, 2010) at 3-8.

[169] See *e.g.*, *R. v. Jonas*, [1981] O.J. No. 2442, 25 C.R. (3d) 325 (Ont. H.C.J.) (ordering detention of unemployed accused with no local ties and who was present in Canada illegally); *R. v. Hall*, [1996] N.J. No. 30, 138 Nfld. & P.E.I.R. 80 (Nfld. C.A.) (upholding detention of accused with no real ties to Newfoundland or roots in any particular area).

[170] See *e.g.*, *R. v. Riach*, [1972] B.C.J. No. 523, 9 C.C.C. (2d) 110 at 111 (B.C.S.C.) (persons "who have previously skipped bail or escaped from lawful custody" should be denied bail because "experience teaches that such record is likely to be of greater significance than any expression of pious future intentions"); *R. v. Demers*, [1988] S.J. No. 446, 69 Sask.R. 210 (Sask. Q.B.) (detention ordered for accused with criminal record including convictions for failing to appear in court); *R. v. Miller*, [1984] S.J. No. 284, 32 Sask.R. 138 (Sask. Q.B.) (same); *R. v. Ashade (No. 1)*, [1992] N.S.J. No. 54, 111 N.S.R. (2d) 375 (N.S.T.D.) (same); *R. v. Benn*, [1993] A.J. No. 626, 141 A.R. 293 (Alta. C.A.) (same).

[171] See *e.g.*, *R. v. Biddle*, [1995] O.J. No. 1211, 82 O.A.C. 107 at para. 6 (Ont. C.A. (In Chambers)) (ordering accused's release despite two dated prior convictions for failing to appear; *R. v. Crane*, [1997] M.J. No. 122 (Man. C.A.) (relevance of convictions for failing to attend court from six years earlier dismissed given passage of time).

[172] *R. v. Brotherston*, [2009] B.C.J. No. 2294, 71 C.R. (6th) 81 at para. 25 (B.C.C.A.).

[173] See *e.g.*, *R. v. McCreery*, [1996] B.C.J. No. 2018, 110 C.C.C. (3d) 561 at para. 35 (B.C.S.C.) ("The more a conviction looks imminent, the less likely the bail possibility becomes."). But see

bail hearing it can be dangerous to place too much weight on the apparent strength of the Crown's case. As Justice Trotter has pointed out, the "expeditious and sometimes informal nature of a bail hearing may reflect an unrealistically strong case for the Crown."[174]

(b) Public Safety: The Secondary Ground

§6.65 The secondary ground, set out in section 515(10)(*b*), allows for detention where "the detention is necessary for the protection or safety of the public, including any victim of or witness to the offence, or any person under the age of 18 years, having regard to all the circumstances including any substantial likelihood that the accused will, if released from custody, commit a criminal offence or interfere with the administration of justice".

§6.66 In *R. v. Morales*,[175] the Supreme Court of Canada declared a portion of an earlier version of this subsection unconstitutional. It permitted pre-trial detention based on either the "public interest" or the "protection or safety of the public". The Court found the former phrase to be unconstitutionally vague and inconsistent with section 11(*e*) of the *Charter*. This aspect of the decision is explained more fully below in Part 4(3). At the same time, however, the Court held that the latter phrase was constitutionally valid. Under amendments enacted after *Morales*, public safety is now the key consideration under section 515(10)(*b*).

§6.67 In *Morales*, the Court explained that the "danger or likelihood that an individual will commit a criminal offence does not in itself provide just cause for detention. In general, our society does not countenance preventive detention of individuals simply because they have a proclivity to commit crime."[176] Instead, as the Court explained:

> [b]ail is denied only for those who pose a "substantial likelihood" of committing an offence or interfering with the administration of justice, and only where this "substantial likelihood" endangers "the protection or safety of the public". Moreover, detention is justified only when it is "necessary" for

---

R. v. Siemans, [1991] M.J. No. 39, 70 Man.R. (2d) 319 (Man. C.A. (In Chambers)) (granting bail for murder despite strong prosecution case where accused turned himself in, had strong family support, had no criminal record, and displayed no propensity for violence, substance abuse or psychiatric difficulties); *R. v. Perron*, [1989] J.Q. no 852, 51 C.C.C. (3d) 518 at 530 (Que. C.A.) ("Strong evidence, even overwhelming evidence, is only one factor to be considered among several others.").

[174] Gary T. Trotter, *The Law of Bail in Canada*, 3d ed. (Toronto: Thomson Carswell, 2010) at 3-7. See also Gary T. Trotter, "Bail Pending Appeal: The Strength of the Appeal and Public Interest Criterion" (2001) 45 C.R. (5th) 267 at 269 ("It is well recognized that the case may seem artificially strong or cogent at the bail hearing, due to the relaxed rules of evidence"); *R. v. Blind*, [1999] S.J. No. 597, 139 C.C.C. (3d) 87 at 94 (Sask. C.A.) (there are "many cases where the strength of the Crown's case appears, at the pre-trial stage, to be overwhelming only to have it unravel as the trial progresses"); Ontario, *Commission on Systemic Racism in the Ontario Criminal Justice System* (Toronto: Queen's Printer for Ontario, 1995) at 123 (finding that 18 per cent of those denied bail were not found guilty).

[175] [1992] S.C.J. No. 98, [1992] 3 S.C.R. 711 (S.C.C.).

[176] *Ibid.*, at para. 37 (S.C.R.).

public safety. It is not justified where detention would merely be convenient or advantageous.[177]

The precise meaning of "substantial likelihood" has been the subject of some controversy.[178] Clearly, speculative assertions that the accused might commit further offences or interfere with the administration of justice are not enough to warrant detention under section 515(10)(*b*). At the same time, as the Supreme Court of Canada acknowledged in *Morales*, it is impossible to make unerring predictions about the potential for recidivism and future dangerousness.[179] Justice Trotter has thus suggested that the provision requires satisfying a slightly enhanced balance of probabilities test.[180] This means that detention should only be ordered if it is clearly more likely than not that, if released, the accused will commit a criminal offence or interfere with administration of justice and thereby endanger the protection or safety of the public.

§6.68 A number of factors will be relevant to a court's assessment of the secondary ground under section 515(10)(*b*).[181] The accused's criminal record is obviously a key consideration. For example, where the charge(s) are serious and the accused already has a long and uninterrupted criminal record, the court may often conclude that there is a substantial likelihood that the accused will commit further offences and thereby endanger public safety.[182] This is especially true where the offence charged appears consistent with a pattern of prior offending.[183]

---

[177] *Ibid.*, at para. 39 (S.C.R.). See also *R. v. Baltovich*, [1991] O.J. No. 2031, 68 C.C.C. (3d) 362 at para. 18 (Ont. C.A.).

[178] See *R. v. Carbone*, [1972] O.J. No. 1226, 20 C.R.N.S. 313 at 313 (Ont. Co. Ct.) (the standard's "meaning is more akin to the balance of probabilities in that the evidence should substantially weigh in favour of the likelihood of a repetition of the offence"); *R. v. Braun*, [1994] S.J. No. 312, 91 C.C.C. (3d) 237 at 253-55 (Sask. C.A.) ("The simple possibility of criminal activity is not sufficient to keep an accused in custody."). But see *R. v. Link*, [1990] A.J. No. 169, 105 A.R. 160 (Alta. C.A.) ("substantial likelihood" only means "substantial risk" and is not synonymous with "probability" in the sense of being more likely to occur or not).

[179] *R. v. Morales*, [1992] S.C.J. No. 98, [1992] 3 S.C.R. 711 at para. 44 (S.C.C.) ("the impossibility of making exact predictions does not preclude a bail system which aims to deny bail to those who likely will be dangerous").

[180] Gary T. Trotter, *The Law of Bail in Canada*, 3d ed. (Toronto: Thomson Carswell, 2010) at 3-16.

[181] See generally, *R. v. Rondeau*, [1996] J.Q. no 1090, 108 C.C.C. (3d) 474 at 478 (Que. C.A.), suggesting the following list of considerations:

> ... (1) the nature of the offence, (2) the relevant circumstances of the offence, which may put in issue events prior to and subsequent to the offence, (3) the likelihood of a conviction, (4) the degree of participation of the accused, (5) the relationship between the accused and the victim, (6) the profile of the accused, *i.e.*, his occupation, his lifestyle, his criminal record, his family situation, his mental state, (7) his conduct prior to the commission of the alleged offence, (8) the danger which the interim release of the accused represents for the community specifically affected by the matter.

[182] See *e.g.*, *R. v. Favel*, [1984] S.J. No. 613, 35 Sask.R. 235 (Sask. Q.B.); *R. v. Squires*, [1996] N.J. No. 353, 161 Nfld. & P.E.I.R. 17 (Nfld. S.C.T.D.); *R. v. Cooke* (1996), 188 N.B.R. (2d) 235, 40 A.P.R. 235 (N.B.C.A.); *R. v. MacLellan*, [1985] P.E.I.J. No. 49, 56 Nfld. & P.E.I.R. 324 (P.E.I.S.C.).

[183] See *e.g.*, *R. v. Carrier*, [1979] M.J. No. 93, 51 C.C.C. (2d) 307 (Man. C.A.) (accused ordered detained where he had a number of prior convictions for offences similar to those charged); *R. v. Groulx* (1974), 17 C.C.C. (2d) 351 (Que. S.C.) (same); *R. v. Pearson (No. 2)*, [1979] Q.J. No.

§6.69 The length of an accused's criminal record may, however, be less important than the nature of previous offences. For example, where the record includes convictions for failing to comply with court orders (such as bail or probation orders) this will weigh strongly in favour of pre-trial detention.[184] In contrast, if an accused does not have a criminal record, the Crown will be hard pressed to justify pre-trial detention under section 515(10)(*b*). Similarly, as Justice Trotter suggests, even where an accused has a criminal record, if it "is somewhat dated, or is comprised of fairly minor offences, [it] should not carry much weight."[185] The same is arguably true with respect to a criminal record that does not include prior convictions for failing to comply with court orders.[186]

§6.70 A further consideration is whether an accused is already on bail when charged. As noted above, this will serve to place the burden on the accused to justify his release.[187] Depending on the circumstances, the onus may prove difficult for the accused to overcome. For example, bail will be especially hard to secure where the accused was already on a number of prior release orders at the time of arrest[188] or where the offence charged is similar to the offence for which the accused was already on bail.[189] Analogous concerns arise under the secondary ground where an accused is on probation at the time of arrest, although in such situations the *Code* does not formally reverse the burden.

§6.71 The nature of the charge is also an important consideration, although its use must be approached with some caution. No matter the offence, the *Code* contemplates the potential for bail.[190] Allowing the nature of the allegations to

---

236, 9 C.R. (3d) 229 (Que. S.C.) (same). See however, *R. v. Larsen*, [1976] B.C.J. No. 1045, 34 C.R.N.S. 399 (B.C.S.C.), where the Court arguably took this principle too far by considering the fact that the accused had twice been *acquitted* of similar allegations.

[184] See *e.g.*, *R. v. C. (P.R.)*, [1996] P.E.I.J. No. 103, 146 Nfld. & P.E.I.R. 240 (P.E.I.S.C. (In Chambers)) (emphasizing accused's lengthy criminal record, which included convictions for violating a mandatory supervision order, failing to attend court, disobeying court order and breach of recognizance, in concluding that detention warranted on secondary ground); *R. v. Robart*, [1993] N.S.J. No. 560, 136 N.S.R. (2d) 72 (N.S.S.C.) (accused detained, in part, on basis of lengthy criminal record, although offences "not of the most serious kind" many committed while awaiting trial for other offences); *R. v. MacLellan*, [1985] P.E.I.J. No. 49, 56 Nfld. & P.E.I.R. 324 (P.E.I.S.C.) (detention ordered due to lengthy criminal record, including offences committed while on earlier forms of release).

[185] Gary T. Trotter, *The Law of Bail in Canada*, 3d ed. (Toronto: Thomson Carswell, 2010) at 3-17, citing *R. v. Hickey*, [1977] N.J. No. 180, 35 C.C.C. (2d) 154 (Nfld. Dist. Ct.).

[186] See *e.g.*, *R. v. Ross*, [2003] P.E.I.J. No. 125, 234 Nfld. & P.E.I.R. 302 at para. 28 (P.E.I.S.C.T.D.) (accused's record did not include any prior convictions for breaching court orders, factor counted toward release under secondary ground).

[187] *Criminal Code*, s. 516(a)(i).

[188] See *e.g.*, *R. v. Menard*, [1972] O.J. No. 2125, 19 C.R.N.S. 6 (Ont. Co. Ct.) (accused ordered detained because on four separate bail orders when arrested).

[189] See *R. v. Hill*, [1973] B.C.J. No. 736, [1973] 5 W.W.R. 382 at 384 (B.C.S.C.) (noting that the most likely basis for detention on the secondary ground "will occur in cases where an accused, while on release on one or more charges, is charged with committing other crimes of a similar nature").

[190] See *R. v. LaFramboise*, [2005] O.J. No. 5785, 203 C.C.C. (3d) 492 at para. 31 (Ont. C.A. (In Chambers)) ("the nature of the offence charged, by itself, cannot justify the denial of bail"; accused charged with first degree murder ordered released); *R. v. Blind*, [1999] S.J. No. 597, 139

control the decision would therefore be at odds with both Parliament's intention and the presumption of innocence.[191] When considered along with other factors, however, the seriousness of the offence may legitimately militate against release. In many cases, for example, detention under the secondary ground would be justified where the accused is charged with a brutal and unexplained crime and the Crown's case seems overwhelming.[192]

Mental illness + addiction

§6.72 Mental illness and addiction may also militate in favour detention under the secondary ground, especially if these problems have resulted in violent or erratic behaviour.[193] In the absence of evidence that the problem can be managed effectively in the community through the use of conditions, an accused facing such challenges may have a difficult time gaining release.

§6.73 Subsection 515(10)(*b*) also contemplates that public safety could be endangered by an accused who poses a substantial likelihood of interfering with the administration of justice if released. Again, speculative concerns that an accused may attempt to interfere with the administration of justice are not enough to justify detention. There must be a concrete foundation for such concerns before pre-trial detention is justified.[194]

C.C.C. (3d) 87 at para. 15 (Sask. C.A.) ("hearing judge must not become so focused on the gravity of the offence and the strength of the Crown's case as to overlook that there are no categories of offences for which bail is not a possibility"; accused charged with murder released).

[191] See *R. v. Braun*, [1994] S.J. No. 312, 91 C.C.C. (3d) 237 at 254-55 (Sask. C.A.) ("appellant is entitled to the benefit of the presumption of innocence...[t]he overwhelming nature of the evidence and the probability of conviction are factors but not determining factors in deciding this question"). But see *R. v. Ghannime*, [1980] J.Q. no 185, 18 C.R. (3d) 186 (Que. S.C.) (seriousness of drug trafficking charge justification for detention on secondary ground); *R. v. Groulx* (1974), 17 C.C.C. (2d) 351 (Que. S.C.) (same).

[192] See *e.g.*, *R. v. Saswirsky*, [1984] O.J. No. 587, 17 C.C.C. (3d) 341 (Ont. H.C.J.) (accused charged with brutal attack on a young woman, case corroborated in several materials respects, detention ordered on secondary ground); *R. v. Squires*, [1996] N.J. No. 353, 161 Nfld. & P.E.I.R. 17 (Nfld. T.D.) (same); *R. v. Rondeau*, [1996] J.Q. no 1090, 108 C.C.C. (3d) 474 (Que. C.A.) (same).

[193] See *e.g.*, *R. v. Squires*, [1996] N.J. No. 353, 161 Nfld. & P.E.I.R. 17 (Nfld. T.D.) (accused with drinking problem who becomes aggressive and belligerent when drunk ordered detained on secondary ground); *R. v. O'Brien*, [1981] A.J. No. 21, 25 C.R. (3d) 168 (Alta. Q.B.) (bizarre allegations involving two counts of pointing a firearm involving an accused who is unstable when drinking results in detention based on secondary ground despite absence of criminal record); *R. v. Litke*, [1976] B.C.J. No. 1259, 34 C.R.N.S. 397 (B.C.S.C.) (heroin addiction emphasized in ordering detention); *R. v. Rondeau*, [1996] J.Q. no 1090, 108 C.C.C. (3d) 474 at 478 (Que. C.A.) (noting that the accused's "mental state" is a relevant consideration under the secondary ground); *R. v. Lehoux*, [1997] B.C.J. No. 2067, 97 B.C.A.C. 52 (B.C.C.A.) (detention ordered on secondary ground where accused suffered from a paranoid personality disorder and was charged with a violent and unprovoked attack on lawyer involved in family dispute); *R. v. Pesic*, [1993] B.C.J. No. 159, 22 B.C.A.C. 170 (B.C.C.A.) (detention ordered of accused charged with murder who displayed "considerable emotional instability", as evidenced in part by 12 prior shoplifting convictions).

[194] See *R. v. Baltovich*, [1991] O.J. No. 2031, 68 C.C.C. (3d) 362 at para. 18 (Ont. C.A.).

§6.74 Courts have ordered detention on this basis, for example, of accused persons who attempted to influence potential witnesses before being arrested,[195] have expressed an intention to interfere with witnesses or destroy evidence if released,[196] have established connections to organized crime[197] or plan to live in close proximity to key Crown witnesses.[198]

(c) Confidence in the Administration of Justice: The Tertiary Ground

§6.75 The most controversial basis for denying bail is the tertiary ground supplied by section 515(10)(c). Its current form results from a recent amendment to the *Code* introduced to correct a constitutional deficiency that the Supreme Court of Canada identified in an earlier version of the provision.[199] In *R. v. Hall*,[200] the Court found what was then the opening phrase of section 515(10)(c) ("on any other just cause being shown") to be unconstitutional because it conferred an open-ended discretion to refuse bail. (The predecessor provision's constitutional infirmities are explained more fully below in Part 4(3)).

§6.76 The current iteration of the tertiary ground retains those aspects from the predecessor provision that the Court in *Hall* upheld as constitutional, while also adding a requirement to consider the role of firearms in the offence(s) for which bail is sought. The provision now provides that a denial of bail is justified:

> if the detention is necessary to maintain confidence in the administration of justice, having regard to all the circumstances, including
>
> (i) the apparent strength of the prosecution's case,
>
> (ii) the gravity of the offence,
>
> (iii) the circumstances surrounding the commission of the offence, including whether a firearm was used, and
>
> (iv) the fact that the accused is liable, on conviction, for a potentially lengthy term of imprisonment or, in the case of an offence that involves, or whose subject-matter is, a firearm, a minimum punishment of imprisonment for a term of three years or more.

---

[195] See *e.g.*, *R. v. Nielsen*, [1982] M.J. No. 95, 17 Man.R. (2d) 109 (Man. C.A.) (accused detained in part because of allegation that he attempted to influence potential evidence of two witnesses who were members of his family).

[196] See *e.g.*, *R. v. O'Neill*, [1973] N.B.J. No. 96, 11 C.C.C. (2d) 240 (N.B.Q.B.) (accused detained where overheard by police officer telling co-accused that if released he would destroy evidence).

[197] See *e.g.*, *R. v. Milton*, [1985] N.S.J. No. 410, 70 N.S.R. (2d) 155 (N.S.T.D.) (admitted member of Hell's Angels detained on basis of likelihood that he would threaten witnesses); *R. v. Giles*, [1985] N.S.J. No. 416, 70 N.S.R. (2d) 176 (N.S.T.D.) (same).

[198] See *e.g.*, *R. v. Daigle*, [1988] N.B.J. No. 1176, 95 N.B.R. (2d) 248 (N.B.Q.B.) (accused charged with second degree murder proposed to live with parents across street from key Crown witness).

[199] See *R. v. Hall*, [2002] S.C.J. No. 65, [2002] 3 S.C.R. 309 (S.C.C.). See also, *Tackling Violent Crime Act*, S.C. 2008, c. 6, s. 37.

[200] *R. v. Hall*, [2002] S.C.J. No. 65, [2002] 3 S.C.R. 309 (S.C.C.).

§6.77 As discussed, many of the factors listed for the tertiary ground are also relevant to the primary and secondary grounds. As Chief Justice McLachlin stressed for the majority in *Hall*, however, denying bail to "maintain confidence in the administration of justice is not a mere 'catch-all' for cases where the first two grounds have failed."[201] "It represents," she explained, "a separate and distinct basis for bail denial not covered by the other two categories."[202]

§6.78 According to the majority in *Hall*, section 515(10)(*c*) "sets out specific factors which delineate a narrow set of circumstances under which bail can be denied on the basis of maintaining confidence in the administration of justice."[203] In explaining its decision upholding (most of) the predecessor provision, the majority emphasized the safeguards built into the provision to guard against the arbitrary denial of bail. As the Chief Justice explained, to deny bail under section 515(10)(*c*):

> The judge must be satisfied that detention is not only advisable but necessary. The judge must, moreover, be satisfied that detention is necessary not just to any goal, but to maintain confidence in the administration of justice. Most importantly, the judge makes this appraisal objectively through the lens of the four factors Parliament has specified. The judge cannot conjure up his own reasons for denying bail; while the judge must look at all the circumstances, he must focus particularly on the factors Parliament has specified. At the end of the day, the judge can only deny bail if satisfied that in view of these factors and related circumstances, a reasonable member of the community would be satisfied that denial is necessary to maintain confidence in the administration of justice. ... the reasonable person making this assessment must be one properly informed about "the philosophy of the legislative provisions, *Charter* values and the actual circumstances of the case"... .[204]

§6.79 The tertiary ground must therefore be approached in light of the strong preference for pre-trial release evinced in both the *Code* and section 11(*e*) of the *Charter*. The decision whether to deny bail under this ground, moreover, should focus on the four specific, enumerated factors. Doing so reduces the danger that the tertiary ground will become a proxy for "a judge's own perspective, resulting in unpredictable and inconsistent bail decisions determined by judicial discretion."[205] As the Ontario Court of Appeal has explained:

---

[201] *Ibid.*, at para. 30 (S.C.R.).

[202] *Ibid.*

[203] *Ibid.*, at para. 40 (S.C.R.).

[204] *Ibid.*, at para. 41(S.C.R.) [emphasis in original]. See also *R. v. Nguyen*, [1997] B.C.J. No. 2121, 119 C.C.C. (3d) 269 at 274 (B.C.C.A. (In Chambers)) [citations omitted].

[205] *R. v. M. (E.W.)*, [2006] O.J. No. 3654, 223 C.C.C. (3d) 407 at para. 28 (Ont. C.A.). See also *R. v. B. (A.)*, [2006] O.J. No. 394, 204 C.C.C. (3d) 490 at para. 26 (Ont. S.C.J.) (reversing order denying bail to accused charged with firearms offences, noting that "it cannot be seriously maintained, that 'today's climate' of public opinion requires that *every* person charged with the commission of an offence involving handguns must be denied bail pending their trial" [emphasis in original]).

The importance of the legislative direction that the court consider these four factors cannot be overstated.

...

No one factor is determinative. The four factors should be analysed together, not separately. Consideration of their combined effect in the context of all the circumstances enables the court to determine whether it is necessary to deny bail in order to maintain public confidence in the administration of justice.[206]

§6.80 *Hall* provides a vivid example of the sort of circumstances that may combine to justify pre-trial detention based on the need to maintain confidence in the administration of justice. In that case, the victim was found savagely murdered in her home, there were 37 slash wounds on her hands, forearms, shoulder, neck and face and her neck was cut to the vertebrae in an apparent effort to decapitate her. There was compelling evidence linking the accused to the murder, including traces of the accused's blood in the deceased's home and footwear impressions found at the crime scene matching the accused's running shoes. Videotape evidence from a convenience store on the night of the murder showed the accused wearing those running shoes. The accused admitted to police that he had been in the convenience store that evening but denied that he had been wearing the shoes. The murder received extensive media coverage and, in the relatively small city of Sault Ste. Marie where the crime occurred, there was considerable public anxiety, including fear on the part of the victim's family. In these circumstances, where the accused faced a mandatory sentence of life imprisonment if convicted, the majority in *Hall* found no error in the bail judge's decision denying bail based on the tertiary ground.

§6.81 Thankfully, cases like *Hall*, involving a brutal crime, overwhelming evidence, the potential for a very long sentence, extensive media coverage and significant public concern, are comparatively uncommon. No doubt, this is what led Justice Cronk to observe that detention under the tertiary ground should be "rare" and limited to only a "narrow category of cases".[207] And while tertiary ground cases very often involve shocking allegations,[208] this factor alone is not enough to justify pre-trial detention on the tertiary ground. When the prosecution presents a weak case, even a brutal crime is unlikely to justify detention.[209]

---

[206] *R. v. M. (E.W.)*, [2006] O.J. No. 3654, 223 C.C.C. (3d) 407 at paras. 30-31 (Ont. C.A.).

[207] *R. v. La Framboise*, [2005] O.J. No. 5785, 203 C.C.C. (3d) 492 at paras. 30, 36 (Ont. C.A. (In Chambers)).

[208] See *e.g.*, *R. v. M. (E.W.)*, [2006] O.J. No. 3654, 223 C.C.C. (3d) 407 at paras. 30-31 (Ont. C.A.).

[209] See *e.g.*, *R. v. LaFramboise*, [2005] O.J. No. 5785, 203 C.C.C. (3d) 492 (Ont. C.A. (In Chambers)) (brutal nature of homicide not enough to warrant detention given the appellant's apparently limited involvement and concerns about strength of Crown's case).

(9) Evidence and Procedure at the Bail Hearing

§6.82 A bail hearing is not a trial. The key aim is to facilitate the timely release of those who are good candidates for bail while ensuring that those who do not meet the criteria for release are detained.[210] Not surprisingly, then, the *Criminal Code* contemplates a largely informal process, foregoing the panoply of evidentiary and procedural safeguards that ordinarily mark a trial.[211] In this Part, we consider the various rules governing evidence and procedure at the bail hearing, while critiquing some of the implications of the expeditious nature of the process.

(a) *Publication Bans*

§6.83 Under section 517 of the *Code*, if an accused requests it, a justice presiding at a bail hearing must impose a publication ban on "the evidence taken, the information given or the representations made" and "the reasons ... given by the justice".[212] If more than one accused is being tried on the same information or indictment and a publication ban is requested by one, the order should be extended to all; otherwise it would be ineffective given the real potential for overlapping evidence.[213] In contrast, if the Crown applies for a publication ban, the justice has a discretion whether or not to grant it.[214] If ordered, a publication ban remains in effect either until the accused is discharged after a preliminary inquiry or at the end of the trial.[215]

§6.84 In *Toronto Star Newspapers Ltd. v. Canada*,[216] the mandatory issuance of the ban at the accused's request was challenged as a violation of the right to freedom of expression and a free press under section 2(*b*) of the *Charter*.[217] In upholding this rule as a reasonable limit under section 1, the Court noted that the purpose of the ban is twofold: to protect the accused's right to a fair trial and promote expeditious bail hearings.[218] Most obviously, the ban insulates prospective jurors from potentially prejudicial information.[219] In addition, mandatory issuance relieves the accused from extending scarce resources (that could be put to better use at trial) to contest opposition from the Crown and media.[220] Such

---

[210] See *Toronto Star Newspapers Ltd. v. Canada*, [2010] S.C.J. No. 21, [2010] 1 S.C.R. 721, 2010 SCC 21 at para. 28 (S.C.C.).

[211] *Ibid.*, at paras. 27-28 (SCC).

[212] *Criminal Code*, s. 517(1).

[213] *Toronto Star Newspapers Ltd. v. Canada*, [2010] S.C.J. No. 21, [2010] 1 S.C.R. 721, 2010 SCC 21 at para. 6 (S.C.C.) (finding that while s. 517 is silent on the point, the justice has jurisdiction at common law to make such an order).

[214] *Ibid.*

[215] *Ibid.*

[216] [2010] S.C.J. No. 21, [2010] 1 S.C.R. 721, 2010 SCC 21 at para. 6 (S.C.C.).

[217] *Ibid.*

[218] *Ibid.*, at para. 23 (SCC).

[219] *Ibid.*, at paras. 30, 37, 54, 60 (SCC).

[220] *Ibid.*, at paras. 35-37, 51, 60 (SCC).

opposition, the Court also noted, would invariably delay the bail hearing at the expense of the accused's liberty.[221]

(b) The Evidentiary Foundation for the Bail Determination

§6.85 The informality of the bail process is reflected in the evidentiary rules applying to bail hearings. Although the *Code* contemplates that bail decisions will be made on the basis of "evidence" (*i.e.*, testimony under oath, either *viva voce* or by affidavit), a number of provisions dispense with the need for sworn evidence and strict compliance with the formal rules of evidence.

§6.86 For example, subject to limitations on questioning the accused regarding the offence with which he is charged (discussed immediately below, in Part 3(9)(*c*)), the justice may "make such inquiries, on oath *or otherwise*, of and concerning the accused as he considers desirable".[222] This appears to give a justice the authority to act on information supplied in response to his or her own inquiries, for example, by questioning the accused, counsel or the police.

§6.87 Apart from such informal inquiries by the justice, the *Code* presumes a need for evidence. As set out in section 518(1)(*c*), the prosecutor may, "in addition to any other relevant evidence, lead evidence" to prove that the accused "has previously been convicted of a criminal offence", "has been charged with and is awaiting trial for another criminal offence," "has previously committed an offence under section 145" (*i.e.*, escape custody, failing to attend court, breaching bail, *etc.*), or "to show the circumstances of the alleged offence, particularly as they relate to the probability of conviction of the accused."[223]

§6.88 How is the prosecutor to go about proving these matters? Section 518(1)(*e*) of the *Code* provides that the justice "may receive and base his decision on evidence considered credible and trustworthy by him in the circumstances of each case."[224] Unfortunately, there is a broad spectrum of opinion on the meaning of this provision.[225] At one end of the spectrum, courts have held that the prosecutor may simply read into the record a police-prepared document (often called a "Show Cause" or "Bail" Report) outlining the allegations and providing background information about the accused.[226] A similarly informal approach suggests that each side can make submissions rather than suffering the attendant delay of insisting on more formal proof.[227] At the other end of the spec-

---

[221] *Ibid.*, at paras. 37, 51 (SCC).

[222] *Criminal Code*, s. 518(1)(*a*) [emphasis added]. See also *Toronto Star Newspapers Ltd. v. Canada*, [2010] S.C.J. No. 21, [2010] 1 S.C.R. 721, 2010 SCC 21 at para. 28 (S.C.C.) (citing this provision in emphasizing the informal and expeditious nature of bail determinations).

[223] *Criminal Code*, s. 518(1)(*c*)(iv).

[224] *Criminal Code*, s. 518(1)(*e*).

[225] See generally, Gary T. Trotter, *The Law of Bail in Canada*, 3d ed. (Toronto: Thomson Carswell, 2010) at 5-51 to 5-57.

[226] See *R. v. Kevork*, [1984] O.J. No. 926 (Ont. H.C.J.); *R. v. Atwal*, [1986] B.C.J. No. 728 (B.C.S.C.).

[227] See *R. v. Courchene*, [1999] M.J. No. 536, 141 C.C.C. (3d) 431, 141 Man.R. (2d) 171 (Man. Q.B.).

trum is a decision holding that the investigating officer or complainant must always testify.[228] In between these extremes, some courts have held that the prosecutor may initially read the police report into the record; but if the defence objects the justice may require affidavit or *viva voce* evidence (though this evidence may be in hearsay form).[229]

§6.89 In our view, section 518(1)(*e*) must be read in conjunction with section 518(1)(*d*). The latter provides that "the justice may take into consideration any relevant matters agreed on by the prosecutor and the accused or his counsel." If Parliament intended section 518(1)(*e*) to allow the Crown to rely on unsworn representations without the accused's consent, section 518(1)(*d*) would have no purpose. We are therefore strongly of the view that unless the parties agree (as contemplated by section 518(1)(*d*)), section 518(1)(*e*) requires evidence, be it in *viva voce* or affidavit form. On this interpretation, section 518(1)(*e*) does not displace the need for evidence; it simply relaxes the formal rules of admissibility that would otherwise govern.[230] This is the view that the Supreme Court of Canada seems to have recently endorsed, albeit in *obiter*, explaining that:

> There are practically no prohibitions as regards the evidence the prosecution can lead to show cause why the detention of the accused in custody is justified. According to s. 518(1)(*e*) ... the prosecutor may lead any evidence that is "credible or trustworthy", which might include evidence of a confession that has not been tested for voluntariness or consistency with the *Charter*, bad character, information obtained by wiretap, hearsay statements, ambiguous post-offence conduct, untested similar facts, prior convictions, untried charges, or personal information on living and social habits.[231]

That said, in practice, accused persons often have a considerable incentive to forego insisting on evidence at their bail hearings. In most jurisdictions, the arresting officer is unlikely to be present when the accused makes his or her initial appearance in bail court. Insisting on evidence will therefore often require an adjournment of the hearing to permit the attendance of an officer briefed with sufficient information to testify about the case. In the interim, the accused re-

---

[228] See *R. v. Hajdu*, [1984] O.J. No. 433, 14 C.C.C. (3d) 563 (Ont. H.C.J.).

[229] See *R. v. Milton*, [1985] N.S.J. No. 410, 70 N.S.R. (2d) 155 (N.S.T.D.); *R. v. Dhindsa*, [1986] B.C.J. No. 1615, 30 C.C.C. (3d) 368 (B.C.S.C.); *R. v. Woo*, [1994] B.C.J. No. 1011, 90 C.C.C. (3d) 404 (B.C.S.C.).

[230] This is the position of the Court in *R. v. Woo*, [1994] B.C.J. No. 1011, 90 C.C.C. (3d) 404 at 411 (B.C.S.C.), which is supported by the analysis in *R. v. West*, [1972] O.J. No. 1962, 9 C.C.C. (2d) 369 at 372-73 (Ont. C.A.). This view has also been endorsed by Justice Trotter in his seminal text. See Gary T. Trotter, *The Law of Bail in Canada*, 3d ed. (Toronto: Thomson Carswell, 2010) at 5-54 to 5-55. It has also been followed by other courts. See *R. v. R. (B.E.)*, [2003] P.E.I.J. No. 125, 234 Nfld. & P.E.I.R. 302 at paras. 12-14 (P.E.I.S.C.); *R. v. Broadbent*, [1996] A.J. No. 296, 182 A.R. 74 (Alta. Q.B.).

[231] *Toronto Star Newspapers Ltd. v. Canada*, [2010] S.C.J. No. 21, [2010] 1 S.C.R. 721, 2010 SCC 21 at para. 28 (S.C.C.). See also *Criminal Code*, s. 518(1)(*d.*1) (specifically authorizing the introduction of "private communication under and within the meaning of Part VI" without the need to comply with ss. 189(5)).

mains in custody.[232] This creates a great deal of pressure on an accused to "consent" (as required by section 518(1)(*d*)), to the Crown reading in details about the allegations and accused from a Show Cause or Bail Report.

§6.90 Unfortunately, the quality of such reports can vary from officer to officer and one police force to the next. Information supplied by witnesses about the allegations, for example, may be synthesized into a narrative that glosses over gaps in the prosecution's case. Mistakes and embellishments are also common.[233] As a consequence, the bail hearing is not a particularly effective forum for exposing weaknesses in the prosecution's case or ensuring that there are reasonable and probable grounds to support the charge(s).[234] This is the main reason why we argued above (see §6.57 and §6.58) in favour of making a showing of reasonable and probable grounds a precondition for denying bail or imposing restrictive release conditions.

(c) Limits on Questioning the Accused

§6.91 An accused cannot be compelled to testify at his or her bail hearing.[235] If the accused chooses to testify, "he generally may be questioned with respect to the issues as defined by s. 515(10) of the *Criminal Code*."[236] As a result, the focus of questioning will be "on the accused as an individual: what kind of person he or she is, and whether he or she is likely to be a danger for society or to appear at trial."[237]

§6.92 The questioning of the accused at the bail hearing is subject to one very important limitation, set out in section 518(1)(*b*):

> the accused shall not be examined by the justice or any other persons except counsel for the accused respecting the offence with which the accused is charged, and no inquiry shall be made of the accused respecting that offence by way of cross-examination unless the accused has testified respecting the offence.

§6.93 The purpose of this prohibition is to provide the accused with protection against self-incrimination.[238] However, if the accused testifies "respecting the

---

[232] As was explained above in Part 3(5), a bail hearing may be adjourned for up to three clear days without the accused's consent. See *Criminal Code*, s. 516(1).

[233] For a critical discussion of how these reports are prepared and of the problem of inaccuracy in the contents of the reports, see Ontario, *Commission on Systemic Racism in the Ontario Criminal Justice System* (Toronto: Queen's Printer for Ontario, 1995) at 151-53. For an example, see *Nolan v. Toronto (Metropolitan) Police Force*, [1996] O.J. No. 1764 (Ont. Gen. Div.).

[234] See §6.64, above, and supporting notes.

[235] See *Canadian Charter of Rights and Freedoms*, Part I of the *Constitution Act, 1982*, being Schedule B to the *Canada Act 1982* (U.K.), 1982, c. 11, s. 11(*c*), which provides that: "Any person charged with an offence has the right not to be compelled to be a witness in proceedings against that person in respect of the offence." This language clearly includes the right not to be so compelled at the bail hearing in respect of the offence.

[236] See *R. v. Mallory*, [2007] O.J. No. 236, 217 C.C.C. (3d) 266 at para. 174 (Ont. C.A.).

[237] *Toronto Star Newspapers Ltd. v. Canada*, [2010] S.C.J. No. 21, [2010] 1 S.C.R. 721, 2010 SCC 21 at para. 52 (S.C.C.).

[238] See *R. v. Mallory*, [2007] O.J. No. 236, 217 C.C.C. (3d) 266 at para. 175 (Ont. C.A.).

offence" the door is opened under section 518(1)(*b*) and the Crown will be entitled to cross-examine the accused on that subject.

§6.94 In most cases whether the accused has testified "respecting the offence" will be obvious. If an accused person says anything in his or her testimony to suggest, "that the wrong person has been arrested or that the alleged offence is somehow excused or justified" then this should undoubtedly "be sufficient to trigger the prosecutor's right to cross-examine".[239]

§6.95 The choice to testify at one's bail hearing may have implications for the accused at trial. It is now clear that an accused may be cross-examined at trial based on his or her prior testimony from the bail hearing.[240] In this respect, section 518(1)(*b*) supplies an important protection. For example, if the prohibition is transgressed at the bail hearing the resulting testimony cannot be used to cross-examine the accused at trial.[241]

(10) Reviewing the Initial Bail Determination

§6.96 The initial bail determination is subject to review. The forum for review will vary depending on whether or not a section 469 offence is charged. The different procedural routes for securing a bail review are outlined immediately below. The uncertainty surrounding the standard for review permeates both categories and is addressed below in Part 3(10)(*c*).

(a) *Review Where a Section 469 Offence is Charged*

§6.97 Recall that when the accused is charged with a section 469 offence, it is a judge of the superior court who initially has exclusive jurisdiction to decide whether or not to grant bail under section 522 (discussed above in Part 3(7)). Reviews of that initial determination may only be made by the court of appeal.[242] Such reviews, however, are not a matter of right. Rather, under section 680 of

---

[239] Gary T. Trotter, *The Law of Bail in Canada*, 3d ed. (Toronto: Thomson Carswell, 2010) at 5-60 to 5-61. Justice Trotter also suggests that if an accused testifies that he intends to plead not guilty, this is in effect a declaration of innocence and should be sufficient to trigger the prosecutor's right to cross-examine. *Ibid.*, at 5-61 n. 260. On this point we disagree with Justice Trotter. In our view, an accused who testifies that he or she intends to plead not guilty is simply expressing the intention of putting the Crown to its proof. This should not be enough to open the door to cross-examination by a prosecutor respecting the offence.

[240] See *R. v. Henry*, [2005] S.C.J. No. 76, [2005] 3 S.C.R. 609 (S.C.C.) (holding that s. 13 of the *Charter* does not insulate an accused from cross-examination based on prior testimony in circumstances where that prior testimony was not compelled). The Court in *Henry* also held, however, that such testimony is not admissible if the accused does not testify at trial. See also *R. v. Mallory*, [2007] O.J. No. 236, 217 C.C.C. (3d) 266 at para. 171 (Ont. C.A.) (after citing *Henry*, implicitly suggesting that it does not offend *Charter* s. 13 to cross-examine accused at trial on bail hearing testimony).

[241] See *R. v. Mallory*, [2007] O.J. No. 236, 217 C.C.C. (3d) 266 at para. 175 (Ont. C.A.); *R. v. Deom*, [1981] B.C.J. No. 1546, 64 C.C.C. (2d) 222 at 223 (B.C.S.C.); *R. v. Paonessa*, [1982] O.J. no. 3209, 66 C.C.C. (2d) 300 at 306-307 (Ont. C.A.), affd [1983] S.C.J. No. 46, 3 C.C.C. (3d) 384 (S.C.C.).

[242] *Criminal Code*, s. 522(4).

the *Code*, they occur only when the chief justice or acting chief justice so direct.[243]

§6.98 Unfortunately, section 680 is silent on the standard to be applied in deciding whether or not to order a review by the court of appeal. As a result, guidance has come incrementally from the courts, which have required the applicant to show that the proposed review has "arguable merit";[244] in other words, that the court of appeal could possibly decide to overturn the initial decision.[245]

§6.99 Should a review by the court of appeal be directed, the standard to be applied in reviewing the merits of the superior court judge's bail decision is discussed below.

(b)   Review in all other Cases Involving Adult Accused

§6.100 For all other offences involving adult accused, bail decisions may be reviewed at any time before trial on the accused's[246] or prosecutor's request.[247] In most jurisdictions such reviews are conducted by a superior court judge.[248] Any aspect of the decision may be reviewed, including whether or not to order an accused person's release from custody, the form of release and any conditions imposed. A bail review may be brought after providing at least two clear days written notice to the other side.[249]

§6.101 Unless ordered by the court or requested by one of the parties, the accused is not required to be present at the review.[250] If the accused is in custody, the judge may order the authorities to bring him or her to the hearing.[251] If an accused on release fails to attend when ordered to do so, the judge may issue a warrant for his or her arrest.[252] The judge may adjourn a bail review. However, if the accused is in custody no adjournment may be for more than three clear days without his or her consent.[253]

§6.102 The same evidentiary and procedural provisions governing the bail hearing itself apply (with necessary modifications) to the review.[254] The rules

---

[243] *Criminal Code*, s. 680(1).

[244] *R. v. Cooper*, [1999] A.J. No. 942, 138 C.C.C. (3d) 292 at para. 12. (Alta. C.A.).

[245] See *R. v. Moore*, [1979] N.S.J. No. 619, 49 C.C.C. (2d) 78 at 79 (N.S.C.A.). This statement of the threshold requirement has been widely followed. See *R. v. Allen*, [2001] N.J. No. 243, 158 C.C.C. (3d) 225 (Nfld. C.A.); *R. v. Sanchez*, [1998] N.S.J. No. 415, 172 N.S.R. (2d) 318 (N.S.C.A.); *R. v. Webster*, [1995] P.E.I.J. No. 100, 132 Nfld. & P.E.I.R. 78 (P.E.I.C.A.); *R. v. Ridley*, [1987] N.B.J. No. 612, 82 N.B.R. (2d) 176 (N.B.C.A.), *United States of America v. Andrews*, [1991] M.J. No. 512, 76 Man.R. (2d) 41 (Man. C.A.).

[246] *Criminal Code*, s. 520(1).

[247] *Criminal Code*, s. 521(1).

[248] *Criminal Code*, ss. 493, 520(1), 521(1).

[249] *Criminal Code*, ss. 520(2), 521(2).

[250] *Criminal Code*, ss. 520(3), 521(3).

[251] *Ibid.*

[252] *Criminal Code*, ss. 520(5), 521(5).

[253] *Ibid.*

[254] See *Criminal Code*, ss. 520(9), 521(10), each providing that ss. 517, 518 and 519 "apply with such modifications as the circumstances require".

respecting publication bans[255] and questioning the accused,[256] for example, apply equally on the bail review. In assessing the application, the reviewing judge may consider the transcript from the initial bail hearing and any earlier review, the exhibits filed and any additional evidence or exhibits tendered by the parties.[257] In some provinces, bail reviews are subject to specific rules of practice prescribing exactly what must be filed in terms of supporting materials, including an affidavit from the accused and any proposed sureties.[258] Finally, after an application for review has been heard, a further application on the same charge(s) cannot be brought for another 30 days absent leave of a judge.[259]

(c) The Standard of Review

§6.103 The standard to be applied to bail reviews is the source of some controversy.[260] This stems from an unfortunate lack of clarity in the relevant legislation and the fact that bail issues rarely persist all the way to the Supreme Court of Canada. For reviews by the superior court, the *Code* instructs the judge to either "dismiss the application",[261] or where either the accused or the prosecutor "show cause, allow the application, vacate the order previously made by the justice and make any other order provided for in section 515 that he considers is warranted".[262] The provision governing reviews by the court of appeal is similarly bereft of meaningful guidance.[263]

§6.104 Consequently, lower courts have largely been left on their own in deciding on the appropriate standard of review. Not surprisingly, divergent approaches have emerged. At one end of the spectrum, some courts have treated bail reviews like ordinary appeals, demanding an identifiable error in principle in the original decision before intervening and only permitting the filing of new material when the stringent rules governing the admission of fresh evidence on appeal are satisfied.[264] At the other end of the spectrum, some courts have

---

[255] *Criminal Code*, s. 517. Publication bans are discussed above in Part 3(9)(*a*).

[256] *Criminal Code*, s. 518(1)(*b*). The rules governing evidence at bail hearings, including limitations on the examination of the accused, are discussed above in Part 3(9)(*b*) and (*c*).

[257] *Criminal Code*, ss. 520(7)(*a*), (*b*), (*c*) and 521(8)(*a*), (*b*), (*c*).

[258] See *e.g.*, *Superior Court of Justice Criminal Proceedings Rules*, SI/92-99, Rule 20, available online at: <http://www.ontariocourts.on.ca/scj/en/about/rules/rules.pdf>.

[259] *Criminal Code*, ss. 520(8) and 521(9).

[260] See Gary T. Trotter, *The Law of Bail in Canada*, 3d ed. (Toronto: Thomson Carswell, 2010) at 8-8 to 8-15.

[261] *Criminal Code*, ss. 520(7)(*d*), 521(5)(*d*).

[262] *Criminal Code*, ss. 520(7)(*e*), 521(5)(*e*).

[263] See *Criminal Code*, s. 680(1), which provides that the court may either "confirm the decision", "vary the decision" or "substitute such other decision as, in its opinion, should have been made".

[264] See *R. v. West*, [1972] O.J. No. 1962, 9 C.C.C. (2d) 369 at 375 (Ont. C.A.) (applying predecessor provision and holding that "review should take the general form of an ordinary appeal and not be a hearing *de novo* or one in which either side has the *right* to submit additional material" [emphasis in original]. See also *R. v. Braun*, [1994] S.J. No. 312, 91 C.C.C. (3d) 237 at 242-43, 252 (Sask. C.A.) (same); *R. v. B. (R.V.)*, [1993] A.J. No. 665, 131 A.R. 175 at 178 (Alta. C.A.) (same); *R. v. Horvat*, [1972] B.C.J. No. 540, 9 C.C.C. (2d) 1 at 1-2 (B.C.S.C.) (same). *R. v.*

envisioned a *de novo* hearing. On this view, no deference is given to the initial determination and the reviewing court is free to substitute its decision for that of the original justice.[265]

§6.105 The approach that has garnered the most jurisprudential support is a middle ground between these extremes. On this view, a bail review is neither an ordinary appeal nor a hearing *de novo*. Rather it is a hybrid between the two. In short, the reviewing judge assesses the record (as amplified by any additional evidence) to decide whether a different order is warranted because of a legal or factual error or material change of circumstances.[266]

§6.106 We share Justice Trotter's view that none of the above approaches is entirely satisfactory. He argues that when the permissive language in the relevant sections of the *Code* is read in light of section 11(e) *Charter* right, a better approach on review would be to vacate an earlier order: "1. on the basis of a material change of circumstances; and/or, 2. by persuading the reviewing judge that a different result ought to have been reached by the justice."[267] In our view, except when it comes to credibility assessments, deference toward the initial bail decision is an idea that is difficult to reconcile with the accused's constitutional right "not to be denied reasonable bail without just cause".

Hunter, [1973] O.J. No. 1334, 24 C.R.N.S. 197 (Ont. Co. Ct.) (concluding that the same standard identified in *West* should apply equally to reviews under what are now ss. 520 and 521).

[265] See *R. v. Powers*, [1972] O.J. No. 902, 9 C.C.C. (2d) 533 at 537 (Ont. H.C.J.) (after reviewing the relevant sections and the statutory scheme, concluding that what is contemplated "is a hearing *de novo*"). See also *R. v. Thompson*, [1972] B.C.J. No. 400, 7 C.C.C. (2d) 70 at 76 (B.C.S.C.) (pointing to the word "review" in the relevant section as justification for a *de novo* determination); *R. v. Sexton*, [1976] N.J. No. 89, 33 C.R.N.S. 307 at 318 (Nfld. Dist. Crim. Ct.) (same). Although some courts have avoided the "*de novo*" terminology, the standard endorsed by them is quite permissive. See *R. v. Smith*, [1973] N.B.J. No. 76, 13 C.C.C. (2d) 374 at 377 (N.B.C.A.) ("The duty of this Court ... would appear to be to examine the record judicially and render the decision which we think 'should have been made' by the Judge of first instance giving proper regard to his findings of fact and the inferences which he has drawn."); *R. v. Cooper*, [2000] A.J. No. 1671, 160 C.C.C. (3d) 420 at para. 29 (Alta. C.A.), Berger J.A., dissenting (in the result) (same).

[266] See *R. v. McCue*, [1998] O.J. No. 4384, 130 C.C.C. (3d) 90 at 94 (Ont. Gen. Div.); *R. v. Hill*, [1973] B.C.J. No. 736, [1973] 5 W.W.R. 382 at 383 (B.C.S.C.); *R. v. Lysyk*, [2003] A.J. No. 447, 341 A.R. 81 at paras. 12-20 (Alta. Q.B.); *R. v. Wilson*, [1998] S.J. No. 610, [1998] 3 W.W.R. 56 at para. 16 (Sask. Q.B.); *R. v. Eiswerth*, [1996] S.J. No. 772, 151 Sask.R. 163 at para. 5 (Sask. Q.B.); *R. v. Nguyen*, [1993] A.J. no. 519, 140 A.R. 317 at paras. 15-16 (Alta. Q.B.); *R. v. Broadbent*, [1996] A.J. No. 296, 182 A.R. 74 at paras. 16-17 (Alta. Q.B.); *R. v. Johnson*, [1984] N.W.T.J. No. 40, 13 C.C.C. (3d) 441 at 444 (N.W.T.S.C.); *R. v. Carrier*, [1979] M.J. No. 93, 51 C.C.C. (2d) 307 at 313 (Man. C.A.); *R. v. Bradley and Bickerdike*, [1977] Q.J. No. 191, 38 C.C.C. (2d) 283 at 287 (Que. S.C.); *R. v. La Chappelle*, [1974] N.S.J. No. 324, 19 C.C.C. (2d) 70 at 78 (N.S.T.D.).

[267] Gary T. Trotter, *The Law of Bail in Canada*, 3d ed. (Toronto: Thomson Carswell, 2010) at 8-15. This is very close to the approach endorsed in *R. v. Smith*, [1973] N.B.J. No. 76, 13 C.C.C. (2d) 374 (N.B.C.A.) and *R. v. Cooper*, [2000] A.J. No. 1671, 160 C.C.C. (3d) 420 at para. 29 (Alta. C.A.).

(11) Revisiting the Bail Determination

§6.107 Beyond a bail review, the *Code* envisions a number of other means to review initial bail decisions. Each of these is briefly detailed below.

(a) Administrative Reviews

§6.108 The *Code* includes an important procedure to ensure a judicial monitoring of most accused persons held in custody.[268] If the trial of such an accused has not begun within a certain specified time, section 525 obliges the jailer to apply to have a date fixed for a hearing to decide whether or not the accused should be released from custody.[269] Once the jailer makes the necessary application to the court a date will be set for the hearing and the prosecutor and accused will be notified.[270] The section 525 hearing is mandatory and it is separate and distinct from any review sought by an accused under section 520 of the *Code*.[271]

§6.109 Section 525 directs that an accused must be ordered released if "the judge is not satisfied that the continued detention of the accused in custody is justified within the meaning of subsection 515(10)".[272] Who bears the burden of satisfying the judge whether continued detention is or is not justified? Unfortunately, there is a lack of consensus on that question. Some courts have held that the burden remains on the party that bore it at the initial bail hearing.[273] Others have taken the position that the Crown always bears the onus.[274]

§6.110 In assessing whether or not to order an accused person's release, the judge must consider whether the prosecutor or the accused has been responsible for any unreasonable delay.[275] But even if the delay cannot be attributed to the accused, release under section 525 is only justified when "the delay is so unreasonable as to outweigh the public interest" and "cannot be satisfactorily remedied under subs. (9)."[276] Subsection (9) empowers the judge to "give directions for expediting the trial of the accused."[277]

---

[268] The procedure does not apply to those charged with a s. 469 offence: *Criminal Code*, s. 525(1).

[269] *Criminal Code*, s. 525(1). Given the delays inherent in contemporary criminal proceedings, the specified timelines are short. For example, the time limit for indictable offences is 90 days and for summary offences, 30 days.

[270] *Criminal Code*, s. 525(2).

[271] See *R. v. Burton*, [1993] B.C.J. No. 892, 84 C.C.C. (3d) 311 at 318 (B.C.C.A.); *R. v. Waine*, [1990] O.J. No. 364, 56 C.C.C. (3d) 61 (Ont. H.C.J.); *R. v. Neill*, [1990] A.J. No. 690, 60 C.C.C. (3d) 26 (Alta. C.A.); *R. v. Johnson*, [1980] O.J. No. 2924, 57 C.C.C. (2d) 49 (Ont. H.C.J.). But see *R. v. Dass*, [1978] M.J. No. 19, 39 C.C.C. (2d) 365 (Man. C.A.) (holding that the section does not apply to those held in custody who have already had a bail review.)

[272] *Criminal Code*, s. 525(4). The judge can order release on an undertaking or recognizance, as per ss. 515(2)(*a*) to (*e*) with such conditions as permitted by s. 515(4) as the judge considers desirable. *Ibid.*

[273] See *e.g.*, *R. v. Thorsteinson*, [2006] M.J. No. 270, 238 C.C.C. (3d) 83 (Man. Q.B.).

[274] See *e.g.*, *R. v. Kuzmaski*, [1981] O.J. No. 3307, 65 C.C.C. (2d) 286 at 287-88 (Ont. Co. Ct.).

[275] *Criminal Code*, s. 525(3).

[276] *R. v. Cordes*, [1976] A.J. No. 577, 31 C.C.C. (2d) 279 at 285 (Alta. C.A.).

[277] See also *Criminal Code*, s. 526.

§6.111 The same procedural and evidentiary provisions governing the initial bail hearing apply (with necessary modifications) to section 525 reviews.[278] The rules respecting publication bans[279] and questioning the accused,[280] for example, apply equally on the bail review.

(b) On Consent

§6.112 If the accused and the prosecutor both consent, the *Code* grants considerable flexibility to vary any aspect of an existing bail order.[281] For example, the parties may agree to the accused's release or detention; vary the form of release; change a surety; increase or decrease the amount pledged; or remove, add, or change a condition of release.

§6.113 The judicial officer asked to formalize any agreed change, however, must have jurisdiction to do so. For offences other than those listed in section 469, the change can be made by the justice who made the original order.[282] But for section 469 offences, only a superior court judge can make the change.[283] In addition, "the court, judge or justice before which or whom an accused is to be tried" can modify the bail where the parties consent.[284]

§6.114 Where the accused is already on bail, the *Code* is silent regarding the accused's custodial status after the parties consent to a change but before the new form of release is finalized. In theory, if the earlier order is simply vacated the accused might be required to step back into custody until the new form of release is executed. To avoid this, the parties often ask the court to order that the earlier release order remain in place until the paperwork reflecting the new terms of release is executed.[285]

§6.115 A final provision that bears mentioning in this Part is section 515.1. It professes to allow for the variation of an undertaking or recognizance entered into under sections 499, 503 (*i.e.*, before the police) or 515 (*i.e.*, before a justice) simply "with the written consent of the prosecutor." As Justice Trotter has pointed out, this provision "is highly problematic" because it ostensibly permits court ordered releases under section 515 to be varied without either the

---

[278] See *Criminal Code*, s. 525(8), providing that ss. 517, 518 and 519 "apply with such modifications as the circumstances require".

[279] *Criminal Code*, s. 517. Publication bans are discussed above in Part 3(9)(*a*).

[280] *Criminal Code*, s. 518(1)(*b*). The rules governing evidence at bail hearings, including limitations on the examination of the accused, are discussed above in Part 3(9)(*b*) and (*c*).

[281] See *Criminal Code*, s. 523(2)(*c*).

[282] See *Criminal Code*, s. 523(2)(*c*)(i).

[283] See *Criminal Code*, s. 523(2)(*c*)(ii).

[284] See *Criminal Code*, s. 523(2)(*c*)(iii). This language has been held to include "both the judge presiding at the actual trial and any judge of a court who might so preside." See *R. v. Patterson*, [1985] A.J. No. 1024, 19 C.C.C. (3d) 149 at 152 (Alta. C.A.).

[285] Although such a request may in fact be unnecessary. See *R. v. Nutbean*, [1980] O.J. No. 1344, 55 C.C.C. (2d) 235 at 238 (Ont. C.A.), suggesting that if an existing order is varied the, "new amended interim judicial release order would not become operative until the required recognizance was entered into or undertaking given which would recognize the terms or conditions of the amended order."

accused's consent or the court's involvement.[286] As a result, it is not surprising that in these circumstances the section been read as also requiring judicial approval.[287]

§6.116 The *Code* makes no mention of sureties when a bail order is varied on consent. Nevertheless, the courts have held that before such variations are ordered sureties should confirm that they are willing to continue under any new or changed conditions.[288]

(c) At the Completion of the Preliminary Inquiry

§6.117 If the accused is ordered to stand trial after a preliminary inquiry, and is not charged with a section 469 offence, the presiding judge or justice may vacate any bail order previously made "on cause being shown" and "make any other order ... for the detention or release of the accused until his trial is completed" that the judge or justice "considers to be warranted".[289] Under this provision, an accused who was initially detained may seek pre-trial release if the prosecution's case seems weaker than at the time of the bail hearing. In contrast, where new and more serious allegations emerge at the inquiry, the prosecutor may seek the detention of an accused who was initially ordered released.[290]

(d) At Trial

§6.118 Under section 523(2)(*a*) of the *Code*, the "court, judge or justice before which or whom an accused is being tried" may vary a previous bail order "on cause being shown" and "make any other order ... for the detention or release of the accused until his trial is completed" that the court or judge "considers to be warranted".[291] Because the provision uses the phrase "is being tried", it has been interpreted to permit variation only after the trial has started. In non-jury trials, the trial begins for this purpose only after the accused is arraigned and enters a plea; it is not sufficient that the trial judge has been assigned and has heard

---

[286] Gary T. Trotter, *The Law of Bail in Canada*, 3d ed. (Toronto: Thomson Carswell, 2010) at 8-64.

[287] See *R. v. Ford*, [1988] O.J. No. 3725, 129 C.C.C. (3d) 189 (Ont. Gen. Div.) (The Court explained the provision as a means of bypassing the need for the earlier order to be formally vacated, so as to avoid the need for an accused to surrender into custody and for sureties to reattend.).

[288] See *R. v. Nutbean*, [1980] O.J. No. 1344, 55 C.C.C. (2d) 235 at 237-38 (Ont. C.A.). See also *Re Millward*, [1998] A.J. No. 922, 128 C.C.C (3d) 67 at 74-77 (Alta. Q.B.) (breach of this requirement cited in refusing to order forfeiture of bail against surety).

[289] *Criminal Code*, s. 523(2)(*b*).

[290] See *R. v. Braithwaite*, [1980] N.S.J. No. 605, 57 C.C.C. (2d) 351 (N.S.C.A.) (suggesting that being committed to stand trial following the preliminary inquiry, without more, is not enough to justify revocation of bail).

[291] *Criminal Code*, s. 523(2)(*a*).

pre-trial motions.[292] For jury trials, it commences when the jury is empanelled and the accused placed in its charge.[293]

§6.119 If an accused charged with a serious offence was released on bail before trial, a prosecutor might rely on section 523(2)(*a*) to seek the accused's detention following a guilty verdict but before sentencing. In contrast, an accused charged with several offences who was initially denied bail may use the provision to request bail pending sentencing if acquitted of the most serious charges.

§6.120 There does not appear to be any right of review from the trial judge's decision under section 523(2)(a) granting or refusing bail.[294]

(12) Revoking Bail

§6.121 Not surprisingly, circumstances may arise that justify revoking an accused's bail. This could include the discovery that the accused is preparing to abscond or the arrest of the accused for further offences while on release. Whatever the reason, the means for revoking bail are found in section 524 of the *Criminal Code*. That provision permits police to arrest the accused without a warrant when they have reasonable grounds to believe that the accused has: (*a*) contravened or is about to contravene a summons, appearance notice, promise to appear, undertaking or recognizance that was issued or given to him or entered into by him; or (*b*) has committed an indictable offence while on any one of these forms of release.[295] (Of course, in the second scenario, the police will also have concurrent authority to arrest for the offence they have reasonable grounds to believe the accused has committed.[296])

§6.122 In some cases, the police may choose to apply for a warrant to arrest an accused on bail. Such a warrant may be issued if a justice is satisfied of the same things described in the previous paragraph.[297] A warrant may be obtained, for example, so that it can be entered into the Canadian Police Information Computer (CPIC), enabling any other police officer who encounters the accused to make the arrest even without firsthand knowledge of the underlying reasons. In

---

[292] See *R. v. Durrani*, [2008] O.J. No. 5118, 242 C.C.C. (3d) 103 at para. 14 (Ont. C.A. (In Chambers)).

[293] See *R. v. McCreery*, [1996] B.C.J. No. 2018, 110 C.C.C. (3d) 561 at 569-70 (B.C.S.C.).

[294] See *R. v. Bukmeier*, [1996] B.C.J. No. 1090, 107 C.C.C. (3d) 272 at paras. 15-20 (B.C.C.A.) (concluding there was no right of review contemplated by the *Code* and intimating that the only potential recourse would be an application to the Supreme Court of Canada under s. 40(1) of the *Supreme Court Act*, R.S.C. 1985, c. S-26).

[295] *Criminal Code*, s. 524(2).

[296] See *Criminal Code*, s. 495(1)(*a*). Police arrest powers are discussed in Chapter 2, Part 4(4).

[297] *Criminal Code*, s. 524(1). See *R. v. Fulton*, [1972] S.J. No. 254, 10 C.C.C. (2d) 120 at 123-24 (Sask. Q.B.) (warrant may issue even though the police have not yet laid an information charging the accused with any new offence); *R. v. Sidorov*, [2001] A.J. No. 36, 160 C.C.C. (3d) 122 at 127-28 (Alta. C.A.) (justice before whom accused fails to appear as required has grounds to issue arrest warrant).

addition, police need such a warrant if they want to obtain further authorization to arrest the accused in a residence.[298]

§6.123 An accused who is arrested under these provisions must thereafter be taken before a justice. If the accused was not on bail for a section 469 offence, the justice will conduct a revocation hearing where he or she is required to "hear the prosecutor and his witnesses, if any, and the accused and his witnesses, if any."[299] If the accused is arrested while on bail for a section 469 offence, the justice must order the accused to be taken before a superior court judge.[300] That judge will conduct the very same type of hearing described immediately above.[301]

§6.124 There are several possible outcomes to a revocation hearing. The judge or justice's first task is to decide whether either (a) the accused contravened or was about to contravene his or her existing release order; or (b) there are reasonable grounds to believe that the accused has committed an indictable offence while on an existing form of release. If either of these questions are answered in the affirmative, the judge or justice must cancel the existing release order and order the accused's detention unless the accused shows cause why detention is not justified within the meaning of section 515(10).[302] If such cause is shown, the accused will be released on an undertaking or by entering into a recognizance on such terms and with any conditions that the judge or justice considers desirable.[303] If the judge or justice does not find either that the accused contravened the existing release order or that there are reasonable grounds to believe the

---

[298] See *Criminal Code*, s. 529.1(*a*). So-called "*Feeney*" warrants are explained in detail in Chapter 2, Part 4(4)(*g*).

[299] *Criminal Code*, s. 524(3)(*b*). The justice has jurisdiction on a revocation application even when the accused was released by the superior court following a review application under s. 520. See *R. v. Kinger*, [1982] A.J. No. 21, 65 C.C.C. (2d) 483 (Alta. C.A.). Also see Gary T. Trotter, *The Law of Bail in Canada*, 3d ed. (Toronto: Thomson Carswell, 2010) at 11-9 to 11-10 (suggesting that the justice can embark on a review with respect to an earlier form of release ordered by any level of court except where that earlier release related to a s. 469 offence). It is somewhat unclear whether a justice can embark on such a review on his or her own initiative or whether arrest for revocation purposes is an essential precondition for the jurisdiction to revoke bail to be engaged. See *R. v. Lafond*, [1975] Q.J. No. 94, 25 C.C.C. (2d) 568 (Que. Sess. Peace) (suggesting justice can raise issue on his or her own after the accused is before the court). But see *R. v. McBride*, [1996] O.J. No. 2226, 49 C.R. (4th) 294 (Ont. Gen. Div.) (suggesting that an arrest under s. 524 is an essential precondition for invoking the revocation procedures). See also *R. v. Kot*, [1983] O.J. No. 1168, 10 C.C.C. (3d) 297 (Ont. H.C.J.) (holding that a judge should not have raised bail revocation on his own motion based on his own observations).

[300] *Criminal Code*, s. 524(3)(*a*).

[301] See *Criminal Code*, s. 524(4). See *R. v. Parsons*, [1997] N.J. No. 337, 124 C.C.C. (3d) 92 (Nfld. C.A.), *per* Green J.A.) (holding that if accused was originally ordered released by court of appeal on review, revocation hearing should take place before single judge of that court). But see *R. v. Kinger*, [1982] A.J. No. 21, 65 C.C.C. (2d) 483 (Alta. C.A.) (holding, correctly in our view, that since judge on revocation hearing not reviewing original order, justice can conduct hearing even though original order issued by superior court).

[302] *Criminal Code*, s. 524(8).

[303] See *Criminal Code*, ss. 524(5) (prescribing powers of judge dealing with accused charged with s. 469 offence) and s. 524(9) (prescribing the powers of a justice dealing with all other accused persons).

accused committed an indictable offence while bound by that order, the accused must be released from custody.[304]

§6.125 As with the other review mechanisms discussed in this chapter, the procedural and evidentiary rules governing the bail hearing itself apply (with necessary modifications) to revocation hearings.[305] The rules respecting publication bans[306] and questioning the accused,[307] for example, apply equally to revocation hearings.

§6.126 The decision on a revocation hearing is subject to review. For section 469 offences, the review is conducted by the court of appeal under section 680 of the *Code*.[308] With all other offences, the review is conducted by the superior court under sections 520 and 521.[309]

§6.127 As a practical matter, it is important to recognize that where the reason for the revocation hearing is that the accused is alleged to have committed an indictable offence while on release, the revocation issue will often be dealt with at the same time that the court is considering whether the accused is entitled to bail on the new charge(s).[310] Invariably, the conclusion to revoke an earlier bail order will be accompanied by a decision detaining the accused with respect to the new offence charged. Conversely, a decision releasing the accused on bail for the new offence will often be accompanied by an order dismissing the revocation application.

(13) Bail Under the *Youth Criminal Justice Act*

§6.128 The provisions in the *Code* dealing with bail, which are found in Part XVI, apply to the detention and release of young persons under the *Youth Criminal Justice Act*[311] except to the extent that they are inconsistent or excluded by that Act.[312] It will be remembered that under Part XVI of the *Code*, a "justice" has jurisdiction to decide questions of bail. Section 2 of the *Code* defines "justice" as including both justices of the peace and provincial court judges.[313] This

---

[304] See *Criminal Code*, s. 524(7) (obligation on judge conducting revocation hearing for s. 469 offence) and s. 524(11) (obligation on justice conducting revocation hearing for all other offences).

[305] See *Criminal Code*, s. 524(12) (providing that ss. 517, 518 and 519 "apply with such modifications as the circumstances require", but exempting s. 518(2) (release pending sentencing after guilty plea) for those charged with s. 469 offences).

[306] *Criminal Code*, s. 517. Publication bans are discussed above in Part 3(9)(*a*).

[307] *Criminal Code*, s. 518(1)(*b*). The rules governing evidence at bail hearings, including limitations on the examination of the accused, are discussed above in Part 3(9)(*b*) and (*c*).

[308] *Criminal Code*, s. 524(6).

[309] *Criminal Code*, s. 524(13).

[310] The two hearings may occur concurrently or separately. See *R. v. Yarema*, [1991] O.J. No. 712, 64 C.C.C. (3d) 260 at 268-71 (Ont. C.A.); *R. v. Gabrielson*, [1991] O.J. No. 196, 62 C.C.C. (3d) 571 at 574-76 (Ont. Gen. Div.); *R. v. Major*, [1990] O.J. No. 345, 76 C.R. (3d) 104 at 113 (Ont. Dist. Ct.).

[311] S.C. 2002, c. 1 [YCJA].

[312] YCJA, s. 28.

[313] *Criminal Code*, s. 2.

definition also applies to the YCJA,[314] with one exception: a young person charged with an offence (such as murder) listed in section 469 of the *Criminal Code* may only be released by a youth justice court judge.[315]

§6.129 The YCJA does deviate from the *Criminal Code*'s bail provisions in recognizing the special position of "young persons"[316] and treating them less harshly than adults.

§6.130 The Supreme Court of Canada has recognized that, compared to adults, young people have heightened vulnerability, less maturity and a reduced capacity for moral judgment. The Court has therefore recognized a presumption that young persons should be treated more leniently than adult offenders. According to the Court, this presumption qualifies as a "principle of fundamental justice" under section 7 of the *Charter*.[317] The philosophy of liberal access to bail embodied in the YCJA is consistent that presumption and the special constitutional obligation owed to young persons.

§6.131 A key directive found in the YCJA is that pre-trial custody should not be used as a "substitute for appropriate child protection, mental health or other social measures".[318] In other words, a young person should only be denied bail when it is necessary to ensure attendance in court, protect the public or maintain confidence in the administration of justice.

§6.132 The YCJA also tweaks the application of section 515(10)(b) of the *Code*: the public safety criterion for denying bail. Section 29(2) of the YCJA provides that "a youth justice court or a justice shall presume that detention is not necessary under that paragraph if the young person could not, on being found guilty, be committed to custody ...."[319]

§6.133 Another important variation is found in section 31 of the YCJA. When a young person would otherwise be detained in custody under section 515 of the Code, the youth justice court or justice may instead order that the young person

---

[314] YCJA, s. 20(1) (providing that "[a]ny proceeding that may be carried out before a justice under the *Criminal Code*, other than a plea, a trial or an adjudication, may be carried out before a justice ...").

[315] YCJA, s. 33(8). Note that when a young person elects to be tried by a judge without a jury, is charged with a s. 469 offence or elects trial by judge and jury, the superior court is deemed to be a youth justice court and for the purposes of the proceeding the superior court judge is deemed to be a youth justice court judge. See YCJA, s. 13.

[316] Under the Act, a "young person" "means a person who is or, in the absence of evidence to the contrary, appears to be twelve years old or older, but less than eighteen years old and, if the context requires, includes any person who is charged under this Act with having committed an offence while he or she was a young person or who is found guilty of an offence under this Act." See YCJA, s. 2.

[317] See *R. v. B. (D.)*, [2008] S.C.J. No. 25, [2008] 2 S.C.R. 3 (S.C.C.).

[318] YCJA, s. 29(1).

[319] Under s. 39(1)(a) to (c) of the YCJA, a young person "shall not" be committed to custody unless he or she "(a)... has committed a violent offence;" "(b) ... has failed to comply with non-custodial sentences;" or "(c) ... has committed an indictable offence for which an adult would be liable to imprisonment for a term of more than two years and has a history that indicates a pattern of findings of guilt under this Act or the *Young Offenders Act* ...".

be placed "in the care of a responsible person". The only preconditions are that "the person is willing and able to take care of and exercise control over the young person" and "the young person is willing to be placed in the care of that person".[320] Both the responsible person and the young person are required to acknowledge their respective responsibilities in writing by way of an undertaking.[321] Further, before ordering a young person's detention, the youth justice court judge or justice must inquire "as to the availability of a responsible person and whether the young person is willing to be placed in that person's care."[322] Finally, even when a young person is denied release under section 31, this conclusion does not foreclose another application based on a different plan of release. There is nothing in the language of the provision limiting a young person to only one chance to secure bail.[323]

§6.134 Release into the care of a responsible person can be undone by bringing an application to the youth justice court or a justice. The application may be granted if the person is "no longer willing to take care of or exercise control over the young person" or "for any other reason, no longer appropriate that the young person remain in the care of the person with whom he or she has been placed."[324] Should this occur, the young person will be arrested and the issue of release will be considered afresh.[325]

§6.135 The rules governing the review of bail decisions for young persons are also more relaxed than those applying to adults. A key variation results from section 33(1) of the YCJA. It provides that where the initial bail determination is made by a justice of the peace, an application may be brought "to a youth justice court for the release from or detention in custody of the young person, as the case may be, and the youth justice court shall hear the matter as an original application."[326] In other words, the application will be considered anew; there is no deference to the justice of the peace's original decision. The only restriction on this jurisdiction is procedural, absent waiver; such an application requires two clear days' written notice to the opposing side.[327] Understandably, given the ease with which an initial bail determination by a justice of the peace can be reviewed by a youth justice court judge, the YCJA forecloses review of such decisions in the superior court under sections 520 or 521 of the *Code*.[328]

---

[320] YCJA, s. 31(1). See also *R. v. S. (T.)*, [2006] A.J. No. 1394, 421 A.R. 370 at paras. 21-31 (Alta. Q.B.) (describing provision as a separate and distinct route to release from s. 515 of the *Code*); *R. v. W. (N.)*, [2008] N.J. No. 293, 279 Nfld. & P.E.I.R. 131 at paras. 120-126 (Nfld. Prov. Ct.) (stressing need for plan of release and impressing on responsible person nature of obligation).
[321] YCJA, s. 31(3).
[322] YCJA, s. 31(2).
[323] See *R. v. S. (T.)*, [2006] A.J. No. 1394, 421 A.R. 370 at para. 33 (Alta. Q.B.).
[324] YCJA, s. 31(4).
[325] YCJA, s. 31(5), (6).
[326] YCJA, s. 33(1).
[327] YCJA, s. 33(2), (3), (4).
[328] YCJA, s. 33(7). See *R. v. M. (I.)*, [2008] O.J. No. 3953 at para. 8. (Ont. S.C.J.).

§6.136 Different procedures apply where a youth justice court judge makes the initial bail determination. In such cases, the rules applicable to the review and revocation of adult bail orders apply equally to young persons.[329] Importantly, this includes the authority governing both the review (sections 520, 521 and 525) and revocation (section 524) of bail orders. There is conflicting case law as to which level of court has jurisdiction under sections 520 and 521 of the *Code* to review an initial bail determination made by a youth justice court judge. One court has suggested that youth justice court judges should have exclusive authority to conduct such reviews.[330] The principal difficulty with this view is that it would have judges from the same level of court reviewing the decisions of one another. We therefore prefer the decisions holding that only a superior court judge should hear a review of an order made by a youth justice court judge.[331]

§6.137 The situation is different when it comes to the automatic review for detained accused mandated by section 525 of the *Criminal Code*. This procedure has been characterized as an inquiry into the reason for the continued incarceration of the accused — not a review of the initial decision to deny bail. Consequently, the problem of having judges of the same court sit in review of each other does not arise. The courts have therefore suggested that youth justice court judges should carry out these reviews.[332]

§6.138 As mentioned, if a young person is charged with a section 469 offence, the initial bail decision must be made by a youth justice court judge.[333] A review of that decision must consequently be conducted by the court of appeal under section 680 of the *Code*.[334] The court of appeal must also conduct the review of any bail decisions made by the superior court when acting as a youth justice court.[335]

---

[329] This follows from s. 28 of the YCJA (providing that the "provisions of Part XVI (compelling appearance of an accused and interim release) of the *Criminal Code* apply to the detention and release of young persons under this Act").

[330] See *R. v. O. (A.J.)*, [2004] O.J. No. 1220, 185 C.C.C. (3d) 120 (Ont. S.C.J.) (making this suggestion more generally, although the issue in the case was 90-day reviews under s. 525).

[331] See *R. v. W.-K. (K.)*, [2006] O.J. No. 2912 (Ont. C.J.); *R. v. M. (I.)*, [2008] O.J. No. 3953 (Ont. S.C.J.) (both in the context of a review under s. 520).

[332] See *R. v. O. (A.J.)*, [2004] O.J. No. 1220, 185 C.C.C. (3d) 120 (Ont. S.C.J.). See also *R. v. M. (I.)*, [2008] O.J. No. 3953 at para. 18 (Ont. S.C.J.) (agreeing that s. 525 raises different considerations).

[333] See §6.128, above.

[334] YCJA, s. 33(9).

[335] YCJA, s. 33(5). The superior court is deemed to be a youth justice court, for example, when a young person elects trial by judge and jury. See YCJA, s. 13; *R. v. W. (E.E.)*, [2004] S.J. No. 538, 188 C.C.C. (3d) 467 (Sask. C.A.); *R. v. F. (M.)*, [2006] O.J. No. 1805, 210 C.C.C. (3d) 146 (Ont. C.J.). See also *R. v. M. (S.)*, [2006] O.J. No. 5486 (Ont. C.J.) (holding that the superior court has exclusive jurisdiction to deal with bail once the Attorney General requires a judge and jury trial pursuant to its authority under s. 67(6) of the YCJA). But see *R. v. H. (B.W.)*, [2005] M.J. No. 398, 202 C.C.C. (3d) 566 (Man. Prov. Ct.). (holding that original jurisdiction over bail remained with provincial court, even after young person elected trial in superior court, until young person was committed to stand trial after preliminary inquiry or young person's arraignment date in superior court).

(14) Bail Pending Appeal

§6.139 Under section 679 of the *Code*, an appellant may apply for release on bail pending the determination of his or her appeal or an application for leave to appeal to the Supreme Court of Canada. A single judge of the court of appeal hears the application. The applicant must establish, on a balance of probabilities, that: (a) the appeal or application for leave to appeal is not frivolous; (b) he or she will surrender into custody in accordance with the terms of the order; and (c) detention is not necessary in the public interest.[336] Each of these requirements is fully explained in Chapter 18, Part 2(1)(*e*), which addresses bail pending appeal.

4.　CONSTITUTIONAL CONSIDERATIONS

§6.140 The reforms ushered in by the *Bail Reform Act*[337] foreshadowed the emphasis on civil liberties that would ultimately culminate in the enactment of the *Charter*. It is therefore not at all surprising that the *Charter* includes a provision that specifically addresses the question of bail. In its entirety, section 11(*e*) of the *Charter* provides that:

> Any person charged with an offence has the right not to be denied reasonable bail without just cause.

(1)　Section 11(*e*) of the *Charter*: Basic Requirements

§6.141 The Supreme Court of Canada has had a number of opportunities to address the meaning of section 11(*e*) of the *Charter*. The Court first defined the purpose and requirements of section 11(*e*) in *R. v. Pearson*.[338] It began by resolving a significant objection to the very idea of pre-trial detention: the presumption of innocence. If a person charged with an offence is presumed innocent then how can detention before trial be justified?[339] According to the Court, the guarantee in section 11(*d*) of the *Charter* "to be presumed innocent until proven guilty", applies only at trial; it has "no application at the bail stage of the criminal process, where the guilt or innocence of the accused is not determined and where punishment is not imposed."[340]

§6.142 This does not mean, however, that the presumption of innocence has no effect at the bail stage. As the Court noted in *Pearson*, the presumption of innocence is a principle of fundamental justice under section 7 of the *Charter* and operates throughout the criminal process. Its requirements at the bail stage, however, are met whenever the requirements of section 11(*e*) are satisfied; that

---

[336] *Criminal Code*, s. 679(3). See also *R. v. Ponak; R. v. Gunn*, [1972] B.C.J. No. 621, [1972] 4 W.W.R. 316 at 317-18 (B.C.C.A.) (burden on applicant to establish all three preconditions on a balance of probabilities).

[337] S.C. 1970-71-72, c. 37.

[338] [1992] S.C.J. No. 99, [1992] 3 S.C.R. 665 (S.C.C.).

[339] See generally, Daniel Kiselbach, "Pre-Trial Criminal Procedure: Preventive Detention and the Presumption of Innocence" (1988-89) 31 Crim. L. Q. 167 at 174-78.

[340] [1992] S.C.J. No. 99, [1992] 3 S.C.R. 665 at para. 42 (S.C.C.).

is, by respecting the right of accused persons not to be denied reasonable bail without just cause.[341] In other words, the presumption of innocence is sufficiently respected by making reasonable bail available where there is an absence of just cause for pre-trial detention.

§6.143 In *Pearson*, the Court explained that section 11(*e*) confers "a basic entitlement to be granted reasonable bail unless there is just cause to do otherwise."[342] This entitlement has two components: first, the right not to be denied release without just cause; and, second, the right to have such release subject to reasonable bail.[343] "Reasonable bail" refers to the terms of bail. In other words, "the quantum of bail and the restrictions imposed on the accused's liberty while on bail must be 'reasonable'."[344] "Just cause" means that the accused cannot be detained in custody unless there are good reasons for doing so.[345] According to the Court, there will be "just cause" for denying bail where two conditions are satisfied. First, bail can be denied only in a narrow set of circumstances. Second, the denial must serve to promote the proper functioning of the bail system and not any other purpose.[346] The Supreme Court has applied these two requirements in assessing the constitutionality of a number of the bail provisions in the *Criminal Code*.

(2) Constitutionality of Reverse Onus Bail

§6.144 *Pearson* involved a challenge to the constitutionality of section 515(6)(*d*), which reversed the ordinary burden of proof in bail hearings for those charged with narcotics trafficking, possession for the purpose of trafficking, importing or exporting, or with conspiracy to commit any of these offences.[347] A majority of the Supreme Court concluded that the provision complied with section 11(*e*). First, it reversed the burden only in a narrow set of circumstances: cases involving those charged with commercial narcotics offences. Second, the majority was satisfied that those charged with such offences, given their profit motive, are more likely to reoffend and to have the resources and criminal connections necessary to abscond. Given this, the majority concluded that reversing the burden in such cases is directly connected to valid bail considerations;

---

[341] *Ibid.*, at para. 45 (S.C.R.).

[342] *Ibid.*, at para. 52 (S.C.R.).

[343] *Ibid.*, at para. 60 (S.C.R.).

[344] *Ibid.*, at para. 46 (S.C.R.).

[345] *Ibid.*

[346] *Ibid.*, at para. 60 (S.C.R.). See also *R. v. Morales*, [1992] S.C.J. No. 98, [1992] 3 S.C.R. 711 at 726 (S.C.C.), where the Court explained that in *R. v. Pearson*, [1992] S.C.J. No. 99, [1992] 3 S.C.R. 665 (S.C.C.)I t held that "pursuant to *Charter* s. 11(*e*), there will be just cause for denial of bail if the denial can occur only in a narrow set of circumstances and if the denial is necessary to promote the proper functioning of the bail system." See also *R. v. Hall*, [2002] S.C.J. No. 65, [2002] 3 S.C.R. 309 at paras. 69-70, 92 (S.C.C.), *per* Iacobucci J., dissenting.

[347] The challenge was to a previous version of the provision that imposed a reverse onus for bail for accused charged with these offences under the *Narcotic Control Act*, R.S.C., 1985, c. N-1. The current provision refers to the successor legislation, the *Controlled Drugs and Substances Act*, S.C. 1996, c. 19, and applies the reverse onus to a slightly more limited range of offences.

namely, reducing the risk that those charged with commercial drug offences will commit further offences or fail to attend court.

§6.145 The Court came to a similar conclusion in *R. v. Morales*[348] with respect to a challenge to section 515(6)(*a*). That provision provides that an accused must justify the granting of bail when he or she is charged with an indictable offence "that is alleged to have been committed while he was at large after being released in respect of another indictable offence". The provision satisfies the first "just cause" requirement under section 11(*e*), the Court reasoned, because it applies only to a relatively small group of accused persons who are alleged to have reoffended while on bail. The second requirement was satisfied because the reverse onus attempts to prevent crime, an important objective of the entire criminal justice process, including the bail system.

§6.146 Courts of appeal have also upheld the reverse onus applying to those charged with murder.[349] As explained in Part 3(7), above, for murder and the other offences listed in section 469 of the *Code*, the justice before whom the accused is brought "shall order that the accused be detained in custody".[350] Thereafter only a superior court judge can order the accused's release,[351] and only where the accused "shows cause why his detention in custody is not justified within the meaning of subsection 515(10)."[352] In upholding the constitutionality of this provision, the Nova Scotia Court of Appeal noted that the category of accused persons to whom the provision applies is sufficiently narrow to satisfy the first "just cause" requirement.[353] In addition, the Court noted that the punishment for murder (automatic life imprisonment) provides a considerable incentive to flee. Given this, the Court concluded that the reverse onus is sufficiently connected to the proper functioning of the bail system to satisfy the second "just cause" requirement.[354]

§6.147 Since *Pearson* and *Morales*, Parliament has been busy expanding the list of offences triggering a reversal of the burden on bail.[355] Given the majority's reasoning in *Pearson*, most of these provisions appear to be consistent with section 11(*e*) of the *Charter*. If it is true that those charged with commercial drug crimes are more likely than the average accused to offend or abscond while on bail, these concerns seem equally powerful for those charged with offences related to terrorism[356] or criminal organizations.[357]

---

[348] [1992] S.C.J. No. 98, [1992] 3 S.C.R. 711 (S.C.C.).

[349] See *R. v. Sanchez*, [1999] N.S.J. No. 142, 136 C.C.C. (3d) 31 (N.S.C.A.); *R. v. Bray*, [1983] O.J. No. 2509, 2 C.C.C. (3d) 325 (Ont. C.A.).

[350] *Criminal Code*, s. 515(11).

[351] *Ibid.*, s. 522(1).

[352] *Ibid.*, s. 522(2).

[353] *R. v. Sanchez*, [1999] N.S.J. No. 142, 136 C.C.C. (3d) 31 at paras. 22-26 (N.S.C.A.).

[354] *Ibid.*, at paras. 27-30 (C.C.C.).

[355] See §6.48, above.

[356] See *Criminal Code*, s. 515(6)(*a*)(ii).

[357] See *Criminal Code*, s. 515(6)(*a*)(iii).

§6.148 In contrast, one is hard-pressed to see a parallel where an accused person is charged with perpetrating a violent crime using a firearm.[358] Coming in the aftermath of a spate of handgun violence in Toronto that captured national headlines, those amendments appear to be driven by punitive considerations: a desire to get those charged with serious gun crimes off the street sooner rather than later.[359] Reversing the burden in bail hearings for such a reason would seem to beyond the scope of what section 11(*e*) of the *Charter* permits.

(3) Constitutionality of Criteria Governing Bail

§6.149 In *R. v. Morales*,[360] the Supreme Court applied the section 11(*e*) *Charter* standards developed in *Pearson* to assess whether the "public interest" and "public safety" criteria in the former version of section 515(10)(*b*) of the *Code* supplied "just cause" for refusing bail. At the time, that provision stated that pre-trial detention is justified where it:

> ... is necessary in the public interest or for the protection or safety of the public, having regard to all the circumstances including any substantial likelihood that the accused will, if he is released from custody, commit a criminal offence or interfere with the administration of justice.

The Court held that the "public interest" criterion was unconstitutional. It reasoned that the term was too "vague and imprecise" to qualify as "just cause" under section 11(*e*) of the *Charter* for refusing to grant bail. In the result, the Court severed the offending clause from the remainder of the provision.

§6.150 In contrast, the Court in *Morales* upheld the "public safety" criterion for denying bail found in section 515(10)(*b*). In doing so, the Court again applied the two-prong test it developed in *Pearson* for assessing whether a legislative provision denies bail for "just cause" under section 11(*e*) of the *Charter*. First, it concluded that the public safety ground was sufficiently narrow because it does not permit detention for all persons who pose some risk of committing an offence or interfering with the administration of justice. Rather, it applies only where there is a "substantial likelihood" that such risks will materialize and where detention is "necessary" for public safety. Second, the Court in *Morales* concluded that the public safety ground promotes the proper functioning of the bail system because it helps to prevent accused persons from committing further crimes or interfering with the administration of justice while awaiting trial.

§6.151 Five years passed before Parliament responded to *Morales* by removing the offending "public interest" clause from section 515(10)(*b*) and adding

---

[358] See *Criminal Code*, s. 515(6)(*a*)(vii).

[359] For judicial recognition of the public uproar in Toronto in the aftermath of a year of unprecedented handgun violence in that city, see *R. v. B.(A.)*, [2006] O.J. No. 394, 204 C.C.C. (3d) 490 at para. 1 (Ont. S.C.J.).

[360] [1992] S.C.J. No. 98, [1992] 3 S.C.R. 711 (S.C.C.).

section 515(10)(*c*) to the *Code*.[361] As initially enacted (it has since been amended), section 515(10)(*c*) provided that detention was justified:

> ... on any other just cause being shown and, without limiting the generality of the foregoing, where the detention is necessary in order to maintain confidence in the administration of justice, having regard to all the circumstances, including the apparent strength of the prosecution's case, the gravity of the nature of the offence, the circumstances surrounding its commission and the potential for a lengthy term of imprisonment.

§6.152 The constitutionality of section 515(10)(*c*) was challenged in *R. v. Hall*.[362] The Supreme Court unanimously concluded that the provision's initial clause ("on any other just cause being shown") violated section 11(*e*) of the *Charter*. In failing to specify any particular basis for refusing bail, this language ran afoul of the *Pearson* requirement that bail can be denied only in narrow and precise circumstances. Consequently, the discretion it conferred was too vague to be consistent with section 11(*e*). The next phrase in the provision ("without limiting the generality of the foregoing") was similarly void because it only served to confirm the generality of the phrase permitting a judge to deny bail "on any other just cause".

§6.153 The Court in *Hall* was sharply divided, however, on the constitutionality of the second half of section 515(10)(c): "where the detention is necessary in order to maintain confidence in the administration of justice, having regard to all the circumstances, including the apparent strength of the prosecution's case, the gravity of the nature of the offence, the circumstances surrounding its commission and the potential for a lengthy term of imprisonment." A five-judge majority held that this ground for denying bail (now commonly referred to as the "tertiary" ground) complied with section 11(*e*) of the *Charter*. For the majority, the tertiary ground was narrower and more precise than the old public interest criterion. In so concluding, it emphasized the limitations that Parliament imposed on the application of this subsection, explaining that:

> The inquiry is narrowed to the reasonable community perception of the necessity of denying bail to maintain confidence in the administration of justice, judicially determined through the objective lens of "all the circumstances, including the apparent strength of the prosecution's case, the gravity of the nature of the offence, the circumstances surrounding its commission and the potential for a lengthy term of imprisonment".[363]

For the majority, public confidence in the administration of justice, as amplified by the four considerations specifically enumerated in section 515(10)(*c*), relates to the proper functioning of both the bail system and the justice system as a whole.

---

[361] See *Criminal Law Improvement Act, 1996*, S.C. 1997, c. 18, s. 59.

[362] [2002] S.C.J. No. 65, [2002] 3 S.C.R. 309 (S.C.C.).

[363] *Ibid.*, at para. 36 (S.C.R.).

§6.154 The four dissenting judges, in contrast, concluded that the tertiary ground added nothing to the criteria already found in sections 515(10)(*a*) and (*b*) and thus did little more than revive the old "public interest" criterion.[364] The enumerated factors found in the second half of section 515(10)(*c*), they asserted, "serve as little more than a facade of precision."[365] The provision was therefore "... ripe for misuse, allowing for irrational public fears to be elevated above the *Charter* rights of the accused."[366] As a result, the dissent would have invalidated the whole of section 515(10)(*c*), concluding that it could not be justified under section 1 of the *Charter*.

---

[364] *R. v. Hall*, [2002] S.C.J. No. 65, [2002] 3 S.C.R. 309 at para. 104 (S.C.C.), *per* Iacobucci J., dissenting.
[365] *Ibid.*, at para. 98 (S.C.R.).
[366] *Ibid.*, at para. 106 (S.C.R.).

Chapter 7

DISCLOSURE

1. INTRODUCTION

§7.1 "Disclosure" refers to the rules and procedures governing the exchange of information between the parties (and occasionally third parties) to facilitate preparation for legal proceedings. In civil proceedings, the parties are considered to be on an equal footing, and disclosure obligations are generally mutually extensive. This is not true for criminal matters, where concerns for fairness to the accused and the avoidance of wrongful convictions have resulted in a decidedly asymmetrical regime: the Crown's disclosure obligations are far broader than the accused's. Complete and timely disclosure benefits everyone involved in the administration of criminal justice: it helps protect the accused's right to make full answer and defence; it is essential to preventing miscarriages of justice; and it stimulates early resolution of cases, thus lessening the burden on the courts and minimizing the impact of the criminal trial process on both victims and the accused.

§7.2 This chapter considers three sets of disclosure rules. First, and most importantly, we outline the Crown's duty to disclose relevant information to the defence. This is sometimes referred to as "first party disclosure".[1] As we will see, as a result of the Supreme Court of Canada's groundbreaking decision in *R. v. Stinchcombe*,[2] this duty is mandated by the *Charter* and is explicitly grounded on the policy of preventing the conviction of the innocent.[3] We also describe the much more limited obligations of the defence to disclose certain information to the prosecution. Lastly, we outline the statutory and common law regimes regulating the production to the court and to the defence of information in the hands of third parties ("third party production").

2. DISCLOSURE BY THE CROWN TO THE DEFENCE (FIRST PARTY DISCLOSURE)

(1) Before the *Charter*

§7.3 Even before the *Charter*, it was long accepted in Canada that the prosecutor's role was supposed to be non-partisan. Justice Rand's judgment in *R. v.*

---

[1] See *R. v. McNeil*, [2009] S.C.J. No. 3, [2009] 1 S.C.R. 66 at para. 14 (S.C.C.) [*McNeil*].
[2] [1991] S.C.J. No. 83, [1991] 3 S.C.R. 326 (S.C.C.).
[3] *Ibid.*

Boucher[4] provided the classic statement of the prosecutor's special function within the Canadian criminal justice system:

> Counsel have a duty to see that all available legal proof of the facts is presented: it should be done firmly and pressed to its legitimate strength but it must also be done fairly. The role of prosecutor excludes any notion of winning or losing; his function is a matter of public duty than which in civil life there can be none charged with greater personal responsibility. It is to be efficiently performed with an ingrained sense of the dignity, the seriousness and the justness of judicial proceedings.[5]

Part and parcel of this duty to act impartially was a long recognized professional obligation on prosecutors "to bring forward evidence of every material fact known to the prosecution whether favourable to the accused or otherwise."[6] Either disclosing the evidence to the defence or actually calling the evidence at trial would seem to have satisfied this duty.

§7.4 Unfortunately, this obligation proved slippery in application. The scope of the duty was determined largely by prosecutors' subjective perceptions of what was "material".[7] Courts rarely intervened, typically holding that materiality was a matter of prosecutorial discretion.[8] As a result, disclosure practices varied not only between jurisdictions but sometimes even between prosecutors within the same office.[9]

§7.5 In addition to prosecutors' ethical disclosure obligations, the *Criminal Code*[10] also provides certain disclosure rights to the accused. These rights, however, are very limited. Section 603 provides that:

> An accused is entitled, after he has been ordered to stand trial or at his trial,
>
> > (*a*) to inspect without charge the indictment, his own statement, the evidence and the exhibits, if any; and

---

[4]   [1954] S.C.J. No. 54, [1955] S.C.R. 16 (S.C.C.).

[5]   *Ibid.*, at 23-24 (S.C.R.). The prosecutor's role is discussed in detail in Chapter 8.

[6]   *R. v. Lemay*, [1951] S.C.J. No. 42, [1952] 1 S.C.R. 232 at 257 (S.C.C.). See also *R. v. Boucher*, [1954] S.C.J. No. 54, [1955] S.C.R. 16 at 19, 23-24 (S.C.C.); *R. v. Chamandy*, [1934] O.J. No. 235, 61 C.C.C. 224 (Ont. C.A.). See also Canadian Bar Association, *Code of Professional Conduct* (Ottawa: Canadian Bar Association, 2009), Chapter IX, comm. 9 ("The prosecutor should .... *to the extent required by law and accepted practice*, make timely disclosure to the accused or defence counsel (or to the court if the accused is not represented) of all relevant facts and known witnesses, whether tending to show guilt or innocence, or that would affect the punishment of the accused.") [emphasis added].

[7]   See generally, Brian A. Grosman, *The Prosecutor: An Inquiry Into the Exercise of Discretion* (Toronto: University of Toronto Press, 1969).

[8]   See Michel Proulx & David Layton, *Ethics and Canadian Criminal Law* (Toronto: Irwin Law, 2001) at 652.

[9]   See *R. v. Stinchcombe*, [1991] S.C.J. No. 83, [1991] 3 S.C.R. 326 at 334 (S.C.C.) ("The extent of disclosure varies from province to province, from jurisdiction to jurisdiction and from prosecutor to prosecutor.").

[10] R.S.C. 1985, c. C-46 [*Code*].

(*b*) to receive, on payment of a reasonable fee determined in accordance with a tariff of fees fixed or approved by the Attorney General of the province, a copy

(i) of the evidence,

(ii) of his own statement, if any, and

(iii) of the indictment;

but the trial shall not be postponed to enable the accused to secure copies unless the court is satisfied that the failure of the accused to secure them before the trial is not attributable to lack of diligence on the part of the accused.

§7.6 This closed list of items, however, precluded a reading of this provision as entitling accused persons to have access to all the relevant information in the state's possession. Note as well, that even this limited right to disclosure applies only to offences prosecuted by way of indictment and only after the accused has been ordered to stand trial at the preliminary inquiry. Neither the common law[11] nor the *Charter*[12] bestows the right to disclosure at the preliminary hearing.

§7.7 Beyond section 603, the *Code* offers little assistance by way of rules dealing with disclosure.[13] It is important not to confuse the *Code*'s provisions relating to "particulars" with the Crown's duty to "disclose". Section 587 of the *Code* provides the court with the discretion to order the Crown to furnish particulars. Particulars function to supplement an indictment with sufficient detail to allow an accused to adequately prepare a defence,[14] for example, particularizing the transaction and the essential elements of the offence.[15] As such, particulars relate to the material facts the Crown seeks to prove at trial. Disclosure on the other hand, generally deals with the evidence the Crown will rely upon in proving the allegations.

§7.8 As many commentators pointed out, neither prosecutors' ethical duties nor the disclosure mechanisms in the *Code* were sufficient to ensure the systematic, fulsome disclosure.[16] The result of this deficiency could be quite tragic, as the case of Donald Marshall Jr. made apparent.[17] Beyond systemic racism within the Nova Scotia justice system toward Native Canadians, one of the other factors identified by the Royal Commission that investigated the causes of Donald

---

[11] *R. v. Patterson*, [1970] S.C.J. No. 7, [1970] S.C.R. 409 (S.C.C.).

[12] *Canadian Charter of Rights and Freedoms*, Part I of the *Constitution Act, 1982*, being Schedule B to the *Canada Act 1982* (U.K.), 1982, c. 11 [*Charter*]; *R. v. Hynes*, [2001] S.C.J. No. 80, [2001] 3 S.C.R. 623 at para. 33 (S.C.C.).

[13] See *e.g.*, s. 605 of the *Code* that allows for the release of an exhibit to either the accused or the Crown for the purpose of scientific or other test or examination.

[14] *R. v. Armour Pharmaceutical Co.*, [2006] O.J. No. 137 at para. 21 (Ont. S.C.J.).

[15] *R. v. Djambazov*, [2007] O.J. No 4738 at para. 14 (Ont. S.C.J.).

[16] See *e.g.*, Stanley Cohen, *Due Process of Law: The Canadian System of Criminal Justice* (Toronto: Carswell, 1977) at 139.

[17] *R. v. Marshall*, [1983] N.S.J. No. 322, 57 N.S.R. (2d) 286 (N.S.C.A.).

Marshall Jr.'s wrongful conviction was the prosecutors' failure to disclose exculpatory information.[18]

(2) First Party Disclosure under the *Charter*: *R. v. Stinchombe*

§7.9 The legal landscape governing the Crown's duty to disclose underwent a revolutionary change with the Supreme Court's landmark decision in *R. v. Stinchcombe*.[19] In that case, the Court pointed to the right to make full answer and defence, which it identified as a principle of fundamental justice under section 7 of the *Charter*, in holding that an accused is entitled to receive, and the Crown has a corresponding duty to provide, disclosure of all relevant information in the Crown's possession or under its control relating to the charge. Disclosure is therefore not merely a matter of prosecutorial discretion; it is also a substantive constitutional right[20] that may be enforced under the remedial provisions of the *Constitution Act, 1982*, including section 24 of the *Charter*.[21]

(a) What Must be Disclosed?

§7.10 The scope of the Crown's duty to disclose was reiterated and summarized by the Supreme Court in *R. v. Taillefer; R. v. Duguay*[22] as follows:

> The Crown must disclose all relevant information to the accused, whether inculpatory or exculpatory, subject to the exercise of the Crown's discretion to refuse to disclose information that is privileged or plainly irrelevant. Relevance must be assessed in relation both to the charge itself and to the reasonably possible defences. ... Moreover, all statements obtained from persons who have provided relevant information to the authorities should be produced notwithstanding that they are not proposed as Crown witnesses.[23]

§7.11 The first important concept in this passage is that of "relevance". It is clear that this is a very low threshold. Rather than simply stating that prosecutors have a duty to pass on "relevant" material, the Court has described their discretion to withhold as applying only to that which is "clearly"[24] or "plainly"[25] *irrelevant*. Accordingly, unless the evidence of information is clearly irrelevant,

---

18 See Royal Commission on the Donald Marshall Jr., Prosecution, *Commissioners' Report: Findings and Recommendations*, Vol. 1 (Halifax: Nova Scotia) (Chair: T. Alexander Hickman*)* at 238-42. Inadequate disclosure has been identified as one of the leading causes of wrongful convictions more generally. See Jon B. Gould & Richard A. Leo, "One-hundred Years of Getting It Wrong? Wrongful Convictions After a Century of Research" (2010) J. Crim. L. & Criminology 825.

19 *R. v. Stinchcombe*, [1991] S.C.J. No. 83, [1991] 3 S.C.R. 326 (S.C.C.) [*Stinchcombe*].

20 *Krieger v. Law Society of Alberta*, [2002] S.C.J. No. 45, [2002] 3 S.C.R. 372 at para. 54 (S.C.C.).

21 These provisions, and their use to remedy *Charter* disclosure violations, are discussed in Chapter 10.

22 [2003] S.C.J. No. 75, [2003] 3 S.C.R. 307 (S.C.C.).

23 *Ibid.*, at para. 59 (S.C.R.).

24 *R. v. Stinchcombe*, [1991] S.C.J. No. 83, [1991] 3 S.C.R. 326 at 336 and 339 (S.C.C.).

25 [2003] S.C.J. No. 75, [2003] 3 S.C.R. 307 at para. 59 (S.C.C.).

the Crown should err on the side of inclusion for disclosure.[26] There is little downside to over-disclosure. At worst, it creates more paper to photocopy and distribute. At best, it could prevent a wrongful conviction.

§7.12 At the most general level, relevance is defined as information that might be useful to the defence.[27] As the Supreme Court has stated, information will be considered relevant if it "can reasonably be used by the accused either in meeting the case for the Crown, advancing a defence or otherwise in making a decision which may affect the conduct of the defence such as, for example, whether to call evidence."[28]

§7.13 Second, relevant information must be disclosed regardless of whether it is considered inculpatory or exculpatory. As Justice Sopinka explained for a unanimous Court in *Stinchcombe*, the distinction between the two is "unworkable" and would lead to "interminable controversy at trial".[29]

§7.14 Third, the duty to disclose extends to witness statements. In some cases, these statements will simply be recorded in notes taken by police, in which case the notes or copies should be produced. If no notes exist, a "will say" statement, summarizing the anticipated evidence of the witness should be produced, based on the information in the possession of the police or the Crown.[30] If no statements or notes are in existence, the Court in *Stinchcombe* suggested that the name, address and occupation of the witness and a summary of any relevant evidence that he or she could give should be supplied.[31]

§7.15 Fourth, beyond information that is clearly irrelevant, the Crown's ability to withhold information in its possession is limited to material protected from

---

[26] *R. v. Chaplin*, [1994] S.C.J. No. 89, [1995] 1 S.C.R. 727 (S.C.C.); *R. v. Dixon*, [1998] S.C.J. No. 17, [1998] 1 S.C.R. 244 at para. 21 (S.C.C.).

[27] *R. v. Stinchcombe*, [1991] S.C.J. No. 83, [1991] 3 S.C.R. 326 at 345 (S.C.C.). See also *R. v. Chaplin*, [1994] S.C.J. No. 89, [1995] 1 S.C.R. 727 at para. 30 (S.C.C.) ("Relevance means that there is a reasonable possibility of being useful to the accused in making full answer and defence.").

[28] *R. v. Egger*, [1993] S.C.J. No. 66, [1993] 2 S.C.R. 451 at 467 (S.C.C.). See also *R. v. Dixon*, [1998] S.C.J. No. 17, [1998] 1 S.C.R. 244 at para. 21 (S.C.C.) ("... the threshold requirement for disclosure is set quite low ... The Crown's duty to disclose is therefore triggered whenever there is a reasonable possibility of the information being useful to the accused in making full answer and defence"). Cases dealing with "relevancy" include *R. v. Mardave Construction (1990) Ltd.*, [1993] O.J. No. 4944, 18 C.R.R. (2d) D-5 (Ont. Prov. Div.), where the Court held that statements of individuals that the Crown does not intend to call as witnesses are disclosable since they are relevant to the defence in determining whether or not to call them as defence witnesses; *R. v. Palman*, [1994] O.J. No. 1150, 22 C.R.R. (2d) 344 (Ont. Gen. Div.), where the Court held that the accused was entitled to disclosure of prior police investigations of allegations made by the complainant against the accused since it was relevant to the validity of the complainant now before the Court; *R. v. Dalude*, [2004] O.J. No. 3576, 189 C.C.C. (3d) 18 (Ont. C.A.), where the Court noted that a security videotape from a police station breathalyzer room could be relevant at a trial involving an allegation of an assault in the room.

[29] *R. v. Stinchcombe*, [1991] S.C.J. No. 83, [1991] 3 S.C.R. 326 at 343 (S.C.C.).

[30] *Ibid.*, at para. 30 (S.C.R.).

[31] *Ibid.*, at para. 33 (S.C.R.).

disclosure by either: (*i*) a form of privilege;[32] or *(ii)* a court order or statute.[33] Privilege has been held to attach to the identity of confidential informants[34] and Crown "work product", including internal Crown counsel notes, legal opinions provided to police and correspondence.[35] In circumstances where the Crown has concerns about disclosing information on the grounds of a specified "public interest", it may invoke section 37 of the *Canada Evidence Act*[36] to withhold disclosure. In such circumstances, the Crown will bear the onus of justifying the non-disclosure.[37]

§7.16 An important statutory exception to the Crown's first party disclosure obligations pertaining to potentially relevant information can be found in the *Code*'s provisions dealing with the disclosure of the personal records of sexual assault complainants,[38] which is discussed below in Part 4(1).

(b)   Timing of Disclosure

§7.17 The disclosure duty is triggered by the defence making a timely request, although the Court recognized in *Stinchcombe* that where an accused person is unrepresented the court should ensure that he or she is aware of this right.[39] Once the request is made, disclosure should be provided before the accused is called upon to elect the mode of trial or to plead. Disclosure is usually provided during the intake period. In some jurisdictions, that can be as early as the first appearance or in the weeks following that appearance. In more serious cases, where the materials are much more extensive, disclosure can take several months to be made.

§7.18 In most summary conviction matters, the accused is given substantial disclosure at his or her first appearance. More serious criminal charges involve staggered disclosure over a few months due to such factors as ongoing investigations and the preparation of expert reports. Nevertheless, the duty remains on the Crown to disclose any additional information as soon as it becomes available and not to unnecessarily delay disclosure for tactical reasons.[40]

---

[32]   This includes the duty to protect the identity of confidential informants. See *R. v. Stinchcombe*, [1991] S.C.J. No. 83, [1991] 3 S.C.R. 326 at 343 (S.C.C.); *R. v. Chaplin*, [1994] S.C.J. No. 89, [1995] 1 S.C.R. 727 at para. 21 (S.C.C.); *R. v. Egger*, [1993] S.C.J. No. 66, [1993] 2 S.C.R. 451 at para. 19 (S.C.C.).

[33]   For an example of a statutory restriction on first party disclosure, see ss. 278.1 to 278.91 of the *Code*, discussed below in Part 4(1).

[34]   *R. v. Stinchcombe*, [1991] S.C.J. No. 83, [1991] 3 S.C.R. 326 (S.C.C.); *R. v. Chaplin*, [1994] S.C.J. No. 89, [1995] 1 S.C.R. 727 at para. 21 (S.C.C.); *R. v. Egger*, [1993] S.C.J. No. 66, [1993] 2 S.C.R. 451 at para. 19 (S.C.C.).

[35]   *R. v. Regan*, [1997] N.S.J. No. 428 (N.S.S.C.); *R. v. Shirose*, [1999] S.C.J. No. 16, [1999] 1 S.C.R. 565 (S.C.C.).

[36]   R.S.C. 1985, c. C-5.

[37]   *R. v. Leipert*, [1997] S.C.J. No. 14, [1997] 1 S.C.R. 281 (S.C.C.); *R. v. Richards*, [1997] O.J. No. 2086, 115 C.C.C. (3d) 377 (Ont. C.A.).

[38]   See *Criminal Code*, ss. 278.1 to 278.91.

[39]   *R. v. Stinchcombe*, [1991] S.C.J. No. 83, [1991] 3 S.C.R. 326 at para. 28 (S.C.C.).

[40]   See *R. v. Girimonte*, [1997] O.J. No. 4961, 121 C.C.C. (3d) 33 at 41-42 (Ont. C.A.).

§7.19 The Crown's obligation to disclose continues even through the appeal process.[41] There is no onus on an appellant to request further disclosure at this stage. Once the Crown comes into possession of relevant information not previously disclosed, it has a legal obligation to disclose it immediately to the defence.[42] Should the information come to light after all appeals have been exhausted, the Crown still bears the duty to disclose. Such evidence may be of assistance in an application pursuant to section 696.1 of the *Code* for ministerial review on the grounds of a miscarriage of justice.

(c) Entities Subject to Stinchcombe

§7.20 In *Stinchcombe*, the Court spoke of the duty to disclose relevant information in the possession or control of the "Crown". It is clear, however, that this duty extends not only to material in the hands of prosecutors, but also that in the possession of the police. The police accordingly have a duty to provide all required material to the prosecution,[43] and the prosecution has a concomitant obligation to request and procure this information from the police.[44] In effect, the prosecution and police are treated as a single entity for these purposes.[45]

§7.21 It is important to note that not all state authorities however, constitute a single entity. As the Court in *McNeil* observed, the Crown's *Stinchcombe* disclosure obligation does not go as far as requiring it to "inquire of every department of the provincial government, every department of the federal government and every police force whether they are in possession of material relevant to the accused's case."[46] Crown entities other than the prosecuting Crown are considered third parties under the *O'Connor* production regime (discussed below in Part 4).[47] Nevertheless, a Crown who is put on notice of the existence of relevant information retains a duty to make reasonable inquiries of other Crown agencies and obtaining the information if it is reasonably feasible to do so.[48]

---

[41] *R. v. Trotta*, [2004] O.J. No. 2439 at paras. 20-25 (Ont. C.A.).

[42] *Ibid.*

[43] *R. v. Jack*, [1992] M.J. No. 1, 70 C.C.C. (3d) 67 (Man. C.A.), affd [1994] S.C.J. No. 44 (S.C.C.); *R. v. Gagné*, [1998] J.Q. no. 3240, 131 C.C.C. (3d) 444 at 455 (Que. C.A.).

[44] See *R. v. T. (L.A.)*, [1993] O.J. No. 1605, 84 C.C.C. (3d) 90 at 94 (Ont. C.A.) ("There is a duty on the Crown to make full disclosure and accordingly the Crown has a duty to obtain from the police — and the police have a corresponding duty to provide for the Crown — all relevant information and material concerning the case.").

[45] See *R. v. McNeil*, [2009] S.C.J. No. 3, [2009] 1 S.C.R. 66 at para. 14 (S.C.C.) ("...[T]he investigating police force, although distinct and independent from the Crown at law, is not a third party.").

[46] *Ibid.*, at paras. 22-23 and 48 (S.C.R.).

[47] *Ibid.*, at para. 13 (S.C.R.).

[48] *Ibid.*, at para. 49 (S.C.R.). See also *R. v. Arsenault*, [1994] N.B.J. No. 417, 1994 CanLII 5244 at para. 15 (N.B.C.A.).

(d) Crown's Obligation to Preserve Information

§7.22 The obligation on the Crown to disclose all relevant information imposes a further duty on prosecutors and police to preserve relevant evidence.[49] Where the Crown is not able to comply with its disclosure obligations because potentially relevant evidence has been lost, sections 7 and 11(*d*) of the *Charter* will be violated unless the Crown can show that the loss was neither deliberate nor the product of unacceptable negligence.[50] In the latter case, the main consideration is whether the Crown and police took reasonable steps to preserve the evidence. As Justice Sopinka noted in *R. v. La*,[51] "...[A]s the relevance of the evidence increases, so does the degree of care for its preservation that is expected of the police."[52]

§7.23 Even where the court finds that the evidence was not lost deliberately or through unacceptable negligence, it must go on to decide whether the loss has prejudiced the ability of the accused to make full answer and defence. The accused must establish, on a balance of probabilities, that there is an "air of reality" to the position that the missing evidence would have materially assisted the defence.[53]

§7.24 Once a violation of the right to make full answer and defence has been found, the court must then consider the appropriate remedy. If there is no way to recover the missing evidence and the accused cannot otherwise receive a fair trial, the proceedings must be stayed, even if police and prosecutors acted without *males fides*.[54] Proceedings may also be stayed where the conduct of police or prosecutors has been so egregious that the prejudice to the integrity of the judicial system could not be remedied if the prosecution were to continue.[55] Conversely, a stay should not be granted where other remedies are capable of curing these defects; such remedies may include: permitting the defence to lead

---

[49] *R. v. La*, [1997] S.C.J. No. 30, [1997] 2 S.C.R. 680 at paras. 16-22 (S.C.C.); *R. v. Bero*, [2000] O.J. No. 4199, 151 C.C.C. (3d) 545 (Ont. C.A.); *R. v. Egger*, [1993] S.C.J. No. 66, [1993] 2 S.C.R. 451 (S.C.C.).

[50] *R. v. La*, [1997] S.C.J. No. 30, [1997] 2 S.C.R. 680 at paras. 20-22 (S.C.C.).

[51] [1997] S.C.J. No. 30, [1997] 2 S.C.R. 680 (S.C.C.).

[52] *Ibid.*, at para. 21 (S.C.R.).

[53] *R. v. La*, [1997] S.C.J. No. 30, [1997] 2 S.C.R. 680 (S.C.C.). Note that this is different than what the Supreme Court had earlier declared in *R. v. Carosella*, [1997] S.C.J. No. 12, 112 C.C.C. (3d) 289 (S.C.C.), where Sopinka J. explicitly held that an accused who alleged a breach of s. 7 of the *Charter* as a result of non-disclosure was not required to demonstrate how the conduct of the defence would be affected by the absence of the evidence. Instead, the question of the degree of prejudice to the accused's right to make full answer and defence was to be addressed when determining the appropriate remedy under s. 24 of the *Charter*. *La* now makes it clear that there is no automatic breach to s. 7 of the *Charter* whenever an accused is deprived of relevant information. Instead, the accused must establish actual prejudice due to the lost or destroyed evidence.

[54] See *R. v. Forster*, [2005] S.J. No. 529 (Sask. C.A.); *R. v. Banford*, [2010] S.J. No. 472 (Sask. Prov. Ct.); *R. v. Monaco*, [2008] O.J. No. 2120 (Ont. C.J.); *R. v. L. (J.A.)*, [2008] B.C.J. No. 2615 (B.C. Prov. Ct.).

[55] See *R. v. Greganti*, [2000] O.J. No. 34 (Ont. S.C.J.). For a detailed discussion of the general requirements for obtaining a stay of proceedings, see Chapter 10, Part 5(1)(*a*)(i).

evidence that the Crown failed in its obligation to preserve critical evidence; permitting the defence to lead evidence as to how forensic testing may have assisted if the evidence had been available;[56] and excluding the results of breathalyzer tests when representative samples had not been provided to the accused for independent testing.[57]

(e) Electronic Disclosure

§7.25 The Crown's discretion with respect to disclosure extends from *what* to disclose, to *how* to disclose the information. The distribution of disclosure has evolved from papers and binders to bytes and hard drives. Disclosure that once filled several bankers boxes now fits easily onto various types of digital storage media. This revolution in portability and efficiency has not fully been embraced by all defence counsel. These lawyers continued to seek disclosure in traditional paper form mainly because it was the only way they had been trained to practice.[58] This argument appears to have run its course. As Justice Martin remarked in *R. v. Rose*,[59] "... [E]lectronic disclosure has now become a fact of life, so I suppose that means that those of us who are not adept had better adapt."[60]

§7.26 In *R. v. Piaskowski*,[61] Justice Sinclair set out the following useful principles for dealing with disclosure in electronic form:

> ...

> 4. The Crown must disclose materials in a manner that the accused can reasonably access.

> 5. Where an accused is represented by counsel, electronic disclosure is not objectionable merely because of counsel's lack of computer skills unless it can be shown that access to the materials would be beyond the competence of the average reasonably skilled person.

> 6. Where the Crown wishes to make electronic disclosure as opposed to paper disclosure, the Crown has a further obligation to assist counsel lacking familiarity with the software utilized, and an unrepresented accused who *bona fide* has limited or no computer skills with reasonable access to materials that form part of the disclosure. This further obligation may range from training on the use of the software through the provision of computer equipment and may include the obligation to provide paper copies of all disclosure. This would depend on the circumstances of each case.

---

[56] *R. v. Bero*, [2000] O.J. No. 4199, 151 C.C.C. (3d) 545 (Ont. C.A.).

[57] *R. v. Vidak*, [1989] O.J. No. 3077, 16 M.V.R. (2d) 72 (Ont. Dist. Ct.).

[58] See *R. v. Amzallag*, [1999] Q.J. No. 6252 (Que. S.C.).

[59] [2002] Q.J. No. 8339 at para. 27 (Que. S.C.).

[60] *Ibid.* See also *R. v. Oszenaris*, [2008] N.J. No. 285 at paras. 19-20 (Nfld. C.A.), leave to appeal refused [2008] S.C.C.A. No. 516 (S.C.C.).

[61] [2007] M.J. No. 94 (Man. Q.B.).

7. Electronic disclosure must permit counsel to be able to print copies of the documents and images in a readable manner so as to be able to communicate effectively with his or her client.

8. The expense to the Crown of providing hard copies of the documents is a factor the court can take into account in determining whether electronic disclosure is reasonable, but it cannot trump the accused's right to a fair trial.

9. If the cost of producing hard copies of the electronic documents interferes with the accused's ability to make full answer and defence, the court can order the Crown to provide hard copies of electronic disclosure at Crown expense.[62]

§7.27 There are no legislative provisions currently addressing the practice of electronic disclosure. The Crown must, however, be cognizant of the principle that electronic disclosure should be in a format that is readily accessible, allowing an accused to meaningfully be able to use the information to exercise his or her right to make full answer and defence.[63] Electronic material that is neither organized nor searchable will not be considered adequate disclosure.[64]

(f) Judicial Review of Non-disclosure

§7.28 The withholding of information by the Crown is reviewable by the court.[65] If the material is withheld on the basis of a claim of privilege or other legal prohibition on disclosure, this fact must be made known to the defence (without revealing the protected information, of course) to give the accused the opportunity to challenge the claim. For example, if the Crown claims informer privilege, an accused can seek disclosure on the basis of the "innocence at stake" exception. In doing so, the accused will first have to demonstrate some basis to support the claim that without the disclosure, his or her innocence is at stake. If such a basis is established, the court may then review the information and determine whether disclosure is necessary to prove the accused's innocence. Before disclosing the information, however, the Crown should be given the option of staying the proceedings in order to protect the identity of the informer.[66]

§7.29 In cases where the Crown does not disclose because it believes the material is clearly irrelevant, Justice Sopinka suggested the following procedures on behalf of the Court in *R. v. Chaplin*.[67] If the material has been identified and is in existence:

> ... the Crown must justify non-disclosure by demonstrating either that the information sought is beyond its control, or that it is clearly irrelevant or

---

[62] *Ibid.*, at para. 84.

[63] See *R. v. Amzallag*, [1999] Q.J. No. 6252 at para. 20 (Que. S.C.).

[64] *R. v. Mah*, [2001] A.J. No. 516 (Alta. Q.B.); *R. v. Dunn*, [2009] O.J. No. 5749, 251 C.C.C. (3d) 384 (Ont. S.C.J.).

[65] *R. v. Stinchcombe*, [1991] S.C.J. No. 83, [1991] 3 S.C.R. 326 at para. 21 (S.C.C.).

[66] *R. v. Leipert*, [1997] S.C.J. No. 14, [1997] 1 S.C.R. 281 at para. 33 (S.C.C.).

[67] *R. v. Chaplin*, [1994] S.C.J. No. 89, [1995] 1 S.C.R. 727 (S.C.C.).

privileged. The trial judge must afford the Crown an opportunity to call evidence to justify such allegation of non-disclosure. As noted in *Stinchcombe, supra*, at 12:

> This may require not only submissions but the inspection of statements and other documents and indeed, in some cases, *viva voce* evidence. A *voir dire* will frequently be the appropriate procedure in which to deal with these matters.[68]

§7.30 If the non-disclosure relates to material, of which its existence is disputed:

> ... the defence must establish a basis which could enable the presiding judge to conclude that there is in existence further material which is potentially relevant .... The existence of the disputed material must be sufficiently identified not only to reveal its nature but also to enable the presiding judge to determine that it may meet the test with respect to material which the Crown is obliged to produce ....

> Although the obligation cast upon the defence which I have characterized as "a basis" is in the nature of an evidentiary burden, I prefer not to call it that because it can, and in many cases will, be discharged not by leading or pointing to evidence but by oral submissions of counsel without the necessity of a *voir dire* ...

> ...

> If the defence establishes a basis in accordance with its obligation in that regard as outlined above, the Crown must then justify a continuing refusal to disclose.[69]

(g) Remedy for Breach of Disclosure Right

§7.31 A failure to provide timely disclosure can contribute to a violation of section 11(*b*) of the *Charter* with the result being that the unreasonable delay in an accused being tried will result in a stay of proceedings.[70] More frequently, late disclosure will lead to claims of a breach of an accused's right to make full answer and defence as guaranteed by section 7 of the *Charter*. The accused must demonstrate "actual prejudice to [his or her] ability to make full answer and defence" to be entitled to a remedy pursuant to section 24(1) of the *Charter*.[71] The most common remedies for such a violation are adjournments and further disclosure orders.[72] However, costs have also been awarded in the face of flagrant and unjustified non-disclosure.[73] In exceptional cases, a trial judge may exclude evidence for late disclosure where its admission would result in an unfair trial or

---

[68] *Ibid.*, at para. 25 (S.C.R.).

[69] *Ibid.*, at paras. 30-33 (S.C.R.).

[70] *R. v. Godin*, [2009] S.C.J. No. 26, [2009] 2 S.C.R. 3 (S.C.C.).

[71] *R. v. O'Connor*, [1995] S.C.J. No. 98, [1995] 4 S.C.R. 411 at para. 74 (S.C.C.).

[72] *R. v. Bjelland*, [2009] S.C.J. No. 38, [2009] 2 S.C.R. 651 at para. 3 (S.C.C.).

[73] *R. v. 974649 Ontario Inc. (c.o.b. Dunedin Construction)*, [2001] S.C.J. No. 79, [2001] 3 S.C.R. 575 (S.C.C.).

would otherwise undermine the integrity of the justice system.[74] The most drastic of remedies, a stay of proceedings, will be appropriate in the "clearest of cases" in which the prejudice to the accused's ability to make full answer and defence or to the integrity of the justice system is irremediable.[75]

§7.32 A different situation exists on appeal where the appellant seeks a new trial by proffering fresh evidence not available to the defence at trial due to the Crown's failure to disclose. The appellant will have an onus to demonstrate on a balance of probabilities that his or her right to make full answer and defence was impaired. This will be achieved by showing either *(i)* that there is a *reasonable possibility* that the non-disclosure affected the outcome at trial; or *(ii)* that the non-disclosure affected the overall fairness of the trial process.[76] With respect to the first prong, the appellate court will determine not whether the undisclosed evidence *would* have made a difference, but whether it *could* have made a difference. Put another way, the question is whether in the context of the trial as a whole, there is a reasonable possibility that the verdict might have been different if the undisclosed evidence had been presented to the jury.[77] With respect to the second inquiry, an appellate need only establish a reasonable possibility that the overall fairness of the trial process was impaired. For example, where the undisclosed evidence could have affected the defence's decision not to call evidence[78] or could have been used to impeach the credibility of a witness.[79]

3.   DISCLOSURE BY THE DEFENCE

§7.33 As mentioned, defence counsel have an important role to play in the first party disclosure process. The defence must be reasonably diligent in making disclosure requests in a timely fashion.[80] Further, requests for disclosure should not be overly broad and should not amount to a fishing expedition.[81]

§7.34 When it comes to the defence disclosing information to the Crown, however, an entirely different set of rules operate. In short, the defence generally has no obligation to disclose information to the Crown. This general rule is subject to a few important exceptions, detailed below.

§7.35 In *Stinchcombe*, Justice Sopinka noted for the Court that the suggestion that disclosure "should be reciprocal may deserve consideration by this Court in the future but is not a valid reason for absolving the Crown of its duty."[82] The absence of a defence duty to disclose can be justified, he explained, by counsel's

---

[74]   *R. v. Bjelland*, [2009] S.C.J. No. 38, [2009] 2 S.C.R. 651 at para. 3 (S.C.C.).

[75]   *R. v. O'Connor*, [1995] S.C.J. No. 98, [1995] 4 S.C.R. 411 at para. 74 (S.C.C.). On *Charter* remedies more generally, see Chapter 10.

[76]   *R. v. Dixon*, [1998] S.C.J. No. 17, [1998] 1 S.C.R. 244 at para. 34 (S.C.C.).

[77]   *R. v. Taillefer; R. v. Duguay*, [2003] S.C.J. No. 75, [2003] 3 S.C.R. 307 at para. 82 (S.C.C.).

[78]   See *R. v. Skinner*, [1998] S.C.J. No. 20, [1998] 1 S.C.R. 298 at para. 12 (S.C.C.).

[79]   *R. v. Taillefer; R. v. Duguay*, [2003] S.C.J. No. 75, [2003] 3 S.C.R. 307 at para. 84 (S.C.C.).

[80]   *R. v. Dixon*, [1998] S.C.J. No. 17, [1998] 1 S.C.R. 244 (S.C.C.).

[81]   See *R. v. Girimonte*, [1997] O.J. No. 4961, 121 C.C.C. (3d) 33 at 40-41 (Ont. C.A.).

[82]   *R. v. Stinchcombe*, [1991] S.C.J. No. 83, [1991] 3 S.C.R. 326 at para. 11 (S.C.C.).

purely adversarial role toward the prosecution.[83] In *R. v. P. (M.B.)*,[84] Chief Justice Lamer echoed this sentiment, stating, "the defence in Canada is under no legal obligation to co-operate with or assist the Crown by announcing any special defence, such as an alibi, or by providing documentary or physical evidence."[85]

(1) Incriminating Physical Evidence

§7.36 While *Stinchcombe* imposes no obligation on the defence to disclose physical evidence to the Crown, a lawyer who actively conceals incriminating physical evidence courts both criminal liability and professional discipline.[86] While discussions about incriminating evidence are protected by solicitor-client privilege, physical evidence is not. Defence lawyers who come into the possession of incriminating physical evidence are therefore faced with an unenviable dilemma. As the Supreme Court of Canada recently held in *R. v. National Post*:[87]

> If a client walks into a lawyer's office and leaves a murder weapon covered with fingerprints and DNA evidence on the lawyer's desk the law would not allow the lawyer to withhold production of the gun on the basis of solicitor-client confidentiality, notwithstanding the thoroughgoing protection that the law affords that relationship. In *R. v. Murray* (2000), 144 C.C.C. (3d) 289 (Ont. S.C.J.), the court affirmed this principle in the case of a lawyer charged with suppressing sexual abuse tapes.[88]

§7.37 A discussion of the options available to defence lawyers in these situations is beyond the scope of this book; reference should be made to the works cited above, as well as the ethical rules promulgated by the provincial law societies.[89]

(2) Alibi

§7.38 Although the defence is never obliged to disclose a defence, including one of alibi, a failure to disclose an alibi may have negative consequences for

---

[83] *Ibid.* See also Canadian Bar Association, *Code of Professional Conduct* (Ottawa: Canadian Bar Association, 2009), Chapter IX, comm. 10 ("When defending an accused person, the lawyer's duty is to protect the client as far as possible from being convicted except by a court of competent jurisdiction and upon legal evidence sufficient to support a conviction for the offence charged....").

[84] [1994] S.C.J. No. 27, [1994] 1 S.C.R. 555 (S.C.C.).

[85] *Ibid.*, at para. 38 (S.C.R.).

[86] See *R. v. Murray*, [2000] O.J. No. 2182, 144 C.C.C. (3d) 289 at para. 113 (Ont. S.C.J.). See also Michel Proulx & David Layton, *Ethics and Canadian Criminal Law* (Toronto: Irwin Law, 2001), Chapter 9; Steven Skurka & James Stribopoulos, "Professional Responsibility in Criminal Practice," in Law Society of Upper Canada, *42nd Bar Admission Course, 2000, Criminal Procedure Reference Materials* (Toronto: Law Society of Upper Canada, 2000) c. 1 at §4.5.

[87] [2010] S.C.J. No. 16, [2010] 1 S.C.R. 477, 2010 SCC 16 (S.C.C.).

[88] *R. v. National Post*, [2010] S.C.J. No. 16, [2010] 1 S.C.R. 477, 2010 SCC 16 at para. 65 (S.C.C.).

[89] See *e.g.*, Law Society of Alberta, *Code of Professional Conduct* (2009), Chapter 10, r. 20(d) ("A lawyer must not counsel or participate in...the concealment of property having potential evidentiary value in a criminal proceeding.").

the accused at trial. Specifically, an adverse inference may be made against the accused if the defence does not give the Crown timely and adequate notice of the alibi before trial.[90] In such cases, the trier of fact will normally be instructed to approach the evidence with caution, effectively diminishing its weight.[91] The rationale for this rule is that false alibis are easily procured and difficult to disprove.[92] To avoid this adverse inference, the defence must provide disclosure "in sufficient time" and "with sufficient particularity" to "enable the authorities to meaningfully investigate".[93] Though technically part of the law of evidence, from a tactical standpoint this rule effectively requires the defence to disclose any alibi evidence that it plans to present at trial.[94]

(3) Constitutional Applications

§7.39 Another exception to the principle that the defence is not required to disclose its case relates to the accused's obligation to give the Crown advance notice of any constitutional relief that will be sought. As a result, if an accused intends to seek the exclusion of evidence or the invalidation of a statute at his or her trial, notice must be served on the Crown and filed with the court.[95] The notice sets out the nature of the application, including the factual foundation for it, the legal grounds to be argued and the relief to be sought.[96] In some provinces, legislation and rules of court dictate the procedure and forms to be used.[97]

---

[90]   See *R. v. Cleghorn*, [1995] S.C.J. No. 73, [1995] 3 S.C.R. 175 at para. 4 (S.C.C.); *R. v. P. (M.B.)*, [1994] S.C.J. No. 27, [1994] 1 S.C.R. 555 at 578 (S.C.C.); *R. v. Hill*, [1995] O.J. No. 2360, 102 C.C.C. (3d) 469 at 476-77 (Ont. C.A.).

[91]   *R. v. Cleghorn*, [1995] S.C.J. No. 73, [1995] 3 S.C.R. 175 (S.C.C.); *R. v. P. (M.B)*, [1994] S.C.J. No. 27, [1994] 1 S.C.R. 555 (S.C.C.).

[92]   *R. v. Cleghorn*, [1995] S.C.J. No. 73, [1995] 3 S.C.R. 175 at para. 22 (S.C.C.). See also *R. v. Letourneau*, [1994] B.C.J. No. 265, 87 C.C.C. (3d) 481 at 535-36 (B.C.C.A.).

[93]   *R. v. Cleghorn*, [1995] S.C.J. No. 73, [1995] 3 S.C.R. 175 at para. 3 (S.C.C.), quoting *R. v. Letourneau*, [1994] B.C.J. No. 265, 87 C.C.C. (3d) 481 at 532 (B.C.C.A.). See also *R. v. Noble*, [1997] S.C.J. No. 40, [1997] 1 S.C.R. 874 at para. 111 (S.C.C.); *R. v. Cones*, [2000] O.J. No. 640, 47 O.R. (3d) 630 at para. 28 (Ont. C.A.); *R. v. Robertson*, [1975] O.J. No. 1658, 21 C.C.C. (2d) 385 at 419 (Ont. C.A.); *R. v. Dunbar*, [1982] O.J. No. 581, 68 C.C.C. (2d) 13 at 62-63 (Ont. C.A.).

[94]   *R. v. Noble*, [1997] S.C.J. No. 40, [1997] 1 S.C.R. 874 (S.C.C.); *R. v. Creighton; R. v. Crawford*, [1995] S.C.J. No. 30, [1995] 1 S.C.R. 858 at para. 38 (S.C.C.).

[95]   See *R. v. Kutynec*, [1992] O.J. No. 347, 70 C.C.C. (3d) 289 (Ont. C.A.); *R. v. Dwernychuk*, [1992] A.J. No. 1058, 77 C.C.C. (3d) 385 (Alta. C.A.), leave to appeal refused [1993] S.C.C.A. No. 30, 79 C.C.C. (3d) vi (S.C.C.); *R. v. D. (D.L.)*, [1992] M.J. No. 541, 77 C.C.C. (3d) 426 at 437-39 (Man. C.A.); *R. v. Pelletier*, [1995] S.J. No. 115, 97 C.C.C. (3d) 139 (Sask. C.A.); *Mohammadi c. R.*, [2006] Q.J. No. 6809, 2006 QCCA 930 at paras. 46-56 (Que. C.A.), leave to appeal refused [2006] C.S.C.R. no 373 (S.C.C.); *R. c. Tsiris*, [2000] J.Q. no 3121 (Que. C.A.); *R. c. Godbout*, [2001] J.Q. no 16, J.E. 2001-236 at paras. 42-54 (Que. C.A.); *R. v. Enden*, [2007] S.J. No. 498, 52 M.V.R. (5th) 92 at para. 20 (Sask. C.A.); *R. v. Gundy*, [2008] O.J. No. 1410, 231 C.C.C. (3d) 26 at paras. 19-24 (Ont. C.A.). The notice requirements for *Charter* obligations are addressed in greater detail in Chapter 10, Part 4.

[96]   See *R. v. Kutynec*, [1992] O.J. No. 347, 70 C.C.C. (3d) 289 (Ont. C.A.); *R. v. Loveman*, [1992] O.J. No. 346, 71 C.C.C. (3d) 123 (Ont. C.A.).

[97]   See *e.g.*, Ontario, *Ontario Court of Justice, Criminal Proceedings Rules*, SI 92/99, r. 27.04(1); *Rules of the Ontario Court of Justice in Criminal Proceedings*, SI 97/133, r. 26.04(1) and

(4) Expert Evidence

§7.40 The *Criminal Code* imposes a disclosure obligation on *both* sides in criminal litigation when a party intends to call an expert witness as part of its case.[98] Specifically, a party must give notice to the other side of its intention to call an expert at least 30 days before trial.[99] That notice must advise the opposing party of the name of the proposed witness, describe the area of his or her expertise in sufficient detail to permit the other party to become informed about that area of expertise and set out a statement of the qualifications of the proposed witness as an expert.[100]

§7.41 The opposing party must also be furnished with a copy of the expert's report, if any.[101] If a report is not prepared, then in its place the opposing party must be given a summary of the opinion evidence that the expert is likely to give and an explanation of its bases.[102] In the case of the Crown, the report or summary must be given to the defence "within a reasonable period before trial".[103] In contrast, the defence must disclose this information "not later than the close of the case for the prosecution".[104]

§7.42 The court has wide discretion in dealing with the failure of a party to comply with these disclosure obligations, including ordering disclosure, granting the opposing party an adjournment and ordering the calling or recalling of any witnesses.[105]

4. THIRD PARTY PRODUCTION

§7.43 In some cases, the defence may seek to obtain information in the possession and control of someone other than the Crown, *i.e.*, a "third party". If the information is provided voluntarily, there is no issue. But if not, the accused may apply for an order compelling its production to the court. If this application is successful, the court will then review the information and decide whether to release it, in whole or in part, to the defence. The rules and procedures governing this process vary depending on whether the information sought is protected under sections 278.1 to 278.91 of the *Criminal Code*, which as detailed below, apply to personal information relating to complainants and witnesses in sexual offence prosecutions. If the information is not so protected, its production and

---

r. 30.04(1); *Constitutional Notice Regulation*, Alta. Reg. 102/99, s.1; *Judicature Act*, R.S.A. 2000, c. J-2, s. 24; *Constitutional Question Act*, R.S.B.C. 1996, c. 68, s. 8. See generally, *Eaton v. Brant County Board of Education*, [1996] S.C.J. No. 98, [1997] 1 S.C.R. 241 at paras. 48 and 54 (S.C.C.).

[98] *Criminal Code*, R.S.C. 1985, c. C-46, s. 657.3(3).
[99] *Criminal Code*, s. 657.3(3)(*a*).
[100] *Criminal Code*, s. 657.3(3)(*a*).
[101] *Criminal Code*, s. 657.3(3)(*b*)-(*c*).
[102] *Criminal Code*, s. 657.3(3)(*b*)-(*c*).
[103] *Criminal Code*, s. 657.3(3)(*b*).
[104] *Criminal Code*, s. 657.3(3)(*c*).
[105] *Criminal Code*, ss. 657.3(4) and 657.3(5).

release is dictated by the common law scheme first developed by the Supreme Court in *R. v. O'Connor*.[106] We consider each of these regimes in turn below.

(1) The Statutory Regime for Sexual Offences

§7.44 In 1997, Parliament enacted legislation to govern applications by the accused for the production of personal records relating to complainants or other witnesses in sexual offence prosecutions. As mentioned, the procedure is codified in sections 278.1 through 278.91 of the *Code*. These provisions replace the common law procedure set out in *O'Connor*, but only in respect of situations covered by the legislation.[107] Faced with the Supreme Court's splintered and contentious decision in *O'Connor*,[108] the challenge faced by Parliament was to create a procedure that would safeguard the privacy interests of complainants and witnesses while not unduly hindering an accused's ability to make full answer and defence. In the view of a strong majority in *R. v. Mills*[109] (where the constitutionality of the legislation was upheld by the Supreme Court), Parliament succeeded in this goal. As we will see, however, any success achieved was at least partly a consequence of the Court's own dexterity in interpreting the legislation to give greater leeway to the defence than the plain language of the statute would have suggested.

§7.45 The legislation applies only if two prerequisites are met. First, it applies only to records containing personal information for which there is "a reasonable expectation of privacy", including medical, psychiatric, therapeutic, counselling, educational, employment, child welfare, adoption and social services records, as well as personal journals and diaries.[110] It does not include, however, "records made by persons responsible for the investigation or prosecution of the offence."[111]

§7.46 Second, the statutory regime applies only to prosecutions of the sexual offences enumerated in section 278.2 of the *Code*. Notably, and in contrast to the majority's position in *O'Connor*, the legislation applies not only to records in the hands of third parties, but also those possessed by the Crown (unless the "complainant or witness to whom the record relates has expressly waived the application of [the legislation]").[112] Where the prerequisites are met, in other words, the process applies to both first party disclosure and third party production.

---

[106] [1995] S.C.J. No. 98, [1995] 4 S.C.R. 411 (S.C.C.) [*O'Connor*].

[107] This procedure also governs the production of third party records as fresh evidence on appeal. See *R. v. Rodgers*, [2000] O.J. No. 1065, 144 C.C.C. (3d) 568 (Ont. C.A.).

[108] For disparate views on *R. v. O'Connor*, 1995] S.C.J. No. 98, [1995] 4 S.C.R. 411 (S.C.C.), see *e.g.*, Karen Busby, "Discriminatory Uses of Personal Records in Sexual Violence Cases" (1997) 9 C.J.W.L. 148; David M. Paciocco, "Bill C-46 Should Not Survive Constitutional Challenge" (1996) 3 Sexual Offences Law Reporter 185.

[109] [1999] S.C.J. No. 68, [1999] 3 S.C.R. 668 (S.C.C.) [*Mills*].

[110] *Criminal Code*, s. 278.1.

[111] *Ibid.*

[112] *Criminal Code*, s. 278.2(2).

§7.47 Should the defence seek access to such records, the first step is to serve a formal application, with at least seven days' notice before the hearing, on the Crown, on the person who has possession or control of the record, on the complainant or witness and any other person to whom the record relates.[113] The accused is also required to serve a subpoena on the person who has possession or control of the records at the same time the application is served.[114]

§7.48 Next, a hearing will be held *in camera* to determine whether to order the person who has possession or control of the record to produce it to the court for review by the judge.[115] At this hearing, the accused bears the onus of demonstrating that the records contain information that is "likely relevant" to an issue at trial or to the competence of a witness to testify *and* that the production of the record is "necessary in the interests of justice." The accused must satisfy both requirements.[116] The statutory process allows for the complainant or a witness, as well as the record holder or custodian, to appear and make submissions at the hearing, but they are not compellable as witnesses at the hearing.[117]

§7.49 The accused is required to set out the specific grounds upon which the records are sought. In addition, section 278.3(4) contains a number of assertions that "cannot on their own" establish that a private record is relevant. That is:

(*a*) that the record exists;

(*b*) that the record relates to medical or psychiatric treatment, therapy or counselling that the complainant or witness has received or is receiving;

(*c*) that the record relates to the incident that is the subject-matter of the proceedings;

(*d*) that the record may disclose a prior inconsistent statement of the complainant or witness;

(*e*) that the record may relate to the credibility of the complainant or witness;

(*f*) that the record may relate to the reliability of the testimony of the complainant or witness merely because the complainant or witness has received or is receiving psychiatric treatment, therapy or counselling;

(*g*) that the record may reveal allegations of sexual abuse of the complainant by a person other than the accused;

(*h*) that the record relates to the sexual activity of the complainant with any person, including the accused;

(*i*) that the record relates to the presence or absence of a recent complaint;

(*j*) that the record relates to the complainant's sexual reputation; or

---

[113] *Criminal Code*, s. 278.3(5).
[114] *Criminal Code*, s. 278.3(5).
[115] *Criminal Code*, s. 278.4(1).
[116] *Criminal Code*, s. 278.5(1)(*b*) and (*c*).
[117] *Criminal Code*, s. 278.4(2).

(*k*) that the record was made close in time to a complaint or to the activity
that forms the subject-matter of the charge against the accused.[118]

Consequently, an accused must point to some "case specific evidence or information" that is not readily available to the defence or has potential impeachment
value.[119] Inconsistencies in the evidence of the complainant respecting only minor matters will not meet the "likely relevant" test.[120] Furthermore, an accused
cannot rely on speculative or stereotypical assumptions to satisfy the onus.[121]

§7.50 It is important to note that oftentimes, accused persons find themselves
hampered in their ability to demonstrate "likely relevance" simply because they
do not know what the records contain. The Court in *R. v. Mills*[122] acknowledged
this "Catch-22" dilemma, but held that there is a sufficient evidentiary basis,
even at this early stage, from which the accused can draw assistance. The Court
noted that this basis can be established from Crown disclosure, defence witnesses, the cross-examination of Crown witnesses at both the preliminary inquiry and the trial, and expert evidence.[123]

§7.51 Before ordering production of the records to the court, the trial judge
must also be satisfied that such an order is "necessary in the interests of justice."[124] Section 278.5(2) provides a checklist of various factors for the judge to
consider in exercising his or her discretion in ordering production to the court.[125]
Ultimately, the test requires a balancing of the salutary and deleterious effects
on the accused's right to make full answer and defence and on the right to privacy and equality of the person to whom the records relate. In borderline cases,

---

[118] *Criminal Code*, s. 278.3(4).

[119] See *R. v. Mills*, [1999] S.C.J. No. 68, [1999] 3 S.C.R. 668 at para. 120 (S.C.C.); *R. v. Batte*,
[2000] O.J. No. 2184, 145 C.C.C. (3d) 449 at 468 (Ont. C.A.).

[120] *R. v. Snipe*, [2003] O.J. No. 4596 at paras. 4-5 (Ont. C.A.).

[121] See *R. v. Batte*, [2000] O.J. No. 2184, 145 C.C.C. (3d) 449 at para. 53 (Ont. C.A.). See also *R.
v. Seaboyer; R. v. Gayme*, [1991] S.C.J. No. 62, [1991] 2 S.C.R. 577 (S.C.C.) for a discussion
(and rejection) of the "twin myths" that unchaste women were more likely to consent to intercourse and in any event, were less worthy of belief.

[122] [1999] S.C.J. No. 68, [1999] 3 S.C.R. 668 (S.C.C.).

[123] See *R. v. Mills*, [1999] S.C.J. No. 68, [1999] 3 S.C.R. 668 at paras. 134-135 (S.C.C.).

[124] *Criminal Code*, s. 278.5(1)(*c*).

[125] These factors are:
      (*a*) the extent to which the record is necessary for the accused to make a full answer
           and defence;
      (*b*) the probative value of the record;
      (*c*) the nature and extent of the reasonable expectation of privacy with respect to the
           record;
      (*d*) whether production of the record is based on a discriminatory belief or bias;
      (*e*) the potential prejudice to the personal dignity and right to privacy of any person
           to whom the record relates;
      (*f*) society's interest in encouraging the reporting of sexual offences;
      (*g*) society's interest in encouraging the obtaining of treatment by complainants of
           sexual offences; and
      (*h*) the effect of the determination on the integrity of the trial process.

the trial judge should err on the side of caution and order production to the court. As the Court observed in *Mills*, "The interests of justice require nothing less."[126]

§7.52 Should the accused meet this initial threshold, the judge will then review the records to determine whether, and to what extent, the records should be disclosed to the accused.[127] In making this determination, the judge will consider the same factors as in stage one above.[128]

§7.53 If production is ordered, the trial judge may order that the record be edited; that a copy, rather than the original record, be produced; that the accused and defence counsel not disclose the contents of the record to any other person; that the record be viewed only at the offices of the court; that no copies of the record be made; and that information regarding any person named in the record (*i.e.*, address, telephone number and place of employment) be deleted from the record.[129] Where production of the record is granted to the accused, the Crown usually is provided a copy, unless the judge determines that it is not in the interests of justice to do so.[130]

§7.54 If the judge refuses to order production to the accused, the record will be kept in a sealed package by the court until the expiry of the time for any appeal. After that period, the record will be returned to the person lawfully entitled to its possession or control.[131]

(2) The Common Law *O'Connor* Regime — Non-sexual Offences

§7.55 If an accused is charged with a non-sexual offence, a court may order production of third party records when the accused has met the common law test first established in *R. v. O'Connor*.[132] This procedure applies to all records not in the possession of the Crown, not simply those of a personal nature.[133] In *R. v. McNeil*,[134] the Supreme Court clarified that any such record is at least initially subject to the *O'Connor* process, even if it is later determined not to attract a reasonable expectation of privacy.[135] However, unlike the *Code* provisions applying to sexual offences, personal records in the possession of the Crown fall under the first party disclosure regime set out in *Stinchcombe*.[136]

---

[126] *R. v. Mills*, [1999] S.C.J. No. 68, [1999] 3 S.C.R. 668 at para. 132 (S.C.C.).

[127] *Criminal Code*, ss. 278.5 and 278.6.

[128] *Criminal Code*, s. 278.7(2); see factors listed in s. 278.5(2)(*a*) to (*h*), above, note 125.

[129] *Criminal Code*, s. 278(3).

[130] *Criminal Code*, s. 278.7(4).

[131] *Criminal Code*, s. 278.7(6).

[132] [1995] S.C.J. No. 98, [1995] 4 S.C.R. 411 (S.C.C.).

[133] See *R. v. M. (B.)*, [1998] O.J. No. 4359, 130 C.C.C. (3d) 353 (Ont. C.A.).

[134] [2009] S.C.J. No. 3, [2009] 1 S.C.R. 66 (S.C.C.).

[135] *Ibid.*, at para. 11 (S.C.R.). See also David Paciocco, "A Primer on the Law of Third Party Records" (2005) 9 Can. Crim. L. Rev. 157.

[136] See *R. v. M. (B.)*, [1998] O.J. No. 4359, 130 C.C.C. (3d) 353 (Ont. C.A.).

§7.56 An important distinction between the statutory regime discussed above in Part 4(1) and the two-stage framework set out in *O'Connor* discussed below is that an equivalent presumption of privacy does not attach in respect of all third party records that fall outside the *Mills* regime.[137] The "likely relevance" standard under *Mills* serves to counter the myths and stereotypes about sexual assault victims and the usefulness of private records in sexual assault proceedings.[138] In contrast, as noted in *McNeil*, the "likely relevance" threshold under *O'Connor* "is intended rather to screen applications to ensure the proper use of state authority in compelling production of third party records and to establish the appropriateness of the application so as to avoid squandering scarce judicial resources."[139] Furthermore, the balancing of competing interests that is exercised at the first stage in determining whether production should be made to the court for inspection in sexual assault proceedings is reserved for the second stage of the *O'Connor* regime, when the court can better consider the nature of the privacy interests.

(a)   The First Stage — Production to the Court for Review

§7.57 At the first stage in the production regime under *O'Connor*, an accused has the onus to satisfy a judge that the information is "likely to be relevant". The judge must be satisfied that there is "a reasonable possibility that the information is logically probative to an issue at trial or the competence of a witness to testify."[140] An "issue at trial" includes evidence relating to the credibility of a witness and to the reliability of other evidence.[141] Acknowledging the Catch-22 position of the accused, who has not seen the documents, Chief Justice Lamer in *O'Connor* noted that this initial threshold to provide a basis for production can be satisfied by oral submissions of counsel standing alone.[142]

§7.58 Material that is relevant to the credibility or reliability of a complainant is particularly important to an accused because the Crown's case may hinge entirely upon that witness. Non-disclosure of evidence relevant to credibility or reliability in such a case impairs the core of the accused's right to make full answer and defence by depriving the accused of the only tools available to him or her to test the Crown's case by cross-examination.[143]

§7.59 In *O'Connor*, Chief Justice Lamer also offered guidelines as to the procedure to be followed in seeking the production of such records. The accused is to bring a formal written application supported by an affidavit setting out the

---

[137] *R. v. McNeil*, [2009] S.C.J. No. 3, [2009] 1 S.C.R. 66 at para. 32 (S.C.C.).
[138] *Ibid.*, at para. 31 (S.C.R.).
[139] *Ibid.*
[140] *R. v. O'Connor*, [1995] S.C.J. No. 98, [1995] 4 S.C.R. 411 at para. 22 (S.C.C.) [emphasis deleted from original]; *R. v. McNeil*, [2009] S.C.J. No. 3, [2009] 1 S.C.R. 66 at para. 33 (S.C.C.).
[141] *R. v. O'Connor*, [1995] S.C.J. No. 98, [1995] 4 S.C.R. 411 at para. 22 (S.C.C.).
[142] *Ibid.*, at para. 19 (S.C.R.); *R. v. McNeil*, [2009] S.C.J. No. 3, [2009] 1 S.C.R. 66 at para. 33 (S.C.C.).
[143] *R. v. Osolin*, [1993] S.C.J. No. 135, [1993] 4 S.C.R. 595 at para. 65 (S.C.C.).

grounds for production. The notice must be given to third parties in possession of the documents as well as to those persons who have a privacy interest in the records. The custodian of the records must be subpoenaed in order to ensure the records are brought to court. The application should be made to the judge seized of the trial.[144]

(b) The Second Stage — Production by the Court to the Accused

§7.60 If the accused is able to demonstrate "likely relevance", the third party record holder may be ordered to produce the records for inspection by the judge in order to determine whether production should be ordered to the accused. At this stage, the judge "must examine and weigh the salutary and deleterious effects of a production order and determine whether a non-production order would constitute a reasonable limit on the ability of the accused to make full answer and defence."[145] In balancing these competing rights, the judge is entitled to consider: "(1) the extent to which the record is necessary for the accused to make full answer and defence; (2) the probative value of the record in question; (3) the nature and extent of the reasonable expectation of privacy vested in that record; (4) whether production of the record would be premised upon any discriminatory belief or bias and (5) the potential prejudice to the complainant's dignity, privacy or security of the person that would be occasioned by production of the record in question."[146]

§7.61 Any additional submissions by counsel at the second stage should be made after the trial judge has had an opportunity to review the records. The trial judge can then direct specific questions to counsel about the issues raised by that inspection.[147] To the extent that these records may contain some private information that is not potentially relevant to an issue at trial, such information could be edited out of the copies produced to the defence in order to minimize any possible prejudice to the personal dignity and privacy of the witness.

(3) Discipline Records of Police Witnesses

§7.62 As a general rule, the Crown has a duty to disclose disciplinary records relevant to the credibility of police officers where the police misconduct could reasonably impact on the case against the accused.[148] In *R. v. McNeil*,[149] the Supreme Court explained that disciplinary records and criminal investigation files in the possession of the police that do not fall within the scope of this first party disclosure category are governed by the *O'Connor* regime for third party production. To streamline this third party application process, the Court indicated

---

[144] *R. v. O'Connor*, [1995] S.C.J. No. 98, [1995] 4 S.C.R. 411 at para. 20 (S.C.C.).
[145] *Ibid.*, at para. 30 (S.C.R.).
[146] *Ibid.*, at para. 31 (S.C.R.).
[147] *Ibid.*, at para. 30 (S.C.R.).
[148] *R. v. McNeil*, [2009] S.C.J. No. 3, [2009] 1 S.C.R. 66 at paras. 57-58 (S.C.C.).
[149] [2009] S.C.J. No. 3, [2009] 1 S.C.R. 66 at paras. 57-58 (S.C.C.).

that there should be automatic production by the police upon request by the Crown of the following information regarding acts of misconduct by a police officer who may be a witness or who was otherwise involved in a case before the Court:

    a.   Any conviction or finding of guilt under the Canadian *Criminal Code* or the *Controlled Drugs and Substances Act* [for which a pardon has not been granted].

    b.   Any outstanding charges under the Canadian *Criminal Code* or the *Controlled Drugs and Substances Act.*

    c.   Any conviction or finding of guilt under any other federal or provincial statute.

    d.   Any finding of guilt for misconduct after a hearing under the *Police Services Act* or its predecessor *Act.*

    e.   Any current charge of misconduct under the *Police Services Act* for which a Notice of Hearing has been issued.[150]

§7.63 Upon receiving this information from police, the Crown will act as "gate-keeper", sorting out what should be disclosed to the defence in compliance with the Crown's obligation under *Stinchcombe* to share all relevant information. Any concerned police officer who was the subject of disciplinary records produced to the Crown should be notified in writing and be given the opportunity to make submissions to the Crown.[151]

(4) Defence Already in Possession of Third Party Records

§7.64 In circumstances where the defence has come into possession of third party records without first complying either with the *Code* provisions or the *O'Connor* procedures, the admissibility of such records is determined by assessing the probative value of the records versus their prejudicial effect.[152] In *R. v. Shearing,*[153] the accused had come into possession of the complainant's diary from many years before. The Court held that the admissibility of the diary was governed by the test for the admissibility of defence evidence as set out in *R. v. Seaboyer; R. v. Gayme.*[154] As such, the trial judge could have limited cross-examination on the diary only if the prejudice to the complainant's privacy interests caused by the extended cross-examination would substantially outweigh its probative value.

---

[150] *Ibid.*, at para. 57 (S.C.R.).
[151] *Ibid.*
[152] *R. v. B. (R.S.)*, [2005] O.J. No. 2845 (Ont. C.A.), leave to appeal refused [2005] S.C.C.A. No. 514 (S.C.C.).
[153] [2002] S.C.J. No. 59, [2002] 3 S.C.R. 33 (S.C.C.).
[154] [1991] S.C.J. No. 62, [1991] 2 S.C.R. 577 (S.C.C.).

Chapter 8

PROSECUTORIAL FUNCTION

1. INTRODUCTION

§8.1 Prosecutors play an extremely important role in the criminal justice process. In addition to conducting the Crown's case at preliminary proceedings, trials, sentencing hearings and appeals, they also make numerous discretionary decisions, such as whether to proceed with or continue charges, enter into plea agreements, proceed (in the case of hybrid offences) by way of summary conviction or indictment,[1] and prefer direct indictments.[2] They also often give legal advice to police in the course of criminal investigations. As we will see, in carrying out many of these tasks prosecutors are subject to only very limited external oversight.

§8.2 As a consequence of their extensive powers, prosecutors bear weighty responsibilities. Unlike defence lawyers, who are ethically mandated to be zealous advocates for their clients,[3] a prosecutor's paramount duty is to ensure that justice is done. It is therefore frequently said that the prosecutor's role is to be a "minister of justice".[4] In an oft-cited passage, Justice Rand outlined the nature of this duty in *R. v. Boucher*[5] as follows:

> ... [T]he purpose of a criminal prosecution is not to obtain a conviction, it is to lay before a jury what the Crown considers to be credible evidence relevant to what is alleged to be a crime. Counsel have a duty to see that all available legal proof of the facts is presented: it should be done firmly and pressed to its legitimate strength but it must also be done fairly. The role of prosecutor excludes any notion of winning or losing; his function is a matter of public duty than which in civil life there can be none charged with greater

---

[1] Hybrid offences are discussed more extensively in Chapter 1, Part 2(3)(*c*).

[2] Direct indictments are discussed more extensively in Chapter 9, Part 4(3).

[3] See Michel Proulx & David Layton, *Ethics and Canadian Criminal Law* (Toronto: Irwin Law, 2001) at 645.

[4] *R. v. Puddick* (1865), 176 E.R. 662 at 663 (it should be remembered that "counsel for the prosecution...are to regard themselves as ministers of justice and not to struggle for a conviction"). See also *Nelles v. Ontario*, [1989] S.C.J. No. 86, [1989] 2 S.C.R. 170 at 191 (S.C.C.); *R. v. Regan*, [2002] S.C.J. No. 14, [2002] 1 S.C.R. 297 at para. 65 (S.C.C.); *R. v. McNeil*, [2009] S.C.J. No. 3, [2009] 1 S.C.R. 66 at para. 49 (S.C.C.); Morris Manning, "Abuse of Power by Crown Attorneys" [1979] L.S.U.C. Lectures 571 at 580.

[5] [1954] S.C.J. No. 54, [1955] S.C.R. 16 (S.C.C.).

personal responsibility. It is to be efficiently performed with an ingrained sense of the dignity, the seriousness and the justness of judicial proceedings.[6]

In short, justice requires that prosecutors seek the truth (keeping in mind that some defendants may in fact be innocent) while respecting the legal and constitutional rights of the accused and others involved in the case.

§8.3 This does not mean that prosecutors must act in an entirely non-adversarial manner. As Justice LeBel stated in *R. v. Regan*,[7] "commitment to the case, belief in the allegations, and the desire to see justice done are not incompatible with objectivity and fairness."[8] Prosecutors must therefore balance their obligations as advocates with their duties as ministers of justice.[9] While most ably mediate this conflict, recent decades have unfortunately witnessed many instances of excessive prosecutorial partisanship. In the worst cases, overreaching by prosecutors has contributed to causing wrongful convictions.[10]

§8.4 In this chapter we outline the key roles that prosecutors play in the criminal justice process and examine the legal rules regulating prosecutorial decision-

---

[6]   *Ibid.*, at 23-24 (S.C.R.), *per* Rand J. See also *R. v. Boucher*, [1954] S.C.J. No. 54, [1955] S.C.R. 16 at 25 (S.C.C.), *per* Locke J. This passage from Rand J.'s reasons quoted in the text is also cited in the following decisions: *R. v. Emkeit*, [1974] S.C.J. No. 114, [1974] S.C.R. 133 at 146 (S.C.C.); *R. v. Biddle*, [1995] S.C.J. No. 22, [1995] 1 S.C.R. 761 at para. 51 (S.C.C.), *per* Gonthier J., concurring; *R. v. Regan*, [2002] S.C.J. No. 14, [2002] 1 S.C.R. 297 at para. 65 (S.C.C.); *Nelles v. Ontario*, [1989] S.C.J. No. 86, [1989] 2 S.C.R. 170 at 192 (S.C.C.); *R. v. Brown*, [2002] S.C.J. No. 35, [2002] 2 S.C.R. 185 at para. 78 (S.C.C.); *Proulx v. Quebec (Attorney General)*, [2001] S.C.J. No. 65, [2001] 3 S.C.R. 9 at para. 41 (S.C.C.); *CanadianOxy Chemicals Ltd. v. Canada (Attorney General)*, [1998] S.C.J. No. 87, [1999] 1 S.C.R. 743 at para. 25 (S.C.C.); *R. v. Stinchcombe*, [1991] S.C.J. No. 83, [1991] 3 S.C.R. 326 at 333 (S.C.C.); *R. v. Bain*, [1992] S.C.J. No. 3, [1992] 1 S.C.R. 91 at 117-18 (S.C.C.), *per* Gonthier J., dissenting; *R. v. Duguay*, [2003] S.C.J. No. 75, [2003] 3 S.C.R. 307 at para. 68 (S.C.C.); *R. v. Trochym*, [2007] S.C.J. No. 6, [2007] 1 S.C.R. 239 at para. 79 (S.C.C.). See also *R. v. Curragh Inc.*, [1997] S.C.J. No. 33, [1997] 1 S.C.R. 537 at para. 121 (S.C.C.), *per* McLachlin and Major JJ., dissenting ("To win is not the role of the prosecutor; to win at all costs is an affront to the Canadian justice system."); *Public Prosecution Service of Canada: Annual Report, 2009-2010* (Ottawa: Attorney General of Canada, 2010) at 4 (the prosecutors' role "is not to win convictions at any cost, but to put before the court all available, relevant, and admissible evidence necessary to enable the court to determine the guilt or innocence of an accused").

[7]   [2002] S.C.J. No. 14, [2002] 1 S.C.R. 297 (S.C.C.).

[8]   *R. v. Regan*, [2002] S.C.J. No. 14, [2002] 1 S.C.R. 297 at para. 89 (S.C.C.). See also *R. v. Cook*, [1997] S.C.J. No. 22, [1997] S.C.R. 1113 at para. 21 (S.C.C.) ("it is both permissible and desirable that [the Crown] vigorously pursue a legitimate result to the best of its ability"); *R. v. Savion*, [1980] O.J. No. 580, 52 C.C.C. (2d) 276 at 289 (Ont. C.A.); Graeme G. Mitchell, "'No Joy in This for Anyone': Reflections on the Exercise of Prosecutorial Discretion in *R. v. Latimer*" (2001) 64 Sask. L. Rev. 491 at 496-97.

[9]   See Michel Proulx & David Layton, *Ethics and Canadian Criminal Law* (Toronto: Irwin Law, 2001) at 639, 645-47.

[10]   See *e.g.*, Manitoba, The Report of the Honourable Peter de C. Cory, *The Inquiry Regarding Thomas Sophonow* (Winnipeg: Government of Manitoba, 2001) at 52; Fred Ferguson, "Prosecutorial Assessment of the Case" (1998) National Criminal Law Program, Federation of Law Societies of Canada; Ontario, Commission on Proceedings Involving Guy Paul Morin, *Report*, vol. 2, by Hon. Fred Kaufman (Toronto: Ministry of the Attorney General, 1998) at 909, 911, 1068; *R. v. Regan*, [2002] S.C.J. No. 14, [2002] 1 S.C.R. 297 at para. 69 (S.C.C.).

making. Discussions of the purely ethical restrictions on prosecutorial conduct may be found elsewhere.[11]

2. PROSECUTORIAL AUTHORITY

(1) Provincial Prosecutions

§8.5 Most criminal prosecutions are conducted by provincial prosecutors.[12] The authority to prosecute most *Criminal Code*[13] offences is granted to the "Attorney General", who is generally defined as the "Attorney General or Solicitor General of the province in which those proceedings are taken and includes his or her lawful deputy."[14] In practice, the provincial attorneys general, who are ministers of government, delegate their prosecutorial authority to provincial Crown counsel.[15] To varying degrees, the provinces have given prosecutors a measure of independence and autonomy from the Attorney General.[16] The Attorney General is ultimately responsible, however, for prosecutions conducted by Crown counsel.[17]

(2) Federal Prosecutions

§8.6 The federal government also plays a role in criminal prosecutions. The federal prosecutorial power vests with the "Attorney General of Canada,"

---

[11] See especially Michel Proulx & David Layton, *Ethics and Canadian Criminal Law* (Toronto: Irwin Law, 2001) Chapter 12.

[12] The Supreme Court of Canada has ruled that while Parliament has exclusive authority under s. 91(27) of the *Constitution Act, 1867* (U.K.), 30 & 31 Vict., c. 3 [Reprinted in R.S.C. 1985, App. II, No. 5] to prosecute *Criminal Code* (and other federal) offences, it may delegate this power to the provinces. See *Canada (Attorney General) v. C.N. Transportation Ltd.*, [1983] S.C.J. No. 73, [1983] 2 S.C.R. 206 (S.C.C.); *R. v. Wetmore*, [1983] S.C.J. No. 74, [1983] 2 S.C.R. 284 (S.C.C.); *R. v. S. (S.)*, [1990] S.C.J. No. 66, [1990] 2 S.C.R. 254 (S.C.C.). See also Chapter 1, Part 5(3).

[13] R.S.C. 1985, c. C-46 [*Code*].

[14] *Criminal Code*, s. 2, definition of "Attorney General", subs. (a).

[15] See *R. v. Harrison*, [1977] S.C.J. No. 22, [1977] 1 S.C.R. 238 (S.C.C.) (power of Attorney General to delegate tasks to Crown counsel implicit in *Criminal Code*).

[16] See *e.g., Crown Counsel Act*, R.S.B.C. 1996, c. 87, ss. 5-6 (directions as to prosecutorial policy and conduct of prosecutions from Attorney General or Deputy Attorney General must be given to head of prosecution service in writing and published in Gazette). See generally, Library of Parliament, Parliamentary Information and Research Service, *The Possible Establishment of a Federal Director of Public Prosecutions in Canada*, PRB 05-67E (March 2, 2006); Nova Scotia, Royal Commission on the Donald Marshall, Jr., Prosecution, *Walking the Tightrope of Justice: An Examination of the Office of the Attorney General in Canada with Particular Regard to its Relationships with the Police and Prosecutors and the Arguments for Establishing a Statutorily Independent Director of Public Prosecutions: A Series of Opinion Papers*, vol. 5 by John Ll. J. Edwards (Halifax: Queen's Printer, 1989).

[17] See generally, *Krieger v. Law Society of Alberta*, [2002] S.C.J. No. 45, [2002] 3 S.C.R. 372 at paras. 25-26 (S.C.C.) [*Krieger*] (describing the Attorney General's historical and constitutional role); *Constitution Act, 1867* (U.K.), 30 & 31 Vict., c. 3 [Reprinted in R.S.C. 1985, App. II, No. 5], s. 135 (continuing pre-Confederation powers of Attorney General). As discussed below, Part 4(1)(*a*), the Attorney General himself or herself also enjoys a measure of independence from the executive in exercising prosecutorial authority.

including "his or her lawful deputy."[18] Federal prosecutions are conducted by counsel from the Public Prosecution Service of Canada, a quasi-independent body responsible to the Attorney General of Canada.[19] Federal Crown attorneys are responsible for prosecuting offences in the territories as well as most offences under federal enactments other than the *Criminal Code*, including the offences of conspiring, attempting or counselling the contravention of such statutes (which are technically *Code* offences).[20] The *Code* provides that for such offences, the Attorney General of Canada is responsible for "proceedings commenced at the instance of the Government of Canada and conducted by or on behalf of that Government".[21] This has been interpreted as permitting provincial Crown counsel to prosecute non-*Code* federal offences if the Attorney General of Canada does not do so.[22] Federal prosecutors are entitled to conduct the case, however, even if the charges were laid by provincial law enforcement officials.[23] Further, the Attorney General of Canada may prosecute *Code* offences under a specific grant of authority from a provincial Attorney General.[24]

---

[18] See *e.g.*, *Criminal Code*, s. 2, definition of "Attorney General", subsection (*b*).

[19] See *Director of Public Prosecutions Act*, S.C. 2006, c. 9, s. 121. See also Chantal Proulx, "The Public Prosecution Service of Canada" (2009) 2 J. Parl. & Pol. Law 521 at 522-23. On a day-to-day basis, the Director of Public Prosecutions (DPP), who has guaranteed tenure, acts independently of the Attorney General of Canada. The Attorney General can direct or take carriage of a prosecution, however, by issuing a notice published in the *Canada Gazette*. Further, the DPP is required to inform the Attorney General of any prosecution or intervention raising "questions of general interest". An exception to this arrangement has been made for prosecutions under the *Canada Elections Act*, S.C. 2000, c. 9, where the DPP acts wholly independently of the Attorney General of Canada. See *Director of Public Prosecutions Act*, S.C. 2006, c. 9, ss. 3(8), 10-15; *Canada Elections Act*, S.C. 2000, c. 9, s. 512(1).

[20] *Criminal Code*, s. 2, definition of "Attorney General", subsection (*b*).

[21] *Criminal Code*, s. 2, definition of "Attorney General", subsection (*b*). See also *Controlled Drugs and Substances Act*, S.C. 1996, c. 19, s. 2, definition of "Attorney General" (conferring general authority to prosecute on Attorney General of Canada but permitting provincial prosecutors to conduct "proceedings commenced at the instance of the government of a province and conducted by or on behalf of that government").

[22] See *R. v. Sacobie*, [1979] N.B.J. No. 303, 51 C.C.C. (2d) 430 (N.B.C.A.), affd [1983] S.C.J. No. 17, [1983] 1 S.C.R. 241 (S.C.C.) (power of provincial attorneys general to prosecute non-*Code* criminal offences derives from what is now s. 34(2) of the *Interpretation Act*, R.S.C. 1985, c. I-21, applying *Criminal Code* to other federal offences unless specified otherwise).

[23] See *R. v. Pelletier*, [1974] O.J. No. 2012, 18 C.C.C. (2d) 516 at 535 (Ont. C.A.); *R. v. King*, [1987] O.J. No. 1080, 40 C.C.C. (3d) 359 at 364 (Ont. C.A.) (at a minimum, municipal police may lay charges under federal narcotic statute pursuant to procedure conferring "general authority...to institute or commence proceedings on behalf of the Government of Canada"); *R. v. Thomas*, [1977] B.C.J. No. 1124, 38 C.C.C. (2d) 344 at 348 (B.C. Co. Ct.), affd [1979] B.C.J. No. 2043, 53 C.C.C. (2d) 472 (B.C.C.A.) ("where the information is laid and agents of the Attorney General of Canada assume conduct of the prosecution...the only rational conclusion is that the Attorney General of Canada has ratified and approved the institution of proceedings and they are therefore instituted at the instance of the Government of Canada"). See also *Canada (Attorney General) v. Canadian National Transportation Ltd.*, [1983] S.C.J. No. 73, [1983] 2 S.C.R. 206 (S.C.C.).

[24] See *R. v. Elliott*, [2003] O.J. No. 4694, 181 C.C.C. (3d) 118 at para. 137 (Ont. C.A.); *R. v. Wilder*, [1994] M.J. No. 207, 23 W.C.B. (2d) 355 (Man. Q.B.).

§8.7 As a matter of practice, most prosecutions of non-*Code* offences, including those under the *Controlled Drugs and Substances Act*,[25] *Income Tax Act*[26] and *Immigration and Refugee Protection Act*,[27] are conducted by federal prosecutors.[28] In Quebec and New Brunswick, however, federal prosecutors only prosecute drug offences investigated by the Royal Canadian Mounted Police (RCMP).[29] In all other provinces, they prosecute drug offences regardless of the investigating agency.[30] Both federal and provincial Crown attorneys prosecute cases where drug or other non-*Code* federal charges are combined in the same indictment with *Criminal Code* offences; carriage of the cases is determined by various formal and informal arrangements between offices.[31]

§8.8 The Attorney General of Canada also has concurrent jurisdiction with the provincial attorneys general over certain *Criminal Code* offences of national or international concern, including crimes involving cultural property, the offence of contravening a non-*Code* federal statute not otherwise punishable, war crimes and crimes against humanity, crimes against United Nations personnel, crimes in space, certain crimes involving financial markets, money laundering and proceeds of crime offences, and certain criminal organization offences.[32] In addition, by issuing a fiat to the attorney general of a province, the Attorney General of Canada may take charge of the prosecution of any federal offence with implications for national security or international relations. Specifically, such a fiat may issue when the Attorney General of Canada believes that the offence: (*i*) constitutes a "threat to the security of Canada within the meaning of the *Canadian Security Intelligence Service Act*;"[33] (*ii*) involves a victim who is "an internationally protected person within the meaning of section 2 of the *Criminal Code*;"[34] or could result in the disclosure of "sensitive information or potentially injurious information".[35] Lastly, some *Code* offences require the Attorney

---

[25] S.C. 1996, c. 19. Drug prosecutions comprise about three-quarters of federal prosecutors' case load. See *Public Prosecution Service of Canada: Annual Report, 2008-2009* (Ottawa: Attorney General of Canada, 2009).

[26] R.S.C. 1985, c 1 (5th Supp.).

[27] S.C. 2001, c. 27.

[28] See Chantal Proulx, "The Public Prosecution Service of Canada" (2009) 2 J. Parl. & Pol. Law 521 at 523. Federal prosecutors are responsible for prosecuting offences under approximately 60 federal statutes. See *Public Prosecution Service of Canada: Annual Report, 2009-2010* (Ottawa: Attorney General of Canada, 2010) at 4.

[29] *Public Prosecution Service of Canada: Annual Report, 2009-2010* (Ottawa: Attorney General of Canada, 2010) at 3.

[30] *Ibid.*

[31] See Chantal Proulx, "The Public Prosecution Service of Canada" (2009) 2 J. Parl. & Pol. Law 521 at 523; *Public Prosecution Service of Canada: Annual Report, 2009-2010* (Ottawa: Attorney General of Canada, 2010) at 4, 6.

[32] See *Criminal Code*, R.S.C. 1985, c. C-46, s. 2, definition of "Attorney General", subsections (*b.*1)-(*g*) and ss. 7(2.32), 126, 462.3(3), and 467.2(1).

[33] *Security Offences Act*, R.S.C. 1985, c. S-7, ss. 2-5, as amended.

[34] *Ibid.*

[35] *Canada Evidence Act*, R.S.C. 1985, s. 38.15. Section 38 of that statute defines "potentially injurious information" to mean "information of a type that, if it were disclosed to the public, could injure international relations or national defence or national security"; it defines "sensitive

General of Canada's consent before they can be prosecuted, regardless of who conducts the Crown's case.[36]

(3) Private Prosecutions

§8.9 Prosecutions initiated by private parties are dealt with in Chapter 5, Part 5. As we explain there, though the private party who laid the information may in theory conduct the prosecution,[37] in practice Crown prosecutors almost always exercise their power to take control of the prosecution, which includes a discretion to discontinue the proceedings.[38]

3. PROSECUTORS' ROLE IN CRIMINAL INVESTIGATIONS

§8.10 The investigation of crime is the responsibility of police and other law enforcement officials, who are independent of both attorneys general and prosecutors' offices.[39] Prosecutors participate in the investigative process, however, both before and after charges are laid.

§8.11 In *R. v. Regan*,[40] the accused (a former premier of Nova Scotia) was charged with sexual offences spanning many years involving several complainants. Before charges were laid, a prosecutor interviewed several alleged victims (who had been previously interviewed by police) to help them decide whether to

---

information" as "information relating to international relations or national defence or national security that is in the possession of the Government of Canada, whether originating from inside or outside Canada, and is of a type that the Government of Canada is taking measures to safeguard."

36 See *e.g.*, *Criminal Code*, ss. 7(2.33) (crimes in space), 7(7) (extraterritorial offences where accused is non-citizen), 54 (assisting a Canadian Forces deserter), 119 (accepting of bribes by judge), 251(3) (unsafe carriage of federally-regulated ships, trains and aircraft), 477.2 (extraterritorial maritime offences committed by non-citizens on ships registered outside Canada).

37 See *Criminal Code*, s. 2, definition of "prosecutor" ("'prosecutor' means the Attorney General or, where the Attorney General does not intervene, means the person who institutes proceedings ...").

38 This power is recognized both at common law as well as in some of the statutes governing Crown attorneys. See *Krieger v. Law Society of Alberta*, [2002] S.C.J. No. 45, [2002] 3 S.C.R. 372 at paras. 25, 46 (S.C.C.); *R. v. Osiowy*, [1989] S.J. No. 379, 50 C.C.C. (3d) 189 (Sask. C.A.); *Crown Counsel Act*, R.S.B.C. 1996, c. 87, s. 4(3)(c).

39 See *R. v. Campbell*, [1999] S.C.J. No. 16, [1999] 1 S.C.R. 565 at para. 29 (S.C.C.); *R. v. Regan*, [2002] S.C.J. No. 14, [2002] 1 S.C.R. 297 at para. 64 (S.C.C.). See also Royal Commission on the Donald Marshall, Jr., Prosecution, vol. 1, *Digest of Findings and Recommendations* (Halifax: The Commission, 1989) at 232; Phillip C. Stenning, *Legal Status of the Police: A Study Paper Prepared for the Law Reform Commission of Canada* (Ottawa: The Commission, 1982) at 101-102; Law Reform Commission of Canada, *Controlling Criminal Prosecutions: The Attorney General and the Crown Prosecutor* (Ottawa: Law Reform Commission of Canada, 1990) at 71-72; Michael Code, "Crown Counsel's Responsibilities When Advising the Police at the Pre-Charge Stage" (1998) 40 Crim. L.Q. 326 at 333-37. Though independent of the executive in day-to-day operations, provincial police agencies are ultimately accountable to the Solicitor General of the province. See *e.g.*, *Police Services Act*, R.S.O. 1990, c. P.15, s. 3(2). The RCMP is similarly accountable to the Minister of Public Safety (known until 2005 as the Solicitor General of Canada). See *Royal Canadian Mounted Police Act*, R.S.C. 1985, c. R-10, s. 5(1).

40 [2002] S.C.J. No. 14, [2002] 1 S.C.R. 297 (S.C.C.).

become involved in the case, assess their credibility as witnesses and prepare for a preliminary inquiry.[41] The accused argued that these interviews violated the principle of police independence and constituted an abuse of process. In denying this claim, the Supreme Court of Canada concluded that prosecutors' independence and objectivity are not necessarily compromised by conducting pre-charge interviews.[42] Nor is it improper, the Court found, for prosecutors to discuss charges with police and recommend whether charges should be laid, even in jurisdictions where police may lay charges without prosecutorial approval.[43] Such interviews and discussions may be especially helpful in sexual assault cases, the Court observed, by helping to screen out "fruitless complaints", "encouraging proper charges to go forward", and by "signalling to the larger society that complainants can bring sexual assault charges to the courts without further undue trauma, and that where charges are properly laid, they will be prosecuted."[44]

§8.12 Prosecutors also assist and cooperate with police in other aspects of criminal investigations. They often provide advice on the legality and constitutionality of investigative methods,[45] apply for or assist police in applying for certain types of search warrants and restraint orders[46] and in some circumstances, even help to direct the course of an investigation. Prosecutors work especially closely with police in investigating sophisticated criminal and terrorist enterprises that are regional, national or international in scope.[47] Federal prosecutors, for example, have been assigned to work in integrated units with police and other law enforcement and intelligence agents to investigate organized crime, terrorism, and offences involving financial markets.[48]

---

[41] *Ibid.*, at para. 13 (S.C.R.).

[42] *Ibid.*, at paras. 64-91 (S.C.R.).

[43] *Ibid.*, at para. 87 (S.C.R.) (noting that police may lay charges based on the prosecutor's recommendation). We discuss responsibility for charging decisions in Part 4, below.

[44] *Ibid.*, at para. 85 (S.C.R.). It may also be helpful for prosecutors to conduct pre-charge interviews in other types of cases, the Court noted, including cases where there is a need to ensure the "protection of *Charter* rights during an investigation," cases "involving jailhouse informants", and cases where there is a "statutory requirement for Crown consent to the laying of charges." *Ibid.*, at para. 86 (S.C.R.).

[45] See Michael Code, "Crown Counsel's Responsibilities When Advising the Police at the Pre-Charge Stage" (1998) 40 Crim. L.Q. 326; *Public Prosecution Service of Canada: Annual Report, 2009-2010* (Ottawa: Attorney General of Canada, 2010) at 4.

[46] See *e.g.*, *Criminal Code*, ss. 185(1) (ministerial consent required for wiretap authorizations made by police), 83.13 (Attorney General must apply for order for seizure and restraint of property). See also *R. v. Ebanks*, [2009] O.J. No. 5168, 2009 ONCA 851 at paras. 48-49 (Ont. C.A.), leave to appeal refused [2010] S.C.C.A. No. 84 (S.C.C.) (though Crown must ensure that wiretap application conforms to statutory requirements, not responsible for thorough review of file; doing so would "blur the line between the mutually independent functions of the police and the Crown").

[47] See Michel Proulx & David Layton, *Ethics and Canadian Criminal Law* (Toronto: Irwin Law, 2001) at 689-90.

[48] See Chantal Proulx, "The Public Prosecution Service of Canada" (2009) 2 J. Parl. & Pol. Law 521 at 524-25; *Public Prosecution Service of Canada: Annual Report, 2008-2009* (Ottawa: Attorney General of Canada, 2009) at 4.

4.   CHARGING DECISIONS

(1)   The Decision to Prosecute

(a)   *General Principles*

§8.13 Perhaps the most important decision that prosecutors make is whether to proceed with or discontinue charges. Two statistics tell the tale. Of all charges laid, only about five per cent result in an acquittal or analogous disposition. The remainder are either withdrawn or stayed by the Crown (about 30 per cent) or result in a finding of guilt (about 65 per cent).[49] The predominant factor determining conviction is therefore prosecutorial discretion.[50] Needless to say, the exercise of this discretion may have monumental consequences for the accused, even those who are not ultimately found guilty at trial.[51]

§8.14 In most jurisdictions, the initial decision to charge a person with a criminal offence is made by police.[52] But in British Columbia, Quebec and New Brunswick, charges are typically approved by a prosecutor before the information is laid.[53] In addition, for a limited number of offences, the Attorney General's consent is required before charges are laid.[54]

---

[49]   Statistics Canada, Canadian Centre for Justice Statistics, *Adult Criminal Court Statistics, 2006/2007*, 28(5) Juristat (Ottawa: Minister of Industry, 2008) at 4 and 14, Table 4.

[50]   See Ontario, *Report of the Attorney General's Advisory Committee on Charge Screening, Disclosure, and Resolution Discussions* (Toronto: Queen's Printer, 1993) at 51.

[51]   See generally, Monroe Freedman, *Lawyers' Ethics in an Adversary System* (Indianapolis: Bobbs-Merrill, 1975) at 29.

[52]   See *e.g.*, *R. v. Regan*, [2002] S.C.J. No. 14, [2002] 1 S.C.R. 297 at para. 67 (S.C.C.); Ontario, Attorney General's Advisory Committee, *Report of the Attorney General's Advisory Committee on Charge Screening, Disclosure, and Resolution Discussion* (Toronto: Queen's Printer, 1993) at 37; Law Reform Commission of Canada, *Controlling Criminal Prosecutions: The Attorney General and the Crown Prosecutor* (Working Paper 62) (Ottawa: Law Reform Commission of Canada, 1990) at 69-76.

[53]   See British Columbia, Ministry of the Attorney General, Criminal Justice Branch, *Crown Counsel Policy Manual*, "Charge Assessment Guidelines," Policy CHA-1 (October 2, 2009) at 2; Quebec, Directeur des poursuites criminelles et pénales, "Accusation — Poursuite des Procédures" (March 31, 2009) § 9; New Brunswick, *Public Prosecution Services Operational Manual*, "Attorney General's Policy — Public Prosecutions" at 2-3 (2007). As the *Criminal Code* permits anyone to swear an information against an accused, it is legally possible for police in these provinces to lay charges without prosecutorial approval. (The process for laying charges is discussed in detail in Chapter 5, Part 2.) The role of prosecutors in approving charges in each province, however, is firmly entrenched in law and policy. See *Krieger v. Law Society of Alberta*, [2002] S.C.J. No. 45, [2002] 3 S.C.R. 372 at para. 46 (S.C.C.); *R. v. Regan*, [2002] S.C.J. No. 14, [2002] 1 S.C.R. 297 at paras. 72-77 (S.C.C.); *Crown Counsel Act*, R.S.B.C. 1996, c. 87, s. 4(3)(c); *An Act Respecting Attorney General Prosecutors*, R.S.Q., c. S-35, s. 4. See also Law Reform Commission of Canada, *Controlling Criminal Prosecutions: The Attorney General and the Crown Prosecutor*, Working Paper 62 (Ottawa: The Commission, 1990) at 74-75.

[54]   See *e.g.*, *Criminal Code*, ss. 83.24 (terrorism offences); 136(3) (giving contrary evidence); 174(3) (public nudity); 283(2) (parental abduction of child); 318(3) (advocating genocide); 319(6) (public incitement of hatred); 347(7) (criminal interest rate).

§8.15 In our view, pre-charge prosecutorial screening is superior to post-charge screening. The high percentage of charges withdrawn or stayed by prosecutors mentioned above strongly suggests that prosecutors regularly differ with police as to the adequacy of the evidence to support an arrest and charge,[55] as does the fact that the percentage of cases stayed or withdrawn in the three provinces requiring prosecutorial approval of charges is substantially lower than in the other provinces.[56] As a consequence, in provinces without pre-charge screening, charges destined for dismissal are discontinued at a later stage in the process. Indeed, as mentioned immediately below, in such provinces this may occur months after the charges are laid. Assuming that a significant proportion of people facing such charges are factually innocent, this delay is most regrettable.

§8.16 In any case, the ultimate decision to proceed with charges in all jurisdictions rests with the Attorney General (whether provincial or federal).[57] In jurisdictions where the decision to charge is made by police, the first step is for a prosecutor to review the investigative file brought forward by police and decide whether to prosecute. Ideally, that review should occur soon after charges are laid[58]; however, logistical impediments may delay this for weeks or even months.[59] The review and decision whether to proceed is usually made by a front-line prosecutor, who may or may not be assigned as the prosecutor for the trial.[60] In exceptional cases, the decision may be made by high level prosecutors,

---

[55] See James Stribopoulos, "Unchecked Power: The Constitutional Regulation of Arrest Reconsidered" (2003) 48 McGill L.J. 225 at 262.

[56] See Jennifer Thomas, "Adult Criminal Court Statistics, 2008/2009," *Juristat* vol. 30, no. 2 at 28, Table 3 (Statistics Canada, 2010) (New Brunswick = 16.4 per cent, Quebec = 9.6 per cent, British Columbia = 26.3 per cent, Ontario = 38.4 per cent, Alberta = 31.4 per cent, Nova Scotia = 30.5 per cent, Manitoba = 34.8 per cent, Saskatchewan = 31.1 per cent).

[57] See *R. v. Dowson*, [1983] S.C.J. No. 68, [1983] 2 S.C.R. 144 (S.C.C.); *Kostuch (Informant) v. Alberta (Attorney General)*, [1995] A.J. No. 866, 101 C.C.C. (3d) 321 (Alta. C.A.); *R. v. Osiowy*, [1989] S.J. No. 379, 50 C.C.C. (3d) 189 (Sask. C.A.); *Quebec (Attorney General) v. Chartrand*, [1987] J.Q. no 1411, 40 C.C.C. (3d) 270 (Que. C.A.).

[58] See *e.g.*, Ontario, Ministry of Attorney General, *Crown Policy Manual*, "Charge Screening" (March 21, 2005) at 1 (requiring that charges be screened "as soon as practicable after the charge arrives at the Crown's office and prior to setting a date for preliminary hearing or trial"); British Columbia, Ministry of the Attorney General, Criminal Justice Branch, *Crown Counsel Policy Manual*, "Charge Assessment Guidelines," Policy CHA-1 (October 2, 2009) at 5 (Crown counsel must "make the charge assessment decision in a timely manner, recognizing the need to expedite the decision where an accused is in custody, where a Report to Crown Counsel requests a warrant, or where the charge involves violence").

[59] See Ontario, *Report of the Attorney General's Advisory Committee on Charge Screening, Disclosure, and Resolution Discussions* (Toronto: Queen's Printer, 1993) at 128-29 (acknowledging that in more complicated matters more time will often prove necessary because "the documentation is not short, simple, and entirely completed upon arrest or shortly thereafter").

[60] See *Krieger v. Law Society of Alberta*, [2002] S.C.J. No. 45, [2002] 3 S.C.R. 372 at para. 42 (S.C.C.) ("it is uncommon for a single prosecution to attract the Attorney General's personal attention"); James Stribopoulos, "Unchecked Power: The Constitutional Regulation of Arrest Reconsidered" (2003) 48 McGill L.J. 225 at 258-61; New Brunswick, *Public Prosecution Services Operational Manual*, "Attorney General's Policy — Public Prosecutions" at 1 (2007); Michael Code, "Crown Counsel's Responsibilities When Advising the Police at the Pre-Charge Stage" (1998) 40 Crim. L.Q. 326 at 351-52.

or (in extraordinarily rare circumstances) persons in the Attorney General's ministry, including the Attorney General himself or herself.[61]

§8.17 Whoever makes the decision must do so without considering its political ramifications, even if the decision-maker occupies a political office (like the Attorney General, who as discussed is a member of Cabinet). As the Supreme Court stated in *Krieger v. Law Society of Alberta*,[62] it is a "constitutional principle in this country that the Attorney General must act independently of partisan concerns when supervising prosecutorial decisions."[63] This function, the Court added, is "quasi-judicial" in nature.[64]

---

[61] See James Stribopoulos, "Unchecked Power: The Constitutional Regulation of Arrest Reconsidered" (2003) 48 McGill L.J. 225 at 258-61; Michael Code, "Crown Counsel's Responsibilities When Advising the Police at the Pre-Charge Stage" (1998) 40 Crim. L.Q. 326 at 353-54; Hon. Marc Rosenberg, "The Attorney General and the Administration of Criminal Justice" (2009) 34 Queen's L.J. 813 at 833-34. See also British Columbia, Ministry of the Attorney General, Criminal Justice Branch, *Crown Counsel Policy Manual*, "Charge Assessment Guidelines," Policy CHA-1 (October 2, 2009) at 2 (requiring discussion with senior officials before decision to prosecute for homicide offences and offences raising public concerns for the administration of justice); Alberta, Department of Justice and Attorney General, *Crown Prosecutors' Policy Manual*, "Decision to prosecute" (May 20, 2008) (recommending consultation with senior prosecutors for "significant or unusual cases"); Nova Scotia, Public Prosecution Service, *Crown Policy Manual*, "The Decision to prosecute" (July 1, 2002) at 11 (consultation mandatory for homicides and charges against public figures and persons involved in the administration of justice).

[62] [2002] S.C.J. No. 45, [2002] 3 S.C.R. 372 (S.C.C.) [*Krieger*].

[63] *Ibid.*, at para. 30 (S.C.R.) [*Krieger*]. See also *Miazga v. Kvello Estate*, [2009] S.C.J. No. 51, [2009] 3 S.C.R. 339, 2009 SCC 51 at para. 46 (S.C.C.); *R. v. Regan*, [2002] S.C.J. No. 14, [2002] 1 S.C.R. 297 at paras. 157-58 (S.C.C.), *per* Binnie J., dissenting. See generally, John Ll. J. Edwards, *The Law Officers of the Crown: A Study of the Offices of Attorney-General and Solicitor-General of England, with an Account of the Office of the Director of Public Prosecutions of England* (London: Sweet and Maxwell, 1964); John Ll. J. Edwards, *The Attorney General, Politics and the Public Interest* (London: Sweet and Maxwell, 1984); Royal Commission Inquiry into Civil Rights in the Province of Ontario, Report No. 1 (1968) at 931-34; Ian Scott, "The Role of the Attorney-General and the Charter of Rights" (1986-87) 29 Crim. L.Q. 187 at 189-92; Law Reform Commission of Canada, *Controlling Criminal Prosecutions: the Attorney General and the Crown Prosecutor* (Ottawa: The Commission), Chapter 1.

[64] *Krieger v. Law Society of Alberta*, [2002] S.C.J. No. 45, [2002] 3 S.C.R. 372 at para. 32 (S.C.C.); Hon. Marc Rosenberg, "The Attorney General and the Administration of Criminal Justice" (2009) 34 Queen's L.J. 813 at 819-25. In practice, however, the independence of the Attorney General from executive government is limited by partisan and ideological affiliations as well as the fact that he or she sits at the pleasure of the Prime Minister or Premier and may therefore be dismissed at any time without cause. See Philip Stenning, *Appearing for the Crown* (Cowansville: Brown Legal Publications, 1986) at 295-96; Hon. Marc Rosenberg, "The Attorney General and the Administration of Criminal Justice" (2009) 34 Queen's L.J. 813 at 825; Michael Code, "Crown Counsel's Responsibilities When Advising the Police at the Pre-Charge Stage" (1998) 40 Crim. L.Q. 326 at 351.

(b) Standard for Decision

§8.18 Whenever the review is conducted, and whoever makes it, the standard for decision is broadly similar across jurisdictions. Official policies[65] dictate that charges may go forward only if: (*i*) the evidence meets a certain threshold relating to the probability of conviction; and (*ii*) it is in the public interest to proceed.[66] It should be stressed that both of these criteria must be satisfied for every charge faced by the accused. In other words, the public interest, however compelling, can never justify a prosecution where the odds of conviction are low; conversely, even a certainty of conviction does not warrant proceeding with a prosecution that is not in the public interest.[67] In addition, the obligation to ensure that these criteria are met continues throughout the prosecution up to any appeal; if at any point it becomes evident that one requirement is no longer satisfied, the prosecution should end.[68]

(i) Evidentiary Threshold

§8.19 The first criterion is especially critical. As discussed in Chapter 5, in most criminal cases there will be no substantial judicial scrutiny of the evidence to determine if it warrants a trial. It is imperative, therefore, that prosecutors assess the prospect of conviction objectively and with as much accurate information about the case as possible. As stated in the Ontario Crown Policy Manual:[69]

> All cases, including child abuse, sexual assaults and spouse/partner offences, must be screened in accordance with the "reasonable prospect of conviction" and "public interest" standards. The personal, professional or "political" consequences of a screening decision should never affect Crown counsel's judgment. Nor should stereotypes about certain categories of witnesses such as child witnesses, witnesses with mental disabilities and

---

[65] It should be stressed that the various Crown prosecutors' policy manuals are advisory policy statements and therefore do not give rise to legally enforceable rights. As discussed in Part 5(2), below, a prosecutor's decision to proceed with or discontinue charges is discretionary and subject to judicial review only in exceptional cases. That said, the courts have made reference to the policy manuals in deciding whether prosecutors have exceeded the bounds of their discretion. See *e.g.*, *Miazga v. Kvello Estate*, [2009] S.C.J. No. 51, [2009] 3 S.C.R. 339 at para. 62 (S.C.C.); *R. v. Regan*, [2002] S.C.J. No. 14, [2002] 1 S.C.R. 297 at para. 72 (S.C.C.).

[66] See generally, Ontario, *Report of the Attorney General's Advisory Committee on Charge Screening, Disclosure, and Resolution Discussions* (Toronto: Queen's Printer, 1993) at 52-55.

[67] See Ontario, Ministry of Attorney General, *Crown Policy Manual*, "Charge Screening" (March 21, 2005) at 2; New Brunswick, *Public Prosecution Services Operational Manual*, "Attorney General's Policy — Public Prosecutions" (2007) at 3.

[68] See *e.g.*, Ontario, Ministry of Attorney General, *Crown Policy Manual*, "Charge Screening" (March 21, 2005) at 1; British Columbia, Ministry of the Attorney General, Criminal Justice Branch, *Crown Counsel Policy Manual*, "Charge Assessment Guidelines," Policy CHA-1 (October 2, 2009) at 2; Alberta, Department of Justice and Attorney General, *Crown Prosecutors' Policy Manual*, "Decision to prosecute" (May 20, 2008); Nova Scotia, Public Prosecution Service, *Crown Policy Manual*, "The Decision to Prosecute" (July 1, 2002) at 10.

[69] Ontario, Ministry of Attorney General, *Crown Policy Manual*, "Charge Screening" (March 21, 2005).

complainants of spouse/partner abuse or sexual offences, affect Crown counsel's judgment.[70]

Unfortunately, heavy caseloads, fragmented responsibilities and partisanship may work against the goal of a through, independent prosecutorial screening of cases.[71]

§8.20 What then is the specific evidentiary threshold that must be met to justify prosecuting a particular charge?[72] The various Crown policy manuals give different answers to this question. In effect there are three distinct standards. The threshold in used in most provinces is a "reasonable likelihood" of conviction.[73] This has been defined as requiring "sufficient evidence to believe that a reasonable jury, properly instructed, is more likely than not to convict the accused of the charge(s) alleged."[74] British Columbia uses an even higher standard — "substantial likelihood" of conviction — which has been defined as "a strong, solid case of substance".[75] The standard used in Quebec is similarly stringent: "Le procureur doit ... être moralement convaincu qu'une infraction a été commise, que c'est le prévenu qui l'a commise et être raisonnablement convaincu de pouvoir établir la culpabilité du prévenu."[76] Ontario, Nova Scotia and the Federal Prosecution Service employ the lowest standard: a reasonable or realistic "prospect" of conviction, which means something more than a *prima facie* case but (at least in some cases) less than a "probability" of conviction.[77]

---

[70] *Ibid.*, at 2.

[71] See James Stribopoulos, "Unchecked Power: The Constitutional Regulation of Arrest Reconsidered" (2003) 48 McGill L.J. 225 at 258-62; H. Richard Uviller, "The Neutral Prosecutor: The Obligation of Dispassion in a Passionate Pursuit" (2000) 68 Fordham L. Rev. 1695 at 1713-16.

[72] To be clear, the criteria must be applied separately to each charge faced by the accused. See Alberta, Department of Justice and Attorney General, *Crown Prosecutors' Policy Manual*, "Decision to prosecute" (May 20, 2008).

[73] This is the standard used in Alberta, Saskatchewan, Manitoba, New Brunswick and Newfoundland and Labrador.

[74] Alberta, Department of Justice and Attorney General, *Crown Prosecutors' Policy Manual*, "Decision to prosecute" (May 20, 2008). See also Newfoundland and Labrador, Office of the Director of Public Prosecutions, *Guide Book of Policies and Procedures for the Conduct of Criminal Prosecutions in Newfoundland and Labrador*, "The Decision to Prosecute" (October 2007) at 5-2. Though New Brunswick uses the word "prospect" instead of "likelihood", it defines the standard in the same way: New Brunswick, *Public Prosecution Services Operational Manual*, "Attorney General's Policy — Public Prosecutions" (2007) at 3 ("an impartial trier of fact ... is more likely than not to convict on the offence charged").

[75] Note, however, that a prosecution may proceed on the lower threshold of a "reasonable prospect" of conviction in "exceptional circumstances" such as "cases of high risk violent or dangerous offenders or where public safety concerns are of paramount consideration." British Columbia, Ministry of the Attorney General, Criminal Justice Branch, *Crown Counsel Policy Manual*, "Charge Assessment Guidelines," Policy CHA-1 (October 2, 2009) at 1-3.

[76] Quebec, Directeur des poursuites criminelles et pénales, "Accusation — Poursuite des Procédures" (March 31, 2009) § 6.

[77] See Ontario, Ministry of Attorney General, *Crown Policy Manual*, "Charge Screening" (March 21, 2005) at 1-2; Nova Scotia, Public Prosecution Service, *Crown Policy Manual*, "The Decision to Prosecute" (July 1, 2002) at 2-4; Canada, Department of Justice, *The Federal Prosecution Service Deskbook*, "The Decision to Prosecute" § 15.3.1 (October 2005). The *prima facie*

§8.21 Whichever standard is used, prosecutors must consider a variety of factors in deciding whether the threshold is met, including the admissibility of the evidence, the weight likely to be given to admissible evidence and the strength of any anticipated defences.[78] The Alberta manual[79] gives some helpful direction on some of the questions that should be asked:

    a. Are there inherent (*e.g.*, as with in-custody informants) or other concerns respecting the accuracy, credibility or reliability of any of the Crown's witness?

        i. Do any of these witnesses have improper motives that may affect his or her credibility?

        ii. Is there evidence that may support or detract from the credibility of any of these witnesses?

    b. If the identity of the offender is in issue, of what strength is the evidence identifying the accused as the offender?

    c. Are there grounds for believing that some inculpatory evidence will likely be excluded?

    d. If the case depends in part on an admission by the accused, is there evidence that might support or detract from the reliability of this statement?

    e. Has the accused attempted to explain his (alleged) conduct or present a defence? If so, is it clear that the explanation or defence (by itself or in the context of other evidence or information) will be sufficient to raise a reasonable doubt?[80]

(ii) Public Interest

§8.22 As mentioned, even if the relevant evidentiary threshold is met, the prosecutor must determine whether it is in the public interest to proceed. Though it is often said that criminal sanctions should be reserved for serious wrongdoing,[81] the reality is that the *Criminal Code* and other criminal statutes capture a great deal of conduct that is not especially serious or deserving of criminal punishment.[82] Given the harsh penal and social consequences that often result from

---

case standard is similar to that used in deciding whether to commit the accused to stand trial at a preliminary inquiry. See Chapter 9, Part 3(6)(*a*).

[78] See British Columbia, Ministry of the Attorney General, Criminal Justice Branch, *Crown Counsel Policy Manual*, "Charge Assessment Guidelines," Policy CHA-1 (October 2, 2009) at 3.

[79] Alberta, Department of Justice and Attorney General, *Crown Prosecutors' Policy Manual*, "Decision to prosecute" (May 20, 2008).

[80] *Ibid.* See also Nova Scotia, Public Prosecution Service, *Crown Policy Manual*, "The Decision to Prosecute" (July 1, 2002) at 4-6; Newfoundland and Labrador, Office of the Director of Public Prosecutions, *Guide Book of Policies and Procedures for the Conduct of Criminal Prosecutions in Newfoundland and Labrador*, "The Decision to Prosecute" (October 2007) at 5-2 to 5-6.

[81] See *e.g.*, Law Reform Commission of Canada, *Our Criminal Law* (Ottawa: Information Canada, 1976) at 28.

[82] See Law Reform Commission of Canada, *Our Criminal Law* (Ottawa: Information Canada, 1976) at 33-35. Efforts to use the *Charter* to invalidate offences claimed to cause insubstantial harm have been unsuccessful. See *e.g.*, *R. v. Malmo-Levine; R. v. Caine*, [2003] S.C.J. No. 79,

being found guilty of a criminal offence, it is therefore entirely appropriate for the Crown to choose not to prosecute in some cases even when the accused is probably guilty. As Hartley (later Lord) Shawcross stated to the House of Commons of the United Kingdom:

> It has never been the rule in this country — I hope it never will be — that suspected criminal offences must automatically be the subject of prosecution. Indeed, the very first regulations under which the Director of Public Prosecutions worked provided that he should ... prosecute, amongst other cases: "wherever it appears that the offence or the circumstances of its commission is or are of such a character that a prosecution in respect thereof is required in the public interest." That is still the dominant consideration.[83]

This principle applies equally in Canada.[84]

§8.23 Many factors may be relevant in deciding whether prosecution is in the public interest. But decisions to discontinuing proceedings are typically driven by one or more of the following considerations:

- a conviction is likely to result in an insignificant penalty;

- there are alternatives to prosecution available (including various "diversion", "alternative measures", and "restorative justice" programs) that are likely to achieve the desired result;

- the offence was committed as a result of a genuine mistake or misunderstanding;

- any harm caused was minor;

- the offence is trivial or technical;

- the law is obsolete or obscure;

- the accused has remedied the loss or harm;

- the accused has demonstrated remorse and has taken steps toward rehabilitation;

- a prosecution could harm confidential informants, ongoing investigations, international relations, or national security.[85]

§8.24 Additional considerations include the personal circumstances of the accused, complainant and witnesses, the expected length and expense of the

---

[2003] 3 S.C.R. 571 (S.C.C.); *Rodriguez v. British Columbia (Attorney General)*, [1993] S.C.J. No. 94, [1993] 3 S.C.R. 519 (S.C.C.); *Reference re ss. 193 and 195.1(1)(c) of the Criminal Code (Can.)*, [1990] S.C.J. No. 52, [1990] 1 S.C.R. 1123 (S.C.C.).

[83] U.K., H.C. Debates, vol. 483, col. 681 (January 29, 1951).

[84] See John Ll. J. Edwards, *The Attorney General, Politics and the Public Interest* (London: Sweet and Maxwell, 1984) at 360; See Ontario, Legislative Assembly, *Official Report of Debates (Hansard)*, No. 3 (February 23, 1978) at 50-52 (statement of Attorney General McMurtry).

[85] See Alberta, Department of Justice and Attorney General, *Crown Prosecutors' Policy Manual*, "Decision to prosecute" (May 20, 2008); British Columbia, Ministry of the Attorney General, Criminal Justice Branch, *Crown Counsel Policy Manual*, "Charge Assessment Guidelines," Policy CHA-1 (October 2, 2009) at 5; New Brunswick, *Public Prosecution Services Operational Manual*, "Attorney General's Policy — Public Prosecutions" (2007) at 3-5.

prosecution, the time elapsed since the alleged commission of the offence and whether due to the passage of time the offence may only be tried on indictment, the willingness and ability of the complainant and witnesses to testify, the accused's past and future cooperation in the investigation and prosecution of others, the availability on prosecution of any compensation, restitution or forfeiture, and the need to maintain public confidence in the administration of justice.[86] Presumably, another factor that may be considered is the accused's decision, as a consequence of plea negotiations, to plead guilty to a lesser or different offence. The prosecutor's role in plea bargaining is discussed below in Part 4(2).

(c) *Withdrawals and Stays*

§8.25 If a decision is made not to proceed with a charge that has been laid (including one laid by a private citizen), the prosecutor has two options. First, he or she may withdraw the charge.[87] A withdrawal terminates the prosecution of that charge. Though there is no *Criminal Code* provision authorizing this process, it is a necessary corollary of the Crown's responsibility to decide whether to proceed with charges.[88] As discussed in Part 5(2), below, the decision to withdraw is a matter of core prosecutorial discretion and is reviewable in only very limited circumstances.[89] A charge may be withdrawn any time after process is issued.[90] Leave of the court may be required, however, if the withdrawal is sought after a

---

[86] See Alberta, Department of Justice and Attorney General, *Crown Prosecutors' Policy Manual*, "Decision to prosecute" (May 20, 2008); British Columbia, Ministry of the Attorney General, Criminal Justice Branch, *Crown Counsel Policy Manual*, "Charge Assessment Guidelines," Policy CHA-1 (October 2, 2009) at 5; Nova Scotia, Public Prosecution Service, *Crown Policy Manual*, "The Decision to Prosecute" (July 1, 2002) at 7-9; Newfoundland and Labrador, Office of the Director of Public Prosecutions, *Guide Book of Policies and Procedures for the Conduct of Criminal Prosecutions in Newfoundland and Labrador*, "The Decision to Prosecute" (October 2007) at 5-7 to 5-10; Quebec, Directeur des poursuites criminelles et pénales, "Accusation — Poursuite des Procédures" (March 31, 2009) § 9; Canada, Department of Justice, *The Federal Prosecution Service Deskbook*, "The Decision to Prosecute" § 15.3.2 (October 2005).

[87] See e.g., *R. v. Karpinski*, [1957] S.C.J. No. 18, [1957] S.C.R. 343 (S.C.C.); *R. v. Garcia*, [1969] O.J. No. 1544, [1970] 3 C.C.C. 124 (Ont. C.A.); *R. v. Osborne*, [1975] N.B.J. No. 84 at para. 17, 25 C.C.C. (2d) 405 (N.B.C.A.). See also *McHale v. Ontario (Attorney General)*, [2010] O.J. No. 2030, 2010 ONCA 361 at paras. 32-33, 57 (Ont. C.A.), leave to appeal refused [2010] S.C.C.A. No. 290 (S.C.C.) (power of Crown prosecutor to withdraw extends to private prosecutions).

[88] See *R. v. Dick*, [1968] O.J. No. 1160, 4 C.R.N.S. 102 at para. 14 (Ont. C.J.) ("Once it is premised that the Attorney-General is under a duty to decide whether or not to prosecute in any given case and, if it is decided to prosecute, to carry out that task, it must follow as a corollary thereof that, in the absence of special circumstances, he not only has the right, but is under a duty to withdraw a charge where, in his opinion, the decision to prosecute has, in the light of later factors, turned out to be ill-conceived."); *McHale v. Ontario (Attorney General)*, [2010] O.J. No. 2030, 2010 ONCA 361 at para. 53 (Ont. C.A.) ("The authority, which is beyond argument, originates in the common law and is preserved by s. 8(2) of the *Criminal Code*.").

[89] See *R. v. Garcia*, [1969] O.J. No. 1544, [1970] 3 C.C.C. 124 at 126 (Ont. C.A.); *McHale v. Ontario (Attorney General)*, [2010] O.J. No. 2030, 2010 ONCA 361 at para. 36 (Ont. C.A.).

[90] *McHale v. Ontario (Attorney General)*, [2010] O.J. No. 2030, 2010 ONCA 361 at paras. 70-77 (Ont. C.A.).

plea has been entered or evidence taken.[91] At this stage the judge may bar the withdrawal on the grounds that it would unfairly prejudice the accused. This could occur, for example, where after calling evidence the prosecutor wished to end the proceedings to re-lay the same or another charge.[92] Absent such prejudice, leave to withdraw would normally be granted.[93] In such a case the prosecution would generally be free to lay a new information.

§8.26 The prosecutor's second option is to enter a stay of proceedings under either section 579 or section 579.1 of the *Criminal Code*.[94] The former applies to provincial prosecutors; the latter to federal prosecutors. These provisions empower the prosecutor to direct a stay to be entered, thereby ending the proceedings,[95] at any time after the laying of the information[96] and before judgment.[97] The decision to enter a stay is administrative, not judicial, and does not therefore require the court's leave or approval.[98] As discussed in Part 5(2), below, this decision lies at the core of prosecutorial discretion and is subject to judicial review only in exceptional circumstances.[99]

---

[91]　See *R. v. Blasko*, [1975] O.J. No. 1239, 29 C.C.C. (2d) 321 at 322 (Ont. H.C.J.); *R. v. Osborne*, [1975] N.B.J. No. 84 at para. 30, 25 C.C.C. (2d) 405 (N.B.C.A.); *R. v. Forrester*, [1976] A.J. No. 575, 37 C.R.N.S. 320 (Alta. S.C.T.D.); *McHale v. Ontario (Attorney General)*, [2010] O.J. No. 2030, 2010 ONCA 361 at para. 32 (Ont. C.A.). The Court in *Blasko* suggested that leave would also be required for withdrawals sought after the indictment has been preferred. But as Professor Salhany has argued, the abolition of grand juries, the prosecutor "should be entitled to withdraw an indictment as of right at any time before the accused is arraigned and his plea taken." Roger E. Salhany, *Canadian Criminal Procedure*, looseleaf (Aurora, ON: Canada Law Book, 1994) § 6.2480.

[92]　See Tim Quigley, *Procedure in Canadian Criminal Law*, looseleaf (Toronto: Carswell, 2005) at para. 16.4(b). If a charge were withdrawn after evidence was called, any attempt to re-lay the charge might be prohibited by the special plea of *autrefois acquit*. See generally, *R. v. Selhi*, [1990] S.C.J. No. 18, [1990] 1 S.C.R. 277 (S.C.C.); *R. v. C. (S.S.)*, [2001] A.J. No. 1427, 2001 ABQB 959 (Alta. Q.B.). *Autrefois acquit* and other aspects of "double jeopardy" are discussed in Chapter 14. Alternatively, an attempt to re-lay a withdrawn charge may constitute an abuse of process leading to a judicial stay of proceedings. See Tim Quigley, *Procedure in Canadian Criminal Law*, looseleaf (Toronto: Carswell, 2005) at para. 16(4)(b). Abuse of process and judicial stays are discussed in Chapter 10.

[93]　*Ibid.*

[94]　The same power is given to prosecutors in summary conviction matters by virtue of s. 795 of the *Code*.

[95]　See *R. v. Smith*, [1992] B.C.J. No. 2730, 79 C.C.C. (3d) 70 (B.C.C.A.), leave to appeal refused [1993] S.C.C.A. No. 7 (S.C.C.).

[96]　See *R. v. Pardo*, [1990] J.Q. no. 2202, 62 C.C.C. (3d) 371 at para. 13 (Que. C.A.) (proceedings may be stayed under s. 579(1) of the *Criminal Code* after an information is laid, even if process has not yet issued); *McHale v. Ontario (Attorney General)*, [2010] O.J. No. 2030, 2010 ONCA 361 at paras. 85-86 (Ont. C.A.) (same).

[97]　See *R. v. Beaudry*, [1966] B.C.J. No. 72, [1967] 1 C.C.C. 272 (B.C.C.A.) (stay permitted after judge issued directed verdict of "not guilty" but before jury rendered verdict).

[98]　See *R. v. Smith*, [1992] B.C.J. No. 2730, 79 C.C.C. (3d) 70 (B.C.C.A.), leave to appeal refused [1993] S.C.C.A. No. 7 (S.C.C.); *R. v. Beaudry*, [1966] B.C.J. No. 72, [1967] 1 C.C.C. 272 at 275 (B.C.C.A.).

[99]　See *e.g.*, *R. v. N. (D.)*, [2004] N.J. No. 271, 188 C.C.C. (3d) 89 (Nfld. C.A.) (no basis to review Crown decision to issue stay where no reasonable prospect of conviction); *R. v. Larosa*, [2002] O.J. No. 3219, 166 C.C.C. (3d) 449 (Ont. C.A.) (no basis to review Crown decision to stay charges to enable extradition)

§8.27 Like a stay issued by the court (discussed in Chapter 10), a prosecutorial stay ends the proceedings and vacates any orders relating to pre-trial detention or release.[100] However, unlike a judicial stay or a withdrawal of charges by the prosecutor, after a prosecutorial stay has been entered, proceedings may be re-commenced under the same information or indictment within one year (or in the case of summary conviction proceedings, before the expiry of the six-month limitation period).[101] The prosecutor may revive the proceedings simply by giving notice to the clerk of the court where the stay was entered.[102] In the vast majority of cases, this does not occur. There is no legal impediment to recommencement, however, as long the time period is respected and there is no abuse of process.[103] Further, as with charges that are withdrawn, absent an abuse of process there is no bar to laying a new information either before[104] or after[105] the expiry of the recommencement period.

(2) Prosecutorial Discretion in Proceeding with Charges and Plea Bargaining

§8.28 Once prosecutors decide to approve of or proceed with certain charges, they may then have to decide precisely how those charges should be prosecuted.[106] Depending on the classification of the offences charged, the prosecutor may choose to proceed by way of summary conviction or indictment; include charges on an indictment for which the accused was not committed to stand trial at the preliminary inquiry; and prefer a direct indictment. The mechanics of these decisions, which are dictated by the *Criminal Code*, are explored in other Chapters in this book.[107] We simply note here that, subject to the limits discussed in Part 5(2), below, a prosecutor's decision on these matters is not reviewable.

§8.29 One important aspect of the prosecutor's charging discretion is not mentioned in the *Code*, however: plea-bargaining. Simply stated, a plea-bargain is an agreement between the accused and the Crown that the former will plead guilty to an offence in exchange for a benefit such as the withdrawal of a more serious

---

[100] See *R. v. Jones*, [1997] O.J. No. 613, 113 C.C.C. (3d) 225 (Ont. C.A.).
[101] *Criminal Code*, ss. 579(2), 579.1(2).
[102] *Ibid.*
[103] See *e.g.*, *R. v. Scott*, [1990] S.C.J. No. 132, [1990] 3 S.C.R. 979 (S.C.C.) (no abuse of process where prosecutor entered stay to prevent disclosure of informer and recommenced before different judge). Abuse of process is discussed in Chapter 10.
[104] See *e.g.*, *R. v. McArthur*, [1995] S.J. No. 503, 102 C.C.C. (3d) 84 (Sask. C.A.); *R. v. Boutilier*, [1995] N.S.J. No. 540, 45 C.R. (4th) 345 (N.S.C.A.).
[105] See *e.g.*, *R. v. Allen*, [2002] N.J. No. 11, 208 Nfld. & P.E.I.R. 250 (Nfld. C.A.), revd [2003] S.C.J. No. 16 (S.C.C.).
[106] See generally, *Krieger v. Law Society of Alberta*, [2002] S.C.J. No. 45, [2002] 3 S.C.R. 372 at para. 47 (S.C.C.) ("what is common to the various elements of prosecutorial discretion is that they involve the ultimate decisions as to <u>whether</u> a prosecution should be brought, continued or ceased, and <u>what</u> the prosecution ought to be for") [emphasis in original].
[107] See Chapter 1, Part 2(3)(*c*) and Chapter 9, Part 4.

charge or a sentence recommendation.[108] As noted in the Federal Prosecution Service Deskbook,[109] prosecutors may not engage in plea discussions over a charge that does not meet the threshold for prosecution discussed in Part 4(1)(*b*), above.[110] As a consequence, prosecutors may not proceed with such charges (or threaten to do so) in an effort to induce an accused to plead guilty to a lesser charge.[111] Absent exceptional circumstances, it is also improper for prosecutors to renege on plea agreements.[112] That said, the decision to repudiate an agreement, like the decision to enter into one, is a matter of core prosecutorial

---

[108] Though sentencing judges are not obliged to accept sentence recommendations by counsel, whether or not arising from plea bargains, absent "an adequate evidential foundation", it is an error for a court to impose a sentence greater than that recommended by the Crown: *R. v. F. (J.K.)*, [2005] O.J. No. 812, 195 O.A.C. 141 at para. 3 (Ont. C.A.), additional reasons at [2005] O.J. No. 2212 (Ont. C.A.). See also *R. v. Verdi-Douglas*, [2002] J.Q. no 418, 162 C.C.C. (3d) 37 at paras. 42-43 (Que. C.A.); *R. v. Closs*, [1998] O.J. No. 172, 105 O.A.C. 392 at para. 11 (Ont. C.A.); *R. v. Druken*, [2006] N.J. No. 326, 215 C.C.C. (3d) 394 at para. 17 (Nfld. C.A.).

[109] Canada, Department of Justice, *The Federal Prosecution Service Deskbook*, "The Decision to Prosecute" October 2005).

[110] *Ibid.*, at § 20.2. See also Alberta, Department of Justice and Attorney General, *Crown Prosecutors' Policy Manual*, "Disposition agreements between Crown and defence" (May 20, 2008) ("The decision to proceed with charges as laid or accept pleas to reduced charges is governed by the criteria respecting the sufficiency of the evidence and the public interest...".); British Columbia, Ministry of the Attorney General, Criminal Justice Branch, *Crown Counsel Policy Manual*, "Resolution Discussions and Stays of Proceedings," Policy RES 1 (October 2, 2009) at 1.

[111] See Canada, Department of Justice, *The Federal Prosecution Service Deskbook*, "The Decision to Prosecute" (October 2005) at § 20.3.1 ("The following practices are not acceptable: instructing or proceeding with unnecessary additional charges to secure a negotiated plea; agreeing to a plea of guilty to an offence not disclosed by the evidence ....").

[112] See *R. v. Nixon*, [2011] S.C.J. No. 34, 2011 SCC 34 at paras. 48-49, 63 (S.C.C.) ("Situations in which the Crown can properly repudiate a resolution agreement are, and must remain, very rare"); *R. v. Obadia*, [1998] J.Q. no 2484, 20 C.R. (5th) 162 at para. 35 (Que. C.A.) ("La vitalité et la légitimité d'un système de 'plea-bargaining' reposent sur la prémisse que les parties jouent 'franc-jeu', c'est-à-dire qu'elles respectent leur engagement: c'est une question d'intérêt public."). See also British Columbia, Ministry of the Attorney General, Criminal Justice Branch, *Crown Counsel Policy Manual*, "Resolution Discussions and Stays of Proceedings," Policy RES 1 (October 2, 2009) at 3 ("Repudiation should be considered only where Regional Crown Counsel and the Assistant Deputy Attorney General are satisfied that the resolution agreement would bring the administration of justice into disrepute. If that test is met, the decision on whether to repudiate should take into account the extent to which the accused could be restored to their original position and whether repudiation would likely bring the administration of justice into disrepute."); Canada, Department of Justice, *The Federal Prosecution Service Deskbook*, "The Decision to Prosecute" § 20.3.8.2 (October 2005) ("All negotiated plea or sentence agreements should be honoured by the Crown unless fulfilling the agreement would clearly be contrary to the public interest."); Ontario, Ministry of Attorney General, *Crown Policy Manual*, "Resolution Discussions" (March 21, 2005) at 2 ("Unless there are exceptional circumstances, Crown counsel must honour all agreements reached during resolution discussions."); Nova Scotia, Public Prosecution Service, *Crown Attorney Manual: Prosecution and Administrative Policies for the PPS*, "Resolution Discussions and Agreements" (November 30, 2007) ("Repudiation of a resolution agreement can occur only if (1) the agreement would bring the administration of justice into disrepute, and (2) the accused can be restored to his or her original position.").

discretion that may be overturned by a court only if it constitutes an abuse of process.[113]

5. REVIEW OF PROSECUTORIAL DISCRETION

(1) General Principles

§8.30 Until quite recently, Crown prosecutors were virtually immune from external oversight and regulation.[114] It is now clear, however, that decisions made by prosecutors may be reviewed both by the courts and law societies. As detailed below, there are three main forms of oversight: judicial review in criminal proceedings, professional regulation, and civil liability for malicious prosecution.

§8.31 The overarching principle governing each type of review, however, is the same. In *Krieger*,[115] the Supreme Court of Canada distinguished between two types of discretion exercised by the Crown in criminal cases: "prosecutorial discretion", which is owed great deference, and the ordinary discretion exercised by counsel in matters of "tactics or conduct before the court", which is not.[116] The Court explained:

> "Prosecutorial discretion" is a term of art. It does not simply refer to any discretionary decision made by a Crown prosecutor. Prosecutorial discretion refers to the use of those powers that constitute the core of the Attorney General's office and which are protected from the influence of improper political and other vitiating factors by the principle of independence.
>
> ...
>
> ...[T]hese powers emanate from the office holder's role as legal advisor of and officer to the Crown. In our theory of government, it is the sovereign who holds the power to prosecute his or her subjects. A decision of the Attorney General, or of his or her agents, within the authority delegated to him or her by the sovereign is not subject to interference by other arms of government. An exercise of prosecutorial discretion will, therefore, be treated

---

[113] *R. v. Nixon*, [2011] S.C.J. No. 34, 2011 SCC 34 at paras. 30-31 (S.C.C.) (in absence of evidence that repudiation prejudiced accused's right to fair trial, good faith determination by senior prosecutor that agreement was contrary to public interest not abuse of process).

[114] See *e.g.*, *R. v. Smythe*, [1971] S.C.J. No. 62, [1971] S.C.R. 680 (S.C.C.). See also Kent Roach, "The Attorney General and the *Charter* Revisited" (2000) 50 U.T.L.J. 1 at 4-5.

[115] *Krieger v. Law Society of Alberta*, [2002] S.C.J. No. 45, [2002] 3 S.C.R. 372 (S.C.C.) [*Krieger*].

[116] *Ibid.*, at paras. 43-47 (S.C.R.). Though the Court in *Krieger* was dealing with an allegation of prosecutorial misconduct sanctioned by the Law Society, this principle applies equally to the scope of judicial review in criminal or civil proceedings. See *Miazga v. Kvello Estate*, [2009] S.C.J. No. 51, [2009] 3 S.C.R. 339 at paras. 6-7 (S.C.C.); *R. v. Nixon*, [2011] S.C.J. No. 34, 2011 SCC 34 at paras. 18, 21 (S.C.C.). See also Hon. Marc Rosenberg, "The Attorney General and the Administration of Criminal Justice" (2009) 34 Queen's L.J. 813 at 840.

with deference by the courts and by other members of the executive, as well as statutory bodies like provincial law societies.[117]

§8.32 What kinds of decisions, then, fall under the aegis of "prosecutorial discretion"? While the Court in *Krieger* did not set out an exhaustive list, it held that the "core elements" of this discretion "involve the ultimate decisions as to <u>whether</u> a prosecution should be brought, continued or ceased, and <u>what</u> the prosecution ought to be for."[118] The specific implications of the distinction between a prosecutor's core and non-core discretion are discussed below.

(2) Judicial Review in Criminal Proceedings

§8.33 Historically, the courts took the position that the exercise of prosecutorial discretion was not subject to judicial review, even if the Crown acted abusively or in a manner likely to induce a miscarriage of justice.[119] As mentioned, this is no longer true. The scope of review, however, differs markedly depending on whether or not the conduct challenged falls within the "core" of prosecutorial discretion (as explained in Part 5(1), above).

§8.34 If challenged conduct is a matter of core discretion, the court may intervene in criminal proceedings only in exceptional cases,[120] for example, where there has been a "flagrant impropriety"[121]; the prosecutor acted "dishonestly," in "bad faith," for an "improper purpose"[122] or with a lack of "objectivity"[123]; or the misconduct amounted to an "abuse of process."[124] No deference is owed to the exercise of prosecutorial discretion in such cases because, by definition, the conduct "will be beyond the scope of [the Attorney General's] office as protected by constitutional principle, and the justification for such deference will

---

[117] *Krieger v. Law Society of Alberta*, [2002] S.C.J. No. 45, [2002] 3 S.C.R. 372 at paras. 43, 45 (S.C.C.).

[118] *Ibid.*, at para. 47 (S.C.R.) [emphasis in original].

[119] See *e.g.*, *R. v. Smythe*, [1971] O.J. No. 1520, 3 C.C.C. (2d) 97 at 107 (Ont. C.A.), affd [1971] S.C.J. No. 62 (S.C.C.), citing *R., on the Prosecution of Gregory v. Allen* (1862), 1 B. & S. 850 at 855 (K.B.); *R. v. Rourke*, [1978] S.C.J. No. 99, [1978] 1 S.C.R. 1021 at 1043 (S.C.C.).

[120] See *Krieger v. Law Society of Alberta*, [2002] S.C.J. No. 45, [2002] 3 S.C.R. 372 at para. 32 (S.C.C.). See also *R. v. D.P.P.; Ex parte Kebilene*, [2000] 2 A.C. 326, [1999] 4 All E. R. 801 at 835 (H.L.).

[121] *Campbell v. Ontario (Attorney General)*, [1987] O.J. No. 338, 35 C.C.C. (3d) 480 (Ont. C.A.). See also *R. v. Power*, [1994] S.C.J. No. 29, [1994] 1 S.C.R. 601 at 624; *Chartrand v. Quebec (Minister of Justice)*, [1987] J.Q. no 1411, 59 C.R. (3d) 388 (Que. C.A.).

[122] *Krieger v. Law Society of Alberta*, [2002] S.C.J. No. 45, [2002] 3 S.C.R. 372 at paras. 51-52 (S.C.C.).

[123] See *R. v. Nixon*, [2011] S.C.J. No. 34, 2011 SCC 34 at para. 68 (S.C.C.); *Krieger v. Law Society of Alberta*, [2002] S.C.J. No. 45, [2002] 3 S.C.R. 372 at para. 48 (S.C.C.) [*Krieger*], citing *R. v. Regan*, [2002] S.C.J. No. 14, [2002] 1 S.C.R. 297 at para. 168 (S.C.C.), *per* Binnie J., dissenting.

[124] See *R. v. Nixon*, [2011] S.C.J. No. 34, 2011 SCC 34 at para. 45 (S.C.C.); *R. v. T. (V.)*, [1992] S.C.J. No. 29, [1992] 1 S.C.R. 749 at 762 (S.C.C.); *Miazga v. Kvello Estate*, [2009] S.C.J. No. 51, [2009] 3 S.C.R. 339 at para. 6 (S.C.C.); *Krieger v. Law Society of Alberta*, [2002] S.C.J. No. 45, [2002] 3 S.C.R. 372 at para. 32 (S.C.C.); *R. v. Power*, [1994] S.C.J. No. 29, [1994] 1 S.C.R. 601 at 615-16 (S.C.C.). The abuse of process doctrine is discussed more extensively in Chapter 10, Part 5(1)(*a*)(iii).

have evaporated."[125] Courts may intervene in matters outside of the prosecutor's core discretion, in contrast, even if there is no evidence of *mala fides*.[126]

§8.35 In *Krieger*, the Court stated that a prosecutor's core discretion includes the decisions to: (*i*) prosecute a charge laid by police; (*ii*) enter a stay of proceedings in private and public prosecutions; (*iii*) accept a guilty plea to a lesser charge; (*iv*) withdraw from criminal proceedings altogether; and (*v*) take control of a private prosecution.[127] As mentioned in Part 4(2), above, the Court concluded in *Nixon* that it also includes the decisions to enter into and repudiate plea agreements.[128] And in keeping with the principle that the core of prosecutorial discretion relates to decisions about whether the accused should be prosecuted for a certain offence, the discretion also likely encompasses the decisions to prefer a direct indictment[129] or prosecute a hybrid offence by way of indictment or summary conviction proceedings.[130]

---

[125] *Krieger v. Law Society of Alberta*, [2002] S.C.J. No. 45, [2002] 3 S.C.R. 372 at para. 49 (S.C.C.). See also *R. v. Power*, [1994] S.C.J. No. 29, [1994] 1 S.C.R. 601 at 621-23 (S.C.C.), *per* L'Heureux-Dubé J.; *Nelles v. Ontario*, [1989] S.C.J. No. 86, [1989] 2 S.C.R. 170 at 211 (S.C.C.), *per* McIntyre J. ("public officers are entitled to no special immunities or privileges when they act beyond the powers which are accorded to them by law in their official capacities"); *Miazga v. Kvello Estate*, [2009] S.C.J. No. 51, [2009] 3 S.C.R. 339 at para. 49 (S.C.C.).

[126] Though the Law Society's review of the prosecutor's conduct in *Krieger* was limited to allegations of dishonesty or bad faith, this limitation stemmed from the scope of the applicable rule of professional conduct. See *Krieger v. Law Society of Alberta*, [2002] S.C.J. No. 45, [2002] 3 S.C.R. 372 at para. 38 (S.C.C.). Because a prosecutor's disclosure obligation is a legal (indeed a constitutional) rule, violations may be sanctioned without a showing of bad faith. See Hon. Marc Rosenberg, "The Attorney General and the Administration of Criminal Justice" (2009), 34 Queen's L.J. 813 at 841.

[127] *Krieger v. Law Society of Alberta*, [2002] S.C.J. No. 45, [2002] 3 S.C.R. 372 at para. 46 (S.C.C.). See also *R. v. T. (V.)*, [1992] S.C.J. No. 29, [1992] 1 S.C.R. 749 at 764 (S.C.C.) (absent abuse of process or specific statutory direction, courts have no power to dismiss charges technically constituting offences on basis that they should not have been brought); *R. v. Phillion*, [2010] O.J. No. 2602, 256 C.C.C. (3d) 63 (Ont. S.C.J.) (requiring Crown to proceed with new trial instead of withdrawing charges in wrongful conviction case would infringe upon core discretion). See also *R. v. Catagas*, [1977] M.J. No. 73, 2 C.R. (3d) 328 (Man. C.A.) (no abuse of process to prosecute Aboriginal despite Crown policy exempting Aboriginals from prosecution for wildlife offence; Crown had no power to exempt group from application of law).

[128] *R. v. Nixon*, [2011] S.C.J. No. 34, 2011 SCC 34 (S.C.C.). See also *R. v. D. (E.)*, [1990] O.J. No. 958, 57 C.C.C. (3d) 151 at 163-64 (Ont. C.A.) (citing cases).

[129] See *R. v. L. (S.J.)*, [2009] S.C.J. No. 14, [2009] 1 S.C.R. 426 at para. 24 (S.C.C.) ("Whether a direct indictment should be preferred is at the Attorney General's discretion, and the courts will intervene in such a case only if there is an abuse of process."). See also *R. v. Stucky*, [2005] O.J. No. 5120 at paras. 44-45 (Ont. S.C.J.); *R. v. Ahmad*, [2008] O.J. No. 5919, 256 C.C.C. (3d) 552, 59 C.R. (6th) 308 at para. 42 (Ont. S.C.J.). Direct indictments are discussed in Chapter 9, Part 4(3).

[130] See *R. v. Lonegren*, [2009] B.C.J. No. 2434, 250 C.C.C. (3d) 377 at para. 197 (B.C.S.C.); *R. v. Nystrom*, [2005] C.M.A.J. No. 8, 2005 CMAC 7 at para. 77 (C.M.A.C.). See also *R. v. Laws*, [1998] O.J. No. 3623, 41 O.R. (3d) 499, 128 C.C.C. (3d) 516 (Ont. C.A.); *R. v. Smythe*, [1971] S.C.J. No. 62, [1971] S.C.R. 680 (S.C.C.); *R. v. Dudley*, [2009] S.C.J. No. 58, [2009] 3 S.C.R. 570, 2009 SCC 58 at paras. 65-66 (S.C.C.), *per* Charron J.; *R. v. De Zen*, [2010] O.J. No. 601, 251 C.C.C. (3d) 547 (Ont. S.C.J.) (power under s. 568 of the *Criminal Code* to override accused's election and require trial by judge and jury not part of core prosecutorial discretion). Section 568 of the *Code* is discussed more extensively in Chapter 9, Part 2(2)(*a*)(iv).

§8.36 Decisions less directly related to the initial bringing or discontinuing of charges, however, may not be protected by prosecutorial discretion. In *R. v. Keyowski*,[131] the Supreme Court ruled that a stay of proceedings may be awarded to prevent an accused from being re-tried after a mistrial or order for a new trial on appeal without a showing of Crown misconduct.[132] There is conflicting jurisprudence, moreover, on whether the decision to seek an enhanced punishment[133] is protected by prosecutorial discretion.

§8.37 There is little doubt, in contrast, that decisions entirely unrelated to charging are owed no special deference.[134] In *Krieger*, for example, the Court found that the prosecutor's decision to delay disclosure of relevant evidence to the defence was not protected by prosecutorial discretion because disclosure was an ethical and legal duty.[135] The courts have also been prepared to scrutinize discretionary decisions occurring in the context of various pre-trial proceedings, including bail hearings[136] and jury selection.[137] Similarly, courts have often sanctioned prosecutors (and awarded various remedies to the accused) for

---

131 [1988] S.C.J. No. 28, [1988] 1 S.C.R. 657 (S.C.C.).

132 See *R. v. Keyowski*, [1988] S.C.J. No. 28, [1988] 1 S.C.R. 657 (S.C.C.) (decision to try accused for third time not an abuse of process in the circumstances, although Court suggested that a fourth trial probably would).

133 See *R. v. Gill*, [2008] O.J. No. 4104, 238 C.C.C. (3d) 465 (Ont. C.J.), affd [2011] O.J. No. 2411 (Ont. S.C.J.) (Crown's election under s. 727(1) of the *Criminal Code* to seek greater punishment where previously convicted of same of offence part of core prosecutorial discretion); *R. v. Haneveld*, [2008] A.J. No. 1487, 100 Alta. L.R. (4th) 257 (Alta. Prov. Ct.), affd [2009] A.J. No. 715 (Alta. C.A.) (election under s. 727(1) of the *Criminal Code* not part of core discretion).

134 *Krieger v. Law Society of Alberta*, [2002] S.C.J. No. 45, [2002] 3 S.C.R. 372 at para. 47 (S.C.C.). It should be noted, however, that in *R. v. Cook*, [1997] S.C.J. No. 22, [1997] 1 S.C.R. 1113 at para. 65 (S.C.C.), the Court held that prosecutors also have a "complete discretion in deciding which witnesses it will call as part of its case." See also *R. v. Yebes*, [1987] S.C.J. No. 51, [1987] 2 S.C.R. 168 (S.C.C.); *R. v. Jolivet*, [2000] S.C.J. No. 28, [2000] 1 S.C.R. 751 (S.C.C.). The extent to which this principle has survived the Court's decision in *Krieger* is open to question. See *R. v. Felderhof*, [2003] O.J. No. 4819, 180 C.C.C. (3d) 498 at paras. 53-54 (Ont. C.A.) (in light of *Krieger*, *Cook* should not be read to impinge upon trial judge's power to "manage the trial, including the power to review the order in which certain evidence may be called, [which] properly falls within the area of the prosecutor's 'tactics or conduct before the court' and thus does not implicate prosecutorial discretion that is reviewable only on the standard of abuse of process, bad faith or improper purpose").

135 *Krieger v. Law Society of Alberta*, [2002] S.C.J. No. 45, [2002] 3 S.C.R. 372 (S.C.C.). See also *R. v. McNeil* [2009] S.C.J. No. 3, [2009] 1 S.C.R. 66 at paras. 48-51 (S.C.C.) (prosecutors must make reasonable inquiries of other Crown entities that could reasonably be considered to be in possession of relevant evidence).

136 See *R. v. Brooks*, [2001] O.J. No. 1563, 153 C.C.C. (3d) 533 at para. 22 (Ont. S.C.J.) ("Opposing bail in every case, or without exception where a particular crime is charged, or because of a victim's wishes without regard to individual liberty concerns of the arrestee, derogates from the prosecutor's role as a minister of justice and as a guardian of the civil rights of all persons."). But see *Picha v. British Columbia (Presiding Coroner)*, [2009] B.C.J. No. 1461, 96 B.C.L.R. (4th) 199 at paras. 15-27 (B.C.C.A.) (prosecutors' decision to consent to release "is at, or very close to, the core of prosecutorial discretion"; prosecutors could not therefore be compelled to testify about decision at coroner's inquiry).

137 See *R. v. Gayle*, [2001] O.J. No. 1559, 154 C.C.C. (3d) 221 (Ont. C.A.), leave to appeal refused [2001] S.C.C.A. No. 359, 159 C.C.C. (3d) vi (S.C.C.) (prosecutor may not use peremptory challenges to exclude potential jurors on basis of race); *R. v. Brown*, [1999] O.J. No. 4867 (Ont. Gen. Div.) (same). Jury selection is examined in detail in Chapter 15.

misconduct occurring during the trial itself,[138] including making inflammatory remarks during opening and closing addresses,[139] alluding to facts not properly in evidence,[140] expressing an opinion on the accused's guilt,[141] expressing an opinion on the accused or a witness's credibility[142] and mistreating the accused or other witnesses during questioning.[143]

(3) Professional Regulation

§8.38 Until the Supreme Court's decision in *Krieger*,[144] it was not clear whether Crown prosecutors were subject to the oversight and discipline of the provincial law societies. In *Kreiger*, the Court held that they are, at least with respect to conduct falling outside the ambit of prosecutorial discretion. Specifically, it concluded that the Law Society had the authority to review and impose discipline on a prosecutor for failing to disclose information to the defence.[145] "As the disclosure of relevant evidence is not a matter of prosecutorial discretion but rather a legal duty," the Court reasoned, the Law Society had the jurisdiction to review it.[146] In contrast, conduct falling within the proper scope of prosecutorial

---

[138] See generally, *R. v. Trochym*, [2007] S.C.J. No. 6, [2007] 1 S.C.R. 239 at para. 79 (S.C.C.) (not necessary to rule on claims of Crown misconduct in cross-examining accused and addressing jury, but noting that "[r]hetorical techniques that distort the fact-finding process, and misleading and highly prejudicial statements, have no place in a criminal prosecution"); Canada, Department of Justice, *The Federal Prosecution Service Deskbook*, "Principles Governing Crown Counsel's Conduct," § 9.3.3-9.3.3.1 (October 2005) (setting out Crown's duty in conducting criminal litigation to be fair and avoid inflammatory remarks); Michel Proulx & David Layton, *Ethics and Canadian Criminal Law* (Toronto: Irwin Law, 2001) at 663-71. For the most part, the rules limiting adversarial excesses apply equally to defence counsel. See *R. v. Finta*, [1992] O.J. No. 823, 73 C.C.C. (3d) 65 at 182-91 (Ont. C.A.), affd [1994] S.C.J. No. 26, [1994] 1 S.C.R. 701 (S.C.C.) (defence counsel should not express personal opinion that accused is innocent); The Law Society of Alberta, *Rules of Professional Conduct* (June 3, 2009), Chapter 10, r. 11, r. 21; Law Society of Upper Canada, *Rules of Professional Conduct* (April 22, 2010), r. 4.01(1) and commentary, r. 4.01(2)(g) and (k).

[139] See *e.g.*, *R. v. Boucher*, [1954] S.C.J. No. 54, [1955] S.C.R. 16 (S.C.C.); *R. v. Romeo*, [1991] S.C.J. No. 6, [1991] 1 S.C.R. 86 (S.C.C.); *R. v. Michaud*, [1995] N.B.J. No. 207, 98 C.C.C. (3d) 121 (N.B.C.A.), affd [1996] S.C.J. No. 73, [1996] 2 S.C.R. 458 (S.C.C.); *R. v. F. (A.)*, [1996] O.J. No. 3033, 30 O.R. (3d) 470 at 472 (Ont. C.A.).

[140] See *e.g.*, *R. v. Emkeit*, [1972] S.C.J. No. 114, [1974] S.C.R. 133 (S.C.C.); *R. v. Rose*, [1998] S.C.J. No. 81, [1998] 3 S.C.R. 262 at para. 107 (S.C.C.); *R. v. Kaufman*, [2000] J.Q. no 5631, 151 C.C.C. (3d) 566 at para. 18 (Que. C.A.); *R. v. Hay*, [1982] S.J. No. 667, 70 C.C.C. (2d) 286 (Sask. C.A.).

[141] See *e.g.*, *R. v. Moubarak*, [1982] C.A. 454 (Que. C.A.); *R. v. Kaufman*, [2000] J.Q. no 5631, 151 C.C.C. (3d) 566 at para. 18 (Que. C.A.); *R. v. F. (A.)*, [1996] O.J. No. 3033, 30 O.R. (3d) 470 at 473 (Ont. C.A.).

[142] See *e.g.*, *R. v. Chambers*, [1990] S.C.J. No. 108, [1990] 2 S.C.R. 1293 at 1308-1309 (S.C.C.).

[143] See *e.g.*, *R. v. Bear*, [2008] S.J. No. 815, 320 Sask. R. 12 at para. 24 (Sask. C.A.), leave to appeal refused [2009] S.C.C.A. No. 76 (S.C.C.); *R. v. Robinson*, [2001] O.J. No. 1072, 153 C.C.C. (3d) 398 at 416 (Ont. C.A.); Michel Proulx & David Layton, *Ethics and Canadian Criminal Law* (Toronto: Irwin Law, 2001) at 672-77.

[144] *Krieger v. Law Society of Alberta*, [2002] S.C.J. No. 45, [2002] 3 S.C.R. 372 (S.C.C.).

[145] *Ibid.*, at para. 3 (S.C.R.).

[146] *Ibid.*, at para. 5 (S.C.R.).

discretion cannot be the subject of professional discipline.[147] As discussed in Part 5(2), above, however, decisions made in bad faith or for an improper purpose may be sanctioned, including by the law society.[148]

(4) Malicious Prosecution

§8.39 Abuses in the exercise of prosecutorial discretion may also expose Crown counsel to liability under the tort of malicious prosecution. Though a detailed discussion of this tort is beyond the scope of this book,[149] it is worth noting that as with criminal and professional disciplinary proceedings, until quite recently prosecutors were absolutely immune from liability in tort for their discretionary decisions.[150] This changed in *Nelles v. Ontario*,[151] where the Supreme Court of Canada held that a prosecutor could be liable for perpetrating what amounts to "a fraud on the process of criminal justice and in doing so has perverted or abused his office and the process of criminal justice."[152] To establish malicious prosecution, a plaintiff must prove that "the prosecution was: (1) initiated by the defendant; (2) terminated in favour of the plaintiff; (3) undertaken without reasonable and probable cause; and (4) motivated by malice or a primary purpose other than that of carrying the law into effect."[153] Essentially, a prosecutor may be liable in tort only for the same kind of egregious misconduct that would extinguish the deference accorded in criminal proceedings to conduct encompassed by core prosecutorial discretion.[154] Conduct not performed in bad faith, even if grossly negligent, is not actionable.[155] As a consequence, successful claims of malicious prosecution are exceptionally rare.[156]

---

[147] *Ibid.*, at paras. 3-4 (S.C.R.).

[148] *Ibid.*, at para. 51 (S.C.R.).

[149] On the tort of malicious prosecution, see Allen M. Linden & Bruce Feldthusen, *Canadian Tort Law*, 9th ed. (Markham, ON: LexisNexis Canada, 2011).

[150] See *e.g.*, *Richman v. McMurtry*, [1983] O.J. No. 3015, 5 C.C.C. (3d) 6 (Ont. H.C.J.); *German v. Major*, [1985] A.J. No. 1055, 20 D.L.R. (4th) 703 (Alta. C.A.).

[151] [1989] S.C.J. No. 86, [1989] 2 S.C.R. 170 (S.C.C.).

[152] *Ibid.*, at para. 45 (S.C.R.).

[153] *Miazga v. Kvello Estate*, [2009] S.C.J. No. 51, [2009] 3 S.C.R. 339 at 341 (S.C.C.). See also *Nelles v. Ontario*, [1989] S.C.J. No. 86, [1989] 2 S.C.R. 170 at 193 (S.C.C.); *Proulx v. Quebec (Attorney General)*, [2001] S.C.J. No. 65, [2001] 3 S.C.R. 9 at para. 123 (S.C.C.).

[154] *Miazga v. Kvello Estate*, [2009] S.C.J. No. 51, [2009] 3 S.C.R. 339 at para. 6 (S.C.C.) ("When taken by a Crown prosecutor, [the decision to initiate or continue with a prosecution] is one of the 'core elements' of prosecutorial discretion, thus lying 'beyond the legitimate reach of the court' under the constitutionally entrenched principle of independence"). See also Hon. Marc Rosenberg, "The Attorney General and the Administration of Criminal Justice" (2009) 34 Queen's L.J. 813 at 844 ("The elements of malicious prosecution, as applied to the Attorney General when acting in the prosecution function, closely mirror the standard of flagrant impropriety for judicial review.").

[155] See *Miazga v. Kvello Estate*, [2009] S.C.J. No. 51, [2009] 3 S.C.R. 339 at paras. 8, 81 (S.C.C.); *Proulx v. Quebec (Attorney General)*, [2001] S.C.J. No. 65, [2001] 3 S.C.R. 9 at para. 35 (S.C.C.).

[156] One of the few exceptions is *Proulx v. Quebec (Attorney General)*, [2001] S.C.J. No. 65, [2001] 3 S.C.R. 9 (S.C.C.), where the prosecutor's decision to lay charges was improperly influenced by the involvement in the prosecution of a police officer who had been sued by the plaintiff for defamation.

Chapter 9

Elections, Preliminary Inquiries and Preferring the Indictment

1. INTRODUCTION

§9.1 Depending on the offence charged, the Crown may have certain choices to make regarding the forum and procedure by which a criminal charge will proceed. In addition, the accused will also often have a choice to make regarding the forum of trial and the procedures that precede it. These choices are referred to as "elections" and they are the focus of the first part of this chapter.

§9.2 The second part of this chapter addresses one of the procedures available to an accused charged with a more serious indictable offence. Where such an accused so elects, he or she may have a preliminary inquiry. The preliminary inquiry serves two functions. First, it provides a timely judicial check on the adequacy of the Crown's evidence; and second, it gives the defence an invaluable discovery opportunity. The purposes of preliminary inquiries, the procedural and evidentiary rules governing their operation, and the process available for reviewing their outcomes, are all addressed in this chapter.

§9.3 Finally, this chapter briefly addresses the authority of a prosecutor to prefer an indictment. While a case remains in provincial court, the "information" is the charging document. The "indictment" replaces the information when an accused is charged with an indictable offence and the case moves to superior court for trial. There are rules governing what charges a prosecutor may include in an indictment, which require consideration of both the evidence heard at a preliminary inquiry as well as the formal outcome of such an inquiry. It is those rules that will provide the focus of this final part. (The rules governing informations and indictments more generally are the focus of Chapter 11.)

2. ELECTIONS

§9.4 The *Criminal Code*[1] often confers choices or elections on the Crown and the accused. This part will explain the elections available to both the Crown and the accused, as well as their interrelationship.

---

[1]   R.S.C. 1985, c. C-46 [*Code*].

(1)   Elections by the Crown

§9.5 As was explained in Part 2(3) of Chapter 1, there are three types of criminal offences: summary offences, indictable offences and hybrid (or "duel procedure") offences. The vast majority of offences found in the *Criminal Code* fall into the third category: hybrid offences. The provisions creating hybrid offences specify that a charge may be prosecuted by way of indictment or on summary conviction. The choice of how to proceed belongs to the Crown.[2] This decision is therefore commonly referred to as the "Crown's election". This election is a matter of Crown discretion and will normally not be interfered with by the court absent an abuse of process.[3] The Crown's election will in turn determine the accused person's trial options, if any. The different options available to the accused are discussed in Part 2(2), below.

(a)   Timing of the Crown's Election

§9.6 As the *Code* is silent on the question, the timing of the Crown's election varies from jurisdiction to jurisdiction. In some places, the Crown makes its election on the first court appearance. In others, the Crown will often not make its formal election until much later in the proceedings (although it usually informally communicates its intention to the accused much earlier in the process).[4] To avoid uncertainty and misunderstanding, the Supreme Court of Canada has suggested that it would be best for the Crown to declare explicitly whether it is proceeding on a hybrid offence summarily or by indictment before the accused is asked to plead.[5]

§9.7 Until the Crown elects to proceed summarily, the *Interpretation Act*[6] deems hybrid offences to be indictable offences.[7] In arresting a person for a

---

[2]   *R. v. Dudley*, [2009] S.C.J. No. 58, [2009] 3 S.C.R. 570 at paras. 1, 17 (S.C.C.). See also *R. v. Smythe*, [1971] S.C.J. No. 62, [1971] S.C.R. 680 at 685-87 (S.C.C.), *per* Fauteux C.J.C.

[3]   See *R. v. Abarca*, [1980] O.J. No. 1581, 57 C.C.C. (2d) 410 at 416-17 (Ont. C.A.). Crown discretion is discussed more extensively in Chapter 8.

[4]   See *R. v. Gougeon*, [1980] O.J. No. 1342, 55 C.C.C. (2d) 218 at 234-35 (Ont.C.A.), leave to appeal refused (1980), 35 N.R. 83*n* (S.C.C.) (specifically rejecting the suggestion that the Crown be required to make its election at the accused's first court appearance, noting that such a rule does not accord with established practice and "may well be harmful to both accused persons and the Crown").

[5]   *R. v. Dudley*, [2009] S.C.J. No. 58, [2009] 3 S.C.R. 570 at para. 19 (S.C.C.).

[6]   R.S.C. 1985, c. I-21.

[7]   *Interpretation Act*, R.S.C. 1985, c. I-21, s. 34(1)(*a*). See also *R. v. Dudley*, [2009] S.C.J. No. 58, [2009] 3 S.C.R. 570 at paras. 21-22 (S.C.C.). See also *R. v. Paul-Marr*, [2005] N.S.J. No. 279, 199 C.C.C. (3d) 424 at para. 20 (N.S.C.A.); *R. v. C. (D.J.)*, [1985] P.E.I.J. No. 78, 21 C.C.C. (3d) 246 at 252 (P.E.I.S.C.); *Canada (Attorney General) v. Trueman, P.C.J.*, [1996] B.C.J. No. 2193, 83 B.C.A.C. 227 at para. 13 (B.C.C.A.); *Trinidad and Tobago (Republic) v. Davis*, [2008] A.J. No. 829, 233 C.C.C. (3d) 435 at para. 14 (Alta. C.A.), leave to appeal refused [2008] S.C.C.A. No. 421 (S.C.C.); *R. v. Huff*, [1979] A.J. No. 846, 50 C.C.C. (2d) 324 at 328 (Alta. C.A.); *R. v. Mitchell*, [1997] O.J. No. 5148, 121 C.C.C. (3d) 139 at para. 4 (Ont. C.A.); *R. v. Gougeon*, [1980] O.J. No. 1342, 55 C.C.C. (2d) 218 at 234 (Ont. C.A.), leave to appeal refused (1980), 35 N.R. 83*n* (S.C.C.); *R. v. Tontarelli*, [2009] N.B.J. No. 294, 247 C.C.C. (3d)

hybrid offence, police may therefore use the more robust arrest powers reserved for indictable offences. (Police arrest powers were explained in Chapter 2, Part 4(4)). As discussed in Chapter 2, Part 4(4)(*a*), police may require persons arrested for indictable offences to appear for fingerprinting and photographing under the *Identification of Criminals Act*.[8] The deeming provision in the *Interpretation Act* authorizes police to do the same for persons arrested for hybrid offences, as long as the Crown has not yet elected to proceed summarily. Further, some courts have held that fingerprinting and photographing may be required for persons arrested for hybrid offences even after an election to proceed by summary conviction; though others have disagreed.[9] Practically speaking, police can easily avoid this uncertainty by requiring the accused to appear for fingerprinting and photographing before his or her first appearance in court, as the Crown can only make its election after this appearance.

(b) Summary Elections and the Six-Month Limitation Period in Summary Cases

§9.8 If the Crown elects to proceed summarily, the hybrid offence is treated in all respects as a summary conviction offence. Summary proceedings, which are governed by Part XXVII of the *Code*, must be instituted within six months "after the time when the subject-matter of the proceedings arose, unless the prosecutor and the defendant so agree."[10] The accused will often consent to an out of time summary prosecution to avoid either the same charge being prosecuted by indictment (which will carry a much lengthier maximum punishment) or a prosecution by indictment for a related offence that covers the same conduct.[11] Such a consent must be "informed, clear and unequivocal".[12]

---

160 at para. 55 (N.B.C.A.); *R. v. D. (S.)*, [1997] N.J. No. 202, 119 C.C.C. (3d) 65 at para. 34 (Nfld. C.A.).

[8] R.S.C. 1985, c. I-1.

[9] See *R. v. Dudley*, [2009] S.C.J. No. 58, [2009] 3 S.C.R. 570 at para. 23 (S.C.C.) (acknowledging the lack of judicial consensus on the question but refraining from resolving it). See also *R. v. Connors*, [1998] B.C.J. No. 41, 121 C.C.C. (3d) 358 at para. 69 (B.C.C.A.) (hybrid offences retain their character as indictable offences for purposes of the *Identification of Criminals Act*, R.S.C. 1985, c. I-1, even after the Crown elects to proceed summarily); *R. v. Abarca*, [1980] O.J. No. 1581, 57 C.C.C. (2d) 410 at 413 (Ont. C.A.) (coming to the opposite conclusion, so that the accused would not be required to attend for fingerprinting and photographing after the Crown elects to proceed summarily).

[10] See *Criminal Code*, R.S.C. 1985, c. C-46 [*Code*], s. 786(2) ("No proceedings shall be instituted more than six months after the time when the subject-matter of the proceedings arose, unless the prosecutor and the defendant so agree."). See also *R. v. Dudley*, [2009] S.C.J. No. 58, [2009] 3 S.C.R. 570 at paras. 2, 29 (S.C.C.); *R. v. Karpinski*, [1957] S.C.J. No. 18, [1957] S.C.R. 343 at 350 (S.C.C.) (interpreting the predecessor provision, which did not allow for waiver, as absolutely barring a prosecution after the time limit had expired).

[11] See *R. v. Dudley*, [2009] S.C.J. No. 58, [2009] 3 S.C.R. 570 at para. 30 (S.C.C.).

[12] See *R. v. Dudley*, [2009] S.C.J. No. 58, [2009] 3 S.C.R. 570 at para. 36 (S.C.C.) (adopting the standard for waiver of procedural rights more generally from the Court's earlier decision in *Korponay v. Canada (Attorney General)*, [1982] S.C.J. No. 111, [1982] 1 S.C.R. 41 at 58 (S.C.C.)).

§9.9 Occasionally, due to oversight, the Crown will fail to make its formal election. In such cases, where the matter has proceeded to trial before a summary conviction court, it will be presumed that the Crown elected to proceed summarily.[13] Similarly, the Supreme Court has explained that "the Crown will be deemed to have elected to proceed by indictment where the accused has been put to the election as to mode of trial required, for example by section 536 of the *Criminal Code*, so long as the proceedings take place in a court having jurisdiction over the alleged offence."[14]

§9.10 Jurisdictional difficulties arise, however, where the Crown fails to make an election and the case proceeds to trial in a summary conviction court and it turns out that the charge was not initiated within six months. If the out of time nature of the proceeding is discovered before the verdict is rendered a mistrial should be declared, unless the parties agree to waive the limitation period.[15] If the parties do agree to waive the limitation period, the trial can proceed to its conclusion.[16] If the defect is discovered after a verdict has been rendered, the appropriate remedy is an appeal to the summary conviction appeal court, which should set aside the conviction on this basis.[17]

§9.11 If discovery of the out of time prosecution results in a mistrial or a new trial being ordered on appeal, the Crown may proceed with the charge by indictment and avoid the limitation period or the need for an accused person's consent to forego it.[18] According to the Supreme Court, such a prosecution would only be barred where "the evidence discloses an abuse of process arising from improper Crown motive, or resulting prejudice to the accused sufficient to violate the community's sense of fair play and decency."[19] Obviously, when the error is discovered after lengthy proceedings have taken place for a charge that the Crown originally considered only serious enough to warrant a summary prosecution, the Crown will need to decide whether it is in the interests of justice to proceed.[20] However, the Supreme Court has emphasized that in most cases the decision whether or not to prosecute "is best left to prosecutorial and not judicial discretion".[21]

---

[13] *R. v. Dudley*, [2009] S.C.J. No. 58, [2009] 3 S.C.R. 570 at paras. 3, 20 (S.C.C.). See also *R. v. Mitchell*, [1997] O.J. No. 5148, 121 C.C.C. (3d) 139 at para. 4 (Ont. C.A.).

[14] *R. v. Dudley*, [2009] S.C.J. No. 58, [2009] 3 S.C.R. 570 at para. 20 (S.C.C.).

[15] *Ibid.*

[16] See *R. v. Dudley*, [2009] S.C.J. No. 58, [2009] 3 S.C.R. 570 at para. 33 (S.C.C.).

[17] *R. v. Dudley*, [2009] S.C.J. No. 58, [2009] 3 S.C.R. 570 at paras. 4-5 (S.C.C.).

[18] *Ibid.*, at paras. 5, 31 (S.C.R.).

[19] *Ibid.*, at para. 44 (S.C.R.). See also *ibid.* at paras. 5, 31 (S.C.R.). Absent a showing of prosecutorial bad faith or actual prejudice to the accused, an abuse of process is unlikely to be found. See *e.g., R. v. Kelly*, [1998] O.J. No. 3236, 128 C.C.C. (3d) 206 at para. 64 (Ont. C.A.) (emphasizing an absence of prosecutorial bad faith or actual prejudice in refusing a stay). But see *e.g., R. v. Parkin*, [1986] O.J. No. 203, 28 C.C.C. (3d) 252 (Ont. C.A.) (where actual prejudice was found and a stay was therefore ordered).

[20] The standards governing the Crown's decision whether or not to prosecute a given charge are discussed in Chapter 8, Part 4(1).

[21] *R. v. Dudley*, [2009] S.C.J. No. 58, [2009] 3 S.C.R. 570 at para. 46 (S.C.C.).

§9.12 The situation is different where an accused is acquitted of an offence that was out of time but nevertheless proceeded to trial before a summary conviction court without consent to forego the limitation period. The Supreme Court has held that the Crown may not seek to overturn an acquittal on appeal on this basis. As the Court explained, "the Crown should not be heard to complain *after an adverse adjudication on the merits* that it neglected to obtain the consent of the accused before the accused was acquitted!"[22]

§9.13 To avoid potential jurisdictional dilemmas, the Supreme Court of Canada has indicated that where the Crown elects to proceed summarily beyond the six-month limitation period, the prosecutor and the defendant should both be required to declare expressly — before the accused enters his or her plea — that they agree to proceed summarily.[23]

§9.14 As we shall see in the next part, if the Crown elects to prosecute a hybrid offence by indictment or where the offence charged is an indictable offence, an accused may have his or her own choices to make.

(2) The Accused's Election

§9.15 An accused charged with an indictable offence may have an election as to his or her mode of trial. Whether or not the accused has an election is usually a function of the type of indictable offence charged. There is no election for summary offences, which as mentioned are tried under the procedures specified by Part XXVII of the *Code*. These charges are tried in provincial court before a judge alone in what is termed a "bench" trial.[24]

(a) Circumstances in Which There is No Election

§9.16 As explained in Part 2(2), below, an accused charged with an indictable offence usually has an election as to his or her mode of trial: (*i*) a bench trial before a provincial court judge; (*ii*) a trial in superior court before a judge and jury; or (*iii*) a trial in superior court before a judge alone. This includes situations where a hybrid offence is charged and the Crown elects to proceed by indictment. There are, however, a number of circumstances in which an accused charged with an indictable offence does not have a choice as to the mode of trial. In some cases, the *Code* denies the accused the opportunity to make an election; in others, the accused's election is overridden by the court or the Attorney General.

---

[22] *Ibid.*, at para. 6 (S.C.R.) [emphasis in original]. See also *ibid.*, at para. 31 (S.C.R.).
[23] *R. v. Dudley*, [2009] S.C.J. No. 58, [2009] 3 S.C.R. 570 at para. 19 (S.C.C.).
[24] See definition of "summary conviction court", *Criminal Code*, R.S.C. 1985, c. C-46, s. 785. See also s. 798.

(i) *Exclusive Jurisdiction (Section 469) Offences*

§9.17 Persons charged with the most serious indictable offences — those listed in section 469 of the *Criminal Code* — are always tried in the superior court. These offences (of which murder is by far the most common) are known as "exclusive jurisdiction" offences.[25] A superior court judge usually tries such offences with a jury[26] after an accused has had a preliminary inquiry in provincial court.[27]

(ii) *Absolute Jurisdiction (Section 553) Offences*

§9.18 The accused also lacks an election with respect to the less serious indictable offences listed in section 553 of the *Criminal Code*. Normally, trials of such offences take place in provincial court before a judge alone (since there are no juries in provincial courts). The *Code* characterizes these as "absolute jurisdiction" offences because they are within the absolute jurisdiction of the provincial court.[28]

§9.19 However, while the provincial court's jurisdiction to try section 553 offences is absolute, it is not exclusive. As the Ontario Court of Appeal has explained, it is absolute "in the sense that it does not depend upon the election of the accused."[29] But it is not exclusive because, under section 468 of the *Code*, the superior court has jurisdiction to try any indictable offence, including those listed in section 553.[30] As a result, should an absolute jurisdiction offence make its way before the superior court, for example because it is charged along with a non-absolute jurisdiction indictable offence for which an accused elects trial in superior court, the superior court will have the authority to deal with both types of indictable offences.

(iii) *Where Provincial Court Judge Intervenes*

§9.20 Irrespective of the accused's election, there is a peculiar provision in the *Code* that grants a provincial court judge presiding at the trial of a charge the authority to transform the trial into a preliminary inquiry.[31] This power may be exercised "at any time before the accused has entered on his defence" if "it

---

[25] See *Criminal Code*, ss. 468, 469.

[26] See *Criminal Code*, s. 471 (which makes a jury compulsory for indictable offences, unless otherwise provided by law) and s. 473(1) (which allows for s. 469 offences to be tried by a superior court judge alone, without a jury, provided both the Crown and the accused consent).

[27] See *Criminal Code*, s. 536(4) (which provides that where a s. 469 offence is charged a preliminary inquiry shall be held where either the accused or the Crown request one in accordance with the rules of court in the particular jurisdiction). As explained more fully in Part 2(2)(*a*)(v), even where the accused has requested one, the Crown may avoid a preliminary inquiry by preferring a direct indictment.

[28] See *Criminal Code*, s. 553.

[29] *R. v. Tucker*, [2006] O.J. No. 3679, 213 C.C.C. (3d) 89 at para. 7 (Ont. C.A.), leave to appeal refused [2006] S.C.C.A. No. 474, [2007] 1 S.C.R. xvi (S.C.C.).

[30] *Ibid.*

[31] *Criminal Code*, s. 555(1).

appears to the provincial court judge that for any reason the charge should be prosecuted by indictment".[32] If the judge decides to do so, he or she "shall thereupon inform the accused of his decision"[33] and the accused will be deemed to have elected to be tried by a superior court judge and jury.[34]

§9.21 Although this language seems to confer a relatively unfettered discretion, the courts have constrained it in the following ways. First, they have construed it as applying only to indictable offences. As a result, where a summary offence is charged, including a hybrid offence that the Crown has elected to prosecute summarily, the provision cannot be invoked to require a prosecution by indictment.[35] It can, however, be invoked for all indictable offences, including so-called "absolute jurisdiction" offences.[36]

§9.22 Second, the courts have instructed that the discretion conferred by this provision must be exercised judiciously. Unless there is a judicial reason for overruling the accused's election to be tried by a provincial court judge then the accused should be entitled to proceed in that way.[37] A wish to clear the docket, for example, would not qualify.[38]

(iv)   Where Attorney General Directs a Jury Trial

§9.23 If an accused elects to be tried by a provincial court judge or a superior court judge without a jury, section 568 of the *Criminal Code* provides that the Attorney General "may require" a trial by judge and jury, but only if the offence is punishable with imprisonment for more than five years. The provision does not contain any criteria governing the Attorney General's use of this authority; it is a matter of prosecutorial discretion.[39] Once the Attorney General exercises this authority, the accused's trial must take place with a jury, even if the Crown consents (before or after the Attorney General's directive) to a trial by judge alone.[40]

---

[32]   *Ibid.* An accused has not "entered upon his defence" until he or she calls witnesses or makes known to the Court after the Crown has closed its case his intention to do so. See *R. v. Nadeau*, [1971] N.B.J. No. 36, 3 C.C.C. (2d) 276 at 278-79. (N.B.C.A.)

[33]   *Criminal Code*, s. 555(1).

[34]   *Criminal Code*, s. 565(1)(*a*).

[35]   See *R. v. Turton*, [1988] A.J. No. 721, 44 C.C.C. (3d) 49 (Alta. C.A.).

[36]   See *R. v. Tucker*, [2006] O.J. No. 3679, 213 C.C.C. (3d) 89 at paras. 7-8 (Ont. C.A.), leave to appeal refused [2006] S.C.C.A. No. 474, [2007] 1 S.C.R. xvi (S.C.C.).

[37]   See *R. v. Babcock*, [1989] O.J. No. 13, 68 C.R. (3d) 285 (Ont. C.A.).

[38]   *Ibid.*

[39]   As discussed in Chapter 8, Part 5, matters of "core" prosecutorial discretion may only be reviewed in exceptional circumstances. One court has held, however, that the decision to invoke s. 568 is not a matter of core discretion and is therefore reviewable under the lower standard of "fairness and objectivity." See *R. v. De Zen*, [2010] O.J. No. 601 (Ont. S.C.J.) (abuse of process when decision to invoke s. 568 based on "partisan considerations"). Note as well that the provision has survived *Charter* challenge. See *R. v. Musitano*, [1982] O.J. No. 3573, 1 C.C.C. (3d) 465 (Ont. H.C.J.), affd 39 O.R. (2d) 732 at 733 (Ont. C.A.) (rejecting a challenge under s. 11(*d*) of the *Charter*); *R. v. Hanneson*, [1987] O.J. No. 8, 31 C.C.C. (3d) 560 (Ont. H.C.J.) (also rejecting challenges under ss. 7 and 15).

[40]   See *R. v. Thompson*, [1987] N.S.J. No. 359, 40 C.C.C. (3d) 365 (N.S.C.A.) (once Attorney General has invoked provision, accused cannot be tried by a judge alone, even with Crown's

§9.24 This provision is most likely to be used where a provincial court judge, faced with differing elections by co-accused, fails to exercise the jurisdiction to decline the recording of any election, which would have the effect of deeming each accused to have elected trial by jury.[41] If that happens, rather than allowing the accused to be severed, section 568 permits the Attorney General to override the decision of those accused who elected not to have a jury trial and ensure a joint trial. There is, however, nothing expressly contained in section 568 to restrict its application to such unusual circumstances.

(v) Direct Indictment

§9.25 Under section 577 of the *Criminal Code*, the prosecutor may prefer a "direct indictment" for any offence "even if the accused has not been given the opportunity to request a preliminary inquiry, a preliminary inquiry has been commenced but not concluded or a preliminary inquiry has been held and the accused has been discharged".[42] This extraordinary power may only be exercised with the personal, written consent of the Attorney General or Deputy Attorney General.[43]

§9.26 A direct indictment has the effect of sending an accused directly to trial in the superior court, thereby depriving the accused of his or her election to have a preliminary inquiry. When a direct indictment is preferred, the accused is deemed both to have elected to be tried by a court composed of a judge and jury and not to have requested a preliminary inquiry.[44] However, such an accused may "re-elect" to be tried by a superior court judge alone.[45]

---

consent); *R. v. Pontbriand*, [1978] Q.J. No. 176, 39 C.C.C. (2d) 145 (Que. S.C.) (authority to require jury trial still available even after Crown had consented to accused's re-election to judge alone trial).

41   A provincial court judge faced with differing elections by co-accused, "may decline to record any election". See *Criminal Code*, s. 567. If the judge does so, then the accused will "be deemed to have elected to be tried by a court composed of a judge and jury". See *Criminal Code*, s. 565(1)(*b*).

42   *Criminal Code*, s. 577. See generally, *R. v. McKibbon*, [1984] S.C.J. No. 8, [1984] 1 S.C.R. 131 (S.C.C.) (direct indictment may be preferred on charge for which accused was discharged at preliminary inquiry); *R. v. Benji*, [2002] S.C.J. No. 5, [2002] 1 S.C.R. 142 (accused committed to stand trial may be added to direct indictment charging another); *R. v. L. (S.J.)*, [2009] S.C.J. No. 14, [2009] 1 S.C.R. 426 (S.C.C.) (direct indictment may be preferred against young person to be tried as adult); *R. v. Ewen*, [2000] S.J. No. 155, 144 C.C.C. (3d) 277 (Sask. C.A.) (direct indictment may be preferred where committal for trial is quashed); *R. v. Charlie*, [1998] B.C.J. No. 1506, 126 C.C.C. (3d) 513 (B.C.C.A.) (same); *R. v. Pal*, [2007] B.C.J. No. 2189, 2007 BCSC 47; 75 W.C.B. (2d) 610 (B.C.S.C.) (direct indictment may be preferred even after accused has elected to be tried in provincial court and is before that court for trial).

43   *Criminal Code*, s. 577(*a*). See also *R. v. Dwyer*, [1978] O.J. No. 3878, 42 C.C.C. (2d) 83 (Ont. C.A.), revd [1979] S.C.J. No. 117 (S.C.C.). For private prosecutions, a direct indictment may also be preferred by court order: *Criminal Code*, s. 577(*b*).

44   *Criminal Code*, s. 565(2).

45   *Ibid.* See also *Criminal Code*, s. 565(3) (setting out procedure for such "re-elections"). It is unclear whether individuals charged with a s. 469 offence would have a similar right of "re-election". A plain reading of s. 565(2) and s. 471 suggests that they would.

§9.27 The preferring of the indictment, including the direct indictment procedure, is explained more fully below in Part 4.

(b)   Election for All Other Indictable Offences

§9.28 With all other indictable offences, an accused has an election as to his or her mode of trial. As mentioned, an accused with an election has three options: (*i*) a bench trial before a provincial court judge; (*ii*) a trial in superior court before a judge and jury; or (*iii*) a trial in superior court before a judge alone.

§9.29 The accused is apprised of these various options through the procedure specified in section 536(2) of the *Criminal Code*. That section provides that where an accused is before a justice and charged with an indictable offence — other than one of those listed in sections 469 or 553:

> the "justice shall, after the information has been read to the accused, put the accused to an election in the following words:

> > You have the option to elect to be tried by a provincial court judge without a jury and without having had a preliminary inquiry; or you may elect to be tried by a judge without a jury; or you may elect to be tried by a court composed of a judge and jury. If you do not elect now, you are deemed to have elected to be tried by a court composed of a judge and jury. If you elect to be tried by a judge without a jury or by a court composed of a judge and jury or if you are deemed to have elected to be tried by a court composed of a judge and jury, you will have a preliminary inquiry only if you or the prosecutor requests one. How do you elect to be tried?"

The failure to read this passage to the accused could vitiate any subsequent conviction.[46] Further, absent waiver, the failure put the accused to his or her election, in terms which substantially comply with the provision, removes jurisdiction to conduct a preliminary inquiry or trial and cannot be corrected on appeal.[47]

---

[46]   The failure to properly arraign the accused is a "procedural error". However, the failure to arraign the accused can, in appropriate circumstances, be cured on appeal through the application of the proviso found in s. 686(1)(*b*)(iv). See *R. v. N. (C.)*, [1992] S.C.J. No. 102, [1992] 3 S.C.R. 471 (S.C.C.), revg [1991] J.Q. no 645, 144 N.R. 294 (Que. C.A.). The key consideration will be whether or not the accused experienced any prejudice, which will turn on whether or not he or she appreciated what the charge(s) were. Relevant considerations will include what the accused was told about the charge(s), whether disclosure was provided and whether counsel represented the accused. See *R. v. Mitchell*, [1997] O.J. No. 5148, 121 C.C.C. (3d) 139 at paras. 125-127 (Ont. C.A.).

[47]   See *R. v. Mitchell*, [1997] O.J. No. 5148, 121 C.C.C. (3d) 139 at paras. 28-30 (Ont. C.A.). See also *R. v. Varcoe*, [2007] O.J. No. 1009, 219 C.C.C. (3d) 397 (Ont. C.A.); *R. v. Spence*, [2001] B.C.J. No. 1842, 46 C.R. (5th) 387 (B.C.C.A.); *R. v. Wiseberg*, [1973] O.J. No. 945, 15 C.C.C. (2d) 26 (Ont. C.A.); *R. v. Sanver*, [1973] N.B.J. No. 52, 6 N.B.R. (2d) 189 (N.B.C.A.); *R. v. Leske*, [1968] A.J. No. 18, [1968] 1 C.C.C. 347 (Alta. C.A.); *R. v. Karpuk*, [1962] O.J. No. 153, 133 C.C.C. 108 (Ont. C.A.); *R. v. Roy*, [1955] O.J. No. 408, 115 C.C.C. 335 (Ont. C.A.); *R. v. Nairn*, [1955] N.J. No. 4, 112 C.C.C. 272 (Nfld. T.D.); *R. v. Dauphinee*, [1935] N.S.J. No. 5, 63 C.C.C. 90 (N.S.S.C., *R. v. Bonnis*, [1927] O.J. No. 18, 47 C.C.C. 193 (Ont. C.A.).

§9.30 After being informed of his or her options, the accused must make an express election on the record in open court — an election cannot be implied.[48] If the accused does not do so, he or she will be deemed to have chosen to be tried by a judge and jury.[49] If an accused is charged with multiple counts, he or she must make a single election applying to all of them.[50] The accused cannot therefore effectively sever the counts by electing different modes of trial on each. And where more than one person is charged in the same information and they cannot agree on an election, the provincial court judge "may decline to record any election".[51] Should this happen, each of the accused will "be deemed to have elected to be tried by a court composed of a judge and jury".[52]

§9.31 As the options outlined above make clear, a preliminary inquiry is only possible where the trial of the charge is to take place in superior court. In such cases, however, the preliminary inquiry is not automatic. Rather, it requires that either the accused or the Crown make a request for a preliminary inquiry in accordance with any applicable rules of court in the particular jurisdiction.[53] The judge who puts the accused to his or her election must record the accused's election on the information, and also record whether the accused or the prosecutor requested a preliminary inquiry.[54] If no such request is made, the accused will be remanded to the superior court to fix a date for trial.[55] (The obligation on an accused who wants a preliminary inquiry to request one is discussed more fully below in Part 3(2).)

(c) Election Under Youth Criminal Justice Act

§9.32 A young person facing a criminal charge is normally tried by a youth justice court judge in a bench trial.[56] However, in certain prescribed circumstances

---

[48] See *R. v. Bobyk*, [1962] A.J. No. 39, [1963] 2 C.C.C. 91 (Alta. C.A.) (holding that accused who, when put to his election, elected trial by jury, did not waive that right when he attended for trial and no jury was present and participating and yet he failed to voice any objection, conviction quashed and new trial ordered for this reason).

[49] *Criminal Code* s. 565(1)(c).

[50] See *R. v. Garcia*, [1990] B.C.J. No. 371, 75 C.R. (3d) 250 (B.C.C.A.).

[51] See *Criminal Code*, s. 567.

[52] See *Criminal Code*, s. 565(1).

[53] *Criminal Code*, s. 536(4). Under s. 482(2), the provincial courts across the country have been conferred authority to create rules of court with the approval of the lieutenant governor in council of the relevant jurisdiction. These rules must be published in the *Canada Gazette* (s. 482(4)). See *e.g.*, *Rules of the Ontario Court of Justice in Criminal Proceedings*, SI/97-33 (see <http://laws-lois.justice.gc.ca/eng/regulations/SI-97-133/FullText.html>).

[54] *Criminal Code*, s. 536(4.1). See *R. v. Sagutch*, [1991] B.C.J. No. 740, 63 C.C.C. (3d) 569 (B.C.C.A.), holding that, under the predecessor provision, the failure to endorse the information amounts to jurisdictional error but also concluding that it was curable under s. 686(1)(b)(iv) of the *Code*. See also *R. v. Squires*, [1977] N.J. No. 4, 35 C.C.C. (2d) 325 (Nfld. C.A.) (holding that it is sufficient if the election is endorsed on the information, silence of the transcript alone does not rebut presumption of regularity created by endorsement).

[55] *Criminal Code*, s. 536(4.3).

[56] See *Youth Criminal Justice Act*, S.C. 2002, c. 1, s. 13(1) [YCJA].

the *Youth Criminal Justice Act*[57] grants a young person an election as to his or her mode of trial.

§9.33 A young person will have an election where: (*i*) it is alleged that the young person, after attaining the age of 14 years, committed first degree murder, second murder, attempted murder, manslaughter or aggravated sexual assault;[58] (*ii*) the Crown has given notice of its intention to seek an adult sentence for an offence committed after the young person has attained the age of 14 years;[59] (*iii*) the young person is charged with having committed first or second degree murder before attaining the age of 14 years;[60] or (*iv*) where it is uncertain whether or not the offence was committed when the accused was a young person and an adult would have an election or a section 469 offence is charged.[61]

§9.34 Where a young person has an election, he or she has three options: (*i*) a bench trial before a youth justice court judge; (*ii*) a trial in superior court before a judge and jury; or (*iii*) a trial in superior court before a judge alone.[62] With the latter two options, a preliminary inquiry is available if requested by either the young person or prosecutor.[63] If co-accused do not all make the same election, a youth justice court judge may decline to record any election, other than an election for trial by judge and jury.[64] Should this happen, the judge must then hold a preliminary inquiry if requested by one of the parties.[65] (If one is held, the provisions in the *Code* related to preliminary inquiries govern its operation.[66])

§9.35 Finally, as in the case of adult accused, the Attorney General may overrule a young person's election for a bench trial and require a trial before a superior court judge and jury.[67]

---

[57] S.C. 2002, c. 1.
[58] YCJA, s. 67(1)(*a*).
[59] YCJA, s. 67(1)(*b*).
[60] YCJA, s. 67(1)(*c*).
[61] YCJA, s. 67(1)(*d*).
[62] YCJA, s. 67(2). The young person is apprised of these various options in the following terms: You have the option to elect to be tried by a youth justice court judge without a jury and without having had a preliminary inquiry; or you may elect to be tried by a judge without a jury; or you may elect to be tried by a court composed of a judge and jury. If you do not elect now, you are deemed to have elected to be tried by a court composed of a judge and jury. If you elect to be tried by a judge without a jury or by a court composed of a judge and jury or if you are deemed to have elected to be tried by a court composed of a judge and jury, you will have a preliminary inquiry only if you or the prosecutor requests one. How do you elect to be tried?
[63] YCJA, s. 67(7).
[64] YCJA, s. 67(5)(*a*).
[65] YCJA, ss. 67(5)(*b*), 67(7.1).
[66] YCJA, s. 67(8).
[67] YCJA, s. 67(6). The authority of the Attorney General to require a jury trial in cases involving adult accused can be found in s. 568 of the *Criminal Code*, which is explained above in Part 2(2)(*a*)(iv).

(d)   Timing of the Accused's Election

§9.36 The *Code* does not specify the precise timing of an accused's election. As noted above, it says only that if an accused "is before a justice" and has an election, "the justice shall, after the information has been read to the accused" put the accused to his or her election.[68] Where a hybrid offence is charged an accused's election will necessarily come after the Crown has chosen to prosecute by indictment.[69] Beyond that, the timing of the election varies. In some jurisdictions the accused will be formally put to his or her election after initial intake procedures (such as bail, disclosure, pre-trial conferences and any Crown election) are completed. In others, a date may be set for a preliminary inquiry or trial on the informal understanding that the accused will only be put to his or her formal election on that date. The latter approach is problematic, however, given that in *R. v. Doyle*[70] the Supreme Court of Canada interpreted the relevant provision as creating a mandatory obligation to put an accused to his or her election soon after he or she first appears in court.[71]

§9.37 In *Doyle*, the Court concluded that an eight-month delay between the accused's first appearance and his opportunity to elect resulted in a loss of jurisdiction over the accused.[72] The information would thereafter be void, the Court explained, but that this would not result in a loss of jurisdiction over the offence. As a result, there was nothing precluding "the laying of another information in the same jurisdiction charging the same offence."[73] Given this, it is not surprising that some lower courts in Ontario (where the practice is to put the accused to his or her election late in the process) have found creative (but in our view unconvincing) ways to avoid the jurisdictional implications of *Doyle*.[74]

§9.38 In rare cases, however, putting the accused to his or her election at a late stage in the process may be unavoidable. Consider the offences of theft, fraud, possession of property obtained by crime and mischief (as well as the offences of counselling, conspiring or attempting to commit any of these offences).

---

68 *Criminal Code*, s. 536(2).
69 On the timing of the Crown's election, see above, Part 2(1)(*a*).
70 [1976] S.C.J. No. 38, [1977] 1 S.C.R. 597 (S.C.C.) [*Doyle*].
71 *R. v. Doyle*, [1976] S.C.J. No. 38, [1977] 1 S.C.R. 597 (S.C.C.). The Court did not, however, set down a definite time requirement. The British Columbia Court of Appeal has sensibly pointed out that *Doyle* and the relevant *Code* provisions do not require that the accused be put to his election on the first court appearance. See *R. v. Geszthelyi*, [1976] B.C.J. No. 1159, 33 C.C.C. (2d) 543 at 548 (B.C.C.A.) ("it would be inappropriate to oblige this accused to make his election on the first appearance" because "little would be known about the case," and "the accused was unrepresented and probably he would not have expected an election proceeding"). See also *R. v. Gougeon*, [1980] O.J. No. 1342, 55 C.C.C. (2d) 218 at 234-35 (Ont. C.A.), leave to appeal refused (1980), 35 N.R. 83*n* (S.C.C.).
72 *R. v. Doyle*, [1976] S.C.J. No. 38, [1977] 1 S.C.R. 597 at 607 (S.C.C.).
73 *Ibid.*, at 610 (S.C.R.).
74 See *e.g.*, *R. v. Chaisson*, [1984] O.J. No. 522, 15 C.C.C. (3d) 50 (Ont. H.C.J.) (jurisdiction over accused lost only if court refuses accused's request to make election at first or subsequent appearance); *R. v. Aiello*, [1977] O.J. No. 205, 33 C.C.C. (2d) 280 (Ont. H.C.J.) (delay resulted only in loss of jurisdiction over the accused and not offence; jurisdiction regained when accused attended court to answer charge).

Where the subject matter is not a testamentary instrument and the alleged value does not exceed $5,000, these offences are all in the absolute jurisdiction of the provincial court.[75] The evidence at trial may reveal, however, that the value of the property exceeds $5,000 or that the subject matter is a testamentary instrument. When this becomes apparent, the judge must to put the accused to his or her election.[76] The accused may then either choose to transform the proceeding into a preliminary inquiry and be tried in the superior court (by a judge or judge and jury) or continue with the trial before the provincial court judge.[77]

(e)   Re-electing

§9.39 An accused's election is not fixed in stone. The *Code* allows a change of mind, subject to limitations informed by logistics and trial fairness. Where it would be administratively feasible to accommodate the accused's request, without any unfairness to the Crown, the *Code* permits re-election without the Crown's consent. Specifically, an accused who elected trial before a provincial court judge or did not request a preliminary inquiry may re-elect up to 14 days before the first day scheduled for the trial.[78] Similarly, an accused who elected (or who was deemed to have elected) trial in the superior court before a judge or a judge and jury, may re-elect his or her mode of trial, other than trial before a provincial court judge, at any time before the completion of the preliminary inquiry or before the fifteenth day following the completion of the preliminary inquiry.[79]

§9.40 In contrast, the *Code* understandably requires the Crown's consent for a re-election closer to trial, as such a re-election may create logistical challenges and unfairness to the prosecution. With such consent, however, the ability to re-elect is quite flexible. For example, if an accused elected trial by a provincial court judge or did not request a preliminary inquiry, with the prosecutor's written consent the accused may re-elect at any time up to the commencement of the trial.[80] Similarly, an accused who elected (or who was deemed to have elected) trial in the superior court before a judge or a judge and jury, may with the prosecutor's written consent re-elect to be tried by a provincial court judge at any

---

[75]   *Criminal Code*, ss. 553(*a*) and 553(*b*)(i).

[76]   *Criminal Code*, s. 555(2).

[77]   *Criminal Code*, s. 555(3). See also *Criminal Code*, s. 554(1), which confers jurisdiction on provincial court judges to try indictable offences not listed in ss. 469 or 553, where an accused elects trial before a judge in that court.

[78]   *Criminal Code*, s. 561(2).

[79]   *Criminal Code*, s. 561(1)(*b*). See also *R. v. Ruston*, [1991] M.J. No. 112, 63 C.C.C. (3d) 419 (Man. C.A.). (The Court rejected a literal interpretation of the time limit where the Crown only disclosed important similar fact evidence to the accused more than 15 days after the completion of the preliminary inquiry. The Court favoured a "broad" reading to preserve the accused's choice to re-elect a jury trial as of right, so it construed the time limitation as only beginning to run *after* the accused was apprised of a "substantial change" in the case against him. Therefore, the Court held that that accused's re-election for trial by jury was effective, despite the Crown's refusal to consent.)

[80]   *Criminal Code*, s. 561(2).

time before or after the completion of the preliminary inquiry.[81] Finally, an accused who elected (or was deemed to have elected) a mode of trial other than by provincial court judge, may with the prosecutor's written consent re-elect any mode of trial on or after the fifteenth day following the completion of the preliminary inquiry.[82]

§9.41 The Crown's decision to consent to re-election is a matter of prosecutorial discretion,[83] the exercise of which is subject to review only on the basis the abuse of process doctrine.[84] The mere fact that a prosecutor perceives a tactical advantage from refusing consent is not enough to constitute an abuse of process.[85] To substantiate such a claim, the accused must show that the decision was arbitrary, capricious or motivated by improper considerations.[86] Given the absence of a duty on the Crown to provide reasons for its decision,[87] it is extraordinarily difficult for an accused to make out an abuse of process claim on this basis.[88]

§9.42 The mechanics of re-election vary with the stage and nature of the proceedings. In short, written notice of the desire to re-elect must be given (along with any required written prosecutorial consent), to the following:

    (i) if the re-election is being made before its completion, to the justice presiding at the preliminary inquiry;[89]

    (ii) if the accused originally elected trial in provincial court, to the provincial court judge before whom the accused appeared and pleaded or to the clerk of that court;[90] or

---

81   *Criminal Code*, s. 561(1)(*a*).

82   *Criminal Code*, s. 561(1)(*c*).

83   The *Code* provisions conferring that discretion on the Crown have survived *Charter* challenge. See *e.g.*, *R. v. Koleff*, [1987] M.J. No. 16, 33 C.C.C. (3d) 460 (Man. Q.B.) (rejecting a challenge under ss. 7 and 15 directed at what is now s. 561(1)(*a*)).

84   See *R. v. E. (L.)*, [1994] O.J. No. 2641, 94 C.C.C. (3d) 228 at 239-42 (Ont. C.A.); *R. v. Ng*, [2003] A.J. No. 489, 173 C.C.C. (3d) 349 at para. 33 (Alta. C.A.), leave to appeal refused [2007] S.C.C.A. No. 205, 183 C.C.C. (3d) vi (S.C.C.). Prosecutorial discretion is discussed more extensively in Chapter 8.

85   See *R. v. Mohammed*, [1990] M.J. No. 515, 60 C.C.C. (3d) 296 at 301 (Man. Q.B.). The abuse of process doctrine is discussed more extensively in Chapter 10.

86   *R. v. E. (L.)*, [1994] O.J. No. 2641, 94 C.C.C. (3d) 228 at 230 (Ont. C.A.). See also *R. v. Ng*, [2003] A.J. No. 489, 173 C.C.C. (3d) 349 at paras. 34-36 (Alta. C.A.), leave to appeal refused [2007] S.C.C.A. No. 205, 183 C.C.C. (3d) vi (S.C.C.).

87   *R. v. Ng*, [2003] A.J. No. 489, 173 C.C.C. (3d) 349 at paras. 67-68 (Alta. C.A.), leave to appeal refused [2007] S.C.C.A. No. 205, 183 C.C.C. (3d) vi (S.C.C.). On the burden on the accused to make a showing of bad faith before a court will delve into an examination of a prosecutor's motives for making a discretionary decision, see generally, *R. v. Durette*, [1992] O.J. No. 1044, 72 C.C.C. (3d) 421 at 437-38 (Ont. C.A.), revd on other grounds [1994] S.C.J. No. 22, [1994] 1 S.C.R. 469 (S.C.C.).

88   For a rare example, see *R. v. McGregor*, [1992] O.J. No. 3040, 14 C.R.R. (2d) 155 (Ont. Gen. Div.), affd [1999] O.J. No. 919, 134 C.C.C. (3d) 570 (Ont. C.A.) (Crown's refusal to consent to a judge alone trial gave rise to appearance that Crown was seeking favourable jury, rather than an impartial one and constituted violation of ss. 7 and 11(*d*) of the *Charter*; remedy granted was to dispense with the Crown's consent under s. 473.)

89   *Criminal Code*, s. 561(3).

90   *Criminal Code*, s. 561(4).

(iii) if the accused is re-electing after the completion of the preliminary inquiry, to the judge or clerk of the court of his or her original election (who will need to make arrangements to have the information and exhibits delivered to a judge or the clerk of the court before whom the accused wishes to be tried).[91]

§9.43 Once the requisite notice is given, a time and place will be set for the re-election in the court where it is to take place, and the accused and prosecutor will be notified accordingly.[92] Ultimately, the charges contained in the information or indictment will be read to the accused and the accused will be asked to indicate how he or she re-elects.[93]

§9.44 The failure to adhere to the procedural requirements governing re-election is not necessarily fatal to the jurisdiction of a court that subsequently tries an accused. Interpreting the relevant predecessor provisions, the Supreme Court of Canada held that an accused may waive these requirements, either personally or through counsel.[94] At the same time, the presiding judge has the authority to insist on strict compliance in order to ensure the integrity of the process.[95] Further, to be valid, any purported waiver must be clear, unequivocal and made with full knowledge of both the rights the procedure was enacted to protect and the effect of the waiver on those rights.[96] In making this assessment, relevant considerations include whether the accused was represented by counsel, counsel's experience and local practice.[97]

(f) Form of Election or Re-Election

§9.45 Due to a recent amendment to the *Criminal Code*, elections and re-elections may be made in the accused's absence. In keeping with the accused's ability to appear by designated counsel in circumstances where evidence is not being heard,[98] elections and re-elections may be made in writing.[99] The accused

---

[91] See *Criminal Code*, s. 561(5).

[92] See *Criminal Code*, s. 561(6).

[93] See *Criminal Code*, s. 561(7) (requiring the accused to be put to his or her re-election in the following words: "You have given notice of your wish to re-elect the mode of your trial. You now have the option to do so. How do you wish to re-elect?").

[94] See *Korponay v. Canada (Attorney General)*, [1982] S.C.J. No. 111, [1982] 1 S.C.R. 41 at 50-53 (S.C.C.).

[95] *Ibid.*, at 48 (S.C.R.).

[96] *Ibid.*, at 49 (S.C.R.).

[97] *Ibid.*, at 49-50 (S.C.R.). Because Korponay was represented by counsel, whose competence did not appear to be in issue, the Court indicated that the presiding judge was justified in assuming that the lawyer had discussed the matter with the accused and that the accused had made an informed decision after receiving the benefit of his lawyer's advice. *Ibid.*, at 52 (S.C.R.).

[98] See *Criminal Code*, s. 650.01.

[99] See *Criminal Code*, s. 536.2.

need only file a "Designation of Counsel" with the court and submit an "election-making document in writing."[100]

(g)   Accused's Loss of Election for Absconding

§9.46 Under section 598 of the *Code*, accused persons who have elected trial by judge and jury and fail to appear or remain in attendance at their trials forfeit their right to a jury trial unless: (*a*) they provide a "legitimate excuse"; [101] or (*b*) the Attorney General requires a jury trial under sections 568 or 569.[102] The hearing contemplated by section 598 may be held before any superior court judge. The trial judge may later reconsider that initial determination, but only if the request is based on new circumstances.[103]

§9.47 This provision has been narrowly construed. The Ontario Court of Appeal has held that "nothing less than an intentional avoidance of appearing at trial for the purpose of impeding or frustrating the trial or with the intention of avoiding its consequences, or failure to appear because of a mistake resulting from willful blindness, should deprive an accused of his constitutional right to trial by jury ...".[104]

§9.48 Although the Supreme Court of Canada has found that section 598 violates the accused's right to a jury trial, as guaranteed by section 11(*f*) of the *Charter*, it upheld the violation as a reasonable limit under section 1.[105]

3.   THE PRELIMINARY INQUIRY

(1)   Introduction

§9.49 At its inception, in sixteenth century England, the preliminary inquiry's purpose was investigatory. It was solely a vehicle by which the Crown could gather evidence against an accused. The accused had no participatory rights in this process, other than to be subject to compulsory questioning by the presiding justice of the peace.[106]

§9.50 By the middle of the nineteenth century, legislative reforms had transformed the preliminary inquiry from an investigative to a judicial process, in which the accused was entitled to be present, to be represented by counsel, to

---

[100] *R. v. Trites*, [2011] N.B.J. No. 12, 2011 NBCA 5 at para. 16 (N.B.C.A.). See also *ibid.*, at para. 22 (N.B.C.A.) (purported election ineffective when made by lawyer acting as agent for designated counsel without filing anything in writing).

[101] *Criminal Code*, s. 598(*a*).

[102] *Criminal Code*, s. 598(*b*). See also *R. v. Brown*, [2000] O.J. No. 2434, 146 C.C.C. (3d) 401 at para. 14 (Ont. C.A.) (onus on accused to satisfy the judge that there was a legitimate excuse for his failure to appear). The authority of the Attorney General to require a jury trial is set out in ss. 568 and 569 of the *Code*. This power is discussed above in Part 2(2)(*a*)(iv).

[103] *R. v. Brown*, [2000] O.J. No. 2434, 146 C.C.C. (3d) 401 at para. 27 (Ont. C.A.).

[104] *R. v. Harris*, [1991] O.J. No. 1509, 66 C.C.C. (3d) 536 at 539 (Ont. C.A.).

[105] See *R. v. Lee*, [1989] S.C.J. No. 125, [1989] 2 S.C.R. 1384 (S.C.C.).

[106] See Silas E. Halyk, "The Preliminary Inquiry in Canada" (1967-1968) 10 Crim. L.Q. 181 at 181-84.

cross-examine witnesses, not to be compelled to testify and to be discharged if the evidence was inadequate to justify a trial.[107] In other words, the preliminary inquiry was converted from a procedure meant to facilitate the investigation and prosecution of crime to a safeguard for the accused.

§9.51 It was the judicial version of the preliminary inquiry that the drafters of Canada's first *Criminal Code* adopted[108] and which continues today.[109] The modern preliminary inquiry is said to serve two purposes. At a formal level, it helps to protect the individual from the ordeal of prosecution where the state lacks sufficient evidence to warrant a trial.[110] On a practical level, it also gives the accused a measure of disclosure of the prosecution's case. This function was especially important in the pre-*Stinchcombe*[111] era, when the defence's ability to obtain disclosure of the prosecution's case prior to trial was limited.[112] Today, however, it is often described as ancillary or incidental to the charge screening function.[113]

(2)   A Preliminary Inquiry Must Be Requested

§9.52 Once automatic, today a preliminary inquiry only occurs if the accused or prosecutor requests one.[114] The request must be made either when the accused is

---

[107] *Ibid.*, at 185-86. The changes were occasioned by the *Indictable Offences Act, 1848*, (U.K.), 11 & 12 Vict., c. 42. See also Law Reform Commission of Canada, *Discovery in Criminal Cases (Working Paper No. 4)* (Ottawa: Queen's Printer, 1974) at 8.

[108] *Criminal Code*, S.C. 1892, c. 29, Part XLV. The preliminary inquiry was also part of Canadian law even before the *Criminal Code*, arriving in Canada in 1851. See David Pomerant & Glenn Gilmour, "Annex D History of the Preliminary Inquiry" in *A Survey of the Preliminary Inquiry in Canada* (Ottawa: Department of Justice, 1993) at 19.

[109] See *Criminal Code*, R.S.C. 1985, c. C-46, Part XVIII.

[110] *Ibid.* See especially *Criminal Code*, s. 548. From time to time the Supreme Court has identified this as the exclusive purpose of the preliminary inquiry. See *R. v. Caccamo*, [1975] S.C.J. No. 58, [1976] 1 S.C.R. 786 at 809-10 (S.C.C.); *R. v. Dubois*, [1986] S.C.J. No. 21, [1986] 1 S.C.R. 366 at para. 12 (S.C.C.); *R. v. Patterson*, [1970] S.C.J. No. 7, [1970] S.C.R. 409 at 412 (S.C.C.).

[111] In *R. v. Stinchcombe*, [1991] S.C.J. No. 83, [1991] 3 S.C.R. 326 (S.C.C.), the Supreme Court recognized that s. 7 of the *Charter* required that the Crown provide full disclosure to the defence of all relevant information in its possession or under its control. Disclosure is the subject of Chapter 7, which discusses in detail *Stinchcombe*'s impact on the criminal justice system in Canada.

[112] For a discussion of the important discovery benefits of the preliminary inquiry during the pre-Charter era, see G. Arthur Martin, Q.C.: "Preliminary Hearings", in *Special Lectures of the Law Society of Upper Canada, 1955* (Toronto: Richard De Boo, 1955) at 1.

[113] See *R. v. Hynes*, [2001] S.C.J. No. 80, [2001] 3 S.C.R. 623 at para. 31 (S.C.C.); *R. v. Skogman*, [1984] S.C.J. No. 32, [1984] 2 S.C.R. 93 at 105-106 (S.C.C.); *R. v. O'Connor*, [1995] S.C.J. No. 98, [1995] 4 S.C.R. 411 at para. 169 (S.C.C.); *R. v. Girimonte*, [1997] O.J. No. 4961, 121 C.C.C. (3d) 33 at para. 27 (Ont. C.A.); *R. v. Arviv*, [1985] O.J. No. 2602, 19 C.C.C. (3d) 395 at 403 (Ont. C.A.), leave to appeal refused [1985] S.C.C.A. No. 74, [1985] 1 S.C.R. v (S.C.C.).

[114] *Criminal Law Amendment Act, 2001*, S.C. 2002, c. 13 [*Criminal Law Amendment Act*], ss. 25-26. The undoubted motivation behind the request requirement was to reduce the incidence of preliminary inquiries. Unfortunately, the requirement does so "by exploiting the disorganization of some lawyers and the ignorance of unrepresented accused": David M. Paciocco, "A Voyage of Discovery: Examining the Precarious Condition of the Preliminary Inquiry" (2004) 48 Crim. L. Q. 151 at 184.

put to his or her election or within a period fixed by the rules of court.[115] In cases involving co-accused, if one or more accused requests it, a preliminary inquiry must be held with respect to all of them.[116]

(3) Specifying the Issues and Witnesses and the Focus Hearing

§9.53 At the same time that it introduced the request requirement, Parliament also made amendments to streamline the preliminary inquiry process.[117] Counsel for the party requesting a preliminary inquiry must now provide the opposing party and the court a statement that identifies: (*a*) the issues on which the requesting party wants evidence to be given at the inquiry; and (*b*) the witnesses that the requesting party wants to hear.[118] This obligation does not apply to unrepresented accused.[119] The statement must be provided within the period fixed by any rules of court or specified by the justice.[120]

§9.54 In addition, on the application of the prosecutor, accused or on the court's own motion, the court may convene what has come to be known as a "focus hearing". Such hearings are available in cases involving both represented and unrepresented accused.[121] The hearing's purpose is to: (*a*) assist the parties to identify the issues on which evidence will be given at the inquiry; (*b*) assist the parties to identify the witnesses to be heard at the inquiry, taking into account the witnesses' needs and circumstances; and (*c*) encourage the parties to consider any other matters that would promote a fair and expeditious inquiry.[122] At the end of hearing the justice must record any admissions of fact agreed to by the parties and any agreement reached by the parties.[123]

§9.55 Finally, section 536.5 of the *Code* states that whether or not a focus hearing is conducted, the parties may agree to limit the scope of the preliminary inquiry to specific issues. If they do, any agreement should either be recorded on the record or reduced to writing and filed with the court.[124]

§9.56 Although some commentators have opined that these amendments have brought an end to the preliminary inquiry's historic charge screening functions,[125] we do not agree. In our view, they simply serve to codify what has long been good practice. In many preliminary inquiries, it is obvious from the outset

---

[115] *Criminal Code*, s. 536(4). The courts within the various provinces and territories are all vested with the authority to make rules of court. See *Criminal Code*, s. 482.

[116] *Criminal Code*, s. 536(4.2).

[117] *Criminal Law Amendment Act, 2001*, S.C. 2002, s. 27.

[118] *Criminal Code*, s. 536.3.

[119] See *R. v. Gallant*, [2009] N.B.J. No. 409, 250 C.C.C. (3d) 29 at para. 41 (N.B.C.A.).

[120] *Criminal Code*, s. 536.3.

[121] *Ibid.*

[122] *Criminal Code*, s. 536.4(1).

[123] *Criminal Code*, s. 536.4(2).

[124] See *Criminal Code*, s. 536.5.

[125] See Stephen Coughlan, *Criminal Procedure* (Toronto: Irwin Law Inc., 2008) at 226-27.

that the accused will be committed to stand trial. In such cases, the defence's primary objective is discovery. And in many other cases where committal is in issue, the outcome will turn on a few discrete issues or even a single issue. The provisions simply encourage the parties to identify the real issues between them and formalize their shared understanding on the record.[126] Ultimately, as the New Brunswick Court of Appeal has noted, there nothing preventing the accused from "stating that all issues are live issues at the preliminary inquiry."[127] Nor, it added, do the amendments alter "the ultimate adjudicative responsibility of the preliminary inquiry justice to determine whether there is sufficient evidence to order the accused to stand trial or whether, on the whole of the evidence, the accused should be discharged."[128]

(4)   Powers and Procedure

§9.57 Part XVIII of the *Criminal Code* contemplates that a "justice" will preside over the preliminary inquiry. The *Code* defines "justice" as including either a justice of the peace or a provincial court judge.[129] In virtually every jurisdiction, however, it is almost always provincial court judges who conduct preliminary inquiries.

§9.58 Justices conducting preliminary inquiries have no inherent jurisdiction.[130] They are entirely creatures of statute and their powers are therefore limited to those expressly granted by the provisions found within Part XVIII of the *Criminal Code* as well any additional powers that flow from these provisions by necessary implication.[131] As explained below, this conclusion has significant constitutional implications.

---

[126]   The New Brunswick Court of Appeal has helpfully explained how this should work:
> If the real issue in a particular case is, for example, identification, an accused might, through counsel, provide the court and the prosecutor with a statement identifying this issue as the one on which evidence is required to be given at the inquiry and listing the witnesses the accused wants to hear (s. 536.3). In doing so, counsel would likely agree under s. 536.5 to limit the scope of the inquiry to the specific issue of identification and would file an agreement with the court to that effect. Thus, the presiding justice would only have to determine if there was some evidence on the issue of identification, which, if believed, could result in a conviction.

See *R. v. Gallant*, [2009] N.B.J. No. 409, 250 C.C.C. (3d) 29 at para. 36 (N.B.C.A.).
[127]   *Ibid.*, at para. 29 (C.C.C.).
[128]   *Ibid.*, at para. 37 (C.C.C.).
[129]   See *Criminal Code*, s. 2.
[130]   See *e.g.*, *R. v. Deschamplain*, [2004] S.C.J. No. 73, [2004] 3 S.C.R. 601 at para. 12 (S.C.C.) ("the jurisdiction of a preliminary inquiry judge is statutory and not inherent").
[131]   See *R. v. Hynes*, [2001] S.C.J. No. 80, [2001] 3 S.C.R. 623 at para. 28 (S.C.C.) ("The powers of a preliminary inquiry justice are entirely statutory, and therefore the power to grant the remedy sought must derive expressly or impliedly from its enabling legislation, namely Part XVIII of the *Criminal Code*."). See also *R. v. Dubois*, [1975] B.C.J. No. 980, 29 C.R.N.S. 220 at para. 14 (B.C.S.C.); *R. v. Mills*, [1986] S.C.J. No. 39, [1986] 1 S.C.R. 863 at 954-55 (S.C.C.); *R. v. Seaboyer; R. v. Gayme*, [1991] S.C.J. No. 62, [1991] 2 S.C.R. 577 at 638-39 (S.C.C.); *R. v. Doyle*, [1976] S.C.J. No. 38, [1977] 1 S.C.R. 597 at 602 (S.C.C.).

§9.59 The boundaries of the justice's authority are consequently strictly delineated by the *Code*. The key provision is section 537, which gives the justice powers to: adjourn the inquiry from time to time;[132] change the location of the hearing where it is desirable to do so, for instance to accommodate a witness;[133] remand an accused, not on bail, in custody;[134] resume the inquiry before its scheduled return date with the consent of the parties;[135] order that an accused be brought before the justice or any other justice for the same territorial division prior to a previously scheduled remand date;[136] grant or refuse permission to the prosecutor to make an opening or closing statement, including summing up in response to any evidence called by an accused;[137] exclude all members of the public from the courtroom where the justice considers that it would serve the ends of justice to do so;[138] where the prosecutor and accused agree, allow the accused to appear by closed-circuit television unless the evidence of a witness is being taken;[139] and permit the accused, on his or her request, to be out of court during the whole or any part of the inquiry on any conditions that the justice considers appropriate.[140]

§9.60 Other powers are scattered throughout Part XVIII, and in a few instances, elsewhere in the *Code*. For example, section 523(2)(*b*) provides that if an

---

[132] *Criminal Code*, s. 537(1)(*a*). With respect to hybrid offences, which are presumed to be indictable until the Crown makes its formal election either way, this provision has been held to confer jurisdiction on a justice to adjourn such matters from time to time. See also *R. v. Gougeon*, [1980] O.J. No. 1342, 55 C.C.C. (2d) 218 at 234-35 (Ont. C.A.), leave to appeal refused (1980), 35 N.R. 83*n* (S.C.C.).

[133] *Ibid.* If the justice orders the inquiry moved to a different territorial division within the province than that in which the justice has jurisdiction, any justice who has jurisdiction in the place to which the hearing is changed may continue the hearing. See *Criminal Code*, s. 537(2).

[134] *Criminal Code*, s. 537(1)(*c*), the justice is to do so by warrant in Form 19.

[135] *Criminal Code*, s. 537(1)(*d*).

[136] *Criminal Code*, s. 537(1)(*e*), the justice is to do so in writing using Form 30.

[137] *Criminal Code*, s. 537(1)(*f*). There is, however, no parallel provision with respect to an accused making either an opening or closing statement. Accordingly, it has been held that a justice has no discretion to refuse counsel for the accused the fundamental right to make submissions. Such a refusal has been characterized as a denial of natural justice and resulted in a committal to trial being quashed on review. See *R. v. Taillefer*, [1978] O.J. No. 968, 42 C.C.C. (2d) 282 (Ont. C.A.).

[138] *Criminal Code*, s. 537(1)(*h*). See also *R. v. S. (N.)*, [2010] O.J. No. 4306, 262 C.C.C. (3d) 4 at para. 33 (Ont. C.A.), leave to appeal granted [2010] S.C.C.A. No. 494 (S.C.C.) (in deciding whether or not to make such an order, "the preliminary inquiry judge will inevitably be required to address values underlying a variety of constitutional rights, potentially including those protected by s. 2(*b*) (freedom of expression), s. 8 (privacy rights), and s. 11(*d*) (fair trial rights)"); *Armstrong v. Wisconsin (State)*, [1972] O.J. No. 1841, 7 C.C.C. (2d) 331 (Ont. H.C.J.) (before excluding public, justice should, if possible, conduct hearing in presence of counsel and accused and ensure record reflects terms of and reasons for any order); *R. v. Sayegh (No. 1)*, [1982] O.J. No. 3648, 66 C.C.C. (2d) 430 (Ont. Prov. Ct.) (public excluded because publication ban alone inadequate to protect accused's fair trial as American media present in courtroom); *R. v. Vaudrin*, [1982] B.C.J. No. 1841, 2 C.C.C. (3d) 214 (B.C.S.C.) (speculation that persons in public gallery will intimidate or communicate with witnesses insufficient basis for order).

[139] *Criminal Code*, s. 537(1)(*j*).

[140] *Criminal Code*, s. 537(1)(*e*), the justice is to do so in writing using Form 30.

accused is ordered to stand trial after a preliminary inquiry, and is not charged with a section 469 offence, the presiding judge or justice may vacate any bail order previously made "on cause being shown" and "make any other order ... for the detention or release of the accused until his trial is completed" that the judge or justice "considers to be warranted".[141] This provision is discussed in further detail in Chapter 6, Part 3(11)(*c*), which deals with bail. Some of the more significant powers possessed by a justice enumerated in section 537, other sections of Part XVIII, and elsewhere in the *Code* are given separate treatment below.

(a)   Publication Bans

§9.61   The *Code* contains several provisions relating to the publishing or broadcasting of evidence or other information relating to a preliminary inquiry. Most important is the standard publication ban that is ordered at almost all preliminary inquiries. Section 539(1) of the *Code* provides that before any evidence is led the justice "may" (if the application is made by the prosecutor)[142] and "shall" (if the application is made by any accused),[143] prohibit the publishing or broadcasting of the evidence taken at the inquiry until the accused is either discharged[144] or, if ordered to stand trial, the trial is ended.[145] Where an accused is unrepresented, the justice must also inform the accused of the right to apply for a publication ban.[146] It is a summary conviction offence to wilfully fail to comply with a publication ban order.[147] The constitutionality of section 539(1) has been upheld as a reasonable limit on the right to freedom of the press guaranteed by section 2(b) of the *Charter*.[148]

automatic ban

§9.62   There is also an automatic ban prohibiting in all cases the publishing or broadcasting of the fact that an admission or confession was tendered in evidence at the preliminary inquiry or a report of the nature of such admission or confession.[149] The purpose of this prohibition is obvious: to protect the fair trial rights of the accused. News of a confession could prejudice prospective jurors, a danger that is especially great when the confession is ultimately excluded at trial. This ban remains in effect until the accused is either discharged[150] or, if

---

[141]   *Criminal Code*, s. 523(2)(*b*).

[142]   *Criminal Code*, s. 539(1)(*a*).

[143]   *Criminal Code*, s. 539(1)(*b*).

[144]   *Criminal Code*, s. 539(1)(*c*).

[145]   *Criminal Code*, s. 539(1)(*d*). If the Crown stays the charges against the accused following the preliminary inquiry, "the trial is ended" and the publication ban is thereafter no longer in effect. See *British Columbia College of Teachers v. British Columbia (Ministry of Attorney General)*, [2010] B.C.J. No. 1152, 256 C.C.C. (3d) 345 (B.C.S.C.) [*College of Teachers*].

[146]   *Criminal Code*, s. 539(2).

[147]   *Criminal Code*, s. 539(4).

[148]   See *R. v. Banville*, [1983] N.B.J. No. 110, 3 C.C.C. (3d) 312 (N.B.Q.B.). See also *Toronto Star Newspapers Ltd. v. Canada*, [2010] S.C.J. No. 21, [2010] 1 S.C.R. 721 (S.C.C.) (upholding analogous provision in s. 517 governing publication bans at bail hearings).

[149]   *Criminal Code*, s. 542(2).

[150]   *Criminal Code*, s. 542(2)(*a*).

ordered to stand trial, the trial is ended.[151] Violating this prohibition is a summary offence.[152]

§9.63 Finally, there are also a number publication ban provisions found elsewhere in the *Code* that confer jurisdiction on a "presiding judge or justice" to order bans on publication or broadcasting in certain enumerated circumstances. For example, a ban can be ordered with respect to information that would identify a complainant or a witness under the age of 18 years in cases where an accused is charged with an enumerated sexual offence.[153] These provisions appear to be equally applicable to a justice who is presiding at a preliminary inquiry.[154] The relevant provisions and the potential orders that can be made are more fully explained in Chapter 16, Part 3(1).

(b) Authority to Regulate the Inquiry

§9.64 To the extent that there is anything in Part XVIII resembling a plenary grant of power to a preliminary inquiry justice, it is found in section 537(1)(*i*), which provides that a justice may:

> regulate the course of the inquiry in any way that appears to the justice to be consistent with this Act and that, unless the justice is satisfied that to do so would be contrary to the best interests of the administration of justice, is in accordance with any admission of fact or agreement recorded under subsection 536.4(2) or agreement made under s. 536.5.[155]

§9.65 As the Ontario Court of Appeal has noted, this section may be invoked "to fill procedural gaps" that may arise during the inquiry.[156] It allows a justice, the Court held, to "implement procedures which are not inconsistent with the Act and will allow the justice to effectively carry out his or her mandate."[157] For example, courts have concluded that the provision grants the presiding justice the authority to: make security arrangements (including ordering the accused to remain shackled during the inquiry);[158] disqualify counsel from acting based on a conflict of interest;[159] compel a witness to testify, answer questions or produce documents for the purpose of cross-examination of that witness;[160] recall

---

[151] *Criminal Code*, s. 542(2)(*b*).

[152] *Criminal Code*, s. 542(2).

[153] See *e.g.*, *Criminal Code*, s. 486.4(1).

[154] See *e.g.*, *British Columbia College of Teachers v. British Columbia (Ministry of Attorney General)*, [2010] B.C.J. No. 1152, 256 C.C.C. (3d) 345 (B.C.S.C.).

[155] *Criminal Code*, s. 537(1)(*i*).

[156] *R. v. Girimonte*, [1997] O.J. No. 4961, 121 C.C.C. (3d) 33 at para. 24 (Ont. C.A.). See also *R. v. Swystun*, [1990] S.J. No. 287, 84 Sask. R. 238 at 239 (Sask. C.A.).

[157] *R. v. Girimonte*, [1997] O.J. No. 4961, 121 C.C.C. (3d) 33 at para. 24 (Ont. C.A.).

[158] See *R. v. McNeil*, [1996] O.J. No. 2488, 108 C.C.C. (3d) 364 (Ont. C.A.) (when issue is raised, justice must conduct hearing to determine, based on evidence and counsel's submissions, what is necessary to strike balance between safety concerns and need to maintain accused's dignity in light of presumption of innocence).

[159] See *R. v. Robillard*, [1986] O.J. No. 261, 28 C.C.C. (3d) 22 (Ont. C.A.) (pointing to predecessor provision in holding that presiding justice has power and duty to prevent conflict of interest).

[160] See *R. v. Girimonte*, [1997] O.J. No. 4961, 121 C.C.C. (3d) 33 at para. 25 (Ont. C.A.).

witnesses because of a malfunction in recording equipment;[161] allow the accused to sit in the public part of the courtroom (in cases where identity is at sue);[162] permit a witness to sit while giving evidence;[163] allow a witness to testify through an interpreter;[164] and direct an inappropriately attired witness to change before giving evidence.[165] In addition, in our view, it is this provision that authorizes a justice to exclude witnesses from the courtroom until they testify.[166]

§9.66 The authority conferred by section 537(1)(*i*) also has its limits. For example, courts have concluded that this provision does not empower a preliminary inquiry justice to: compel production of a witness's police statement;[167] sever co-accused;[168] exclude some members of the public from the courtroom but not others;[169] order particulars;[170] appoint counsel;[171] direct the Crown to call particular witnesses;[172] prevent the Crown from calling further witnesses once the justice concludes a *prima facie* case is established;[173] and, as explained more fully immediately below, grant constitutional remedies.

---

[161] *R. v. Swystun*, [1990] S.J. No. 287, 84 Sask. R. 238 (Sask. C.A.).

[162] See *R. v. Vaudrin*, [1982] B.C.J. No. 1841, 2 C.C.C. (3d) 214 (B.C.S.C.) (recognizing this discretion but concluding that refusal to allow it does not amount to jurisdictional error justifying review by superior court on application for *certiorari*). See also *R. v. Dubois*, [1975] B.C.J. No. 980, 29 C.R.N.S. 220 (B.C.S.C.) (outlining the mechanics of such procedure when allowed). But see *R. v. Grant*, [1973] O.J. No. 2363, 13 C.C.C. (2d) 495 (Ont. H.C.J.) (disapproving of the practice).

[163] *R. v. S. (N.)*, [2010] O.J. No. 4306, 262 C.C.C. (3d) 4 at para. 39 (Ont. C.A.), leave to appeal granted [2010] S.C.C.A. No. 494 (S.C.C.).

[164] *Ibid.*

[165] *Ibid.*, at para. 40 (C.C.C.).

[166] The case law makes clear that such an order should be made upon request of counsel unless grounds are shown why the justice should not make the order. See *R. v. Learn*, [1981] O.J. No. 922, 63 C.C.C. (2d) 191 (Ont. H.C.J.) See also *R. v. Collette*, [1983] O.J. No. 1111, 6 C.C.C. (3d) 300 (Ont. H.C.J.), affd [1983] O.J. No. 3332, 7 C.C.C. (3d) 574 (Ont. C.A.) (order should be made when requested and unopposed and credibility is in issue). But note that in *Collette* the Court pointed to the predecessor to s. 537(1)(*h*) as supplying authority to make such an order. On a plain reading, the current provision only supplies the authority to exclude *all* members of the public, contemplating, as it does, that the "the prosecutor, the accused and their counsel" will be exempt from the order made. In our view, the provision that is more sensibly construed as authorizing the exclusion of witnesses is s. 537(1)(*i*).

[167] See *R. v. Patterson*, [1970] S.C.J. No. 7, [1970] S.C.R. 409 (S.C.C.) (under the predecessor provision).

[168] See *R. v. Poitras*, [1976] M.J. No. 199, 32 C.C.C. (2d) 184 (Man. Q.B.) (under the predecessor provision).

[169] See *R. v. Sayegh (No. 2)*, [1982] O.J. No. 3649, 66 C.C.C. (2d) 432 (Ont. Prov. Ct.) (under predecessor provision, excluding American journalists from courtroom who would not have been bound by publication ban). But see *R. v. Sayegh (No. 1)*, [1982] O.J. No. 3648, 66 C.C.C. (2d) 430 (Ont. Prov. Ct.) (ordering exclusion of all members of public).

[170] See *R. v. Chew*, [1967] O.J. No. 1092, [1968] 2 C.C.C. 127 (Ont. C.A.) (under the predecessor provision).

[171] See *R. v. Farewell*, [2006] O.J. No. 2282, 81 O.R. (3d) 375 (Ont. C.J.).

[172] See *R. v. Brass*, [1981] S.J. No. 1030, 64 C.C.C. (2d) 206 (Sask. Q.B.) (nothing in *Code* supplied such authority). See also *R. v. Caccamo*, [1975] S.C.J. No. 58, [1976] 1 S.C.R. 786 at 810 (S.C.C.) ("Crown has the discretion to present only that evidence which makes out *a prima facie* case").

[173] See *R. v. Schreder*, [1987] N.W.T.J. No. 84, 36 C.C.C. (3d) 216 at 222-23 (N.W.T.S.C.) (rejecting claim that what is now s. 537(1)(*i*) supplied such authority).

(c) Not a "Court of Competent Jurisdiction" for Charter Purposes

§9.67 The Supreme Court of Canada has twice considered whether a justice presiding at a preliminary inquiry qualifies as a "court of competent jurisdiction" for section 24 *Charter* purposes.[174] On both occasions, a majority of justices concluded that they are not courts of competent jurisdiction for any purpose under section 24 and therefore cannot grant stays of proceedings under section 24(1)[175] or exclude unconstitutionally obtained evidence under section 24(2).[176] This conclusion was reached despite the fact that preliminary inquiry justices frequently apply common law exclusionary rules, including the confessions rule.[177] Similarly, a justice presiding at a preliminary inquiry lacks the authority to strike down legislation under section 52(1) of the *Constitution Act, 1982*.[178]

§9.68 Despite their legislated authority to "regulate the course of the inquiry"[179] (discussed above), this lack of jurisdiction to grant constitutional remedies means that a justice presiding at a preliminary inquiry cannot order disclosure,[180] award costs for late disclosure,[181] compel the production of third party records[182] or order the appointment of counsel.[183]

§9.69 Although preliminary inquiry justices lack authority to order constitutional remedies, this does not mean that they operate in a *Charter*-free zone. The Ontario Court of Appeal has held that they must exercise their statutory powers "in accordance with the *Charter*" and "render decisions that reflect an

---

[174] See *R. v. Mills*, [1986] S.C.J. No. 39, [1986] 1 S.C.R. 863 (S.C.C.) and *R. v. Hynes*, [2001] S.C.J. No. 80, [2001] 3 S.C.R. 623 (S.C.C.). See also *R. v. Conway*, [2010] S.C.J. No. 22, [2010] 1 S.C.R. 765 at paras. 24, 25, 38 (S.C.C.) (summarizing this jurisprudence). We discuss the "court of competent jurisdiction" issue generally in Chapter 10, Part 3(4).

[175] See *R. v. Mills*, [1986] S.C.J. No. 39, [1986] 1 S.C.R. 863 at 889 (S.C.C.), *per* Lamer J.; 954-56 (S.C.R.), *per* McIntyre J., 970-71 (S.C.R.), *per* La Forest J.

[176] See *R. v. Hynes*, [2001] S.C.J. No. 80, [2001] 3 S.C.R. 623 at paras. 33-43 (S.C.C.).

[177] See *Criminal Code*, s. 542(1); *R. v. Hynes*, [2001] S.C.J. No. 80, [2001] 3 S.C.R. 623 at paras. 32, 47 (S.C.C.); *R. v. Mills*, [1986] S.C.J. No. 39, [1986] 1 S.C.R. 863 at 889-90 (S.C.C.), Lamer J., dissenting; *R. v. R. (L.)*, [1995] O.J. No. 1381, 100 C.C.C. (3d) 329 at 340 (Ont. C.A.).

[178] *Canadian Charter of Rights and Freedoms*, Part I of the *Constitution Act, 1982*, being Schedule B to the *Canada Act 1982* (U.K.), 1982, c. 11 [*Charter*]. See *R. v. Seaboyer; R. v. Gayme*, [1991] S.C.J. No. 62, [1991] 2 S.C.R. 577 at 637-39 (S.C.C.).

[179] *Criminal Code*, s. 537(1)(*i*).

[180] See *R. v. Girimonte*, [1997] O.J. No. 4961, 121 C.C.C. (3d) 33 (Ont. C.A.).

[181] See *R. v. Howard*, [2009] P.E.I.J. No. 66, 250 C.C.C. (3d) 102 (P.E.I.C.A.).

[182] See *R. v. O'Connor*, [1995] S.C.J. No. 98, [1995] 4 S.C.R. 411 (S.C.C.), *per* L'Heureux-Dubé J. But see *R. v. R. (L.)*, [1995] O.J. No. 1381, 100 C.C.C. (3d) 329 (Ont. C.A.). See also *R. v. Verma*, [1996] O.J. No. 2621, 1 C.R. (5th) 177 (Ont. Gen. Div.) (observing that *O'Connor* effectively overruled *R. (L.)* on this question). See also *Criminal Code*, where the application relates to a "record" as defined in s. 278.1, s. 278.3(2) expressly precludes such applications being made to a judge or justice presiding at a preliminary inquiry.

[183] *R. v. Farewell*, [2006] O.J. No. 2282, 81 O.R. (3d) 375 (Ont. C.J.). See *contra*, *Canada (Attorney General) v. Garand*, [1992] Y.J. No. 184 (Y.K.S.C.).

appropriate reconciliation" of competing *Charter* values."[184] In *R. v. S. (N.)*,[185] the Court found that section 537(1)(*i*) empowers justices to make orders directed at witnesses, including an order to remove a face covering. In deciding whether to make such an order, however, justices must consider the accused's right to make full answer and defence (including the right to fully cross-examine the witness) in light of the witness's right to freedom of religion.[186]

§9.70 Finally, it should be remembered that although a preliminary inquiry justice lacks jurisdiction to grant constitutional remedies, superior courts have "constant, complete and concurrent jurisdiction"[187] under the *Charter*. The Supreme Court of Canada has cautioned, however, that the superior court should decline to intervene unless it is better suited than the trial court to assess and grant a just and appropriate remedy. In that regard, the Court has in mind cases "where there is as yet no trial court within reach and the timeliness of the remedy or the need to prevent a continuing violation of rights is shown, and those where it is the process below itself which is alleged to be in violation of the *Charter*'s guarantees."[188] For example, though the preliminary inquiry justice lacks jurisdiction to order disclosure, he or she may adjourn the inquiry to allow a disclosure application to be brought in the superior court.[189]

(d)   *Continuing in Absence of an Absconding Accused*

§9.71 Should an accused "abscond during the course of a preliminary inquiry" the *Code* deems the accused to have waived his or her right to be present[190] and entitles the presiding justice to either continue the inquiry in the accused's

---

[184] *R. v. S. (N.)*, [2010] O.J. No. 4306, 262 C.C.C. (3d) 4 at para. 36 (Ont. C.A.), leave to appeal granted [2010] S.C.C.A. No. 494 (S.C.C.).

[185] [2010] O.J. No. 4306, 262 C.C.C. (3d) 4 (Ont. C.A.), leave to appeal granted [2010] S.C.C.A. No. 494 (S.C.C.).

[186] *Ibid.*

[187] *R. v. Mills*, [1986] S.C.J. No. 39, [1986] 1 S.C.R. 863 at para. 61 (S.C.C.), Lamer J., dissenting.

[188] *R. v. Rahey*, [1987] S.C.J. No. 23, [1987] 1 S.C.R. 588 at 603-604 (S.C.C.). See also *R. v. Smith*, [1989] S.C.J. No. 119, [1989] 2 S.C.R. 1120 (S.C.C.). This issue is discussed more extensively in Chapter 10, Part 3(2).

[189] In *R. v. Girimonte*, [1997] O.J. No. 4961, 121 C.C.C. (3d) 33 at para. 42 (Ont. C.A.), the Court explained the available options where there are difficulties with disclosure as follows:

> In rare cases, the Crown will not have provided sufficient disclosure to allow the accused to make a reasonably informed election. If the Crown takes the position that the requested disclosure will be made, but requests further time to make that disclosure, a justice should adjourn the taking of the election and allow the Crown a reasonable time to fulfill its disclosure obligations. If the time needed to make proper disclosure is inordinate, any delay in the proceedings will count against the Crown. If there is a true disclosure dispute, that is the Crown refuses to produce material which the defence claims should be produced and is essential to the making of an informed election, a justice may adjourn the taking of the election to allow the accused to seek the appropriate remedy in the superior court. If it turns out that the Crown has improperly withheld disclosure, any delay caused by the bringing of that application in the superior court will count against the Crown.

[190] *Criminal Code*, s. 544(1)(*a*).

absence[191] or issue a warrant for the accused's arrest and adjourn the inquiry pending his or her appearance.[192] The use of the verb "abscond" has been held to restrict the availability of this section "to the accused who voluntarily absents himself or herself from a preliminary inquiry."[193] Nevertheless, the British Columbia Court of Appeal has held that once an accused makes his or her election, the failure thereafter to attend on the date scheduled for the preliminary inquiry is sufficient to trigger this section.[194] The *Code* also directs the justice to draw an adverse inference against the absconding accused.[195] Should the accused reappear at the preliminary inquiry, the *Code* precludes the reopening of those portions of the inquiry that occurred in the accused's absence unless the justice "is satisfied that because of exceptional circumstances it is in the interest of justice to re-open the inquiry."[196]

§9.72 Where the accused who absconds is represented by counsel and the inquiry continues in the accused's absence, counsel may "continue to act for the accused in the proceedings."[197] This specifically includes the right to "call witnesses on behalf of the accused."[198] The lawyer may nevertheless feel ethically compelled to withdraw in such circumstances given that he or she will be unable to obtain instructions from the accused.

(5) Witnesses and Evidence

§9.73 There are a number of provisions in Part XVIII bearing on the testimony of witnesses at the preliminary inquiry and the admissibility of their evidence. Some of these apply equally to both parties; others are specifically directed at either the prosecution or the accused.

(a) *Testimony Under Oath and Recorded*

§9.74 Witnesses at the preliminary inquiry must testify under oath or affirmation[199] and their evidence must be recorded.[200] Although the *Code* permits testimony by deposition[201] (a written statement signed by the witness), this method is obsolete. Instead, the evidence is recorded by a court reporter (by stenography or audio recording), who later produces a certified transcript of the proceeding that can be used at trial.[202]

---

191 *Criminal Code*, s. 544(1)(*b*)(i).
192 *Criminal Code*, s. 544(1)(*b*)(ii).
193 *R. v. Sokoluk*, [1992] A.J. No. 24, 128 A.R. 120 at para. 25 (Alta. Q.B.).
194 See *R. v. Plummer*, [1983] B.C.J. No. 2308, 5 C.C.C. (3d) 17 (B.C.C.A.).
195 *Criminal Code*, s. 544(2).
196 *Criminal Code*, s. 544(3).
197 *Criminal Code*, s. 544(4).
198 *Criminal Code*, s. 544(5).
199 See *Criminal Code*, s. 540(1)(*a*) and s. 541(5).
200 See *Criminal Code*, s. 540(1)(*b*).
201 See *Criminal Code*, s. 540(1)(*b*)(i).
202 See *Criminal Code*, ss. 540(5), (6).

(b) Measures to Assist Witnesses

§9.75 Parliament has recently made explicit a power that preliminary inquiry justices have long exercised as part of their authority to regulate the course of the inquiry.[203] Section 537(1.1) states that a justice "shall order the immediate cessation of any part of an examination or cross-examination of a witness that is, in the opinion of the justice, abusive, too repetitive or otherwise inappropriate."

§9.76 Because preliminary inquiries constitute "proceedings against an ac-cused", the various measures found in the *Code* for easing the ordeal of child witnesses apply equally at these hearings. Child witnesses may therefore testify behind a protective screen or outside the courtroom via a video link.[204] They may also have a support person present while giving evidence.[205] Under these provi-sions, adult witnesses may be treated similarly where the presiding justice is satisfied that it is "necessary to obtain a full and candid account from the witness of the acts complained of."[206]

(c) Measures for Dealing with Recalcitrant Witnesses

§9.77 Finally, because preliminary inquiries are creatures of statute, the presid-ing justice has no inherent power to summarily punish a recalcitrant witness for contempt of court.[207] Instead, the justice's authority to deal with such a witness is limited and defined by section 545 of the *Code*, which empowers the justice to adjourn the proceedings and jail the witness for a period not exceeding eight clear days.[208] If the witness continues to refuse to cooperate after being brought back before the justice, the justice may commit the person to custody again for a period not exceeding eight clear days.[209] This process may continue "until the person consents to do what is required of him".[210] Alternatively, the justice may proceed with the inquiry without the recalcitrant witness and commit the ac-cused to stand trial on any other sufficient evidence that is taken.[211]

§9.78 A witness committed to custody under this provision may not be subse-quently prosecuted for contempt of court or obstructing justice.[212] But where the

---

[203] See §9.64, above.

[204] See *Criminal Code*, s. 486.2(1). This provision has been upheld as constitutional by the Su-preme Court of Canada. See *R. v. Levogiannis*, [1993] S.C.J. No. 70, [1993] 4 S.C.R. 475 (S.C.C.).

[205] See *Criminal Code*, s. 486.1(1).

[206] See *Criminal Code*, ss. 486.1(2) and 486.2(2).

[207] See *R. v. Bubley*, [1976] A.J. No. 553, 32 C.C.C. (2d) 79 (Alta. C.A.).

[208] *Criminal Code*, s. 545(1) (authorizing committal to prison where witness "(*a*) refuses to be sworn, (*b*) having been sworn, refuses to answer the questions that are put to him, (*c*) fails to produce any writings that he is required to produce, or (*d*) refuses to sign his deposition, with-out offering a reasonable excuse for his failure or refusal"). The committal is in Form 20.

[209] *Criminal Code*, s. 545(2).

[210] *Ibid.*

[211] *Ibid.*

[212] See *R. v. McKenzie*, [1978] A.J. No. 968, 41 C.C.C. (2d) 394 (Alta. C.A.); *R. v. Mercer*, [1988] A.J. No. 709, 43 C.C.C. (3d) 347 (Alta. C.A.).

justice refrains from jailing the witness such a prosecution would not be barred by the double jeopardy principle.[213]

(d) Defence Cross-Examining Crown Witnesses

§9.79 The *Code* specifically authorizes the accused (or his or her counsel) to cross-examine Crown witnesses at the preliminary inquiry.[214] This has been characterized as a "fundamental right",[215] entitling the accused to conduct a "full, detailed and careful cross-examination".[216] Such cross-examination is not limited to testing the adequacy of the evidence in terms of committal. Rather, as Justice Arbour has explained, "the right to explore, at that early stage, the credibility of the Crown's witnesses and the availability of potential defences is still an important aspect of the right to make full answer and defence."[217]

§9.80 The case law therefore makes clear that an accused may cross-examine to lay the foundation for securing the exclusion of evidence at trial. For example, where the Crown decides to forego reliance on an accused's statement, the defence may still cross-examine the police officers as to the circumstances surrounding the taking of the statement.[218] Similarly, the accused may cross-examine Crown witnesses to lay the foundation for a *Charter* argument at trial.[219] As the Ontario Court of Appeal has noted, "[i]t is now commonplace to have examinations of witnesses at preliminary hearings on all aspects of potential *Charter* violations."[220] For example, it has been held that an accused may cross-examine the complainant at the preliminary inquiry to lay the foundation for a third-party records application at trial.[221] The accused is not, however, permitted

---

[213] See *R. v. Lacroix*, [1987] S.C.J. No. 17, [1987] 1 S.C.R. 244 (S.C.C.). Double jeopardy is discussed in Chapter 14, Part 3.

[214] *Criminal Code*, s. 540(1)(*a*).

[215] *R. v. B. (E.)*, [2002] O.J. No. 75, 162 C.C.C. (3d) 451 at para. 46 (Ont. C.A.), leave to appeal refused [2003] 1 S.C.R. xvi (S.C.C.).

[216] *R. v. Durette*, [1979] O.J. No. 862, 47 C.C.C. (2d) 170 at 172 (Ont. H.C.J.). So, for example, a magistrate's decision to set an arbitrary time limit on the length of counsel's cross-examination was held to constitute a refusal to exercise jurisdiction and led to the issuance of a writ of *mandamus*. See *R. v. Roulette*, [1972] M.J. No. 109, 7 C.C.C. (2d) 244 (Man. Q.B.).

[217] *R. v. R. (L.)*, [1995] O.J. No. 1381, 100 C.C.C. (3d) 329 at para. 13 (Ont. C.A.). See also *R. v. McGrath*, [2007] N.S.J. No. 363, 225 C.C.C. (3d) 1 (N.S.S.C.).

[218] See *Barnett v. Williams*, [1970] O.J. No. 1719, 2 C.C.C. (2d) 298 (Ont. H.C.J); *R. v. Bélanger*, [1988] J.Q. no 2012, 68 C.R. (3d) 67 (Que. C.A.).

[219] See *R. v. Dawson*, [1998] O.J. No. 1039, 123 C.C.C. (3d) 385 (Ont. C.A.) (same rules applying to cross-examination of wiretap affiant at trial apply at preliminary inquiry); *R. v. George*, [1991] O.J. No. 1704, 69 C.C.C. (3d) 148 at 152 (Ont. C.A.) ("It is now recognized that an accused is entitled to cross-examine Crown witnesses at a preliminary hearing relating to such matters as *Charter* defences which are not of concern to the judge conducting the hearing."). But see *R. v. Pham*, [2008] B.C.J. No. 2041, 178 C.R.R. (2d) 262 at para. 32 (B.C.S.C.) ("cross-examination of Crown witnesses at a preliminary inquiry directed exclusively to discovering evidence that might be useful on a *Charter* application for exclusion of evidence at trial is not appropriate").

[220] *R. v. Dawson*, [1998] O.J. No. 1039, 123 C.C.C. (3d) 385 at para. 13 (Ont. C.A.).

[221] See *R. v. B. (E.)*, [2002] O.J. No. 75, 162 C.C.C. (3d) 451 at para. 46 (Ont. C.A.), leave to appeal refused [2003] 1 S.C.R. xvi (S.C.C.) (noting limits on extent of permissible probing). See

to call the record holder at the preliminary inquiry and thereby circumvent the legislative regime for gaining access to such records at trial.[222]

§9.81 The right to cross-examine is also limited by provisions in other parts of the *Code*. For example, under section 486.3, an order may be granted in "proceedings against an accused" (which include preliminary inquiries) prohibiting the accused from personally cross-examining child or adult witnesses.[223]

(e) Address to the Unrepresented Accused

§9.82 After the prosecution finishes calling its witnesses,[224] the justice must address an accused not represented by counsel as follows:

[handwritten margin note: A not represented by counsel]

> Do you wish to say anything in answer to these charges or to any other charges which might have arisen from the evidence led by the prosecution? You are not obliged to say anything, but whatever you do say may be given in evidence against you at your trial. You should not make any confession or admission of guilt because of any promise or threat made to you but if you do make any statement it may be given in evidence against you at your trial in spite of the promise or threat.[225]

This address to the accused is read only once no matter how many offences the accused is charged with.[226] To give the accused fair notice of his or her jeopardy, the justice may also apprise the accused of the other charges that the justice believes might have arisen from the evidence led by the prosecution.[227] After reading the address and ensuring that anything said is recorded,[228] the justice must also ask the accused if he or she wishes to call any witnesses.[229]

§9.83 In practice, it is extraordinarily rare for an accused to make a statement in response to this address. This is understandable, given the absence of any benefit in doing so. For example, though anything incriminating said by the accused

---

also *R. v. O'Connor*, [1995] S.C.J. No. 98, [1995] 4 S.C.R. 411 at para. 146 (S.C.C.), *per* L'Heureux-Dubé J. ("In establishing the required evidentiary basis, the applicant may resort to the Crown's disclosure, to its own witnesses, and to cross-examination of the Crown witnesses at both the preliminary inquiry and the trial."); *R. v. Mills*, [1999] S.C.J. No. 68, [1999] 3 S.C.R. 668 at para. 124 (S.C.C.).

[222] See *R. v. B. (S.A.)*, [1998] B.C.J. No. 3087 (B.C.S.C.).

[223] See *Criminal Code*, 486.3. This provision displaces case law holding that an accused had the right, even if represented by counsel, to personally cross-examine witnesses at the preliminary inquiry. See *e.g.*, *R. v. Zaor*, [1984] J.Q. no 171, 12 C.C.C. (3d) 265 (Que. C.A.).

[224] See *R. v. Jenkins*, [1996] O.J. No. 2674, 108 C.C.C. (3d) 565 (Ont. Gen. Div.) (justice committed jurisdictional error by reading the warning to the accused once he concluded that the prosecution had adduced sufficient evidence to establish a *prima facie* case). See also *R. v. Ulrich*, [1977] A.J. No. 775, 38 C.C.C. (2d) 1 (Alta. T.D.) (after warning is read Crown precluded from calling further evidence). But see *Criminal Code*, s. 537(1)(g), which expressly allows for reply evidence.

[225] *Criminal Code*, s. 541(2).

[226] See *R. v. Eusler*, [1978] N.B.J. No. 2646, 43 C.C.C. (2d) 501 (N.B.C.A.).

[227] See *R. v. Melaragni*, [1992] O.J. No. 4179, 73 C.C.C. (3d) 356 (Ont. H.C.J.).

[228] The justice is obligated to record anything said by the accused in response. See *Criminal Code*, s. 541(3).

[229] *Criminal Code*, s. 541(2).

could be adduced by the Crown at trial, the accused would be precluded from eliciting evidence regarding his prior denial.[230]

(f) Defence Witnesses Must be Heard

§9.84 After the prosecution has finished calling its witness, the *Code* directs the justice to "hear each witness called by the accused who testifies to any matter relevant to the inquiry".[231] This provision imposes a mandatory obligation on a justice. Even though the main purpose of the preliminary inquiry is to decide whether there is enough evidence to warrant a committal to stand trial, the defence is entitled to present evidence even if the justice believes that the Crown's evidence has crossed the threshold for committal.[232] In fulfilling this obligation, the justice may need to adjourn the inquiry; for example, where the need for an adjournment arises through no fault of the accused.[233]

§9.85 The ability of an accused to compel witnesses to testify at the preliminary inquiry is an invaluable discovery tool. Absent such a power the accused might otherwise be denied the opportunity to access material evidence. Unlike the police, whose status and official role will provide most witnesses with an incentive to cooperate, the accused may have very little leverage in dealing with reluctant witnesses beyond a subpoena and the ability to subject the witness to questioning under oath at the preliminary inquiry.

(g) Recalling Witnesses

§9.86 Section 537(1)(g) of the *Code* authorizes a justice presiding at a preliminary inquiry to "receive evidence on the part of the prosecutor or the accused, as the case may be, after hearing any evidence that has been given on behalf of either of them." The provision has been held not only to entitle the parties to

---

[230] Under the rules of evidence a witness's prior consistent statements are presumptively inadmissible; this includes prior statements made by an accused. See *R. v. Béland*, [1987] S.C.J. No. 60, [1987] 2 S.C.R. 398 at 409-10 (S.C.C.); *R. v. Ellard*, [2009] S.C.J. No. 27, [2009] 2 S.C.R. 19 at paras. 31-33 (S.C.C.); *R. v. Stirling*, [2008] S.C.J. No. 10, [2008] 1 S.C.R. 272 at para. 5 (S.C.C.).

[231] *Criminal Code*, s. 541(5). See s. 541(1), which also provides that "the justice shall ... hear the witness called by the accused."

[232] See *R. v. Ward*, [1976] O.J. No. 807, 31 C.C.C. (2d) 466 (Ont. H.C.J.), aff'd 31 C.C.C. (2d) 466n (Ont. C.A.). There is also case law suggesting that discovery is a purpose "relevant to the inquiry" and that an accused is thus entitled to call witnesses to uncover evidence of potential *Charter* claims. See *R. v. McGrath*, [2007] N.S.J. No. 363, 225 C.C.C. (3d) 1 (N.S.S.C.). But see *R. v. Tran*, [2008] A.J. No. 1331, 63 C.R. (6th) 345 (Alta. Prov. Ct.).

[233] See *R. v. Lena*, [2001] B.C.J. No. 1906, 158 C.C.C. (3d) 415 (B.C.C.A.) (refusal of adjournment to enable accused to call witnesses amounted jurisdictional error where day's proceedings had ended and accommodating accused's request to call witness necessitated adjournment); *R. v. Giroux*, [2003] A.J. No. 1551, 349 A.R. 146 (Alta. Q.B.) (same). But see *R. v. McKenzie*, [1989] B.C.J. No. 1804, 51 C.C.C. (3d) 285 (B.C.S.C.) (failure to obtain subpoena for witness cited in refusing adjournment request, no loss of jurisdiction resulted); *R. v. Hiebert*, [2007] B.C.J. No. 3120, 2007 BCCA 614 (B.C.C.A.) (same).

elicit rebuttal evidence, but also to allow them to recall witnesses to elaborate upon, correct or clarify their previous evidence.[234]

(h) Application of the Rules of Evidence

§9.87 The Supreme Court of Canada has recognized that "Parliament equipped the preliminary inquiry with a structure that shares broad similarities with that of the trial court."[235] A key parallel is that the "traditional rules governing the admissibility of evidence apply."[236] In other words, the rules of evidence that ordinarily determine the admissibility of evidence at trial operate equally at the preliminary inquiry, subject to an important legislated exception that was recently added to the *Code* (which is explained below).

(i) Admissibility of Admission, Confession or Statement

§9.88 One of the rules of evidence applied by a preliminary inquiry justice is the voluntary confessions rule. A preliminary inquiry justice must exclude statements made by an accused to persons in authority if they were not made voluntarily.[237] Parliament directly alludes to this power in section 542(1) of the *Code*, which contemplates that a prosecutor may lead evidence of "any admission, confession or statement made at any time by the accused that by law is admissible against him." Voluntariness must be established at the preliminary inquiry to the same standard of proof applicable at trial: beyond a reasonable doubt.[238] This determination must be made on a *voir dire*,[239] although an accused or his or her counsel may waive the need for one, provided the waiver is express and informed.[240]

(ii) Admitting Credible or Trustworthy Information

§9.89 As part of the package of changes made to the preliminary inquiry in 2004, Parliament added sections 540(7), (8) and (9) to the *Code*.[241] These provisions have been characterized as "an attempt to streamline the preliminary inquiry procedures to make them more focused and efficient without diminishing

---

[234] See *Ponak v. Jones*, [1969] B.C.J. No. 382, [1970] 1 C.C.C. 250 (B.C.C.A.), affg [1969] B.C.J. No. 381, 7 C.R.N.S. 82 (B.C.S.C.).

[235] *R. v. Hynes*, [2001] S.C.J. No. 80, [2001] 3 S.C.R. 623 at para. 32 (S.C.C.).

[236] *Ibid.* See also *R. v. Deschamplain*, [2004] S.C.J. No. 73, [2004] 3 S.C.R. 601 at para. 17 (S.C.C.); *R. v. Chabot*, [1980] S.C.J. No. 108, [1980] 2 S.C.R. 985 at 1005 (S.C.C.).

[237] *R. v. Hynes*, [2001] S.C.J. No. 80, [2001] 3 S.C.R. 623 at paras. 37, 47 (S.C.C.). The confessions rule is discussed in detail in Chapter 4, Part 2.

[238] See *R. v. Picket*, [1975] O.J. No. 675, 28 C.C.C. (2d) 297 (Ont. C.A.); *R. v. Pearson*, [1957] A.J. No. 45, 117 C.C.C. 249 (Alta. C.A.), affd [1959] S.C.J. No. 14 (S.C.C.).

[239] See *R. v. Jenkins*, [1996] O.J. No. 2674, 108 C.C.C. (3d) 565 at para. 39 (Ont. Gen. Div.).

[240] *R. v. Park*, [1981] S.C.J. No. 63, [1981] 2 S.C.R. 64 (S.C.C.).

[241] See *Criminal Law Amendment Act, 2001*, S.C. 2002, c. 13.

the twofold purpose of the preliminary inquiry as a screening mechanism and discovery opportunity."[242]

§9.90 Section 540(7) confers discretion on the presiding justice to loosen the rules of evidence. It permits the admission of "any information that would not otherwise be admissible" (including "a statement made by a witness in writing or otherwise") if the justice considers it to be "credible or trustworthy in the circumstances of the case".[243] This language is almost identical to that found in section 518(1)(*e*) of the *Code* relating to the admission of evidence at bail hearings. As explained in Chapter 6, Part 3(9)(*b*), there is a lack of consensus in the bail context regarding the meaning of the bail provision; similar ambiguity persists with respect to section 540(7). What is clear is that a justice presiding at a preliminary inquiry enjoys considerable discretion in deciding whether to admit evidence under section 540(7).[244] In *R. v. Francis*,[245] Justice Ratushny concluded that the judge should not engage in the "ultimate" consideration of the credibility or weight as "that is to be left for the trier of fact at trial after all of the trial evidence has been heard."[246] Instead, the information need only have "*prima facie* air of reliability" — a standard that he fixed below the need for "circumstantial guarantees of trustworthiness" that controls admissibility under the principled exception to the hearsay rule.[247]

§9.91 In order to rely on section 540(7), the party proffering the information must have "given to each of the other parties reasonable notice" of the party's "intention to tender it, together with a copy of the statement," unless the judge orders otherwise.[248] What constitutes "reasonable notice" is left to the discretion of the justice.[249]

§9.92 Importantly, even where information is admitted under section 540(7), *viva voce* evidence from the source of the information may still be adduced. Subsection 540(9) provides that the "justice shall, on application of a party,

---

[242] *R. v. Francis*, [2005] O.J. No. 2864, 202 C.C.C. (3d) 147 at para. 25 (Ont. S.C.J.). See also *R. v. M. (P.)*, [2007] J.Q. no 2195, 222 C.C.C. (3d) 393 at para. 78 (Que. C.A.), leave to appeal refused [2007] C.S.C.R. no 287, 380 N.R. 394*n* (S.C.C.) ("exploratory role of the preliminary inquiry, though ancillary, was not diminished by Bill C-15A"); see *R. v. Gallant*, [2009] N.B.J. No. 409, 250 C.C.C. (3d) 29 at para. 35 (N.B.C.A.).

[243] *Criminal Code*, s. 540(7).

[244] See *R. v. Gallant*, [2009] N.B.J. No. 409, 250 C.C.C. (3d) 29 at para. 52 (N.B.C.A.) (noting that s. 540(7) "vests in the justice the discretion to admit evidence he or she considers credible or trustworthy in the circumstances of the case").

[245] [2005] O.J. No. 2864, 202 C.C.C. (3d) 147 (Ont. S.C.J.).

[246] *Ibid.*, at para. 27 (C.C.C.).

[247] *Ibid.*, at para. 26 (C.C.C.).

[248] *Criminal Code*, s. 540(8).

[249] See *R. v. Gallant*, [2009] N.B.J. No. 409, 250 C.C.C. (3d) 29 at para. 52 (N.B.C.A.) ("The determination of what constitutes reasonable notice is left to the judgment of the presiding justice as is the discretion to order the evidence be admitted without the required notice."). See also *R. v. Francis*, [2005] O.J. No. 2864, 202 C.C.C. (3d) 147 at para. 32 (Ont. S.C.J.) ("Fairness in one case might not be fairness in another depending on the particular circumstances, and Parliament has given complete discretion to the preliminary inquiry justice to determine the length and nature of the notice.").

require any person whom the justice considers appropriate to appear for examination or cross-examination".[250] In *R. v. M. (P.)*,[251] after reviewing the legislative record that culminated in these amendments, the Quebec Court of Appeal concluded that they did not occasion a "radical reform".[252] Accordingly, before requiring *viva voce* evidence from a witness, the justice should be satisfied that the witness's testimony would be relevant, not in the strict sense, but in terms of the appropriateness of having the witness appear.[253] The Court rejected the Crown's suggestion that an accused should be required to establish "justiciable cause" before being allowed to cross-examine, for example, by pointing to contradictions in a statement filed under section 540(7). Such a reading, the Court concluded, would add "requirements to subsection 540(9) that are not formulated in it."[254] It therefore rejected the notion that the amendments were meant to make cross-examination at the preliminary inquiry exceptional.[255] Ultimately, in deciding whether or not to allow cross-examination, the judge should consider, on the one hand, the accused's legitimate interest in preparing his or her defence and bringing out the insufficiency or weakness in the Crown's evidence and, on the other hand, relevance in light of the particular situation of the person whose appearance is requested and all of the circumstances of the case.[256]

(6) Committal or Discharge

§9.93 The preliminary inquiry's protective role stems from the justice's obligation to assess the adequacy of the Crown's evidence in support of each charge. Once all the evidence has been taken, the justice must make one of the determinations set out in section 548. If, "there is sufficient evidence to put the accused on trial for the offence charged or any other indictable offence in respect of the same transaction," the justice must order the accused to stand trial.[257] If "no sufficient case is made out to put the accused on trial for the offence charged or any other indictable offence in respect of the same transaction," the justice must discharge the accused.[258]

(a) Test

§9.94 The Supreme Court has repeatedly held that the standard for committal is the same as that governing a motion for a directed verdict at trial or the decision to extradite a fugitive. The test is "whether or not there is any evidence upon

---

[250] *Criminal Code*, s. 540(9).
[251] [2007] J.Q. no 2195, 222 C.C.C. (3d) 393 at para. 78 (Que. C.A.), leave to appeal refused [2007] C.S.C.R. no 287, 380 N.R. 394*n* (S.C.C.).
[252] *Ibid.*, at para. 72 (C.C.C.).
[253] *Ibid.*, at paras. 50, 63, 75 (C.C.C.).
[254] *Ibid.*, at para. 76 (C.C.C.).
[255] *Ibid.*, at paras. 52-53, 64-66, 85 (C.C.C.).
[256] *Ibid.*, at para. 86 (C.C.C.).
[257] *Criminal Code*, s. 548(1)(*a*).
[258] *Criminal Code*, s. 548(1)(*b*).

which a reasonable jury properly instructed could return a verdict of guilt."[259] The accused will accordingly be committed to stand trial "in any case in which there is admissible evidence which could, if it were believed, result in a conviction."[260]

§9.95 In applying this test, the justice's mandate is tightly circumscribed. He or she is not permitted to assess the quality, credibility or reliability of the evidence.[261] Those sorts of assessments are reserved exclusively for the trier-of-fact at trial.[262] The test remains the same whether the Crown's case consists of direct or circumstantial evidence.[263] Nevertheless, the nature of the presiding justice's task varies with the type of evidence. If there is direct evidence for every element of the offence, the accused must be committed.[264] In such a case the only remaining question is whether the evidence should be believed (which is a decision reserved for trial).[265] The justice's task becomes more difficult where the prosecution's case relies in part on circumstantial evidence. In such a case, the Supreme Court has explained that the justice must:

> ... weigh the evidence, in the sense of assessing whether it is reasonably capable of supporting the inferences that the Crown asks the jury to draw. This weighing, however, is limited. The judge does not ask whether she herself would conclude that the accused is guilty. Nor does the judge draw factual inferences or assess credibility. The judge asks only whether the evidence, <u>if believed</u>, could reasonably support an inference of guilt.[266]

§9.96 The impact of defence evidence turns on the nature of the Crown's case. As the Supreme Court has explained, if the Crown has adduced "direct evidence on all the elements of the offence, the case must proceed to trial, regardless of the existence of defence evidence, as by definition the only conclusion that needs to be reached is whether the evidence is true."[267] But where the Crown's case includes circumstantial evidence, "the judge must engage in a limited weighing of the whole of the evidence (*i.e.*, including any defence evidence) to determine whether a reasonable jury properly instructed could return a verdict of

---

[259] *United States of America v. Shephard*, [1977] S.C.J. No. 106, [1977] 2 S.C.R. 1067 at 1080 (S.C.C.).

[260] *Ibid.* See also *R. v. Sazant*, [2004] S.C.J. No. 74, [2004] 3 S.C.R. 635 at para. 16 (S.C.C.); *R. v. Arcuri*, [2001] S.C.J. No. 52, [2001] 2 S.C.R. 828 at para. 21 (S.C.C.); *R. v. Monteleone*, [1987] S.C.J. No. 52, [1987] 2 S.C.R. 154 at 160 (S.C.C.).

[261] See *R. v. Deschamplain*, [2004] S.C.J. No. 73, [2004] 3 S.C.R. 601 at para. 15 (S.C.C.); *R. v. Sazant*, [2004] S.C.J. No. 74, [2004] 3 S.C.R. 635 at para. 18 (S.C.C.); *R. v. Arcuri*, [2001] S.C.J. No. 52, [2001] 2 S.C.R. 828 at para. 30 (S.C.C.).

[262] *R. v. Deschamplain*, [2004] S.C.J. No. 73, [2004] 3 S.C.R. 601 at para. 15 (S.C.C.).

[263] See *R. v. Arcuri*, [2001] S.C.J. No. 52, [2001] 2 S.C.R. 828 at para. 22 (S.C.C.); *R. v. Monteleone*, [1987] S.C.J. No. 52, [1987] 2 S.C.R. 154 at 161 (S.C.C.). See also *R. v. Mezzo*, [1986] S.C.J. No. 40, [1986] 1 S.C.R. 802 at 842-43 (S.C.C.).

[264] *R. v. Arcuri*, [2001] S.C.J. No. 52, [2001] 2 S.C.R. 828 at para. 22 (S.C.C.).

[265] *Ibid.*

[266] *Ibid.*, at para. 23 (S.C.R.) [emphasis in original].

[267] *Ibid.*, at para. 29 (S.C.R.). See also *R. v. Sazant*, [2004] S.C.J. No. 74, [2004] 3 S.C.R. 635 at para. 16 (S.C.C.).

guilty."[268] If the evidence adduced is capable of supporting competing inferences, the justice is *not* to choose between them. Rather, as the Supreme Court has explained, "where more than one inference can be drawn from the evidence, only the inferences that favour the Crown are to be considered."[269] In other words, at the preliminary inquiry, unlike at trial, the benefit of the doubt is given to the Crown, not the accused.

§9.97 The justice may also commit the accused to stand trial on any offences "included" in those charged in the information.[270] That power exists independently from the authority in section 548(1)(*a*) to commit an accused to stand trial for "any other indictable offences in respect of the same transaction" which we deal with next.

(b)   Committal for "any other indictable offence in respect of the same transaction"

§9.98 As mentioned, section 548(1)(*a*) states that where the evidence is sufficient, the justice must commit the accused to stand trial not only for the offence charged but also "any other indictable offence in respect of the same transaction". Consequently, an accused could very well emerge from the preliminary inquiry facing more charges than when the hearing began. For any accused who may have been under-charged, this is undoubtedly an important consideration in deciding whether to forego a preliminary inquiry.

§9.99 For section 548(1)(*a*) to apply, the other offence must form part of a series of acts or occurrences extending over a period of time which, the Crown alleges, prove the commission of the offence charged in the information.[271] Consequently, as the Ontario Court of Appeal has explained, "the other offence will, of necessity, be closely interwoven with or related to the offence charged in the information".[272] To satisfy this test it is not enough that the offences are

---

[268]   *R. v. Arcuri*, [2001] S.C.J. No. 52, [2001] 2 S.C.R. 828 at para. 29 (S.C.C.).

[269]   *R. v. Sazant*, [2004] S.C.J. No. 74, [2004] 3 S.C.R. 635 at para. 18 (S.C.C.). See also *R. v. Deschamplain*, [2004] S.C.J. No. 73, [2004] 3 S.C.R. 601 at para. 15 (S.C.C.).

[270]   See *R. v. Chabot*, [1980] S.C.J. No. 108, [1980] 2 S.C.R. 985 at 1009 (S.C.C.) (coming to this conclusion under predecessor provision before the "same transaction" language was added, given that "included offences necessarily form part of the original charge"). See also *Re Walker*, [1974] O.J. No. 899, 20 C.C.C. (2d) 539 (Ont. H.C.J.) (accused may be committed to stand trial on included offence even where that offence is in absolute jurisdiction of provincial court). See §9.19, above, which explains the authority of the superior court to try absolute jurisdiction offences.

[271]   See *R. v. Goldstein*, [1988] O.J. No. 549, 42 .C.C.C. (3d) 548 at 554, 557 (Ont. C.A.), leave to appeal refused [1988] S.C.C.A. No. 286, [1988] 2 S.C.R. v (S.C.C.). See also *R. v. Stewart*, [1988] O.J. No. 1699, 44 C.C.C. (3d) 109 at 111-12 (Ont. C.A.); *R. v. Do*, [2005] S.J. No. 247, 196 C.C.C. (3d) 210 (Sask. C.A.).

[272]   *R. v. Goldstein*, [1988] O.J. No. 549, 42 C.C.C. (3d) 548 at 557 (Ont. C.A.), leave to appeal refused [1988] S.C.C.A. No. 286, [1988] 2 S.C.R. v (S.C.C.).

temporally connected. Rather, the additional offence must form a "component part" of the transaction that makes up the offence charged in the information.[273]

§9.100 Section 548(1)(*a*) has been challenged under section 11(*a*) of the *Charter*. That provision of the *Charter* guarantees any person charged with an offence the right "to be informed without unreasonable delay of the specific offence." In *R. v. Cancor Software Corp.*,[274] the Ontario Court of Appeal concluded that section 11(*a*) requires that once a charge is laid, the accused must be provided without unreasonable delay with the information necessary to enable him to proceed appropriately with his defence.[275] This requirement was met in *Cancor* because before the preliminary inquiry began, the Crown had informed the accused of its intention to seek committal on specific charges that it anticipated would be revealed by the evidence called at the preliminary inquiry. In our view, an accused who has received full disclosure before the preliminary inquiry will similarly have received adequate notice for the purposes of section 11(*a*) of the *Charter*.

(7) Committal on Consent

§9.101 At any stage of a preliminary inquiry, with the consent of the accused and the prosecutor, the presiding justice may order the accused to stand trial without taking or recording any or further evidence.[276] In addition, where the accused and prosecutor agree under section 536.5 to limit the inquiry to specific issues, the justice, without recording evidence on any other issues, may order the accused to stand trial.[277]

(8) Review

§9.102 There is no statutory right of appeal against the decisions of a preliminary inquiry justice. To the extent that such decisions can be reviewed, the

---

[273] *R. v. Stewart*, [1988] O.J. No. 1699, 44 C.C.C. (3d) 109 at 113 (Ont. C.A.). In *Stewart*, the accused was charged with assaulting A. The evidence showed that in the course of the assault on A the accused had also assaulted V. According to the Court, the assault on V did not form part of the same transaction as the offence charged in relation to A. As such, the Court refused to interfere on appeal with the preliminary inquiry justice's decision not to commit the accused to stand trial with respect to the assault on V. But see *R. v. Panzevecchia*, [1997] O.J. No. 1454, 115 C.C.C. (3d) 476 (Ont. C.A.) (accused charged with assaulting victim, evidence revealed that at end of protracted assault accused also uttered death threat against potential witness, committal on threatening upheld as stemming from same transaction); *R. v. Brown*, [1990] O.J. No. 493, 54 C.C.C. (3d) 561 (Ont. H.C.J.) (accused charged with assault on one victim, evidence disclosing that accused pushed head of first victim into head of second, committal for assault on second victim upheld as forming part of same transaction as assault on first victim). See also *R. v. Do*, [2005] S.J. No. 247, 196 C.C.C. (3d) 210 (Sask. C.A.) (although accused discharged on charge of conspiracy presiding justice justified in committing accused to stand trial on underlying substantive offences).

[274] [1990] O.J. No. 1287, 58 C.C.C. (3d) 53 at 61 (Ont. C.A.).

[275] *Ibid.*, at 61 (C.C.C.) (Ont. C.A.).

[276] *Criminal Code*, s. 549(1).

[277] *Criminal Code*, s. 549(1.1.).

venue for doing so is the superior court and the mechanism (at least historically) was the prerogative writ. Prerogative writs only issue to remedy jurisdictional error. Each writ serves a different but related purpose: *prohibition* prevents a justice from embarking on a course of conduct for which the justice lacks jurisdiction; *mandamus* directs a justice to discharge his or her jurisdictional obligations; and *certiorari* overturns a decision made in excess of jurisdiction.[278] Given that reviews of preliminary inquiry decisions almost always occur after an accused has been committed to stand trial or discharged, *certiorari* is by far the writ resorted to most often.

§9.103 Although the term *"certiorari"* is far from extinct, today it is used interchangeably with the phrase "judicial review". Regardless of the label, the basis for review remains the same. As the Supreme Court of Canada has explained, *"certiorari*, or the newer term of judicial review, runs largely to jurisdictional review or surveillance by a superior court of statutory tribunals, the term 'jurisdiction' being given its narrow or technical sense."[279]

§9.104 Although jurisdictional error amounts to legal error, the converse is not true. Every legal error does not amount to jurisdictional error. As the Supreme Court has explained, *"certiorari* review does not authorize a superior court to reach inside the functioning of the statutory tribunal for the purpose of challenging a decision reached by that tribunal within its assigned jurisdiction on the ground that the tribunal committed an error of law in reaching that decision, or reached a conclusion different from that which the reviewing tribunal might have reached."[280] Consequently, as the Court has noted, "situations in which there can be a loss of jurisdiction in the course of a preliminary inquiry are few indeed."[281]

§9.105 Nevertheless, the Supreme Court of Canada has made clear that jurisdiction will be lost where a justice conducting a preliminary inquiry fails to observe a mandatory provision of the *Criminal Code*.[282] A denial of natural justice has been characterized as having the same effect, depriving the justice of jurisdiction and warranting intervention by the superior court on review.[283]

---

[278] See generally, Gilles Létourneau, *The Prerogative Writs in Canadian Criminal Law and Procedure* (Toronto: Butterworths, 1976).

[279] *R. v. Skogman*, [1984] S.C.J. No. 32, [1984] 2 S.C.R. 93 at 99 (S.C.C.). See also *R. v. Russell*, [2001] S.C.J. No. 53, [2001] 2 S.C.R. 804 at para. 19 (S.C.C.).

[280] *R. v. Skogman*, [1984] S.C.J. No. 32, [1984] 2 S.C.R. 93 at 100 (S.C.C.).

[281] *R. v. Forsythe*, [1980] S.C.J. No. 66, [1980] 2 S.C.R. 268 at 271-72 (S.C.C.).

[282] *Ibid.*, 271-72 (S.C.R.). See also *R. v. Dubois*, [1986] S.C.J. No. 21, [1986] 1 S.C.R. 366 at 377 (S.C.C.); *R. v. Doyle*, [1976] S.C.J. No. 38, [1977] 1 S.C.R. 597 at 607 (S.C.C.); *R. v. Deschamplain*, [2004] S.C.J. No. 73, [2004] 3 S.C.R. 601 at paras. 12-13, 19 (S.C.C.).

[283] *R. v. Forsythe*, [1980] S.C.J. No. 66, [1980] 2 S.C.R. 268 at 271-72 (S.C.C.). See also *R. v. Dubois*, [1986] S.C.J. No. 21, [1986] 1 S.C.R. 366 at 377 (S.C.C.) (acknowledging "that rulings in the course of a preliminary hearing on evidentiary questions as to the extent of limitation on the basic right to cross-examine or to call witnesses, may develop into a violation of natural justice and fall within the condemnation of *Forsythe, supra*, and hence be subject to judicial review").

(a)   Decisions During the Course of the Preliminary Inquiry

§9.106 As explained above, a justice has considerable authority when it comes to regulating the course of the preliminary inquiry. There are therefore few legal errors that a justice can make during a preliminary inquiry that will warrant intervention. The case law provides a useful catalogue of the sorts of errors that qualify. For example, reviewable error has been found where the presiding justice: completely denies the accused the opportunity to cross-examine prosecution witnesses[284] or the right to call witnesses;[285] directs the Crown to call particular witnesses;[286] prevents the Crown from calling further witnesses (because he or she believes *prima facie* case has already been established);[287] fails, at the completion of the Crown's evidence, to inquire whether the accused has anything to say or wishes to call evidence[288] (an obligation now only applicable where an accused is unrepresented); or refuses to hear submissions from the accused on whether or not there should be a committal or discharge.[289]

§9.107 In contrast, merely disallowing "a question or questions on cross-examination or other rulings on proffered evidence would not ... amount to a jurisdictional error."[290] As the Supreme Court has explained, "*certiorari* lies only for lack of jurisdiction and a decision concerning the admissibility of evidence, even if erroneous, does not affect jurisdiction."[291]

---

[284] See *R. v. Patterson*, [1970] S.C.J. No. 7, [1970] S.C.R. 409 at 411, 413, 416 (S.C.C.); *R. v. Forsythe*, [1980] S.C.J. No. 66, [1980] 2 S.C.R. 268 at 271-72 (S.C.C.). See also *R. v. Churchman*, [1954] O.J. No. 316, 110 C.C.C. 382 (Ont. H.C.J.) (failure to allow counsel for the accused to cross-examine important Crown witness); *R. v. Durette*, [1992] O.J. No. 1044, 72 C.C.C. (3d) 421 (Ont. C.A.), revd on other grounds [1994] S.C.J. No. 22, [1994] 1 S.C.R. 469 (S.C.C.) (proceeding with examination of Crown witness in absence of counsel).

[285] See *R. v. Forsythe*, [1980] S.C.J. No. 66, [1980] 2 S.C.R. 268 at 272 (S.C.C.); *R. v. Ward*, [1976] O.J. No. 807, 31 C.C.C. (2d) 466 (Ont. H.C.J.), affd 31 C.C.C. (2d) 466n (Ont. C.A.); *R. v. Brooks*, [1964] A.J. No. 21, 45 C.R. 318 (Alta. T.D.); *R. v. Mishko*, [1945] O.J. No. 396, 85 C.C.C. 410 (Ont. H.C.J.); *R. v. LaFleur*, [1994] O.J. No. 1416, 32 C.R. (4th) 188 (Ont. C.A.). See also *R. v. Lena*, [2001] B.C.J. No. 1906, 158 C.C.C. (3d) 415 (B.C.C.A.) (refusal of adjournment to enable accused to call witnesses amounted to jurisdictional error).

[286] See *R. v. Brass*, [1981] S.J. No. 1030, 64 C.C.C. (2d) 206 (Sask. Q.B.).

[287] See *R. v. Schreder*, [1987] N.W.T.J. No. 84, 36 C.C.C. (3d) 216 (N.W.T.S.C.).

[288] See *R. v. Bayne*, [1970] A.J. No. 67, 14 C.R.N.S. 130 (Alta. C.A.); *R. v. Paton*, [1985] M.J. No. 300, 31 Man. R. (2d) 79 (Man. Q.B.) (same).

[289] See *R. v. Taillefer*, [1978] O.J. No. 968, 42 C.C.C. (2d) 282 at 284 (Ont. C.A.) ("To refuse counsel for the accused the right to make submissions before a committal is made is a denial of natural justice.").

[290] *R. v. Forsythe*, [1980] S.C.J. No. 66, [1980] 2 S.C.R. 268 at 272 (S.C.C.) (refusal to allow accused's counsel to cross-examine police officer on interview notes). See also *R. v. Martin*, [1977] O.J. No. 2532, 41 C.C.C. (2d) 308 at 341 (Ont. C.A.) (refusal to order police witness to produce notebook for inspection by defence).

[291] *Québec (Attorney General) v. Cohen*, [1979] S.C.J. No. 50, [1979] 2 S.C.R. 305 at 310 (S.C.C.). See also *R. v. Deschamplain*, [2004] S.C.J. No. 73, [2004] 3 S.C.R. 601 at para. 17 (S.C.C.); *R. v. Depagie*, [1976] A.J. No. 439, 32 C.C.C. (2d) 89 (Alta. C.A.), leave to appeal refused [1976] S.C.C.A. No. 1 (S.C.C.).

(b)   Decisions Relating to Committal or Discharge

§9.108 The justice's decision to either commit or discharge the accused will be open to review by way of *certiorari* where it results from jurisdictional error. According to the Supreme Court of Canada, such an error arises when the accused is committed to stand trial in the absence of evidence of an essential ingredient of the offence.[292] Should this happen, the committal of the accused to stand trial can be quashed.[293] The Supreme Court has extended this reasoning to the sentence classification scheme that controls whether murder will be characterized as first degree murder under section 231(5) of the *Code*.[294] Consequently, if a justice commits an accused to stand trial for first degree murder where there is no evidence in the record capable of satisfying the preconditions for such an elevation, this will constitute jurisdictional error and justify quashing the committal.[295]

§9.109 The Court has expressed a need for caution, however, when reviewing the preliminary inquiry justice's assessment of the evidence. The justice's "determination of sufficiency is entitled to the greatest deference" and a committal may be vacated "only if there is no evidence on an element of the offence, or on an essential condition of s. 231(5)."[296]

§9.110 Jurisdictional error may also manifest itself in the decision to discharge an accused. For example, it is a jurisdictional error for a justice to discharge an accused: on the basis of the "proof beyond a reasonable doubt standard";[297] without considering the "whole of the evidence" as required by section 548(1)(*b*) of the *Code*;[298] after misidentifying the elements of the offence charged;[299] preferring the inference favourable to the accused when an inference favourable to the Crown was possible;[300] or after assessing the credibility of witnesses or the reliability of the evidence.[301]

---

[292] *R. v. Skogman*, [1984] S.C.J. No. 32, [1984] 2 S.C.R. 93 at 104 (S.C.C.) ("'No evidence' on an essential element of the charge cannot amount to 'sufficient evidence' under [what is now s. 548(1)(*a*) of the *Code*").

[293] *Ibid.*, at 106 (S.C.R.).

[294] See *R. v. Russell*, [2001] S.C.J. No. 53, [2001] 2 S.C.R. 804 (S.C.C.).

[295] *Ibid.*, at paras. 22-25 (S.C.R.).

[296] *Ibid.*, at para. 48 (S.C.R.).

[297] *R. v. Dubois*, [1986] S.C.J. No. 21, [1986] 1 S.C.R. 366 (S.C.C.).

[298] See *R. v. Deschamplain*, [2004] S.C.J. No. 73, [2004] 3 S.C.R. 601 at paras. 18-19 (S.C.C.). See also *R. v. Sazant*, [2004] S.C.J. No. 74, [2004] 3 S.C.R. 635 at paras. 22, 25 (S.C.C.).

[299] See *R. v. Sazant*, [2004] S.C.J. No. 74, [2004] 3 S.C.R. 635 at para. 25 (S.C.C.). But see *Quebec (Attorney General) v. Girouard*, [1988] S.C.J. No. 74, [1988] 2 S.C.R. 254 (S.C.C.) (overturning [1984] Q.J. No. 4, 43 C.R. (3d) 92 (Que. C.A.)), where the Supreme Court found that a mistake by the justice as to the elements of the offence of robbery was not jurisdictional in nature. This inconsistency was noted by the dissenting judges in *R. v. Sazant*, [2004] S.C.J. No. 74, [2004] 3 S.C.R. 635 at para. 46 (S.C.C.), *per* Bastarache and Fish JJ. dissenting.

[300] *R. v. Sazant*, [2004] S.C.J. No. 74, [2004] 3 S.C.R. 635 at para. 25 (S.C.C.).

[301] *Ibid.*, at para. 18 (S.C.R.).

(c)   Timing

§9.111 Decisions made by the preliminary inquiry justice may be judicially reviewed at any time before the indictment is lodged with the trial court at the beginning of the accused's trial.[302] Consequently, the fact that an accused has already appeared in superior court for the purpose of setting a trial date does not deprive him or her of the right to seek prerogative relief against jurisdictional errors relating to the preliminary inquiry.[303]

(9)   Re-laying Charges after Discharge

§9.112 On a formal level at least, the main purpose of a preliminary inquiry is to safeguard the individual against unwarranted criminal charges.[304] This purpose would be undermined if the Crown were free to charge the accused again with the same offence.[305] In recent years, courts have held that unless the preliminary inquiry justice made a significant legal error, the re-laying of a charge for which the accused was discharged would in most circumstances constitute an abuse of process.[306] But where a justice has made a legal error in discharging an accused, the Supreme Court of Canada has sent mixed messages on whether re-laying the charge would amount to an abuse of process.[307] (As explained above, a legal

---

[302] See *R. v. Chabot*, [1980] S.C.J. No. 108, [1980] 2 S.C.R. 985 at 999-1000 (S.C.C.). The formal start of the trial is marked by the accused being arraigned and pleading to the charge(s).

[303] *Ibid.*

[304] See §9.51, above.

[305] As was explained above in Part 2(2)(*a*)(v) and as detailed more fully below in Part 4(3), pursuant to s. 577 of the *Code*, with the personal consent in writing of the Attorney General or the Deputy Attorney General, a direct indictment can be preferred even after an accused was discharged following a preliminary inquiry.

[306] See *R. v. Oshaweetok*, [1984] N.W.T.J. No. 26, 16 C.C.C. (3d) 392 (N.W.T.S.C.) (re-laying of same charge based on same evidence following discharge at preliminary inquiry characterized as abuse of process and found to violate s. 7 of the *Charter*, charge stayed); *R. v. Sheehan*, [1973] O.J. No. 835, 14 C.C.C. (2d) 23 (Ont. H.C.J.) (characterizing second prosecution as an abuse of process and issuing an order of prohibition to preclude the holding of a second preliminary inquiry on the charge). See also *R. v. Tapaquon*, [1993] S.C.J. No. 133, [1993] 1 S.C.R. 535 at 538 (S.C.C.) (remarking that re-laying charge in such circumstances may "constitute in some circumstances an abuse of process"); *R. v. Hamm*, [1984] S.J. No. 476, [1984] 5 W.W.R. 696 (Sask. C.A.) (no abuse of process where no evidence heard at preliminary inquiry and accused discharged after Crown adjournment refused, but acknowledging that under certain circumstances the laying of a new information might amount to abuse of process). Not surprisingly, before the widespread acceptance of the abuse of process doctrine courts typically rejected this argument. See *e.g.*, *R. v. Fields*, [1979] B.C.J. No. 1664, 12 C.R. (3d) 273 (B.C.C.A.) (characterizing the laying of the second information as potentially abusive and questioning the sensibility of so proceeding, but based on the state of the law governing abuse of process at that time, questioning the court's authority to intervene); *R. v. Ewanchuk*, [1974] A.J. No. 139, 16 C.C.C. (2d) 517 (Alta. C.A.), affd [1976] 2 W.W.R. 576n (S.C.C.) (finding no impediment to the laying of the same charge based on the same evidence following a discharge). For a discussion of the abuse of process in Canadian criminal procedure, see Chapter 10, Part 5(1)(*a*)(iii).

[307] See *R. v. Dubois*, [1986] S.C.J. No. 21, [1986] 1 S.C.R. 366 at para. 27 (S.C.C.) (acknowledging the "possibility" that relaying the charge(s) in such circumstances "may be held to amount to abuse of process"); *R. v. Russell*, [2001] S.C.J. No. 53, [2001] 2 S.C.R. 804 at para. 29

error falling short of a jurisdictional error would not be reviewable by way of *certiorari*.)

(10) The Future of the Preliminary Inquiry

§9.113 In the aftermath of *Stinchcombe*, the preliminary inquiry has come under attack. Given that accused persons now receive full disclosure as a matter of course, the Supreme Court of Canada has suggested that "the incidental function of the preliminary inquiry as a discovery mechanism has lost much of its relevance."[308] Given the minimal evidentiary threshold for committal, the inquiry's effectiveness at protecting against unjustified charges is also questionable. The toll on victims, who are often required to testify twice, first at the preliminary inquiry and then again at trial, is also cause for concern. This is especially so in cases involving child witnesses and victims of sexual violence. Lastly, it should be recalled that a great many criminal cases, including summary conviction matters, indictable offences within the absolute jurisdiction of the provincial court, do not involve a preliminary inquiry. Given all of this, it has been argued that the preliminary inquiry does more harm than good and that the dedication of scarce time and resources toward maintaining it is no longer justified.[309]

§9.114 Nevertheless, defence lawyers continue to champion the preliminary inquiry. To the extent that it is currently an ineffective device for ending unjustified prosecutions,[310] they argue that the solution is to make the standard for committal more onerous. Disclosure is also said to be a poor substitute for the sort of detailed information gleaned from questioning witnesses under oath. The preliminary inquiry also gives rise to a number of tactical benefits. It enables the defence to flesh out a Crown witness's story and commit the witness to a specific and detailed account. If a witness's testimony at trial conflicts with his or her evidence at the preliminary inquiry, such inconsistencies will provide a basis for impeachment.[311]

(S.C.C.) (suggesting that when faced with a discharge resulting from legal error, " the Crown is free, subject to the requirements of s. 577 of the *Criminal Code*, to lay a new information or prefer an indictment").

[308] *R. v. L. (S.J.)*, [2009] S.C.J. No. 14, [2009] 1 S.C.R. 426 at para. 23 (S.C.C.).

[309] See John Arnold Epp, "Abolishing Preliminary Inquiries in Canada" (1996) 38 Crim. L. Q. 495; Canada (Department of Justice), *Do We Still Need Preliminary Inquiries?: Options for Changes to the Criminal Code: A Consultation Paper* (Ottawa: Department of Justice, 1994). See also *R. v. O'Connor*, [1995] S.C.J. No. 98, [1995] 4 S.C.R. 411 at paras. 170-171 (S.C.C.), per L'Heureux-Dubé J. (approving of a provincial court judge's concern that the experience had become "a living hell for victims of crime and witnesses" and suggesting that inquiry's discovery function should be reconsidered).

[310] The validity of this assumption is questionable. See David M. Paciocco, "A Voyage of Discovery: Examining the Precarious Condition of the Preliminary Inquiry" (2004) 48 Crim. L.Q. 151 at 154-55 (observing that between 10-15 per cent of preliminary inquiries result in discharges, with at least some of the charges being rejected in up to 10 per cent of those cases where accused persons are committed to stand trial).

[311] See Alan D. Gold & Jill R. Presser, "Let's Not Do Away with the Preliminaries: A Case in Favour of Retaining the Preliminary Inquiry" (1996) 1 Can. Crim. L.R. 145; Marvin Bloos &

§9.115 In recent years, Parliament has amended the *Criminal Code* to erode the importance of the preliminary inquiry. Above, we discussed a variety of procedural and evidentiary amendments aimed at reducing their incidence and expediting those that do take place.[312] Even more significantly, in 1994 Parliament increased the maximum summary conviction sentence for certain commonly charged hybrid offences (assault causing bodily harm, assault with a weapon and sexual assault) from six to 18 months' imprisonment.[313] This has enabled prosecutors to keep such charges in provincial court, thereby avoiding a preliminary inquiry and superior court trial, while still seeking significant jail sentences. As a result, preliminary inquiries have become less common than they once were.

§9.116 If Parliament did decide to eliminate preliminary inquiries altogether, it would not likely face any constitutional impediment. "There is no constitutional right to a preliminary inquiry," the Supreme Court has stated, "or to the outcome of such an inquiry."[314]

§9.117 That said, we are not convinced that preliminary inquiries have outlived their usefulness. With recent legislative amendments, preliminary inquiries are typically reserved for the most serious cases, where the stakes for both the accused and the state are greatest. It is in these very cases that the need for a timely judicial vetting of the adequacy of the prosecution's evidence is at its height. The infamous case of Susan Nelles demonstrates that, despite the low threshold for committal, the preliminary inquiry can sometimes spare an innocent person the ordeal of an unjustified criminal trial.[315]

§9.118 Nor should the preliminary inquiry's discovery benefits be underestimated. It strikes us as strange that civil litigants involved in disputes over money

---

Michael Plaxton, "An Almost-Eulogy for the Preliminary Inquiry: 'We Hardly Knew Ye'" (2000) 43 Crim. L.Q. 516.

[312] See *Criminal Law Amendment Act, 2001*, S.C. 2002, c. 13, ss. 24-33. For a review and critique of these measures, see David M. Paciocco, "A Voyage of Discovery: Examining the Precarious Condition of the Preliminary Inquiry" (2004) 48 Crim. L.Q. 151.

[313] See *Criminal Law Amendment Act, 1994*, S.C. 1994, c. 44, ss. 17-19.

[314] *R. v. L. (S.J.)*, [2009] S.C.J. No. 14, [2009] 1 S.C.R. 426 at para. 21 (S.C.C.) (citing with approval *R. v. Ertel*, [1987] O.J. No. 516, 35 C.C.C. (3d) 398 (Ont. C.A.), leave to appeal refused [1987] S.C.C.A. No. 354, [1987] 2 S.C.R. vii (S.C.C.); *R. v. Moore*, [1986] M.J. No. 56, 26 C.C.C. (3d) 474 (Man. C.A.)). This still leaves open the possibility of case-specific remedies in individual cases. For example, in *R. v. Ertel*, [1987] O.J. No. 516, 35 C.C.C. (3d) 398 at 414 (Ont. C.A.), leave to appeal refused [1987] S.C.C.A. No. 354, [1987] 2 S.C.R. vii (S.C.C.), the Ontario Court of Appeal noted that, "a contravention of s. 7 of the Charter may result if the combination of the direct indictment with the failure of the Crown to make adequate disclosure results in the inability of the accused to make full answer and defence at trial." If such circumstances are made out, however, the remedy will undoubtedly be an order for further disclosure and not an opportunity to cross-examine the Crown's witnesses. As the Supreme Court of Canada has made clear, the Crown's disclosure duty "does not extend to producing its witnesses for oral discovery." *R. v. Khela*, [1995] S.C.J. No. 95, [1995] 4 S.C.R. 201 at para. 18 (S.C.C.). See also *R. v. L. (S.J.)*, [2009] S.C.J. No. 14, [2009] 1 S.C.R. 426 at para. 23 (S.C.C.); *R. v. Girimonte*, [1997] O.J. No. 4961, 121 C.C.C. (3d) 33 at para. 37 (Ont. C.A.).

[315] See *R. v. Nelles*, [1982] O.J. No. 3654, 16 C.C.C. (3d) 97 (Ont. Prov. Ct.) (nurse discharged on four counts of first degree murder in relation to mysterious deaths of four infant children at The Hospital for Sick Children in Toronto).

are afforded the opportunity to examine material witnesses under oath, while (with the elimination of the preliminary inquiry) the accused and the Crown would be denied the same opportunity when the liberty of the subject is at stake.

§9.119 The preliminary inquiry also serves an important role in preserving evidence for trial should a material witness abscond, become ill or die.[316] Depending on the circumstances, this can inure to the benefit of both sides, although there is little doubt that the Crown will more often enjoy the advantage of this sort of evidence preservation.

§9.120 Finally, we believe that the administration of justice benefits from affording the parties involved an opportunity to size up their respective cases. In practice, cases often resolve following a preliminary inquiry, either because the accused comes to realize that the Crown's witnesses will deliver and his or her "goose is cooked" or because after hearing and seeing its witnesses the Crown recognizes that there is no reasonable prospect of conviction. In each scenario, the time, expense, and ordeal of a full-blown trial are avoided.

4. PREFERRING THE INDICTMENT

§9.121 The indictment is the document filed with the superior court that sets out the details of the charge an accused is facing. In other words, it is the charging document for criminal allegations in the superior court. This part explains how the indictment comes into existence and how it supplies the basis for a criminal trial in the superior court.

(1) Mechanics

§9.122 While a criminal charge proceeds through the provincial court, the charging document before the court throughout is the information.[317] This is the case whether the offence charged is summary or indictable. Where a preliminary inquiry is held the presiding justice's decision to discharge or commit the accused to stand trial is recorded on the information.[318] If the accused foregoes a preliminary inquiry and elects a trial in superior court or has a preliminary inquiry and is committed to stand trial, the entire provincial court file (*i.e.*, the information and all exhibits) is transferred to the superior court.

§9.123 Before the accused makes his or her first appearance in superior court a prosecutor will prepare an indictment.[319] Unlike the information, the indictment is not a sworn document. Rather, it is simply a piece of paper that, like the

---

[316] See *Criminal Code*, s. 715.

[317] See *Criminal Code*, s. 506, 788(1) and Form 2.

[318] See *Criminal Code*, s. 548(2), which, rather strangely, only expressly requires the justice to endorse on the information with respect to any charges "other than or in addition to the one with which the accused was charged" on which he or she orders the accused to stand trial. Be that as it may, in practice the information notes the charges upon which the accused was either committed to stand trial or discharged.

[319] See *Criminal Code*, s. 580 and Form 4.

information, names the accused and sets out the particulars of the offence(s) charged (typically the "who", "when", "where" and "what" of the allegation).[320] The document is ordinarily signed by the prosecutor on behalf of the Attorney General and filed with the court shortly before (or even on) the date of the accused's first appearance in superior court. The preparing and filing of the indictment with the court is referred to as "preferring and presenting" the indictment.[321] The prosecutor who signs the indictment is not thereafter obligated to personally prosecute the case. Rather, any prosecutor authorized to act by the Attorney General may take carriage of it.[322]

§9.124 As explained in Chapter 5, the *Code* contemplates the possibility of privately laid charges. In the unlikely event that the Crown does not assume carriage of such a prosecution, the written order of a superior court judge is required before a private prosecutor may prefer an indictment.[323]

(2) Charges that May be Included

§9.125 The charges that may be included in the indictment are a function of a number of variables, including the charges in the information, whether or not there was a preliminary inquiry, the evidence at that inquiry and the justice's decision with respect to committal and discharge. If an accused did not request a preliminary inquiry and opted instead to go directly to trial in the superior court, a prosecutor may only include in the indictment a charge that was contained in the information or any included offence to that charge.[324]

§9.126 If an accused has a preliminary inquiry, the prosecutor's options are more expansive. Under section 574(1) of the *Criminal Code*, a prosecutor may include in an indictment (whether the charges were contained in one information or not[325]): (*a*) any charge on which the person was ordered to stand trial; or (*b*) any charge founded on the facts disclosed by the evidence taken on the preliminary inquiry in addition to or in substitution for any charge on which the person was ordered to stand trial.[326] Charges may be included in the indictment under

---

[320] *Ibid.* See also *Criminal Code*, s. 566. The technical requirements of informations and indictments are explained in Chapter 11.

[321] See generally, *R. v. Chabot*, [1980] S.C.J. No. 108, [1980] 2 S.C.R. 985 (S.C.C.).

[322] See *R. v. Alward*, [1976] N.B.J. No. 220, 32 C.C.C. (2d) 416 at 427-28 (N.B.C.A.), affd [1977] S.C.J. No. 63 (S.C.C.).

[323] *Criminal Code*, s. 574(3).

[324] See *Criminal Code*, s. 574(1.1). See also s. 566(3), which makes s. 574 applicable to judge alone trials in the superior court.

[325] In other words, an individual charged separately in different informations with different offences may see those charges joined in the same indictment. The rules governing indictments and severance of counts are detailed in Chapter 11. Further, under s. 574(2) the prosecutor may join together in the same indictment charges for which the accused did not have a preliminary inquiry and charges for which the accused did.

[326] See *Criminal Code*, s. 574(1). See generally, *R. v. Barbeau*, [1992] S.C.J. No. 72, [1992] 2 S.C.R. 845 (S.C.C.). See also s. 566(3), which makes s. 574 applicable to judge alone trials in the superior court. The inclusion of any charges in the indictment beyond what is contemplated by s. 577(1) requires the accused's consent. See *Criminal Code*, s. 574(2).

section 574(1) "at any time from the day after committal at the conclusion of the preliminary inquiry until the time when the accused is called upon to plead to the preferred indictment on the day that the trial commences."[327]

§9.127 The Supreme Court of Canada has interpreted section 574(1)(*b*) as permitting a prosecutor to include in an indictment, "any charge founded on facts disclosed in the evidence taken at the preliminary hearing, provided that it is not an offence charged and in respect of which the accused was not ordered to stand trial."[328] In other words, if the justice, after hearing the evidence at the preliminary inquiry, concludes that a committal to stand trial on a particular charge is not justified, section 574(1)(*b*) does not empower the prosecutor to overrule the justice's decision and proceed with that charge.[329]

§9.128 Section 574(1)(*b*) is controversial. Based solely on a prosecutor's assessment of the evidence, an accused can face trial on additional and potentially more serious offences than those charged at the preliminary inquiry. The provision has nonetheless survived constitutional challenge. In *R. v. Garcia*,[330] the accused argued that the provision violated his right to trial by jury guaranteed in section 11(*f*) of the *Charter* by requiring him to make an election without knowing precisely what additional charges he might face as a result of the evidence heard at the preliminary inquiry.[331] In rejecting this claim, the British Columbia Court of Appeal concluded that it is sufficient that the accused "is making his election on the footing that after the preliminary inquiry the Crown may exercise its right to add such additional counts as may be founded on the evidence given at the preliminary inquiry".[332]

(3) Direct Indictment

§9.129 Under section 577 of the *Code* the Attorney General may prefer a "direct indictment". This extraordinary procedure sends an accused directly to trial in the superior court and trumps any entitlement to a preliminary inquiry that an accused might otherwise have. Specifically, the provision states that an indictment may be preferred "even if the accused has not been given the opportunity to request a preliminary inquiry, a preliminary inquiry has been commenced but

---

[327] *R. v. Tapaquon*, [1993] S.C.J. No. 133, [1993] 4 S.C.R. 535 at 553-54 (S.C.C.).

[328] *Ibid.*, at 538 (S.C.R.).

[329] But see *R. v. Hyde*, [1990] M.J. No. 108, 55 C.C.C. (3d) 251 (Man. C.A.), holding that the refusal of the justice presiding at the preliminary inquiry to order the accused to stand trial with respect to another offence founded on the evidence that forms part of the same transaction but that was not charged in the information, pursuant to the justice's authority under s. 548(1)(*a*), does not preclude the Crown from including that charge in the indictment under s. 574(1)(*b*). In our view, this conclusion is entirely reconcilable with *R. v. Tapaquon*, [1993] S.C.J. No. 133, [1993] 4 S.C.R. 535 (S.C.C.). There would seem to be a clear difference between a justice discharging an accused with respect to a charge set out in the information and a justice simply refusing to commit an accused in relation to additional offences.

[330] [1990] B.C.J. No. 371, 75 C.R. (3d) 250 (B.C.C.A.).

[331] *Ibid.*

[332] *Ibid.*, at 254 (C.R.).

not concluded or a preliminary inquiry has been held and the accused has been discharged." For prosecutions undertaken by the Attorney General, a direct indictment cannot be preferred unless the "personal consent in writing" of the Attorney General or Deputy Attorney General is filed with the court.[333] For privately conducted prosecutions, the indictment cannot be preferred unless "a judge of the court so orders".[334]

§9.130 Efforts to interpret section 577 in a technical manner to limit the scope of the Attorney General's authority have rarely met with success. Instead, the courts have read it purposively, granting the Attorney General a vast power to avoid the consequences (actual or potential) of a preliminary inquiry. Specifically, the Supreme Court of Canada has held that the provision does not set out a closed list of circumstances in which a direct indictment may be preferred. As a result, the courts have found that a direct indictment may be preferred: if the accused was committed to stand trial at a preliminary inquiry;[335] on a charge for which an earlier committal to stand trial had been quashed;[336] and where a young person would otherwise have been entitled to a preliminary inquiry under the *Youth Criminal Justice Act.*[337]

§9.131 Technical arguments focusing on the precise role to be played by the Attorney General or the Deputy Attorney General have also met with failure. For example, several courts have rather sensibly rejected the argument that in order to rely on the provision the Attorney General must not only sign the indictment but must personally appear in court in order to present it.[338] Similarly, the claim that a direct indictment becomes invalid where a different person has assumed the office of Attorney General since consent was first obtained has also rightly been rejected.[339]

§9.132 In deciding whether to authorize a direct indictment, the Attorney General is not required to afford the accused a hearing, even where the Attorney General is contemplating preferring a direct indictment partway through the

---

[333] *Criminal Code*, s. 577(*a*).
[334] *Criminal Code*, s. 577(*b*).
[335] See *R. v. Benji*, [2002] S.C.J. No. 5, [2002] 1 S.C.R. 142 (S.C.C.) (permitting Crown to use a direct indictment to join two accused together for trial where the second accused's preliminary inquiry had been adjourned).
[336] See *R. v. Ewen*, [2000] S.J. No. 144 C.C.C. (3d) 277 (Sask. C.A.). Courts had taken a similarly permissive view of the triggering language found in predecessor provisions. See *R. v. Charlie*, [1988] B.C.J. No. 1506, 126 C.C.C. (3d) 513 (B.C.C.A.); *R. v. Stewart*, [1977] O.J. No. 706, 35 C.C.C. (2d) 281 (Ont. C.A.).
[337] S.C. 2002, c. 1. See *R. v. L. (S.J.)*, [2009] S.C.J. No. 14, [2009] 1 S.C.R. 426 (S.C.C.).
[338] See *R. v. Philbin*, [1977] A.J. No. 764, 37 C.C.C. (2d) 528 (Alta. C.A.); *R. v. Dwyer*, [1978] O.J. No. 3787, 42 C.C.C. (2d) 83 at 95-96 (Ont. C.A.), revd on other grounds [1979] S.C.J. No. 117, [1980] 1 S.C.R. 481 (S.C.C.); *R. v. Balderstone*, [1983] M.J. No. 207, 8 C.C.C. (3d) 532 at 536 (Man. C.A.). But see *R. v. Arseneau*, [1974] N.B.J. No. 103, 21 C.C.C. (2d) 432 (N.B.Q.B.) (holding that the Attorney General's failure to personally appear when the accused was arraigned and pleaded rendered the indictment invalid).
[339] See *R. v. Rooke*, [1988] B.C.J. No. 104, 40 C.C.C. (3d) 484 (B.C.C.A.).

accused's preliminary hearing.[340] Nor is the Crown required to provide disclosure to the accused of the "recommendation package" forwarded by the local prosecutors to the Attorney General when requesting a direct indictment. This is because such materials are subject to solicitor and client privilege.[341]

§9.133 Appellate courts have repeatedly upheld the constitutionality of the procedure for preferring a direct indictment, holding that there is no constitutional right to a preliminary inquiry.[342] The Supreme Court of Canada has acknowledged, however, that like all prosecutorial decisions, the courts may intervene if the decision amounts to an abuse of process.[343] The Ontario Court of Appeal has also pointed out that, "a contravention of s. 7 of the *Charter* may result if the combination of the direct indictment with the failure of the Crown to make adequate disclosure results in the inability of the accused to make full answer and defence at his trial."[344] As mentioned above, however, in such a case the remedy will undoubtedly be an order for further disclosure and not an opportunity to cross-examine the Crown's witnesses.[345] As the Supreme Court of Canada has made clear, the Crown's disclosure duty "does not extend to producing its witnesses for oral discovery."[346]

§9.134 As mentioned, section 577(*b*) allows for a direct indictment in private prosecutions if "a judge of the court so orders". Because the Attorney General almost always either stays or takes carriage of private prosecutions, this provision is rarely invoked. Consequently, there is very little case law to guide a judge's exercise of discretion. It has been suggested, however, that consent should not be granted too readily.[347]

---

[340] See *R. v. Saikaly*, [1979] O.J. No. 94, 48 C.C.C. (2d) 192 (Ont. C.A.); *R. v. Stolar*, [1983] M.J. No. 25, 4 C.C.C. (3d) 333 (Man. C.A.).

[341] See *R. v. Ahmad* [2008] O.J. No. 5915 (Ont. S.C.J.).

[342] See *R. v. Arviv*, [1985] O.J. No. 2602, 19 C.C.C. (3d) 395 at 404 (Ont. C.A.), leave to appeal refused [1985] S.C.C.A. No. 74, [1985] 1 S.C.R. v (S.C.C.); *R. v. Ertel*, [1987] O.J. No. 516, 35 C.C.C. (3d) 398 (Ont. C.A.), leave to appeal refused [1987] S.C.C.A. No. 354, [1987] 2 S.C.R. vii (S.C.C.); *R. v. Stolar*, [1983] M.J. No. 25, 4 C.C.C. (3d) 333 (Man. C.A.); *R. v. Sterling*, [1993] S.J. No. 354, 84 C.C.C. (3d) 65 (Sask. C.A.); *R. v. Guimond*, [2003] J.Q. no 7603, 177 C.C.C. (3d) 315 (Que. C.A.).

[343] See *R. v. L. (S.J.)*, [2009] S.C.J. No. 14, [2009] 1 S.C.R. 426 at para. 24 (S.C.C.) ("Whether a direct indictment should be preferred is at the Attorney General's discretion, and the courts will intervene in such a case only if there is an abuse of process."). See also *R. v. Ertel*, [1987] O.J. No. 516, 35 C.C.C. (3d) 398 at 414 (Ont. C.A.), leave to appeal refused [1987] S.C.C.A. No. 354, [1987] 2 S.C.R. vii (S.C.C.). The review of prosecutorial discretion under the abuse of process doctrine is discussed more generally in Chapter 10, Part 5(1)(*a*)(iii).

[344] *R. v. Ertel*, [1987] O.J. No. 516, 35 C.C.C. (3d) 398 at 414 (Ont. C.A.), leave to appeal refused [1987] S.C.C.A. No. 354, [1987] 2 S.C.R. vii (S.C.C.).

[345] See *R. v. Stolar*, [1983] M.J. No. 25, 4 C.C.C. (3d) 333 (Man. C.A.), which held that a superior court judge has no power to compel potential Crown witnesses to attend to be questioned by defence counsel where a direct indictment has been preferred.

[346] *R. v. Khela*, [1995] S.C.J. No. 95, [1995] 4 S.C.R. 201 at para. 18 (S.C.C.) 18. See also §9.116 and the cases cited in the accompanying footnote.

[347] See *Garton v. Whelan*, [1984] O.J. No. 3325, 14 C.C.C. (3d) 449 (Ont. H.C.J.) (judge should not give consent merely because preliminary inquiry justice made an error of law; consent should only be granted to prevent miscarriage of justice); *Johnson v. Inglis*, [1980] O.J. No. 1108, 52 C.C.C. (2d) 385 (Ont. H.C.J.) (where no preliminary hearing has been held consent

§9.135 The *Code* contains no explicit instruction on the question of bail for those subject to direct indictments. The Ontario Court of Appeal has thankfully provided guidance on this question.[348] It has explained that once a direct indictment is preferred, it constitutes new proceedings distinct from any previous proceedings relating to the same charges.[349] As a result, a direct indictment triggers the bail provisions in Part XVI of the *Code*. Accordingly, the accused may be brought before the trial court for the purposes of a bail hearing in at least three ways. First, if the accused is in custody he or she may be brought to court on a judge's order. Second, if the accused is not in custody, a judge of the trial court may also issue a summons or warrant for his or her arrest. Third, a police officer who has reasonable and probable grounds to believe the accused has committed the offence alleged in the indictment may arrest the accused and take him or her before a justice for a bail hearing.[350] But if an accused was already on bail on charges included in the direct indictment, any existing bail order attaching to the information containing those charges remains effective until the Crown either withdraws or stays the charges in the information. Finally, a judge in the superior court where the accused will be tried should deal with the question of bail.[351]

---

should only be granted where there is a compelling reason to deprive the person of a such a hearing).

[348] *R. v. Jones*, [1997] O.J. No. 613, 113 C.C.C. (3d) 225 (Ont. C.A.).
[349] *Ibid.*, at 232 (C.C.C.).
[350] *Ibid.*, at 233-34 (C.C.C.).
[351] *Ibid.*

Chapter 10

CHARTER REMEDIES

1. INTRODUCTION

§10.1 When a rule of criminal procedure is breached, the person suffering the breach (usually a suspect or defendant) will often (but not always[1]) be able to seek a remedy. A right without a remedy, it is often said, is of little value.[2] These remedies stem from three sources: common law,[3] statute and the Constitution. In this book, the most important common law and statutory remedies are discussed in tandem with the rules they attach to.[4] Constitutional remedies stem from two sources: section 52(1) of the *Constitution Act, 1982*[5] and section 24 of the *Canadian Charter of Rights and Freedoms*.[6] Typically, section 52(1) is invoked when the claimant challenges the constitutionality of the law itself, and section 24 when the challenge is to the constitutionality of the discretionary acts of government agents acting pursuant to constitutional laws.[7]

§10.2 Section 52(1) declares the Constitution to be the "supreme law of Canada" and deems any law inconsistent with it to be "to the extent of the

---

[1]   *Criminal Code*, R.S.C. 1985, c. C-46, s. 495(3).
[2]   *R. v. Therens*, [1983] S.J. No. 325, 5 C.C.C. (3d) 409 at 426-27 (Sask. C.A.), affd [1985] S.C.J. No. 30 (S.C.C.); *R. v. Mills*, [1986] S.C.J. No. 39, [1986] 1 S.C.R. 863 at 881 (S.C.C.), *per* Lamer J., at 971 (S.C.R.), *per* La Forest J.; *R. v. 974649 Ontario Inc.*, [2001] S.C.J. No. 79, [2001] 3 S.C.R. 575 at para. 20 (S.C.C.); *Nelles v. Ontario*, [1989] S.C.J. No. 86, [1989] 2 S.C.R. 170 at 196 (S.C.C.).
[3]   By "common law", we include the various prerogative remedies historically available from courts of equity.
[4]   See *e.g.*, Chapter 3, Part 3(3)(*e*) (return of seized material); Chapter 4, Part 2 (confessions rule).
[5]   Being Schedule B to the *Canada Act 1982* (U.K.), 1982, c. 11, Part VII.
[6]   Part I of the *Constitution Act, 1982*, being Schedule B to the *Canada Act 1982* (U.K.), 1982, c. 11 [*Charter*].
[7]   See *R. v. Ferguson*, [2008] S.C.J. No. 6, [2008] 1 S.C.R. 96 at paras. 35, 60 (S.C.C.); *Eldridge v. British Columbia (Attorney General)*, [1997] S.C.J. No. 86, [1997] 3 S.C.R. 624 (S.C.C.); *R. v. 974649 Ontario Inc.*, [2001] S.C.J. No. 79, [2001] 3 S.C.R. 575 at para. 14 (S.C.C.); *Doucet-Boudreau v. Nova Scotia (Minister of Education)*, [2003] S.C.J. No. 63, [2003] 3 S.C.R. 3 at para. 43 (S.C.C.); *Schachter v. Canada*, [1992] S.C.J. No. 68, [1992] 2 S.C.R. 679 at 719-20(S.C.C.); Peter W. Hogg, *Constitutional Law of Canada*, 5th ed. (supplemented), vol. 2, looseleaf (Toronto: Thomson Carswell, 2007) § 40.1(c). On occasion, both provisions may be relied on, for example, where police are alleged to have obtained evidence by relying on an unconstitutional power. If the court finds the power to be unconstitutional in such a case it will declare it to be of no force or effect under s. 52(1) of the *Constitution Act, 1982* and go on to decide whether the evidence should be excluded under s. 24(2) of the *Charter*.

inconsistency, of no force or effect."[8] The Constitution includes, *inter alia*, the division of legislative powers set out in the *Constitution Act, 1867* and the rights and freedoms enshrined in the *Charter*.[9] In other chapters of this book we discuss several criminal procedural laws struck down under section 52(1), such as the search powers found to violate section 8 of the *Charter* in *Hunter v. Southam Inc. (sub nom. Canada (Combines Investigation Acts, Director of Investigation and Research) v. Southam Inc.)*.[10] We leave the detailed treatment of section 52(1), however, for other works.[11]

§10.3 This chapter focuses on the criminal procedural remedies provided by the *Charter* itself. As mentioned, these remedies exist by virtue of section 24 of the *Charter*, which, in its entirety, states:

> (1) Anyone whose rights or freedoms, as guaranteed by this *Charter*, have been infringed or denied may apply to a court of competent jurisdiction to obtain such remedy as the court considers appropriate and just in the circumstances.

> (2) Where, in proceedings under subsection (1), a court concludes that evidence was obtained in a manner that infringed or denied any rights or freedoms guaranteed by this Charter, the evidence shall be excluded if it is

---

[8]   The specific remedies flowing from a finding of invalidity under s. 52(1) may include nullification, temporary validity, severance, reading in and reading down. See Peter W. Hogg, *Constitutional Law of Canada*, 5th ed. (supplemented), vol. 2, looseleaf (Toronto: Thomson Carswell, 2007) § 40.1; *R. v. Ferguson*, [2008] S.C.J. No. 6, [2008] 1 S.C.R. 96 at paras. 39, 49 (S.C.C.); *Schachter v. Canada*, [1992] S.C.J. No. 68, [1992] 2 S.C.R. 679 (S.C.C.). In limited circumstances, it may also be possible to receive a "constitutional exemption" relieving an accused from the application of a law that does not violate the *Charter* as applied generally, but did so in the particular circumstances of the case. In *R. v. Ferguson*, [2008] S.C.J. No. 6, [2008] 1 S.C.R. 96 (S.C.C.), however, the Court ruled that constitutional exemptions are not available (under either s. 52 of the *Constitution Act, 1982* or s. 24(1) of the *Charter*) as a remedy for mandatory minimum sentencing provisions that violate the right against cruel and unusual punishment in s. 12 of the *Charter*. The *Ferguson* Court also strongly suggested (at paras. 62-66 (S.C.R.)) that, on its own, s. 24(1) can never be used as a remedy for *Charter* violations stemming from legislation (as opposed to government acts). See also *Downtown Eastside Sex Workers United Against Violence Society v. Canada (Attorney General)*, [2010] B.C.J. No. 1983, 2010 BCCA 439 at para. 35 (B.C.C.A.) (s. 24(1) remedy not available when challenging legislation, as opposed to state action). In the legislative context, s. 24 remedies may be used only to supplement s. 52(1) declarations of invalidity when such relief "is necessary to provide the claimant with an effective remedy." *Ibid.*, at para. 63 (B.C.C.A.). See also *R. v. Demers*, [2004] S.C.J. No. 43, [2004] 2 S.C.R. 489 at paras. 61-64 (S.C.C.).

[9]   See *Constitution Act, 1982*, s. 52(2).

[10] See Chapter 3, Part 2(5)(*a*) - (*b*); *Hunter v. Southam Inc. (sub nom. Canada (Combines Investigation Acts, Director of Investigation and Research) v. Southam Inc.)*, [1984] S.C.J. No. 36, [1984] 2 S.C.R. 145 (S.C.C.).

[11] See Peter W. Hogg, *Constitutional Law of Canada*, 5th ed. (supplemented), vol. 2, looseleaf (Toronto: Thomson Carswell, 2007) § 40.1; Kent Roach, *Constitutional Remedies in Canada*, looseleaf (Aurora: Canada Law Book, 2008) c. 14; Hon. Robert J. Sharp & Kent Roach, *The Charter of Rights and Freedoms*, 3d ed. (Toronto: Irwin Law, 2005) at 347-58; Andrew K. Lokan & Christopher M. Dassios, *Constitutional Litigation in Canada*, looseleaf (Toronto: Thomson Carswell, 2006) 6-8.1-6-19.

established that, having regard to all the circumstances, the admission of it in the proceedings would bring the administration of justice into disrepute.[12]

§10.4 Section 24 therefore provides for two different types of remedies: (*i*) any remedy that the court considers "appropriate and just in the circumstances"; and (*ii*) the exclusion of evidence. Before either type of remedy can be ordered, however, two preliminary issues must be determined: (*i*) whether the applicant has standing to apply for a remedy; and (*ii*) whether the court has the authority to grant it. As discussed immediately below, the jurisprudence on these questions applies equally to sections 24(1) and 24(2).

2. STANDING

§10.5 As mentioned, section 24(1) permits anyone "whose [*Charter*] rights or freedoms ... have been infringed" to apply for a remedy. A plain reading of this phrase suggests, firstly, that the infringement must have occurred before a remedy can be sought; and second, that a remedy cannot be awarded for the violation of the rights of anyone other than the applicant. On the first point, however, the Supreme Court of Canada has not insisted that the infringement precede the remedy. Standing may accordingly be granted to persons alleging apprehended *Charter* violations.[13] This will only occur, however, when the application is ripe, *i.e.*, when sufficient facts are available to permit a proper adjudication on both violation and remedy.[14]

§10.6 The Court's position on the second point, in contrast, has been strict: only persons whose own *Charter* rights have been violated may seek remedies under sections 24(1) or 24(2).[15] Thus in *R. v. Edwards*,[16] the Supreme Court of Canada

---

[12] As discussed below, Part 5(1)(*a*)(vi), the Supreme Court has sometimes granted remedies directly under various *Charter* rights provisions, such as ss. 7 and 11(*d*).

[13] See *Operation Dismantle Inc. v. Canada*, [1985] S.C.J. No. 22, [1985] 1 S.C.R. 441 (S.C.C.); *R. v. Vermette*, [1988] S.C.J. No. 47, [1988] 1 S.C.R. 985 (S.C.C.); *R. v. A.*, [1990] S.C.J. No. 43, [1990] 1 S.C.R. 995 (S.C.C.); *R. v. Mills*, [1999] S.C.J. No. 68, [1999] 3 S.C.R. 668 (S.C.C.); *New Brunswick (Minister of Health and Community Services) v. G.(J.)*, [1999] S.C.J. No. 47, [1999] 3 S.C.R. 46 (S.C.C.); *United States of America v. Kwok*, [2001] S.C.J. No. 19, [2001] 1 S.C.R. 532 (S.C.C.).

[14] See *R. v. Vermette*, [1988] S.C.J. No. 47, [1988] 1 S.C.R. 985 (S.C.C.); *Danson v. Ontario (Attorney General)*, [1990] S.C.J. No. 92, [1990] 2 S.C.R. 1086 (S.C.C.).

[15] See *R. v. Rahey*, [1987] S.C.J. No. 23, [1987] 1 S.C.R. 588 at 619 (S.C.C.), *per* Wilson J.; *R. v. Wijeshina*, [1995] S.C.J. No. 49, [1995] 3 S.C.R. 422 at 449 (S.C.C.); *R. v. Edwards*, [1996] S.C.J. No. 11, [1996] 1 S.C.R. 128 at paras. 45, 51-56 (S.C.C.); *R. v. Belnavis*, [1997] S.C.J. No. 81, [1997] 3 S.C.R. 341 at para. 20 (S.C.C.); *R. v. Ferguson*, [2008] S.C.J. No. 6, [2008] 1 S.C.R. 96 at para. 61 (S.C.C.); *Borowski v. Canada (Attorney General)*, [1989] S.C.J. No. 14, [1989] 1 S.C.R. 342 at 367 (S.C.C.). In this s. 24 differs from s. 52(1), under which any person with standing in the proceeding, including persons charged with an offence, may apply to strike down a law, even if only third parties suffer its unconstitutional effects. The rationale for this rule is that an unconstitutional law is null and void in its entirety and therefore cannot be validly applied against anyone. See *R. v. Ferguson*, [2008] S.C.J. No. 6, [2008] 1 S.C.R. 96 at para. 59 (S.C.C.); *R. v. Big M Drug Mart Ltd.*, [1985] S.C.J. No. 17, [1985] 1 S.C.R. 295 at 313 (S.C.C.); Peter Sankoff, "Constitutional Exemptions: Myth or Reality?" (1999-2000) 11 N.J.C.L. 411 at 432-34; Kent Roach, *Constitutional Remedies in Canada*, looseleaf (Aurora: Canada Law Book, 2008) at paras. 5.40-5.355.

held that evidence that may have been obtained in violation of the defendant's girlfriend's section 8 *Charter* rights could not be excluded at his trial.[17]

§10.7 While restricting section 24's scope to personal remedies may be justifiable as a matter of constitutional interpretation,[18] it limits the capacity of courts to deter investigative abuses. As *Edwards* illustrates, the standing rule permits police to obtain admissible evidence against a suspect who lacks a reasonable expectation of privacy in the location searched by committing (potentially serious) violations of the section 8 rights of third parties.[19] Because non-accused victims of *Charter* violations rarely seek legal redress, police may commit such violations with relative impunity.[20]

§10.8 Fortunately, there may be ways to surmount this problem.[21] One is to interpret the relevant procedural right so as to protect the interests of third parties.[22] Another, discussed in Part 5(1)(*a*)(vi), below, is to find that admitting evidence obtained by violating a non-defendant's rights would be "unfair" or constitute an abuse of process. Whatever method is used, courts should have some way to discourage violations of the rights of third parties.[23] To focus exclusively on the accused's rights gives "greater protection to ...the accused or other wrongdoer than to a person against whom there may be no reasonable suspicion of wrongdoing."[24]

§10.9 Lastly, third parties in criminal trial proceedings (*i.e.*, persons other than the accused or Crown) may in limited circumstances have standing to apply for section 24 remedies for violations of their own rights. This may occur where the

---

16   [1996] S.C.J. No. 11, [1996] 1 S.C.R. 128 (S.C.C.).

17   *Ibid*. The application of this rule to s. 24(2) flows from that provision's opening clause ("Where, in proceedings under subsection (1)..."). See *R. v. Hynes*, [2001] S.C.J. No. 80, [2001] 3 S.C.R. 623 at para. 15 (S.C.C.).

18   See Kent Roach, *Constitutional Remedies in Canada*, looseleaf (Aurora: Canada Law Book, 2008) at para. 5.390.

19   See generally, *R. v. Edwards*, [1996] S.C.J. No. 11, [1996] 1 S.C.R. 128 (S.C.C.), La Forest J., dissenting.

20   See Kent Roach, *Constitutional Remedies in Canada*, looseleaf (Aurora.: Canada Law Book, 2008) at paras. 10.450-10.570. See also Jonathan Dawe, "Standing to Challenge Searches and Seizures Under the *Charter*: The Lessons of the American Experience and Their Application to Canadian Law" (1993) 52 U.T. Fac. L. Rev. 39 at 68-71.

21   See Steven Penney, "Taking Deterrence Seriously: Excluding Unconstitutionally Obtained Evidence Under Section 24(2) of the *Charter*" (2004) 49 McGill L.J. 105 at 125-26.

22   See *R. v. A.*, [1990] S.C.J. No. 43, [1990] 1 S.C.R. 995 at 1003 (S.C.C.), *per* Sopinka J.; *R. v. Belnavis*, [1997] S.C.J. No. 81, [1997] 3 S.C.R. 341 at paras. 61, 65 (S.C.C.), *per* La Forest J., dissenting; Jonathan Dawe, "Standing to Challenge Searches and Seizures Under the *Charter*: The Lessons of the American Experience and Their Application to Canadian Law" (1993) 52 U.T. Fac. L. Rev. 39 at 53-56, 60-61; Kent Roach, *Constitutional Remedies in Canada*, looseleaf (Aurora: Canada Law Book, 2008) at paras. 5.410-5.420.

23   As discussed in Chapter 3, Part 2(5)(*c*)(i), if the applicant does have standing, the effect of the alleged violation on third parties' *Charter* rights may be considered in deciding whether there has been a violation of the applicant's rights. See *R. v. Thompson*, [1990] S.C.J. No. 104, [1990] 2 S.C.R. 1111 (S.C.C.); *R. v. Martin*, [2010] N.B.J. No. 198, 2010 NBCA 41 at paras. 47-48.

24   *R. v. Edwards*, [1996] S.C.J. No. 11, [1996] 1 S.C.R. 128 at para. 64 (S.C.C.), *per* La Forest J., dissenting.

media wishes to vindicate its *Charter* rights or challenge a publication ban,[25] when a third party wishes to exclude evidence from proceedings[26] or when a witness wishes to suppress records or information obtained in violation of a *Charter* right.[27] Alternatively, such a party may seek a *Charter* remedy by way of an originating motion in superior court.[28]

3. COURT OF COMPETENT JURISDICTION
(1) General Principles

§10.10 Section 24's remedies, including the exclusion of evidence under subparagraph (2), may only be granted by a "court of competent jurisdiction".[29] According to the Supreme Court, this refers to a court that has jurisdiction over the person, subject matter and remedy.[30] Whether a tribunal has jurisdiction over either the person applying for the remedy or the subject matter of the dispute is rarely contentious.[31] The key question is thus whether it has jurisdiction to award *Charter* remedies. The Court has held that this remedial power must stem from "a source other than the *Charter* itself".[32] As discussed in Part 3(2), below, the superior courts have an inherent jurisdiction to award *Charter* remedies. For other tribunals, the power to award *Charter* remedies derives exclusively from statute.[33] Legislatures may expressly authorize a tribunal to grant *Charter* remedies, but as most enabling statutes predate the *Charter*, this will be rare.[34] More

---

[25] *Dagenais v. Canadian Broadcasting Corp.*, [1994] S.C.J. No. 104, [1994] 3 S.C.R. 835 (S.C.C.).

[26] *R. v. Shayesteh*, [1996] O.J. No. 393, 31 O.R. (3d) 161 (C.A.); *R. c. Rendon*, [1999] J.Q. no 4124, 140 C.C.C. (3d) 12 (Que. C.A.), affd *(sub nom. R. v. Peters; R. v. Rendon)* [2001] S.C.J. No. 35 (S.C.C.). See also *R. v. Guilbride*, [2003] B.C.J. No. 1258, 10 C.R. (6th) 243 (B.C. Prov. Ct.) (exclusion of evidence obtained from third parties flowing from *Charter* breaches against accused).

[27] *R. v. Mack*, [2006] A.J. No. 494, 2006 ABQB 324 (Alta. Q.B.).

[28] See *Re Southam Inc. and The Queen (No. 1)*, [1983] O.J. No. 2962, 41 O.R. (2d) 113 (Ont. C.A.); *Canadian Newspapers Co. v. Attorney-General for Canada*, [1985] O.J. No. 2485, 49 O.R. (2d) 557 (Ont. C.A.), revd [1988] S.C.J. No. 67 (S.C.C.); *R. v. S. (N.)*, [2010] O.J. No. 4306, 2010 ONCA 670 (Ont. C.A.).

[29] *R. v. Hynes*, [2001] S.C.J. No. 80, [2001] 3 S.C.R. 623 at para. 15 (S.C.C.).

[30] *Singh v. Canada (Minister of Employment and Immigration)*, [1985] S.C.J. No. 11, [1985] 1 S.C.R. 177 (S.C.C.); *R. v. Mills*, [1986] S.C.J. No. 39, [1986] 1 S.C.R. 863 at 890 (S.C.C.), Lamer J. dissenting; *R. v. 974649 Ontario Inc.*, [2001] S.C.J. No. 79, [2001] 3 S.C.R. 575 at para. 15 (S.C.C.); *Weber v. Ontario Hydro*, [1995] S.C.J. No. 59, [1995] 2 S.C.R. 929 (S.C.C.); *Mooring v. Canada (National Parole Board)*, [1996] S.C.J. No. 10, [1996] 1 S.C.R. 75 at para. 22 (S.C.C.).

[31] See *R. v. Conway*, [2010] S.C.J. No. 22, [2010] 1 S.C.R. 765 at para. 40 (S.C.C.) (noting that courts have not defined "jurisdiction over the parties" and "jurisdiction over the subject matter" and that decisions always turn on whether the tribunal has remedial jurisdiction).

[32] *R. v. 974649 Ontario Inc.*, [2001] S.C.J. No. 79, [2001] 3 S.C.R. 575 at para. 26 (S.C.C.). See also *Singh v. Minister of Employment and Immigration*, [1985] S.C.J. No. 11, [1985] 1 S.C.R. 177 at 222 (S.C.C.).

[33] *R. v. Mills*, [1986] S.C.J. No. 39, [1986] 1 S.C.R. 863 at 952 (S.C.C.), *per* McIntyre J.

[34] *R. v. 974649 Ontario Inc.*, [2001] S.C.J. No. 79, [2001] 3 S.C.R. 575 at para. 27 (S.C.C.).

commonly, the question is whether the legislation implicitly grants the power to order remedies under section 24.

§10.11 Previously, the Supreme Court had held that the answer to this question turned on whether the tribunal's "function and structure" revealed that it is "an appropriate forum for ordering the *Charter* remedy in question."[35] However, in *R. v. Conway*,[36] the Court departed from this approach, ruling that the decision hinges on whether the tribunal has "jurisdiction to grant *Charter* remedies *generally*".[37] This in turn depends on whether the tribunal has explicit or implied jurisdiction to decide questions of law.[38] If it does, and the legislature has not "clearly" prohibited it from deciding *Charter* claims, the tribunal is a court of competent jurisdiction.[39] The Court added:

> The tribunal must then decide, given this jurisdiction, whether it can grant the particular remedy sought based on its statutory mandate. The answer to this question will depend on legislative intent, as discerned from the tribunal's statutory mandate.[40]

§10.12 *Conway*'s significance is not yet clear. Writing for the Court, Justice Abella did signal a preference for permitting tribunals to award *Charter* remedies. "Over two decades of jurisprudence has confirmed," she wrote, "the practical advantages and constitutional basis for allowing Canadians to assert their *Charter* rights in the most accessible forum available, without the need for bifurcated proceedings between superior courts and administrative tribunals."[41] That said, Justice Abella confirmed that in deciding whether a court of competent jurisdiction can grant it, the remedy sought must be one that "the legislature intended would fit within the statutory framework of the particular tribunal."[42] To divine this legislative intent, she added, courts should continue to focus on factors identified in previous case law, including "the tribunal's statutory mandate, structure and function."[43] Under this jurisprudence, the factors relevant to "function" include: the tribunal's role the legislative scheme; whether

---

[35] *Ibid.*, at para. 35 (S.C.R.). See also *R. v. Hynes*, [2001] S.C.J. No. 80, [2001] 3 S.C.R. 623 at para. 27 (S.C.C.).

[36] [2010] S.C.J. No. 22, [2010] 1 S.C.R. 765 at para. 40 (S.C.C.).

[37] *R. v. Conway*, [2010] S.C.J. No. 22, [2010] 1 S.C.R. 765 at para. 22 (S.C.C.) [emphasis added].

[38] *R. v. Conway*, [2010] S.C.J. No. 22, [2010] 1 S.C.R. 765 at paras. 22, 81 (S.C.C.). This holding mirrors the Court's decision in *Nova Scotia (Workers' Compensation Board) v. Martin*, [2003] S.C.J. No. 54, [2003] 2 S.C.R. 504 at para. 36 (S.C.C.), where it held that (subject to express statutory direction to the contrary) tribunals may determine constitutional validity under s. 52(1) of the *Constitution Act, 1982* if they are statutorily empowered to decide question of law. See also *Paul v. British Columbia (Forest Appeals Commission)*, [2003] S.C.J. No. 34, [2003] 2 S.C.R. 585 at para. 39 (S.C.C.); *Douglas/Kwantlen Faculty Assn. v. Douglas College*, [1990] S.C.J. No. 124, [1990] 3 S.C.R. 570 (S.C.C.); *Cuddy Chicks Ltd. v. Ontario (Labour Relations Board)*, [1991] S.C.J. No. 42, [1991] 2 S.C.R. 5 (S.C.C.); Kent Roach, *Constitutional Remedies in Canada*, looseleaf (Aurora, ON: Canada Law Book, 2008) at paras. 6.130-6.204.

[39] *R. v. Conway*, [2010] S.C.J. No. 22, [2010] 1 S.C.R. 765 at paras. 22, 81 (S.C.C.).

[40] *Ibid.*, at para. 22 (S.C.R.) [citations omitted].

[41] *Ibid.*, at para. 79 (S.C.R.) [citations omitted].

[42] *Ibid.*, at para. 82 (S.C.R.).

[43] *Ibid.*, at para. 82 (S.C.R.) [citations omitted].

jurisdiction to order the remedy would "frustrate or enhance this role"; the importance of the remedial power to the tribunal's "effective and efficient functioning"; the tribunal's function in the "broader legal system"; and the availability of another, more appropriate forum to redress the violation.[44] The factors relevant to "structure" include: the "judicial or quasi-judicial" nature of the proceedings; the "role of counsel"; the applicability of "traditional rules of proof and evidence"; whether the tribunal "can issue subpoenas"; whether evidence is "offered under oath"; the decision maker's expertise; the tribunal's "institutional experience" with the remedy in question; its workload; the "time constraints it operates under"; and its ability to "compile an adequate record for a reviewing court".[45]

§10.13 In the following paragraphs, we outline the jurisdictional limits on the courts and tribunals most relevant to the criminal process.

(2) Superior Courts

§10.14 Superior courts, *i.e.*, those established under section 96 of the *Constitution Act, 1867*,[46] are always courts of competent jurisdiction under section 24 of the *Charter*.[47] They have an inherent jurisdiction to award *Charter* remedies that cannot be ousted by statute.[48] Accordingly, the framework set out in *Conway* and its predecessors for deciding whether a tribunal is a "court of competent jurisdiction" does not apply to superior courts.[49] Section 24 also gives superior courts much broader powers to review and reverse orders of other superior courts than they possessed before the *Charter*.[50]

§10.15 While section 24 does not impose any jurisdictional limits on superior courts, as detailed in Part 5(1), below, it may still be argued that a requested

---

[44] *R. v. 974649 Ontario Inc.*, [2001] S.C.J. No. 79, [2010] 3 S.C.R. 575 at para. 44 (S.C.C.).

[45] *Ibid.*, at para. 45 (S.C.R.).

[46] (U.K.), 30 & 31 Vict., c. 3.

[47] *R. v. Rahey*, [1987] S.C.J. No. 23, [1987] 1 S.C.R. 588 at 598 (S.C.C.), *per* Lamer J., 616 (S.C.R.), *per* Le Dain J., 618 (S.C.R.), *per* Wilson J.; *R. v. Smith*, [1989] S.C.J. No. 119, [1989] 2 S.C.R. 1120 (S.C.C.); *Doucet-Boudreau v. Nova Scotia (Minister of Education)*, [2003] S.C.J. No. 63, [2003] 3 S.C.R. 3 at para. 49 (S.C.C.).

[48] *Doucet-Boudreau v. Nova Scotia (Minister of Education)*, [2003] S.C.J. No. 63, [2003] 3 S.C.R. 3 at paras. 46, 48 (S.C.C.); *R. v. Mills*, [1986] S.C.J. No. 39, [1986] 1 S.C.R. 863 at 956 (S.C.C.), *per* McIntyre J., 892-93 (S.C.R.), *per* Lamer J., dissenting.

[49] *Doucet-Boudreau v. Nova Scotia (Minister of Education)*, [2003] S.C.J. No. 63, [2003] 3 S.C.R. 3 at para. 48 (S.C.C.).

[50] See *Kourtessis v. Canada (Minister of National Revenue - M.N.R.)*, [1993] S.C.J. No. 45, [1993] 2 S.C.R. 53 (S.C.C.); *R. v. Dersch*, [1993] S.C.J. No. 116, [1993] 3 S.C.R. 768 (S.C.C.); *R. v. Garofoli*, [1990] S.C.J. No. 115, [1990] 2 S.C.R. 1421 (S.C.C.); *R. v. Zito*, [1990] S.C.J. No. 114, [1990] 2 S.C.R. 1520 (S.C.C.); *R. v. Lachance*, [1990] S.C.J. No. 116, [1990] 2 S.C.R. 1490 (S.C.C.); *Dagenais v. Canadian Broadcasting Corp.*, [1994] S.C.J. No. 104, [1994] 3 S.C.R. 835 (S.C.C.). See also Kent Roach, *Constitutional Remedies in Canada*, looseleaf (Aurora: Canada Law Book, 2008) at paras. 6.270-6.300; Michael Code, "American Cadillacs or Canadian Compacts: What is the Correct Criminal Procedure for S. 24 Applications under the Charter of Rights? (Part II)" (1991) 33 Crim. L.Q. 407 at 437-38.

remedy would not be "appropriate and just in the circumstances."[51] Further, where a matter is before an inferior court (such as a provincial court trying a criminal offence), the superior court should normally decline to exercise its power to award *Charter* remedies.[52] As discussed in the next section, trial courts are the preferred forum for section 24 applications. Consequently, when not serving as the trial court, the superior court should generally decide *Charter* claims only when the trial court: (*i*) has not yet been assigned;[53] (*ii*) lacks the power to order the remedy sought;[54] or (*iii*) is implicated in the alleged violation.[55] For the purposes of section 24, superior courts (when they are not acting as trial courts) are the courts of last resort — they are always competent, but should step aside unless no other court is fit to award the remedy.

(3) Criminal Trial Courts

§10.16 All courts conducting criminal trials, including inferior courts of criminal jurisdiction, may issue section 24 remedies.[56] Indeed, because trial courts are usually best situated to assess the relevant circumstances, they are presumed to be the best forum to redress *Charter* breaches.[57] The decision to award or refuse a *Charter* remedy may be made before or during trial[58] and may be appealed as a

---

[51] *Doucet-Boudreau v. Nova Scotia (Minister of Education)*, [2003] S.C.J. No. 63, [2003] 3 S.C.R. 3 at para. 50 (S.C.C.).

[52] See *R. v. Mills*, [1986] S.C.J. No. 39, [1986] 1 S.C.R. 863 at 892, 894 (S.C.C.), *per* Lamer J., dissenting; *R. v. S. (N.)*, [2010] O.J. No. 4306, 2010 ONCA 670 at paras 17-18 (Ont. C.A.). This limitation is derived from the direction in s. 24(1) that any remedy awarded must be one that the "court considers appropriate and just in the circumstances." See *Doucet-Boudreau v. Nova Scotia (Minister of Education)*, [2003] S.C.J. No. 63, [2003] 3 S.C.R. 3 at para. 52 (S.C.C.).

[53] *R. v. Mills*, [1986] S.C.J. No. 39, [1986] 1 S.C.R. 863 at 958 (S.C.C.), *per* La Forest J.; *R. v. Rahey*, [1987] S.C.J. No. 23, [1987] 1 S.C.R. 588 at 603-604 (S.C.C.), *per* Lamer J.; *R. v. Smith*, [1989] S.C.J. No. 119, [1989] 2 S.C.R. 1120 at 1128-29 (S.C.C.) (application for stay under s. 11(*b*) properly before superior court where preliminary inquiry not yet held and delay already considerable); *Kourtessis v. Canada (Minister of National Revenue - M.N.R.)*, [1993] S.C.J. No. 45, [1993] 2 S.C.R. 53 (S.C.C.) (application to superior court to quash search warrant and declare authorizing statute permitted invalid as no trial judge assigned).

[54] See above, Part 3(2).

[55] *R. v. Rahey*, [1987] S.C.J. No. 23, [1987] 1 S.C.R. 588 at 603-604 (S.C.C.), *per* Lamer J., 630 (S.C.R.), *per* La Forest J. (trial judge failed to render decision on motion for directed verdict in timely fashion). See also *R. v. Mills*, [1986] S.C.J. No. 39, [1986] 1 S.C.R. 863 at 972-73 (S.C.C.), *per* La Forest J.

[56] *R. v. Mills*, [1986] S.C.J. No. 39, [1986] 1 S.C.R. 863 at 955 (S.C.C.), *per* McIntyre J.

[57] *R. v. Mills*, [1986] S.C.J. No. 39, [1986] 1 S.C.R. 863 at 955 (S.C.C.), *per* McIntyre J., 894-96 (S.C.R.), *per* Lamer J., dissenting, 970-71 (S.C.R.), *per* La Forest J.; *R. v. Rahey*, [1987] S.C.J. No. 23, [1987] 1 S.C.R. 588 at 603 (S.C.C.), *per* Lamer J.; *R. v. Smith*, [1989] S.C.J. No. 119, [1989] 2 S.C.R. 1120 at 1128-30 (S.C.C.). As mentioned above, Part 3(2), an application to the superior court may be required when the trial court has not yet been assigned, lacks the power to award the remedy sought or is itself the source of the *Charter* violation.

[58] *R. v. Mills*, [1986] S.C.J. No. 39, [1986] 1 S.C.R. 863 at 957-58 (S.C.C.).

question of law under the usual *Criminal Code* procedures.[59] As with other trial court decisions, interlocutory appeals generally are not permitted.[60]

§10.17 The range of remedies available to inferior criminal courts, moreover, is not absolute. Though they are not limited to the specific remedies set out in their enabling statues, they may not award remedies falling outside the ambit of the criminal law powers set out in the Constitution.[61] Consequently, while they may order traditionally "criminal" remedies (such as stays,[62] the exclusion of evidence,[63] the appointment of counsel,[64] publication bans,[65] disclosure of evidence[66] and costs[67]), they may not order either civil remedies[68] or prerogative relief.[69] Applications for such orders must be made to the superior court.

(4) Preliminary Inquiries

§10.18 The Supreme Court of Canada has twice considered whether preliminary inquiry justices are courts of competent jurisdiction. Though the specific issue in *R. v. Mills*[70] was whether a stay of proceedings could be awarded for a violation of the right to be tried within a reasonable time, a majority of the Court concluded that preliminary inquiry justices were not courts of competent jurisdiction for *any* purpose under section 24, including the exclusion of unconstitutionally obtained evidence under section 24(2).[71]

---

[59] *R. v. Mills*, [1986] S.C.J. No. 39, [1986] 1 S.C.R. 863 at 958-60 (S.C.C.), *per* McIntyre J. See also Chapter 18.

[60] *R. v. Mills*, [1986] S.C.J. No. 39, [1986] 1 S.C.R. 863 at 958-60 (S.C.C.), *per* McIntyre J. See also *Tingley v. R.*, [2011] N.B.J. No. 22, 2011 NBCA 8 (N.B.C.A.).

[61] *R. v. Mills*, [1986] S.C.J. No. 39, [1986] 1 S.C.R. 863 at 955 (S.C.C.), *per* McIntyre J.

[62] *R. v. Mills*, [1986] S.C.J. No. 39, [1986] 1 S.C.R. 863 (S.C.C.).

[63] *R. v. Therens*, [1985] S.C.J. No. 30, [1985] 1 S.C.R. 613 (S.C.C.); *R. v. Stillman*, [1997] S.C.J. No. 34, [1997] 1 S.C.R. 607 (S.C.C.).

[64] *Legal Services Society v. British Columbia (Provincial Court, Judge)*, [1983] B.C.J. No. 1772, 5 C.C.C. (3d) 404 (B.C.S.C.); *Re White and The Queen*, [1976] A.J. No. 574, 1 Alta. L.R. (2d) 292 (Alta. T.D.); *R. v. Cote*, [2002] S.J. No. 517, [2002] 11 W.W.R. 706 (Sask. Q.B.).

[65] *Dagenais v. Canadian Broadcasting Corp.*, [1994] S.C.J. No. 104, [1994] 3 S.C.R. 835 (S.C.C.); *Criminal Code*, R.S.C. 1985, c. C-46, ss. 517, 539, 631(6).

[66] *R. v. O'Connor*, [1995] S.C.J. No. 98, [1995] 4 S.C.R. 411 (S.C.C.).

[67] *R. v. 974649 Ontario Inc.*, [2001] S.C.J. No. 79, [2001] 3 S.C.R. 575 at para. 80 (S.C.C.); *R. v. Ouellette*, [1980] S.C.J. No. 12, [1980] 1 S.C.R. 568 (S.C.C.); *R. v. Taylor*, [2008] N.S.J. No. 14, 230 C.C.C. (3d) 504 (N.S.C.A.); *R. v. Caron*, [2009] A.J. No. 70, 241 C.C.C. (3d) 296 (Alta. C.A.), affd [2011] S.C.J. No. 5, [2011] 1 S.C.R. 78 (S.C.C.) (quasi-criminal proceedings).

[68] However, as discussed in Part 5(1)(*a*)(v), below, an individual whose *Charter* rights are violated can seek damages in a separate civil proceeding. See generally, *Vancouver (City) v. Ward*, [2010] S.C.J. No. 27, [2010] 2 S.C.R. 28 (S.C.C.).

[69] *R. v. Mills*, [1986] S.C.J. No. 39, [1986] 1 S.C.R. 863 at 884-86 (S.C.C.), *per* Lamer J., at 955-56 (S.C.R.), *per* McIntyre J., 971 (S.C.R.), *per* La Forest J. The prerogative remedies, which include *mandamus, certiorari*, prohibition and *habeas corpus* are discussed in Chapter 1, Part 5(2).

[70] [1986] S.C.J. No. 39, [1986] 1 S.C.R. 863 (S.C.C.).

[71] *R. v. Mills*, [1986] S.C.J. No. 39, [1986] 1 S.C.R. 863 at 889 (S.C.C.), *per* Lamer J., 954-56 (S.C.R.), *per* McIntyre J., 970-71 (S.C.R.), *per* La Forest J. See also *R. v. Carter*, [1986] S.C.J. No. 36, [1986] 1 S.C.R. 981 (S.C.C.). In *R. v. Seaboyer; R. v. Gayme*, [1991] S.C.J. No. 62, [1991] 2 S.C.R. 577 at 637-39 (S.C.C.), the Court held that preliminary inquiry justices also

§10.19 These holdings were reaffirmed in *R. v. Hynes*,[72] where the Court found in a 5:4 decision that section 24(2) does not apply at preliminary inquiries.[73] Preliminary inquiry justices serve a limited function (deciding whether to commit the accused to stand trial), the Court reasoned, and do not have jurisdiction to order the usual panoply of criminal remedies.[74] Allowing evidence obtained in violation of the *Charter* would lengthen preliminary inquiries and make them more complex, it added.[75] Trial courts are in a better position, moreover, to assess "all the circumstances" relevant to the section 24(2) decision.[76] This conclusion was reached despite the fact that preliminary inquiry justices frequently apply common law exclusionary rules, including the confessions rule.[77] Most lower courts have also concluded that preliminary inquiry justices are not competent to award any other type of remedy under section 24 of the *Charter*.[78]

(5) Other Pre-Trial Proceedings

§10.20 As discussed, the trial judge is the preferred "court of competent jurisdiction" under section 24 of the *Charter*. However, in addition to the preliminary inquiry (discussed in the section immediately above), inferior criminal courts preside over many other proceedings before a trial judge is assigned. As discussed in Part 3(2), above, section 24 applications may always be brought before the superior court. The question remains, however, whether *Charter* remedies may also be ordered at any of these pre-trial proceedings. To date, courts have answered this question in the negative, holding that provincial court judges presiding over arraignments,[79] bail hearings[80] and pre-trial conferences,[81]

---

lack the power to strike down legislation under s. 52(1) of the *Constitution Act, 1982*. The vitality of this holding is questioned in Peter W. Hogg, *Constitutional Law of Canada*, 5th ed. (supplemented), vol. 2, looseleaf (Toronto: Thomson Carswell, 2007) § 40.3(c).

[72] [2001] S.C.J. No. 80, [2001] 3 S.C.R. 623 (S.C.C.).

[73] *Ibid.*

[74] *Ibid.*, at paras. 33, 36 (S.C.R.).

[75] *Ibid.*, at paras. 38-42 (S.C.R.).

[76] *Ibid.*, at paras. 38, 40 (S.C.R.).

[77] See *Criminal Code*, R.S.C. 1985, c. C-46, s. 542(1); *R. v. Hynes*, [2001] S.C.J. No. 80, [2001] 3 S.C.R. 623 at paras. 32, 47 (S.C.C.); *R. v. Mills*, [1986] S.C.J. No. 39, [1986] 1 S.C.R. 863 at 889-90 (S.C.C.), *per* Lamer J., dissenting; *R. v. R. (L.)*, [1995] O.J. No. 1381, 100 C.C.C. (3d) 329 at 340 (Ont. C.A.).

[78] See *e.g.*, *R. v. Girimonte*, [1997] O.J. No. 4961, 121 C.C.C. (3d) 33 (Ont. C.A.) (disclosure); *R. v. Canada (Attorney-General)*, [1992] P.E.I.J. No. 25, 98 Nfld. & P.E.I.R. 277 (P.E.I.S.C.) (stay of proceedings); *R. v. Farewell*, [2006] O.J. No. 2282, 81 O.R. (3d) 375 (Ont. C.J.) (appointment of counsel); *R. v. S. (N.)*, [2010] O.J. No. 4306, 2010 ONCA 670 at paras. 28-30 (Ont. C.A.) (no jurisdiction under *Charter* to order witness to remove veil, but justice had statutory power to make such an order, which order must be consistent with *Charter* values). See *contra*, *Canada (Attorney General) v. Garand*, [1992] Y.J. No. 184, [1992] Y.J. No. 184 (Y.T.S.C.) (appointment of counsel). Preliminary inquiry justices also lack jurisdiction to stay proceedings for abuses of process in non-*Charter* cases: *Argentina (Republic) v. Mellino*, [1987] S.C.J. No. 25, [1987] 1 S.C.R. 536 at 550 (S.C.C.).

[79] See *R. v. Wilson*, [1997] N.S.J. No. 473, 121 C.C.C. (3d) 92 (N.S.C.A.).

[80] See *R. v. Menard*, [2008] B.C.J. No. 2438, 240 C.C.C. (3d) 1 (B.C.C.A.).

[81] See *R. v. Commanda*, [2007] Q.J. No. 6991, 3 C.N.L.R. 311, 2007 QCCA 947 (Que. C.A.); *R. v. S. (S.S.)*, [1999] O.J. No. 1922, 136 C.C.C. (3d) 477 (Ont. S.C.J.).

who are not the judge seized with the trial of a case, cannot order *Charter* remedies. A solution to this jurisdictional challenge is for the accused to be arraigned and enter a plea before the presiding judge, thereby making him or her the trial judge.

(6) Regulatory Offence Trial Courts

§10.21 Regulatory prosecutions are usually conducted in a similar manner to criminal trials.[82] They typically follow the rules of evidence and procedure applying to criminal trials and involve the possibility of (sometimes substantial) penal sanctions.[83] It was not surprising, then, that the Supreme Court of Canada held that a provincial court presiding over a trial of a provincial regulatory offence was a court of competent jurisdiction for the purposes of awarding costs against the Crown for a violation of its *Charter* disclosure obligations.[84] Indeed, like criminal trial courts, regulatory trial courts "are the preferred forum for issuing *Charter* remedies in the cases originating before them".[85]

(7) Extradition Judges

§10.22 In 1987, the Supreme Court of Canada held in *Argentina [Republic] v. Mellino*[86] that, under the *Extradition Act*,[87] as it then read, extradition judges were not courts of competent jurisdiction under section 24 of the *Charter*.[88] Consequently, the only way for fugitives to make *Charter* claims was to file a writ of *habeas corpus* in the superior court, which (as discussed in Part 3(2), above) is always a court of competent jurisdiction.[89] This procedure was required even when the extradition judge was a superior court judge, which was often the case.[90]

§10.23 Recognizing the inefficiency and delay caused by this process, Parliament responded by amending the *Extradition Act* to confer express jurisdiction on extradition judges, who are now always superior court judges, to exercise their competence under the *Constitution Act, 1982* "with respect to the functions that the judge is required to perform in applying" the Act.[91] As a result, as the

---

[82] *R. v. 974649 Ontario Inc.*, [2001] S.C.J. No. 79, [2001] 3 S.C.R. 575 at paras. 78, 90 (S.C.C.).

[83] *Ibid.*, at para. 90 (S.C.R.).

[84] This conclusion was reached despite the fact that the governing statute contemplated a much more limited jurisdiction to award costs: *R. v. 974649 Ontario Inc.*, [2001] S.C.J. No. 79, [2001] 3 S.C.R. 575 at paras. 94-97 (S.C.C.). See also *R. v. Makaruk*, [2011] O.J. No. 1873, 2011 ONCJ 214 at para. 22 (Ont. C.J.).

[85] *R. v. 974649 Ontario Inc.*, [2001] S.C.J. No. 79, [2001] 3 S.C.R. 575 at para. 79 (S.C.C.).

[86] [1987] S.C.J. No. 25, [1987] 1 S.C.R. 536 (S.C.C.).

[87] R.S.C. 1985, c. E-23.

[88] *Argentina [Republic] v. Mellino*, [1987] S.C.J. No. 25, [1987] 1 S.C.R. 536 (S.C.C.). See also *United States v. Allard*, [1987] S.C.J. No. 20, [1987] 1 S.C.R. 564 (S.C.C.).

[89] *Argentina [Republic] v. Mellino*, [1987] S.C.J. No. 25, [1987] 1 S.C.R. 536 at 557(S.C.C.).

[90] *Ibid.*, at 553-54 (S.C.R.).

[91] *Extradition Act*, R.S.C. 1985, c. E-23, as amended by S.C. 1992, c. 13, s. 9(3). Today, see *Extradition Act*, S.C. 1999, c. 18, s. 25, which provides:

Supreme Court of Canada has since explained, an extradition judge is "competent to grant *Charter* remedies, including a stay of proceedings, on the basis of a *Charter* violation but only insofar as the *Charter* breach pertains directly to the circumscribed issues relevant at the committal stage of the extradition process."[92]

(8) Administrative Tribunals

§10.24 As mentioned in Part 3(1), above, unless their enabling legislation states otherwise, administrative tribunals are courts of competent jurisdiction under section 24 of the *Charter* if they have the power to decide questions of law. Whether they may award a particular *Charter* remedy continues to turn on the "function and structure" inquiry. Because such tribunals vary so widely, it is particularly important to examine their enabling statutes.[93] Tribunals with statutory authority to grant the type of remedy sought are likely to have jurisdiction to grant the remedy under the *Charter*.[94]

§10.25 In *Weber v. Ontario Hydro*,[95] for example, the Supreme Court of Canada held that a labour arbitrator could award *Charter* damages because the Board's enabling statute contemplated damage awards.[96] It concluded in *Mooring v. Canada (National Parole Board)*,[97] in contrast, that the Parole Board had no jurisdiction to exclude unconstitutionally obtained evidence.[98] The informal and inquisitorial character of the Board's proceedings, the Court reasoned, was not well suited to the "balancing of factors that s. 24(2) demands."[99] And in *R. v. Conway*,[100] the Court held that while the Ontario Review Board was a court of

---

> For the purposes of the *Constitution Act, 1982*, a judge has, with respect to the functions that the judge is required to perform in applying this Act, the same competence that that judge possesses by virtue of being a superior court judge.

92 *United States of America v. Cobb*, [2001] S.C.J. No. 20, [2001] 1 S.C.R. 587 at para. 26 (S.C.C.) (affirming stay of proceedings ordered by extradition judge for s. 7 abuse of process). See also *United States of America v. Kwok*, [2001] S.C.J. No. 19, [2001] 1 S.C.R. 532 at para. 57 (S.C.C.) (same).

93 *R. v. 974649 Ontario Inc.*, [2001] S.C.J. No. 79, [2001] 3 S.C.R. 575 at para. 65 (S.C.C.).

94 *Ibid.*, at para. 66 (S.C.R.).

95 [1995] S.C.J. No. 59, [1995] 2 S.C.R. 929 (S.C.C.).

96 *Weber v. Ontario Hydro*, [1995] S.C.J. No. 59, [1995] 2 S.C.R. 929 at 965 (S.C.C.). See also *Okwuobi c. Commission scolaire Lester B. Pearson*, [2002] J.Q. no 1130, 116 A.C.W.S. (3d) 46 (Que. C.A.) (Tribunal administratif du Québec may grant *Charter* remedies).

97 [1996] S.C.J. No. 10, [1996] 1 S.C.R. 75 (S.C.C.).

98 *Mooring v. Canada (National Parole Board)*, [1996] S.C.J. No. 10, [1996] 1 S.C.R. 75 (S.C.C.). While questioning expressly *Mooring*'s correctness, the Court in *Conway* appeared to sympathize with Major J.'s dissenting reasons in the former case. See *R. v. Conway*, [2010] S.C.J. No. 22, [2010] 1 S.C.R. 765 at paras. 31-33 (S.C.C.).

99 *Mooring v. Canada (National Parole Board)*, [1996] S.C.J. No. 10, [1996] 1 S.C.R. 75 at para. 26 (S.C.C.). See also *Thomson v. Alberta (Transportation and Safety Board)*, [2003] A.J. No. 1115, 178 C.C.C. (3d) 508 (Alta. C.A.) (concession that Transportation and Safety Board not empowered to grant *Charter* remedies); *Ayangma v. Prince Edward Island Eastern School Board*, [2000] P.E.I.J. No. 50, 187 Nfld. & P.E.I.R. 154 (P.E.I.C.A.) (provincial human rights commission not statutorily enabled to grant s. 24(1) *Charter* remedies).

100 [2010] S.C.J. No. 22, [2010] 1 S.C.R. 765 (S.C.C.).

competent jurisdiction,[101] it could not grant remedies under section 24(1) of the *Charter* that were not available in the circumstances under the statutory remedial scheme.[102]

4. PROCEDURE AND PRACTICE

§10.26 In addition to establishing standing before a court of competent jurisdiction, applicants for *Charter* remedies must also follow certain rules of practice and procedure to ensure that their claims are heard on the merits.[103] To begin, they must provide timely written notice to the Crown and the court of their intention to apply for a *Charter* remedy; if not, the application may be refused.[104] Though such notice should be ideally given before the trial, courts may entertain later applications in appropriate circumstances.[105] In exercising this discretion, the applicant's right to raise constitutional claims must be balanced against the Crown's need for an adequate opportunity to meet those claims. Factors to be considered include the existence of any statutory notice rules[106] or practice

---

[101] *R. v. Conway*, [2010] S.C.J. No. 22, [2010] 1 S.C.R. 765 at para. 84 (S.C.C.) (the Board is "unquestionably authorized to decide questions of law" because of its statutory authority over mentally disordered offenders and fact that its decisions are appealable on questions of law, fact or mixed law and fact).

[102] *R. v. Conway*, [2010] S.C.J. No. 22, [2010] 1 S.C.R. 765 at paras. 97-102 (S.C.C.) (refusing to order either that the offender be discharged absolutely despite a finding that he was dangerous or that he be provided with a particular treatment).

[103] For a more expansive discussion, see Anil K. Kapoor, "Speak Up or Forever Hold Your Peace: The Timing of Section 24 Charter Applications" (1991) 10 Advocates' Soc. J. 25; Michael Code, "American Cadillacs or Canadian Compacts: What is the Correct Criminal Procedure for s. 24 Applications under the Charter of Rights? (Part I)" (1990-1991) 33 Crim. L.Q. 298; Wayne Gorman, "A Review and Analysis of Procedural Issues in Charter Applications Involving Criminal Causes or Matters: Pre-Trial, Trial and Post-Trial" (1994-1995) 37 Crim. L.Q. 154 at 160-69.

[104] See *R. v. Kutynec*, [1992] O.J. No. 347, 70 C.C.C. (3d) 289 (Ont. C.A.); *R. v. Dwernychuk*, [1992] A.J. No. 1058, 77 C.C.C. (3d) 385 (Alta. C.A.), leave to appeal refused [1993] S.C.C.A. No. 30, 79 C.C.C. (3d) 385 (S.C.C.); *R. v. D. (D.L.)*, [1992] M.J. No. 541, 77 C.C.C. (3d) 426 at 437-39 (Man. C.A.); *R. v. Pelletier*, [1995] S.J. No. 115, 97 C.C.C. (3d) 139 (Sask. C.A.); *Mohammadi c. R.*, [2006] Q.J. No. 6809, 2006 QCCA 930 at paras. 46-56 (Que. C.A.); *R. c. Tsiris*, [2000] J.Q. no 3121 (Que. C.A.); *R. c. Godbout*, [2001] J.Q. no 16, J.E. 2001-236 at paras. 42-54 (Que. C.A.); *R. v. Enden*, [2007] S.J. No. 498, 52 M.V.R. (5th) 92 at para. 20 (Sask. C.A.); *R. v. Gundy*, [2008] O.J. No. 1410, 231 C.C.C. (3d) 26 at paras. 19-24 (Ont. C.A.).

[105] See *R. v. Loveman*, [1992] O.J. No. 346, 71 C.C.C. (3d) 123 at 126-27 (Ont. C.A.); *R. v. Dwernychuk*, [1992] A.J. No. 1058, 77 C.C.C. (3d) 385 (Alta. C.A.), leave to appeal refused [1993] S.C.C.A. No. 30, 79 C.C.C. (3d) 385 (S.C.C.).

[106] See *e.g.*, *Rules of the Ontario Court of Justice in Criminal Proceedings*, SI/97-133, r. 26 (for applications in provincial court, notice to Attorney General of Ontario for ss. 24(2) and 523(1) applications), r. 30 (for applications in provincial court, notice to court and Crown for s. 24(2) applications required); *Courts of Justice Act*, R.S.O. 1990, c. C.43, s. 109 (for applications in superior courts, notice of ss. 24(1) and 52(1) applications to Attorneys General of Ontario and Canada); *Constitutional Notice Regulation*, Alta. Reg. 102/99, s. 1 (for applications in provincial court, notice to court and prosecutor for ss. 24(1), 24(2), and 52(1) applications); *Judicature Act*, R.S.A. 2000, c. J-2, s. 24 (for applications challenging constitutionality of legislation in superior courts, notice to Attorneys General of Alberta and Canada); *Constitutional Question Act*, R.S.B.C. 1996, c. 68, s. 8 (notice to Attorneys General of British Columbia and Canada for

directions,[107] Crown objections at time of the application, the timing of the application,[108] the nature of the claim,[109] the extent of any prejudice to the Crown,[110] whether the trial is in provincial or superior court, whether there has been a preliminary inquiry and the impact of the application on the course of the trial.[111] Applications for exclusion under section 24(2) will rarely be entertained after the evidence is admitted, however, absent unforeseeable subsequent developments.[112]

§10.27 Applicants must also provide a proper factual foundation for their claims.[113] If they do not, the court may again refuse to hear them.[114] This obligation stems from the fact that applicants bear the burden to prove (on a balance of probabilities) both the violation of one of their *Charter* rights and their entitlement to a remedy under section 24.[115]

§10.28 *Charter* applications should typically be decided at the end of the trial. There may be cases, however, where "the interests of justice necessitate an immediate decision" or where the issue may be resolved expeditiously before the trial without reference to evidence to be elicited at trial.[116]

§10.29 Appeals of *Charter* decisions follow the usual *Criminal Code* procedures;[117] that is, the verdict may be appealed and allegations that the trial judge erred in making those decisions will be grounds of appeal.[118]

---

applications in superior court for ss. 24(1) or 52(1) remedies). See generally, *Eaton v. Brant County Board of Education*, [1997] 1 S.C.R. 241 at paras. 48 and 54.

[107] See *R. v. Loveman*, [1992] O.J. No. 346, 71 C.C.C. (3d) 123 (Ont. C.A.).

[108] See *R. v. Saulnier*, [2006] N.B.J. No. 3, 205 C.C.C. (3d) 245 at para. 22 (N.B.C.A.); *Price v. R.*, [2010] N.B.J. No. 418, 2010 NBCA 84 (N.B.C.A.).

[109] *R. v. Loewen*, [1997] M.J. No. 649, 122 C.C.C. (3d) 198 at 207 (Man. C.A.), affd [1998] M.J. No. 553 (Man. C.A.).

[110] *R. v. Byron*, [2001] M.J. No. 245, 156 C.C.C. (3d) 312 (Man. C.A.).

[111] *R. v. Loveman*, [1992] O.J. No. 346, 71 C.C.C. (3d) 123 (Ont. C.A.).

[112] *R. v. Dwernychuk*, [1992] A.J. No. 1058, 77 C.C.C. (3d) 385 at 398-99 (Alta. C.A.), leave to appeal refused [1993] S.C.C.A. No. 30, 79 C.C.C. (3d) 385 (S.C.C.); *R. v. Kutynec*, [1992] O.J. No. 347, 70 C.C.C. (3d) 289 at 297, 302 (Ont. C.A.).

[113] See *R. v. L. (W.K.)*, [1991] S.C.J. No. 40, [1991] 1 S.C.R. 1091 (S.C.C.); *R. v. Dwernychuk*, [1992] A.J. No. 1058, 77 C.C.C. (3d) 385 at 400 (Alta. C.A.), leave to appeal refused [1993] S.C.C.A. No. 30, 79 C.C.C. (3d) 385 (S.C.C.); *R. v. Kutynec*, [1992] O.J. No. 347, 70 C.C.C. (3d) 289 at 301 (Ont. C.A.); *R. v. Hamill*, [1984] B.C.J. No. 3148, 13 D.L.R. (4th) 275 at 302-303 (B.C.C.A.), affd [1987] S.C.J. No. 12, [1987] 1 S.C.R. 301 (S.C.C.); *R. v. D. (D.L.)*, [1992] M.J. No. 541, 77 C.C.C. (3d) 426 at 439 (Man. C.A.); *R. v. Feldman*, [1994] B.C.J. No. 722, 67 W.A.C. 31 at 35-37 (B.C.C.A.), affd [1994] S.C.J. No. 103 (S.C.C.); *R. v. Enden*, [2007] S.J. No. 498, 52 M.V.R. (5th) 92 (Sask. C.A.).

[114] See *R. v. L. (W.K.)*, [1991] S.C.J. No. 40, [1991] 1 S.C.R. 1091 (S.C.C.); *R. v. Dwernychuk*, [1992] A.J. No. 1058, 77 C.C.C. (3d) 385 at 393, 400 (Alta. C.A.), leave to appeal refused [1993] S.C.C.A. No. 30, 79 C.C.C. (3d) 385 (S.C.C.); *R. v. Kutynec*, [1992] O.J. No. 347, 70 C.C.C. (3d) 289 at 298 (Ont. C.A.); *R. v. Felderhof*, [2003] O.J. No. 4819, 68 O.R. (3d) 481 at para. 88 (Ont. C.A.).

[115] *R. v. Collins*, [1987] S.C.J. No. 15, [1987] 1 S.C.R. 265 at 277-78 (S.C.C.).

[116] *R. v. DeSousa*, [1992] S.C.J. No. 77, [1992] 2 S.C.R. 944 at 954. (S.C.C.) See also *R. v. Curtis*, [1998] O.J. No. 467, 123 C.C.C. (3d) 178 at para. 8 (Ont. C.A.).

[117] For appeals to the Court of Appeal, see *Criminal Code*, R.S.C. 1985, c. C-46, ss. 675-676. Appeals to the Supreme Court of Canada follow the grounds outlined in ss. 691-693 of the *Criminal Code*, R.S.C. 1985, c. C-46. Where the *Criminal Code* confers no right of appeal, an

§10.30 On appeal, trial judges' section 24 rulings will be afforded deference, though appellate intervention is warranted when the trial judge erred in law or principle, gave inadequate weight to relevant factors, failed to find or mischaracterized a *Charter* violation, made unreasonable factual findings, provided inadequate reasons or was "so clearly wrong as to amount to an injustice."[119] *Charter* claims not raised at trial will rarely be considered on appeal without an adequate factual foundation in the record.[120]

5. TYPES OF REMEDIES

§10.31 As discussed in Part 3, above, a person with standing to apply for a particular remedy under section 24 of the *Charter* must first establish that the court has the jurisdiction to do so. If it does, the court must decide whether to grant the remedy sought (or any other remedy). It is here that the distinction between sections 24(1) and 24(2) becomes relevant. Applicants seeking the exclusion of evidence obtained in violation of the *Charter* must follow the route prescribed in section 24(2); all other remedies flow from section 24(1).[121] Evidence not *obtained* in violation of the *Charter* may be excluded under section 24(1), however, if its *admittance in the proceedings* would violate the *Charter*.[122]

---

applicant may seek leave to appeal directly to the Supreme Court of Canada under s. 40 of the *Supreme Court Act*, R.S.C. 1985, c. S-26. See Chapter 18, Part 2(2).

[118] See *R. v. Mills*, [1986] S.C.J. No. 39, [1986] 1 S.C.R. 863 at 958-59 (S.C.C.). For a more extensive discussion of appellate procedures, see Chapter 18. See also Kent Roach, *Constitutional Remedies in Canada*, looseleaf (Aurora, ON: Canada Law Book, 2008) at paras. 6.370-6.436.

[119] See *R. v. Bjelland*, [2009] S.C.J. No. 38, [2009] 2 S.C.R. 651 at para. 15 (S.C.C.), *per* Rothstein J., at paras. 42, 57-58 (S.C.C.), *per* Fish J., dissenting; *R. v. Grant*, [2009] S.C.J. No. 32, [2009] 2 S.C.R. 353 at para. 129 (S.C.C.); *R. v. Grant*, [1993] S.C.J. No. 98, [1993] 3 S.C.R. 223 at 256-57 (S.C.C.), *per* Sopinka J.; *R. v. Carosella*, [1997] S.C.J. No. 12, [1997] 1 S.C.R. 80 at paras. 48-49 (S.C.C.); *R. v. Regan*, [2002] S.C.J. No. 14, [2002] 1 S.C.R. 297 at paras. 117-118 (S.C.C.); *Canada (Minister of Citizenship and Immigration) v. Tobiass*, [1997] S.C.J. No. 82, [1997] 3 S.C.R. 391 at para. 87 (S.C.C.); *Doucet-Boudreau v. Nova Scotia (Minister of Education)*, [2003] S.C.J. No. 63, [2003] 3 S.C.R. 3 at paras. 86-87 (S.C.C.).

[120] See *R. v. Broyles*, [1991] S.C.J. No. 95, [1991] 3 S.C.R. 595 (S.C.C.); *R. v. Ullrich*, [1991] B.C.J. No. 3721, 69 C.C.C. (3d) 473 at 477-78 (B.C.C.A.); *R. v. Seo*, [1986] O.J. No. 178, 25 C.C.C. (3d) 385 (Ont. C.A.). In *R. v. Brown*, [1993] S.C.J. No. 82, [1993] 2 S.C.R. 918 (S.C.C.), however, the Court allowed the appeal for the reasons of Harradance J.A. in the Alberta Court of Appeal, who had explained that:

> Where the court has a sufficient factual foundation to appraise the issue without prejudice to the parties and particularly where *refusing* to do so will result in unfairness, then in my view it is proper for the appeal court to hear and determine the question put before it. [Emphasis in original.]

R. v. Brown, [1992] A.J. No. 602, 73 C.C.C. (3d) 481 at 488 (Alta. C.A.), revd [1993] S.C.J. No. 82, [1993] 2 S.C.R. 918 (S.C.C.). See also *R. v. Lewis*, [2007] O.J. No. 1784, 219 C.C.C. (3d) 427 at para. 28 (Ont. C.A.) (emphasizing the absence of any apparent tactical reason for the failure to raise the *Charter* issue below as a relevant consideration); *R. v. Hogg*, [2010] N.S.J. No. 335, 2010 NSCA 53 at paras. 52-62 (N.S.C.A.) (refusing to grant leave to raise *Charter* challenge for the first time on appeal).

[121] *R. v. Therens*, [1985] S.C.J. No. 30, [1985] 1 S.C.R. 613 at 647-48 (S.C.C.), *per* Le Dain J., dissenting.

[122] *R. v. White*, [1999] S.C.J. No. 28, [1999] 2 S.C.R. 417 (S.C.C.).

(1)   Section 24(1) Remedies

§10.32 Section 24(1) authorizes any remedy that a court with jurisdiction to award it "considers appropriate and just in the circumstances."[123] As Justice McIntyre of the Supreme Court of Canada once observed, "[i]t is difficult to imagine language which could give the court a wider and less fettered discretion."[124] Novel and creative remedies may be necessary to "meet the challenges and circumstances" of the case at hand.[125] Nonetheless, the discretion must be exercised with the following considerations in mind: (*i*) the need to effectively vindicate the *Charter* right in question; (*ii*) the separation of functions among the state's legislative, executive and judicial branches; (*iii*) the particular capacities and competence of courts and the judicial function; and (*iv*) ensuring fairness to the party against whom the order is made.[126]

§10.33 Little more can be said about the general principles animating this discretion. It is more helpful to examine the particular remedies sought most commonly in criminal cases.

(a)   Stay of Proceedings

(i)   General Principles

§10.34 Judicial stays of proceedings may be awarded in both *Charter* and non-*Charter* cases.[127] A judicial stay permanently terminates proceedings against the accused, usually before the case has been decided on the merits.[128] Further prosecutions for the same conduct are barred by the double jeopardy rules.[129]

---

[123] As mentioned, above, Part 3(2), the court may decide that another tribunal is better placed to decide the matter.

[124] *R. v. Mills*, [1986] S.C.J. No. 39, [1986] 1 S.C.R. 863 at 965 (S.C.C.), *per* McIntyre J. See also *R. v. Bjelland*, [2009] S.C.J. No. 38, [2009] 2 S.C.R. 651 at para. 18 (S.C.C.); *Vancouver (City) v. Ward*, [2010] S.C.J. No. 27, [2010] 2 S.C.R. 28 at para. 17 (S.C.C.).

[125] *Doucet-Boudreau v. Nova Scotia (Department of Education)*, [2003] S.C.J. No. 63, [2003] 3 S.C.R. 3 at para. 59 (S.C.C.).

[126] *Ibid.*, at paras. 55-58 (S.C.R.). See also *Canada (Prime Minister) v. Khadr*, [2010] S.C.J. No. 3, [2010] 1 S.C.R. 44, 2010 SCC 3 at paras. 30-33 (S.C.C.); *Vancouver (City) v. Ward*, [2010] S.C.J. No. 27, [2010] 2 S.C.R. 28 at para. 20 (S.C.C.); Peter W. Hogg, *Constitutional Law of Canada*, 5th ed. (supplemented), vol. 2, looseleaf (Toronto: Thomson Carswell, 2007) § 40.2(g).

[127] Prosecutors also have the power under the *Criminal Code* to enter a stay of proceedings. Unlike judicial stays, however, prosecutorial stays may be lifted and proceedings recommenced up to one year after the entry of the stay. See *Criminal Code*, R.S.C. 1985, c. C-46, ss. 579, 579.1 and 795. See also Chapter 8, Part 4(1)(*c*).

[128] See *Canada (Minister of Citizenship and Immigration) v. Tobiass*, [1997] S.C.J. No. 82, [1997] 3 S.C.R. 391 at para. 86 (S.C.C.); *R. v. Regan*, [2002] S.C.J. No. 14, [2002] 1 S.C.R. 297 at para. 53 (S.C.C.); *Charkaoui v. Canada (Minister of Citizenship and Immigration)*, [2008] S.C.J. No. 39, [2008] 2 S.C.R. 326 at para. 76 (S.C.C.). See also *R. v. Mack*, [1988] S.C.J. No. 91, [1988] 2 S.C.R. 903 (S.C.C.) (stay tantamount to acquittal for appeal purposes); *R. v. Jewitt*, [1985] S.C.J. No. 53, [1985] 2 S.C.R. 128 at 147-48 (S.C.C.) (same); *R. v. Dias*, [2010] A.J. No. 1426, 2010 ABCA 382 at para. 32 (Alta. C.A.) (stay is a permanent, prospective remedy).

[129] See *R. v. Jewitt*, [1985] S.C.J. No. 53, [1985] 2 S.C.R. 128 at 146-47 (S.C.C.). See also Chapter 14, Part 3.

Because a stay is tantamount to an acquittal, it will usually be awarded only when other remedies cannot adequately redress the wrong at issue.[130]

§10.35 Judicial stays may be grouped into three categories. The first consists of those awarded under section 24(1) of the *Charter* for violations of section 11(*b*): the right to be tried within a reasonable time. We discuss this right in detail in Chapter 13, Part 3. It is sufficient to note here that stays are the minimum remedy for section 11(*b*) violations.[131] In other words, while other section 24(1) remedies may also be awarded, a stay is automatically ordered once a section 11(*b*) violation is found.

§10.36 The second category consists of stays awarded as remedies for entrapment. As with violations of section 11(*b*), stays flow automatically from a finding of entrapment.[132] Such stays do not hinge on the violation of any *Charter* right, however.[133] Instead, they stem from the courts' inherent power to control procedural abuses.[134] Entrapment is similar to a substantive defence in that it forecloses conviction despite proof of the elements of the offence.[135] Canadian courts have treated entrapment, however, as a procedural remedy that limits police power without regard to culpability.[136] We thus detail its requirements below.

---

[130] See *e.g.*, *Canada (Minister of Citizenship and Immigration) v. Tobiass*, [1985] S.C.J. No. 53, [1997] 3 S.C.R. 391 at para. 86 (S.C.C.); *Charkaoui v. Canada (Minister of Citizenship and Immigration)*, [2008] S.C.J. No. 39, [2008] 2 S.C.R. 326 at paras. 75-77 (S.C.C.).

[131] *R. v. Rahey*, [1987] S.C.J. No. 23, [1987] 1 S.C.R. 588 at 614-15 (S.C.C.), *per* Lamer J., 617-18 (S.C.R.), *per* Le Dain J., 618-22 (S.C.R.), *per* Wilson J. See also *R. v. Askov*, [1990] S.C.J. No. 106, [1990] 2 S.C.R. 1199 at 1226 (S.C.C.); *R. v. Mills*, [1986] S.C.J. No. 39, [1986] 1 S.C.R. 863 at 948 (S.C.C.), *per* Lamer J.; *R. v. W. (R.E.)*, [2011] N.S.J. No. 81, 2011 NSCA 18 at para. 75 (N.S.C.A.); *R. v. Taylor*, [2010] N.J. No. 147, 2010 NLCA 26 at para. 21 (N.L.C.A.); *R. v. Lanteigne*, [2010] N.B.J. No. 423, 2010 NBCA 91 (N.B.C.A.).

[132] *R. v. Mack*, [1988] S.C.J. No. 91, [1988] 2 S.C.R. 903 at 967, 975-77 (S.C.C.). See also *R. v. Clothier*, [2011] O.J. No. 102, 2011 ONCA 27 (Ont. C.A.). The Ontario Court of Appeal has suggested (without deciding) that it would be inappropriate to exclude evidence under s. 24(2) of the *Charter* as a remedy for entrapment: *R. v. Imoro*, [2010] O.J. No. 586, 2010 ONCA 122 at paras. 25-28 (Ont. C.A.), supp. reasons [2011] O.J. No. 996 (Ont. S.C.J.), affd [2010] S.C.J. No. 50, [2010] 3 S.C.R. 62 (S.C.C.).

[133] That said, in *R. v. Mack*, [1988] S.C.J. No. 91, [1988] 2 S.C.R. 903 at 939-40 (S.C.C.), Lamer J. (as he then was) noted for the Court that concerns about law enforcement abuses underlay both the defence of entrapment and the legal rights provisions in the *Charter*. See also *R. v. Imoro*, [2008] O.J. No. 2519, 59 C.R. (6th) 109, 235 C.C.C. (3d) 86 at para. 25 (Ont. S.C.J.) (suggesting that entrapment violates s. 7 of the *Charter*), revd on other grounds, [2010] O.J. No. 586, 2010 ONCA 122 (Ont. C.A.), affd [2010] S.C.J. No. 50, [2010] 3 S.C.R. 62 (S.C.C.).

[134] See *R. v. Campbell*, [1999] S.C.J. No. 16, [1999] 1 S.C.R. 565 at para. 21 (S.C.C.); *R. v. Mack*, [1988] S.C.J. No. 91, [1988] 2 S.C.R. 903 at 939-41 (S.C.C.); *R. v. Schacher*, [2003] A.J. No. 1341, 179 C.C.C. (3d) 561 at para. 11 (Alta. C.A.). It has also been suggested that entrapment stems from s. 8(3) of the *Criminal Code*, R.S.C. 1985, c. C-46, which preserves the courts' power to recognize common law criminal defences. See *R. v. Amato*, [1982] S.C.J. No. 72, [1982] 2 S.C.R. 418 (S.C.C.), *per* Estey J., dissenting.

[135] See Morris Manning & Peter Sankoff, *Manning, Mewett & Sankoff, Criminal Law*, 4th ed. (Markham, ON: LexisNexis Canada, 2009) at 501-502, 511.

[136] See *R. v. Mack*, [1988] S.C.J. No. 91, [1988] 2 S.C.R. 903 at 942-52 (S.C.C.). *R. v. Jewitt*, [1985] S.C.J. No. 53, [1985] 2 S.C.R. 128 at 148 (S.C.C.), *per* Dickson C.J.C.; *R. v. Pearson*, [1998] S.C.J. No. 86, [1998] 3 S.C.R. 620 at paras. 5-13 (S.C.C.).

§10.37 The third category consists of stays awarded as a remedy for other abuses of process. Where the abuse involves the violation of a *Charter* right,[137] the stay is awarded under section 24(1).[138] Where it does not, it flows from the court's inherent power to control abuses of process.[139] In either case, a stay will only be granted in the "clearest of cases."[140] An application for stay will meet this standard where "compelling an accused to stand trial would violate those fundamental principles of justice which underlie the community's sense of fair play and decency" or where a stay is necessary "to prevent the abuse of a court's process through oppressive or vexatious proceedings."[141] Stays for abuses of process are also discussed in more detail below.

(ii) Entrapment

§10.38 As with other procedural remedies, defendants bear the burden of proving entrapment (on a balance of probabilities).[142] The question is decided by the

---

[137] Stays have been sought to remedy a variety of alleged *Charter* violations. See *e.g.*, *R. v. Kalanj*, [1989] S.C.J. No. 71, [1989] 1 S.C.R. 1594 (S.C.C.) (pre-charge delay (s.7)); *R. v. O'Connor*, [1995] S.C.J. No. 98, [1995] 4 S.C.R. 411 (S.C.C.) (non-disclosure (s.7)); *R. v. Chaplin*, [1994] S.C.J. No. 89, [1995] 1 S.C.R. 727 (S.C.C.) (same); *R. v. Khela*, [1995] S.C.J. No. 95, [1995] 4 S.C.R. 201 (S.C.C.) (same); *R. v. La*, [1997] S.C.J. No. 30, [1997] 2 S.C.R. 680 (S.C.C.) (loss of evidence (s. 7)); *R. v. Carosella*, [1997] S.C.J. No. 12, [1997] 1 S.C.R. 80 (S.C.C.) (same); *R. v. Bero*, [2000] O.J. No. 4199, 39 C.R. (5th) 291 (Ont. C.A.) (same); *R. v. Rowbotham*, [1988] O.J. No. 271, 41 C.C.C. (3d) 1 (Ont. C.A.) (legal assistance (s. 7)), *R. v. Cai*, [2002] A.J. No. 1521, 2002 ABCA 299 (Alta. C.A.) (same); *R. v. Gostick*, [1991] O.J. No. 178, 62 C.C.C. (3d) 276 (Ont. C.A.) (courthouse conditions (s. 7)); *R. v. P. (T.G.)*, [1996] B.C.J. No. 2445, 112 C.C.C. (3d) 171 (B.C.C.A.) (poor health of accused (s. 7)); *R. v. Neil*, [2002] S.C.J. No. 72, [2002] 3 S.C.R. 631 (S.C.C.) (lawyer's conflict of interest (s. 7)); *United States of America v. Maydak*, [2004] B.C.J. No. 1937, 2004 BCCA 478 (B.C.C.A.) (extradition, improper exercise of ministerial discretion (s. 7)); *R. v. Regan*, [2002] S.C.J. No. 14, [2002] 1 S.C.R. 297 (S.C.C.) (prosecutorial and police misconduct (s. 7)); *R. v. Conway*, [1989] S.C.J. No. 70, [1989] 1 S.C.R. 1659 (S.C.C.) (prosecutorial misconduct (s. 7)); *R. v. Arcand*, [2008] O.J. No. 3294, 92 O.R. (3d) 444 (Ont. C.A.) (same); *Canada (Minister of Citizenship and Immigration) v. Tobiass*, [1997] S.C.J. No. 82, [1997] 3 S.C.R. 391 (S.C.C.) (judicial misconduct (s. 7)); *R. v. Cheba*, [1993] S.J. No. 17, 105 Sask. R. 256 (Sask. C.A.) (interpreter (s. 14)); *R. v. Simpson*, [1995] S.C.J. No. 12, [1995] 1 S.C.R. 449 (S.C.C.), revg [1994] N.J. No. 69, 117 Nfld. & P.E.I.R. 110 (Nfld. C.A.) (arbitrary detention (s. 9)); *R. v. Iseler*, [2004] O.J. No. 4332, 190 C.C.C. (3d) 11 (Ont. C.A.) (same); *R. v. Mangat*, [2006] O.J. No. 2418, 209 C.C.C. (3d) 225 (Ont. C.A.) (same).

[138] See *R. v. O'Connor*, [1995] S.C.J. No. 98, [1995] 4 S.C.R. 411 at paras. 59-72 (S.C.C.); *United States of America v. Cobb*, [2001] S.C.J. No. 20, [2001] 1 S.C.R. 587 at para. 28 (S.C.C.); *United States of America v. Shulman*, [2001] S.C.J. No. 18, [2001] 1 S.C.R. 616 at para. 33 (S.C.C.); *R. v. Campbell*, [1999] S.C.J. No. 16, [1999] 1 S.C.R. 565 (S.C.C.).

[139] See *R. v. Jewitt*, [1985] S.C.J. No. 53, [1985] 2 S.C.R. 128 at 131-37 (S.C.C.); *R. v. Keyowski*, [1988] S.C.J. No. 28, [1988] 1 S.C.R. 657 (S.C.C.); *R. v. Conway*, [1989] S.C.J. No. 70, [1989] 1 S.C.R. 1659 (S.C.C.).

[140] *R. v. O'Connor*, [1995] S.C.J. No. 98, [1995] 4 S.C.R. 411 at para. 68 (S.C.C.).

[141] *R. v. Jewitt*, [1985] S.C.J. No. 53, [1985] 2 S.C.R. 128 at 136-37 (S.C.C.), quoting *R. v. Young*, [1984] O.J. No. 3229, 40 C.R. (3d) 289 at 329 (Ont. C.A.). See also *R. v. Keyowski*, [1988] S.C.J. No. 28, [1988] 1 S.C.R. 657 (S.C.C.); *R. v. Conway*, [1989] S.C.J. No. 70, [1989] 1 S.C.R. 1659 (S.C.C.).

[142] *R. v. Mack*, [1988] S.C.J. No. 91, [1988] 2 S.C.R. 903 at 973-76 (S.C.C.).

judge[143] after guilt has been determined.[144] As mentioned, when entrapment is proved proceedings are automatically stayed. Unlike other abuses of process, once entrapment is established there is no need to show that it is one of the few "clearest of cases" warranting a stay.[145]

§10.39 Broadly stated, the entrapment defence discourages police from causing crime that would not have been committed otherwise.[146] Such conduct may be considered to unfairly intrude upon the individual's liberty and privacy interests[147] and waste law enforcement resources.[148]

§10.40 In *R. v. Mack*,[149] the Supreme Court of Canada held that there were two species of entrapment.[150] The first arises where state agents[151] "provide a person with an opportunity to commit an offence": (*i*) "without acting on a reasonable suspicion that this person is already engaged in criminal activity;" or (*ii*) "pursuant to a bona fide inquiry."[152] The second occurs when "having such a reasonable

---

[143] *R. v. Mack*, [1988] S.C.J. No. 91, [1988] 2 S.C.R. 903 at 967 (S.C.C.) (the question is "one of law, or mixed law and fact"). See also *R. v. Jewitt*, [1985] S.C.J. No. 53, [1985] 2 S.C.R. 128 at 145 (S.C.C.), *per* Dickson C.J.C.; *R. v. Amato*, [1982] S.C.J. No. 72, [1982] 2 S.C.R. 418 at 448 (S.C.C.), *per* Estey J., dissenting.

[144] *R. v. Mack*, [1988] S.C.J. No. 91, [1988] 2 S.C.R. 903 at 972-73 (S.C.C.). Entrapment may thus be raised, and a stay awarded, even after the accused enters a guilty plea. See *R. v. Maxwell*, [1990] O.J. No. 2320, 3 C.R. (4th) 31 (Ont. C.A.). In our view, where a solid foundation for entrapment exists, judges should have the discretion (on the accused's application) to decide the matter before or during the trial. See Morris Manning & Peter Sankoff, *Manning, Mewett & Sankoff, Criminal Law*, 4th ed. (Markham.: LexisNexis Canada, 2009) at 512. Though this proposal would (where the defence is successful) prevent the waste of court resources, it has not yet been accepted by the courts. See *R. v. Imoro*, [2010] O.J. No. 586, 2010 ONCA 122 at paras. 21-24 (Ont. C.A.), affd [2010] S.C.J. No. 50, [2010] 3 S.C.R. 62 (S.C.C.) ("Whatever the mode of trial, the judge ought to consider entrapment only after a finding of guilt").

[145] See *R. v. Swan*, [2009] B.C.J. No. 623, 244 C.C.C. (3d) 108 at para. 47 (B.C.C.A.); Don Stuart, *Canadian Criminal Law*, 5th ed. (Toronto: Thomson Carswell, 2007) at 614. But see *R. v. Clothier*, [2011] O.J. No. 102, 2011 ONCA 27 at para. 16 (Ont. C.A.) ("[a]s with other aspects of the abuse of process doctrine, a stay is granted only if the accused meets the 'clearest of cases' standard")

[146] See generally, *R. v. Mack*, [1988] S.C.J. No. 91, [1988] 2 S.C.R. 903 at 941 (S.C.C.) (outlining suite of policies underlying entrapment).

[147] See Paul M. Hughes, "Temptation and Culpability in the Law of Duress and Entrapment" (2006) 51 Crim. L.Q. 342; *R. v. Mack*, [1988] S.C.J. No. 91, [1988] 2 S.C.R. 903 at 942, 960-61 (S.C.C.).

[148] See Richard A. Posner, "An Economic Theory of the Criminal Law" (1985) 85 Colum. L. Rev. 1193 at 1220 (resources used to apprehend and convict accused who would not have committed offence but for police efforts "socially wasted, because they do not prevent any crimes").

[149] [1988] S.C.J. No. 91, [1988] 2 S.C.R. 903 S.C.C.).

[150] *Ibid.*, at 964-65 (S.C.R.). See also *R. v. Barnes*, [1991] S.C.J. No. 17, [1991] 1 S.C.R. 449 at 460 (S.C.C.); *R. v. Campbell*, [1999] S.C.J. No. 16, [1999] 1 S.C.R. 565 at para. 21 (S.C.C.); *R. v. Clothier*, [2011] O.J. No. 102, 2011 ONCA 27 at paras. 13-20 (Ont. C.A.).

[151] See *R. v. Pearson*, [1998] S.C.J. No. 86, [1998] 3 S.C.R. 620 at para. 11 (S.C.C.) ("Entrapment concerns the conduct of the police and the Crown."); *R. v. Carson*, [2004] O.J. No. 1530, 185 C.C.C. (3d) 541 at paras. 29 (Ont. C.A.) ("For entrapment to apply, the court must conclude that the appellant was convicted of an offence that was the work of the state."); Morris Manning & Peter Sankoff, *Manning, Mewett & Sankoff, Criminal Law*, 4th ed. (Markham.: LexisNexis Canada, 2009) at 504; Kate Hofmeyr, "The Problem of Private Entrapment" [2006] Crim. L. Rev. 319.

[152] *R. v. Mack*, [1988] S.C.J. No. 91, [1988] 2 S.C.R. 903 at 964-65 (S.C.C.).

suspicion or acting in the course of a bona fide inquiry, they go beyond providing an opportunity and induce the commission of an offence."[153]

§10.41 To make out the first type of entrapment, defendants must first show that police gave them an "opportunity" to commit the offence. The Supreme Court has not elaborated on this requirement — in most cases it will be obvious. But the Ontario Court of Appeal has stressed the need to distinguish between "legitimately investigating a tip and giving an opportunity to commit a crime."[154] In *R. v. Imoro*,[155] the accused approached an undercover police officer (who was following up on an anonymous tip that a man was selling drugs on the twelfth floor of an apartment building) as the officer exited the elevator on the twelfth floor.[156] The accused said, "Come with me" and the officer replied, "You can hook me up?" After the accused answered positively and the officer saw him sell drugs to another, the officer bought drugs from the accused. The trial judge held that when the officer first spoke to the accused, he did not have reasonable suspicion and thus entrapped him.[157] The Ontario Court of Appeal agreed that he did not have reasonable suspicion at this time but held that he did not give him an opportunity by asking him to "hook [him] up."[158] "The question was simply a step in the police's investigation of the anonymous tip," the court concluded.[159] The officer did not give the accused an opportunity to sell him drugs until he had established reasonable suspicion.

§10.42 If the "opportunity" requirement is satisfied, the next step for the first type of entrapment is to show that police lacked both reasonable suspicion and *bona fides*. The Supreme Court has said little about the meaning of "reasonable suspicion" in this context. As discussed in other chapters in this book,[160] in the context of police powers to detain and search, it means "something more than a mere suspicion and something less than a belief based upon reasonable and probable grounds."[161] Presumably the same definition applies to entrapment. The Court has stated that a suspect's known criminal propensity may be considered in entrapment cases, but only if it "can be linked to other factors leading the police to a reasonable suspicion that the individual is engaged in a criminal activity."[162] There must also be logical and temporal connections between the

---

[153] *Ibid.*, at 964-65 (S.C.R.).

[154] *R. v. Imoro*, [2010] O.J. No. 586, 2010 ONCA 122 at para. 15 (Ont. C.A.), affd [2010] S.C.J. No. 50, [2010] 3 S.C.R. 62 (S.C.C.). See also *R. v. Benedetti*, [1997] A.J. No. 536, 51 Alta. L.R. (3d) 16 (Alta. C.A.); *R. v. Milley*, [1995] N.J. No. 12, 389 A.P.R. 97 at para. 12 (Nfld. C.A.).

[155] [2010] O.J. No. 586, 2010 ONCA 122 (Ont. C.A.), affd [2010] S.C.J. No. 50, [2010] 3 S.C.R. 62 (S.C.C.).

[156] *Ibid.*, at paras. 2-5 (ONCA).

[157] *Ibid.*, at paras. 6, 13 (ONCA).

[158] *Ibid.*, at paras. 4-17 (ONCA).

[159] *Ibid.*, at para. 16 (ONCA).

[160] See Chapter 2, Part 4(3)(*a*)(i) and Chapter 3, Part 4(4).

[161] *R. v. Kang-Brown*, [2008] S.C.J. No. 18, [2008] 1 S.C.R. 456 at para. 75 (S.C.C.), *per* Binnie J. and at paras. 164-165 (S.C.R.), *per* Deschamps J., dissenting.

[162] See *R. v. Mack*, [1988] S.C.J. No. 91, [1988] 2 S.C.R. 903 at 953-58 (S.C.C.).

crime under investigation and suspects' past crimes.[163] Propensity will only be relevant, in other words, where police give suspects an opportunity to commit the same type of crime they have committed in the not-too-distant past.[164] The fact that the suspect had been convicted of possessing illegal drugs, for example, would not help show that he or she is trafficking.[165]

§10.43 The Court has said much more about the meaning of *bona fides*. In *R. v. Mack*, Justice Lamer (as he then was) explained that police exceed the boundaries of a *bona fide* inquiry when they target a suspect either: (*i*) for "dubious motives unrelated to the investigation and repression of crimes;" or (*ii*) as part of a program of "random virtue-testing."[166] An example of (*i*), he suggested, would be a police officer offering prostitutes to recently-released parolees to "get them to commit an offence and so have their parole revoked."[167] As an example of (*ii*), he invoked the following hypothetical:

> ...[A police officer] plants a wallet with money in an obvious location in a park, and ensures that the wallet contains full identification of the owner. Someone may walk up, take the money and throw away the wallet and the identification; he would then arrest and charge that person. In my opinion, whether or not we are willing to say the average person would steal the money, this policeman has acted without any grounds, and his conduct carries the unnecessary risk that otherwise law-abiding people will commit a criminal offence.[168]

§10.44 In practice, courts rarely find that police lacked *bona fides*. Perniciously-motivated inquiries are (hopefully) infrequent and (in any case) difficult to prove. And courts have defined random virtue testing narrowly. In *Mack*, Justice Lamer noted that police may provide criminal opportunities in a "particular location ... where it is reasonably suspected that certain criminal activity is occurring"[169] as long as that location is defined with "sufficient precision."[170]

---

[163] *Ibid.*, at 958 (S.C.R.).

[164] See *R. v. Mack*, [1988] S.C.J. No. 91, [1988] 2 S.C.R. 903 at 958 (S.C.C.).

[165] *R. v. Mack*, [1988] S.C.J. No. 91, [1988] 2 S.C.R. 903 at 958 (S.C.C.). See also *R. v. Fortin*, [1989] O.J. No. 123, 33 O.A.C. 123 (Ont. C.A.). But see *R. c. Lebrasseur*, [1995] J.Q. no 633, 102 C.C.C. (3d) 167 (Que. C.A.) (no entrapment where accused involved in "drug milieu" offered opportunity to traffic despite absence of specific evidence of trafficking).

[166] *R. v. Mack*, [1988] S.C.J. No. 91, [1988] 2 S.C.R. 903 at 956 (S.C.C.).

[167] *Ibid.*, at 956-57 (S.C.R.).

[168] *Ibid.*, at 956 (S.C.R.).

[169] *Ibid.*, at 956-57 (S.C.R.) (noting that entrapment would not arise where police planted a handbag in an obvious location in a bus terminal where there had been several complaints of handbag theft).

[170] *R. v. Barnes*, [1991] S.C.J. No. 17, [1991] 1 S.C.R. 449 at 463 (S.C.C.). See also *R. v. Kenyon*, [1990] B.C.J. No. 2684, 61 C.C.C. (3d) 538 (B.C.C.A.) (no reasonable suspicion that drug dealing taking place at pub); *R. v. Benjamin*, [1994] O.J. No. 1373 (Ont. C.A.) (area targeted too large); *R. v. Swan*, [2009] B.C.J. No. 623, 244 C.C.C. (3d) 108 (B.C.C.A.) (suggesting that geographic precision may not be feasible in context of "dial-a-dope" investigations but finding that cold calling of cell phones without efforts to substantiate suspicion was not *bona fide*). Some courts have suggested that entrapment may not arise when officials enforcing certain regulatory schemes randomly provide opportunities to commit offences. See *R. v. Au Canada Monetary Exchange Inc.*, [1999] B.C.J. No. 455, 41 W.C.B. (2d) 367 (B.C.S.C.) (police do not

§10.45 The degree of precision required is illustrated by the Supreme Court's decision in *R. v. Barnes.*[171] There, police conducted a "buy-and-bust" operation over a six-block area. Though police had no reason (beyond his "scruffy" appearance) to suspect the accused of selling drugs,[172] the Court held that they acted with *bona fides* because they reasonably believed that drug trafficking was occurring throughout the area.

§10.46 In her dissenting opinion, Justice McLachlin (as she then was) chided the majority for discounting innocent people's interest in "being able to go about their daily lives without courting the risk that they will be subjected to the clandestine investigatory techniques of agents of the state."[173] In applying the *bona fide* inquiry test, she argued, judges should consider "not only the motive of the police and whether there is crime in the general area, but also other factors relevant to the balancing process, such as the likelihood of crime at the particular location targeted, the seriousness of the crime in question, the number of legitimate activities and persons who might be affected, and the availability of other less intrusive investigative techniques."[174]

§10.47 As the Supreme Court has observed, claims of the first type of entrapment are unlikely to succeed.[175] To defeat them, the prosecution need only show that police reasonably suspected either that a particular individual is committing a particular offence *or* that a particular offence is being committed by unknown individuals in a particular place. This is as it should be. Short of inducement, few argue that police should be not be able to give persons already reasonably suspected of committing offences opportunities to commit them so that evidence of their guilt can be obtained. As the Supreme Court has recognized, prohibiting this investigative technique would severely hamper efforts to combat "consensual" crimes like drug trafficking and prostitution.[176] And while the targeting of broadly-defined locations does raise the risk of targeting the innocent, short of inducement such importuning is a relatively minor intrusion on liberty. Further, the nuanced, *ex post* balancing of interests contemplated by Justice McLachlin in *Barnes* would be very difficult for police to apply *ex ante*.

---

require reasonable suspicion to provide opportunity to commit record-keeping offence under proceeds of crime legislation); *R. v. Clothier*, [2011] O.J. No. 102, 2011 ONCA 27 at para. 33 (Ont. C.A.) (no reasonable suspicion required to check if vendors would sell tobacco to underage buyer). See also Morris Manning & Peter Sankoff, *Manning, Mewett & Sankoff, Criminal Law*, 4th ed. (Markham.: LexisNexis Canada, 2009) at 504-505.

[171]   *R. v. Barnes*, [1991] S.C.J. No. 17, [1991] 1 S.C.R. 449 (S.C.C.).
[172]   *Ibid.*, at 456, 460 (S.C.R.).
[173]   *Ibid.*, at 480 (S.C.R.), *per* McLachlin J., dissenting.
[174]   *Ibid.*, at 483 (S.C.R.), *per* McLachlin J., dissenting.
[175]   See *R. v. Mack*, [1988] S.C.J. No. 91, [1988] 2 S.C.R. 903 at 959 (S.C.C.).
[176]   *Ibid.*, at 956 (S.C.R.). See also *Kirzner v. R.*, [1977] S.C.J. No. 123, [1978] 2 S.C.R. 487 at 492-93 (S.C.C.), *per* Laskin C.J.C.; *R. v. Imoro*, [2010] O.J. No. 586, 2010 ONCA 122 at para. 8 (Ont. C.A.), affd [2010] S.C.J. No. 50, [2010] 3 S.C.R. 62 (S.C.C.). This begs the larger question of whether, and in what circumstances, such activities ought to be criminalized. See Don Stuart, *Canadian Criminal Law*, 5th ed. (Toronto: Thomson Carswell, 2007) at 620-21.

§10.48 It is thus not surprising that most cases focus on the second type of entrapment. As mentioned, this arises when police go beyond providing a criminal opportunity and "induce" the commission of an offence. It is this form of entrapment, after all, that squarely implicates the policy concerns underlying the defence: the moral impropriety and waste of resources caused by the creation of crimes that would not have otherwise occurred. Unfortunately, it is not always easy to decide whether the accused would have committed the offence but for the importuning of state agents. In each case, the court must consider the "totality of the circumstances",[177] including the following:

- the type of crime being investigated and the availability of other techniques for the police detection of its commission;

- whether an average person, with both strengths and weaknesses, in the position of the accused would be induced into the commission of a crime;

- the persistence and number of attempts made by the police before the accused agreed to committing the offence;

- the type of inducement used by the police including: deceit, fraud, trickery or reward;

- the timing of the police conduct, in particular whether the police have instigated the offence or became involved in ongoing criminal activity;

- whether the police conduct involves an exploitation of human characteristics such as the emotions of compassion, sympathy and friendship;

- whether the police appear to have exploited a particular vulnerability of a person such as a mental handicap or a substance addiction;

- the proportionality between the police involvement, as compared to the accused, including an assessment of the degree of harm caused or risked by the police, as compared to the accused, and the commission of any illegal acts by the police themselves;

- the existence of any threats, implied or express, made to the accused by the police or their agents;

- whether the police conduct is directed at undermining other constitutional values.[178]

§10.49 In *R. v. Mack*,[179] for example, the Supreme Court found that the persistent, lengthy and threatening requests of a police agent to entice a former drug trafficker to sell drugs constituted entrapment.[180] The average person in the accused's position, Justice Lamer wrote, "might also have committed the offence, if only to finally satisfy this threatening informer and end all further

---

[177] *R. v. Mack*, [1988] S.C.J. No. 91, [1988] 2 S.C.R. 903 at 964 (S.C.C.).
[178] *R. v. Mack*, [1988] S.C.J. No. 91, [1988] 2 S.C.R. 903 at 966-67 (S.C.C.). See also *R. v. Amato*, [1982] S.C.J. No. 72, [1982] 2 S.C.R. 418 (S.C.C.), *per* Estey J., dissenting.
[179] [1988] S.C.J. No. 91, [1988] 2 S.C.R. 903 (S.C.C.).
[180] *Ibid.*, at 977-79 (S.C.R.).

contact."[181] In *R. v. Showman,*[182] in contrast, the fact that the agent made several requests of the accused and referred to their "friendship" was not enough to make out entrapment.[183] There was no exploitation of a "close personal relationship", the requests were non-threatening and were made over a brief period of time.[184]

(iii)   Abuse of Process

§10.50 As a remedy for abuses of process other than entrapment, a stay of proceedings may be ordered to remedy two types of "prejudice": first, prejudice to the defendant's right to a fair trial or to make "full answer and defence"; and second, prejudice to the integrity of the justice system.[185] When stays are awarded, the Supreme Court of Canada has stated, it will usually be as a consequence of the first type[186] ("fairness prejudice"). Though this type of prejudice has not been authoritatively defined or explained, it appears to encompass concerns about adjudicative reliability[187] and inhumane treatment of the accused.[188] Notably, fairness prejudice does not require a showing of abusive state conduct.[189]

---

[181]   *Ibid.,* at 979 (S.C.R.). See also *R. v. Meuckon,* [1990] B.C.J. No. 1552, 57 C.C.C. (3d) 193 (B.C.C.A.) (open to trial judge to find entrapment based on "making gifts, by persistent importuning, and by relying on compassion, sympathy and friendship through a fabricated story about failing to gain a job if he did not supply cocaine to his prospective employer's son"); *R. v. S. (J.),* [2001] O.J. No. 104, 152 C.C.C. (3d) 317 (Ont. C.A.) (pressing of 14-year-old accused to sell marijuana to bigger, larger, police officers constituted inducement).

[182]   [1988] S.C.J. No. 93, [1988] 2 S.C.R. 893 (S.C.C.).

[183]   *Ibid.,* at 901 (S.C.R.).

[184]   *Ibid.,* at 901-902 (S.C.R.). See also *R. v. Voustis,* [1989] S.J. No. 76, 47 C.C.C. (3d) 451 (Sask. C.A.).

[185]   See *R. v. O'Connor,* [1995] S.C.J. No. 98, [1995] 4 S.C.R. 411 at paras. 75-92 (S.C.C.); *Canada (Minister of Citizenship and Immigration) v. Tobiass,* [1997] S.C.J. No. 82, [1997] 3 S.C.R. 391 at para. 89 (S.C.C.); *R. v. Regan,* [2002] S.C.J. No. 14, [2002] 1 S.C.R. 297 at para. 55 (S.C.C.).

[186]   *Canada (Minister of Citizenship and Immigration) v. Tobiass,* [1997] S.C.J. No. 82, [1997] 3 S.C.R. 391 at para. 89 (S.C.C.).

[187]   *Charkaoui v. Canada (Minister of Citizenship and Immigration),* [2008] S.C.J. No. 39, [2008] 2 S.C.R. 326 at para. 48 (S.C.C.), quoting *R. v. Stinchcombe,* [1991] S.C.J. No. 83, [1991] 3 S.C.R. 326 at 336 (S.C.C.) ("The right to make full answer and defence is one of the pillars of criminal justice on which we heavily depend to ensure that the innocent are not convicted."). See generally, *R. v. G. (S.G.),* [1997] S.C.J. No. 70, [1997] 2 S.C.R. 716 (S.C.C.), *per* McLachlin J., dissenting.

[188]   See *R. v. O'Connor,* [1995] S.C.J. No. 98, [1995] 4 S.C.R. 411 at para. 80 (S.C.C.) (noting that adjournments caused by breach of Crown's disclosure obligations may "have physical, psychological and economic consequences upon the accused, particularly if the accused is incarcerated pending trial"); *R. v. Tran,* [2010] O.J. No. 2785, 2010 ONCA 471 (Ont. C.A.) (stay awarded for physical abuse of accused by police).

[189]   See *R. v. O'Connor,* [1995] S.C.J. No. 98, [1995] 4 S.C.R. 411 at para. 79 (S.C.C.) ("while a finding of flagrant and intentional Crown misconduct may make it significantly more likely that a stay of proceedings will be warranted, it does not follow that a demonstration of *mala fides* on the part of the Crown is a necessary precondition to such a finding"); *R. v. MacDonnell,* [1995] N.S.J. No. 224, 141 N.S.R. (2d) 266 (N.S.S.C.), revd [1996] N.S.J. No. 65, 148 N.S.R. (2d) 289 (N.S.C.A.), affd [1997] S.C.J. No. 16, [1997] 1 S.C.R. 305 (S.C.C.) (despite absence of abusive conduct, trial judge correct to find that stay warranted by 31-year delay between alleged offence and trial); *R. v. Neil,* [2002] S.C.J. No. 72, [2002] 3 S.C.R. 631 at para. 43 (S.C.C.) (suggesting

§10.51 The second type ("integrity prejudice") will only very rarely justify a stay.[190] The Supreme Court has defined this form of prejudice as addressing the "panoply of diverse and sometimes unforeseeable circumstances in which a prosecution is conducted in such a manner as to connote unfairness or vexatiousness of such a degree that it contravenes fundamental notions of justice."[191] This misconduct need not have affected the accused's rights or interests.[192] Where both types of prejudice are present, their cumulative effect may be considered in deciding whether to grant a stay.[193]

§10.52 Whatever the type (or combination of types) of prejudice, a stay will only be appropriate if two additional criteria are met: first, the prejudice must be "manifested, perpetuated or aggravated through the trial's conduct or outcome;" and second, there must no other remedy capable of removing that prejudice.[194] If (and only if) it remains unclear whether a stay should issue after considering these criteria, courts may also balance society's interest in an adjudication on the merits against the interests that would be furthered by awarding a stay.[195]

§10.53 For fairness prejudice, the first two criteria effectively merge into one: a stay will be appropriate when the prejudice cannot otherwise be remedied, *i.e.,* when continuing the proceeding would perpetuate the prejudice.[196] When there

---

that state action not required where incompetent representation by counsel creates risk of injustice).

[190] *Canada (Minister of Citizenship and Immigration) v. Tobiass*, [1997] S.C.J. No. 82, [1997] 3 S.C.R. 391 at para. 89 (S.C.C.).

[191] *R. v. O'Connor*, [1995] S.C.J. No. 98, [1995] 4 S.C.R. 411 at para. 73 (S.C.C.).

[192] *R. v. O'Connor*, [1995] S.C.J. No. 98, [1995] 4 S.C.R. 411 at para. 73 (S.C.C.). It is not clear whether, or in what circumstances, a stay may be awarded on this ground when the abuse has been committed by a non-state actor. In *R. v. Carosella*, [1997] S.C.J. No. 12, [1997] 1 S.C.R. 80 at para. 56 (S.C.C.), the Court upheld a stay granted for the deliberate destruction of evidence by a non-state agency. Though the stay was based primarily on fairness prejudice, the majority suggested that a stay was also warranted by the agency's conduct, noting that it was subject to governmental oversight and financial support. See also *R. v. Neil*, [2002] S.C.J. No. 72, [2002] 3 S.C.R. 631 at para. 43 (S.C.C.).

[193] See *R. v. O'Connor*, [1995] S.C.J. No. 98, [1995] 4 S.C.R. 411 at para. 64 (S.C.C.); Kent Roach, *Constitutional Remedies in Canada*, looseleaf (Aurora, ON: Canada Law Book, 2008) at paras. 9.108-9.109.

[194] *R. v. O'Connor*, [1995] S.C.J. No. 98, [1995] 4 S.C.R. 411 at para. 75 (S.C.C.); *R. v. Regan*, [2002] S.C.J. No. 14, [2002] 1 S.C.R. 297 at paras. 54, 56 (S.C.C.); *Canada (Minister of Citizenship and Immigration) v. Tobiass*, [1997] S.C.J. No. 82, [1997] 3 S.C.R. 391 at para. 90 (S.C.C.); *Charkaoui v. Canada (Minister of Citizenship and Immigration)*, [2008] S.C.J. No. 39, [2008] 2 S.C.R. 326 at para. 74 (S.C.C.). See also David M. Paciocco, "The Stay of Proceedings as a Remedy in Criminal Cases: Abusing the Abuse of Process Concept" (1991) 15 Crim. L.J. 315 at 341.

[195] *R. v. Regan*, [2002] S.C.J. No. 14, [2002] 1 S.C.R. 297 at paras. 57, 105 (S.C.C.) (trial court erred when it failed to apply the first two criteria before considering the balancing test); *Canada (Minister of Citizenship and Immigration) v. Tobiass*, [1997] S.C.J. No. 82, [1997] 3 S.C.R. 391 at para. 92 (S.C.C.) (third factor "merely recognizes that in certain cases, where it is unclear whether the abuse is sufficient to warrant a stay, a compelling societal interest in having a full hearing could tip the scales in favour of proceeding").

[196] See *e.g.*, *R. v. Taillefer*, [2003] S.C.J. No. 75, [2003] 3 S.C.R. 307 (S.C.C.) (prosecution would perpetuate unfairness where accused had already served two-thirds of sentence he would have received if found guilty).

has been prejudice to the integrity of the justice system, however, the criteria remain somewhat distinct. The "perpetuation" criterion suggests that past misconduct will in itself rarely warrant a stay. As the Supreme Court of Canada stated in *Canada (Minister of Citizenship and Immigration) v. Tobiass*,[197] a stay will not be appropriate unless the misconduct "is likely to continue in the future" or the continuation of the prosecution "will offend society's sense of justice."[198] The Court explained further:

> Ordinarily, the latter condition will not be met unless the former is as well — society will not take umbrage at the carrying forward of a prosecution unless it is likely that some form of misconduct will continue. There may be exceptional cases in which the past misconduct is so egregious that the mere fact of going forward in the light of it will be offensive.[199]

§10.54 As Kent Roach has noted, however, it will be very rare to find abuses that have continued up to the time of a stay application.[200] Equally uncommon are cases in which the courts have found past misconduct so egregious as to warrant a stay.[201] As the Court stated in *Tobiass*, "only an exceedingly serious abuse could ever bring such continuing disrepute upon the administration of justice."[202]

§10.55 The "alternative remedies" criterion has had a similar effect. Courts have typically found that these remedies — such as adjournments,[203] orders for disclosure[204]

---

[197] [1997] S.C.J. No. 82, [1997] 3 S.C.R. 391 (S.C.C.).

[198] *Ibid.*, at para. 91 (S.C.R.).

[199] *Ibid.*, at para. 91 (S.C.R.).

[200] Kent Roach, *Constitutional Remedies in Canada*, looseleaf (Aurora, ON: Canada Law Book, 2008) at paras. 9.115-9.119.5.

[201] See *e.g.*, *Canada (Minister of Citizenship and Immigration) v. Tobiass*, [1997] S.C.J. No. 82, [1997] 3 S.C.R. 391 at para. 97 (S.C.C.) (judicial misconduct not serious enough for stay); *R. v. Curragh Inc.*, [1997] S.C.J. No. 33, [1997] 1 S.C.R. 537 (S.C.C.) (stay awarded by trial judge for whom there was reasonable apprehension of bias overturned and new trial ordered); *R. v. Regan*, [2002] S.C.J. No. 14, [2002] 1 S.C.R. 297 at para. 55 (S.C.C.) ("a stay of proceedings is only appropriate when the abuse is likely to continue or be carried forward"); *R. v. Latimer*, [1997] S.C.J. No. 11, [1997] 1 S.C.R. 217 (S.C.C.) (flagrant interference with prospective jurors did not warrant stay); *Charkaoui v. Canada (Minister of Citizenship and Immigration)*, [2008] S.C.J. No. 39, [2008] 2 S.C.R. 326 at para. 77 (S.C.C.) (destruction of evidence was not so egregious to warrant stay); *R. v. Svekla*, [2010] A.J. No. 1443, 2010 ABCA 390 (Alta. C.A.) (lost evidence did not justify stay); *R. v. Carosella*, [1997] S.C.J. No. 12, [1997] 1 S.C.R. 80 at para. 56 (S.C.C.), *per* Sopinka J., at paras. 133, 139 (S.C.R.), *per* L'Heureux-Dubé J., dissenting (stay granted for deliberate destruction of evidence by third party subject to governmental oversight and support). See also Kent Roach, *Constitutional Remedies in Canada*, looseleaf (Aurora: Canada Law Book, 2008) at paras. 9.118-9.119. But see *R. v. Tran*, [2010] O.J. No. 2785, 2010 ONCA 471 (Ont. C.A.) (stay awarded for physical abuse of accused by police).

[202] *Canada (Minister of Citizenship and Immigration) v. Tobiass*, [1997] S.C.J. No. 82, [1997] 3 S.C.R. 391 at para. 96 (S.C.C.). See also *R. v. Regan*, [2002] S.C.J. No. 14, [2002] 1 S.C.R. 297 at para. 55 (S.C.C.).

[203] See *e.g.*, *R. v. O'Connor*, [1995] S.C.J. No. 98, [1995] 4 S.C.R. 411 at paras. 76-77 (S.C.C.); *R. v. Leboeuf*, [2005] Q.J. No. 8452, 2005 QCCA 637 (Que. C.A.); *R. v. Wicksted*, [1996] O.J. No. 1576, 29 O.R. (3d) 144 (Ont. C.A.), affd [1997] S.C.J. No. 17 (S.C.C.).

[204] See *R. v. O'Connor*, [1995] S.C.J. No. 98, [1995] 4 S.C.R. 411 at para. 76 (S.C.C.) ("Although it is not a precondition to a disclosure order that there be a *Charter* violation, a disclosure order *can* be a remedy under s. 24(1).") [emphasis in original]

or costs,[205] recalling witnesses for cross-examination,[206] ordering a mistrial[207] or new trial[208] and ordering that further proceedings be held in front of a different judge[209] — have been sufficient to remove prejudice to the integrity of the system.

§10.56 Several aspects of this jurisprudence are in need of clarification or reform. First, the courts should be more specific about the meaning of "fairness prejudice". As mentioned, the cases reveal that this form of prejudice arises from concerns about wrongful convictions or inhumane treatment. The courts should thus clarify that stays should be granted under section 24(1) when, considering the ameliorative effects of alternative remedies, continuing with the proceedings would either: (*i*) create an undue risk of wrongful conviction; or (*ii*) cause undue harm to the applicant.

§10.57 The courts should also provide more guidance on how these two types of prejudice interact with concerns about state abuse and society's interest in adjudication on the merits. When there is a significant risk of wrongful conviction, neither of these concerns should be relevant. If this risk cannot be ameliorated by other remedies, proceedings should be stayed even if the accused is charged with a serious offence and there is no state misconduct. A stay might be justified in such circumstances, for example, by the loss of exculpatory evidence.[210]

§10.58 It may sometimes be appropriate to consider state misconduct and offence seriousness, in contrast, when wrongful convictions are not a concern, *i.e.*, when the only type of "fairness prejudice" is inhumane treatment. While abuse is not required to justify a stay on this ground, its presence may strengthen the case for one.[211] Conversely, in deciding whether continuing with the proceeding would cause too much harm to the applicant, it may be appropriate to consider

---

[205] See *R. v. Cole*, [2000] N.S.J. No. 84, 2000 NSCA 42 (N.S.C.A.); *R. v. Leboeuf*, [2005] Q.J. No. 8452, 2005 QCCA 637 (Que. C.A.); *R. v. McKillip*, [1996] O.J. No. 747, 35 C.R.R. (2d) 172 (Ont. Gen. Div.).

[206] See *R. v. O'Connor*, [1995] S.C.J. No. 98, [1995] 4 S.C.R. 411 at para. 77 (S.C.C.).

[207] *Ibid.*

[208] See *R. v. O'Connor*, [1995] S.C.J. No. 98, [1995] 4 S.C.R. 411 at paras. 57, 77 (S.C.C.); *R. v. Latimer*, [1997] S.C.J. No. 11, [1997] 1 S.C.R. 217 (S.C.C.); *R. v. Bero*, [2000] O.J. No. 4199, 151 C.C.C. (3d) 545 (Ont. C.A.); *R. v. Antinello*, [1995] A.J. No. 214, 165 A.R. 122 (Alta. C.A.); *Canada (Minister of Citizenship and Immigration) v. Tobiass*, [1997] S.C.J. No. 82, [1997] 3 S.C.R. 391 (S.C.C.); *R. v. Curragh Inc.*, [1997] S.C.J. No. 33, [1997] 1 S.C.R. 537 (S.C.C.); *R. v. Hobbs*, [2010] N.S.J. No. 386, 2010 NSCA 62 at paras. 40-44 (N.S.C.A.), leave to appeal refused [2010] S.C.C.A. No. 370 (S.C.C.); *R. v. Henry*, [2011] N.B.J. No. 136, 2011 NBCA 40 (N.B.C.A.).

[209] *Canada (Minister of Citizenship and Immigration) v. Tobiass*, [1997] S.C.J. No. 82, [1997] 3 S.C.R. 391 (S.C.C.).

[210] See *e.g.*, *R. v. MacDonnell*, [1995] N.S.J. No. 224, 141 N.S.R. (2d) 266 (N.S.S.C.), revd [1996] N.S.J. No. 65, 148 N.S.R. (2d) 289 (N.S.C.A.), affd [1997] S.C.J. No. 16, [1997] 1 S.C.R. 305 (S.C.C.) (stay in murder case justified, *inter alia*, by loss of medical examiner's potentially exculpatory evidence).

[211] See *e.g.*, *R. v. Tran*, [2010] O.J. No. 2785, 2010 ONCA 471 (Ont. C.A.) (stay granted where police inflicted severe beating on accused).

the seriousness of the offence and other factors bearing on society's interest in resolving the case on the merits.[212]

§10.59 Lastly, like many other commentators,[213] in our estimation the courts have been too reluctant to grant stays to preserve the integrity of the justice system. By referring to this form of prejudice as an exceptional, "residual" ground for a stay,[214] and by imposing virtually unattainable requirements, the Supreme Court has severely limited the ability of courts to sanction authorities for gross misconduct. This approach also conflicts with the Court's approach to entrapment, which as discussed in Part 5(1)(*a*)(ii), is merely a specific iteration of the abuse of process doctrine. To establish entrapment (and obtain the automatic stay it triggers), an accused need not demonstrate that continuing the proceedings would perpetuate prejudice to the integrity of the justice system.[215]

§10.60 We agree, of course, that stays must be used with restraint. But in a small (but not trivial) proportion of cases, alternative remedies will simply not do enough to remove the stain on the system's integrity and discourage future abuse. For example, in *R. v. Tran*,[216] the Ontario Court of Appeal substituted a stay of proceedings for the sentence reduction awarded by the trial judge where police severely beat the accused during an interrogation (leaving him with permanent injuries), doggedly attempted to conceal their abuse and continued to assist the prosecution at trial after the judge found that they had beaten the accused.[217]

§10.61 As detailed in Part 5(2)(*c*), below, in its section 24(2) jurisprudence the Court has repeatedly stressed the importance of excluding evidence obtained by serious misconduct, even if factually guilty defendants are sometimes acquitted as a result. Though a greater range of remedies is available under section 24(1) than section 24(2), and though evidentiary exclusion may not prevent

---

[212] *R. v. Regan*, [2002] S.C.J. No. 14, [2002] 1 S.C.R. 297 at paras. 57, 105 (S.C.C.) (trial court erred when it failed to apply first two criteria before considering balancing test); *Canada (Minister of Citizenship and Immigration) v. Tobiass*, [1997] S.C.J. No. 82, [1997] 3 S.C.R. 391 at para. 92 (S.C.C.) (third factor "merely recognizes that in certain cases, where it is unclear whether the abuse is sufficient to warrant a stay, a compelling societal interest in having a full hearing could tip the scales in favour of proceeding").

[213] See Kent Roach, *Constitutional Remedies in Canada*, looseleaf (Aurora: Canada Law Book, 2008) at paras. 9.107-9.125; Kent Roach, "The Evolving Test for Stays of Proceedings" (1998) 40 Crim. L.Q. 400; Don Stuart, *Charter Justice in Canadian Criminal Law*, 5th ed. (Toronto: Thomson Carswell, 2010) at 175-79; David MacAlister, "Does the Residual Category for Abuse of Process Still Exist?" (2000) 28 C.R. (5th) 72.

[214] *R. v. O'Connor*, [1995] S.C.J. No. 98, [1995] 4 S.C.R. 411 at para. 73 (S.C.C.); *Canada (Minister of Citizenship and Immigration) v. Tobiass*, [1997] S.C.J. No. 82, [1997] 3 S.C.R. 391 at para. 89 (S.C.C.).

[215] See generally, Don Stuart, *Canadian Criminal Law*, 5th ed. (Toronto: Thomson Carswell, 2007) at 614.

[216] [2010] O.J. No. 2785, 2010 ONCA 471 (Ont. C.A.).

[217] The state misconduct was further exacerbated, the Court found, by the unexplained decision of the authorities that there were no grounds for disciplinary or criminal proceedings against the officers involved: *R. v. Tran*, [2010] O.J. No. 2785, 2010 ONCA 471 at paras. 100-102 (Ont. C.A.).

adjudication on the merits, the same reasoning should apply to misconduct in other aspects of the criminal justice process. As in section 24(2) cases, stays should thus be imposed when (considering the ameliorative effects of other remedies), continuing with the proceedings would bring the administration of justice into disrepute, having regard to the seriousness of the violation, the impact of the violation on the applicant's *Charter*-protected interests and society's interest in obtaining a decision on the merits.[218]

(iv) Costs

§10.62 Costs may be awarded against the prosecution in both criminal and regulatory prosecutions.[219] Unlike in civil proceedings, however, costs awards are exceptional: they do not flow as a matter of routine to defendants successful on the merits.[220] In most cases, costs may only be awarded when there has been "a marked and unacceptable departure from the reasonable standards expected of the prosecution."[221]

§10.63 That said, costs awards are not rare; they have played a particularly important role, for example, in enforcing the Crown's disclosure obligations.[222] Further, the "marked and unacceptable departure" standard may be relaxed where the applicant is not a criminal defendant. In *R. v. Ciarniello*,[223] the Ontario

---

[218] See *R. v. Grant*, [2009] S.C.J. No. 32, [2009] 2 S.C.R. 353 at para. 71 (S.C.C.). See also *R. v. Campbell*, [1999] S.C.J. No. 16, [1999] 1 S.C.R. 565 (S.C.C.) (suggesting that illegal sale of drugs by police in reverse sting operation could warrant a stay, depending on further findings on good faith); *United States of America v. Cobb*, [2001] S.C.J. No. 20, [2001] 1 S.C.R. 587 (S.C.C.) (upholding stay of extradition proceedings ordered because U.S. prosecutor had threatened fugitives with bodily harm if they resisted extradition).

[219] See *R. v. 974649 Ontario Inc.*, [2001] S.C.J. No. 79, [2001] 3 S.C.R. 575 (S.C.C.); *R. v. Curragh*, [1997] S.C.J. No. 33, [1997] 1 S.C.R. 537 at para. 13 (S.C.C.); *R. v. Robinson*, [1999] A.J. No. 1469, 142 C.C.C. (3d) 303 (Alta. C.A.); *R. v. Pawlowski*, [1993] O.J. No. 554, 12 O.R. (3d) 709 (C.A.), leave to appeal refused [1993] S.C.C.A. No. 187, [1993] 3 S.C.R. viii (S.C.C.); *R. v. Pang*, [1994] A.J. No. 935, 35 C.R. (4th) 371 (Alta. C.A).

[220] See *R. v. M. (C.A.)*, [1996] S.C.J. No. 28, [1996] 1 S.C.R. 500 at para. 97 (S.C.C.); *R. v. Ciarniello*, [2006] O.J. No. 3444, 81 O.R. (3d) 561 at paras. 31-33 (Ont. C.A.), leave to appeal refused [2006] S.C.C.A. No. 424 (S.C.C.).

[221] *R. v. 974649 Ontario Inc.*, [2001] S.C.J. No. 79, [2001] 3 S.C.R. 575 at para. 87 (S.C.C.). See also *R. v. Arcand*, [2008] O.J. No. 3294, 2008 ONCA 595 at paras. 77-78 (Ont. C.A.); *R. v. Cole*, [2000] N.S.J. No. 84, 2000 NSCA 42 at para. 18 (N.S.C.A.); *R. v. Robinson*, [1999] A.J. No. 1469, 1999 ABCA 367 at para. 30 (Alta. C.A.); *R. v. Tran*, [1994] S.C.J. No. 16, [1994] 2 S.C.R. 951 at 1010 (S.C.C.); *R. v. Cameron*, [2006] O.J. No. 1928, 208 C.C.C. (3d) 481 at para. 18 (Ont. C.A.); *R. v. Taylor*, [2008] N.S.J. No. 14, 2008 NSCA 5 at paras. 48, 52 (N.S.C.A.); *R. v. Sweeney*, [2003] M.J. No. 358, 179 C.C.C. (3d) 225 at paras. 47-49 (Man. C.A.); *R. v. Leboeuf*, [2005] Q.J. No. 8452, 2005 QCCA 637 at para. 61 (Que. C.A.). See generally, Kenneth Jull, "Costs, the *Charter* and Regulatory Offences: The Price of Fairness" (2002) 81 Can. Bar Rev. 646.

[222] See *R. v. 974649 Ontario Inc.*, [2001] S.C.J. No. 79, [2001] 3 S.C.R. 575 at paras. 80-81 (S.C.C.); *R. v. Pawlowski*, [1993] O.J. No. 554, 12 O.R. (3d) 709 (Ont. C.A.), leave to appeal refused [1993] S.C.C.A. No. 187, [1993] 3 S.C.R. viii (S.C.C.); *R. v. Pang*, [1994] A.J. No. 935, 35 C.R. (4th) 371 (Alta. C.A). See also Chapter 7.

[223] [2006] O.J. No. 3444, 81 O.R. (3d) 561 (Ont. C.A.), leave to appeal refused [2006] S.C.C.A. No. 424 (S.C.C.).

Court of Appeal awarded costs to a non-accused person who had sued for the return of unconstitutionally seized property, despite the absence of serious prosecutorial misconduct.[224] Compared to criminal defendants, the Court reasoned, non-accused persons face greater barriers to the pursuit of *Charter* claims and are clothed with fewer procedural protections (such as the prospect of evidentiary exclusion).[225] The possibility of costs awards may thus encourage such persons to vindicate their rights.

(v) Damages

§10.64 Damages may be awarded under section 24(1) as a remedy for *Charter* violations when: (*i*) the application is made to a court or tribunal empowered to do so; and (*ii*) damages would be an "appropriate and just" remedy in the circumstances. Under the first requirement, it is clear that claimants may pursue damages before the superior courts in a civil lawsuit brought against state actors who allegedly perpetrated the violation.[226] Such a suit may be brought in conjunction with a tort claim, but applicants are not required to exhaust private law remedies before pursuing a claim for damages under section 24(1) of the *Charter*.[227] As a consequence of the Supreme Court of Canada's ruling in *Vancouver (City) v. Ward*,[228] it is also clear that damages are not available in provincial criminal (*i.e.*, inferior) courts.[229] Such courts, the Court stated in *Ward*, have neither the statutory nor inherent authority to award damages.[230] Though the Court in *Ward* did not expressly resolve the question, it would appear from its decision that damages may be sought in criminal proceedings before the superior courts. Following *R. v. Conway*,[231] the Court in *Ward* stated simply that "[g]enerally, the appropriate forum for an award of damages under s. 24(1) is a court which has the power to consider *Charter* questions and which by statute or inherent

---

[224] *Ibid.*

[225] *Ibid.*, at paras. 39-41 (O.R.), leave to appeal refused [2006] S.C.C.A. No. 424 (S.C.C.).

[226] See *Vancouver (City) v. Ward*, [2010] S.C.J. No. 27, [2010] 2 S.C.R. 28 (S.C.C.) (damages awarded in civil action for unconstitutional strip search) [*Ward*]. See also *Samimifar v. Canada (Minister of Citizenship and Immigration)*, [2006] F.C.J. No. 1626, [2007] 3 F.C.R. 663 (F.C.), affd [2007] F.C.J. No. 926 (F.C.A.) (damages awarded for unreasonably delay, negligence, abuse of process); *Du-lude v. Canada*, [2000] F.C.J. No. 1454, [2001] 1 F.C. 545 at para. 18 (F.C.A.); *Auton (Guardian ad litem of) v. British Columbia (Minister of Health)*, [2001] B.C.J. No. 215, 197 D.L.R. (4th) 165 (B.C.S.C.), vard (*sub nom. Auton (Guardian ad litem of) v. British Columbia (Attorney General)*) [2002] B.C.J. No. 225 8, 220 D.L.R. (4th) 411 (B.C.C.A.), revd [2004] S.C.J. No. 71, [2004] 3 S.C.R. 657 (S.C.C.) ("symbolic damages" awarded for unequal treatment under healthcare regime); *Lahaie v. Canada (Attorney General)*, [2008] O.J. No. 5276, 303 D.L.R. (4th) 213 (Ont. S.C.J.), revd [2010] O.J. No. 3100 (Ont. C.A.). See generally, Peter W. Hogg & Patrick J. Monahan, *Liability of the Crown*, 3d ed. (2000) sec. 6.5(d); Peter W. Hogg, *Constitutional Law of Canada*, 5th ed. (supplemented), vol. 2, looseleaf (Toronto: Thomson Carswell, 2007) § 40.2(g).

[227] See *Vancouver (City) v. Ward*, [2010] S.C.J. No. 27, [2010] 2 S.C.R. 28 at para. 59 (S.C.C.).

[228] [2010] S.C.J. No. 27, [2010] 2 S.C.R. 28 (S.C.C.).

[229] See *Vancouver (City) v. Ward*, [2010] S.C.J. No. 27, [2010] 2 S.C.R. 28 (S.C.C.).

[230] See *ibid.*, at para. 58 (S.C.R.).

[231] [2010] S.C.J. No. 22, [2010] 1 S.C.R. 765 (S.C.C.).

jurisdiction has the power to award damages".[232] Superior courts of criminal jurisdiction fulfill both of these criteria and therefore presumably may award *Charter* damages when it is "appropriate and just" to do so.[233]

§10.65 Some courts have questioned, however, whether damages can ever be an appropriate and just remedy in criminal proceedings.[234] The criminal trial process, the reasoning goes, lacks the procedural mechanisms (such as pleadings and discovery) necessary to fairly and accurately assess damages. We strongly disagree. Indeed, like many other commentators, we think that all criminal trial courts (including the provincial courts) should be able to award *Charter* damages.[235] Damages may sometimes be the best way to provide meaningful compensation for the harms caused by *Charter* breaches and deter future infringements.[236] Victims in such cases should not be expected to pursue separate civil claims, especially when the quantum of expected damages is modest.[237] Procedural fairness concerns may be taken into account in deciding, on a case by case basis, whether damages would be an "appropriate and just" remedy.

§10.66 The general considerations for deciding whether damages are appropriate and just under section 24(1) of the *Charter* were set out in *Ward*. Damages should be only awarded, the Court held, to the extent that they "serve the objectives of (1) compensating the claimant for loss and suffering caused by the breach; (2) vindicating the right by emphasizing its importance and the gravity of the breach; and (3) deterring state agents from committing future breaches."[238] Even if damages would serve one or more of these purposes, however, they may

---

[232] *Vancouver (City) v. Ward*, [2010] S.C.J. No. 27, [2010] 2 S.C.R. 28 at para. 58 (S.C.C.).

[233] See *R. v. F. (R.G.)*, [1991] N.J. No. 20, 90 Nfld. & P.E.I.R. 113 (Nfld. T.D.) ($1,000 damages awarded for arbitrary detention); *R. v. Kenny*, [1992] N.J. No. 189, 99 Nfld. & P.E.I.R. 107 (Nfld. T.D.) (superior court of criminal jurisdiction may award damages pursuant to its inherent jurisdiction using procedural rules of its choosing).

[234] See *R. v. Mills*, [1986] S.C.J. No. 39, [1986] 1 S.C.R. 863 at 884-86 (S.C.C.), *per* Lamer J., 971 (S.C.R.), *per* La Forest J.; *R. v. Pang*, [1994] A.J. No. 935, 162 A.R. 24 at para. 27 (Alta. C.A.); *R. c. Dufresne*, [1990] J.Q. no 73, 75 C.R. (3d) 117 (Que. C.A.); *R. v. McGillivary*, [1990] N.B.J. No. 324, 56 C.C.C. (3d) 304 (N.B.C.A.).

[235] See Kent Roach, *Constitutional Remedies in Canada*, looseleaf (Aurora: Canada Law Book, 2008) at paras. 11.210-11.285; Marilyn Pilkington, "Monetary Redress for Charter Infringement," in Robert Sharpe, ed. *Charter Litigation* (Toronto: Butterworths, 1987) 326. See also *R. v. Agat Laboratories Ltd.*, [1998] A.J. No. 304, 218 A.R. 160 (Alta. Prov. Ct.) (when *quantum* can be expeditiously determined, both superior and inferior criminal courts have jurisdiction to award pecuniary (but not general) damages).

[236] See *Doucet-Boudreau v. Nova Scotia (Department of Education)*, [2003] S.C.J. No. 63, [2003] 3 S.C.R. 3 at paras. 52-59 (S.C.C.); *R. v. 974649 Ontario Inc.*, [2001] S.C.J. No. 79, [2001] 3 S.C.R. 575 at 587-88 (S.C.C.); *Vancouver (City) v. Ward*, [2010] S.C.J. No. 27, [2010] 2 S.C.R. 28 at paras. 20-21 (S.C.C.); *Hawley v. Bapoo*, [2005] O.J. No. 4328, 76 O.R. (3d) 649 at paras. 195, 198 (Ont. S.C.J.), vard on other grounds [2007] O.J. No. 2695, 227 O.A.C. 81 (Ont. C.A.); *Auton (Guardian ad litem of) v. British Columbia (Minister of Health)*, [2001] B.C.J. No. 215, 197 D.L.R. (4th) 165 at para. 64 (B.C.S.C.), vard (*sub nom. Auton (Guardian ad litem of) v. British Columbia (Attorney General)*) [2002] B.C.J. No. 2258, 220 D.L.R. (4th) 411 (B.C.C.A.), revd on merits [2004] S.C.J. No. 71, [2004] 3 S.C.R. 657 (S.C.C.).

[237] See *e.g.*, *Vancouver (City) v. Ward*, [2010] S.C.J. No. 27, [2010] 2 S.C.R. 28 at para. 73 (S.C.C.) (upholding award of $5,000 for unconstitutional strip search).

[238] *Vancouver (City) v. Ward*, [2010] S.C.J. No. 27, [2010] 2 S.C.R. 28 at para. 31 (S.C.C.).

not be appropriate if they are trumped by "countervailing considerations", including "the existence of alternative remedies and concerns for good governance."[239] On the question of quantum, the Court stressed that the award must "reflect what is required to functionally serve the objects of compensation, vindication of the right and deterrence of future breaches, insofar as they are engaged in a particular case, having regard to the impact of the breach on the claimant and the seriousness of the state conduct," keeping in mind the need to avoid the duplication of any damages awarded under private law causes of action.[240]

(vi) Exclusion of Evidence

§10.67 The exclusion of evidence takes place mainly under section 24(2) of the *Charter*. In his reasons for a majority of the Court on this point in *R. v. Therens*,[241] Justice Le Dain expressed the view that "in making explicit provision for the remedy of exclusion of evidence in s. 24(2), following the general terms of s. 24(1), the framers of the *Charter* intended that this particular remedy should be governed entirely by the terms of s. 24(2)."[242] On this view, the exclusion of evidence could never be an "appropriate and just remedy" under section 24(1).

§10.68 The Supreme Court has since modified this position slightly. Justice Le Dain's approach has been retained in cases where the impugned evidence was, as expressed in section 24(2), "obtained in a manner" that violated the *Charter*.[243] When applicants allege that authorities infringed their *Charter* rights in *obtaining* the evidence (for example, when police obtain a confession after violating a suspect's right to counsel), the only route to exclusion is section 24(2). The applicant would accordingly be required to show that the admission of the evidence could "bring the administration of justice into disrepute."[244] It would not be sufficient to show that exclusion would be an "appropriate and just remedy." Evidence may be excluded under section 24(1), however, as a remedy for *Charter* violations unconnected to the acquisition of the evidence. This may only occur where "admission would result in an unfair trial or would otherwise

---

239 *Vancouver (City) v. Ward*, [2010] S.C.J. No. 27, [2010] 2 S.C.R. 28 at para. 33 (S.C.C.). Other remedies, the Court stated at para. 34, include "private law remedies for actions for personal injury, other *Charter* remedies like declarations under s. 24(1), and remedies for actions covered by legislation permitting proceedings against the Crown." Good governance considerations may prevail, the Court added at para. 42, if damages might "deter state agents from doing what is required for effective governance".

240 *Vancouver (City) v. Ward*, [2010] S.C.J. No. 27, [2010] 2 S.C.R. 28 at paras. 55, 57 (S.C.C.).

241 [1985] S.C.J. No. 30, [1985] 1 S.C.R. 613 (S.C.C.).

242 *R. v. Therens*, [1985] S.C.J. No. 30, [1985] 1 S.C.R. 613 at 647 (S.C.C.). See also *R. v. Collins*, [1987] S.C.J. No. 15, [1987] 1 S.C.R. 265 at 276 (S.C.C.); *R. v. Strachan*, [1988] S.C.J. No. 94, [1988] 2 S.C.R. 980 at 1000 (S.C.C.).

243 See discussion below, Part 5(2)(*b*).

244 See discussion below, Part 5(2)(*c*).

undermine the integrity of the justice system" and a "less intrusive remedy cannot be fashioned to safeguard [these interests]."[245]

§10.69 In *R. v. White*,[246] the Supreme Court held that the admission of a criminal defendant's statutorily compelled statements would violate the right to silence protected by section 7 of the *Charter*.[247] Because police did not violate the *Charter* in taking the statements (which were made under a provincial law mandating the reporting of certain motor vehicle accidents), section 24(2) did not apply. Instead, the Court held that since it was the admission of the statements (or any evidence derived from them) at trial that would violate the *Charter*, they could be excluded under section 24(1).[248]

§10.70 It is also likely that evidence may be excluded under section 24(1) when it is obtained in circumstances where the *Charter* does not apply. In a series of decisions on the extraterritorial application of the *Charter* in transnational criminal investigations, the Supreme Court has held that evidence collected improperly outside the territorial ambit of the *Charter* could nonetheless be excluded to prevent an unfair trial.[249] The Court has similarly suggested that evidence obtained in Canada by non-state actors may be excluded when its admission would be unfair to the accused.[250] Though the majorities in these cases have stated that the power to exclude in these circumstances derives directly from either the common law or sections 7 and 11(*d*) of the *Charter*, the better view is that it derives (in *Charter* cases) from section 24(1). Though the practical consequences are the same (evidence is excluded when its admission would render the trial unfair), this approach preserves the distinction between rights and remedies.[251]

§10.71 Evidence may also be excluded under section 24(1) as a remedy for untimely disclosure in violation of defendants' section 7 rights to full answer and

---

[245] *R. v. Bjelland*, [2009] S.C.J. No. 38, [2009] 2 S.C.R. 651 at paras. 3, 19 (S.C.C.).
[246] [1999] S.C.J. No. 28, [1999] 2 S.C.R. 417 (S.C.C.).
[247] *Ibid.*
[248] *R. v. White*, [1999] S.C.J. No. 28, [1999] 2 S.C.R. 417, at para. 89 (S.C.C.). See also *R. v. Osmar*, [2007] O.J. No. 244, 217 C.C.C. (3d) 174 (Ont. C.A.); *R. v. Kakegamic*, [2010] O.J. No. 5671, 2010 ONCA 903 at para. 45 (Ont. C.A.); *R. v. Powers*, [2006] B.C.J. No. 2650, 213 C.C.C. (3d) 351 (B.C.C.A.), leave to appeal refused [2006] S.C.C.A. No. 452 (S.C.C.).
[249] See *R. v. Harrer*, [1995] S.C.J. No. 81, [1995] 3 S.C.R. 562 at paras. 21-24 (S.C.C.); *R. v. Terry*, [1996] S.C.J. No. 62, [1996] 2 S.C.R. 207 at para. 25 (S.C.C.); *R. v. Hape*, [2007] S.C.J. No. 26, [2007] 2 S.C.R. 292 at paras. 108-113 (S.C.C.). These cases are discussed in detail in Chapter 1, Part 4(3)(*d*).
[250] *R. v. Buhay*, [2003] S.C.J. No. 30, [2003] 1 S.C.R. 631 at para. 40 (S.C.C.). See also Chapter 1, Part 4(3)(*e*).
[251] See *R. v. Harrer*, [1995] S.C.J. No. 81, [1995] 3 S.C.R. 562 (S.C.C.), McLachlin J. (as she then was) (evidence not obtained by a *Charter* breach but which would render the trial unfair may be excluded either at common law or pursuant to s. 24(1) of the *Charter*); *Schreiber v. Canada (Attorney General)*, [1998] S.C.J. No. 42, [1998] 1 S.C.R. 841 at para. 24 (S.C.C.), Lamer C.J.C. ("if use of the evidence obtained on the strength of foreign laws affected the fairness of a trial held in Canada, it could be excluded under a combination of ss. 7 and 24(1) of the *Charter*").

defence.[252] This will only be appropriate, however, when lesser remedies (such as orders for disclosure, adjournments, a mistrial and costs) would not cure the prejudice to either trial fairness or the integrity of the justice system.[253] Exclusion may thus be warranted where "evidence is produced mid-trial after important and irrevocable decisions about the defence have been made by the accused" and the accused can demonstrate "how the late disclosed evidence would have affected" such decisions.[254] Similarly, exclusion may be justified to protect the integrity of the justice system where adjournment would "significantly prolong" pre-trial custody or where the "Crown has withheld evidence through deliberate misconduct amounting to an abuse of process."[255] As with the remedy of a stay of proceedings, before ordering exclusion on this basis courts must consider society's interest in a reliable adjudication on the merits, especially for serious offences.[256]

(vii) Reduction in Sentence

§10.72 For many years, most courts accepted that sentence reductions could be ordered under section 24(1).[257] They differed, however, on when they would be "appropriate and just in the circumstances." Some courts held that sentences should be reduced only when the *Charter* violation mitigated the seriousness of the offence or "resulted in some form of punishment or added hardship."[258] Other courts were less restrictive, stressing that reductions may sometimes be the only meaningful remedy available.[259]

§10.73 The Supreme Court of Canada has recently taken a different (and even broader) approach. In *R. v. Nasogaluak*,[260] it concluded that state misconduct should generally be considered in sentencing without resort to the *Charter*.[261]

---

[252] *R. v. Bjelland*, [2009] S.C.J. No. 38, [2009] 2 S.C.R. 651 (S.C.C.); *R. v. Buric*, [1996] O.J. No. 1657, 106 C.C.C. (3d) 97 (Ont. C.A.), affd [1997] S.C.J. No. 38, [1997] 1 S.C.R. 535 (S.C.C.).

[253] *R. v. Bjelland*, [2009] S.C.J. No. 38, [2009] 2 S.C.R. 651 (S.C.C.).

[254] *Ibid.*, at para. 26 (S.C.R.).

[255] *Ibid.*, at para. 27 (S.C.R.).

[256] *Ibid.*

[257] See *e.g.*, *R. v. Mills*, [1986] S.C.J. No. 39, [1986] 1 S.C.R. 863 at 974 (S.C.C.), *per* La Forest J.

[258] See *R. v. Glykis*, [1995] O.J. No. 2212, 41 C.R. (4th) 310 at para. 27 (Ont. C.A.). See also *R. v. Carpenter*, [2002] B.C.J. No. 1037, 4 C.R. (6th) 115 at para. 26 (B.C.C.A.) (sentence reduced as remedy for unlawful pre-trial detention); *R. v. MacPherson*, [1995] N.B.J. No. 277, 100 C.C.C. (3d) 216 (N.B.C.A.) (same).

[259] See *R. v. Dennison*, [1990] N.B.J. No. 856, 60 C.C.C. (3d) 342 (N.B.C.A.), leave to appeal refused [1990] S.C.C.A. No. 448 (S.C.C.) (sentence reduced as remedy for failure to provide fair hearing during sentencing); *R. v. Zwicker*, [1995] N.B.J. No. 502, 169 N.B.R. (2d) 350 (N.B.C.A.) (sentence reduced where prosecutor in conflict of interest); *R. v. Stannard*, [1989] S.J. No. 582, 52 C.C.C. (3d) 544 (Sask. C.A.) (sentence reduced for breaches of ss. 8 and 10(*b*) of the *Charter*); *R. v. Charles*, [1987] S.J. No. 489, 36 C.C.C. (3d) 286 (Sask. C.A.) (sentence reduced for violation of s. 9).

[260] [2010] S.C.J. No. 6, [2010] 1 S.C.R. 206 (S.C.C.).

[261] *Ibid.* See also *R. v. Pigeon*, [1992] B.C.J. No. 1198, 73 C.C.C. (3d) 337 (B.C.C.A.) (assaults by police mitigated sentence without consideration of *Charter*); *R. v. Potts*, [2011] B.C.J. No. 38, 2011 BCCA 9 at paras. 3, 7-8, 65-74 (B.C.C.A.); *R. v. Punko*, [2010] B.C.J. No. 1551, 2010

Writing for the Court, Justice LeBel held that misconduct (whether or not constituting a *Charter* breach) is a mitigating factor in sentencing as long as it relates to the "circumstances of the offence or the offender."[262] Misconduct unconnected to these circumstances, in contrast, cannot reduce the sentence.[263] Remedies for such misconduct must be sought outside of the sentencing process.[264]

§10.74 *Nasogaluak* thus rejects the view that had been endorsed by some courts that reducing sentences for state misconduct conflicts with proportionality.[265] Sentencing, Justice LeBel wrote, "includes consideration of society's collective interest in ensuring that law enforcement agents respect the rule of law and the shared values of society."[266] Like other mitigating factors, state misconduct may thus reduce the offender's sentence below the usual range set out in the case law.[267] A sentence "falling outside the regular range of appropriate sentences," he wrote, "is not necessarily unfit. Regard must be had," he continued, "to all the circumstances of the offence and the offender, and to the needs of the community in which the offence occurred."[268]

§10.75 Absent exceptional circumstances, however, the sentence imposed must adhere to any minimums or other statutory restrictions.[269] Consequently, the Court in *Nasogaluak* held that the sentencing judge correctly treated the police's use of excessive force in arresting the accused as mitigating but erred in failing to impose the statutory minimum.[270]

(viii) Trial Process Remedies

§10.76 Criminal defendants and third parties may seek a variety of section 24(1) remedies to protect their liberty, trial fairness and other *Charter*-protected interests. Remedies of this nature include orders to: ban the publication of court

---

BCCA 365 at paras. 26-42 (B.C.C.A.); *R. v. Tran*, [2010] O.J. No. 2785, 2010 ONCA 471 at para. 82 (Ont. C.A.). This issue is discussed further in Chapter 17, Part 6(6).

[262] *R. v. Nasogaluak*, [2010] S.C.J. No. 6, [2010] 1 S.C.R. 206 at paras. 3, 47, 55 (S.C.C.).

[263] *Ibid.*, at para. 4 (S.C.R.).

[264] *Ibid.*

[265] See *R. v. Carpenter*, [2002] B.C.J. No. 1037, 4 C.R. (6th) 115 at para. 26 (B.C.C.A.); *R. v. Glykis*, [1995] O.J. No. 2212, 41 C.R. (4th) 310 at paras. 26-27 (Ont. C.A.).

[266] *R. v. Nasogaluak*, [2010] S.C.J. No. 6, [2010] 1 S.C.R. 206 at para. 49 (S.C.C.).

[267] *Ibid.*, at para. 44 (S.C.R.). See also Kent Roach, *Constitutional Remedies in Canada*, looseleaf (Aurora: Canada Law Book, 2008) at para. 9.1036; Alan Manson, "Charter Violations in Mitigation of Sentence" (1995) 41 C.R. (4th) 318; *R. v. Kim*, [2010] B.C.J. No. 2586, 2010 BCCA 590 at para. 39 (B.C.C.A.); *R. v. Oxford*, [2010] N.J. No. 232, 2010 NLCA 45 at para. 76 (N.L.C.A.).

[268] *R. v. Nasogaluak*, [2010] S.C.J. No. 6, [2010] 1 S.C.R. 206 at para. 44 (S.C.C.).

[269] *R. v. Nasogaluak*, [2010] S.C.J. No. 6, [2010] 1 S.C.R. 206 at paras. 6, 63-64 (S.C.C.) ("I...do not foreclose the possibility that, in some exceptional cases, a sentence reduction outside statutory limits may be the sole effective remedy for some particularly egregious form of misconduct by state agents in relation to the offence and the offender."). See also *Québec (Procureur général) c. Chabot*, [1992] J.Q. no 1651, 77 C.C.C. (3d) 371 (Que. C.A.); *R. v. Ferguson*, [2008] S.C.J. No. 6, [2008] 1 S.C.R. 96 (S.C.C.).

[270] *R. v. Nasogaluak*, [2010] S.C.J. No. 6, [2010] 1 S.C.R. 206 at para. 7 (S.C.C.).

proceedings, prohibit access to evidence or enjoin media broadcasts;[271] produce or disclose evidence in possession of the Crown or a third party; [272] provide an interpreter;[273] require the Crown to pay for legal representation;[274] adjourn proceedings;[275] recall witnesses for cross-examination;[276] grant a mistrial[277] or new

---

[271] Defendants typically seek publication bans to prevent future jurors from prejudging the case based on prejudicial (and potentially inadmissible) information. Prosecutors may also seek publication bans pursuant to statute or inherent judicial powers. When a publication ban is ordered, media organizations and others may apply to quash it under section 24(1) on the basis that it violates their rights to free expression under section 2(*b*) of the *Charter*. See *Dagenais v. Canadian Broadcasting Corp.*, [1994] S.C.J. No. 104, [1994] 3 S.C.R. 835 (S.C.C.) (before ordering ban, court must consider whether alternative measures sufficient to ensure fair trial); *R. v. Mentuck*, [2001] S.C.J. No. 73, [2001] 3 S.C.R. 442 (S.C.C.) (restrictions on publication should only be granted if the order would not affect the administration of justice, and the salutary effects of publication restrictions outweigh its deleterious effects); *Toronto Star Newspapers Ltd. v. Ontario*, [2005] S.C.J. No. 41, [2005] 2 S.C.R. 188 (S.C.C.) (courts considering restrictions on media access should weigh a number of factors, including the privacy interests of the parties affected, the right to freedom of expression, open court principles and the public interest, the effect on the administration of justice and the right to a fair trial); *Re Vancouver Sun*, [2004] S.C.J. No. 41, [2004] 2 S.C.R. 332 (S.C.C.) (same balancing test applied to any discretionary judicial decision). See also *Toronto Star Newspapers Ltd. v. Canada*, [2010] S.C.J. No. 21, [2010] 1 S.C.R. 721 (S.C.C.) (mandatory publication restriction on bail proceedings where requested by accused upheld); *National Post Co. v. Canada (Attorney General)*, [2003] O.J. No. 2238, 176 C.C.C. (3d) 432 (Ont. S.C.J.) (access to intercepted private communication used to obtain a warrant restricted); *R. v. Canadian Broadcasting Corp.*, [2006] O.J. No. 1685, 208 C.C.C. (3d) 257 (Ont. S.C.J.) (court refusal to provide blurred videotaped statements of young offenders upheld); *R. v. Hogg [re CTV Television Inc.]*, [2006] M.J. No. 403, 214 C.C.C. (3d) 70 (Man. C.A.) ("common sense and logic" insufficient grounds to restrict access to videotaped statement); *R. v. Casement*, [2009] S.J. No. 201, 2009 SKQB 105 (Sask. Q.B.) (court refusal to provide copies, but allows the review of, video and audio exhibits over concerns of exposing police undercover techniques); *R. v. Fry*, [2010] B.C.J. No. 590, 2010 BCCA 169 (B.C.C.A.) (refusal to release court exhibit over concerns of the safety and privacy of undercover officers overturned); *Vickery v. Nova Scotia Supreme Court (Prothonotary)*, [1991] S.C.J. No. 23, [1991] 1 S.C.R. 671 (S.C.C.) (exhibits not subject to same level of public access as court record, requirement of public trial is met if public is permitted to attend and report on trial).

[272] See *R. v. Stinchcombe*, [1991] S.C.J. No. 83, [1991] 3 S.C.R. 326 at para. 29 (S.C.C.); *R. v. Horan*, [2008] O.J. No. 3167, 2008 ONCA 589 at para. 26 (Ont. C.A.); *R. v. Bjelland*, [2009] S.C.J. No. 38, [2009] 2 S.C.R. 651 at para. 20 (S.C.C.). See also Chapter 7.

[273] Section 14 of the *Charter* guarantees the right to an interpreter in legal proceedings to witnesses and parties. See *R. v. Tran*, [1994] S.C.J. No. 16 at para. 43, [1994] 2 S.C.R. 951 (S.C.C.) (accused is entitled, where vital interest is involved, to interpretation which meets standard of "continuity, precision, impartiality, competency and contemporaneousness"); *R. v. Cheba*, [1993] S.J. No. 17, 105 Sask. R. 256 (Sask. C.A.) (mistrial appropriate where accused's lack of competency in English discovered midway through trial).

[274] Rather than directly ordering the government to pay for the accused's counsel, courts have typically stayed proceedings until it does so. See *e.g.*, *R. v. Rowbotham*, [1988] O.J. No. 271, 41 C.C.C. (3d) 1 (Ont. C.A.). However, in *New Brunswick (Minister of Health and Community Services) v. G. (J.)*, [1999] S.C.J. No. 47, [1999] 3 S.C.R. 46 (S.C.C.), the Supreme Court ordered the provision of state-funded counsel in child protection proceedings. The adoption of this principle in the criminal context has been mixed. See *R. v. Hayes*, [2002] N.B.J. No. 356, 253 N.B.R. (2d) 299 at para. 13 (N.B.C.A.) (government may be compelled to provide counsel). But see *R. v. Peterman*, [2004] O.J. No. 1758, 185 C.C.C. (3d) 352 at para. 21 (Ont. C.A.) (stay of proceedings is the appropriate remedy).

[275] See *R. v. O'Connor*, [1995] S.C.J. No. 98, [1995] 4 S.C.R. 411 at paras. 76-77 (S.C.C.) (adjournment generally an appropriate remedy where non-disclosure can be cured by disclosure order); *R. v. Leboeuf*, [2005] Q.J. No. 8452, 2005 QCCA 637 (Que. C.A.) (adjournment

trial;[278] require the return of seized goods;[279] require further proceedings be held in front of a different judge;[280] require the accused to be tried by a judge without a jury;[281] substitute a lesser charge;[282] and have detainees brought to court to determine the lawfulness of their detention by way of *habeas corpus*.[283] Some of

---

appropriate remedy where accused became aware of non-disclosure at *voir dire*); *R. v. Wicksted*, [1996] O.J. No. 1576, 29 O.R. (3d) 144 (Ont. C.A.), affd [1997] S.C.J. No. 17 (S.C.C.) (adjournment for late disclosure of allegations made by key witness appropriate remedy, stay ordered by trial judge overturned).

[276] See *R. v. O'Connor*, [1995] S.C.J. No. 98, [1995] 4 S.C.R. 411 at para. 77 (S.C.C.).

[277] *Ibid.*

[278] See *R. v. Taillefer*, [2003] S.C.J. No. 75, [2003] 3 S.C.R. 307 at para. 121 (S.C.C.) (new trial minimum remedy on appeal for serious infringement of right to full answer and defence by non-disclosure); *R. v. O'Connor*, [1995] S.C.J. No. 98, [1995] 4 S.C.R. 411 at paras. 57, 77 (S.C.C.) (mistrial acceptable remedy where non-disclosure revealed late in proceedings); *R. v. Latimer*, [1997] S.C.J. No. 11, [1997] 1 S.C.R. 217 (S.C.C.) (Crown interference with jury); *R. v. Bero*, [2000] O.J. No. 4199, C.C.C. (3d) 545 (Ont. C.A.) (loss or destruction of evidence); *R. v. Antinello*, [1995] A.J. No. 214, 165 A.R. 122 (Alta. C.A.) (untimely disclosure); *Canada (Minister of Citizenship and Immigration) v. Tobiass*, [1997] S.C.J. No. 82, [1997] 3 S.C.R. 391 (S.C.C.) (judicial misconduct); *R. v. Curragh Inc.*, [1997] S.C.J. No. 33, [1997] 1 S.C.R. 537 (S.C.C.) (apprehension of judicial bias).

[279] As long as the owner did not obtain the goods illegally, their return may be awarded either under ss. 489.1(1), 490(9) or 490.01 of the *Criminal Code* or s. 24(1) of the *Charter*. See *Lagiorgia v. Canada*, [1987] F.C.J. No. 438, [1987] 3 F.C. 28 (F.C.A.) (returning goods seized in violation of s. 8 is most appropriate remedy except where initial possession was illicit); *Re Harkat*, [2009] F.C.J. No. 659, 2009 FC 659 (F.C.) (documents retrieved from overbroad search must be returned and copies destroyed); *R. v. Spindloe*, [2001] S.J. No. 266, 154 C.C.C. (3d) 8 (Sask. C.A.) (drug paraphernalia used for illegal purposes not returned since doing so would bring administration of justice into disrepute); *Re Chapman and The Queen*, [1984] O.J. No. 3178, 12 C.C.C. (3d) 1 (Ont. C.A.) (Court has discretion to return seized items even where required by Crown as evidence); *Re Dobney Foundry Ltd. v. Canada (Attorney General)*, [1985] B.C.J. No. 2252, 19 C.C.C. (3d) 465 at 474 (B.C.C.A.) (documents obtained under quashed warrant to be returned unless Crown can obtain a new warrant); *Canada (Deputy Minister of National Revenue, Customs, Excise and Taxation) v. Millar*, [2007] B.C.J. No. 1668, 2007 BCCA 401 (B.C.C.A.) (return of seized funds not appropriate remedy where applicant intended to hide them from authorities).

[280] *Canada (Minister of Citizenship and Immigration) v. Tobiass*, [1997] S.C.J. No. 82, [1997] 3 S.C.R. 391(S.C.C.) (judicial misconduct on part of previous judge would be remedied with new trial in front of a different judge).

[281] See *R. v. Strebakowski*, [1997] B.C.J. No. 1335, 93 B.C.A.C. 139 (B.C.C.A.) (pre-trial publicity alone insufficient to require trial with judge alone); *R. v. E. (L.)*, [1994] O.J. No. 2641, 94 C.C.C. (3d) 228 at 241-43 (Ont. C.A.) (oppressive conduct by Crown in refusing to consent to judge alone trial required); *R. v. McGregor*, [1992] O.J. No. 3040, 14 C.R.R. (2d) 155 (Ont. Gen. Div.) (apprehension of bias in jury could not be corrected by other means, allowing the Crown to exercise discretion in refusing to consent to judge only trial would violate ss. 11(*d*) and 7 of the *Charter*); *R. v. Muise (No. 1)*, [1993] N.S.J. No. 309, 124 N.S.R. (2d) 81 (S.C.) (same).

[282] See *R. v. Burlingham*, [1995] S.C.J. No. 39, [1995] 2 S.C.R. 206 at para. 136 (S.C.C.) (remedy awarded for violation of fair trial right in s. 7 of the *Charter* when Crown and police acted in bad faith in plea bargaining).

[283] See *Charter*, s. 10(*c*); *R. v. Gamble*, [1988] S.C.J. No. 87, [1988] 2 S.C.R. 595 (S.C.C.) (writ of *habeas corpus* should be interpreted flexibly as remedy under s. 24(1) of *Charter*); *R. v. Sarson*, [1996] S.C.J. No. 63, [1996] 2 S.C.R. 223 at para. 41 (S.C.C.) (same); *R. v. Pearson*, [1992] S.C.J. No. 99, [1992] 3 S.C.R. 665 at 680-81 (S.C.C.) (availability of other remedies does not bar a claim for *habeus corpus* as part of claim under the *Charter*); *Steele v. Mountain*

these remedies are examined in more detail in other parts of this book;[284] extended discussions of others may be found in other works.[285]

(2) Section 24(2) Remedies

(a) Introduction

§10.77 The most frequently sought *Charter* remedy is the exclusion of evidence under section 24(2). The enactment of section 24(2) was a watershed moment in Canadian law. Before 1982, there was no mechanism (apart from the confessions rule) to exclude evidence obtained by improper or illegal means.[286] Reformers had long argued that the absence of such a mechanism rendered courts impotent to sanction police misconduct[287] and defied developments in comparable jurisdictions.[288] These arguments went unheeded, however, on the grounds that the exclusion of reliable evidence would weaken the truth-seeking process and prevent the conviction of factually guilty defendants.

§10.78 Though initially reluctant to do so, the *Charter*'s framers eventually acceded to these pressures.[289] As worded, however, section 24(2) stops well short

---

Institution, [1990] S.C.J. No. 111, [1990] 2 S.C.R. 1385 at 1418 (S.C.C.) (remedy of *habeus corpus* should not create costly parallel to existing systems of judicial review).

284 See especially Chapter 7.

285 See Kent Roach, *Constitutional Remedies in Canada*, looseleaf (Aurora: Canada Law Book, 2008) at paras. 9.120-9.125, 9.134-9.190, 9.225-9.292, 9.780-9.960, 9.1100-9.1230.

286 See *Quebec (Attorney General) v. Begin*, [1955] S.C.J. No. 37, [1955] S.C.R. 593 (S.C.C.) (improperly obtained blood samples not subject to exclusion under confessions rule); *R. v. Wray*, [1970] S.C.J. No. 80, [1971] S.C.R. 272, 11 D.L.R. (3d) 673 (S.C.C.) (rejecting discretion to exclude reliable, improperly obtained evidence); *R. v. Rothman*, [1981] S.C.J. No. 55, [1981] 1 S.C.R. 640 (S.C.C.) (same); *R. v. Hogan*, [1974] S.C.J. No. 116, [1975] 2 S.C.R. 574 (S.C.C.) (no power to exclude evidence obtained in violation of the *Canadian Bill of Rights*). See generally, Don Stuart, *Charter Justice in Canadian Criminal Law*, 5th ed. (Toronto: Thomson Carswell, 2010) at 563-66.

287 See Law Reform Commission of Canada, *Report on Evidence* (Ottawa: Information Canada, 1975) at 61-62 (proposing a statutory discretionary rule under which judges could exclude unfairly obtained evidence if its admission would bring the administration of justice into disrepute).

288 See *Lawrie v. Muir*, [1950] J.C.A., [1949] S.L.T. 58 (H.C.J. Scot.) (in a regulatory prosecution, evidence obtained during an illegal search excluded as "inspectors ought to know the precise limits of their authority and should be held to exceed these limits at their peril"); *Bunning v. Cross* (1978), 19 A.L.R. 641 (H.C.A.) (judge has discretion, if evidence obtained unlawfully, to exclude it based on a weighing of "the public need to bring to conviction those who commit criminal offenses" and "the public interest in the protection of the individual from unlawful and unfair treatment"); *R. v. Sang*, [1980] A.C. 402 (H.L.) (court has inherent power to exclude illegally obtained evidence if necessary to preserve trial fairness). See generally, Steven Penney, "Unreal Distinctions: The Exclusion of Unfairly Obtained Evidence Under s. 24(2) of the *Charter*" (1994) 32 Alta. L. Rev. 782 at 784-95. For a contemporary account of exclusionary powers in comparable jurisdictions, see William van Caenegem, "New Trends in Illegal Evidence in Criminal Procedure: General Report — Common Law" Law Papers, in *XIII World Congress of Procedural Law* (2007) online: <http://works.bepress.com/w_v_caen/12>.

289 See A. Anne McClellan & Bruce P. Elman, "The Enforcement of the *Canadian Charter of Rights and Freedoms*: An Analysis of Section 24" (1983) 21 Alta. L. Rev. 205 at 206-208; Don Stuart, *Charter Justice in Canadian Criminal Law*, 5th ed. (Toronto: Thomson Carswell, 2010) at 573-74; David M. Paciocco, "The Judicial Repeal of s. 24(2) and the Development of the

of the more robust "exclusionary rule" applying to unconstitutionally obtained evidence in the United States.[290]

§10.79 To have evidence excluded[291] under section 24(2), defendants must prove that: (*i*) one of their own *Charter* rights was violated; (*ii*) the evidence was "obtained in a manner" that violated this right; and (*iii*) the admission of the evidence could "bring the administration of justice into disrepute."[292] The first of these requirements ("standing") is discussed in Part 2, above. We examine the second and third in Parts 5(2)(*b*) and 5(2)(*c*), below.

§10.80 Before doing so, it will be helpful to ask: "What is the purpose of excluding unconstitutionally obtained evidence?" According to the Supreme Court, it is not to punish police[293] or compensate defendants.[294] Rather, it is to maintain the "integrity of, and public confidence in, the justice system".[295] Despite the risk that it will distort truth-finding, courts may need to exclude unconstitutionally obtained evidence in order to "dissociate themselves" from "state

---

Canadian Exclusionary Rule" (1990) 32 Crim. L.Q. 326 at 354; Martin L. Friedland, "Controlling the Administrators of Criminal Justice" (1989) 31 Crim. L.Q. 280 at 292; James Stribopoulos, "Lessons From the Pupil: A Canadian Solution to the American Exclusionary Rule Debate" (1999) 22 B.C. Int'l. & Comp. L. Rev. 77 at 117-19.

[290] First applied only to evidence unconstitutionally acquired by federal law enforcement agents, the exclusionary rule was applied to the States in *Mapp v. Ohio*, 367 U.S. 643 (1961). The rule is subject, however, to several exceptions. See *e.g.*, *United States v. Leon*, 468 U.S. 897 (1984) (exclusionary rule did not apply to evidence obtained by police acting in good faith reliance on a facially valid search warrant that had in fact issued without probable cause); *Hudson v. Michigan*, 547 U.S. 586 (2006) (evidence obtained following a violation of the "knock and announce" rule could not be excluded on the basis of that breach alone).

[291] In *R. v. Calder*, [1996] S.C.J. No. 30, [1996] 1 S.C.R. 660 at para. 35 (S.C.C.), the Court stated that defendants' statements excluded under s. 24(2) for the purposes of establishing guilt may be admitted to impeach their credibility, but only in "very limited" and "very special" cases where there has been a "material change in circumstances" after the initial s. 24(2) ruling. It is not known what these circumstances could entail, and in subsequent decisions the Court has hinted that evidence excluded under s. 24(2) is never admissible for any purpose at trial. See *R. v. Cook*, [1998] S.C.J. No. 68, [1998] 2 S.C.R. 597 at para. 76 (S.C.C.); *R. v. G. (B.)*, [1999] S.C.J. No. 29, [1999] 2 S.C.R. 475 at para. 44 (S.C.C.). It has also been suggested that evidence excluded under s. 24(2) is not admissible at sentencing: *R. v. Craig*, [2003] O.J. No. 3263, 177 C.C.C. (3d) 321 (Ont. C.A.).

[292] *R. v. Therens*, [1985] S.C.J. No. 30, [1985] 1 S.C.R. 613 at 648 (S.C.C.). The accused bears the burden of proof (on a balance of probabilities) for each of these requirements. For the first two, this conclusion flows from the language of s. 24(1), discussed above, Part 4. For the third, it flows also from the phrase "if it is established that" in s. 24(2). See *R. v. Collins*, [1987] S.C.J. No. 15, [1987] 1 S.C.R. 265 at 280 (S.C.C.). Though the English version states "*would* bring the administration of justice into disrepute," in *Collins*, at 287 (S.C.C.), the Court determined that the correct translation of the French version of the provision ["*est susceptible de déconsidérer l'administration de la justice*"] is "*could* bring the administration of justice into disrepute" [emphasis added]. It is doubtful that much turns on this distinction.

[293] *R. v. Grant*, [2009] S.C.J. No. 32, [2009] 2 S.C.R. 353 at para. 69 (S.C.C.). See also *R. v. Collins*, [1987] S.C.J. No. 15, [1987] 1 S.C.R. 265 at 280-81 (S.C.C.) (while it "often has some effect on the repute of the administration of justice, ... s. 24(2) is not a remedy for police misconduct").

[294] *R. v. Grant*, [2009] S.C.J. No. 32, [2009] 2 S.C.R. 353 at paras. 69-70 (S.C.C.), *per* McLachlin C.J.C. and Charron J. and 201, *per* Deschamps J., dissenting.

[295] *R. v. Grant*, [2009] S.C.J. No. 32, [2009] 2 S.C.R. 353 at para. 68 (S.C.C.).

deviation from the rule of law".[296] This will be necessary when the "reasonable person, informed of all relevant circumstances and the values underlying the *Charter*" would conclude that admission would cause "further damage" to the repute of the justice system.[297] Further, while its primary aim is not to deter *Charter* breaches,[298] the Court has recognized that exclusion encourages police to "respect the exigencies of the *Charter*" and promotes "the decency of investigatory techniques."[299] Notably, the Court has stressed that in deciding whether to exclude, courts should focus "less on the particular case than on the impact over time of admitting the evidence obtained by infringement of the constitutionally protected rights of the accused."[300]

(b) "Obtained in a Manner"

§10.81 As mentioned, evidence cannot be excluded unless it is found to have been "obtained in a manner" that infringed the *Charter*. In other words, it is not enough to show that police: (*i*) violated one of the defendant's *Charter* rights; and (*ii*) obtained the impugned evidence. There must also be a sufficient connection between these two events. The Supreme Court has not insisted, however, on a causal connection. In *R. v. Strachan*,[301] it considered whether drugs found during a lawful search could be excluded because police violated the defendant's right to counsel. There was no causal connection as police would have found the drugs even had they complied with the *Charter*. The Court nevertheless held that the drugs were "obtained in a manner" that infringed the *Charter*. A causation inquiry, it reasoned, would require undue speculation and lead to a "narrow view of the relationship between a *Charter* violation and the discovery of evidence."[302]

---

[296] *Ibid.*, at para. 72 (S.C.R.). See also *R. v. Collins*, [1987] S.C.J. No. 15, [1987] 1 S.C.R. 265 at 281 (S.C.C.) (s. 24(2)'s purpose is to prevent the further disrepute occasioned by the "admission of evidence that would deprive the accused of a fair hearing, or from judicial condonation of unacceptable conduct by the investigatory and prosecutorial agencies"). The idea that admitting illegally obtained evidence stains the integrity of the judiciary first gained prominence in the dissents of Justices Holmes and Brandeis in *Olmstead v. United States*, 277 U.S. 438 (1928). See also Robert M. Bloom, "Judicial Integrity: A Call for its Re-emergence in the Adjudication of Criminal Cases" (1993) 84 J. Crim. L. & Criminology 462.

[297] *R. v. Grant*, [2009] S.C.J. No. 32, [2009] 2 S.C.R. 353 at paras. 68-69 (S.C.C.).

[298] *R. v. Grant*, [2009] S.C.J. No. 32, [2009] 2 S.C.R. 353 at para. 73 (S.C.C.) ("The concern... is not to punish the police or to deter *Charter* breaches, although deterrence of *Charter* breaches may be a happy consequence.").

[299] *R. v. Burlingham*, [1995] S.C.J. No. 39, [1995] 2 S.C.R. 206 at paras. 25 and 50 (S.C.C.). See also *R. v. Kokesch*, [1990] S.C.J. No. 117, [1990] 3 S.C.R. 3 at 35 (S.C.C.); *R. v. Stillman*, [1997] S.C.J. No. 34, [1997] 1 S.C.R. 607 at para. 126 (S.C.C.); *R. v. Feeney*, [1997] S.C.J. No. 49, [1997] 2 S.C.R. 13 at para. 82 (S.C.C.); *R. v. Buhay*, [2003] S.C.J. No. 30, [2003] 1 S.C.R. 631 at para. 70 (S.C.C.).

[300] *R. v. Morelli*, [2010] S.C.J. No. 8, [2010] 1 S.C.R. 253 at para. 108 (S.C.C.).

[301] *R. v. Strachan*, [1988] S.C.J. No. 94, [1988] 2 S.C.R. 980 (S.C.C.). See also *R. v. Therens*, [1985] S.C.J. No. 30, [1985] 1 S.C.R. 613 at 649 (S.C.C.), *per* Le Dain J., dissenting.

[302] *R. v. Strachan*, [1988] S.C.J. No. 94, [1988] 2 S.C.R. 980 at 1002 (S.C.C.).

§10.82 The Court instead adopted an approach focussing on "the entire chain of events during which the *Charter* violation occurred and the evidence was obtained."[303] It explained:

> A temporal link between the infringement of the *Charter* and the discovery of the evidence figures prominently in this assessment, particularly where the *Charter* violation and the discovery of the evidence occur in the course of a single transaction. The presence of a temporal connection is not, however, determinative. Situations will arise where evidence, though obtained following the breach of a *Charter* right, will be too remote from the violation to be "obtained in a manner" that infringed the *Charter*. In my view, these situations should be dealt with on a case by case basis. There can be no hard and fast rule for determining when evidence obtained following the infringement of a *Charter* right becomes too remote.[304]

§10.83 The "obtained in a manner" requirement may be satisfied, in other words, by a non-remote, temporal connection between the two events.[305] In a series of cases decided after *Strachan*, for example, the Court held that evidence found during the execution of search warrants obtained in reliance on unconstitutional perimeter searches was "obtained in manner" even though the warrants could have been issued (and the evidence found) without the tainted evidence.[306] In each case, the violation and the obtaining of the evidence were considered to comprise a single transaction.[307]

§10.84 We agree that causation should not be a prerequisite for exclusion. Such a requirement would blunt the ability of courts to dissociate themselves from

---

[303] *R. v. Strachan*, [1988] S.C.J. No. 94, [1988] 2 S.C.R. 980 at 1005 (S.C.C.).

[304] *Ibid.*

[305] *R. v. Strachan*, [1988] S.C.J. No. 94, [1988] 2 S.C.R. 980 at 1005-1006 (S.C.C.). See also *R. v. Therens*, [1985] S.C.J. No. 30, [1985] 1 S.C.R. 613 at 649 (S.C.C.), *per* Le Dain J., dissenting; *R. v. Kokesch*, [1990] S.C.J. No. 117, [1990] 3 S.C.R. 3 at 19 (S.C.C.); *R. v. Grant*, [1993] S.C.J. No. 98, [1993] 3 S.C.R. 223 at 254-55 (S.C.C.); *R. v. Wiley*, [1993] 3 S.C.J. No. 96, [1993] 3 S.C.R. 263 at 278 (S.C.C.); *R. v. Plant*, [1993] S.C.J. No. 97, [1993] 3 S.C.R. 281 at 299 (S.C.C.); *R. v. Bartle*, [1994] S.C.J. No. 74, [1994] 3 S.C.R. 173 at 208 (S.C.C.); *R. v. Goldhart*, [1996] S.C.J. No. 76, [1996] 2 S.C.R. 463 at paras. 33-36 (S.C.C.); *R. v. Grant*, [2009] S.C.J. No. 32, [2009] 2 S.C.R. 353 at para. 131 (S.C.C.); *R. v. Weaver*, [2005] A.J. No. 235, [2005] 363 A.R. 253 at para. 20 (Alta. C.A.); *R. v. Smith*, [2008] O.J. No. 623, 229 C.C.C. (3d) 117 at paras. 24-25 (Ont. C.A.)). Though the violation will typically precede the obtaining of the evidence, the requirement may also be met if the violation occurs after the evidence is acquired. See *R. v. Brydges*, [1990] S.C.J. No. 8, [1990] 1 S.C.R. 190 at 208 (S.C.C.) ("s. 24(2) is implicated as long as a *Charter* violation occurred in the course of obtaining the evidence"). See also Kent Roach, *Constitutional Remedies in Canada*, looseleaf (Aurora, ON: Canada Law Book, 2008) at para. 10.780.

[306] *R. v. Grant*, [1993] S.C.J. No. 98, [1993] 3 S.C.R. 223 at 253-54 (S.C.C.); *R. v. Wiley*, [1993] S.C.J. No. 96, [1993] 3 S.C.R. 263 at 277 (S.C.C.); *R. v. Plant*, [1993] S.C.J. No. 97, [1993] 3 S.C.R. 281 at 299 (S.C.C.).

[307] As Paciocco and Stuesser have argued, a sufficient temporal connection may sometimes arise even when the evidence is obtained *before* the *Charter* breach. They point to the situation, for example, where police find drugs in the course of a lawful pat-down search and proceed to conduct an unconstitutional strip search. See David M. Paciocco & Lee Stuesser, *The Law of Evidence*, 5th ed. (Toronto: Irwin Law, 2008) at 363-64. See also *R. v. Therens*, [1985] S.C.J. No. 30, [1985] 1 S.C.R. 613 at 649 (S.C.C.), *per* Le Dain J. dissenting.

state misconduct.[308] It would also give police little reason to forego abuses unlikely to produce evidence. Consider again the facts of *Strachan*, assuming a causation requirement. If police thought that suspects might make self-incriminating statements during the search, they would have good reason to comply with section 10(*b*) (since the statements would not have been made "but for" the violation and be eligible for exclusion).[309] Now suppose that police either did not need a confession to make their case or were more interested in what the suspect could tell them for use as criminal intelligence rather than for admission in court. Since a violation in such circumstances would not have contributed to the discovery of the drugs, police could violate section 10(*b*) with impunity.[310]

§10.85 For the same reason, a causation requirement would encourage unconstitutional intrusions on privacy or bodily integrity when there is little expectation of discovering evidence, such as strip searches of suspects arrested for impaired driving.[311] It would similarly encourage police to use constitutionally dubious methods of obtaining evidence to support warrant applications (such as the perimeter searches mentioned above). If an issuing justice or reviewing court later declares the method unconstitutional, police would be no worse off than they would have been had they not used it. The same calculus would apply to the use of excessive force in executing otherwise lawful searches. If police would have obtained the evidence without using excessive force, it would not be eligible for exclusion.[312]

§10.86 While a causal connection is a not a *necessary* condition for fulfilling the "obtained in a manner" requirement, after *Strachan* many assumed it would be *sufficient* one.[313] This assumption was upturned in *R. v. Goldhart*.[314] There, the

---

[308] See Steven Penney, "Taking Deterrence Seriously: Excluding Unconstitutionally Obtained Evidence Under Section 24(2) of the *Charter*" (2004) 49 McGill L.J. 105 at 126-28; Peter Sankoff, "Routine Strip Searches and the Charter: Addressing Conceptual Problems of Right and Remedy" (1998) 16 C.R. (5th) 266 at 272. See also *R. v. Burlingham*, [1995] S.C.J. No. 39, [1995] 2 S.C.R. 206 at para. 36 (S.C.C.).

[309] The Court has been very reluctant to find that self-incriminating evidence would have been obtained even if police had complied with section 10(*b*), casting the burden to establish this on the prosecution. See *R. v. Bartle*, [1994] S.C.J. No. 74, [1994] 3 S.C.R. 173 at 211-13 (S.C.C.); *R. v. Harper*, [1994] S.C.J. No. 71, [1994] 3 S.C.R. 343 at 354 (S.C.C.).

[310] See *R. v. Strachan*, [1988] S.C.J. No. 94, [1988] 2 S.C.R. 980 at 1003-1005 (S.C.C.).

[311] See *R. v. Flintoff*, [1998] O.J. No. 2337, 16 C.R. (5th) 248 at para. 30 (Ont. C.A.) ("breathalyzer test was tainted by the humiliating and unconstitutional strip search, which formed an integral part of a single investigatory transaction").

[312] See *R. v. Strachan*, [1988] S.C.J. No. 94, [1988] 2 S.C.R. 980 at 1002-1003 (S.C.C.), citing *R. v. Cohen*, [1983] B.C.J. No. 2306, 5 C.C.C. (3d) 156 (B.C.C.A.); *R. v. Schedel*, [2003] B.C.J. No. 1430, 175 C.C.C. (3d) 193 at para. 78 (B.C.C.A.) (evidence "obtained in a manner" when acquired during otherwise lawful search executed with excessive force).

[313] See *e.g.*, *R. v. Black*, [1989] S.C.J. No. 81, [1989] 2 S.C.R. 138 at 162-63 (S.C.C.); *R. v. Church of Scientology of Toronto (No. 2)*, [1992] O.J. No. 3756, 74 C.C.C. (3d) 341 (Ont. Gen. Div), affd [1997] O.J. No. 1548, 116 C.C.C. (3d) 1 (Ont. C.A.), leave to appeal refused [1997] S.C.C.A. No. 683 (S.C.C.); *R. v. Goldhart*, [1996] S.C.J. No. 76, [1996] 2 S.C.R. 463 (S.C.C.), *per* La Forest J., dissenting.

[314] [1996] S.C.J. No. 76, [1996] 2 S.C.R. 463 (S.C.C.).

Court confronted an unusual scenario. In searching a residence used for marijuana cultivation, the defendant was arrested along with Mayer, a person previously unknown to police. At his preliminary inquiry months later, Mayer pleaded guilty, explaining that he had undergone a religious conversion and wished to atone for his misdeeds. This plea was accepted despite his lawyer's advice that he could be acquitted on the basis of a section 24(2) application to exclude the marijuana. Indeed, at the accused's trial the search was found to violate section 8 of the *Charter* and the marijuana excluded. The prosecution then proposed to call Mayer as witness. The accused's lawyer objected, asserting that Mayer's testimony was "obtained in a manner" that violated the *Charter* and should be excluded under section 24(2).

§10.87 Though this testimony may not have been available "but for" the violation,[315] the Court concluded that it was not "obtained in a manner" that violated the *Charter*. The mere existence of a causal nexus, it reasoned, was not sufficient. As with temporal connections, causal connections may be too "remote" or "weak" to satisfy the requirement.[316] Courts must consider the presence and strength of both temporal and causal connections in deciding "on a case-by-case basis" whether the discovery of the evidence was linked closely enough to the violation to justify exclusion.[317] Justice Sopinka explained as follows for the majority:

> If both the temporal connection and the causal connection are tenuous, the court may very well conclude that the evidence was not obtained in a manner that infringes a right or freedom under the *Charter*. On the other hand, the temporal connection may be so strong that the *Charter* breach is an integral part of a single transaction. In that case, a causal connection that is weak or even absent will be of no importance.[318]

§10.88 In the case at hand, the Court concluded, both the temporal and causal connections were tenuous. The evidence was only "obtained", Justice Sopinka reasoned, when Mayer decided to testify, not when police first discovered him (as the Court of Appeal had found).[319] This decision was made long after the

---

[315] The trial judge concluded that Mayer's testimony would likely not have been available but for the breach. See *R. v. Goldhart*, [1996] S.C.J. No. 76, [1996] 2 S.C.R. 463 at para. 41 (S.C.C.).

[316] *R. v. Goldhart*, [1996] S.C.J. No. 76, [1996] 2 S.C.R. 463 at para. 40 (S.C.C.).

[317] *Ibid*. See also *R. v. Luu*, [2006] B.C.J. No. 347, 36 C.R. (6th) 337 at para. 33 (B.C.C.A.) (real evidence not "obtained in a manner" as it was within police control and knowledge prior to breach of section 10(*b*), giving rise to no temporal or causal connection); *R. v. LaChapelle*, [2007] O.J. No. 3613, 52 C.R. (6th) 175 at para. 47 (Ont. C.A.) (blood test evidence not "obtained in a manner" as it left the accused's control prior to alleged breach of s. 10(*b*) rights); *R. v. Pettit*, [2003] B.C.J. No. 2380, 179 C.C.C. (3d) 295 at para. 20 (B.C.C.A.) (evidence not "obtained in a manner" as no temporal or causal link where breaches of ss. 8 and 10(*b*) occur after evidence lawfully obtained).

[318] *R. v. Goldhart*, [1996] S.C.J. No. 76, [1996] 2 S.C.R. 463 at para. 40 (S.C.C.).

[319] *Ibid.*, at paras. 42-45 (S.C.R.). See also *R. v. Hyatt*, [2003] B.C.J. No. 63, 171 C.C.C. (3d) 409 at para. 23 (B.C.C.A.).

search and stemmed largely from his voluntary, religiously-inspired guilty plea.[320]

§10.89 In measuring the strength of temporal and causal connections courts have considered several factors. The most obvious "temporal" factor is the duration of the period between the violation and the obtaining of the evidence. The shorter the period, the more likely the court will find that the evidence was acquired during the same transaction as the violation. That said, in some circumstances courts have found that evidence was "obtained in a manner" despite a lengthy gap,[321] or, conversely, that it was not "obtained in a manner" despite a very short one.[322]

§10.90 Indeed, the duration of the gap between the violation and the acquisition of the evidence will often be less important than the (non-causal) circumstances surrounding it. In *R. v. Wittwer*,[323] the Supreme Court referred to these circumstances as comprising the "contextual connection" between the two events.[324] As noted in *Strachan*, the "obtained in a manner" requirement will be met when the two events are characterized as forming a "single transaction".[325] For example, while the unconstitutional search in *R. v. Grant*[326] was not causally connected to the evidence, it formed "an integral component in a series of investigative tactics" that led to its discovery.[327]

§10.91 Conversely, the "obtained in a manner" requirement may not be met if the violation is "severable" from the "investigatory process which culminated in discovery of the impugned evidence;"[328] in other words, if the temporal or causal

---

[320] *R. v. Goldhart*, [1996] S.C.J. No. 76, [1996] 2 S.C.R. 463 at para. 42 (S.C.C.). In his dissenting reasons (at para. 63), La Forest J. characterized the situation differently: "Mayer's exercise of free will cannot be viewed separately from his arrest. While it may be capable of being so characterized, any independent decision undertaken by Mayer after the arrest was necessarily affected by the arrest."

[321] See *e.g.*, *R. v. Wittwer*, [2008] S.C.J. No. 33, [2008] 2 S.C.R. 235 at para. 22 (S.C.C.) (evidence "obtained in a manner" despite five-month gap because statement made immediately after accused confronted with inadmissible self-incriminating statement made at time of violation); *R. v. Grant*, [1993] S.C.J. No. 98, [1993] 3 S.C.R. 223 at 254 (S.C.C.) (one-day gap did not sever temporal connection since evidence obtained as part of single investigative transaction).

[322] See *R. v. Henrikson*, [2005] M.J. No. 110, 196 C.C.C. (3d) 440 (Man. C.A.) (voluntary and spontaneous statements made shortly after failure to reiterate s. 10(*b*) caution after change in jeopardy not "obtained in a manner"); *R. v. Whitaker*, [2008] B.C.J. No. 725, 170 C.R.R. (2d) 309 (B.C.C.A.) (despite temporal connection, causal connection extremely tenuous).

[323] [2008] S.C.J. No. 33, [2008] 2 S.C.R. 235 (S.C.C.).

[324] *Ibid.*, at paras. 21-22 (S.C.C.). See also *R. v. Plaha*, [2004] O.J. No. 3484, 188 C.C.C. (3d) 289 at paras. 45-57 (Ont. CA.); *R. v. S. (S.)*, [2008] O.J. No. 3072, 176 C.R.R. (2d) 68 at para. 65 (Ont. C.A.). While courts have long stressed, as part of the "temporal connection" inquiry, the importance of looking at the context in which the violation and evidence arose, presumably the *Wittwer* Court thought that the phrase "contextual connection" better captured the need consider factors other than duration and causation.

[325] *R. v. Strachan*, [1988] S.C.J. No. 94, [1988] 2 S.C.R. 980 at 1005 (S.C.C.). See also *R. v. Schaeffer*, [2005] S.J. No. 144, 257 Sask. R. 219 at para. 58 (Sask. C.A.).

[326] [1993] S.C.J. No. 98, [1993] 3 S.C.R. 223 (S.C.C.).

[327] *Ibid.*, at 254 (S.C.R.).

[328] *Ibid.*, at 255 (S.C.R.). See also *R. v. Plaha*, [2004] O.J. No. 3484, 188 C.C.C. (3d) 289 at para. 51 (Ont. CA.).

link was "broken by any intervening events."[329] In *Goldhart*, for instance, Mayer's religious conversion and "sincere desire to cooperate" rendered the causal link between his testimony and the unconstitutional search "extremely tenuous".[330] In *R. v. Church of Scientology of Toronto*,[331] in contrast, testimony from witnesses discovered during an unconstitutional search was found to have been "obtained in a manner" because incriminating documents found during the search were a "key factor" in their decision to testify.[332]

§10.92 The "obtained in a manner" issue often arises when, after initially violating a *Charter* right (typically section 10(*b*)) and obtaining a confession, police belatedly fulfil their *Charter* obligations and obtain further admissions. In deciding whether the post-compliance statements were "obtained in a manner" that violated the *Charter*, courts engage in analysis similar to the "derived confession rule" discussed in Chapter 4, Part 2(5)(*c*)(i).[333] To reiterate, a confession will be inadmissible under that rule if "either the tainting features which disqualified the first confession continued to be present or if the fact that the first statement was made was a substantial factor contributing to the making of the second statement."[334]

§10.93 The two rules are not identical, however. To begin, unlike statements derived from involuntary confessions, evidence obtained in violation of the *Charter* is not always excluded; it must also be shown that admission would bring the administration of justice into disrepute. Further, as mentioned in Chapter 4, Part 2(5)(*c*)(i), the second branch of the derived confession rule hinges on causation, *i.e.*, whether the second confession would have been made "but for" the first.[335] As we know, causation is not a prerequisite for exclusion under

---

329   *R. v. Kokesch*, [1990] S.C.J. No. 117, [1990] 3 S.C.R. 3 at 19 (S.C.C.). See also *R. v. Plant*, [1993] S.C.J. No. 97, [1993] 3 S.C.R. 281 at 299 (S.C.C.).

330   *R. v. Goldhart*, [1996] S.C.J. No. 76, [1996] 2 S.C.R. 463 at paras. 42, 45 (S.C.C.).

331   [1997] O.J. No. 1548, 116 C.C.C. (3d) 1 (Ont. C.A.), leave to appeal refused [1997] S.C.C.A. No. 683 (S.C.C.).

332   *Ibid.*, at para. 85 (C.C.C.). In his majority reasons in *R. v. Goldhart*, [1996] S.C.J. No. 76, [1996] 2 S.C.R. 463 at para. 42 (S.C.C.) Sopinka J. criticized the trial judge in *Church of Scientology* for concluding that the evidence was "obtained in a manner" based solely on the existence of a causal connection. He noted, however, that the connection between the violation and the testimony was stronger in that case than in *Goldhart*. The Court of Appeal relied on this *dictum* in its decision in *Church of Scientology* (at para. 85 (S.C.R.)).

333   See *R. v. Wittwer*, [2008] S.C.J. No. 33, [2008] 2 S.C.R. 235 at paras. 23-24 (S.C.C.) (referring to derived confessions rule in concluding that accused's statement obtained in a manner). See also *R. v. I. (L.R.) and T. (E.)*, [1993] S.C.J. No. 132, [1993] 4 S.C.R. 504 at paras. 31, 40 (S.C.C.) (first involuntary statement substantial factor leading to second).

334   *R. v. I. (L.R.) and T. (E.)*, [1993] S.C.J. No. 132, [1993] 4 S.C.R. 504 at 526 (S.C.C.). See also *R. v. G. (B.)*, [1999] S.C.J. No. 29, [1999] 2 S.C.R. 475 (S.C.C.); *R. v. McIntosh*, [1999] O.J. No. 4842, 141 C.C.C. (3d) 97 at para. 22 (Ont. C.A.).

335   *R. v. McIntosh*, [1999] O.J. No. 4842, 141 C.C.C. (3d) 97 at paras. 64-65 (Ont. C.A), leave to appeal refused [2000] S.C.C.A. No. 81, [2000] 1 S.C.R. xvii (S.C.C.); *R. v. Caputo*, [1997] O.J. No. 857, 98 O.A.C. 30 at para. 37 (Ont. C.A.).

section 24(2) of the *Charter*.[336] Writing for the Court in *Wittwer*, Justice Fish accordingly considered the temporal and contextual links, as well as the causal nexus, between the breach and the proffered statement. There, police twice violated the accused's right to counsel, each time obtaining incriminating statements. Knowing that the statements would likely be inadmissible, they interviewed him again five months later, hoping to make a "fresh start" by complying with section 10(*b*) and telling him not to be influenced by any previous statements.[337] After four hours of fruitless interrogation, he confessed upon being confronted with one of his previous admissions. In concluding that this final confession was "obtained in a manner" that violated the *Charter*, Justice Fish explained:

> In this case, I am satisfied that the connection is *temporal*, in the sense that mention of the first inadmissible statement ... was followed *immediately* by the appellant's statement to Sergeant Skrine. The connection is causal as well, in the sense that the impugned statement was elicited after more than four hours of resistance by the appellant and – as the interrogator expected – as a result of the interrogator's reference to the [earlier] statement. ... Finally, I am satisfied that the connection between the impugned statement and its inadmissible predecessors is to some extent *contextual*, in that any prior gap between the two was intentionally and explicitly bridged by Sergeant Skrine's association of one with the other ....[338]

§10.94 To summarize, the "obtained in a manner" requirement will be satisfied if any temporal, contextual or causal connection (or any combination of such connections) is sufficiently strong.[339] Conversely, connections that are "merely 'remote' or 'tenuous' will not suffice."[340]

§10.95 In our view, courts should be reluctant to conclude that any of these connections is too weak to engage section 24(2). A generous interpretation of "obtained in a manner" allows courts to address misconduct that does not directly or immediately lead to the discovery of evidence.[341] Such a reading is also supported by the fact that evidence meeting the "obtained in manner" standard

---

[336] See *R. v. I. (L.R.) and T. (E.)*, [1993] S.C.J. No. 132, [1993] 4 S.C.R. 504 at 528 (S.C.C.) (noting that derived confessions may be excluded under s. 24(2) "irrespective of any causal relationship between the breach and the obtaining of the evidence").

[337] *R. v. Wittwer*, [2008] S.C.J. No. 33, [2008] 2 S.C.R. 235 at paras. 2-12 (S.C.C.).

[338] *R. v. Wittwer*, [2008] S.C.J. No. 33, [2008] 2 S.C.R. 235 at para. 22 (S.C.C.) [emphasis in original].

[339] *Ibid.*, at para. 21 (S.C.R.). See also *R. v. Plaha*, [2004] O.J. No. 3484, 189 O.A.C. 376 at para. 45 (Ont. C.A.).

[340] *R. v. Wittwer*, [2008] S.C.J. No. 33, [2008] 2 S.C.R. 235 at para. 21 (S.C.C.).

[341] See *e.g.*, *R. v. Therens*, [1985] S.C.J. No. 30, [1985] 1 S.C.R. 613 at 645 (S.C.C.), *per* Le Dain J. (the "obtained in a manner" inquiry must give "adequate recognition to the intrinsic harm that is caused by a violation of a Charter right or freedom, apart from its bearing on the obtaining of evidence"); *R. v. Flintoff*, [1998] O.J. No. 2337, 16 C.R. (5th) 248 at para. 33 (Ont. C.A.) ("We cannot appear to condone a flagrant violation of the Charter occurring minutes before evidence was obtained by refusing to engage in the s. 24(2) inquiry because the evidence would have been obtained regardless of the violation.").

may still be admitted under section 24(2)'s second branch, which allows courts to balance the competing interests implicated by the exclusionary remedy.

§10.96 In some cases, however, the connection between the violation and the acquisition of the evidence may be so tenuous that exclusion would be counter-productive. If the purpose of exclusion is to dissociate courts from police misconduct (and at least secondarily, promote *Charter* compliance), it is sensible to require a modest nexus between the violation and the evidence.[342] Otherwise police may not perceive any connection between their behaviour and exclusion and continue to use unconstitutional methods. Excluding evidence unconnected to overreaching may also weaken their incentive to rectify violations. In *R. v. Upston*,[343] for example, police failed to inform a suspect of his section 10(*b*) rights immediately after detaining him. They did so later, however, and he subsequently confessed. The Supreme Court decided that the statement was not "obtained in a manner" because there was no causal connection.[344] A better justification for admission, however, is that exclusion would have discouraged future compliance in similar circumstances. If violations always taint the acquisition of subsequently obtained evidence, police would have little reason to correct their errors and fulfil their *Charter* obligations.[345] While it may be difficult to judge when the relevant connections are too tenuous to justify exclusion, focussing on exclusion's effect on police behaviour may provide more guidance than the evasive concept of remoteness.[346]

(c) *Repute of the Administration of Justice*

(i) *Introduction*

§10.97 The most contentious aspect of section 24(2) is deciding whether the admission of evidence would "bring the administration of justice into disrepute". Given the ambiguity of this phrase[347] and the divisiveness of the policy concerns

---

[342] See generally, Kent Roach, *Constitutional Remedies in Canada*, looseleaf (Aurora, ON: Canada Law Book, 2008) at para. 10.780; *R. v. Simon*, [2008] O.J. No. 3072, 2008 ONCA 578 at paras. 72-74 (Ont. C.A.).

[343] [1988] S.C.J. No. 51, [1988] 1 S.C.R. 1083 (S.C.C.).

[344] This holding is inconsistent with the Court's later decision in *R. v. Strachan*, [1988] S.C.J. No. 94, [1988] 2 S.C.R. 980 (S.C.C.), which held that exclusion does not always require defendants to establish a causal connection between the violation and the discovery of the evidence.

[345] See *R. v. S. (S.)*, [2008] O.J. No. 3072, 176 C.R.R. (2d) 68 at paras. 72-74 (Ont. C.A.) (evidence not obtained in a manner where police rectified earlier s. 10(*b*) breach and obtained fully informed consent before acquiring bodily samples). See also Kent Roach, *Constitutional Remedies in Canada*, looseleaf (Aurora: Canada Law Book, 2008) at para. 10.780 (if *Charter's* "purposes have been met by subsequent compliance or are not implicated in obtaining the evidence, then a court can safely conclude that the evidence was not obtained in a manner").

[346] See Steven Penney, "Taking Deterrence Seriously: Excluding Unconstitutionally Obtained Evidence Under Section 24(2) of the *Charter*" (2004) 49 McGill L.J. 105 at 126-28.

[347] See *R. v. Grant*, [2009] S.C.J. No. 32, [2009] 2 S.C.R. 353 at para. 60 (S.C.C.) (describing s. 24(2)'s language as "broad and imprecise").

underlying it,[348] this is unsurprising. Nor is it surprising that the decisions of the Supreme Court interpreting and applying section 24(2) have often been complex and unpredictable. Until recently, this jurisprudence was subjected to trenchant criticism.[349] Responding to this criticism, in 2009 the Court issued its decision in *R. v. Grant*,[350] which promises to provide more coherent and defensible guidance to trial courts in deciding whether admission would bring the administration of justice into disrepute.

§10.98 Before examining *Grant*, however, we must trace the circuitous path that led to it.[351] The story begins with *R. v. Collins*.[352] In his majority reasons, Justice Lamer (as he then was) suggested, as "a matter of personal preference", that the factors bearing on whether unconstitutionally obtained evidence should be excluded could be grouped into three categories: (*i*) those affecting the "fairness of the trial"; (*ii*) those "relevant to the seriousness of the *Charter* violation"; and (*iii*) those relating to the "effect of excluding the evidence" on the repute of the system.[353] Trial fairness is compromised, he explained, by the admission of evidence obtained when the accused "is conscripted against himself through a confession or other evidence emanating from him."[354]

§10.99 The categories were not of equal importance. The admission of evidence affecting trial fairness "would tend to bring the administration of justice into disrepute and, subject to a consideration of the other factors, the evidence generally should be excluded."[355] Evidence not affecting trial fairness, in contrast, was not presumptively inadmissible; its admissibility was determined by balancing the factors in the second and third categories.[356]

§10.100 *Collins* generated two interpretive problems. First, courts struggled to decide whether certain types of evidence "emanated" from the accused so as to trigger trial fairness concerns.[357] Statements were almost always held to do so,

---

[348] See also Kent Roach, *Constitutional Remedies in Canada*, loose-leaf (Aurora, ON: Canada Law Book, 2008) at paras. 10.20-10.150.

[349] See David M. Paciocco, "The Judicial Repeal of s. 24(2) and the Development of the Canadian Exclusionary Rule" (1990) 32 Crim. L.Q. 326; Don Stuart, *Charter Justice in Canadian Criminal Law*, 4th ed. (Toronto: Thomson Carswell, 2005) at 547-82; Steven Penney, "Taking Deterrence Seriously: Excluding Unconstitutionally Obtained Evidence Under Section 24(2) of the *Charter*" (2004) 49 McGill L.J. 105.

[350] [2009] S.C.J. No. 32, [2009] 2 S.C.R. 353 (S.C.C.).

[351] See also Kent Roach, *Constitutional Remedies in Canada*, looseleaf (Aurora, ON: Canada Law Book, 2008) at paras. 10.250-10.440, 10.840-10.1560; Don Stuart, *Charter Justice in Canadian Criminal Law*, 4th ed. (Toronto: Thomson Carswell, 2005) at 547-76.

[352] [1987] S.C.J. No. 15, [1987] 1 S.C.R. 265 (S.C.C.).

[353] *Ibid.*, at 284-86 (S.C.R.).

[354] *Ibid.*, at 284 (S.C.R.). See also *R. v. Ross*, [1989] S.C.J. No. 2, [1989] 1 S.C.R. 3 at 16 (S.C.C.).

[355] *Ibid.*, at 284 (S.C.R.).

[356] *Ibid.*, at 285-86 (S.C.R.). See also *R. v. Buhay*, [2003] S.C.J. No. 30, [2003] 1 S.C.R. 631 at para. 51 (S.C.C.).

[357] See Steven Penney, "Unreal Distinctions: The Exclusion of Unfairly Obtained Evidence Under s. 24(2) of the *Charter*" (1994) 32 Alta. L. Rev. 782 at 797-806; Alan W. Bryant, Sidney N. Lederman & Michelle K. Fuerst, *Sopinka, Lederman & Bryant, The Law of Evidence in Canada*, 3d ed. (Markham: LexisNexis Canada, 2009) at 568-71.

unless it was shown that they would have been made despite *Charter* compliance.[358] Physical evidence was often more difficult to classify. After a period of uncertainty,[359] the Supreme Court concluded that bodily samples compelled from the accused affected trial fairness, while bodily samples obtained without compulsion did not.[360] The Court also found that participation in an identification line-up implicated trial fairness,[361] but electronic surveillance did not.[362] And in *R. v. Mellenthin*,[363] it decided that trial fairness was implicated by the accused's participation in the discovery of physical evidence that would not otherwise have been available.[364] Many commentators found these distinctions unconvincing.[365]

§10.101 The second interpretive problem stemmed from the inconsistent treatment of evidence found to affect trial fairness. In some cases this evidence was excluded after considering all three categories;[366] in others it was excluded on the basis of trial fairness alone (although sometimes with mention of the other factors);[367] and in a few it was admitted without an explanation as to how the

---

[358] See *R. v. Harper*, [1994] S.C.J. No. 71, [1994] 3 S.C.R. 343 at 354 (S.C.C.) (evidence emanating from accused, including statements, not affecting trial fairness if otherwise discoverable). See also *R. v. Bartle*, [1994] S.C.J. No. 74, [1994] 3 S.C.R. 173 (S.C.C.) (same).

[359] See *R. v. Pohoretsky*, [1987] S.C.J. No. 26, [1987] 1 S.C.R. 945 (S.C.C.) (excluding blood sample without express reference to trial fairness); *R. v. Dyment*, [1988] S.C.J. No. 82, [1988] 2 S.C.R. 417 (S.C.C.) (excluding blood sample because of seriousness of violation); *R. v. Dersch*, [1993] S.C.J. No. 116, [1993] 3 S.C.R. 768 (S.C.C.) (same).

[360] See *R. v. Colarusso*, [1994] S.C.J. No. 2, [1994] 1 S.C.R. 20 (S.C.C.); *R. v. Borden*, [1994] S.C.J. No. 82, [1994] 3 S.C.R. 145 (S.C.C.); *R. v. Bartle*, [1994] S.C.J. No. 74, [1994] 3 S.C.R. 173 (S.C.C.). Foreign objects extracted from bodily cavities were not considered to affect trial fairness. See *R. v. Greffe*, [1990] S.C.J. No. 32, [1990] 1 S.C.R. 755 at 763-64 (S.C.C.), *per* Dickson C.J.C., dissenting.

[361] *R. v. Ross*, [1989] S.C.J. No. 2, [1989] 1 S.C.R. 3 (S.C.C.).

[362] See *R. v. Wise*, [1992] S.C.J. No. 16, [1992] 1 S.C.R. 527 at 540-44 (S.C.C.); *R. v. Wijesinha*, [1995] S.C.J. No. 49, [1995] 3 S.C.R. 422 at para. 55 (S.C.C.); *R. v. Fliss*, [2002] S.C.J. No. 15, [2002] 1 S.C.R. 535 at paras. 76-83 (S.C.C.).

[363] [1992] S.C.J. No. 100, [1992] 3 S.C.R. 615 (S.C.C.).

[364] *R. v. Mellenthin*, [1992] S.C.J. No. 100, [1992] 3 S.C.R. 615 (S.C.C.). See also *R. v. Burlingham*, [1995] S.C.J. No. 39, [1995] 2 S.C.R. 206 (S.C.C.) (admission of weapon discovered though unconstitutionally obtained confession would compromise trial fairness).

[365] See Steven Penney, "Unreal Distinctions: The Exclusion of Unfairly Obtained Evidence Under s. 24(2) of the *Charter*" (1994) 32 Alta. L. Rev. 782 at 797-806; David M. Paciocco, "The Judicial Repeal of s. 24(2) and the Development of the Canadian Exclusionary Rule" (1990) 32 Crim. L.Q. 326 at 360-61; Tim Quigley & Eric Colvin, "Developments in Criminal Law and Procedure: The 1990-91 Term" (1992) 3 Sup. Ct. L. Rev. (2d) 121 at 182; Tim Quigley & Eric Colvin, "Developments in Criminal Law and Procedure: The 1988-89 Term" (1990) 1 Sup. Ct. L. Rev. (2d) 187 at 233; R.J. Delisle, "*Collins*: An Unjustified Distinction" (1987) 56 C.R. (3d) 216 at 218; Bruce Elman, "*Collins v. The Queen*: Further Jurisprudence on Section 24(2) of the *Charter*" (1986-87) 25 Alta. L. Rev. 477.

[366] See *e.g.*, *R. v. Hebert*, [1990] S.C.J. No. 64, [1990] 2 S.C.R. 151 at 187-89 (S.C.C.); *R. v. Broyles*, [1991] S.C.J. No. 95, [1991] 3 S.C.R. 595 at 617-20 (S.C.C.); *R. v. Bartle*, [1994] S.C.J. No. 74, [1994] 3 S.C.R. 173 at 218-20 (S.C.C.).

[367] See *e.g.*, *R. v. Mellenthin*, [1992] S.C.J. No. 100, [1992] 3 S.C.R. 615 at 629 (S.C.C.); *R. v. Elshaw*, [1991] S.C.J. No. 68, [1991] 3 S.C.R. 24 at 44-46 (S.C.C.).

inadmissibility presumption was rebutted.[368] This disparate treatment puzzled many commentators, who noted that neither the language nor history of section 24(2) supported an exclusionary presumption.[369]

§10.102 In its 1997 decision in *R. v. Stillman*,[370] the Supreme Court tried to resolve these difficulties and give more concrete guidance to trial judges. First, Justice Cory proclaimed for the majority that trial fairness was compromised only by evidence that is both "conscriptive" and "non-discoverable".[371] Only four types of evidence were considered "conscriptive": (*i*) statements; (*ii*) compelled bodily samples; (*iii*) compelled uses of the body as evidence;[372] and (*iv*) evidence causally derived from evidence in categories (*i*), (*ii*) or (*iii*).[373] Evidence was "non-discoverable" if it could not have been obtained by legal, nonconscriptive means.[374] He noted, however, that the admission of conscriptive, non-discoverable evidence would not always render the trial unfair; this was only a "general rule"[375] that may be subject to exceptions for "minimally intrusive" forms of conscription.[376] Second, he stated emphatically that evidence affecting trial fairness should be excluded without considering the other *Collins* factors.[377]

§10.103 *Stillman* was not well received.[378] Criticism again focused on the seemingly arbitrary definition of the trial fairness category and the presumptive

---

[368] See *R. v. Tremblay*, [1987] S.C.J. No. 59, [1987] 2 S.C.R. 435 (S.C.C.); *R. v. Mohl*, [1989] S.C.J. No. 51, [1989] 1 S.C.R. 1389 (S.C.C.); *R. v. Dewald*, [1996] S.C.J. No. 5, [1996] 1 S.C.R. 68 (S.C.C.); *R. v. Smith*, [1991] S.C.J. No. 24, [1991] 1 S.C.R. 714 at 731-32 (S.C.C.).

[369] See e.g., David M. Paciocco, "The Judicial Repeal of s. 24(2) and the Development of the Canadian Exclusionary Rule" (1990) 32 Crim. L.Q. 326 at 338-39; Tim Quigley, *Procedure in Canadian Criminal Law*, 2d ed. looseleaf (Toronto: Thomson Carswell, 2005) at 4-24.2; David M. Paciocco, "Evidence About Guilt: Balancing the Rights of the Individual and Society in Matters of Truth and Proof" (2001) 80 Can. Bar Rev. 433 at 451-52; Don Stuart, "Welcome Flexibility and Better Criteria for Section 24(2)" (2009) 66 C.R. (6th) 82.

[370] [1997] S.C.J. No. 34, [1997] 1 S.C.R. 607 (S.C.C.).

[371] *Ibid.*, at paras. 80-119 (S.C.R.).

[372] This refers to the use of a suspect's body for identification purposes (including the taking of bodily impressions) and not the mere participation of the accused in the discovery of pre-existing "real" evidence. *R. v. Stillman*, [1997] S.C.J. No. 34, [1997] 1 S.C.R. 607 (S.C.C.) thus implicitly overruled *R. v. Mellenthin*, [1992] S.C.J. No. 100, [1992] 3 S.C.R. 615 (S.C.C.) on this point. See *R. v. Stillman*, [1997] S.C.J. No. 34, [1997] 1 S.C.R. 607 at paras. 77, 94, 98, 113 (S.C.C.). See also *R. v. Feeney*, [1997] S.C.J. No. 49, [1997] 2 S.C.R. 13 at para. 64 (S.C.C.); *R. v. Fliss*, [2002] S.C.J. No. 15, [2002] 1 S.C.R. 535 at para. 77 (S.C.C.); *R. v. Law*, [2002] S.C.J. No. 10, [2002] 1 S.C.R. 227 at para. 34 (S.C.C.); *R. v. Buhay*, [2003] S.C.J. No. 30, [2003] 1 S.C.R. 631 at para. 49 (S.C.C.); *R. v. Mann*, [2004] S.C.J. No. 49, [2004] 3 S.C.R. 59 at para. 73 (S.C.C.).

[373] *R. v. Stillman*, [1997] S.C.J. No. 34, [1997] 1 S.C.R. 607 at paras. 80, 99-101 (S.C.C.).

[374] See *R. v. Stillman*, [1997] S.C.J. No. 34, [1997] 1 S.C.R. 607 at paras. 108-10 (S.C.C.); *R. v. Feeney*, [1997] S.C.J. No. 49, [1997] 2 S.C.R. 13 at para. 65 (S.C.C.).

[375] *R. v. Stillman*, [1997] S.C.J. No. 34, [1997] 1 S.C.R. 607 at paras. 92, 93, 98, 119 (S.C.C.).

[376] *Ibid.*, at para. 90 (S.C.R.).

[377] *Ibid.*, at paras. 72, 110, 118-19 (S.C.R.).

[378] See David M. Paciocco, "*Stillman*, Disproportion and the Fair Trial Dichotomy under Section 24(2)" (1997) 2 Can. Crim. L.R. 163; Richard Mahoney, "Problems with the Current Approach to s. 24(2) of the *Charter*: An Inevitable Discovery" (1999) 42 Crim. L.Q. 443; Don Stuart, *Charter Justice in Canadian Criminal Law*, 4th ed. (Toronto: Thomson Carswell, 2005) at 566-

exclusion of evidence falling within it.[379] More surprisingly, within a few years some lower courts,[380] as well as some newly appointed members of the Supreme Court itself,[381] began resisting the rule that evidence affecting trial fairness should always be excluded.

§10.104 This resistance culminated in *Grant*, where the Court candidly accepted much of the criticism directed at the *Collins/Stillman* framework[382] and unanimously jettisoned the trial fairness category.[383] In their majority reasons, Chief Justice McLachlin and Justice Charron promulgated a new approach, holding that admissibility should be assessed by considering:

(1) "the seriousness of the *Charter*-infringing state conduct";

(2) "the impact of the breach on the *Charter*-protected interests of the accused"; and

(3) "society's interest in the adjudication of the case on its merits."[384]

§10.105 These three factors must be weighed and balanced without the aid of any "overarching rule",[385] including any rule of automatic exclusion for any type of *Charter* violation or class of evidence.[386] That said, the majority attempted to add a "measure of certainty" to the decision making process by giving guidance as to how section 24(2) should be applied to "particular types of evidence."[387]

§10.106 In what follows we examine first how the *Grant* majority described the three factors, and secondly, how it applied them to four evidentiary types: (*i*) statements; (*ii*) bodily evidence; (*iii*) non-bodily physical evidence; and (*iv*) derivative evidence. We discuss the continued relevance (or irrelevance) of the pre-*Grant* jurisprudence throughout.

76, 578-82; Steven Penney, "Taking Deterrence Seriously: Excluding Unconstitutionally Obtained Evidence Under Section 24(2) of the *Charter*" (2004) 49 McGill L.J. 105 at 129-33.

[379] See *R. v. Grant*, [2009] S.C.J. No. 32, [2009] 2 S.C.R. 353 at para. 64 (S.C.C.) (noting that courts generally interpreted *Stillman* "as creating an all-but-automatic exclusionary rule for non-discoverable conscriptive evidence").

[380] See *e.g.*, *R. v. Grant*, [2006] O.J. No. 2179, 209 C.C.C. (3d) 250 at paras. 47, 49-50 (Ont. C.A.), revd on other grounds [2009] S.C.J. No. 32, [2009] 2 S.C.R. 353 (S.C.C.); *R. v. Dolynchuk*, [2004] M.J. No. 135, 184 C.C.C. (3d) 214 at paras. 47-48 (Man. C.A.); *R. v. Richfield*, [2003] O.J. No. 3230, 14 C.R. (6th) 77 at para. 18 (Ont. C.A.); *R. v. Janzen*, [2006] S.J. No. 629, 285 Sask. R. 296 at para. 7 (Sask. C.A.); *R. v. Lotozky*, [2006] O.J. No. 2516, 210 C.C.C. (3d) 509 at para. 44 (Ont. C.A.); *R. v. Shepherd*, [2007] S.J. No. 119, 45 C.R. (6th) 213 at paras. 95, 111 (Sask. C.A.), affd [2009] S.C.J. No. 35 (S.C.C.).

[381] *R. v. Orbanski*, [2005] S.C.J. No. 37, [2005] 2 S.C.R. 3 at paras. 87, 92-93 (S.C.C.), *per* Le Bel J.

[382] *R. v. Grant*, [2009] S.C.J. No. 32, [2009] 2 S.C.R. 353 at paras. 62-65, 101-107 (S.C.C.), *per* McLachlin C.J.C. and Charron J. and paras. 206-208 (S.C.R.), *per* Deschamps J.

[383] *R. v. Grant*, [2009] S.C.J. No. 32, [2009] 2 S.C.R. 353 at para. 65 (S.C.C.), *per* McLachlin C.J.C. and Charron J. ("trial fairness is better conceived as an overarching systemic goal than as a distinct stage of the s. 24(2) analysis") and 206 (S.C.R.), *per* Deschamps J.

[384] *R. v. Grant*, [2009] S.C.J. No. 32, [2009] 2 S.C.R. 353 at para. 71 (S.C.C.). Writing only for herself, Deschamps J. proposed a framework placing less emphasis on the culpability of police and greater emphasis on society's interest in deciding the case on the merits.

[385] *R. v. Grant*, [2009] S.C.J. No. 32, [2009] 2 S.C.R. 353 at para. 86 (S.C.C.).

[386] *Ibid.*, at paras. 85-86 (S.C.R.).

[387] *Ibid.*, at para. 86 (S.C.R.).

(ii) The Grant Factors

a.   Seriousness of the *Charter*-infringing State Conduct

§10.107 In the *Collins/Stillman* era, when trial fairness was not affected, the "seriousness of the violation" factors were usually the most influential drivers of the section 24(2) decision. Now that the trial fairness category is gone, these factors have become even more critical. Under *Grant*, they have been distributed into two categories: (*i*) the seriousness of the *Charter*-infringing state conduct; and (*ii*) the impact of the breach on the accused's *Charter*-protected interests.[388] We discuss the first category immediately below, and the second in the section that follows.

§10.108 Put simply, the court's task in assessing the seriousness of the *Charter*-infringing state conduct is to situate that conduct on a scale of culpability. Chief Justice McLachlin and Justice Charron explained:

> At one end of the spectrum, admission of evidence obtained through inadvertent or minor violations of the *Charter* may minimally undermine public confidence in the rule of law. At the other end of the spectrum, admitting evidence obtained through a wilful or reckless disregard of *Charter* rights will inevitably have a negative effect on the public confidence in the rule of law, and risk bringing the administration of justice into disrepute.[389]

§10.109 Where there is evidence that police (or other state actors) have wilfully violated the *Charter*, the case for exclusion will be strong.[390] Where such evidence is lacking, the culpability of the violation may sometimes be more difficult to measure. Courts have typically found violations to be less serious when police acted in "good faith".[391] Early on, courts often defined good faith as a subjective belief that conduct was lawful.[392] Recognizing that such a rule would

---

[388] See *R. v. Beaulieu*, [2010] S.C.J. No. 7, [2010] 1 S.C.R. 248 at para. 8 (S.C.C.) (noting that these considerations mirror the pre-*Grant* "seriousness of the violation" factors).

[389] *R. v. Grant*, [2009] S.C.J. No. 32, [2009] 2 S.C.R. 353 at para. 74 (S.C.C.). See also *R. v. Kitaitchik*, [2002] O.J. No. 2476, 166 C.C.C. (3d) 14 at para. 41 (Ont. C.A.), quoted with approval in *R. v. Harrison*, [2009] S.C.J. No. 34, [2009] 2 S.C.R. 494 at para. 23 (S.C.C.) ("police conduct can run the gamut from blameless conduct, through negligent conduct, to conduct demonstrating a blatant disregard for *Charter* rights ... What is important is the proper placement of the police conduct along that fault line, not the legal label attached to the conduct.").

[390] See *R. v. Grant*, [2009] S.C.J. No. 32, [2009] 2 S.C.R. 353 at para. 75 (S.C.C.) ("It follows that deliberate police conduct in violation of established *Charter* standards tends to support exclusion of the evidence.").

[391] *R. v. Collins*, [1987] S.C.J. No. 15, [1987] 1 S.C.R. 265 at 285 (S.C.C.); *R. v. Therens*, [1985] S.C.J. No. 30, [1985] 1 S.C.R. 613 at 652 (S.C.C.), *per* Le Dain J.

[392] See *e.g.*, *R. v. Wise*, [1992] S.C.J. No. 16, [1992] 1 S.C.R. 527 at 545, 70 C.C.C. (3d) 193 (S.C.C.) (use of expired search warrant indicated "carelessness," but not bad faith); *R. v. Grant*, [1993] S.C.J. No. 98, [1993] 3 S.C.R. 223 at 253 (S.C.C.) (police "inadvertently" failed to inform issuing justice of previous warrantless perimeter search; no evidence of "bad faith"); *R. v. Plant*, [1993] S.C.J. No. 97, [1993] 3 S.C.R. 281 at 298 (S.C.C.) (misstatement to issuing justice exaggerating specificity of informant's tip was "good faith, albeit erroneous, attempt to draft the information concisely", not "deliberate attempt to mislead").

encourage ignorance of *Charter* obligations,[393] the Supreme Court eventually held that good faith errors must also be reasonable.[394] *Grant* confirms this position; violations will be considered serious (and likely result in exclusion) if they are either deliberate or negligent.[395] "Ignorance of *Charter* standards," the majority stated, "must not be rewarded or encouraged and negligence or wilful blindness cannot be equated with good faith."[396]

§10.110 How then have courts gone about deciding whether state conduct was negligent? A key factor is whether authorities have reasonably relied on standards set out in legislation,[397] policy,[398] practices,[399] legal advice[400] or case law.[401] Violations have usually been excused, for example, when police relied on statutory or common law powers not yet found to violate the *Charter*. Thus in *R. v. Duarte*[402] and *R. v. Wong*,[403] the Supreme Court found that police acted in good faith when they used surveillance techniques complying with then-existing *Criminal Code* standards. As Justice La Forest stated in *Wong*, police "acted in accordance with what they had good reason to believe was the law, and before

---

[393] Kenneth Jull, "Remedies for Non-Compliance with Investigative Procedures: A Theoretical Overview" (1985) 17 Ottawa L. Rev. 525 at 549; Don Stuart, "Eight Plus Twenty-Four Two Equals Zero" (1998) 13 C.R. (5th) 50 at 62-63; Steven Penney, "Taking Deterrence Seriously: Excluding Unconstitutionally Obtained Evidence Under Section 24(2) of the *Charter*" (2004) 49 McGill L.J. 105 at 122.

[394] See *e.g.*, *R. v. Duarte*, [1990] S.C.J. No. 2, [1990] 1 S.C.R. 30 at 60 (S.C.C.) (police misunderstanding of law was "entirely reasonable"); *R. v. Wong*, [1990] S.C.J. No. 118, [1990] 3 S.C.R. 36 at 59 (S.C.C.); *R. v. Genest*, [1989] S.C.J. No. 5, [1989] 1 S.C.R. 59 at 87(S.C.C.) (no evidence of bad faith but "defects in the search warrant were serious and the police officers should have noticed them"); *R. v. Dyment*, [1988] S.C.J. No. 82, [1988] 2 S.C.R. 417 at 440 (S.C.C.) ("no evidence that the respondent's rights were knowingly breached," but "lax police procedures cannot be condoned"); *R. v. Kokesch*, [1990] S.C.J. No. 117, [1990] 3 S.C.R. 3 at 32 (S.C.C.) ("Either the police knew they were trespassing, or they ought to have known. Whichever is the case, they cannot be said to have proceeded in good faith, as that term is understood in s. 24(2) jurisprudence."); *R. v. Buhay*, [2003] S.C.J. No. 30, [2003] 1 S.C.R. 631 at para. 59 (S.C.C.) ("[T]he officer's subjective belief that the appellant's rights were not affected does not make the violation less serious, unless his belief was reasonable."); *R. v. Therens*, [1985] S.C.J. No. 30, [1985] 1 S.C.R. 613 at 652 (S.C.C.).

[395] See also *R. v. Harrison*, [2009] S.C.J. No. 34, [2009] 2 S.C.R. 494 at para. 22 (S.C.C.) (violation serious when "departure from *Charter* standards was major in degree, or where the police knew (or should have known) that their conduct was not *Charter*-compliant").

[396] *R. v. Grant*, [2009] S.C.J. No. 32, [2009] 2 S.C.R. 353 at para. 75 (S.C.C.). See also *R. v. Morelli*, [2010] S.C.J. No. 8, [2010] 1 S.C.R. 253 at paras. 100-103 (S.C.C.) (state misconduct judged to be serious and evidence excluded because officer who prepared warrant application "was neither reasonably diligent nor mindful of his duty to make full and frank disclosure").

[397] See *R. v. Sieben*, [1987] S.C.J. No. 11, [1987] 1 S.C.R. 295 at 299 (S.C.C.); *R. v. Hamill*, [1987] S.C.J. No. 12, [1987] 1 S.C.R. 301 at 308 (S.C.C.); *R. v. Grant*, [1993] S.C.J. No. 98, [1993] 3 S.C.R. 223 at 259-60 (S.C.C.); *R. v. Wiley*, [1993] S.C.J. No. 96, [1993] 3 S.C.R. 263 at 279 (S.C.C.); *R. v. Plant*, [1993] S.C.J. No. 97, [1993] 3 S.C.R. 281 at 300 (S.C.C.).

[398] See *R. v. Simmons*, [1988] S.C.J. No. 86, [1988] 2 S.C.R. 495 at 534-35 (S.C.C.); *R. v. Jacoy*, [1988] S.C.J. No. 83, [1988] 2 S.C.R. 548 at 560 (S.C.C.); *R. v. Caslake*, [1998] S.C.J. No. 3, [1998] 1 S.C.R. 51 at para. 34 (S.C.C.).

[399] See *R. v. Colarusso*, [1994] S.C.J. No. 2, [1994] 1 S.C.R. 20 at 76-77 (S.C.C.), *per* La Forest J.

[400] See *R. v. Wong*, [1990] S.C.J. No. 118, [1990] 3 S.C.R 36 at 59 (S.C.C.).

[401] See *R. v. Thompson*, [1990] S.C.J. No. 104, [1990] 2 S.C.R. 1111 at 1155 (S.C.C.).

[402] [1990] S.C.J. No. 2, [1990] 1 S.C.R. 30 (S.C.C.).

[403] [1990] S.C.J. No. 118, [1990] 3 S.C.R 36 (S.C.C.).

they had had a reasonable opportunity to assess the consequences of the *Charter* on their established practices."[404]

§10.111 Courts have also sometimes found good faith when police err in applying established but indeterminate legal standards. In *Grant*, for example, the majority noted that "the point at which an encounter becomes a detention is not always clear, and is something with which courts have struggled."[405] Since police were "operating in circumstances of considerable legal uncertainty," their failure to comply with section 10(*b*) was "understandable," tipping the "balance in favour of admission."[406]

§10.112 Conversely, exclusion should generally follow when police break an unambiguous rule, even if it was a benign and isolated mistake.[407] And once uncertain legal standards are clarified, any failure to abide by them will no longer be reasonable. "While police are not expected to engage in judicial reflection on conflicting precedents," the majority noted in *Grant*, "they are rightly expected to know what the law is."[408]

§10.113 The Court's focus on the reasonableness of the state conduct comprising the *Charter* violation is laudable. Reasonable mistakes are inherently less culpable than negligent ones. Accordingly, they do not warrant the judicial dissociation implied by exclusion.[409] Excluding evidence generated by non-negligent errors also does little to encourage compliance with *Charter* standards. If police cannot be expected to know that an investigative method violates the *Charter*, the prospect of exclusion is not likely to dissuade them from using it.[410]

§10.114 One unresolved question is whether police act in good faith when they reasonably rely on the advice or authority of other state actors.[411] In our view, courts should not find good faith unless every authority implicated in the

---

[404] *Ibid.*, at 59 (S.C.R.). See also *R. v. Wijesinha*, [1995] S.C.J. No. 49, [1995] 3 S.C.R. 422 at paras. 55-56 (S.C.C.); *R. v. B. (B.W.)*, [2002] B.C.J. No. 1391, 4 C.R. (6th) 24 (B.C.C.A.).

[405] *R. v. Grant*, [2009] S.C.J. No. 32, [2009] 2 S.C.R. 353 at para. 133 (S.C.C.).

[406] *Ibid.*, at paras. 133, 140 (S.C.C.).

[407] See *R. v. Harrison*, [2009] S.C.J. No. 34, [2009] 2 S.C.R. 494 at paras. 24-25 (S.C.C.) (exclusion warranted for blatant violation of well-known rules even though conduct not "deliberate" or product of "systemic or institutional abuse").

[408] *R. v. Harrison*, [2009] S.C.J. No. 34, [2009] 2 S.C.R. 494 at para. 133 (S.C.C.). See also *R. v. Kokesch*, [1990] S.C.J. No. 117, [1990] 3 S.C.R. 3 at 34 (S.C.C.) (where powers are "already constrained by statute or judicial decisions, it is not open to a police officer to test the limit by ignoring the constraint"). This suggests that courts should take care to craft constitutional criminal procedure rules as precisely as possible, avoiding the indeterminacy endemic to *ex post facto*, "all of the circumstances" inquiries.

[409] See *R. v. Harrison*, [2009] S.C.J. No. 34, [2009] 2 S.C.R. 494 at para. 22 (S.C.C.).

[410] Steven Penney, "Taking Deterrence Seriously: Excluding Unconstitutionally Obtained Evidence Under Section 24(2) of the *Charter*" (2004) 49 McGill L.J. 105 at 136-38.

[411] See *R. v. Goncalves*, [1993] S.C.J. No. 41, [1993] 2 S.C.R. 3 (S.C.C.), revg [1992] A.J. No. 476, 81 C.C.C. (3d) 240 (Alta. C.A.) (violations less serious when police acted on what they believed were valid search warrants); *R. v. Erickson*, [1993] S.C.J. No. 71, [1993] 2 S.C.R. 649 (S.C.C.), affg [1992] A.J. No. 221, 72 C.C.C. (3d) 75 (Alta. C.A.) (same); *R. v. Blake*, [2010] O.J. No. 48, 2010 ONCA 1 at paras. 24-33 (Ont. C.A.) (reasonable reliance on defective search warrant not serious misconduct).

violation (including prosecutors giving advice to police and justices issuing search and arrest warrants) honestly and reasonably attempted to comply with the *Charter*. Constitutional criminal procedure is complex and police often rely on others to define the boundaries of their powers. If these actors know that their intentional or negligent errors could result in exclusion, they will be better able to resist pressure to give police maximum investigative liberty.[412]

§10.115 Though the isolated nature of a *Charter* violation is not mitigating,[413] systemic violations are more serious,[414] as is a pattern of cumulative violations.[415] Violations are similarly aggravated by accompanying misconduct that may not in itself infringe the *Charter*. The violation in *R. v. Harrison*,[416] for example, was compounded by misleading police testimony.[417]

§10.116 Another factor affecting the seriousness of the *Charter*-infringing state conduct is the extent to which police had objective grounds to suspect wrongdoing. In *Harrison*, the Court held that the violation was aggravated by the absence of reasonable suspicion for the unconstitutional detention and search.[418] In some circumstances, however, the presence of reasonable suspicion may also exacerbate the violation's seriousness. This may be the case when the presence of the requisite grounds for suspicion would have allowed police to obtain the evidence legally.[419] Proceeding with such an unnecessary violation may be characterized

---

[412] In the United States, the "good faith" exception to the exclusionary rule does not apply to judges and magistrates issuing warrants. In *United States v. Leon*, 468 U.S. 897 at 916 (1984), the Court reasoned that there was no basis "for believing that exclusion of evidence seized pursuant to a warrant will have a significant deterrent effect on the issuing judge or magistrate." The argument in favour of requiring prosecutorial reasonableness is admittedly stronger than that requiring magisterial reasonableness. Unlike prosecutors, justices issuing warrants are required to be independent and impartial. Empirical evidence suggests, however, that the *ex parte* nature of warrant applications may result in systemic bias in favour of police interests. See Casey Hill, Scott Hutchison & Leslie Pringle, "Search Warrants: Protection or Illusion?" (2000) 28 C.R. (5th) 89; Wayne R. LaFave, "The Seductive Call of Expediency: *United States v. Leon*, Its Rationale and Ramifications" [1984] U. Ill. L. Rev. 895 at 906-909. Subjecting issuing justices to the possibility of the exclusionary remedy seems likely to attenuate this bias. It also dissuades police from judge-shopping and from uncritically relying on justices' determinations of probable grounds. See generally, *United States v. Leon*, 468 U.S. 897 at 955-56 (1984), Brennan J., dissenting, and 974-76, Stevens J., dissenting; Stewart J. at 1403.

[413] *R. v. Harrison*, [2009] S.C.J. No. 34, [2009] 2 S.C.R. 494 at para. 25 (S.C.C.).

[414] See *R. v. Harrison*, [2009] S.C.J. No. 34, [2009] 2 S.C.R. 494 at para. 25 (S.C.C.); *R. v. Strachan*, [1988] S.C.J. No. 94, [1988] 2 S.C.R. 980 at 1007-1008 (S.C.C.); *R. v. Greffe*, [1990] S.C.J. No. 32, [1990] 1 S.C.R. 755 at 796 (S.C.C.). See also *R. v. Schedel*, [2003] B.C.J. No. 1430, 12 C.R. (6th) 207 (B.C.C.A.); *R. v. Lau*, [2003] B.C.J. No. 1307, 12 C.R. (6th) 296 (B.C.C.A).

[415] See *R. v. Chiasson*, [2006] S.C.J. No. 11, [2006] 1 S.C.R. 415; (S.C.C.) *R. v. Stillman*, [1997] S.C.J. No. 34, [1997] 1 S.C.R. 607 at para. 123 (S.C.C.); *R. v. Feeney*, [1997] S.C.J. No. 49, [1997] 2 S.C.R. 13 at para. 80 (S.C.C.).

[416] [2009] S.C.J. No. 34, [2009] 2 S.C.R. 494 (S.C.C.).

[417] *Ibid.*, at para. 26 (S.C.R.). See also *R. v. Stillman*, [1997] S.C.J. No. 34, [1997] 1 S.C.R. 607 at para. 124 (S.C.C.).

[418] *R. v. Harrison*, [2009] S.C.J. No. 34, [2009] 2 S.C.R. 494 at para. 24 (S.C.C.).

[419] See *R. v. Law*, [2002] S.C.J. No. 10, [2002] 1 S.C.R 227 at para. 38 (S.C.C.); *R. v. Buhay*, [2003] S.C.J. No. 30, [2003] 1 S.C.R. 631 at paras. 52, 56, 63 (S.C.C.).

as a "blatant disregard for the *Charter*."[420] Conversely, the fact that there was no other way to obtain the evidence has in some cases been held diminish the breach's seriousness.[421]

§10.117 In our view, these factors should be relevant only insofar as they illuminate the reasonableness of the state's conduct. In *Harrison*, for instance, the complete absence of grounds for suspicion (when such grounds were clearly required) highlighted the officer's negligence. But in *R. v. Duarte*, where police conducted consent surveillance in compliance with then-existing statutory rules, the presence of reasonable grounds was mitigating.[422] If police had properly understood the law, they would have been able to get a warrant to acquire the evidence in compliance with the *Charter*.[423]

§10.118 Similarly, when the legality of an intrusion was uncertain *ex ante*, the existence of an obviously lawful alternative indicates that the violation was deliberate or negligent. Police are expected to forego constitutionally questionable methods in favour of clearly legal ones. Conversely, when there are no apparent legal alternatives, a court is more likely to determine that the violation was inadvertent and reasonable. This does not mean that courts should overlook blatant improprieties when there is no other means of obtaining evidence.[424] Nor is it an excuse for inadequate training.[425] It simply recognizes that even well-trained officers will encounter situations in which the bounds of legality are not clearly marked, and that when alternative legal means are unavailable the prospect of exclusion is unlikely to prevent violations.[426]

---

[420] *R. v. Collins*, [1987] S.C.J. No. 15, [1987] 1 S.C.R. 265 at 285 (S.C.C.).

[421] See *R. v. Thompson*, [1990] S.C.J. No. 104, [1990] 2 S.C.R. 1111 at 1155 (S.C.C.); *R. v. Wong* [1990] S.C.J. No. 118, [1990] 3 S.C.R. 36 at 59 (S.C.C.).

[422] *R. v. Duarte*, [1990] S.C.J. No. 2, [1990] 1 S.C.R. 30 at 59-60 (S.C.C.). See also *R. v. Wong* [1990] S.C.J. No. 118, [1990] 3 S.C.R. 36 at 59 (S.C.C.).

[423] *R. v. Duarte*, [1990] S.C.J. No. 2, [1990] 1 S.C.R. 30 at 60 (S.C.C.).

[424] See *R. v. Kokesch*, [1990] S.C.J. No. 117, [1990] 3 S.C.R. 3 at 29 (S.C.C.) ("Where the police have nothing but suspicion and no legal way to obtain other evidence, it follows that they must leave the suspect alone, not charge ahead and obtain evidence illegally and unconstitutionally.")

[425] See generally, *R. v. Clayton*, [2007] S.C.J. No. 32, [2007] 2 S.C.R. 725 at para. 97 (S.C.C.) (emphasizing importance of police training to "successful utilization of their common law powers of detention and search"). In *Clayton*, Abella J. suggested for the majority (at paras. 51-53) that the focus of the section 24(2) inquiry should be "police conduct, not police training." "To go further and examine the training behind such conduct," she continued, "would risk transforming the inquiry into a protracted pedagogical review of marginal relevance to whether the police conduct itself represented a breach of sufficient severity to warrant excluding the evidence." It would be regrettable if this *obiter* comment were interpreted to mean that inadequate training can never aggravate the seriousness of the violation. The better interpretation is that (as Abella J. found) there was no evidence of improper training on the facts of the case. See also Don Stuart, *Charter Justice in Canadian Criminal Law*, 4th ed. (Toronto: Thomson Carswell, 2005) at 576 (evidence should be excluded where there has been an "institutional failure to equip officers with the training necessary to perform their duties").

[426] See Steven Penney, "Taking Deterrence Seriously: Excluding Unconstitutionally Obtained Evidence Under Section 24(2) of the *Charter*" (2004) 49 McGill L.J. 105 at 140-41.

§10.119 Less defensible is the principle that violations may be mitigated by exigent circumstances.[427] If in particular circumstances an investigative intrusion that would normally infringe the *Charter* is justified by countervailing interests, that right should be interpreted to permit the intrusion. As discussed in Chapters 2 and 3, exigent circumstances exceptions have been incorporated into the definition of *Charter* rights; warrantless entries to arrest and search are allowed, for example, to prevent physical harm or the imminent loss of evidence.[428] But if circumstances are not urgent enough to justify what would otherwise be a violation, perceived exigency should not weigh in favour of admission.[429] Otherwise, exclusion loses its capacity to discourage intrusions *ex ante* that courts would find unjustified *ex post*. It is precisely when police feel the need to act urgently that exclusion is most needed to minimize overreaching. The only exceptions to this principle should arise when the constitutional rules governing police conduct in the circumstances are unclear. In urgent circumstances, police who are unsure about the legality of an intrusion are especially unlikely to be influenced by the prospect of exclusion.

b.   Impact on Accused's *Charter*-protected Interests

§10.120 Under this category, courts measure the extent to which the *Charter* breach "actually undermined the interests protected by the right infringed."[430] "The more serious the impact on the accused's protected interests," the majority in *Grant* stated, "the greater the risk that admission of the evidence may signal to the public that *Charter* rights, however high-sounding, are of little actual avail to the citizen, breeding public cynicism and bringing the administration of justice into disrepute."[431] Section 8 violations are considered more serious, for example, if they invade a realm protected by a "high expectation of privacy"[432]

---

[427] See *R. v. Grant*, [2009] S.C.J. No. 32, [2009] 2 S.C.R. 353 at para. 75 (S.C.C.); *R. v. Silveira*, [1995] S.C.J. No. 38, [1995] 2 S.C.R. 297 at para. 150 (S.C.C.); *R. v. Wong*, [1990] S.C.J. No. 118, [1990] 3 S.C.R. 36 at 59 (S.C.C.); *R. v. Genest*, [1989] S.C.J. No. 5, [1989] 1 S.C.R. 59 at 84 (S.C.C.).

[428] See *e.g.*, *R. v. Grant*, [1993] S.C.J. No. 98, [1993] 3 S.C.R. 223 (S.C.C.) (warrantless search power read down to require exigent circumstances); *R. v. Feeney*, [1997] S.C.J. No. 49, [1997] 2 S.C.R. 13 (S.C.C.) (hot pursuit exception to warrant requirement for residential arrests); *R. v. Godoy*, [1998] S.C.J. No. 85, [1999] 1 S.C.R. 311 (S.C.C.) (warrantless entry of residence to ensure safety permitted in response to emergency calls). See also *R. v. Strachan*, [1988] S.C.J. No. 94, [1988] 2 S.C.R. 980 at 999 (S.C.C.) (immediate s. 10(*b*) warning requirement may be deferred until police achieve control over "potentially volatile situation").

[429] See Steven Penney, "Taking Deterrence Seriously: Excluding Unconstitutionally Obtained Evidence Under Section 24(2) of the *Charter*" (2004) 49 McGill L.J. 105 at 141; Alan W. Bryant, Sidney N. Lederman & Michelle K. Fuerst, *Sopinka, Lederman & Bryant, The Law of Evidence in Canada*, 3d ed. (Markham.: LexisNexis Canada, 2009) at 599.

[430] *R. v. Grant*, [2009] S.C.J. No. 32, [2009] 2 S.C.R. 353 at para. 76 (S.C.C.).

[431] *Ibid.*

[432] See *R. v. Grant*, [2009] S.C.J. No. 32, [2009] 2 S.C.R. 353 at paras. 78, 109, 113-14 (S.C.C.); *R. v. Morelli*, [2010] S.C.J. No. 8, [2010] 1 S.C.R. 253 at para. 104 (S.C.C.); *R. v. Dyment*, [1988] S.C.J. No. 82, [1988] 2 S.C.R. 417 at 439 (S.C.C.), *per* La Forest J.; *R. v. Greffe*, [1990] S.C.J. No. 32, [1990] 1 S.C.R. 755 at 795 (S.C.C.); *R. v. Pohoretsky*, [1987] S.C.J. No. 26, [1987] 1 S.C.R. 945 at 949 (S.C.C.); *R. v. Buhay*, [2003] S.C.J. No. 30, [2003] 1 S.C.R. 631 at

(such as one's body, [433] home [434] or personal computer. [435]) Conversely, violations of lesser expectations of privacy, such as that pertaining to vehicles, have sometimes been discounted. [436] The Court warned in *Harrison*, however, that such violations may still have profoundly negative effects. [437] "Being stopped and subjected to a search by the police without justification," it wrote, "impacts on the motorist's rightful expectation of liberty and privacy in a way that is much more than trivial."[438]

c.   Society's Interest in an Adjudication on the Merits

§10.121 Under the third *Collins/Stillman* category, courts considered the effect of exclusion on the reputation of the justice system. When trial fairness was affected, admission would diminish that reputation. [439] When it was not, the system's repute would be harmed by exclusion, especially if the evidence was needed to prove a serious offence. [440]

§10.122 In *Grant*, the third category operates quite differently: courts must ask whether truth-seeking would be better served by admission or exclusion. [441] If the reliability of the evidence is questionable, exclusion is favoured; if not,

---

para. 52 (S.C.C.); *R. v. Simmons*, [1988] S.C.J. No. 86, [1988] 2 S.C.R. 495 at 516-17 (S.C.C.), *per* Dickson C.J.C.; *R. v. Golden*, [2001] S.C.J. No. 81, [2001] 3 S.C.R. 679 at para. 87 (S.C.C.).

[433] See *e.g.*, *R. v. Grant*, [2009] S.C.J. No. 32, [2009] 2 S.C.R. 353 at paras. 78, 109, 113-14 (S.C.C.); *R. v. Dyment*, [1988] S.C.J. No. 82, [1988] 2 S.C.R. 417 at 439 (S.C.C.), *per* La Forest J.; *R. v. Greffe*, [1990] S.C.J. No. 32, [1990] 1 S.C.R. 755 at 795 (S.C.C.); *R. v. Pohoretsky*, [1987] S.C.J. No. 26, [1987] 1 S.C.R. 945 at 949 (S.C.C.); *R. v. Simmons*, [1988] S.C.J. No. 86, [1988] 2 S.C.R. 495 at 516-17 (S.C.C.), *per* Dickson C.J.C.; *R. v. Golden*, [2001] S.C.J. No. 81, [2001] 3 S.C.R. 679 at para 87 (S.C.C.).

[434] See *e.g.*, *R. v. Morelli*, [2010] S.C.J. No. 8, [2010] 1 S.C.R. 253 at para. 105 (S.C.C.); *R. v. Kokesch*, [1990] S.C.J. No. 117, [1990] 3 S.C.R. 3 at 29 (S.C.C.).

[435] See *e.g.*, *R. v. Morelli*, [2010] S.C.J. No. 8, [2010] 1 S.C.R. 253 at para. 105 (S.C.C.) ("Computers often contain our most intimate correspondence. They contain the details of our financial, medical, and personal situations. They even reveal our specific interests, likes, and propensities, recording in the browsing history and cache files the information we seek out and read, watch, or listen to on the Internet.").

[436] See *R. v. Caslake*, [1998] S.C.J. No. 3, [1998] 1 S.C.R. 51 at para. 34 (S.C.C.); *R. v. Belnavis*, [1997] S.C.J. No. 81, [1997] 3 S.C.R. 341 at para. 40 (S.C.C.).

[437] *R. v. Harrison*, [2009] S.C.J. No. 34, [2009] 2 S.C.R. 494 at paras. 30-32 (S.C.C.).

[438] *Ibid.*, at para. 31 (S.C.R.). See also *R. v. Mann*, [2004] S.C.J. No. 49, [2004] 3 S.C.R. 59 at para. 56 (S.C.C.).

[439] See *e.g.*, *R. v. Evans*, [1991] S.C.J. No. 31, [1991] 1 S.C.R 869 at 898-99 (S.C.C.); *R. v. Collins*, [1987] S.C.J. No. 15, [1987] 1 S.C.R. 265 at 286 (S.C.C.); *R. v. Burlingham*, [1995] S.C.J. No. 39, [1995] 2 S.C.R. 206 at 242 (S.C.C.).

[440] See *e.g.*, *R. v. Buhay*, [2003] S.C.J. No. 30, [2003] 1 S.C.R. 631 at para. 51 (S.C.C.); *R. v. Grant*, [1993] S.C.J. No. 98, [1993] 3 S.C.R. 223 at 261 (S.C.C.); *R. v. Colarusso*, [1994] S.C.J. No. 2, [1994] 1 S.C.R. 20 at 78 (S.C.C.). See also David M. Paciocco, "*Stillman*, Disproportion and the Fair Trial Dichotomy under Section 24(2)" (1997) 2 Can. Crim. L. Rev. 163 at 172-73; Kent Roach, "The Evolving Fair Trial Test Under Section 24(2) of the Charter" (1996) 1 Can. Crim. L. Rev. 117 at 119; David M. Paciocco & Lee Stuesser, *The Law of Evidence*, 5th ed. (Toronto: Irwin Law, 2008) at 386-89.

[441] *R. v. Grant*, [2009] S.C.J. No. 32, [2009] 2 S.C.R. 353 at para. 79 (S.C.C.).

admission is favoured.[442] The importance of the evidence to the prosecution's case also figures into this analysis. If dubious evidence "forms the entirety of the case against the accused," it is likely to be excluded.[443] The exclusion of highly reliable evidence, in contrast, "may impact more negatively on the repute of the administration of justice where the remedy effectively guts the prosecution."[444] That said, where the first two factors work in favour of the accused, exclusion may be warranted even if it would "leave the prosecution with essentially no case against the accused."[445]

§10.123 The seriousness of the offence may also be considered, but as the Court stated in *Grant*, "it has the potential to cut both ways."[446] "[W]hile the public has a heightened interest in seeing a determination on the merits where the offence charged is serious," it concluded, "it also has a vital interest in having a justice system that is above reproach, particularly where the penal stakes for the accused are high."[447] This suggests that offence seriousness will play only a modest role in section 24(2) analyses. Where the state misconduct is grave and the impact on the accused's interests substantial, a serious offence will (at best) buttress an already strong case for exclusion. Similarly, it is unlikely that the characterization of the offence as more or less serious will do much to persuade courts to exclude in cases of minor misconduct and trivial harm. Indeed, the majority found in *Grant* itself that the seriousness of the offence (gun possession) militated in favour of neither exclusion nor admission.[448]

§10.124 In our view, offence seriousness should play little or no role in section 24(2) decisions, though not for the reasons articulated by the majority in *Grant*. As Justice Deschamps asserted in her dissent, the majority's reasoning "place[s] value in the benefit derived by the accused from the exclusion of reliable evidence."[449] However, allowing offence seriousness to weigh heavily in favour of admission (as she would prefer) would signal that there is a lesser need to respect constitutional rights when police perceive *ex ante* that they are investigating a "serious" offence. As the majority put it in *R. v. Harrison*:[450]

> ... allowing the seriousness of the offence and the reliability of the evidence to overwhelm the s. 24(2) analysis "would deprive those charged with serious crimes of the protection of the individual freedoms afforded to all Canadians under the *Charter* and, in effect, declare that in the administration of the criminal law 'the ends justify the means.'"[451]

---

[442] *Ibid.*, at para. 81 (S.C.R.).
[443] *Ibid.*, at para. 83 (S.C.R.).
[444] *Ibid.*
[445] *R. v. Morelli*, [2010] S.C.J. No. 8, [2010] 1 S.C.R. 253 at para. 107 (S.C.C.).
[446] *R. v. Grant*, [2009] S.C.J. No. 32, [2009] 2 S.C.R. 353 at para. 84 (S.C.C.).
[447] *Ibid.*
[448] *Ibid.*, at para. 139 (S.C.R.).
[449] *Ibid.*, at para. 218 (S.C.R.).
[450] [2009] S.C.J. No. 34, [2009] 2 S.C.R. 494 (S.C.C.).
[451] *Ibid.*, at para. 40 (S.C.R.) [citation omitted].

§10.125 It must be kept in mind, moreover, that many of the persons suffering *Charter* breaches are innocent; as the Court put it in *Grant*, "for every *Charter* breach that comes before the courts, many others may go unidentified and unredressed because they did not turn up relevant evidence leading to a criminal charge."[452]

d. Application to Types of Evidence

Statements of the Accused

§10.126 Though the Court discarded the trial fairness test in *Grant*, it proclaimed a "presumptive general, although not automatic" exclusionary rule for statements of the accused.[453] This presumption, Chief Justice McLachlin and Justice Charron reasoned, was justified by each of the three factors: because of the strong constraints on police questioning, *Charter* breaches producing statements are often serious; the self-incrimination interests harmed by such violations are particularly "fundamental"; and improper questioning often results in unreliable confessions.[454]

§10.127 Exclusion may not be appropriate, however, in at least two circumstances. First, minor breaches may be excused, where an accused is still "clearly informed of his or her choice to speak to the police, despite a technical breach of section 10(*b*)."[455] Second, as before *Grant*, admission may be appropriate when a "statement is made spontaneously following a *Charter* breach, or in the exceptional circumstances where it can confidently be said that the statement in question would have been made notwithstanding the *Charter* breach".[456]

§10.128 The argument that breaches producing confessions are categorically more serious, harmful or likely to thwart accurate adjudication than breaches producing other types of evidence is not persuasive.[457] However, as noted in *Grant*, many of the rules regulating interrogation are clear and should be easy for police to follow. Apart from cases where courts retrospectively amend these rules,[458] violations should rarely be excused as honest, non-negligent errors. But other types of violations may sometimes be excusable, for example, where police make reasonable mistakes about whether suspects are detained and thus

---

[452] *R. v. Grant*, [2009] S.C.J. No. 32, [2009] 2 S.C.R. 353 para. 75 (S.C.C.). See also *R. v. Crocker*, [2009] B.C.J. No. 1816, 2009 BCCA 388 at para. 109 (B.C.C.A.); *R. v. Osolsky*, [2009] O.J. No. 3962, 2009 ONCJ 445 at para. 15 (Ont. C.J.); Steven Penney, "Taking Deterrence Seriously: Excluding Unconstitutionally Obtained Evidence Under Section 24(2) of the *Charter*" (2004) 49 McGill L.J. 105 at 134-35.

[453] *R. v. Grant*, [2009] S.C.J. No. 32, [2009] 2 S.C.R. 353 at para. 92 (S.C.C.).

[454] *Ibid.*, at paras. 93-98 (S.C.R.).

[455] *Ibid.*, at para. 96 (S.C.R.).

[456] *Ibid.*, at para. 96 (S.C.R.).

[457] Steven Penney, "Taking Deterrence Seriously: Excluding Unconstitutionally Obtained Evidence Under Section 24(2) of the *Charter*" (2004) 49 McGill L.J. 105 at 129-33.

[458] See *e.g.*, *R. v. Broyles*, [1991] S.C.J. No. 95, [1991] 3 S.C.R. 595 (S.C.C.); *R. v. Bartle*, [1994] S.C.J. No. 74, [1994] 3 S.C.R. 173 (S.C.C.); *R. v. Prosper*, [1994] S.C.J. No. 72, [1994] 3 S.C.R. 236 (S.C.C.).

entitled to be cautioned.[459] Where police have acted reasonably, and there are no concerns about reliability, courts should generally find that the presumption of exclusion has been rebutted.

§10.129 On the other hand, the fact that a statement would have been made despite the violation is not a good reason to admit it. Exclusion is not intended to compensate defendants for past harms or put them in the position they would have been in "but for" the violation.[460] To achieve the purposes of section 24(2) — preserving judicial integrity and encouraging *Charter* compliance — evidence obtained through deliberate or negligent misconduct should generally be excluded, even if it was otherwise "discoverable".[461]

Bodily Evidence

§10.130 Under *Stillman*, bodily samples taken from the accused by state actors were "conscriptive" evidence and (if not otherwise discoverable) almost always excluded. In *Grant*, the Court sharply criticized this rule, rightly noting that *Charter* breaches producing such evidence were not necessarily any more serious or intrusive than breaches generating non-conscriptive evidence.[462] "Plucking a hair from the suspect's head may not be intrusive," it noted, but "a body cavity or strip search may be intrusive, demeaning and objectionable."[463] They accordingly held that bodily evidence should receive the same treatment under section 24(2) as non-bodily physical evidence, which we examine immediately below.[464]

---

[459] See *R. v. Grant*, [2009] S.C.J. No. 32, [2009] 2 S.C.R. 353 at para. 133 (S.C.C.) (describing unlawful detention as "understandable" mistake, as "the point at which an encounter becomes a detention is not always clear, and is something with which courts have struggled").

[460] See *R. v. Grant*, [2009] S.C.J. No. 32, [2009] 2 S.C.R. 353 at paras. 69-70 (S.C.C.), *per* McLachlin C.J.C and Charron J. and 201, *per* Deschamps J., dissenting; Steven Penney, "Taking Deterrence Seriously: Excluding Unconstitutionally Obtained Evidence Under Section 24(2) of the *Charter*" (2004) 49 McGill L.J. 105 at 129-30; Richard Mahoney, "Problems with the Current Approach to s. 24(2) of the Charter: An Inevitable Discovery" (1999) 42 Crim. L.Q. 443 at 472-73; Don Stuart, *Charter Justice in Canadian Criminal Law*, 5th ed. (Toronto: Thomson Carswell, 2010) at 600-601.

[461] See generally, *R. v. Grant*, [2009] S.C.J. No. 32, [2009] 2 S.C.R. 353 at para. 75 (S.C.C.) ("It should also be kept in mind that for every *Charter* breach that comes before the courts, many others may go unidentified and unredressed because they did not turn up relevant evidence leading to a criminal charge.").

[462] *R. v. Grant*, [2009] S.C.J. No. 32, [2009] 2 S.C.R. 353 at paras. 100-107 (S.C.C.). See also Steven Penney, "Taking Deterrence Seriously: Excluding Unconstitutionally Obtained Evidence Under Section 24(2) of the *Charter*" (2004) 49 McGill L.J. 105 at 130-33.

[463] *R. v. Grant*, [2009] S.C.J. No. 32, [2009] 2 S.C.R. 353 at para. 103 (S.C.C.).

[464] *Ibid.*, at para. 107 (S.C.R.). Somewhat curiously, the Court suggested (at para. 111) that breath sample evidence should often be admitted because of its reliability and the relatively non-intrusive means by which it is collected. Hopefully, lower courts will not take this as invitation to admit bodily samples where police have carelessly failed to adhere to well-understood *Charter* obligations.

Non-bodily Physical Evidence

§10.131 There are no special rules associated with this category. The three *Grant* factors should thus be given equal weight. The admissibility of physical evidence typically arises in the context of section 8 violations. As discussed in Part 5(2)(*c*)(iii), above, in such cases a key consideration will be the extent to which the intrusion invaded a reasonable expectation of privacy.[465]

Derivative Evidence

§10.132 Under the *Collins/Stillman* framework, evidence *derived* from conscriptive evidence (*i.e.*, evidence that would not have been otherwise discoverable) was considered to affect trial fairness and almost always excluded.[466] *Grant* abandons this rule.[467] However, discoverability may be considered "in assessing the actual impact of the breach on the protected interests of the accused."[468] It appeared to limit this consideration to situations where physical evidence is derived from an unconstitutionally obtained statement. The majority explained:

> The more likely it is that the evidence would have been obtained even without the statement, the lesser the impact of the breach on the accused's underlying interest against self-incrimination. The converse, of course, is also true. On the other hand, in cases where it cannot be determined with any confidence whether evidence would have been discovered in absence of the statement, discoverability will have no impact on the s. 24(2) inquiry.[469]

§10.133 For the reasons set out above in this Part, in our view the discoverability or non-discoverability of evidence should play no role in section 24(2) decisions. Derivative evidence should thus be treated in the same manner as other types of evidence. If it was "obtained in a manner" that violated the *Charter*, its admissibility should turn primarily on the seriousness of the violation.

---

[465] *R. v. Grant*, [2009] S.C.J. No. 32, [2009] 2 S.C.R. 353 at paras. 113-114 (S.C.C.). See also *R. v. Nolet*, [2010] S.C.J. No. 24, [2010] 1 S.C.R. 851 at para. 54 (S.C.C.) (unconstitutional inventory search had "minimal" impact on accused as police had already lawfully searched vehicle incident to arrest).

[466] Technically, there were two stages to this analysis. First, to be classified as conscriptive derivative evidence, the applicant had to show that "but for" the violation, the evidence would not have been available to police, whether by constitutional or unconstitutional means. The burden then fell to the prosecution to show that the evidence was not "discoverable" by constitutional means. See *R. v. Feeney*, [1997] S.C.J. No. 49, [1997] 2 S.C.R. 13 at paras. 62, 69 (S.C.C.). However, since the same "but for" test was used at both stages, non-derivative evidence could never be "discoverable". In practice, discoverability analysis was thus only needed in dealing with non-derivative conscriptive evidence, such as statements, bodily samples, and uses of the body as evidence. On the treatment of derivative evidence before *Stillman*, see Mark D. Wiseman, "The Derivative Imperative: An Analysis of Derivative Evidence in Canada" (1997) 39 Crim. L.Q. 435.

[467] *R. v. Grant*, [2009] S.C.J. No. 32, [2009] 2 S.C.R. 353 at para. 121 (S.C.C.).

[468] *Ibid.*, at para. 122 (S.C.R.). See also *R. v. Nolet*, [2010] S.C.J. No. 24, [2010] 1 S.C.R. 851 at para. 54 (S.C.C.) (evidence obtained through unconstitutional inventory search would have been lawfully discoverable if police had continued search incident to arrest).

[469] *R. v. Grant*, [2009] S.C.J. No. 32, [2009] 2 S.C.R. 353 at para. 122 (S.C.C.).

§10.134 A particular danger of admitting derivative evidence is that it signals to police that they may be able to obtain highly incriminating, admissible evidence despite the use of coercive interrogation methods. As discussed in Chapter 3, this risk may be particularly acute when police believe that lawful tactics will not be productive. In such circumstances they may think that they have "nothing to lose" by non-compliance. The majority in *Grant* was thankfully alive to this risk, stressing that judges should "refuse to admit evidence where there is reason to believe the police deliberately abused their power to obtain a statement which might lead them to such evidence."[470]

---

[470] *R. v. Grant*, [2009] S.C.J. No. 32, [2009] 2 S.C.R. 353 at para. 128 (S.C.C.).

PART IV

THE TRIAL

Chapter 11

INFORMATIONS AND INDICTMENTS

1. INTRODUCTION

§11.1 "Informations" and "indictments" are the documents used at trial to set out the charges against the accused. We accordingly refer to them collectively in this chapter as "charging documents". As we saw in Chapter 5, a prosecution normally begins when a police officer (or any other person) lays an information before a justice, swearing that he or she has "personal knowledge" or "believes on reasonable grounds" that the person to be charged committed the offence(s) specified.[1] For offences tried in provincial court (whether summary conviction or indictable), this information also serves as the charging document at trial.[2]

§11.2 For trials in superior court, the information is replaced by an "indictment",[3] which is prepared and signed by a Crown prosecutor, usually after the accused is committed to stand trial at a preliminary inquiry.[4] The superior court obtains jurisdiction to try the matter when the prosecutor "prefers" the indictment and formally lodges it with the court.[5] (We discuss the charges that may be included on an indictment after the preliminary inquiry in Chapter 9, Parts 3(6) and 4.) However, under section 577 of the *Criminal Code*,[6] the prosecutor may prefer a "direct indictment" for any offence "even if the accused has not been given the opportunity to request a preliminary inquiry, a preliminary inquiry has been commenced but not concluded or a preliminary inquiry has been held and the accused has been discharged."[7] Direct indictments are discussed in Chapter

---

[1] *Criminal Code*, R.S.C. 1985, c. C-46, s. 504, Form 2 [*Code*]. See also *R. v. Kamperman*, [1981] N.S.J. No. 494, 48 N.S.R. (2d) 317 (N.S.T.D.). As discussed below in this Part, the only exception arises when a prosecutor prefers a direct indictment against the accused before any information is laid.

[2] See *Criminal Code*, ss. 553 (indictable offences within "absolute jurisdiction" of provincial court judge), 554 (indictable offences where accused has elected to be tried in provincial court) and 788(1) (summary conviction offences).

[3] *Criminal Code*, ss. 566, 580.

[4] *Criminal Code*, ss. 566(1), 574(1), 580, Form 4. In the unlikely event that a private prosecution is neither taken over nor discontinued by the Crown, the indictment may not be preferred without the order of the court. See *Criminal Code*, s. 574(3). On private prosecutions, see Chapter 5, Parts 2 and 5 and Chapter 8, Part 2(3).

[5] See *Criminal Code*, ss. 566(2), 574; *R. v. Chabot*, [1980] S.C.J. No. 108, [1980] 2 S.C.R. 985 at 999 (S.C.C.).

[6] R.S.C. 1985, c. C-46.

[7] *Criminal Code*, s. 577. See generally, *R. v. McKibbon*, [1984] S.C.J. No. 8, [1984] 1 S.C.R. 131 (S.C.C.) (direct indictment may be preferred on charge for which accused was discharged at preliminary inquiry); *R. v. Benji*, [2002] S.C.J. No. 5, [2002] 1 S.C.R. 142 (S.C.C.) (accused committed to stand trial may be added to direct indictment charging another accused; *R. v. L.*

9, Part 4(3). If a direct indictment is preferred before any information is laid, the indictment serves as the charging document throughout — no information will be laid. Absent an abuse of process, the decision to prefer a direct indictment is not subject to judicial review.[8] A direct indictment may only be preferred, however, with the personal, written consent of the Attorney General.[9]

§11.3 Regardless of their form, charging documents serve the same purpose: to give defendants adequate notice of the charges against them.[10] As we elaborate below, if this "golden rule"[11] is satisfied, a charge should not be quashed even if it is defective in some way. In contrast to an earlier era, judges now have considerable discretion to either ignore or correct defects in charging documents to permit the case to continue and be decided on the merits.[12]

§11.4 This chapter is accordingly organized into two major Parts. In the first, we detail the rules directing the structure and content of charging documents; in the second, we examine the remedies available for defective charges. Note that while the provisions setting out these rules typically refer to indictments and appear in parts of the *Code* dealing with trials in superior court, by virtue of

---

(S.J.), [2009] S.C.J. No. 14, [2009] 1 S.C.R. 426 (S.C.C.) (direct indictment may be preferred against young person to be tried as adult); *R. v. Ewen*, [2000] S.J. No. 155, 144 C.C.C. (3d) 277 (Sask. C.A.) (direct indictment may be preferred where committal for trial is quashed); *R. v. Charlie*, [1998] B.C.J. No. 1506, 126 C.C.C. (3d) 513 (B.C.C.A.) (same); *R. v. Pal*, [2007] B.C.J. No. 2189, 75 W.C.B. (2d) 610 (B.C.S.C.) (direct indictment may be preferred even after accused has elected trial in provincial court and is before that court for trial); *R. v. Poloni*, [2009] B.C.J. No. 942, 190 C.R.R. (2d) 162 (B.C.S.C.) (direct indictment may be preferred before commencement of new trial).

[8] See *R. v. L. (S.J.)*, [2009] S.C.J. No. 14, [2009] 1 S.C.R. 426 at para. 24 (S.C.C.). See also Chapter 8, Part 5(2).

[9] *Criminal Code*, s. 577(a). See also *R. v. Dwyer*, [1978] O.J. No. 3787, 42 C.C.C. (2d) 83 (Ont. C.A.). For private prosecutions, a direct indictment may also be preferred by court order: *Criminal Code*, s. 577(b).

[10] See *R. v. R. (G.)*, [2005] S.C.J. No. 45, [2005] 2 S.C.R. 371 at paras. 11-15 (S.C.C.).

[11] *R. v. Côté*, [1977] S.C.J. No. 37, [1978] 1 S.C.R. 8 at 13 (S.C.C.) ("the golden rule is for the accused to be reasonably informed of the transaction alleged against him, thus giving him the possibility of a full defence and a fair trial").

[12] See *e.g.*, *R. v. Sault Ste. Marie (City)*, [1978] S.C.J. No. 59, [1978] 2 S.C.R. 1299 at 1307 (S.C.C.) where Dickson J. (as he then was) stated the following for the Court:

> The rule [against multiplicity and duplicity] developed during a period of extreme formality and technicality in the preferring of indictments and laying of informations. It grew from the humane desire of judges to alleviate the severity of the law in an age when many crimes were still classified as felonies, for which the punishment was death by the gallows. The slightest defect made an indictment a nullity. That age passed. Parliament has made it abundantly clear in those sections of the *Criminal Code* having to do with the form of indictments and informations that the punctilio of an earlier age is no longer to bind us. We must look for substance and not petty formalities.

See also *R. v. B. (G.) (No.2)*, [1990] S.C.J. No. 58, [1990] 2 S.C.R. 30 at 42 (S.C.C.); *R. v. Vézina*, [1986] S.C.J. No. 2, [1986] 1 S.C.R. 2 at 25 (S.C.C.); *R. v. Leclaire*, [1956] O.J. No. 162, 115 C.C.C. 297 (Ont. C.A.); Roger E. Salhany, *Canadian Criminal Procedure*, 6th ed., looseleaf (Aurora, ON: Canada Law Book, 2001) at paras. 6.800-6.840.

sections 2 and 795 of the *Code*, they apply equally to proceedings in provincial court, including those prosecuted by way of summary conviction.[13]

2. STRUCTURE AND CONTENT

(1) Structure of Charges ("Joinder")

§11.5 Police and prosecutors enjoy great flexibility in structuring charges against one or more accused.[14] As detailed in Part 2(2)(*b*) below, a series of incidents may be characterized as comprising either one charge or many. A single information or indictment may thus contain multiple charges against one accused. [15] Alternatively, charges against one accused may be distributed among several charging documents, in which case a separate trial will normally be held for each document. Where an offence is alleged to have been committed by more than one person, a single charging document may also contain charges against each of those persons.[16] In such cases there will be only one trial on all charges against all accused. The practice of including multiple "counts" (whether relating to one accused or several) in the same charging document is known as "joinder".

§11.6 The Crown's freedom to join counts, however, is not unbounded. The *Code* specifies that no count alleging an offence other than murder may be included in the same indictment as a murder count unless it "arises out of the same transaction" as the murder or the accused consents.[17] In addition, a summary

---

[13] Section 2 of the *Code* defines "indictment" to include an "information". Section 795 of the *Code* provides that unless specified otherwise, the provisions of Part XX of the *Code* setting out the rules for charging documents in indictable matters apply equally to summary conviction proceedings.

[14] See generally, *R. v. Last*, [2009] S.C.J. No. 45, [2009] 3 S.C.R. 146 at para. 1 (S.C.C.) ("The Crown enjoys a large discretion in deciding to include more than one count in an indictment."); *R. v. Mazur*, [1986] Y.J. No. 11, 27 C.C.C. (3d) 359 (Y.T.C.A.), leave to appeal refused [1986] S.C.C.A. No. 165 (S.C.C.) (subject to statutory rules, structuring of charges matter of prosecutorial discretion subject to review only for abuse of process). On prosecutorial discretion in charging decisions, see Chapter 8, Part 4.

[15] *Criminal Code*, s. 591(1).

[16] This rule stems from the common law. See *R. v. L. (S.J.)*, [2009] S.C.J. No. 14, [2009] 1 S.C.R. 426 at para. 48 (S.C.C.); *R. v. Phillips*, [1983] S.C.J. No. 70, [1983] 2 S.C.R. 161 at 164-65 (S.C.C.); *R. v. Clunas*, [1992] S.C.J. No. 17, [1992] 1 S.C.R. 595 at 610-11 (S.C.C.). The power to join accused is also recognized in various provisions of the *Code*. See *e.g.*, *Criminal Code*, R.S.C. 1985, c. C-46, s. 591(3)(*b*) (referring to power to require separate trials for jointly-charged accused); s. 567 ("if two or more persons are jointly charged in an information, unless all of them elect or re-elect or are deemed to have elected the same mode of trial, the justice, provincial court judge or judge may decline to record any election, re-election or deemed election for trial by a provincial court judge or a judge without a jury"); and s. 536(4.2) ("If two or more persons are jointly charged in an information and one or more of them make a request for a preliminary inquiry ... a preliminary inquiry must be held with respect to all of them").

[17] *Criminal Code*, s. 589. See also *R. v. Melaragni*, [1992] O.J. No. 2294, 72 C.C.C. (3d) 339 (Ont. Gen. Div.) (charges of discharging firearm, aggravated assault and careless use of firearm against one accused included in same indictment as charge of murder against co-accused because offenses arose out of same transaction involving same victim); *R. v. Jackson*, [2007] O.J.

conviction offence cannot be tried by a judge and jury, even if it is alleged to have been committed during the same transaction as an indictable offence.[18] However, for non-jury trials, summary conviction and indictable offences may be tried together (whether contained on the same charging document or separate ones) when it is "in the interests of justice" to do so and "the offences or accuseds could initially have been jointly charged."[19] Joint trials of summary and indictable offences should be conducted on the basis of indictable offence procedures.[20] Where there are appeals on both summary and indictable charges, the parties may appeal the disposition of the summary charges (along with the indictable charges) directly to the court of appeal (with leave of that court).[21] It has also been held that a summary conviction regulatory offence may be tried together with a summary conviction criminal offence arising out of the same transaction.[22] However, persons under the age of 18 cannot be tried jointly with adults.[23]

No. 58, 230 C.C.C. (3d) 569 (Ont. S.C.J.) (charge of accessory after the fact severed from murder charge as two incidents did not form single transaction).

[18] *R. v. Clunas*, [1992] S.C.J. No. 17, [1992] 1 S.C.R. 595 at 612-13 (S.C.C.); *R. v. L. (S.J.)*, [2009] S.C.J. No. 14, [2009] 1 S.C.R. 426 at para. 60 (S.C.C.).

[19] *R. v. Clunas*, [1992] S.C.J. No. 17, [1992] 1 S.C.R. 595 at 610 (S.C.C.). Unfortunately, two aspects of this rule are subject to debate. First, though the rule has been cast in subsequent cases to permit joinder of summary and indictable offences based solely on the accused's consent (see *e.g.*, *R. v. L. (S.J.)*, [2009] S.C.J. No. 14, [2009] 1 S.C.R. 426 at para. 60 (S.C.C.)), that is not what the Court stated in *Clunas*. There, the Court stated that when joinder is being considered, "the court should seek the consent of both the accused and the prosecution." "If consent is withheld," the Court continued, "the reasons should be explored." Ultimately, however, the Court held that "*[w]hether the accused consents or not*, joinder should only occur when, in the opinion of the court, it is in the interests of justice and the offences or accuseds could initially have been jointly charged." [Emphasis added].

It is also not entirely certain whether a joint trial of summary and indictable offences can take place in superior court. The confusion stems from a passage in *Clunas* approving a recommendation by the Law Reform Commission of Canada that "joinder may occur only where trial on the indictable offence is to take place before the provincial court." *Clunas*, *ibid.*, at 612 (S.C.R.). Immediately after this quotation, however, the Court states that such a joinder "will occur only when on the indictable offence the accused either will have chosen a trial by provincial court judge under Part XIX *or, having chosen a trial by judge under Part XIX, has waived his preliminary*" [emphasis added]. Being a clear and direct statement of the Court itself, the latter passage should be taken as authoritative. See also *R. v. L. (S.J.)*, [2009] S.C.J. No. 14, [2009] 1 S.C.R. 426 (S.C.C.) (describing *Clunas* as having "opened the door to trying summary conviction offences and indictable offences together where the trial is to take place, without a preliminary inquiry, in a provincial court *or before a judge without a jury*, provided that the accused consents to the joinder or that joinder is in the interests of justice" [emphasis added]). For a contrary view, see Roger E. Salhany, *Canadian Criminal Procedure*, 6th ed., looseleaf (Aurora, ON: Canada Law Book, 2001) at para. 6.1450.

[20] *R. v. Clunas*, [1992] S.C.J. No. 17, [1992] 1 S.C.R. 595 at 612-13 (S.C.C.).

[21] *Criminal Code*, ss. 675(1.1), 676(1.1).

[22] *R. v. Massick*, [1985] B.C.J. No. 1986, 21 C.C.C. (3d) 128 (B.C.C.A.). But see *R. v. Krisza*, [2007] O.J. No. 4018, 2007 ONCJ 471 (Ont. C.J.) (denying prosecution's motion to join summary criminal and summary regulatory charges arising out of same hunting incident but directing that same judge hear both matters).

[23] *R. v. L. (S.J.)*, [2009] S.C.J. No. 14, [2009] 1 S.C.R. 426 (S.C.C.).

(2) Content of Charges

§11.7 The format for an information is set out in Form 2 of the *Criminal Code*;[24] the format for indictments in Form 4.[25] Other than the directive to "state the offence", neither states how the charges should be described. Some guidance is provided, however, by section 581 of the *Code*, which states that "[e]ach count in an indictment shall in general apply to a single transaction and shall contain in substance a statement that the accused or defendant committed an offence therein specified."[26] The provision goes on to specify that the statement of the charge may be:

(*a*) in popular language without technical averments or allegations of matters that are not essential to be proved;

(*b*) in the words of the enactment that describes the offence or declares the matters charged to be an indictable offence; or

(*c*) in words that are sufficient to give to the accused notice of the offence with which he is charged.[27]

§11.8 Further, each count must "contain sufficient detail of the circumstances of the alleged offence to give to the accused reasonable information with respect to the act or omission to be proved against him and to identify the transaction referred to, but otherwise the absence or insufficiency of details does not vitiate the count."[28]

§11.9 As the Supreme Court of Canada emphasized in *R. v. R. (G.)*,[29] these provisions impose two distinct notice requirements: first, the charging document must properly "specify the charge"; and second, it must provide "sufficient supporting detail of the underlying transaction or circumstances."[30] Like many other jurists, we refer to these requirements as "legal sufficiency" and "factual sufficiency", respectively.[31] As we explain in the sections that follow, legal sufficiency ensures that the accused has prior knowledge of the legal elements of the offence. Legal sufficiency, in our view, should also be understood to include the "rule against duplicity", which forbids the prejudicial characterization of a charge as encompassing multiple offences with different legal elements. Factual sufficiency ensures that the accused has sufficient notice of the alleged facts

---

[24] *Criminal Code*, s. 506. See also Chapter 5, Part 2.

[25] *Criminal Code*, ss. 566(2), 580.

[26] *Criminal Code*, s. 581(1). As mentioned above in Part 1, s. 2 of the *Code* defines "indictment" to include an "information". See also *Criminal Code*, s. 789(1)(*b*) (for summary conviction matters, information "may charge more than one offence or relate to more than one matter of complaint, but where more than one offence is charged or the information relates to more than one matter of complaint, each offence or matter of complaint, as the case may be, shall be set out in a separate count").

[27] *Criminal Code*, s. 581(2).

[28] *Criminal Code*, s. 581(3).

[29] [2005] S.C.J. No. 45, [2005] 2 S.C.R. 371 (S.C.C.).

[30] *Ibid.*, at para. 15 (S.C.R.).

[31] See *e.g.*, Tim Quigley, *Procedure in Canadian Criminal Law*, 2d ed. (Toronto: Thomson Carswell, 2005) § 17.2.

undergirding the legal elements of the offence.[32] In brief, the requirements of legal and factual sufficiency are designed to ensure that the accused is able to prepare for and make "full answer and defence" at trial.[33]

(a) Legal Sufficiency (Including Duplicity)

§11.10 As stated in *R. (G.)*, legal sufficiency requires that "the accused be able clearly to ascertain from the offence charged (as described in the enactment creating it or as charged in the count or as expressly stated to be an included offence in the *Criminal Code* itself), the charges for which he or she risks conviction."[34] Legal sufficiency is rarely an issue, but at least three types of problems occasionally arise. The first occurs when the document inadequately identifies the offence charged. As mentioned, section 581(2)(*a*) states that the charge may be worded in "popular language" without "technical averments". It is not necessary, in other words, to either use the language describing the offence set out in the *Criminal Code* or list the legal elements of the offence.[35] But if statutory language is used, it may derive either from the provision describing the offence or any separate provision setting out the punishment.[36] Further, in determining the sufficiency of the charge, the court may consider the fact that the document refers to the statutory section number.[37] Lastly, section 582 of the *Code* specifies that an accused cannot be convicted of first degree murder or treason "unless in the indictment charging the offence he is specifically charged with that offence."

§11.11 The second problem is often referred to as "duplicity". At common law, the rule against duplicity prevented a single count in a charging document from encompassing more than one offence.[38] The rule was designed to help defendants prepare their defence and bar subsequent prosecutions arising from the

---

[32] It should be noted, however, that there is no consistent usage of these phrases in the cases or commentary.

[33] See *R. v. Brodie*, [1936] S.C.J. No. 15, [1936] S.C.R. 188 at 194 (S.C.C.); *R. v. Côté*, [1977] S.C.J. No. 37, [1978] 1 S.C.R. 8 at 13 (S.C.C.); *R. v. Douglas*, [1991] S.C.J. No. 16, [1991] 1 S.C.R. 301 at 314 (S.C.C.); *R. v. B. (G.)*, [1990] S.C.J. No. 58, [1990] 2 S.C.R. 30 at 42 (S.C.C.); *R. v. Wis Development Corp.*, [1984] S.C.J. No. 23, [1984] 1 S.C.R. 485 at 493 (S.C.C.); *R. v. R.(G.)*, [2005] S.C.J. No. 45, [2005] 2 S.C.R. 371 at para. 58 (S.C.C.), *per* Abella J. dissenting.

[34] *R. v. R. (G.)*, [2005] S.C.J. No. 45, [2005] 2 S.C.R. 371 at para. 15 (S.C.C.).

[35] See *e.g.*, *R. v. Henyu*, [1979] B.C.J. No. 2060, 48 C.C.C. (2d) 471 (B.C.C.A.) (upholding use of "did stab" instead of statutory language of "causing bodily harm"); *R. v. Allen*, [1974] N.B.J. No. 44, 17 C.C.C. (2d) 549 (N.B.C.A.) (upholding use of "heifer" instead of statutory term "cattle"). See also *Criminal Code*, s. 794(1) (prescribing that for summary conviction matters, no "exception, exemption, proviso, excuse or qualification prescribed by law is required to be set out or negatived, as the case may be, in an information").

[36] *Criminal* Code, s. 581(2)(*b*). See also *R. v. McKenzie*, [1971] S.C.J. No. 120, [1972] S.C.R. 409 (S.C.C.) (reference to "theft" interpreted to refer to punishment provision; existence of multiple provisions defining theft did not therefore invalidate charge).

[37] *Criminal Code*, s. 581(5). See *e.g.*, *R. v. Côté*, [1977] S.C.J. No. 37, [1978] 1 S.C.R. 8 at 13 (S.C.C.) (absence of statutory phrase "without reasonable excuse" could not have misled accused because charge referred to relevant *Code* section number).

[38] See *R. v. Kipp*, [1964] S.C.J. No. 52, [1965] S.C.R. 57 (S.C.C.).

same transaction.[39] As Professor Coughlan notes, the rule differs from the "single transaction" rule set out in section 581(1) of the *Code* (mentioned in Part 2(2), above and examined further in Part 2(2)(*b*), below) in that the latter rule "limits a count to a single factual situation, while the duplicity rule limits it to a single legal issue."[40]

§11.12 The duplicity rule remains alive under the *Criminal Code*,[41] but its rationale and scope have both been attenuated. While the rule continues to reflect a concern for fair notice, any future prosecution arising from the same transaction would today be prohibited by double jeopardy principles.[42] Modern courts have accordingly interpreted the rule to apply only when the accused is "prejudiced in the preparation of his defence by ambiguity in the charge".[43] This interpretation is buttressed by section 590(1) of the *Code*, which provides that a "count is not objectionable by reason only that (*a*) it charges in the alternative several different matters, acts or omissions that are stated in the alternative in an enactment that describes as an indictable offence the matters, acts or omissions charged in the count; or (*b*) it is double or multifarious." In other words, if a statutory provision states that a single offence may be committed in different ways, it is not duplicitous.[44]

§11.13 In *R. v. Sault Ste. Marie (City)*,[45] for example, the information alleged that the City "did discharge, or cause to be discharged, or permitted to be discharged" deleterious materials. The City argued that the statute created three separate offences and the charge failed to specify which of them it was alleged to have committed. In rejecting the claim that the charge was duplicitous and prejudicial, the Supreme Court concluded that statute merely set out different modes of committing the same, generic offence: "polluting".[46] "There is nothing wrong," it stated, "in specifying alternative methods of committing an offence, or in embellishing the periphery, provided only one offence is to be found at the focal point of the charge."[47]

---

[39] See *R. v. Sault Ste. Marie (City)*, [1978] S.C.J. No. 59, [1978] 2 S.C.R. 1299 at 1307 (S.C.C.); Roger E. Salhany, *Canadian Criminal Procedure*, 6th ed., looseleaf (Aurora, ON: Canada Law Book, 2001) at para. 6.1020.

[40] Stephen Coughlan, *Criminal Procedure* (Toronto: Irwin Law, 2008) at 310. It should be noted that the courts have not always maintained this distinction, sometimes characterizing as duplicitous charges that, while encompassing multiple transactions, involve only one type of criminal offence. See *e.g.*, *Canada (Attorney General) v. ITT Industries of Canada Ltd.*, [1987] B.C.J. No. 1865, 39 C.C.C. (3d) 268 at 277 (B.C.C.A.).

[41] See *Criminal Code*, ss. 590(1), 789(1).

[42] See *R. v. Kienapple*, [1974] S.C.J. No. 76, [1975] 1 S.C.R. 729 (S.C.C.). The "*Kienapple*" rule and other aspects of double jeopardy are discussed in Chapter 14.

[43] *R. v. Sault Ste. Marie (City)*, [1978] S.C.J. No. 59, [1978] 2 S.C.R. 1299 at 1308 (S.C.C.).

[44] See Roger E. Salhany, *Canadian Criminal Procedure*, 6th ed., looseleaf (Aurora, ON: Canada Law Book, 2001) at para. 6.1060.

[45] [1978] S.C.J. No. 59, [1978] 2 S.C.R. 1299 (S.C.C.).

[46] *R. v. Sault Ste. Marie (City)*, [1978] S.C.J. No. 59, [1978] 2 S.C.R. 1299 at 1308 (S.C.C.).

[47] *Ibid.* See also *R. v. Fischer*, [1987] S.J. No. 53, 31 C.C.C. (3d) 303 (Sask. C.A.) (indictment referring to two modes of committing theft set out in different *Code* provisions not duplicitous); *R. v. Brewer*, [1988] N.B.J. No. 127, 84 N.B.R. (2d) 357 (N.B.C.A.) (duplicity rule not engaged

§11.14 A count that appears to state only one offence, however, may be duplicitous in the context of the evidence. In *R. v. Sharpe*,[48] the accused was charged with indecent assault occurring between January 1, 1978 and January 3, 1983.[49] Because the complainant turned 14 years of age during that period, it was not clear whether the prosecution needed to prove that she did not consent (at the time, consent was an element of the offence for complainants over 13 years of age but not for those under 14 years of age). In effect, the count alleged two distinct offences and should accordingly have been divided at the beginning of trial.[50] (We discuss division of counts as a remedy for duplicitous charges in Part 3(3)(*a*), below). Though the accused was not misled in preparing his defence, the Court ruled, the failure to divide the count created a risk that the jury would convict without unanimity as to the elements of the offence.[51]

§11.15 The third type of problem, similar to duplicity, arises from the rules regarding "included" offences. If offence Y is included within offence X, then despite the absence of an express reference to Y in the document charging X, the accused may be convicted of Y even if acquitted of X. To qualify as an included offence, however, the charging document must adequately convey to the accused the risk of conviction for Y. If not, the document is legally insufficient and cannot support a conviction for Y.

§11.16 An offence is "included" in another offence if it: (*i*) is expressly included by statute (*e.g.*, the offences set out in sections 660 and 662(2) to (6) of the *Code*); (*ii*) is necessarily committed when the offence charged is committed (*e.g.*, common assault in a charge of sexual assault); or (*iii*) becomes included through the addition of words of description to the principal charge.[52] But as the Supreme Court explained in *R. (G.)*, an offence cannot become included as a consequence of the facts of a particular case. The issue there was whether an accused acquitted of the charged offence of incest with his underage daughter

---

by use of word "alternatively" where clear that information contained two separate counts); *R. v. Gatto*, [1938] N.S.J. No. 1, 70 C.C.C. 1 (N.S.S.C.), affd [1938] S.C.J. No. 22, [1938] S.C.R. 423 (S.C.C.) (no duplicity in charge that defendants assisted in unlawful "importing, unshipping, landing, removing, transporting or harbouring" of spiritous liquors).

48   [2007] B.C.J. No. 626, 219 C.C.C. (3d) 187 (B.C.C.A.).
49   *Ibid.*
50   *Ibid.*, at para. 26.
51   *Ibid.*, at para. 36 ("certain jurors could have convicted the appellant on the basis that the indecent acts were performed ...when C.M. was 13 years old and consent was no defence; others could have had a reasonable doubt that the sexual acts took place when C.M. was 13 years old, but concluded that he did not consent to the acts when he was 14 years old"). Note, however, that where they all agree that the prosecution has proven the elements of the offence, jurors need not be unanimous in deciding how, as a matter of fact, the accused committed the offence. See *R. v. Thatcher*, [1987] S.C.J. No. 22, [1987] 1 S.C.R. 652 (S.C.C.) (unanimity not required in deciding whether accused committed murder as principal or aider and abettor); *R. v. M. (G.L.)*, [1999] B.C.J. No. 1838, 138 C.C.C. (3d) 383 (B.C.C.A.) (where series of transactions charged as one continuous offence, jury need not be unanimous in finding which incident or incidents occurred).
52   See *Criminal Code*, s. 662(1); *R. v. Simpson (No. 2)*, [1981] O.J. No. 23, 58 C.C.C. (2d) 122 (Ont. C.A.), affd [1981] O.J. No. 34 (Ont. C.A.); *R. v. R. (G.)*, [2005] S.C.J. No. 45, [2005] 2 S.C.R. 371 at para. 29 (S.C.C.).

could be convicted of the allegedly included offence of sexual assault. In answering "no," the majority noted that the elements of the two offences are different; specifically, incest (which never requires proof of non-consent) may be committed without committing sexual assault (which, unless the complainant was underage, does require proof of non-consent).[53] Sexual assault could only be considered an included offence to incest, the court stated, if the charge had been supplemented by "words of description in the count itself of facts which put an accused on notice that, if proven, such facts taken together with the elements of the charge, disclose the commission" of a sexual assault.[54] In this case, it concluded, there was nothing in wording of the count that described a sexual assault or "gave any information from which an issue of non-consent could fairly be inferred, or suggested that the victim was underage and therefore was incapable of consenting."[55] As Justice Abella noted in her dissent, because the accused knew his daughter's age, any act of incest would necessarily have involved a sexual assault.[56] This does not alter the fact, however, that the indictment did not notify the accused before trial that he was in jeopardy of being convicted of this offence. With such notice, he might have taken a different approach to his defence.

(b) *Factual Sufficiency*

§11.17 As mentioned, to be factually sufficient the charging document must give the accused adequate notice of the "transaction or circumstances" underlying the charge.[57] Broadly speaking, the document must describe the offence with enough precision to "lift it from the general to the particular."[58]

§11.18 The first question is whether the document properly identifies the specific transaction(s) alleged to constitute the offence. Recall that section 581(1) of the *Criminal Code* states that each count "shall in general apply to a single transaction". However, as in cases of ongoing sexual abuse, it is sometimes difficult to say whether a given offence comprises one transaction or several. Courts have accordingly interpreted the "in general" caveat in section 581(1) to grant the Crown considerable leeway in deciding whether to charge a series of incidents as a single count or lay separate charges for each.[59] However, as discussed in Part 3(3)(*a*), below, if the accused claims prejudice by the inclusion of

---

[53] *R. v. R. (G.)*, [2005] S.C.J. No. 45, [2005] 2 S.C.R. 371 at para. 31 (S.C.C.).

[54] *Ibid.*, at para. 32 (S.C.R.).

[55] *Ibid.*, at para. 39 (S.C.R.). The Court noted, however, that since the accused was not at risk of being convicted of sexual assault, any subsequent prosecution for that offence would not constitute double jeopardy. *Ibid.*, at para. 41 (S.C.R.). Double jeopardy is discussed in Chapter 14, Part 3.

[56] *R. v. R. (G.)*, [2005] S.C.J. No. 45, [2005] 2 S.C.R. 371 at paras. 45-46, 66-67 (S.C.C.), *per* Abella J. dissenting.

[57] *Ibid.*, at para. 15 (S.C.R.).

[58] *R. v. Brodie*, [1936] S.C.J. No. 15, [1936] S.C.R. 188 at 198 (S.C.C.). See also *R. v. B. (G.)*, [1990] S.C.J. No. 58, [1990] 2 S.C.R. 30 at 41 (S.C.C.).

[59] See *e.g.*, *R. v. Barnes*, [1975] N.S.J. No. 331, 5 A.P.R. 272 at 281 (N.S.S.C.).

multiple transactions in a single count, he or she may apply for an order dividing it into separate charges.

§11.19 The second question is whether, as required by section 581(3) of the *Code*, the charging document contains "sufficient detail of the circumstances of the alleged offence" to "identify the transaction" and give the accused "reasonable information" about it.[60] Section 583 further provides that:

> No count in an indictment is insufficient by reason of the absence of details where, in the opinion of the court, the count otherwise fulfils the requirements of section 581 and, without restricting the generality of the foregoing, no count in an indictment is insufficient by reason only that
>
> (*a*) it does not name the person injured or intended or attempted to be injured;
>
> (*b*) it does not name the person who owns or has a special property or interest in property mentioned in the count;
>
> (*c*) it charges an intent to defraud without naming or describing the person whom it was intended to defraud;
>
> (*d*) it does not set out any writing that is the subject of the charge;
>
> (*e*) it does not set out the words used where words that are alleged to have been used are the subject of the charge;
>
> (*f*) it does not specify the means by which the alleged offence was committed;
>
> (*g*) it does not name or describe with precision any person, place or thing; or
>
> (*h*) it does not, where the consent of a person, official or authority is required before proceedings may be instituted for an offence, state that the consent has been obtained.[61]

§11.20 Charging documents typically contain little detail beyond the time and place of the alleged offence. In most cases, moreover, even these facts need not be set out precisely. "[P]articularity as to the exact time of the alleged offence," the Supreme Court stated in *R. v. B. (G.)*, "is not in the usual course necessary for this purpose."[62] Given the nature of the offence (sexual assault) and the young age of the complainant, the Court ruled, it was sufficient to allege that the assault occurred during a 19-day span.[63] Moreover, unless the time or place is

---

[60] *Criminal Code*, s. 581(3). Section 581(4) of the *Code* also specifies that for the offences of high treason, alarming Her Majesty, assisting an alien enemy to leave Canada, failing to prevent treason, committing violence in order to intimidate a legislature, sabotage and inciting to mutiny, the Crown must state "every overt act that is to be relied on" in the indictment.

[61] See also *Criminal Code*, ss. 584-586 (listing details that do not necessarily need to be included for libel; obscenity; committing or procuring perjury, making a false oath or statement or fabricating evidence; or fraud).

[62] *R. v. B. (G.)*, [1990] S.C.J. No. 58, [1990] 2 S.C.R. 30 at 45 (S.C.C.). See also *R. v. Douglas*, [1991] S.C.J. No. 16, [1991] 1 S.C.R. 301 at 314 (S.C.C.) ("Time is not required to be stated with exact precision unless it is an essential part of the offence charged and the accused is not misled or prejudiced by any variation in time that arises.").

[63] *R. v. B. (G.)*, [1990] S.C.J. No. 58, [1990] 2 S.C.R. 30 at 45 (S.C.C.).

either an element of the offence or "crucial to the defence," a variance between the charging document and the evidence does not invalidate the charge.[64]

§11.21 In rare cases factual sufficiency may demand more than the time and place of the alleged offence. In *R. v. Wis Development Corp.*,[65] for example, the Supreme Court found that a count alleging that the defendant operated a "commercial air service" without the requisite licence at a specified time and place did not provide sufficient detail of the circumstances of the offence, as the statute's definition of "commercial air service" contemplated "many diverse and unrelated uses".[66]

§11.22 If details are included in a charge, then as a general rule they must be proved to gain a conviction.[67] This rule is subject to two exceptions. First, as discussed in Part 3(2), below, if the details are not necessary for factual sufficiency, they may be deleted by amendment.[68] Second, absent amendment, the court may find that the details are mere "surplusage", in which case failure to prove them is not fatal to conviction.[69] Details will be surplus if their inclusion in

---

[64] See *Criminal Code*, s. 601(4.1) ("A variance between the indictment or a count therein and the evidence taken is not material with respect to (*a*) the time when the offence is alleged to have been committed, if it is proved that the indictment was preferred within the prescribed period of limitation, if any; or (*b*) the place where the subject-matter of the proceedings is alleged to have arisen, if it is proved that it arose within the territorial jurisdiction of the court."). See also *R. v. B. (G.)*, [1990] S.C.J. No. 58, [1990] 2 S.C.R. 30 at 45-53 (S.C.C.); *R. v. Douglas*, [1991] S.C.J. No. 16, [1991] 1 S.C.R. 301 at 314 (S.C.C.); *R. v. Ryan*, [1985] O.J. No. 232, 23 C.C.C. (3d) 1 (Ont. C.A.) (failure to identify precise time and location of alleged impaired driving did not invalidate charge); *R. v. C. (R.I.)*, [1986] O.J. No. 1087, 32 C.C.C. (3d) 399 at 403 (Ont. C.A.) (given duration of alleged sexual abuse and youth of child, "full particularity with respect to ... dates, is likely impossible and to require it would make prevention of a serious social problem exceedingly difficult").

[65] [1984] S.C.J. No. 23, [1984] 1 S.C.R. 485 (S.C.C.).

[66] *R. v. Wis Development Corp.*, [1984] S.C.J. No. 23, [1984] 1 S.C.R. 485 at 492 (S.C.C.). The Court proceeded to quash the charge on the basis that it was void *ab initio* and thus could not be amended or particularized. This conclusion, however, was driven by since-repealed *Code* provisions severely limiting the availability of amendment and particularization for summary offences. As explained in Part 3(2), below, the rules regarding amendment and particularization are now the same for summary and indictable matters and are much more permissive than the rules applying to *Wis Development*. See also *R. v. Gotfried*, [1964] M.J. No. 6, 2 C.C.C. 382 (Man. C.A.) (charge of selling underweight goods lacked sufficient detail because it did not permit isolation of specific transactions at issue).

[67] See *R. v. Little*, [1974] S.C.J. No. 135, [1976] 1 S.C.R. 20 (S.C.C.); *R. v. Daoust*, [2004] S.C.J. No. 7, [2004] 1 S.C.R. 217 at para. 22 (S.C.C.); *R. v. Saunders*, [1990] S.C.J. No. 22, [1990] 1 S.C.R. 1020 (S.C.C.); *R. v. Morozuk*, [1986] S.C.J. No. 3, [1986] 1 S.C.R. 31 (S.C.C.).

[68] See *R. v. Daoust*, [2004] S.C.J. No. 7, [2004] 1 S.C.R. 217 at para. 22 (S.C.C.); *R. v. Morozuk*, [1986] S.C.J. No. 3, [1986] 1 S.C.R. 31 (S.C.C.), *per* Lamer J.; *R. v. Elliott*, [1977] S.C.J. No. 122, [1978] 2 S.C.R. 393 at 427 (S.C.C.), *per* Ritchie J.; *R. v. Saunders*, [1990] S.C.J. No. 22, [1990] 1 S.C.R. 1020 (S.C.C.).

[69] *R. v. Vézina*, [1986] S.C.J. No. 2, [1986] 1 S.C.R. 2 at 23-24 (S.C.C.); *R. v. Van Hees*, [1957] O.J. No. 342, 119 C.C.C. 129 at 135 (Ont. C.A.). See also *R. v. McConnell*, [2005] O.J. No. 1613, 75 O.R. (3d) 388 at para. 12 (Ont. C.A.).

the charge could not have misled the accused as to the nature of the charge or the identity of the transaction.[70]

3. REMEDIES FOR DEFICIENT CHARGES

§11.23 As explained above, charges are unlikely to be found deficient unless they are misleading or otherwise prejudicial to the accused. Further, as we elaborate in the remainder of this chapter, even when a charge is found deficient, it is very unlikely to be quashed. In most cases, the prejudice caused by the defect can be cured by one of the remedies discussed below.

(1) Particulars

§11.24 Under section 587 of the *Criminal Code*, the court may order the prosecutor to "furnish particulars" to ensure a fair trial. Typically particulars will be ordered when the charging document fails to provide enough detail to meet the standard of factual sufficiency discussed in Part 2(2)(*b*), above.[71] Section 587(1) states that the prosecution may be ordered to provide particulars:

(*a*) of what is relied on in support of a charge of perjury, the making of a false oath or a false statement, fabricating evidence or counselling the commission of any of those offences;

(*b*) of any false pretense or fraud that is alleged;

(*c*) of any alleged attempt or conspiracy by fraudulent means;

(*d*) setting out the passages in a book, pamphlet, newspaper or other printing or writing that are relied on in support of a charge of selling or exhibiting an obscene book, pamphlet, newspaper, printing or writing;

(*e*) further describing any writing or words that are the subject of a charge;

(*f*) further describing the means by which an offence is alleged to have been committed; or

(*g*) further describing a person, place or thing referred to in an indictment.[72]

---

[70] See *e.g.*, *R. v. Vézina*, [1986] S.C.J. No. 2, [1986] 1 S.C.R. 2 (S.C.C.) (specifying particular bank as victim of attempted fraud was surplusage and thus no need to prove identity of victim); *R. v. Little*, [1974] S.C.J. No. 135, [1976] 1 S.C.R. 20 (S.C.C.) (fact that legal name of owner of stolen goods misidentified on indictment not fatal to conviction where accused had sufficient notice of circumstances of offence); *R. v. Hanna*, [1991] N.S.J. No. 377, 109 N.S.R. (2d) 338 (N.S.S.C.) (no possibility accused could have been misled by misidentification of owner of stolen gravel); *R. v. Hundt*, [1971] A.J. No. 45, 3 C.C.C. (2d) 279 (Alta. C.A.) (no obligation on Crown to prove unnecessary statements in charge negativing qualifications of accused for exemptions under regulatory statute); *R. v. Reynolds*, [2010] O.J. No. 3908, 2010 ONCA 576 at paras. 33-43 (Ont. C.A.), revd on other grounds [2011] S.C.J. No. 19, [2011] 1 S.C.R. 693 (S.C.C.) (particularized count containing essential averments regarding nature and date of offence, identity of witness and manner of commission of *actus reus* not surplus).

[71] See *R. v. Douglas*, [1991] S.C.J. No. 16, [1991] 1 S.C.R. 301 at 312 (S.C.C.) ("In cases where confusion exists as to the indictment, a provision is made for the accused person to obtain particulars.").

[72] This list, it should be noted, is not exhaustive. See *Criminal Code*, s. 587(1) ("without restricting the generality of the foregoing").

§11.25 A request for particulars, however, may not be used to restrict the prosecution to only one theory of the case.[73] Further, in deciding whether to order particulars, the court may consider the evidence taken at trial up to that point.[74]

§11.26 Though the matter is not entirely clear, the cases suggest that only the trial judge has the power to order particulars.[75] When particulars are ordered, they become part of the information or indictment.[76] Subject to any amendment[77] or a finding of surplusage,[78] the particulars must therefore be proved for conviction.[79] But allegations in the prosecutor's opening address, argument or theory of the case cannot particularize the count so as to require proof of such allegations.[80]

(2) Quashing or Amending

§11.27 At common law, the trial judge could not amend even trivial, technical errors in the indictment without the consent of the grand jury that presented it.[81] As a consequence, it was common for charges to be quashed or dismissed before a decision on the merits. Today, deficient charges are very rarely quashed; the *Criminal Code* now gives courts very broad powers to amend deficient charges.[82] The governing rules are set out in section 601. Section 601(1) provides as follows:

---

[73] See *R. v. Govedarov*, [1974] O.J. No. 1837, 16 C.C.C. (2d) 238 at 269 (Ont. C.A.). See also *R. v. Thatcher*, [1986] S.J. No. 19, 24 C.C.C. (3d) 449 (Sask. C.A.), affd [1987] S.C.J. No. 22, [1987] 1 S.C.R. 652 (S.C.C.).

[74] *Criminal Code*, s. 587(2).

[75] See *R. v. Croal*, [1995] S.J. No. 377, 133 Sask. R. 86 (Sask. Q.B.). See also *R. v. Hynes*, [2001] S.C.J. No. 80, [2001] 3 S.C.R. 623 at para. 33 (S.C.C.) (preliminary inquiry justice may not order particulars); *R. v. Haney*, [1924] O.J. No. 125, 43 C.C.C. 297 (Ont. S.C.); *R. v. Litchfield*, [1993] S.C.J. No. 127, [1993] 4 S.C.R. 333 (S.C.C.) (since indictment is not preferred until lodged with trial judge, application to sever counts cannot be brought at any earlier stage of proceedings); Roger E. Salhany, *Canadian Criminal Procedure*, 6th ed. looseleaf (Aurora, ON: Canada Law Book, 2001) at para. 6.970 (application should be made at earliest possible opportunity).

[76] *Criminal Code*, s. 587(3)(*c*).

[77] See *R. v. Cox*, [1963] S.C.J. No. 51, [1963] S.C.R. 500 at 511 (S.C.C.).

[78] Surplusage is discussed above, Part 2(2)(*b*).

[79] *Criminal Code*, s. 601(2) (power to make the "indictment, count or particular conform to the evidence"). See also *R. v. Reynolds*, [2010] O.J. No. 3908, 2010 ONCA 576 at para. 16 (Ont. C.A.), revd on other grounds [2011] S.C.J. No. 19, [2011] 1 S.C.R. 693 (S.C.C.). Amendment is discussed below, Part 3(2).

[80] See *R. v. Bengert*, [1980] B.C.J. No. 721, 15 C.R. (3d) 114 (B.C.C.A.); *R. v. Govedarov*, [1974] O.J. No. 1837, 16 C.C.C. (2d) 238 (Ont. C.A.); *R. v. McCune*, [1998] B.C.J. No. 2925, 131 C.C.C. (3d) 152 at paras. 35-38 (B.C.C.A.).

[81] See *R. v. Moore*, [1988] S.C.J. No. 58, [1988] 1 S.C.R. 1097 at 1106 (S.C.C.), *per* Dickson C.J.C., dissenting; Roger E. Salhany, *Canadian Criminal Procedure*, 6th ed., looseleaf (Aurora, ON: Canada Law Book, 2001) at para. 6.1190 (common law rule based on "theory that, since the grand jurors were the true accusers, they alone had the power to amend a defect in their accusation").

[82] See *R. v. Moore*, [1988] S.C.J. No. 58, [1988] 1 S.C.R. 1097 at 1128 (S.C.C.) ("Since the enactment of our Code in 1892 there has been, through case law and punctual amendments to

An objection to an indictment or to a count in an indictment for a defect apparent on the face thereof shall be taken by motion to quash the indictment or count before the accused has pleaded, and thereafter only by leave of the court before which the proceedings take place, and the court before which an objection is taken under this section may, if it considers it necessary, order the indictment or count to be amended to cure the defect.

Section 601 goes on to set out two specific amendment powers. First, under section 601(2), the court may amend an "indictment, count, or particular" to "conform to the evidence" when there is a "variance" between the two. Second, section 601(3) allows an indictment or count therein to be amended where it appears:

> *(a)* that the indictment has been preferred under a particular Act of Parliament instead of another Act of Parliament;
>
> *(b)* that the indictment or a count thereof
>
> > (i) fails to state or states defectively anything that is requisite to constitute the offence,
> >
> > (ii) does not negative an exception that should be negatived,
> >
> > (iii) is in any way defective in substance,
>
> and the matters to be alleged in the proposed amendment are disclosed by the evidence taken on the preliminary inquiry or on the trial; or
>
> *(c)* that the indictment or a count thereof is in any way defective in form.

§11.28 Section 601(4) states that in deciding whether to amend under either of these provisions, courts may consider:

> *(a)* the matters disclosed by the evidence taken on the preliminary inquiry;[83]
>
> *(b)* the evidence taken on the trial, if any;
>
> *(c)* the circumstances of the case;
>
> *(d)* whether the accused has been misled or prejudiced in his defence by any variance, error or omission mentioned in subsection (2) or (3); and
>
> *(e)* whether, having regard to the merits of the case, the proposed amendment can be made without injustice being done.

§11.29 Section 601(5) further provides that if an accused has been misled or prejudiced by a deficiency in the charging document, the court may adjourn the proceedings (and order the Crown to pay any associated costs) if "the misleading or prejudice may be removed" by the adjournment.

§11.30 An application under section 601 results in one of three outcomes: quashing the charge, amending it, or leaving it as written. If the charge as written does not prejudice the accused and is supported by the evidence, it will not

---

s. 529 and its predecessor sections, a gradual shift from requiring judges to quash to requiring them to amend in the stead; in fact, there remains little discretion to quash.").

[83] See *R. v. Geary*, [1960] A.J. No. 33, 126 C.C.C. 325 (Alta. C.A.) (failure to consider evidence from preliminary inquiry vitiates amendment).

be quashed and need not be amended.[84] If any prejudice or variance can be cured by amendment (and any necessary adjournment), the charge must be amended rather than quashed.[85] A charge should only be quashed if: (*i*) proceeding with it would cause the accused "irreparable prejudice"; or (*ii*) as amended, it would not be supported by the evidence.[86]

§11.31 Charges found to be legally insufficient because they lack an "essential averment", for example, may usually be cured by amendment. In *R. v. Moore*,[87] the Supreme Court of Canada held that an unlawful possession charge that failed to specify that the property was obtained from the commission of an indictable offence should have been amended rather than quashed.[88] Since the defect was noticed at the beginning of trial, it could easily have been amended to include the averment without prejudice to the accused.[89] Indeed, even when the accused has been convicted on a charge lacking an essential averment, the conviction should not be vacated on appeal unless the accused could have been misled by the error.[90]

§11.32 The power to amend legally insufficient counts, however, does not go so far as to allow the substitution of a different offence for the one originally charged.[91] Such amendments may only change the "particulars" of the offence.[92] Thus in *R. v. Daoust*,[93] the Court refused the prosecutor's application to amend the indictment to plead an attempt to commit the offence charged. "To allow the Crown to make out a different offence," it reasoned, "would infringe on the accused's right 'to be reasonably informed of the transaction alleged against him, thus giving him the possibility of a full defence and fair trial'."[94] Similarly, it has

---

[84] See *R. v. Moore*, [1988] S.C.J. No. 58, [1988] 1 S.C.R. 1097 at 1129-30 (S.C.C.), *per* Lamer J.; *R. v. Irwin*, [1998] O.J. No. 627, 123 C.C.C. (3d) 316 at para. 26 (Ont. C.A.).

[85] See *R. v. Moore*, [1988] S.C.J. No. 58, [1988] 1 S.C.R. 1097 at 1128-29 (S.C.C.), *per* Lamer J. and at 1109 (S.C.R.), *per* Dickson C.J.C. dissenting; *R. v. Webster*, [1992] S.C.J. No. 92, [1993] 1 S.C.R. 3 at paras. 13-14 (S.C.C.). See also *R. v. Henyu*, [1979] B.C.J. No. 2060, 48 C.C.C. (2d) 471 (B.C.C.A.). The only exceptions are for charges of treason and certain related offences, which under s. 601(9) of the *Criminal Code* cannot be amended to add the "overt acts" that must be specified by virtue of s. 581(4). Note, however, that while "overt acts" must be specified for the offences in ss. 47 and 49-53, the ban on amendment applies only to the offences in ss. 49, 50, 51 and 53.

[86] *R. v. Moore*, [1988] S.C.J. No. 58, [1988] 1 S.C.R. 1097 at 1128-30 (S.C.C.); *R. v. Tremblay*, [1993] S.C.J. No. 85, [1993] 2 S.C.R. 932 at para. 49 (S.C.C.).

[87] [1988] S.C.J. No. 58, [1988] 1 S.C.R. 1097 (S.C.C.).

[88] *Ibid.*, at 1126 (S.C.R.), *per* Lamer J. and 1110-11(S.C.R.), *per* Dickson C.J.C., dissenting.

[89] *Ibid.* See also *R. v. Stewart*, [1979] B.C.J. No. 2047, 7 C.R. (3d) 165 (B.C.C.A.).

[90] *R. v. Moore*, [1988] S.C.J. No. 58, [1988] 1 S.C.R. 1097 at 1107 (S.C.C.). See also *R. v. Major*, [1975] N.S.J. No. 317, 10 N.S.R. (2d) 348 (N.S.S.C.), revd [1976] S.C.J. No. 48, [1977] 1 S.C.R. 826 (S.C.C.); *R. v. Morozuk*, [1986] S.C.J. No. 3, [1986] 1 S.C.R. 31 (S.C.C.).

[91] See *R. v. Daoust*, [2004] S.C.J. No. 7, [2004] 1 S.C.R. 217 at para. 22 (S.C.C.); *R. v. Dupont*, [1958] J.Q. no 5, 28 C.R. 146 (Que. C.A.); *R. v. Elliot*, [1969] O.J. No. 1561, [1970] 3 C.C.C. 233 (Ont. C.A.).

[92] *R. v. Daoust*, [2004] S.C.J. No. 7, [2004] 1 S.C.R. 217 at para. 22 (S.C.C.).

[93] [2004] S.C.J. No. 7, [2004] 1 S.C.R. 217 (S.C.C.).

[94] *Ibid.*, at para. 70, citing *R. v. Côté*, [1977] S.C.J. No. 37, [1978] 1 S.C.R. 8 at 13 (S.C.C.).

been held that a charge cannot be amended to add an included offence that was not originally included in the charging document.[95]

§11.33 A variance between a charge and the evidence may also usually be rectified by amendment. In *R. v. P. (M.B.)*,[96] for example, the Supreme Court upheld the trial judge's decision to amend the indictment (after the close of the prosecution's case) to extend the time period during which the sexual assaults were alleged to have occurred.[97] Because the accused knew the allegations related to the period during which he was residing in the complainant's home, the amendment caused him no "irreparable prejudice".[98] Similarly, in *R. v. Morozuk*,[99] the Court referred to the absence of prejudice in amending the indictment on appeal to reflect the fact that the substance found in the accused's possession was cannabis resin and not marijuana as stated in the indictment.[100] And in *R. v. Melo*,[101] the Ontario Court of Appeal ruled that the trial judge should have allowed the prosecution's request to amend a charge of unlawfully discharging a weapon to delete the name of the alleged victim and replace it with the anonymous "male person".[102] Since the victim's identity was irrelevant to whether the accused committed the offence, the amendment could not have caused him prejudice.

§11.34 In *R. v. Tremblay*,[103] in contrast, the Supreme Court upheld the trial judge's decision to refuse the prosecutor's request to amend the information.[104] The defendants were charged with keeping a common bawdy-house, which is defined by the *Criminal Code* as a place used for either prostitution or indecent acts.[105] The information mentioned acts of indecency but not prostitution. The prosecution applied, after most of its witnesses had testified, to amend the charge by either deleting the reference to indecency or adding a reference to prostitution. As the defendants' strategy was to challenge the claim that the impugned conduct was indecent, the Court reasoned, the amendment would have caused them "irreparable prejudice".[106] Similarly, in *R. v. Saunders*,[107] the Court refused to amend the indictment after the accused was erroneously convicted of conspiring to import heroin when the evidence showed only a conspiracy to

---

[95] *R. v. Rinnie*, [1969] A.J. No. 21, [1970] 3 C.C.C. 218 (Alta. C.A.).

[96] [1994] S.C.J. No. 27, [1994] 1 S.C.R. 555 (S.C.C.).

[97] *Ibid.*

[98] *Ibid.*, at para. 15 (S.C.R). The Court did find, however, that the trial judge should not have allowed the prosecution to re-open its case after the accused had revealed that he would be calling evidence.

[99] [1986] S.C.J. No. 3, [1986] 1 S.C.R. 31 (S.C.C.).

[100] *Ibid.*, at 38 (S.C.R.).

[101] [1986] O.J. No. 278, 29 C.C.C. (3d) 173 (Ont. C.A.).

[102] *Ibid.*

[103] [1993] S.C.J. No. 85, [1993] 2 S.C.R. 932 (S.C.C.).

[104] *Ibid.* See also *R. v. Charlton*, [1976] B.C.J. No. 1273, 30 C.C.C. (2d) 372 (B.C.C.A.) (trial judge erred in amending indictment at close of prosecution's case to include allegations of theft unrelated to original charges; had allegations been included from the start defence would have conducted case differently).

[105] *Criminal Code*, s. 197(1).

[106] *R. v. Tremblay*, [1993] S.C.J. No. 85, [1993] 2 S.C.R. 932 at para. 51 (S.C.C.).

[107] [1990] S.C.J. No. 22, [1990] 1 S.C.R. 1020 (S.C.C.).

import cocaine.[108] Unlike in *Morozuk*, in *Saunders* prejudice was established by the fact that one of the accused, relying on the particularization of the charge to refer only to heroin, admitted to conspiring to import other drugs.

§11.35 As mentioned, absent leave, an application to quash must be made before pleading.[109] However, charges may be amended under section 601(3) of the *Code* (on the application of one of the parties or on the court's own motion) "at any stage of the proceedings",[110] including at the arraignment,[111] preliminary inquiry[112] and appeal.[113] Section 601(2) states that amendments to correct a variance between a charge and the evidence may be made "on the trial of" the charging document. Though it is certain that such amendments may be made during trial and on appeal,[114] it is not as clear whether they can be made before the trial begins or before evidence is heard.[115]

§11.36 If the court orders an amendment, it becomes part of the record and the proceedings continue "as if the indictment or count had been originally preferred as amended."[116] If a charge is quashed, in contrast, it is void *ab initio*. In other words, it is a nullity and is treated as if it had never been laid. As a consequence,

---

[108] *Ibid.*

[109] *Criminal Code*, s. 601(1). See also *R. v. Leclaire*, [1956] O.J. No. 162, 115 C.C.C. 297 (Ont. C.A.) (application to quash cannot be made for first time on appeal unless court finds that accused misled or prejudiced).

[110] *Criminal Code*, s. 601(3), (11).

[111] See also *R. v. Volpi*, [1987] O.J. No. 530, 34 C.C.C. (3d) 1 (Ont. C.A.), leave to appeal refused [1987] S.C.C.A. No. 317 (S.C.C.) (application to quash may be made before provincial court judge on arraignment before putting accused to election as to mode of trial).

[112] *Criminal Code*, s. 601(11). See also *R. v. Webster*, [1992] S.C.J. No. 92, [1993] 1 S.C.R. 3 (S.C.C.) (preliminary inquiry justice has jurisdiction to determine validity of information and decision not generally subject to judicial review); *R. v. Volpi*, [1987] O.J. No. 530, 34 C.C.C. (3d) 1 (Ont. C.A.) (same).

[113] See *R. v. Morozuk*, [1986] S.C.J. No. 3, [1986] 1 S.C.R. 31 (S.C.C.). See also *Criminal Code*, s. 683(1)(*g*) (giving appeal court power to amend indictment unless "the accused has been misled or prejudiced in his defence or appeal").

[114] See *e.g.*, *R. v. Morozuk*, [1986] S.C.J. No. 3, [1986] 1 S.C.R. 31 (S.C.C.). See also *Criminal Code*, s. 683(1)(*g*) (giving appeal court power to amend indictment unless "the accused has been misled or prejudiced in his defence or appeal"); *R. v. Irwin*, [1998] O.J. No. 627, 123 C.C.C. (3d) 316 (Ont. C.A.); *R. v. Reynolds*, [2010] O.J. No. 3908, 2010 ONCA 576 at paras. 48-56 (Ont. C.A.), revd on other grounds [2011] S.C.J. No. 19 (S.C.C.); *R. v. D. (A.)*, [2007] M.J. No. 235, 222 C.C.C. (3d) 217 at para. 31 (Man. C.A.).

[115] See *R. v. McConnell*, [2005] O.J. No. 1613, 75 O.R. (3d) 388 (Ont. C.A.) (no power to amend charge to correct variance before evidence heard); *R. v. M. (E.A.D.)*, [2008] M.J. No. 465, 234 C.C.C. (3d) 292 at para. 15 (Man. C.A.) (amendment to correct variance must be made during trial); *R. v. Griffin*, [1981] N.S.J. No. 493, 63 C.C.C. (2d) 111 (N.S.S.C.) (amendment permitted on basis of prosecutor's representation that he would be calling evidence in support of amendment). Section 601(4)(*a*) would appear to give the court the power to order an amendment under s. 601(2) based on the evidence taken at the preliminary inquiry. Note as well that even if it is an error to correct a variance before evidence is heard, absent prejudice, such an error does not warrant reversing a conviction on appeal. See *R. v. McConnell*, [2005] O.J. No. 1613, 75 O.R. (3d) 388 at para. 20 (Ont. C.A.); *R. v. Fiore*, [1962] O.J. No. 44, 132 C.C.C. 213 (Ont. C.A.). See also *R. v. Seath*, [1997] B.C.J. No. 451, 114 C.C.C. (3d) 356 (B.C.C.A.) (amendment not supported by evidence erroneously granted by trial judge, however appeal dismissed because no prejudice).

[116] *Criminal Code*, s. 601(7).

a new information may be laid or new indictment preferred against the accused for the same offence without triggering double jeopardy.[117] Decisions on whether to quash or amend are questions of law and may thus be appealed after the conclusion of the trial by either party.[118] Interlocutory applications for judicial review, however, are permitted only in exceptional circumstances.[119]

(3) Division and Severance

§11.37 As mentioned in Part 2(1), above, one count in a charging document may encompass a series of incidents and one charging document may include several counts (against one or more accused). If an accused claims that the structuring of charges is prejudicial, he or she may apply for an order to: (*i*) divide counts in a single charging document ("division of counts"); (*ii*) sever counts against one accused into separate charging documents ("severance of counts"); and (*iii*) sever counts against one accused from those against co-accused ("severance of accused"). These applications must be made to the trial judge, though they may be made as soon as that judge is assigned.[120] We deal with each in turn below.

(a) Division of Counts

§11.38 If the accused demonstrates prejudice by the inclusion of multiple transactions in one count, section 590(2) of the *Criminal Code* empowers the court to amend the count or divide it into two or more counts.[121] In *R. v. Lilly*,[122] for example, the Supreme Court ruled that the trial judge should have divided a charge of theft into two counts because the accused had distinct defences relating to two separate incidents.[123] Such a division, the Court reasoned, would have ensured that the jury considered each defence independently from the other. In *R. v. Litchfield*,[124] in contrast, the Court ruled that the trial judge wrongly divided (and severed) a sexual assault count based on the body parts of the complainants.[125] "This arbitrary distinction," the Court stated, "greatly amplified the difficulties

---

[117] *R. v. Moore*, [1988] S.C.J. No. 58, [1988] 1 S.C.R. 1097 at 1128 (S.C.C.). This principle is subject to claims that new charges are statute-barred (see Chapter 13, Part 2) or would constitute an abuse of process (see Chapter 10, Part 5(1)(*a*)(iii)).
[118] See *Criminal Code*, ss. 675(1)(a)(i), 676(1)(*a*)-(c). See also Chapter 18.
[119] *R. v. Webster*, [1992] S.C.J. No. 92, [1993] 1 S.C.R. 3 (S.C.C.) (*certiorari* may be available when the judge declines to quash charge that fails to disclose offence or where evidence reveals that offence took place outside court's jurisdiction).
[120] See *R. v. Litchfield*, [1993] S.C.J. No. 127, [1993] 4 S.C.R. 333 (S.C.C.); *R. v. Sapara*, [2001] A.J. No. 256, 91 Alta. L.R. (3d) 28 at para. 66 (Alta. C.A.).
[121] *Criminal Code*, s. 590(2)-(3) (requiring accused to show that count as written "embarrasses him in his defence" and that amendment or division required by "the ends of justice"). See also *R. v. M. (G.L.)*, [1999] B.C.J. No. 1838, 138 C.C.C. (3d) 383 at para. 24 (B.C.C.A.) (no division where no prejudice to accused).
[122] [1983] S.C.J. No. 57, [1983] 1 S.C.R. 794 (S.C.C.).
[123] *Ibid.*
[124] [1993] S.C.J. No. 127, [1993] 4 S.C.R. 333 (S.C.C.).
[125] *Ibid.*

in assessing the alleged sexual assaults in the context of all of the circumstances surrounding the conduct by creating an evidentiary problem which would not have existed but for the order."[126]

§11.39 Unless the court ordering a count to be divided also severs it from the charging document, the charges will still be tried together. Severance of counts is discussed next.

(b) Severance of Counts

§11.40 When faced with a multi-count charging document, an accused may apply to be tried separately on one or more counts.[127] Severance is normally sought to either avoid exposing the trier of fact to incriminating evidence admissible on one charge but not others or allow the accused to testify on one charge but not others. An application to sever a count should normally be made at the start of trial, though severance may be ordered subsequently on the basis of prejudice that was not apparent at the outset.[128]

§11.41 Severance may be ordered where the accused establishes that "the interests of justice" require it.[129] This standard encompasses both the accused's right to be tried on admissible evidence and society's interests in truth seeking and trial economy.[130] In balancing these interests, courts must consider a number of factors, including "the general prejudice to the accused; the legal and factual nexus between the counts; the complexity of the evidence; whether the accused intends to testify on one count but not another; the possibility of inconsistent verdicts; the desire to avoid a multiplicity of proceedings; the use of similar fact evidence at trial; the length of the trial having regard to the evidence to be called; the potential prejudice to the accused with respect to the right to be tried within a reasonable time; and the existence of antagonistic defences as between co-accused persons."[131]

§11.42 In *R. v. Last*,[132] the Supreme Court held that to justify severance, an accused's desire to testify selectively must be objectively justifiable.[133] Such justification could consist, it noted, "of the type of potential defences open to the

---

[126] *Ibid.*, at para. 31.

[127] *Criminal Code*, s. 591(3)-(6).

[128] See *R. v. R. v. C. (D.A.)*, [1996] B.C.J. No. 583, 106 C.C.C. (3d) 28 at para. 10 (B.C.C.A.), affd [1997] S.C.J. No. 4, [1997] 1 S.C.R. 8 (S.C.C.).

[129] *Criminal Code*, s. 591(3)(a). See also *R. v. B. (M.O.)*, [1998] B.C.J. No. 560, 123 C.C.C. (3d) 270 at para. 26 (B.C.C.A.) (accused has onus to establish that "interests of justice" warrant severance on balance of probabilities).

[130] See *R. v. Last*, [2009] S.C.J. No. 45, [2009] 3 S.C.R. 146 at paras. 16-17 (S.C.C.).

[131] *Ibid.*, at para. 18 (S.C.R.). See also *R. v. E. (L.)*, [1994] O.J. No. 2641, 94 C.C.C. (3d) 228 at 238 (Ont. C.A.); *R. v. Cross*, [1996] J.Q. no 3761, 112 C.C.C. (3d) 410 at 419 (Que. C.A.); *R. v. C. (D.A.)*, [1996] B.C.J. No. 583, 106 C.C.C. (3d) 28 at para. 9 (B.C.C.A.), affd [1997] S.C.J. No. 4, [1997] 1 S.C.R. 8 (S.C.C.); *R. v. Eng*, [1995] B.C.J. No. 329, 56 B.C.A.C. 18 (B.C.C.A.); *R. v. Jeanvenne*, [2010] O.J. No. 4537, 261 C.C.C. (3d) 462 at para. 29 (Ont. C.A.).

[132] [2009] S.C.J. No. 45, [2009] 3 S.C.R. 146 (S.C.C.)

[133] *R. v. Last*, [2009] S.C.J. No. 45, [2009] 3 S.C.R. 146 at para. 26 (S.C.C.).

accused or the nature of his testimony."[134] Even an objectively justifiable basis for selective testimony, however, is not determinative; it can be "counterbalanced by other circumstances that the judge finds may prevent the accused from testifying, or be outweighed by factors that demonstrate that the interests of justice require a joint trial."[135] In *Last*, for example, the Court found that the accused's desire to testify selectively was "objectively justifiable".[136] In light of the considerable tactical pressure he faced to testify on both counts, however, this was not a "significant factor" favouring severance.[137]

§11.43 The Court in *Last* ultimately concluded, however, that the trial judge erred in refusing the accused's application for severance. Severance was justified, it held, by the "extremely thin" factual and legal connections between the two allegations[138] and the risk that the jury would engage in impermissible credibility bolstering and propensity reasoning.[139] Further, because there was no overlap in evidence or witnesses between the two counts and no danger of inconsistent verdicts, a joint trial would do nothing to further the search for truth and bring only "minimal" benefits to trial economy.[140]

§11.44 The Court in *Last* also commented on the relationship between severance and the similar fact evidence rule. "In many cases," it noted, "a ruling allowing similar fact evidence will favour a joint trial since the evidence on all incidents would have to be introduced in any event."[141] Conversely, as in *Last*, the fact that evidence tendered on one count is inadmissible as similar fact evidence on the other militates in favour of separate trials.[142] That said, the two

---

[134] *Ibid.*, at para. 26 (S.C.R.). See also *R. v. Cross*, [1996] J.Q. no 3761, 112 C.C.C. (3d) 410 at 421 (Que. C.A.).

[135] *R. v. Last*, [2009] S.C.J. No. 45, [2009] 3 S.C.R. 146 at para. 27 (S.C.C.). See also *R. v. Papequash*, [1987] S.J. No. 797, 61 Sask. R. 222 at 224 (Sask. C.A.); *R. v. McMath*, [1997] B.C.J. No. 2772, 121 C.C.C. (3d) 174 (B.C.C.A.); *R. v. Steele*, [2006] B.C.J. No. 492, 206 C.C.C. (3d) 327 (B.C.C.A.), affd [2007] S.C.J. No. 36, [2007] 3 S.C.R. 3 (S.C.C.).

[136] *R. v. Last*, [2009] S.C.J. No. 45, [2009] 3 S.C.R. 146 at para. 30 (S.C.C.).

[137] *Ibid.*, at paras. 29-30 (S.C.R.).

[138] *Ibid.*, at paras. 32-35 (noting that the two sexual assault allegations occurred a month apart, involved different victims, and were contested by the defence on different theories — consent in the first and identity in the second). See also *R. v. Racco (No. 1)*, [1975] O.J. No. 1659, 23 C.C.C. (2d) 201 (Ont. Co. Ct.) (close temporal and geographic nexus between charges, evidence on one relevant to other).

[139] *R. v. Last*, [2009] S.C.J. No. 45, [2009] 3 S.C.R. 146 at paras. 36-40 (S.C.C.) (noting the risks that the jury would "inevitably wonder why two complainants who did not know each other would independently accuse Mr. Last of sexual assault" and might conclude, if convinced that he committed one assault, that he "had the propensity for committing this type of offence and convict on the other"). The Court further noted (at paras. 45-46 (S.C.R.)) that limiting instructions will not always be sufficient to mitigate the risks of a joint trial. See also *R. v. M. (B.)*, [1998] O.J. No. 4359, 130 C.C.C. (3d) 353 at para. 27 (Ont. C.A.) ("Joining the bestiality counts with the other counts served only to invite the jury to engage in the forbidden line of reasoning that the appellant was the type of person likely to commit acts of sexual misconduct.").

[140] *R. v. Last*, [2009] S.C.J. No. 45, [2009] 3 S.C.R. 146 at paras. 41-44 (S.C.C.).

[141] *Ibid.*, at para. 33 (S.C.R.). See also *R. v. B. (M.O.)*, [1998] B.C.J. No. 560, 123 C.C.C. (3d) 270 at para. 33 (B.C.C.A.) (joint trial warranted where evidence on counts mutually admissible as similar fact evidence).

[142] See also *R. v. Rose*, [1997] O.J. No. 1947, 100 O.A.C. 67 at paras. 16-18 (Ont. C.A.).

issues are distinct and cast different burdens on the parties. As the Supreme Court stated in *R. v. Arp*,[143] "notwithstanding the trial judge's refusal to sever the counts in a multi-count indictment, it remains open to him or her, as the evidence progresses at trial, to determine as a matter of law that evidence on one count is not admissible as similar fact evidence on the other counts."[144]

§11.45 The decision whether or not to sever counts is discretionary and should not be overturned on appeal unless it is exercised "unjudicially" or results in an "injustice".[145] As the Court held in *Last*, "the determination of whether the judge acted unjudicially calls for an inquiry into the circumstances prevailing at the time it was made, the review of whether the ruling resulted in an injustice will usually entail scrutiny that includes the unfolding of the trial and of the verdicts."[146] An "unjudicial" decision, the Court added, is one that was either unreasonable or involved an error of law.[147]

(c) Severance of Accused

§11.46 An accused may apply to be tried separately from a co-accused on one or more counts.[148] As with severance of counts, the accused must demonstrate on a balance of probabilities that it is in the "interests of justice" to do so.[149] The interests of justice include "those of the accused, the co-accused, and the community as represented by the prosecution."[150] Where accused persons are alleged to have acted in concert, there is a strong presumption in favour of joint trials.[151] This presumption is grounded on concerns for trial economy, a desire to avoid inconsistent verdicts, and the fact that "the full truth about an incident is much

---

[143] [1998] S.C.J. No. 82, [1988] 3 S.C.R. 339 at para. 52 (S.C.C.).

[144] *Ibid.*, at para. 52 (S.C.R.).

[145] *R. v. Litchfield*, [1993] S.C.J. No. 127, [1993] 4 S.C.R. 333 at 353-54 (S.C.C.). See also *R. v. Last*, [2009] S.C.J. No. 45, [2009] 3 S.C.R. 146 at para. 14 (S.C.C.).

[146] *R. v. Last*, [2009] S.C.J. No. 45, [2009] 3 S.C.R. 146 at para. 15 (S.C.C.). See also *R. v. Rose*, [1997] O.J. No. 1947, 100 O.A.C. 67 at para. 17 (Ont. C.A.).

[147] *R. v. Last*, [2009] S.C.J. No. 45, [2009] 3 S.C.R. 146 at para. 21 (S.C.C.).

[148] *Criminal Code*, ss. 591(3)(*b*), (4)-(6).

[149] *Criminal Code*, s. 593(3)(*b*). And as with the decision to sever or not sever counts, the trial judge's decision is discretionary and will be overturned on appeal only if he or she erred in principle or applied the correct principles in an unreasonable manner. See *R. v. Savoury*, [2005] O.J. No. 3112, 200 C.C.C. (3d) 94 at para. 26 (Ont. C.A.). See also *R. v. Unger*, [1993] M.J. No. 363, 83 C.C.C. (3d) 228 (Man. C.A.).

[150] *R. v. Savoury*, [2005] O.J. No. 3112, 200 C.C.C. (3d) 94 at para. 22 (Ont. C.A.).

[151] See *R. v. Crawford; R. v. Creighton*, [1995] S.C.J. No. 30, [1995] 1 S.C.R. 858 at para. 19 (S.C.C.) (referring to "a uniform stream of authority in this country in favour of joint trials"); *R. v. Chow*, [2005] S.C.J. No. 22, [2005] 1 S.C.R. 384 at para. 47 (S.C.C.) ("It is well established that separate trials for alleged co-conspirators are the exception, not the rule."); *R. v. Torbiak*, [1978] O.J. No. 580, 40 C.C.C. (2d) 193 at 199 (Ont. C.A.) (referring to the "well established [rule] that ... where the essence of the case is that the accused were acting in concert, they should be jointly indicted and tried, and an appellate court will not interfere with the discretion of the trial judge unless he has failed to exercise it judicially or his decision has caused a miscarriage of justice"); *R. v. Boulet*, [1987] J.Q. no 2057, 40 C.C.C. (3d) 38 at 45 (Que. C.A.), leave to appeal refused [1989] 1 S.C.R. vi (S.C.C.); *R. v. Kematch*, [2010] M.J. No. 58, 252 C.C.C (3d) 349 at paras. 22-23 (Man. C.A.).

more likely to emerge if every alleged participant gives his account on one occasion."[152] An accused should not be severed, therefore, unless he or she can show that a joint trial would cause an "injustice".[153] The most common grounds invoked to justify severance were outlined in *R. v. Weir*[154] as follows:

(1) That the defendants have antagonistic defences;

(2) That important evidence in favour of one of the defendants which would be admissible on a separate trial would not be allowed on a joint trial;

(3) That evidence which is incompetent against one defendant, to be introduced against another, and that it would work prejudicially to the former with the jury;

(4) That a confession made by one of the defendants, if introduced and proved, would be calculated to prejudice the jury against the other defendants; and

(5) That one of the defendants could give evidence for the whole or some of the other defendants and would become a competent and compellable witness on the separate trials of such other defendants.[155]

§11.47 None of these factors is determinative. For example, in and of itself, the fact that co-accused have antagonistic or "cut-throat" defences is not enough to justify severance.[156] Indeed, as the Supreme Court stressed in *R. v. Crawford; R. v. Creighton*,[157] in such circumstances the risk of inconsistent verdicts is especially acute.[158] Similarly, courts have found that the intention of one accused to cross-examine another on the latter's involuntary confession does not necessarily justify severance.[159]

§11.48 That said, courts have been prepared to sever accused in a variety of circumstances. Separate trials may be necessary, for example, when a voluntary confession or other evidence admissible against an accused is inadmissible against a co-accused and would cause the latter irreparable prejudice.[160] Such prejudice is especially likely in conspiracy cases where the evidence against one

---

[152] *R. v. Crawford; R. v. Creighton*, [1995] S.C.J. No. 30, [1995] 1 S.C.R. 858 at para. 30 (S.C.C.), quoting D.W. Elliot, "Cut Throat Tactics: The Freedom of an Accused to Prejudice a Co-Accused" [1991] Crim. L. Rev. 5 at 17. See also *R. v. McFall*, [1979] S.C.J. No. 108, [1980] 1 S.C.R. 321 (S.C.C.), *per* Estey J. dissenting.

[153] *R. v. Crawford; R. v. Creighton*, [1995] S.C.J. No. 30, [1995] 1 S.C.R. 858 at para. 31 (S.C.C.). See also *R. v. Boulet*, [1987] J.Q. no 2057, 40 C.C.C. (3d) 38 (Que. C.A.), leave to appeal refused [1989] 1 S.C.R. vi (S.C.C.).

[154] [1899] Q.J. No. 3, 3 C.C.C. 351 (Que. Q.B.).

[155] *Ibid.*, at para. 8 (C.C.C.).

[156] *R. v. Crawford; R. v. Creighton*, [1995] S.C.J. No. 30, [1995] 1 S.C.R. 858 at para. 31 (S.C.C.).

[157] [1995] S.C.J. No. 30, [1995] 1 S.C.R. 858 (S.C.C.).

[158] *R. v. Crawford; R. v. Creighton*, [1995] S.C.J. No. 30, [1995] 1 S.C.R. 858 at paras. 30-31 (S.C.C.). See also *R. v. Unger*, [1993] M.J. No. 363, 83 C.C.C. (3d) 228 (Man. C.A.) (where co-accused have antagonistic defences, joint trial often more advantageous to the innocent).

[159] See *R. v. Pelletier*, [1986] B.C.J. No. 480, 29 C.C.C. (3d) 533 (B.C.C.A.).

[160] See *R. v. Guimond*, [1979] S.C.J. No. 16, [1979] 1 S.C.R. 960 (S.C.C.); *R. v. Vaas*, [1982] A.J. No. 614, 30 C.R. (3d) 277 (Alta. Q.B.). See also *R. v. McFall*, [1979] S.C.J. No. 108, [1980] 1 S.C.R. 321 (S.C.C.), *per* Estey J., dissenting.

accused is much stronger than another.[161] The general presumption, however, is that the risk of prejudice can be mitigated by an instruction to the trier of fact to disregard evidence inadmissible against a co-accused.[162]

§11.49 Separate trials may also be ordered when an accused wishes to compel a co-accused to testify, as an accused cannot be compelled to testify (by either the prosecution or a co-accused) at his or her own trial.[163] In deciding whether to sever on this basis, the trial judge must consider two questions: (*i*) is there a "reasonable possibility that the co-accused, if made compellable by severance, would testify"; and (*ii*) if such a possibility exists, "is there a reasonable possibility that the co-accused's evidence could affect the verdict in a manner favourable to the accused seeking severance."[164] Some courts have held that even if these questions are answered positively, the trial judge may refuse to sever where countervailing factors outweigh the potential impairment of the accused's right to a fair trial.[165] Others have stated, correctly in our view, that severance is mandatory when the accused shows that a co-accused's proposed evidence is likely to raise a reasonable doubt.[166] While the mere assertion of a desire to call a co-accused is not sufficient to justify severance,[167] the trial judge should not generally weigh the co-accused's credibility in making the decision as this would usurp the function of the jury.[168]

---

[161] *R. v. Guimond*, [1979] S.C.J. No. 16, [1979] 1 S.C.R. 960 (S.C.C.).

[162] See *R. v. McLeod*, [1983] O.J. No. 81, 6 C.C.C. (3d) 29 (Ont. C.A.), affd *(sub nom. R. v. Farquharson)* [1986] S.C.J. No. 32, [1986] 1 S.C.R. 703 (S.C.C.).

[163] See *Charter*, s. 11(*c*) ("[a]ny person charged with an offence has the right...not to be compelled to be a witness in proceedings against that person in respect of the offence."); *R. v. Clunas*, [1992] S.C.J. No. 17, [1992] 1 S.C.R. 595 (S.C.C.).

[164] *R. v. Savoury*, [2005] O.J. No. 3112, 200 C.C.C. (3d) 94 at para. 28 (Ont. C.A.). See also *R. v. Chow*, [2005] S.C.J. No. 22, [2005] 1 S.C.R. 384 at para. 51 (S.C.C.); *R. v. Torbiak*, [1978] O.J. No. 580, 40 C.C.C. (2d) 193 (Ont. C.A.).

[165] See *e.g.*, *R. v. Savoury*, [2005] O.J. No. 3112, 200 C.C.C. (3d) 94 at para. 29 (Ont. C.A.).

[166] See *e.g.*, *R. v. Boulet*, [1987] J.Q. no 2057, 40 C.C.C. (3d) 38 at 43, *per* Beauregard J.A. and 45-47, *per* Vallerand J.A. (Que. C.A.), leave to appeal refused [1989] C.S.C.R. no 43, 26 Q.A.C. 79*n*, [1989] 1 S.C.R. vi (S.C.C.).

[167] See *R. v. Torbiak*, [1978] O.J. No. 580, 40 C.C.C. (2d) 193 at 199 (Ont. C.A.); *R. v. Agawa*, [1975] O.J. No. 2556, 28 C.C.C. (2d) 379 (Ont. C.A.); *R. v. Quiring*, [1974] S.J. No. 319, 19 C.C.C. (2d) 337 at 349 (Sask. C.A.), leave to appeal refused (1974), 19 C.C.C. (2d) 337*n*; *R. v. Boulet*, [1987] J.Q. no 2057, 40 C.C.C. (3d) 38 at 42 (Que. C.A.), leave to appeal refused [1989] C.S.C.R. no 43, 26 Q.A.C. 79*n*, [1989] 1 S.C.R. vi (S.C.C.); Roger E. Salhany, *Canadian Criminal Procedure*, 6th ed. looseleaf (Aurora, ON: Canada Law Book, 2001) at para. 6.1550.

[168] *R. v. Savoury*, [2005] O.J. No. 3112, 200 C.C.C. (3d) 94 at para. 28 (Ont. C.A.). But see *R. v. Agawa*, [1975] O.J. No. 2556, 28 C.C.C. (2d) 379 at 388 (Ont. C.A.) (severance denied where co-accused's proposed evidence was "patently unbelievable"); *R. v. Szczerba*, [2002] A.J. No. 513, 314 A.R. 114 at para. 14 (Alta. Q.B.) ("a separate trial should be refused where the testimony which is sought to be elicited from the co-accused would be totally incredible so that no reasonable jury could possibly have a reasonable doubt as to the guilt of the accused as a result of such testimony").

Chapter 12

TERRITORIAL LIMITS

1. INTRODUCTION

§12.1 This chapter addresses the territorial limits that govern Canadian criminal proceedings. It explains the circumstances in which a court in a particular place will have jurisdiction to try a specific criminal charge. In the vast majority of cases territorial jurisdiction is not at all controversial. For example, where an accused is alleged to have committed a crime in a particular locale, is apprehended there, and is then brought before a court in that location, the authority of that court to try the charge is entirely straightforward. Greater complexity arises, however, when the connection between an alleged crime and the place of a proposed trial is more tenuous. This chapter explains the rules that govern the resolution of questions regarding territorial jurisdiction. It also explains the means by which an accused may seek to have his or her trial moved to a different locale from where it would ordinarily be tried, a procedure known as a change of venue application.

2. EXTRATERRITORIAL LIMITS

(1) Generally

§12.2 The concept of territorial jurisdiction is the subject of a number of provisions in the *Criminal Code*.[1] The starting point is section 6(2), which provides that:

> Subject to this Act or any other Act of Parliament, no person shall be convicted or discharged under section 730 of an offence committed outside Canada.

This provision codifies a well-established rule of international law known as the principle of territoriality. That principle requires that states only apply their laws within their territorial boundaries.[2] The rule has a long history at common law.[3]

---

[1] R.S.C. 1985, c. C-46 [*Code*].

[2] See *R. v. Finta*, [1994] S.C.J. No. 26, [1994] 1 S.C.R. 701 at para. 170 (S.C.C.), noting that the provision: "reflects the principle of sovereign integrity, which dictates that a state has exclusive sovereignty over all persons, citizens or aliens, and all property, real or personal, within its own territory." See generally, Luzius Wildhaber, "Sovereignty and International Law" in Ronald St. J. Macdonald and Douglas M. Johnston, eds., *The Structure and Process of International Law: Essays in Legal Philosophy, Doctrine, and Theory* (Boston: Kluwer, 1983) 425.

[3] See *e.g.*, *R. v. Keyn* (1876), 2 Ex. Div. 63 at 239 (C.C.R.) (the inherent jurisdiction of criminal courts "extends no further than the limits of the realm ... [which] consisted of the lands within

Its rationale is obvious. Without it, Canadian courts might be expected to assert their jurisdiction over crimes committed anywhere in the world, a possibility that would be practically unworkable and at odds with the principle of international comity.[4]

§12.3 According to the Supreme Court of Canada, all that is necessary to make an offence subject to the jurisdiction of Canadian courts "is that a significant portion of the activities constituting that offence [take] place in Canada. ... it is sufficient that there be a 'real and substantial link' between an offence and this country".[5] In *R. v. Libman*,[6] the Supreme Court concluded that the requisite link was present where the appellant was charged with conspiracy to defraud arising out of conduct originating from a Toronto telephone solicitation room. From that location, at the appellant's direction, sales staff telephoned U.S. residents and attempted to convince them to buy shares in two Central American mining companies by making material misrepresentations with respect to their identity, where they were telephoning from and to the quality and value of the shares being sold. Promotional materials were then mailed from Central America. Customers who took the bait and bought the essentially valueless shares sent payment to Central America, where the appellant received his share of the proceeds before returning the money to Canada. Based on these facts, without parsing the evidence, Justice La Forest simply concluded that "[t]here were ample links here."[7]

§12.4 The Ontario Court of Appeal applied the "real and substantial link" test in *R. v. Greco*.[8] In *Greco*, the accused savagely beat his girlfriend while the couple was vacationing in Cuba. He was not prosecuted for this conduct there. Instead, he was convicted of breaching a probation order issued by an Ontario court that required him to "keep the peace and be of good behaviour". On appeal, the Court rejected his claim that the order ceased to operate at Canada's borders. Rather, after emphasizing that an Ontario court issued the probation order, Justice Moldaver noted that the *Libman* test was satisfied because "Canada is the only country that has an interest in ensuring compliance with orders made by Canadian Courts".[9] In other words, the fact that the order being enforced originated in Ontario provided the real and substantial link required for Canadian criminal law to apply, even though the conduct that occasioned the breach took

---

the body of the country"). See also *Macleod v. Attorney-General for New South Wales*, [1891] A.C. 455 at 458 (P.C.). See generally, Edward M. Morgan, "Criminal Process, International Law, and Extraterritorial Crime" (1988) 38 U.T. L.J. 245.

[4] See *R. v. Libman*, [1985] S.C.J. No. 56, [1985] 2 S.C.R. 178 at para. 11 (S.C.C.) [*Libman*] ("States ordinarily have little interest in prohibiting activities that occur abroad and they are, as well, hesitant to incur the displeasure of other states by indiscriminate attempts to control activities that take place wholly within the boundaries of those other countries").

[5] *R. v. Libman*, [1985] S.C.J. No. 56, [1985] 2 S.C.R. 178 at 213 (S.C.C.). See also *R. v. Larche*, [2006] S.C.J. No. 56, [2006] 2 S.C.R. 762 at para. 59 (S.C.C.).

[6] [1985] S.C.J. No. 56, [1985] 2 S.C.R. 178 (S.C.C.).

[7] *Ibid.*, at para. 76 (S.C.R.).

[8] [2001] O.J. No. 4147, 159 C.C.C. (3d) 146 (Ont. C.A.) [*Greco*].

[9] *Ibid.*, at para. 42 (C.C.C.).

place in another country. This reasoning has since been extended to other types of court orders.[10]

§12.5 In contrast, in *R. v. B. (O.)*,[11] the Ontario Court of Appeal overturned the appellant's conviction for sexual assault. In that case, a Canadian trucker sexually assaulted his 13-year-old Canadian granddaughter in his Canadian registered vehicle while travelling through the U.S. en route back to Canada. Applying *Libman*, the Court overturned the conviction, reasoning that there "must be more than Canadian residence or vehicular ownership; there must be a significant link between Canada and the formulation, initiation, or commission of the offence."[12]

(2) Exceptions Prefaced on Universality and Nationality Principles

§12.6 Although international law generally restricts states from applying their criminal laws extraterritorially, there are a number of well-established exceptions that, as we shall see below, are also reflected in Canadian law.

§12.7 The crime of piracy on the high seas emerged as an early exception to the territoriality principle. The rationale for this extension of jurisdiction was the idea that pirates were enemies of all states and therefore undeserving of the protection of any.[13] Under international law, universal jurisdiction was ultimately extended to include a number of other offences that were also considered to be of concern to the whole of humanity. For example, any state that obtains custody of an individual who is alleged to have committed genocide, a crime against humanity or a war crime, is entitled to try and punish such an accused.[14]

§12.8 Another well-recognized exception to the territoriality principle is known as the nationality principle. Under international law, a state may regulate and adjudicate regarding actions committed by its nationals abroad, provided enforcement of the rules takes place when those nationals are within the state's own borders.[15]

---

[10] See *R. v. Rattray*, [2008] O.J. No. 359, 229 C.C.C. (3d) 496 (Ont. C.A.) (upholding the appellant's convictions for breaching a weapons prohibition, a probation order and a recognizance, as a result of his purchase of a firearm in the State of Michigan).

[11] [1997] O.J. No. 1850, 116 C.C.C. (3d) 189 (Ont. C.A.).

[12] *Ibid.*, at para. 12 (C.C.C.).

[13] See *Re Piracy Jur Gentium*, [1934] A.C. 586 at 589 (P.C.). The extraterritorial application of Canadian criminal law to acts of piracy is maintained by the current *Criminal Code*, which makes it an offence to engage in acts of piracy "in or out of Canada". See *Criminal Code*, s. 74(2).

[14] See generally, Gillian Triggs, "Australia's War Crimes Trials: A Moral Necessity or Legal Minefield?" (1987) Mel. U. L. Rev. 382 at 389; Ian Brownlie, *Principles of Public International Law*, 6th ed. (Oxford: Oxford University Press, 2003) at 303. See also *R. v. Hape*, [2007] S.C.J. No. 26, [2007] 2 S.C.R. 292 at para. 61 (S.C.C.).

[15] See generally, Ian Brownlie, *Principles of Public International Law*, 6th ed. (Oxford: Oxford University Press, 2003) at 306, 428-32; Oscar Schachter, *International Law in Theory and Practice* (Boston: Norwell, 1991) at 254. See also *R. v. Hape*, [2007] S.C.J. No. 26, [2007] 2 S.C.R. 292 at para. 60 (S.C.C.); *R. v. Cook*, [1998] S.C.J. No. 68, [1998] 2 S.C.R. 597 at para. 28 (S.C.C.).

§12.9 Canadian law extends its reach beyond our national boundaries through a combination of the universality and nationality principles. So, for example, the *Crimes Against Humanity and War Crimes Act*[16] makes it an offence to commit, *outside* Canada genocide, a crime against humanity or a war crime.[17] Section 8 of the Act provides that a person may be prosecuted for such offences if:

> (*a*) at the time the offence is alleged to have been committed,
>
> > (i) the person was a Canadian citizen or was employed by Canada in a civilian or military capacity,
> >
> > (ii) the person was a citizen of a state that was engaged in an armed conflict against Canada, or was employed in a civilian or military capacity by such a state,
> >
> > (iii) the victim of the alleged offence was a Canadian citizen, or
> >
> > (iv) the victim of the alleged offence was a citizen of a state that was allied with Canada in an armed conflict; or
>
> (*b*) after the time the offence is alleged to have been committed, the person is present in Canada.

§12.10 Section 7 of the *Code* also sets out a number of exceptions to the territoriality requirement. These exceptions are mostly prefaced on there being some nexus to Canada. For example, the perpetrator or victim is either a citizen or permanent resident of Canada, an aircraft or vessel registered in Canada is involved or the alleged perpetrator is ultimately found in Canada. The various exceptions must be read closely. They are far too lengthy to be excerpted here, but by way of a very general overview they include: offences committed on an aircraft registered in Canada;[18] offences committed on an aircraft where the flight is terminated in Canada;[19] hijacking and other offences aimed at aviation and its infrastructure;[20] offences involving cultural property;[21] offences involving acts of piracy;[22] offences committed in space;[23] offences involving internationally protected persons;[24] hostage taking;[25] offences involving nuclear materials;[26] offences against United Nations or associated personnel;[27] offences involving explosives;[28] offences relating to terrorism;[29] and sexual offences involving children.[30]

---

[16] S.C. 2000, c. 24.
[17] *Ibid.*, s. 6(1). Section 4 of the Act makes these same acts crime if committed in Canada.
[18] *Criminal Code*, s. 7(1)(*a*).
[19] *Criminal Code*, s. 7(1)(*b*).
[20] *Criminal Code*, s. 7(2)(*a*)-(*e*).
[21] *Criminal Code*, s. 7(2.01).
[22] *Criminal Code*, ss. 7(2.1), (2.2).
[23] *Criminal Code*, ss. 7(2.3), (2.31), (2.32), (2.33).
[24] *Criminal Code*, s. 7(3).
[25] *Criminal Code*, s. 7(3.1).
[26] *Criminal Code*, ss. 7(3.2)-(3.7).
[27] *Criminal Code*, s. 7(3.71).
[28] *Criminal Code*, s. 7(3.72).
[29] *Criminal Code*, ss. 7(3.73), (3.74), (3.75).
[30] *Criminal Code*, ss. 7(4.1), (4.3).

§12.11 With some of these provisions, the consent of the Attorney General of Canada is necessary to institute proceedings.[31] If one of these subsections is the basis for jurisdiction, the *Code* permits the proceedings to be commenced in any territorial division in Canada.[32]

§12.12 The *Code* also contains an exception vesting Canadian courts with jurisdiction to try criminal accusations for crimes committed in the exclusive economic zone of Canada, above Canada's continental shelf and even in international waters, at least in certain specified circumstances; for example, when the offence takes place on a ship registered in Canada or is committed by a Canadian citizen or takes place in hot pursuit.[33]

(3) Offences Defined so as to Apply Extraterritorially

§12.13 There are also a number of offences in the *Code* that are defined in such a way as to extend the reach of Canada's criminal laws beyond its borders. So, for example, the *Code* makes it an offence to conspire in Canada to commit an offence in another country[34] or to conspire abroad to commit an offence in Canada.[35] Similarly, the offence of piracy is defined to permit the prosecution of piratical acts no matter where they take place.[36] The same is true of treason,[37] torture,[38] proceeds of crime,[39] and forging or using a false passport.[40] In addition, it is an offence to possess property in Canada that was obtained through the commission of an offence elsewhere.[41] It is also a crime for a Canadian citizen or resident to leave Canada in order to commit bigamy.[42] These provisions do not operate to the exclusion of the real and substantial connection test from *Libman* (which was explained above). Rather, they supply a further and alternative basis for Canadian courts to assume jurisdiction.[43]

---

[31] See *e.g.*, *Criminal Code*, s. 7(2.33) (relating to offences in space).
[32] *Criminal Code*, s. 7(5).
[33] *Criminal Code*, s. 477.1. The Attorney General of Canada must, however, consent to such a prosecution. *Criminal Code*, s. 477.2. The *Code* also extends police powers of search and arrest in order to facilitate such investigations. *Criminal Code*, s. 477.3.
[34] *Criminal Code*, s. 465(3).
[35] *Criminal Code*, s. 465(4).
[36] *Criminal Code*, s. 74.
[37] *Criminal Code*, s. 46(3).
[38] *Criminal Code*, s. 269.1(2).
[39] *Criminal Code*, ss. 462.3, 463.31.
[40] *Criminal Code*, s. 57(1).
[41] *Criminal Code*, s. 354.
[42] *Criminal Code*, s. 290(1)(b).
[43] See *R. v. Rowbotham*, [1993] S.C.J. No. 136, [1993] 4 S.C.R. 834 (S.C.C.).

3.   INTERPROVINCIAL LIMITS

(1)   Generally

§12.14 Canada is a federal state, with different court systems operating in the various provinces and territories. The *Code* contemplates a division of jurisdiction over criminal matters based on Canada's political boundaries. Section 478(1) of the *Code* provides that:

> Subject to this Act, a court in a province shall not try an offence committed entirely in another province.

(2)   Exceptions Where Offence Transcends Provincial Boundaries

§12.15 Obviously, the effective enforcement of criminal law could too easily be thwarted if an offender could structure his or her criminal activities to take advantage of Canada's territorial boundaries. The *Code* recognizes this possibility and redresses it through the various subsections found in section 476. That provision refers to "territorial divisions", which are defined expansively to include "any province, county, union of counties, township, city, town, parish or other judicial division or place to which the context applies".[44] The provision supplies concurrent authority to courts in different territorial divisions in a variety of circumstances where an offence implicates the interests of more than one jurisdiction within Canada.[45]

§12.16 So, for example, where an offence is committed on a bridge between territorial divisions, it can be prosecuted in either one of them.[46] Similarly, where an offence is committed on the boundary between two territorial divisions, or within 500 metres of such a boundary, the courts in either place have jurisdiction.[47] In addition, where an offence is committed in a vehicle or on a vessel, it is deemed to be committed within any territorial division through which the vehicle or vessel passes during its journey.[48] The same is true of offences committed

---

[44]   *Criminal Code*, s. 2.

[45]   See *R. v. B. (O.)*, [1997] O.J. No. 1850, 116 C.C.C. (3d) 189 at para. 9 (Ont. C.A.) (explaining that the expansive definition of "territorial division" must be read in light of s. 6(2) of the *Code* and therefore must be restricted to the sorts of places specified that are within Canada).

[46]   *Criminal Code*, s. 476(*a*).

[47]   *Criminal Code*, s. 476(*b*).

[48]   *Criminal Code*, s. 476(*c*). See *R. v. Moore*, [1970] B.C.J. No. 608, 1 C.C.C. (2d) 521 (B.C.C.A.) (holding that this subsection does not create a rebuttable presumption; in short, proof that the vehicle was actually in a different territorial division than the one particularized in the charge is of no consequence because of this subsection). See also *R. v. B. (O.)*, [1997] O.J. No. 1850, 116 C.C.C. (3d) 189 (Ont. C.A.), in holding that s. 476(*c*) must be read in light of s. 6(2), which means that the provision does not supply jurisdiction unless the location through which the vehicle happened to be travelling when the offence was committed was in Canada. The fact that the vehicle eventually made its way into Canada from the United States, after the offence was completed, did not provide a basis for jurisdiction under this subsection. *Ibid.*, at paras. 9-10 (C.C.C.).

on aircraft, with the courts in the territorial division where the flight commenced, over which it passed or where it ended, all having concurrent jurisdiction.[49] Offences involving the mails are treated the same way: they are deemed to have been committed in any territorial division through which a letter or package was carried in the course of being delivered.[50]

§12.17 The most expansive grant of jurisdiction stems from subsection 476(*b*). Beyond addressing offences committed on or near the boundary of two territorial divisions, it also provides that where "the offence was commenced within one territorial division and completed within another, the offence shall be deemed to have been committed in any of the territorial divisions". As the Ontario Court of Appeal observed, Canadian courts have evidenced a willingness to construe this provision "flexibly and sensibly and to avoid restricting its operation by interpreting it narrowly or technically."[51]

§12.18 In *R. v. Bigelow*,[52] the Ontario Court of Appeal noted that the jurisprudence has recognized three bases for conferring jurisdiction under section 476(*b*). First, where there is a continuity of operation extending over more than one province, any province where a component of the offence took place may exercise jurisdiction.[53] Second, where an overt act that forms an element of the offence takes place in a province, the courts in that province will also have jurisdiction to try the offence.[54] Finally, where the act of an accused in one province generates effects in another, section 476(*b*) confers jurisdiction on the second province.[55]

§12.19 In *Bigelow* the Court of Appeal held that Ontario had jurisdiction to try a charge of denying a custodial parent of lawful custody of a child. The accused resided in Alberta. His wife, who lived in Ontario, had custody of their child. Pursuant to a court order, the accused had a right of access every second week-

---

[49] *Criminal Code*, s. 476(*d*).

[50] *Criminal Code*, s. 476(*e*).

[51] *R. v. Bigelow*, [1982] O.J. No. 3314, 69 C.C.C. (2d) 204 at 213 (Ont. C.A.), leave to appeal refused [1982] S.C.C.A. No. 105, 45 N.R. 534*n* (S.C.C.). See also *R. c. Gélinas*, [1994] J.Q. no 631, 94 C.C.C. (3d) 69 (Que. C.A.).

[52] [1982] O.J. No. 3314, 69 C.C.C. (2d) 204 at 213 (Ont. C.A.), leave to appeal refused [1982] S.C.C.A. No. 105, 45 N.R. 534*n* (S.C.C.).

[53] *Ibid.*, at 209-10 (C.C.C.). See *e.g.*, *R. v. Hogle* (1896), 5 C.C.C. 53 (Que. Q.B.) and *R. v. Solloway*, [1933] O.J. No. 396, 61 C.C.C. 297 (Ont. C.A.), both involving frauds where the scheme began in one province but was completed in another. See also *R. v. L. (D.A.)*, [1996] B.C.J. No. 930, 107 C.C.C. (3d) 178 (B.C.C.A.) (same).

[54] *R. v. Bigelow*, [1982] O.J. No. 3314, 69 C.C.C. (2d) 204 at 210-12 (Ont. C.A.), leave to appeal refused [1982] S.C.C.A. No. 105, 45 N.R. 534*n* (S.C.C.). See *e.g.*, *R. v. Horbas*, [1968] M.J. No. 14, [1969] 3 C.C.C. 95 (Man. C.A.), receipt of package in Manitoba was sufficient to give courts there jurisdiction, even though conspiracy occurred mostly in Alberta. See also *R. v. Shulman*, [1946] J.Q. no 14, 2 C.R. 153 (Que. K.B.) (overt acts of conspiracy initiated in Quebec, although proceeds obtained elsewhere, sufficient to give Quebec court jurisdiction).

[55] *R. v. Bigelow*, [1982] O.J. No. 3314, 69 C.C.C. (2d) 204 at 212-13 (Ont. C.A.), leave to appeal refused [1982] S.C.C.A. No. 105, 45 N.R. 534*n* (S.C.C.). See *e.g.*, *The Queen v. Gillespie* (1898), 1 C.C.C. 551 (Que. Q.B.) (a false prospectus was prepared in Ontario but mailed to Quebec; this was sufficient to also give courts in Quebec jurisdiction).

end. After exercising that right, he then flew the child to Calgary and subsequently refused to return the child home. The Court concluded that the Ontario courts had jurisdiction to try the charge on two bases. First, the Court characterized the accused's boarding of the plane with the child as an overt act that took place in Ontario, which alone supplied the courts in that province with jurisdiction. An even more compelling basis for conferring jurisdiction on Ontario, the Court found, was the fact that the effects of the accused's acts in keeping the child in Alberta were felt in Ontario where the mother was deprived of custody.[56]

§12.20 In our view, the three bases identified in *Bigelow* for assuming jurisdiction under section 476(*b*) of the *Code* are merely (non-exhaustive) examples of the more general "real and substantial link" principle discussed in Part 2(1), above in the context of extraterritorial jurisdiction.[57] There is no reason why the principles governing extraterritorial jurisdiction should not also apply in the interprovincial context.

(3)   Transfer for Guilty Plea

§12.21 Another exception to the general rule restricting provinces to crimes committed within their boundaries is found in subsection 478(3). That subsection allows anyone who intends to plead guilty to an offence, other than an offence listed in section 469 (*e.g.*, murder), to have the case dealt with in a province other than the province where the offence was committed. The transfer may only occur, however, with the consent of the appropriate Attorney General in the province where the proceedings were initiated.[58] Once the charge is transferred, the accused must plead to the offence as charged — the charge cannot be pled down in the second province.[59] Nor can the accused proceed to trial in the receiving province. Rather, the jurisdiction of the second province is contingent on the accused pleading guilty. Failing that, the charge must be returned to the original province. (As we will see below, there is a parallel provision for the transfer and resolution of charges within a province.)

---

[56]   *R. v. Bigelow*, [1982] O.J. No. 3314, 69 C.C.C. (2d) 204 at 212-13 (Ont. C.A.), leave to appeal refused [1982] S.C.C.A. No. 105, 45 N.R. 534*n* (S.C.C.).

[57]   *R. v. Libman*, [1985] S.C.J. No. 56, [1985] 2 S.C.R. 178 at 213 (S.C.C.). See also *R. v. Hammerbeck*, [1993] B.C.J. No. 685, 26 B.C.A.C. 1 at para. 22 (B.C.C.A.) ("The test in *Libman* encompasses the test in *Bigelow* ...."); *R. v. Doer*, [1999] M.J. No. 40, [1999] 12 W.W.R. 684 at paras. 89-90 (Man. Q.B.) (applying "real and substantial link" test to interprovincial jurisdiction); *R. v. Edwards*, [2008] N.B.J. No. 312, 337 N.B.R. (2d) 206 at paras. 12-14 (N.B. Prov. Ct.) (same).

[58]   If it is a *Criminal Code* offence, the provincial Crown in the originating jurisdiction must consent. For other federal crimes, like drug charges, it will be the federal Crown. On the division of prosecutorial responsibilities, see Chapter 8, Part 2.

[59]   Nevertheless, the court in the receiving province is not necessarily bound by any joint position agreed upon by way of plea-bargain in the sending province. See *R. v. Shaw*, [2005] B.C.J. No. 1648, 199 C.C.C. (3d) 93 (B.C.C.A.) (allowing appeal where sentence excessive by British Columbia standards); *R. v. Lister*, [2003] B.C.J. No. 1078, 175 C.C.C. (3d) 528 (B.C.C.A.) (sentence reduced on appeal because agreement resulted in excessive sentence under both Saskatchewan and British Columbia standards).

4. INTRA-PROVINCIAL LIMITS

(1) Generally

§12.22 By comparison to those rules that govern the extraterritorial and inter-provincial application of the criminal law, the rules governing intra-provincial jurisdiction are far more permissive. Though there is a longstanding presumption that a person charged with an offence should be tried in the place where the crime allegedly occurred,[60] given the permissive way in which the *Code* now grants jurisdiction to criminal courts in the province, today this is more of an expectation than a legal presumption. In practice, the championing of that idea as a firm presumption tends to occur when the accused seeks to change the trial venue.

(2) Territorial Jurisdiction of Courts within Province: Section 470 of the *Code*

§12.23 Section 470 of the *Code* gives all the criminal courts within a province an expansive jurisdiction to try offences no matter where they are alleged to have been committed within the province.[61] Because of section 470, the key determinant is no longer where the offence occurred but where the accused happens to be. Section 470 provides:

> Subject to this Act, every superior court of criminal jurisdiction and every court of criminal jurisdiction that has power to try an indictable offence is competent to try an accused for that offence
>
> (*a*) if the accused is found, is arrested or is in custody within the territorial jurisdiction of the court; or
>
> (*b*) if the accused has been ordered to be tried by
>
> (i) that court, or
>
> (ii) any other court, the jurisdiction of which has by lawful authority been transferred to that court.

§12.24 There are two conflicting lines of authority interpreting subsection 470(*a*). The vast majority of decisions read the provision literally, so that once an accused is before a particular criminal court (because he is "found", "arrested" or "in custody" in that court's territorial division), that court has jurisdiction

---

[60] This was a rule at common law. See *Rex v. Harris* (1762), 97 E.R. 858 at 860 (K.B.) ("There was no rule better established than 'that all causes shall be tried in the county, and by the neighbourhood of the place, where the fact is committed.'"). See also *R. v. Ponton*, [1898] O.J. No. 206, 2 C.C.C. 192 at 197 (Ont. H.C.J.); *R. v. O'Gorman*, [1909] O.J. No. 50, 15 C.C.C. 173 at 178 (Ont. C.A.); *The King v. Lynn*, [1910] S.J. No. 1, 19 C.C.C. 129 at 136-37 (Sask. S.C.).

[61] Beyond s. 470, it is also important to bear in mind s. 504 (discussed in greater detail in Chapter 5, Part 2). That provision essentially permits a justice to receive an information charging an offence that was committed "anywhere" provided that it "may be tried in the province in which the justice resides". See *Criminal Code*, s. 504. In short, s. 504 is entirely permissive on the question of territorial jurisdiction; it leaves for other sections (those discussed in this chapter) the thornier questions of what offences courts can try.

regardless of where in the province the offence was allegedly committed.[62] On this interpretation, "the common law rule has been abrogated by section 470 of the *Criminal Code*."[63]

§12.25 In a small minority of cases, however, the court has taken a far narrower view of the subsection. These decisions emphasize the common law presumption that trials should occur in the locale where an offence was allegedly committed to resist the plain wording of section 470(*a*). The plain language reading of the provision, these courts have reasoned, would allow the Crown to unfairly select a venue of its choosing.[64] Unfortunately, these decisions fail to offer a convincing explanation as to the purpose and effect of section 470(*a*). Without that, the plain meaning of the provision would seem to control. Nevertheless, where the Crown's choice of venue takes an accused far away from potential witnesses and thereby interferes with the ability to make full answer and defence, relief under the *Charter*[65] would surely be available.[66]

---

[62] See *Re Seeley*, [1908] S.C.J. No. 49, 14 C.C.C. 270 at 280 (S.C.C.) (interpreting an earlier version of the section and concluding that "when an offence is committed *within the limits of a province* any presence, however transitory, of the accused in any part of that province will justify the exercise of as full and complete jurisdiction as if the offence was committed where the offender is apprehended, leaving to the magistrate a discretionary power to send the prisoner for further inquiry or for trial before the justice having jurisdiction over the locus where the offence was committed") [emphasis in original]. See also *R. v. Thornton* (1915), 26 C.C.C. 120 (Alta. S.C.) (Court had jurisdiction to try offence allegedly committed in different territorial division because accused was in custody within its territorial division); *The King v. Lynn*, [1910] S.J. No. 1, 19 C.C.C. 129 at 136-37 (Sask. S.C.) (same); *R. v. Nevison*, [1919] B.C.J. No. 32, 31 C.C.C. 116 (B.C.C.A.) (same); *R. v. Roberts* (1928), 49 C.C.C. 171 (Sask. C.A.) (same); *R. v. Abbot*, [1944] O.J. No. 436, 81 C.C.C. 174 (Ont. C.A.), leave to appeal refused [1944] S.C.J. No. 25, [1944] S.C.R. 264 (S.C.C.) (same); *R. v. Falkner*, [1977] B.C.J. No. 1122, 37 C.C.C. (2d) 330 (B.C.C.A.), affd [1978] B.C.J. No. 1113 (B.C.C.A.) (same). See also *Katz v. Rice*, [1967] M.J. No. 4, [1968] 3 C.C.C. 85 at para. 15 (Man. C.A.) (by appearing before the court and entering a plea, the accused was "in custody within the territorial jurisdiction of the court", so that under what is now s. 470(*a*) a court in Winnipeg had jurisdiction to try accused for offence allegedly committed in St. Boniface).

[63] Roger E. Salhany, *Canadian Criminal Procedure*, 6th ed., looseleaf (Aurora, ON: Canada Law Book, 1994) at para. 2.370.

[64] See *R. v. O'Gorman*, [1909] O.J. No. 50, 15 C.C.C. 173 (Ont. C.A.) (interpreting an earlier version of the subsection and concluding that the accused were not in custody or apprehended within the jurisdiction where they were ultimately tried, given that they were compelled there by legal process); *R. v. Sarazin*, [1978] P.E.I.J. No. 63, 39 C.C.C. (2d) 131 at 135 (P.E.I.S.C.) (the words "is in custody within the territorial jurisdiction of the court" do not give the court in one region jurisdiction where an accused was arrested in a different region, "otherwise it would be open to the Crown to select jurisdiction for trial by the simple process of arranging to have an accused held in custody in the jurisdiction of its choice" concluding that this "was never the intent of the legislature"). See also *R. v. Simons*, [1967] O.J. No. 152, 30 C.C.C. (2d) 162 (Ont. C.A.) (acknowledging the dominant strand of authority, but noting that police have no power when releasing accused on promise to appear to direct him to appear in court in different locale than where the offence allegedly occurred).

[65] *Canadian Charter of Rights and Freedoms*, Part I of the *Constitution Act, 1982*, being Schedule B to the *Canada Act 1982* (U.K.), 1982, c. 11 [*Charter*].

[66] See *R. v. Ittoshat*, [1970] Q.J. No. 26, [1970] 5 C.C.C. 159 (Que. Sess.) (stay of proceedings where Crown moved trial to location far removed from potential witnesses). Given the *Charter* jurisprudence governing stays of proceedings (see Chapter 10, Part 5(1)), it is rather unlikely that a stay would be ordered today. It is much more likely that the court would order that the

§12.26 Section 470(*b*) takes things even further. It permits a justice presiding over a preliminary inquiry in one territorial region to order the accused to stand trial before a court located in a different territorial region within the province; there is no requirement that the accused be present in that second region at the time of the committal.[67]

§12.27 Thankfully, practical constraints inhibit the Crown from using section 470 to engage in forum shopping. Just like the accused, the Crown usually has a vested interest in keeping the prosecution in the location where the crime is alleged to have occurred. That is where the victim, witnesses and investigating police officers will ordinarily be located. Nevertheless, the Crown may occasionally have practical or tactical reasons for moving a case elsewhere in the province. Given that an accused who wishes to change the venue of trial must first convince a judge that doing so is expedient to the ends of justice, the use of this prosecutorial power is troubling. (Change of venue applications are discussed in Part 4(4), below.)

(3) Transfer for Guilty Plea

§12.28 Section 479 of the *Code* permits an accused charged with an offence, other than an offence listed in section 469 (*e.g.*, murder), to have a charge dealt with in a territorial division within the province other than the one that would ordinarily have jurisdiction. A precondition is that the appropriate Attorney General must consent.[68] If such consent is obtained, the accused may plead guilty to the offence in the receiving region. Once the charge is transferred, the accused must plead to the offence as charged, the charge cannot be pled down or tried in the second region. Rather, the jurisdiction of the court in the receiving territorial division is contingent on the accused pleading guilty. Failing that, the charges must be returned to the original court. (As we saw in Part 3(3), above, there is a parallel provision for the transfer and resolution of charges between provinces.)

(4) Change of Venue

§12.29 As noted above, there is a longstanding presumption that criminal cases should be tried in the locale where the offence was allegedly committed.[69] As the Ontario Court of Appeal has explained: "The theory still is that local offences shall be tried locally, and not alone out of consideration for the prisoner, but in order that each locality may in this way be made to bear its proper share of

---

trial be relocated or that the Crown be required to cover the expense of transporting and accommodating defence witnesses.

[67] See *e.g.*, *R. v. McMorris*, [1971] O.J. No. 1931, 4 C.C.C. (2d) 268 at 270 (Ont. Co. Ct.).

[68] If it is a *Criminal Code* offence, the provincial Crown in the territorial division where the charge was initially laid. For other federal crimes, like drug charges, it will be the federal Crown. On the division of prosecutorial responsibility see Chapter 8, Part 2.

[69] See Part 4(1), above.

enforcing the criminal law against the local offender."[70] Most often, both the accused and Crown will prefer the trial to remain in the locale where a charge originates.[71] The accused person's family, friends and potential witnesses are likely to be close by, as are the complainant, the investigating police officers and the Crown's other witnesses.

§12.30 Nevertheless, it is easy to imagine circumstances in which a party may want to avoid a trial in the jurisdiction where the offence allegedly occurred. For example, imagine a small town where there has been extensive, sustained and prejudicial pre-trial publicity and the community's mood is hostile toward the accused.[72] Changing the trial venue requires an application under section 599 of the *Criminal Code*.[73] That section provides, in part:

> (1) A court before which an accused is or may be indicted, at any term or sittings thereof, or a judge who may hold or sit in that court, may at any time before or after an indictment is found, on the application of the prosecutor or the accused, order the trial to be held in a territorial division in the same province other than that in which the offence would otherwise be tried if
>
> > (*a*) it appears expedient to the ends of justice, or
> >
> > (*b*) a competent authority has directed that a jury is not to be summoned at the time appointed in a territorial division where the trial would otherwise by law be held.

§12.31 The key subsection is 599(1)(*a*). To succeed, the moving party (usually the accused)[74] must demonstrate that it would be "expedient to the ends of justice" to relocate the trial to a different territorial division within the province.[75] What does this mean?

---

[70]   *R. v. O'Gorman*, [1909] O.J. No. 50, 15 C.C.C. 173 at 178 (Ont. C.A.).

[71]   See *R. v. Suzack*, [2000] O.J. No. 100, 141 C.C.C. (3d) 449 at para. 30 (Ont. C.A.) (Noting that "[t]his principle serves both the interests of the community and those of the accused").

[72]   See *e.g.*, *R. v. MacNeil*, [1993] N.S.J. No. 406, 125 N.S.R. (2d) 346 (N.S.S.C.) (application granted in a case involving a notorious triple murder at a McDonald's restaurant in a small town in Nova Scotia).

[73]   The Ontario Court of Appeal concluded in *R. v. Suzack*, [2000] O.J. No. 100, 141 C.C.C. (3d) 449 at para. 44 (Ont. C.A.) that established change of venue procedures are consistent with the fair trial right guaranteed to accused persons by s. 11(*d*) of the *Charter*. As Doherty J. explained, "[T]he right to a fair trial [does not] require a change of venue wherever pre-trial publicity poses a risk to that right. The risk will exist to some extent in virtually every case where there has been pre-trial publicity. The right to a fair trial is compromised where despite the available safeguards there is a reasonable likelihood that an accused cannot receive a fair trial in the local venue."

[74]   But see *R. v. Fatt*, [1986] N.W.T.J. No. 29, 30 C.C.C. (3d) 69 (N.W.T.S.C.) (Crown change of venue application granted where only 300 people lived in community and evidence established that residents were biased against victim and in favour of accused).

[75]   The language of s. 599(1) ("to be held in a territorial division in the same province") does not permit a case to be moved to another province. See *R. v. Threinen*, [1976] S.J. No. 399, 30 C.C.C. (2d) 42 (Sask. Q.B.).

§12.32 The courts have consistently held that this determination is one that lies within the discretion of the judge hearing the motion.[76] In exercising that discretion a judge is required to consider whether a change of venue is necessary in order to ensure that an accused has a fair trial with an impartial jury.[77] In making this decision the judge is to weigh those factors that are for and against granting the motion,[78] including the ameliorative effects of established trial safeguards, such as challenges for cause, the oath taken by jurors, the rules of evidence and the trial judge's instructions to the jury.[79] As the Ontario Court of Appeal explained: "If a judge is satisfied, having regard to the various mechanisms available to protect an accused's right to a fair trial, that an accused cannot receive a fair trial in the assigned venue, then the interests of justice would clearly require a change of venue under s. 599(1)(a)."[80]

§12.33 The motivation for most change of venue applications is publicity adverse to the accused.[81] Such applications, however, are rarely successful. The cases make clear that extensive publicity, even of a sensationalistic nature, does not necessarily justify a change of venue. To succeed, there typically must be "very strong evidence of a general prejudicial attitude in the community as a whole."[82] The reporting of the allegations alone is therefore usually not enough to warrant a change of venue.[83] Similarly, the courts have distinguished between hostility toward a particular crime and prejudice toward the accused — only the latter militates in favour of changing the venue.[84] Further, courts have often

---

[76] See *R. v. Collins*, [1989] O.J. No. 488, 48 C.C.C. (3d) 343 at 350 (Ont. C.A.) ("the decision is one that lies within the discretion of the judge hearing the motion"). See also in *R. v. Suzack*, [2000] O.J. No. 100, 141 C.C.C. (3d) 449 at para. 31 (Ont. C.A.) (same); *R. v. Hutchison*, [1975] N.B.J. No. 108, 26 C.C.C. (2d) 423 at para. 22 (N.B.S.C.), affd [1976] S.C.J. No. 92 (S.C.C.) (same).

[77] *R. v. Collins*, [1989] O.J. No. 488, 48 C.C.C. (3d) 343 at 350-51 (Ont. C.A.) ("The fundamental consideration is whether the change of venue is necessary in order to ensure that an accused has a fair trial with an impartial jury."). See also *R. v. Adams*, [1946] O.J. No. 607, 86 C.C.C. 425 at 428 (Ont. H.C.J.) (same); *R. v. Suzack*, [2000] O.J. No. 100, 141 C.C.C. (3d) 449 at para. 31 (Ont. C.A.) (same); *R. v. Charest*, [1990] J.Q. no 405, 57 C.C.C. (3d) 312 (Que. C.A.) (same); *R. v. Proulx*, [1992] J.Q. no 1400, 76 C.C.C. (3d) 316 (Que. C.A.) (same).

[78] *R. v. Suzack*, [2000] O.J. No. 100, 141 C.C.C. (3d) 449 at para. 31 (Ont. C.A.).

[79] See *R. v. Fitzgerald*, [1981] O.J. No. 823, 23 C.R. (3d) 163 at 171-72 (Ont. H.C.J.); *R. v. Suzack*, [2000] O.J. No. 100, 141 C.C.C. (3d) 449 at paras. 35-36 (Ont. C.A.); *R. v. Sandham*, [2008] O.J. No. 5806 at para. 45 (Ont. S.C.J.).

[80] *R. v. Suzack*, [2000] O.J. No. 100, 141 C.C.C. (3d) 449 at para. 42 (Ont. C.A.).

[81] But see *R. v. Falkner*, [1979] B.C.J. No. 1123, 45 C.C.C. (2d) 146 (B.C. Co. Ct.) (change of venue granted to location where preponderance of offence-related events occurred and accused resided).

[82] *R. v. Alward*, [1976] N.B.J. No. 220, 32 C.C.C. (2d) 416 at 427 (N.B.S.C.), affd on other grounds [1977] S.C.J. No. 63, [1977] 1 S.C.R. 559 (S.C.C.). See also *R. v. Proulx*, [1992] J.Q. no 1400, 76 C.C.C. (3d) 316 at 335-36 (Que. C.A.) (same).

[83] *R. v. Suzack*, [2000] O.J. No. 100, 141 C.C.C. (3d) 449 at para. 38 (Ont. C.A.), noting that: "Where the real potential for prejudice lies in the evidence which the jury eventually selected to try the case will hear, a change of venue does not assist in protecting an accused's right to a fair trial." See also *R. v. Tremblay*, [1978] J.Q. no. 242, 45 C.C.C. (2d) 238 (Que. S.C.) (prior knowledge of facts and accused on the part of prospective jurors not enough).

[84] See *R. v. Turvey*, [1970] N.S.J. No. 115, 1 C.C.C. (2d) 90 at 95 (N.S.T.D.), explaining that: "I have been satisfied only that any prejudice likely to exist arises out of the very nature of the

denied change of venue applications on the basis that concerns about adverse publicity can be adequately addressed by the trial safeguards mentioned above, especially where counsel are permitted to challenge potential jurors for cause because of such publicity.[85]

§12.34 That said, change of venue applications have been allowed where the publicity was extensive and included prejudicial and likely inadmissible information.[86] They have similarly succeeded where there is overwhelming and widespread sympathy toward the alleged victim of a crime in the community.[87]

§12.35 Lastly, it should be noted that there is a further basis to change the trial venue set out in section 531 of the *Criminal Code*, which relates to the right of accused persons to be tried in one of Canada's official languages. A change of venue is mandatory under this provision when the accused wishes to be tried in his or her own official language (*i.e.*, English or French), but that request cannot be conveniently complied with in the region where the trial is scheduled to occur.

---

offence and nothing else. I am not satisfied that such would be a proper reason for the decision that it is probable that there could not be a fair and impartial trial in Kings County and that there could be elsewhere. I find that this alone could not be a ground upon which the motion could be granted." See also *R. v. Vaillancourt*, [1973] O.J. No. 2375, 14 C.C.C. (2d) 136 at 138 (Ont. H.C.J.), affd on other grounds [1974] O.J. No. 91, 16 C.C.C. (2d) 137 (Ont. C.A.), affd [1975] S.C.J. No. 23 (S.C.C.)

[85]   See *e.g.*, *R. v. Munson*, [2003] S.J. No. 161, 172 C.C.C. (3d) 515 at para. 23 (Sask. C.A.); *R. v. Badgerow*, [2009] O.J. No. 3721 at para. 39 (Ont. S.C.J.); *R. v. Sandham*, [2008] O.J. No. 5806 at paras. 39, 48 (Ont. S.C.J.). Challenges for cause are discussed in detail in Chapter 15, Part 1(2)(*d*).

[86]   See *R. v. Frederick*, [1978] O.J. No. 549, 41 C.C.C. (2d) 532 (Ont. H.C.J.); *R. v. Kully*, [1973] O.J. No. 2278, 15 C.C.C. (2d) 488 (Ont. H.C.J.); *R. v. Upton*, [1922] O.J. No. 705, 37 C.C.C. 15 (Ont. S.C.); *R. v. DeBruge*, [1927] O.J. No. 30, 47 C.C.C. 311 (Ont. S.C.); *R. v. Proulx*, [1992] J.Q. no 1400, 76 C.C.C. (3d) 316 (Que. C.A.); *R. v. Bridson*, [1994] M.J. No. 307, 99 Man. R. (2d) 6 (Man. Q.B.).

[87]   See *e.g.*, *R. v. Talbot*, [1977] O.J. No. 2596, 38 C.C.C. (2d) 555 (Ont. H.C.J.).

Chapter 13

TEMPORAL LIMITS

1. INTRODUCTION

§13.1 The idea that "justice delayed is justice denied" can be traced back through the "mists of time".[1] As long ago as 1215, King John promised in the *Magna Carta*[2] that "To no one will we sell, to no one will we refuse *or delay, right or justice.*"[3] Timely adjudication of criminal matters serves the interests of many. The public is assured that criminals are being dealt with promptly; victims receive a measure of closure; and accused persons do not languish in jail or carry the stigma of a criminal charge for an extended period of time. As we will see in this chapter, the temporal limits prescribed both by statute and the *Charter*[4] strive to meet all of these needs. Because limitation periods are usually associated with civil actions, it is important to begin by pointing out the distinction between the two systems. Civil limitation periods typically act to bar remedies, while temporal limits in criminal law create a bar to the prosecution itself.

2. STATUTORY LIMITATION PERIODS

§13.2 Unlike in many American states where "statutes of limitation" are common, there is only one true limitation period in Canadian criminal law.[5] Section 786(2) of the *Criminal Code*[6] provides that for summary conviction offences, "[n]o proceedings shall be instituted more than six months after the time when the subject-matter of the proceedings arose, unless the prosecutor and the defendant so agree." With respect to true summary offences, section 786(2) does indeed create a limitation period. However, as noted in Chapter 1, Part 2(3)(*b*), there are very few offences that fall into this category and all of them are comparatively minor. Subsection 786(2) also serves as a bar to the Crown electing to

---

[1]   *Blencoe v. British Columbia (Human Rights Commission)*, [2000] S.C.J. No. 43, [2000] 2 S.C.R. 307 at para. 146 (S.C.C.), *per* LeBel J., dissenting in part. See also *R. v. Rahey*, [1987] S.C.J. No. 23, [1987] 1 S.C.R. 588 at 636 (S.C.C.), *per* La Forest J.(the right to a speedy trial has been "a right known to the common law ... for more than 750 years").

[2]   9 Hen. III, c. 29.

[3]   *Magna Carta*, cl. 40 (1215) [emphasis added]. See also 9 Hen. III, c. 29, s. 2 ("We will sell to no man, we will not deny, *or defer*, to any man, either justice or right.") [emphasis added]).

[4]   *Canadian Charter of Rights and Freedoms*, Part I of the *Constitution Act, 1982*, being Schedule B to the *Canada Act 1982* (U.K.), 1982, c. 11 [*Charter*].

[5]   In contrast, it is not unusual to see time limitations in non-criminal contexts, including in regulatory matters. See *e.g.*, *Provincial Offences Act*, R.S.O. 1990, c. P.33, s. 76(1).

[6]   R.S.C. 1985, c. C-46 [*Code*].

proceed summarily with respect to a hybrid offence where the charge is laid more than six months after the events that give rise to the charge.

§13.3 It is hard to imagine why a defendant would consent to an out-of-time prosecution for a pure summary offence.[7] In the case of hybrid offences, however, the incentive for both the prosecutor and the defendant to consent, at least where the offence is relatively minor, is considerable. For the prosecutor, proceeding summarily avoids a preliminary hearing and the possibility of a jury trial.[8] For the defendant, it avoids exposure to a much lengthier maximum punishment and some of the harsher consequences that can accompany a conviction for an indictable offence.

§13.4 Where the offence is punishable only on summary conviction and the defendant declines to consent[9] to the proceedings continuing, the prosecution cannot proceed in any form. If the fact that the proceeding is statute-barred is discovered before the trial commences, the court should simply dismiss the information.[10] If it is discovered after the trial has commenced but before an adjudication on the merits, the judge should declare a mistrial.[11] And if it is discovered on the appeal of a conviction, the conviction should be set aside.[12]

§13.5 Where consent is denied for a hybrid matter, in contrast, the Crown may simply choose to proceed by indictment,[13] so long as there is no evidence that discloses an "abuse of process arising from improper Crown motive, or resulting prejudice to the accused sufficient to violate the community's sense of fair play and decency."[14] Before the trial commences, the Crown may simply "re-elect" to proceed by indictment — the original information remains valid and the proceedings will continue as an indictable matter.[15] If the trial has already commenced, the proceedings may not continue. As mentioned above, if it becomes apparent that the charge is statute-barred before an adjudication on the merits, a

---

7 One possibility was mooted by the Court in *R. v. Dudley*, [2009] S.C.J. No. 58, [2009] 3 S.C.R. 570 at para. 30 (S.C.C.) ("[T]he accused may nonetheless agree to proceed beyond the limitation period to avoid prosecution by indictment for a related offence that covers the same conduct.").

8 The differences between summary and indictable proceedings are discussed in Chapter 1, Part 2.

9 See *R. v. Dudley*, [2009] S.C.J. No. 58, [2009] 3 S.C.R. 570 at para. 35 (S.C.C.), where Fish J. explained, "The consent of the parties, I repeat, can be given at any time during the proceedings before the verdict. The prosecutor will always be deemed to have consented by virtue of his or her election to try the hybrid offence summarily. The defendant must consent to the proceedings in a manner consistent with the reasons of the Court in *Korponay v. Attorney General of Canada*, [1982] S.C.J. No. 111, [1982] 1 S.C.R. 41. That is to say, the consent of the defendant to continue with the proceedings must be 'informed, clear and unequivocal': *Korponay*, at p. 58."

10 *R. v. Dudley*, [2009] S.C.J. No. 58, [2009] 3 S.C.R. 570 at paras. 37-38 (S.C.C.). See also *R. v. Belair*, [1988] O.J. No. 239, 41 C.C.C. (3d) 329 (Ont. C.A.).

11 *R. v. Dudley*, [2009] S.C.J. No. 58, [2009] 3 S.C.R. 570 at para. 3 (S.C.C.).

12 *Ibid.*, at paras. 4-5 (S.C.R.).

13 *Ibid.*, at paras. 5, 31(S.C.R.); *R. v. Karpinski*, [1957] S.C.J. No. 18, [1957] S.C.R. 343 (S.C.C.).

14 *R. v. Dudley*, [2009] S.C.J. No. 58, [2009] 3 S.C.R. 570 at para. 44 (S.C.C.), quoting the decision of the court below, [2008] A.J. No. 209, 2008 ABCA 73 at para. 1 (Alta. C.A.). See also Chapter 9, Part 2(1)(*b*).

15 *Ibid.*

mistrial must be declared; if this becomes apparent on a conviction appeal, the court must set aside the conviction. But in either case the Crown may lay a new information and proceed by indictment (absent an abuse of process).

§13.6 The prosecution will not be able to prosecute a hybrid offence again, however, when the court determines on an appeal of an acquittal that the matter was statute-barred.[16] "Having elected to proceed by way of summary conviction," the Supreme Court of Canada held in *R. v. Dudley*,[17] "... the Crown should not be heard to complain *after an adverse adjudication on the merits* that it neglected to obtain the consent of the accused before the accused was acquitted!"[18] Any attempt to try the accused again on indictment would be barred by the principle of double jeopardy, since the accused would have been finally acquitted of the offence. It does not constitute double jeopardy, in contrast, to prosecute the accused again after a mistrial or conviction is set aside on appeal.[19]

3. UNREASONABLE DELAY (SECTION 11(*B*) OF THE *CHARTER*)

§13.7 Section 11(*b*) of the *Charter* guarantees that any person charged with an offence has the right to be tried within a reasonable time. As mentioned above, as a general rule, speedy trials serve the interests of everyone involved in the criminal justice process, including the accused and society at large. The purpose of section 11(*b*) is to ensure that these interests are vindicated. As the Supreme Court of Canada explained in *R. v. Morin*,[20] the provision protects the accused by minimizing "the anxiety, concern and stigma of exposure to criminal proceedings," minimizing "exposure to the restrictions on liberty which result from pretrial incarceration and restrictive bail conditions," and ensuring "that proceedings take place while evidence is available and fresh."[21] The right serves society, the Court noted, by "ensuring that those who transgress the law are brought to trial and dealt with according to the law."[22]

§13.8 Early jurisprudence on section 11(*b*) propelled the *Charter* to the forefront of society's consciousness, perhaps unlike any other section. The Supreme Court of Canada's decision in *R. v. Askov*[23] had an unprecedented and seismic impact on the administration of justice. Trial judges throughout the country began applying mechanical formulae in staying charges deemed to have violated

---

16   *Ibid.*, at paras. 7, 31.
17   [2009] S.C.J. No. 58, [2009] 3 S.C.R. 570 (S.C.C.).
18   *Ibid.*, at para. 6 (S.C.R.). [emphasis in original].
19   *Ibid.*, at para. 5 (S.C.R.). Double jeopardy is discussed more extensively in Chapter 14, Part 3.
20   [1992] S.C.J. No. 25, [1992] 1 S.C.R. 771 (S.C.C.) [*Morin*].
21   *Ibid.*, at 786-87 (S.C.R.).
22   *Ibid.*, at 787 (S.C.R.), quoting *R. v. Askov*, [1990] S.C.J. No. 106, [1990] 2 S.C.R. 1199 at 1219-20 (S.C.C.).
23   [1990] S.C.J. No. 106, 59 C.C.C. (3d) 449 (S.C.C.) [*Askov*].

the six-to-eight-month rule purportedly set out in *Askov*.[24] Public outcry mounted as charges by the thousands were "thrown out of court" in the wake of the decision.[25]

§13.9 Consequently, the Supreme Court moved uncharacteristically quickly to revisit the issue, issuing its decision in *Morin*[26] a mere 17 months after *Askov*. In *Morin*, the Court acknowledged the fallout from *Askov*'s perceived *dicta*, and stated in much clearer language that the approach to determining whether an individual's right to trial within a reasonable time has been infringed "is not by the application of a mathematical or administrative formula but rather by a judicial determination balancing the interests which the section is designed to protect against factors which either inevitably lead to delay or are otherwise the cause of delay."[27] Since the uncharted waters of *Askov* and *Morin*, the development of the jurisprudence relating to section 11(*b*) has been much less turbulent. Trial judges have become accustomed to their duties of balancing the factors having an impact on both an individual accused and the public at large in determining whether section 11(*b*) has been breached. Further calming the waters, appellate courts have afforded a high degree of deference to trial judges' section 11(*b*) rulings.

§13.10 The accused has the onus of proving a breach of section 11(*b*) of the *Charter* on a balance of probabilities. If an accused is successful in discharging its burden, "[n]o flexibility exists; a stay of proceedings must be ordered."[28] As discussed in more detail in Chapter 10, Part 5(1)(*a*)(i), this distinguishes section 11(*b*) from all other *Charter* rights; stays of proceedings are awarded for violations of other *Charter* rights only in the "clearest of cases".[29]

(1) Applicable Factors

§13.11 In *Askov* and *Morin*, the Supreme Court of Canada identified the factors to be considered in deciding section 11(*b*) claims as: *(i)* the length of the delay; *(ii)* waiver of time periods; *(iii)* the reasons for the delay (including inherent

---

24   See *R. v. Bennett*, [1991] O.J. No. 884, 6 C.R. (4th) 22 at para. 6 (Ont. C.A.), affd [1992] S.C.J. No. 58 (S.C.C.) (describing impact of [1990] S.C.J. No. 106, [1990] 2 S.C.R. 1199 (S.C.C.) in Ontario as "staggering"). See also Don Stuart, *Charter Justice in Canadian Criminal Law*, 5th ed. (Toronto: Thomson Carswell, 2010) at 400-402.

25   Gene Allen, "32,000 charges stayed since Askov ruling — Hampton says 60,000 counts still at risk" *The Globe and Mail* (March 27, 1991) A10; Editorial, "Supreme Court gets a black eye" *The Toronto Star* (July17, 1991) A20; Paul Wells, "The Charter in Action — How court decisions have changed real lives; The Askov ruling brought more grief for a dead man's parents" *The Gazette* (April 18, 1992) B2.

26   *R. v. Morin*, [1992] S.C.J. No. 25, [1992] 1 S.C.R. 771 (S.C.C.).

27   *Ibid.*, at para. 31 (S.C.R.).

28   *R. v. Rahey*, [1987] S.C.J. No. 23, [1987] 1 S.C.R. 588 at 615 (S.C.C.); *R. v. Kporwodu*, [2005] O.J. No. 1405, 195 C.C.C. (3d) 501 at para. 2 (Ont. C.A.).

29   *R. v. O'Connor*, [1995] S.C.J. No. 98, [1995] 4 S.C.R. 411 at para. 68 (S.C.C.). Stays of proceedings are also awarded automatically as a remedy for entrapment; entrapment claims, however, do not hinge on the violation of any *Charter* rights. Entrapment is discussed more fully in Chapter 10, Part 5(1)(*a*)(ii).

time requirements of the case, actions of the accused, actions of the Crown, limits on institutional resources); and *(iv)* prejudice to the accused.[30]

(a) Length of the Delay

§13.12 A claim made under section 11(*b*) begins with the accused demonstrating that the total length of the delay is exceptional so as to warrant further inquiry by the court. As the Court stated in *Morin*, if "the length of the delay is unexceptional, no inquiry is warranted and no explanation for the delay is called for unless the applicant is able to raise the issue of reasonableness of the period by reference to other factors such as prejudice."[31]

§13.13 The relevant time period starts when the accused was charged with an offence[32] and continues until the completion of the trial, including sentencing.[33] Accordingly, neither pre-charge[34] nor appellate delay[35] is reviewable under section 11(*b*). In exceptional circumstances, however, either of these types of delay may amount to an abuse of process under section 7 of the *Charter*.[36] Though section 11(*b*) claims are usually based on the period of delay between the charge and the beginning of the trial, on occasion the time taken to complete the trial itself may result in unreasonable delay.[37]

---

[30] *R. v. Askov*, [1990] S.C.J. No. 106, [1990] 2 S.C.R. 1199 at 1231-32 (S.C.C.); *R. v. Morin*, [1992] S.C.J. No. 25, [1992] 1 S.C.R. 771 (S.C.C.).

[31] *R. v. Morin*, [1992] S.C.J. No. 25, [1992] 1 S.C.R. 771 at 789 (S.C.C.).

[32] A person is "charged with an offence" within the meaning of s. 11(*b*) "when an information is sworn alleging an offence against him, or where a direct indictment is laid against him when no information is sworn." *R. v. Kalanj*, [1989] S.C.J. No. 71, [1989] 1 S.C.R. 1594 at 1607-1608 (S.C.C.).

[33] See *R. v. MacDougall*, [1998] S.C.J. No. 74, 128 C.C.C. (3d) 483 (S.C.C.); *R. v. Gallant*, [1998] S.C.J. No. 73, 128 C.C.C. (3d) 509 (S.C.C.). See also *R. v. Teskey*, [2003] A.J. No. 648 (Alta. Q.B.); *R. v. Dvorak*, [2002] B.C.J. No. 3032 (B.C.S.C.).

[34] Although in *R. v. L. (W.K.)*, [1991] S.C.J. No. 40, [1991] 1 S.C.R. 1091 (S.C.C.), the Supreme Court left open the availability of a stay of proceedings based on pre-charge delay where there has been an abuse of process. The Court did not, however, define what circumstances would make delay abusive. Successful applications to stay historical prosecutions are rather unusual. For a rare example, see *R. v. MacDonnell*, [1997] S.C.J. No. 16, [1997] 1 S.C.R. 305 (S.C.C.), reversing [1996] N.S.J. No. 65, 47 C.R. (4th) 97 (N.S.C.A.) and thereby restoring the stay of proceedings that had been ordered by the trial judge. See also *R. v. Carter*, [1986] S.C.J. No. 36, [1986] 1 S.C.R. 981 at para. 11 (S.C.C.), *per* Lamer J. (as he then was) ("In passing, I might add that I say 'generally' because there might be exceptional circumstances under which the time might run prior to the actual charge on which the accused will be tried. As an example, if the Crown withdraws the charge to substitute a different one but for the same transaction, the computation of time might well commence as of the first charge.").

[35] *R. v. Potvin*, [1993] S.C.J. No. 63, [1993] 2 S.C.R. 880 (S.C.C.).

[36] *R. v. Kalanj*, [1989] S.C.J. No. 71, [1989] 1 S.C.R. 1594 at 1610-11 (S.C.C.) (pre-charge delay); *R. v. Potvin*, [1993] S.C.J. No. 63, [1993] 2 S.C.R. 880 at 915-16 (S.C.C.) (appellate delay).

[37] See *e.g.*, *R. v. Rahey*, [1987] S.C.J. No. 23, [1987] 1 S.C.R. 588 (S.C.C.) (unreasonable delay where trial judge reserved judgment on a motion for a directed verdict for 11 months; a matter that should have been resolved in a few days).

(b) Waiver

§13.14 If the accused has waived in whole or in part any time periods between the laying of the charge and the end of the trial, the period of time waived will be discounted in deciding whether section 11(*b*) was violated. Justice Sopinka made clear in *Morin*, however, that an accused's waiver must be clear and unequivocal with full knowledge of the rights being waived and of the effect of the waiver on those rights. In the face of such a high standard, the failure of an accused to assert the right, his or her silence, or lack of objection cannot constitute a lawful waiver. For example, an agreement by the accused's counsel to a future trial date that amounts to "mere acquiescence in the inevitable" does not constitute a waiver.[38] Importantly, the Crown has the onus to establish that the accused action's amounted to a waiver of the delay.[39]

(c) Reasons for the Delay

§13.15 If the accused's application is not defeated by waiver, the court must go on to consider other reasons for the delay. As Justice Arbour stated in *R. v. Bennett*,[40] "[u]ltimately, it is the reasonableness of the total period of time that has to be assessed, in the light of the reasons that explain its constituent parts."[41] When taking into account the reasons for delay, the following factors are to be considered: *(i)* inherent time requirements; *(ii)* actions of the accused; *(iii)* actions of the Crown; *(iv)* limits on institutional resources; and *(v)* other reasons for the delay. In brief, factors (*i*) and (*ii*) do not count toward the total time period assessed for reasonableness under section 11(*b*); factors (*iii*) and (*iv*) do count. The significance of factor (*v*), of course, depends on the nature of any "other" reasons for the delay.

§13.16 This process inevitably leads to a minute examination of the particular time periods. But as Justice Cromwell noted in *R. v. Godin*,[42] it is important "not to lose sight of the forest for the trees".[43] In the end, the court must balance the individual's rights to liberty, security of the person and a fair trial against society's interests in seeing that laws are enforced.[44]

(i) Inherent Time Requirements

§13.17 All criminal cases involve inevitable delay. Intake procedures such as bail applications, retaining counsel and preparation of disclosure are necessary aspects of most criminal matters. In *Morin*, the Supreme Court declined to set

---

[38] *R. v. Morin*, [1992] S.C.J. No. 25, [1992] 1 S.C.R. 771 at 790 (S.C.C.).

[39] *R. v. Sapara*, [2001] A.J. No. 256 at para. 33 (Alta. C.A.).

[40] [1991] O.J. No. 884, 64 C.C.C. (3d) 449 (Ont. C.A.), affd [1992] S.C.J. No. 58, 74 C.C.C. (3d) 384 (S.C.C.).

[41] *Ibid.*, at 467 (C.C.C.) (Ont. C.A.).

[42] [2009] S.C.J. No. 26, [2009] 2 S.C.R. 3 (S.C.C.) [*Godin*].

[43] *Ibid.*, at para. 18 (S.C.R.).

[44] See *R. v. Morin*, [1992] S.C.J. No. 25, [1992] 1 S.C.R. 771 at 787 (S.C.C.).

out guidelines for how long these "intake" requirements should take; *de facto* guidelines would emerge in practice, it predicted, based on local conditions.[45]

§13.18 Some types of cases, moreover, will occasion more inherent delay than others, including complex cases, cases with multiple accused and cases involving a preliminary inquiry.[46] Other factors considered to be inherent features of the criminal litigation, despite being beyond the accused's control, include adjournments due to the illness of a principal Crown witness;[47] adjournments resulting from a trial judge's illness;[48] delay caused by the actions of a co-accused;[49] original trial estimates that prove to be inaccurate ,which result in adjournments;[50] and delay attributed to mistrials declared to preserve the fairness of a trial.[51]

§13.19 As the Supreme Court of Canada has stressed, inherent delay also includes the fact that "counsel for the prosecution and the defence cannot be expected to devote their time exclusively to one case."[52] Thus in *Godin*, the Court ruled that the accused's lawyer did not waive the delay occasioned by an adjournment simply because he was not available on the first date offered for a preliminary inquiry.[53] The Court explained:

> Scheduling requires reasonable availability and reasonable cooperation; it does not, for s. 11(b) purposes, require defence counsel to hold themselves in a state of perpetual availability. Here, there is no suggestion that defence counsel was unreasonable in rejecting the earlier date. Indeed, his prior conduct in seeking earlier dates for the preliminary inquiry – efforts which were ignored – suggests that he wished to proceed expeditiously. I respectfully agree with Glithero R.S.J., dissenting in the Court of Appeal, at para. 53, that: "To hold that the delay clock stops as soon as a single available date is offered to the defence and not accepted, in circumstances where the Crown is responsible for the case having to be rescheduled, is not reasonable."[54]

(ii) Actions of the Accused

§13.20 This category addresses the delay caused by the direct acts of the accused. Such acts are not blameworthy; they may be entirely justified by the need to prepare a proper defence. But since they are within the accused's control, they

---

[45] *Ibid.*, at 792-93 (S.C.R.).

[46] *Ibid.*, at 791-93 (S.C.R.); *R. v. Horgan*, [2007] O.J. No. 4844 at para. 22 (Ont. C.A.), leave to appeal to S.C.C. refused [2008] S.C.C.A. No. 62 (S.C.C.); *R. v. Satkunananthan*, [2001] O.J. No. 1019, 152 C.C.C. (3d) 321 at para. 38 (Ont. C.A.).

[47] *R. v. Hoffner*, [2005] O.J. No. 3862 (Ont. S.C.J.).

[48] *R. v. MacDougall*, [1998] S.C.J. No. 74, 128 C.C.C. (3d) 483 (S.C.C.).

[49] *R. v. G. (L.)*, [2007] O.J. No. 3611 at para. 62 (Ont. C.A.).

[50] *R. v. Allen*, [1996] O.J. No. 3175, 110 C.C.C. (3d) 331 (Ont. C.A.), affd without reasons [1997] S.C.J. No. 91, 119 C.C.C. (3d) 1 (S.C.C.).

[51] *R. v. Pizzardi*, [1994] O.J. No. 552 (Ont. C.A.), affd *(sub nom. R. v. Pizzardi; R. v. Levis)*, [1994] S.C.J. No. 109.

[52] *R. v. Morin*, [1992] S.C.J. No. 25, [1992] 1 S.C.R. 771 at 792 (S.C.C.).

[53] *R. v. Godin*, [2009] S.C.J. No. 26, [2009] 2 S.C.R. 3 at paras. 21-23 (S.C.C.).

[54] *Ibid.*, at para. 23 (S.C.R.).

do not count against the Crown in assessing the reasonableness of the delay.[55] Actions of the accused include applications for a change of venue; attacks on wiretap packets; adjournment requests; attacks on search warrants; changes of counsel; re-election; and refusal to set a date where an expert report is not available.[56] Except where the accused's intent to cause delay is readily apparent, the Crown bears the onus of proving that accused is responsible for the delay.[57]

(iii) Actions of the Crown

§13.21 As with the actions of the defence, actions of the Crown causing delay are not necessarily blameworthy.[58] However, since it is the Crown's duty to bring accused persons to trial in a timely manner, and since the Crown's conduct is beyond the accused's control, the period of delay attributable to the Crown counts toward the assessment of reasonableness under section 11(b).[59] Crown conduct considered under this category includes untimely disclosure;[60] adjournment requests; giving priority to other cases;[61] staying and then re-instituting proceedings;[62] deciding to proceed against multiple accused;[63] and failing to try the accused separately from his or her co-accused.[64] Disclosure poses a unique challenge for the Crown, especially in complex fraud trials where the disclosure is extensive and includes expert reports to be prepared by third parties.[65] And with forensic science evidence playing an increasing role in criminal cases, the Crown faces added pressure to obtain expert reports from crime labs in a timely fashion.[66] Where, however, the defence makes a tactical decision to not pursue further disclosure with a view of advancing a section 11(b) claim, the courts have spared the Crown full responsibility for the delay.[67]

(iv) Limits on Institutional Resources

§13.22 Undoubtedly the most common source of delay, institutional or systemic delay, arises when the Crown and the defence are ready to proceed to trial but

---

[55] See *R. v. Morin*, [1992] S.C.J. No. 25, [1992] 1 S.C.R. 771 at 793-94 (S.C.C.).

[56] *Ibid.*, at 793-94 (S.C.R.); *R. v. B. (W.)*, [2000] O.J. No. 2186, 145 C.C.C. (3d) 498 (Ont. C.A.); *R. v. Kovacs-Tatar*, [2004] O.J. No. 4756 (Ont. C.A.).

[57] *R. v. Askov*, [1990] S.C.J. No. 106, [1990] 2 S.C.R. 1199 at paras. 62-63 (S.C.C.).

[58] *R. v. Morin*, [1992] S.C.J. No. 25, [1992] 1 S.C.R. 771 at 794 (S.C.C.).

[59] *Ibid.*, at 794 (S.C.R.); *R. v. Askov*, [1990] S.C.J. No. 106, [1990] 2 S.C.R. 1199 at 1225 (S.C.C.); *R. v. Godin*, [2009] S.C.J. No. 26, [2009] 2 S.C.R. 3 at para. 11 (S.C.C.).

[60] *R. v. Godin*, [2009] S.C.J. No. 26, [2009] 2 S.C.R. 3 (S.C.C.).

[61] *R. v. Whylie*, [2006] O.J. No. 1127, 207 C.C.C. (3d) 97 (Ont. C.A.).

[62] *R. v. Condello*, [1997] O.J. No. 3798 (Ont. Gen. Div.).

[63] *R. v. Whylie*, [2006] O.J. No. 1127, 207 C.C.C. (3d) 97 (Ont. C.A.).

[64] *R. v. Topol*, [2008] O.J. No. 535 (Ont. C.A.); *R. v. Kern*, [1994] B.C.J. No. 2994 (B.C.S.C.).

[65] *R. v. Atkinson*, [1991] O.J. No. 1913, 68 C.C.C. (3d) 109 (Ont. C.A.), affd [1992] S.C.J. No. 91, 76 C.C.C. (3d) 288 (S.C.C.).

[66] See e.g., *R. v. Godin*, [2009] S.C.J. No. 26, [2009] 2 S.C.R. 3 (S.C.C.) (long, unexplained delay in obtaining and disclosing exculpatory DNA analysis contributed to s. 11(b) violation).

[67] *R. v. MacPherson*, [1999] B.C.J. No. 1675 (B.C.C.A.).

the system cannot accommodate them.[68] Like the inherent time requirements to have a criminal matter prepared to proceed to trial, a certain amount of institutional delay is to be expected. However, unlike inherent delay, institutional delay is not discounted from "reasonable time" required by section 11(*b*). For example, Canada's multicultural society may present language barriers to some defendants. Although a brief delay in securing a qualified interpreter in a rare language may be tolerated,[69] the failure of the system to provide any interpreter at all should be delay attributable to the Crown.[70] Indigent accused also add to the strain of institutional resources. While time spent to obtain legal aid may be part of the inherent time needed to retain a lawyer, excessive delays in issuing legal aid certificates may amount to institutional delay.[71]

§13.23 It was the Supreme Court's attempt in *Askov* to set out quantitative guidelines for the maximum amount of institutional delay permitted by section 11(*b*) that caused the turmoil discussed in Part 3, above. As mentioned, in *Morin* the Court clarified that the *Askov* guidelines were to be treated a "suggested period", not a "fixed ceiling".[72]

§13.24 What then are the periods suggested in *Askov* and *Morin* and what are the circumstances that may permit them to be exceeded without violating section 11(*b*)? In provincial court, the suggested period of institutional delay ranges from six to 10 months.[73] This includes matters that are tried in provincial court as well as matters to be tried in the superior court after a preliminary inquiry. The guideline will be exceeded, for example, if the trial or preliminary inquiry concludes more than 10 months after the parties indicated that they were prepared for trial (or in the case of the Crown, the time when it should have been prepared), plus any additional time waived by or attributable to the defence. Once the accused is committed to stand trial at the preliminary inquiry, the suggested period is six to eight months.[74] This guideline will be exceeded, for example, if the trial concludes more than eight months after committal, plus any additional time waived by or attributable to the defence.

§13.25 Beyond the guidelines, two other factors must be considered in deciding whether the quantum of institutional delay violates section 11(*b*). The first is prejudice to the defence. If the accused has been significantly prejudiced, "the period of acceptable institutional delay may be shortened to reflect the court's concern."[75] (We discuss the meaning of prejudice in Part 3(1)(*d*), below.) Unfortunately, the Supreme Court has not made clear whether prejudice may lower

---

[68] *R. v. Morin*, [1992] S.C.J. No. 25, [1992] 1 S.C.R. 771 at 794-95 (S.C.C.).

[69] *R. v. Tamang*, [1998] N.S.J. No. 289 (N.S.C.A.).

[70] *R. v. Sidhu*, [2005] O.J. No. 4881, 203 C.C.C. (3d) 17 at para. 366 (Ont. S.C.J.); *R. v. Satkunananthan*, [2001] O.J. No. 1019, 152 C.C.C. (3d) 321 at 343 (Ont. C.A.).

[71] *R. v. Chatwell*, [1998] O.J. No. 206, 122 C.C.C. (3d) 162 (Ont. C.A.); *R. v. Schiewe*, [1992] A.J. No. 490, 72 C.C.C. (3d) 353 (Alta. C.A.), affd [1993] S.C.J. No. 32 (S.C.C.).

[72] *R. v. Morin*, [1992] S.C.J. No. 25, [1992] 1 S.C.R. 771 at 795 (S.C.C.).

[73] *Ibid.*, at 798-99 (S.C.R.).

[74] *Ibid.*; *R. v. Askov*, [1990] S.C.J. No. 106, [1990] 2 S.C.R. 1199 at 1240 (S.C.C.).

[75] *R. v. Morin*, [1992] S.C.J. No. 25, [1992] 1 S.C.R. 771 at 798 (S.C.C.).

the period acceptable for delay beyond the lower bound of the relevant range (*i.e.*, eight months for provincial court and six months after committal). Conversely, "in a case in which there is no prejudice or prejudice is slight, the guideline may be applied to reflect this fact."[76] Presumably, this means that minimal prejudice will sometimes stretch the tolerable period of inherent delay beyond the maximum bound of the guideline.[77]

§13.26 The second factor that must be considered alongside the quantum of institutional delay is the existence of local conditions that might warrant departing from the guidelines. The Court explained the effect of these conditions in *Morin* as follows:

> [The guideline] is the result of the exercise of a judicial discretion based on experience and taking into account the evidence of the limitations on resources, the strain imposed on them, statistics from other comparable jurisdictions and the opinions of other courts and judges, as well as any expert opinion. With respect to the use of statistics, care must be taken that a comparison of jurisdictions is indeed a comparative analysis. ... Comparison with other jurisdictions is therefore to be applied with caution and only as a rough guide. ...
>
> ... Rapidly changing conditions may place a sudden and temporary strain on resources. ... Such changing conditions should not result in an amnesty for persons charged in that region. Rather this fact should be taken into account in applying the guideline. On the other hand, when the case load has been constant over a substantial period of time the delay envisaged by the guideline may be regarded as excessive. In this appeal, the Court of Appeal purported to apply a transitional period to accommodate the situation in Durham .... The use of a transitional period implies a fixed period during which unreasonable delay will be tolerated while the system adjusts to a new set of rules. It imposes a general moratorium on certain Charter rights. ... It appears to me undesirable to impose a moratorium on Charter rights every time a region of the country experiences unusual strain on its resources. It is preferable to simply treat this as one factor in the overall decision as to whether a particular delay is unreasonable.[78]

§13.27 Trial courts have the primary responsibility for periodically adjusting the guidelines to reflect local conditions, the Court added, with the courts of appeal imposing a measure of province-wide uniformity.[79] That said, the Supreme Court retains ultimate responsibility for ensuring that "the right to trial within a reasonable time is being respected" across the country.[80]

---

[76] *Ibid.*, at 798 (S.C.R.).

[77] *R. v. Seegmiller*, [2004] O.J. No. 5004, 191 C.C.C. (3d) 347 at para. 25 (Ont. C.A.), leave to appeal refused [2005] S.C.C.A. No. 64 (S.C.C.); *R. v. Sychterz*, [2005] O.J. No. 2722 at para. 50 (Ont. S.C.J.).

[78] *R. v. Morin*, [1992] S.C.J. No. 25, [1992] 1 S.C.R. 771 at 797-98 (S.C.C.).

[79] *Ibid.*, at 799 (S.C.R.).

[80] *Ibid.*, at 799-800 (S.C.R.).

(v) Other Reasons for Delay

§13.28 Reasons for delay that do not neatly fit into any of the categories described above will also be considered in determining the reasonableness of the delay.[81] An extreme example, highlighted by the Court in *Morin*, occurred in *R. v. Rahey*,[82] where the trial judge instigated nineteen adjournments during the course of the trial.[83]

(d) Prejudice

§13.29 Where the length of institutional delay is not in itself determinative of whether section 11(*b*) has been violated, the decision will often turn on the degree of prejudice to the accused occasioned by the delay. As Justice Prowse remarked in *R. v. Stewart*,[84] "the degree of prejudice suffered by the accused is a significant, if not overriding, factor in the s. 11(b) analysis."[85] Notably, this does not include prejudice arising from the fact of being charged with a crime. The focus is instead on prejudice arising from the delay.[86] In other words, the accused will have to tender proof that his or her plight worsened as a result of the institutional delay in disposing of the charge.

§13.30 This proof may relate to one or more of three forms of prejudice: (*i*) prejudice to the accused's liberty interests (as it relates to pre-trial custody or bail conditions); (*ii*) prejudice to the security of the accused's person (in the sense of being free from the stress and cloud of suspicion accompanying a criminal charge); or (*iii*) prejudice to the accused's right to make full answer and defence (insofar as delay can prejudice the ability of the accused to lead evidence, cross-examine witnesses, or otherwise to raise a defence).[87]

§13.31 In some cases, prejudice may be inferred simply from the length of delay.[88] Indeed, as the Supreme Court noted in *Godin*, the very question of prejudice "cannot be considered separately from the length of the delay."[89] The longer

---

[81] *Ibid.*, at 800 (S.C.R.).

[82] [1987] S.C.J. No. 23, [1987] 1 S.C.R. 588 (S.C.C.).

[83] *R. v. Morin*, [1992] S.C.J. No. 25, [1992] 1 S.C.R. 771 at 800 (S.C.C.).

[84] [2000] B.C.J. No. 1333 (B.C.C.A.).

[85] *Ibid.*, at para. 88. Examples of appellate decisions in which lengthy delays did not result in s. 11(*b*) violations due to a lack of specific prejudice include *R. v. Chatwell*, [1998] O.J. No. 206, 122 C.C.C. (3d) 162 (Ont. C.A.); *R. v. Bijelic*, [2001] O.J. No. 3853 (Ont. C.A.); *R. v. Miller*, [2000] B.C.J. No. 2535 (B.C.C.A.); *R. v. Fleet*, [2001] N.S.J. No. 434, 163 C.C.C. (3d) 177 (N.S.C.A.). In contrast, cases in which actual prejudice existed resulted in charges being stayed in *R. v. Maracle*, [1998] S.C.J. No. 7, [1998] 1 S.C.R. 86 (S.C.C.); *R. v. Eizenga*, [2002] O.J. No. 3902 (Ont. C.A.); *R. v. Christie*, [2001] N.S.J. No. 390, 160 C.C.C. (3d) 192 (N.S.C.A.).

[86] *R. v. Kovacs-Tatar*, [2004] O.J. No. 4756 (Ont. C.A.); *R. v. Pusic*, [1996] O.J. No. 3329 (Ont. Gen. Div.).

[87] See *R. v. Godin*, [2009] S.C.J. No. 26, [2009] 2 S.C.R. 3 at para. 30 (S.C.C.); *R. v. Morin*, [1992] S.C.J. No. 25, [1992] 1 S.C.R. 771 at 802-803 (S.C.C.). See also *R. v. Rego*, [2005] O.J. No. 4768 (Ont. C.A.); *R. v. White*, [2006] A.J. No. 179 (Alta. C.A.).

[88] *R. v. B. (W.)*, [2000] O.J. No. 2186, 145 C.C.C. (3d) 498 (Ont. C.A.); *R. v. Satkunananthan*, [2001] O.J. No. 1019, 152 C.C.C. (3d) 321 at para. 38 (Ont. C.A.).

[89] *R. v. Godin*, [2009] S.C.J. No. 26, [2009] 2 S.C.R. 3 at para. 31 (S.C.C.).

the delay, of course, "the more likely that an inference of prejudice will be drawn."[90] In *Godin*, for example, the Court inferred prejudice based on the very lengthy, unexplained delay in bringing a simple case to trial. Proof of actual prejudice to the right to make full answer and defence, it held, was "not invariably required to establish a s. 11(*b*) violation."[91]

§13.32 Whatever the basis of the defence's claim of prejudice, the prosecution may counter that the accused was not in fact prejudiced by the delay. As the courts have long recognized, some defendants may not actually want a speedy trial. Indeed, some may desire the proceedings to fester in the hope that the court will find a section 11(*b*) violation and issue a stay.[92] As the Court stated in *Morin*, conduct by an accused "inconsistent with a desire for a timely trial" will thus work against a finding of prejudice.[93] Evidence that the defence sought an early trial date, in contrast, will work in the opposite direction.[94]

(2) Standard of Review

§13.33 There has been some debate among appellate courts regarding the standard of review of a trial judge's discretion in ruling on a section 11(*b*) claim. Appeal courts in Manitoba and British Columbia have taken the view that the standard of review of a judge's discretion is a high one, requiring an error on a question of law or an error as to the proper weight to be given to one of the relevant factors, such that the decision is unreasonable.[95]

§13.34 The Ontario Court of Appeal, however, has held that a trial judge's ultimate decision whether the delay was unreasonable is to be reviewed on a standard of correctness. In addition, the standard of correctness also applies to the review of the trial judge's characterization of various periods of time. However, the underlying findings of fact are to be reviewed on the standard of palpable and overriding error.[96] If one considers the Supreme Court of Canada judgment in *Housen v. Nikolaisen*,[97] it can be argued that the Ontario approach to an appellate court's standard of review should prevail. As the majority in *Housen v. Nikolaisen* dictates, the more inextricably tied a question of fact and law is to a

---

90 *Ibid.*
91 *Ibid.*, at para. 38 (S.C.R.).
92 See *R. v. Morin*, [1992] S.C.J. No. 25, [1992] 1 S.C.R. 771 at 802 (S.C.C.).
93 *Ibid.*, at 802 (S.C.R.).
94 For example, in *R. v. Godin*, [2009] S.C.J. No. 26, [2009] 2 S.C.R. 3 at para. 27 (S.C.C.), the Court noted that the only person who appeared to have made effort to move the matter ahead more quickly was defence counsel. His effort to set earlier dates for a preliminary inquiry was met by "radio silence". See also *R. v. Morin*, [1992] S.C.J. No. 25, [1992] 1 S.C.R. 771 at 803 (S.C.C.).
95 See *R. v. Byron*, [2001] M.J. No. 245, 156 C.C.C. (3d) 312 at para. 10 (Man. C.A.); *R. v. Guilbride*, [2006] B.C.J. No. 2047, 211 C.C.C. (3d) 465 at para. 84 (B.C.C.A.).
96 *R. v. Schertzer*, [2009] O.J. No. 4425 at para. 71 (Ont. C.A.), leave to appeal refused [2010] S.C.C.A. No. 3 (S.C.C.); *R. v. Cranston*, [2008] O.J. No. 4414 at para. 35 (Ont. C.A.), leave to appeal refused [2009] S.C.C.A. No. 326 (S.C.C.); *R. v. Quereshi*, [2004] O.J. No. 4711, 190 C.C.C. (3d) 453 (Ont. C.A.).
97 [2002] S.C.J. No. 31, [2002] 2 S.C.R. 235 (S.C.C.).

question of law, the more likely it will be that the standard of review to be applied is one of correctness.[98] It is also worth noting that in *Godin*, the Court ultimately held that the trial judge was "correct" to conclude that the delay in that case, which was attributable virtually all to the Crown, was unreasonable.[99]

---

[98] *Ibid.*, at paras. 27-37 (S.C.R.).
[99] *R. v. Godin*, [2009] S.C.J. No. 26, [2009] 2 S.C.R. 3 at para. 2 (S.C.C.).

Chapter 14

THE PLEA

1. INTRODUCTION

§14.1 At arraignment, the defendant is called upon to enter a plea. The defendant has three options: (*i*) a plea of guilty; (*ii*) a plea of not guilty; or (*iii*) one of the special pleas of *autrefois acquit, autrefois convict* or pardon.[1] However, with the Crown's consent, the defendant may plead not guilty to the offence charged, but guilty to any other offence arising out of the same transaction, whether or not it is an included offence.[2] If the Crown refuses to consent, the guilty plea to the lesser offence is void and the court will record only the plea of not guilty for the greater offence. Where there is more than one count in the charging document, the accused must enter a plea with respect to each. If a defendant refuses to enter a plea, the trial judge must direct that a plea of not guilty be entered.[3] In the absence of any plea at all, any resulting conviction or acquittal constitutes a nullity.[4]

§14.2 This chapter begins with an overview of the most common form of resolution in the criminal justice system: the guilty plea.[5] An examination then follows of the rarer forms of pleas — the special pleas of *autrefois acquit* and *autrefois convict*. The chapter concludes with a discussion on *res judicata* and the rule against multiple convictions.

2. GUILTY PLEAS

§14.3 An accused may plead guilty to a criminal offence for a variety of reasons, including genuine remorse, a desire to be released from custody or an agreement with the prosecutor to plead guilty in exchange for a charging or

---

[1]   *Criminal Code*, R.S.C. 1985, c. C-46, s. 606(1) [*Code*]. Note that there is no ability to enter a "conditional" guilty plea, for example, one conditional on an appellate court upholding a trial judge's *Charter* ruling (*Canadian Charter of Rights and Freedoms*, Part I of the *Constitution Act, 1982*, being Schedule B to the *Canada Act 1982* (U.K.), 1982, c. 11 [*Charter*]) (See *R. v. Fegan*, [1993] O.J. No. 733, 80 C.C.C. (3d) 356 (Ont. C.A.)).

[2]   *Criminal Code*, s. 606(4). Note, however, that the court is not bound to accept the guilty plea where the facts support guilt of the full offence (See *R. v. Naraindeen*, [1990] O.J. No. 1645, 80 C.R. (3d) 66 (Ont. C.A.); *R. v. Pentiluk*, [1974] O.J. No. 964, 21 C.C.C. (2d) 87 (Ont. C.A.), affd [1977] S.C.J. No. 33 (S.C.C.)).

[3]   *Criminal Code*, s. 606(2).

[4]   *R. v. Atkinson*, [1977] S.C.J. No. 97, [1978] 1 S.C.R. 1018 (S.C.C.).

[5]   In 2008/2009, 66 per cent of adult cases resulted in a guilty decision with the accused pleading guilty in 59 per cent of all completed cases (See "Adult criminal court statistics" at Statistics Canada: <http://www.statcan.gc.ca/daily-quotidien/100728/dq100728b-eng.htm>).

sentencing benefit.[6] Whatever the motivation, the consequences are dramatic. In *R. v. Adgey*,[7] Justice Laskin observed that a guilty plea "carries an admission that the accused so pleading has committed the crime charged and a consent to a conviction being entered without any trial."[8] In pleading guilty, he added, the accused "relieves the Crown of the burden to prove guilt beyond a reasonable doubt, abandons his non-compellability as a witness and his right to remain silent and surrenders his right to offer full answer and defence to a charge."[9]

§14.4 At the hearing of a typical guilty plea, the facts are "read in" by the Crown. If the facts are substantially admitted by the defence and the judge is satisfied that there is proof of all the essential elements of the offence,[10] the judge records a finding of "guilt" and the hearing then proceeds to sentencing. However, should the defendant dispute any of the material facts, an evidentiary hearing must be held. Aggravating facts beyond the essential elements of the offence must be proven by the Crown on a beyond a reasonable doubt standard.[11]

(1)   The Plea Inquiry

§14.5 If a defendant pleads guilty, the court may accept it only if it is satisfied that the defendant is making it voluntarily and understands: (*i*) that the plea is an admission of the essential elements of the offence; (*ii*) the nature and consequences of the plea; and (*iii*) that the court is not bound by any agreement made between the defendant and the prosecutor.[12] The court usually will satisfy itself of the validity of the guilty plea by asking the defendant a series of questions specifically relating to the matters listed in section 606(1.1) of the *Code*. The inquiry is conducted in open court and the questions are put to, and answered by, the defendant. This minimizes the risk of an appeal on the basis that the plea was not valid due to a lack of understanding on the part of the defendant, particularly in cases of unrepresented defendants. The timing of the plea inquiry is not prescribed in section 606(1.1). In practice, the plea inquiry varies amongst judges. Some judges conduct the inquiry immediately after the facts are read into the record and the defendant formally enters a guilty plea. In these cases, should the trial judge not be satisfied that the conditions of section 606(1.1) are met, the guilty plea will be struck and the matter will proceed to trial. Other judges conduct the inquiry just prior to the plea being formally entered. In these cases, a

---

[6]   See *R. v. Fegan*, [1993] O.J. No. 733, 80 C.C.C. (3d) 356 at para. 11 (Ont. C.A.). The effect of a guilty plea on sentencing is discussed more extensively in Chapter 17, Part 3(3)(*a*).

[7]   [1973] S.C.J. No. 159, [1975] 2 S.C.R. 426 (S.C.C.).

[8]   *R. v. Adgey*, [1973] S.C.J. No. 159, [1975] 2 S.C.R. 426 at 440 (S.C.C.).

[9]   *Ibid.*

[10]   If the judge is not satisfied that the facts support a guilty plea, the plea is to be rejected (See *R. v. Adgey*, [1973] S.C.J. No. 159, [1975] 2 S.C.R. 426 at 440 (S.C.C.) and *R. v. Lucas*, [1983] O.J. No. 158, 9 C.C.C. (3d) 71 (Ont. C.A.)).

[11]   *R. v. Gardiner*, [1982] S.C.J. No. 71, 68 C.C.C. (2d) 477 (S.C.C.). See also *Criminal Code*, s. 724(3)(*e*).

[12]   *Criminal Code*, s. 606(1.1).

judge will refuse to take the plea should he or she not be satisfied that the pre-conditions under section 606(1.1) are met and will proceed to trial.

§14.6 Nevertheless, the failure of the court to fully inquire whether the conditions of section 606(1.1) of the *Code* have been met does not affect the validity of the plea.[13] This is especially true when the defendant is represented by counsel at the time he or she enters the guilty plea.[14]

(2) Striking the Guilty Plea

§14.7 A guilty plea is presumed to be valid.[15] However, a defendant may attempt to demonstrate (on a balance of probabilities) that his or her plea was not valid.[16] An application to strike or "withdraw" a plea should be brought before the completion of the sentencing hearing, since a judge has no jurisdiction to strike a plea after sentence has been imposed.[17] After sentencing, a defendant may seek to have the conviction quashed on appeal on the basis of an invalid guilty plea.[18]

§14.8 A guilty plea is valid only when it is voluntary, unequivocal and informed.[19] To be an informed decision, the defendant must be aware of the nature of the allegations, the effect of the plea and the consequences resulting from the plea.[20] Whether striking a plea on the trial judge's own accord or on the basis of an application by the defendant to withdraw the guilty plea, it is ultimately a matter for the discretion of the trial judge.[21] In *R. v. Bertram*,[22] Justice Watt provides a useful list of factors to be considered when exercising this discretion:

> There is no fixed or closed list of matters which may constitute a sufficient basis upon which to set aside a plea of guilty in criminal proceedings, but it has been recognized that where it appears that
>
> i   the accused did not appreciate the nature of the charge to which the plea of guilty was entered;
>
> ii   the accused did not appreciate the nature and/or effect of a plea of guilty;
>
> iii the accused never intended to enter a plea of guilty;

---

13 *Criminal Code*, s. 606(1.2). See also *R. v. Adgey*, [1973] S.C.J. No. 159, [1975] 2 S.C.R. 426 at 429 (S.C.C.) ("This Court has decided in *Brosseau v. The Queen*...that a trial judge is not bound, as a matter of law, in all cases to conduct an inquiry after a guilty plea has been entered."); *R. v. MacDonald*, [2009] O.J. No. 5750 at para. 9 (Ont. C.A.).

14 *R. v. Moser*, [2002] O.J. No. 552, 163 C.C.C. (3d) 286 (Ont. S.C.J.).

15 *R. v. Eastmond*, [2001] O.J. No. 4353 at para. 6 (Ont. C.A.).

16 *R. v. Easterbrook*, [2005] O.J. No. 1486 (Ont. C.A.).

17 *R. v. Atlay*, [1992] B.C.J. No. 283, 70 C.C.C. (3d) 553 (B.C.C.A.).

18 See Chapter 18, Part 3(3) for further discussion on striking a guilty plea on appeal.

19 *R. v. T. (R.)*, [1992] O.J. No. 1914, 10 O.R. (3d) 514 (Ont. C.A.).

20 *Ibid.*

21 See *R. v. Atlay*, [1992] B.C.J. No. 283, 70 C.C.C. (3d) 553 (B.C.C.A.).

22 [1989] O.J. No. 2123 (Ont. H.C.J.).

iv the accused never intended to admit a fact, proof of which is an essential element of the offence, to which the plea of guilty has been entered; or,

v the facts admitted do not disclose the commission of the offence to which the plea of guilty has been entered.

§14.9 A common complaint advanced by defendants seeking to strike their pleas is that they were coerced or under duress to plead guilty. There is no doubt that improper coercion or duress may vitiate the plea.[23] However, the reality is that many defendants feel considerable pressure to plead guilty. For example, a defendant may wish to be released from custody as soon as possible to maintain employment or face pressure to make an immediate decision on the morning of trial due to last minute plea bargain negotiations. However, as Justice Doherty explained in *R. v. T.(R.)*,[24] "Absent credible and competent testimony that those emotions reached a level where they impaired the appellant's ability to make a conscious volitional choice, the mere presence of these emotions does not render the pleas involuntary."[25]

§14.10 At times, unfortunately, a guilty plea that meets the legal requirements of "voluntary, unequivocal and informed" may nonetheless lead to a miscarriage of justice. The future costs for a defendant who is indeed factually innocent may be too high to resist. As one commentator puts it, "[A] day of freedom today is worth more than a day of freedom ten years from now."[26] The dilemma is poignantly highlighted in two recent cases in Ontario. In *R. v. Hanemaayer*,[27] the defendant was charged with break and enter and committing an assault. The defendant had spent eight months in jail awaiting trial and after the complainant and a key eyewitness testified on the first day of his trial, he changed his plea to guilty. In short, "he lost his nerve" because his lawyer advised him that the witnesses were very convincing and he would most certainly be convicted and sentenced to at least six years' imprisonment. Upon pleading guilty, the defendant was sentenced to two years less one day imprisonment. Nearly 20 years after the defendant pleaded guilty, it was determined that someone else had committed the crime. The Ontario Court of Appeal recognized the "terrible dilemma" facing the defendant and despite the traditional tests for a valid guilty plea were present in this case, the court "retains a discretion, to be exercised in the interests of justice, to receive fresh evidence to explain the circumstances that led to the plea and that demonstrates a miscarriage of justice occurred."[28] Consequently, the court set aside the defendant's guilty plea and entered acquittals.

---

[23] For example, where a defendant is unduly pressured by defence counsel to plead guilty (See *R. c. Lamoureux*, [1984] J.Q. no 289, 13 C.C.C. (3d) 101 (Que. C.A.); *R. v. Toussaint*, [1984] J.Q. no 657, 40 C.R. (3d) 230 (Que. C.A.)).

[24] [1992] O.J. No. 1914, 10 O.R. (3d) 514 (Ont. C.A.).

[25] *Ibid.*, at para. 18 (O.J.).

[26] Stephanos Bibas, "Plea Bargaining Outside the Shadow of Trial" (2004) 117 Harv. L. Rev. 2464 at 2504.

[27] [2008] O.J. No. 3087, 234 C.C.C. (3d) 3 (Ont. C.A.).

[28] *Ibid.*, at para. 19 (O.J.).

§14.11 In *R. v. Sherret-Robinson*,[29] the defendant was charged with the first degree murder of her four-month-old son in 1996. In 1999, she reached an agreement with the Crown to have the murder charge withdrawn and instead a charge of infanticide laid. In return, the defendant agreed not to contest a set of facts that included an allegation that she smothered her child. The agreement was premised on the strength of the evidence of a pathologist whom, given his stature at the time, the defence did not believe could successfully contest. Many years later, it was determined that the pathologist's evidence was flawed and the Ontario Court of Appeal held that the defendant was wrongfully convicted and entered an acquittal.

§14.12 It is fair to say that there are many innocent defendants who falsely plead guilty.[30] Indeed, it may be within the ethical boundaries for counsel to act on a guilty plea for a client who maintains innocence if there is a likelihood of conviction due to the strength of the Crown's case.[31] This is implicit in the decisions of *Hanemaayer* and *Sherret-Robinson*, where the court was in no way critical of defence counsel for advising their clients in the manner that they did due to the circumstances. It is unknown, however, how pervasive false guilty pleas are in the criminal justice system. As Professor Gross observes, "Some innocent defendants who plead guilty are exonerated, but not many."[32]

3. THE SPECIAL PLEAS (DOUBLE JEOPARDY)

§14.13 It is a basic tenet of the criminal law that defendants may not be prosecuted on charges similar to ones for which they had previously been acquitted or convicted. This "double jeopardy" principle is entrenched in section 11(*h*) of the *Charter* and codified in section 607 of the *Criminal Code*, which deals with the special pleas of *autrefois acquit, autrefois convict* and pardon.

§14.14 When the defendant makes one of the special pleas, the trial judge must rule on the matter (without the jury) before the defendant is called on to plead further.[33] If the plea is accepted, the defendant will be discharged in respect of that count.[34] If the pleas are disposed of against the defendant, then he or she may plead guilty or not guilty.[35]

§14.15 The plea of pardon is the most straightforward, albeit the rarest, where the defendant offers proof of a pardon for the same offence before the court.

---

[29] [2009] O.J. No. 5312 at paras. 8-9 (Ont. C.A.).
[30] Samuel R. Gross, "Convicting the Innocent" (2008) 4 Annual Review of Law and Social Science 173 at 181.
[31] See Michel Proulx & David Layton, *Ethics and Canadian Criminal Law* (Toronto: Irwin Law, 2001) at 452-53.
[32] Samuel R. Gross, "Convicting the Innocent" (2008) 4 Annual Review of Law and Social Science 173 at 181.
[33] *Criminal Code*, s. 607(3).
[34] *Criminal Code*, s. 609.
[35] *Criminal Code*, s. 607(4).

§14.16 The special pleas of *autrefois acquit* and *autrefois convict* can be raised in respect of both indictable and summary conviction proceedings,[36] but not at a preliminary inquiry.[37]

§14.17 In pleading *autrefois acquit* or *autrefois convict*, the defendant must: (*i*) state that he or she has been lawfully acquitted, convicted or discharged of the offence charged in the count to which the plea relates; and (*ii*) indicate the time and place of the acquittal, conviction or discharge.[38] Further, the defendant must show that: (*i*) there was a final adjudication on the prior charge on its merits;[39] and (*ii*) the matter is the same, in whole or in part, and the new count must be the same as the first trial, or be implicitly included in that of the first trial, either in law or on account of the evidence presented if it had been legally possible at that time to make the necessary amendments.[40]

§14.18 The plea of *autrefois acquit* has been found not to apply in cases where the first charge did not result in a final adjudication due to a withdrawal of a previous information by the Crown at the outset of the trial;[41] a discharge at a preliminary inquiry;[42] a stay of proceedings;[43] or an appeal that resulted in a new trial.[44] In contrast, *autrefois acquit* is available to a charge relating to an offence for which the defendant was found not criminally responsible on account of mental disorder[45] or where a trial judge quashes an indictment or information after arraignment and plea on a prior same or similar charge.[46]

§14.19 Section 609 of the *Code* sets out an "identity" test that must be met in order to establish that the "matter" in both charges is the same, thereby triggering the operation of *autrefois acquit* or *autrefois convict*. In *R. v. Van Rassel*,[47] Justice McLachlin (as she then was) explained the test as follows:

> Despite the technical form of the relevant sections of the *Criminal Code* the substantive point is a simple one: could the accused have been convicted at the first trial of the offence with which he is now charged? If the differences between the charges at the first and second trials are such that it must be concluded that the charges are different in *nature*, the plea of *autrefois acquit* is not appropriate. On the other hand, the plea will apply if, despite the differences between the earlier and the present charges, the offences are the same.[48]

---

36 *R. v. Riddle*, [1979] S.C.J. No. 111, [1980] 1 S.C.R. 380 (S.C.C.).
37 *Canada v. Schmidt*, [1987] S.C.J. No. 24, [1987] 1 S.C.R. 500 at 515-17 (S.C.C.).
38 *Criminal Code*, s. 607(5).
39 *Rex v. Purcell*, [1933] N.S.J. No. 5, 61 C.C.C. 261 (N.S.S.C.); *R. v. Taylor*, [1914] A.J. No. 32, 22 C.C.C. 234 (Alta. S.C.).
40 *R. v. Van Rassel*, [1990] S.C.J. No. 11, [1990] 1 S.C.R. 225 (S.C.C.).
41 *R. v. Selhi*, [1990] S.C.J. No. 18, [1990] 1 S.C.R. 277 (S.C.C.).
42 *R. v. Sommervill*, [1963] S.J. No. 151, [1963] 3 C.C.C. 240 at para. 31 (Sask. C.A.).
43 *R. v. Tateham*, [1982] B.C.J. No. 1941, 70 C.C.C. (2d) 565 (B.C.C.A.).
44 *Rex v. Purcell*, [1933] N.S.J. No. 5, 61 C.C.C. 261 (N.S.S.C.).
45 *Criminal Code*, s. 672.35(*a*).
46 *R. v. Moore*, [1988] S.C.J. No. 58, [1988] 1 S.C.R. 1097 (S.C.C.).
47 [1990] S.C.J. No. 11, [1990] 1 S.C.R. 225 (S.C.C.).
48 *Ibid.*, at 234-35 (S.C.R.) [emphasis added].

Further, section 610 provides for the application of a special plea in the following circumstances:

(1) Where an indictment charges substantially the same offence as that charged in an indictment on which an accused was previously convicted or acquitted, but adds a statement of intention or circumstances of aggravation tending, if proved, to increase the punishment, the previous conviction or acquittal bars the subsequent indictment.

(2) A conviction or an acquittal on an indictment for murder bars a subsequent indictment for the same homicide charging it as manslaughter or infanticide, and a conviction or acquittal on an indictment for manslaughter or infanticide bars a subsequent indictment for the same homicide charging it as murder.

(3) A conviction or an acquittal on an indictment for first degree murder bars a subsequent indictment for the same homicide charging it as second degree murder, and a conviction or acquittal on an indictment for second degree murder bars a subsequent indictment for the same homicide charging it as first degree murder.

(4) A conviction or an acquittal on an indictment for infanticide bars a subsequent indictment for the same homicide charging it as manslaughter, and a conviction or acquittal on an indictment for manslaughter bars a subsequent indictment for the same homicide charging it as infanticide.

4. RES JUDICATA

§14.20 Closely associated with the special pleas of *autrefois acquit* and *autrefois convict* is the common law defence of *res judicata* or "a matter adjudged". The doctrine of *res judicata* encapsulates two branches: double jeopardy and issue estoppel.[49] As Chief Justice McLachlin highlighted in *R. v. Mahalingan*,[50] there is an important distinction between the two concepts:

While double jeopardy is concerned with the total cause of action and the ultimate result of the litigation, issue estoppel is concerned with particular issues arising in two different pieces of litigation.

...

I conclude that, properly understood, issue estoppel in Canadian criminal law operates to prevent the Crown from relitigating an issue that has been determined in the accused's favour in a prior criminal proceeding, whether on the basis of a positive finding or reasonable doubt.[51]

§14.21 Since *res judicata* is not a special plea, the defence must be raised under a plea of not guilty.[52] The onus is on the defendant to satisfy the court that a particular issue was decided in his or her favour in a previous proceeding.

---

[49] *R. v. Mahalingan*, [2008] S.C.J. No. 64, [2008] 3 S.C.R. 316 at paras. 14-16 (S.C.C.).
[50] [2008] S.C.J. No. 64, [2008] 3 S.C.R. 316 (S.C.C.).
[51] *Ibid.*, at paras. 17 and 31 (S.C.R.).
[52] *Rex v. Sweetman*, [1939] O.J. No. 455, 71 C.C.C. 171 (Ont. C.A.).

However, only those issues that were expressly resolved or had to be resolved for there to be an acquittal are the subject of issue estoppel.[53] In addition, "the protection is not available where the acquittal has been obtained by fraud and the evidence of that fraud was not available to the Crown at the time of the first trial through the exercise of reasonable diligence."[54]

5. THE *KIENAPPLE* PRINCIPLE

§14.22 *Res judicata* also relates to the rule against multiple convictions, as first articulated by the Supreme Court of Canada in *R. v. Kienapple*.[55] There the Court applied the common law theory of *res judicata* in holding that an accused cannot be convicted for more than one offence arising out of the same "delict". Otherwise, the accused could be punished twice for essentially the same offence.[56] For the *Kienapple* principle to apply, there must be a sufficient factual and legal nexus between the charges. The factual nexus will be established if the same act of the accused undergirds each of the charges.[57] The legal nexus will be satisfied if "there is no additional and distinguishing element that goes to guilt contained in the offence for which a conviction is sought to be precluded by the *Kienapple* principle."[58]

§14.23 The most common application of *Kienapple* is found in drinking and driving cases where findings of guilt with respect to offences of "impaired driving" and "over 80" routinely lead to a conditional stay of the conviction of one of the charges. Other examples of *Kienapple* can usually be found in cases involving robbery and aggravated assault arising out of the same incident[59] and cases involving sexual assault and sexual interference.[60]

§14.24 Where the *Kienapple* principle applies, the trial judge will enter a conviction for the offence that best captures the delict of the case and enter a conditional stay for any remaining convictions arising from the same delict. If the accused does not appeal from the conviction of the non-*Kienapple*d offence, then the conditionally stayed *Kienapple*d offence becomes a permanent stay tantamount to a verdict of acquittal.[61] However, if the accused successfully appeals the conviction of the non-*Kienapple*d offence, the conditional stay dissolves and the appellate court can make an order remitting to the trial judge the count that was conditionally stayed.[62] It should be noted that the operation of the

---

53   *R. v. Mahalingan*, [2008] S.C.J. No. 64, [2008] 3 S.C.R. 316 at paras. 22-23 (S.C.C.).
54   *R. v. F. (F.D.J.)*, [2005] O.J. No. 2148, 197 C.C.C. (3d) 365 at para. 20 (Ont. C.A.), leave to appeal refused [2005] S.C.C.A. No. 477 (S.C.C.). See also *R. v. Grdic*, [1985] S.C.J. No. 41, [1985] 1 S.C.R. 810 at paras. 13-15 (S.C.C.).
55   [1974] S.C.J. No. 76, [1975] 1 S.C.R. 729 (S.C.C.) [*Kienapple*].
56   *Ibid.*, at 747-48 (S.C.R.).
57   *R. v. Prince*, [1986] S.C.J. No. 63, [1986] 2 S.C.R. 480 at para. 20 (S.C.C.).
58   *Ibid.*, at para. 32 (S.C.R.).
59   *R. v. Doliente*, [1997] S.C.J. No. 48, [1997] 2 S.C.R. 11 (S.C.C.).
60   *R. v. M. (R.M.)*, [1998] O.J. No. 255, 122 C.C.C. (3d) 563 (Ont. C.A.).
61   *R. v. Provo*, [1989] S.C.J. No. 77, [1989] 2 S.C.R. 3 at 19-20 (S.C.C.).
62   *Ibid.*

Kienapple rule has little practical impact on an accused. As Justice Doherty observed in *R. v. Ramage*,[63] the rule against multiple convictions "is often of academic interest only, as its outcome has no impact on the actual sentence to be served by the accused."[64] This is so because even where the *Kienapple* principle is not applied, a judge must still remain cognizant of the "one transaction rule" in which concurrent sentences may be imposed for multiple offences occurring as part of the same episode.[65]

---

[63] [2010] O.J. No. 2970, 257 C.C.C. (3d) 261 (Ont. C.A.).
[64] *Ibid.*, at para. 59 (C.C.C.).
[65] See Chapter 17, Part 5(1)(*a*)(i).

Chapter 15

JURY SELECTION

1. INTRODUCTION

§15.1 Most criminal trials are tried by a judge sitting without a jury. As explained in Chapter 1, a great proportion of trials take place in provincial and territorial courts, which do not use juries. Many trials in the superior courts, moreover, are conducted by a judge alone. That said, jury trials are by no means rare. Defendants charged with many offences may (and often do) choose to be tried by a judge and jury.[1] And for a few offences (chiefly murder) juries are mandatory unless the parties consent to a trial by a judge alone.[2]

§15.2 The Constitution also guarantees a limited right to a jury trial. Section 11(*f*) of the *Charter*[3] gives persons charged with an offence the right "except in the case of an offence under military law tried before a military tribunal, to the benefit of trial by jury where the maximum punishment for the offence is imprisonment for five years or a more severe punishment."[4] There is no converse right, however, to a trial by a judge alone.[5]

---

[1] *Criminal Code*, R.S.C. 1985, c. C-46, s. 536(2) [*Code*].

[2] *Criminal Code*, ss. 469, 471, 473.

[3] *Canadian Charter of Rights and Freedoms*, Part I of the *Constitution Act, 1982*, being Schedule B to the *Canada Act 1982* (U.K.), 1982, c. 11 [*Charter*].

[4] See generally, *R. v. Mack*, [1988] S.C.J. No. 91, [1988] 2 S.C.R. 903 at 972-73 (S.C.C.) (no violation arising from judge deciding entrapment as guilt or innocence not in issue); *R. v. Lyons*, [1987] S.C.J. No. 62, [1987] 2 S.C.R. 309 (S.C.C.) (no violation arising from judge deciding dangerous offender status as guilt or innocence not in issue); *R. v. Lee*, [1989] S.C.J. No. 125, [1989] 2 S.C.R. 1384 (S.C.C.) (s. 598 power to mandate judge-alone trial where accused fails to appear violates s. 11(*f*) but justified by s. 1); *R. v. L. (R.)*, [1986] O.J. No. 249, 26 C.C.C. (3d) 417 (Ont. C.A.) (no violation arising from lack of juries in young offender proceedings as maximum punishment three years' custody); *R. v. Brown*, [1995] C.M.A.J. No. 1, 35 C.R. (4th) 318 (Court Martial Appeal Court) (no violation arising from lack of juries in military cases); *R. v. B. (S.)*, [1989] S.J. No. 388, 50 C.C.C. (3d) 34 (Sask. C.A.) (same); *PPG Industries Canada Ltd. v. Canada (Attorney General)*, [1983] B.C.J. No. 2260, 3 C.C.C. (3d) 97 (B.C.C.A.) (corporation not "person" for purposes of s. 11(*f*) as not subject to imprisonment); *R. v. Cohn*, [1984] O.J. No. 3344, 15 C.C.C. (3d) 150 (Ont. C.A.) (no violation from judge finding person guilty of common law offence of contempt as punishment always less than two years); *MacMillan Bloedel Ltd. v. Simpson*, [1994] B.C.J. No. 670, 89 C.C.C. (3d) 217 (B.C.C.A.), affd [1995] S.C.J. No. 101, [1995] 4 S.C.R. 725 (S.C.C.) (same); *Manitoba (Attorney General) v. Groupe Quebecor Inc.*, [1987] M.J. No. 306, 37 C.C.C. (3d) 421 (Man. C.A.) (contempt not "offence" under s. 11(*f*)).

[5] *R. v. Turpin*, [1989] S.C.J. No. 47, [1989] 1 S.C.R. 1296 at 1321 (S.C.C.) ("An accused may repudiate his or her s. 11(*f*) right but such repudiation does not, in my view, transform the constitutional right to a jury trial into a constitutional right to a non-jury trial so as to overcome the

§15.3 Jury selection thus remains an important part of the pre-trial criminal process. The jury's role is to follow the judge's legal directives, resolve the factual issues in dispute and decide whether the accused is guilty, not guilty or not criminally responsible for each of the offences charged.[6] While judges perform this function in judge-alone trials, the use of juries in at least a minority of cases is often thought to foster public confidence in the criminal justice system. As the Supreme Court of Canada has put it, the jury "through its collective decision making, is an excellent fact finder; due to its representative character, it acts as the conscience of the community; the jury can act as the final bulwark against oppressive laws or their enforcement; it provides a means whereby the public increases its knowledge of the criminal justice system and it increases, through the involvement of the public, societal trust in the system as a whole."[7]

§15.4 In light of these roles, the law governing jury selection is designed to ensure that the jury is impartial and representative of the community.[8] The process is therefore divided into two steps,[9] each of which is described in detail below. The first is to assemble a group of potential jurors. This is known as assembling the array.[10] The second is to select a group of 12 jurors from the array to form the jury. This is known as empanelling the jury. Very generally, representativeness is achieved by provincial legislation governing the assembly of the array, while impartiality is secured by the *Criminal Code*'s provisions on empanelling the jury.

2. ASSEMBLING THE ARRAY

§15.5 The provincial statutes governing the assembly of the array find their constitutional authority in section 92(14) of the *Constitution Act, 1867* ("The

---

mandatory jury trial provisions of the *Criminal Code*"). See generally, Benjamin Berger, "Peine Forte et Dure: Compelled Jury Trials and Legal Rights in Canada" (2003) 48 Crim. L.Q. 205.

[6] See *R. v. Finta*, [1992] O.J. No. 823, 73 C.C.C. (3d) 65 at 173-74 (Ont. C.A.), affd [1994] S.C.J. No. 26, [1994] 1 S.C.R. 701 (S.C.C.) ("It is hornbook law that in a trial by a court composed of a judge and jury, the judge decides questions of law and instructs the jury as to the relevant law. The jury weighs the evidence, determines the facts, applies the law to those facts and renders a verdict.").

[7] *R. v. Sherratt*, [1991] S.C.J. No. 21, [1991] 1 S.C.R. 509 at 523-24 (S.C.C.). See also *R. v. Church of Scientology of Toronto*, [1997] O.J. No. 1548 at para. 140, 116 C.C.C. (3d) 1 (Ont. C.A.), leave to appeal refused [1997] S.C.C.A. No. 683 (S.C.C.).

[8] *R. v. Sherratt*, [1991] S.C.J. No. 21, [1991] 1 S.C.R. 509 (S.C.C.). See also *Nishnawbe Aski Nation v. Eden*, [2011] O.J. No. 988 at paras. 28-29 (Ont. C.A.) (representativeness of coroner's jury).

[9] See generally, *R. v. Find*, [2001] S.C.J. No. 34, [2001] 1 S.C.R. 863 at para. 19 (S.C.C.); *R. v. Yumnu*, [2010] O.J. No. 4163, 260 C.C.C. (3d) 421 at paras. 13-19 (Ont. C.A.).

[10] In certain provisions of the provincial jury statutes and the *Criminal Code*, the array is referred to as the "panel". See *e.g.*, *Criminal Code*, s. 629. This is not to be confused with the "panel" of jurors ultimately selected to try the case, which is sometimes referred to as the "petit jury". See *e.g.*, *R. v. Church of Scientology of Toronto*, [1997] O.J. No. 1548 at para. 158, 116 C.C.C. (3d) 1 (Ont. C.A.), leave to appeal refused [1997] S.C.C.A. No. 683 (S.C.C.).

Administration of Justice in the Province").[11] This jurisdiction is recognized in section 626 of the *Criminal Code*, which provides that a "person who is qualified as a juror according to, and summoned as a juror in accordance with, the laws of a province is qualified to serve as a juror in criminal proceedings in that province."[12] Each provincial statute sets out qualifications for jury service and dictates how arrays are to be summoned.

§15.6 Though qualifications vary among the provinces,[13] all require jurors to be of the age of majority and residents of the province. Most also require jurors to be Canadian citizens.[14] Each statute also disqualifies or permits exemptions for persons with certain occupations. Law enforcement officials, legislators, judges, court workers, lawyers and students-at-law are typically disqualified; people

---

[11] *Constitution Act, 1867* (U.K.), 30 & 31 Vict., c. 3 [Reprinted in R.S.C. 1985, App. II, No. 5] , s. 92(14). See *R. v. Barrow*, [1987] S.C.J. No. 84, [1987] 2 S.C.R. 694 at 712-13 (S.C.C.) ("the provincial power for the administration of justice stops and the federal power over criminal procedure begins when the judge's activity is not concerned with the assembly of an array of eligible citizens, but with the precautions necessary to ensure an impartial jury"). See also *R. v. Sherratt*, [1991] S.C.J. No. 21, [1991] 1 S.C.R. 509 at 519-20 (S.C.C.); *R. v. Teerhuis-Moar*, [2010] M.J. No. 342, 263 C.C.C. (3d) 100 at paras. 134-35 (Man. C.A.), leave to appeal refused [2011] S.C.C.A. No. 18 (S.C.C.). Despite these seemingly authoritative pronouncements, some have suggested that jury selection is entirely a matter of "Criminal Procedure" under s. 91(27) of the *Constitution Act, 1867* (U.K.), 30 & 31 Vict., c. 3 [Reprinted in R.S.C. 1985, App. II, No. 5] and that Parliament has delegated to the provinces (through s. 626 of the *Criminal Code*) responsibility over the assembly of the array. See *R. v. Church of Scientology of Toronto*, [1997] O.J. No. 1548 at para. 98, 116 C.C.C. (3d) 1 (Ont. C.A.), leave to appeal refused [1997] S.C.C.A. No. 683 (S.C.C.); David Pomerant, *Multiculturalism, Representation and the Jury Selection Process in Canadian Criminal Cases* (Ottawa: Department of Justice Canada, 1994). Following *Barrow*, in our view the provinces do have independent authority to set juror qualifications and establish the process for summoning the array. Parliament retains control, however, over aspects of the process affecting impartiality and trial fairness. Though their constitutional position obviously differs from that of the provinces, the three territories have each passed similar legislation. In this chapter, all references to the provinces and their jury statutes should be read to include the territories and their statutes.

[12] Section 626(2) of the *Code* also states that "[n]otwithstanding any law of a province referred to in subsection (1), no person may be disqualified, exempted or excused from serving as a juror in criminal proceedings on the grounds of his or her sex."

[13] The rules governing qualification, disqualification, and exemption of persons from jury service are set out in the following: *Jury Act*, R.S.A. 2000, c. J-3, ss. 3-6; *Jury Act*, R.S.B.C. 1996, c. 242, ss. 3-7, 13; *Jury Act*, C.C.S.M. c. J30, ss. 3-4, 25-28; *Jury Act, 1991*, S.N.L. 1991, c. 16, s. 4-10, 19; *Jury Act*, S.N.B. 1980, c. J-3.1, ss. 2-5.1; *Jury Act*, R.S.N.W.T. 1988, c. J-2, ss. 4-7; *Juries Act*, S.N.S. 1998, c. 16, ss. 3-6; *Jury Act*, R.S.N.W.T. (Nu.) 1988, c. J-2, ss. 4-7, 17; *Juries Act*, R.S.O. 1990, c. J.3, ss. 2-4, 19(2), 23; *Jury Act*, R.S.P.E.I. 1988, c. J-5.1, ss. 5-6; *Jurors Act*, R.S.Q., c. J-2, ss. 3-6, 29-30; *Jury Act, 1998*, S.S. 1998, c. J-4.2, ss. 5-6, 10-12; *Jury Act*, R.S.Y. 2002, c. 129, ss. 4-7, 14, as am. by *Act to Amend the Jury Act*, S.Y. 2005, c. 11.

[14] In the Northwest Territories and Nunavut, jurors must be either citizens or permanent residents: *Jury Act*, R.S.N.W.T. 1988, c. J-2, s. 4(*b*); *Jury Act*, R.S.N.W.T. (Nu.) 1988, c. J-2, s. 4(*b*). Manitoba does not require either citizenship or permanent residency. See *Charter Compliance Statute Amendment Act*, R.S.M. 1987 Supp., c. 4, s. 14. Courts have rejected claims that excluding non-citizens violates the *Charter*. See *R. v. Church of Scientology of Toronto*, [1997] O.J. No. 1548 at para. 152, 116 C.C.C. (3d) 1 (Ont. C.A.), leave to appeal refused [1997] S.C.C.A. No. 683 (S.C.C.) ("no evidence that non-citizens as a group share any common thread or basic similarity in attitude, ideas or experience that would not be brought to the jury process by citizens"); *R. v. Laws*, [1998] O.J. No. 6323, 41 O.R. (3d) 499 (Ont. C.A.) (no violation despite citizenship requirement slightly reducing likelihood of black persons being on jury).

working in various "essential services" are often either disqualified or eligible for exemption.[15] People who have been convicted (and not pardoned of) criminal offences are also often ineligible.[16] The statutes also typically disqualify or allow exemptions for people unable to serve because of physical, mental or linguistic difficulties.[17] Lastly, they often provide for exemptions based on religious objection, recent jury service, personal hardship and other factors.

§15.7 As with qualifications, the provinces have adopted differing procedures for summoning arrays. Typically the task is performed by a court official, usually known as a sheriff. This official must choose people at random from a representative database.[18] Some provinces have specified the source or sources to be used;[19] others leave it to the official's discretion.[20]

§15.8 Under section 629 of the *Criminal Code*, both the accused and the prosecutor may challenge the array based on "partiality, fraud or wilful misconduct on the part of the sheriff or other officer by whom the panel was returned."[21] If the judge upholds the challenge, he or she must order the summoning of a new array.[22] The accused can also allege that the process violated the *Charter*. Such claims have been brought under sections 11(*d*) (the right to a fair trial conducted by an "impartial tribunal"), 11(*f*) (the principles of impartiality and representativeness inhering in the right to a jury trial) and 15 (the right to equal protection and equal benefit of the law without discrimination). Courts may issue remedies for violations (including ordering the assembly of a new array, declaring a mistrial and ordering a new trial) under section 24(1) of the *Charter*.[23] Sections 670(*a*) and 671 of the *Code* state that irregularities in assembling the array are

---

[15] In *R. v. Church of Scientology of Toronto*, [1997] O.J. No. 1548 at paras. 160-164, 116 C.C.C. (3d) 1 (Ont. C.A.), leave to appeal refused [1997] S.C.C.A. No. 683 (S.C.C.), the Court rejected *Criminal Code* and *Charter* challenges to the exclusion of physicians, veterinarians and coroners, as well as the (since repealed) exclusion of judges', lawyers' and law enforcement officials' spouses.

[16] See *R. v. Teerhuis-Moar*, [2007] M.J. No. 257, 223 C.C.C. (3d) 74 at paras. 86-97 (Man. Q.B.) (though Aboriginals disproportionately affected, exclusion of convicted offenders does not violate accused's s. 11 *Charter* rights).

[17] Some provincial statutes provide that people with visual, auditory, or other physical difficulties may serve as jurors if adequate assistance can be provided. See *e.g.*, *Jury Act*, R.S.B.C. 1996, c. 242, s. 5; *Jury Act*, S.N.B. 1980, c. J-3.1, s. 5.1. Section 627 of the *Criminal Code* also specifies that the judge "may permit a juror with a physical disability who is otherwise qualified to serve as a juror to have technical, personal, interpretive or other support services."

[18] In some provinces people are periodically selected for inclusion on a "jury roll" from which persons are chosen to be summoned to the array as needed. See *e.g.*, *Jury Act*, C.C.S.M. c. J30, ss. 1, 5-21; *Juries Act*, R.S.O. 1990, c. J.3, ss. 5-11.

[19] See *e.g.*, *Jury Act Regulation*, Alta. Reg. 68/83, s. 2(2); *Juries Act*, R.S.O. 1990, c. J.3, s. 6(2); *Jury Act, General Regulation*, N.B. Reg. 95-126, s. 4; *Jury Regulation*, Man. Reg. 320/87 R, s. 6.

[20] See *e.g.*, *Jury Act*, R.S.B.C. 1996, c. 242, s. 8.

[21] In this provision, "panel" is equivalent to "array".

[22] *Criminal Code*, s. 630.

[23] See *e.g.*, *R. v. Buckingham*, [2007] N.J. No. 196, 221 C.C.C. (3d) 568 at paras. 21-24 (Nfld. T.D.).

not appealable. This rule, however, only applies to errors in form;[24] errors of substance (as when the accused is deprived of a statutory or constitutional right) may be appealed.[25]

§15.9 The broad principle emerging from this jurisprudence (under both the *Code* and *Charter*) is that the array must be "selected at random from sources which will furnish a representative cross-section of the community."[26] The measure of representativeness required, however, is limited. As explained by Justice Rosenberg for the Ontario Court of Appeal in *R. v. Church of Scientology of Toronto*:[27]

> The right to a representative jury roll is not absolute in the sense that the accused is entitled to a roll representative of all of the many groups that make up Canadian society. This level of representativeness would be impossible to obtain. There are a number of practical barriers inherent in the selection process that make complete representativeness impossible. The roll is selected from a discrete geographical district which itself may or may not be representative of the broader Canadian society.

> Further, the critical characteristic of impartiality in the petit jury is ensured, in part, by the fact that the roll and the panel are produced through a random selection process. To require the sheriff to assemble a fully representative roll or panel would run counter to the random selection process. The sheriff would need to add potential jurors to the roll or the panel based upon perceived characteristics required for representativeness. The selection process would become much more intrusive since the sheriff, in order to carry out the task of selecting a representative roll, would require information from potential jurors as to their race, religion, country of origin and other characteristics considered essential to achieve representativeness ....[28]

§15.10 Justice Rosenberg went on to suggest, however, that in some cases the "exclusion of certain segments of society from jury service would infringe the requirement of a representative cross-section."[29] Though there is no bright line

---

[24] See *e.g.*, *R. v. Singh*, [1996] B.C.J. No. 1410, 108 C.C.C. (3d) 244 (B.C.C.A.) (replacement of juror before evidence heard in possible violation of *Code* formal error not requiring new trial); *R. v. Rushton*, [1974] O.J. No. 763, 20 C.C.C. (2d) 297 (Ont. C.A.) (ineligible juror's presence on jury error of form not requiring new trial).

[25] See *R. v. Barrow*, [1987] S.C.J. No. 84, [1987] 2 S.C.R. 694 at 716-17 (S.C.C.); *R. v. James*, [1968] B.C.J. No. 89, 64 W.W.R. 659 (B.C.C.A.).

[26] *R. v. Sherratt*, [1991] S.C.J. No. 21, [1991] 1 S.C.R. 509 at 526 (S.C.C.), citing P. Schulman & E. Meyers, "Jury Selection," in Criminal Law Series (Law Reform Commission of Canada), Anthony N. Doob, *Studies on the Jury* (Ottawa: The Commission, 1979) at 408. See also *R. v. Church of Scientology of Toronto*, [1997] O.J. No. 1548 at paras. 143-144, 116 C.C.C. (3d) 1 (Ont. C.A.), leave to appeal refused [1997] S.C.C.A. No. 683 (S.C.C.).

[27] [1997] O.J. No. 1548, 116 C.C.C. (3d) 1 at paras. 143-144 (Ont. C.A.), leave to appeal refused [1997] S.C.C.A. No. 683 (S.C.C.).

[28] *Ibid.*, at paras. 146-147 (O.J.).

[29] *Ibid.*, at para. 149 (O.J.) (referring to American jurisprudence and noting that historically certain "distinctive groups" had been excluded from jury service). See also *R. v. Sherratt*, [1991] S.C.J. No. 21, [1991] 1 S.C.R. 509 at 524 (S.C.C.) (noting historic ineligibility of women, people who did not own real property, and racial minorities).

marking such infringements, he added, cases should be decided with reference to the purpose of the representativeness requirement: bringing to the jury "the possibility of different perspectives from a diverse group of persons."[30] "The representativeness requirement," he added, "seeks to avoid the risk that persons with these different perspectives, and who are otherwise available, will be systematically excluded from the jury roll."[31]

§15.11 A deliberate policy of excluding members of distinctive groups (such as those based on race or sex) clearly violates this requirement.[32] But courts have rejected claims that arrays and juries must include members of such groups (including members of groups that the accused belongs to[33]). Nor does the accused have any right to a jury including members of any particular community or geographic area.[34] Moreover, the calculated inclusion of a particular group constitutes partiality. In *R. v. Born With A Tooth*,[35] for example, the prosecutor successfully challenged the array under section 629 of the *Code* on the grounds that the sheriff intentionally included 52 members of the accused's race.[36] Further, despite evidence that members of certain disadvantaged groups are less likely to be eligible for jury duty, selected for arrays and appear when summoned for jury selection,[37] courts have rejected *Code* and *Charter* claims based

---

[30] *Ibid.*, at para. 151 (C.C.C.).

[31] *Ibid.*

[32] See *R. v. Butler*, [1984] B.C.J. No. 1775, 3 C.R. (4th) 174 (B.C.C.A.) (deliberate policy of excluding Aboriginal people from the array violated s. 629). See also *R. v. Smoke*, [1984] 2 C.N.L.R. 178 (Ont. H.C.J.) (government ruling not to provide list of names of persons living in two Aboriginal reserves to sheriff may have violated *Code*, but no remedy awarded in circumstances); *R. v. Church of Scientology of Toronto*, [1997] O.J. No. 1548 at para. 155, 116 C.C.C. (3d) 1 (Ont. C.A.), leave to appeal refused [1997] S.C.C.A. No. 683 (S.C.C.) ("The deliberate exclusion of distinctive groups based on characteristics such as race, sex, colour, religion or national origin might well infringe the requirement of a jury selected from a fair cross-section of the community.").

[33] See *R. v. Kent*, [1986] M.J. No. 239, 27 C.C.C. (3d) 405 (Man. C.A.); *R. v. LaForte*, [1975] M.J. No. 31, 25 C.C.C. (2d) 75 (Man. C.A.); *R. v. Lamirande*, [2002] M.J. No. 133, 164 C.C.C. (3d) 299 at para. 152 (Man. C.A.); *R. v. Bradley (No. 1)*, [1973] O.J. No. 1337, 23 C.R.N.S. 33 (Ont. H.C.J.); *R. v. Fowler*, [2005] B.C.J. No. 3035, 211 C.C.C. (3d) 401 (B.C.S.C); *R. v. Bear*, [1993] M.J. No. 636, 90 Man. R. (2d) 286 (Man. Q.B.); *R. v. Pigeon*, [2009] B.C.J. No. 764 at para. 27 (B.C.S.C.).

[34] See *R. v. F. (A.)*, [1994] O.J. No. 1392, [1994] 4 C.N.L.R. 99 (Ont. Gen. Div.); *R. v. Redhead*, [1995] M.J. No. 243, 99 C.C.C. (3d) 559 (Man. Q.B.); *R. v. Teerhuis-Moar*, [2007] M.J. No. 257, 49 C.R. (6th) 90 (Man. Q.B.), leave to appeal refused [2007] M.J. No. 354, 226 C.C.C. (3d) 105 (Man. C.A.); *R. v. Bear*, [1993] M.J. No. 636, 90 Man. R. (2d) 286 (Man. Q.B.); *R. v. Yooya*, [1995] S.J. No. 584, [1995] 2 W.W.R. 135 (Sask. Q.B.).

[35] [1993] A.J. No. 397, 22 C.R. (4th) 232 (Alta. Q.B.).

[36] *Ibid.* See also *R. v. Brown*, [2006] O.J. No. 5077, 45 C.R. (6th) 22 at paras. 17-29 (Ont. C.A.) (method used by trial judge to divide and present array for selection to jury, which gave temporal priority to groups with members of same race as accused, was ill advised but not reversible error as selected jury was representative of racial make-up of community).

[37] See Manitoba (Public Inquiry into the Administration of Justice and Aboriginal People), *Report of the Aboriginal Justice Inquiry of Manitoba*, vol. 1, c. 9 (Winnipeg: The Inquiry, 1991); Commission on Systemic Racism in the Ontario Criminal Justice System, *Report of the Commission on Systemic Racism in the Ontario Criminal Justice System* (Toronto: Queen's Printer for Ontario, 1995) at 250-53; Lynn Smith, "Charter Equality Rights: Some General Issues and Specific Applications in British Columbia to Elections, Juries and Illegitimacy" (1984) 18

on mere statistical under-representation.[38] As Justice Monnin observed in *R. v. Teerhuis-Moar*,[39] the achievement of "full statistical representativeness" is constrained by numerous social, logistical, and geographic factors.[40] Courts have consequently found violations for non-deliberate exclusion only when officials choose prospective jurors from databases very substantially under-representing groups defined by race, sex or age.[41]

3. EMPANELLING THE JURY

(1) General Procedure

§15.12 The process for empanelling a jury is governed by sections 631 to 644 of the *Criminal Code*. Absent a successful challenge to the array, the judge[42] will typically begin by "pre-screening" the prospective jurors summoned to the court for partiality and hardship. Specifically, section 632 authorizes the judge to excuse jurors on the following grounds:

> *(a)* personal interest in the matter to be tried;

U.B.C. L. Rev. 351 at 387-97; Cynthia Petersen, "Institutionalized Racism: The Need for Reform of the Criminal Jury Selection Process" (1993) 38 McGill L.J. 147.

[38] See *R. v. Teerhuis-Moar*, [2007] M.J. No. 257, 49 C.R. (6th) 90 (Man. Q.B.), leave to appeal refused [2007] M.J. No. 354, 226 C.C.C. (3d) 105 (Man. C.A.) (diminished chance that Aboriginals will respond to summons, given their greater mobility, does not violate the *Charter*); *R. v. Nepoose [No. 2]*, [1991] A.J. No. 1220, 128 A.R. 258 (Alta. Q.B.) (no violation where diminished chance, based on use of utility records, that young people and people living more than 60 kilometres from judicial centre would be selected to array); *R. v. Fowler*, [2005] B.C.J. No. 3035, 211 C.C.C. (3d) 401 (B.C.S.C.) (use of voter's list with disproportionately few Aboriginals to assemble array does not constitute partiality).

[39] [2007] M.J. No. 257, 49 C.R. (6th) 90 at para. 84 (Man. Q.B.), leave to appeal refused [2007] M.J. No. 354, 226 C.C.C. (3d) 105 (Man. C.A.).

[40] *Ibid.*, at para. 84 (C.R.) (noting that "full statistical representativeness may require a larger catchment area from more remote locations, thereby leading to increased travel costs and hardships to jurors who have to travel distances in order to serve"). See also *R. v. Poucette*, [1993] A.J. No. 1058 at para. 19 (Alta. Q.B.); *R. v. Nepoose [No. 2]*, [1991] A.J. No. 1220, 128 A.R. 258 at para. 22 (Alta. Q.B.); *R. v. Teerhuis-Moar*, [2010] M.J. No. 342, 263 C.C.C. (3d) 100 at para. 143 (Man. C.A.), leave to appeal refused [2011] S.C.C.A. No. 18 (S.C.C.); Law Reform Commission of Canada, *Report on the Jury* (Ottawa: The Commission, 1982) at 35.

[41] See *R. v. Nahdee*, [1993] O.J. No. 2425, 26 C.R. (4th) 109 at para. 24 (Ont. Gen. Div.) (sheriff's failure to secure list of Aboriginal residents in accordance with provincial legislation violated s. 629 of the *Criminal Code*); *R. v. Nepoose [No. 1]*, [1991] A.J. No. 1219, 128 A.R. 250 (Alta. Q.B.), affd [1993] A.J. No. 335 (Alta. C.A.) (use of utility records to select array resulted in substantially disproportionate number of males in violation of s. 11(*f*) of the *Charter*); *R. v. Buckingham*, [2007] N.J. No. 196, 221 C.C.C. (3d) 568 (Nfld. T.D.) (use of outdated vehicle registration list violated ss. 11(*d*) and 11(*f*) of the *Charter* because eligible persons under a certain age as well as those who have recently moved to the district systematically excluded). See also *R. v. Francis*, [2007] N.S.J. No. 143, 2007 NSSC 108 (N.S.S.C.) (change of venue to courthouse affording access to persons with disabilities required to ensure that disabled persons would have reasonable prospect of serving as jurors).

[42] Though the trial judge usually presides over jury selection, under s. 626.1 of the *Criminal Code* it may be any judge of the same court.

(b) relationship with the judge presiding over the jury selection process, the judge before whom the accused is to be tried, the prosecutor, the accused, the counsel for the accused or a prospective witness; or

(c) personal hardship or any other reasonable cause[43] that, in the opinion of the judge, warrants that the juror be excused.[44]

§15.13 The judge will usually address the entire array *en masse* and ask any potential jurors who wish to be excused on hardship grounds or have any of the conflicts of interest set out in subsections 632(*a*) or (*b*) to identify themselves.[45] Such persons may be excused summarily or after questioning on the basis for their exemption.[46] Potential jurors should be excused for partiality at this stage only in "obvious" cases, as when they have a personal interest in the matter or relationship with a trial participant.[47] Non-obvious cases (such as those based on pre-trial publicity or racial bias) must be dealt with under the "challenge for cause" process discussed in Part 3(5), below.[48]

§15.14 The next step is to select people, one by one, for further vetting from those remaining after pre-screening. First, the names, assigned numbers and addresses of each member of the array are written on cards.[49] The court clerk then puts the cards in a box, shakes them and draws one from the box, reading

---

[43] In *R. v. B. (A.)*, [1997] O.J. No. 1578, 115 C.C.C. (3d) 421 at para. 105 (Ont. C.A.), leave to appeal refused [1997] S.C.C.A. No. 461 (S.C.C.), the court interpreted "any other reasonable cause" to include "matters of obvious partiality not mentioned specifically in subsections (a) and (b)". See also *R. v. Krugel*, [2000] O.J. No. 354, 143 C.C.C. (3d) 367 (Ont. C.A.) (same interpretation of identical phrase in s. 633); *R. v. Holcomb*, [1973] S.C.J. No. 45, 15 C.C.C. (2d) 239 (S.C.C.), affg [1973] N.B.J. No. 75, 12 C.C.C. (2d) 417 (N.B.C.A.) (same interpretation of identical phrase in what is now s. 644(1)). A prospective juror might be excluded on this basis, for example, when his or her spouse has already been sworn as a juror. See *R. v. Fournier*, [2002] N.B.J. No. 326, 173 C.C.C. (3d) 566 at paras. 16-18 (N.B.C.A.) (spouses serving together "should be discouraged" but no evidence that trial fairness compromised in this case).

[44] *Criminal Code*, s. 632. While the *Code* does not expressly require pre-screening (s. 632 merely states that potential jurors may be excluded "at any time before the commencement" of the trial), it has become commonplace. See *R. v. Find*, [2001] S.C.J. No. 34, [2001] 1 S.C.R. 863 at paras. 22-23 (S.C.C.). See also *R. v. Douglas*, [2002] O.J. No. 4734, 170 C.C.C. (3d) 126 at paras. 28-33 (Ont. C.A.) (pre-screening should occur whenever it is likely that significant number of potential jurors will ultimately be excused for personal hardship or obvious partiality).

[45] See *R. v. Find*, [2001] S.C.J. No. 34, [2001] 1 S.C.R. 863 at para. 22 (S.C.C.). To help identify potential conflicts, judges will typically introduce themselves, counsel, and read a list of witnesses. See David M. Tanovich, David M. Paciocco & Steven Skurka, *Jury Selection in Criminal Trials: Skills, Science, and the Law* (Concord, ON: Irwin Law, 1997) at 78.

[46] See *R. v. B. (A.)*, [1997] O.J. No. 1578, 115 C.C.C. (3d) 421 at para. 79 (Ont. C.A.), leave to appeal refused [1997] S.C.C.A. No. 461 (S.C.C.) (in sexual assault cases, judges should alert panel to nature of charges, invite those who would find it too difficult to serve to identify themselves and excuse them on account of personal hardship without follow-up questioning).

[47] See *R. v. Find*, [2001] S.C.J. No. 34, [2001] 1 S.C.R. 863 at para. 23 (S.C.C.); *R. v B. (A.)*, [1997] O.J. No. 1578, 115 C.C.C. (3d) 421 (Ont. C.A.), leave to appeal refused [1997] S.C.C.A. No. 461 (S.C.C.).

[48] *R. v. B. (A.)*, [1997] O.J. No. 1578, 115 C.C.C. (3d) 421 at paras. 103-106 (Ont. C.A.), leave to appeal refused [1997] S.C.C.A. No. 461 (S.C.C.). See also *R. v. Sherratt*, [1991] S.C.J. No. 21, [1991] 1 S.C.R. 509 at 534 (S.C.C.) (deciding, under previous version of *Criminal Code* not expressly authorizing judicial exemption, that judge could nonetheless exempt jurors in "such clear-cut cases of partiality that ... the consent of counsel is and can be presumed").

[49] *Criminal Code*, s. 631(1).

the name and panel number on the card.[50] At this point, as detailed in Parts 3(2)-(5), below, the prospective juror may be excused or "stood aside" by the judge, successfully challenged for cause by one of the parties, or peremptorily challenged by one of the parties. If none of these things happens, the person will be sworn as the first juror. This process continues until the judge decides that a sufficient number have been called to comprise a full jury and any alternates.[51] The number of jurors for criminal trials is set at 12.[52] If the trial judge considers it to be in the interests of justice, he or she may also order that one or two additional jurors be selected as alternates before the cards are drawn.[53]

§15.15 If the array is exhausted without enough jurors sworn to constitute a full jury and alternates, the judge can order the sheriff (at the prosecutor's request) to "summon without delay as many persons, whether qualified jurors or not, as the court directs".[54] These "talesmen", as they are known, may be assembled from any place and are selected to the jury in the same manner as members of the initial array.[55] The sheriff may not, however, pre-screen prospective talesmen.[56]

(2) Excusing

§15.16 Whether or not the array has been pre-screened, when prospective jurors' cards are drawn, the judge may excuse them on one of the grounds set out in section 632 (discussed in Part 3(1), above).[57] As mentioned in Part 4, below, sworn jurors may also be excused under this provision at any time before the trial begins.[58]

(3) Stand Asides

§15.17 Instead of excusing persons whose names have been drawn, the judge may direct them to "stand by for reasons of personal hardship or any other

---

[50] *Criminal Code*, ss. 631(2)-(3).

[51] *Criminal Code*, s. 631(3).

[52] *Criminal Code*, ss. 631(5), 642.1(1). Formerly juries in the Yukon and the Northwest Territories could consist of six jurors. After this was held to violate s. 15 of the *Charter* in *R. v. Emile*, [1988] N.W.T.J. No. 196, 65 C.R. (3d) 135 (N.W.T.C.A.), the *Code* was amended to provide for 12-person juries throughout Canada: *An Act to amend the Criminal Code (jury)*, S.C. 1992, c. 41, s. 2.

[53] *Criminal Code*, s. 631(2.1).

[54] *Criminal Code*, s. 642(1). See also *R. v. Rowbotham*, [1988] O.J. No. 271, 63 C.R. (3d) 113 (Ont. C.A.) (talesmen need not be qualified jurors but judge should specify number to be summoned).

[55] *Criminal Code*, s. 642(3). See also *R. v. Mid Valley Tractor Sales Ltd.*, [1995] N.B.J. No. 396, 101 C.C.C. (3d) 253 at paras. 5-6 (N.B.C.A.) (assembling talesmen from government buildings did not violate accused's right to a random selection); *R. v. Lawrence*, [2001] N.S.J. No. 83, 192 N.S.R. (2d) 43 at para. 93 (N.S.C.A.) (sheriff may assemble people from streets).

[56] *R. v. Mid Valley Tractor Sales Ltd.*, [1995] N.B.J. No. 396, 101 C.C.C. (3d) 253 at para. 17 (N.B.C.A.).

[57] *Criminal Code*, s. 632.

[58] *Ibid.*

reasonable cause."[59] This is commonly known as the "stand aside" power. Persons stood aside will be called for possible selection only if the array is exhausted before 12 jurors (and any alternates) are selected.[60]

§15.18 For many decades, only the prosecutor (and not the judge or accused) could exercise stand asides.[61] As persons stood aside are often not called for selection, prosecutors could use their stand asides to exclude large numbers of potential jurors.[62] In *R. v. Bain*,[63] the Supreme Court of Canada held that this unilateral power violated the accused's right to a fair trial from an impartial tribunal under section 11(*d*) of the *Charter* because it provided a "tempting means to obtain a jury that appears to be favourable to the Crown."[64] Parliament subsequently amended the *Code* to allow only the trial judge to order stand asides.[65]

§15.19 Though the current legislation does not refer to partiality as a ground for standing aside prospective jurors, in *R. v. Krugel*[66] the Ontario Court of Appeal interpreted "other reasonable cause" to include it.[67] Thus, potential jurors who may (or may not) ultimately be dismissed for partiality may be stood aside until the array is exhausted. If the array is not exhausted, their partiality becomes moot.

(4) Challenges for Cause

(a) General Procedure

§15.20 If prospective jurors whose names are drawn are neither excused nor stood aside, both the prosecutor and accused may challenge them "for cause". This process, governed by sections 635 through 640 of the *Code*, occurs in two stages. The challenging party (usually the accused) must first convince the judge that the claim has an "air of reality".[68] As detailed below, most challenges allege that some (usually unspecified) potential jurors are partial to the other side. If the air of reality threshold is met, the challenging party may question jurors about their possible partiality (or other challengeable ground).[69] The questions

---

59   *Criminal Code*, s. 633. See *R. v. Krugel*, [2000] O.J. No. 354,143 C.C.C. (3d) 367 (Ont. C.A.) (no authority to stand aside jurors before names are drawn, though doing so did not cause prejudice in this case).

60   *Criminal Code*, s. 641.

61   See *Criminal Code*, R.S.C. 1970, c. C-34, s. 563 (granting prosecutor 48 stand asides).

62   See *e.g.*, *R. v. Pizzacalla*, [1991] O.J. No. 2008, 69 C.C.C. (3d) 115 (Ont. C.A.) (new trial ordered where prosecutor used stand asides to create all-female jury in a sexual assault case). The issue of sex discrimination in jury selection is discussed below in Part 3(5)(*b*).

63   [1992] S.C.J. No. 3, [1992] 1 S.C.R. 91 (S.C.C.).

64   *Ibid.*, at 103 (S.C.R.), *per* Cory J. See also *ibid.*, at 148-62 (S.C.R.), *per* Stevenson J.

65   *An Act to amend the Criminal Code (jury)*, S.C. 1992, c. 41, s. 2.

66   [2000] O.J. No. 354, 143 C.C.C. (3d) 367 (Ont. C.A.).

67   *Ibid.*

68   *R. v. Sherratt*, [1991] S.C.J. No. 21, [1991] 1 S.C.R. 509 at 535 (S.C.C.). See also *R. v. Yumnu*, [2010] O.J. No. 4163, 260 C.C.C. (3d) 421 at para. 70 (Ont. C.A.) (applicant must show "'realistic potential' that the jury pool may contain people who are not impartial").

69   See *R. v. Guérin*, [1984] J.Q. no 696, 13 C.C.C. (3d) 231 (Que. C.A.) (trial judge erred in conducting questioning). In Alberta, it is common for judges to conduct the questioning, especially

must be approved by the judge and are generally limited in scope.[70] Challenges for cause, the Supreme Court stated in *R. v. Sherratt*,[71] are not meant to be a "'fishing expedition' in order to obtain personal information about the juror."[72]

§15.21 Curiously, though trial judges decide whether challenges for cause should proceed, with one minor exception[73] they do not decide the merits of challenges of specific jurors. Rather, this decision is made by the "two jurors who were last sworn", who are commonly known as the "triers" of the challenge.[74] Subject to the rules set out in the following two paragraphs, this process is mandatory; the challenge cannot be decided by the judge[75] or persons not among the last two to be sworn as jurors.[76]

§15.22 If two jurors have not yet been sworn (as is usually the case before the challenges begin), the judge appoints any "two persons present" to decide the challenge.[77] It is common practice (but not mandatory) for the judge to randomly choose two members of the array for this purpose.[78] These triers may not themselves be challenged for cause.[79] Some courts require the first person sworn to the jury to replace the first trier, who then returns to the array to await possible

---

for challenges based on racial bias. See *R. v. McLeod*, [2005] A.J. No. 1572, 2005 ABQB 846 at para. 24 (Alta. Q.B.).

[70] *R. v. Sherratt*, [1991] S.C.J. No. 21, [1991] 1 S.C.R. 509 (S.C.C.).

[71] [1991] S.C.J. No. 21, [1991] 1 S.C.R. 509 (S.C.C.).

[72] *Ibid.*, at 533 (S.C.R.).

[73] The only exception is for challenges alleging that the prospective juror's name is not on the panel. In such cases the judge decides the challenge by "inspection of the panel, and such other evidence as the judge thinks fit to receive": *Criminal Code*, s. 640(1).

[74] *Criminal Code*, s. 640(2). At common law and under early versions of the *Criminal Code*, challenges to the array were also decided by triers. See Roger E. Salhany, *Canadian Criminal Procedure*, 6th ed., looseleaf (Aurora, ON: Canada Law Book, 1994) at para. 6.2810.

[75] See *R. v. Barrow*, [1987] S.C.J. No. 84, [1987] 2 S.C.R. 694 at 714 (S.C.C.) ("The judge's role is to supervise trials of partiality, not to decide them."); *R. v. Sherratt*, [1991] S.C.J. No. 21, [1991] 1 S.C.R. 509 at 534-35 (S.C.C.) ("There is absolutely no room for a trial judge to increase further his/her powers and take over the challenge process by deciding controversial questions of partiality."); *R. v. Guérin*, [1984] J.Q. no 69613 C.C.C. (3d) 231 at 246 (Que. C.A.) *per* Bisson J.A. (trial judge erred in questioning and deciding partiality of potential jurors on basis of exposure to pre-trial publicity, judge's capacity to pre-screen jurors for obvious cases of partiality cannot usurp challenge for cause process); *R. v. Pietrangelo*, [2001] O.J. No. 868, 152 C.C.C. (3d) 475 (Ont. C.A.) (accused's right to challenge for cause usurped by judicial screening for partiality on basis of pre-trial publicity). But see *R. v. Katoch*, [2009] O.J. No. 3456, 246 C.C.C. (3d) 423 (Ont. C.A.) (no jurisdictional error where judge withdrew decision from triers based on answers to first questions asked; answers clearly revealed lack of bias and failure of challenge effectively conceded by party bringing it).

[76] See *R. v. V. (W.)*, [2007] O.J. No. 3247 (Ont. C.A.), leave to appeal refused [2007] S.C.C.A. No. 615 (S.C.C.).

[77] *Criminal Code*, s. 640(2). See also *R. v. Sampson* (1935), 63 C.C.C. (3d) 24 (N.S.C.A.).

[78] See *R. v. Brown*, [2002] O.J. No. 2562, 166 C.C.C. (3d) 570 at para. 7 (Ont. C.A.).

[79] See *R. v. English*, [1993] N.J. No. 252, 84 C.C.C. (3d) 511 (Nfld. C.A.); *R. v. Brown*, [2002] O.J. No. 2562, 166 C.C.C. (3d) 570 (Ont. C.A.). At least one court has held, however, that the judge may screen prospective jurors for suitability to serve as the initial triers: *R. v. Riley*, [2009] O.J. No. 1851, 247 C.C.C. (3d) 517 at paras. 21-24 (Ont. S.C.J.).

selection to the jury.[80] In other courts, the first two triers continue in that role until two jurors are sworn and replace them.[81]

§15.23 Under a 2008 amendment to the *Criminal Code*, the accused may apply for an order removing other sworn jurors and prospective jurors from the courtroom while the triers decide the challenges.[82] The judge may make this order when it is "necessary to preserve the impartiality of the jurors."[83] In such cases the first two triers decide all of the challenges and never become jurors.[84]

§15.24 Before the challenges begin, the judge should tell the triers that: they can deliberate either in court or in the jury room; their decision must be unanimous and based on a balance of probabilities; and they should inform the judge if they cannot agree within a reasonable time.[85] The judge should also instruct them on the meaning of partiality and "the importance and purpose of the challenge for cause process."[86] The judge may also allow counsel to make submissions to the triers before they make their decision.[87] Once the decision is in the triers' hands it must be decided by them; the challenge may not be withdrawn or

---

[80] See *R. v. Brown*, [2002] O.J. No. 2562, 166 C.C.C. (3d) 570 (Ont. C.A.) (approving of this procedure); *R. v. English*, [1993] N.J. No. 252, 84 C.C.C. (3d) 511 (Nfld. C.A.) (suggesting that this is the preferable procedure but declining to find that trial judge's adoption of the alternative approach was in error). See also Austin M. Cooper, "The ABC's of Challenge for Cause in Jury Trials: To Challenge or Not to Challenge and What to Ask if You Get It" (1994) 37 Crim. L.Q. 62 at 68 (suggesting that this is the preferable procedure).

[81] See *R. v. Brigham*, [1988] J.Q. no. 1027, 44 C.C.C. (3d) 379 (Que. C.A.) (first two triers must continue until two jurors are sworn).

[82] *Criminal Code*, s. 640(2.1).

[83] *Criminal Code*, s. 640(2.1). See also *R. v. White*, [2009] O.J. No. 3348 at para. 26 (Ont. S.C.J.) (noting that this process avoids "the risk that a prospective juror might make a comment during the challenge for cause process which could taint both sworn and prospective jurors"); *R. v. Riley*, [2009] O.J. No. 1851, 247 C.C.C. (3d) 517 at paras. 11-13 (Ont. S.C.J.) (comparing advantages and disadvantages of "rotating" and "static" triers); *R. v. Swite*, [2011] B.C.J. No. 175, 2011 BCCA 54 at paras. 16-31 (B.C.C.A.) (trial judge erred interpreting s. 640 as requiring the use of static triers on a challenge for cause when accused made it clear that he wanted rotating triers).

[84] *Criminal Code*, s. 639(2.2). Before this amendment, courts had held that the judge had a discretion to exclude from the courtroom prospective jurors other than the triers and the individual being challenged. See *R. v. Moore-McFarlane*, [2001] O.J. No. 4646, 160 C.C.C. (3d) 493 at para. 85 (Ont. C.A.); *R. v. English*, [1993] N.J. No. 252, 84 C.C.C. (3d) 511 (Nfld. C.A.). It is not clear whether that discretion has been superseded by ss. 639(2.1)-(2.2) of the *Code*. If it has, then the only way to exclude prospective or sworn jurors is through s. 639(2.1); and in such cases, the two initial triers must decide every challenge. See *R. v. Riley*, [2009] O.J. No. 1851, 247 C.C.C. (3d) 517 (Ont. S.C.J.). If not, then judges may still exclude prospective or sworn jurors during the traditional procedure where the triers are continually replaced. See *R. v. Huard*, [2009] O.J. No. 3142, 247 C.C.C. (3d) 526 (Ont. S.C.J.); *R. v. White*, [2009] O.J. No. 3348 (Ont. S.C.J.); *R. v. Sandham*, [2009] O.J. No. 1853, 248 C.C.C. (3d) 46 (Ont. S.C.J.).

[85] See *R. v. Hubbert*, [1975] O.J. No. 2595, 29 C.C.C. (2d) 279 at 294 (Ont. C.A.), affd [1977] S.C.J. No. 4, [1977] 2 S.C.R. 267 (S.C.C.); *R. v. Douglas*, [2002] O.J. No. 4734, 170 C.C.C. (3d) 126 at paras. 7-23 (Ont. C.A.); *R. v. Moore-McFarlane*, [2001] O.J. No. 4646, 160 C.C.C. (3d) 493 at para. 85 (Ont. C.A.). For efficiency's sake, these instructions may be imparted to groups of potential jurors/triers as they are brought into court for selection: *R. v. Douglas*, [2002] O.J. No. 4734, 170 C.C.C. (3d) 126 at para. 20 (Ont. C.A.).

[86] *R. v. Moore-McFarlane*, [2001] O.J. No. 4646, 160 C.C.C. (3d) 493 at para. 88 (Ont. C.A.).

[87] *Ibid.*, at para. 89 (C.C.C.).

conceded by the parties.[88] As mentioned, the triers' decision must be unanimous, and if they cannot agree within a reasonable time the judge may direct others to decide the challenge.[89] If the challenge is upheld, the prospective juror is dismissed; if not, then subject to either party exercising a peremptory challenge (discussed below), he or she will be sworn and join the jury.[90] There is no appeal from the decision of the triers.[91]

(b) Applying to Challenge for Cause

§15.25 Challenges for cause must be based on at least one of the following grounds set out in section 638(1) of the *Criminal Code*:

    (a) the name of the juror does not appear on the panel;

    (b) the juror is not indifferent between the Queen and the accused;

    (c) the juror has been convicted of an offence for which he or she was sentenced to death or imprisonment exceeding 12 months;

    (d) the juror is an alien;

    (e) the juror is physically unable to properly perform the duties of a juror; and

    (f) the juror does not speak the language in which the trial will be conducted.[92]

Most of these are fact-based and uncontroversial.[93] The ground generating the overwhelming proportion of litigation is section 638(1)(*b*): non-indifference between the accused and the Crown. "Not indifferent", according to the Supreme Court of Canada, means "not impartial" or "prejudiced".[94] As mentioned in Part 3, above, by this point potential jurors with obvious conflicts of interest will usually have been excused or stood aside.[95] If not, and a party has reason to think that particular potential jurors may be biased, the party may apply to challenge them.[96] Most often, however, the parties will not have such knowledge. Challenges for cause are thus usually grounded on the potential partiality of unspecified members of the entire array.

---

[88] See *R. v. Wade*, [1990] O.J. No. 1768, 11 W.C.B. (2d) 229 (Ont. C.A.).

[89] *Criminal Code*, s. 640(4). See also *R. v. Brigham*, [1988] J.Q. no 1027, 44 C.C.C. (3d) 379 (Que. C.A.).

[90] *Criminal Code*, s. 640(3).

[91] *R. v. Sherratt*, [1991] S.C.J. No. 21, [1991] 1 S.C.R. 509 at 521-22 (S.C.C.).

[92] This list is exhaustive: *Criminal Code*, s. 638(2) ("No challenge for cause shall be allowed on a ground not mentioned in subsection (1).").

[93] But see *R. v. Seenivasam*, [2004] O.J. No. 4888, 34 C.R. (6th) 200 (Ont. S.C.J.) (permitting challenge under s. 638(*f*) on basis of potential jurors' ability to speak English; significant proportion of population not native English speakers and self-assessment of linguistic competence based on written questionnaire not sufficient to guarantee fair trial).

[94] *R. v. Williams*, [1998] S.C.J. No. 49, [1998] 1 S.C.R. 1128 at para. 10 (S.C.C.).

[95] *Criminal Code*, ss. 632-633.

[96] See *R. v. Rasmussen*, [1934] N.B.J. No. 1, 62 C.C.C. 217 (N.B.C.A.).

§15.26 Potential jurors are presumed to be impartial.[97] According to the Supreme Court in *Sherratt*, the party applying to challenge must therefore show that there is a "realistic potential for . . . partiality."[98] That said, the Court also stressed that challenges for cause should not be regarded as "extraordinary" or "exceptional"; the right to challenge, it added, "is an important one designed to ensure a fair trial."[99] And in *R. v. Williams*,[100] the Court noted that since the test speaks of the "potential" for partiality, a "reasonably generous approach is appropriate."[101] The trial judge's decision to allow or refuse the challenge is discretionary and accorded deference on appeal.[102]

§15.27 To convince the court to approve the challenge, the party must generally show that: (*i*) "a widespread bias exists in the community"; and (*ii*) that some jurors "may be incapable of setting aside this bias, despite trial safeguards, to render an impartial decision."[103] The first criterion requires proof that some people in the community harbour a bias that could "incline a juror to a certain party or conclusion in a manner that is unfair" and that such bias is "sufficiently pervasive in the community to raise the possibility that it may be harboured by one or more members of a representative jury pool."[104] The second requires a

---

[97]   *R. v. Sherratt*, [1991] S.C.J. No. 21, [1991] 1 S.C.R. 509 at 527 (S.C.C.); *R. v. Spence*, [2005] S.C.J. No. 74, [2005] 3 S.C.R. 458 at para. 21 (S.C.C.). See also *R. v. Vermette*, [1988] S.C.J. No. 47, [1988] 1 S.C.R. 985 (S.C.C.); *R. v. Hubbert*, [1975] O.J. No. 2595, 29 C.C.C. (2d) 279 at 289-96 (Ont. C.A.), affd [1977] S.C.J. No. 4, [1977] 2 S.C.R. 267 (S.C.C.) (Ont. C.A.); *R. v. Williams*, [1998] S.C.J. No. 49, [1998] 1 S.C.R. 1128 at para. 13 (S.C.C.).

[98]   *R. v. Sherratt*, [1991] S.C.J. No. 21, [1991] 1 S.C.R. 509 at 536 (S.C.C.). See also *R v. Yumnu*, [2010] O.J. No. 4163, 260 C.C.C. (3d) 421 at para. 70 (Ont. C.A.).

[99]   *R. v. Sherratt*, [1991] S.C.J. No. 21, [1991] 1 S.C.R. 509 at 536 (S.C.C.).

[100]   [1998] S.C.J. No. 49, [1998] 1 S.C.R. 1128 (S.C.C.).

[101]   *Ibid.*, at para. 32 (S.C.R.). See also *R. v. Find*, [2001] S.C.J. No. 34, [2001] 1 S.C.R. 863 at para. 45 (S.C.C.).

[102]   See *R. v. Williams*, [1998] S.C.J. No. 49, [2008] 1 S.C.R. 1128 at paras. 13-14 (S.C.C.) (noting, however, that judges "exercising the discretion to permit or refuse challenges for cause must act on the evidence and in a way that fulfills the purpose of s. 638(1)(*b*) — to prevent persons who are not indifferent between the Crown and the accused from serving on the jury"); *R. v. Barnes*, [1999] O.J. No. 3296, 27 C.R. (5th) 290 at para. 30 (Ont. C.A.); *R. v. Parks*, [1993] O.J. No. 2157, 15 O.R. (3d) 324 at 335-36 (C.A.), leave to appeal refused [1993] S.C.J. No. 481, [1994] 1 S.C.R. x (S.C.C.); *R. v. Hubbert*, [1975] O.J. No. 2595, 29 C.C.C. (2d) 279 at 291 (Ont. C.A.), affd [1977] S.C.J. No. 4, [1977] 2 S.C.R. 267 (S.C.C.); *R. v. Zundel [No. 1]*, [1987] O.J. No. 52, 31 C.C.C. (3d) 97 at 135 (Ont. C.A.), leave to appeal refused [1987] S.C.C.A. No. 116, [1987] 1 S.C.R. xii (S.C.C.).

[103]   *R. v. Find*, [2001] S.C.J. No. 34, [2001] 1 S.C.R. 863 at para. 32 (S.C.C.). See also *R. v. Sherratt*, [1991] S.C.J. No. 21, [1991] 1 S.C.R. 509 at 536 (S.C.C.) (the "threshold question is not whether the ground of alleged partiality will create such partiality in a juror, but rather whether it could create that partiality which would prevent a juror from being indifferent as to the result"); *R. v. Spence*, [2005] S.C.J. No. 74, [2005] 3 S.C.R. 458 at paras. 23-26 (S.C.C.).

[104]   *R. v. Find*, [2001] S.C.J. No. 34, [2001] 1 S.C.R. 863 at paras. 36-39 (S.C.C.). The Court mentioned in *R. v. Williams*, [1998] S.C.J. No. 49, [2008] 1 S.C.R. 1128 at para. 43 (S.C.C.), that prejudice that is "less than widespread" might "in some circumstances" be sufficient. In *R. v. Find*, [2001] S.C.J. No. 34, [2001] 1 S.C.R. 863 at para. 39 (S.C.C.), the Court characterized these circumstances as "exceptional". But see *R. v. Katoch*, [2009] O.J. No. 3456, 246 C.C.C. (3d) 423 (Ont. C.A.) (though anti-police bias not widespread, questioning of prospective jurors on affiliation with anti-police advocacy group warranted in case where police officer accused of assaulting group member).

demonstration that some jurors may be "unable to set aside their bias despite the cleansing effect of the judge's instructions and the trial process".[105] The nature of the evidence required to meet these conditions depends on the type of partiality alleged. The three most common challenges are based on: (*i*) exposure to pre-trial publicity; (*ii*) racial bias; and (*iii*) bias against people accused of certain types of offences.[106] We examine each in turn below.

(i)   Pre-trial Publicity

§15.28 This type of challenge aims to mitigate the risk that jurors will be biased by exposure to information about the case before trial. The leading decision is *R. v. Sherratt*, where the media had reported widely on the grisly details of a murder before trial.[107] In upholding the trial judge's denial of the challenge, the Supreme Court held that mere reporting of facts about the case would not normally justify a challenge for cause.[108] Rather, the reporting must itself be biased or misleading, as where "the media misrepresents the evidence, dredges up and widely publicizes discreditable incidents from an accused's past or engages in speculation as to the accused's guilt or innocence."[109] This threshold was not met in *Sherratt* because the reporting occurred months before trial and focused not on the accused but on the victim's reputation and the search for his body.[110]

§15.29 Later cases have confirmed that widespread publicity alone does not justify a challenge for cause.[111] While no single factor is determinative, successful challenges often involve extensive publicity that is critical of the accused and extends close to the beginning of trial. Courts are less likely to approve challenges based on objective reporting or critical publicity ceasing long before trial. In reversing the trial judge's decision to deny a challenge in *R. v. Zundel*,[112] for example, the court characterized the widespread media reports of the accused's Holocaust denials as "generally adverse" to the accused.[113] And in holding that a

---

[105] *R. v. Find*, [2001] S.C.J. No. 34, [2001] 1 S.C.R. 863 at para. 40 (S.C.C.).

[106] Where the judge approves more than one type of challenge, the questions related to each challenge should be clearly separated from one another. See *R. v. Glasgow*, [1996] O.J. No. 3026, 110 C.C.C. (3d) 57 at paras. 7-35 (Ont. C.A.) (reference to accused's race in question directed at pre-trial publicity not sufficient to address racial prejudice).

[107] *R. v. Sherratt*, [1991] S.C.J. No. 21, [1991] 1 S.C.R. 509 (S.C.C.).

[108] *Ibid.*, at 527 (S.C.R.). See also *R. v. Hubbert*, [1975] O.J. No. 2595, 29 C.C.C. (2d) 279 at 291-92 (Ont. C.A.), affd [1977] S.C.J. No. 4, [1977] 2 S.C.R. 267 (S.C.C.).

[109] *R. v. Sherratt*, [1991] S.C.J. No. 21, [1991] 1 S.C.R. 509 at 535-36 (S.C.C.). See also *R. v. Zundel [No. 1]*, [1987] O.J. No. 52, 31 C.C.C. (3d) 97 at 135 (Ont. C.A.), leave to appeal refused [1987] S.C.C.A. No. 116, [1987] 1 S.C.R. xii (S.C.C.).

[110] *R. v. Sherratt*, [1991] S.C.J. No. 21, [1991] 1 S.C.R. 509 at 537 (S.C.C.).

[111] See *R. v. Smith*, [1993] O.J. No. 865, [1993] 63 O.A.C. 181 (Ont. C.A.); *R. v. Merz*, [1999] O.J. No. 4309, 140 C.C.C. (3d) 259 at para. 35 (Ont. C.A.).

[112] [1987] O.J. No. 52, 31 C.C.C. (3d) 97 (Ont. C.A.), leave to appeal refused [1987] S.C.C.A. No. 116, [1987] 1 S.C.R. xii (S.C.C.).

[113] *Ibid.*, at 132 (C.C.C.).

challenge should have been allowed in *R. v. Keegstra*,[114] the Court stressed that widespread adverse publicity (including remarks by the Premier and parliamentarians) "continued unceasingly" right up to the beginning of the trial.[115] In *R. v. Merz*,[116] in contrast, the Court upheld the trial judge's refusal to permit a challenge where all but a few of many "mostly factual" articles about the case were published more than a year before trial.[117] Though one article revealed negative and inadmissible information about the accused, the passage of two years between its publication and trial "provided an adequate antidote against any realistic possibility of prejudice".[118]

(ii) Racial Bias

§15.30 Until quite recently, applications to challenge prospective jurors for racial bias were invariably rejected.[119] While trial judges would sometimes warn the jury to guard against the influence of racial prejudice in cases with visible minority accused, they refused to allow questioning on the issue.[120]

§15.31 The situation is very different today, where racial bias challenges are common. The turning point was *R. v. Parks*,[121] where the Ontario Court of Appeal overturned the trial judge's refusal to allow a race-based challenge in the trial of a black defendant in Toronto.[122] In his decision for the court, Justice Doherty canvassed an extensive body of social science evidence (not introduced by counsel) documenting the pervasive nature of racism, especially against blacks. He wrote:

> ... Racism, and in particular anti-black racism, is a part of our community's psyche. A significant segment of our community holds overtly racist views. A much larger segment subconsciously operates on the basis of negative racial stereotypes. Furthermore, our institutions, including the criminal justice system, reflect and perpetuate those negative stereotypes. These elements combine to infect our society as a whole with the evil of racism. Blacks are among the primary victims of that evil.

---

[114] [1991] A.J. No. 232, 63 C.C.C. (3d) 110 at 116 (Alta. C.A.) (supplementing [1988] A.J. No. 501, 43 C.C.C. (3d) 150 (Alta. C.A.), revd [1990] S.C.J. No. 131, [1990] 3 S.C.R. 697 (S.C.C.)), leave to appeal refused [1991] S.C.C.A. No. 188 (S.C.C.).

[115] *Ibid.*, at 116 (63 C.C.C.).

[116] [1999] O.J. No. 4309, 140 C.C.C. (3d) 259 (Ont. C.A.).

[117] *Ibid.*, at paras. 30-35 (C.C.C.). See also *R. v. Smith*, [1993] O.J. No. 865, [1993] 63 O.A.C. 181 (Ont. C.A.) (upholding trial judge's denial of challenge despite intense and sensational media coverage lasting only one week, 18 months before trial).

[118] *R. v. Merz*, [1999] O.J. No. 4309, 140 C.C.C. (3d) 259 at para. 36 (Ont. C.A.).

[119] See *e.g.*, *R. v. Racco (No. 2)*, [1975] O.J. No. 1660, 23 C.C.C. (2d) 205 at 208 (Ont. Co. Ct.); *R. v. Crosby*, [1979] O.J. No. 4569, 49 C.C.C. (2d) 255 (Ont. H.C.J.).

[120] See *e.g.*, *R. v. Crosby*, [1979] O.J. No. 4569, 49 C.C.C. (2d) 255 at 256 (Ont. H.C.J.) ("to permit challenges of this kind to go forward simply on the ground that man is prejudiced and that black and white may frequently be prejudiced against each other is to admit to a weakness in our nation and in our community which I do not propose to acknowledge").

[121] [1993] O.J. No. 2157, 84 C.C.C. (3d) 353 (Ont. C.A.), leave to appeal refused [1993] S.C.J. No. 481, [1994] 1 S.C.R. x (S.C.C.).

[122] *Ibid.*

In my opinion, there can be no doubt that there existed a realistic possibility that one or more potential jurors drawn from the Metropolitan Toronto community would, consciously or subconsciously, come to court possessed of negative stereotypical attitudes toward black persons.[123]

§15.32 The safeguards available in the trial process to mitigate such bias,[124] Justice Doherty reasoned, could not ensure that subtle and invidious stereotypes would not influence jurors' decisions.[125] This risk led him to conclude that the trial judge should have allowed counsel to ask prospective jurors if their "ability to judge the evidence in the case without bias, prejudice or partiality [would] be affected by the fact that the person charged is ... black ... and the deceased is a white man?"[126] He further held that it would be "the better course" to permit this question to be asked "in any trial held in Metropolitan Toronto involving a black accused."[127] Such a procedure would, he added, help to prevent some biased people from joining the jury, sensitize accepted jurors on "the need to confront potential racial bias and ensure that it does not impact on their verdict," and enhance the "appearance of fairness in the mind of the accused."[128]

§15.33 Courts outside of Ontario (and some within) did not rush to follow *Parks*.[129] Many construed it as applying only to black defendants in the Toronto area.[130] This is how the trial judge in *R. v. Williams*[131] read *Parks* in refusing to

---

[123] *Ibid.*, at 369 (C.C.C.).

[124] See *R. v. Parks*, [1993] O.J. No. 2157, 84 C.C.C. (3d) 353 at 370-71 (Ont. C.A.), leave to appeal refused [1993] S.C.J. No. 481, [1994] 1 S.C.R. x (S.C.C.) (noting salutary effects on racial bias of juror's oath or affirmation, solemnity of proceedings, jury's diversity, collective decision-making and judicial directions).

[125] *R. v. Parks*, [1993] O.J. No. 2157, 84 C.C.C. (3d) 353 at 371 (Ont. C.A.), leave to appeal refused [1993] S.C.J. No. 481, [1994] 1 S.C.R. x (S.C.C.) (because much racism is "engrained in an individual's subconscious", it will "prove more resistant to judicial cleansing" than exposure to pre-trial publicity).

[126] The original question proposed also referred to the accused's status as a "Jamaican immigrant". Justice Doherty ruled that this reference should have been omitted as there was no indication that the accused's nationality or immigration status would be made known to the jury. *R. v. Parks*, [1993] O.J. No. 2157, 84 C.C.C. (3d) 353 at 359 (Ont. C.A.), leave to appeal refused [1993] S.C.J. No. 481, [1994] 1 S.C.R. x (S.C.C.). Following *Parks*, courts have typically omitted references to nationality and immigration status in race-based challenges. See *R. v. Koh*, [1998] O.J. No. 5425, 131 C.C.C. (3d) 257 (Ont. C.A.); *R. v. Bishop*, [1999] O.J. No. 3155 (Ont. C.A.); *R. v. Barnes*, [1999] O.J. No. 3296, 138 C.C.C. (3d) 500 (Ont. C.A.); *R. v. Phung*, [2006] O.J. No. 5661 (S.C.).

[127] *R. v. Parks*, [1993] O.J. No. 2157, 84 C.C.C. (3d) 353 (Ont. C.A.), leave to appeal refused [1993] S.C.J. No. 481, [1994] 1 S.C.R. x (S.C.C.). See also *R. v. Wilson*, [1996] O.J. No. 1158 (Ont. C.A.) (extending application of *Parks* to black defendants anywhere in Ontario).

[128] *R. v. Parks*, [1993] O.J. No. 2157, 84 C.C.C. (3d) 353 at 379-80, 15 O.R. (3d) 324 at 335-36 (Ont. C.A.), leave to appeal refused [1993] S.C.J. No. 481, [1994] 1 S.C.R. x (S.C.C.). See also *R. v. Spence*, [2005] S.C.J. No. 74, [2005] 3 S.C.R. 458 at para. 25 (S.C.C.).

[129] See David M. Tanovich, "Rethinking Jury Selection: Challenges for Cause and Peremptory Challenges" (1994) 30 C.R. (4th) 310.

[130] See *e.g.*, *R. v. Drakes*, [1998] B.C.J. No. 127, 122 C.C.C. (3d) 498 (B.C.C.A.); *R. v. Cinous*, [2000] J.Q. no 6, 143 C.C.C. (3d) 397 at paras. 31-41 (Que. C.A.), revd on other grounds [2002] S.C.J. No. 28, [2002] 2 S.C.R. 3 (S.C.C.) (refusing to take judicial notice of anti-black bias in Montreal).

allow an Aboriginal accused to challenge prospective jurors for racial prejudice. In overturning this decision, the Supreme Court of Canada largely adopted the approach taken in *Parks*.[132] Writing for the Court in *Williams*, Justice McLachlin (as she then was) noted that racial bias is often subtle and subconscious and thus difficult to counter with judicial directions.[133] Where widespread bias is shown, she reasoned, it will be reasonable to infer that "some people will have difficulty identifying and eliminating their biases."[134] It follows that racial challenges should be allowed on the basis of widespread bias alone; the second element of the "air of reality" test need not be addressed.[135]

§15.34 Justice McLachlin noted, however, that widespread bias cannot be presumed in every case where the accused is a member of a racial minority.[136] The accused must show that such bias actually exists in the "community from which the jury pool is drawn."[137] This can be established either by evidence or judicial notice.[138] And when a finding of widespread racial prejudice has been made in one case, "judges in subsequent cases may be able to take judicial notice of the fact."[139]

§15.35 Lastly, Justice McLachlin noted that trial judges have "a wide discretion" to control the challenge process to minimize its duration and intrusiveness.[140] The decision by the judge at Williams's first trial to limit the challenge to two questions (with a few "tightly controlled" subsidiary questions) was a

---

131 [1994] B.C.J. No. 1301, 90 C.C.C. (3d) 194 (B.C.S.C.), affd [1996] B.C.J. No. 926, 106 C.C.C. (3d) 215 (B.C.C.A.), revd [1998] S.C.J. No. 49, [2008] 1 S.C.R. 1128 (S.C.C.). A race-based challenge for cause had been permitted at Williams's first trial, which ended in a mistrial. See *R. v. Williams*, [1998] S.C.J. No. 49, [2008] 1 S.C.R. 1128 at paras. 3-7 (S.C.C.).

132 *R. v. Williams*, [1998] S.C.J. No. 49, [1998] 1 S.C.R. 1128 (S.C.C.).

133 *R. v. Williams*, [1998] S.C.J. No. 49, [1998] 1 S.C.R. 1128 at paras. 20-25 (S.C.C.) ("We should not assume that instructions from the judge or other safeguards will eliminate biases that may be deeply ingrained in the subconscious psyches of jurors."). See also Jerry Kang, "Trojan Horses of Race" (2004) 118 Harv. L. Rev. 1489 at 1499-1520 (reviewing experimental psychological and other empirical evidence of subtlety and pervasiveness of racial stereotyping).

134 *R. v. Williams*, [1998] S.C.J. No. 49, [1998] 1 S.C.R. 1128 at para. 23 (S.C.C.).

135 See *R. v. Williams*, [1998] S.C.J. No. 49, [1998] 1 S.C.R. 1128 at para. 57 (S.C.C.) (for racial bias challenges, "the judge should exercise his or her discretion to permit challenges for cause if the accused establishes widespread racial prejudice in the community"). The Court in *Williams* also held that there need not be a link between the nature of the prejudice and any specific aspect of the trial (such as an interracial element to the crime or a belief that members of the accused's race are more likely to commit the offence charged). These issues may be determinative, however, in the triers' decision to accept or reject a particular proposed juror: *R. v. Williams*, [1998] S.C.J. No. 49, [1998] 1 S.C.R. 1128 at paras. 26-31 (S.C.C.).

136 *R. v. Williams*, [1998] S.C.J. No. 49, [1998] 1 S.C.R. 1128 at para. 41 (S.C.C.).

137 *R. v. Williams*, [1998] S.C.J. No. 49, [1998] 1 S.C.R. 1128 at para. 41 (S.C.C.) (no bias against Aboriginals likely, for example, in "a community where aboriginals are in a majority position," though generally "where widespread prejudice against people of the accused's race is demonstrated at a national or provincial level, it will often be reasonable to infer that such prejudice is replicated at the community level").

138 *Ibid.*, at para. 54 (S.C.R.).

139 *Ibid.*

140 *Ibid.*, at para. 55 (S.C.R.).

"practice to be emulated," she stated.[141] The questions were: (*i*) "[w]ould your ability to judge the evidence in the case without bias, prejudice or partiality be affected by the fact that the person charged is an Indian?"; and (*ii*) "[w]ould your ability to judge the evidence in the case without bias, prejudice, or partiality be affected by the fact that the person charged is an Indian and the complainant is white?"[142]

§15.36 Lower courts have generally followed this practice and limited the types of questions that may be asked in racial challenges.[143] Some defendants have sought approval for a lengthy list of "attitudinal" questions designed to ferret out racial bias. A few courts have permitted this,[144] but most have not.[145] After reviewing expert evidence and studies on the issue, the Ontario Court of Appeal in *R. v. Gayle*[146] concluded that this kind of questioning, while not required, may be appropriate in some cases.[147] It held, however, that the trial judge did not err in limiting the challenge to the types of questions approved in *Parks* and *Williams*.[148]

§15.37 Courts have since expanded *Parks* and *Williams* to apply to prejudice against any racial minority. In *R. v. Koh*,[149] the Ontario Court of Appeal took judicial notice of discrimination against visible minorities, holding that non-white defendants have a "right" to challenge for cause without calling evidence.[150] Courts in other provinces also commonly permit visible minority accused to make race-based challenges, often with the prosecutor's consent.[151]

---

[141] *Ibid.*

[142] *Ibid.*, at para. 3 (S.C.R.).

[143] See *e.g.*, *R. v. Sandham*, [2009] O.J. No. 1853, 248 C.C.C. (3d) 46 at paras. 3-9 (Ont. S.C.J.); *R. v. VandenElsen*, [2005] O.J. No. 1359, 29 C.R. (6th) 316 at para. 18 (Ont. S.C.J.); *R. v. McLeod*, [2005] A.J. No. 1572, 2005 ABQB 846 at para. 23 (Alta. Q.B.).

[144] See *e.g.*, *R. v. Griffis*, [1993] O.J. No. 1939, 16 C.R.R. (2d) 322 (Ont. Gen. Div.).

[145] See *e.g.*, *R. v. Dhillon*, [2001] B.C.J. No. 1946, 158 C.C.C. (3d) 353 at paras. 44-54 (B.C.C.A.); *R. v. McKenzie*, [2001] O.J. No. 4858, 49 C.R. (5th) 123 (Ont. S.C.J.); *R. v. Douse*, [2009] O.J. No. 2874, 246 C.C.C. (3d) 227 (Ont. S.C.J.). See also *R. v. Spence*, [2005] S.C.J. No. 74, [2005] 3 S.C.R. 458 at para. 1 (S.C.C.) (referring to courts' "broad acceptance" of the *Parks* question).

[146] [2001] O.J. No. 1559, 154 C.C.C. (3d) 221 (Ont. C.A.), leave to appeal refused [2001] S.C.C.A. No. 359, 159 C.C.C. (3d) vi (S.C.C.).

[147] *Ibid.*, at para. 34 (154 C.C.C.).

[148] *Ibid.*, at para. 34 (154 C.C.C.). See also *R. v. Douse*, [2009] O.J. No. 2874, 246 C.C.C. (3d) 227 at para. 281 (Ont. S.C.J.) (permitting "multiple-choice" response to standard *Parks/Williams* question as follows: "(a) I would not be able to judge the case fairly; (b) I might be able to judge the case fairly; (c) I would be able to judge the case fairly; (d) I do not know if I would be able to judge the case fairly"); *R. v. Valentine*, [2009] O.J. No. 5961 at para. 11 (Ont. S.C.J.) (same).

[149] [1998] O.J. No. 5425, 131 C.C.C. (3d) 257 (Ont. C.A.).

[150] *R. v. Koh*, [1998] O.J. No. 5425, 131 C.C.C. (3d) 257 (Ont. C.A.). See also *R. v. P. (V.)*, [1999] O.J. No. 3294, 124 O.A.C. 54 (Ont. C.A.).

[151] See *e.g.*, *R. v. Fleury*, [1998] S.J. No. 538, [1998] 3 C.N.L.R. 160 (Sask. Q.B.); *R. v. Hummel*, [2001] Y.J. No. 4, 2001 YKSC 3 (Y.K.S.C.); *R. v. Le*, [2008] M.J. No. 111, 2008 MBQB 81 at para. 2 (Man. Q.B.); *R. v. Cho*, 1998 CarswellBC 2991 (B.C.S.C.); *R. c. Kabli*, 2008 CarswellQue 1785 (Que. S.C.). See also *R. v. Spence*, [2005] S.C.J. No. 74, [2005] 3 S.C.R. 458 at para. 5 (S.C.C.) ("The courts have acknowledged that racial prejudice against visible minorities is so notorious and indisputable that its existence will be admitted without any need of evidence.").

Following *Parks*, courts have also allowed inquiries about the heightened potential for partiality where the accused is a visible minority and the complainant or victim is white.[152] Courts have also allowed prosecutors to challenge for racial bias when white accused are charged with offences against minorities.[153]

§15.38 Questioning about other forms of racial or ethnic bias, however, has rarely been permitted. Courts have rejected challenges from accused who are predominately white in appearance, for example, even if they are recent immigrants or have foreign accents.[154] And in *R. v. Spence*,[155] the Supreme Court of Canada upheld the trial judge's refusal to allow the accused to ask prospective jurors whether they could impartially decide the guilt of "a black man *charged with robbing an East Indian person?*"[156] Though the reference to the accused's race was proper, the Court ruled, there was no evidence that the complainant's race was relevant. As discussed above, the Court recognized that "bias against a black accused may be aggravated where the accused is said to have 'crossed the colour line' against a victim who belongs to the white majority."[157] But there was no evidence, the Court ruled, that such bias is compounded when the victim belongs to another visible minority.[158] The idea that jurors might unduly sympathize with victims of their own race, it reasoned, had no evidentiary basis and was not a proper subject of judicial notice.[159]

§15.39 Courts have also been reluctant to apply *Parks* and *Williams* to prejudice arising from other personal characteristics. They have refused, for example, to permit challenges on the basis of the accused's sex,[160] youth,[161] homosexuality[162]

---

[152] *R. v. C. (D.)*, [1999] O.J. No. 3568, 139 C.C.C. (3d) 258 at paras. 2-7 (Ont. C.A.) ("The interracial nature of the crime increases the possibility of partiality.").

[153] See *R. v. Rogers*, [2000] O.J. No. 3009, 38 C.R. (5th) 331 (Ont. S.C.J.).

[154] See *R. v. Shchavinsky*, [2000] O.J. No. 3357, 148 C.C.C. (3d) 400 at paras. 37-38 (Ont. C.A.), leave to appeal refused [2001] S.C.C.A. No. 318, 157 O.A.C. 400 (S.C.C.) (Russian defendants not "part of a visible minority immigrant group"); *R. v. Gonzalez*, [2007] O.J. No. 4328, 75 W.C.B. (2d) 697 (Ont. S.C.J.) (Ecuadorian with Spanish accent and "European" appearance not "visible minority" and thus not entitled to question for racial bias).

[155] [2005] S.C.J. No. 74, [2005] 3 S.C.R. 458 (S.C.C.).

[156] *Ibid.*, at para. 1 (S.C.R.) [emphasis in original].

[157] *Ibid.*, at para. 3 (S.C.R.).

[158] *Ibid.*, at paras. 39-47 (S.C.R.).

[159] *Ibid.*, at paras. 52-69 (S.C.R.). See also *R. v. Hummel*, [2002] Y.J. No. 63, 166 C.C.C. (3d) 30 at paras. 11-22 (Y.T.C.A.), leave to appeal dismissed [2002] S.C.C.A. No. 434 (S.C.C.) (upholding trial judge's decision to refuse defence counsel's request to ask potential jurors if they believed that a "white woman is less likely to consent to sex with an Aboriginal man than a Caucasian man?"); *R. v. Murrin*, 1999 CarswellBC 3053 (S.C.) (white accused of offence against Asian complainant not permitted to inquire about anti-white or pro-Asian bias).

[160] See *e.g.*, *R. v. Francis*, [2006] O.J. No. 356, 68 W.C.B. (2d) 409 (Ont. S.C.J.).

[161] See *R. v. McLeod*, [2005] A.J. No. 1572, 2005 ABQB 846 at para. 10 (Alta. Q.B.); *R. v. Phung*, [2006] O.J. No. 5661 at para. 11 (Ont. S.C.J.).

[162] See *R. v. Alli*, [1996] O.J. No. 3032, 110 C.C.C. (3d) 283 (Ont. C.A) (no evidentiary foundation for claim of bias against homosexual accused); *R. v. Paterson*, [1998] B.C.J. No. 126, 122 C.C.C. (3d) 254 at paras. 70-73 (B.C.C.A.), leave to appeal refused [1999] S.C.C.A. No. 54, 134 C.C.C. (3d) iv (S.C.C.) (same).

and HIV positive status.[163] One court concluded, however, that there was a realistic possibility of bias against "the poor and homeless" where the accused were charged with offences during an anti-poverty demonstration.[164]

(iii) Offence-based Challenges

§15.40 Accused persons have also attempted to question potential jurors on biases relating to the nature of the offence. In *Williams*, the Supreme Court suggested that prejudice could arise from the "nature of the crime itself"[165] and in the years following some courts permitted such challenges.[166] But in *R. v. Find*,[167] the Supreme Court of Canada upheld the trial judge's decision to refuse a challenge based on bias against persons charged with the sexual assault of children.[168] Writing for the Court, Chief Justice McLachlin noted that despite high rates of victimization by sexual violence, widespread criticism of the law as being too accommodating of alleged sexual offenders, and the likelihood of strong emotional reactions to child sexual assault allegations, there was no evidence that people with these experiences, beliefs and reactions would be more likely to be biased against defendants in child sexual assault cases than those accused of other serious crimes.[169] She similarly rejected the contention that the existence of widespread bias was proven by the fact that many potential jurors had been dismissed in Ontario after such applications had been permitted to proceed. "[T]he number of prospective jurors disqualified," she reasoned, "... is equally consistent with the conclusion that the challenge processes, despite the best intentions of the participants, disqualified prospective jurors for acknowledging the intense emotions, beliefs, experiences and misgivings anyone might experience when confronted with the prospect of sitting as a juror on a case involving charges of sexual assault of children."[170] The Chief Justice was similarly unconvinced that social science evidence suggestive of widespread negative attitudes toward

---

[163] See *R. v. Aziga*, [2008] O.J. No. 2431, 78 W.C.B. (2d) 87 at para. 17 (Ont. S.C.J.) (finding "no evidentiary basis to support an assertion that there exists within the community a widespread bias against HIV positive individuals that would render jurors incapable of delivering an impartial decision despite trial safeguards").

[164] *R. v. Clarke*, 2003 CarswellOnt 5782 at para. 20 (Ont. S.C.). See also *R. v. Coates*, [2002] O.J. No. 155, 49 C.R. (5th) 139 (Ont. S.C.J.) (permitting questions on bias against members of Hells Angels gang in context of recent, unrelated negative publicity toward club in community).

[165] *R. v. Williams*, [1998] S.C.J. No. 49, [1998] 1 S.C.R. 1128 at para. 10 (S.C.C.).

[166] See *R. v. B. (A.)*, [1997] O.J. No. 1578, 115 C.C.C. (3d) 421 (Ont. C.A.), leave to appeal refused [1997] S.C.C.A. No. 461 (S.C.C.) (collecting cases from lower courts).

[167] [2001] S.C.J. No. 34, [2001] 1 S.C.R. 863 (S.C.C.).

[168] *R. v. Find*, [2001] S.C.J. No. 34, [2001] 1 S.C.R. 863 (S.C.C.). See also *R. v. B. (A.)*, [1997] O.J. No. 1578, 115 C.C.C. (3d) 421 (Ont. C.A.), leave to appeal refused [1997] S.C.C.A. No. 461 (S.C.C.); *R. v. K. (A.)*, [1999] O.J. No. 3280, 137 C.C.C. (3d) 225 (Ont. C.A.), leave to appeal quashed [2000] S.C.C.A. No. 16 (S.C.C.).

[169] *R. v. Find*, [2001] S.C.J. No. 34, [2001] 1 S.C.R. 863 at paras. 55-73 (S.C.C.). See also *R. v. B. (A.)*, [1997] O.J. No. 1578, 115 C.C.C. (3d) 421 at 447 (Ont. C.A.), leave to appeal refused [1997] S.C.C.A. No. 461 (S.C.C.).

[170] *R. v. Find*, [2001] S.C.J. No. 34, [2001] 1 S.C.R. 863 at paras. 74-82 (S.C.C.).

sexual assault defendants was indicative of widespread bias.[171] Finally, she held that even if widespread bias were established, bias resulting from the nature of the charge "may be more susceptible to cleansing by the rigours of the trial process."[172] Unlike racial bias, she concluded, the "aversion, fear, abhorrence, and beliefs alleged to surround sexual assault offences" do not "point a finger at a particular accused."[173]

§15.41 The Chief Justice left open the possibility that offence based challenges might succeed on better evidence.[174] But such cases, she predicted, "may prove exceptional."[175] This prediction was prescient; since *Find*, courts have rarely accepted challenges based on the generic nature of the offence, including cases involving drugs,[176] guns,[177] sexual violence[178] and domestic violence.[179]

§15.42 Courts have sometimes been willing to permit challenges, however, based on more specific aspects of the case. In *R. v. Cansanay*,[180] for example, the Court permitted questions regarding prospective jurors' animosity toward specific street gangs active (and subject to widespread media coverage) in local neighbourhoods.[181] And in *R. v. Katoch*,[182] a police officer was accused of assaulting a member of an anti-police advocacy group.[183] Because there was a realistic potential for anti-police bias among members of this group, the Ontario Court of Appeal upheld the trial judge's decision allowing prospective jurors to be asked if they or any of their family members supported the group.[184]

---

[171]   *Ibid.*, at paras. 83-87 (S.C.R.).

[172]   *Ibid.*, at paras. 95-108 (S.C.R.).

[173]   *Ibid.*, at para. 94 (S.C.R.).

[174]   *Ibid.*, at para. 108 (S.C.R.).

[175]   *Ibid.*, at para. 108 (S.C.R.).

[176]   See *e.g.*, *R. v. Duguay*, [2004] N.B.J. No. 478 (N.B.Q.B.); *R. v. Huynh*, 2001 BCSC 1731 at para. 19 (B.C.S.C.). See also *R. v. Parks*, [1993] O.J. No. 2157 at para. 16, 84 C.C.C. (3d) 353 (Ont. C.A.), leave to appeal refused [1993] S.C.J. No. 481, [1994] 1 S.C.R. x (S.C.C.) ("no merit" in proposed question inquiring as to partiality based on "the fact that there are people involved in cocaine and other drugs"); *R. v. Barnes*, [1999] O.J. No. 3296, 138 C.C.C. (3d) 500 (Ont. C.A.) (trial judge's decision to excise reference to drug-related nature of crime from standard, race-based *Parks* question not in error).

[177]   See *e.g.*, *R. v. Lucas*, [2009] O.J. No. 5328, 86 W.C.B. (2d) 49 (Ont. S.C.J.); *R. v. Le*, [2008] M.J. No. 111, 2008 MBQB 81 (Man. Q.B.). But see *R. v. Riley*, [2009] O.J. No. 1516 at para. 15 (Ont. S.C.J.) (permitting question relating to general media coverage of "street gangs, guns and violence"); *R. v. Egonu*, [2007] O.J. No. 2994, 2007 CarswellOnt 6282 (Ont. S.C.) (permitting question relating to "gun-related offences").

[178]   See *e.g.*, *R. v. F. (K.)*, [2007] B.C.J. No. 30, 2007 BCSC 31 (B.C.S.C.); *R. v. Johnson*, [2009] M.J. No. 451, 2009 MBQB 267 (Man. Q.B.); *R. v. W. (K.)*, 2009 CarswellOnt 4448 (Ont. S.C.J). But see *R. v. Eastman*, [2004] O.J. No. 2841, 62 W.C.B. (2d) 295 (Ont. S.C.J.) (permitting challenge based on bias against persons accused of sexual murder).

[179]   See *e.g.*, *R. v. Griecken*, [2009] O.J. No. 5036 (Ont. S.C.J.); *R. v. Kimpe*, [2007] O.J. No. 4500, 75 W.C.B. (2d) 474 (Ont. S.C.J.).

[180]   [2010] M.J. No. 126, 2010 MBQB 48 (Man. Q.B.).

[181]   *R. v. Cansanay*, [2010] M.J. No. 126, 2010 MBQB 48 (Man. Q.B.).

[182]   [2009] O.J. No. 3456, 246 C.C.C. (3d) 423 (Ont. C.A.).

[183]   *R. v. Katoch*, [2009] O.J. No. 3456, 246 C.C.C. (3d) 423 (Ont. C.A.).

[184]   *R. v. Katoch*, [2009] O.J. No. 3456, 246 C.C.C. (3d) 423 (Ont. C.A.). But see *R. v. Smith*, [2007] O.J. No. 2584, 74 W.C.B. (2d) 548 (Ont. S.C.J.) (defendant accused of killing taxi driver not permitted to question on affiliations with taxi drivers).

Similarly, courts have often permitted jurors to be questioned about their relationships with or views about police in cases where the accused or complainant is a police officer.[185] Courts have typically rejected questioning on pro-police bias, however, in other cases.[186]

(5) Peremptory Challenges

(a) General Procedure

§15.43 Under section 634 of the *Criminal Code*, the accused and prosecutor may challenge an equal, limited number of potential jurors peremptorily. Peremptory challenges may be exercised without cause or explanation.[187] Where the accused is charged with high treason or first degree murder, the number of peremptory challenges is 20; for any other offence with a maximum sentence of more than five years, the number of peremptory challenges is 12; and in all other cases, four.[188] If the judge decides to choose alternate jurors, each party's allocation increases by the number of alternates to be selected.[189] If there are multiple counts against one accused, the total number of peremptory challenges is that attaching to the most serious offence.[190] In joint trials, defendants have the number they would have if tried alone, with the prosecutor receiving the sum of all defendants' challenges.[191]

§15.44 Before the selection process begins, the parties are supplied with the names, occupations and addresses of potential jurors.[192] Unless a prospective juror is challenged for cause, the decision to exercise a peremptory challenge will normally be based solely on this information as well as any information gleaned from the appearance and demeanour of the prospective jurors. Attempts by the parties to obtain additional information before the selection process begins are generally forbidden. In *R. v. Latimer*,[193] for example, a prosecutor and police officers distributed a questionnaire to prospective jurors designed to gauge their sympathy for the accused, who had committed an alleged "mercy killing" of his disabled child.[194] The Supreme Court of Canada characterized this

---

[185] See *R. v. Dagenais*, [2008] S.J. No. 602, 323 Sask. R. 258 (Sask. Q.B.).

[186] See *R. v. Barnes*, [1999] O.J. No. 3296, 138 C.C.C. (3d) 500 (Ont. C.A.); *R. v. T. (M.)*, 2009 CarswellOnt 4834 (Ont. S.C.); *R. c. Colalillo*, [2006] Q.J. No. 414, 41 C.R. (6th) 21 (Que. S.C.); *R. v. Egonu*, [2007] O.J. No. 2994, 2007 CarswellOnt 6282 (Ont. S.C.).

[187] See *R. v. Cloutier*, [1979] S.C.J. No. 67, [1979] 2 S.C.R. 709 at 720-21 (S.C.C.).

[188] *Criminal Code*, s. 634(2).

[189] *Criminal Code*, s. 634(2.1). Despite any statutory authority, it has also been held that when sworn jurors are dismissed and replaced under s. 644(1.1) (discussed in Part 4, below), the parties should gain an additional peremptory challenge for each substitute: *R. v. Cazzetta*, [2003] J.Q. no 43, 173 C.C.C. (3d) 144 (Que. C.A.).

[190] *Criminal Code*, s. 634(3).

[191] *Criminal Code*, s. 634(4).

[192] See Roger E. Salhany, *Canadian Criminal Procedure*, 6th ed., looseleaf (Aurora, ON: Canada Law Book, 1994) at para. 6.2780.

[193] [1997] S.C.J. No. 11, [1997] 1 S.C.R. 217 (S.C.C.).

[194] *Ibid.*

practice as a "flagrant abuse of process and interference with the administration of justice" and ordered a new trial.[195] Similarly, in *R. v. Emms*[196] and *R. v. Yumnu*,[197] prosecutors asked police to determine whether any persons from a list of prospective jurors had criminal records and provide comments "concerning any disreputable persons we would not want as a juror."[198] The Ontario Court of Appeal found that while the disclosure of criminal record information to prosecutors was acceptable (since convictions for certain offences make a person ineligible or unqualified for jury service), it should have been disclosed to the defence.[199] The request for comments about "disreputable persons", the Court stated, should not have been made at all.[200]

§15.45 If the judge has permitted a challenge for cause, it must be decided before the parties exercise their peremptory challenges.[201] In this way the parties avoid wasting peremptory challenges on potential jurors who would be dismissed in any case.[202] If the first potential juror is not successfully challenged for cause, the accused must choose whether to use a peremptory challenge.[203] If not, the prosecution may do so. For the second juror the prosecutor must choose first, and so on in alternating order, until the parties' peremptory challenges are exhausted.[204]

(b)   Rationale and Limits on Use

§15.46 The rationale for peremptory challenges is somewhat obscure. In England, the common law gave the prosecutor an unlimited number of peremptory

---

[195]   *Ibid.*, at para. 43 (S.C.R.).

[196]   [2010] O.J. No. 5195, 2010 ONCA 817 at para. 36 (Ont. C.A.), leave to appeal granted [2011] S.C.C.A. No. 52 (S.C.C.).

[197]   [2010] O.J. No. 4163, 260 C.C.C. (3d) 421 (Ont. C.A.).

[198]   See *R. v. Emms*, [2010] O.J. No. 5195, 2010 ONCA 817 at paras. 36, 60 (Ont. C.A.), leave to appeal granted [2011] S.C.C.A. No. 52 (S.C.C.); *R. v. Yumnu*, [2010] O.J. No. 4163, 260 C.C.C. (3d) 421 at paras. 29, 93 (Ont. C.A.).

[199]   *R. v. Emms*, [2010] O.J. No. 5195, 2010 ONCA 817 at para. 55 (Ont. C.A.), leave to appeal granted [2011] S.C.C.A. No. 52 (S.C.C.); *R. v. Yumnu*, [2010] O.J. No. 4163, 260 C.C.C. (3d) 421 at paras. 74, 85, 93 (Ont. C.A.). See also *R. v. Hobbs*, [2010] N.S.J. No. 386, 257 C.C.C. (3d) 411 (N.S.C.A.), leave to appeal refused [2010] S.C.C.A. No. 370 (S.C.C.).

[200]   *R. v. Emms*, [2010] O.J. No. 5195, 2010 ONCA 817 at para. 61 (Ont. C.A.), leave to appeal granted [2011] S.C.C.A. No. 52 (S.C.C.); *R. v. Yumnu*, [2010] O.J. No. 4163, 260 C.C.C. (3d) 421 at para. 92 (Ont. C.A.).

[201]   See *R. v. Cloutier*, [1979] S.C.J. No. 67, [1979] 2 S.C.R. 709 (S.C.C.); *R. v. Bernardo*, [2000] O.J. No. 949, 144 C.C.C. (3d) 260 at paras. 46-57 (Ont. C.A.).

[202]   *R. v. Douglas*, [2002] O.J. No. 4734, 170 C.C.C. (3d) 126 at para. 33 (Ont. C.A.).

[203]   *Criminal Code*, s. 635(1).

[204]   *Criminal Code*, s. 635(1). Section 635(2) specifies that for joint trials "all of the accused shall exercise the challenges of the defence in turn, in the order in which their names appear in the indictment or in any other order agreed on by them, (*a*) in respect of the first juror, before the prosecutor; and (*b*) in respect of each of the remaining jurors, either before or after the prosecutor, in accordance with subsection (1)." See also *R. v. Suzack*, [2000] O.J. No. 100, 30 C.R. (5th) 346 (Ont. C.A.), leave to appeal refused [2000] S.C.C.A. No. 583, 80 C.R.R. (2d) 376 (S.C.C.) (any tactical disadvantage suffered by earlier named defendants under this process does not violate s. 11(*d*) *Charter* right to fair trial).

challenges; the accused had only 35.[205] To curtail abuses of this advantage, a statute was passed in 1305 effectively eliminating Crown peremptory challenges and replacing them with an unlimited number of stand asides.[206] The prosecutor retained an unlimited number of stand asides under our first *Criminal Code*, which also gave the accused a certain number of peremptory challenges that increased with the seriousness of the offence.[207] Parliament later gave the prosecutor four peremptory challenges and reduced its complement of stand asides to 48.[208] As mentioned in Part 3(3), above, in response to *R. v. Bain*,[209] Parliament abolished prosecutorial stand asides and implemented the symmetrical peremptory challenge regime described in the preceding paragraph.[210]

§15.47 Until recently, peremptory challenges were thus used mainly by defendants. Their purpose, courts and commentators suggested, was to allow defendants to dismiss jurors who they suspect may be inclined against them based on subtle factors (like the prospective juror's dress, manner, whether or not they look at the accused and answers given to questions posed during a challenge for cause) but cannot otherwise exclude.[211] This reasoning presumably applies equally to the prosecution in the contemporary regime.[212] Given the limited scope of the challenge for cause process, peremptory challenges may therefore help to promote the perception of impartiality and, therefore, the appearance of fairness.[213]

---

[205] The history of peremptory challenges and stand asides is detailed in *R. v. Bain*, [1992] S.C.J. No. 3, [1992] 1 S.C.R. 91 at 150-52 (S.C.C.), *per* Stevenson J., concurring.

[206] *An Ordinance for Inquests*, 33 Edw. 1, stat. 4.

[207] *Criminal Code*, S.C. 1892, c. 29, s. 668(9) (providing 20 challenges for offences punishable by death; 12 for those punishable by imprisonment for more than five years).

[208] *An Act to amend the Criminal Code (respecting jurors)*, S.C. 1917, c. 13, s. 1.

[209] [1992] S.C.J. No. 3, [1992] 1 S.C.R. 91 (S.C.C.).

[210] *An Act to amend the Criminal Code (jury)*, S.C. 1992, c. 41, s. 2.

[211] See W.D. Lewis, ed., *Commentaries on the Laws of England*, vol. 4 (Philadelphia: Rees Welsh & Co., 1897) at 1738 (accused should be able to dismiss a prospective juror "against whom he has conceived a prejudice, even without being able to assign a reason for his dislike"). See also *R. v. Bain*, [1992] S.C.J. No. 3, [1992] 1 S.C.R. 91 at 115 (S.C.C.), *per* Cory J. and 153 (S.C.R.), *per* Stevenson J.; *R. v. Cloutier*, [1979] S.C.J. No. 67, [1979] 2 S.C.R. 709 at 720 (S.C.C.); Law Reform Commission of Canada, Working Paper 27, "The Jury in Criminal Trials" (Ottawa: Law Reform Commission of Canada, 1980).

[212] See *R. v. Sherratt*, [1991] S.C.J. No. 21, [1991] 1 S.C.R. 509 at 532-33 (S.C.C.); *R. v. Gayle*, [2001] O.J. No. 1559, 154 C.C.C. (3d) 221 at paras. 59-60 (Ont. C.A.), leave to appeal refused [2001] S.C.C.A. No. 359, 159 C.C.C. (3d) vi (S.C.C.); *R. v. Bellas*, [2002] O.J. No. 5372 at para. 16 (Ont. S.C.J.). See also David M. Tanovich, David M. Paciocco & Steven Skurka, *Jury Selection in Criminal Trials: Skills, Science, and the Law* (Concord, ON: Irwin Law, 1997) at 172.

[213] Attempts to challenge the existing peremptory challenge regime on *Charter* grounds have failed. See *R. v. Oliver*, [2005] O.J. No. 596, 194 C.C.C. (3d) 92 (Ont. C.A.), leave to appeal refused [2005] S.C.C.A. No. 458 (S.C.C.) (rejecting defence argument that lesser number of challenges for second degree murder as compared to first degree murder violates *Charter*); *R. v. Bellas*, [2002] O.J. No. 5372 (Ont. S.C.J.) (same). See also *R. v. Bain*, [1992] S.C.J. No. 3, [1992] 1 S.C.R. 91 at 159 (S.C.C.), *per* Stevenson J. (peremptory challenges may be "used under partisan considerations, and so long as the right of exercise is proportionate neither the Crown nor the accused can be said to have an unconstitutional advantage").

§15.48 Peremptory challenges may also be exercised, however, on the basis of discriminatory stereotypes.[214] Some courts have accordingly held that prosecutors may not exclude prospective jurors because of their race.[215] In *R. v. Gayle*, the prosecutor used peremptory challenges to remove two blacks in a case involving a black accused.[216] The resulting jury had two visible minorities but no blacks.[217] Because the accused's lawyer at trial did not object to these challenges, the Court denied the accused's claim of discrimination.[218] It held, however, that the prosecutor's discretion in exercising peremptory challenges is constrained by both their quasi-judicial role and the *Charter*.[219] In light of evidence that prosecutors have sometimes disproportionately excluded members of certain racial minorities, the court concluded that exercising peremptory challenges on racial or ethnic grounds undermines "public confidence in the administration of justice".[220] In our view, the discriminatory use of peremptory challenges by the accused is also prohibited by the *Charter*.[221]

§15.49 It is exceptionally difficult to show, however, that any particular peremptory challenge has been used discriminatorily.[222] Without a requirement to explain or justify the use of peremptory challenges, successful claims of racial discrimination will be extraordinarily rare. We thus recommend that where a pattern of dismissals reveals *prima facie* discrimination, counsel should be required to provide a non-discriminatory explanation for each dismissal.[223] Such a

---

[214] See *Report of the Aboriginal Justice Inquiry of Manitoba* (Winnipeg: Queen's Printer, 1991) c. 9 (recommending abolition of peremptory challenges); Cynthia Petersen, "Institutional Racism: The Need for Reform of the Criminal Jury Selection Process" (1993) 38 McGill L.J. 147 at 175 (same); David M. Tanovich, "Rethinking Jury Selection: Challenges for Cause and Peremptory Challenges" (1994) 30 C.R. (4th) 310 (same); *Criminal Justice Act, 1988* (U.K.), c. 33, s. 118 (abolishing peremptory challenges). See also Alan W. Mewett, "The Jury Stand-By" (1988) 30 Crim. L.Q. 385 at 386.

[215] See *R. v. Gayle*, [2001] O.J. No. 1559, 154 C.C.C. (3d) 221 (Ont. C.A.), leave to appeal refused [2001] S.C.C.A. No. 359, 159 C.C.C. (3d) vi (S.C.C.); *R. v. Brown*, [1999] O.J. No. 4867 (Ont. Gen. Div.).

[216] *R. v. Gayle*, [2001] O.J. No. 1559, 154 C.C.C. (3d) 221 (Ont. C.A.), leave to appeal refused [2001] S.C.C.A. No. 359, 159 C.C.C. (3d) vi (S.C.C.).

[217] *Ibid.*

[218] *Ibid.*, at paras. 68-70 (C.C.C.).

[219] *Ibid.*, at para. 61 (C.C.C.). See also *R. v. Brown*, [1999] O.J. No. 4867 at para. 5 (Ont. Gen. Div.). On prosecutors' quasi-judicial role, see Chapter 8.

[220] *R. v. Gayle*, [2001] O.J. No. 1559, 154 C.C.C. (3d) 221 at para. 66 (Ont. C.A.), leave to appeal refused [2001] S.C.C.A. No. 359, 159 C.C.C. (3d) vi (S.C.C.).

[221] Specifically, the discriminatory exclusion of minority prospective jurors should be held to violate the s. 15 equality rights of prospective jurors. The *Charter* applies to criminal defendants in this context, we submit, because in exercising peremptory challenges to promote juror impartiality and ensure a fair trial, they are carrying out a specific governmental objective. See *Eldridge v. British Columbia (Attorney General)*, [1997] S.C.J. No. 86, [1997] 3 S.C.R. 624 at paras. 41-51 (S.C.C.). See also *Georgia v. McCollum*, 505 U.S. 42 (1992) (race-based peremptory challenges by defendants constitute state action and violate equal protection clause of the Fourteenth Amendment to the United States Constitution).

[222] See *R. v. Amos*, [2007] O.J. No. 3732, 75 W.C.B. (2d) 528 (Ont. C.A.) (no evidence that dismissal of only black prospective juror motivated by race).

[223] See *Batson v. Kentucky*, 476 U.S. 79 at 100 (1986) (where pattern of dismissals shows "prima facie, purposeful discrimination," burden shifts to prosecution to provide race-neutral explanation).

rule would mitigate discrimination without unduly constraining the parties' discretion in exercising peremptorily challenges.

§15.50 Surprisingly, it is less certain whether potential jurors may be dismissed on the basis of sex. As mentioned, in *R. v. Pizzacalla*,[224] the Ontario Court of Appeal ordered a new trial because the prosecutor improperly used stand asides to ensure an all-female jury.[225] However, in *R. v. Biddle*,[226] the same court later decided in similar circumstances that no reasonable apprehension of bias arose.[227] When *Biddle* was appealed to the Supreme Court, only three of nine justices addressed the issue.[228] Justice McLachlin (as she then was) found no evidence that the prosecution's discretion was exercised to achieve a "favourable" jury.[229] "It is at least equally open to infer ...," she wrote, that "its aim was to secure a jury which would be capable of judging the issues in an impartial and unbiased manner."[230] Justice L'Heureux-Dubé agreed with Justice McLachlin on this issue.[231] In Justice Gonthier's view, in contrast, the prosecutor's pursuit of an all-female jury undermined the jury's impartiality.[232]

§15.51 Of course, these decisions dealt with the now-repealed Crown stand aside power, not peremptory challenges. With each party having an equal (and more limited) number of peremptory challenges, it is now more difficult to empanel a jury comprised entirely of one sex. Given the roughly equal proportion of men and women in most arrays, all-male or all-female juries are also far less attainable than either all-white juries or juries excluding members of a certain race. Nevertheless, while any particular jury made up entirely of men or entirely of women may be capable of acting impartially, deliberate attempts to exclude members of either sex should be held to violate the principles of impartiality and representativeness inhering in sections 11(*d*) and 11(*f*) of the *Charter* as well as prospective jurors' equality rights under section 15. If it is improper and

---

See also Wayne R. LaFave, Jerold H. Israel & Nancy J. King, *Criminal Procedure*, 3d ed. (St. Paul, Minn.: West Group, 2000) § 22.3; David M. Tanovich, David M. Paciocco & Steven Skurka, *Jury Selection in Criminal Trials: Skills, Science, and the Law* (Concord, ON: Irwin Law, 1997) at 234.

[224] [1991] O.J. No. 2008, 69 C.C.C. (3d) 115 (Ont. C.A.)

[225] *Ibid.* In his plurality reasons in *R. v. Bain*, [1992] S.C.J. No. 3, [1992] 1 S.C.R. 91 at 513 (S.C.C.), Cory J. remarked that *Pizzacalla* was a case where the prosecution had "abused" its stand aside power.

[226] [1993] O.J. No. 1833, 14 O.R. (3d) 756 (Ont. C.A.), revd [1995] S.C.J. No. 22, [1995] 1 S.C.R. 761 (S.C.C.).

[227] *Ibid.*

[228] The majority declined to do so because the repeal of the Crown stand aside power rendered the issue moot: *R. v. Biddle*, [1995] S.C.J. No. 22, [1995] 1 S.C.R. 761 at para. 34 (S.C.C.).

[229] *R. v. Biddle*, [1995] S.C.J. No. 22, [1995] 1 S.C.R. 761 at para. 59 (S.C.C.), *per* McLachlin J., concurring.

[230] *Ibid.*, at para. 59 (S.C.R.), *per* McLachlin J., concurring.

[231] *Ibid.*, at para. 42 (S.C.R.), *per* L'Heureux-Dubé J., dissenting.

[232] *Ibid.*, at paras. 48-53 (S.C.R), *per* Gonthier J., concurring.

unconstitutional to exclude on the basis of race, then it is equally improper and unconstitutional to do so on the basis of sex.[233]

4.   REMOVAL AND REPLACEMENT OF SWORN JURORS

§15.52 There are several ways for judges to dismiss and replace sworn jurors under the *Criminal Code*.[234] Jurors may be dismissed at any time before or during trial on grounds of partiality, personal hardship or other reasonable cause. Before the "commencement of a trial" (which has been interpreted in this context to occur when the accused is put in the charge of the jury[235]), the judge may excuse sworn jurors under section 632, which we discussed in Part 3(1), above. This provision applies equally to sworn and unsworn jurors.[236] After the trial begins, jurors may only be discharged under section 644. While the only grounds for dismissal specified in this provision are "illness or other reasonable cause," courts have interpreted the latter phrase to include personal hardship[237] and potential partiality.[238]

§15.53 In deciding whether to discharge a juror under this provision, the judge should exclude the other jurors from the courtroom and conduct an inquiry in open court, on the record, with all counsel present.[239] Though counsel may suggest questions to the judge, most courts have held that the juror should not be put on oath or cross-examined.[240] Questioning that would violate the confidentiality of jury deliberations and should also be avoided.[241]

---

[233]   See *J.E.B. v. Alabama ex rel. T. B.*, 511 U.S. 127 (1994) (use of peremptory challenges based solely on sex unconstitutional). See also Stephen Coughlan, *Criminal Procedure* (Toronto: Irwin Law, 2008) at 289; *Criminal Code*, s. 626(2) ("Notwithstanding any [provincial jury selection law], ... no person may be disqualified, exempted or excused from serving as a juror in criminal proceedings on the grounds of his or her sex.").

[234]   See also *R. v. Walizadah*, [2003] O.J. No. 284 at paras. 10, 17 (Ont. S.C.J.) (suggesting that courts may also have an inherent jurisdiction to exempt sworn jurors); *R. v. Parker*, [1981] O.J. No. 3297, 62 C.C.C. (2d) 161 (Ont. H.C.J.) (same).

[235]   See *R. v. Basarabas*, [1982] S.C.J. No. 96, [1982] 2 S.C.R. 730 (S.C.C.); *R. v. Hatton*, [1978] O.J. No. 460, 39 C.C.C. (2d) 281 at 289 (Ont. C.A.); *R. v. Walizadah*, [2003] O.J. No. 284 (Ont. S.C.J.).

[236]   See *R. v. Walizadah*, [2003] O.J. No. 284 at para. 8 (Ont. S.C.J.).

[237]   See *R. v. Walizadah*, [2003] O.J. No. 284 at paras. 9-10 (Ont. S.C.J.).

[238]   See *R. v. Pan; R. v. Sawyer*, [2001] S.C.J. No. 44, [2001] 2 S.C.R. 344 at paras. 94, 96 (S.C.C.); *R. v. Holcomb*, [1973] N.B.J. No. 75, 12 C.C.C. (2d) 417 (N.B.C.A.), affd (1973), 15 C.C.C. (2d) 239 (S.C.C.); *R. v. Tsoumas*, [1973] O.J. No. 296, 11 C.C.C. (2d) 344 (Ont. C.A.); *R. v. Andrews*, [1984] B.C.J. No. 1690, 13 C.C.C. (3d) 207 (B.C.C.A.); *R. v. Gargan*, [2010] N.W.T.J. No. 85, 265 C.C.C. (3d) 132 at para. 23 (N.W.T.C.A.).

[239]   See *R. v. Hanna*, [1993] B.C.J. No. 961, 80 C.C.C. (3d) 289 at 312 (B.C.C.A.), leave to appeal refused [1994] S.C.C.A. No. 246, 91 C.C.C. (3d) vi (S.C.C.).

[240]   See *R. v. Hanna*, [1993] B.C.J. No. 961, 80 C.C.C. (3d) 289 (B.C.C.A.), leave to appeal to S.C.C. refused [1994] S.C.C.A. No. 246, 91 C.C.C. (3d) vi (S.C.C.); *R. v. Giroux*, [2006] O.J. No. 1375, 207 C.C.C. (3d) 512 (Ont. C.A.), leave to appeal refused [2006] S.C.C.A. No. 211, 212 C.C.C. (3d) vi (S.C.C.). But see *R. v. Sophonow*, [1985] M.J. No. 10, 25 C.C.C. (3d) 415 (Man. C.A.), leave to appeal refused [1986] 1 S.C.R. xiii, 44 Man.R. (2d) 80*n* (S.C.C.) (permitting cross-examination).

[241]   Roger E. Salhany, *Canadian Criminal Procedure*, 6th ed., looseleaf (Aurora, ON: Canada Law Book, 1994) at para. 6.3170. It has also been suggested that when a juror is dismissed in the

§15.54 Jurors who have been discharged or are otherwise unavailable may be replaced at any time before the jury has begun hearing evidence. If jurors are excused before the trial begins, they may be replaced by randomly selecting from: (*i*) members of the array whose cards have not yet been drawn; (*ii*) stand asides; or (*iii*) summoned talesmen.[242] In addition, if there is not a full jury of 12 immediately before the trial begins, the judge may substitute any alternate jurors chosen.[243] The trial must commence with exactly 12 jurors, even if the accused consents to fewer.[244] Lastly, jurors discharged after the commencement of trial, but before the jury has heard evidence may be replaced with anyone still available from the initial array or by summoning talesmen.[245] While trial judges may elect not to replace a juror after the trial begins, they must at least consider doing so, keeping in mind that the accused "should not be lightly deprived" of a full jury.[246] Once evidence has been heard, jurors may not be replaced, even with alternate jurors.[247] After commencement, the trial may continue with as few as 10 jurors unless the judge orders otherwise.[248] If the number of jurors drops below 10, the judge must declare a mistrial.

---

midst of the trial, the judge should explain the dismissal to the remaining jurors to avoid speculation prejudicial to the accused. See *R. v. MacKay*, [1980] B.C.J. No. 478, 53 C.C.C. (2d) 366 at 376-77 (B.C.C.A.).

[242] See *R. v. Ladouceur*, [1998] O.J. No. 1680, 124 C.C.C. (3d) 269 (Ont. C.A.).

[243] *Criminal Code*, s. 642.1(1) ("Alternate jurors shall attend at the commencement of the presentation of the evidence on the merits and, if there is not a full jury present, shall replace any absent juror, in the order in which their cards were drawn under subsection 631(3)."). If the alternative jurors are not used, they are discharged: *Criminal Code*, s. 642.1(2). Anticipating that sworn jurors may often need to be excused, courts sometimes defer putting the accused in the charge of the jury for a period of time to allow alternate jurors to be substituted before the trial commences. See *R. v. Walizadah*, [2003] O.J. No. 284 at paras. 26-27 (Ont. S.C.J.).

[244] See *R. v. Wellman*, [1996] B.C.J. No. 1478, 108 C.C.C. (3d) 372 (B.C.C.A.). See also *R. v. Walizadah*, [2003] O.J. No. 284 at para. 24 (Ont. S.C.J.) (accused must be put in charge of 12 jurors, not 12 jurors plus alternates).

[245] *Criminal Code*, s. 644(1.1). This provision was added to the *Code* in response to decisions holding that jurors could not be replaced after commencement, but before the hearing of evidence. See *R. v. Piche*, [1997] B.C.J. No. 219, 113 C.C.C. (3d) 149 (B.C.C.A.); *R. v. S. (R.J.)*, [1996] N.S.J. No. 387, 110 C.C.C. (3d) 535 (N.S.C.A.); *R. v. Gargan*, [2010] N.W.T.J. No. 85, 265 C.C.C. (3d) 132 at para. 25 (N.W.T.C.A.).

[246] *R. v. Hazlett*, [2005] O.J. No. 5540, 205 O.A.C. 298 at para. 4 (Ont. C.A.).

[247] See *R. v. Walizadah*, [2003] O.J. No. 284 at para. 26 (Ont. S.C.J.).

[248] *Criminal Code*, s. 644(2). See also *R. v. Peters*, [1999] B.C.J. No. 1587, 137 C.C.C. (3d) 26 (B.C.C.A.) (juror may be discharged and trial may continue even after jury has begun deliberating); *R. c. Lessard*, [1992] J.Q. no 821, 74 C.C.C. (3d) 552 (Que. C.A.) (continuing trial with fewer than 12 jurors does not infringe s. 11(*f*) of the *Charter*); *R. v. Genest*, [1990] J.Q. no 1609, 61 C.C.C. (3d) 251 (Que. C.A.) (same).

Chapter 16

TRIAL PROCEDURE

1. INTRODUCTION

§16.1 A trial is a dynamic process in which rules of criminal procedure intersect with rules of evidence in an adversarial setting. This chapter provides an overview of some of the more common procedural rules, not covered in other chapters, governing the pre-trial and trial process. Trial procedure is governed by both statute (federal and provincial) and common law. Most of the procedural rules applying to criminal trials are set out in the *Criminal Code*.[1] However, the *Canada Evidence Act*,[2] the *Controlled Drugs and Substances Act*,[3] the *Youth Criminal Justice Act*[4] and other statutes may also play a role. And as we will see, many of the most important trial process rules, such as the trial judge's power to exclude witnesses and grant adjournments, are based on the court's common law authority to control its own process.

§16.2 As explained in Chapter 1 and further discussed in Chapter 15, criminal trials are tried either by judge alone or by a judge sitting with a jury. In either case, it is the trial judge's responsibility to "manage the trial and control the procedure to ensure that the trial is effective, efficient and fair to both sides."[5] Also in both cases, questions of law are decided by the trial judge, usually in the absence of jurors in jury trials. In jury trials, jurors are the triers of fact but follow the judge's instructions as to the applicable legal rules and principles.

2. BURDEN AND STANDARD OF PROOF

§16.3 The most fundamental tenet of the criminal trial is that the prosecution must prove the guilt of the accused beyond a reasonable doubt. This tenet may in turn be broken down into two, inextricably intertwined principles: the presumption of innocence and the standard of proof beyond a reasonable doubt.[6] In

---

[1]   R.S.C. 1985, c. C-46 [*Code*].
[2]   R.S.C. 1985, c. C-5.
[3]   S.C. 1996, c. 19.
[4]   S.C. 2002, c. 1.
[5]   *R. v. Snow*, [2004] O.J. No. 4309, 190 C.C.C. (3d) 317 at para. 24 (Ont. C.A.).
[6]   These principles are protected by s. 11(*d*) of the *Canadian Charter of Rights and Freedoms*, Part I of the *Constitution Act, 1982*, being Schedule B to the *Canada Act 1982* (U.K.), 1982, c. 11 [*Charter*]. See *R. v. Oakes*, [1986] S.C.J. No. 7, [1986] 1 S.C.R. 103 (S.C.C.); *R. v. Whyte*, [1988] S.C.J. No. 63, [1988] 2 S.C.R. 3 (S.C.C.); *R. v. Keegstra*, [1990] S.C.J. No. 131, [1990] 3 S.C.R. 697 (S.C.C.); *R. v. Chaulk*, [1990] S.C.J. No. 139, [1990] 3 S.C.R. 1303 (S.C.C.). See

R. v. Lifchus,[7] the Supreme Court of Canada suggested that these principles be explained to jurors in the following manner:

> The accused enters these proceedings presumed to be innocent. That presumption of innocence remains throughout the case until such time as the Crown has on the evidence put before you satisfied you beyond a reasonable doubt that the accused is guilty.
>
> What does the expression "beyond a reasonable doubt" mean?
>
> The term "beyond a reasonable doubt" has been used for a very long time and is a part of our history and traditions of justice. It is so engrained in our criminal law that some think it needs no explanation, yet something must be said regarding its meaning.
>
> A reasonable doubt is not an imaginary or frivolous doubt. It must not be based upon sympathy or prejudice. Rather, it is based on reason and common sense. It is logically derived from the evidence or absence of evidence.
>
> Even if you believe the accused is probably guilty or likely guilty, that is not sufficient. In those circumstances you must give the benefit of the doubt to the accused and acquit because the Crown has failed to satisfy you of the guilt of the accused beyond a reasonable doubt.
>
> On the other hand you must remember that it is virtually impossible to prove anything to an absolute certainty and the Crown is not required to do so. Such a standard of proof is impossibly high.
>
> In short if, based upon the evidence before the court, you are sure that the accused committed the offence you should convict since this demonstrates that you are satisfied of his guilt beyond a reasonable doubt.

§16.4 In *R. v. Starr*,[8] Justice Iacobucci further suggested that the jury be told that the reasonable doubt standard "falls much closer to absolute certainty than to proof on a balance of probabilities."[9] Today, most trial judge's instructions to the jury track the language in *Lifchus*, while the supplemental language in *Starr* remains optional.[10]

3.   PROCEDURAL ORDERS

(1)   Publication Bans

§16.5 Court proceedings operate on the presumption of openness.[11] The public has the right to attend court[12] and the media has the right to disseminate

---

also Don Stuart, *Charter Justice in Canadian Criminal Law*, 5th ed. (Toronto: Thomson Carswell, 2010) at 416-36.

[7]   [1997] S.C.J. No. 77, [1997] 3 S.C.R. 320 at para. 39 (S.C.C.).

[8]   [2000] S.C.J. No. 40, [2000] 2 S.C.R. 144 (S.C.C.).

[9]   *Ibid.*, at para. 242 (S.C.R.).

[10]   See *e.g.*, *R. v. Hall*, [2004] O.J. No. 5007 at paras. 34-36 (Ont. C.A.).

[11]   See *Nova Scotia (Attorney General) v. MacIntyre*, [1982] S.C.J. No. 1, [1982] 1 S.C.R. 175 (S.C.C.); *Canadian Broadcasting Co. v. New Brunswick (Attorney General)*, [1996] S.C.J. No. 38, [1996] 3 S.C.R. 480 (S.C.C.); *Toronto Star Newspapers Ltd v. Ontario*, [2005] S.C.J. No. 41, [2005] 2 S.C.R. 188 (S.C.C.).

information about what occurs there. The open court principle, however, may be curtailed by publication bans imposed under common law and statutory authority. There are two types of publication bans: mandatory and discretionary. Common law powers to order publication bans are always discretionary. Statutory powers may be mandatory or discretionary.

§16.6 When the judge has a discretion to order a publication ban under the *Criminal Code* or common law, the decision must be made with reference to the test formulated by the Supreme Court in *R. v. Mentuck*.[13] Broadening the framework it had established in *Dagenais v. Canadian Broadcasting Corp.*,[14] the Court in *Mentuck* explained that a publication ban should only be ordered when: (*i*) necessary to prevent a serious risk to the proper administration of justice because reasonably alternative measures will not prevent the risk; and (*ii*) the salutary effects of the publication ban outweigh the deleterious effects on the rights and interests of the parties and the public, including the effects on the right to free expression, the right of an accused to a fair and public trial, and the efficacy of the administration of justice.[15]

§16.7 The following sections discuss the most common forms of publication bans.

(a) Young Persons

§16.8 The *Youth Criminal Justice Act* (YCJA) prohibits the publication of the name of a young person charged with a criminal offence or any other information that would identify the young person.[16] While a young person can apply to set aside a publication ban, the court must be satisfied that the publication "would not be contrary to the young person's best interests or the public interest."[17] A publication ban is not available to a young person who receives an adult

---

[12] Except where an order is made pursuant to s. 486(1) of the *Code* banning the attendance of the public and media. See Part 3(2), below.

[13] [2001] S.C.J. No. 73, [2001] 3 S.C.R. 442 (S.C.C.).

[14] [1994] S.C.J. No. 104, [1994] 3 S.C.R. 835 (S.C.C.).

[15] [2001] S.C.J. No. 73, [2001] 3 S.C.R. 442 (S.C.C.) at para. 32.

[16] YCJA, s. 110(1). One exception to the prohibition under s. 110(1) is where "publication of information is made in the course of the administration of justice, if it is not the purpose of the publication to make the information known in the community" (see s. 110(2)(*c*)). Further, s. 110(4) provides that a peace officer can apply *ex parte* to a youth justice court judge for an order permitting publication of the identity of a young person where there is reason to believe that the young person is a danger to others and the publication of the information is necessary to assist in apprehending the young person. Subsection 111(1) also prohibits the publication of the "the name of a child or young person, or any other information related to a child or a young person, if it would identify the child or young person as having been a victim of, or as having appeared as a witness in connection with, an offence committed or alleged to have been committed by a young person." However, pursuant to s. 111(2), information relating to young victims or witnesses may be caused to be published by (*a*) that young person after he or she attains the age of 18 years or before that age with the consent of his or her parents; or (*b*) the parents of that young person if he or she is deceased.

[17] YCJA, s. 110(6).

sentence.[18] In addition, if the court imposes a youth sentence for a young person convicted of one of a class of "presumptive" offences,[19] or a young person has been convicted of one of another class of such offences and the Attorney General has given notice of an intention to seek an adult sentence,[20] the YCJA provides that the court "shall at the sentencing hearing inquire whether the young person or the Attorney General wishes to make an application...for a ban on publication."[21] If such an application is made, the judge may order a publication ban if "the court considers it appropriate in the circumstances, taking into account the importance of rehabilitating the young person and the public interest."[22] While this provision places the burden on the applicant to justify the ban, the Supreme Court of Canada held in *R. v. B. (D.)*[23] that the provision is inconsistent with section 7 of the *Charter* and not saved by section 1 to the extent that it imposes a reverse onus on the young person.[24] As a result, the Crown must justify the loss of a publication ban.

(b)   Pre-Trial Stage

§16.9 A justice presiding at a bail hearing is required, if the accused asks for one, to order a publication ban on "the evidence taken, the information given or the representations made and the reasons, if any, given or to be given by the justice".[25] The publication ban remains in effect until either (*i*) the accused is discharged after a preliminary inquiry; or (*ii*) the end of the trial.[26] In *Toronto*

---

[18]   YCJA, s. 110(2)(*a*).

[19]   This class is defined in paragraph (*a*) of the definition of "presumptive offence" in s. 2 of the YCJA as follows:

> ... an offence committed, or alleged to have been committed, by a young person who has attained the age of fourteen years, or, in a province where the lieutenant governor in council has fixed an age greater than fourteen years under section 61, the age so fixed, under one of the following provisions of the *Criminal Code*:
> (i)   section 231 or 235 (first degree murder or second degree murder within the meaning of section 231),
> (ii)   section 239 (attempt to commit murder),
> (iii) section 232, 234 or 236 (manslaughter), or
> (iv)   section 273 (aggravated sexual assault)....

[20]   This class is defined in paragraph (*b*) of the definition of "presumptive offence" in s. 2 of the YCJA as follows:

> ... a serious violent offence for which an adult is liable to imprisonment for a term of more than two years committed, or alleged to have been committed, by a young person after the coming into force of section 62 (adult sentence) and after the young person has attained the age of fourteen years, or, in a province where the lieutenant governor in council has fixed an age greater than fourteen years under section 61, the age so fixed, if at the time of the commission or alleged commission of the offence at least two judicial determinations have been made under subsection 42(9), at different proceedings, that the young person has committed a serious violent offence.

[21]   YCJA, s. 75(1).

[22]   YCJA, s. 75(3).

[23]   [2008] S.C.J. No. 25, [2008] 2 S.C.R. 3 (S.C.C.).

[24]   *Ibid.*

[25]   *Criminal Code*, s. 517(1).

[26]   *Criminal Code*, s. 517(1)(*a*) and (*b*).

Star Newspapers Ltd. v. Canada,[27] the Supreme Court of Canada held that while the statutory mandatory publication ban contained in section 517 of the *Code* limits freedom of expression as protected by section 2(*b*) of the *Charter*, that limit is justified under section 1 of the *Charter*. The Court held that the mandatory publication ban is an important safeguard to the right to a fair trial in preventing the dissemination of prejudicial and largely untested evidence heard at the bail hearing. Further, the ban is not absolute in either scope or time. With respect to bail proceedings under a publication ban, the media is still able to publish "the identity of the accused, comment on the facts and the offence that the accused has been charged with, and that an application for bail has been made, as well as report on the outcome of the application ... [and to] the legal conditions attached to the release of the accused."[28] In addition, the ban merely defers the publication of the bail hearing evidence to a later time.

§16.10 Publication bans are also very common at the preliminary hearing stage. At a preliminary hearing, an order for a publication ban is mandatory if requested by the defence[29] and discretionary if the application is made by the Crown.[30] The ban on publishing any evidence taken at the preliminary hearing will last until either the accused is discharged, or — if he or she is ordered to stand trial — until the trial has ended.[31]

(c) Trial Stage

§16.11 The *Criminal Code* also offers protection for the identity of complainants and witnesses in sexual cases. Section 486.4(1) automatically prohibits the disclosure of any information that could identify the complainant or a witness on the application of the complainant, the witness or the prosecutor.[32] In child pornography cases, the court must ban the publication of the identity of persons depicted in the offending material and any witnesses under the age of 18 regardless of whether any person applies for a ban.[33]

§16.12 In all other cases, upon an application by the prosecutor, a victim or a witness, the judge may ban the publication of information that could identify the victim or witness if the judge is "satisfied that the order is necessary for the proper administration of justice."[34] The party seeking the ban must apply for the ban in writing and provide notice to the Crown, the accused and any other person affected by the order that the judge specifies.[35] The judge may hold a hearing

---

[27]   [2010] S.C.J. No. 21, [2010] 1 S.C.R. 721 (S.C.C.).
[28]   *Ibid.*, at para. 38 (S.C.R.).
[29]   *Criminal Code*, s. 539(1)(*b*).
[30]   *Criminal Code*, s. 539(1)(*a*).
[31]   *Criminal Code*, s. 539(1)(*c*) and (*d*).
[32]   *Criminal Code*, s. 486.4(2)(*b*).
[33]   *Criminal Code*, s. 486.4(3).
[34]   *Criminal Code*, s. 486.5(1).
[35]   *Criminal Code*, s. 486.5(4).

to determine whether an order should be made, and the hearing may be held in private.[36]

§16.13 In determining whether to make the order, the judge must consider: (*a*) the right to a fair and public hearing; (*b*) whether there is a real and substantial risk that the victim, witness or justice system participant would suffer significant harm if their identity were disclosed; (*c*) whether the victim, witness or justice system participant needs the order for their security or to protect them from intimidation or retaliation; (*d*) society's interest in encouraging the reporting of offences and the participation of victims, witnesses and justice system participants in the criminal justice process; (*e*) whether effective alternatives are available to protect the identity of the victim, witness or justice system participant; (*f*) the salutary and deleterious effects of the proposed order; (*g*) the impact of the proposed order on the freedom of expression of those affected by it; and (*h*) any other factor that the judge considers relevant.[37] Although the *Criminal Code* does not speak to the removal of a publication ban, the Supreme Court of Canada has held that a ban may be revoked on the consent of both the Crown and the subject of the ban.[38]

§16.14 In jury trials, section 648(1) of the *Criminal Code* prohibits the publication or broadcast of "any portion of the trial at which the jury is not present ... before the jury retires to consider its verdict." Most courts have held that this ban extends to pre-trial motions and applications heard prior to a jury being empanelled.[39]

(2) Exclusion of the Public and Media

§16.15 In addition to publication bans, the trial judge has discretion to exclude the public and the media from the proceedings. Subsection 486(1) of the *Criminal Code* provides, "[a]ny proceedings against an accused shall be held in open court, but the presiding judge or justice may order the exclusion of all or any members of the public from the court room for all or part of the proceedings if the judge or justice is of the opinion that such an order is in the interest of public morals, the maintenance of order or the proper administration of justice or is necessary to prevent injury to international relations or national defence or national security."[40] While privacy interests continue to gain prominence in the

---

[36]   *Criminal Code*, s. 486.5(6).

[37]   *Criminal* Code, s. 486.5(7).

[38]   *R. v. Adams*, [1995] S.C.J. No. 105, [1995] 4 S.C.R. 707 at para. 32 (S.C.C.). See also *R. v. B. (A.)*, [1997] O.J. No. 1578, 115 C.C.C. (3d) 421 (Ont. C.A.) (ban may be revoked on appeal with Crown and subject's consent).

[39]   See, for example, *R. v. Bernardo*, [1995] O.J. No. 247 (Ont. Gen. Div.); *R. v. Regan*, [1997] N.S.J. No. 427, 124 C.C.C. (3d) 77 (N.S.S.C.); *R. v. Brown*, [1998] O.J. No. 482, 126 C.C.C. (3d) 187 (Ont. Gen. Div.). For a contrary view, see *Canada (Attorney General) v. Cheung*, [2000] A.J. No. 1463, 150 C.C.C. (3d) 192 (Alta. Q.B.).

[40]   The constitutionality of s. 486(1) was upheld in *Canadian Broadcasting Corp. v. New Brunswick (Attorney General)*, [1996] S.C.J. No. 38, [1996] 3 S.C.R. 480 (S.C.C.). See also s. 132(1)(*b*) of the YCJA, which grants the court the power to exclude the public from the

criminal courts, mere offence or embarrassment will not suffice for the exclusion of the public and media from the courtroom. As Justice La Forest observed in *Canadian Broadcasting Corp. v. New Brunswick (Attorney General)*:[41]

> It must be remembered that a criminal trial often involves the production of highly offensive evidence, whether salacious, violent or grotesque. Its aim is to uncover the truth, not to provide a sanitized account of facts that will be palatable to even the most sensitive human spirit. The criminal court is an innately tough arena.[42]

§16.16 In exercising its discretionary power to exclude the public and media, the trial judge should draw from the *Dagenais/Mentuck* principles[43] and: (*i*) consider the available options and consider whether there are any other reasonable and effective alternatives available; (*ii*) consider whether the order is limited as much as possible; and (*iii*) weigh the importance of the objectives of the order and its probable effects against the importance of openness and the particular expression that will be limited in order to ensure that the positive and negative effects of the order are proportionate.[44] The burden of displacing the general rule of openness lies on the party seeking the exclusion of the public.[45]

(3) Exclusion of Witnesses

§16.17 A trial judge has a common law discretion to order the exclusion of witnesses during the trial. Excluding witnesses mitigates the risk that a proposed witness's testimony will be influenced by hearing other witness's evidence. This benefit is especially great for unsavoury witnesses who would otherwise be able to prepare for (and shape their answers to) cross-examination. The exclusion order will apply to all witnesses proposed to be called by both the Crown[46] and the defence. Typically, a witness must remain outside the courtroom until all of the evidence, including that given in rebuttal, is completed.[47] A witness bound by an exclusion order who nevertheless remains in the courtroom during other evidence may affect the weight to be given to his or her evidence but does not necessarily disqualify him or her as a witness.[48]

---

courtroom where "it would be in the interest of public morals, the maintenance of order or the proper administration of justice".

[41] [1996] S.C.J. No. 38, [1996] 3 S.C.R. 480 (S.C.C.).

[42] *Ibid.*, at para. 40 (S.C.R.).

[43] *Ibid.*, at paras. 50-51 (S.C.R.); *Re Vancouver Sun*, [2004] S.C.J. No. 41, [2004] 2 S.C.R. 332 at para. 31 (S.C.C.).

[44] *Canadian Broadcasting Corp. v. New Brunswick (Attorney General)*, [1996] S.C.J. No. 38, [1996] 3 S.C.R. 480 at para. 69 (S.C.C.).

[45] *Ibid.*, at para. 71 (S.C.R.).

[46] It is common, however, to except from the order the investigating officer assisting the prosecutor at trial.

[47] *R. v. Dobberthien*, [1974] S.C.J. No. 115, 18 C.C.C. (2d) 449 (S.C.C.).

[48] *Ibid.*

(4) Compelling Attendance of Witnesses

§16.18 The parties in criminal cases often resort to the *Criminal Code*'s subpoena provisions to ensure the attendance of witnesses. A subpoena may be issued and served upon a person who "is likely to give material evidence in a proceeding".[49] The subpoena may also require the witness "to bring with him anything that he has in his possession or under his control relating to the subject-matter of the proceedings."[50] Unless excused by the judge, the subpoena compels the witness to remain in attendance for the duration of the particular proceeding for which it was issued.[51] A subpoena issued for a preliminary inquiry, for example, would expire at the end of that hearing and a new subpoena would have to be issued to compel the witness's attendance at trial.

§16.19 Where a person is required to attend to give evidence before a superior court, a court of appeal or a court of criminal jurisdiction other than a provincial court judge acting under Part XIX, a subpoena must be issued out of the court requiring the person's attendance.[52] Such a subpoena has effect anywhere in Canada.[53]

§16.20 If a person is required to give evidence before a provincial court judge acting under Part XIX, a summary conviction court under Part XXVII or in proceedings over which a justice has jurisdiction, a subpoena must be issued by: (*a*) a provincial court judge or a justice, where the person is within the province in which the proceedings were instituted; or (*b*) by a provincial court judge or out of a superior court of criminal jurisdiction of the province in which the proceedings were instituted, where the person is not within the province.[54]

§16.21 A prospective witness may move to quash a subpoena on the basis that he or she does not have "material evidence" to give.[55] When a subpoena is challenged, the party who obtained it must prove, on a balance of probabilities, that the person is likely to give material evidence.[56]

(5) Testimony Outside the Courtroom or Behind a Screen

§16.22 The *Criminal Code* allows certain witnesses to testify outside the courtroom or behind a screen in order not to see the accused. Witnesses under the age of 18 and witnesses who have difficulty in communicating by reason of a mental or physical disability are entitled to testify outside the courtroom or behind a

---

[49]   *Criminal Code*, s. 698(1).
[50]   *Criminal Code*, s. 700(1). Such a subpoena is also known as a subpoena *duces tecum* and is common in the context of third party applications (See Chapter 7, Part 4).
[51]   *Criminal Code*, s. 700(2).
[52]   *Criminal Code*, s. 699(1).
[53]   *Criminal Code*, s. 702(1).
[54]   *Criminal Code*, s. 699(2).
[55]   A motion to quash a subpoena should typically be brought at trial before the presiding judge. See *R. v. Logan*, [1988] O.J. No. 1360, 43 C.C.C. (3d) 567 (Ont. C.A.).
[56]   *R. v. Yarema*, [1996] O.J. No. 42, 27 O.R. (3d) 177 (Ont. Gen. Div.); *R. v. Baltovich [Finkle v. Ontario]*, [2007] O.J. No. 3506 at para. 72 (Ont. S.C.J.).

screen, unless doing so would "interfere with the proper administration of justice."[57] Witnesses in a criminal organization or terrorism related trial may also testify behind a screen or outside the courtroom when necessary to protect the safety of the witness or obtain a full and candid account from the witness.[58]

§16.23 For all other witnesses, the Crown must satisfy the judge "that the order is necessary to obtain a full and candid account from the witness of the acts complained of."[59] In deciding the issue, the judge must consider "the age of the witness, whether the witness has a mental or physical disability, the nature of the offence, the nature of any relationship between the witness and the accused, and any other circumstance that the judge or justice considers relevant."[60]

§16.24 If an order is made allowing a witness to testify outside the courtroom or behind a screen, arrangements must be made for the accused, the judge and the jury to watch the testimony of the witness by means of closed-circuit television or equivalent means and the accused must be permitted to communicate with counsel while watching the testimony.[61]

§16.25 The Supreme Court of Canada upheld the predecessor section to section 486.2 under sections 7 and 11(*d*) of the *Charter* in *R. v. Levogiannis*.[62] The screening of a complainant's testimony, the Court reasoned, does not impair the accused's ability to cross-examine, since the screen does not obstruct the view of the complainant by the accused, defence counsel, the Crown or the judge. Further, the Court held, a properly informed jury would not draw an adverse inference from the fact that a witness testified behind a screen or outside the courtroom.

(6) Adjournments

§16.26 One of the most commonly exercised of the court's discretionary powers to control its own process is the granting of adjournments. As long as this discretion is exercised judicially and does not cause a miscarriage of justice, it will not be interfered with on appeal.[63] In deciding whether to grant an adjournment, the court should consider, *inter alia*, the gravity of the charges, the number of previous adjournments and the consequences of an adjournment for the Crown and accused.[64]

---

[57] *Criminal Code*, s. 486.2(1).
[58] *Criminal Code*, s. 486.2(4) and (5).
[59] *Criminal Code*, s. 486.2(2).
[60] *Criminal Code*, s. 486.2(3) and s. 486.1(3).
[61] *Criminal Code*, s. 486.2(7).
[62] [1993] S.C.J. No. 70, [1993] 4 S.C.R. 475 (S.C.C.).
[63] *R. v. Olbey*, [1977] O.J. No. 1199, 38 C.C.C. (2d) 390 at p. 398 (Ont. C.A.), affd [1979] S.C.J. No. 137 (S.C.C.); *R. v. Barette*, [1976] S.C.J. No. 59, [1977] 2 S.C.R. 121 at 125 (S.C.C.). Also see discussion in Chapter 13, Part 3(1)(*c*) as to the treatment of adjournments in the context of an unreasonable delay application pursuant to s. 11(*b*) of the *Charter*.
[64] *R. v. White*, [2010] A.J. No. 208, 2010 ABCA 66 at para. 16 (Alta. C.A.).

§16.27 Where a party seeks an adjournment to procure the attendance of a witness, it must show that: (*i*) the witness is a material witness; (*ii*) it has not been guilty of laches or neglect in failing to ensure the witness's attendance; and (*iii*) the witness can reasonably be expected to attend on the date that the trial would recommence if adjourned.[65]

§16.28 As with many other aspects of trial procedure, adjournment applications present additional complications when brought by unrepresented accused. In such cases, courts have considered the following factors: "(*a*) whether or not there have been prior adjournments due to the unavailability of counsel and the accused was warned well in advance of trial that the trial would be proceeding on the scheduled date with or without counsel ...; (*b*) the accused's criminal record which reflects on the accused's degree of familiarity with the criminal justice system and legal aid programmes ...; (*c*) whether the charge against the accused is simple or complex which fact impacts on the critical question whether or not the accused can get a fair trial without counsel ...; (*d*) the public interest in the orderly and expeditious administration of justice ....; and (*e*) if the accused has been refused legal aid and when the refusal was communicated to the accused."[66]

4. THE TRIAL PROCESS

(1) Presence of the Accused

(a) *Indictable Matters*

§16.29 Section 650 of the *Criminal Code* gives an accused the right to be "present in court during the whole of his or her trial." This right, however, is not absolute. The court may order the removal of the accused when he or she "misconducts himself by interrupting the proceedings so that to continue the proceedings in his presence would not be feasible."[67] Removal may also be ordered to determine whether the accused is unfit to stand trial when the accused's presence "might have an adverse effect on [his or her] mental condition".[68] The judge may also "permit the accused to be out of court during the whole or any part of his trial on such conditions as the court considers proper."[69]

§16.30 The right to be present is also limited to proceedings constituting part of the "trial". In *R. v. Hertrich*,[70] Justice Martin interpreted this to include any proceeding affecting the accused's vital interests, such as the arraignment and plea, jury selection, reception of evidence (including *voir dires* held to decide the admissibility of evidence), rulings on evidence, arguments of counsel, addresses to

---

[65] *R. v. Darville*, [1956] S.C.J. No. 82, 116 C.C.C. 113 at 117 (S.C.C.).
[66] *R. v. Beals*, [1993] N.S.J. No. 436, 126 N.S.R. (2d) 130 at para. 29 (N.S.C.A.).
[67] *Criminal Code*, s. 650(2)(*a*).
[68] *Criminal Code*, s. 650(2)(*c*).
[69] *Criminal Code*, s. 650(2)(*b*).
[70] [1982] O.J. No. 496, 67 C.C.C. (2d) 510 (Ont. C.A.).

the jury, the judge's charge to the jury (including requests by the jury for further instructions), the receipt of the verdict and sentencing.[71]

§16.31 A fairly recent amendment to the *Criminal Code* permits an accused to attend certain court proceedings by way of a "designated counsel".[72] Once a formal designation is filed with the court,[73] an accused may be absent for any part of the proceedings, other than: (*i*) a part during which oral evidence of a witness is taken; (*ii*) a part during which jurors are being selected; and (*iii*) an application for a writ of *habeas corpus*.[74] In addition, a plea of guilty may be made, and a sentence may be pronounced, only in the attendance of the accused, unless the court orders otherwise.[75]

(b) Summary Conviction Matters

§16.32 In summary conviction proceedings, a defendant may appear personally or by counsel or agent, although the court may require the defendant to appear personally.[76] Where a defendant appears represented by an agent who is not a lawyer, a trial judge should ensure that the choice is an informed one by: (*i*) making inquiries to determine that the defendant is aware that the agent is not a lawyer and that the defendant will not have recourse to various remedies that might be available to him or her if the agent were a lawyer and performed inadequately; (*ii*) informing the defendant that provincial laws may not require that agents receive any training or demonstrate any level of expertise before being allowed to take money in return for representing persons in criminal matters; and (*iii*) advising the defendant that while the law expects certain minimum standards of competence from lawyers it imposes no such standards on those who are not lawyers.[77]

§16.33 While there is no similar mandatory obligation on the trial judge to inquire into the competency of an agent appearing on behalf of the defendant, the trial judge retains the authority to refuse to permit an agent to represent an accused where the agent's participation in the proceedings would either damage

---

[71] *Ibid.*, at 537 (C.C.C.). This test was later endorsed by the Supreme Court of Canada. See *R. v. Vézina*, [1986] S.C.J. No. 2, [1986] 1 S.C.R. 2 (S.C.C.); *R. v. Barrow*, [1987] S.C.J. No. 84, [1987] 2 S.C.R. 694 (S.C.C.).

[72] *Criminal Code*, s. 650.01 [as am. S.C. 2002, c. 13, s. 61]. There is conflicting authority on whether the designation may authorize a lawyer to sub-delegate to an agent to appear on the behalf of the accused. For a decision holding that it can, see *R. v. Golyanik*, [2003] O.J. No. 346 at para. 18 (Ont. S.C.J.). But see *R. v. Trites*, [2011] N.B.J. No. 12, 2011 NBCA 5 at para. 26 (N.B.C.A.), holding that such sub-delegation is simply not permitted under s. 650.01.

[73] A designation must contain the name and address of the designated counsel and be signed by the accused and the designated counsel: See *Criminal Code*, s. 650.01(2).

[74] *Criminal Code*, s. 650.01(3)(*a*).

[75] *Criminal Code*, s. 650.01(3)(*c*).

[76] *Criminal Code*, s. 800(2).

[77] *R. v. Romanowicz*, [1999] O.J. No. 3191, 138 C.C.C. (3d) 225 at paras. 41-43 (Ont. C.A.).

the fairness of those proceedings, impair the ability of the tribunal to perform its function or otherwise undermine the integrity of the process.[78]

(2) Arraignment

§16.34 The trial begins with the person who is charged being "arraigned". The arraignment consists of the charge(s) being formally read to the accused person or defendant in order to ensure: (*i*) that an accused is aware of the exact charges when he or she elects and pleads; and (*ii*) that all parties to the proceeding have a common understanding of the charges that are to be the subject-matter of the proceedings.[79] In a jury trial, arraignment generally takes place before the jury is selected in the presence of the jury panel, unless to do so would be impractical.[80] In summary conviction matters, the substance of the information is read to the defendant by the clerk or registrar of the court and the defendant is asked whether he or she pleads guilty or not guilty to the charges contained in the information.[81]

(3) Opening Statement or Address of Counsel

§16.35 In order to provide an outline of the case, counsel will make an "opening statement" in a trial by judge alone, or most typically, an "opening address" in a jury case. While the *Criminal Code* is silent on the Crown's right to make an opening address, custom and tradition has cemented the practice to a *de facto* right.[82] However, there are limits to the scope of the Crown's opening address. As the Ontario Court of Appeal observed in *R. v. Mallory*,[83] "[i]t is well established that the opening address is not the appropriate forum for argument, invective, or opinion."[84] Instead, the prosecutor should use the opening address to "introduce the parties, explain the process, and provide a general overview of the evidence that the Crown anticipates calling in support of its case".[85]

§16.36 As for defence's opportunity to make an opening statement, section 651(2) of the *Code* provides that defence counsel "is entitled, if he thinks fit, to open the case for the defence, and after the conclusion of that opening to examine such witnesses as he thinks fit ...". Consequently, where the defence wishes to make an opening statement, it typically occurs at the close of the Crown's case. However, the defence may seek leave of the court to address the jury

---

[78] *Ibid.*, at para. 61 (C.C.C.).

[79] *R. v. Mitchell*, [1997] O.J. No. 5148, 121 C.C.C. (3d) 139 at para. 27 (Ont. C.A.).

[80] See *R. v. Sandham*, [2008] O.J. No. 5810 (Ont. S.C.J.) where the trial judge ruled that the arraignment of the six co-accused would take place after the jury was selected because it was "not practical or sensible" to arraign the accused before each of the 10 jury panels.

[81] *Criminal Code*, s. 801.

[82] See *R. v. Vitale*, [1987] O.J. No. 1607, 40 C.C.C. (3d) 267 at 268 (Ont. Dist. Ct.); *R. v. C. (J.)*, [2002] O.J. No. 4042 (Ont. S.C.J.).

[83] [2007] O.J. No. 236, 217 C.C.C. (3d) 266 (Ont. C.A.).

[84] *Ibid.*, at para. 338 (C.C.C.).

[85] *Ibid.*

immediately following the Crown's opening address, but will have to establish that there are special circumstances that may impair the accused's right to a fair trial if not permitted to do so.[86]

(4) Admissions at Trial

§16.37 Section 655 of the *Criminal Code* permits an accused to "admit any fact alleged against him for the purpose of dispensing with proof thereof." Such an admission must be made formally,[87] however; counsel's informal acknowledgment that the Crown has proved an issue does not constitute an admission.[88] An accused cannot admit a fact, moreover, until the allegation has been made and the prosecutor consents.[89] That said, prosecutors may not refuse consent for the sole purpose of keeping an "issue alive artificially."[90]

(5) Examination of Witnesses

§16.38 The rules respecting the examination of witnesses stem from both evidentiary and procedural law. Indeed, in many cases it is difficult to categorize a rule as a rule of evidence or procedure. In this section we examine some of the most basic rules governing the process. More extensive treatments may be found in other works.[91]

(a) Direct Examination

§16.39 A witness at a trial will first be questioned by the party who called the witness. Generally, the party calling a witness will be restricted to asking non-leading questions. However, there are two exceptions to this rule. Firstly, it is acceptable, and usually encouraged for the sake of trial efficiency, to lead one's own witness through non-contentious matters.[92] Further, a party may employ leading questions or cross-examine its own witness where the witness has been declared "hostile" at common law or "adverse" under section 9 of the *Canada Evidence Act.*[93]

---

[86] *R. v. Dalzell*, [2003] O.J. No. 4900, 180 C.C.C. (3d) 319 (Ont. S.C.J.).

[87] Usually made in writing and entered as an exhibit.

[88] See *R. v. Desjardins*, [1998] B.C.J. No. 1707, 110 B.C.A.C. 33 at para. 29 (B.C.C.A.), *per* Huddart J.A., concurring.

[89] *R. v. Castellani*, [1969] S.C.J. No. 85, [1970] S.C.R. 310 at. 315-16 (S.C.C.).

[90] *R. v. Proctor*, [1992] M.J. No. 32, 69 C.C.C. (3d) 436 (Man. C.A.).

[91] See generally, Earl J. Levy, *The Examination of Witnesses in Criminal Cases*, 5th ed. (Toronto: Thomson Carswell, 1999); Alan W. Mewett & Peter Sankoff, *Witnesses*, looseleaf (Toronto: Carswell, 1991); David M. Paciocco & Lee Stuesser, *The Law of Evidence*, 5th ed. (Toronto: Irwin Law, 2008).

[92] See *Reference re R. v. Coffin*, [1956] S.C.J. No. 1, 114 C.C.C. 1 at 22 (S.C.C.).

[93] See David M. Paciocco & Lee Stuesser, *The Law of Evidence*, 5th ed. (Toronto: Irwin Law, 2008) at 506-509.

(b)   Cross-examination of Witnesses

§16.40 Cross-examination has been described as "a faithful friend in the pursuit of justice and an indispensable ally in the search for truth."[94] Indeed, the courts have recognized that the right to cross-examine is protected by sections 7 and 11(*d*) of the *Charter*.[95] The right though, is neither absolute nor unfettered. Trial judges enjoy a broad discretion to prevent harassment, misrepresentation, repetitiousness or the asking of questions that have a greater prejudicial effect than probative value.[96] Further, while a question can be put to a witness in cross-examination regarding a matter that need not be proven independently, counsel must have a "good faith basis" for asking the question.[97] Apart from a judge's common law power to control cross-examination, the *Criminal Code* provides that a preliminary hearing judge "shall order the immediate cessation of any part of an examination or cross-examination of a witness that is, in the opinion of the justice, abusive, too repetitive or otherwise inappropriate."[98]

(c)   Re-examination of Witnesses

§16.41 Also deeply entrenched in trial procedure is the common law right to re-examine one's own witness.[99] Re-examination is generally restricted to having the witness explain or clarify new matters that arose in cross-examination. It is not an opportunity to raise new facts or issues not previously covered in the examination-in-chief. Re-examination may also serve to rehabilitate the credibility of the witness that was harmed during cross-examination.[100] For example, in *R. v. Linklater*,[101] the Crown was entitled to re-examine the witness on prior consistent statements to police to rebut the defence cross-examination that focussed on impeaching the witness on only parts of his statement to police.[102]

(d)   Questioning of Witnesses by Judge

§16.42 As a general rule, trial judges may ask questions of witnesses for the purposes of clarification and amplification. However, judicial intervention

---

[94] *R. v. Lyttle*, [2004] S.C.J. No. 8, [2004] 1 S.C.R. 193 at para. 1 (S.C.C.).

[95] *Ibid.*, at para. 43 (S.C.R.); *R. v. Osolin*, [1994] S.C.J. No. 135, [1993] 4 S.C.R. 595 at 665 (S.C.C.).

[96] *R. v. Lyttle*, [2004] S.C.J. No. 8, [2004] 1 S.C.R. 193 at para. 44 (S.C.C.).

[97] *Ibid.*, at para. 48 (S.C.R.) ("In this context, a 'good faith basis' is a function of the information available to the cross-examiner, his or her belief in its likely accuracy, and the purpose for which it is used. Information falling short of admissible evidence may be put to the witness. In fact, the information may be incomplete or uncertain, provided the cross-examiner does not put suggestions to the witness recklessly or that he or she knows to be false.").

[98] *Criminal Code*, s. 537(1.1).

[99] See *Queen's Case* (1820), 129 E.R. 976 at 981.

[100] See John Sopinka, Sidney N. Lederman & Alan W. Bryant, *The Law of Evidence in Canada* (Markham: Butterworths, 1998) at 879.

[101] [2009] O.J. No. 771 (Ont. C.A.).

[102] *Ibid.*, at para. 14.

should not usurp the function of counsel.[103] If a trial judge wishes to ask a question, prudence dictates that he or she waits until both counsel have finished their questioning. At the least, the intervention should not be made until counsel has completed a particular line of inquiry. As noted by Lord Greene M.R. in *Yuill v. Yuill*,[104] "[i]t must always be borne in mind that the judge does not know what is in counsel's brief and has not the same facilities as counsel for an effective examination-in-chief or cross-examination."[105]

§16.43 Excessive interventions by a trial judge may compromise the appearance of fairness and raise concerns of bias. In assessing the propriety of judicial intervention, Justice Martin held in *R. v. Valley*[106] that "[t]he ultimate question to be answered is not whether the accused was in fact prejudiced by the interventions but whether he might reasonably consider that he had not had a fair trial or whether a reasonably minded person who had been present throughout the trial would consider that the accused had not had a fair trial."[107]

(6) Expert Evidence

§16.44 With the growing reliance of expert testimony in criminal trials, Parliament has enacted legislation to assist in the orderly and efficient presentation of the evidence. Subsections 657.3(1) and (2) of the *Code* provide a statutory exception to the hearsay rule by allowing the evidence of an expert to be given by "means of a report accompanied by the affidavit or solemn declaration of the person, setting out, in particular, the qualifications of the person as an expert" as long as the court recognizes that person as an expert and the party intending to produce the report has given the other party a copy of the affidavit and reasonable notice of the intention to produce it in evidence.[108] The trial judge does retain the discretion to require the expert to appear for examination or cross-examination.[109]

§16.45 Subsections 657.3(3) and (4) set out the notice requirements for parties intending to call an expert witness. At least 30 days before the beginning of the trial, the party must provide: (*i*) the name of the proposed witness; (*ii*) a description of the witness's area of expertise sufficient to permit the other parties to inform themselves about that area of expertise; and (*iii*) a statement of the qualifications of the proposed witness as an expert.[110] In addition, the prosecutor is required, within a "reasonable period before trial", to provide to the defence:

---

[103] See *R. v. Brouillard*, [1985] S.C.J. No. 3, 17 C.C.C. (3d) 193 at 195-96 (S.C.C.); *R. v. Osolin*, [1993] S.C.J. No. 135, 86 C.C.C. (3d) 481 at 542-43 (S.C.C.).

[104] [1945] 1 All E.R. 183 (C.A.).

[105] *Ibid.*, at 185.

[106] [1986] O.J. No. 77, 26 C.C.C. (3d) 207 (Ont. C.A.), leave to appeal refused [1986] S.C.C.A. No. 298 (S.C.C.).

[107] *Ibid.*, at 232 (C.C.C.).

[108] *Criminal Code*, s. 657.3(1).

[109] *Criminal Code*, s. 657.3(2).

[110] *Criminal Code*, s. 657.3(3)(*a*).

(*i*) a copy of the report, if any, prepared by the proposed witness for the case; and (*ii*) if no report is prepared, a summary of the opinion anticipated to be given by the proposed witness and the grounds on which it is based.[111] The defence is required to provide the Crown with that same material "not later than the close of the case for the prosecution".[112]

§16.46 If either the Crown or the defence fails to comply with the notice requirements of section 657.3(3), the trial judge must, at the aggrieved party's request: (*i*) grant an adjournment of the proceedings to allow the affected party to prepare for cross-examination of the expert witness; (*ii*) order the party who called the expert witness to provide the other party with more fulsome material; or (*iii*) order the calling or recalling of any witness for the purpose of giving testimony on matters related to those raised in the expert witness's testimony.[113] The courts have held that, on request, an adjournment is the minimum remedy for improper notice.[114] The trial judge is not empowered, however, to refuse to allow the expert witness to testify.[115]

(7) Mental Disorder Issues

§16.47 When an accused is alleged to suffer from a mental disorder, two key questions may arise: whether the accused is "unfit to stand trial"; and (*b*) whether the accused is not "criminally responsible".[116] This section examines the procedural rules associated with these issues; the meanings of "unfit to stand trial" and "not criminally responsible" are dealt with more extensively in other works on the substantive criminal law.[117]

(a) Fitness to Stand Trial

§16.48 Section 2 of the *Criminal Code* defines "unfit to stand trial" as being:

> unable on account of mental disorder to conduct a defence at any stage of the proceedings before a verdict is rendered or to instruct counsel to do so, and, in particular, unable on account of mental disorder to

---

[111] *Criminal Code*, s. 657.3(3)(*b*).

[112] *Criminal Code*, s. 657.3(3)(*c*).

[113] *Criminal Code*, s. 657.3(4).

[114] See *R. v. Apolinario*, [2007] O.J. No. 4788 at para. 112 (Ont. S.C.J.); *R. v. Nandlal*, [2004] O.J. No. 3284 (Ont. C.J.); *R. v. Turner*, [2004] B.C.J. No. 2869 (B.S.S.C.); *R. v. Mousseau*, [2003] A.J. No. 934 (Alta. Q.B.).

[115] *R. v. Horan*, [2008] O.J. No. 3167, 237 C.C.C. (3d) 514 at para. 29 (Ont. C.A.).

[116] The rules applying to these determinations are set out in Part XX.1 of the *Criminal Code*. This Part was added to the *Code* after the Supreme Court of Canada found in *R. v. Swain*, [1991] S.C.J. No. 32, [1991] 1 S.C.R. 933 (S.C.C.), that the previous legislation dealing with mentally disordered accused violated ss. 7 and 9 of the *Charter* and could not be saved by s. 1 because of its procedural defects.

[117] See Morris Manning, Q.C. & Peter Sankoff, *Manning, Mewett & Sankoff Criminal Law*, 4th ed. (Markham.: LexisNexis Canada, 2009), c. 11; Don Stuart, *Canadian Criminal Law*, 5th ed. (Toronto: Thomson Carswell, 2007) at 385-430; Eric Colvin & Sanjeev Anand, *Principles of Criminal Law*, 3d ed. (Toronto: Thomson Carswell, 2007) at 425-67; Kent Roach, *Criminal Law*, 4th ed. (Toronto: Irwin Law, 2009), c. 8.

(*a*) understand the nature or object of the proceedings,

(*b*) understand the possible consequences of the proceedings, or

(*c*) communicate with counsel.

An accused is presumed fit to stand trial unless the contrary is proved on a balance of probabilities.[118]

§16.49 The issue of the fitness to stand trial may be raised by either party or on the court's own motion at any time before the verdict.[119] The party making the application has the onus to prove that the accused is unfit to stand trial.[120] The court may order an assessment of the accused's mental condition to assist in deciding the issue.[121] Such an order may be made at any stage of the proceedings on the court's own motion or on application by one of the parties.[122] However, in summary conviction matters, an assessment order may only be granted at the prosecution's request if: (*i*) the accused raised the issue of fitness; or (*ii*) the Crown satisfies the Court that there are reasonable grounds to doubt that the accused is fit to stand trial.[123] Assessment orders remain in force for no more than 30 days[124] and cannot direct the accused to undergo treatment.[125]

§16.50 After the completion of an assessment, the court will determine whether the accused is fit to stand trial. If the accused is found to be fit, the trial proceeds as if the issue had never arisen.[126] Where the accused is found to be unfit to stand trial, any pleas that had been made will be set aside and any jury discharged.[127] An accused initially found to be unfit may be tried if he or she becomes fit.[128] The party alleging that the accused has become fit must prove it on a balance of probabilities.[129]

§16.51 If the accused is found unfit, the court may proceed directly to a disposition hearing and order the accused to either be released (subject to conditions) or placed in custody.[130] Alternatively, the court may defer the disposition to the Review Board, *i.e.*, the committee established in each province to make or review dispositions for accused found unfit or not criminally responsible.[131]

---

[118] *Criminal Code*, s. 672.22.
[119] *Criminal Code*, s. 672.3(1).
[120] *Criminal Code*, s. 672.23(2).
[121] *Criminal Code*, s. 672.11(*a*).
[122] *Criminal Code*, s. 672.12(1).
[123] *Criminal Code*, s. 672.12(2)(*a*).
[124] *Criminal Code*, s. 672.14(1). However, s. 672.14(3) allows for an assessment for up to 60 days where "compelling circumstances exist that warrant it."
[125] *Criminal Code*, s. 672.19.
[126] *Criminal Code*, s. 672.28.
[127] *Criminal Code*, s. 672.31.
[128] *Criminal Code*, s. 672.32(1).
[129] *Criminal Code*, s. 672.32(2).
[130] *Criminal Code*, s. 672.45(1).
[131] *Criminal Code*, s. 672.45(1.1).

(b)   Not Criminally Responsible by Reason of Mental Disorder

§16.52 An accused may be found not criminally responsible if, at the time of the offence, he or she suffered from a mental disorder that prevented him or her from either: (*i*) appreciating the nature and quality of a criminal act; or (*ii*) knowing that it was wrong.[132] The party claiming that the accused is not criminally responsible must prove these elements on a balance of probabilities.[133]

§16.53 The accused is entitled to raise the issue of not criminally responsible by reason of mental disorder at any stage of the trial. In contrast, the prosecutor may normally raise the issue only after a finding of guilt (but before the entry of a conviction). However, where the accused's own evidence tends to put his or her mental capacity for criminal intent into question, the prosecutor may raise the issue without awaiting a guilty verdict.[134]

§16.54 As with fitness to stand trial, the court may order an assessment, for up to 30 days, of the accused's mental condition to help it decide the issue.[135] If the accused is found not criminally responsible, the judge must "render a verdict that the accused committed the act or made the omission but is not criminally responsible on account of mental disorder."[136] The judge may then either proceed directly to a disposition hearing[137] or defer the disposition issue to the Review Board.[138]

5.   CLOSING OF THE CASE

(1)   Reply and Re-opening the Case

§16.55 At the close of the Crown's case, the accused is entitled to present a defence.[139] Should an accused avail himself or herself of this right, the Crown may be permitted with leave of the court to present "reply" or "rebuttal" evidence in response to new matters raised by the defence. Reply evidence, however, is not an opportunity for the Crown to "split its case" and present further evidence to support its case.[140] Generally, reply evidence is admissible where the matter arises out of the defence's case, where it is not collateral, and where the Crown could not have foreseen its development.[141]

---

[132]   *Criminal Code*, s. 16(1).
[133]   *Criminal Code*, ss. 16(2)-(3). The reverse onus placed on the defence by way of this section was held to be constitutionally valid by the Supreme Court of Canada in *R. v. Chaulk*, [1990] S.C.J. No. 139, [1990] 3 S.C.R. 1303 (S.C.C.).
[134]   See *R. v. Swain*, [1991] S.C.J. No. 32, [1991] 1 S.C.R. 933 (S.C.C.).
[135]   *Criminal Code*, ss. 672.11(*b*) and 672.14(1).
[136]   *Criminal Code*, s. 672.34.
[137]   *Criminal Code*, s. 672.45(1).
[138]   *Criminal Code*, s. 672.45(1.1).
[139]   *Criminal Code*, s. 650(3).
[140]   See *R. v. Krause*, [1986] S.C.J. No. 65, [1986] 2 S.C.R. 466 at 472-73 (S.C.C.).
[141]   *R. v. G. (S.G.)*, [1997] S.C.J. No. 70, [1997] 2 S.C.R. 716 at para. 39 (S.C.C.).

§16.56 It is important to distinguish between reply evidence and "re-opening the case". Sometimes counsel fails to adduce particular evidence during its turn to present evidence for various reasons and seeks permission of the court to re-open its case. A trial judge may permit the re-opening of the evidence at any time before sentence is passed, but only if the proposed evidence is material and where the other side will not suffer any prejudice.[142] The later the stage of the proceedings, the less likely the request to re-open the case will be granted. In *R. v. P. (M.B.)*,[143] Chief Justice Lamer offered three examples of the narrow circumstances in which the Crown should be allowed to re-open its case after the defence has commenced to answer the Crown's case: (*i*) where the conduct of the defence has either directly or indirectly contributed to the Crown's failure to adduce certain evidence before closing its case; (*ii*) where the Crown's omission or mistake was over a non-controversial issue to do with purely formal procedural or technical matters, having nothing to do with the substance or merits of a case; and (*iii*) where the interests of the accused warrant re-opening the Crown's case.

§16.57 An accused who has been convicted but not yet sentenced may apply to re-open the defence, but will have to meet the test for the admission of fresh evidence established in *R. v. Palmer*.[144] To meet this test, the accused must show that the evidence: (*i*) could not, in the exercise of due diligence, have been adduced at trial; (*ii*) is relevant and bears upon a potentially decisive issue in the trial; (*iii*) is credible; and (*iv*) if believed, could reasonably have affected the result.[145]

(2) Final Submissions and Closing Addresses of Counsel

§16.58 After all the evidence has been presented, counsel will alternate in making "final submissions" in a judge alone trial or "closing addresses" in jury trials. An important factor for the defence to consider in deciding whether to call evidence is the impact it may have on the order of presenting these submissions. If the defence does not call any witnesses, then it is entitled to present after the prosecution.[146] However, if the defence, or any co-accused in a joint trial, calls witnesses, the defence must present first.[147] In *R. v. Rose*,[148] the Supreme Court of Canada rejected the argument that this rule infringed the accused's right to make full answer and defence under sections 7 and 11(*d*) of the *Charter*.[149] Though the

---

[142] See *R. v. Lessard*, [1976] O.J. No. 74, 30 C.C.C. (2d) 70 at 74-75 (Ont. C.A.); *R. v. Hayward*, [1993] O.J. No. 2939, 86 C.C.C. (3d) 193 (Ont. C.A.).

[143] [1994] S.C.J. No. 27, [1994] 1 S.C.R. 555 (S.C.C.).

[144] [1979] S.C.J. No. 126, [1980] 1 S.C.R. 759 (S.C.C.). See *R. v. Kowall*, [1996] O.J. No. 2715, 108 C.C.C. (3d) 481 at 493-94 (Ont. C.A.). See also *R. v. Arabia*, [2008] O.J. No. 2960, 235 C.C.C. (3d) 354 (Ont. C.A.).

[145] *R. v. Palmer*, [1979] S.C.J. No. 126, [1980] 1 S.C.R. 759 (S.C.C.).

[146] *Criminal Code*, s. 651(3).

[147] *Criminal Code*, ss. 651(3) and (4).

[148] [1998] S.C.J. No. 81, [1998] 3 S.C.R. 262 (S.C.C.).

[149] *Ibid.*

rule "may just not be the most desirable", the Court reasoned, it was nonetheless fair.[150] Since the trial judge must instruct the jury that the Crown has the burden to prove the accused's guilt beyond a reasonable doubt, there is no danger that jurors would presume guilt from the fact that the defence addresses them first.

§16.59 While counsel are afforded much latitude in forcefully advancing their respective positions to the trier of fact, closing submissions — especially in jury trials — should be "limited to reviewing and commenting on the evidence and to the making of submissions which may properly be supported by the evidence adduced."[151]

(3) Charge to the Jury

§16.60 In jury trials, at the conclusion of closing addresses to the jury by both parties, a trial judge will provide instructions to the jury before jurors begin their deliberations. While there is no particular formula in charging the jury, the majority of the Court in *R. v. Daley*[152] set out the following elements that should be covered:

1. instruction on the relevant legal issues, including the charges faced by the accused;

2. an explanation of the theories of each side;

3. a review of the salient facts which support the theories and case of each side;

4. a review of the evidence relating to the law;

5. a direction informing the jury they are the masters of the facts and it is for them to make the factual determinations;

6. instruction about the burden of proof and presumption of innocence;

7. the possible verdicts open to the jury; and

8. the requirements of unanimity for reaching a verdict.[153]

Counsel will be given an opportunity to raise objections to the jury charge in the absence of the jury and the trial judge retains a discretion as to whether to re-charge the jury upon consideration of the objections.

6.   THE VERDICT

(1) Directed Verdict

§16.61 At the close of the Crown's case, an accused may decide to bring a motion for a directed verdict (also known as a "no-evidence" or "non-suit" motion).

---

[150] *Ibid.*, at para. 118 (S.C.R.).
[151] *Ibid.*, at para. 104 (S.C.R.), quoting *Gray v. Alanco Developments Ltd.*, [1967] O.J. No. 704, [1967] 1 O.R. 597 at 601 (Ont. C.A.).
[152] [2007] S.C.J. No. 53, [2007] 3 S.C.R. 523 (S.C.C.).
[153] *Ibid.*, at para. 29 (S.C.R.). See also *R. v. MacKinnon*, [1999] O.J. No. 346, 132 C.C.C. (3d) 545 at para. 27 (Ont. C.A.).

In making such a motion, the accused asserts that the prosecution has failed to make out a *prima facie* case to meet and he or she should therefore be acquitted without having to decide whether to call evidence. The test for a directed verdict was first articulated by the Supreme Court of Canada in *United States of America v. Sheppard*,[154] where the Court held that a trial judge must determine "whether or not there is any evidence upon which a reasonable jury properly instructed could return a verdict of guilty."[155] The Court elaborated on this test in *R. v. Monteleone*[156] as follows:

> Where there is before the court any admissible evidence, whether direct or circumstantial, which, if believed by a properly charged jury acting reasonably, would justify a conviction, the trial judge is not justified in directing a verdict of acquittal. It is not the function of the trial judge to weigh the evidence, to test its quality or reliability once a determination of its admissibility has been made. It is not for the trial judge to draw inferences of fact from the evidence before him. These functions are for the trier of fact, the jury.[157]

§16.62 The existence of evidence on every essential element will result in dismissal of the directed verdict motion.[158] The trial judge's assessment of the evidence will vary, however, depending on whether the Crown's evidence is direct or circumstantial. Where there is direct evidence on each element of the offence, no weighing of the evidence will be required by the trial judge. However, where the Crown's case involves circumstantial evidence, the trial judge must engage in a limited weighing of the evidence to determine whether the evidence can reasonably support an inference of guilt.[159]

(2) Trial by Judge Alone vs. Jury Trial

§16.63 In non-jury trials, the responsibility to decide the case rests with the trial judge. The trial judge must provide reasons, whether orally or in writing, that demonstrate a sufficient basis for the judgment and allow for meaningful appellate review.[160] In contrast, a jury is only required to arrive at a "verdict" of "guilty" or "not guilty"; it does not provide reasons.[161] The jury must be unanimous in its verdict of "guilty" or "not guilty", although it need not be unanimous in the evidentiary route each juror takes to this decision.[162] There are times, however, when a jury cannot arrive at a unanimous verdict. In these situations, a trial

---

[154] [1976] S.C.J. No. 106, [1977] 2 S.C.R. 1067 (S.C.C.).

[155] *Ibid.*, at 1080 (S.C.R.).

[156] [1987] S.C.J. No. 52, [1987] 2 S.C.R. 154 (S.C.C.).

[157] *Ibid.*, at 161 (S.C.R.).

[158] *R. v. Charemski*, [1998] S.C.J. No. 23, [1998] 1 S.C.R. 679 at para. 22 (S.C.C.).

[159] *R. v. Arcuri*, [2001] S.C.J. No. 52, [2001] 2 S.C.R. 828 at paras. 22 and 32 (S.C.C.).

[160] See *R. v. Sheppard*, [2002] S.C.J. No. 30, [2002] 1 S.C.R. 869 (S.C.C.).

[161] See *R. v. Tuckey*, [1985] O.J. No. 142, 20 C.C.C. (3d) 502 (Ont. C.A.). See also *Criminal Code*, s. 649 (making it a criminal offence for jurors to disclose any information relating to their deliberations).

[162] See *R. v. Thatcher*, [1987] S.C.J. No. 22, [1987] 1 S.C.R. 652 (S.C.C.).

judge will decide whether to exhort the jury to try to make a decision.[163] Should the jury remain deadlocked, the trial judge has the discretion to declare a mistrial, discharge the jury and direct that a new jury be empanelled for a new trial.[164]

7. MISTRIAL

§16.64 As we have seen in this chapter, a trial judge retains much control in ensuring that a trial runs efficiently without compromising fairness or running afoul *Charter* principles. Sometimes, however, an incident occurs at trial that poses "a 'real danger' of prejudice to the accused or danger of a miscarriage of justice" that requires a judge to declare a mistrial.[165] Courts have recognized though, that a mistrial should be a measure of last resort and that the trial judge should first consider other corrective means of remedying the situation.[166] Examples in which mistrials have been declared due to a fatal wounding of the trial process include where jurors have been exposed to prejudicial media coverage;[167] counsel's closing address to the jury exceeds the bounds of propriety due to "inflammatory invective";[168] and where delayed disclosure deprives the accused of an opportunity to make full answer and defence.[169] It should be noted that the trial judge's jurisdiction to declare a mistrial becomes narrowly restricted at the post-verdict stage of a trial. At this juncture, a trial judge is generally *functus officio* and the verdict cannot be altered except on appeal. In a jury trial, a judge retains a residual discretion to correct a mistaken verdict where the jury did not render the verdict it intended. However, where the mistake is discovered after the jury is discharged, the trial judge will recall the jurors for an inquiry. If the inquiry establishes a reasonable apprehension of bias, then a trial judge may order a mistrial in order to prevent a miscarriage of justice.[170] However, in a judge alone trial, a judge is not *functus officio* following a finding of guilt until he or she has imposed sentence. Therefore, the trial judge may vacate the adjudication of guilt at any time before the imposition of sentence, albeit only in exceptional circumstances.[171]

163	See *R. v. G. (R.M.)*, [1996] S.C.J. No. 94, [1996] 3 S.C.R. 362 at para. 48 (S.C.C.) (providing example of exhortation).

164	*Criminal Code*, s. 653(1).

165	See *R. v. Burke*, [2002] S.C.J. No. 56, [2002] 2 S.C.R. 857 at para. 74 (S.C.C.).

166	See *R. v. Siu*, [1998] B.C.J. No. 812, 124 C.C.C. (3d) 301 at 327 (B.C.C.A.); *R. v. Lessard*, [1992] J.Q. no 821, 74 C.C.C. (3d) 552 at 559-63 (Que. C.A.); *R. v. Arabia*, [2008] O.J. No. 2960, 235 C.C.C. (3d) 354 at paras. 51-52 (Ont. C.A.).

167	*R. v. CHBC Television*, [1999] B.C.J. No. 219, 132 C.C.C. (3d) 390 (B.C.C.A.).

168	*R. v. Karaibrahimovic*, [2002] A.J. No. 527 at para. 54, 164 C.C.C. (3d) 431 (Alta. C.A.).

169	*R. v. Antinello*, [1995] A.J. No. 214, 97 C.C.C. (3d) 126 (Alta. C.A.). See also *R. v. T. (L.A.)*, [1993] O.J. No. 1605, 84 C.C.C. (3d) 90 (Ont. C.A.) (where the failure to order a mistrial in such circumstances led to a successful appeal).

170	*R. v. Burke*, [2002] S.C.J. No. 56, [2002] 2 S.C.R. 857 at para. 23 (S.C.C.).

171	*R. v. Lessard*, [1976] O.J. No. 74, 30 C.C.C. (2d) 70 at 78 (Ont. C.A.); *R. v. Henderson*, [2004] O.J. No. 4157, 189 C.C.C. (3d) 447 at 457 (Ont. C.A.), leave to appeal refused [2005] S.C.C.A. No. 12 (S.C.C.).

PART V

POST-TRIAL PROCEDURES

Chapter 17

SENTENCING

1. INTRODUCTION

§17.1 Sentencing was once described as an art in which a judge blended the primary principles of deterrence, denunciation and rehabilitation to craft an appropriate sentence.[1] Today, the art has become more akin to a paint-by-number kit where the sentencing judge's discretion is guided mainly by the "true penological code" within the *Criminal Code*.[2] As we will see in this chapter, many of the common law principles associated with sentencing have been codified in sections 718 to 718.2 of the *Code*. Statutory mandatory minimum sentences have further curtailed the discretion of judges. The codification of principles has also seen an expanded role for the participation of victims in the sentencing process. Nevertheless, sentencing remains a highly individualized process and counsel must be prepared to deal with factors extrinsic to the offence. This chapter will explore these factors along with the statutory and common law principles that govern the sentencing process.[3]

§17.2 The chapter begins with an overview of the general principles of sentencing — both codified (*e.g.*, denunciation, deterrence and rehabilitation) and at common law (*e.g.*, the "gap principle" and the "jump effect") — and discusses two of the more common mitigating factors at sentencing: the guilty plea and the age of the offender. The second part of the chapter examines four specific types of offenders (young persons, Aboriginal offenders, dangerous and long-term offenders, and corporate offenders) who engage special sentencing considerations. The chapter then looks at various custodial dispositions (imprisonment, consecutive and concurrent sentences, minimum sentences, intermittent sentences and conditional sentences) and non-custodial dispositions (discharges, suspended sentences, probation, fine, restitution and forfeiture), as well as the ancillary orders relating to DNA Data Bank orders, *Sex Offender Information Registration Act*[4] orders, driving prohibitions and firearms prohibitions. The chapter reviews the use of diversion and peace bonds as common alternatives to criminal sanctions. Other factors that have impacts on sentencing will also be

---

[1] *R. v. Willaert*, [1953] O.J. No. 658, 105 C.C.C. 172 at 176 (Ont. C.A.).

[2] *R. v. Angelillo*, [2006] S.C.J. No. 55, [2006] 2 S.C.R. 728 at para. 21 (S.C.C.); *Criminal Code*, R.S.C. 1985, c. C-45 [*Code*].

[3] Note that a discussion regarding the range of sentences applicable to various offences is beyond the scope of this chapter. In that regard, see R. Paul Nadin-Davis & Clarey B. Sproule, *Canadian Sentencing Digest Quantum Service*, looseleaf (Toronto: Carswell, 1988).

[4] S.C. 2004, c. 10.

covered (joint submissions, pre-sentence custody, immigration status and pa-role). The chapter concludes with a summary of the types of evidence that is typically presented at sentencing hearings, including the criminal record of the offender, pre-sentence reports and victim impact statements.

2. CONCEPT OF PUNISHMENT

§17.3 Inextricably linked with the theory of criminal justice is the concept of punishment. From the beginning of time, people have punished one another, but a universally accepted theory for subjecting an individual to punishment has remained elusive. Two distinct schools of thought have emerged from the debate regarding punishment: utilitarianism *versus* retributive justice.[5] The nature of the utilitarian theory is forward looking — it strives to reduce crime through the mechanisms of rehabilitation, incapacitation and deterrence. Conversely, retributivists focus on past crimes and maintain that punishment should be imposed when it is deserved. Both theories are not without shortcomings. For example, the deterrence literature has failed to produce decisive evidence that harsh sentences have a significant impact on the crime rate.[6] Similarly, a retributivist's "just deserts" approach may be criticized due to the inability to assess exactly how much punishment is "deserved" in a given situation.[7] As we shall see, while the utilitarian theory seems to have been the prevailing principle for most of the twentieth century, the trend in current sentencing legislation appears to favour retributive notions of punishments.

3. SENTENCING PRINCIPLES

§17.4 Parliament has identified the main objectives and principles of sentencing. Section 718 of the *Criminal Code* provides:

> The fundamental purpose of sentencing is to contribute, along with crime prevention initiatives, to respect for the law and the maintenance of a just, peaceful and safe society by imposing just sanctions that have one or more of the following objectives:
>
> (*a*) to denounce unlawful conduct;
>
> (*b*) to deter the offender and other persons from committing offences;
>
> (*c*) to separate offenders from society, where necessary;
>
> (*d*) to assist in rehabilitating offenders;
>
> (*e*) to provide reparations for harm done to victims or to the community; and

---

[5]   See generally, James Rachels, *The Elements of Moral Philosophy*, 5th ed. (New York: McGraw Hill, 2007) for a review and discussion of both these theories.

[6]   J. Braithwaite & P. Petit, *Not Just Deserts: A Republican Theory of Criminal Justice* (Oxford: Clarendon Press, 1990) at 57-58.

[7]   *Ibid.*, at 57.

(*f*) to promote a sense of responsibility in offenders, and acknowledgment of the harm done to victims and to the community.

§17.5 By virtue of section 718.1 of the *Code*, Parliament has designated proportionality as the fundamental principle in sentencing. The section states that "[a] sentence must be proportionate to the gravity of the offence and the degree of responsibility of the offender."[8] The sentencing judge is also obliged to take into consideration the following principles listed in section 718.2:

(*a*) a sentence should be increased or reduced to account for any relevant aggravating or mitigating circumstances relating to the offence or the offender, and, without limiting the generality of the foregoing,

   (i) evidence that the offence was motivated by bias, prejudice or hate based on race, national or ethnic origin, language, colour, religion, sex, age, mental or physical disability, sexual orientation, or any other similar factor,

   (ii) evidence that the offender, in committing the offence, abused the offender's spouse or common-law partner,

   (ii.1) evidence that the offender, in committing the offence, abused a person under the age of eighteen years,

   (iii) evidence that the offender, in committing the offence, abused a position of trust or authority in relation to the victim,

   (iv) evidence that the offence was committed for the benefit of, at the direction of or in association with a criminal organization, or

   (v) evidence that the offence was a terrorism offence

shall be deemed to be aggravating circumstances;

(*b*) a sentence should be similar to sentences imposed on similar offenders for similar offences committed in similar circumstances;

(*c*) where consecutive sentences are imposed, the combined sentence should not be unduly long or harsh;

(*d*) an offender should not be deprived of liberty, if less restrictive sanctions may be appropriate in the circumstances; and

(*e*) all available sanctions other than imprisonment that are reasonable in the circumstances should be considered for all offenders, with particular attention to the circumstances of aboriginal offenders.

§17.6 Building on this statutory framework, the courts have provided further guidance as to how these sentencing principles are to be applied in practice. In contrast to the United States, where quantitative guidelines have been adopted in

---

[8] *R. v. Nasogaluak*, [2010] S.C.J. No. 6, [2010] 1 S.C.R. 206 at para. 40 (S.C.C.) ("Thus, whatever weight a judge may wish to accord to the objectives listed [in s. 718], the resulting sentence *must* respect the fundamental principle of proportionality."[emphasis in original]).

many jurisdictions,[9] the Supreme Court of Canada has interpreted the *Code*'s qualitative sentencing provisions as providing judges with a wide measure of discretion. As Justice LeBel stated in *R. v. Nasogaluak*:[10]

> [t]he language in ss. 718 to 718.2 of the *Code* is sufficiently general to ensure that sentencing judges enjoy a broad discretion to craft a sentence that is tailored to the nature of the offence and the circumstances of the offender. The determination of a "fit" sentence is, subject to some specific statutory rules, an individualized process that requires the judge to weigh the objectives of sentencing in a manner that best reflects the circumstances of the case .... No one sentencing objective trumps the others and it falls to the sentencing judge to determine which objective or objectives merit the greatest weight, given the particulars of the case.[11]

§17.7 Justice LeBel also commented on the relationship between the general sentencing principles and "aggravating" and "mitigating factors" as follows:

> The relative importance of any mitigating or aggravating factors will then push the sentence up or down the scale of appropriate sentences for similar offences. The judge's discretion to decide on the particular blend of sentencing goals and the relevant aggravating or mitigating factors ensures that each case is decided on its facts, subject to the overarching guidelines and principles in the *Code* and in the case law.[12]

(1)   The Parity Principle

§17.8 Section 718.2(*b*) of the *Code* requires a sentencing judge to consider that "a sentence should be similar to sentences imposed on similar offenders for similar offences". Typically referred to as "parity", this principle encourages courts to impose similar sentences for co-accused convicted for joint ventures and order a sentence for an offender that is broadly similar to sentences ordered for similar offenders who have committed similar offences. Parity, however, is not an absolute principle. As Justice LeBel observed in *R. v. M. (L.)*,[13] "[o]wing to the very nature of an individual sentencing process, sentences imposed for offences of the same type will not always be identical."[14] The parity principle, he added, "does not preclude disparity *where warranted by the circumstances*, because of the principle of proportionality."[15] As a consequence, an offender is not automatically entitled to the benefit of a more lenient sentence imposed on a co-accused. A more severe sentence may be justified, for example, by a more significant criminal record or a more active role in the commission of the offence.

---

9   See *e.g.*, United States Sentencing Commission, *Guidelines Manual* (Nov. 2010). Once considered mandatory, the United States Supreme Court has now ruled that the federal sentencing guidelines are advisory only. See *United States v. Booker*, 543 U.S. 220 (2005).
10   [2010] S.C.J. No. 6, [2010] 1 S.C.R. 206 (S.C.C.).
11   [2010] S.C.J. No. 6, [2010] 1 S.C.R. 206 at para. 43 (S.C.C.).
12   *Ibid.*
13   [2008] S.C.J. No. 31, [2008] 2 S.C.R. 163 (S.C.C.).
14   *Ibid.*, at para. 36 (S.C.R.).
15   *Ibid.* [emphasis in original].

(2) The Effect of a Criminal Record: The Gap Principle and Jump Effect

§17.9 A criminal record often serves as an aggravating factor in sentencing since it indicates the offender is a recidivist. Though not expressly mentioned in the *Code* as a sentencing principle, the courts have held that the presence or absence of a criminal record, as well as its content, are relevant to many of the codified sentencing principles, including proportionality, deterrence and rehabilitation.[16] The more dated the record, however, the less likely it is to be considered aggravating. The "gap principle", as it is known, recognizes that the long period of time since the offender's last transgression demonstrates an effort at rehabilitation.[17] The principle also makes allowances for periods when the offender committed only relatively minor crimes.[18] Courts are less inclined to apply it, however, for offences causing death or serious bodily harm.[19] The same holds for drinking and driving cases where there is evidence of ongoing alcohol abuse.[20]

§17.10 The courts have also recognized that "sentences for a repeat offender should increase gradually, rather than by large leaps."[21] Like the gap principle, the "jump effect" rests on the principles of rehabilitation and proportionality. The idea here is to give the offender a second chance without "a dead weight on his [or her] future life."[22] The jump effect is generally applied where the offences are "at the relatively less serious end of the criminal conduct spectrum."[23] It has little or no application, however, where the severity of the offender's crime shows a "dramatic increase in violence and seriousness."[24] In these cases, the need for denunciation and deterrence outweigh rehabilitation considerations and public safety becomes paramount.[25]

(3) Mitigating Factors

§17.11 The *Criminal Code* does not set out the specific factors that may be considered by the sentencing judge to mitigate the culpability of the offender. The courts have not hesitated, however, to recognize mitigating factors under the

---

[16] See *e.g.*, *R. v. Wright*, [2010] M.J. No. 272, 2010 MBCA 80 at paras. 7, 11 (Man. C.A.); *R. v. Taylor*, [2004] O.J. No. 3439, 189 O.A.C. 388 at para. 39 (Ont. C.A.).

[17] *R. v. Harrell*, [1973] O.J. No. 570, 12 C.C.C. (2d) 480 at 482 (Ont. C.A.); *R. v. Adam*, [2007] B.C.J. No. 1189 at para. 109 (B.C.S.C.); *R. v. Kubbernus*, [2000] A.J. No. 1054 at para. 36 (Alta. Q.B.).

[18] *R. v. Graveline*, [1958] O.J. No. 79, 120 C.C.C. 367 (Ont. C.A.); *R. v. Letourneau*, [1996] A.J. No. 941 (Alta. C.A.).

[19] *R. v. Lockyer*, [2000] N.J. No. 306 at paras. 142-145 (Nfld. C.A.).

[20] *R. v. MacLeod*, [2004] N.S.J. No. 58, 182 C.C.C. (3d) 470 at paras. 26-27 (N.S.C.A.).

[21] *R. v. O. (E.)*, [2003] O.J. No. 563 at para. 15 (Ont. C.A.).

[22] *R. v. Robitaille*, [1993] B.C.J. No. 1404 at para. 8 (B.C.C.A.).

[23] *R. v. Muyser*, [2009] A.J. No. 323 at para. 9 (Alta. C.A.).

[24] *R. v. B. (Q.)*, [2003] O.J. No. 354, 172 C.C.C. (3d) 225 at para. 39 (Ont. C.A.).

[25] *R. v. G. (J.)*, [2005] O.J. No. 4599 at paras. 44-45 (Ont. S.C.J.); *R. v. Manning*, [2007] O.J. No. 1205 (Ont. S.C.J.).

common law such as good character, family responsibilities, employment record and mental health issues. We examine two of the most commonly-invoked mitigating circumstances below: guilty pleas and age.

(a) Guilty Plea

§17.12 A guilty plea has long been considered a significant mitigating factor because it saves resources and (generally) indicates remorse. In *R. v. Layte*,[26] Justice Salhany noted that while the "discount" to be applied to a guilty plea will vary with the circumstances, the general rule at common law was it should attract a one-quarter to one-third discount.[27] The timing of a guilty plea will also factor into how much discount is applied. An early guilty plea may avoid a lengthier sentence, even in the face of a strong Crown case.[28]

(b) Age

§17.13 Youth is generally considered a mitigating sentencing factor. As discussed in Part 4(1), below, persons between the ages of 12 and 17 are subject to the special sentencing provisions of the *Youth Criminal Justice Act*.[29] But even for younger adults, specific deterrence and rehabilitation are generally considered to be the paramount sentencing objectives, at least for first time offenders. These objectives can usually be achieved by a suspended sentence and probation.[30] If a sentence of imprisonment is to be imposed, it should be "the shortest possible sentence [in order to] achieve the relevant objectives."[31] However, where the offence is serious and involves violence, general deterrence and denunciation become the primary concerns.[32]

4.   TYPE OF OFFENDER

§17.14 While the circumstances of the offender are always relevant to sentencing, Parliament has also set out specific rules and sentencing principles that apply to specific types of offender: young persons, Aboriginals, dangerous and long-term offenders, and organizations.

---

[26] [1983] O.J. No. 2415 (Ont. Co. Ct.).

[27] *Ibid.*, at paras. 2 and 8.

[28] *R. v. Reid*, [2009] O.J. No. 5205 (Ont. C.J.); *R. v. Manning*, [2007] O.J. No. 1205 (Ont. S.C.J.); *R. v. Dos Santos*, [2005] O.J. No. 1788 (Ont. C.J.). See also Gregory Lafontaine & Vincenzo Rondinelli, "Plea Bargaining and the Modern Criminal Defence Lawyer: Negotiating Guilt and the Economics of 21st Century Criminal Justice" (2005) 50 Crim. L.Q. 108 (noting that offenders may effectively be subject to an "entertainment tax" by insisting on proceeding to trial and delaying the inevitable).

[29] S.C. 2002, c. 1 [YCJA].

[30] *R. v. Stein*, [1974] O.J. No. 93, 15 C.C.C. (2d) 376 at p. 377 (Ont. C.A.); *R. v. B. (Q.)*, [2003] O.J. No. 354, 172 C.C.C. (3d) 225 at para. 36 (Ont. C.A.); *R. v. Priest*, [1996] O.J. No. 3369, 110 C.C.C. (3d) 289 at 296-97 (Ont. C.A.).

[31] *R. v. Priest*, [1996] O.J. No. 3369, 110 C.C.C. (3d) 289 at 296-97 (Ont. C.A.).

[32] *Ibid.*

(1) Young Persons

§17.15 The *Youth Criminal Justice Act*[33] came into force in April 2003, replacing the *Young Offenders Act*. The fundamental objective of the YCJA — which governs the sentencing of persons between the ages of 13 and 17 — is to curb the use of custody for young offenders.[34]

(a) Codified Principles

§17.16 Like the *Criminal Code*, the YCJA contains a number of principles that animate the sentencing of youths. Section 3 of the YCJA provides in part:

3. (1) The following principles apply in this Act:

(*a*) the youth criminal justice system is intended to

(i) prevent crime by addressing the circumstances underlying a young person's offending behaviour,

(ii) rehabilitate young persons who commit offences and reintegrate them into society, and

(iii) ensure that a young person is subject to meaningful consequences for his or her offence

in order to promote the long-term protection of the public;

(*b*) the criminal justice system for young persons must be separate from that of adults and emphasize the following:

(i) rehabilitation and reintegration,

(ii) fair and proportionate accountability that is consistent with the greater dependency of young persons and their reduced level of maturity,

(iii) enhanced procedural protection to ensure that young persons are treated fairly and that their rights, including their right to privacy, are protected,

(iv) timely intervention that reinforces the link between the offending behaviour and its consequences, and

(v) the promptness and speed with which persons responsible for enforcing this Act must act, given young persons' perception of time;

(*c*) within the limits of fair and proportionate accountability, the measures taken against young persons who commit offences should

(i) reinforce respect for societal values,

(ii) encourage the repair of harm done to victims and the community,

(iii) be meaningful for the individual young person given his or her needs and level of development and, where appropriate,

---

[33] S.C. 2002, c. 1 [YCJA].

[34] *R. v. D. (C.); R. v. K. (C.D.)*, [2005] S.C.J. No. 79, [2005] 3 S.C.R. 668 at para. 45-49 (S.C.C.).

> involve the parents, the extended family, the community and social or other agencies in the young person's rehabilitation and reintegration, and
>
> (iv) respect gender, ethnic, cultural and linguistic differences and respond to the needs of aboriginal young persons and of young persons with special requirements.

§17.17 Subsection 38(2) of the YCJA contains further principles to be considered when sentencing a young person:

> (*a*) the sentence must not result in a punishment that is greater than the punishment that would be appropriate for an adult who has been convicted of the same offence committed in similar circumstances;
>
> (*b*) the sentence must be similar to the sentences imposed in the region on similar young persons found guilty of the same offence committed in similar circumstances;
>
> (*c*) the sentence must be proportionate to the seriousness of the offence and the degree of responsibility of the young person for that offence;
>
> (*d*) all available sanctions other than custody that are reasonable in the circumstances should be considered for all young persons, with particular attention to the circumstances of aboriginal young persons; and
>
> (*e*) subject to paragraph (*c*), the sentence must
>
>   (i) be the least restrictive sentence that is capable of achieving the purpose set out in subsection (1),
>
>   (ii) be the one that is most likely to rehabilitate the young person and reintegrate him or her into society, and
>
>   (iii) promote a sense of responsibility in the young person, and an acknowledgement of the harm done to victims and the community.

§17.18 And further in section 38(3):

> (3) In determining a youth sentence, the youth justice court shall take into account
>
> (*a*) the degree of participation by the young person in the commission of the offence;
>
> (*b*) the harm done to victims and whether it was intentional or reasonably foreseeable;
>
> (*c*) any reparation made by the young person to the victim or the community;
>
> (*d*) the time spent in detention by the young person as a result of the offence;
>
> (*e*) the previous findings of guilt of the young person; and
>
> (*f*) any other aggravating and mitigating circumstances related to the young person or the offence that are relevant to the purpose and principles set out in this section.

§17.19 Notably, the objectives of specific and general deterrence are not mentioned. In *R. v. P. (B.W.); R. v. N. (B.V.),*[35] the Supreme Court of Canada held that deterrence is not a sentencing principle to be considered under the YCJA. Ultimately, the purpose of sentencing a young person is to hold him or her accountable through meaningful consequences while at the same time promoting rehabilitation and reintegration into society, thereby contributing to the long-term protection of the public.[36]

(b) Extrajudicial Measures

§17.20 The YCJA contains a number of extrajudicial measures that the police or the Crown may take instead of instituting formal court proceedings.[37] The police or the Crown must first determine whether an extrajudicial measure is appropriate, having regard to the needs of the young person and the interests of society.[38] The measures range from a formal warning to participation in a community program.[39] To take advantage of an extrajudicial sanction, the young person must acknowledge involvement in the commission of the offence and waive his or her right to have the charge dealt with in court.[40]

(c) Custodial Sentences

§17.21 The only offence for which a custodial sentence is mandatory under the YCJA is murder.[41] Otherwise, section 39(1) of the YCJA provides that a youth can be committed to custody only where: (*a*) the young person has committed a violent offence; (*b*) the young person has failed to comply with non-custodial sentences; (*c*) the young person has committed an indictable offence for which an adult would be liable to imprisonment for a term of more than two years and has a history that indicates a pattern of findings of guilt under the YCJA; or (*d*) in an exceptional case, where the young person has committed an indictable offence and the aggravating circumstances of the offence warrant the imposition of a custodial sentence.

§17.22 While the YCJA does not define "violent offence" for the purpose of section 39(1), the Supreme Court of Canada has defined it as "an offence in the commission of which a young person causes, attempts to cause or threatens to cause bodily harm."[42]

---

[35] [2006] S.C.J. No. 27, [2006] 1 S.C.R. 941 (S.C.C.).
[36] *Ibid.,* at para. 4 (S.C.R.). See also YCJA, s. 38(1).
[37] YCJA, ss. 4 to 12.
[38] YCJA, s. 6(1) and s. 10(1)(*b*).
[39] YCJA, ss. 61(1) and s. 10(1).
[40] YCJA, s. 10(3).
[41] YCJA, ss. 42(2)(*q*) and (*r*). See also *Criminal Code*, s. 745.1.
[42] *R. v. D. (C.); R. v. K. (C.D.),* [2005] S.C.J. No. 79, [2005] 3 S.C.R. 668 at para. 17 (S.C.C.).

(d)   Adult Sentences

§17.23 Since the enactment of the YCJA, all proceedings involving young persons have been conducted in youth court. However, a youth court judge may still impose an adult sentence in certain cases. Section 62 of the YCJA provides that a young person older than 14 "shall" be sentenced as an adult if the young person is found guilty of a "presumptive offence" of murder, attempted murder, manslaughter or aggravated sexual assault.[43] In addition, a third "serious violent offence" ("an offence in the commission of which a young person causes or attempts to cause serious bodily harm") is also considered a "presumptive offence".[44]

§17.24 However, section 63(1) allows the young person to "make an application for an order that he or she is not liable to an adult sentence and that a youth sentence must be imposed." In *R. v. B. (D.)*,[45] the Supreme Court of Canada held that the presumptive sections of the YCJA violated section 7 of the *Charter*.[46] Placing the onus on the young person, the Court concluded, is inconsistent with the principle of fundamental justice that young people are entitled to a presumption of diminished moral culpability. It may well be that the seriousness of the offence and the circumstances of the offender call for an adult sentence, but it should be for the Crown to demonstrate that an adult sentence is justified. In deciding whether it has met this burden, the judge must consider "the seriousness and circumstances of the offence, and the age, maturity, character, background and previous record of the young person and any other factors that the court considers relevant."[47]

(2)   Aboriginal Offenders

§17.25 As mentioned, when sentencing Aboriginal offenders, the court must pay particular attention to all available sanctions, other than imprisonment, that are reasonable in the circumstances.[48] This does not mean that Aboriginals receive preferential treatment by the criminal justice system or that Aboriginal status is a mitigating factor on sentence.[49] Rather, as the Supreme Court of Canada emphasized in *R. v. Gladue*,[50] particular attention is paid to the circumstances of aboriginal offenders "*because those circumstances are unique, and*

---

[43]   "Presumptive offence" is defined in s. 2. Under the YCJA, the maximum sentence for first degree murder is 10 years, with no more than six of those years being a custodial sentence. If sentenced as an adult, the mandatory life sentence applies, but the period of parole ineligibility is between five and seven years for those individuals under the age of 16 at the time of the offence and 10 years for those who were 16 or 17 years old.

[44]   *Ibid.*

[45]   [2008] S.C.J. No. 25, [2008] 2 S.C.R. 3 (S.C.C.).

[46]   *Ibid.*

[47]   YCJA, s. 72(1).

[48]   *Criminal Code*, s. 718.2(e). See also YCJA, s. 38(2)(*d*), which provides for a similar consideration for Aboriginal young persons.

[49]   *R. v. Kakekagamick*, [2006] O.J. No. 3346, 211 C.C.C. (3d) 289 at para. 34 (Ont. C.A.).

[50]   [1999] S.C.J. No. 19, [1999] 1 S.C.R. 688 (S.C.C.).

different from those of non-aboriginal offenders."[51] A restorative approach to sentencing Aboriginal offenders may go some way to ameliorating the serious problem of over-representation of Aboriginal people in prisons in Canada.[52] Further, sentences for aboriginals should not necessarily be different than those for non-Aboriginals.[53] As noted in *Gladue*, as a general rule "the more violent and serious the offence the more likely it is as a practical reality that the terms of imprisonment for aboriginals and non-aboriginals will be close to each other or the same."[54]

§17.26 As interpreted by the Supreme Court in *Gladue*, *Code* section 718.2(*e*) thus requires a sentencing judge to conduct a three-step inquiry in determining whether an Aboriginal offender should be imprisoned. He or she must: (*a*) consider the unique systemic or background factors common to Aboriginal offenders as a group; (*b*) consider the factors that may have played a part in bringing the particular Aboriginal offender before the courts; and (*c*) then decide upon a fit sentence, having regard to the information obtained in steps (*a*) and (*b*).[55] This must be performed in all cases involving Aboriginal offenders, whether in urban or reserve communities,[56] and regardless of the seriousness of the offence.[57]

§17.27 In *R. v. Laliberte*,[58] the Saskatchewan Court of Appeal suggested that the following information be provided to a sentencing judge at a *"Gladue* hearing":

(i) Whether the offender is aboriginal, that is, someone who comes within the scope of section 25 of the *Charter* and s. 35 of the *Constitution Act, 1982*;

(ii) What band or community or reserve the offender comes from and whether the offender lives on or off the reserve or in an urban or rural setting. This information should also include particulars of the treatment facilities, the existence of a justice committee, and any alternative measures or community-based programs;

(iii) Whether the offender has been affected by:

    a) substance abuse in the community;

    b) alcohol abuse in the community;

    c) poverty;

    d) overt racism;

    e) family or community breakdown;

(iv) Whether imprisonment would effectively deter or denounce crime in the subject community. Within this heading it would be useful for the Court

---

[51] *Ibid.*, at para. 37 (S.C.R.) [emphasis added].

[52] *Ibid.*, at para. 64 (S.C.R.).

[53] *R. v. Laliberte*, [2000] S.J. No. 138, 143 C.C.C. (3d) 503 at para. 56 (Sask. C.A.).

[54] *R. v. Gladue*, [1999] S.C.J. No. 19, [1999] 1 S.C.R. 688 at para. 79 (S.C.C.).

[55] *R. v. Laliberte*, [2000] S.J. No. 138, 143 C.C.C. (3d) 503 at para. 59 (Sask. C.A.).

[56] *R. v. Gladue*, [1999] S.C.J. No. 19, [1999] 1 S.C.R. 688 at para. 91 (S.C.C.).

[57] *R. v. Kakekagamick*, [2006] O.J. No. 3346, 211 C.C.C. (3d) 289 at para. 38 (Ont. C.A.); *R. v. Abraham*, [2000] A.J. No. 645 (Alta. C.A.).

[58] [2000] S.J. No. 138, 143 C.C.C. (3d) 503 (Sask. C.A.).

to determine whether or not crime prevention can be better served by principles of restorative justice or by imprisonment;

(v) What sentencing options exist in the community at large and in the offender's community. For example, does an alternative measures program exist in the offender's community if he lives on a reserve?;

...[G]eneral information concerning systemic poverty, alcohol and substance abuse, cultural and racial bias in the community at large; and

[I]nformation concerning the particular circumstances surrounding the offence.[59]

§17.28 Even where the above information is not provided by counsel, it remains incumbent on the sentencing judge to try to acquire the information in other ways, including a pre-sentence report and a request for witnesses to testify as to reasonable alternatives to a custodial sentence.[60]

§17.29 It is important to note that an offender may not wish to have such evidence adduced and may waive the right to have particular attention paid to his or her circumstances as an Aboriginal offender. This waiver must be express and made on the record.[61]

(3) Dangerous and Long-term Offenders

§17.30 In dealing with habitual violent offenders with the highest risk of recidivism, Parliament has enacted special provisions, set out in Part XXIV of the *Code*, that aim to protect the public by enabling lengthy prison terms and enhanced post-release supervision. These provisions create two classes of offenders: "dangerous" offenders and "long-term" offenders.

§17.31 To obtain a dangerous or long-term offender designation, the Crown must first advise the court, after a finding of guilt[62] of a predicate offence[63] and before the sentence being imposed, that it intends to make an application to have an assessment conducted by corrections or mental health experts and have a report prepared for the use at a designation hearing.[64] The court will order an assessment if there are reasonable grounds to believe that an offender who is convicted of a serious personal injury offence might be found to be a dangerous offender or a long-term offender.[65] The offender will be remanded for a period not exceeding 60 days in order for the assessment to take place.[66] The report is

---

[59] *R. v. Laliberte*, [2000] S.J. No. 138, 143 C.C.C. (3d) 503 at paras. 59 and 60 (Sask. C.A.).
[60] *R. v. Kakekagamick*, [2006] O.J. No. 3346, 211 C.C.C. (3d) 289 at para. 45 (Ont. C.A.).
[61] *Ibid.*, at para. 44 (C.C.C.).
[62] However, an application can be made up to six months after sentencing if new evidence arises. See *Criminal Code*, ss. 753(2)(*b*), 753(3) and 753(4.2).
[63] The predicate offence is "a serious personal injury offence that is a designated offence." See *Criminal Code*, s. 752.01.
[64] *Criminal Code*, s. 752.01.
[65] *Criminal Code*, s. 752.1(1).
[66] *Ibid.*

to be filed with the court no later than 30 days after the end of the assessment period.[67]

§17.32 Once a report is filed, the Crown may seek to proceed with a dangerous offender or long-term offender application, but must first: (*a*) obtain the consent of the provincial Attorney General; (*b*) give the offender at least seven days' notice of the application, outlining the basis on which it is intended to found the application; and (*c*) file a notice of the application with the court.[68] The application can be heard by either a provincial court judge or a superior court judge without a jury.[69]

(a) Dangerous Offender Designation

§17.33 Dangerous offenders are subject to the most severe punishment in the *Criminal Code*: a prison term of indeterminate length.[70] Although Parliament has made a "diligent attempt" to restrict the dangerous offender designation to "a very small group of offenders whose personal characteristics and particular circumstances militate strenuously in favour of preventive incarceration,"[71] the number of dangerous offenders has increased steadily over the last 30 years.[72] Given recent amendments designating the types of offenders as eligible for dangerous offender status, it is likely that these numbers will increase even more rapidly in the future.[73]

§17.34 There are two routes to a dangerous offender designation. Normally, the Crown must prove all of the requirements applying under each route beyond a reasonable doubt.[74] However, offenders who have been convicted for a third time for a "primary designated offence"[75] for which they received sentences of

---

[67] *Criminal Code*, s. 752.1(2).
[68] *Criminal Code*, s. 754(1).
[69] *Criminal Code*, s. 754(2).
[70] See *Criminal Code*, s. 753(4)(a). After serving seven years, however, dangerous offenders must be considered for parole on a periodic basis, though any offender released remains subject to supervision for the rest of his or her life: *Criminal Code*, s. 761. The dangerous offender scheme has been held to be constitutionally sound. See *R. v. Lyons*, [1987] S.C.J. No. 62, [1987] 2 S.C.R. 309 (S.C.C.).
[71] *R. v. Lyons*, [1987] S.C.J. No. 62, [1987] 2 S.C.R. 309 at para. 44 (S.C.C.).
[72] The number of offenders designated as dangerous has grown from an average of nine per year (between 1978 and 1991) to 20 per year (between 1992 and 2005). See "The Dangerous Offender and Long-term Offender Regime" (Parliamentary Information and Research Service, November 4, 2008). Available at: <http://www2.parl.gc.ca/content/LOP/ResearchPublications/prb0613-e.pdf>.
[73] See Bill C-2: *An Act to amend the Criminal Code and to make consequential amendments to other Acts*, S.C. 2008, c. 6, which came into force on July 2, 2008. The amendments allow a dangerous offender application to be brought in respect of an offence that would be subject to two years' imprisonment (rather than 10 years, as previously required). The legislation also introduced a presumption that an offender who has committed three designated offences is a dangerous offender.
[74] See *R. v. Neve*, [1999] A.J. No. 753, 137 C.C.C. (3d) 97 (Alta. C.A.); *R. v. Read*, [1994] B.C.J. No. 1491 (B.C.C.A.).
[75] The definition of "primary designated offence" in s. 752(*a*) of the *Code* contains the following offences: s. 151 (sexual interference), s. 152 (invitation to sexual touching), s. 153 (sexual

at least two years' imprisonment are presumed to meet these requirements unless they can rebut the presumption with contrary evidence on a balance of probabilities.[76]

§17.35 The first route is typically used when the predicate offence is non-sexual and the second when it is sexual. Under the first route, the Crown must first prove that the offender was convicted of a "serious personal injury" as defined in subparagraph (*a*) of the definition of that term in section 752 of the *Code*.[77] It must next demonstrate that the offender constitutes "a threat to the life, safety or physical or mental well-being of other persons" on the basis of evidence establishing one of the following:

(*i*)   a pattern of repetitive behaviour by the offender, of which the offence for which he or she has been convicted forms a part, showing a failure to restrain his or her behaviour and a likelihood of causing death or injury to other persons, or inflicting severe psychological damage on other persons, through failure in the future to restrain his or her behaviour,

(*ii*)   a pattern of persistent aggressive behaviour by the offender, of which the offence for which he or she has been convicted forms a part, showing a substantial degree of indifference on the part of the offender respecting the reasonably foreseeable consequences to other persons of his or her behaviour, or

(*iii*) any behaviour by the offender, associated with the offence for which he or she has been convicted, that is of such a brutal nature as to compel the conclusion that the offender's behaviour in the future is unlikely to be inhibited by normal standards of behavioural restraint. ...[78]

Under the second route, the Crown must again first prove that the offender was convicted of a "serious personal injury offence," in this case within the meaning of subparagraph (*b*) of the definition of that phrase.[79] Next, it must show that the offender, "by his or her conduct in any sexual matter including that involved in the commission of the offence for which he or she has been convicted, has

---

exploitation), s. 155 (incest), s. 239 (attempt to commit murder), s. 244 (discharging firearm with intent), s. 267 (assault with weapon or causing bodily harm), s. 268 (aggravated assault), s. 271 (sexual assault), s. 272 (sexual assault with weapon, threats to third party or causing bodily harm), s. 273 (aggravated sexual assault), and s. 279(1) (kidnapping). Subsections 752(*b*) and (*c*) also include a list of historical sexual offences.

[76]   *Criminal Code*, s. 753(1.1).

[77]   This provision defines "serious personal injury offence" to mean

an indictable offence, other than high treason, treason, first degree murder or second degree murder, involving

(i)   the use or attempted use of violence against another person, or

(ii) conduct endangering or likely to endanger the life or safety of another person or inflicting or likely to inflict severe psychological damage on another person,

and for which the offender may be sentenced to imprisonment for ten years or more ....

[78]   *Criminal Code*, s. 753(1)(*a*) and (*b*).

[79]   This provision defines "serious personal injury offence" to mean "an offence or attempt to commit an offence mentioned in ss. 271 (sexual assault), 272 (sexual assault with a weapon, threats to a third party or causing bodily harm) or 273 (aggravated sexual assault).

shown a failure to control his or her sexual impulses and a likelihood of causing injury, pain or other evil to other persons through failure in the future to control his or her sexual impulses."[80]

§17.36 For each type of dangerous offender application, the court must be satisfied beyond a reasonable doubt that there is a "likelihood" — or "reasonable possibility"[81] — that the offender will cause death or injury or inflict severe psychological damage on other persons in the future.[82] In determining the potential risk of re-offending, the court may consider the offender's past conduct along with the expert opinion.[83] The expert opinion will often contain actuarial measures such as the *Violent Risk Appraisal Guide* (VRAG),[84] the *Sexual Offender Risk Appraisal Guide* (SORAG)[85] and the *Psychopathy Checklist Revised* (PCL-R).[86]

§17.37 If the court finds an offender to be a dangerous offender, it must: (*a*) impose a sentence of detention in a penitentiary for an indeterminate period; (*b*) impose a sentence for the offence for which the offender has been convicted — which must be a minimum of two years' imprisonment — and order that the offender be subject to long-term supervision for a period that does not exceed ten years; or (*c*) impose a sentence for the predicate offence for which the offender has been convicted.[87] Lastly, before ordering indefinite detention, the court must consider whether a lesser sentence can be reasonably expected to protect the public.[88]

§17.38 If the court does not find an offender to be a dangerous offender, the court may: (*a*) treat the dangerous offender application as an application to find the offender to be a long-term offender and may either find the offender to be a long-term offender or hold another hearing for that purpose; or (*b*) impose a sentence for the offence for which the offender has been convicted.[89]

---

[80] *Criminal Code*, s. 753(1)(*b*).

[81] *R. v. Tremblay*, [2010] O.J. No. 3450 at para. 99 (Ont. S.C.J.).

[82] *Ibid.*

[83] *R. v. Lyons*, [1987] S.C.J. No. 62, [1987] 2 S.C.R. 309 at para. 94 (S.C.C.).

[84] See V. L. Quinsey, G. T. Harris, M. E. Rice & C. A. Cormier, *Violent Offenders: Appraising and Managing Risk*, 2d ed. (Washington, D.C.: American Psychological Association, 2006).

[85] *Ibid.*

[86] R. D. Hare, *The Psychopathy Checklist – Revised*, 2d ed. (Toronto: Multi-Health Systems, 2003).

[87] *Criminal Code*, s. 753(4).

[88] *Criminal Code*, s. 753(4.1). This section codifies the Supreme Court of Canada's decision in *R. v. Johnson*, [2003] S.C.J. No. 45, [2003] 2 S.C.R. 357 (S.C.C.), where the Court held that a judge retains the discretion to not declare an offender dangerous and impose a sentence that fits the individual circumstances of a given case, even where the statutory requirements for the designation are met.

[89] *Criminal Code*, s. 753(5).

(b)   Long-term Offender Designation

§17.39 The long-term offender category was introduced in 1997.[90] A court may make a long-term offender designation if it is satisfied beyond a reasonable doubt that: (*a*) it would be appropriate to impose a sentence of at least two years' imprisonment for the predicate offence; (*b*) there is a substantial risk that the offender will re-offend; and (*c*) there is a reasonable possibility of eventual control of the risk in the community.[91] The criterion of "substantial risk" of re-offending will be met if the offender has been convicted of an enumerated sexual offence[92] and has shown a pattern of repetitive behaviour demonstrating a likelihood of causing death or injury or severe psychological damage to other persons in the future.[93]

§17.40 If the court finds an offender to be a long-term offender, it must: (*a*) impose a sentence of at least two years' imprisonment for the offence for the predicate offence; and (*b*) order that the offender be subject to long-term supervision for a period not exceeding 10 years.[94] If the court does not find an offender to be a long-term offender, it must impose a sentence for the predicate offence.[95]

(c)   Appeal

§17.41 Both the offender and the Crown may appeal to the court of appeal from dangerous and long-term offender decisions. The offender may appeal on any ground of law or fact or mixed law and fact,[96] whereas the Crown can only appeal on a ground of law.[97] If the court allows the appeal, it can impose a new sentence or order a new hearing.[98]

(4)   Organizations

§17.42 Like individuals, corporations and other organizations may be subject to criminal punishment.[99] As with individuals, the *Criminal Code* sets out factors that must be considered in sentencing organizations:

---

[90]   *An Act to amend the Criminal Code (high-risk offenders)*, S.C. 1997, c. 17 (came into force August 1, 1997).

[91]   *Criminal Code*, s. 753.1(1).

[92]   *Criminal Code*, s. 753.1(2)(*a*) lists the following offences: s. 151 (sexual interference), s. 152 (invitation to sexual touching), s. 153 (sexual exploitation), s. 163.1(2) (making child pornography), s. 163.1(3) (distribution, *etc.*, of child pornography), s. 163.1(4) (possession of child pornography), s. 163.1(4.1) (accessing child pornography), s. 172.1 (luring a child), s. 173(2) (exposure), s. 271 (sexual assault), s. 272 (sexual assault with a weapon) and s. 273 (aggravated sexual assault).

[93]   *Criminal Code*, s. 753.1(2)(*a*) and (*b*).

[94]   *Criminal Code*, s. 753.1(3).

[95]   *Criminal Code*, s. 753.1(6).

[96]   *Criminal Code*, s. 759(1).

[97]   *Criminal Code*, s. 759(2).

[98]   *Criminal Code*, s. 752(3).

[99]   See *Criminal Code*, ss. 2 (definition of "organization"), 22.1-22.2.

(*a*) any advantage realized by the organization as a result of the offence;

(*b*) the degree of planning involved in carrying out the offence and the duration and complexity of the offence;

(*c*) whether the organization has attempted to conceal its assets, or convert them, in order to show that it is not able to pay a fine or make restitution;

(*d*) the impact that the sentence would have on the economic viability of the organization and the continued employment of its employees;

(*e*) the cost to public authorities of the investigation and prosecution of the offence;

(*f*) any regulatory penalty imposed on the organization or one of its representatives in respect of the conduct that formed the basis of the offence;

(*g*) whether the organization was — or any of its representatives who were involved in the commission of the offence were — convicted of a similar offence or sanctioned by a regulatory body for similar conduct;

(*h*) any penalty imposed by the organization on a representative for their role in the commission of the offence;

(*i*) any restitution that the organization is ordered to make or any amount that the organization has paid to a victim of the offence; and

(*j*) any measures that the organization has taken to reduce the likelihood of it committing a subsequent offence.[100]

§17.43 Deterrence and denunciation will be of paramount importance in sentencing an organization.[101] That is not to say that rehabilitation does not play a role. As Justice Bourassa observed in *R. v. Panarctic Oils Ltd.*:[102]

> Reformation and rehabilitation of a defendant must remain an element for the Court's consideration, even where the defendant is a corporation. Indeed, I believe this may be an area where it is most fruitful and most fertile for the concept of rehabilitation to be explored because of the instrumental nature of the crime and because I believe it can be assumed that corporations, such as Panarctic Oils Limited, are rational beings. A fine may deter, but it can also be passed on to others and leave the corporation unaffected. If true rehabilitation can be effected, then I believe society has ultimate protection--society will benefit, and the corporation will benefit .... I have no doubt that Panarctic Oils Limited needs to some degree to regain the public confidence and public trust that it has enjoyed in the past and that it has now lost to a degree.[103]

§17.44 For obvious reasons, the range of sentences available to sanction organizations differs from that available to individuals; organizations, for example, cannot be incarcerated. The primary sanction imposed on an organization will

---

[100] *Criminal Code*, s. 718.21.
[101] *R. v. Hoffmann-LaRoche Ltd. (No. 2)*, [1980] O.J. No. 3782, 56 C.C.C. (2d) 563 (Ont. H.C.J.), affd [1981] O.J. No. 3075 (Ont. C.A.).
[102] [1983] N.W.T.J. No. 17, 43 A.R. 199 (N.W.T. Terr. Ct.).
[103] *Ibid.*, at para. 34 (N.W.T.J.).

almost always be a fine. The *Code* limits the maximum fine to be imposed for a summary conviction offence to $100,000.[104] There is no corresponding maximum for an indictable offence — the determination of the fine amount remains within the discretion of the court.[105] While the size of a fine should not be so minimal as to amount to a mere "licensing fee" or "cost of doing business",[106] it should not be so high as to put the economic viability of the organization in question and be akin to a corporate death sentence.[107]

§17.45 Recognizing the ability of an organization to be rehabilitated, Parliament has authorized judges to order probation. In addition to the conditions of probation that may be imposed on individuals,[108] a judge may prescribe that the organization: (*a*) make restitution to a person for any loss or damage that they suffered as a result of the offence; (*b*) establish policies, standards and procedures to reduce the likelihood of the organization committing a subsequent offence; (*c*) communicate those policies, standards and procedures to its representatives; (*d*) report to the court on the implementation of those policies, standards and procedures; (*e*) identify the senior officer who is responsible for compliance with those policies, standards and procedures; (*f*) provide, in the manner specified by the court, information to the public of the offence of which the organization was convicted, the sentence imposed and the measures the organization is taking to reduce the likelihood of re-offending; and (*g*) comply with any other reasonable conditions that the court considers desirable to prevent the organization from committing subsequent offences or to remedy the harm caused by the offence.[109] Before prescribing a condition that the organization establish policies, the court must consider whether another regulatory body is better suited to supervise the development of the policies.[110]

5. DISPOSITIONS

§17.46 In this Part, we examine the dispositions available under the *Criminal Code* to sanction offenders. We look first at the rules governing custodial dispositions (imprisonment and conditional sentences) and next at those governing non-custodial dispositions (discharges, suspended sentences, probation, fines, restitution and forfeiture). We then discuss a number of "ancillary" orders that may flow from conviction or discharge: DNA data bank orders, sex offender registry orders, driving prohibitions, and firearms and explosives prohibitions.

---

[104] *Criminal Code*, s. 735(1)(*b*).

[105] *Criminal Code*, s. 735(1)(*a*).

[106] *R. v. Cotton Felts Ltd.*, [1982] O.J. No. 178, 2 C.C.C. (3d) 287 at para. 10 (Ont. C.A.); *R. v. General Scrap Iron and Metals Ltd.*, [2003] A.J. No. 13 at para. 112 (Alta. Q.B.).

[107] *Criminal Code*, s. 718.21(*d*). See also *R. v. United Keno Hill Mines*, [1980] Y.J. No. 10, 10 C.E.L.R. 43 at 49-50 (Y.T. Terr. Ct.).

[108] See *Criminal Code*, s. 732.1(2) and (3).

[109] *Criminal Code*, s. 732(3.1).

[110] *Criminal Code*, s. 732.1(3.2).

Lastly, we examine two alternatives to formal criminal sanctions: diversion and peace bonds.

(1) Custodial Dispositions

(a) Imprisonment

§17.47 As we have seen, section 718(*c*) of the *Code* provides that offenders should be separated from society "where necessary". Adult offenders sentenced to a term of custody of two years or more will serve their sentences in a federal penitentiary,[111] while offenders receiving terms of custody of less than two years will fall under the provincial system. Offenders serving a provincial sentence will be transferred to the penitentiary if he or she subsequently receives another sentence that, in combination with the unexpired provincial sentence, amounts to over two years or more.[112] In 2008/2009, there were 57 correctional facilities across Canada that were under federal jurisdiction and 177 that were run by provinces and territories.[113] During that same period, there were 13,343 inmates in federal penitentiaries and 9,964 in provincial and territorial facilities.[114] The National Parole Board is the agency that manages the decisions respecting the conditional release of inmates, including parole. The agency acts at both the federal and provincial level.[115]

(i) Consecutive and Concurrent Sentences

§17.48 Judges must frequently sentence an accused for multiple offences. Under section 719(1) of the *Code*, a sentence begins when it is imposed. As a result, sentences imposed for each offence will be deemed to run concurrently unless the sentencing judge orders them to be served consecutively. Generally speaking, offences arising from a single transaction will attract concurrent sentences,[116] whereas separate criminal acts involving different victims will call for consecutive sentences. This principle, however, has not been universally applied.[117] *R. v. McDonnell*,[118] for example, the offender committed two unrelated sexual offences on two different victims occurring years apart.[119] The sentencing

---

[111] *Criminal Code*, s. 743.1(1)(*a*) and (*b*). Combined sentences with an aggregate length of custody of more than two years will also be served in a penitentiary (s. 743.1(1)(*c*)).

[112] *Criminal Code*, s. 743.1(5).

[113] See Text box 6: Correctional facilities in *Juristat: Adult Correctional Services in Canada, 2008/2009*. Available at: <http://www.statcan.gc.ca/pub/85-002-x/2010003/article/11353-eng.htm>.

[114] *Ibid.*, Table 3: Average counts of persons in adult correctional services, by program and jurisdiction, 2008/2009).

[115] Except for Ontario and Quebec, which have their own parole boards.

[116] *R. v. Crocker*, [1991] N.J. No. 303, 93 Nfld. & P.E.I.R. 222 at paras. 38-43 (Nfld. C.A.); *R. v. Newhook*, [2008] N.J. No. 258, 276 Nfld. & P.E.I.R. 190 at para. 9 (Nfld. C.A.).

[117] In *R. v .P. (E.T.)*, [2002] M.J. No. 64, 162 C.C.C. (3d) 481 at para. 24 (Man. C.A.), Philp J., in dissent, noted some of the inconsistency in the jurisprudence.

[118] [1997] S.C.J. No. 42, [1997] 1 S.C.R. 948 (S.C.C.).

[119] *Ibid.*

judge imposed concurrent sentences, the Court of Appeal substituted consecutive sentences and the Supreme Court of Canada restored the original sentence.[120] An appellate court's disagreement with the original sentence, the Supreme Court reasoned, does not justify interference; intervention is warranted only where there is an error in principle, a failure to consider applicable factors or a sentence that is demonstrably unfit.[121]

§17.49 Sentencing judges thus have a broad discretion in choosing between concurrent and consecutive sentences.[122] In crafting a cumulative sentence for multiple offences, however, judges are bound by the so-called "totality" principle, which requires that in ordering consecutive sentences, the judge must ensure that the "cumulative sentence rendered does not exceed the overall culpability of the offender."[123] This principle is codified in section 718.2(*c*) of the *Code* which mandates that combined sentences "should not be unduly long or harsh."

§17.50 The discretion to choose between concurrent and consecutive sentences is further curtailed by a few specific *Code* provisions. Consecutive sentences are mandatory for certain offences relating to terrorism,[124] criminal organizations[125] and the use of a firearm or imitation firearm in the commission of an offence.[126] The *Code* also prescribes that a term of imprisonment imposed in default of a payment of a fine made in lieu of forfeiture of proceeds of crime[127] must be served consecutively to any other term of imprisonment ordered.[128] Lastly, section 718.3(4) gives the sentencing judge the discretion to order that a sentence be served consecutively when the offender is sentenced while under sentence for another offence.

(ii) Minimum Sentences

§17.51 Once exceedingly rare, the *Criminal Code* now contains several minimum sentences.[129] The most severe are reserved for murder — both first and second degree murder have minimum sentences of life imprisonment.[130] Minimum

---

[120] *Ibid.*

[121] *Ibid.*, at para. 46 (S.C.R.).

[122] See *R. v. Paul*, [1982] S.C.J. No. 32, [1982] 1 S.C.R. 621 at 633-34 (S.C.C.). See also Clayton C. Ruby, *Sentencing*, 6th ed. (Toronto: Butterworths, 2004) at 465.

[123] *R. v. M. (C.A.)*, [1996] S.C.J. No. 28, [1996] 1 S.C.R. 500 at para. 42 (S.C.C.).

[124] *Criminal Code*, s. 83.26.

[125] *Criminal Code*, s. 467.14.

[126] *Criminal Code*, s. 85(4).

[127] *Criminal Code*, s. 462.37.

[128] *Criminal Code*, s. 462.37(4)(*b*).

[129] See generally, *R. v. Nasogaluak*, [2010] S.C.J. No. 6, [2010] 1 S.C.R. 206 at para. 45 (S.C.C.) ("A relatively new phenomenon in Canadian law, the minimum sentence is a forceful expression of governmental policy in the area of criminal law.").

[130] See *Criminal Code*, s. 235(1). See also *R. v. Latimer*, [2001] S.C.J. No. 1, [2001] 1 S.C.R. 3 (S.C.C.) (mandatory minimum sentence for second degree murder does not amount to cruel and unusual punishment within the meaning of s. 12 of the *Charter*).

sentences are also prescribed for child pornography offences[131] and many firearms offences.[132] Minimum penalties are circumscribed by section 12 of the *Charter*, which prohibits "cruel and unusual" punishment. A minimum sentence will amount to cruel and unusual punishment if it is grossly disproportionate to the sentence that would have been imposed absent the minimum.[133] The analysis under section 12 involves two stages. First, the court conducts a "particularized inquiry" considering the "gravity of the offence, the personal characteristics of the offender and the particular circumstances of the case" to determine the range of sentences necessary to "punish, rehabilitate or deter this particular offender or to protect the public ....".[134] In considering whether a mandatory minimum sentence is "grossly disproportionate", Justice Lamer (as he then was) suggested in *R. v. Smith*,[135] resort to the criteria outlined by Professor Tarnopolsky: (1) Is the punishment such that it goes beyond what is necessary to achieve a legitimate penal aim?; (2) Is it unnecessary because there are adequate alternatives?; (3) Is it unacceptable to a large segment of the population?; (4) Is it such that it cannot be applied upon a rational basis in accordance with ascertained or ascertainable standards?; (5) Is it arbitrarily imposed?; (6) Is it such that it has no value in the sense of some social purpose such as reformation, rehabilitation, deterrence or retribution?; (7) Is it in accord with public standards of decency or propriety?; (8) Is the punishment of such a character as to shock general conscience or as to be intolerable in fundamental fairness?; (9) Is it unusually severe and hence degrading to human dignity and worth?[136]

---

[131] See *e.g.*, s. 163.1(2) (making: minimum of one year by indictment and 90 days by summary conviction); s. 163.1(3) (distributing: same); s. 163.1(4) (possession: minimum of 45 days by indictment and 14 days by summary conviction); s. 163.1(4.1) (accessing: same).

[132] For example, s. 85 (using a firearm or imitation firearm in the commission of an offence: minimum of one year for first offence and three years for subsequent offences); s. 92(2) (possession of firearm knowing its possession is unauthorized: minimum of one year); s. 95(2) (possession of prohibited or restricted firearm with ammunition: minimum of three years for first offence and five years for subsequent offence); s. 96(2) (possession of firearm obtained by commission of offence: minimum of one year); s. 99(2) (firearms trafficking: minimum of three years for first offence and five years for subsequent offence); s. 100(2) (possession for purpose of firearms trafficking: minimum of threeyears for first offence and five years for subsequent offence); s. 103(2) (unauthorized importing or exporting a firearm: minimum of three years for first offence and five years for subsequent offence); s. 244(2)(*b*) (discharging firearm with intent to wound, maim or disfigure: minimum of four years); and s. 244.2(*b*) (recklessly discharging firearm: minimum of four years). Also, the following offences carry minimum terms of imprisonment of four years if a firearm is used in the commission of the offence: s. 220(*a*) (causing death by criminal negligence); s. 236(*a*) (manslaughter); s. 239(1)(*a*.1) (attempt murder); s. 272(2)(*a*.1) (sexual assault with a weapon); s. 273(2)(*a*.1) (aggravated assault); s. 279(1.1)(*a*.1) (kidnapping); s. 344(1)(*a*.1) (robbery); and s. 346(1)(*a*.1) (extortion).

[133] *R. v. Smith*, [1987] S.C.J. No. 36, [1987] 1 S.C.R. 1045 at para. 54 (S.C.C.).

[134] *Ibid.*, at para. 55 (S.C.R.).

[135] [1987] S.C.J. No. 36, [1987] 1 S.C.R. 1045 (S.C.C.).

[136] *Ibid.*, at para. 55 (S.C.R.) (referring to W. S. Tarnopolsky "Just Deserts or Cruel and Unusual Treatment or Punishment? Where Do We Look for Guidance?" (1978) 10 Ottawa L. Rev. 1). See also *R. v. Nasogaluak*, [2010] S.C.J. No. 6, [2010] 1 S.C.R. 206 at para. 41 (S.C.C.); *R. v. Ferguson*, [2008] S.C.J. No. 6, [2008] 1 S.C.R. 96 at para. 14 (S.C.C.); *R. v. Morrisey*, [2000]

§17.52 If this inquiry reveals that the sentence is grossly disproportionate, then a *prima facie* violation of section 12 has been made out and the inquiry proceeds to a section 1 *Charter* analysis to determine whether the violation is justified. If the court finds no infringement as a result of the particularized inquiry, "there may remain another aspect to be examined, namely a *Charter* challenge or constitutional question as to the validity of a statutory provision on grounds of gross disproportionality as evidenced in *reasonable hypothetical circumstances*, as opposed to far-fetched or marginally imaginable cases."[137] The focus must be on "imaginable circumstances" that could arise in everyday life.[138]

§17.53 Thus far, constitutional challenges to mandatory minimum sentences have been met with mixed results.[139] As Parliament continues its trend to enact more mandatory minimum sentences, further *Charter* challenges may reasonably be expected in the future. Any anticipated success however, should be tempered by the Supreme Court of Canada's caution in *Steele v. Mountain Institution*[140] that a court will find a sentence so grossly disproportionate that it violates section 12 of the *Charter* in only "rare and unique occasions".[141]

(iii) Intermittent Sentences

§17.54 Where a court imposes a sentence of imprisonment of 90 days or less, the court may, "having regard to the age and character of the offender, the nature of the offence and the circumstances surrounding its commission," order that the sentence be served intermittently.[142] In practice, this usually means that the offender serves the sentence in a custodial institution on weekends. When not in confinement, the offender will be bound by the conditions prescribed in a probation order during the period that the sentence is being served.[143]

§17.55 Although an intermittent sentence allows the offender more freedom than does a custodial sentence served uninterrupted, it would be improper to

---

S.C.J. No. 39, [2000] 2 S.C.R. 90 at para. 26 (S.C.C.); *R. v. Wiles*, [2005] S.C.J. No. 53, [2005] 3 S.C.R. 895 at para. 4 (S.C.C.).

[137] *R. v. Goltz*, [1991] S.C.J. No. 90, [1991] 3 S.C.R. 485 at 506 (S.C.C.) [emphasis in original].

[138] *Ibid.*, at 520 (S.C.R.).

[139] For example, see *R. v. Smith*, [1987] S.C.J. No. 36, [1987] 1 S.C.R. 1045 (S.C.C.) (minimum sentence of seven years for importing or exporting a narcotic violated s. 12 because it failed to take into account nature and quantity of substance, reason for offence and absence of previous convictions). Conversely, see *R. v. Morrisey*, [2000] S.C.J. No. 39, [2000] 2 S.C.R. 90 (S.C.C.) (minimum sentence of four years' imprisonment for criminal negligence causing death, where a firearm was used, did not infringe s. 12 since offence a wanton and reckless disregard for life and safety).

[140] [1990] S.C.J. No. 111, [1990] 2 S.C.R. 1385 (S.C.C.).

[141] *Ibid.*, at 1417 (S.C.R.).

[142] *Criminal Code*, s. 732(1)(*a*). Note that two separate intermittent sentences cannot be made consecutive to each other if the aggregate sentence exceeds the *Code*'s 90-day maximum. See *R. v. Drost*, [1996] N.B.J. No. 23, 104 C.C.C. (3d) 389 (N.B.C.A.); *R. v. Fletcher*, [1982] O.J. No. 188, 2 C.C.C. (3d) 221 (Ont. C.A.); *R. v. Aubin*, [1992] J.Q. no. 239, 72 C.C.C. (3d) 189 (Que. C.A.).

[143] *Criminal Code*, s. 732(1)(*b*).

consider an intermittent sentence as "an indulgence".[144] As Justice Meiklem observed in *R. v. Wood*,[145] for some people "an intermittent sentence which extends the sentencing period considerably and involves repeated surrender into custody is more harsh than an equivalent single term."[146] An intermittent sentence serves a dual purpose. It seeks to deter the offender of future transgression by giving him or her a "taste of jail", while at the same time fostering rehabilitation by enabling the offender to maintain employment or schooling.[147] Further, should the offender be subsequently imprisoned for another offence while still being subject to an intermittent sentence, section 732(3) of the *Code* grants the court a discretion to order that the unexpired portion of the intermittent sentence be served on consecutive days.

(b) Conditional Sentence

§17.56 Conditional sentences became a sentencing option in September 1996.[148] Though styled as a form of "imprisonment" (and thus conceptually a type of custodial sentence) an offender who successfully fulfills the requirements of a conditional sentence will not spend any time in prison.[149] Instead, he or she will "serve the sentence in the community".[150] In giving sentencing judges the option of imposing a conditional sentence in certain circumstances, Parliament sought to emphasize the virtues of restorative justice and alternative measures of punishment, even for relatively serious crimes.[151] In effect, conditional sentences provide judges with a sentencing option halfway between probation and imprisonment. While probation, the Supreme Court stressed in *R. v. Proulx*,[152] has primarily a rehabilitative ends, conditional sentences are designed to denounce and deter as well as rehabilitate and restore.[153] Conditional sentences thus typically include punitive conditions (such as house arrest) that substantially restrict the offender's liberty.[154]

---

[144] *R. v. MacKinnon*, [2005] O.J. No. 6274 at para. 57 (Ont. S.C.J.).

[145] [1993] B.C.J. No. 2761 at para. 24 (B.C.S.C.).

[146] *Ibid.*, at para. 24. Also, s. 732(2) of the *Code* provides the offender serving an intermittent sentence with the option to apply to the court to allow the sentence to be served on consecutive days.

[147] In *R. v. Middleton*, [2009] S.C.J. No. 21, [2009] 1 S.C.R. 674 (S.C.C.), the Court held that an intermittent sentence can be combined with a conditional sentence. Combining these two types of sentences "harmonizes" the differing correctional advantages of conditional and intermittent sentences.

[148] Conditional sentences were introduced by Bill C-41, now S.C. 1995, c. 22, proclaimed in force on September 3, 1996.

[149] *Criminal Code*, ss. 742-742.7. See also *R. v. Proulx*, [2000] S.C.J. No. 6, [2000] 1 S.C.R. 61 at para. 40 (S.C.C.).

[150] *Criminal Code*, s. 742.1.

[151] *R. v. Proulx*, [2000] S.C.J. No. 6, [2000] 1 S.C.R. 61 at paras. 15, 18-22 (S.C.C.). As discussed in Part 5(1)(*b*)(i)a, below, however, Parliament has since removed the conditional sentence option for certain specified offences.

[152] [2000] S.C.J. No. 6, [2000] 1 S.C.R. 61 (S.C.C.).

[153] *Ibid.*, at paras. 22-39 (S.C.R.).

[154] *Ibid.*, at paras. 36, 103, 117, 127 (S.C.R.).

§17.57 As detailed below, the *Criminal Code* sets out the pre-conditions for imposing a conditional sentence,[155] the types of conditions that can be imposed as part of the sentence[156] and the procedure for dealing with breaches.[157] It does not, however, attribute to either party the onus of establishing whether or not the offender should receive a conditional sentence. In *Proulx*, the Court held that as a consequence, "the judge can take into consideration all the evidence, no matter who adduces it" to inform his or her decision about the appropriateness of a conditional sentence.[158]

(i) Prerequisites to Imposing a Conditional Sentence

§17.58 Before imposing a conditional sentence, a judge must consider the following five statutory pre-requisites:

(1) The offender must not be convicted of a serious personal injury offence as defined in s. 752 of the *Code*, a terrorism offence or a criminal organization offence prosecuted by way of indictment for which the maximum term of imprisonment is 10 years or more;

(2) The offender must be convicted of an offence that has no minimum term of imprisonment;

(3) The court must impose a sentence of imprisonment of less than two years;

(4) The court must be satisfied that the service of the sentence in the community would not endanger the safety of the community; and

(5) The court must be satisfied that the conditional sentence would be consistent with the fundamental purpose and principles of sentencing set out in ss. 718 to 718.2.[159]

§17.59 We deal with the first two requirements immediately below under the heading of "Statutory Exclusions". Under the approach in *Proulx*, the remaining factors (discussed in Part 5(1)(*b*)(i)b, below) are considered together as a part of a "purposive two-stage approach".

a. Statutory Exclusions

§17.60 When originally enacted, the conditional sentencing provisions excluded only offences carrying a minimum term of imprisonment.[160] In 2007, Parliament added the exclusions for "serious personal injury" offences as well as terrorism and criminal organization offences prosecuted by way of indictment for which

---

[155] *Criminal Code*, s. 742.1.
[156] *Criminal Code*, s. 742.3.
[157] *Criminal Code*, s. 742.6.
[158] See *R. v. Proulx*, [2000] S.C.J. No. 6, [2000] 1 S.C.R. 61 at para. 120 (S.C.C.).
[159] *Criminal Code*, s. 742.1.
[160] *R. v. Proulx*, [2000] S.C.J. No. 6, [2000] 1 S.C.R. 61 at para. 81 (S.C.C.) ("...[I]t would be both unwise and unnecessary to establish judicially created presumptions that conditional sentences are inappropriate for specific offences.").

the maximum term of imprisonment is 10 years or more.[161] The exclusion of serious personal injury offences casts a particularly wide brush. It encompasses the various sexual assault offences (including attempts) as well as any indictable offence (other than those already excluded by virtue of a minimum sentence) with a maximum punishment of 10 years or more involving either: (*i*) "the use or attempted use of violence against another person"; or (*ii*) "conduct endangering or likely to endanger the life or safety of another person or inflicting or likely to inflict severe psychological damage on another person."[162]

b.   Purposive Two-stage Approach

§17.61 The final three factors require a two-stage purposive approach. At the first stage, the sentencing judge's task is to narrow the range of possible sentences.[163] If a non-custodial sentence such as a suspended sentence with probation is appropriate, then a conditional sentence should not be imposed. If the sentencing judge comes to the conclusion that a penitentiary sentence (*i.e.*, a sentence of two years or more) is required then a conditional sentence is unavailable. In either of these cases, the inquiry would stop here and the offender would be sentenced to either a non-custodial sentence or a penitentiary term of imprisonment.

§17.62 However, if the sentencing judge determines the appropriate range to be somewhere between a non-custodial sentence and a penitentiary term, the second stage of the inquiry is triggered. Here, the judge considers the "safety of the community" as well as the sentencing principles set out in the *Code*.[164] In deciding whether a conditional sentence would endanger the safety of the community, the judge must consider two factors: (*i*) the risk of the offender re-offending; and (*ii*) the gravity of the damage that could ensue in the event of re-offence.[165] Community safety, the Court stressed in *Proulx*, includes the risk of economic harm as well as physical and psychological harm.[166]

§17.63 If satisfied that the offender would not endanger the community, the sentencing judge must then consider whether a conditional sentence would be consistent with statutory sentencing principles. As Chief Justice Lamer suggested in *Proulx*:

> ... [S]entencing judges should consider which sentencing objectives figure most prominently in the factual circumstances of the particular case before them. Where a combination of both punitive and restorative objectives may

---

[161] *An Act to amend the Criminal Code (conditional sentence of imprisonment)*, S.C. 2007, c. 12, s. 1.

[162] *Criminal Code*, s. 742.1. See also *R. v. Lebar*, [2010] O.J. No. 1133, 252 C.C.C. (3d) 411 (Ont. C.A.) (conditional sentence unavailable where offender held knife to cashier's neck and demanded money without explicitly threatening or physically injuring her).

[163] See *R. v. Proulx*, [2000] S.C.J. No. 6, [2000] 1 S.C.R. 61 at para. 58 (S.C.C.).

[164] *Ibid.*

[165] *Ibid.*, at paras. 66-76 (S.C.R.).

[166] *Ibid.*, at paras. 75-76 (S.C.R.).

be achieved, a conditional sentence will likely be more appropriate than incarceration. In determining whether restorative objectives can be satisfied in a particular case, the judge should consider the offender's prospects of rehabilitation, including whether the offender has proposed a particular plan of rehabilitation; the availability of appropriate community service and treatment programs; whether the offender has acknowledged his or her wrongdoing and expresses remorse; as well as the victim's wishes as revealed by the victim impact statement (consideration of which is now mandatory pursuant to s. 722 of the *Code*). This list is not exhaustive.[167]

§17.64 Before imposing a conditional sentence, the judge must also consider whether a firearms prohibition order is applicable.[168] A sentencing judge may also impose a conditional sentence consecutive to another conditional sentence as long as the total sentence, including pre-trial custody,[169] does not exceed 24 months.[170] Further, a conditional sentence can be blended with an intermittent sentence[171] or another sentence of incarceration provided it does not exceed 24 months.[172]

(c)   Conditions Imposed

§17.65 If a conditional sentence is imposed, the following five conditions are compulsory: (*a*) keep the peace and be of good behaviour; (*b*) appear before the court as required; (*c*) report to a supervisor as required; (*d*) remain within the jurisdiction of the court unless written permission is obtained from the court or the supervisor; and (*e*) notify the court or the supervisor of any change in name, address or employment.[173] In addition, the judge may add the following optional conditions: (*a*) abstain from the consumption of alcohol or drugs; (*b*) abstain from owning or possessing a weapon; (*c*) provide for the support of dependants; (*d*) perform community service; (*e*) attend a treatment program; (*f*) comply with any other reasonable conditions as the court considers desirable.[174] Further, as the Court directed in *Proulx*, punitive, liberty-restraining conditions such house arrest or strict curfews "should be the norm, not the exception."[175]

---

[167] *Ibid.*, at para. 113 (S.C.R.).

[168] *Criminal Code*, s. 742.2(1).

[169] See *R. v. Fice*, [2005] S.C.J. No. 30, [2005] 1 S.C.R. 742 (S.C.C.) (discussing the relationship between pre-trial custody and the availability of a conditional sentence). This issue is examined in Part 6(2), below.

[170] *R. v. Frechette*, [2001] M.J. No. 197, 154 C.C.C. (3d) 191 (Man. C.A.).

[171] See *R. v. Middleton*, [2009] S.C.J. No. 21, [2009] 1 S.C.R. 674 (S.C.C.).

[172] *R. v. R. (R.A.)*, [2000] S.C.J. No. 9, [2000] 1 S.C.R. 163 (S.C.C.); *R. v. Ploumis*, [2000] O.J. No. 4731, 150 C.C.C. (3d) 424 (Ont. C.A.); *R. v. Alfred*, [1998] O.J. no 70, 122 C.C.C. (3d) 213 (Ont. C.A.).

[173] *Criminal Code*, s. 742.3(1).

[174] *Criminal Code*, s. 742.3(2).

[175] See *R. v. Proulx*, [2000] S.C.J. No. 6, [2000] 1 S.C.R. 61 at para. 36 (S.C.C.).

(2) Non-custodial Dispositions

(a) Discharges

§17.66 A discharge — either absolute or conditional — is the least severe sentence available under the *Criminal Code*. Discharges are available only with respect to offences that: (*i*) have no minimum punishment; and (*ii*) are punishable by imprisonment for less than 14 years.[176] While the *Code* does not restrict the availability of a discharge to trivial offences, in practice the more serious the offence the less likely a discharge will be ordered.

§17.67 The sentencing judge has the discretion to direct that the accused be discharged absolutely or on conditions prescribed in a probation order.[177] No conviction is entered, and therefore no permanent criminal record results from receiving either a conditional or absolute discharge.[178] Consequently, neither an absolute nor a conditional discharge may be combined with a fine, since a fine cannot be imposed without convicting the accused.[179]

§17.68 In exercising its discretion to grant a discharge, the sentencing judge is required to consider whether it is in the best interests of the accused and the public.[180] A discharge would certainly be in the accused's best interests in the majority of cases. However, the Alberta Court of Appeal in *R. v. M. (B.J.)*[181] observed that "a short term of imprisonment and the supervision of probation may in the long run be in the accused's best interests as deterring him from further criminal activity and removing him, at least for a time, from the very environment which may have generated such activity".[182] With respect to the public interest, the Court noted that discharges should be used "sparingly" since "one of the strongest deterrents to criminal activity, particularly in the case of those who have no records, is the fear of the acquisition of a criminal record."[183]

(b) Suspended Sentence

§17.69 For offences with no minimum punishment, section 731(1)(*a*) of the *Criminal Code* permits a sentencing judge to "suspend the passing of sentence" and instead place the accused on a period of probation. The sentencing judge must be satisfied that a suspended sentence is appropriate having regard "to the age and character of the offender, the nature of the offence and the circumstances

---

[176] *Criminal Code*, s. 730(1).

[177] *Criminal Code*, s. 730(1).

[178] See *Criminal Code*, s. 730(1) and (3). Technically, a record of an absolute discharge will remain on the Government of Canada's automated criminal conviction records retrieval system for one year before being erased. A conditional discharge will remain for three years. See *Criminal Records Act*, R.S.C. 1985, c. C-47, s. 6.1.

[179] *R. v. Leonard*, [1973] O.J. No. 205, 11 C.C.C. (2d) 527 (Ont. C.A.).

[180] *Criminal Code*, s. 730(1). See also *R. v. Fallofield*, [1973] B.C.J. No. 559, 13 C.C.C. (2d) 450 (B.C.C.A.); *R. v. M. (B.J.)*, [1976] A.J. No. 429 (Alta. C.A.).

[181] [1976] A.J. No. 429 (Alta. C.A.).

[182] *Ibid.*, at para. 11.

[183] *Ibid.*, at para. 13.

surrounding its commission."[184] In *R. v. Ursel*,[185] Justice Finch explained suspended sentences as follows:

> Where a suspended sentence is granted, in conjunction with a probation order, the court does not pronounce any sentence. The form of penalty to be imposed remains unknown, and if the offender complies with the conditions of the probation order, may never be imposed. If a condition of a probation order is breached, the offender may be charged with breach of the probation order, which is a separate offence. Proof of that offence must be made to the usual criminal standard, that is, beyond a reasonable doubt. The court may, as well, on proof of the breach, revoke the earlier order suspending sentence and impose the penalty it would have imposed for the original offence had the sentence not been suspended.[186]

§17.70 Like a discharge, a suspended sentence mainly finds application in relatively non-serious offences. Unlike a discharge, however, a suspended sentence does result in a criminal record since it is the passing of sentence that is suspended, not the conviction.

(c) Probation

§17.71 As we have seen, probation orders must attach to conditional discharges and suspended sentences. A sentencing judge may also order probation in addition to a fine or sentence of imprisonment not exceeding two years.[187] There is no authority, however, to order probation plus a fine plus imprisonment.[188] Probation orders may last no more than three years.[189]

§17.72 When considering the rule against attaching a probation order to a sentence of more than two years, special attention must be made to section 139 of the *Corrections and Conditional Release Act*,[190] which provides that "[w]here a person who is subject to a sentence that has not expired receives an additional sentence, the person is ... deemed to have been sentenced to one sentence commencing at the beginning of the first of those sentences to be served and ending on the expiration of the last of them to be served." Courts have accordingly quashed probation orders issued after an earlier sentence already being served where the merged sentence totalled over two years' imprisonment.[191]

---

[184] *Criminal Code*, s. 731(1).

[185] [1997] B.C.J. No. 1853, 117 C.C.C. (3d) 289 (B.C.C.A.).

[186] *Ibid.*, at 314 (C.C.C.).

[187] *Criminal Code*, s. 731(1)(*b*).

[188] *R. v. Kelly*, [1995] N.J. No. 377, 104 C.C.C. (3d) 95 at para. 3 (Nfld. C.A.). See also *R. v. Blacquiere*, [1975] O.J. No. 443, 24 C.C.C. (2d) 168 (Ont. C.A.). Similarly, a suspended sentence plus probation plus a fine is unavailable. See *R. v. Polywjanyj*, [1982] O.J. No. 143, 1 C.C.C. (3d) 161 (Ont. C.A.).

[189] *Criminal Code*, s. 732.2(2)(*b*).

[190] S.C. 1992, c. 20 [CCRA], as am. by S.C. 1995, c. 42, s. 54; S.C. 1995, c. 22, s. 18 (Sch. IV, Item 9), s. 139.

[191] *R. v. Pawlak*, [2005] B.C.J. No. 2251 (B.C.C.A.); *R. v. Amyotte*, [2005] B.C.J. No. 32, 192 C.C.C. (3d) 412 (B.C.C.A.); *R. v. Maloney*, [2006] B.C.J. No. 2993 (B.C.C.A.); *R. v. Hendrix*,

§17.73 A probation order must contain the following three conditions: (*i*) keep the peace and be of good behaviour; (*ii*) appear before the court when required to do so by the court; and (*iii*) notify the court or probation officer of any change of name, address, or employment.[192] The judge has the discretion to order the following optional conditions:

> (*a*) report to a probation officer ...;
>
> (*b*) remain within the jurisdiction of the court unless written permission to go outside that jurisdiction is obtained from the court or the probation officer;
>
> (*c*) abstain from
>
> > (i) the consumption of alcohol or other intoxicating substances, or
> >
> > (ii) the consumption of drugs except in accordance with a medical prescription;
>
> (*d*) abstain from owning, possessing or carrying a weapon;
>
> (*e*) provide for the support or care of dependants;
>
> (*f*) perform up to 240 hours of community service over a period not exceeding eighteen months;
>
> (*g*) if the offender agrees, and subject to the program director's acceptance of the offender, participate actively in a treatment program approved by the province;
>
> (*g.1*) where the lieutenant governor in council of the province in which the probation order is made has established a program for curative treatment in relation to the consumption of alcohol or drugs, attend at a treatment facility, designated by the lieutenant governor in council of the province, for assessment and curative treatment in relation to the consumption by the offender of alcohol or drugs that is recommended pursuant to the program;
>
> (*g.2*) where the lieutenant governor in council of the province in which the probation order is made has established a program governing the use of an alcohol ignition interlock device by an offender and if the offender agrees to participate in the program, comply with the program; and
>
> (*h*) comply with such other reasonable conditions as the court considers desirable ... for protecting society and for facilitating the offender's successful reintegration into the community.[193]

There is no authority, in contrast, to require the accused to submit to drug testing without his or her consent;[194] impose terms effectively banishing an accused

---

[1999] N.J. No. 181, 137 C.C.C. (3d) 445 (Nfld. C.A.); *R. v. Miller*, [1987] O.J. No. 753, 36 C.C.C. (3d) 100 (Ont. C.A.).

[192] *Criminal Code*, s. 732.1(2).

[193] *Criminal Code*, s. 732.1(3).

[194] *R. v. Shoker*, [2006] S.C.J. No. 44, [2006] 2 S.C.R. 399 (S.C.C.).

from a jurisdiction or province;[195] or require an accused to comply with conditions imposed in unrelated family court proceedings.[196]

§17.74 Although the primary purpose of probation is rehabilitation, it also has a punitive aspect. In *R. v. Prieduls*,[197] Justice Dubin (as he then was) observed that "a person on probation is not a free man ... [h]e is under supervision and must earn his ultimate freedom."[198]

(d) Fines

§17.75 A fine is undoubtedly one of the most common sanctions imposed by courts. Fines have many advantages over other sanctions: they are simple to administer, place little burden on the public purse and cause less disruption and stigma to the accused.[199] Courts have recognized that a fine has the ability to achieve both denunciation and deterrence.[200] Section 734(1)(*a*) of the *Code* allows a sentencing judge to impose a fine "in addition to or in lieu of any other sanction that the court is authorized to impose", such as a conditional sentence or probation,[201] as long as the offence does not include a minimum term of imprisonment. If the offence includes a minimum term of imprisonment, then a fine can only be made in addition to any other sanction imposed.[202] Because a conviction is a pre-condition for a fine, a criminal record does result from the imposition of a fine.

§17.76 Before imposing a fine, section 734(2) requires the sentencing judge to consider the offender's ability to pay it, unless the offence includes a minimum fine or a fine is imposed in lieu of a forfeiture order.[203] If the sentencing judge is satisfied that the offender has the ability to pay the fine, the burden to show otherwise shifts to the offender.[204] As Justice Bastarache observed in *R. v. Desjardins*:[205]

> ... Courts are not ignorant of the ease with which many convicted persons can prove their financial incapacity by showing their lack of legal financial resources at the moment of sentencing. It is for this reason that, where traffickers are concerned, the courts will infer financial capacity on the basis of

---

[195] *R. v. Rowe*, [2006] O.J. No. 3738, 212 C.C.C. (3d) 254 at paras. 4-8 (Ont. C.A.).

[196] *R. v. Saari*, [2006] B.C.J. No. 1473 at para. 17 (B.C.C.A.).

[197] [1975] O.J. No. 589 (Ont. C.A.).

[198] *Ibid.*, at para. 8.

[199] Clayton C. Ruby, *Sentencing*, 6th ed. (Toronto: Butterworths, 2004) at 407.

[200] *R. v. Doherty*, [1972] O.J. No. 706, 9 C.C.C. (2d) 115 (Ont. C.A.); *R. v. Dunton*, [1973] O.J. No. 825 (Ont. C.A.).

[201] A fine and a probation order may be imposed at the same time. See *R. v. Polywjanyj*, [1982] O.J. No. 143, 1 C.C.C. (3d) 161 (Ont. C.A.).

[202] *Criminal Code*, s. 734(1)(*b*).

[203] The discretion of a sentencing judge to impose a fine in lieu of forfeiture under s. 462.37 of the *Code* is discussed below in Part 5(2)(*d*).

[204] *R. v. Grimberg*, [2002] O.J. No. 526, 163 C.C.C. (3d) 310 at para. 18 (Ont. C.A.); *R. v. Desjardins*, [1996] N.B.J. No. 467 at para. 29 (N.B.C.A.).

[205] [1996] N.B.J. No. 467 (N.B.C.A.).

the illegal profits realized from trafficking and impose a term of imprisonment in default of payment.[206]

§17.77 When the offender is fined, a term of imprisonment will be deemed to be imposed in default of payment.[207] The length of imprisonment is calculated pursuant to the formula set out in section 734(5); that is, the product of the sum of the unpaid amount of the fine plus the costs of committing and conveying the accused to prison (if the amount of such costs are set out in provincial regulations[208]), divided by eight times the provincial minimum hourly wage at the time of the default. For example, a fine with a remaining unpaid portion of $8,000 (and assuming no regulations concerning committal and conveyance charges) divided by 80 (being eight times a hypothetical $10 minimum wage) would result in 100 days of imprisonment. The deemed period of imprisonment cannot, however, exceed the maximum term of imprisonment that the court could itself impose on conviction.[209] If the punishment for the offence does not include a term of imprisonment, the maximum deemed period is five years for indictable offences or six months' imprisonment for summary conviction offences.[210]

§17.78 In addition to any other punishment, a judge must impose a victim fine surcharge, unless the offender satisfies the court that it would cause undue hardship personally or to his or her dependants.[211]

(e) Restitution

§17.79 Section 718(*e*) of the *Criminal Code* speaks to the sentencing objective of providing "reparations for harm done to victims or to the community." This objective may be achieved by ordering restitution under sections 738 or 739 of the *Code*. It is important to note, however, that a restitution order is not a substitute for a civil remedy.[212] As the Ontario Court of Appeal observed in *R. v. Popert*,[213] "[T]he focus must remain on the offence and the offender – it ought not to be shifted to complicated accounting issues."[214]

§17.80 Perhaps the most important factor to consider before ordering restitution is the ability of the offender to pay. This is so because a restitution order remains

---

[206] *Ibid.*, at para. 29. See also *R. v. Jung*, [1976] B.C.J. No. 147, 1 C.R. (3d) S. 1 (B.C.C.A.); *R. v. Dow*, [1976] B.C.J. No. 228, 1 C.R. (3d) S-9 (B.C.C.A.).

[207] *Criminal Code*, s. 734(4).

[208] *Criminal Code*, s. 734(7).

[209] *Criminal Code*, s. 734(5)(*b*). For example, in *R. v. DiGiuseppe*, [2008] O.J. No. 1107 at para. 27 (Ont. C.J.), affd [2010] O.J. No. 426 (Ont. C.A.), the sentencing judge noted that the Crown's request for a fine of $3.5 million for a fraud conviction would result in a deemed term of imprisonment of approximately 150 years pursuant to the formula referenced in s. 734(5) of the *Code*.

[210] *Criminal Code*, s. 734(5)(*b*).

[211] *Criminal Code*, s. 737.

[212] See *R. v. Zelensky*, [1978] S.C.J. No. 48, 41 C.C.C. (2d) 97 (S.C.C.).

[213] [2010] O.J. No. 401, 251 C.C.C. (3d) 30 (Ont. C.A.).

[214] *Ibid.*, at para. 39 (C.C.C.).

with the offender for life, even after a declaration of bankruptcy.[215] Courts have accordingly recognized that a restitution order should not result in a lifetime obstacle to rehabilitation.[216] Generally speaking, then, the lengthier the term of imprisonment, the less likely that restitution should be ordered due to the offender's diminished capacity to comply with the order.[217] Restitution orders may nevertheless be appropriate for impecunious offenders in egregious circumstances, as in cases involving a breach of trust.[218]

§17.81 Restitution may be granted for: (*a*) lost, damaged or destroyed property (not exceeding its replacement value); (*b*) pecuniary damages for bodily or psychological harm; (*c*) moving-related expenses incurred by members of the accused's household in domestic violence cases; and (*d*) expenses associated with identity theft.[219] It may not be ordered in any of these situations, however, unless the "amount is readily ascertainable."[220] Restitution should not therefore be granted "when it would require the criminal court to interpret written documents to determine the amount of money sought through the order."[221]

§17.82 The *Code* gives priority to restitution over fines and forfeiture orders. That is, a sentencing judge "shall first make the order of restitution and shall then consider whether and to what extent an order of forfeiture or an order to pay a fine is appropriate in the circumstances."[222]

(f) Forfeiture

§17.83 Where an accused is convicted or receives a discharge for a "designated offence" under section 462.3(1) of the *Code*,[223] the Crown may bring an application for a forfeiture order.[224] The sentencing judge must make such an order if it is satisfied, "on a balance of probabilities", that "any property is proceeds of crime and that the designated offence was committed in relation to that property".[225] The sentencing judge may order forfeiture even if the property is not directly connected with the offence for which an offender is being sentenced.

---

215 See *Bankruptcy and Insolvency Act*, R.S.C. 1985, c. B-3, s. 178(1)(*a*).

216 See *R. v. Biegus*, [1999] O.J. No. 4963, 141 C.C.C. (3d) 245 at para. 15 (Ont. C.A.).

217 *R. v. Siemens*, [1999] M.J. No. 285, 136 C.C.C. (3d) 353 at para. 8 (Man. C.A.).

218 See *R. v. Yates*, [2002] B.C.J. No. 2415, 169 C.C.C. (3d) 506 at para. 17 (B.C.C.A.).

219 *Criminal Code*, s. 738(1).

220 *Criminal Code*, s. 738(1).

221 See *R. v. Devgan*, [1999] O.J. No. 1825, 44 O.R. (3d) 161 at 168 (Ont. C.A.). See also *R. v. Hirnschall*, [2003] O.J. No. 2296, 176 C.C.C. (3d) 311 at para. 33 (Ont. C.A.).

222 *Criminal Code*, s. 740.

223 "Designated offence" is defined in s. 462.3(1) as: "(*a*) any offence that may be prosecuted as an indictable offence under this or any other Act of Parliament, other than an indictable offence prescribed by regulation; or (*b*) a conspiracy or an attempt to commit, being an accessory after the fact in relation to, or any counselling in relation to, an offence referred to in paragraph (*a*)."

224 *Criminal Code*, s. 462.37(1).

225 *Criminal Code*, s. 462.37(1).

However, the judge must be satisfied "beyond a reasonable doubt" that the property is proceeds of crime.[226]

§17.84 For criminal organization offences punishable by five or more years' imprisonment and certain offences under the *Controlled Drugs and Substances Act*[227] prosecuted by indictment,[228] the Crown may seek a forfeiture order of "any property of the offender". The sentencing judge must be satisfied "on a balance of probabilities"[229] that: (*a*) within 10 years before the proceedings were commenced in respect of the offence, the offender "engaged in a pattern of criminal activity for the purpose of directly or indirectly receiving a material benefit, including a financial benefit";[230] or (*b*) the offender's income cannot reasonably account for the value of all the property of the offender.[231] A court "shall not" make a forfeiture order in respect of any property that the offender establishes, "on a balance of probabilities", is not proceeds of crime.[232]

§17.85 A sentencing judge may impose a fine in lieu of forfeiture if the property or any part of or interest in the property: (*a*) cannot, on the exercise of due diligence, be located; (*b*) has been transferred to a third party; (*c*) is located outside Canada; (*d*) has been substantially diminished in value or rendered worthless; or (*e*) has been commingled with other property that cannot be divided without difficulty.[233] The amount of the fine is to be equal to the value of the property or the part of or interest in the property.[234] Unlike the discretion to impose fines under section 734 of the *Code*, a sentencing judge cannot take into account the offender's ability to pay when determining the amount of a fine in lieu of forfeiture — although the amount of time given to the offender to pay the fine will be considered.[235] This is to ensure that Parliament's message that "crime does not pay" is heard loud and clear.[236]

---

[226] *Criminal Code*, s. 462.37(2). In *R. v. Hape*, [2005] O.J. No. 3188 at para. 40 (Ont. C.A.), affd [2007] S.C.J. No. 26 (S.C.C.), the Ontario Court of Appeal explained, "that s. 462.37(2) contemplates a nexus between the offence which was the subject of the trial giving rise to the conviction and sentencing proceedings and the property the Crown seeks forfeited. That is not to say that the property must be the proceeds of the crime for which the accused was convicted. If that were the case, the property would be properly forfeited under s. 462.37(1). The property must, however, have been the subject matter of the allegations made at trial. If at the end of the trial the property that was the subject matter of the allegations on which the trial was based is determined to fall within the definition of proceeds of crime, but is not the proceeds of the offence for which the accused was convicted at trial, s. 462.37(2) may have application."

[227] S.C. 1996, c. 19.

[228] See s. 462.37(2.02). The applicable sections of the *Controlled Drugs and Substances Act*, S.C. 1996, c. 19, are s. 5 (trafficking), s. 6 (importing and exporting) and s. 7 (production of substance).

[229] *Criminal Code*, s. 462.37(2.03).

[230] *Criminal Code*, s. 462.37(2.01(*a*).

[231] *Criminal Code*, s. 462.37(2.01).

[232] *Criminal Code*, s. 462.37(2.03).

[233] *Criminal Code*, s. 462.37(3).

[234] *Ibid.*

[235] See *R. v. Lavigne*, [2006] S.C.J. No. 10, [2006] 1 S.C.R. 392 at paras. 10, 37 and 47 (S.C.C.).

[236] *Ibid.*, at para. 10 (S.C.R.).

§17.86 Where a sentencing judge orders a fine in lieu of forfeiture, the judge must also impose a term of imprisonment in default of payment.[237] The default term of imprisonment is to be served consecutively to any other term of imprisonment imposed on the offender or that the offender may already be serving.[238]

§17.87 A similar forfeiture scheme as provided for proceeds of crime in section 462.37 is found in section 490.1 of the *Criminal Code*, which is broader in scope as it deals with forfeiture in relation to "offence-related property".[239] This provision applies to offenders convicted of an indictable offence under the *Criminal Code* or the *Corruption of Foreign Public Officials Act*.[240] The sentencing judge must order forfeiture when he or she is satisfied, "on a balance of probabilities", that any property is offence-related property and that the offence was committed in relation to that property. If the sentencing judge is not so satisfied, the judge may still make an order of forfeiture if it is satisfied, "beyond a reasonable doubt", that the property is offence-related property.

(3) Ancillary Orders

(a) *DNA Data Bank Orders*

§17.88 As discussed in Chapter 3, Part 3(7)(*a*), the *Criminal Code* authorizes bodily samples to be taken from offenders convicted of designated offences to be included in the National DNA Data Bank. A DNA data bank order flows automatically from convictions or discharges for any of the offences listed in paragraph (*a*) of the definition of "primary designated offence" in section 487.04 of the *Code*.[241] For offences listed in paragraph (*a*.1), a DNA data bank order will presumptively issue unless the sentencing judge is satisfied that the impact on the offender's privacy and security of the person would be "grossly disproportionate to the public interest in the protection of society and the proper administration of justice, to be achieved through the early detection, arrest and conviction of offenders."[242] Orders are rarely denied under this category.[243]

---

[237] *Criminal Code*, ss. 462.37(4).
[238] *Criminal Code*, s. 467.37(4)(*b*).
[239] "Offence-related property" is defined in s. 2 of the *Code* as "any property, within or outside Canada, (*a*) by means or in respect of which an indictable offence under this Act or the *Corruption of Foreign Public Officials Act* is committed, (*b*) that is used in any manner in connection with the commission of such an offence, or (*c*) that is intended to be used for committing such an offence."
[240] S.C. 1998, c. 34.
[241] *Criminal Code*, s. 487.051(1).
[242] *Criminal Code*, s. 487.051(2). Though this provision does not, unlike the provision dealing with secondary designated offences, refer judges to any specific factors to consider in making this decision, courts have held that they should consider the same factors. See *R. v. C. (R.)*, [2005] S.C.J. No. 62, [2005] 3 S.C.R. 99 at para. 30 (S.C.C.); *R. v. Jordan*, [2002] N.S.J. No. 20, 162 C.C.C. (3d) 385 at para. 62 (N.S.C.A.).
[243] *R. v. Hendry*, [2002] O.J. No. 5084, 161 C.C.C. (3d) 275 at 289-90 (Ont. C.A.).

§17.89 In the case of a secondary designated offence, the Crown must make an application for the order.[244] The order may be granted if the sentencing judge is satisfied that it is in the best interests of the administration of justice to do so.[245] In making this decision, the sentencing judge must consider the criminal record of the offender, the nature of the offence, the circumstances surrounding its commission, and the impact such an order would have on the person's privacy and security in their person.[246] Like orders under section 487.051(2), orders for secondary designated offences will be made in most cases.[247]

(b) Sex Offender Registration Orders

§17.90 Similar to DNA data bank orders, certain "designated" offences trigger the application of the *Sex Offender Information Registration Act*.[248] Depending on the maximum sentence for the predicate offence, SOIRA orders are effective for 10 years,[249] 20 years[250] or life.[251]

§17.91 The conditions to be met before registration under SOIRA is required depending on the predicate offence. For offences listed in section 490.011(1)(*a*), (*c*), (*c.1*), (*d*) and (*e*) of the *Criminal Code*,[252] registration will be ordered on the prosecutor's request, subject to the exception discussed in the following paragraph.[253] For designated offences listed in section 490.011(1)(*b*) and (*f*), registration requires the prosecutor to prove "beyond a reasonable doubt that the person committed the offence with the [further] intent to commit an offence referred to in [section 490.011(1)(*a*), (*c*), (*c.1*), (*d*) or (*e*)]."[254]

§17.92 For either category of designated offences, the sentencing judge may decline to make the order when the offender establishes that its impact on him or her, including on his or her privacy or liberty, would be "grossly disproportionate" to the public interest in protecting society through the effective

---

[244] *Criminal Code*, s. 487.051(3).

[245] *Criminal Code*, s. 487.051(3).

[246] *Criminal Code*, s. 487.051(3).

[247] See Chapter 3, Part 3(7)(*a*)(ii).

[248] The *Sex Offender Information Registration Act* [SOIRA], S.C. 2004, c. 10 and its associated amendments to the *Criminal Code* came into force on December 15, 2004 requiring offenders convicted of a designated sex offence to report and register personal information to be held in a database of sex offenders. See *Criminal Code*, s. 490.011(1)(*a*) to (*f*). Note that the requirements under the SOIRA are similar to those under Ontario's *Christopher's Law (Sex Offender Registry), 2000*, S.O. 2000, c. 1. The Ontario law was endorsed as being constitutionally valid by the Ontario Court of Appeal in *R. v. Dyck*, [2008] O.J. No. 1567, 232 C.C.C. (3d) 450 (Ont. C.A.).

[249] *Criminal Code*, s. 490.013(1)(*a*) (*i.e.*, where the matter was prosecuted summarily or if the maximum term of imprisonment for the offence is two or five years).

[250] *Criminal Code*, s. 490.013(1)(*b*) (*i.e.*, if the maximum term of imprisonment for the offence is 10 or 14 years).

[251] *Criminal Code*, s. 490.013(1)(*c*) (*i.e.*, if the maximum term of imprisonment for the offence is life).

[252] These sections list the most serious of sexual offences as well as historical sexual offences.

[253] *Criminal Code*, s. 490.012(1).

[254] *Criminal Code*, s. 490.012(2).

investigation of sexual crimes.[255] This standard, the courts have stressed, is "very stringent and demanding" and "not easily satisfied".[256] In addition to the offender's privacy and liberty interests, the judge should consider any personal handicap that would hamper reporting, stigma, the effect of registration in undermining rehabilitation and reintegration in the community, and the potential for police harassment.[257] Although SOIRA is not limited to likely recidivists or sexual predators,[258] it is important to focus the inquiry on the offender's present and possible future circumstances, rather than on the offence itself.[259]

(c) Driving Prohibitions

§17.93 If convicted of a driving offence under the *Criminal Code*, an accused can expect to be prohibited from driving for a period of time. The *Code* contains both mandatory and discretionary driving prohibitions. Convictions for impaired driving or "over 80" attract automatic driving prohibitions ranging from a minimum of one year (and a maximum of three years) for a first time offender to a minimum of three years (and no maximum) after a third offence.[260] However, offenders who register in alcohol ignition interlock programs (where they exist), may have the period of driving ineligibility reduced.[261] Driving offences committed while street racing[262] also result in mandatory driving prohibitions,[263] ranging from a minimum one-year prohibition for a first offence[264] to a mandatory life prohibition for an accused previously convicted of causing death by criminal negligence or dangerous operation of a vehicle while street racing.[265]

§17.94 Discretionary prohibitions may be ordered with respect to convictions or discharges for criminal negligence causing bodily harm or death by means of a motor vehicle, manslaughter, dangerous driving, flight from police and failure to stop at a scene of an accident.[266] The prohibition can be for any period of time up to various maximums depending on the period of imprisonment that the offender is liable to in respect of the underlying offence.[267]

§17.95 Where a court makes a driving prohibition order, it must ensure that: (*a*) the order is read by or to the offender; (*b*) a copy of the order is given to the

---

[255] *Criminal Code*, s. 490.012(4).
[256] *R. v. Debidin*, [2008] O.J. No. 5219, 241 C.C.C. (3d) 152 at para. 63 (Ont. C.A.).
[257] *R. v. Redhead*, [2006] A.J. No. 273, 206 C.C.C. (3d) 315 at para. 31 (Alta. C.A.), leave to appeal refused [2006] S.C.C.A. No. 187 (S.C.C.).
[258] *Ibid.*, at para. 21 (C.C.C.); *R. v. Debidin*, [2008] O.J. No. 5219, 241 C.C.C. (3d) 152 at para. 70 (Ont. C.A.).
[259] *R. v. Redhead*, [2006] A.J. No. 273, 206 C.C.C. (3d) 315 at para. 28 (Alta. C.A.), leave to appeal refused [2006] S.C.C.A. No. 187 (S.C.C.).
[260] *Criminal Code*, s. 259(1).
[261] *Criminal Code*, s. 259(1.1) and (1.2).
[262] *Criminal Code*, ss. 249.2 to 249.4.
[263] *Criminal Code*, s. 259(3.1) to (3.4).
[264] *Criminal Code*, s. 259(3.1)(*a*).
[265] *Criminal Code*, s. 259(3.4).
[266] *Criminal Code*, s. 259(2).
[267] *Criminal Code*, s. 259(2)(*a*) to (*c*).

offender; and (*c*) the offender is informed if he or she is found guilty of driving while disqualified he or she may be imprisoned for up to five years.[268] The offender is then given the opportunity to endorse the order, acknowledging that the order has been explained and that he or she has received a copy of it.[269] A failure of the offender to endorse the order does not invalidate it.[270]

(d) Firearms and Explosive Prohibitions

§17.96 A sentencing judge must prohibit offenders from possessing "any firearm, cross-bow, prohibited weapon, restricted weapon, prohibited device, ammunition, prohibited ammunition and explosive substance"[271] when they have been convicted or discharged of: (*a*) an indictable offence in the commission of which violence was used, threatened or attempted for which the person may be imprisoned for 10 years or more; (*b*) an enumerated firearm offence or criminal harassment;[272] (*c*) a listed offence under the *Controlled Drugs and Substances Act*;[273] or (*d*) an offence that involves a firearm, prohibited weapon or explosive during a time the offender was already bound by a prohibition order. For first time offenders, the prohibition lasts for life with respect to any prohibited firearm, restricted firearm, prohibited weapon, prohibited device or prohibited ammunition.[274] For any other firearm, the mandatory duration of the prohibition is 10 years.[275] Subsequent offences will, however, attract lifetime bans.[276]

§17.97 A sentencing judge also has the discretion to make a prohibition order when the offender was convicted or discharged of: (*a*) an offence not covered in section 109 but the commission of which involved the use, threat or attempt of violence;[277] or (*b*) an offence involving a firearm, prohibited weapon or explosive.[278] In deciding whether to make the order, the court must "consider whether it is desirable, in the interests of the safety of the person or of any other person,

---

[268] *Criminal Code*, s. 260(1).

[269] *Criminal Code*, s. 260(2).

[270] *Criminal Code*, s. 260(3).

[271] *Criminal Code*, s. 109(1).

[272] An offence under s. 85(1) (using firearm in commission of offence), s. 85(2) (using imitation firearm in commission of offence), s. 95(1) (possession of prohibited or restricted firearm with ammunition), s. 99(1) (weapons trafficking), s. 100(1) (possession for purpose of weapons trafficking), s. 102(1) (making automatic firearm), s. 103(1) (importing or exporting knowing it is unauthorized), or s. 264 (criminal harassment).

[273] The applicable offences under the *Controlled Drugs and Substances Act*, S.C. 1996, c. 19, are s. 5 (trafficking), s. 6 (importing and exporting) and s. 7 (production of substance).

[274] *Criminal Code*, s. 109(2)(b).

[275] *Criminal Code*, s. 109(2)(a).

[276] *Criminal Code*, s. 109(3).

[277] *Criminal Code*, s. 110(1)(*a*). Note however, that the use of a firearm in the commission of an offence is not required for a discretionary prohibition under s. 110(1)(*a*). See *R. v. Coleman*, [2000] N.S.J. No. 30 at para. 11 (N.S.C.A.).

[278] *Criminal Code*, s. 110(1)(*b*).

to make an order ...".[279] The maximum duration of the prohibition order under this section is 10 years.[280]

(4) Alternatives to Criminal Sanctions

(a) Diversion

§17.98 In 1996, Parliament introduced alternative measures, also known as "diversion", to deal with minor offences outside of formal criminal proceedings.[281] Section 717 of the *Code* allows for diversion "only if it is not inconsistent with the protection of society" and where: (*a*) the diversion is part of a program authorized by the province; (*b*) it is appropriate, having regard to the needs of the accused and the interests of society and of the victim; (*c*) the accused "fully and freely" consents to participate in the program; (*d*) the accused has been advised of the right to be represented by counsel prior to consenting to participate in diversion; (*e*) the accused accepts responsibility for the alleged acts; (*f*) there is sufficient evidence to proceed with the prosecution of the offence; and (*g*) the prosecution of the offence is not barred at law.[282] No admission, confession or statement made by an accused participating in a diversion program is admissible against the accused in any civil or criminal proceedings.[283] Diversion is not available where the accused denies involvement in the commission of the crime, or expresses the wish to have the charge dealt with by a court.[284]

§17.99 Generally, the discretion to offer diversion rests with the Crown prosecutor. While the *Code* does not restrict diversion to any particular offences, alternative measures are typically thought to be "most suitable for younger adult offenders and those with no criminal record, who have committed minor offences."[285] Typically, the alternative measure may include a letter of apology, community service or a donation to charity.[286] Offences involving domestic violence, threats or assault that are more than merely transient or trifling in nature, and drug trafficking offences involving youths are generally precluded from diversion.[287]

---

[279] *Criminal Code*, s. 110(1).

[280] *Criminal Code*, s. 110(2).

[281] Bill C-41, *An Act to amend the Criminal Code (sentencing) and other Acts in consequence thereof*, 1st Sess., 35th Parl., 1994 (assented to July 13, 1995, S.C. 1995, c. 22), came into force on September 3, 1996.

[282] *Criminal Code*, s. 717(1).

[283] *Criminal Code*, s. 717(3).

[284] *Criminal Code*, s. 717(2).

[285] See the *Federal Prosecution Service Deskbook*, "Alternative and Extrajudicial Measures," 14.2.1. (<http://sppc.gc.ca/eng/fps-sfp/fpd/ch14.html>).

[286] See Alberta, *Crown Prosecutors' Policy Manual*, "Adult Alternative Measures Program" (<http://justice.alberta.ca/programs_services/criminal_pros/crown_prosecutor/Pages/AdultAlter nativeMeasuresProgram.aspx>).

[287] See *Federal Prosecution Service Deskbook*, "Alternative and Extrajudicial Measures," 14.2.1. (<http://sppc.gc.ca/eng/fps-sfp/fpd/ch14.html>); Alberta, Alberta, *Crown Prosecutors' Policy*

§17.100 If the accused completes the alternative measures program success-fully, which usually occurs within a three-month time frame, the charge is with-drawn and the accused avoids a criminal record.[288] If not, criminal proceedings may be instituted, though the court may dismiss the charge if it finds that the prosecution "would be unfair, having regard to the circumstances and that per-son's performance with respect to the alternative measures."[289]

(b) Peace Bonds

§17.101 Another alternative to prosecution and punishment is the peace bond. Though designed to prevent anticipated crimes, a prosecutor may seek a peace bond to resolve existing charges, "[o]ften as a result of concerns including those for the strength of the Crown's case, the availability of witnesses, the views of the complainant, the best interest of the administration of justice and/or over-crowded court dockets".[290] A peace bond can be ordered at common law or pur-suant to section 810 of the *Criminal Code*. The main differences between the two types of peace bonds are that a section 810 peace bond is based on a sworn information, based on a complainant's fears on reasonable grounds that the ac-cused will cause personal injury to him or her or to his or her spouse or common law partner or child or will damage his or her property, and has a maximum du-ration of 12 months; a common law peace bond does not require a sworn infor-mation, is broader in scope, encompassing a reasonably apprehended breach of the peace and has no maximum duration period.[291]

§17.102 A peace bond is not a finding of guilt and does not result in a criminal record. The accused does not enter a guilty plea or make any admission of criminal liability. Before entering into the peace bond, the accused has the op-tion to show cause why he or she should not enter the bond or not show cause but contest a proposed condition of the bond.

§17.103 The incentives for an accused to enter into a peace bond are obvious. However, it is important to note that a peace bond nevertheless places restriction on the liberty of the accused, albeit fairly minor in nature.[292] Further, a breach of a peace bond can result in criminal liability.[293]

Manual, "Adult Alternative Measures Program" (<http://justice.alberta.ca/programs_services/criminal_pros/crown_prosecutor/Pages/AdultAlternativeMeasuresProgram.aspx>).

[288] *Ibid.*

[289] *Criminal Code*, s. 717(4)(*b*).

[290] *R. v. Musoni*, [2009] O.J. No. 1161, 243 C.C.C. (3d) 17 at para. 26 (Ont. S.C.J.), affd [2009] O.J. No. 4935 (Ont. C.A.). See also *R. v. Soungie*, [2003] A.J. No. 899 (Alta. Prov. Ct.).

[291] *R. v. Musoni*, [2009] O.J. No. 1161, 243 C.C.C. (3d) 17 at para. 21 (Ont. S.C.J.), affd [2009] O.J. No. 4935 (Ont. C.A.).

[292] See *R. v. MacKenzie*, [1945] O.J. No. 547, 85 C.C.C. 233 (Ont. C.A.); *R. v. Budreo*, [2000] O.J. No. 72, 142 C.C.C. (3d) 225 (Ont. C.A.).

[293] Section 811 of the *Code* creates a hybrid offence for breaching a peace bond issued under s. 810. The maximum penalty is two years' imprisonment if proceeding by indictment and six months when prosecuted summarily. An individual who breaches a common law peace bond

6.   OTHER FACTORS THAT HAVE IMPACTS ON SENTENCE

(1)   Joint Submissions

§17.104   As a result of plea negotiations, the accused and prosecutor sometimes agree to make a joint submission as to sentence. Though the sentencing judge is not bound by the submission, the courts have recognized that for plea bargaining to be effective, they must have a high degree of confidence that their resolution will be respected by the court. To depart from a joint submission, the sentencing judge must meet a high threshold. As Justice Fish stated in *R. v. Douglas*:[294]

> Canadian appellate courts have expressed in different ways the standard for determining when trial judges may properly reject joint submissions on sentence accompanied by negotiated admissions of guilt.

> Whatever the language used, the standard is meant to be an exacting one. Appellate courts, increasingly in recent years, have stated time and again that trial judges should not reject jointly proposed sentences unless they are "unreasonable", "contrary to the public interest", "unfit", or "would bring the administration of justice into disrepute".[295]

§17.105   Before rejecting a joint submission, a sentencing judge should afford both defence counsel and the Crown an opportunity to make further submissions.[296] If the sentencing judge is still reluctant to accept the agreement, the court must then consider fully the circumstances of the offence and the offender in determining a fit sentence.[297]

---

can be charged under s. 127 of the *Code* for disobeying a court order that has the same penalties as prescribed in s. 811.

[294]   [2002] J.Q. no 418, 162 C.C.C. (3d) 37 (Que. C.A.).

[295]   *Ibid.*, at paras. 42-43 (C.C.C.). See also *R. v. Cerasuolo*, [2001] O.J. No. 359, 151 C.C.C. (3d) 445 at para. 8 (Ont. C.A.) (The judge should reject a joint submission only where it "is contrary to the public interest and the sentence would bring the administration into disrepute."); *R. v. F. (J.K.)*, [2005] O.J. No. 812, 195 O.A.C. 141 at para. 3 (Ont. C.A.), additional reasons at [2005] O.J. No. 2212 (Ont. C.A.) (absent "an adequate evidential foundation", it is an error for a court to impose a sentence greater than that recommended by the Crown); *R. v. Guignard*, [2005] N.B.J. No. 132, 195 C.C.C. (3d) 145 at para. 18 (N.B.C.A.) ("joint recommendation on sentence should be followed unless it is unreasonable"); *R. v. C. (G.W.)*, [2000] A.J. No. 1585, 150 C.C.C. (3d) 513 (Alta. C.A.) (sentencing judge is to accept a joint submission unless it is "unfit" or "unreasonable"); *R. v. Chartrand*, [1998] M.J. No. 508, 131 C.C.C. (3d) 122 at para. 9 (Man. C.A.) (joint submission should be accepted by the judge unless it is "so unfit that it demands rejection"). But see *R. v. Bezdan*, [2001] B.C.J. No. 808 at para. 15 (B.C.C.A.) (in referring to the standard articulated in *Cerasuolo*, stating that it is not clear that "these two circumstances cover all situations in which a sentencing judge might conclude that the sentence proposed was 'unfit'").

[296]   *R. v. Tsicos*, [2006] O.J. No. 4041 at para. 4 (Ont. C.A.).

[297]   *Ibid.*, at para. 6.

(2) Pre-Trial Custody

§17.106 In determining sentence, a judge may take into account any time spent in custody awaiting trial and sentencing.[298] Although the language authorizing the judge to consider pre-sentence custody in section 719(3) is permissive rather than mandatory, the courts have held that credit should normally be given for pre-sentence custody unless there is a good reason to conclude otherwise.[299] In *R. v. Francis*,[300] the Ontario Court of Appeal set out the rationale for enhanced credit for pre-sentence custody as follows:

> Three considerations inform the rationale for giving enhanced credit for pre-sentence custody. They are: (1) that other than for life sentences, legislative provisions for parole eligibility and statutory release do not take into account time spent in pre-sentence custody; (2) that there are few rehabilitative, educational or retraining programs available in detention centres; and (3) that the conditions in detention facilities are often more crowded and more onerous than in correctional facilities.[301]

§17.107 Before February 22, 2010,[302] courts typically applied a two-for-one credit for pre-sentence custody.[303] The *Criminal Code* now limits "any credit for that time to a maximum of one day for each day spent in custody" unless the "circumstances justify" a greater credit up to a maximum of 1.5 days.[304] The *Code*, however, does not provide guidance as to the types of circumstances justifying enhanced credit. In *R. v. Kravchov*,[305] a case decided before the one-for-one presumption came into force, Justice Kenkel summarized the range of factors that were relevant in determining the appropriateness of enhanced credit as follows:

- the effect of pre-trial custody on a particular prisoner due to age, infirmity, mental illness ... ;

- incarceration at a facility that houses primarily men where that has resulted in isolation of a female prisoner ... ;

- lengthy pre-trial custody ... ;

- significant pre-trial custody where the accused has never been incarcerated before ... ;

- the unavailability of rehabilitative or education programs at the detention centre ... ;

---

[298] *Criminal Code*, s. 719(3).
[299] *R. v. Wust*, [2000] S.C.J. No. 19, [2000] 1 S.C.R. 455 at paras. 44-45 (S.C.C.); *R. v. Rezaie*, [1996] O.J. No. 4468, 112 C.C.C. (3d) 97 at 104 (Ont. C.A.).
[300] [2006] O.J. No. 1287, 207 C.C.C. (3d) 536 (Ont. C.A.).
[301] *Ibid.*, at para. 14 (C.C.C.).
[302] *Truth in Sentencing Act*, S.C. 2009, c. 29.
[303] *R. v. Wust*, [2000] S.C.J. No. 19, [2000] 1 S.C.R. 455 at para. 45 (S.C.C.); *R. v. McDonald*, [1998] O.J. No. 2990, 127 C.C.C. (3d) 57 at 83 (Ont. C.A.).
[304] *Criminal Code*, ss. 719(3)-(3.1). A judge may never impose greater than one-for-one credit, however, where pre-trial detention was ordered in the circumstances set out in s. 719(3.1).
[305] [2002] O.J. No. 2172 (Ont. C.J.).

- whether a jail is "overcrowded" and engaging in practices such as "triple bunking" ... ;

- the frequency of "lockdowns" and other measures denying the prisoner exercise and access to areas outside his or her cell ... ;

- waiver of a preliminary hearing along with conditions of detention ... ;

- the prevalence of disease and any other conditions which endanger the health of the prisoner ... ;

- custody during a public service strike where that labour disruption affected the care of the prisoners and prevented their transportation to court ... ; and

- any unusual delays in the progress of the case attributable to the Crown.[306]

Whether any of these factors continue to be relevant under the new regime remains to be determined. But it seems clear that Parliament intended that one-for-one credit should be the norm; with greater credit ordered only in exceptional cases.[307]

§17.108 Apart from its influence in deciding the duration of imprisonment, the courts have also considered the effect of pre-sentence custody on the availability of various sentencing options. In *R. v. Wust*,[308] the Supreme Court held that a sentencing judge may take pre-sentence custody into account in imposing a sentence that is less than the mandatory minimum. Pre-sentence custody, it reasoned is "in effect, deemed part of the punishment following the offender's conviction, by the operation of s. 719(3)."[309] In *R. v. Fice*,[310] however, the Court ruled that credit for pre-sentence custody cannot reduce a sentence to two years or less and thereby make it eligible for a conditional sentence. A conditional sentence cannot be imposed if the "total punishment", including any credit for pre-sentence custody, is two years or greater.[311]

§17.109 Most recently, the Court declared in *R. v. Mathieu*,[312] that pre-trial custody is not to be considered in determining the availability of probation under section 731(1)(*b*) of the *Code*.[313] As discussed in Part 5(2)(*c*), above, that provision states that probation is available when the offender is sentenced to a term of

---

[306] *Ibid.*, at para. 12.
[307] See *R. v. C. (A.W.)*, [2010] B.C.J. No. 1763 at para. 20 (B.C. Prov. Ct.) ("Presumably if Parliament had meant simply to reduce the previously generally applied credit of two-for-one to one and a half-for-one, the legislative drafters could have said this.").
[308] [2000] S.C.J. No. 19, [2000] 1 S.C.R. 455 (S.C.C.).
[309] *Ibid.*, at para. 41 (S.C.R.). At the time, s. 719 stated simply that "[i]n determining the sentence to be imposed on a person convicted of an offence, a court may take into account any time spent in custody by the person as a result of the offence." The amendments imposing the maximum limits on the credit that may be awarded (referred to at §17.107, above) should not be interpreted as disrupting this holding.
[310] [2005] S.C.J. No. 30, [2005] 1 S.C.R. 742 (S.C.C.).
[311] *Ibid.*, at paras. 21-22 (S.C.R.).
[312] [2008] S.C.J. No. 21, [2008] 1 S.C.R. 723 (S.C.C.).
[313] *Ibid.*

imprisonment of less than two years. The Court interpreted this in *Mathieu* to refer to the "the actual term of imprisonment imposed by the court after taking into account any time spent in pre-sentence custody."[314] For the same reasons, the Court also held that pre-sentence custody cannot be considered in deciding whether to lengthen the offender's period of parole ineligibility under section 743.6(1.2) of the *Code*.[315] As a consequence, sentencing judges may not delay the parole eligibility of offenders sentenced to less than two years' imprisonment after taking into account credit for pre-sentence custody.

§17.110 The Supreme Court of Canada has not yet decided whether pre-sentence custody should be counted in determining the availability of suspended sentences, discharges, fines or intermittent sentences.[316]

(3) Immigration Status

§17.111 For non-citizens, a conviction and sentence may also have adverse immigration consequences. Under section 36(1)(*a*) of the *Immigration and Refugee Protection Act*,[317] a permanent resident or a foreign national becomes inadmissible and therefore removable from Canada if convicted of either: (*i*) a federal offence carrying a maximum punishment of imprisonment least 10 years; or (*ii*) a federal offence for which a term of imprisonment of more than six months was imposed. A removal order may not be appealed if the offender received a sentence of two years' imprisonment or more for any single offence.[318]

§17.112 While sentencing judges may not usurp the role of the Immigration Board, appellate courts have held that "the certainty of deportation may justify some reduction in the term of imprisonment for purely pragmatic reasons."[319] However, immigration consequences should not be the deciding factor.[320] It is also important to note that even where an offender is convicted of multiple offences, as long as the totality of the sentence is within the acceptable range for

---

[314] *Ibid.*, at para. 19 (S.C.R.).

[315] *Ibid.*, at paras. 23-29 (S.C.R.). This power is discussed below, Part 6(5).

[316] However, in *R. v. Peebles*, [2010] M.J. No. 164, 2010 MBCA 47 at para. 54 (Man. C.A.), the Manitoba Court of Appeal held, "Pre-sentence custody is a factor to be taken into account in determining the sentence to be imposed and the sentence commences when it is imposed. Thus, the 'ninety days or less' requirement for an intermittent sentence means the sentence imposed after taking into account any credit for pre-sentence custody."

[317] S.C. 2001, c. 27, s. 64 [IRPA].

[318] *Ibid.*, at s. 64. For the purpose of s. 64(2) of IRPA, the "term of imprisonment" includes any time the accused spent in pre-trial custody. See *Sherzad v. Canada (Minister of Citizenship and Immigration)*, [2005] F.C.J. No. 954, 2005 FC 757 at para. 44 (F.C.); *Atwal v. Canada (Minister of Citizenship and Immigration)*, [2004] F.C.J. No. 63 (F.C.); *Canada (Minister of Citizenship and Immigration) v. Smith*, [2004] F.C.J. No. 2159, 2004 FC 63 (F.C.); *Cheddesingh v. Canada (Minister of Citizenship and Immigration)*, [2005] F.C.J. No. 847, 2005 FC 667 (F.C.).

[319] *R. v. Hamilton*, [2004] O.J. No. 3252, 72 O.R. (3d) 1 at para. 156 (Ont. C.A.). See also *R. v. C. (B.R.)*, [2010] O.J. No. 3571 at para. 8 (Ont. C.A.); *R. v. Kanthasamy*, [2005] B.C.J. No. 517, 195 C.C.C. (3d) 182 (B.C.C.A.).

[320] *R. v. Wisniewski*, [2002] M.J. No. 268 (Man. C.A.).

the type of offences, a sentence of less than two years for each conviction may be appropriate.[321]

(4) Notice to Seek Greater Punishment

§17.113 Section 727 of the *Criminal Code* provides that "where an offender is convicted of an offence for which a greater punishment may be imposed by reason of previous convictions, no greater punishment shall be imposed on the offender...unless the prosecutor satisfies the court that the offender, before making a plea, was notified that a greater punishment would be sought...". In practice, this provision finds most application in drinking and driving cases due to the graduating scale of punishment for each subsequent conviction.[322] Of course, a sentencing judge may take into account the offender's criminal record in crafting a sentence, regardless of whether notice under section 727 had been given to the offender. However, notice under section 727 serves to fix the "bottom limit" of the sentencing judge's sentencing discretion.[323]

(5) Parole

§17.114 For the most part, the eligibility of parole for federal prisoners is governed by the CCRA.[324] Sentencing judges, in other words, cannot generally dictate when an offender should be eligible to apply for parole.[325] This principle admits of two exceptions. The first relates to the offences of high treason and murder. For persons convicted of high treason or first degree murder, the sentence is always life imprisonment without eligibility for parole for 25 years.[326] The same sentence must be imposed on persons convicted of second degree murder where that person has previously been convicted of either: (*i*) first or second degree murder; or (*ii*) "an offence under section 4 or 6 of the *Crimes Against Humanity and War Crimes Act* that had as its basis an intentional killing, whether or not it was planned and deliberate".[327] In all other cases of second

---

[321] *R. v. Kanthasamy*, [2005] B.C.J. No. 517, 195 C.C.C. (3d) 182 at para. 23 (B.C.C.A.); *R. v. Hennessey*, [2007] O.J. No. 3204 (Ont. C.A.); *R. v. Curry*, [2005] O.J. No. 3763 at paras. 34-35 (Ont. C.A.).

[322] For example, the punishment for impaired driving for a first offence is a minimum fine of $1,000, while a second conviction carries a term of imprisonment for at least 30 days. See *Criminal Code*, s. 255(1)(*a*).

[323] *R. v. Norris*, [1988] N.W.T.J. No. 195, 41 C.C.C. (3d) 441 at para. 22 (N.W.T.C.A.).

[324] *Corrections and Conditional Release Act*, S.C. 1992, c. 20, s. 120.

[325] See generally, *R. v. Smith*, [2008] S.J. No. 97, 232 C.C.C. (3d) 176 at para. 58 (Sask. C.A.) ("Historically, the courts had been unable to consider the parole factor when determining sentence, and roles and functions in the process were sharply divided: the courts determined sentence and the Correctional system executed sentence and the National Parole Board determined eligibility for remission of sentence.").

[326] *Criminal Code*, s. 745(*a*). However, after serving at least 15 years of a life sentence, an offender convicted of first degree murder or high treason may apply for judicial review pursuant to s. 745.6, commonly referred to as the "faint hope clause", for a reduction of the parole ineligibility period.

[327] *Criminal Code*, s. 745(*b.1*).

degree murder, the judge must set a parole ineligibility period between 10 and 25 years, considering "the character of the offender, the nature of the offence and the circumstances surrounding its commission, and to the recommendation, if any, made [by the jury] pursuant to section 745.2".[328] The *Criminal Code* also provides special exception for calculating the period of imprisonment for murder. For parole purposes, the term of imprisonment begins on the day that the accused was arrested and taken into custody in respect of the first or second degree murder charge.[329]

§17.115 The second exception applies to sentences of imprisonment of two years or more on conviction for: (*a*) an offence set out in Schedule I or II of the *Corrections and Conditional Release Act*;[330] (*b*) a criminal organization offence;[331] or (*c*) a terrorism offence.[332] In such cases, the sentencing judge may prohibit the eligibility of parole until one half of the total sentence is served or 10 years, whichever is less. In ordering a delay in parole, the sentencing judge must be satisfied that "having regard to the circumstances of the commission of the offence and the character and circumstances of the offender, that the expression of society's denunciation of the offence or the objective of specific or general deterrence" deem the order appropriate.[333]

§17.116 In *R. v. Zinck*,[334] the Supreme Court of Canada clarified some of the procedural aspects associated with this scheme.[335] First, the judge is to arrive at an "appropriate sentence" by evaluating the facts of the case and the factors set out in section 718 of the *Code*. Then, the judge must review the same facts and give priority to the objectives of deterrence and denunciation. If, "after due consideration of all the relevant facts, principles and factors at the first stage, it appears at the second stage that the length of the jail term would not satisfy the imperatives of denunciation and deterrence," then an order delaying parole is required.[336] While the two-stage process does not require a special and distinct hearing, the accused should be "informed clearly that he [or she] is at risk in this respect" and should be given a reasonable opportunity to make submissions and adduce additional evidence.[337] The Court in *Zinck* further cautioned that a

---

[328] *Criminal Code*, ss. 745(*c*) and 745.4. Note that the maximum periods of parole ineligibility for first and second degree murder are shorter for persons under 18 years of age: *Criminal Code*, s. 745.1.

[329] *Criminal Code*, s. 746.

[330] Schedule I includes a multitude of *Criminal Code* offences, while Schedule II lists offences under the *Controlled Drugs and Substances Act*, S.C. 1996, c. 19 and *Food and Drugs Act*, R.S.C. 1985, c. F-27.

[331] *Criminal Code*, s. 743.6(1.1).

[332] *Criminal Code*, s. 743.6(1.2).

[333] *Criminal Code*, s. 743.6(1).

[334] [2003] S.C.J. No. 5, [2003] 1 S.C.R. 41 (S.C.C.).

[335] *Ibid.*

[336] *Ibid.*, at para. 33 (S.C.R.).

[337] *Ibid.*, at paras. 33 and 36 (S.C.R.).

delayed parole order is not "an ordinary measure" and should be invoked only on the basis of "demonstrated need."[338]

(6) Sentence Reduction to Remedy State Misconduct

§17.117 In *R. v. Nasogaluak*,[339] the Supreme Court held that state misconduct, including *Charter* breaches, may be considered in sentencing. As explained more fully in Chapter 10, Part 5(1)(*a*)(vii), such misconduct may be treated as a mitigating factor if it relates to the "circumstances of the offence or the offender."[340] Save in "exceptional cases", however, the sentence imposed must adhere to any minimums or other statutory restrictions.[341]

7. EVIDENCE PRESENTED AT SENTENCING

§17.118 In order to "fit the sentence to the offender rather than to the crime,"[342] a sentencing judge will wish to have as much information concerning the background of the offender as possible. As long as it is credible and trustworthy, hearsay evidence may be accepted.[343] Evidence adduced at a sentencing hearing is adduced largely by way of counsel's oral submissions.

(1) Burden of Proof

§17.119 While the traditional strict rules governing trials do not slavishly apply at a sentencing hearing, the resolution of contested facts does require proof. If the Crown wishes to rely on a fact in dispute alleged to be aggravating, it must prove that fact beyond a reasonable doubt. First recognized by the Supreme Court of Canada in *R. v. Gardiner*,[344] this principle has since been codified. Section 724(3) of the *Criminal Code* provides as follows:

> Where there is a dispute with respect to any fact that is relevant to the determination of a sentence,
>
> > (*a*) the court shall request that evidence be adduced as to the existence of the fact unless the court is satisfied that sufficient evidence was adduced at the trial;

---

[338] *Ibid.*, at para. 31 (S.C.R.). See also *R. v. Cheddesingh*, [2002] O.J. No. 3176, 168 C.C.C. (3d) 310 at para. 20 (Ont. C.A.), affd [2004] S.C.J. No. 15, 182 C.C.C. (3d) 37 (S.C.C.). ("If the offence is one of unusual violence, brutality or degradation, then the need to strongly express society's denunciation of the offence may make a s. 741.2 order appropriate.").

[339] [2010] S.C.J. No. 6, [2010] 1 S.C.R. 206, 2010 SCC 6 (S.C.C.).

[340] *Ibid.*, at paras. 3, 47, 55 (S.C.R.).

[341] *Ibid.*, at paras. 6, 63-64 (S.C.R.) ("I...do not foreclose the possibility that, in some exceptional cases, a sentence reduction outside statutory limits may be the sole effective remedy for some particularly egregious form of misconduct by state agents in relation to the offence and the offender."). See also *R. v. Chabot*, [1992] J.Q. no 1651, 77 C.C.C. (3d) 371 (Que. C.A.); *R. v. Ferguson*, [2008] S.C.J. No. 6, [2008] 1 S.C.R. 96 (S.C.C.).

[342] *R. v. Gardiner*, [1982] S.C.J. No. 71, [1982] 2 S.C.R. 368 at 414 (S.C.C.).

[343] *Ibid.*, at 414 (S.C.R.).

[344] *Ibid.*, at 414-15 (S.C.R.).

(b) the party wishing to rely on a relevant fact, including a fact contained in a presentence report, has the burden of proving it;

(c) either party may cross-examine any witness called by the other party;

(d) subject to paragraph (e), the court must be satisfied on a balance of probabilities of the existence of the disputed fact before relying on it in determining the sentence; and

(e) the prosecutor must establish, by proof beyond a reasonable doubt, the existence of any aggravating fact or any previous conviction by the offender.

(2) Criminal Record

§17.120 As discussed in Part 3(2), above, the existence (or lack of) a criminal record is an important factor to be considered by a sentencing judge since it provides insight on the offender's character and prospects for rehabilitation. A criminal record is usually tendered at sentencing by the Crown in the form of a record produced by the Canadian Police Information Centre (CPIC). Typically, the accused, through counsel, consents to the admission of the record and acknowledges it to be substantially accurate. However, where the record is not admitted by the accused, the Crown is required to prove the record by way of section 667 of the *Code*. Generally, a certificate signed by a judge, court clerk or a designated fingerprint examiner will be sufficient to prove the record.[345]

(3) Pre-sentence Report

§17.121 If a sentencing judge believes it would be of assistance, he or she may order the preparation of a pre-sentence report under section 721 of the *Code*. The report will be prepared by a probation officer and contain information on "the offender's age, maturity, character, behaviour, attitude and willingness to make amends."[346] The content of the report sometimes becomes an issue. As Chief Justice MacKeigan noted in *R. v. Rudyk*,[347] it should not contain "the investigator's impressions of the facts relating to the offence charged, whether based on information received from the accused, the police, or other witnesses, and whether favourable or unfavourable to the accused".[348] Further, details of the commission of an offence should not be included in the report.[349] It is similarly inappropriate for the report to include self-serving statements by the offender.[350]

---

[345] *Criminal Code*, s. 667(1)(a) and (2).
[346] *Criminal Code*, s. 721(3)(a).
[347] [1975] N.S.J. No. 33, 1 C.R. (3d) S. 26 (N.S.C.A.).
[348] *Ibid.*, at 31 (C.R.). See also *R. v. Donovan*, [2004] N.B.J. No. 273, 188 C.C.C. (3d) 193 (N.B.C.A.).
[349] *R. v. Martell*, [1984] P.E.I.J. No. 67 (P.E.I.S.C.); *R. v. Craig*, [1975] N.S.J. No. 358 (N.S.C.A.).
[350] See *R. v. Urbanovich; R. v. Brown*, [1985] M.J. No. 119, 19 C.C.C. (3d) 43 at 52 (Man. C.A.), affd [1987] S.C.J. No. 96 (S.C.C.).

§17.122 Under section 724 of the *Code*, if an objection is taken to any of the assertions contained in the pre-sentence report, the party wishing to rely on that assertion has the burden of proving it.[351] Cross-examination of the probation officer may be necessary to confirm that the report is "an accurate, independent and balanced assessment of an offender, his background and his prospects for the future."[352]

(4) Victim Impact Statements

§17.123 The conventional view of our criminal justice system is that crimes are committed against the state and the function of the system is to protect society.[353] Victims of crime may be the ones to set the judicial process in motion, but they are soon relegated to the back seat while the police focus on apprehending the offender, the Crown prepares its case, defence counsel acts in the best interests of the client and corrections personnel protect the public and facilitate the offender's rehabilitation. The *Charter* too focuses largely on the due process rights of criminal suspects and accused as balanced against the state's crime control interests.

§17.124 This system reserves little room for the victim. This has led to what some commentators call a secondary victimization. As Nils Christie observes, "[t]he victim is a double loser: his property may have been stolen by the offender, but his conflict has been stolen by the state."[354]

§17.125 Sentencing is one of the few stages of the criminal justice system where victims are entitled to participate, even in a limited way. Section 722 of the *Criminal Code* allows for the introduction of victim impact statements at the sentencing hearing. Victim impact statements provide victims with the opportunity to describe "the harm done to, or loss suffered by, the victim arising from the commission of the offence."[355] Section 722 makes it mandatory, rather than permissive, for the sentencing judge to consider a victim impact statement "[f]or the purpose of determining the sentence to be imposed". Pursuant to section 722(2.1), a victim has the right to request to read the victim impact statement in court. The "victim" need not be the direct complainant. Section 722(4)(*a*) defines "victim" as "*a* person to whom harm was done or who suffered physical or emotional loss",[356] recognizing that indirect victims are frequently affected by crime.

§17.126 Allowing victim input at the sentencing stage has raised concerns over the possibility of increased sentencing disparity based on "the resiliency, vindictiveness

---

[351] *Criminal Code*, s. 724(3)(*b*).
[352] *R. v. Junkert*, [2010] O.J. No. 3387 at para. 59 (Ont. C.A.).
[353] See *R. v. Antler*, [1982] B.C.J. No. 1705, 69 C.C.C. (2d) 480 at 480 (B.C.S.C.).
[354] Nils Christie, "Conflicts as Property" (1977) 17 Brit. J. Crim. 1.
[355] *Criminal Code*, s. 722(1).
[356] Emphasis added.

or other personality attributes of the victim."[357] That is, by shifting the focus from the offender to the victim, the sentencing judge may be influenced by a heart-wrenching victim impact statement rather than objectively focusing on the severity of the crime. Courts have been wary of this potential and have attempted to curb the use of inflammatory content within victim impact statements. In *R. v. Gabriel*,[358] Justice Hill cautioned that victim impact statements should not contain "criticisms of the offender, assertions as to the facts of the offence, or recommendations as to the severity of punishment."[359] A victim impact statement is not a vehicle to augment the facts of the offence. In dealing with prejudicial content, a sentencing judge has the discretion to excise inadmissible material from the statement.[360] Furthermore, a judge retains a discretion to allow cross-examination on the victim impact statement.[361]

§17.127 The consideration of a victim impact statement will inevitably involve some human emotional reaction. Judges are not machines capable of functioning without emotion. However, they are constantly exposed to stirring situations and placed in situations requiring them to disabuse their minds of inadmissible evidence. Dealing with an overzealous victim impact statement would require the same discipline as having to deal with inadmissible evidence. Nevertheless, an appellate court can always provide a remedy in situations where a judge improperly gave undue weight to a victim impact statement and imposed a sentence outside the appropriate range for the offence. For example, in *R. v. Bremner*,[362] the British Columbia Court of Appeal varied a custodial sentence to a conditional sentence where the victim impact statements adversely affected the sentencing proceeding.[363] The Court found that the victim impact statements contained inappropriate material, particularly with regard to recommendations for sentence and the use of psychiatric diagnostic terms such as "pedophile".

(5) Opportunity for Offender to Speak

§17.128 Section 726 of the *Code* provides that "[b]efore determining the sentence to be imposed, the court shall ask whether the offender, if present, has anything to say." The question is to be put to the offender after argument and just before sentence is imposed. As the Alberta Court of Appeal noted in *R. v. Gouthro*,[364] "what s. 726 calls for is more argument, not evidence".[365] This may

---

[357] P.N. Grabosky, "Victims" in G. Zdenkowski *et al.*, eds., *The Criminal Injustice System* (Sydney: Pluto Press, 1987) at 147.

[358] [1999] O.J. No. 2579, 137 C.C.C. (3d) 1 (Ont. S.C.J.).

[359] *Ibid.*, at para. 29 (C.C.C.).

[360] See *R. v. Talbot*, [1995] O.J. No. 4304 at para. 9 (Ont. Gen. Div.).

[361] *R. v. Lafleche*, [2001] A.J. No. 1504 at para. 23 (Alta. C.A.); *R. v. Shaban*, [2004] A.J. No. 1310 at para. 20 (Alta. Q.B.).

[362] [2000] B.C.J. No. 1096, 146 C.C.C. (3d) 59 (B.C.C.A.).

[363] *Ibid.*

[364] [2010] A.J. No. 656, 256 C.C.C. (3d) 432 (Alta. C.A.).

[365] *Ibid.*, at para. 40 (C.C.C.).

include, the Court suggested, "an expression of remorse or intention, or an apology."[366]

§17.129 While the language of section 726 is obligatory, the courts have held that a failure to comply does not invalidate the sentencing proceeding.[367] Where counsel has had the opportunity to make full submissions on behalf of the offender at the sentencing hearing, appellate courts have viewed the failure to comply an "inadvertent slip"[368] and "harmless error."[369]

---

[366] *Ibid.*

[367] *R. v. Spath*, [2003] A.J. No. 141 (Alta. C.A.); *R. v. Haug*, [2002] S.J. No. 210 (Sask. C.A.); *R. v. Senek*, [1998] M.J. No. 477, 130 C.C.C. (3d) 473 (Man. C.A.).

[368] *R. v. Haug*, [2002] S.J. No. 210 (Sask. C.A.).

[369] *R. v. Ratt*, [2006] S.J. No. 590 at para. 8 (Sask. C.A.).

Chapter 18

APPEALS

1. INTRODUCTION

§18.1 The appeal process serves to both correct errors and provide precedential value to lower courts. Provincial courts of appeal not only intervene to correct errors made by trial judges but also remain vigilant in redressing wrongful convictions and miscarriages of justice. However, when the appeal process reaches the Supreme Court of Canada, the interest of the Court is not in error correction but in legal issues of national importance.

§18.2 As we have discussed, the *Charter*[1] guarantees many rights and freedoms. On its face, at least, a right of appeal is not one of them.[2] This chapter will examine the appeal process as shaped by statute and common law. An important starting point is that courts of appeal are creatures of statute acquiring their jurisdiction entirely by way of legislation.[3] As Justice La Forest observed in *Kourtessis v. Canada (Minister of National Revenue - M.N.R.)*,[4] "this basic proposition tends at times to be forgotten."[5]

§18.3 There are essentially three types of appeals in criminal cases: (*i*) appeals of indictable matters (as of right) to the provincial or territorial courts of appeal;

---

[1]   *Canadian Charter of Rights and Freedoms*, Part I of the *Constitution Act, 1982*, being Schedule B to the *Canada Act 1982* (U.K.), 1982, c. 11 [*Charter*].

[2]   Although there is no express constitutional right to appellate review, such a right may arguably qualify as a "principle of fundamental justice" under s. 7 of the *Charter*. See *R. v. Farinacci*, [1993] O.J. No. 2627, 86 C.C.C. (3d) 32 at 42 (Ont. C.A.), suggesting, in *obiter*, that: "It is arguable, but it does not fall to be decided in this case, that the principles of fundamental justice in Canada, as they had evolved at the time the *Charter* was enacted, provide an entitlement to some form of review of convictions resulting in imprisonment." But see *R. v. Robinson*, [1989] A.J. No. 950, 51 C.C.C. (3d) 452 at 462 (Alta. C.A.), noting that: "As a constitutional postulate, the right of appeal is very much in doubt. It is a right that only derives from statute, and traditionally, has never been regarded as inherent."

[3]   *Kourtessis v. Canada (Minister of National Revenue - M.N.R.)*, [1993] S.C.J. No. 45, [1993] 2 S.C.R. 53 at 69-70 (S.C.C.); *R. v. Meltzer*, [1989] S.C.J. No. 75, [1989] 1 S.C.R. 1764 at 1773 (S.C.C.). See also *Criminal Code*, R.S.C. 1985, c. C-46, s. 674 ("No proceedings other than those authorized by this Part and Part XXVI shall be taken by way of appeal in proceedings in respect of indictable offences.").

[4]   [1993] S.C.J. No. 45, [1993] 2 S.C.R. 53 (S.C.C.).

[5]   *Ibid.* Note that in contrast, superior courts have inherent jurisdiction to deal with matters not expressly conferred by statute since they are appointed under s. 96 of the *Constitution Act, 1867* (U.K.), 30 & 31 Vict., c. 3 [Reprinted in R.S.C. 1985, App. II, No. 5]: see *R. v. DeJong*, [1996] B.C.J. No. 682, 1996 CanLII 1388 (B.C.C.A.). That is, for example, provincial superior courts have the inherent jurisdiction to hear applications for extraordinary remedies such as *certiorari*, *mandamus* and prohibition: see *Dagenais v. Canadian Broadcasting Corp.*, [1994] S.C.J. No. 104, [1994] 3 S.C.R. 835 at para. 38 (S.C.C.).

(*ii*) appeals of summary matters, initially (as of right) to the summary conviction appeal court and from there (with leave) to the court of appeal; and (*iii*) appeals to the Supreme Court of Canada, primarily with leave. We first deal with the specific rules attaching to each type of appeal; we then discuss the general principles applying to all of them.

2. TYPES OF APPEALS

(1) Appeals of Indictable Matters to the Court of Appeal

§18.4 The *Criminal Code* gives both the accused and the Crown the right to appeal decisions of the trial court in indictable matters to the provincial court of appeal. Under section 675 of the *Code*, a person who is convicted in proceedings by indictment[6] (whether tried in provincial or superior court) may appeal to the court of appeal against conviction on any ground of appeal involving: (*i*) a question of law alone; or (*ii*) a question of fact or a question of mixed law and fact, with leave of the court.

§18.5 Under section 686(1)(*a*) of the *Code*, an appeal against conviction may be allowed only on the basis that: (*i*) the verdict is unreasonable or cannot be supported by the evidence; (*ii*) an error of law was committed; or (*iii*) a miscarriage of justice occurred. A discussion of each of these grounds follows.

(a) Overturning a Conviction

(i) Unreasonable Verdict (Section 686(1)(a)(i))

§18.6 The test to be applied by the appellate court under section 686(1)(*a*)(i) of the *Code* has been established by the Supreme Court of Canada as whether "the verdict is one that a properly instructed jury acting judicially, could reasonably have rendered."[7] The test is equally applicable to a judge sitting at trial without a jury.[8] Where the verdict rests primarily on circumstantial evidence, Justice Doherty noted in *R. v. Mars*[9] that "the question becomes: could a trier-of-fact acting judicially be satisfied that the accused's guilt was the only reasonable conclusion available on the totality of the evidence?"[10] In considering whether a verdict is unreasonable, an appellate court is required to analyze and to some extent, reweigh the evidence adduced at trial. The court will do so through the "lens of judicial experience", which serves as an additional safeguard against unsafe

---

[6] It is the nature of the proceedings, not the nature of the conviction, which governs the procedure on appeal. Proceedings by way of indictment call for an appeal route to the court of appeal, even in situations where an accused is convicted of a summary conviction offence, but acquitted of an indictable offence that was tried together with the summary conviction offence: see *R. v. Yaworski*, [1959] M.J. No. 7, 124 C.C.C. 151 (Man. C.A.).

[7] *R. v. Yebes*, [1987] S.C.J. No. 51, [1987] 2 S.C.R. 168 at para. 16 (S.C.C.).

[8] *R. v. Biniaris*, [2000] S.C.J. No. 16, [2000] 1 S.C.R. 381 at para. 37 (S.C.C.).

[9] [2006] O.J. No. 472, 205 C.C.C. (3d) 376 (Ont. C.A.).

[10] *Ibid.*, at para. 4 (C.C.C.).

convictions.[11] The burden on the appellant in establishing an unreasonable verdict has been described as "high"[12] and "difficult".[13] Practically speaking, "at the end of the day this is a judgment call [by the court] and not a precise science. A subjective element is invariably involved in the global assessment of the case."[14]

(ii) Error of Law (Section 686(1)(a)(ii))

§18.7 The claim that the trial judge erred in law is the most common basis for appealing a conviction. Before the court of appeal will quash a conviction under section 686(1)(a)(ii) of the *Code*, three questions that must be answered in the appellant's favour are: (*i*) is there a "question of law"; (*ii*) was there a "wrong decision"; and (*iii*) should the curative proviso found in section 686(1)(b)(iii) be applied?[15]

§18.8 In *R. v. Shepherd*,[16] the Supreme Court of Canada reiterated that a question of law involves the application of a legal standard to the facts of the case.[17] Without comprising an exhaustive list of what constitutes a "question of law", typical examples include:

(*i*)   the admissibility of evidence;[18]

(*ii*) the interpretation of a statute;[19]

(*iii*) the sufficiency of a trial judge's reasons;[20]

(*iv*) the misapprehension of evidence;[21]

(*v*)   whether the facts as found by a trial judge amount at law to reasonable and probable grounds to make a breath demand;[22]

(*vi*) the mental state or condition that constitute a "disease of the mind";[23] and

(*vii*) a misdirection of law in charging the jury.[24]

§18.9 Not all errors of law, however, warrant appellate intervention. The court may resort to the curative proviso found in section 686(1)(b)(iii) of the *Code* to uphold the conviction despite finding an error in law if "it is of the opinion that

---

11   *R. v. Biniaris*, [2000] S.C.J. No. 16, [2000] 1 S.C.R. 381 at para. 40 (S.C.C.).

12   *R. v. Clark*, [2004] O.J. No. 1516 at para. 3 (Ont. C.A.).

13   *R. v. R. (M.)*, [2010] O.J. No. 1547 at para. 9 (Ont. C.A.).

14   *R. v. Sterling*, [1995] S.J. No. 612, 102 C.C.C. (3d) 481 at para. 295 (Sask. C.A.).

15   See Gil D. McKinnon, *The Criminal Lawyers' Guide to Appellate Court Practice* (Aurora, ON: Canada Law Book, 1997) at 47.

16   [2009] S.C.J. No. 35, [2009] 2 S.C.R. 527 (S.C.C.).

17   *Ibid.*, at para. 20 (S.C.R.).

18   See *R. v. B. (G.) (No. 3)*, [1990] S.C.J. No. 57, [1990] 2 S.C.R. 57 at 71 (S.C.C.).

19   *L. (H.) v. Canada (Attorney General)*, [2005] S.C.J. No. 24, [2005] 1 S.C.R. 401, 2005 SCC 25 at para. 57 (S.C.C.).

20   See *R. v. Sheppard*, [2002] S.C.J. No. 30, [2002] 1 S.C.R. 869 (S.C.C.); *R. v. M. (R.E.)*, [2008] S.C.J. No. 52, [2008] 3 S.C.R. 3 (S.C.C.).

21   See *R. v. Morrissey*, [1995] O.J. No. 639, 97 C.C.C. (3d) 193 (Ont. C.A.).

22   See *R. v. Shepherd*, [2009] S.C.J. No. 35, [2009] 2 S.C.R. 527 at para. 20 (S.C.C.).

23   See *R. v. Rabey*, [1977] O.J. No. 2356 (Ont. C.A.), affd [1980] S.C.J. No. 88 (S.C.C.).

24   See *R. v. Guyatt*, [1997] B.C.J. No. 2185, 119 C.C.C. (3d) 304 (B.C.C.A.).

no substantial wrong or miscarriage of justice has occurred." It is the Crown who bears the onus to demonstrate to the court that either: *(i)* the error was so harmless that it could not have affected the verdict; or *(ii)* that the error, albeit serious, did not result in a miscarriage of justice or a substantial wrong, because the case against the appellant was so overwhelming that a conviction would have been inevitable even if the error had not been committed.[25]

§18.10 The application of the curative proviso in Canadian law was poignantly described in the notorious serial murder case of Robert Pickton. Justice LeBel stated:

> Some errors may be so innocuous or so irrelevant to the questions at issue that there is little likelihood that they would have had any impact on the verdict. Other errors may be more serious, but the proviso will also apply because there is overwhelming evidence of the guilt of the accused and, on that evidence, a properly instructed jury would necessarily return a verdict of guilty .... In my view, this is the case in the instant appeal. As mentioned above, there were serious errors in relation to a key issue at trial, criminal participation in the offences, in both the instructions to the jury and in response to its question. Nevertheless, in order to assess the possible impact of these errors, the context of the trial as a whole must be kept in mind.
>
> The trial was all about the participation of Mr. Pickton in the murders of the six victims. I will not attempt to review here all of the evidence offered by the Crown during what was a very long trial. However, on a review of the record, in my opinion, the Crown presented compelling, overwhelming evidence of the participation of Mr. Pickton in the murders. From whichever perspective we consider the participation of Mr. Pickton, on the evidence, he was necessarily either a principal or an aider or abettor. It would surpass belief that a properly instructed jury would not have found him guilty of murder in the presence of such cogent evidence of his involvement. Indeed, this properly instructed jury would likely have convicted Mr. Pickton of first degree rather than second degree murder.[26]

An important procedural point relating to the curative proviso is that it is for the Crown to make a request of the court, either in its factum or in oral submissions, to consider applying section 686(1)(*b*)(iii). The court cannot apply the proviso on its own intitiative, that is *proprio motu.*[27]

(iii) Miscarriage of Justice (Section 686(1)(a)(iii))

§18.11 The reach of section 686(1)(*a*)(iii) goes beyond errors characterized as errors of law, fact, or mixed fact or law. Instead, "[a]ny error which occurs at

---

25   See *R. v. Jaw*, [2009] S.C.J. No. 42, [2009] 3 S.C.R. 26 (S.C.C.); *R. v. Trochym*, [2007] S.C.J. No. 6, [2007] 1 S.C.R. 239 at paras. 80-81 (S.C.C.); *R. v. Khan*, [2001] S.C.J. No. 83, [2001] 3 S.C.R. 823 (S.C.C.).

26   *R. v. Pickton*, [2010] S.C.J. No. 32, [2010] 2 S.C.R. 198 at paras. 85-87 (S.C.C.).

27   *R. v. McMaster*, [1996] S.C.J. No. 31, [1996] 1 S.C.R. 740 at para. 37 (S.C.C.); *R. v. Pétel*, [1994] S.C.J. No. 1, [1994] 1 S.C.R. 3 at 17 (S.C.C.).

trial that deprives the accused of [a fair trial] is a miscarriage of justice."[28] Judicial and Crown misconduct in the course of a trial will obviously jeopardize the fairness of a trial and would fall under the scope of section 686(1)(*a*)(iii). For example, the repetitive and improper cross-examination of the accused by the Crown,[29] or where a trial judge makes an express assessment of the accused's credibility during the course of the trial.[30] Two other claims commonly pursued within the concept of a miscarriage of justice relate to the competence of trial counsel[31] and challenging a guilty plea.[32] We deal with these claims in Parts 3(2) and 3(3), below.

(b) Available Remedies

§18.12 Where the court of appeal quashes a conviction under section 686(1)(*a*)(i) of the *Code* for unreasonableness, the court will enter an acquittal.[33] Where however, the appeal is allowed under section 686(1)(*a*)(ii) due to a legal error or under section 686(1)(*a*)(iii) for a miscarriage of justice, the customary order is for a new trial.[34] In dismissing an appeal under section 686(1)(*b*)(i), the court has the further power to substitute a guilty verdict on an included offence.[35] In doing so, the court can affirm the sentence passed by the trial court, impose a sentence on its own accord or remit the matter to the trial court for sentencing.[36]

(c) Crown Appeals

§18.13 Unique amongst common law countries is the fact that in Canada, the Crown has a right to appeal acquittals in indictable matters. However, that right is limited to questions of law alone.[37] Importantly, the Crown is not entitled to appeal from an "unreasonable acquittal".[38] The parameters of such appeals are further circumscribed by the heavy onus the Crown has to meet in order to obtain a new trial. The Crown must satisfy the appellate court that the verdict would not necessarily have been the same if no error had been made at trial. In *R. v. Morin*,[39] Justice Sopinka held:

> [T]he onus is a heavy one and ... the Crown must satisfy the court with a reasonable degree of certainty. An accused who has been acquitted once

---

28 *Per* McIntyre J.in *R. v. Fanjoy*, [1985] S.C.J. No. 55, 21 C.C.C. (3d) 312 at 317-18 (S.C.C.).
29 *Ibid.*
30 *R. v. Stewart*, [1991] O.J. No. 81, 62 C.C.C. (3d) 289 (Ont. C.A.).
31 *R. v. B. (G.D.)*, [2000] S.C.J. No. 22, [2000] 1 S.C.R. 520 (S.C.C.).
32 *R. v. Hoang*, [2004] A.J. No. 1555, 182 C.C.C. (3d) 69 (Alta. C.A.); *R. v. Nevin*, [2006] N.S.J. No. 235, 210 C.C.C. (3d) 81 (N.S.C.A.).
33 *Criminal Code*, s. 686(2)(*a*).
34 *Criminal Code*, s. 686(2)(*b*).
35 *Criminal Code*, s. 686(3).
36 *Criminal Code*, s. 686(3)(*a*) and (*b*).
37 *Criminal Code*, s. 676(1)(*a*).
38 See *R. v. B. (G.) [No. 3]*, [1990] S.C.J. No. 57, [1990] 2 S.C.R. 57 at 67-68 (S.C.C.); *R. v. Sunbeam Corp. (Canada) Ltd.*, [1969] S.C.J. No. 94, [1969] S.C.R. 221 at para. 31 (S.C.C.).
39 [1988] S.C.J. No. 80, [1988] 2 S.C.R. 345 (S.C.C.).

should not be sent back to be tried again unless it appears that the error at the first trial was such that there is a reasonable degree of certainty that the outcome may well have been affected by it. Any more stringent test would require an appellate court to predict with certainty what happened in the jury room. That it cannot do.[40]

§18.14 In *R. v. Graveline*,[41] Justice Fish observed that the Crown must "satisfy the appellate court that the error (or errors) of the trial judge might reasonably be thought, in the concrete reality of the case at hand, to have had a material bearing on the acquittal".[42]

(d)   Sentence Appeals

§18.15 Where an accused is convicted by a trial court in proceedings by indictment, he or she may appeal against the sentence imposed at trial.[43] While leave of the court is required to appeal sentence, the usual procedure by appellate courts is for the leave to appeal sentence to be argued at the same time as the sentence appeal proper.

§18.16 Under section 687 of the *Code*, a court of appeal has the power to vary a sentence on appeal. The reviewing court must, however, heed to the guiding principle of deference. As Justice Doherty noted in *R. v. Ramage*:[44]

> Sentencing is a fact-specific exercise of judicial discretion. It is anything but an exact science. In the vast majority of cases, there is no single sentence that is clearly preferable to all others. Instead, there is a range of reasonable options from which the trial judge must make his or her selection. That selection is driven by the judge's evaluation of the sentence that best reflects his or her assessment of the combined effect of the many variables inevitably at play when imposing a sentence. Absent the discipline of deference, sentence appeals would invite the appellate court to repeat the same exercise performed by the trial judge, with no realistic prospect that the appellate court would arrive at a more appropriate sentence. Appellate repetition of the exercise of judicial discretion by the trial judge, without any reason to think that the second effort will improve upon the results of the first, is a misuse of judicial resources. The exercise also delays the final resolution of the criminal process, without any countervailing benefit to the process.[45]

§18.17 Consequently, it has become a well established principle that an appellate court will not interfere with the sentence imposed unless the sentencing judge: *(i)* has made an error in principle; *(ii)* failed to consider a relevant factor

---

[40]   *Ibid.*, at para. 80 (S.C.R.). See also *R. v. Vézeau*, [1977] S.C.J. No. 71, [1977] 2 S.C.R. 277 at 292 (S.C.C.); *R. v. Evans*, [1993] S.C.J. No. 30, [1993] 2 S.C.R. 629 (S.C.C.).

[41]   [2006] S.C.J. No. 16, [2006] 1 S.C.R. 609 (S.C.C.).

[42]   *Ibid.*, at para. 14 (S.C.R.).

[43]   *Criminal Code*, s. 675(1)(*b*). For more extensive discussions of sentence appeals, see Clayton C. Ruby *et al.*, *Sentencing* (Markham: LexisNexis Canada, 2008), c. 4; Allan Manson, *The Law of Sentencing* (Toronto: Irwin Law, 2001), c. 12.

[44]   [2010] O.J. No. 2970, 2010 ONCA 488 (Ont. C.A.).

[45]   *Ibid.*, at para. 70 (ONCA).

or overemphasized appropriate factors; *(iii)* or has imposed a sentence that is demonstrably unfit.[46]

(e) Bail Pending Appeal

§18.18 Under section 679 of the *Code*, an appellant may apply to a court of appeal for judicial interim release pending the determination of his or her appeal or an application for leave to appeal to the Supreme Court of Canada. The application is heard by a single judge of the court. The applicant must establish, on a balance of probabilities, that: *(a)* the appeal or application for leave to appeal is not frivolous; *(b)* he or she will surrender into custody in accordance with the terms of the order; and *(c)* detention is not necessary in the public interest.[47]

§18.19 The first requirement, a lack of frivolousness, is a relatively low threshold. It has two aspects. An appeal may be considered frivolous if it is brought for some purpose other than succeeding on appeal or if it has no reasonable prospect of success.[48] With respect to this second requirement, it is only necessary for the applicant to show that "there is at least some arguable point to be made."[49] This same standard applies where the application is for bail pending the determination of a leave application to the Supreme Court of Canada.[50]

§18.20 The second requirement is concerned with whether an appellant poses a flight risk. Just like in the pre-trial bail context (see Chapter 6), roots in the community are key. A job, a residence and family and friends willing to act as sureties, all weigh in favour of release. In contrast, the absence of these things make continued detention far more probable. Of course, an important variable will often be the length of the sentence the appellant is facing should the appeal

---

[46] See *R. v. M. (L.)*, [2008] S.C.J. No. 31, [2008] 2 S.C.R. 163 at para. 14 (S.C.C.); *R. v. W.(L.F.)*, [2000] S.C.J. No. 7, [2000] 1 S.C.R. 132 at para. 25 (S.C.C.); *R. v. W. (G.)*, [1999] S.C.J. No. 37, [1999] 3 S.C.R. 597 at para. 19 (S.C.C.); *R. v. McDonnell*, [1997] S.C.J. No. 42, [1997] 1 S.C.R. 948 at paras. 15-17 (S.C.C.); *R. v. M. (C.A.)*, [1996] S.C.J. No. 28, [1996] 1 S.C.R. 500 at para. 90 (S.C.C.); *R. v. Shropshire*, [1995] S.C.J. No. 52, [1995] 4 S.C.R. 227 at paras. 46-50 (S.C.C.).

[47] *Criminal Code*, s. 679(3). See *R. v. Ponak; R. v. Gunn*, [1972] B.C.J. No. 621, [1972] 4 W.W.R. 316 at 317-18 (B.C.C.A.) (holding that the burden is on the applicant to establish all three of these preconditions on a balance of probabilities).

[48] *R. v. McPherson*, [1999] B.C.J. No. 2489, 140 C.C.C. (3d) 316 at 318-19 (B.C.C.A.). See also *R. v. Ilina*, [2003] M.J. No. 41, 172 C.C.C. (3d) 568 at para. 7 (Man. C.A.).

[49] *R. v. Davison*, [1974] O.J. No. 2145, 20 C.C.C. (2d) 422 at 423 (Ont. H.C.J.). See also *R. v. Baltovich*, [1993] O.J. No. 2118, 10 O.R. (3d) 737 at 738 (Ont. C.A.); *R. v. Parsons*, [1994] N.J. No. 72, 30 C.R. (4th) 169 at 173 (Nfld. C.A.); *R. v. Hanna*, [1991] B.C.J. No. 2551, 3 B.C.A.C. 57 at 59 (B.C.C.A.); *R. v. Mian*, [1996] N.S.J. No. 95, 148 N.S.R. (2d) 155 at 157 (N.S.C.A.). See *R. v. P. (D.M.)*, [1997] A.J. No. 1151, 121 C.C.C. (3d) 444 at 447 (Alta. C.A.) ("the applicant need only show that his or her ground of appeal would not necessarily fail"). See also *R. v. McPherson*, [1999] B.C.J. No. 2489, 140 C.C.C. (3d) 316 at 319 (B.C.C.A.) ("that the appeal has so little chance of success that no one could possibly believe that it could succeed").

[50] See *R. v. Ilina*, [2003] M.J. No. 41, 172 C.C.C. (3d) 568 (Man. C.A.). See also *France v. Ouzghar*, [2009] O.J. No. 573, 95 O.R. (3d) 187 at para. 13 (Ont. C.A.), in arriving at this same conclusion, Doherty J. indicated: "I do not think that an applicant who has shown himself otherwise entitled to bail should be held in custody based on my speculative and somewhat uninformed assessment of the likelihood of the applicant obtaining leave to appeal."

prove unsuccessful. For example, where an appeal does not seem especially strong and life imprisonment will be the outcome if it is dismissed, such considerations alone may be sufficient to justify a denial of bail pending appeal.[51]

§18.21 The third requirement, the "public interest" consideration, is less straightforward. Although that term has been characterized as unconstitutionally vague in the context of pre-trial bail,[52] its use in section 679(3)(*c*) has been specifically upheld as constitutional.[53] The cases emphasize the importance of two variables: protection of the public and public confidence in the administration of justice.[54] So, for example, courts have concluded that detention pending appeal will be necessary where an appellant has been convicted of a serious violent crime and the grounds of appeal are not especially strong. In contrast, the public interest will favour release where the grounds of appeal have considerable merit and the delay until an appeal will be heard is inordinate.[55] In short, as Justice Ryan explained on behalf of the British Columbia Court of Appeal, "public interest" under section 679(3) encompasses many variables:

> Depending on the demonstrated strength of the grounds, other factors, such as the circumstances of the offence — for example, premeditated violence — and, inordinate delay will be matters to weigh in the balance. The essential question, however, will be whether the appellant has been able to establish that enforceability is outweighed by reviewability.[56]

---

[51]	See *e.g.*, *R. v. Baltovich*, [1993] O.J. No. 2118, 10 O.R. (3d) 737 (Ont. C.A.).

[52]	See *R. v. Morales*, [1992] S.C.J. No. 98, [1992] 3 S.C.R. 711 (S.C.C.), which is discussed in detail in Chapter 6.

[53]	See *R. v. Farinacci*, [1993] O.J. No. 2627, 86 C.C.C. (3d) 32 (Ont. C.A.), holding that s. 11(*e*) of the *Charter* does not apply in this context as a person convicted and sentenced is no longer "charged with an offence" under s. 11. In addition, rejecting that the term, as used in this context, is unconstitutionally vague under s. 7.

[54]	*Ibid.*, at 47 (C.C.C.). See also *R. v. Rhyason*, [2006] A.J. No. 376, 208 C.C.C. (3d) 193 at para. 11 (Alta. C.A.).

[55]	See *R. v. Demyen*, [1975] S.J. No. 402, 26 C.C.C. (2d) 324 at 326 (Sask. C.A.), suggesting that in assessing the "public interest", public concern is a key consideration, such that where an individual has been convicted of a serious violent crime this criterion assumes added weight. See also *R. v. Pabani*, [1991] O.J. No. 3462, 10 C.R. (4th) 381 at 383-84 (Ont. C.A.), pointing to these same concerns in denying bail pending appeal to the appellant who had been convicted of a brutal murder. But noting that: "There will no doubt be cases where the hearing of an appeal will be so long delayed and the probability of success on the appeal so strong that it would be contrary to the public interest to refuse a release and a fortiori an applicant's detention would not be necessary in the public interest. A strong probability of success on the appeal may be sufficient grounds in itself to establish that an appellant's detention is not necessary in the public interest."
See also *R. v. Rhyason*, [2006] A.J. No. 376, 208 C.C.C. (3d) 193 at paras. 15-18 (Alta. C.A.); *R. v. Baltovich*, [2000] O.J. No. 987, 144 C.C.C. (3d) 233 at para. 20 (Ont. C.A.); *R. v. Parsons*, [1994] N.J. No. 72, 30 C.R. (4th) 169 at 186-87 (Nfld. C.A.); *R. v. Morin*, [1993] O.J. No. 267, 19 C.R. (4th) 398 (Ont. C.A.) (ordering the release of an appellant convicted of first degree murder).

[56]	*R. v. Mapara*, [2001] B.C.J. No. 1774, 158 C.C.C. (3d) 312 at para. 36 (B.C.C.A.). See also *R. v. Farinacci*, [1993] O.J. No. 2627, 86 C.C.C. (3d) 32 at 47-48 (Ont. C.A.) ("The concerns reflecting public interest, as expressed in the case law, relate both to the protection and safety of the public and to the need to maintain a balance between the competing dictates of enforceability and reviewability .... Ideally, judgments should be reviewed before they have been enforced.

§18.22 Where an individual appeals only his or her sentence, the test for release is more onerous. The applicant is required to establish that: *(a)* the appeal has sufficient merit that, in the circumstances, it would cause unnecessary hardship if he or she were detained in custody; *(b)* he or she will surrender into custody in accordance with the terms of the order; and *(c)* detention is not necessary in the public interest. In addition, a judge must first hear and determine the application for leave to appeal the sentence before deciding on bail.[57]

§18.23 Almost all applications for bail pending appeal will be brought after sentencing. However, there is a very limited jurisdiction for an appellate court to release an individual from custody upon being convicted but while waiting to be sentenced.[58] Some of the factors to be considered are whether it is clear the appeal will be successful; whether there is overwhelming hardship in being detained; and whether there is a lengthy delay between conviction and sentencing.[59]

§18.24 Successive applications under section 679 for bail pending appeal are generally not permitted. A further application is only allowed where there has been a *material* change in circumstances since the original application was brought. That is, a change that could affect the court's assessment of one or more of the statutory factors.[60] Otherwise, further review requires an application to the court, a step that depends upon the applicant first obtaining a direction from the chief justice or acting chief justice of the court of appeal.[61] Such a review operates like an appeal rather than a *de novo* hearing, meaning that the panel will only interfere if the original justice failed to exercise his or her discretion judicially.[62]

§18.25 Finally, where an appeal is allowed and a new trial is ordered, either by a court of appeal or the Supreme Court of Canada, a judge of the court of appeal has the authority to release an accused person pending his or her new trial. The criteria that govern in such situations (where an accused is once again presumed to be innocent) are the same factors that control with respect to bail in the

---

When this is not possible, an interim regime may need to be put in place which must be sensitive to a multitude of factors including the anticipated time required for the appeal to be decided and the possibility of irreparable and unjustifiable harm being done in the interval.").

[57] *Criminal Code*, s. 679(4).

[58] See *R. v. Morris*, [1985] O.J. No. 170, 21 C.C.C. (3d) 242 at 244 (Ont. C.A.); *R. v. H. (W. A.)*, [1998] N.S.J. No. 313 (N.S.C.A.).

[59] See Gary T. Trotter, *The Law of Bail in Canada*, 2d ed. (Toronto: Carswell, 1999) at 373.

[60] See *R. v. Daniels*, [1997] O.J. No. 4023, 119 C.C.C. (3d) 413 (Ont.C.A.); *R. v. Baltovich*, [2000] O.J. No. 987, 144 C.C.C. (3d) 233 (Ont. C.A.).

[61] *Criminal Code*, s. 680. See *R. v. Baltovich*, [2000] O.J. No. 987, 144 C.C.C. (3d) 233 at 236 (Ont. C.A.) (noting that applications to the chief justice or acting chief justice "are relatively rare and are rarely granted").

[62] *R. v. Perron*, [1989] J.Q. no 852, 51 C.C.C. (3d) 518 (Que. C.A.) at 541-42. See also *R. v. West*, [1972] O.J. No. 1962, 20 C.R.N.S. 15 (Ont. C.A.); *R. v. Smith*, [1973] N.B.J. No. 76, 13 C.C.C. (2d) 374 (N.B.C.A.); *R. v. Desjarlais*, [1984] M.J. No. 173, 14 C.C.C. (3d) 77 (Man. C.A.); *R. v. Parsons*, [1994] N.J. No. 97, 30 C.R. (4th) 189 (Nfld. C.A.).

pre-trial context.[63] Once such an accused is back before the trial court, however, a judge in that court also enjoys jurisdiction to deal with the question of bail.[64]

(f)   Fresh Evidence

§18.26 Section 683(1) of the *Code* permits a court of appeal to receive fresh evidence "where it considers it in the interests of justice." Fresh evidence tendered pursuant to section 683(1) generally falls under two categories. The first deals with proposed evidence that goes to challenge an issue decided at trial.[65] The second type deals with matters directed at the regularity of the process[66] or to a request for an original remedy in the appellate court.[67]

§18.27 With respect to the first category of proposed fresh evidence, the preconditions for its admission were established by the Supreme Court of Canada in *R. v. Palmer*[68] as follows:

> (1) The evidence should generally not be admitted if, by due diligence, it could have been adduced at trial provided that this general principle will not be applied as strictly in a criminal case as in civil cases. (2) The evidence must be relevant in the sense that it bears upon a decisive or potentially decisive issue in the trial. (3) The evidence must be credible in the sense that it is reasonably capable of belief. (4) It must be such that if believed it could reasonably, when taken with the other evidence adduced at trial, be expected to have affected the result.[69]

An identical test was adapted by the Supreme Court in *R. v. Lévesque*[70] in the context of fresh evidence applications on sentence appeals.

§18.28 Under the *Palmer* test, the factor of due diligence plays a prominent role since the criterion "is designed to preserve the integrity of the process" and "[w]ere it otherwise, the finality of the trial process would be lost and cases would be retried on appeal whenever more evidence was secured by a party prior to the hearing of the appeal."[71] Nevertheless, the due diligence criterion may be relaxed "[i]f the evidence is compelling and the interests of justice

---

[63]   *Criminal Code*, s. 679(7.1), which specifically makes s. 515 or s. 522 applicable in such circumstances. Bail at the pre-trial stage is explained in detail in Chapter 6.

[64]   See *R. v. Barbeau*, [1998] Q.J. No. 3766, 131 C.C.C. (3d) 350 at 351-52 (Que. C.A.). See also *R. v. F. (D.P.)*, [1999] N.J. No. 353, 141 C.C.C. (3d) 391 (Nfld. C.A.).

[65]   For example, the credibility of a witness (see *R. v. Hurley*, [2010] S.C.J. No. 18, [2010] 1 S.C.R. 637, 2010 SCC 18 (S.C.C.), where the new evidence showing the accused's DNA on three items in the hotel room in which the murder was committed had an impact on the jury's assessment of the credibility of a Crown witness).

[66]   For example, claims of ineffective assistance of counsel or involuntary guilty pleas.

[67]   For example, a stay of proceedings due to an abuse of process. See *United States of America v. Shulman*, [2001] S.C.J. No. 18, [2001] 1 S.C.R. 616 at 636 (S.C.C.), where fresh evidence of threats made by a U.S. prosecutor was admitted and the extradition proceedings were stayed.

[68]   [1979] S.C.J. No. 126, [1980] 1 S.C.R. 759 (S.C.C.).

[69]   *Ibid.*, at 775 (S.C.R.).

[70]   [2000] S.C.J. No. 47, [2000] 2 S.C.R. 487 at para. 35 (S.C.C.).

[71]   *R. v. M. (P.S.)*, [1992] O.J. No. 2410, 77 C.C.C. (3d) 402 at 411 (Ont. C.A.).

require that it be admitted."[72] It makes sense as a matter of fairness that the due diligence criterion yield where its rigid application might lead to a miscarriage of justice.[73]

§18.29 As for the second type of proposed fresh evidence that goes to the integrity of the trial process, the requirements for admission are more lax than set out in *Palmer*.[74] In *R. v. Truscott*,[75] the Ontario Court of Appeal noted:

> The second category of fresh evidence that may be tendered on appeal is not directed at re-litigating factual findings made at trial, but instead is directed at the fairness of the process that produced those findings. Where an appellant proffers this kind of evidence on appeal, he or she attempts to demonstrate that something happened in the trial process that materially interfered with his or her ability to make full answer and defence. An appellant claims that the verdict is rendered unreliable because the unfairness of the process denied the appellant the opportunity to fully and effectively present a defence and to challenge the Crown's case. When this kind of fresh evidence is received and acted on in the court of appeal, the conviction is quashed as a miscarriage of justice. The miscarriage of justice lies in the unreliability of a verdict produced by a fatally flawed process.[76]

§18.30 The decision to admit fresh evidence under this category will depend on the context and nature of the issue raised. For example, where an appellant alleges that he or she received ineffective assistance by trial counsel, the fresh evidence will be received where it demonstrates that the conduct of trial counsel fell below the standard of reasonable professional judgment and a miscarriage of justice resulted.[77]

(g) Appeals Relating to Extraordinary Remedies

§18.31 Section 784(1) of the *Code* provides an avenue to appeal to the court of appeal a decision granting or refusing the relief sought in proceedings by way of *mandamus*, *certiorari* or prohibition. Appeals under this section most often involve *certiorari* challenges to decisions of a preliminary hearing judge regarding committal for trial. The scope of review on *certiorari* is limited to jurisdictional

---

[72] See *R. v. Warsing*, [1998] S.C.J. No. 91, [1998] 3 S.C.R. 579 at para. 51 (S.C.C.); *R. v. Lévesque*, [2000] S.C.J. No. 47, [2000] 2 S.C.R. 487 at para. 15 (S.C.C.).

[73] See *R. v. Maciel*, [2007] O.J. No. 1034, 219 C.C.C. (3d) 516 at para. 47 (Ont. C.A.), leave to appeal refused [2007] S.C.C.A. No. 258 (S.C.C.). However, see *contra*, *R. v. Knight*, [2010] A.J. No. 9, 2010 ABCA 2 at para. 8 (Alta. C.A.) (for precedential reasons "[w]e cannot follow any suggestion ... in *R. v. Maciel*...that evidence showing innocence must be received for the first time on appeal despite non-compliance with some or all of the usual tests in *R. v. Palmer*...").

[74] See *R. v. Rajaeefard*, [1996] O.J. No. 108, 104 C.C.C. (3d) 225 (Ont. C.A.).

[75] [2007] O.J. No. 3221, 225 C.C.C. (3d) 321 (Ont. C.A.).

[76] *Ibid.*, at para. 85 (C.C.C.).

[77] See generally, *R. v. B. (G.D.)*, [2000] S.C.J. No. 22, [2000] 1 S.C.R. 520 (S.C.C.). See also *R. v. W. (W.)*, [1995] O.J. No. 2383, 100 C.C.C. (3d) 225 at 232-33 (Ont. C.A.); *R. v. Joanisse*, [1995] O.J. No. 2883, 102 C.C.C. (3d) 35 at 430-44 (Ont. C.A.); *R. v. McKellar*, [1994] O.J. No. 2046, 19 O.R. (3d) 796 at para. 12 (Ont. C.A.).

error. Thus, a reviewing court will overturn a committal for trial decision only where the preliminary hearing judge acts in excess of its assigned statutory jurisdiction or has acted in breach of the principles of natural justice. For example, a preliminary hearing judge commits a jurisdictional error by committing a defendant for trial under section 548(1)(*a*) of the *Code* when an essential element of the offence is not made out.[78] The test on review of a committal for trial was articulated by Justice Martin in *R. v. Tuske*[79] as follows:

> [T]he reviewing court is not empowered to determine whether in its opinion there is any evidence upon which a properly instructed jury acting judicially could convict, but is confined to considering whether there is any evidence before the committing justice upon which acting judicially he could form an opinion that the evidence is sufficient to put the accused on trial.[80]

The reviewing court will not interfere merely because the preliminary hearing judge committed an error of law or reached a conclusion different than a reviewing court would have reached.[81]

(2) Summary Conviction Appeals

(a) *Appeals to the Summary Conviction Appeal Court*

§18.32 Summary conviction appeals are governed by the provisions of Part XXVII of the *Criminal Code*. A summary conviction appeal can be brought either under section 813 or section 830.

§18.33 Appeals under section 813 are heard by a provincial superior court. Both the accused and the Crown can appeal as of right pursuant to this section. The accused may appeal against conviction, sentence or a verdict of unfit to stand trial or not criminally responsible on account of mental disorder.[82] The Crown may appeal from an order that stays proceedings on an information or dismisses an information, against sentence, or against a verdict of not criminally responsible on account of mental disorder or unfit to stand trial.[83] Unlike in indictable matters, the Crown is not limited under section 813 to questions of law alone, and may appeal on questions of fact.[84] Subsection 822(1) of the *Code* imports sections 683 to 689 of the *Code* in dealing with appeals under section 813. Therefore, a summary conviction appeal court will only interfere with a trial judge's decision where the conviction is unreasonable or cannot be supported by

---

[78] See *R. v. Skogman*, [1984] S.C.J. No. 32, 13 C.C.C. (3d) 161 at 170-71 (S.C.C.); *R. v. Dubois*, [1986] S.C.J. No. 21, 25 C.C.C. (3d) 221 at 229 (S.C.C.).

[79] [1978] O.J. No. 1253 (Ont. C.A.).

[80] *Ibid.*, at para. 3.

[81] See *R. v. Russell*, [2001] S.C.J. No. 53, [2001] 2 S.C.R. 804 at para. 19 (S.C.C.).

[82] *Criminal Code*, s. 813(*a*).

[83] *Criminal Code*, s. 813(*b*).

[84] *R. v. Wilke*, [1980] O.J. No. 1417, 56 C.C.C. (2d) 61 at 64 (Ont. C.A.), affd [1981] O.J. No. 3277 (Ont. Dist. Ct.); *R. v. Gillis*, [1981] N.S.J. No. 368, 60 C.C.C. (2d) 169 (N.S.C.A.).

the evidence;[85] where there is an error of law;[86] or there has been a miscarriage of justice.[87] As with indictable appeals, the summary conviction appeal court may dismiss the appeal, allow the appeal or set aside the verdict and order a new trial.[88]

§18.34 The second mode of summary conviction appeals set out in Part XXVII of the *Code* is titled "Summary Appeal on Transcript or Agreed Statement of Facts" and encompasses sections 829 to 838. This mode allows for a more streamlined appeal that permits an agreed statement of facts to be filed in lieu of a trial transcript.[89] However, in proceeding under section 830, the accused must be prepared to extinguish his or her right to challenge questions of fact or the fitness of sentence.[90] Appeals under section 830 are heard by the "superior court of criminal jurisdiction" as defined by section 2 of the *Code*.[91] Subsection 830(1) permits the accused or the Crown to appeal against "a conviction, judgment, verdict of acquittal or verdict of not criminally responsible on account of mental disorder or of unfit to stand trial or other final order or determination of a summary conviction court" on the basis of an error of law; an excess of jurisdiction; or a refusal or failure to exercise jurisdiction. Pursuant to section 834, the summary conviction appeal court may affirm, reverse or modify the conviction, judgment, verdict or other final order or determination; or remit the matter to the summary conviction court judge with the opinion of the appeal court; and may make any other order it considers proper.

(b) Appeal from Summary Conviction Appeal

§18.35 Pursuant to section 839 of the *Code*, an appeal lies to a court of appeal from a summary conviction appeal court on a question of law alone. Leave of the appeal court however, is required. This leave is granted sparingly, at least in Ontario,[92] due to the test established in *R. v. R. (R.)*.[93] In that case, Justice Doherty observed that "[n]ot all questions of law merit a second appeal"[94] and detailed the two categories of cases for which leave to appeal would be appropriate: *(i)* the proposed question of law has significance to the administration of justice beyond the four corners of the case; and *(ii)* where there appears to be a "clear" error even if it cannot be said that the error has significance to the administration of justice beyond the specific case.[95]

---

85   *Criminal Code*, s. 686(1)(*a*)(i).
86   *Criminal Code*, s. 686(1)(*a*)(ii).
87   *Criminal Code*, s. 686(1)(*a*)(iii).
88   *Criminal Code*, s. 686(4).
89   *Criminal Code*, s. 830(2).
90   *Criminal Code*, s. 836.
91   In most instances, either the provincial superior court or the provincial appeal court.
92   Although there appears to be a similar movement afoot in other provinces. See *R. v. Harper*, [2008] A.J. No. 1045 (Alta. C.A.); *R. v. Snow*, [2008] M.J. No. 315 at para. 17 (Man. C.A.).
93   [2008] O.J. No. 2468, 234 C.C.C. (3d) 463 at para. 32 (Ont. C.A.).
94   *Ibid.*, at para. 24 (C.C.C.).
95   *Ibid.*, at para. 32 (C.C.C.).

(3) Appeals to the Supreme Court of Canada

§18.36 The last available stop on the appellate ladder is the Supreme Court of Canada. Getting there is not an easy journey. Careful attention must be made of the practice and procedures set out in the *Supreme Court Act*[96] and the *Rules of the Supreme Court of Canada*.[97] Even after navigating the procedural obstacles, the chances of being granted leave to appeal has hovered around 10 per cent over the last decade.[98]

§18.37 An individual's right to appeal to the Supreme Court of Canada against conviction or a reversal of an acquittal is governed by section 691 of the *Code* and is restricted to questions of law. An appeal lies as of right where a court of appeal affirms a conviction but a judge of the court dissents on any question of law,[99] where the court of appeal sets aside an acquittal and either enters a verdict of guilty[100] or if a judge of the court dissents on any question of law.[101] Otherwise, leave is required.[102]

§18.38 The Crown may appeal to the Supreme Court of Canada against a successful appeal by an accused person;[103] an unsuccessful crown appeal against acquittal;[104] or the quashing or staying of an indictment.[105] Where a judge of the court of appeal dissents on a question of law in any of the above situations, the Crown may appeal as of right.[106]

§18.39 In situations where the Supreme Court's jurisdiction is not derived from any specific right of appeal found in the *Code*, section 40 of the *Supreme Court Act* governs. The section allows the Court to serve as a "general court of appeal for Canada", stating:

> 40(1) Subject to subsection (3), an appeal lies to the Supreme Court from any final or other judgment of the Federal Court of Appeal or of the highest court of final resort in a province, or a judge thereof, in which judgment can be had in the particular case sought to be appealed to the Supreme Court, whether or not leave to appeal to the Supreme Court has been refused by any other court, where, with respect to the particular case sought to be appealed, the Supreme Court is of the opinion that any question involved therein is, by reason of its public importance or the importance of any issue of law or any issue of mixed law and fact involved in that question, one that ought to be decided by the Supreme Court or is, for any other reason, of

---

[96]   R.S.C. 1985, c. S-26.
[97]   SOR/2002-156, as amended by SOR/2006-203.
[98]   See Bulletin of Proceedings: Special Edition — Supreme Court of Canada, Statistics 2000 to 2010 (<http://www.scc-csc.gc.ca/stat/pdf/doc-eng.pdf>) at 4.
[99]   *Criminal Code*, s. 691(1)(*a*).
[100]   *Criminal Code*, s. 691(2)(*b*).
[101]   *Criminal Code*, s. 691(2)(*a*).
[102]   *Criminal Code*, ss. 691(1)(*b*) and 691(2)(*c*).
[103]   *Criminal Code*, s. 675.
[104]   *Criminal Code*, s. 676(1)(*a*).
[105]   *Criminal Code*, s. 676(1)(*b*) and (*c*).
[106]   *Criminal Code*, s. 693(1)(*a*).

such a nature or significance as to warrant decision by it, and leave to appeal from that judgment is accordingly granted by the Supreme Court.

. . .

(3) No appeal to the Court lies under this section from the judgment of any court acquitting or convicting or setting aside or affirming a conviction or acquittal of an indictable offence or, except in respect of a question of law or jurisdiction, of an offence other than an indictable offence.

§18.40 The Supreme Court has taken a purposive approach to section 40, and unless specifically barred from entertaining an appeal by section 40(3), the Court will "fill the void" and expand the breadth of its authority to grant leave to hear any appeal from the decision of any "court of final resort".[107] Appeals of sentence and challenges to interlocutory orders are routinely pursued under section 40(1). The prospect of obtaining leave to appeal in the latter is rather bleak. As Justice McIntyre observed in *R. v. Mills*,[108] "It has long been a settled principle that all criminal appeals are statutory and that there should be no interlocutory appeals in criminal matters."[109] However, this rule is not absolute. For example, the Court has established that a third party can seek leave to appeal pursuant to section 40 of a trial judge's interlocutory order for the production of private records in a sexual assault criminal proceeding,[110] a publication ban ruling[111] or a ruling denying the quashing of a witness subpoena.[112]

§18.41 Under section 40(1), the Court's jurisdiction is confined to grant leave only to those cases that are of sufficient public importance. Justice Dickson (as he then was) stated in *R. v. Gardiner*:[113]

> The function of this Court is ... to settle questions of law of national importance in the interests of promoting uniformity in the application of the law across the country, especially with respect to matters of federal competence. To decline jurisdiction is to renounce the paramount responsibility of an ultimate appellate court with national authority.[114]

Unfortunately, since the Court does not provide reasons for either granting or denying leave, no clear guidelines exist in defining "public importance".

---

[107] *R. v. Mentuck*, [2001] S.C.J. No. 73, [2001] 3 S.C.R. 442 at para. 20 (S.C.C.); see also *R. v. Shea*, [2010] S.C.J. No. 26, [2010] 2 S.C.R. 17, 2010 SCC 26 (S.C.C.).

[108] [1986] S.C.J. No. 39, [1986] 1 S.C.R. 863 (S.C.C.).

[109] *Ibid.*, at para. 272 (S.C.C.).

[110] *A. (L.L.) v. B. (A.)*, [1995] S.C.J. No. 102, [1995] 4 S.C.R. 536 (S.C.C.).

[111] See *Dagenais v. Canadian Broadcasting Corp.*, [1994] S.C.J. No. 104, [1994] 3 S.C.R. 835 (S.C.C.); *R. v. Adams*, [1995] S.C.J. No. 105, [1995] 4 S.C.R. 707 (S.C.C.).

[112] *R. v. Primeau*, [1995] S.C.J. No. 33, [1995] 2 S.C.R. 60 (S.C.C.); *R. v. Jobin*, [1995] S.C.J. No. 31, [1995] 2 S.C.R. 78 (S.C.C.).

[113] [1982] S.C.J. No. 71, [1982] 2 S.C.R. 368 (S.C.C.).

[114] *Ibid.*, at 397 (S.C.R.). Although it is important to note that while not "of national importance" in a strict sense, the Supreme Court does also deal with cases arising from Quebec's civil law.

3.   GENERAL PRINCIPLES

(1)   Standard of Review

§18.42 The standard of review undertaken by appellate courts varies depending on whether the issue involves a question of fact or law. As will be further discussed below, for questions of fact, the standard of review is that of "palpable and overriding error".[115] Questions of law in contrast, require a standard of correctness.[116] In particular, the application of a legal standard to the facts of the case is a mixed question of law and fact, thus engaging a standard of correctness.[117] However, it is important to note that the Supreme Court appears to have adopted a somewhat modified test in reviewing a trial judge's ruling with respect to the exclusion of evidence pursuant to section 24(2) of the *Charter*. In *R. v. Law*,[118] the Court held that "[w]hile the decision to exclude must be a reasonable one, a reviewing court will not interfere with a trial judge's conclusions on section 24(2) absent an 'apparent error as to the applicable principles or rules of law' or an 'unreasonable finding'...".[119]

(a)   Attacking Findings of Fact

§18.43 The findings of facts made by a trial judge attract an almost impenetrable degree of deference. In *Housen v. Nikolaisen*,[120] the Supreme Court held:

> ... [I]t is not the role of appellate courts to second-guess the weight to be assigned to the various items of evidence. If there is no palpable and overriding error with respect to the underlying facts that the trial judge relies on to draw the inference, then it is only where the inference-drawing process itself is palpably in error that an appellate court can interfere with the factual conclusion ....
>
> ... The essential point is that making a factual conclusion, of any kind, is inextricably linked with assigning weight to evidence, and thus attracts a deferential standard of review."[121]

§18.44 Findings based on a misapprehension of evidence and findings based on speculation rather than inference are examples of "palpable" errors.[122] To meet

---

[115] See *Housen v. Nikolaisen*, [2002] S.C.J. No. 31, [2002] 2 S.C.R. 235 at para. 21 (S.C.C.); *R. v. Shepherd*, [2009] S.C.J. No. 35, [2009] 2 S.C.R. 527 at para. 18 (S.C.C.).

[116] *R. v. Shepherd*, [2009] S.C.J. No. 35, [2009] 2 S.C.R. 527 at para. 18 (S.C.C.).

[117] For example, a trial judge's ruling as to whether the facts are sufficient, at law, to constitute reasonable and probable grounds to make a breath demand (see *R. v. Shepherd*, [2009] S.C.J. No. 35, [2009] 2 S.C.R. (S.C.C.)); a trial judge's ruling as to whether a confession was voluntary (see *R. v. Oickle*, [2000] S.C.J. No. 38, [2000] 2 S.C.R. 3 at para. 22 (S.C.C.)); and a review of a wiretap authorization (see *R. v. Araujo*, [2000] S.C.J. No. 65, [2000] 2 S.C.R. 992 at para. 18 (S.C.C.)).

[118] [2002] S.C.J. No. 10, [2002] 1 S.C.R. 227, 2002 SCC 10 (S.C.C.).

[119] *Ibid.*, at para. 32 (S.C.R.). See also *R. v. Buhay*, [2003] S.C.J. No. 30, [2003] 1 S.C.R. 631 at paras. 44-45 (S.C.C.).

[120] [2002] S.C.J. No. 31, [2002] 2 S.C.R. 235 (S.C.C.).

[121] *Ibid.*, at paras. 23-24 (S.C.R.).

the "overriding" standard, an appellant would have to demonstrate that the error "goes to the root of the challenged finding of fact such that the fact cannot safely stand in the face of that error".[123]

(b) *Attacking Credibility*

§18.45 Courts have long been weary to interfere with convictions resting upon a trier of fact's assessment of credibility. This is understandable in light of the trial judge or jury's advantageous position in assessing the credibility of a witness or accused who testifies before them in court. A lifeless transcript provides little opportunity for an appellate court to evaluate the appearance and manner in which the witness testified. Nevertheless, section 686(1)(*a*)(i) of the *Code* grants the appellate court the power to overturn a conviction where the assessment of credibility made at trial is not supported by the evidence. Justice Sopinka noted in *R. v. Burke*:[124]

> I acknowledge that this is a power which an appellate court will exercise sparingly. This is not to say that an appellate court should shrink from exercising the power when, after carrying out its statutory duty, it concludes that the conviction rests on shaky ground and that it would be unsafe to maintain it. In conferring this power on appellate courts to be applied only in appeals by the accused, it was intended as an additional and salutary safeguard against the conviction of the innocent.[125]

Importantly, even with respect to trials free of legal error or in the face of some evidence inculpating the defendant, appellate intervention may be necessary to avoid an injustice.[126]

---

[122] *Waxman v. Waxman*, [2004] O.J. No. 1765 at para. 296 (Ont. C.A.), leave to appeal refused [2004] S.C.C.A. No. 291 (S.C.C.), reconsideration allowed [2004] O.J. No. 6013 (Ont. C.A.).

[123] *Ibid.*, at para. 297.

[124] [1996] S.C.J. No. 27, 105 C.C.C. (3d) 205 (S.C.C.).

[125] *Ibid.*, at paras. 4-7 (S.C.C.); see also *R. v. W. (R.)*, [1992] S.C.J. No. 56, [1992] 2 S.C.R. 122 at 131-32 (S.C.C.).

[126] See *R. v. G. (A.)*, [1998] O.J. No. 4031, 130 C.C.C. (3d) 30 at paras. 15 and 19 (Ont. C.A.), affd [2000] S.C.J. No. 18 (S.C.C.); *R. v. Tat*, [1997] O.J. No. 3579, 117 C.C.C. (3d) 481 at 515 (Ont. C.A.); *R. v. Malcolm*, [1993] O.J. No. 967, 81 C.C.C. (3d) 196 (Ont. C.A.); *R. v. Stewart*, [1994] O.J. No. 811, 18 O.R. (3d) 509 (Ont. C.A.), leave to appeal refused [1994] S.C.C.A. No. 290 (S.C.C.). As Carthy J. (dissenting, but not on this point) warned in *R. v. Francois*, [1993] O.J. No. 1419, 82 C.C.C. (3d) 441 at para. 35 (Ont. C.A.), affd [1994] S.C.J. No. 66 (S.C.C.): "The appellant urges that in our reassessment of the evidence, we should not seek support for the verdict under appeal from the fact that it was open to the jury to believe the complainant and she was believed; that is always the case when unreasonable verdict is argued in a case depending upon findings of credibility. I accept that and direct my mind to the evidence itself, with all of its frailties, for a determination of whether another person or group of persons, having the advantage of seeing and hearing the evidence, could be considered unreasonable in not having a reasonable doubt as to the guilt of the appellant."

(2)　Ineffective Assistance of Counsel

§18.46 An accused person who is represented by counsel at trial is entitled to receive the effective assistance of counsel. That entitlement has common law and statutory roots. As Justice Major noted in *R. v. B. (G.D.)*,[127] "While the early history of the common law shows that society had little interest in permitting anyone charged with a felony the assistance of counsel, times have changed."[128] Today, because of sections 7 and 11(*d*) of the *Charter*, it has been elevated to a constitutional right.[129]

§18.47 Appellate claims of incompetent representation tend to centre around two main arguments. Firstly, in seeking to introduce fresh evidence on appeal, an appellant may advance the argument that although the evidence was available at trial, it was not introduced due to the incompetence of counsel.[130] Or secondly, counsel's conduct caused a miscarriage of justice.[131]

§18.48 The Supreme Court of Canada has adopted a two-pronged approach for assessing claims of ineffective assistance of counsel. Justice Major explained in *B. (G.D.)*: "For an appeal to succeed, it must be established, first, that counsel's acts or omissions constituted incompetence and second, that a miscarriage of justice resulted."[132]

§18.49 On appeal, an appellant will have a hefty onus to establish a claim of ineffective assistance of counsel. Courts are loathe to perform "forensic autopsies of counsel's performance at trial"[133] and are cognizant of the ease of an appellant to fabricate these allegations as a last-ditch effort to overturn a conviction. In addition, reconstructing an accurate record of counsel's challenged conduct may be difficult. A lawyer whose professional integrity is being attacked may, perhaps subconsciously, prove to be a revisionist historian. Similarly, an appellant "[l]ooking backwards through the bars of a jail cell is not the most reliable of vantage points from which to see events that culminated in the conviction."[134]

§18.50 Under the performance prong of the analysis, the Supreme Court of Canada instructed in *B. (G.D.)* that "[i]ncompetence is determined by a reasonableness standard".[135] That component is assessed in light of a "strong

---

[127]　[2000] S.C.J. No. 22, [2000] 1 S.C.R. 520 (S.C.C.).

[128]　*Ibid.*, at para. 23 (S.C.R.).

[129]　See generally, *R. v. B. (G.D.)*, [2000] S.C.J. No. 22, [2000] 1 S.C.R. 520 at paras. 24-25 (S.C.C.). See also *R. v. Joanisse*, [1995] O.J. No. 2883, 102 C.C.C. (3d) 35 at 57 (Ont. C.A.).

[130]　As in *R. v. Appleton*, [2001] O.J. No. 3338, 55 O.R. (3d) 321 (Ont. C.A.), where the appellant's main contention was that his trial counsel's failure to call available evidence that would have supported his explanation at trial about the source of his knowledge that the murder weapon was a handmade gun.

[131]　As in *R. v. Cook*, [1980] O.J. No. 506, 53 C.C.C. (2d) 217 (Ont. C.A.), where the Court dealt with an allegation of a lawyer being incompetent by reason of alcohol consumption.

[132]　*R. v. B. (G.D.)*, [2000] S.C.J. No. 22, [2000] 1 S.C.R. 520 at para. 26 (S.C.C.).

[133]　*R. v. Joanisse*, [1995] O.J. No. 2883, 102 C.C.C. (3d) 35 at 58 (Ont. C.A.).

[134]　*R. v. Archer*, [2005] O.J. No. 4348, 202 C.C.C. (3d) 60 at para. 142 (Ont. C.A).

[135]　*R. v. B. (G.D.)*, [2000] S.C.J. No. 22, [2000] 1 S.C.R. 520 at para. 27 (S.C.C.).

presumption that counsel's conduct fell within the wide range of reasonable professional assistance."[136] Recognizing the "highly individualized art" of advocacy,[137] the court will have to determine whether the acts or omissions of trial counsel fell below the standard of "reasonable professional judgment."[138]

§18.51 The prejudice prong of the analysis focuses on the effects of trial counsel's incompetence. It is only when trial counsel's acts or omissions occasion a "miscarriage of justice" that appellate relief is warranted. In elaborating on what must be demonstrated, in *B. (G.D.)*, Justice Major explained that:

> Miscarriages of justice may take many forms in this context. In some instances, counsel's performance may have resulted in procedural unfairness. In others, the reliability of the trial's result may have been compromised.[139]

§18.52 A miscarriage of justice can therefore be demonstrated on alternative basis, either by showing: (*i*) that counsel's incompetence undermined the fairness of the appellant's trial;[140] or (*ii*) that there is a reasonable probability that because of counsel's incompetence, the verdict cannot be taken as a reliable assessment of an appellant's culpability.[141]

§18.53 In *B. (G.D.)*, the Supreme Court noted that an assessment of an ineffective assistance of counsel claim is best served by beginning with the prejudice component. Should the appellant fail to show prejudice, there will be no need to consider trial counsel's competence.[142]

(3) Guilty Pleas

§18.54 In challenging a guilty plea on appeal, the appellant has the onus of establishing that the guilty plea was not valid. A "valid" guilty plea is one that is voluntary, unequivocal and informed.[143]

---

[136] *Ibid.*

[137] *R. v. White*, [1997] O.J. No. 961, 114 C.C.C. (3d) 225 at 247 (Ont. C.A.).

[138] *R. v. B. (G.D.)*, [2000] S.C.J. No. 22, [2000] 1 S.C.R. 520 at para. 27 (S.C.C.).

[139] *Ibid.*, at para. 28 (S.C.R.). See also *R. v. Joanisse*, [1995] O.J. No. 2883, 102 C.C.C. (3d) 35 at 62 (Ont. C.A.).

[140] See *R. v. Joanisse*, [1995] O.J. No. 2883, 102 C.C.C. (3d) 35 at 62 (Ont. C.A.), explaining that "[a] reliable verdict may still be the product of a miscarriage of justice if the process through which that verdict was reached was unfair". See *e.g.*, *R. v. Silvini*, [1991] O.J. No. 1931, 68 C.C.C. (3d) 251 (Ont. C.A.), where a claim of ineffective assistance of counsel was made out because trial counsel was in a conflict of interest in jointly representing the appellant and a co-accused at trial. The Court concluded that a verdict resulting from a trial lacking in fairness could not be relied upon.

[141] See generally, *R. v. Joanisse*, [1995] O.J. No. 2883, 102 C.C.C. (3d) 35 at 6264 (Ont. C.A.). See *e.g.*, *R. v. B. (M.)*, [2009] O.J. No. 2653, 68 C.R. (6th) 55 (Ont. C.A.), where the Court found that defence counsel's failure, in preparation for cross-examination, to ensure that the appellant was afforded a meaningful opportunity to review his statements made to police materially prejudiced the appellant in his defence.

[142] *R. v. B. (G.D.)*, [2000] S.C.J. No. 22, [2000] 1 S.C.R. 520 at paras. 26-29 (S.C.C.).

[143] *R. v. T. (R.)*, [1992] O.J. No. 1914, 10 O.R. (3d) 514 (Ont. C.A.).

§18.55 An appellant who demonstrates that he or she was "pressured" by counsel to plead guilty cannot be seen to have acted voluntarily.[144] In terms of being informed, the appellant must have had knowledge of the nature of the allegations, the effect of the plea and the consequences of the plea. A misapprehension of any of these factors could result in the plea being struck.[145]

§18.56 Even in cases where a guilty plea appears to meet all the traditional tests for a valid guilty plea, the court of appeal retains a discretion to strike the plea where the interests of justice call for righting a miscarriage of justice.[146]

---

[144] *R. c. Lamoureux*, [1984] J.Q. no 289, 13 C.C.C. (3d) 101 (Que. C.A.); *R. v. Stork*, [1975] B.C.J. No. 1049, 24 C.C.C. (2d) 210 (B.C.C.A.).

[145] *R. v. Meers*, [1991] B.C.J. No. 759, 64 C.C.C. (3d) 221 (B.C.C.A.).

[146] See *e.g.*, *R. v. Hanemaayer*, [2008] O.J. No. 3087, 234 C.C.C. (3d) 3 (Ont. C.A.), where the Court allowed an appeal from an accused who had pleaded guilty to a break and enter and assault at trial. The Court entered an acquittal since the fresh evidence established that someone else committed the offence.

INDEX